Strategic Management

Theory and Application

Dr Adrian Haberberg
Senior Lecturer, Westminster Business School University of Westminster, UK

Professor Alison Rieple
Professor of Strategic Management, Harrow Business School, University of Westminster, UK

OXFORD
UNIVERSITY PRESS

OXFORD

UNIVERSITY PRESS

Great Clarendon Street, Oxford OX2 6DP

Oxford University Press is a department of the University of Oxford.
It furthers the University's objective of excellence in research, scholarship,
and education by publishing worldwide in

Oxford New York

Auckland Cape Town Dar es Salaam Hong Kong Karachi
Kuala Lumpur Madrid Melbourne Mexico City Nairobi
New Delhi Shanghai Taipei Toronto

With offices in

Argentina Austria Brazil Chile Czech Republic France Greece
Guatemala Hungary Italy Japan Poland Portugal Singapore
South Korea Switzerland Thailand Turkey Ukraine Vietnam

Oxford is a registered trade mark of Oxford University Press
in the UK and in certain other countries

Published in the United States
by Oxford University Press Inc., New York

© Adrian Haberberg and Alison Rieple 2008

The moral rights of the authors have been asserted
Database right Oxford University Press (maker)

First published 2008

British Library Cataloguing in Publication Data

Data available

Library of Congress Cataloging in Publication Data

Data available

Typeset in Albertina MT by Graphicraft Limited, Hong Kong
Printed in Spain
on acid-free paper by
Gráficas Estella

ISBN 978-0-19-921646-8

1 3 5 7 9 10 8 6 4 2

Strategic Management

Dedication

To our families: Gordon, Manuela, Claudia and Julia

About the authors

About the

Adrian Haberberg is Senior Lecturer in Strategic Management at the University of Westminster's Westminster Business School. He has a PhD in Strategic Decision-Making from Cass Business School. His current research interests are in the way in which strategic practices are adopted within organizations, and populations of organizations, with particular reference to corporate social responsibility. This builds upon earlier published work on the theory of strategic groups and strategic alliances. He has a particular interest in the food retailing and information technology industries. He worked for several years as a corporate planner with Rank Xerox before becoming a management consultant, most recently with Price Waterhouse. His consultancy clients have included the World Bank, the European Commission and a number of major UK corporations and public sector organisations.

Alison Rieple is Professor of Strategic Management at the University of Westminster's Harrow Business School, until recently as Director of Research. She has an MBA and a PhD from Cranfield School of Management, which examined the micro-politics of organizational change. Her research is now focused on the management of design, innovation and change; especially in the creative and cultural industries. She consults in the areas of design and innovation management, change management and business planning for both public and private sector organizations in the UK and internationally, especially in the USA and South Korea. Recent publications have included articles in journals such as the Journal of Organizational Behavior, Design Management Review and the Journal of Cultural Economics.

About the book

Before we took the decision to commit to a successor to our first book, *The Strategic Management of Organisations*, we had to be sure that there was still a place for it in an increasingly crowded market. We concluded that there *was* still space for a book which addressed the needs of, in particular, undergraduate students in a way that was readable, rigorous, up-to-date, and stimulating to readers of all ability levels.

We continue to believe that the key challenge of teaching strategic management lies in presenting complex ideas, spanning many theoretical disciplines, in a way that encourages readers to embrace that complexity, rather than resort to simplification and generalization. Only then are they able to penetrate into the soul of an organization, to gain a deep understanding of its competitive advantage, to develop considered analyses and diagnoses rather than simplistic 'SWOTs', and to present strategic proposals that address the key issues in a coherent fashion.

This emphasis on application, reflected in the title of this book, sets us apart, we believe, from our competitors. The ability to apply strategic management theory in deep and rigorous analysis, however, comes naturally to few people. This has led us to include a feature on 'Using Evidence,' to help students home in on the data, both qualitative and quantitative, that they will need to feed into their theoretical analyses. We have also made our Worked Examples far longer and more detailed than any that we have seen elsewhere. We hope that, if students have proper models to follow, they will be less tempted to cut corners in their own analyses.

The text is also interspersed with Real-life Applications, some classic but mostly very recent, which show the relevance of particular elements of theory to the understanding of real managerial issues. The case studies at the end of each chapter and the longer cases on our companion web site provide further opportunities for applying the theory to real-life situations.

Good analysis, of course, requires the ability to critique the actions of managers and strategies that result. Intelligent students can be strangely reluctant to find any fault with an apparently successful firm, or to confront the possibility that a strategy that has succeeded in the past might not be well adapted to the future. Most strategy texts, in our view, feed this tendency by focusing unduly on successful strategies. We aim to counter it in each chapter, with 'What Can Go Wrong', where recent difficulties encountered by well-known organizations such as Vodafone, Airbus, and BP, are laid bare and discussed. This enables readers to see how the messiness of real life can disrupt plausible decisions by highly qualified executives.

This emphasis on well-known firms is a consistent feature in this book. In our experience, familiarity breeds confidence. Undergraduates, in particular, are far better able to grapple with an unfamiliar concept if it is presented in the context of an organization whose products or services they have used. We have taken four well-known international firms – Sony, McDonald's, H&M, and British Airways – as running examples that we refer to frequently throughout the book, in Real-life Applications and, particularly, Worked Examples. There are real benefits to allowing students to gain a rounded picture of a firm's strategy in this way. For example, it enables us, when discussing the potential obstacles to change in one of our four firms in Chapter 16, to show how these relate to that firm's business environment (analyzed in Chapter 3) and culture (in Chapter 8).

We choose international firms because, even for the smallest organizations, strategy is now, in our view, an international discipline. While we have a chapter on Strategy in a

Global Context, which brings together the key concepts of international strategy, we have tried to retain a balance throughout the book between national and global aspects of the discipline. We also draw our readers' attention to lesser-known organizations in developing countries, such as Mexico's CEMEX, Egypt's Orascom, India's Ranbaxy, or Bangladesh's Grameen Bank; in a globalizing world, these are the household names of the future.

Along with critical thinking and analytical rigour, the key intellectual requirement for a strategist is creativity. We have tried to stimulate this by including exercises in Creative Strategizing, where the reader is invited to consider strategic issues from a different point of view and to consider unusual approaches to strategic problems.

None of this will work, however, unless the body of theory in the book is comprehensive and up-to-date. The tendency with many of our competitors is to update only selected portions of the book between one edition and the next. Their treatment of topics like positioning, for example, may rest on a single source from the 1980s. We believe that the scholarship in this book, and the currency of our sources, stands comparison with any other in the field. All major advances in theory up to early 2007 have, we believe, been incorporated.

Strategic management theory draws on many disciplines, notably sociology, organization theory, and economics. Most competing authors have a background in one of those disciplines that influences their approach. We, however, strive to give a balanced and rigorous account that combine insights from them all. For example, when discussing structure and architecture in Chapter 8, we bring together agency theory and game theory with organizational culture. But theory is not cut and dried, and each of our chapters incorporates at least one Theoretical Debate, in which contending views on an important topic are compared and discussed in a style similar to that of the literature review in a refereed article. Not all students will be drawn to this feature, but we hope that those that are will gain some appreciation of the cut and thrust of academic argument.

We hope that, whether you approach strategic management from a practical or from a theoretical standpoint, you will find something to stimulate you. We also hope that you will find it set out in an approachable way. Our aim is that every sentence in this book should be understandable, at first reading, by any student, even if English is not their first language. If we fail in this aim, tell us!

Adrian Haberberg (A.B.Haberberg@wmin.ac.uk) and Alison Rieple
(A.Rieple@westminster.ac.uk). London, September 2007.

How to use this book

There are several features that are designed to help you learn strategic management. We have developed features to help you organise the information. Many features emphasise how theory is applied in real organisations, others help you to develop deeper understanding and to think like a strategist.

Organizing the information

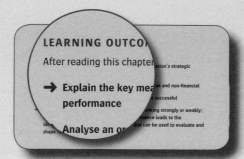

Learning outcomes
Each chapter opens with a bulleted outline of the main concepts and ideas. These serve as helpful signposts to what you can expect to learn from each chapter.

Key terms and glossary
Key terms are highlighted in green where they first appear; they are also defined in a glossary at the end of the book.

Cross references
There is a myriad of connections linking the topics within strategic management. Cross references help you to appreciate these connections.

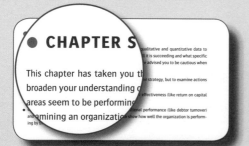

Chapter Summary
The key points of the chapter, summarized in a form that helps fix them in your mind; this feature also serves as a useful revision aid.

Further Reading

These are books or articles that serve as a starting point to gain a deeper appreciation of key concepts in each chapter. We aim to give a mixture of readings aimed at the practising manager and more scholarly articles.

Strategy in action

Real-life Application

These examples show you how the key concepts in each chapter apply to real-life organizations, and can be used to understand their situations and their managers' strategic responses.

What Can Go Wrong?

These show you how, in the real, unpredictable, world, managers can take decisions that result in serious organizational problems. They demonstrate the implications of such factors as principal-agent conflicts, volatile or unfamiliar environments, overcommitment, and undue flexibility or inflexibility.

End-of-chapter Case Study

These are extended examples that give you the opportunity to practice the skills relating to each chapter. They can be used as seminar exercises.

Thinking like a strategist

Theoretical Debate

Written in a style close to that of a literature review in a learned article, these sections aim to enhance your critical thinking skills, serving as an antidote to notions that management theory is cut and dried. They might also be useful as models for literature reviews in dissertations.

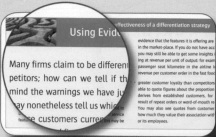

Using Evidence

'Using Evidence' points you to the quantitative and qualitative data you can invoke to support your arguments and make your conclusions robust.

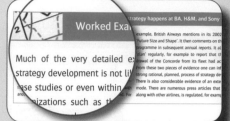

Worked Example

These extended sections walk you through the process of rigorous, full-scale strategic analysis. They show how relevant theory can be used to structure and interpret data, and derive a range of conclusions.

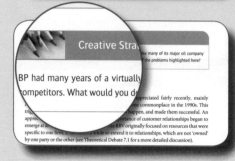

Creative Strategizing

These take, as a starting point, a strategic challenge or dilemma from one of the Real-life Applications and invite you to think creatively about how you would respond to it.

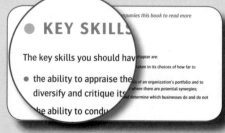

Key Skills

The test of an understanding of strategic management theory is the ability to apply it. This feature lists the main applied skills that you will have acquired in the course of each chapter.

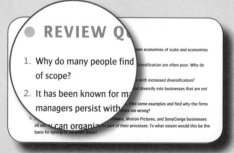

Review Questions

These questions are designed to test your understanding of the main concepts in each chapter – and to stimulate awareness and discussion of the limitations of those concepts.

How to use the Online Resource Centre

 http://www.oxfordtextbooks.co.uk/orc/haberberg_rieple/

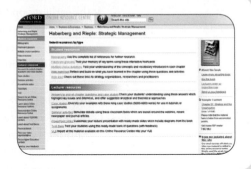

The Online Resource Centre that accompanies this book provides students and instructors with ready-to-use teaching and learning resources. They are free-of-charge and designed to complement the textbook. All these resources can be downloaded and incorporated into a virtual learning environment.

For students

Multiple choice questions
Self-test multiple choice questions are available for each chapter, giving you the opportunity to test your understanding of key concepts and vocabulary.

Web links
A series of annotated web links to key researchers, practitioners and organizations in the field of strategic management provide a guide to helpful, as well as controversial material.

Flashcard glossary
Interactive flashcards to help you commit key concepts and key terms to memory, or to refresh your memory if it falters!

Web exercises
Questions and activities that extend and update the Creative Strategizing, Theoretical Debates and Using Evidence features in the book, taking into account of new developments in the business world. These offer you an opportunity to self-test, allowing a greater degree of reflection and discussion than the multiple-choice questions.

Bibliography
A complete list of references from the book to help you explore the primary literature and recent advances in the field.

For lecturers

Test bank
For each chapter, a ready-made bank of questions has been devised. The test bank can be downloaded to a virtual learning environment and customised to test students' progress.

Seminar activities
Seminar activities, including exercises based around the weblinks and recent newspaper and journal articles, that can be used as case studies or the basis for discussion.

Case studies
A collection of relevant and engaging case studies has been provided for use in tutorials or assignments. Written by the authors and contributing authors, these include the music and mobile phone industries.

Answers
Suggested answers to all the end-of-chapter questions and case studies; offering analytical and theoretical approaches and highlighting key issues and dilemmas.

PowerPoint slides
A suite of customisable PowerPoint slides have been provided for use in lecture preparation. The slides include diagrams from the text.

Acknowledgements

Every effort has been made to trace and contact copyright holders but this has not been possible in every case. If notified, the publisher will undertake to rectify any errors or omissions at the earliest opportunity.

A project of this magnitude requires the input of many people, and we owe a debt of gratitude to all of them. Our Commissioning Editors, Sacha Cook and Jim Collins, and our Development Editor, Lucy Hyde have been constant sources of encouragement, support, and advice. The work of the Production Editors, Heidi Young and Anna Reeves, the copy-editor Katia Hamza and the design team of Charlotte Dobbs and Claire Dickinson has also commanded our respect and gratitude.

Although we are fierce critics of each other's work, we rely upon others to ensure that our ideas resonate with a wider audience and have been clearly expressed. We are indebted to our reviewers for their time and constructive input.

We have also been able to call upon friends, colleagues, and students past and present for concrete input into the book. In particular, we would like to acknowledge the contributions of Clive Helm for the end-of-chapter case studies for Chapters 3 and 7, Roger Lewis and Mark Hopwood of c2c for Real-life Application 17.2, Peral Hussein for Real-life Application 17.3, and Jon Gander for sections of Theoretical Debate 10.1.

Last, but not least, we would like to thank our long-suffering families for their support during the long and difficult days (and sometimes nights) that we have given over to this book. We owe them more than we can say.

Brief contents

Detailed contents

PART FOUR From Strategic Analysis to Strategy Formulation   451

PART ONE

Core Concepts

In this first part of the book, we lay the foundations for a broad understanding of strategy and strategic management. We show you what strategy is, and how it develops within organizations. We place this discussion in the context of the ways in which organizations function, and the people who manage and work in them behave. Human frailties and idiosyncrasies have a great deal of influence on strategy.

In the process, we bring in most of the key concepts and vocabulary of strategic management. In particular, we introduce you to the criteria that a strategy must meet in order to be successful: it must fit the environment, give the organization something distinctive from its competitors and also, ideally, resources or other attributes that will make its advantage sustainable. These three concepts—fit, distinctiveness, and sustainability—are developed further in the following two parts.

We examine some of the dilemmas and trade-offs that managers confront when developing a strategy, including the strategic role of ethics and social responsibility. We also look at how strategies can go wrong, and how success can turn to failure.

CHAPTER ONE

Strategy and the Organization

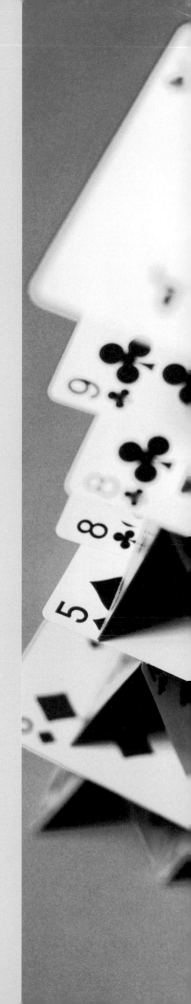

LEARNING OUTCOMES

After reading this chapter you should be able to:

→ Describe what strategy is and what organizations are, and explain the bases of those definitions

→ Distinguish between five different ways of looking at an organization—as a legal entity, an economic actor, a collection of people, an accumulation of knowledge and learning, and a bundle of resources—and explain how these views, separately and together, impact upon strategic management

→ Explain how organizations develop over time, and why this is relevant to understanding their strategies

→ Debate the extent to which strategies can be expected to be rational.

INTRODUCTION

This book is about organizations and the way in which they adapt to the world around them. The things they do to adapt over time are what we call strategies, and the process of shaping this adaptation is strategic management. We start this chapter with a definition of strategy. Understanding this definition requires an appreciation of what organizations are, and how they interact with the world around them. For this reason, the rest of the chapter is given over to an exploration of different aspects of organizations and organizing. In the process, we introduce you to many of the key concepts of strategic management, which we shall discuss in detail in the later chapters.

1.1 The basics—organizations and strategies

Organizations are collections of people that come together and are *organized* for a particular set of purposes. These are usually regulated by some sort of legal framework that says what they can and cannot do. Many of the organizations that we will discuss in this book are firms or companies, legally allowed to trade. Others are charitable trusts set up to fulfil a social need, and not expected to make profits, or public sector units such as schools or government departments set up by governments to act as their agents. There are many legal forms. There are also a variety of reasons why organizations come to exist. Sometimes they are created by entrepreneurs who see an opportunity to meet an unfulfilled need in the market-place (and perhaps to become rich in the process!). Sometimes they are formed to fight poverty or injustice, or to play music or football. Sometimes they are brought together by governments to educate, administer justice, build roads, empty dustbins, or regulate banks and insurance companies.

In a nutshell, a strategy is the path taken by one of these collections of people on its way to becoming an effective economic performer.

A strategy is the set of actions through which an organization, by accident or design, develops resources and uses them to deliver services or products in a way which its users find valuable, while meeting the financial and other objectives and constraints imposed by key stakeholders. Most successful strategies give an organization:

- some property that is unique, or at least distinctive;
- the means for renewing its competitive advantage as the environment changes.

Using Evidence 1.1 Understanding what an organization's strategy actually is

In order to identify an organization's strategy, you might be tempted to only look at pronouncements by the CEO and the board, at its written strategic plan, or at its mission statement. These give valuable clues about what influential people would like the strategy to be, and about the organization's culture. But to understand what its strategy *is*, and how this has come about, you need to do more. You should look at what the organization actually *does*. So examine the customers it is targeting and the products or services it is offering them. Is it trying to differentiate its products or is it relying on low prices to attract customers? How does it attract and motivate its members? Does it give the biggest rewards to its innovators or its operations managers? Does it develop new ➜

➜ products by doing what it has always done, perhaps slightly differently, or does it hunt for opportunities out in the world and develop new ideas and ways of working to try to capitalize on those prospects. Is it driven by government edicts, or can its managers do virtually what they want? What has happened to it during its history?

All of these will, when brought together, give you a good idea of what strategies an organization has chosen, and why, and those that have been imposed on it. It will give you a sense of why it exists, and who have been the most important stakeholders. All of these give very strong clues as to what it may do from now on—its future strategy.

We can look at each element of this definition in turn.

1.1.1 Strategy as a set of actions arrived at by accident or design

You may notice that words like 'planning' are missing from the definition of strategy that we are developing here. In fact, we talk of strategies happening 'by accident or design'. This does not mean that planning does not, or should not, happen in firms. But because, as we discuss in Section 1.6, many organizations are complex social systems operating in unpredictable environments, not all plans are implemented, and people in the organization may end up acting in ways that are opportunistic or otherwise unplanned. The organization's eventual strategy is what theorists call its realized strategy—what it ends up doing—which may not be what it starts out wanting to do.

➜ We discuss the relationship between managerial intentions and realized strategies in greater depth in Section 2.1.2.

1.1.2 The development of resources

The knowledge and other resources that the organization acquires over time—we discuss how this happens in Sections 1.4 and 1.5, and again in Chapters 7 and 10—are vital elements in its strategy. As we shall see, they are the result of the collective learning experiences of the people in the organization, interacting with their environment and with each other. Because no two social systems are precisely alike, these interactions are subtly different in every firm, so that every organization has the opportunity to develop distinctive resources that it can employ to add value to its users. However, not all organizations succeed in doing this, or in motivating their people so that users and customers are satisfied.

Resource
Something that an organization owns, controls, or has access to on a semi-permanent basis. It may be a physical object, a person, money, or something intangible, such as a capability or reputation.[1]

1.1.3 Delivering products and services that users find valuable

If an organization is to survive, it must find a way of justifying its existence. It must develop products or services, and find customers who think these are worth buying or, as with a charity or a public sector organization, find those who are willing to advance money to the organization so that it can carry on providing them for its users. Alternatively, as is the case for internet-based firms, like YouTube or Google, and free newspapers, like Metro, it must attract enough users—visitors or readers—to make it attractive to the advertisers who are its potential customers.

Customers
The people or other organizations that pay for an organization's services or products.

Users
The people or other organizations who actually use an organization's products or services.

Stakeholders
People with an interest in
an organization's success,
failure, or activities, and
therefore a desire to
influence its behaviour.

➜ We review appropriate
ways to assess an
organization's performance
against its objectives in
Chapter 11.

1.1.4 Meeting stakeholder objectives and constraints

Through satisfying the needs of its customers, the organization will aim to fulfil the personal and economic goals of its controlling stakeholders. If it is a commercial concern—a business—it must meet the financial expectations of its founders or investors. If it is a club, charity, or government body, it may not be expected to make a profit, but will have to survive within a limited budget.

As we shall see in Section 1.6, the organization may also at the same time be fulfilling a number of other, non-economic objectives, set by a variety of stakeholders, many of whom will have influence over the path that it follows.

1.1.5 Unique or distinctive features

An organization is unlikely to survive for long, and highly unlikely to become a leader in its field, unless there is something distinctive about it. Often, this will take the form of a clear reason for some people to buy its offerings in preference to those of its competitors—a better product or superior customer service. Organizations may also have distinctive value chains (Section 1.3.4) that enable them to make more profit than competitors with comparable offerings. We explore this idea in greater depth in Section 2.4.2 and again in Chapters 4 and 6.

As we mentioned in Section 1.1.2, most organizations have distinctive resources that enable them to be unique in some fashion. And different customers or users will value different aspects of the product or service—which is what makes it possible for different organizations to co-exist profitably even if there are only small differences in what they offer and how they operate.

1.1.6 Renewing advantage as the environment changes

As the environment changes, with new technologies emerging, customer tastes evolving, and new competitive threats appearing, organizations must change as well. If they rely upon established areas of distinctiveness in their products, value chains, and resources, they risk being left with products and services that nobody thinks are valuable, or being outflanked by competitors.

This implies that organizations need to have mechanisms for detecting how their environment is changing and for adapting to those changes, so that they can sustain their advantage (see Section 2.4.3). Some go further and try, through innovation, to influence environmental change in ways that fit with their capabilities.

1.1.7 Introducing four interesting organizations

The following sections of this chapter explore these ideas about organizations and strategy in greater depth, introducing you along the way to some of the key concepts and vocabulary of strategic management. They use a number of examples, many drawn from the companies that we introduce in Real-life Application 1.1, and which we shall be drawing upon as illustrations throughout the book.

Each of these companies shows a track record of success along with a number of instructive setbacks. We chose them for a number of reasons. Firstly, we believe that in our modern interconnected world, where students come from all over the globe, it is important to show that the points we make apply to companies from very different cultural backgrounds—so we have deliberately chosen firms representing four different countries: Japan, the USA,

Britain, and Sweden. But these companies are not only representative of their national backgrounds, they are also extremely well known on the international scene and will, we hope, be familiar and recognizable to many of you, wherever in the world you are from.

They also represent very different industries—manufacturing, food services (in fact food service manufacturing), clothes retailing, and transport. These different industries have different critical factors for success and different structures, which can provide contrasting examples of how strategic priorities can vary from industry to industry.

In addition, although these are all well known firms with a strong track record, they illustrate how even such large, successful firms have to face, and solve, testing strategic problems along the way.

Real-life Application 1.1 Four interesting organizations

Sony Corporation is one of the world's leading manufacturers of consumer electronics. *Sony Corporation*

Sony Corporation is one of the word's leading manufacturers of consumer electronics. It was founded just after World War II by Akio Morita and Masura Ikuba. It came to prominence by being the first company to make a pocket-sized radio, using transistor technology licensed from the USA. This was followed by the world's first transistorized TV, and the Trinitron colour television system. It became one of the world's premier suppliers of high-quality TVs, videos, and audio equipment to home and corporate users, with production and R&D facilities on four continents. It cemented a reputation for innovation when in 1979 it introduced the Walkman, a portable cassette player designed to be clipped to a belt and worn while walking or skating. It moved into the business of making the music and film 'software' to be played on its consumer 'hardware' with the 1988 acquisition of CBS Records (now Sony Music) and its 1989 acquisition of the US entertainment combine, Columbia Pictures Entertainment. In 2004 its music division announced its intention to merge with BMGE, the music and entertainment division of the German conglomerate Bertelsmann. Its most recent successes have been its PlayStation videogames console, launched in 1994, which outsold the products of established players such as Sega and Nintendo, the Walkman telephones produced by its Sony-Ericsson subsidiary, and its Bravia flat-screen televisions. In 2006 it was the world's 65th largest company (ranked by turnover), with revenues of $66 billion, profits of $1.1 billion and 158,500 employees.[2] It also appeared (again) on the *Fortune* Magazine list of the world's most admired companies.[3]

McDonald's Inc. is the world's largest restaurant chain, serving 38 million customers each day in 32,000 outlets in over 100 countries. It came into being in 1948 when Dick and Sam McDonald worked out how to redesign their kitchen along mass-production lines, producing high volumes of a limited menu for sale at low prices. The firm grew slowly until Ray Kroc, a milkshake-machine salesman intrigued by the brothers' high ➜

➜ milkshake sales, saw the concept's potential and became the exclusive franchising agent for the USA. Through tireless promotion, he grew the business 16-fold in four years. Its restaurants, with their distinctive golden arch insignia, are now a common sight throughout the world. Apart from its food, the chain is famous for the way that all staff are trained in its distinctive operating procedures, at the company's own 'Hamburger University'. In 2006, it had 447,000 employees worldwide and was number 108 in the Fortune 500 list of the largest American companies. It made profits of over $3.5 billion on a turnover of $21.6 billion.[4] It is one of the most recognized brands in the world.

H&M AB is a Swedish retailer of fashionable clothing. It was founded by Erling Persson in 1947 in Västerås Sweden to sell women's-wear (the H stands for 'Hennes', women in Swedish). After the purchase of Mauritz Widfors in 1968, the company started selling men's clothing and changed its name to Hennes & Mauritz. H&M has enjoyed impressive international growth during its life, and especially during the past decade. Turnover rose by an average of 50 per cent annually throughout the 1990s. In 1964 it opened its first store abroad—in Norway—followed by outlets in most other countries in western Europe. Since 2000 H&M has followed a consistent policy of geographic expansion, including its first openings in the USA in 2000, eastern Europe in 2003, Canada in 2004, and China in 2007. The company launched ranges of children's wear in 1968, cosmetics in 1975, and clothes for teenagers in 1976, has since expanded into baby wear, and since the 1980s has also had a mail order arm. H&M is now Europe's second largest fashion retailer with over 60,000 employees, 1,400 stores, and 2006 profits of 10.8 billion Swedish Kronor (SEK) on sales of 68 billion SEK[5] (about US$10 billion). In December 2000 it was named Best International Retailer by the USA's National Retail Federation, the world's biggest retail trade body. Although Erling Persson died recently, he was an executive director of the company for many years, and his son Stefan, Managing Director from 1982–98, is now executive chairman.

British Airways plc is the world's seventh-largest airline measured by flight miles and was for many years its largest international passenger airline, until KLM and Air France merged to form a larger entity. Since being sold off into the private sector by the UK government in 1984, it has become one of the world's most profitable airlines. For much of the 1980s and 1990s it moved faster than competitors in controlling its cost base, and its customer service gained such high ratings from travel magazines that it was legitimately able to claim in its strap-line to be the 'world's favourite airline'. Although it has experienced difficulties since then with its internal industrial relations and with new, low-cost competitors, in 2007 it was to be found (again) in the Fortune list of Global most admired companies.[6] It controls a large share (40.6 per cent in 2006[7]) of the traffic at Heathrow, one of the world's busiest airports and an important international air transport hub. In 2006 it had revenues of £8.2 billion ($15.2 billion)—giving it a ranking of 442 amongst the world's largest firms—profits of £468m ($800m), and just under 50,000 employees.[8]

A Swedish company, H&M is now Europe's second largest fashion retailer. *H&M AB*

1.2 **Organizations as legal entities**

The legal forms that organizations can take are broadly similar in different countries, though the legislation governing how these forms are interpreted or regulated can vary slightly.

Most of the ones that we discuss in this book are firms, businesses, or enterprises (the three terms mean much the same thing) set up to trade and produce profits for their owners. In order to allow the owners to keep their own assets distinct from those of the firm, and to make it easier for outside investors to put in money and participate in the profits, firms are often legally constituted ('incorporated') as companies. If a company goes bankrupt, then the owners only lose what they have invested, rather than being liable for the company's debts. In return for this concession, they can, in most countries, be prosecuted or sued like people, if they do wrong. They are governed by laws about how they are managed and structured, and their income and accounts have to be published at least once a year.

As companies grow, they may decide to list their shares on one of the world's many stock markets, so that a broader public can buy and sell shares in them. This gives them access to a larger pool of investment capital, and may also allow the founding investors to turn some of their shares into cash, and so enjoy the fruits of their success. In order to attract stock-market investors, however, the firm must publish regular information so that people can judge whether to buy the shares, how much they are worth, and whether the company, of which they will become part owners, is being well managed. Unlike the original shareholders, these new investors are not always well acquainted with the firm or its managers, and may even be located on a different continent. This means that such public companies or corporations face more stringent requirements than privately owned firms. Typically they have to supply accounts more often, conform to agreed accounting standards, hold open shareholders' meetings, and communicate major trading events to the various stock markets and national and international regulatory bodies that are set up to monitor and control them.

All four of the companies that we introduce in Real-life Application 1.1 are publicly quoted corporations. They are also multinationals: they have operations in many countries. Sony, in particular, qualifies as a conglomerate: a large company that has a number of different business areas within its overall portfolio, some of which may be separate legal entities in their own right.

In addition to companies, there are a number of other legally-defined types of organizations. In a partnership, two or more individuals each agree formally to share costs and meet any debts incurred jointly. If the partnership is also a firm, then the partners will share the profits according to an agreed formula. Partnerships may, however, be set up to achieve other goals—perhaps to travel or play music.

Not-for-profits (NFPs), a broad heading which includes charities and voluntary organizations, are typically set up to solve social problems or for cultural or educational purposes. Although their main aim is not to make profits, they may act in ways that are quite similar to firms. They may charge fees or have commercial activities, such as shops, which generate funds for their chosen cause. Because there is usually some sort of societal benefit from these organizations they are often offered special treatment, such as lower taxes. Governments, in return, usually expect charities and NFPs to conform to specific laws detailing what they can and cannot do, and to undergo regular inspections.

➔ We examine not-for-profit and public sector organizations in greater depth in Chapter 15.

Governments also have a strong role in controlling and managing the bodies that they themselves set up to fulfil their public duties. These are public sector organizations, and they are regulated in a different way from commercial firms, although, like charities, they sometimes behave commercially. Hospitals not only have to fulfil their government's responsibility to care for its people, they have to manage their funds in a cost-effective manner.

In some countries, this means that they sell their medical services to other countries, negotiate contracts to buy and supply services with other organizations, often companies, and generally act in a very commercial way. Sometimes the line between publicly owned hospitals and private ones is blurred: some hospitals act like businesses. However, there are considerable national differences in how public sector organizations are regulated and how commercial they can be, and, similarly, there are differences in what the various types of public sector units can and cannot do.

1.3 **Organizations as economic actors**

All of these types of legal entity have to function effectively as economic units and achieve the financial objectives of their key stakeholders (see Table 1.1).

If they fail, the management team may be sacked, or the business sold or closed down. If they succeed, on the other hand, people can be rewarded. They may benefit financially from increased salaries, bonuses or stock options, or more indirectly from improvements to the working environment. They may also gain in self-esteem from working for a successful organization, as well as taking satisfaction from a job well done.

In order to achieve their economic objectives, organizations need to carry out a range of activities. They have to generate revenue, by providing products and services that satisfy the needs of customers and users, and deliver them at an acceptable cost. In order to do this they develop a value chain and architecture that enable them to operate effectively, and they interact, as a buyer, seller, or competitor, with individuals and other firms in industries and markets. In order to judge whether these activities are working effectively, managers need good information about their competitors' actions and intentions, about their own cost structures and about the likely reaction of consumers to changes in prices and product quality. They also need the time, technology, and mental capacity to process that information, so as to determine the best action to take.

Table 1.1 Organizations, stakeholders, and their financial objectives

Organization	Controlling stakeholder	Financial objective
Sony	Japanese banks	Sufficient profits to satisfy expectations of banks (typically lower than those of Western shareholders)
McDonald's	US shareholders	Profit maximization
H&M	Persson family and long-standing directors	Cash flow to fund expansion
British Airways	British and US financial institutions	Profit maximization
A medical research charity	Sponsors and donors	Break-even between income from donations, sponsorship and commercial activities, and expenditure to fund research
A state prison	Government	To use up allocated budget, but not overspend it

1.3.1 Products, services, and software

If organizations are to meet their stakeholders' financial objectives, they must serve their users effectively. This is what gives businesses revenues from customers, keeps donations and sponsorship income flowing into a charity's bank account, and persuades governments to keep open, or even expand, a prison or a university.

Organizations serve users by taking inputs and *adding value* to them, i.e. transforming them into outputs that customers are willing to pay for. The inputs may be raw materials, information, or human labour. Outputs may be:

- Tangible products, such as computers or clothing or hamburgers.

- Software, which includes not only programs that run on computers, but also music and films. Although these often have a tangible form, such as a CD or video cassette, the valuable element is the intangible intellectual property, which may be the result of many person-years of creative effort. The stock-market value of Microsoft, the dominant force in computer software, now exceeds those of most of the oil firms and automobile manufacturers that have been America's largest companies for many decades.

- Services, like a restaurant meal, a retail transaction, or an airline flight. Services are intangible and are consumed at the point of production. One of the main trends of the late twentieth century has been the decline in importance of manufacturing industries and the growth of services in the developed economies. Services account for over 80 per cent of the economic output of the USA and the UK.

The differences between products and services can be exaggerated. Almost all services rely on the efficient manipulation of physical items: a McDonald's restaurant is a small masterpiece of carefully designed mass production, and a British Airways flight depends on aircraft maintenance facilities that are managed and equipped like a factory. Many physical products are sold as a package with a bundle of services, such as design, delivery, and after-sales maintenance. Increasingly, they also have software built into them, and the reliability of that software and the quality of the user interface have become important factors when considering which car, washing machine, or mobile phone to buy. It is best to think of organizations as producing a mixture of physical outputs, intellectual property, and services, and in this book we shall often use the words 'outputs', 'products', and 'services' interchangeably to cover all parts of this mix.

1.3.2 Effectiveness and efficiency

If the organization is to succeed, it needs to be effective: physical products or software must do what users expect them to and have the other attributes, such as price, appearance, or reliability, that customers desire. Services, similarly, must be available when needed and meet customers' requirements in terms of speed, courtesy, or other factors.

Many organizations also strive to be efficient, and keep their costs as low as possible. They may try to reduce the variable costs of obtaining the inputs and converting them into outputs. They may also try to minimize their fixed costs: plant, buildings, web servers, and overheads such as sales and administration. Where high fixed costs are unavoidable, the firm may try to utilize its assets as intensively as possible, to minimize the unit costs of its outputs. It may do this by producing individual products in large quantities, to try to gain economies of scale. It may also try to use parts of its fixed cost base, such as warehouses, websites, and invoice processing systems, for a variety of products, to gain economies of scope.

Effectiveness
An output or activity is effective if it does what the intended user or beneficiary, inside or outside the organization, requires it to do.

Efficiency
Getting or keeping the cost of an output or process as low as possible, minimizing wastage and unnecessary activities.

→ We discuss economies of scale and scope in more detail in Section 5.2.3.

Organizations that at first sight seem very efficient are not always the most successful—keeping costs low can sometimes interfere with innovation or customer service, which may in some industries be vitally important to a firm's effectiveness. However, any organization must meet a minimum standard of efficiency—it must keep the cost of the inputs plus the costs of the conversion process below what it receives as income. Normally, of course, there needs to be a surplus to allow a firm to renew its assets and show the required level of profit to distribute to its stakeholders.

1.3.3 Transaction and agency costs

Transaction costs
The costs (many of which may be hidden) of doing business with other organizations.

Agency costs
The cost to an organization of making sure that its employees are acting in its interests and those of its owners, together with any profits lost because of ineffective control.

However efficient an organization may be, it will spend a significant amount on administrative costs. Some of these are linked to producing outputs and serving customers: responding to enquiries, dealing with suppliers, and producing invoices, for example. Others are incurred in order to produce information for investors, or simply to pass information around the organization. The people who are dealing with customers need to know which products are available, and which ones managers believe should be promoted most enthusiastically for a given type of customer. The managers, in turn, need information about sales and costs so they can monitor how well their strategy is working.

Not all administrative costs, however, are unavoidable, and there are two particular types of avoidable cost that are important in strategic management: transaction costs and agency costs.

Transaction costs

→ Transaction costs are examined in more detail in Section 8.2.1.

When a firm uses outside firms, such as suppliers, contractors, retailers, or distributors, it runs the risk that they will try to cheat it in some way. For example, a supplier might lie about its costs to try to inflate its prices. A distributor might pretend to have sold more than it really has, to obtain a greater discount or commission than it is entitled to.

Transaction costs incorporate the costs to an organization of being exploited by independent suppliers and distributors, or the costs of the administration and control systems needed to avoid such exploitation. These may include the costs of setting up contracts and agreements, of legal proceeding if things go wrong with these contracts, and of staff to monitor the performance of outside contractors.

There are various ways that organizations can seek to reduce their transaction costs. They can do as much as possible in-house (see Real-life Application 1.2 below). They can try to do business only with firms that they know and trust, or that have strong reputations for fair dealing. Or they can try to put control systems in place to police the relationship, although the costs of those systems themselves count as transaction costs.

Agency costs

It is possible that a firm's managers and employees may use its resources to further their own ambitions rather than to do what their owners, shareholders or controlling stakeholders require. Economists term this a principal–agent problem (the owners are the principals, the managers are the agents). Managers may, for example, use corporate jets for personal holidays or carry on their own businesses using the firm's equipment. They may purchase unnecessarily luxurious offices in order to boost their status and self-esteem at the organization's expense.

→ We discuss control systems again in Chapter 10.

Agency costs include such items as: the writing of employment contracts; the salaries of administrators and managers who monitor employees' performance; the costs of control and audit systems and of the people that run them; and excessive expense claims by managers who are trying to 'milk' their company for a few extra euros.

Agency costs can be reduced by setting up a supervisory structure and a set of control systems that make it difficult for employees to cheat. They can also be minimized if an organization develops a culture in which such cheating is socially unacceptable.

1.3.4 Value chain and architecture

An organization's operations have to be configured so that its outputs are produced efficiently and effectively and its transaction and agency costs minimized. These configurations together constitute its value chain and architecture.

The value chain

An organization's value chain determines how effectively it serves its users, and at what cost. It includes:

- The way that it develops new products and services—for example through intensive prior research and test-marketing of a small number of products, or by launching a lot of new products and seeing which ones become popular with customers.

- The way that outputs are produced. Products or services may be highly standardized to keep costs down, like the service in a chain of budget-priced hotels or a mass-produced product like a TV set. Alternatively, they may be highly customized, like a prestige office building or a luxury car. Outputs may be processed along traditional mass-production lines, with inputs being purchased cheaply in bulk and processed in long production runs. Or a firm may have more flexible 'lean production' methods, with suppliers delivering the inputs 'just-in-time' to be processed, inventories being kept low and the process structured so as to allow frequent changeovers between one product line and another.

- The way in which products are distributed and marketed. A firm may sell its products through specialist dealers, or general retailers such as supermarkets, or use its own salesforce or sell direct via mail order or the internet. Each of these may be an effective way of reaching a particular market segment. A firm may choose to invest heavily in advertising to make a lot of people aware of its services, target a narrower group of customers by direct mail, or rely upon word-of-mouth.

- The way in which customers are looked after once they have bought the product, for example through maintenance and repair services, customer help-lines and complaints-handling procedures.

The design of the value chain is one way in which an organization can make itself different from its competitors.

An important set of decisions within the value chain relates to an organization's degree of vertical integration: what it produces in-house, how it can control delivery times and quality to its own requirements; what it buys in from outside; and whether to use the firm's own resources or third parties to distribute outputs. Other important decisions within the value chain (Real-life Application 1.2) relate to:

- the scale of operations—large to try to gain lower costs through economies of scale, or small to gain flexibility;

- the scope of operations—whether to direct them towards a few products, markets, or activities, or spread them across a broader range;

- location—for example, close to customers, to give them fast service, or far away, in a country where labour costs are low.

Value chain
The way an organization decides to undertake the important activities at each stage in the development, production, and delivery of its products and services.

Vertical integration
The extent to which an organization extends control over its activities 'forwards' towards the customer or end user, and 'backwards' or 'upstream' towards the production of its raw materials.

➜ We discuss vertical integration and other aspects of the value chain in more detail in Chapter 6.

Real-life Application 1.2 Value chains and architectures in fashion retailing

H&M's senior management team is based at its head office in Stockholm. Stockholm is also where the main functions for design and buying, finance, expansion, shop fitting and display, advertising, communications, human resources, logistics, security, and IT are located. H&M has 13 country offices that are responsible for the various functions in each country in which it has stores. It sources its products from 700-odd suppliers in Europe, Asia, Africa, and the USA. All are managed by a network of 22 production offices, ten each in Europe and Asia, one in Central America and one in Africa. Although it does not own its suppliers, all have to abide by its code of practice in respect of quality and safety, and H&M exercises what appears to be tight control over the behaviour and standards of its suppliers.

In contrast, one of its major competitors, Zara (a subsidiary of Europe's largest fashion chain, the Spanish company Inditex), chooses to produce around 50 per cent of its clothing in its own factories and to outsource much of the sewing to trusted small suppliers, many of them in Spain and Portugal, close to its head office and home base. Inditex cements these suppliers' loyalty with technical and financial support. This exceptionally tight control over production is said to give it an advantage in terms of the speed with which it can bring new clothes designs to stores, and respond to fast-changing consumer trends. In March 2006 it overtook H&M to become Europe's largest clothes' retailer.

Zara owns the majority of its retail outlets, although it also has a number of franchisees. This is similar to many other fashion chains, such as Benetton, Karen Millen, and Whistles, which have a mixture of wholly owned and franchised stores. These firms sell their clothes through franchised outlets so that they can benefit from local management and knowledge, and also spread the risk of international expansion. Although The Gap, another leading competitor, has shied away from franchising in the past, it recently announced that it would contemplate using franchises as well as licensing or partnership arrangements abroad, rather than continue its current policy of opening company-owned stores.[9] H&M, however, has chosen to own all its shops, and therefore has tight control over their design and the service quality that customers experience from sales staff. It appears to have no plans to change this policy.

Other fashion brands choose to sell their clothes through independently owned retail outlets such as Selfridges, David Jones, El Corte Inglés, or Macy's department stores. Sometimes these brands are allowed to design their own space within these stores, although their control over their environment is generally less than if the clothes were sold through their own outlets. However, these brands benefit from generally lower costs, and are able to reach a wider customer base using this route.

In March 2006, Zara overtook H&M to become Europe's largest fashion retailer. *Zara*

Architecture

An organization's architecture is the way it structures the relationships between its different elements. As it grows more complex, an organization needs more managers to supervise the different parts of its operations, and systems to help them. Its architecture includes its structure and its control and reward systems, which shape the motivation of people to share information and process and act upon it. This has an important effect upon its agency costs.

The concept of architecture also embraces the relationships between the organization and others in its immediate environment, such as its customers, suppliers, and distributors. Architecture is an important influence on transaction costs. Recently, structures involving networks of independently owned and managed firms have become common in certain industries, for example biotechnology and pharmaceuticals. This reflects the need to develop close-knit relationships with suppliers of specialist technologies that do better if they retain their separate cultures.

Architecture
The structures, systems, and practices that shape information flow into and out of the organization, and the way that decisions are taken (or avoided) on the basis of that information.

→ Different aspects and types of architecture are discussed in Chapters 8 and 9.

1.3.5 **The business environment**

A firm's value chain can be viewed as a link in a more extensive chain in which basic raw materials, such as wood, iron ore, silicon, petrochemicals, water, and electricity, are transformed, through the addition of labour and more raw materials, into products and services. These may then be incorporated into other customers' products, and so on down the chain (Figure 1.1). The end point of the chain is a product like a stereo, or a service like a retail transaction or an education, which is paid for by individual consumers, either as a private transaction or through their taxes.

Figure 1.1 illustrates some important things about the organization's environment:

- It is a complex system: you cannot understand it fully just by looking at one or two elements. Anything that happens to any part of the system may affect the demand for an organization's services, or the prices of its inputs.

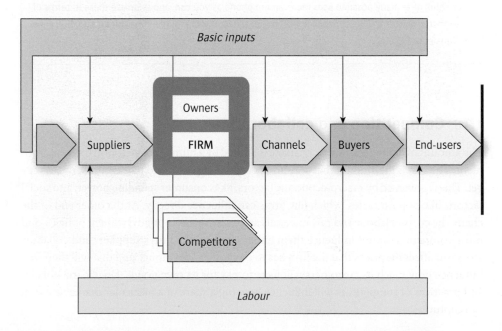

Figure 1.1 A production chain

- It is unpredictable (see Real-life Application 1.3): not only because of the large number of components, but also because each component is in itself a complex social system full of unpredictable human beings.

Real-life Application 1.3 The unpredictable environment: the market for video phones

When telephone technology advanced to the point where cameras could be incorporated into mobile phones, and the pictures sent to other phones, the cellular networks, such as Vodafone, launched new handsets and services designed to profit from what they saw as a huge opportunity. They had a clear idea of who would buy the phones: their advertisements were full of young people sending their friends pictures of other friends in embarrassing situations, or of themselves in the company of an attractive member of the opposite sex.

However, the take-up of the services has been disappointing—people seem to prefer to share their photos over the internet—and the users have often been different from the ones the phone companies expected. Construction industry professionals, for example, found them handy for sending pictures to their offices of the condition of a site or a building, to help prepare quotes for repair or renovation.

As a planner working for one of the service providers, you might just, if you had a good imagination or some friends who were surveyors or engineers, have thought of these professional markets. But what other groups of people would you have thought could be important users of this service?

Would you have thought of deaf people? Deaf people have never been able to use phones that were not specially adapted—so there are no historical reasons why a phone service strategist should give them a second thought. But it turns out that they *can*—and do—use *video* phones, to read the lips of the person they are talking to, or to communicate in sign language.

What about doctors, police, and ambulance staff? These phones might be useful in the case of road accidents where photos could be immediately beamed to experts located in a hospital some distance away. They could give advice about the best sort of treatment locally, on, for example, whether the victim could be safely moved. And the importance of phone cameras to news reporting was highlighted by the London tube and bus bombings of July 2005. Television screens were filled with images taken by passengers with their phones, in the immediate aftermath, in a place where no television cameras or their crews could reach. Some of these images are the most compelling you could ever see.

Creative Strategizing 1.1

So—if you were a camera phone company boss, where would you now be targeting your advertising? Think of as many possible uses for a camera phone as you can, and prioritize these in terms of 1) expected sales and 2) user needs (for example, speed of recharging a flash, picture quality, ease of transfer to PC, etc.).

1.3.6 Competition and collaboration

The amount of money that firms can make is limited by a number of factors in their environment. The first is the amount that consumers are willing or able to pay for the services they get. This is governed by macro-economic factors, like consumer spending power, and social factors, like popular tastes, which few firms can influence directly. At the other end of the chain, the costs of labour and raw materials are set by markets or government policies, and most companies cannot influence them either. Second, the firm's suppliers and collaborators can affect the prices that the firm has to pay for its own inputs, and that will therefore influence how much its customers will have to pay for its own goods. Finally, the policies and practices of competitors will influence how big a share of a particular market the firm can capture.

So, if a firm wants to make more money, it has a limited number of options on which to base its strategies:

1. It can become more efficient, reducing the quantities of raw materials and labour that it uses, or finding ways of using cheaper ones.

2. It can make its products more attractive so that its customers are willing to pay more for them, or buy more of them. Sometimes this will be because they are more attractive than other items of expenditure or competing products. Sometimes it will be because using the firm's services actually saves the customer money (for example, using an energy consultant can save money spent on fuel). This type of strategy is known as differentiation.

3. It can use power over the other firms in the chain to drive down the prices it pays for its inputs or to drive up the prices it charges for its outputs.

4. It can collaborate with other firms in the chain to drive down the *total cost* of delivering services to the final consumer, so that all can share the benefits.

None of these options is inherently superior to any of the others, so organizations may choose any of them, or a combination. Which one is chosen will depend in part on their culture—some organizations are more competitive by nature than others. It will also depend upon their perceptions of the industry in which they operate, and the likely reactions of suppliers, competitors, and customers to the moves they make.

Industry
A group of firms (competitors) that produce a set of similar outputs—products and services that fulfil the same broad function.

1.3.7 Industries and markets

The size of an industry is measured in terms of the total sales of the outputs of the businesses competing in it. These may be single-product firms, or they may be divisions of larger companies. A firm may compete in several industries.

An industry's products may be sold in a range of markets. The size of each market is represented by the total purchases made by these customers, and may be measured in terms of volume (quantity of outputs sold), value (sales turnover), or sometimes numbers of customers. (Market size is also sometimes used to mean *potential* sales or customers.)

Market
A group of customers.

➜ We examine the issues involved in selecting which markets an organization should address, and how it should match its offerings to its customers and users, in Chapter 4.

Markets can be further subdivided into segments—buyers who are linked by some common characteristic. It may be that they are located in the same place (a geographic segment) or are similar in terms of age or purchasing behaviour. You will sometimes see geographic segments referred to as geographic markets (e.g. 'the UK market for fast food'). You may also see references to vertical markets. These are groups of firms or consumers with similar characteristics, such as 'financial services firms' or 'retired people'.

One market may be served by several industries. For example, the market for people seeking holidays is served by tour operators, who buy airline seats and hotel rooms in bulk and put them into packages aimed at different types of holidaymaker, and by travel agents who sell their products. But it is also served by the hotels that independent travellers seek out for themselves, the banks and outlets that buy and sell foreign currency, the websites that provide information about destinations or the means of booking hotels or flights, and many other industries of different sizes and importance. The holidaymaker market absorbs part of the output of all of these industries (Figure 1.2).

The outputs of different industries serving the same market are said to be substitutes for one another. If they perform very much the same task, they can be said to be close substitutes. For example, for travel between major cities in Europe, rail services are close substitutes for air services—they offer the traveller similar journey times and degrees of comfort. On the other hand, for a journey from Europe to the United States, a cruise on a ship is not a close substitute for an airline journey.

➜ We look at industries and substitutes in more detail in Chapter 3.

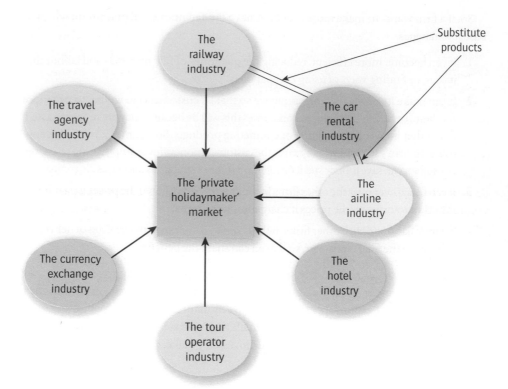

Figure 1.2 Industries serving the private holidaymaker market

The use of the term 'substitute' in strategic management theory may be different from the one you have met if you have studied economics. Some economics textbooks say that nearly identical products from different firms (such as Sony and Philips televisions) are substitutes for one another. We, however, would refer to them as competing products. Strategic management theory would class a trip to the cinema, a hi-fi, and a personal computer as substitutes for a TV set.

Just as one market may be served by many industries, one industry may serve several markets. The airline, hotel, and car-hire industries do not just sell to holidaymakers. For most of them, the business travel market is more important. Some of them develop specialized products tailored to the needs of the business traveller, such as business class air travel. However, business class travel cannot usefully be considered a separate industry. Its users will travel on the same planes as holiday travellers and be served by the same crew, while the aircraft may also carry mail and freight—two other services offered by the airline industry.

Not all airline firms serve all these markets. Some carry only packages or freight, some are low-cost airlines that carry very few business travellers. Such firms form discrete parts of an industry, which some writers confusingly refer to as segments (e.g. the 'charter airline segment'). In this book, we shall refer to a part of an industry as a sub-sector, and use segment to denote a part of a market.

1.3.8 **Globalization**

European firms in the nineteenth century faced few competitors from North America or Asia, because transport costs were higher and consumer awareness of alternatives much narrower. Nowadays, however, almost all organizations may face competition from anywhere in the world. Well-travelled consumers have a much greater awareness of choice, and the internet allows all kinds of products, services, and software to be procured quickly and cheaply across national boundaries.

Most of the world's largest companies have operations in many different countries, and have global brands that would be recognized the world over. Think of Sony, McDonald's, Nokia, or Pepsi. They are also quite likely to manufacture their products in locations far away from where they are finally sold, or source their raw supplies from wherever in the world they can be found most cheaply—this is termed a global strategy.

However, although operations may be in any corner of the world, not all firms have or should have global products. Other international companies have products that are different in each of the markets where they operate. These companies feel that consumers have specific local needs that cannot be met by a single, global, offering. Examples here are to be found particularly in retailing, food, and service industries. The world's largest retailer, the US firm Wal-Mart, experienced significant problems in adapting to the tastes of consumers and staff in Germany, and after nine years sold its operations there to Metro, a local company that is the German market leader.[10]

The economics of an industry may also be such that a global firm has no significant advantages over a local one. A bus company, for example, has to deliver its services on a local basis and cannot use cheap labour in developing countries to bring down its operating costs in developed ones, or gain greater economies of scale than local operators.

So although organizations have to be prepared to deal with international issues in their everyday lives, not all are, or should be, global. Many, in fact, operate at a regional level, with local or regional brands, and manage some aspects of their business locally and others on a global or regional basis—what is termed a transnational strategy.

Global strategy
Where a firm uses a single set of brands worldwide, sources key inputs internationally, and exerts strong central control over many aspects of the business.

➔ We discuss globalization and the various international strategic options for organizations in detail in Chapter 14.

Transnational strategy
When a firm uses regional brands for its otherwise global products, and allows its businesses considerable local autonomy—but exerts central control over key aspects of the business.

1.3.9 **The impact of the environment**

It is important for managers to understand the environments in which they operate, since these are a major influence on what their organizations need to do in order to survive and succeed. In some industries, global firms have an advantage, in others they do not. In some industries, firms that are able to keep costs and prices low have the best chance of success, in other industries it will be those that are the most creative or innovative. In some markets, success may come from an architecture that keeps a firm close to changing customer tastes, in others it may be good contacts with the government that are vital. Environmental factors also influence where the firm is able to source its raw materials (whether these are physical goods or skills and knowledge), how it distributes its goods, and the impact that its competitors and stakeholders have on what the organization does. Understanding these factors can make the difference between success and failure.

The idea of fit between an organization's strategy and the survival and success factors in its environment is a fundamental one that we shall explore later in the book. However, even if they have achieved a measure of fit, organizations differ in their ability to succeed in particular industries or markets. One important reason for this is differences in their ability to accumulate, and make use of, relevant knowledge and resources, and these are the factors that we discuss in the next two sections.

➔ We introduce ways of analysing an organization's environment in Chapter 3, and review strategies in different types of environment in Chapter 13.

1.4 **The organization as an accumulation of knowledge and learning**

1.4.1 **Experience and knowledge**

Most organizations change over time: some start small and grow bigger; some start small and happily stay that way; and others may even start large and get smaller. But even if they do not alter in size and shape over the years, what they do changes over time. Companies that begin by making one product branch out and make something else, or sell their existing product in a different market that requires people with different skills.

So organizations *evolve*. And the ones that you are now assessing, or perhaps are employed by, have evolved as the result of doing certain things and finding out what did or did not work. Although organizations come into being to fulfil particular purposes, they do not always start out with clearly defined methods for achieving them.

They often build upon existing practices in their industry and on the personal experience of their members. People will develop solutions to particular operational problems, some after much thought and rehearsal, others on the spur of the moment. They will share these solutions with other people inside the organization over a cup of coffee or in a formal training session.

In this way, organizations *learn* ways of coping with the situations that they meet most often, which develop into routines. Some routines may be written down and widely understood within the organization. The knowledge that they employ is explicit knowledge—it can be packaged and transferred easily. Other routines may have been built up over time from a variety of experiences, have never been written down and may not even be capable of being put into words. This is tacit knowledge.

Learning and knowledge are not just about internal problems and solutions. Organizations also learn about patterns in their environment. McDonald's has learnt what types of food are most in demand in particular seasons of the year and at particular times of day. British Airways has learnt, for each particular destination, when to expect surges of demand and what types of food to serve to cater for the cultural and religious preferences of its customers. H&M has learnt which colours and styles appeal to particular groups of consumers, and which to avoid in a particular market.

Sometimes, they have learnt about these things by thinking ahead—BA and McDonald's would both have been able to predict surges of demand in their home markets around the holiday seasons. However, to learn how to meet the dietary requirements of Muslim or Hindu customers, or about holiday periods in other parts of the world, they will have needed careful research, or may simply have learnt from making mistakes and then addressing the complaints.

1.4.2 **Organizational learning**

→ We explore organizational learning and the learning organization in Chapter 10.

Learning is not automatic. Some businesses learn only how to deal with a particular set of customers at a particular point in time, and then stop. This leaves them very vulnerable when the environment changes—when there is a recession, for example, or when customers suddenly insist upon being able to place their orders through the internet.

First, people must be able to gather data about what is going on in the organization and its environment. They then need to analyse the data for patterns that tell them something important about the organization's efficiency, or about customer behaviour. Effective learning thus requires sources, inside and outside the organization, from which to gather information, and the technology to process and distribute it.

For example, many airlines have set up code-sharing alliances with other airlines. Originally these alliances were simply a means of sharing flight codes, i.e. flight numbers, allowing passengers to move seamlessly from one airline to another when they were travelling on complex multi-stop journeys. Increasingly, however, the alliance partners now exchange much more than simple code-sharing data. British Airways' network now links the computer terminals in airports across the world with those of its oneworld alliance partners, its own central computers, and computerized air ticket reservation systems.

Information from all of these sources allows it to issue e-tickets and improve its operating efficiency and customer responsiveness.[11]

With time and effort this information can be turned into knowledge. British Airways' staff start to know what patterns of booking can be expected on a particular route at a particular time of year, which oneworld flights the passengers may want to connect to, and perhaps what meals the passengers are likely to prefer. This helps them to schedule the right aircraft at the right times, enhance the quality of their service, and also be alert to the implications if one of their alliance partners changes the times of a connecting flight.

For this kind of learning to occur, it is important that the organizational culture is favourable. People must be motivated to make the effort to gather data and convert them into information and knowledge. And if they are to make the effort, they need to be fairly confident that their colleagues will listen to what they have learnt, and want to share it. Without the right culture, individuals will be unable or unwilling to transfer their learning to colleagues, so that it will never become part of the organization's routines and so will never 'belong' to it rather than the employee.

1.4.3 Knowledge management

The effective use of data allowed British Airways to improve its operations to the benefit of both its own bottom-line profits and its customers. In this case raw data has been transformed into knowledge that has allowed the airline to change what it does and improve its competitive performance. How knowledge can be retained and used effectively throughout an organization has been the subject of much research in recent years, leading to a whole body of theory, loosely entitled knowledge management.

➜ We discuss knowledge management in Chapter 10.

Much of this theory has focused on the computerization of data, which is then widely accessible through the use of corporate databases. However, other aspects of this body of theory have focused on how people use knowledge, and the barriers that prevent this from happening effectively.

1.5 Organizations as bundles of resources

An important part of strategy theory in recent years has focused on how some firms appear able to out-perform some of their competitors, despite each having access in theory to the same supplies of raw materials and the same customer base. The differences in performance have been ascribed to the type and strength of the resources that a firm controls—a body of theory that is known as the resource-based view of the firm (RBV).

➜ We return to the resource-based view of the firm in more detail in Chapter 7.

There are a large number of things that can be described as resources. They include knowledge and routines as well as the perhaps more conventional ones like money, or physical artefacts such as buildings and plant. A key aspect of the resource-based view of the firm is that superior competitive performance comes from resources that are valuable to the paying customer, rare, and difficult to find substitutes for. Not all resources have these characteristics to the same extent. Those that give a firm the potential for exceptional performance over the long term are termed strategic resources; those that a firm has to have simply to compete in an industry, are threshold resources. These resources can be grouped into six main categories:

1. Physical assets
2. Financial assets
3. Human assets

4. Intellectual assets

5. Reputational assets

6. Relational resources

1.5.1 Physical assets

Most organizations acquire physical locations, such as offices, laboratories, and factories, together with the furniture, computers, and other equipment that go inside them. Many of these resources will simply be the usual things that organizations need to stay in business.

More interesting to the strategist are the rarer ones, such as specialized equipment or important locations for retail stores, which can give an organization the edge over its competitors. British Airways' slots at Heathrow Airport, which give it the right to take off or land at popular times of the day, can be considered examples of this kind of resource. Of course, a take-off slot is not a 'physical' resource, like a building, but, for strategic purposes, a slice of time (the ownership of a time-slot at an airport) can be considered in the same way as a slice of space (the ownership of a piece of land).

1.5.2 Financial assets

One of the rewards of success can be strong cash flow and cash reserves. These give organizations the ability to survive temporary setbacks, such as downturns in demand or strategic mistakes. They also enable them to purchase other types of resource if needed, or to launch lawsuits or takeover bids against awkward competitors.

1.5.3 Human assets

It is a cliché, echoed in many company reports, that an organization's most important resource is its people. Like most clichés, it contains an element of truth. Machines cannot work without people to design, operate, and maintain them. Learning cannot take place unless the people have the intelligence and the skills to use the information. No organizational culture can take hold unless the people are susceptible to the type of motivation that the organization favours.

1.5.4 Intellectual assets

Intellectual resources are based upon the organization's knowledge, and can be manifested as patents, research programmes, and various types of intellectual property. Knowledge can also show up more subtly within capabilities and competences—things that an organization knows how to do, which make a difference to its ability to do business. For example, Sony has the capability consistently to produce innovative electronics products.

Many contemporary theorists believe that intellectual resources are the most important source of enduring competitive advantage. British Airways flies the same aircraft as many of its competitors, but the one thing that has historically distinguished it from most of them is its capability to deliver good, consistent in-flight service.

1.5.5 Reputation

As a result of their capabilities, organizations may build a reputation. This may be a brand built deliberately, using market campaigns such as McDonald's Ronald McDonald promotion. Or it may arise from word-of-mouth as a result of good products or excellent service.

Reputation can be important in giving organizations access to sources of finance or to good staff. In a competitive industry, it can be useful to have a reputation as the kind of company that will fight back if provoked.

1.5.6 Relational resources

Not all resources reside within a single organization, and those that cross organizational boundaries are increasingly important. BA's relationships with its partners in oneworld are crucial in enabling it to compete effectively with Lufthansa and its fellow members of the Star Alliance. If you look back to Real-life Application 1.2, you will see that competition between H&M and Zara is not just a two-firm affair. It is more useful to think of it as between H&M and its supplier partners on the one hand, and Zara together with its supplier network on the other. British Airways and H&M can look upon these relationships with these partners as resources in their own right.

It is not just formalized and contractual relationships that can be resources, however. Less formal relationships can also be crucial, particularly in a country such as China, where they have a special name, 'guanxi'. Organizations may have well-developed understandings with their governments or local administrations that give them a degree of influence that their competitors must try to match. Many airlines have benefited from measures taken by their national governments to keep them from going bankrupt, or to make it difficult for competitors to gain a foothold in a key hub.

1.5.7 The durability of resources

Not all resources retain their value over time. Some, for example reputation, can be quite durable. Sony's reputation for quality and innovation in laptop computers and televisions is unsurpassed, and it would probably take a succession of disasters over a long period of time for this to be damaged. IBM was 'fundamentally rocked' by changes in the way that customers used and purchased computers in the early 1990s, and recorded a record loss of $8 billion in 1993,[12] but its reputation as a supplier of quality computing solutions remained extremely high, and was a major factor in its subsequent revival.

However, some resources may lose value over time:

- *The environment is likely to change.* New technologies will appear, customer tastes and needs will change, and new competitors may enter the fray. These changes may threaten the organization's existing sources of advantage. The value of McDonald's carefully honed ability to produce hamburgers quickly and reliably has been diminished by changing consumer tastes: an increasing desire to eat foods with less salt, saturated fat, and refined carbohydrates. McDonald's has made some changes to its product ranges and advertising, but it does not as yet have the same dominance with these new products that it enjoys with burgers.

- *Competitors are not stupid.* They will be looking at ways to copy and improve upon the strategies that a successful organization has followed. Unless something about a firm's resources makes them distinctive and difficult to imitate, any advantage that they confer is likely to be short-lived. Samsung, a Korean competitor in the consumer electronics industry, has developed competences in innovation that some observers rank alongside Sony's, and a reputation to match.[13]

Therefore, a great deal of emphasis is placed by some theorists upon innovation as a means of anticipating environmental change and ensuring that resources can be adapted.

1.6 **Organizations as collections of people**

It should by now be clear that organizations are not homogeneous; they vary widely in what they do, how they are managed, and how they are regulated. Why people work in one type of organization or another also varies widely. Entrepreneurs set up firms to exploit an underdeveloped business niche. Others set up firms to provide a living and employment for themselves and their families. Yet others wish to work voluntarily to help others.

They also vary widely in the size and scope of their activities. Some tiny businesses may employ no more than the family members, while others, as we have seen, may be very large multinational conglomerates. The thing that is common to all, is that they are social systems, run by and for people with ambitions that they look to the organization to help them fulfil, or at least not to block. And understanding how people behave and influence what their organizations do is fundamental to understanding how strategy happens.

These people have the usual spread of human strengths, frailties, and peculiarities. They have reserves of energy and creativity that the organization can tap, but they are limited in their attention span and in their capacity to absorb and process information. They may also, on a bad day or in the wrong environment, be apathetic or demotivated. They form relationships with each other and with users and suppliers—friendships, dislikes, sometimes even romances. These personal relationships have important consequences. They shape the way in which different parts of an organization work (or fail to work) together, and decisions about which firms they will buy from or collaborate with.

1.6.1 **Stakeholders**

→ Methods of identifying stakeholders and assessing their influence are discussed in Sections 2.7 and 16.2.2.

All the people in an organization, and most of those who interact with it, are stakeholders—a concept we introduced in Section 1.1.4. Stakeholders shape what an organization does. They set its objectives and the yardsticks that are used to assess their success or failure—see Table 1.2 for examples. Different stakeholder groups can also be a powerful influence on the extent to which the organization can change its strategy.[14]

a. Internal stakeholders

In businesses where the owners or founders are in charge, they are usually the dominant stakeholders. In most public sector organizations, the owner, in this case the government,

Table 1.2 Examples of stakeholders

Internal stakeholders	External stakeholders	Mixed internal and external stakeholders
Owners/founders	Users of products and services	Unions
Managers	Customers	Employees' families
Staff	Distributors	Communities where the organization is based
Board of directors	Suppliers	Network partners
	Bankers Shareholders Investment fund managers Pension fund trustees Regulatory bodies Governments	Franchisees

has a great deal of influence. In larger concerns, it is common for there to be a variety of distinct stakeholder groups, such as the different types of staff working in the various divisions and functions, each with differing views and aspirations. The effective management of these different viewpoints is an important strategic challenge.

b. External stakeholders

Attitudes to other outside stakeholders vary from country to country. The traditional western attitude to *suppliers* has been to seek the cheapest source and not to let long-standing relationships stand in the way of getting the lowest quote. This attitude has softened as Japanese companies, notably automobile manufacturer Toyota, have shown how long-term collaborative relationships can lead to better quality and lower costs. McDonald's has strong links with its suppliers of key inputs such as French fried potatoes. British Airways has been involved in helping its main aircraft supplier, Boeing, to design a new generation of airliners.

The relative importance of financial stakeholders, such as banks and shareholders, also differs between countries. In Anglo-Saxon cultures, shareholders are held, as the owners of a company, to be the most important stakeholders of all. Other models of capitalism start out from the view that companies exist for the benefit of the societies that they belong to, and give unions and employees legal rights to consultation on key decisions or representation on a supervisory board. Under any model of capitalism, there is a risk that managers may try to divert the firm's resources for their own benefit. Systems of 'corporate governance' have been developed to ensure that firms are run for the benefit of the proper stakeholders, whether they be shareholders alone or some wider group.

But those providing the finance are not the only significant external stakeholders. Also important are an organization's users and customers, on whom it depends for survival.

➜ Different attitudes to financial stakeholders, and different forms of corporate ownership and governance, are reviewed in Chapter 2.

c. Mixed internal and external stakeholders

Some stakeholders, while not really part of the organization, may nevertheless have strong personal links with its members, which give them an interest in its affairs. Unions can be influential in some countries and firms, though they have lost power in Anglo-Saxon cultures over the last 20 years. Where a company is a major local employer, it can face strong pressure from its community not to reduce its staffing levels and to contribute time and money to its neighbourhood. Sometimes the pressure is in the other direction. A number of European airports offered a variety of inducements to Ryanair and other low-cost carriers to use them as a hub. Landing fees were reduced or waived altogether, office space was offered at low rates, and upfront payments offered for each route opened. In doing so, they hoped not just to generate revenue from people using the airports, but bring tourists to their region and make themselves attractive to other airlines.[15]

Other examples of mixed stakeholders occur in organizations that have developed as networks, such as Toyota in Japan. Here, it is difficult to draw a neat boundary to show which stakeholders are 'inside' the organization and which are 'outside'. For example, many companies even outside Japan nowadays have strong relationships with other independent companies. Although they are all separate entities, they are nonetheless dependent on one another for supplies of raw materials or specialist technology. In these cases it is hard to say whether they are insider stakeholders or outside ones.

1.6.2 Stakeholder power and politics

Because different stakeholder groups in organizations often have different interests, there will sometimes be tension between them. Such tension can be destructive, but it can also stimulate creativity and help the organization to develop. These tensions are resolved through political processes (sometimes called micro-politics to distinguish them from governmental politics), which are an important influence on strategic management and the decisions that strategy-makers take. Decisions will depend upon how much information the decision-makers have at their disposal, how well the different arguments are presented, and the decision-makers' desire to further their personal interests.[16] Decision-makers may also be influenced by their past experiences (see Section 1.2.3). They may be more inclined to listen to people from parts of the company where they themselves have spent a substantial part of their career. They may be influenced by sentimental attachments, or because those people know how to put their arguments in language which will appeal to the decision-maker. Some of these considerations are illustrated in Real-life Application 1.4.

Real-life Application 1.4 Stakeholders, power, and strategy

a. British Airways and aircraft

For many years, British Airways has bought aeroplanes from Boeing, the US manufacturer that was the market leader in commercial aircraft for over a decade. Boeing's aircraft have an excellent reputation, and there are good arguments for sourcing from a single manufacturer, since it saves on the costs of spares and training. However, the European Commission has been a strong lobbyist on behalf of Boeing's main rival, Airbus Industrie, a company that was formed from aerospace firms from four different European countries. In July 1998, British Airways announced its decision to purchase aircraft from Airbus for the first time. The quality of the planes obviously influenced its decision, but it is entirely possible that British Airways also wanted to create a good impression with the European Commission, which was due that same month to announce its decision on whether to permit BA to set up a strategic alliance with American Airlines, the largest US carrier, and the terms it would demand for allowing the alliance.

In fact, during the last decade, Airbus has steadily gained market share at Boeing's expense. In 2003, Airbus took more orders than Boeing, the fourth time in five years that it had achieved this, and in 2004, overtook its rival as the world's largest manufacturer of commercial aircraft measured by numbers of aircraft actually delivered. As of 31 December 2005, the two firms were vying strongly for industry leadership. Boeing led on new orders, with 58 per cent of the estimated $144 billion of new orders in 2005, compared with 42 per cent for Airbus. In terms of actual sales in 2005, it is likely that Airbus is still ahead.[17] And Airbus assessed its performance as 'continuing its industry leadership in terms of market share, deliveries, order intake and profitability'.[18]

How much of this performance is due to the quality of the aircraft, and how much to the influence of government over their former or current nationally owned flag carriers, such as Lufthansa, KLM/Air France, and BA, is a moot point. Orders have also come in from airlines such as Emirates, Qantas, Singapore Virgin Atlantic, and Korean Air, suggesting that the quality of the aircraft is the key issue. But in October 2004, Boeing registered a complaint with the World Trade Organization (WTO) claiming that European governments have given a huge amount of financial support to aid Airbus' fight to take market share from Boeing. The European Union responded with a similar complaint to the WTO, claiming that Boeing had benefited for many years from unfair tax breaks and development funding from the US government.[19]

Both sides have good reason to argue their case. A contract to buy Airbus planes was a major discussion point during a trip to France in July 2004 by the Turkish prime minister Recep Tayyip Erdoğan. Turkey has received the backing of the French government for Turkey's entry to the European Union. Some commentators have suggested that this is no coincidence, although Airbus denied this.[20] The French government part-owns Airbus Industrie via its holding of shares in EADS, which in turn owns 80 per cent of Airbus Industrie.[21] On the other side, in 1998 commercial jets accounted for nearly 85 per cent of Boeing's revenue. By 2003, 54 per cent came from military contracts, such as aerial refuelling tankers. In January 2004, an article in the *Economist* claimed that in a 'blatant attempt to curry favour with the British government', Boeing said that if it won a contract to supply military tankers, it would increase the civil sub-contracting work for wing manufacturing that it already places with BAE.[22] At the time of writing, many commentators believe that it is quite possible that this dispute may develop into a full-blown trade war between the EU and the USA.

b. Volkswagen

Volkswagen (VW) is a German car maker, whose marques include the iconic Beetle. In 2005 it was hit by a series of sex and corruption scandals and declining profits, and, to compound its woes, fell to near the bottom of a poll which measured brands by quality.[23] ➜

The New Beetle

11/05 www.volkswagenpressoffice.co.uk
For more information call 01908 601187

© Copyright free for editorial purposes only

Press and Public Relations

Volkswagen's marques include the iconic Beetle. *Volkswagen*

➡ In July 2005, Peter Hartz, VW's personnel director and a friend of Germany's then chancellor, Gerhard Schröder, resigned over allegations of the misuse of company money in his department. It was said that this money had been used to attempt to influence worker representatives on VW's supervisory board, by, for example, providing them with prostitutes and luxury foreign travel.[24]

Some have suggested that VW's problems lie with Germany's system of 'co-determination', under which companies with more than 2,000 workers must draw at least half of their supervisory board members either from the workforce or from trade unions. As VW has over 300,000 employees it has to have seven members from the workforce and three from the unions on its 21-member board. As two further board members are political appointees, those who are there to represent private shareholders are outnumbered.[25]

Critics of this system say that such co-determinism can lead to bosses failing to take the tough measures necessary to improve a company's performance, such as sacking poorly performing staff or shutting down inefficient factories, but which may alienate the board's worker or union representatives. And—as was alleged in VW's case—it may tempt managers to try to buy their support.

The counter-argument is made by those who suggest that problems are less likely to materialize if all stakeholders have a real say in what goes on in an organization.[26]

1.6.3 The influences on behaviour in organizations

The interplay of power and politics can result in strategic decisions that seem irrational to an outside observer. Such decisions may, however, make perfect sense to people who are conditioned to the way in which the organization sees the world. It is important to keep this in mind when considering some of the economic models that you will meet later in this book. We examine the extent to which strategies can be considered to be rational in Theoretical Debate 1.1.

Theoretical Debate 1.1 Rationality and strategy

One of the most important differences of opinion in the strategy literature relates to the extent to which strategic decisions can be considered to be rational—see Zouboulakis (2001) for an example.

At one level, this highlights a difference between the two different disciplines that lie at the heart of strategic management theory: economics and organization theory. Economists tend to play up the rational aspects of human thinking, and seek models that enable us to predict outcomes. Although organization theory also started out looking for predictable and regular patterns, modern organization theorists, whose roots tend to lie in sociology and anthropology, place more emphasis upon the unpredictable and idiosyncratic nature of human behaviour. The argument also has a geographic dimension. By and large, journals from the United States tend to favour the application of economic theory to strategy, and quantitative studies based on large samples of firms: a model of scholarship based upon economics. European journals tend to be more sympathetic to sociological and anthropological explanations of strategic behaviour, and to studies based on deeper observation of small numbers of firms.

This is, of course, a massive generalization: much of the sociological theory of organizations originates from the United States, as do the most influential studies of organizational power and politics. But it is nonetheless remarkable that almost all strategy textbooks written in the United States portray strategy development as a logical, linear process, and find little room for the analysis of power, politics, and culture, whereas many European and Canadian writers emphasize how politics can influence, or even derail, decision-making, and give cultural analysis a much more prominent role.

So, how different, and how compatible, are the two viewpoints? First of all, it needs to be emphasized that economists are not unanimous in their attitudes to rationality. One of the major economics-based theories of why organizations exist and are the shape they are, transaction cost theory, was developed by the American economist Oliver Williamson. Transaction cost theory is based on the idea that costs are incurred when organizations have to protect themselves against the possibility that the people that they conduct business with may attempt to take advantage of them. A fundamental element underlying this theory is that those attempting to protect themselves against this opportunistic behaviour, through the writing of legal contracts or setting in place protective measures, cannot fully anticipate all the possible behaviours of the parties concerned—that is, they are boundedly rational. Bounded rationality comes from the fact that individuals are necessarily limited in their ability to 'receive, store, retrieve and process information without error' (Williamson, 1973: 317). It has to be said that Williamson's interpretation of this term is somewhat different from other peoples', but it shows that

some economic reasoning is perfectly at home with imperfect rationality.

However, when it comes to the study of industries and markets, economic thinking largely ignores these imperfections, and assumes that individuals behave as rational profit maximizers with perfect information. The economist's excuse for sticking with these simplifying assumptions is that they have been shown to give such good predictions of how large populations of firms and people behave, on average, that there is no reason to use more detailed, and hence more complicated models.

This, however, is where a difference in emphasis between strategic management and economic theory becomes important. In strategic management, we are less interested in how the *average* person or organization is likely to behave than in understanding how *particular* groups of people behave in *specific* organizational contexts, and how that behaviour can influence success or failure in *particular* industries. For example, economic theory shows that in an oligopoly—an industry dominated by a few firms—the rational path for those firms to take is to collude, tacitly, to avoid price wars or other behaviour that would eventually reduce everyone's profits. And it may well be that, in most oligopolies, that is what happens. However, as we show in Chapter 3, there are also cases where, for various historical and cultural reasons, firms in oligopolies compete very fiercely on price and in other ways. The strategist has to recognize those situations and deal with them as they arise.

This leaves open the questions of how far managerial and firm behaviour will deviate from what economists see as rational, and for how long. Boundedly rational behaviour is not the same as irrational behaviour; managers are probably taking the most rational decisions they are capable of, given their perceptual limitations. But part of the problem is that economic rationality assumes a single, objectively best, choice, and influential theorists such as Herbert Simon (1947), and Richard Cyert and James March (1963) have suggested that there is no single right answer out there for us all to aspire to.

Moreover, a number of writers, some quite famous, have proposed, or observed deviations from the economist's ideal that go far beyond any presumption of rationality. Cohen et al. (1972) modelled decision-making in certain types of organization as essentially a random process in which people, problems, and solutions were shaken around in a 'garbage can' until they came together. Mezias and Starbuck (2003) observed some quite startling gaps in managers' knowledge of their own firms. Firms have blind spots that affect the way that they understand competitors' actions (Zajac and Bazerman, 1991) and may simply fail to act even when they know it would be rational to do so (Powell, 2004).   →

→ Meyer and Rowan (1977) put forward the idea that managers were primarily motivated by the desire for 'legitimation'—to be seen by others as good managers and human beings—so that they might pursue fashionable policies, that earned them kudos with their peers, even if such policies were not in the best economic interests of their organization. And researchers such as Jeffery Pfeffer (1992) and Andrew Pettigrew (1973) observed cases where strategic decisions seemed largely driven by micro-political processes, which allowed powerful individuals to direct resources to their own parts of the organization, and increase their own influence.

So far, no researcher has found an organization that behaves in quite the random fashion that Cohen et al. discussed. However, there is no doubt that legitimation, politics, and power play a role in decision-making, and there are cases of firms in which decisions taken on those grounds were not the ones that were best for the firm's long-term economic welfare. But do these factors *systematically* lead to irrational decisions? If, by pursuing policies that make the organization look legitimate in the eyes of finan-cial institutions or governments, the firm can gain access to funds or contracts, then this may be as rational a decision as one aimed at lowering costs or increasing market share. While some theorists undoubtedly see micro-politics as a wasteful activity that leads to poorer decisions, others see it as part and parcel of normal organizational life and one of the ways in which contrasting views are debated before decisions are made (see Eisenhardt and Zbaracki, 1992 and Theoretical Debate 17.1).

In the end, it comes down to a clash of views about what will happen over time. Economists believe that firms that do not take economically rational decisions will eventually be forced out of business or taken over by those that do, so that in the end rationality will prevail. Those on the other side believe that a combination of imperfect information, human weaknesses on the part of managers, and political behaviour in organizations is sufficient to prevent any firm from acting rationally for long enough for this competitive mechanism to take effect. Brunsson (1982) has gone so far as to argue that rationality actually gets in the way of effective decision-making.

Selection and socialization

What organizations do is shaped by the people that work there. Their selection is not a random process; employees are appointed because they have certain attributes that are believed to be valuable. Often managers will employ people with backgrounds and attitudes similar to their own because they believe that such people will fit in easily and will quickly become effective. Alternatively, through recruiting people with different ways of seeing the world, different skills, and different experiences, organizations can hope to learn new ways of approaching a problem. They also lose people: employees can move away from the area, they can be sacked, or they can simply decide that working there is not for them.

What people do is also the result of socialization processes: the ways in which new employees learn what they can and cannot do. Observing how existing employees themselves behave, and learning through trial and error what behaviour they will tolerate are examples of these processes. People also learn about past experiences of what works and what doesn't—whether this takes place in formal training sessions or simply around the coffee machine. The passing on of traditional ways of doing things and the telling of stories about successes and failures make it likely that over time people in organizations will develop similar world views and think about things in a similar way.

Together, these socialization, selection, and retention processes, along with the experience that employees gather along the way, shape behaviours. Over time, repeated behaviour patterns emerge that are distinctive—no two organizations' patterns are precisely alike. They are most often known as routines, a term which covers a wide range of behaviours by both individuals and groups (see Real-life Application 1.5). Other terms you may encounter are rituals (regular behaviours that do not specifically contribute to the organization's operations) and institutions (long-standing repeated activities). These ingrained ways of doing things distinguish one organization from another and from random collections of people, and persist even though the employees that developed them may leave and be replaced by new faces.[27]

Real-life Application 1.5   Examples of routines

Sony and H&M's designers both have routines for developing new products. These include the development of prototypes that can be used to experiment with certain aspects of functionality or look, procedures for testing them with retailers or members of the general public, such as fashion shows, and routines for selecting which designs should go into production—meetings, for example, where the merits of each option are discussed and production budgets agreed.

The factory workers in those same companies, or their suppliers, have routines that enable them to manufacture products quickly and with minimum waste. These procedures, and the rules which govern them, allow the product to be transferred on a moving production line from one specialist worker to another, and by scheduling the movement of raw materials and components allow them to arrive when they are needed at precise times and locations.

McDonald's has developed a series of finely tuned kitchen routines to make sure that freshly prepared food is ready when the people at the counter call for it, with minimum delay even during busy periods, but also keeping waste as low as possible. These routines are the same whichever McDonald's you go into worldwide.

British Airways' ground crew have routines for checking in baggage, for getting people on to the aircraft and settled in their seats, for informing passengers of the safety arrangements on the aircraft, for loading food for the flight and baggage into the hold, and for refuelling the aircraft as quickly as possible. The flight crew have comprehensive routines for checking that the aircraft is safe to fly. The cabin crew use very carefully developed routines for serving food and drinks to a plane-load of passengers—quite tricky to fit in on a short flight!

1.6.4 Bounded rationality

An organization's routines are simplifying mechanisms—they spare employees the effort of deciding from scratch what to do at every point in their working life. This need to simplify a complex world also leads to another important influence on what people do. Even the most gifted employees are fallible human beings. They cannot process all available information and reach a perfectly rational decision. They are too busy, or too tired, to deal with all the stimuli hitting their various senses, and to think deeply about each and every decision. They are predisposed to accept information that reinforces their view of the world and their existing patterns of behaviour. Conversely, they tend to filter out information that challenges their beliefs and behaviour patterns.

In deciding what they need to notice, people give priority to what has been important in the past, and devise simplifying rules (known as heuristics) based on their previous experience, to help them to decide what to do. Rather than optimizing—trying to reach the very best decision in the circumstances—people satisfice, a word that combines satisfy and suffice: they settle for the first proposal that appears to give an acceptable outcome. For example, rather than maximizing profits, managers simply look for a way of meeting acceptable profit targets. This kind of decision-making is said to be *boundedly rational*.

Bounded rationality provides the academic underpinning for huge tracts of strategy theory that we shall return to in this book, such as those relating to strategic decision-making, organizational change, as well as transaction and agency costs.[28]

Under ideal circumstances, heuristics, satisficing, and routines allow people to focus their attention and energy on new and important problems, rather than on mundane ones for which acceptable solutions already exist. However, sometimes managers come to rely too much upon familiar decision rules and routines, and will ignore evidence that they are no

Bounded rationality
A reasoning process determined—or *bounded*—by factors such as preconceptions, or lack of time or information, which make particular ways of problem-solving much more likely than others.

longer relevant. This can lead to an organization becoming misaligned with its environment if it changes, a phenomenon called strategic slip or drift.[29] It may take an outsider, who does not share the same experiences, to perceive things in a new way and bring about the necessary change.

a. Experience, upbringing, and emotions

People's upbringing and past experience are important influences that shape the kinds of decisions that they will prefer.[30] Younger people, and those with higher levels of education, have been shown, on average, to have a greater liking for entrepreneurial, innovative strategies than others. Managers with finance backgrounds are likely to pursue unrelated diversification or conglomerate strategies; managers with marketing or production backgrounds are likely to pursue vertical integration or single-business strategies; and managers who have been with their firms a relatively short time are likely to choose diversification strategies. Managers are also likely to incline towards re-using strategies that have worked for them in the past.

→ We discuss diversification in Chapter 5, vertical integration in Chapter 6, and innovation in Chapter 10.

More recently, there has been an increasing awareness that other factors, such as emotions, can play an important part in strategic processes.[31] The example of Enron discussed in What Can Go Wrong 1.1 is a good instance of where emotions and other psychological processes can shape organizational behaviour—in Enron's case with disastrous results.

b. Belief systems and organizational culture

People tend to recruit and mix with like-minded individuals. Socialization processes such as training, the passing on of traditional ways of doing things, and the telling of stories about successes and failures also ensure that over time people in organizations develop similar world views and think about things in a similar way.

Organizational culture
Culture is 'how things are done around here'. It is what is typical of the organization, the habits, the prevailing attitudes, the grown-up pattern of accepted and expected behaviour.[32]

Thus, over time, employees acquire a set of values and assumptions about the world, their industry, and their organization. This belief system or 'paradigm' forms a standard against which all new activities are measured, consciously or unconsciously, to determine how credible they are, or indeed whether they are to be considered at all. The belief system is a central element in an organization's culture.

The belief system is shaped by a variety of factors (see Table 1.3):

- The company's leaders, past and present, have a pervasive and lasting influence on what the organization does and how it does it.[33]
- Events in the history of the organization will shape how it responds to current and future events.
- The industrial environment in which it developed will encourage certain sorts of behaviours and attitudes from the organization's employees.
- The national environment in which the organization developed will also shape the attitudes and behaviours of the people within it.

Culture is fundamental to understanding organizations—to quote Karl Weick, a famous organization theorist, 'Organizations do not have cultures—they are cultures.'[34] It affects the activities of an organization's staff and its strategies in many ways:

→ We look at ways of analysing how culture contributes to a firm's competitiveness in Chapter 8, and the way it affects an organization's capacity to change in Chapter 16.

- It shapes how its members behave and conditions their attitude towards others—colleagues, employees, and stakeholders—both inside and outside.[35]
- It encourages certain sorts of behaviour, for example the ethical stance that the organization adopts, that influence the purchasing decisions of customers, and the extent to which suppliers, customers, and financiers will co-operate with the organization.

Table 1.3 Four companies, four cultures

	Sony	McDonald's	H&M	British Airways
Leaders	Both Ibuka and Morita shaped Sony as an innovator. Morita instilled a regard for the importance of good marketing	Ray Kroc laid down basic values of Quality, Service, Cleanliness, Value which are still central to McDonald's culture and strategy	H&M's founder Erling Persson created a company that explicitly espouses social responsibility. Company literature often refers to H&M's core business concept of 'fashion and quality at the best price'	Lord King and Colin Marshall, Chairman and CEO after privatization, shaped BA's pugnacious attitude to competition and its marketing-driven culture
History	The loss of control of the standard for video cassettes to arch-rival Matsushita almost certainly engendered in Sony a fear of losing control over future standards, and contributed to Sony's desire to acquire CBS and Columbia			BA's history as the UK's flag carrier has shaped its attitude towards the UK government, which it hopes will fight its cause with other companies and governments[a]
Industry	The virtues of innovation and technological progress are deeply ingrained in many consumer electronics firms		The idea of constant updating of product lines and appearing fresh and up-to-the-minute is central to the mindset of H&M and its competitors	Many airlines drew flight staff from the military. This is reflected in the airline's uniforms and job titles of the flight crew
National culture	Typically Japanese in the long-term commitment it gives and expects from employees (though atypical in other respects)	Very American in the values it portrays to outside world and its aggressive, capitalist stance to competition	Sweden, where H&M was founded, is famous for its national culture of social inclusion, equality, and its (supposedly) feminine values of caring and concern for others. It has also produced more multinational firms per head of population than any other country	

Notes
a See for example, BA 2007 Annual Report, p. 4

Second, culture shapes the *motivation* of people. In order for it to prosper, the people within need to be motivated to put the organization's interests alongside (or even ahead of) their own. People can be given incentives with high commission on sales or with share options to behave in certain ways. They can be coaxed through fear of losing their jobs, or of ridicule from their bosses or fellow workers. But there are numerous case studies suggesting that getting them to share the organization's values and identify with its culture has the greatest impact on organizational effectiveness.

The third important way in which culture influences strategy is by affecting organizations' capacities to react and change. People's patterns of behaviour, and the ways in which they view the world, develop gradually over time, and may alter only slowly. If managers are confronted with a problem, then the solutions they tend to favour are conditioned by experience of what has worked in the past. To use the examples in Table 1.3, if confronted with a competitive problem, Sony or H&M might tend to look for a solution based upon product innovation or design, while McDonald's and British Airways might favour aggressive pricing or marketing. The stronger the organization's culture, the more difficult it can be for people to force themselves to consider new types of strategy. However, new strategies may be needed if, for example, new technologies are developed or economic conditions change.

1.7 How the five views of the organization interact

The five views of the organization—as a legal entity, an economic actor, an accumulation of knowledge and learning, a bundle of resources, and a collection of people—are not alternatives, but complementary. If you want fully to understand an organization's strategy, and why it succeeds or fails, you need to understand all five aspects, and how they interact.

In order for an organization to be operationally viable at any point in time, it must be a viable economic actor, otherwise its controlling stakeholders will close it down or sell it off. In order to do this, it needs to deploy its resources within its value chain so as to generate value for its users. In this way, it will generate financial resources and a good reputation.

The legal form adopted does not directly influence its ability to generate value. Well-run organizations can do this whether they are privately owned, publicly quoted, or part of the public sector. However, at certain stages in their development, firms may find it easier to gain access to financial resources if they are quoted on a stock market—if they are prepared to bear the administrative costs of reporting to shareholders.

For an organization to *continue* to be viable as the environment *changes* over time, it must adapt or innovate. This implies that it must learn effectively, so that it can build new capabilities and adjust its value chain to the changing requirements of its users. Information must be brought in, processed, absorbed, and distributed as knowledge. This in turn makes the architecture important.

Underlying all of this is the way the organization operates as a social system. If this social system fails, then it may frighten away its customers and its staff, or spend too much time on internal conflict to fulfil its original purpose. If it works well, then the people who encounter the organization will enjoy the experience and it is likely to prosper.

If people are motivated to further the aims of the organization, then they are more likely to make the effort to ensure that products and services are delivered on time and at the desired level of quality. Less well-motivated people take fewer pains to achieve top-quality results, and leave urgent jobs unfinished at the end of the working day.

The way it functions as a social system will also affect how well an organization learns. People who like and believe in their organization are more likely to make the effort to ensure that information is accurate and reaches the person who can use it most effectively. In a poorly functioning social system, information is used as a political weapon by one department against another.

The final interaction relates to an organization's ability to change. Nearly all writers on the topic seem to agree that this is hard to do. Political manoeuvring to preserve the interests of powerful stakeholders can slow down change processes. Sometimes, it can require the threat of bankruptcy or takeover to overcome these factors. Organizations that are effective learning systems suffer less from this than others, because they become accustomed to a constant rhythm of gradual adaptation.

Here, the legal form of the company can be a consideration. Not-for-profit and public sector organizations may have many powerful stakeholders—governments, donors, sponsors, public users of the services—that need to be satisfied before change can occur. And businesses that are shielded from the threat of takeover, because they are owned by the

➜ We examine the challenges of effecting change in organizations in Chapter 16.

state or by a small group of private individuals—perhaps a family—may be able to ignore pressures for change. This is not always a bad thing, because sometimes such firms are able to persist with a far-sighted strategy that only pays off after a long delay—probably too long for the average stock market investor. But on the other hand, these organizations may end up ignoring signals from the market place, indicating that their products and services are not truly competitive, that a more accountable set of managers would have had to respond to.

What Can Go Wrong? 1.1 The influences on organizational (mis)behaviour in Enron

Enron had, until its spectacular failure, been one of the USA's most successful companies; the fifth largest, and *Fortune* magazine's 'most admired company' six years in a row. It was the world's biggest energy trader and a major player in the global oil and gas industry. During the 1990s it had embarked on an ambitious series of acquisitions into, for example, water utility companies and broadband telephony. However, in 2001, Enron filed for bankruptcy—one of the world's largest—and many of its directors have subsequently been prosecuted for serious crimes such as fraud and false accounting.[36]

Part of this problem was an over-strong focus on Enron as an economic actor. It was a company where fear of failing to produce regularly increasing profits for its major shareholders led senior managers to embark on the unethical actions that helped to contribute to its collapse. Its 2000 annual report describes the company as being 'laser-focused' on earnings per share (EPS—a widely-used stock market performance indicator) and intending to continue its policy of achieving a strong earnings performance. EPS, however, is also quite easy to manipulate, and hence Enron's managers began to look for ways—some of them illegal—that would make it look like its EPS was increasing. Chuck Watson, the CEO of Dynegy, a company that at one point planned to take over Enron after its bankruptcy appeared inevitable, suggested that Enron's managers refused to be open about its financial position, even to its potential rescuer.[37]

And this refusal to be open shows Enron to have been a very 'human' place in which power, emotions, and bounded rationality also appear to have been important influences on what it did. It seems to have been a highly charged and emotional workplace—in all sorts of ways. It was clearly an exciting and motivating place to work for much of its history, but a number of articles about its collapse also describe a culture of fear and intimidation, in which there was 'widespread knowledge of the company's tenuous finances, but no one felt confident enough to confront [the company's president Jeffrey] Skilling or other senior officials, about it'.[38] Potential whistleblowers failed to report their concerns to outside authorities because of fear that they would lose their jobs. The *Economist* also talks of Mr Skilling allegedly disliking criticism.[39] Being 'unable to take the heat', he resigned in August 2000.

An American lawyer and writer, John Cohan, has discussed[40] the 'failure of knowledge conditions', or what he calls 'information myopia', that arose from the Enron 'implosion'—a problem of knowledge-resource management which itself has an emotional component. He describes Kenneth Lay, the company's chairman who is said to have been unaware of all the financial details of the company, as being optimistic about the company's performance, even at the time that he was being confronted with evidence that things were going seriously wrong.[41] In a large hierarchical firm, senior managers are dependent for information about lower-level dealings on filtered information that is provided by trusted staff. If this is inaccurate, and worse, is inappropriately filtered through heightened emotions, there is clear potential for poor strategic decision-making.

● CHAPTER SUMMARY

A strategy is the manner in which a social system—an organization—develops and uses resources to achieve its economic and other goals.

This chapter has introduced you to five different ways of thinking about organizations—as legal entities, economic actors, accumulations of knowledge and learning, bundles of resources, and collections of people. Each of these interacts and overlaps with the others, and will need to be taken into account when strategies are developed.

Organizations have legally defined forms. Most of the ones that we discuss in this book are firms, but others include charities, or not-for-profits, and government or public sector organizations, such as hospitals or universities.

These legal entities function as economic actors. All organizations have to satisfy the financial objectives of stakeholders, although what these are can vary widely. Companies are likely to be required to generate profits for their shareholders, while public sector organizations may be required to spend no more than the budget the government allocates them. In order to be economically viable all organizations have to have a value chain that allows inputs to be sourced, transformed into finished products or services, and distributed to customers or users, at a cost lower than customers or funders will be willing to pay for the finished output, in an environment that may be dynamic or stable.

Whether this is achieved effectively and efficiently is also a measure of the amount of transaction and agency costs accrued as the result of administering and coordinating activities, and protecting the organization against unscrupulous behaviour. The organization's architecture—the structures, control systems, and information systems that influence the way in which people gather information and are motivated to use it—has a strong influence on such behaviour. Different organizational priorities, such as local responsiveness to market demands versus the need for economies of scale, will result in different types of structure.

Over time, organizations accumulate knowledge and learning. They have learned what works and does not work; and as a result they develop knowledge about the best way of doing things. Often this learning and knowledge leads to the accumulation of resources, of which there are six main types:

- physical assets like freehold sites in the centre of towns or airport landing slots;
- financial assets—cash flow and cash reserves;
- human assets—people with rare skills;
- intellectual resources, such as brands or the patents that come out of R&D labs. These are what the organization *has*, but other resources are what it *does*—competences and capabilities that its staff collectively demonstrates extraordinarily well;
- reputation with key stakeholders, and brands;
- relationships with partner organizations, governments, and other key stakeholders.

The type, strength, and durability of an organization's resources are major factors in its long-term success.

Organizations, crucially, are also collections of people, who come together to interact, and achieve objectives that they could not achieve by themselves. Everyone that works in an organization is a stakeholder, but this classification also includes people who may have something to say about how it is run—they may be the firm's neighbours, customers, suppliers, or government. Stakeholders vary in the amount of power they have. Some can have a considerable influence on what the organization does, and political manoeuvring between stakeholders has a strong impact on strategic decision-making.

Who chooses to work in an organization—and who is selected or allowed to work there—is an important factor in the development of its culture. Another is the socialization process that all new recruits go through. These result in behaviours that are characteristic of each organization, many of which occur on a regular basis. Because people are boundedly rational—they do not have the capacity to absorb and process all available information, and work out how to react to each new situation as it arises—together they develop routines for handling work situations, which become the basis of its resources and also its culture. These and other psychological features such as emotions shape the choices that managers make about what the organization should do, and which strategies to adopt.

 Online Resource Centre
www.oxfordtextbooks.co.uk/orc/haberberg_rieple

Visit the Online Resource Centre that accompanies this book to read more information relating to strategy and the organization.

● KEY SKILLS

The key skills you should have developed after reading this chapter are:

- the ability to utilize key elements of the vocabulary of strategy precisely and confidently;

- the ability to identify key elements of an organization's strategy—the industries in which it operates, the markets, customers, and users it is targeting, the key decisions it has taken about its value chain, the knowledge and other sources it has accumulated, and its main stakeholders;

- the ability to analyse how organizations develop over time and the effect that this has on how they are likely to perform in the future.

● REVIEW QUESTIONS

1. Greenpeace (<http://www.greenpeace.org>) is a campaigning not-for-profit organization whose main objective is to defend the environment. Who are its users? Who are its customers? What are its economic objectives? Is it possible to define its strategy in a way that makes financial or economic matters irrrelevant?

2. Which of the five views of organizations is the most important for the strategic manager? Which is the least important—and why?

3. Should an organization formulate its strategy as a reaction to its environment, or should it aim to use its resources to create an environment that is favourable to itself?

4. What can an organization do to extend the limits of its managers' bounded rationality? What would be the possible drawbacks of putting these ideas into practice?

5. Do strategies come about because of factors beyond any individual's control? If so, which factors are most important? Why? Can anything be done to change them?

● FURTHER READING

There are a few books whose authors, like us, encourage you to look at strategy and organizations from a variety of viewpoints. Among these, we would particularly recommend:

- Morgan, G. (2006). *Images of Organization*. Thousand Oaks, CA: Sage Publications. This book by a genuinely original thinker, is aimed at practitioners as well as students, and aims to stimulate creativity as well as insight.

- Ambrosini, V. and Jenkins, M. with Collier, N. (2007). *Advanced Strategic Management: A Multi-perspective Approach*. 2nd edition. Basingstoke: Palgrave MacMillan. A more scholarly work that invokes a number of theoretical lenses that can be used to understand strategy.

- Tsoukas, H. and Knudsen, C. (eds) (2005). *The Oxford Handbook of Organization Theory*. Oxford: Oxford University Press. This is designed more for researchers in organizations but is an excellent work of reference.

Alongside these, there are a number of books and articles on key elements of the theory we have reviewed in this chapter:

- Nonaka, I. and Takeuchi, H. (1995). *The Knowledge Creating Company: How Japanese Companies Create the Dynamics of Innovation*. Oxford: Oxford University Press. This book was a major influence in establishing the importance of knowledge in strategic management.

- Barney, J. B. (2001). 'Resource-based theories of competitive advantage: A ten-year retrospective on the resource-based view'. *Journal of Management*, 27(6): 643–50. An authoritative review of the role of resources in strategy by one of the most influential theorists in the field.

- Hodgkinson, G. and Sparrow, P. (2002). *The Competent Organization*. Buckingham: Open University Press. A comprehensive review of how managerial thinking processes affect organizations and strategies.

- Foss, N. (2003). 'Bounded rationality in the economics of organization: "Much cited and little used" '. *Journal of Economic Psychology*, 24(2): 245–64. A review of how the theory of bounded rationality has developed since its inception.

- Pfeffer, J. (1992). *Managing with Power: Politics and Influence in Organizations*. Boston, MA: Harvard Business School Press. A key book on power, and what it does to strategic decision-making.

- Starbuck, W. (2006) *Organizational Realities: Studies of Strategizing and Organizing*. Oxford: Oxford University Press. A collection of articles by one of the most original and provocative theorists and writers active in the field.

- Starbuck, W. (2007). 'Living in mythical spaces'. *Organization Studies*, 28(1): 21–5. A short piece by the same writer, in which he questions whether the whole idea of 'the organization' is anything more than a myth.

- March, J. (2006). 'Rationality, foolishness, and adaptive intelligence'. *Strategic Management Journal*, 27: 201–14. A discussion on the role of rationality in strategic thinking, by one of the deepest and most original thinkers in the field of management and organization studies. Note March's writing style—not a word is wasted.

● REFERENCES

Ashkanasy, N. M., Härtel, C. E. J., and Daus, C. S. (2002). 'Advances in organizational behavior: diversity and emotions'. *Journal of Management*, 28: 307–38.

Boeker, W. (1997). 'Strategic change: The influence of managerial characteristics and organizational growth'. *Academy of Management Journal*, 40/1: 152–70.

Brickson, S. (2007). 'Organizational identity orientation: the genesis of the role of the firm and distinct forms of social value'. *Academy of Management Review*, 32/3: 864–88.

Brunsson, N. (1982). 'The irrationality of action and action rationality: decisions, ideologies and organizational actions'. *Journal of Management Studies*, 19: 29–44.

Child, J. (1972). 'Organizational structure, environment and performance: the role of strategic choice'. *Sociology*, 6: 1–22.

Coff, R. (1999). 'When competitive advantage doesn't lead to performance: the resource-based view and stakeholder bargaining power'. *Organization Science*, 10/2: 119–213.

Cohan, J. A. (2002). ' "I didn't know" and "I was only doing my job": has corporate governance careened out of control? A case study of Enron's information myopia'. *Journal of Business Ethics*, 40: 275–99.

Cohen, M. D., March, J. G., and Olsen, J. P. (1972). 'A garbage can model of organizational choice'. *Administrative Science Quarterly*, 17: 1–25.

Crick, F. (1994). *The Astonishing Hypothesis: The Scientific Search for the Soul*. New York: Scribner.

Cyert, R. M., and March, J. G. (1963). *A Behavioral Theory of the Firm*. Englewood Cliffs, NJ: Prentice-Hall.

Daniels, K. (1998). 'Towards integrating emotions into strategic management research: trait affect and perceptions'. *British Journal of Management*, 9/3: 163–8.

Dawe, A. (1970). 'The two sociologies'. *British Journal of Sociology*, 21: 207–18.

Drennan, D. (1992). *Transforming Company Culture*. London: McGraw-Hill.

Economist, The (1998). 'Bertelsmann's Bismarck', 7 November: 103–4.

Economist, The (2005). 'An icon under fire—Volkswagen', 9 July: 54.

Eisenhardt, K. M. and Zbaracki, M. J. (1992). 'Strategic decision making'. *Strategic Management Journal*, 13: 17–37.

Fineman, S. (ed.) ([1993] 2000). *Emotions in Organizations*. 2nd edn. London: Sage.

Finkelstein, S. and Hambrick, D. C. (1996). *Strategic Leadership: Top Executives and their Effects on Organizations*. Minneapolis/St Paul: West.

Foss, N. (2003). 'Bounded rationality in the economics of organization: "Much cited and little used"'. *Journal of Economic Psychology*, 24/2: 245–64.

Gibbons, R. (2003). 'Team theory, garbage cans and real organizations: some history and prospects of economic research on decision-making in organizations'. *Industrial & Corporate Change*, 12/4: 753–87.

Goleman, D. (1995). *Emotional Intelligence: Why it Can Matter More than IQ*. New York: Bantam Books.

Hambrick, D. and Mason, P. (1984). 'Upper echelons: the organization as a reflection of its top managers'. *Academy of Management Review*, 9/3: 193–206.

Harris, L. C. and Ogbonna, E. (1999). 'The strategic legacy of company founders'. *Long Range Planning*, 32/3: 333–43.

Helfat, C. and Peteraf, M. (2003). 'The dynamic resource-based view: Capability lifecycles'. *Strategic Management Journal*, 24/10: 997–1010.

Hjelt, P. (2005). 'The world's most admired companies'. *Fortune* (Europe edition), 151/4.

Kassinis, G. and Vafeas, N. (2006). 'Stakeholder pressures and environmental performance'. *Academy of Management Journal*, 49/1: 145–59.

Kuvaas, B. and Kaufmann, G. (2004). 'Individual and organizational antecedents to strategic-issue interpretation'. *Scandinavian Journal of Management*, 20/3: 245–75.

March, J. G. (1991). 'How decisions happen in organizations'. *Human–Computer Interaction*, 6/2: 95.

Marshall, A. (1890). *The Principles of Economics*. London: Macmillan.

Meyer, J. W. and Rowan, B. (1977). 'Institutional organizations: formal structure as myth and ceremony'. *American Journal of Sociology*, 83: 340–63.

Mezias, J. and Starbuck, W. (2003). 'Studying the accuracy of managers' perceptions: The odyssey continues'. *British Journal of Management*, 14: 3–17.

Miles, R. E. and Snow, C. C. (1978). *Organizational Structure, Strategy, Process*. New York: McGraw Hill.

Mintzberg, H. and Westley, F. (2001). 'Decision making: it's not what you think'. *MIT Sloan Management Review*, 42/3: 89–93.

Morse, G. (2006). 'Decisions and desire'. *Harvard Business Review*, 84/1: 42, 44–51.

Olsen, J. P. (2001). 'Garbage cans, new institutionalism, and the study of politics'. *American Political Science Review*, 95/1: 191.

Pajunen, K. (2006). 'Stakeholder influences in organizational survival'. *Journal of Management Studies*, 43/6: 1261–88.

Pettigrew, A. (1973). *The Politics of Organisational Decision Making*. London, Tavistock.

Pfeffer, J. (1992). *Managing with Power: Politics and Influence in Organizations*. Boston, MA: Harvard Business School Press.

Powell, T. (2004). 'Strategy, execution and idle rationality'. *Journal of Management Research*, 4/2: 77–98.

Powell, W. W. and DiMaggio, P. J. (1991). Introduction. In Powell, W. W. and DiMaggio, P. J. (eds), *The New Institutionalism in Organizational Analysis*. Chicago: University of Chicago Press, 1–38.

Rivkin, J. (2000). 'Imitation of complex strategies'. *Management Science*, 46/6: 824–44.

Roome, N. and Wijen, F. (2006). 'Stakeholder power and organizational learning in corporate environmental management'. *Organization Studies*, 27/2: 235–63.

Schein, E. (1992). *Organizational Culture and Leadership*. 2nd edn. San Franciso: Jossey-Bass.

Simon, H. A. (1947). *Administrative Behavior*. New York: Macmillan.

Sterman, J., Henderson, R., Beinhocker, E., and Newman, L. (2007). 'Getting big too fast: strategic dynamics with increasing returns and bounded rationality'. *Management Science*, 53/4: 683–96.

Weick, K. (1983). 'Letters to Fortune'. *Fortune*, 14 November: 17.

Wiersema, M. and Bantel, K. (1992). 'Top management team demography and corporate strategic change'. *Academy of Management Journal*, 35: 91–121.

Williamson, O. (1973). 'Markets and hierarchies: some elementary considerations'. *The American Economic Review Papers and Proceedings of the Eighty-fifth Meeting of the American Economic Association*, 63/2: 316–25.

Zajac, E. and Bazerman, M. (1991). 'Blind spots in industry and competitor analysis: implications of interfirm (mis)perceptions for strategic decisions'. *Academy of Management Review*, 16/1: 37–56.

Zouboulakis, M. S. (2001). 'From Mill to Weber: the meaning of the concept of economic rationality'. *European Journal of the History of Economic Thought*, 8/1: 30–42.

End-of-chapter Case Study 1.1 Bertelsmann AG[42]

Bertelsmann is a privately owned company that is one of the world's largest media conglomerates. It has nearly 80,000 employees working for the 500 or so companies across 63 countries in its portfolio. Its divisions include RTL, Europe's top television and radio company; the world's biggest book-publishing group, Random House; Europe's top magazine publisher, Gruner & Jahr; one of the world's four major music companies, Sony BMG Music Entertainment; book and music clubs; and Arvato, a business services division that focuses on logistics and distribution, service centres, customer relationship management, storage, media production, and IT management.

Origins and early development

The firm started life in 1835 when Carl Bertelsmann established Bertelsmann House as a printing business in Gütersloh, a small town (population <100,000) in north-western Germany. The company's head office is still there. Early publications concentrated on religious texts, and the company's operations remained relatively modest (<400 employees) for the following 100 years. Reinhard Mohn, whose grandfather had married Carl's daughter, took over from his father Heinrich Mohn in 1947, and began to transform the small family firm. The younger Mohn's first strategic move was to start a 'Lesering', Germany's first book club. The book club and the sales that it generated drove the company's early growth during the 1950s. In the 1960s Dr Mohn took the first step in creating a media company by buying a controlling interest in UFA, a German TV/film production company. The 1970s saw further evidence of Mohn's media ambitions with the acquisition of Gruner & Jahr, a German magazine and newspaper company. In 1977, he took the company's interests outside Germany with the purchase of an American company, Bantam Books, and in 1979 the acquisition of Arista, a US record company.

Before retiring Reinhard Mohn ensured that the company would remain private by transferring around 70 per cent of his shares in the company to the specially created Bertelsmann Foundation, a non-profit organization that funds charitable works. It continues to own the majority of the shares to this day. In 1981, he stepped down as CEO, leaving Mark Wössner to carry on transforming the family concern into one of the world's biggest media and publishing conglomerates. Dr Wössner's reign lasted until October 1998, when he retired at the obligatory age of 60 to be replaced by Thomas Middelhoff, a 45-year-old.

Thomas Middelhoff challenges the status quo

Dr Middelhoff had huge ambitions for the company and made some spectacular deals to double Bertelsmann's turnover to around €20 billion per annum in the next four years. Industry peers described this period as 'audacious and innovative'.[43] Bertelsmann made €2.8 billion in January 2002 from selling its 50 per cent stake in AOL Europe back to AOL's parent company at the height of the internet bubble. But Middelhoff was also responsible for allying the company with Napster at the time that it was threatened with legal action from the five major record companies, including Bertelsmann's own BMG (prior to its 2004 merger with Sony). Dr Middelhoff's decision caused conflict with his own BMG executives, many of whom quit soon afterwards, citing 'strategic differences'.[44]

Although Dr Middelhoff was initially seen as 'a low-key administrator in the tradition of the Mohn family',[45] he soon gained a reputation as someone with a desire for a high profile. He once described himself as an American with a German passport who drew his inspiration from a US management style. But behind his back, his German colleagues were rather less keen on what they saw as his fondness for being photographed by the media.[46] His personal style did not help his relationship with key stakeholders such as the Mohn family, who still retained huge influence over the company through their shareholding and seats on the supervisory board. He was said to be confrontational with his senior managers and publicly criticized his own executives during the series of annual 'town hall meetings' which he held in an attempt to 'emotionally connect' with his firm's 25,000 employees.[47]

Dr Middelhoff also apparently got into trouble over his restructuring of the company.[48] Enshrined within Bertelsmann's ethos was a commitment to a decentralized structure. This went back many years to Reinhard Mohn's belief in the advantages of a corporation made up of independent entrepreneurs—the ➜

→ company's core values are described in its written constitution as 'decentralized, pluralistic and participatory'.[49] The result of translating these values into operating principles was a flat and decentralized organizational structure that conferred a wide degree of autonomy on to divisional managers, who were encouraged to behave like 'the owner of any mid-sized company'.[50] Each of the divisions could source their supplies from wherever they chose. Whilst they were encouraged to collaborate on specific projects, such co-operation was only entered into if both partners felt that the arrangement suited their individual business needs. At one time 35 per cent of BMG's CDs were produced by competitors. And when asked if he would promote one of BMG's artists, the head of the newspaper and magazine division said no, 'we do it only if it's interesting for our readers'.[51]

When Thomas Middelhoff arrived, he decided that more collaboration between the divisions was needed, particularly given the increasing convergence in media content. He had some success. In 2002, the US operations of Gruner & Jahr tried, unsuccessfully, to resist after being told they had to use Bertelsmann's own printer rather than their traditional supplier. In 1999, he set up a 'Corporate University' with the aim of encouraging cross-company learning and cooperation. Other initiatives included the Executive Network which links around 1,400 managers through interactive communication technologies.

However, other initiatives were more problematic. He created a seven-member Executive Council, which was to advise the eight-strong Vorstand, or management board. He created three new divisions: content, media services, and direct-to-consumer businesses, and appointed a chief operating officer, whose brief included control of operations, as well as the achievement of synergy and integration, and the steering of strategic alliances. This was modelled on the role of a US chief operating officer and was a marked departure from traditional German management practice. The COO had a seat on both the Vorstand and the Executive Council.

This structure was in line with his intention to take the privately-owned company public, but the creation of a more centralized management structure annoyed the independently minded divisions. Moreover, it appears that the move towards a public listing caused concern for the Mohn family, even though they had initially gone along with the idea. In 2001 Middelhoff had persuaded the Mohn family to give up 25 per cent of Bertelsmann in order to acquire a larger stake in the European TV company RTL. After this deal 57.6 per cent of Bertelsmann's shares were held by the Bertelsmann Foundation, 17.3 per cent by the Mohn family directly, and 25.1 per cent by Groupe Bruxelles Lambert (GBL), a Belgian investment company. Unfortunately for the Mohn family, part of the deal allowed GBL to 'demand' a stock exchange listing of Bertelsmann's shares in 2005/2006. This would make the company into a public corporation for the first time in its history. In fact, it was agreed in May 2006 that Bertelsmann would buy back GBL's stake; the funds were raised through debt and the sale of the company's music publishing arm.[52]

Gunter Thielen replaces Middelhoff

So in July 2003, Thomas Middelhoff was replaced by Gunter Thielen, a 59-year-old who was persuaded out of semi-retirement at 24 hours' notice to take over as chief executive. His contract has been recently extended until 2007, despite Reinhard Mohn's previous decree that executives should retire at 60. Dr Thielen used to head the group's Arvato printing and business services division. He is apparently lacking in vanity, preferring to drive himself in his company Mercedes. He is also said to be sceptical about a share flotation.[53] Having previously chaired the Bertelsmann Foundation, the charity created by Reinhard Mohn, he is close to the Mohn family.[54]

Through Reinhard Mohn's wife, Liz, the family's spokesperson since 2002, and their children Christoph and Brigitte, the family retains enough members on the eight-member shareholders committee to be able to block strategic decisions.[55] In November 2006, the two children joined Liz on the company's supervisory board. Liz, who argues that 'emotional intelligence' is essential, and that the purpose of a firm is to 'offer a home to its workers',[56] holds no executive post within the firm. Some suggest that Mrs Mohn nonetheless exerts a great deal of power, in particular over key appointments such as those of Dr Thielen and of Harmut Ostrowski, his designated successor as CEO.[57]

On taking office Dr Thielen said that his main objective was to boost operational profitability, and to foster strong organic growth. In 2003 he initiated a programme entitled Growth and Innovation (GAIN). Since it began more than 100 new business ideas with strong growth potential have been identified and are being developed. He also quickly dismantled his predecessor's structure, abolishing the post of chief operating officer and the 15-strong 'office of the chairman', and downsizing the head office. His plans appear to be working. In March 2005, Bertelsmann announced increases in its 2004 operating profits to €1,429m from €1,026m in 2003 (a 40 per cent increase). In 2005 it saw a 5.1 per cent increase in sales to €17.9 billion, and a 13 per cent in profits to €1.6 billion.

Case study questions

1. What was Bertelsmann's strategy under Thomas Middelhoff? Which elements have changed under Gunter Thielen? Use the definition in Section 1.1 to structure your answer.

2. Use each of the five ways of thinking about organizations to analyse the strategic actions that Middelhoff took, or tried to take, as CEO of Bertelsmann.

3. Who are Bertelsmann's major stakeholders? How can you tell? How have the interactions between them affected strategic decisions and decision-making?

4. Were the strategic decisions taken under Middelhoff more or less rational than those taken under Thielen?

5. How do Bertelsmann's early values and beliefs influence its present-day strategy?

● NOTES

1 This definition is adapted from that in Helfat and Peteraf (2003).

2 Sony News and Information—press release 06-035E dated 27 April 2006.

3 Hjelt (2005).

4 <http://money.cnn.com/magazines/fortune/fortune500/2007/full_list/101_200.html>, accessed 1 June 2007.

5 <http://www.hm.com/gb/abouthm/factsabouthm/hminbrief__hminbreif.nhtml> and H&M Annual Report 2006: 50, both accessed on 1 June 2007.

6 *Fortune* Europe Edition, 26 March 2007: 45.

7 <http://media.corporateir.net/media_files/irol/69/69499/bafactbook/2007/Section2_March2007.pdf>: 10, accessed on 1 June 2007.

8 Sterling financial figures and employee numbers from BA Factbook 2007 (<http://media.corporateir.net/media_files/irol/69/69499/bafactbook/2007/FinancialStatements_March2007.pdf>: 82; <http://media.corporateir.net/media_files/irol/69/69499/bafactbook/2007/Section2_March2007.pdf>: 45). US$ equivalents from <http://money.cnn.com/magazines/fortune/global500/2006/full_list/401_500.html>. All sources accessed on 1 June 2007.

9 Moin, D. (2005). 'Gap Inc.'s recovery plan: new format, markets and décor'. *Women's Wear Daily*, 189/86: 1–2; <http://www.gapinc.com/public/Media/Press_Releases/med_pr_FranchiseMiddleEast041806.shtml>, accessed 20 April 2006.

10 Norton, K. (2006). 'Wal-Mart's German retreat'. *BusinessWeek Online* (31 July); *Economist* (2006). 'Heading for the exit' (5 August); Birchall, J. (2006). 'Wal-Mart hit by first profit fall in a decade'. *Financial Times* (16 August): 20.

11 BA Annual Report and interim results, 2006.

12 <http://www-03.ibm.com/ibm/history/history/decade_1990.html>, accessed on 8 June 2007.

13 Davidson, A. (2005). 'Driving Samsung to digital supremacy'. *Sunday Times*, 28 August: Business, 7; *Guardian Unlimited* (2005). 'Samsung sees brand value soar', 22 July; Hunt, B. (2006). 'Samsung attracted to birds' beauty'. *Financial Times*, 23 November, Surveys DEU1: 9.

14 For a discussion of how stakeholders shape key facets of a strategy see Kassinis and Vafeas (2006), Pajunen (2006), and Roome and Wijen (2006).

15 Clark, A. (2003). 'Lost weekends?' *GuardianUnlimited*. 23 September; BBC News Online (2004a). 'Q&A—Ryanair's Charleroi knockback', 3 February; BBC News Online (2004b). 'Depressed region fears Ryanair exit', 3 February; all accessed on 5 June 2007.

16 See, for example, Eisenhardt and Zbaracki (1992), and Mintzberg and Westley (2001).

17 Laing, J. (2006). 'Behind Boeing's comeback: the right stuff'. *Barrons*, 13 March.

18 <http://www.airbus.com/en/airbusfor/analysts/>, accessed 12 June 2006.

19 Mergent Industry Reports (2005). *Aviation—Europe*, 1 October, MIRAUS; Wall, R. (2005). 'In the race; Airbus launches A350-800/-900, with government aid on hold'. *Aviation Week & Space Technology*, 163: 22.

20 *Business Brief* (2004). 'European voice', 22 July; Boland, V. and Munir, M. (2004). 'Hopes are high for the future of THY'. *Financial Times*, 17 August: 27; Wall, R. (2005). 'In the race; Airbus launches A350-800/-900, with government aid on hold'. *Aviation Week & Space Technology*, 163: 22.

21 European Aeronautic Defence & Space Company (EADS) owns 80% of Airbus; UK-based BAE Systems owns the other 20% (although in April 2006 it announced that it hopes to sell its share). EADS consists of DaimlerChrysler Aerospace (Germany), Aerospatiale Matra (France), and CASA (Spain). DaimlerChrysler owns about 30% of EADS; the French government (SOGEPA), France-based Lagardère, BNP Paribas, and AXA together own about 30%; Spain's state-owned SEPI owns 5.5%. Source: *Economist* (2004a). 'Boeing down, again—Boeing loses again', 24 January.

22 *Economist* (2004a) op. cit.

23 Milne, R. and Williamson, H. (2005). 'Tarnished: a scandal at VW could signal a reversal in Germany's worker power'. *Financial Times*, 12 July: 17; Evans-Pritchard, A. (2005). 'Sex row claims key driver at VW'. *The Daily Telegraph*, 14 July: 37; Simon, B. (2005). 'VW plans N American sales incentives drive'. *Financial Times*, 22 July: 27.

24 Economist (2005a). 'Together they stand—Scandal at Volkswagen', 16 July; Hall, A. (2007). 'MP's sex, bribes and VW—Car-maker embroiled in scandal'. *The Daily Telegraph*, 1 June (City Edition): 23;

25 *Economist* (2005a) op. cit.

26 *Economist* (2005b). 'Dark days for Volkswagen—German business', 16 July.

27 See, for example, Powell and DiMaggio (1991).

28 For a review, see Foss (2003).

29 Sterman et al. (2007) show how bounded rationality can be a particular issue in fast-moving industries.

30 Writers who have identified links between particular strategic preferences and the individual characteristics or background of the organization's key decision-makers include Kuvaas and Kaufmann (2004), Boeker (1997), Finkelstein and Hambrick (1996), and Hambrick and Mason (1984).

31 See Morse (2006), Fineman ([1993] 2000), Ashkanasy et al. (2002), Daniels (1998), and Goleman (1995). There are also editions of the *European Journal of Work and Organizational Psychology*, 8/3 (September 1999), *Organizational Behaviour and Human Decision Processes*, 86/1 (2001), and the *Journal of Organizational Behaviour*, 21/3 (2000) devoted entirely to the issue of emotions in organizations.

32 Drennan (1992).

33 See, for example, Harris and Ogbonna (1999) and also Edgar Schein's hugely influential 1992 book *Organizational Culture and Leadership*.

34 Weick (1983).

35 For a review of how an organization's sense of identity affects its attitudes towards internal and external stakeholders, see Brickson (2007).

36 Kay, K. (2002). 'Aides defend Bush over Enron debacle'. *The Times*, 15 January: 15; Larsen, P. (2002). 'Enron estimates $14bn writedown'. *Financial Times*, 23 April: 18; Teather, D. (2006). 'Trial in Texas: Four years on, Enron men face their day of reckoning'. *The Guardian*, 26 January: 28.

37 *Economist* (2001), The amazing disintegrating firm, Vol. 361, Issue 8251 (8 December).

38 *Economist* (2001) op. cit.; Cohan (2002).

39 *Economist* (2001) op. cit.

40 Cohan (2002).

41 Cohan (2002).

42 Based on numerous articles, including: *Economist* (2002). 'Logging off', 9 July, 364/8289: 56–8; Benoit, B. (2003). 'Media chief determined to keep it in the family. Interview—Günter Thielen, chief executive of Bertelsmann'. *Financial Times*, 24 March; Benoit, B. (2002). 'Bertelsmann set to overhaul old structure'. *Financial Times*, 5 February; Landler, M. (2006). 'Bertelsmann weighs end to its privacy'. *New York Times*, 23 March; Wiesmann, G. (2006). 'Frere faces a dynastic fighter at Bertelsmann'. *Financial Times*, 30 January; various corporate press releases and annual reports from Bertelsmann.com, accessed on 22 March 2006.

43 Politi, J. (2002). 'Middelhoff's roller-coaster ride ends: driven by deal-making'. *National Post*, 29 July.

44 Peers, M., Rose, M., and Karnitschnig, M. (2002). 'Digital divide: at Bertelsmann, another blow to futuristic media visions'. *Wall Street Journal*, 29 July.

45 Burt, T. (2002). 'Back to earth'. *Financial Times*, 30 July: 14.

46 Peers et al. (2002) op. cit.

47 Burt (2002) op. cit.

48 Ibid.; Peers et al. (2002) op. cit.; Benoit (2003) op. cit.

49 Bertelsmann AG 1997/8 Annual Report.

50 Ibid.

51 *Economist*, 7 November 1998.

52 Esterl, M. (2006). 'Bertelsmann will buy out investor'. *Wall Street Journal*, 26 May: A7; Maurer, H. (2006). 'A Bertelsmann buyout'. *BusinessWeek*, 12 June: 27; Sabbagh, D. (2006). 'Why the song had to come to an end for Bertelsmann'. *The Times*, 2 September: 63.

53 Benoit, B. (2003) op. cit.

54 Benoit, B. (2003) op. cit.; Wiesmann, G. (2007). 'Bertelsmann selects board member as new chief'. *Financial Times*, 19 January: 22; Ewing, J. (2004). 'Reckoning at Bertelsmann'. *BusinessWeek*, 9 February: 44; Wassener, B. (2003). 'Departures from Bertelsmann signal a deeper malaise'. *Financial Times*, 21 November: 31.

55 Benoit, B. (2003) op. cit.; Lottman, H. (2003). 'The family strikes back'. *The Bookseller*, 18 April: 10; Tech Europe (2003). 'Dispute erupts within Bertelsmann'. 27 February; Karnitschnig, M. (2003). 'Bertelsmann spat threatens firm—claim by Patriarch Mohn to keep blocking minority has executives on defensive'. *Wall Street Journal*, 18 February: B13.

56 *Economist* (2004b). 'In the court of Queen B'. 3 June, 370/8365: 61.

57 *Economist* (2004b) op. cit.; Edgecliffe-Johnson, A. and Wiesmann, G. (2006). 'The court of Queen Liz: Europe's largest media group puts family first'. *Financial Times*, 16 October: 15; Ewing (2004) op. cit.; Wiesmann, G. (2007), op.cit.; Ritter, J. (2007). 'Bertelsmann to appoint Hartmut Ostrowski as new head (Liz Mohns Favorit)'. *Frankfurter Allgemeine Zeitung*, 19 January: 16; Carvajal, D. (2007). 'Bertelsmann is days away from naming a new chief'. *New York Times*, 15 January, Late Edition—Final: 5.

CHAPTER TWO

What is Strategic Management?

INTRODUCTION

This chapter builds on our understanding of what an organization is from Chapter 1. Knowing what an organization is, and why it exists, helps us to understand how managing strategy effectively can vary in different contexts. Because different organizations have different priorities, how strategy is managed, and the strategies that are appropriate, will differ.

In addition, as we saw in Section 1.6.1, organizations have various stakeholders, each of whom may have different things that they want from the organization. In this chapter, we go more deeply into the nature of some of these stakeholders and their likely influence on the strategy development process, and discuss some of the ways that strategy comes about in organizations as they compete to have their objectives adopted.

We also introduce you to some of the ways in which the strategy process can go wrong, leading to poor performance, and in some cases the demise of the organization.

2.1 Strategy—basic concepts

In Chapter 1 we defined strategy, but this left some questions unanswered. In this section, we look at two of them:

- How can you tell the difference between strategic decisions and what are often called 'tactical' or 'operational' decisions?

- Can unplanned, opportunistic, or forced decisions or actions really be called strategies?

2.1.1 Strategic decisions

Not all decisions made within an organization contribute equally to its strategy. A strategic decision can be distinguished from other types of decision in three ways:

- Magnitude: Strategic decisions are big decisions. They affect an entire organization or a large part of it, such as a whole division or a major function. And they entail a significant degree of interaction with the world around it—the organization's competitors, suppliers, and customers.

- Time-scale: Strategic decisions set the direction for the organization over the medium to long term. But they will have a short-term impact as well—the medium term may finish in several years' time, but it starts at the end of this sentence! What constitutes medium or long term will depend on the organization and the industries in which it operates. In a fast-moving industry, such as computer software or consumer goods, 18 months may be a long time to think ahead. In capital goods industries like electricity generation or oil production, where new facilities take several years to plan and bring on stream, 10–15 years may be a realistic time horizon. It is helpful to measure time-scales in terms of product life-cycles, with the short term being one product life-cycle and the medium term two. For most industries, this gives a time horizon for the strategist of around 3–5 years.

- Commitment: Strategic decisions involve making choices, and committing resources in ways that cannot be reversed cheaply or easily. This may mean investing large amounts of money in buildings or high-profile, long-term, marketing campaigns, or large amounts of management time in changing the way an organization operates. We go into more depth on this topic in Section 2.5.

It is not always easy to tell what is and what is not a strategic decision. When a clothing company launches a new line of clothing, as H&M did when it started a new designer brand in conjunction with Madonna, that is not necessarily a strategic decision. Companies like H&M launch new product ranges all the time, and are not surprised if some of them do not find favour with the customer. The investment in advertising and new manufacturing skills may be tens of thousands of euros, but this may be small change to a firm like H&M. The failure of that one product is unlikely seriously to affect its profits or future viability. This is a short-term decision requiring little commitment.

However, for a relatively small clothing company with only one established line of products, as H&M was in 1968, launching itself into the men's and children's clothing markets certainly was a strategic decision. In absolute terms, the smaller firm might have spent less on these new product launches than H&M would today on its product extension. But, measured in relation to the size of the firm, the degree of impact of commitment is far higher. Similarly, when an aircraft manufacturer such as Airbus or Boeing decides to launch a new product, that *is* a strategic decision. The investment in design, new manufacturing facilities and marketing will be millions of euros or dollars. The product will be expected to make returns over ten years or more—the Boeing 747 has been in service for over thirty years. If this type of product fails in the market-place, it will hit the organization's reputation as well as its financial security. Customers, banks, and shareholders may start to have doubts about the future of the company, which will affect the sales of their other products, and also their ability to raise funds. So, these are examples of long-term, high-commitment decisions.

Worked Example 2.1 Identifying strategic and non-strategic decisions in H&M

H&M was founded by Erling Persson in 1947 in Västerås, Sweden. It started off life as a retailer of women's clothing, Hennes. In 1968 it acquired another Swedish clothing retailer, Mauritz Widfors, which sold menswear, and changed its name to Hennes & Mauritz.

- *This was a strategic decision: it involved a major outlay of capital, it increased the size and complexity of the business; and it involved most of the company. And it brought Hennes into contact with a whole new customer segment —men!*

In 1974 it went public and was quoted on the Stockholm stock exchange.

- *This is not a strategic decision. It was a means of obtaining funds for expansion. The expansion may well have been a strategic decision, but going public in itself was not. Similarly, later statements that H&M makes about expansion being financed entirely from the firm's own internal funds are an indication of how it intends to implement any strategies it adopts, but are not themselves strategies.*

Each year, for the past several years, H&M has expanded into a new international market or markets.

- *For other companies, that have not previously expanded internationally, and H&M in the 1960s when it opened its first store abroad (in Norway), this would almost certainly be a strategic decision; for H&M nowadays it is arguably not always. Expanding into new geographic areas is part of its current strategy—it opens new shops regularly. Sometimes these are in countries where it already has a presence, sometimes in totally new markets. But expanding geographically into a smallish country like Slovenia may be considered an incremental development of its existing European business. Even entry into a major market like Canada, one of the world's largest economies, might only be an incremental move if it were done slowly, using logistics already in place to serve the US. On the other hand, at the point at which expansion in Canada (or any other market) involves major investments in warehouses or in a country-wide campaign of major store openings, it does become a strategic decision.*

Practical dos and don'ts

In exams or case study analyses you will often be asked to develop a strategy (or strategic *options* which we discuss in much →

The recent opening of H&M's Shanghai store; expanding into new geographic areas is part of its strategy. *H&M AB*

more detail in Chapter 12) for an organization. The key things to look for when trying to decide whether your recommendations can be considered strategic are:

- Scope and scale—is your suggestion going to affect a significant part of the organization's activities and value chain.

- Is your suggestion going to involve a significant commitment of resources. This could mean a reallocation of existing resources such as manpower or plant and machinery, but may also involve the need to find new resources such as finance or staff. Putting an absolute figure on this is difficult, but if your recommendation involves, say, the reallocation of more than 20 per cent of existing plant and machinery, or using finance equivalent to 5 per cent or more of its shareholders' funds, then this is likely to be a strategic decision.

- Does your suggestion pose a significant risk to the organization as a whole? —perhaps because it involves a large commitment of resources that cannot be reallocated elsewhere if things don't work out as planned, or perhaps because it is something entirely new.

- Is your recommendation likely to affect what the organization as a whole does over the *long term*? What the long term means varies from industry to industry, but anything over two years can probably be thought of as a strategic decision. If the organization can quickly reverse the decision then it is unlikely to be strategic.

Finally, you may wish to recommend that the organization carries on doing exactly what it is already doing. This may not conform to some of our tests of 'strategicness', such as obtaining new resources, but is nevertheless strategic because it involves the whole organization, a large commitment of resources (the total amount!) and certainly will affect what it does over the long term. Some opportunities for expansion or innovation may not exist in a few years' time, or might require massive investment to catch up with competitors.

2.1.2 Deliberate, emergent, imposed, and realized strategies

In our definition of strategy at the start of Chapter 1, we referred to actions coming about 'by accident or design'. This is, as we shall see, rather controversial. Surely a strategy is something thought out in advance by a chief executive and his or her top management team, and passed down the organization for carefully planned implementation. After all, the word 'strategy' is derived from the Greek term *strategos*, meaning a carefully formulated military-style plan of campaign. Deliberate, planned, or intentional strategies of this kind occur in organizations as well. But, as we suggested in Section 1.6, there has been increasing recognition that strategic direction of the whole organization can be shaped by opportunistic decisions that can happen at any level in the organization. These have been termed *emergent* strategies.

There are two significant problems with the deliberate/planned view of strategy development:[1]

- Not all the strategies that the top team wants to happen will happen in practice. Products may not sell because of changing customer tastes; economies may go into recession; and political environments can change suddenly.

- The strategies that are actually implemented are often not those that are developed through the planning processes.

And sometimes the strategies that an organization adopts are not what it would have wanted to do itself, but have been forced on it.

Figure 2.1 illustrates this. Strategies that are decided on in advance by the leadership of the organization are intended strategies. Those that are put into operation are deliberate strategies. For example, H&M's expansion into new geographical markets has happened in a systematic and deliberate way, and its move into the cosmetics business was clearly an intentional one. These were deliberate strategies that were carefully planned in advance.

Those intended or deliberate strategies that do not happen become unrealized strategies. Strategies which are not intentionally planned, and which can come about from lower levels in an organization, are emergent strategies. For example, an enterprising salesperson may discover that a product that is intended to be sold to schools is also attractive to banks or hospitals, and passes this information on to some of his colleagues. This is recognized to be a good idea, and as a result the firm ends up entering the financial services or medical markets. New strategies can also be the unintended consequences of organizational policies such as control or rewards systems. For example, if branch managers are given profit targets and start to cut corners on quality, then the company may 'accidentally' move down-market.

Deliberate strategy
A strategy conceived by senior managers as a planned response to the challenges confronting an organization. Often the result of a systematic analysis of the organization's environment and resources.

Emergent strategy
A strategy that 'emerges' from lower down the organization without direct senior management intervention.

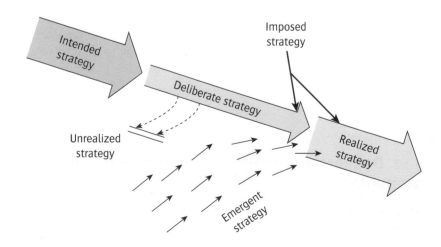

Figure 2.1 Strategy development processes (Mintzberg and Waters, 1985)

In the documentary film *Super Size Me* the filmmaker shows himself eating nothing but McDonald's products for 30 days.
Super Size Me

Those that are *imposed* on an organization are strategies about which the members of an organization have little effective choice. When McDonald's updated its range to incorporate products with lower fat and salt content, and withdrew the 'supersize' option on some of its products, this appeared to be in some way an imposed strategy. It had been (unsuccessfully) sued in the US courts by people who accused it of making them obese.[2] And in a documentary film, *Super Size Me*, the filmmaker showed himself suffering unpleasant side-effects from eating nothing but McDonald's products for 30 days. Although the firm could legitimately argue that it was not doing anything illegal or immoral, it seemed under considerable pressure to respond to the concerns of these newly voluble stakeholders.[3] Other common types of imposed strategy are those forced upon an organization by government policies.

The imposed strategies, *plus* some emergent strategies, *plus* those intended strategies that are, in the end, deliberately adopted, together constitute the realized strategies—i.e. what the organization as a whole does in practice.

As Real-life Application 2.1 shows, it can often be very difficult for even experienced academics and consultants to tell whether a realized strategy was originally deliberate or emergent.

Imposed strategy
A strategy that an organization's managers would not otherwise have chosen, but is forced on them.

Realized strategy
The strategy the organization actually ends up implementing. It may be deliberate, emergent or imposed.

Real-life Application 2.1 Honda's strategy—deliberate or emergent?

In 1975, the Boston Consulting Group (BCG), an influential management consultancy specializing in strategy, wrote a report for the UK government setting out alternatives for the British motorcycle industry. Within that report[4] they analysed Honda's success in the US market. They painted a picture of how Honda had cleverly planned its penetration into the USA with small motorcycles sold to ordinary households, at a time when US producers focused on selling large machines to motorcycle enthusiasts. Honda then used this initial breakthrough to build volume in the USA, and gain reputation and economies of scale, which enabled them to gradually move up-market and to expand internationally.

In 1980, Richard Pascale, a US academic, decided on a whim to interview the Japanese executives who had managed Honda's US operations at the time. The picture they painted was very different from the calculated strategy described by BCG. They suggested that Honda's US success was the result of a set of happy accidents. The managers had started by trying to sell Honda's larger bikes, which however were not robust enough for American road conditions. The move to smaller motorcycles happened partly because there was nothing else for them to sell, partly because US retailers had expressed interest after the Japanese managers had been spotted using the bikes to travel around. Henry Mintzberg, a very influential Canadian academic and author, was most taken with Pascale's account, and used it extensively to support his ideas about emergent strategy. According to him, Honda's success came about because, rather than planning everything in advance, they adapted to market conditions as they encountered them.[5]

Andrew Mair, a British academic who made a long study of Honda, did not dispute the details of Pascale's account. However, he found documents suggesting that it was always Honda's intention to market their smaller motorcycles in the US, and that the manufacturing capacity to support those sales was planned well in advance. He suggests that the real basis of Honda's success, in the US and elsewhere, was not its use of avoidance of planning, but in its ability to handle ambiguity.[6]

Using Evidence 1.1 Assessing modes of strategy development

For the Honda case example above both Richard Pascale and Andrew Mair had access to real company data. When you are looking at a case study, whose data are much more superficial, you may have even more difficulty in finding evidence of strategy processes. But there are some things you should be looking for if you can.

First, you need to look at the organization over a period of time—you cannot assess whether a strategy was planned or emergent until after it has happened! The fact that there is a planning process in place does not necessarily mean that it will play a major role in the organization's actual strategy.

Then you need to compare actual organizational activities with those that were earlier expressed as intentions by the CEO or chairman—usually these will be found in a company's annual report or the organization's strategic plan. Or if you have access to real company information, memos or letters are often good indicators of intentions.

Furthermore, you might look for indicators, such as systems to encourage employees to come up with suggestions, that point to an organization where the top team are not considered as all-seeing and all-knowing.

Table 2.1 Modes of strategy-making

Descriptors	Style	Role of top management	Role of organizational members
Rational	*Analytical* Strategy driven by formal structure and planning systems	*Boss* Evaluate and control	*Subordinate* Follow the system
Command	*Imperial* Strategy driven by leader or small top team	*Commander* Provide direction	*Soldier* Obey orders
Symbolic	*Cultural* Strategy driven by mission and a vision of the future	*Coach* Motivate and inspire	*Player* Respond to challenge
Transactive	*Procedural* Strategy driven by internal process and mutual adjustment	*Facilitator* Empower and enable	*Participant* Learn and improve
Generative	*Organic* Strategy driven by organizational actors' initiative	*Sponsor* Endorse and sponsor	*Entrepreneur* Experiment and take risks
Muddling through	*Political* Strategy driven by bargaining between powerful interest groups	*Umpire* Arbitrate and enforce order	*Onlooker* Bend with the wind
Externally dependent	*Enforced choice* Strategy driven by prescriptive external pressures	*Buffer* Moderate pressures as far as possible	*Sensor* Detect and transmit key environmental changes

Adapted from Hart (1992) and Bailey and Johnson (1995)

2.2 **How strategy happens**

Studies of how organizations actually go about developing and implementing strategies have now, in Europe particularly, developed into a major stream of research relating to micro-strategy and strategy as practice (see Section 2.2.6 below).[7] Researchers have identified several modes of strategy-making, summarized in Table 2.1. They also found that few organizations were locked into a single way of strategizing: in most cases, a number of modes tended to operate in parallel.[8]

2.2.1 **The rational mode**

Perhaps the most traditional view on strategy is that of a *rational*, thought-out, planned process. Strategic planning involves a process of analysis, the setting of goals and targets as a result, and the measurement of performance outcomes against these. Analytical tools,[9] many of which we shall cover in this book, are used to identify suitable opportunities or problem areas that need to be tackled, leading eventually to a final selection of strategy.

This style allows as much data as possible to be taken into account when devising strategy. The organization's functional and geographic units will submit data on their sales, costs, quality, and other important aspects of performance, alongside their assessment of environmental conditions and future market prospects. Central planning units may add their own data about key markets, and sometimes consultants will be asked to gather or collate the information.

There then follows a period of contemplation, discussion and negotiation between the team whose job it is to write the plan and the operational managers who will be expected to implement it. Following this, the new plan will be written and communicated to unit managers. These strategic plans set out what the organization intends to achieve over, typically, a five-year period. They are often an important guide to what the senior management believe are the priorities for the organization, and act as an aid to financial planning and budgeting for large-scale projects.

Although planning processes like this are less fashionable than in the 1970s, many large firms or public sector units still have planning departments, and almost all organizations will have some sort of strategic or business plan that sets in place what they intend to do and how they will do it. Many strategy courses and textbooks (including this one, even though we think that planning is not necessarily the most important element in strategic management) implicitly or explicitly accept the importance of planning techniques.

Strategic plans have a role in helping an organization's managers to make sense of what is happening around them and plan for major items of expenditure, but they work best in predictable, stable environments where things do not change much from one year to the next. They are often too bulky to be used as a guide for managers in their day-to-day activities, and become out of date as soon as there is any major unexpected development in the organization or its environment.[10]

2.2.2 The command mode

Another traditionally important view of strategy, the command mode, focuses on the role of the leader or top management team.[11] The earliest thinkers on strategy took it for granted that strategy development was the prerogative of the chief executive who would make a decision that had been evaluated against alternatives in a rational manner, its outcomes assessed down to the last detail. In other words, they assumed strategy-making was a combination of the command mode and the rational mode we discussed in the previous section.

It is natural to expect top managers to play a significant role in deciding, at least, what the overall intended strategy ought to be, so that the command mode is likely to feature in many organizations. But research shows that it is not just the chief executive and the top management team who shape strategy, while many top managers spend very little time thinking about it (less than 10 per cent, by one estimate). Much of senior managers' time is devoted to other high-profile tasks, like communicating inside and outside the organization, and solving operational problems. And not all leaders see it as their role to make strategy. Some, for example, believe that if they focus on bringing the right people into the organization, or on framing the right kinds of rules and values to help those people in their decisions, the strategy will essentially take care of itself.[12]

➜ We examine different styles of leadership, and the leadership role of middle management, in Section 17.1.

So the extent to which the command mode influences strategic decision-making will depend upon the nature of the firm, and the personality of the leader. In a small or a young firm, it would be usual for the founding entrepreneurs to exert a dominant influence on strategy, but this happens in larger firms as well. In H&M the influence of the founder remained strong until his recent death. Sometimes, when a firm is drifting strategically, a new leader arrives who finds that he has to impose his strategic view in order to turn the organization around, as did Michael Eisner when he became CEO of the Walt Disney Company in 1984.[13]

Values
The philosophical principles that the great majority of an organization's members hold in common.

2.2.3 The symbolic mode

We showed in Section 1.6.4 how the people in an organization come over time to share a set of core values. These values typically stem from, and are sustained by, the organization's founder and leaders, but may be much more widespread than this. In the symbolic mode of strategy-making, an organization possesses clear and compelling values that are so widely shared that they exert a major influence over which strategies are adopted.

The name 'symbolic mode' derives from the important role played by the symbols of these values: the organization's vision and mission. Although the definitions of values, vision, and mission given here will be recognizable to most managers, the three concepts overlap, and different authors use conflicting terminology. Americans James Collins and Jerry Porras, who are two of the most prolific writers in this area, use 'vision' as an overall term that encompasses mission and values. You may also encounter other terms, such as 'strategic intent' (for vision) and 'superordinate goals' (for core values).

Many organizations make great play of their mission and vision statements in their annual reports. Here are a sample:

McDonald's

Vision for Diversity

Mission

To leverage the unique talents, strengths and assets of our diversity in order to be the World's best quick service restaurant experience.

Vision

- Ensure that our employees, owner operators and suppliers reflect and represent the diverse populations McDonald's serves around the world.
- Harness the multi-faced qualities of our diversity—individual and group differences among our people—as a combined, complementary force to run great restaurants.
- Maximize investments in the quality of community life in the diverse markets we serve.
- Expanding the range of opportunities for all our people—employees, owner operators and suppliers—to freely invest human capital, ideas, energies, expertise and time.[14]

H&M

Fashion and quality at the best price.

H&M also expand on their values throughout their public communications, for example in a 61-page corporate social responsibility report, and a 6-page code of conduct guide for its suppliers.[15]

EasyJet

Value airline and the new owner of Go, BA's former venture into the value airline sector.

To provide our customers with safe, good value, point to point air services. To effect and to offer a consistent and reliable product and fares appealing to leisure and business markets on a range of European routes. To achieve this we will develop our people and establish lasting relationships with our suppliers.[16]

If an organization's mission, vision, and values are clear and inspiring, as is clearly the intention in the statements reproduced above, they will help drive the organization forward by giving employees a shared objective to which all can aspire. It also gives them a clear

---

Vision
A description of what an organization's leaders aspire to achieve over the medium/long term, and of how it will feel to work in or with the organization once this has taken effect.

Mission
The set of goals and purposes that an organization's members and other major stakeholders agree that it exists to achieve. It is often expressed in a formal, public mission statement.

→ In Section 8.3.2 we discuss the importance of mission and vision to an organization's competitiveness.

reference point for their decisions, both short term and long term. This helps to avoid unnecessary costs that might arise if objectives were constantly being renegotiated or if policies on products, service levels, customers, and markets were continually being altered. This means that formal, written strategies become less necessary—the organization progresses more or less spontaneously. And the organization's values in respect of ethics and social responsibility (issues to which we return in Section 2.7) will strongly influence the extent to which employees act with honesty and compassion when carrying out their work —written rules and procedures are not sufficient to ensure this.[17]

Many writers suggest that a strong sense of mission and corporate purpose is important for an organization's success.[18] However, if a firm develops a very strong sense of purpose, it paradoxically may risk blinding itself to opportunities that are outside this remit.

➜ We look again at how shared values can act as barriers to change in Chapter 16.

2.2.4 The transactive mode

If the rational and command modes emphasized deliberate strategy-making, this and the next mode are very much about emergent strategy. In the transactive mode, the organization is feeling its way forward, trying out different strategies to find out what works best for it in its particular environment, a process that has been described as 'logical incrementalism'.[19]

This mode of strategy-making depends crucially on input from lower-level and middle managers.[20] They feed detailed technological and market knowledge into the strategy process, and influence top managers' strategic thinking by making them aware of issues that operational staff think are important. They also use their influence to promote proposals made by junior employees, perhaps to be adopted in a mainstream way when they are shown to work on a smaller scale. Strategies built this way are often the result of employees sharing ideas and practices among themselves, through the organizational and individual learning processes that we outlined in Section 1.4.

Henry Mintzberg wrote a number of articles in the 1990s in which he suggested that strategies developed in this way were more likely to take root and succeed than those developed using rational planning processes. However, more recent research has suggested that organizations benefit from using both modes: that planning leaves organizations better prepared to learn about their environment, and that learning, in turn, feeds back into better plans.[21]

2.2.5 The generative mode

In the transactive mode, strategic change comes about as the result of small, quite cautious moves. Strategy-making in the generative mode, on the other hand, is characterized by more substantial, innovative leaps that emerge spontaneously from all levels in the organization. For this mode to operate, the organization must have a culture and architecture that foster innovation and corporate entrepreneurship[22]—individuals acting, on the organization's behalf, as though they were entrepreneurs working for themselves.

➜ We look at the management of innovation in depth in Chapter 10.

This means that strategy-making in the generative mode has a deliberate as well as an emergent element. The deliberate part involves putting in place, and nurturing, the appropriate cultural norms and the control and reward systems, so that employees feel able to pursue projects on their own initiative and to take risks on the firm's behalf without fearing punishment if those risks do not pay off.

A number of authors, including Tom Peters and Robert Waterman, have suggested that this form of strategy-making is inherently superior to others, because of the degree of innovation that it stimulates.[23] Some theorists believe that, given the right culture and architecture, organizations can become self-organizing,[24] resulting in a constant flow of innovative competitive moves, while reducing the need for costly monitoring and control structures. However, even highly innovative firms eventually need to get down to the dull but important business of making and selling their innovative products in the most efficient manner. For this, strategy-making in one of the other modes may be more appropriate.

2.2.6 Muddling through mode

This mode of strategy-making, like the transactive mode, involves the organization feeling its way forward in small incremental steps, but here the driving force tends to be political manoeuvring by powerful individuals and groups, who may be pursuing their own aims rather than those of the organization.

As we mentioned in Section 1.6.2, the use of power and influence by stakeholders at all levels both inside and outside an organization is what allows strategies to emerge, so that this mode of strategy-making is commonly found alongside the others. Which ideas are adopted by the organization as a whole depends on whether the person initiating the idea has the power to make others 'buy into' it and take it up. A person's power affects how many decisions they can take, or how much they can control a decision that someone else takes, and therefore how important they are to the strategy development processes in an organization.

All stakeholders in an organization have some degree of power, but some have more power than others. Power often comes from factors such as the ability to do some critically important things better than other people can, or control of access to funds or other vital resources, but it is often very closely associated with authority. The most powerful people in most organizations tend to be the board of directors, the chief executive, and the senior management team. However some people—perhaps those with strong personalities, or those who have been with the organization a long time, and have earned the respect of others—have influence over their colleagues even though they may have little formal authority.

Although power and politics are part of everyday life in most organizations, there are dangers if muddling through[26] becomes the dominant mode of strategy-making. In such cases, strategies tend to persist unchanged for long periods, while powerholders squabble over the correct direction to take. Furthermore, the organization tends to look inwards, focusing on its own internal routines rather than the outside world, so it may lose touch with its environment; Real-life Application 2.2 provides an example.

Power
The ability of one person to *induce* another to do something they would not otherwise do.[25]

Authority
The formal hierarchical position to which society (the organization itself or the wider social environment) has allocated certain power elements.

Influence
The ability to *persuade* someone to do something that they would not otherwise have done.

➡ We look at power in more detail when we look at the management of change and strategy implementation in Chapters 16 and 17.

Strategizing
The processes of strategy development, and in particular the way in which the practices that make up organizational life contribute to them and their outcomes.

Real-life Application 2.2 Strategizing in a British symphony orchestra[27]

British orchestras operate in a climate of uncertain funding and changing public tastes in music. Fewer people go to concerts and those that do go are more likely to go to a pop concert than to hear classical music performed by a symphony orchestra, especially one that wants to experiment with less popular works. Since the invention of the CD, which needs replacing less often than tapes or vinyl records, sales of recorded classical music have fallen.

One orchestra needed to address these issues—but how? One of its funders, the Arts Council of England, had some thoughts on the matter—as did its new principal conductor, a new chief executive, and the members of the orchestra. All that these groups really agreed on was that it needed a new artistic strategy—and fast.   ➡

→ A number of problems led to increasing despair at a lack of a coherent artistic policy or market position. First, there was no-one with clear responsibility for developing a strategy in the orchestra. Should the (part-time) conductor be responsible for its artistic strategy, or the chief executive, or the artistic director (who was not the chief executive nor the conductor), or the funders—the Arts Council, the orchestra's members, or its audience? People simply passed the buck, deflecting responsibility away from themselves and their own areas of accountability, and blaming others for the lack of progress. A second problem was that no-one agreed what was the root cause of the crisis. The people who selected music for the concerts complained that they did not have a commercially viable strategy in areas like ticket pricing. Those with commercial and financial responsibilities attributed the organization's problems to an incoherent artistic product. As a result the orchestra struggled from one crisis to the next, managers left, and the orchestra failed to develop a sustainable artistic strategy, despite years of trying.

2.2.7 Externally dependent mode

Outside stakeholders, such as governments or trades unions, also frequently have a degree of power over an organization. In the externally dependent mode of strategy-making, this power is exerted, resulting in the imposed strategies we discussed in section 2.1.2. It is quite commonly found alongside other modes. Many public sector units, or organizations that receive a proportion of their income from public sources, such as the orchestra described in Real-life Application 2.2, are subject to the control of government agencies. Commercial organizations can also be limited in what they do, or may be forced to do things they would not otherwise have done. British Airways is constrained by UK and European legislation and by international treaties that dictate to some extent where it can fly, as well as to what extent it can collaborate with other airlines.

The externally dependent mode becomes particularly noticeable when the organization's environment is unstable or hostile, reducing its scope for strategic manoeuvre. Legislation on greenhouse gas emissions has forced some companies to restructure their manufacturing processes. Even competitors can sometimes influence matters. British Airways has had to respond to the low-price strategies of 'no-frills' competitors such as Ryanair, while Sony has needed to find a response to competitors' developments of TVs with LCD and plasma screens.

Worked Example 2.2 Assessing how strategy happens at BA, H&M, and Sony

Much of the very detailed examination of the processes of strategy development is not likely to be readily available within case studies or even within the publicly available literature on organizations such as their press releases or annual reports. Hence you may have to infer what the dominant mode of strategy development is in any setting from the limited data that you have available.

Sometimes you do this through a process of triangulation[28]—finding one piece of evidence and bringing it together with another to make a judgement about what has happened. For

example, British Airways mentions in its 2002 annual report a 'Future Size and Shape'. It then comments on the progress of this programme in subsequent annual reports. It also uses the word 'plan' regularly, for example to report that the planned withdrawal of the Concorde from its fleet had actually happened. From these two pieces of evidence one can infer that there is a strong rational, planned, process of strategy development in BA. There is also considerable evidence of an externally-dependent mode. There are numerous press articles that discuss how BA, along with other airlines, is regulated, for example in terms of →

→ safety standards, landing and take-off slots, and who it can and cannot merge with.[29] Proposals for a merger between BA and American Airlines, came to nothing because of tough conditions imposed by EU and US regulators.[30] There have also been numerous discussions in the press about the effect that the unions have had on shaping BA's pension arrangements and working practices.[31]

There is indirect evidence of the command mode at BA. The two sections at the beginning of the annual reports in which both the chairman and chief executive outline their view of the company's performance and prospects indicate that they have a strong role to play. One tip is to look at who owns the shares of a company; if they are mostly in one name, there is a likelihood that that person will be exercising a considerable degree of control, although you will find cases where a majority investor is content to take a passive role.

If the symbolic mode is important in an organization, there will normally be a fair amount of evidence available, though you will need to weigh it carefully. Despite the fact that we have shown a number of mission and vision statements above, these are not necessarily the best indicators of an organization's core values. They are sometimes statements of aspirations—and in any case may be put out into the public domain by a chief executive who does not actually understand what the organization's core values are.[32] So you need to look elsewhere. Press articles and books are a good starting point. These are often based on interviews with key personnel, whose quotes and attitudes may well show what really matters. In H&M's case, it is the company itself that describes how staff in established stores work alongside staff in new stores, particularly in new countries. This is a way of training people in necessary skills, but it is also a way of imparting core values—which H&M themselves say is a motive. From these various pieces of evidence one may infer that H&M is a company with a strong set of core values, and a focus on socially sensitive, symbolic, strategy development processes, a company in which meaning as well as action is important, and which shapes employees' behaviour without formal instruction.

Transactive and generative modes of strategy development are less apparent than other modes in both BA and H&M. For evidence on these modes, we turn to Sony, and the efforts that Ken Kutaragi, the driving force behind the PlayStation, one of the company's most successful products, had to put in to get the product off the ground, working for several years without official backing.[33] Whether this was a semi-deliberate, generative move that senior managers had put in place, and which allowed him the freedom to work autonomously, or whether it was the transactive action of a 'fiercely independent engineering visionary'[34] is almost impossible to tell from the secondary data that we have available.

2.3 **Where strategy happens**

In the previous section we outlined the ways in which strategy happens. Now we will look at the different types of strategic decisions that can be taken—according to which part of the organization they relate to. It is common to refer to three levels of strategy (Figure 2.2).

As organizations grow and sometimes diversify, the levels at which strategic decisions are taken can multiply. When the first airlines started operating in the early days of flying, many would have had a single plane, with a single person who might have been responsible for advertising the firm's services, piloting the aeroplane, and possibly servicing it as well. However, as the number of destinations and passengers multiplied, and the technology became more complicated, the need arose for the different specialized functions that can be seen in most modern airlines: ticketing, reservations, and marketing staff to sell the services; specialist planners to schedule them; engineers to maintain them; aircrew to fly them; purchasing staff to obtain the food needed in-flight; finance staff to keep control of costs; human resources specialists to make sure that appropriate staff are recruited and trained; IT specialists to run the computing services, etc. Often these individuals work together in the same functional department. For them, the strategic decisions that they take will be functional ones.

But organizations also operate as businesses, where all the functions act together to achieve a particular objective. Such decisions relate to the types of customers that are served, or the geographical markets where the company's products are sold. These are business-level strategic decisions.

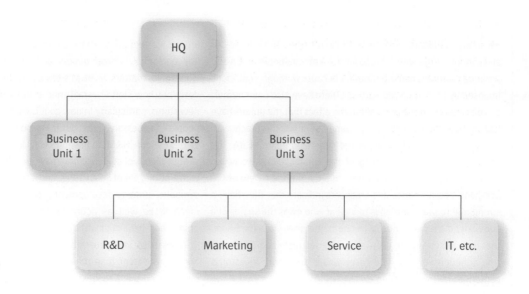

Corporate strategy
— where to invest
— adding value by
  linking units

Business strategy
— what we sell to
  whom
— competitive
  advantage

Functional strategies

Figure 2.2 The three
levels of strategy

Over time, businesses often diversify into different areas; perhaps they develop a new type of product or move into a number of different geographical areas, each of which may have the need for a slightly different type of management. Sometimes these businesses are related to one another, sometimes they are not. Sometimes they are separate legal entities, sometimes not. But when an organization has a range of different types of business within its portfolio, its managers have to take decisions about how these businesses work together, and how many and what sort of businesses should be in its portfolio. These are corporate-level strategic decisions.

2.3.1 **Functional-level strategy**

➜ Functional strategies
have an important influence
on the organization's value
chain, which we discuss in
Chapter 6.

Each of an organization's individual functions will have its own functional strategy. For example, British Airways might have a marketing strategy to increase customer recognition of its Club World brand with specific targets to be achieved over the next two years, or to increase direct mail activity to certain market segments. A maintenance strategy might be to reduce the frequency of unplanned aircraft breakdowns, again with specific targets to be achieved in a given time period. Because functional strategies are not of particularly great magnitude, and are likely to be short-term, we do not discuss them in great detail in this book.

2.3.2 **Business-level strategy**

A modern airline such as British Airways has all the functions outlined in Section 2.3, and more. The crucial task of its managers is to knit these disparate groups of specialists together into a coherent whole that delivers an all-round service to its customers. The planes must be ready to fly at the scheduled time, with motivated, helpful, and well-trained staff on board, serving palatable food in planes which are as full as possible of fare-paying passengers. A failure by any one function, however remote from the user, can lead to poor service and customer dissatisfaction: for example, an IT failure can lead to long check-in queues.

This linking together of different activities to add value to users is the essence of business-level strategy. Business-level strategies relate to:

- choosing which users an organization should serve and which services it should offer them. They may decide to develop specialized outputs so as to focus on the needs of a small group or niche of customers. Alternatively, they may opt for less specialized products that serve a larger, mass market, hoping to gain economies of scale. They may choose to differentiate their products on the basis of a low price relative to competitors', or to offer levels of service or features that competing products do not have;

- obtaining inputs through an effective supply chain and then utilizing the organization's resources within a value chain that delivers those services effectively and reasonably efficiently;

- developing an architecture that enables information to flow into, out of and around the organization, to allow the value chain to function effectively and the organization to learn and adapt.

A supply chain is the way that the organization is configured to obtain the inputs it needs at the place and time that it needs them to operate efficiently and effectively. For many organizations this requires close linkage with the value chain of key suppliers, often extending to the development of common computer systems that exchange information on the sales of specific products or ranges. For industries, such as retailing or manufacturing, obtaining supplies quickly and reliably can be an important source of competitive advantage.

→ We look at supply chains and their part in an organization's value chain in more detail in Chapter 6.

Contemporary theory places a lot of emphasis on business-level strategies, since they determine how well an organization competes in its chosen markets (they are sometimes referred to as *competitive strategies*). We cover them in some detail throughout the book, particularly in Chapters 4, 6, and 7.

2.3.3 Corporate-level strategy

Many organizations diversify their activities as they grow. They gather a portfolio of more or less related businesses. Sony started off as a single business company which sold rice-makers, voltmeters, and other basic electronic products. It soon diversified into wireless, audio, and telecommunications equipment, and has since steadily increased in size and scope. It now has five main business areas (electronics, games, music, pictures, and financial services), and numerous subdivisions in each of these.

→ We examine the issues relating to growth and diversification in Chapter 5.

A firm with a diverse portfolio of business units is referred to as a corporation, and it has an additional level of strategies that do not relate directly to serving users in individual markets. These corporate-level strategies, the uppermost level in Figure 2.2, relate mainly to establishing appropriate architectures, looking at which businesses to enter and exit, and managing relationships between them. Each of the businesses may be a significant concern in its own right, pursuing its own business-level strategies. However, resources may be shared across a number of businesses, and there may be common elements in the different businesses' architectures as a result of their common ownership.

→ We examine the issues relating to the management of diversified corporations in Chapter 9.

Not all organizations diversify to the extent that they have or need corporate-level strategies. Some very large firms, such as McDonald's, are essentially single businesses.

2.4 What makes for a good strategy

As we discussed in Chapter 1, organizations can have a number of reasons for existing and what types of strategy are chosen will depend on the organization's key stakeholders' objectives. Nonetheless, there are three tests that we believe can be applied to most strategies.

These are whether they fit the environment in which the organization finds itself, so that they correspond to the survival factors in that environment. They should also allow the organization to be distinctive—to provide something different that customers will want to buy, or to function more efficiently than its competitors. They should also ensure that the organization is able to survive and thrive over the long term—they should be sustainable. We will return to these concepts in more detail in Chapters 4–10.

2.4.1 Fit

→ The analysis of fit and survival and success factors in an industry is developed in more detail in Chapter 3. The idea of fit between strategy and structure is also discussed in Section 8.1, and the concept of coherence in strategy is reviewed in Chapter 12.

The concept of fit actually has two elements. The first of these relates to fit with the environment. Different environments have different characteristics: some, for example, are faster-changing than others, or more vulnerable to government interference. A firm's strategy must be compatible with that environment. H&M's customers expect a new 'look' at least twice a year, and its strategy necessarily involves making sure that it is constantly alert to changes in taste. Sony's world changes as quickly as H&M's, but for different reasons: new technologies are constantly emerging. If Sony is to avoid being driven out of business by Matsushita or Samsung, it has to have a strategy which enables it quickly to incorporate those technologies into new, desirable products—and perhaps to invent some technologies for itself.

BA's world changes more slowly in some ways: people do not expect to see a new type of aircraft or airline seat every time they fly, although their willingness or ability to fly is dependent on changing economic circumstances or perceptions of how safe air travel is. But BA's business is very sensitive to governmental policies on safety, and to inter-governmental agreements that set down, for example, which US airlines are allowed to fly to Heathrow, whether other European airlines are allowed to compete in the UK market (they are), and whether BA and other European airlines are allowed to carry passengers internally within the world's largest airline market, the US (they are not). So it makes sense for BA's strategy to involve building strong links with the UK, EU, and US authorities, and to lobby them strongly and constantly. For a firm like H&M to match BA's effort in this area would be largely a waste of time and resources.

So a firm's strategy must be adapted to—must 'fit'—the context in which it finds itself. But it must also be internally consistent. Every one of the many products sold under the Sony brand must be of a standard that matches the company's carefully nurtured reputation—it cannot sell unreliable and outdated televisions or mobile phones at the same time as it prides itself on producing innovative laptops. In fact, Sony makes a point of ensuring not just that these products are built to similarly high standards, but that they work together as well. But this need for consistency extends to its other ventures, such as the financial services it sells in Japan—it should not launch any product that might damage its brand values.

There is another dimension to internal consistency, or fit: the need for the organization's architecture to match its strategy. Research[35] has shown that firms that are successful over a sustained period of time link three decisions in a coherent way:

- the marketing decision about which products to sell in which markets—what we have called 'competitive stance';
- the manufacturing decision—broadly equivalent to the choice of value chain;
- the administrative decision—broadly equivalent to what we have called architecture.

For example, if, like H&M or Sony, you are trying to foster creativity or innovation, then you must create an atmosphere in which creative people feel at home. You cannot burden them with too many bureaucratic procedures, for example. On the other hand, for McDonald's, whose strategy emphasizes efficiency and value for money, tight cost controls and strict procedures for preparing and serving food are essential.

2.4.2 Distinctiveness

It is not enough for an organization's strategy just to fit the environment and to be internally consistent, however, if it is to stand any chance of success or long-term survival. Our second vital test of whether a strategy is a good one is whether it gives the organization something different from its competitors.

Having a distinctive position in the market-place allows a firm to develop an identity that customers can notice, and which will save them time and money when looking for products. The whole of the theory of brands is based on this notion of distinctiveness. Choosing specific market segments to focus on, or levels of technology to build into products, also allows an organization to become specialized in fulfilling the needs of its chosen customer groups. So distinctiveness relates to the parts of the strategy that the organization's customers can see—its competitive stance.

But distinctiveness can also be hidden—in the configuration of its value chain and in the way that a firm brings its divisions or external partners together. Being distinctive in how it organizes itself can allow a firm to be more efficient or effective at what it does, and because these elements are often hidden from competitors, they may not be able to imitate it and appropriate any good ideas for themselves. A well-configured organization can lead to a number of benefits:

- It can allow an organization to reduce its costs, for example by reducing the amount of stock it holds. This enables it to reduce prices, or keep the same prices and enhance profit margins.

- It allows an organization to get its products to its customers where and when they want them.

- It enhances flexibility in sourcing its raw materials from suppliers.

- It can help an organization to develop innovative technologies by bringing together different types of knowledge both from within the organization and from other firms outside.

In the end, all the different ways in which organizations can be distinctive boil down to two things: they may make an organization more efficient, so that it gains cost advantage and/or they give its products or services a degree of differentiation in the market-place. These are two fundamental concepts in the understanding of competitive success and failure. There is a widely publicized theory that organizations must choose between cost and differentiation advantage—that if they do not opt for one or the other, they risk being 'stuck in the middle'.[36] However, empirical studies[37] have shown that successful firms can, and in fact do, mix the two.

An important combined test of fit and distinctiveness lies in the firm's performance. A strategy may look plausible—if it did not, the firm's management would not consider it—but unless it is leading to good performance—above all, a good return on capital employed—then either fit or distinctiveness is lacking.

2.4.3 Sustainability

Cost and differentiation advantage only explain how an organization can achieve competitive advantage at one moment in time. The third, and toughest, test of a good strategy is

---

Position
The choices that an organization makes about the price and quality levels of its products and services, as well as the ways and places in which they are sold.

Competitive stance
The visible aspects of a strategy that customers and users see when dealing with an organization. It comprises the organization's chosen markets, products, and services, and their positioning.

➡ We look at distinctiveness factors, notably competitive stance, corporate scope, and value chain configuration, in more detail in Chapters 4–6.

➡ We return to differentiation and cost advantage in more depth in Chapter 4.

➡ We look at the measurement of strategic performance in Chapter 11.

whether it leads to the organization developing the attributes that will allow it to survive and thrive over the long term. The four companies that we have used as our examples have all passed this test—each has a history that reaches back for 40 years or more. But the average life-span of a commercial firm is less than 30 years.[38] And each of our companies could point to competitors (see Real-life Application 2.3 and What Can Go Wrong 2.1) that flourished as a significant force in the industry, only to be undone, either by their own internal problems, by having an inappropriate business model, or by changes in their environment. We discuss in more detail some of the reasons why strategies can go wrong in Section 2.7 below.

Business model
The combination of competitive stance, value chain, and administrative structure (architecture) of an organization.

Real-life Application 2.3 Problems at SAS

For much of the 1980s, the Scandinavian Airline System (SAS) was seen as a model for its competitors to follow, winning praise for its customer service. Along with BA, it was a pioneer in putting the customer first, rather than being driven by the engineering side of the business. It did so by giving a great deal of autonomy to its staff, empowering them to respond to customer needs. This made it a much-cited story of how to turn around an unprofitable business, and Jan Carlzon, the chief executive who presided over it, became a much-admired leader.[39]

Carlzon based his strategy on a vision of SAS as one of only five survivors in the European airline industry by 1995, expanding his firm's interest in the hotels business and pursuing alliances with other airlines, in Europe and elsewhere, in which SAS took equity stakes.[40]

However, this strategy encountered a number of obstacles. In 1990, US airline Continental Airlines, sought protection from its creditors in the USA. SAS had to write off most of its $100m equity stake in that firm, although Continental continued to operate, and to feed passengers on to SAS's network.[41] In 1992, it wrote off a further $300m when it sold its stake in Intercontinental Hotels to Saison, its Japanese joint-venture partner.[42] These setbacks came at a time when the airline industry was experiencing problems as a result of increases in fuel prices and a recession that hit demand for air travel. Although SAS did better than many of its competitors in sustaining demand, it still made losses for three years at the beginning of the 1990s.[43] In 1990, after negotiations with the unions in Sweden, Denmark, and Norway, Carlzon

initiated moves designed to reduce costs, but according to local analysts, by 1993, when he left the company, these had not been fully implemented.[44] When negotiations on 'Alcazar', a merger of SAS, KLM, Swissair, and Austrian Airlines—to which Carlzon had devoted much attention when at SAS, and which he left to head—collapsed in November 1993,[45] it was unclear what SAS's next move would be.

In the event, the cost cuts, combined with a resurgence in demand, were sufficient to return SAS to profitability in 1994.[46] It remained profitable until 2001, when a combination of falling global demand and unexpectedly fast penetration of the Scandinavian market by low-cost airlines led to further losses.[47] The business-class market, which Carlzon had made an SAS stronghold, was particularly hard hit.[48] In a 2004 interview, the company's president, Anders Lindegaard, said: 'Nothing had really happened for the last 10, 15 years. . . . If you are a monopoly, you don't need to. But we were caught in a terrible situation of yields going down and volumes falling, and not being able to do anything about it. . . . We simply didn't realise how rapidly budget operations would happen in Scandinavia.'[49]

SAS fought back. Its own low-cost airline, 'Snowflake', was launched in 2003 but then withdrawn after further customer research; the airline now offers no-frills service to the lowest-fare passengers in the economy-class cabins of its regular flights.[50] Turnaround 2005, a renewed cost reduction programme, was also instrumental in returning SAS to profitability in 2005.[51]

Creative Strategizing 2.1

Imagine you were a senior manager in SAS when problems are just becoming apparent. What would you do to try to prevent the continuing decline of the company. Think of as many possible reasons for the decline as you can. Prioritize these in terms of a) the scale of the problem and b) the likely difficulties in redressing it. Now try to think of how you might start to tackle the most important issues. (Incidentally, we examine the management of change in Chapter 16 and turnarounds in Chapter 17.)

A strong reputation is one example of an asset that is likely to deliver advantage over a long period. And the ability constantly to develop new products or ways of working—to be innovative—is another, which in industries such as biotechnology and pharmaceuticals is critical to a firm's success. Some innovative firms, like Sony, periodically come up with new, 'blockbuster' innovations, while in other cases innovation shows up as consistent small improvements that keep the organization just that little bit ahead of its competitors.

Both reputations and innovation capabilities are examples of what are known as strategic resources. Others include competences and capabilities that allow the firm to develop new areas and perceive new opportunities.

Strong reputations depend upon an organization possessing the routines and knowledge that enable it to deliver good products or service, time after time. Similarly, sustained innovation and other strategic resources come back to the organization has possessing the right routines and knowledge, and using them effectively day after day. This means that in the end, many aspects of sustainable advantage can be traced back to the way it operates as a social system. In particular:

→ We look at sustainability factors, notably culture, architecture, organizational learning, knowledge management, and strategic resources, in more detail in Chapters 7–10.

- its culture. The particular habits and ways of interacting that a social system develops over time are unique. So any capabilities or knowledge that depend particularly on these social interactions are likely to be difficult to copy. Alternatively, sustainable advantage may come from a culture in which people are motivated to make extra effort, giving their firm lasting superiority in areas like customer service or innovation;

- its architecture. By helping people communicate and share knowledge—and therefore learn from one another—architecture can foster knowledge assets that can give enduring advantage.

2.5 The management of risk, trade-offs, commitment, and paradox

Practising managers face many sources of uncertainty in their strategic decisions. They are trying to make decisions that enable their organizations to cope with an uncertain environment and the unpredictable reactions of human beings inside their organization. And they have to face the near certainty that they will be wrong, at least some of the time. Successful organizations therefore need some way of addressing risk.

There is an important difference between *managing* risk and *avoiding* it. In the 1960s, several firms developed corporate-level strategies that were aimed at diversifying away their risk. They deliberately bought businesses that they thought would generate high profits in economic circumstances that would reduce returns from their core businesses. This strategy was intended to let the corporation generate stable, high returns from its portfolio.

These risk-avoidance strategies were rarely successful. They were based on earlier strategic theories that tended to overestimate the ability of managers to add value to unrelated businesses, and to underestimate the costs of diversification. These strategies also overlooked the economic relationship between risk and reward—by diminishing their exposure to risk, these firms also reduced the probability of their making exceptionally high returns.

→ We analyse the costs of diversification in Section 5.2.

Risk management strategies, by contrast, involve acquiring a detailed knowledge of the risks involved in a range of businesses. Managers then try to ensure that the firm has sufficient cash and other resources to remain viable when the environment is unfavourable, and that it can make exceptional profits in favourable circumstances.

One factor that distinguishes successful risk management from risk avoidance is making the right strategic commitments. The 'right' level of strategic commitment, and the degree of diversification of risk that is appropriate, will vary across different firms in different industries. Strategic decisions involve commitment in the following ways:[52]

- They 'lock in' resources so that they cannot easily be redeployed. For example, when firms decide to launch a new generation of products or introduce new technologies, they will commit cash, expertise, and management time. They may need to build new, specialized research and production facilities. If the original product or technology concept is wrong, then this time and money is likely to have been wasted (although there may occasionally be profitable spin-offs from the research activity) and another firm will take the market. This kind of commitment can be seen in its most extreme form in firms like Intel, the microprocessor manufacturer, or Boeing, the aircraft maker. In both cases, the investment required for a new generation of products is so large that a product failure might bankrupt the firm—yet if they do not make the investment, rivals are likely to emerge to threaten their position.

- They 'lock out' alternative opportunities. A decision *not* to do something—to pull back from an investment, or to exit from an industry—is as strategic as a decision to go ahead. For example, automobile firms that had not entered the Chinese market by 1997 knew that they would not be able to do so for the foreseeable future. The Chinese government had already announced that no new entrants would be permitted after that time, and Chinese culture tends to favour people and organizations that are prepared to build relationships over a long period. Although China represents a vast potential market for cars, firms are finding it difficult to operate there at present. It is quite possible that a decision to stay out of the market there is correct—but it is certain that it is irrevocable.

- They commit resources to changing the organization. This may involve cash spent on training and consultancy, management time spent developing and implementing change programmes, and staking the organization's reputation with customers and employees on getting the change right. If the change fails, the cash and time will have been wasted and the firm's reputation damaged.

Here we see a paradox. On the one hand flexibility—the avoidance of premature commitments—can be valuable in reducing risk, and authors such as Hamel and Prahalad (1994) advocate a phased approach to investment in key capabilities and technologies. On the other hand, some form of commitment is essential to a viable strategy (Real-life Application 2.4 and Table 2.2). There are two main reasons for this:

- Without commitment of time, cash, or other resources, it is impossible for an organization to do anything that cannot easily and quickly be copied by a competitor. Strategies that are simple to copy afford no prospect of lasting advantage.

- Commitment sends important messages to stakeholders. It tells customers, employees, and host governments that the organization is committed to a long-term presence. It tells competitors that the firm will not easily be brushed aside, or that it is intent upon taking a major slice of a market. Simulations show that sometimes, by signalling intent in this way, a firm may persuade less committed competitors to withdraw from a sector.

→ We discuss competitive signalling and strategic collaborations in Section 3.5.6.

Many theorists, most notably Michael Porter,[53] believe that in order to arrive at a sustainable competitive position an organization has to make trade-offs. It must decide which users it wishes to focus its efforts upon, and set up all its systems and processes, and its structure to deliver the services that those users desire, in the way that they want to receive it.

The organization may have to decide that it cannot serve users whose needs are different from those of its core customers, or that it will only take them on its own terms—at a premium price, or by making them wait longer for service than the primary clients. This tailoring of organizational resources and value chains is a form of commitment. Sometimes it may be possible for a firm to straddle a number of customer groups, using the same resources to serve them all. But it must be very careful, in trying to satisfy everyone, that it does not end up diluting its service to its core customers and satisfying no one.

Real-life Application 2.4 Trade-offs and commitment in airliner manufacture

Boeing and Airbus have both committed enormous quantities of resources to the development of major new aircraft. Both have been in anticipation of changes to the airline industry. But there are profound differences in how they see the future developing.

Airbus has invested in a 'super-jumbo', the A380, which will carry 555 passengers. It anticipates that air travel will continue to expand, but that airlines in future will be constrained by limited landing slots at key international airport hubs, which will themselves become fewer and more concentrated in location. It offers its customers a way of dealing with this problem, by allowing them to process the same number of passengers with fewer landing slots.

Boeing, on the other hand, does not see the future in quite the same way. It has committed its resources to the development of smaller mid-sized, fuel-efficient aircraft such as the 200–250 passenger 787 Dreamliner, which is expected to be launched in 2008. Boeing hopes to exploit what it believes will be a fragmentation of airline markets. It envisages that increasing numbers of passengers will choose direct, non-stop journeys with frequent flights, rather than being channelled to their final destinations via huge inter-connecting hubs.

Each firm originally opted for a trade-off, reserving its major commitments to its chosen strategy, while looking for low-commitment ways of providing a rival aircraft in the other segment. Boeing is proposing a stretched version of its existing jumbo aircraft, the 747.[54] Airbus's original idea for the A350, its proposed competitor to the 787, was very similar to the existing A330,[55] but it has since announced a more substantially redesigned aircraft, the A350XWB, that will match the Boeing's key features more closely.[56]

Airbus is finding it challenging to manage these different commitments. The A380 has suffered delays[57] and the A350 will not enter service before 2010.[58] The A340, a slightly larger plane than the A350, is attracting many fewer orders than the rival Boeing 777, but it is not clear if Airbus has the resources to upgrade it; the A350XWB will partially address this issue.[59]

Not all theorists accept Porter's ideas about trade-offs,[60] and even where they do exist, advances in technology and theory may enable organizations to find ways around them. For example, for at least fifty years people believed that there was a trade-off between production costs and number of defects. Improvements in product quality were thought to require more elaborate and expensive production and quality control procedures. However, the total quality movement established that it was often possible to have both highly reliable production processes and low production costs. The savings from not having to find and rectify faulty output more than paid for any extra costs associated with the newer manufacturing procedures.

Similarly, some authors[61] now believe that the trade-off described in Table 2.2 between global operations and local cultural sensitivity is similarly a false one—that it is possible for 'transnational' corporations to get the best of both worlds.

→ Transnational strategies are discussed in Chapter 5.

Table 2.2 Common trade-offs and paradoxes

Trade-off	On the one hand . . .	. . . but on the other hand
Flexibility versus commitment	Premature commitment can waste resources. Prolonged commitment can lock resources into unproductive areas. Flexibility helps diminish risk	Failure to commit sufficient resources early enough may lead to markets being lost to more adventurous or committed players
Diversification versus focus	Too much reliance on one set of customers and markets can render an organization vulnerable to their whims	Too wide a spread can leave each constituent business vulnerable to more focused competitors
Efficiency versus innovation[1]	Small efficiency gains can be the difference between success and failure in highly competitive industries. Innovation can give world-beating products, or big-step gains in customer service or efficiency	If a firm commits too much time and attention to refining its core competences, it may overlook changes in the environment that make them worthless. But if it commits all its attention to innovation, it may never become efficient enough at anything to make money from its new developments
Control versus empowerment	Rigid controls can lead to slow, expensive decision-making. Empowerment can improve innovation and customer responsiveness	Lax controls can lead to agency problems or to maverick entrepreneurial behaviour that undermines corporate image
Globalization versus local responsiveness	Unified global products, brands and management can generate economies of scale and learning	Products designed to be acceptable in every country may end up being second best everywhere. Global managers may overlook the needs of local employees and customers

1 In the literature, this trade-off is more commonly referred to as 'exploitation versus exploration' (March, 1991). We look at it in greater depth in Chapter 6

2.6 For whom strategy happens

In Sections 1.1.4 and 1.6.1 we introduced you to the relationship between strategies and stakeholders' objectives, and summarized the different kinds of stakeholder. In this section, we look at the different kinds of objective that drive particular stakeholder groups. We explore the extent to which different stakeholder groups should be, and are, taken into consideration during the strategy process. We examine the extent to which firms do, and should, take matters other than profit into account in their decision-making. And finally, we review current trends in the ways in which firms are governed to avoid unethical or even criminal behaviour.

2.6.1 Different stakeholders and their objectives

In many firms, the owners—shareholders for example—are not the people who work in them, or who are dependent on them, or who are affected by them in other ways. As we summarize in Table 2.3, the internal stakeholders who work in a firm, and some external stakeholders, may have very different objectives from the owners.

Main stakeholders

Privately owned firms make up a large proportion of employment in most countries of the world (of the 2 million registered companies in the UK in 2004, for example, only 12,000

Table 2.3 Different stakeholder objectives

Stakeholder	Typical financial objectives	Possible other objectives
Private owners	High personal salaries and/or share dividends	Build a monument to personal achievement
	Fringe benefits and pensions	Ensure employment for extended family
		Create employment for local people
External shareholding institutions	Dividends and share price growth (driven by profits)	Retain reputation with investors, so avoid ethical dilemmas or bad publicity
	Eventual exit through sale of shares	
Private funding bodies	Interest payments and recovery of principal	Increase personal power and influence
Governments and regulatory bodies	Tax revenues	Ensure employment for local people
	Minimize cost to taxpayer	Enhance quality of life: • low pollution • efficient and effective infrastructure—transport, energy, telecommunications, water, education, culture
Senior management	High personal salaries and/or share dividends	Be recognized and esteemed by peer group (perhaps leading to lucrative outside appointments)
	Fringe benefits and pensions	Personal power and influence
		Security of employment
Junior employees	Secure, growing income	Security of employment
		Health and safety
		Promotion
		Feel valued by employers and colleagues
Unions	Large body of fee-paying members	Health, safety, and security of employment for members
		Increasing income for members
		Personal power and influence

were PLCs—less than 1 per cent, and this ignores the large numbers of firms that are not registered companies). Their owners often have particular personal objectives and values—wealth, fame, ethical standards, the welfare of their native region—that play a significant role in the firm's strategy. In addition to the owners, internal stakeholders such as employees, managers, and directors, have an interest in what the firm does, and have an influence on the choice of strategy. However, the only stakeholders that have the power to enforce major changes in management or strategy, or to close down an organization, fall into three main categories: shareholding institutions and stock markets; government and regulatory bodies; major funding bodies.

Shareholding institutions have particular significance in Anglo-Saxon economies and a growing influence in continental Europe and Japan. Pension funds and insurance companies own the vast majority of all traded equities in those economies, and they employ specialist fund managers who select the shares for them. Companies like McDonald's and British Airways that are quoted on the UK and US stock markets often invest considerable time and effort in keeping these stakeholders informed and happy. Most such outside share-holders hold shares as financial investments, and are required to generate a return on these investments. They therefore tend to look above all for steadily increasing profits and share prices, and also in some cases for a steady flow of dividends.

Governments, legislators and regulators, such as the UK's Charities' Commission and Strategic Rail Authority, or the Food and Drug Administration (FDA) and the Securities & Exchange Commission in the USA, are relevant to both public sector organizations, where they are likely to be the controlling stakeholders, and commercial firms, where they may also be hugely influential. In some parts of the world, such as the UK, regulators have a par-ticularly strong role in firms that are now privatized but were previously in the public sector. In such cases, it has been government practice to set up regulators to ensure that firms do not abuse local monopoly positions.

Major funding bodies' requirements are most often relevant to the public sector or non-profit organizations, which rely on them for sponsorship or revenue. These types of stake-holders include large private or corporate donors as well as semi-autonomous government bodies, termed quangos in the UK, which are set up specifically to fund and manage certain kinds of organization. For example, the UK government's Arts Council funds many different sorts of arts activities such as theatre groups or opera companies, and as a condition of funding requires them to do certain things. A theatre company may be required to put on a certain minimum number of productions, to make a certain number of tickets available at prices affordable by people with low incomes, or to arrange sessions in local schools to help to give young people an interest in live theatre. Such organizations are also likely to seek and receive funding from other sources, such as private donors, who may have their own (potentially conflicting) objectives.

Main types of stakeholder objective

As Table 2.3 shows, almost every stakeholder has, alongside financial objectives, non-financial ones that relate to their individual needs and ambitions.

Organizations survive and grow by attracting resources, such as people, raw materials, and money. The external stakeholders that control those resources, and the internal stake-holders that control access to them, have, if they choose to exercise it, a great deal of power within organizations and influence on its strategy. In order for the organization to gain those resources, stakeholders must perceive it as a legitimate body to work with.

If an organization is not seen as legitimate, then suppliers and customers will hesitate to do business with it, people may be reluctant to work for it, and financial institutions may decide that it is too risky to lend money to. If government bodies doubt its legitimacy, they may burden it with costly extra inspections or reporting requirements. This means that many things that organizations do are directed towards achieving legitimacy with key stakeholders. But legitimacy cuts both ways—it is used by stakeholders to assess the organization but is also used by managers to evaluate which stakeholders they should give priority to. The pro-cess of winning legitimacy is known as 'legitimation'. Legitimacy takes three main forms.

Moral legitimacy comes from doing, or appearing to do, the 'right thing' to enhance social welfare. Organizations that make much of their ethical standards, or the way in which they treat their employees or minimize pollution, are trying to win moral legitimacy—which does not necessarily mean that they do not sincerely believe in what they are doing. However, as we discuss later in this chapter, there is a considerable debate about how far down the path of Corporate Social Responsibility an organization should go to win moral legitimacy.

Pragmatic legitimacy comes when an organization provides some benefit to those that have a relationship with it, even though in other circumstances there is unlikely to be a

Legitimacy
'[A] generalized perception or assumption that the actions of an entity are desirable, proper or appropriate within some socially constructed system of norms, values, beliefs and definitions' (Suchman, 1995: 574).

relationship. Even if you were vehemently opposed to European unity, you might still try to have a good working relationship with the European Commission, which has a great deal of influence over business regulations in Europe and, because of its power to veto mergers and acquisitions with a European dimension, world wide. The Commission has pragmatic legitimacy, even in the eyes of people who doubt its legitimacy on other fronts.

To achieve cognitive legitimacy, organizations or people must 'fit in' by acting in the ways that people expect from respectable members of society. Most people like to be accepted, or better still respected, by those around them, because it makes everyday life easier and more pleasant. It may also help in getting promoted, finding a better job, or becoming a member of an exclusive sports club. When you wear smart clothes to a job interview, even if you normally wear, and work better in, scruffy jeans, then you are looking for cognitive legitimacy in the eyes of your future employer. Firms expect their suppliers to observe laws and norms on health and safety, and suppliers expect to see some signs of creditworthiness before agreeing to take the firm on as a customer. This does not mean you must never challenge the beliefs and assumptions of the social system in which you are operating—but you need to be aware that, in doing so, you may create a credibility problem that you have to work hard to overcome.

People often find that, if the organization they work for is successful or prestigious, some of the glory will rub off on them, so that their social and family life will benefit. This gives them a motive for acting in ways that will bring legitimacy to their employer. Sometimes, however, considerations of personal legitimacy may override the interests of the firm.

Cognitive and moral legitimacy depend greatly, of course, on the society where the organization or person lives, or is trying to do business. In some countries, certain amounts of tax evasion, bribery, or nepotism (hiring friends and relatives even though there may be better people for the job) are regarded as normal things that help keep the wheels of commerce turning. In others, these practices are not tolerated, even in small doses. Expectations and norms also vary from industry to industry.

There are two reasons why the pursuit of legitimacy as an end in itself may be problematic or controversial. One is that it may tempt managers to 'follow the herd' and put in place fashionable practices, or hire fashionable advisers, without calculating the costs and benefits carefully enough, or think through whether the benefits are actually achievable for their firm. Some firms have quality management systems because they believe that quality is important to being competitive, and some because they believe that it is morally wrong to put imperfect products on the market. But others do so because government or other customers have made it clear that they expect them, or perhaps even because all their friends in prestigious firms have systems of that kind. Some theorists believe that a number of management fads, such as total quality management, have spread this way.[62]

The second reason is that at some stage a trade-off is reached between legitimacy and profitability, at least in the short term. A corporate social responsibility (CSR) programme to help unemployed people in the area, for example, may win moral legitimacy but prove expensive. There is a considerable debate about how much an organization should commit to CSR; we go into this in more depth later in the chapter.

2.6.2 Which stakeholders are important

The debate over CSR is strongly rooted in a debate over who an organization *really* belongs to. Is it the property of the shareholders, or is it managed for the benefit of the society in which it is based? This summarizes two different philosophies of the firm: shareholder value and stakeholder capitalism.

Shareholder value
Shareholder value theory states that organizations belong to their shareholders, whose interests supersede those of any other stakeholders, and that it is the managers' duty to maximize the firm's economic value.

a. Shareholder value

In Anglo-Saxon cultures, great importance is attached to the idea that the shareholders are the owners, or principals of the company, so that their interests take precedence over those of other stakeholders.[53] This implies that the agents (managers and staff) that they employ to run the firm on their behalf should manage it solely to increase shareholder value.

The measure of whether they are performing this duty is the firm's stock market value, which is held to express the net present value of the firm's resources and all profits likely to flow from them, resulting in a capital gain as the share price rises. Firms may also choose to issue dividends if they believe that their own ability to generate returns from this money is less than the shareholder could obtain from investing it elsewhere. Increases in shareholder value are measured on the basis of increases in share price plus dividends paid in a particular period.

Focusing on shareholder value has its detractors, however. James Collins and Jerry Porras[64] compared a portfolio of 18 'visionary' firms, and compared their performance from 1926 to 1990 against a matched set of 18 companies that claimed to maximize shareholder value and another group of 'normal' public corporations. The visionary firms appreciated over six times more than the shareholder value claiming firms, and 15 times more than the normal firms. Their conclusion was that shareholder-value methods do not maximize shareholder value.

One reason for this is that it has proved difficult to find a good measure of shareholder value. An earlier, crude indicator, earnings per share, has fallen out of fashion in the light of evidence that it can lead to poor management decisions, but alternatives, such as 'economic value added', have also proved controversial and difficult to calculate.

➡ We examine the different methods of measuring shareholder value in Theoretical Debate 11.1.

b. Stakeholder capitalism

Criticisms of the shareholder value philosophy are reflected in an alternative body of thinking that regards it as oversimplified, and holds that corporate decision-making should take account of other shareholders. It emerged from the Stanford Research Institute in the 1960s, and was popularized by Edward Freeman,[65] who also coined the definition of a stakeholder that we and most other writers use.

In practice, this alternative philosophy, stakeholder capitalism, is most deeply embedded in Japan and continental European countries, notably France and Germany. All these countries were devastated by the Second World War, and their people needed to marshal a huge effort to rebuild their economies. They came to adopt a version of capitalism in which firms assumed partial responsibility for the welfare of their workers and local communities, and the supremacy of the equity shareholder is regarded as less obvious.[66] Long-term bank lending plays a greater role in the firm's capital than is usual in the UK or the USA, and the bank is an influential stakeholder with board representation.

In countries such as France or Germany, the culture and the legal system give more weight to the interests of employees and communities than to those of shareholders. Workers' representatives are entitled to participate in key decisions, and local and national governments often have considerable influence on decisions like plant openings and closures.

Shareholders in these countries seemed content to live with lower returns on their investment than they might have obtained in, say, the United States. Firms instead spent money on salaries for employees they did not always need, and on government taxes that funded a comprehensive social welfare system. This gave individuals some kind of guarantee of personal security—they would not usually lose their jobs, and if they did, they would still not live in poverty. This guarantee helped motivate them for the task of economic reconstruction. Over the four decades following the Second World War, the Japanese, German, and French economies grew much faster than those of the UK or the USA, and gave rise to innovative and highly competitive companies such as Toyota, Sony, Daimler, and Alcatel. Proponents of this model of capitalism also point to the lower crime rates and higher degree of social cohesion in these countries.

More recently, however, economic growth in these countries has slowed and unemployment has risen sharply. This has led some of their business leaders and politicians to question whether the firms' social obligations have become too burdensome, raising their costs and slowing their adjustment to change in the competitive environment. There is some evidence that they are now gradually moving towards the Anglo-Saxon shareholder value model.[67]

Meanwhile, customers and consumers have, for their part, suddenly found that they have considerable power to influence the decisions made by organizations, even those that espouse shareholder value. In 1999, a Europe-wide consumer revolt against genetically modified (GM) foodstuffs resulted in many retailers and fast-food chains committing themselves to phase out food items containing GM ingredients.[68] The European Union put a moratorium on the approval of new GM crops that was only lifted in 2004.[69] Monsanto, the market leader in GM technology, modified its marketing of GM produce and brought in a new CEO, less evangelical in his approach than his predecessor.[70] Lending institutions and pension fundholders in their turn are reflecting consumers' ethical concerns in their lending and investment policies towards companies.

c. The principal-agent problem

A further problem that has emerged with shareholder value is that managers who espouse it have not always acted in external shareholders' long-term interests. These can be viewed as managers putting their personal needs for wealth, power, or legitimacy above those of other stakeholders, and are instances of what we referred to in Section 1.3.3 as the principal–agent problem.

There is a danger that in public companies, chief executives and other board members may be able to profit from the firm at the expense of shareholders and other stakeholders. In the UK recently, and previously in the USA, there has been controversy because senior executive remuneration has been increasing much faster than general salary levels, and often bears no relationship to profits or share prices.[71] US directors have also been criticized for putting in place 'poison pills'—legal devices to protect their firms from hostile takeover bids—and 'golden parachutes'—provisions to give them large payments if their firms are taken over. Many theorists believe that these provisions work against the interests of shareholders, by protecting managers from the consequences of poor decisions, though some recent studies cast doubt upon this.[72]

In the UK, this led to the Greenbury Report, which investigated the level and structure of remuneration schemes for senior executives of public companies and recommended that directors' pay should be disclosed in annual reports and set by independent committees. Other remedies designed to improve corporate governance were implemented at the same time and are discussed in Section 2.7.2b.

Some other practices have been recommended to help marry the objectives of organizational managers and shareholders. One of the best known is the paying of executives in the form of share options rather than in the form of a salary. In this way, it is thought, they will be encouraged to achieve the highest levels of shareholder value, rather than taking payment in the form of high levels of perks or wages—money which is taken off the bottom line and never finds its ways to shareholders. However, share options eventually have to be paid for through the issuing of shares, diluting other shareholders' own holdings. There have been examples of executives attempting artificially to boost share prices through buying back their company's own equity with borrowed money, in order to increase the value of their share options in the short term (see Section 2.7 below).

➜ We return to the issues of shareholder value and the role of reward systems in shaping strategic behaviour in Chapters 8 and 12 respectively.

➜ We look at mergers and acquisitions in Chapter 17.

Principal–agent problems are not unique to the societies that have espoused shareholder value. Some observers believe, for example, that the German system has led to complacent directors whose conservative policies and high remuneration are rarely questioned by the union representatives on the board, and who in return have been generous in the pay and benefits offered to union members.

d. Which stakeholders are given priority in practice

So far, our discussion of stakeholder importance has focused at the level of the society in which the organization is located. For managers, however, life is always more complicated than these theories suggest. Even in societies where shareholders are the most important stakeholder in theory, in practice there are always others competing for managerial attention. In practice, therefore, managers appear to use three criteria to judge which stakeholder demands are most pressing:[73]

- The power of the stakeholder to enforce its claims on the organization or individual managers, by giving or withholding resources.

- The legitimacy of the stakeholder and of the particular claim it is making. Stakeholders with low cognitive legitimacy, such as ethnic minority employees or environmental pressure groups, may have particular difficulties in getting managers to take their demands seriously, unless they can get power, for example by lobbying the government or the press. On the other hand, managers may give a sympathetic hearing to their firm's pensioners, people whom they may know personally and whose ranks they will eventually join, even though those people may have little formal power.

➜ We look in greater detail at how to analyse stakeholder power, legitimacy, and urgency in Worked Example 15.1 and Section 16.2.2.

- The urgency of the claim. Other things being equal, managers will give priority to the stakeholders who need quick attention.

As Figure 2.3 shows, the more of these characteristics a stakeholder has, the more attention it is likely to command.

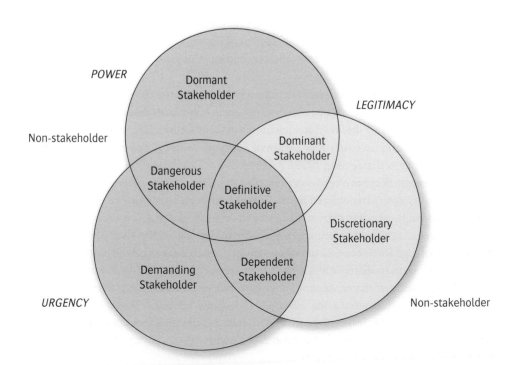

Figure 2.3 Stakeholder typology (Mitchell et al., 1997)

2.7 Corporate social responsibility and business ethics

One of the pressing questions in management theory relates to the lengths to which managers should go to satisfy, or even to anticipate, stakeholder demands. One school of thought suggests that executives' only responsibility is to make profits for shareholders; any activity that is not clearly to do with this should be avoided. At its most extreme, this ethos can be summarized in the famous phrase of the Chicago monetarist economist Milton Friedman:[74] 'the business of business is business', although Friedman made it clear that managers should act, 'in open and free competition, without deception or fraud'. In fact a recent *Economist* article claimed that socially responsible corporate behaviour, unless it was profitable as well, was actually *unethical*—because money was being spent on good causes and thus diverted away from the rightful recipients—shareholders.[75]

The question then arises as to how far an organization should go to win business and avoid unprofitable obligations. Profit-seeking behaviour is sometimes taken too far, the result of the competitive nature of companies; striving to win is necessary for a manager to get to the top in most companies. In fact the last decade has been exceptional in the number and size of corporate fraud cases. These have been particularly prevalent in the USA, in the cases of WorldCom, Enron, and Tyco, but there have also been cases in Europe and Asia— Parmalat in Italy and PetroVietnam in Vietnam.[76] All of these examples appear to have been encouraged by inherent aspects of the capitalist system, particularly its requirement for profits and for returns to be made to shareholders.

In September 2004, three years after the company went bankrupt, charges of conspiracy, fraud, and insider trading and the manipulation of corporate accounts were brought against Enron's top executives (see also What Can Go Wrong 1.1). They were accused of using fraudulent schemes to deceive investors about the true performance of the firm's businesses and to line their own pockets. These schemes helped Enron to meet its financial targets and its executives to earn bonuses.[77] Although these practices were not necessarily illegal, as they exploited inconsistencies in the different rules for tax and book accounting, they have been used to argue that Enron's corporate culture was one where sharp practices were commonplace.

Parmalat, Italy's largest dairy firm, had debts of €14bn when it collapsed, leaving tens of thousands of small investors with worthless bonds. Although its former chief executive has been charged with market-rigging, fraudulent bankruptcy, making false statements, and false accounting, the scandal is said to have gone much deeper to include the company's banks and auditors, against some of whom lawsuits have been filed. In addition lawsuits seeking €10bn in damages have been launched against two international auditing firms that for years oversaw the accounts of the firm. It accuses them of improper auditing that allowed huge sums to be 'stolen, squandered or wasted' by the firms' managers.[78] As a result, in 2004, the Italian government took the first steps to overhaul regulation of the country's financial institutions by stripping the central bank of many of its powers, and to increase the role of the main stock-market regulator, Consob.[79]

There has therefore been considerable soul-searching, in the USA and Italy at least, about the regulatory and cultural framework that has allowed these scandals to develop. In each case there appears to have been a widespread systemic failure on the part of the boards of directors, auditors, and regulators to exercise appropriate control, allowing cultures where sharp practice and loose accounting practices were commonplace. Thus another school of thought says that organizations have obligations to a much broader group of stakeholders than shareholders, particularly those that may be disadvantaged and have little formal power. Those who fall below the normal standards of legal or ethical behaviour are relatively rare, and a more relevant topic for discussion is how much should companies contribute to the wider society in which they operate.

2.7.1 **Corporate social responsibility**

Corporate social responsibility (CSR)
An umbrella term for corporate policies to ensure ethical behaviour and address social problems inside and outside the organization.

The term 'social responsibility' was coined in the 1950s,[80] but the practice of corporate social responsibility (CSR) is much older than that. Medieval trades' guilds endowed schools and hospitals for their members and their families. In the nineteenth century, companies such as Lever Brothers (now part of Unilever) and Cadburys (part of Cadbury-Schweppes) set up company towns where workers were offered a clean, pleasant environment with a wide range of social and educational facilities.

As we pointed out in Section 2.6.1, CSR can boost profits by winning legitimacy for the organization in the eyes of customers and other important stakeholders. The FTSE and Dow Jones have recently set up indices of socially responsible companies. Indeed, there is some evidence that ethical behaviour can help firms survive longer.[81] However, there comes a point at which the balance of costs and benefits to shareholders becomes unclear. Therefore a real question for managers is how much weight they should give to competing obligations, to society and to shareholders.

A wide range of activities come under CSR's umbrella. Some may be targeted at specific stakeholder groups, for example:

- charitable donations in cash or in kind;

- providing child care or other social services to employees or local communities;

- paying higher than average wages to employees with little bargaining power;

- providing goods or services, over and above what is on offer for the firm's typical customer, for customers with low incomes or disabilities.

Some examples are shown below:

- The Co-operative Bank in the UK has positioned itself entirely as the ethical bank, assuring customers that their bank deposits will never be lent onwards to firms that manufacture arms or pollute the environment. Lending institutions and pension fund-holders in their turn are reflecting consumers' ethical concerns in their lending and investment policies towards companies that, for example, promote GM foods.

- Companies that place a lot of production work in developing countries, such as Disney and Mattel, the world's leading toy manufacturer, have taken the initiative in making sure that their own personnel management practices are above criticism. They have set up codes of conduct for their managers and subcontractors and have their plants inspected by independent auditors.[82]

- Mining companies Placer Dome and RTZ have helped the World Health Organization to develop and fund a 'business plan for health' in Papua. One scheme helps to train local villagers to treat malaria and deliver babies. The payoff to the contributors comes partly in increased goodwill, and partly in having a happier, healthier, and so more productive workforce.

- De Beers, the diamond producer, contributed $2.7m to a World Health Organization programme to eliminate polio in Angola. It also insists on its local employees using their marketing skills to raise awareness of the campaign.

Many firms have explicit policies on protecting the natural environment.[83] BP, the world's largest oil company, spent $45m to purchase Solarex, a solar energy firm and has started to fit solar panels to generate electricity at its filling stations. It was the first major oil firm to support the aims, agreed in 1997 at the UN's Kyoto summit, to reduce emissions of greenhouse gases.

And firms also do things intended to benefit a broad swathe of society. They may decide to hold down prices for products in short supply, or go above legal requirements in order to preserve the natural environment. They may also, voluntarily, decide to place more information in the public domain than they are legally compelled to, even though this means extra costs and gives competitors data that can be used against them. They may put in place extra internal controls to ensure compliance with laws or ethical codes, or undertake not to take on business which might involve unethical or environmentally damaging behaviour—for example, in countries where bribery is common or environmental standards are lax (see Real-life Application 2.5).

Real-life Application 2.5 H&M's ethical policies

H&M has had a Code of Conduct for its 900 or so suppliers (who are mainly in East Asia) since 1997, and started producing an annual CSR report in 2002. The 2003 version runs to some 60 pages and is widely referred to in many of the company's public statements. In addition, the department that is responsible for environment and CSR issues reports directly to the managing director. From this one can infer that H&M takes its social responsibilities seriously.

H&M is a Swedish company and therefore comes from a culture where social issues have a higher priority than almost any other nation. It is also operating in an industry where customers (mainly young women) are not afraid to demand socially responsible behaviour from their retailers, and where some of their major competitors have had their fingers rather severely burnt when their treatment of juvenile workers in developing countries was called into question. So H&M is obviously an organization which takes its ethical responsibilities extremely seriously, and is clearly investing a lot of money in various CSR schemes. However, this is unlikely to be doing it much harm commercially at the moment either. It acknowledges this: 'Good relations with the world around us and long-term profitability depend on H&M taking responsibility for how people and the environment are affected by their activities.'[84]

The Code of Conduct says that every supplier must: observe the laws of the country, abstain from using child labour, maintain good working conditions and safety, provide reasonable pay and working hours, and allow freedom of association (which in effect is to allow trade unions). The supplier also agrees to regular factory inspections—both announced and unannounced—by H&M. Those suppliers that do not currently meet all requirements must sign a declaration stating that they will implement the necessary improvements. To enforce compliance, H&M has a team of 30 inspectors and 110 quality controllers, all of whom have responsibility for reporting any infringements they find. H&M say that they carry out two thousand inspections each year. It also says they have appointed environmental representatives in all the countries in which it does business, and for its central office, and set detailed environmental targets each year.

H&M also has explicit policies concerning the impact of its business on the environment. In this it has a number of concerns:

- To ensure that chemicals that may be harmful to health and the environment are not used in the production or selling of their goods. The restrictions now cover around 150 substances, including lead, cadmium, mercury, PVC, certain dyes, organotins, and brominated flame retardants. Restriction on these substances also allows their products and fittings to be recycled more easily.

- To reduce the consumption of energy, for example through low-energy lighting, new production routines to improve heat exchange, insulation to reduce heat loss, and recycling.

- To ensure a clean production chain including water treatment, the storage and use of chemicals, and the disposal of hazardous waste—an especial problem during the dyeing stage of clothes production.

- To reduce the impact of its transportation on the environment through increasing load capacity, the use of rail rather than road vehicles, and through the introduction of policies on the type of road vehicle and fuel to be used, and driver training in fuel-efficient driving.

H&M also makes use of a number of external verifiers of its CSR policies. It follows the OECD's guidelines for multinational enterprises and is a member of the Swedish Amnesty Business Group's Business Forum. It is included in the Dow Jones World, STOXX, FTSE4Good, and Ethibel sustainability indexes. It recently signed a worldwide agreement with Union Network International, the international umbrella trade union organization for the retail and services sector (UNI). H&M also supports the UN Global Compact, a United Nations-driven initiative that 'seeks to advance responsible corporate citizenship through the power of collective action'. In so doing H&M says that it wants to 'signify' that it respects human rights and contributes to sustainable development'.[85] In July 2004, UNICEF announced that H&M had donated $1.5m towards girls' education programmes worldwide and HIV/AIDS prevention programmes in Cambodia. This partnership is UNICEF's Swedish Committee's first global initiative.

Main stimulus for CSR	Outside firm	Normative CSR	Competitive CSR Coercive CSR
	Inside firm	Philanthropic CSR Inertial CSR	Enlightened self-interest
		Unclear (ethical CSR)	*Clear (strategic CSR)*
		Economic benefits from CSR	

Figure 2.4 Different reasons for corporate social responsibility (Haberberg and Mulleady, 2004)

There are a number of different reasons why firms and managers practise CSR. These are summarized in Figure 2.4. The nineteenth-century philanthropists in charge of Lever Brothers and Cadbury were very religious people who acted, at least in part, from their own deeply held principles. This was philanthropic CSR. But they would not have been human if they had not realized that a sober and well-educated workforce was likely to be more productive than the alternative, and mixed in with that philanthropy there was likely to have been a healthy dose of enlightened self-interest. This same mix of principles and enlightened self-interest motivates many business people today. And once a charismatic leader has introduced a culture of CSR, then succeeding generations of managers are likely to maintain it—inertial CSR becomes part of the organization's paradigm.

But not all managers that practise CSR necessarily have that degree of internal belief. Sometimes they do so because it is the norm in their profession or social group. This is normative CSR. Sometimes firms are pushed into CSR by the activities of outside stakeholders. Where most firms in an industry have strong policies on the environment or high-profile charitable activities, their competitors may feel compelled to follow, for fear of losing customers: this is competitive CSR. And sometimes socially responsible policies are forced upon organizations by outside pressure groups, or by retailers that will not sell products made using child labour or timber from non-renewable sources. This is coercive CSR.

The notion of coercive CSR brings us to our next section, and also highlights some of the problems in defining absolute standards of CSR. Monsanto, the market leader in GM technology, is a firm that takes considerable pride in its ethical standards, and also deeply believes in the social benefits of its products.[86] Nevertheless, as we mentioned in Section 2.6.2, it has felt it necessary to respond to the concerns over GM of its customers and the wider society in which it operates.

Theoretical Debate 2.1 Should organizations adopt corporate social responsibility programmes?

Scholars such as Milton Friedman (1962, 1996) and Theodore Levitt (1983), a well-known marketing theorist, hold that businesses have no special social responsibility other than to operate within the law. These views tend to proceed from the idea that corporations are created by individuals rather than by society. The argument is that companies should have the same freedoms as individuals do to set their own moral standards and to use their property as they see fit.   →

➔ Those who disagree with this view tend to argue that businesses are so intertwined with the rest of society that they cannot act without considering its obligations to it. According to these arguments, businesses have obligations to stakeholders or constituents, on whom they depend for their survival and who are affected by their actions. Organizations' social power brings social responsibilities as well, and if they want to focus upon shareholders to the exclusion of all other stakeholders, then they should not attempt to influence political processes or government policy (Reich, 1998).

However, the ethics of CSR are not clear-cut. A recent *Economist* article (*Economist*, 2004), as we noted in Section 2.7, argued that socially responsible corporate behaviour might actually be *unethical*. Certainly, if CSR-style activities are being undertaken primarily for the benefit of people inside the organization—to increase their *personal* legitimacy, or to make them feel good about themselves—then, unless this increased self-esteem feeds back into higher productivity or better customer service, the *Economist* argument may have some force.

This indicates how these philosophical arguments are intertwined with more practical ones about the extent to which CSR adds to or subtracts from shareholder value. The early advocates of CSR believed (Bowen, 1953; Carroll, 1999) that there was a trade-off between short-term profit and social responsibility. However, there are counter-arguments, already mentioned in this chapter, that CSR contributes to competitive advantage, for example by winning legitimacy for the firm. Some theorists argue that these positive effects are so great that social responsibility should actually take priority over short-term considerations of shareholder wealth. The theorist who has gone furthest down this route is Thomas Jones of the University of Washington, who has also proposed an extension of principal–agent theory to take in multiple stakeholders (Hill and Jones, 1992; Jones, 1995; Quinn and Jones, 1995).

There have been over 120 empirical studies (Margolis and Walsh, 2003) of the relationship between organizations' financial performance and their adoption of CSR practices, and the results are indeterminate. While almost half the studies found that CSR practices appeared to be associated with better than average performance, and only a handful found the opposite, many showed neutral or mixed results. However, it seems clear, on the balance of evidence, that Bowen was mistaken, and that CSR does not hurt financial performance.

The answer of the opponents of corporate social responsibility is that, although corporate social responsibility programmes *look* as if they are benefiting society, in fact they are hurting it in ways that are not easy to see. One such harmful effect is that organizations, in pursuing CSR, end up making poorer decisions. Jensen (2001) criticizes CSR because it introduces ambiguity into corporate decision-making—he believes that managers need a single, clear target to guide them, and that that should be profit. Henderson (2001) argues that considerations of CSR dull the edge of competition in markets and therefore make the economy as a whole less efficient. He believes that this ends up making everybody poorer. He also worries that, in being too ready to accept stakeholder concerns on issues like globalization, managers shy away from putting the case for business and commerce as a force for progress that increases welfare.

Another potentially harmful effect, highlighted by Henderson and also by Freeman and Liedtka (1991), is that managers end up taking decisions in areas well outside their areas of expertise. They may have no expertise in education, yet end up taking decisions about educational programmes for their local community —or even running them themselves. And how many corporate executives, however committed and intelligent, are *really* qualified to decide on the correct response to African poverty or global warming?

2.7.2 Stakeholder controls on strategic choices

The Monsanto case in the previous section is an example of stakeholders other than managers or shareholders having influence over a company's strategy. It is quite common for different sets of stakeholders to hold differing views about a firm's direction. External shareholders' desire for growth in both profits and the share price may be in conflict with the costs of implementing government legislation. The founder's desire to reinvest profits to secure a long-term future for the firm and jobs for his or her children may be at odds with employees' or unions' desire for higher wages in the short term.

There are several mechanisms that stakeholders, including external ones, can use to control what happens, and to influence managers and other stakeholders to comply with their objectives. These mechanisms will vary according to the norms in the organization's home country.

- In Anglo-Saxon countries, and increasingly elsewhere, control may be exerted through the stock market. Dissatisfied shareholders sell their shares in the market until the price falls to a point where another firm will find it worthwhile to acquire the firm and reform its strategy, or senior managers are forced to resign. This mechanism is also known as the market for corporate control.

- Elsewhere, shareholders and bankers may exert their influence on strategy more directly, through the fact that they have seats on the board or processes for direct lobbying of management.

- A bank or other major funding body also has the option of withdrawing its funding, or refusing new loans, forcing the firm into bankruptcy, or a change of direction or senior management.

- Infringements of legal and regulatory requirements may lead to organizations facing fines, having changes imposed in their management systems, or being forced to close.

a. Regulation

In most industrialized countries governmental stakeholders monitor and control firms through laws and regulations (see Real-life Application 2.6). The types of requirement that they impose will vary from sector to sector. For example:

- Firms may face regulations on the health and safety of employees, laws which prescribe what emissions and effluents may be discharged into the environment, and legislation on the use and abuse of proprietary knowledge.

- Retailers are frequently regulated on their location and their hours of opening.

- Financial services firms must meet international standards on the financial reserves they carry to back up their activities, and local regulations in terms of what they are allowed to sell, and to what types of customer.

- Educational organizations are frequently regulated in terms of what must, as a minimum, be included in their curriculum, the qualification levels of the staff they employ, and sometimes the standards of their internal administration.

- Transport firms may have to meet standards in terms of frequency of service, reliability (number of timetabled services that actually run), and punctuality.

All of these constrain the choices that are available to organizations, and the profits they can accrue.

 Real-life Application 2.6 Regulation in the airline industry

The airline industry is one of the most regulated in the world. International regulations cover areas such as aircraft safety, the instruments and flight manuals on board, the provision of lockable flight decks, pilot training, landing slots at airports, the allocation of routes, and especially which airlines are allowed to enter a country's airspace. The industry is subject to rules from national and supra-national governments such as the EU, as well as industry-specific agencies that control particular aspects of airline operations. These include: both the Civil Aviation Authority in the UK and the Federal Aviation Authority in the USA, which are responsible for, amongst other things, supervising aircraft safety standards, the allocation of airport slots, the collection of passenger and fare data, and air traffic control; as well as the ICAO (International Civil Aviation Organization), an inter-governmental agency which coordinates airline standards and technical procedures internationally.

In the past almost every country's air traffic was heavily regulated. States had their own national airline, which was government owned and which was used for both symbolic and practical purposes—transporting presidents on overseas visits, for example, →

→ as well as supporting the state's defence needs. Since 1978 in the USA, from 1987 to 1997 in the European Union, and patchily elsewhere, the airline industry has been deregulated. Deregulation loosened the previously strict controls over where airlines could fly or how much they could charge. It allowed new airlines to emerge, serving new routes and with new pricing and competitive strategies. It also meant that some inefficient airlines, which had previously been propped up by their governments, went bankrupt—a process that continues to this day. However, strict controls are still maintained over many aspects of the industry.

Partial deregulation has encouraged mergers and alliances in the industry, as airlines have tried to find ways to overcome the remaining areas of government restriction. For example, ownership is still regulated in many parts of the world, with the home government often the majority shareholder. Even the USA, which has no single state carrier, prevents foreign firms from owning more than 25 per cent of any of its airlines' shares. Although it has recently been proposed that this percentage should be increased to 49 per cent, this is still less than would be needed for a foreign company to achieve full control. The restriction appears to stay in force because of trades union concerns about loss of jobs, and fears about loss of control of a key area of national security. In the 2004 Iraq war, the military relied heavily on domestic airlines for transportation; almost all routine travel by military personnel utilizes civilian flights, and domestic carriers are moving an increasing amount of military supplies and equipment.

World-wide routes are also governed by a series of bilateral agreements between nations/regions, which basically consist of allowing country A's airline to operate a flight to country B, and vice versa. But problems of balance arise when a domestic market is not of a comparable size and activity to the partner's—typically the USA. Prime landing slots at key airports are also usually still held by the former national airline—BA in the case of Heathrow, the main London airport in the UK.

International alliances between airlines have therefore allowed them to bypass regulatory restrictions, as have mergers such as the recent one between the Netherlands' KLM and Air France, who can now access each others' international routes. Some alliances are basically a route-sharing and reservation systems agreement, others are more complex, establishing joint commercial and marketing activities and/or physical operations. The first major alliance SkyTeam, initially involving Delta, Singapore, and Swissair, included the coordination of international fares and flight schedules, joint frequent flyer programmes, and the sharing of routes and aircraft. This alliance has since been followed by others including oneworld (including BA, American, and Qantas) and Star (including United, Lufthansa, and Air Canada).

Other bodies may also have regulatory powers delegated to them by law or by consent of their member firms. Professional associations often dictate who is allowed to practise law, medicine, or architecture, or to audit company accounts. Stock exchanges and sporting associations have the power to insist that their member firms meet certain reporting standards. All of these groupings, along with bodies such as sporting associations, can insist that firms' individual employees conform to certain standards of behaviour. They can fine or expel individuals who infringe those standards, for example by taking drugs or abusing

The oneworld alliance includes BA, American Airlines, and Qantas. *oneworld*

privileged information, by taking bets on sporting fixtures in which they are involved, or by 'insider trading'—buying or selling securities that they know, because of information that is not yet public knowledge, will rise or fall.

One of the most important external constraints on strategy-making is related to the abuse of monopolistic positions. Monopolies allow firms to make extraordinary profits, at the expense of the customers who have to pay for essential services. Monopolistic firms also tend to be inefficient, or can become so, as there is little incentive for managers to strive to innovate, minimize costs, or achieve high levels of quality. It is the goal of most profit-maximizing firms to achieve this position, however. The closer they get to a dominant market position, the more profits they are likely to make, and, unless they are controlled, powerful firms tend to become more powerful, as they can set the basis of competition to favour themselves.

➜ The concept of increasing returns is discussed in Section 3.5.6.

Indeed, the recent development of thinking on increasing returns suggests that, in some industries, an initial dominance will never be lost unless deliberately controlled by forces external to the industry. It is this that led the US courts to order remedies against the software giant Microsoft, on the grounds that it acted illegally to maintain a monopoly in the face of threats from Netscape's web browser and Sun Microsystems' Java software.[87]

Because most industrialized countries appear to see monopolies as a bad thing, the majority have legal frameworks which act to minimize the power of dominant firms, through blocking their ability to buy up competing firms, or regulating the price they can charge for their products. In the EU, this is carried out under the aegis of the European Commission and through such country agencies as the Office of Fair Trading in the UK, or the Bundeskartellamt in Germany.

b. Corporate governance

Thus, almost all organizations are regulated in some way. Their executives are subject to legal constraints on what they can do and how they can do it. In the case of some sorts of organizations, such as companies and charities, they are also required to fulfil certain conditions in terms of who manages them, and how they disclose information to the public. There needs to be some mechanism whereby a firm's managers can be monitored to make sure that they are fulfilling their legal obligations, and are meeting the owner's objectives for the company. The systems for doing this are known as corporate governance procedures.

Corporate governance procedures are often discussed in terms of the principals making sure that the agents are doing what is required of them, and not exploiting their position. However, a number of recent corporate scandals, such as Parmalat (see Section 2.7 above), have featured principals—individuals and families with large shareholdings in a corporation—exploiting other principals, notably outside shareholders, by using corporate assets for their private ends. Others have involved owners exploiting the agents, by raiding employee pension funds. So corporate governance procedures are really intended to police the behaviour of principals and agents alike.

In many parts of the world organizations are managed by a board of directors, whose composition, roles, and responsibilities differ greatly between countries. In the UK and the USA, these boards usually comprise both executive and non-executive directors (directors who are not at the same time managers in the company). In other European countries, for example Germany and Holland, the boards are divided into two tiers: the upper tier supervises the lower tier, is separate from it and often includes representatives of the workforce.

This is a way of ensuring a greater distribution of power than would be the case if companies were managed only by internal boards of directors—who could be appointed by existing board members, with the effect of narrowing decision-making to a small and self-selected group of people.

The Cadbury Committee in the UK, the Dey Report in Canada, the Hilmer Report in Australia, and the Veinot Report in France were all official commissions that looked into the issues of corporate board membership and disclosure of information. The various recommendations included the separation of the roles of chairman and chief executive, the inclusion of more non-executive directors and the setting up of codes of best practice, such as those which govern the appointment of auditors. All are concerned to protect small shareholders and weaker organizational stakeholders whose interests may be too fragmented to be powerful. However, researchers have questioned the effectiveness of these measures.[88]

Having strong independent directors can risk breaking up a strong and united management team and weakening the authority of the chief executive. However, the formal involvement of other stakeholder groups in the management of a company can help avoid potentially harmful actions by top managers who have privileged access to corporate 'insider' information. The legal requirement to allow unions in a workplace is another way of limiting top management power.

In Anglo-Saxon economies, major shareholders and institutions such as pension funds or insurance companies, can also, in theory, moderate the power of executives. However, small investors tend to be relatively powerless, unless they can band together, and large investors often find that the benefits in actively managing the companies that they invest in are low, and the costs high. The professional investment managers employed by the major fund-holding institutions potentially could exert a lot of influence on the strategies of the companies that they invest in. However they may also be bidding to run those same companies' pension funds, and so be unwilling to challenge the decisions of their senior managers. Nonetheless, there is some evidence that shareholders are becoming more willing to act. In Britain there have been a number of shareholder revolts over executives' salaries or severance pay in cases of poor performance.

There are other differences in what organizations can and cannot do in different countries across the world, although globalization appears to be leading to convergence in some areas. There has been a recent move to developing comparable accounting standards in the USA and Europe, for example.[89] This means that financial data will be calculated and presented in public accounts in a standardized format, which allows international investors, including shareholders and companies themselves, to assess the relative performance of firms more accurately. Needless to say, there have been a number of problems in deciding whose standards should be adopted as the international norm, and there are many other aspects of business, such as employment laws, where international differences remain profound. Some of these are shown in Table 2.4.

For example, corporate governance in France and Germany during the 1980s involved networked relationships between major firms, in which key shareholders such as banks and other industrial companies (who cross-owned shares in each others' firms) tended to protect executives from the market-controlling effects of the stock market. The role of corporate management was to balance the interests of the firm's different stakeholders.

Both countries have seen these economic/industrial structures break down in the last ten years. In France, the reason appears to be due to changes in financing, whereas in Germany it appears to be due to the more competitive nature of the industrial environment. Thirty-five per cent of French shares are now owned by foreign investors, particularly American fund managers who require regular returns on their capital. At the same time the major French financial groups have begun to demand a focus on shareholder value from their investment companies. In Germany, the recession in the early 1990s highlighted the vulnerability of German manufacturing and the desirability of higher rates of return.[90]

Table 2.4 Corporate-governance practices in the G7 countries

	Britain	Canada	France	Germany	Italy	Japan	United States
Auditors have to be independent from management consultancy arm							
	Recommended	Yes	Voluntary	No	Yes	Yes	Yes
Rotation of auditors							
	Voluntary: 5–7 years	Yes: 7 years	No[a]	No	Yes: 9 years	Yes: 7 years	Yes:[b] 5 years
Shareholders vote on executive pay							
	Advisory	Yes	No	No	Yes	Yes	No
Shareholders may elect own slate of independent directors							
	No	No	No	No[c]	Yes	Yes	No
Independent directors in a majority on board							
	Recommended	No	Voluntary	Recommended	No	No	Yes
Separate chairman and CEO?							
	Recommended	Voluntary	Voluntary	Yes[d]	Voluntary	Voluntary	Voluntary

Notes
a Auditors have maximum term of 6 years, but it can be renewed by the board
b Partners, not firm
c According to company's size, shareholders nominate all, two-thirds, or one-half of the supervisory board
d Refers to the separation of chairman of the supervisory board and the management board
Source: OECD, quoted in 'Beyond shareholder value'. *Economist*, 28 June 2003, 367/8330: 9–13

2.8 How strategies go wrong

Although sometimes managers can behave in ways that lead to the demise of their firm, or the loss of their own jobs, this is not common, and almost all of the previous discussion in this chapter has considered strategic processes that are intended to be beneficial for the organization and its main stakeholders. Unfortunately, they do not always end up that way in practice. In this final section we consider how well-intentioned strategies can sometimes go wrong; how good intentions can lead to competitive disadvantage, and how strategies which once were a source of considerable strength to a firm can lead to its decline and even death.

As we saw in Chapter 1, an organization can be considered to be the outcome of previous strategies that have proved successful. Future strategies are selected at least in part because of:

➡ We discussed the impact of culture, power, learning, and bounded rationality on strategy in Sections 1.4–1.6.

- the organization's culture, which has developed over time and become increasingly homogeneous;

- the organization's considerable investment of time and resources in learning how to do some things very well;

- the organization's information and gathering systems, which are focused on specific, previously important, environmental features;

- the organization's existing stake- and power-holders, who are likely to want to retain their status quo.

The interplay between these various factors means that organizations' strategies sometimes become inappropriate to their environment if it changes. We will now look at some of the ways in which this can happen.

2.8.1 Organizational inertia

One important reason why strategies can go wrong concerns the size and systematization of many organizations. Over time they develop structures and systems which are intimately intertwined with other systems and structures. For example, organizations often have processes for assessing monthly performance figures. These are dependent on other systems that gather raw data (perhaps from customers' own computer systems) and pass these to those responsible for doing the calculations. These performance figures are then entered into a system that eventually collates all twelve months' figures and puts this information into an annual report. This is just one, relatively simple and easy to understand example. Other organizational systems can be much more complex. But even this straightforward example illustrates how each part of these systems is part of a chain of dependencies that may be quite hard to break or restructure without major disruption or cost.

The recognition that it is extremely hard to move large organizations far from the path that they are already on has led to some theorists questioning whether organizations *can* change at all. If they cannot, they will only survive if they happen, by chance, to be suited to their environment. The clear parallels with the Darwinian theory about the survival of species led some researchers to study patterns in the birth and death of organizations in the same way that biologists study patterns in populations of plants and animals. These writers, notably Michael Hannan, John Freeman, and their associates, are known as the population ecology school.

2.8.2 Bounded decision-making

The bounded rationality of decision-makers (see Section 1.6.4) means that the decisions they take are always limited by their ability to perceive the options that are available. Inevitably, therefore, some of the best strategic options are not considered. Worse than this, sometimes even options that would enable a firm to survive are not noticed or are ignored, even though colleagues may make strenuous efforts to bring these to the attention of the decision-maker (see What Can Go Wrong 2.1).

2.8.3 Strategic drift

The process by which a company's strategies become increasingly distanced from the needs of its customers or the environment in which it operates is called strategic drift or strategic slip.[91]

Strategic drift happens gradually for three reasons. First, an organization's homogeneous values and belief system shut out 'deviant' strategies, which are rejected as being 'not what the organization does'. These deviant strategies, however, may be those which would allow the organization to adjust to its customers' changing needs or seek out new customers. Second, managers are constrained in their reactions to changes they perceive in their environment by their own limited expectations of what change should be. Third, existing powerholders within the organization are likely to reject novel strategic suggestions, since any changes involved might undermine their own power positions. We return to this issue in Chapter 16.

➜ The concept of the belief system is defined in Section 1.6.4 and discussed in depth in Section 8.4.2.

Some changes may be implemented and improve performance to some extent, thus deluding the company's managers that they are managing change effectively. Over time, however, the firm's financial performance becomes increasingly weak and it becomes apparent that something radical needs to be done. Sometimes the necessary change is achieved through the takeover of the firm, or it may require a new executive to be brought in from outside to 'turn the company around'. Occasionally existing managers can themselves bring about this change, as they realize the seriousness of their position. However, because their beliefs will be strongly shaped by the organization's belief system, which is, after all, one of the reasons why the company found itself in its predicament in the first place, this can be quite hard for them to achieve.

This state of affairs—periods of relative organizational stability interspersed with periods of significant change—is known as punctuated equilibrium, a term that comes from chaos theory. Research suggests that it is quite common in organizations. However, certain high technology organizations have been found to proceed through a process of time-paced evolution, a form of continuous product and organizational development which results in regular, but quite radical, strategic leaps.[92]

2.8.4 Competency traps, core rigidities, and the Icarus paradox

Another distinguished academic, who has written on the apparent inevitability of strategic decline and the increasing inappropriateness of strategic decisions over time, is Danny Miller. He suggests that the seeds of decline are actually sown in the very success of past strategies. These successes have the potential to lead to a lack of diversity in an organization's skills base and organization structures or belief systems, which can lead to failure. Miller termed this decline the Icarus paradox, in acknowledgement of the Greek myth which tells of Icarus, whose father Daedalus built them both wings of wax and feathers in order to escape their imprisonment on the island of Crete. Because the wings were so successful Icarus used them to fly too close to the sun: the wax melted and he fell to earth. The parable is clear: organizations which are successful can fall from grace, seduced into excess or complacency by their very strengths.

This process happens as an extension of strategic drift. Success appears able to add a layer of complacency or arrogance to the desire to repeat what has worked well in the past. Thus the rejection of deviant strategies is strengthened to the point where even sensible suggestions which identify external threats are rejected.

Another way of describing this is in terms of competency traps or core rigidities.[93] Both occur when an organization gets good results as a result of doing something in a particular way, leading it to persist with, or overuse, those routines. As a result, the perception builds that it is difficult or risky for the firm to adopt better routines that competitors, or even people within the organization, might have developed.

 What Can Go Wrong 2.1   **The punctuation of equilibrium in Marks & Spencer**

Marks & Spencer is a British retailer of clothes, food, and homewares. For many years now it has been something of a British institution. It has been said that you can always tell where the centre of any British town is by where Marks & Spencer is to be found. But from 1990 onwards it suffered increasing criticism in the press, and a decline in its profits and market share.[94] Profits before tax fell from over £1bn in 1998 to less than half that level in 1999, and then continued to decline; in 2001, they were below £145m.[95] A slow recovery began in 2002, but only in 2006 did profits return to the levels of the late 1990s.[96]

The problems were triggered, as so often happens in business, by a combination of events, not all within M&S's control. Economies in Asia, where the company was expanding, experienced problems that hit demand. Dealing with these problems absorbed management time at a point when the company was committed to an ambitious expansion in the UK, having acquired 19 stores from Littlewoods. The building work associated with this expansion was making the stores unattractive—just as established rivals such as Next and Debenhams were improving their offerings, newer entrants such as Jigsaw were appearing on the ➜

→ UK high street, and UK retail sales experienced a downturn. The currency depreciation associated with Asia's economic situation actually helped competing firms, which sourced their clothes there, to price their offerings keenly.[97]

This would have mattered less, however, had M&S's own offerings been more attractive. However, the clothes themselves were described as 'dull' by CEO Peter Salsbury in explaining the 1999 results and by others as 'frumpy' and 'boring'.[98] The layout of the stores in which they were displayed also came in for criticism.[99] Meanwhile, mainstream supermarkets such as Tesco had begun to match M&S's chill-cooked meals, a product category which it had practically invented.[100] With fewer customers for the core offerings, market share in homewares, a subsidiary line, also suffered.[101]

The poor 1999 results shook the firm out of the state of equilibrium that had existed during the profitable mid-1990s. Salsbury trimmed the size of the board, made 200 head office staff redundant, and formed the company's first centralized marketing department, which presided over its first ever TV advertising campaign.[102] But when it came to improving what was on offer to the public, it became clear that the firm had problems in understanding what its core customers, in particular those for its key womenswear ranges, would buy, in what quanitities and at what price.[103] For example, a company spokeswoman gave the following account of the 1998 autumn season: 'Grey was the fashion colour so we bought into it, but the mistake was that we bought it for everybody. Older customers wanted colour and we were missing it . . . By the time we realised, it was too late to buy more colour. We'd had a very successful year previously, so we were confident and bullish about buying. On reflection we bought too much fashion and too much grey . . . It meant that we bought overcautiously for spring and as a result, the bestselling items sold out very early.'[104] Other commentators confirmed that the firm had found it difficult to establish the right point in the trade-off in women's clothing, so that some ranges were too zany for the traditional M&S customer while others were too conservatively styled, and others appeared overpriced.[105]

By 2006, however, the firm, under a new management team headed by Stuart Rose, and with the aid of focus groups and other market research, appeared to have rediscovered its grasp for what the public wanted to buy. It had emulated H&M and other competitors in developing sub-brands to appeal to particular market segments, and had also benefited from some inspired advertising for its food and clothing.[106]

The root cause of the company's apparent inability to foresee and handle the setbacks of the turn of the century is a matter of debate. Sir Richard Greenbury, Salsbury's predecessor as CEO, was one of the most respected retailers of his generation,[107] but in contrast with previous chairmen, he was said to have stopped visiting rivals' stores, or asking colleagues what new developments there were.[108] This may have contributed to a degree of introversion in M&S; according to one strategy consultant in 1999: 'A number of competitors in both food and clothing have damaged M&S but I doubt it even picked them up on its radar screen until it was too late.'[109] Other commentators wrote that the firm's prolonged success had engendered 'corporate hubris: the idea that there is no need to change a winning team' and complacency—which Salsbury himself admitted was a problem.[110] But as we have already noted, both Salsbury and his successor, Luc Vandervelde, took action aimed at arresting the decline; however, once an equilibrium is disturbed, it takes time to build the routines to create a new one.

● CHAPTER SUMMARY

In this chapter we have described strategy formulation as a multi-headed process. Sometimes it is the formal, rational, planned process that it has traditionally been seen as. But we have also introduced you to the idea that strategies can come about, not exactly by accident (although that can also happen), but through experimentation and the purposeful activities of all employees in an organization, not just the chief executive or top management team.

A strategic decision is one that involves a significant commitment of resources, throughout a substantial part of the organization, and will have a long-term impact on the organization as a whole. The various types of strategy have been characterized as:

- deliberate—planned actions resulting from careful analysis;
- emergent—from the spontaneous actions of employees solving particular problems or responding to unforeseen opportunities;
- imposed—by governments, customers, or other powerful stakeholders;

- realized—the strategy that actually materializes, and which may have deliberate, emergent, and imposed elements.

Seven types of strategy development processes have been identified: rational, command, symbolic, transactive, generative, muddling through, and externally dependent. Most organizations will use some or even all of these processes at some time, but will tend to use one or two more than the others.

Strategy can happen at three levels in the organization:

- functional;
- business—decisions about competitive stance (which products to offer in which markets) and about how to configure value chains;
- corporate—how to link together portfolios of products or businesses levels.

Each will involve different types of decision, but only business and corporate-level decisions can be considered truly strategic as we have defined the concept here.

Some strategies are inherently likely to be better than others. They are most likely to succeed if they display:

- fit with the environment, and between the different elements of the strategy;
- distinctiveness—including actions that competitors are not carrying out;
- sustainability—involving elements that competitors are unable to copy in the short term.

Organizations' stakeholders are likely to be influential in shaping what an organization does, but will differ in their objectives. The most influential ('salient') will be those that have power, legitimacy, and urgency. Because stakeholders can include a wide section of the population, there has been some debate about how far companies should go in behaving ethically or being socially responsible beyond the narrow confines of their immediate surroundings. Corporate social responsibility, or business ethics, is an important topic in contemporary strategy.

Strategy processes in organizations can sometimes go drastically wrong. As their size and degree of systematization increases, inertia may take hold. Bounded rationality on the part of managers may contribute to sub-optimal decisions. Both these factors may contribute to strategic drift, where the organization's focus turns inwards and gradually loses touch with its markets and competitors. And finally, the organization may suffer the Icarus paradox, where it repeats the actions that made it successful until it suddenly discovers that the formula no longer works.

● KEY SKILLS

The key skills you should have developed after reading this chapter are:

- the ability to discriminate between strategic and non-strategic decisions;
- the ability to recognize and distinguish between different modes of strategy-making in organizations;
- the ability to identify corporate-level, business-level, and functional strategies in an organization;
- the capacity to analyse, at a basic level, the extent to which an organization's strategy fits its environment and confers disctinctiveness and sustainable advantage;
- the ability to recognize the main stakeholders in an organization and their objectives and to analyse the extent to which they are salient to decision-making in the organization;
- the capacity to recognize the extent to which considerations of corporate social responsibility affect an organization's strategy;
- the ability to identify the symptoms of strategies going wrong and analyse the reasons.

● REVIEW QUESTIONS

1. Are the following functional, business, or corporate strategic decisions for a large firm?

   * entering a new market in Greece
   * moving to an expensive office building close to where major customers are located
   * launching a major advertising campaign for a product
   * changing the supplier of an important component that has a major impact on the quality of the finished product
   * buying the new supplier

2. Would your answers change if these same strategies applied to a small, single-product, firm?

3. In an ideal world, would all strategies be deliberate?

4. Under what circumstances might an organization be advised to make the rational mode the dominant form of strategy-making, and under what circumstances would the other modes be preferable?

5. When might an organization opt for a strategy that did not clearly fit its environment, and what are the risks involved?

6. Should organizations strive to be more ethical than their competitors?

7. What can organizations do to avoid succumbing to the Icarus Paradox?

● FURTHER READING

● Mintzberg, H. (1994). *The Rise and Fall of Strategic Planning: Reconceiving Roles for Planning, Plans, Planners*. New York: The Free Press is a good review of many of the issues that we have discussed in this chapter, by an extremely influential theorist on strategy development processes.

● Brews, P. and Hunt, M. (1999). 'Learning to plan and planning to learn: resolving the planning school/learning school debate'. *Strategic Management Journal*, 20/10: 889–913 is an example of how empirical research can illuminate debates of the kind that Mintzberg initiates.

● Whittington, R. (2001). *What is Strategy and Does it Matter?* 2nd edn. Thomson Learning; and Mintzberg, H., Joseph Lampel, J., and Ahlstrand B. (2005). *Strategy Safari*. New York: Free Press. These two books provide a nice overview of strategic concepts and the history of strategic thinking.

● Kayes, D., Stirling, D., and Nielsen, T. (2007). 'Building organizational integrity'. *Business Horizons*, 50/1: 61–70 is a readable introduction to corporate values and how to build them.

● Freeman, R. and McVea, J. (2005). 'A stakeholder approach to strategic management'. In Hitt, M., Freeman, R., and Harrison, J., *The Blackwell Handbook of Strategic Management*. Oxford: Blackwell, 189–207 summarizes current theoretical debates in stakeholder theory.

● Margolis, J. D. and Walsh, J. P. (2003). 'Misery loves companies: Rethinking social initiatives by business'. *Administrative Science Quarterly*, 48: 268–305. A good summary of what we actually know about the impact of corporate social responsibility.

● Friedman, M. (1996). 'The social responsibility of business is to increase profits'. In Rae, S. B. and Wong, K. L. (eds), *Beyond Integrity: A Judeo-Christian Approach*. Grand Rapids, MI: Zondervan Publishing House, 246–54.

● REFERENCES

Anand, V., Ashforth, B., and Joshi, M. (2005). 'Business as usual: The acceptance and perpetuation of corruption in organizations'. *Academy of Management Executive*, 19/4: 9–23.

Bailey, A. and Johnson, G. (1995). 'Strategy development processes: a configurational approach'. *Academy of Management Journal*, Best Paper Proceedings: 2–6.

Bebchuk, L. and Grinstein, Y. (2005). 'The growth of executive pay'. *Oxford Review of Economic Policy*, 21/2: 283–303.

Bevan, J. (2002). *The Rise and Fall of Marks and Spencer*. London: Profile Books.

Boston Consulting Group (1975). *Strategy Alternatives for the British Motorcycle Industry*. London: HMSO.

Bowen, H. R. (1953). *Social Responsibilities of the Businessman*. New York: Harper and Row.

Boyd, B., Norburn, D., and Fox, M. (1997). 'Who wins in governance reform? Conventional Wisdom 1, Shareholders 0'. In Thomas, H. and O'Neal, D. (eds), *Strategic Discovery: Competing in New Arenas*. Chichester: Wiley, 237–59.

Brews, P. and Hunt, M. (1999). 'Learning to plan and planning to learn: resolving the planning school/learning school debate'. *Strategic Management Journal*, 20/10: 889–913.

Brick, I., Palmon, O., and Wald, J. (2006). 'CEO compensation, director compensation, and firm performance: Evidence of cronyism?' *Journal of Corporate Finance*, 12/3: 403–23.

Brown, S. and Eisenhardt, K. (1997). 'The art of continuous change: linking complexity theory and time-paced evolution in relentlessly shifting organizations'. *Administrative Science Quarterly*, 42/1: 1–34.

Carroll, A. (1999). 'Corporate Social Responsibility', *Business & Society*, 38/3: 268–95.

Clegg, S., Kornberger, M., and Rhodes, C. (2007). 'Business ethics as practice'. *British Journal of Management*, 18/2: 107–22.

Collins, J. and Porras, J. (1994). *Built to Last*. New York: HarperCollins.

Dahl, R. (1957). 'The concept of power'. *Behavioral Science*, 2: 202–10.

Danielson, M. and Karpoff, J (2006). 'Do pills poison operating performance?' *Journal of Corporate Finance*, 12/3: 536–59.

Economist, The (2004). 'Two-faced capitalism: the future of corporate social responsibility'. 24 January.

Floyd, S. and Wooldridge, B. (1994). 'Dinosaurs or dynamos? Recognizing middle management's strategic role'. *Academy of Management Executive*, 8/4: 47–57.

Freeman, R. (1984). *Strategic Management: A Stakeholder Approach*. Boston, MA: Pitman Publishing.

Freeman, R. and Liedtka, J. (1991). 'Corporate social responsibility: a critical approach'. *Business Horizons*, July–August: 92–6.

Freeman, R. and McVea, J. (2005). 'A stakeholder approach to strategic management'. In Hitt, M., Freeman, R., and Harrison, J., *The Blackwell Handbook of Strategic Management*. Oxford: Blackwell, 189–207.

Friedman, M. (1962). *Capitalism and Freedom*. Chicago: University of Chicago Press.

Friedman, M. (1996). 'The social responsibility of business is to increase profits'. In Rae, S. B. and Wong, K. L. (eds), *Beyond Integrity: A Judeo-Christian Approach*. Grand Rapids, MI: Zondervan Publishing House, 246–54.

Ghemawat, P. (1991). *Commitment: The Dynamic of Strategy*. New York: Free Press.

Haberberg, A. and Mulleady, F. (2004). 'Understanding the practice of corporate social responsibility: A research agenda'. *Proceedings of British Academy of Management Annual Conference St Andrews*, September.

Hales, C. (1999). 'Why do managers do what they do? Reconciling evidence and theory in accounts of managerial work'. *British Journal of Management*, 10/4: 335–50.

Hales, C. (2001). 'Does it matter what managers do?' *Business Strategy Review*, 12/2: 50–56.

Hambrick, D. and Mason, P. (1984). 'Upper echelons: the organization as a reflection of its top managers'. *Academy of Management Review*, 9: 193–206.

Hamel, G. and Prahalad, C. K. (1994). *Competing for the Future*. Boston, MA: Harvard Business Press.

Hart, S. (1992). 'An integrative framework for strategy-making processes'. *Academy of Management Review*, 17: 327–51.

Hart, S. and Banbury, C. (1994). 'How strategy-making processes can make a difference'. *Strategic Management Journal*, 15: 251–69.

Hebb, G. and MacLean, S. (2006). 'Canadian firms and poison pill adoption: the effects on financial performance'. *Journal of Business & Economic Studies*, 12/1: 40–53.

Henderson, D. (2001). 'The case against "Corporate Social Responsibility"'. *Policy*, 17/2: 28–32.

Heron, R. and Lie, E. (2006). 'On the use of poison pills and defensive payouts by takeover targets'. *Journal of Business*, 79/4: 1783–1807.

Hill, C. and Jones, T. (1992). 'Stakeholder-agency theory'. *Journal of Management Studies*, 29/2: 131–54.

Jensen, M. C. (2001). 'Value maximisation, stakeholder theory and the corporate objective function'. *European Financial Management*, 7/3: 297–317.

Johnson, G. (1987). *Strategic Change and the Management Process*. Oxford: Blackwell.

Jones, T. M. (1995). 'Instrumental stakeholder theory: a synthesis of ethics and economics'. *Academy of Management Review*, 20: 404–37.

Kayes, D., Stirling, D., and Nielsen, T. (2007). 'Building organizational integrity'. *Business Horizons*, 50/1: 61–70.

Lencioni, P. (2002). 'Make Your Values Mean Something'. *Harvard Business Review*, 80/7: 113–17.

Levitt, T. (1983). 'The dangers of social responsibility'. In Beauchamp, T. L. and Bowie, N. E. (eds), *Ethical Theory and Business*. 2nd edn. Englewood Cliffs, NJ: Prentice-Hall.

Mair, A. (1999). 'Learning from Honda'. *Journal of Management Studies*, 36/1: 25–44.

Maitlis, S. and Lawrence, T. B. (2003). 'Orchestral manoeuvres in the dark: understanding failure in organizational strategizing'. *Journal of Management Studies*, 40/1: 109–40.

March, J. (1991). 'Exploration and exploitation in organizational learning'. *Organization Science*, 2: 71–87.

Margolis, J. D. and Walsh, J. P. (2003). 'Misery loves companies: rethinking social initiatives by business'. *Administrative Science Quarterly*, 48, 268 J.P. 305.

Miles, R. E. and Snow, C. C. (1978). *Organizational Structure, Strategy, Process*. New York: McGraw Hill.

Mintzberg, H. (1973). *The Nature of Managerial Work*. New York: Harper and Row.

Mintzberg, H. (1983). 'The case for corporate social responsibility'. *Journal of Business Strategy*, 4/2: 3–15.

Mintzberg, H. (1994). *The Rise and Fall of Strategic Planning: Reconceiving Roles for Planning, Plans, Planners*. New York: The Free Press.

Mintzberg, H. and Waters, J. (1985). 'Of strategies, deliberate and emergent'. *Strategic Management Journal*, July–September: 257–72.

Mitchell, R. K., Agle, B. R., and Wood, D. J. (1997). 'Toward a theory of stakeholder identification and salience: defining the principle of who and what really counts'. *Academy of Management Review*, 22: 853–86.

Norburn, D., Boyd, B., Fox, M., and Muth, M. (2000). 'International corporate governance reform'. *European Business Journal*, 12/3: 116–33.

Pascale, R. (1990). *Managing on the Edge*. New York: Simon and Schuster.

Pearce, J. and Robinson, R. (2004). 'Hostile takeover defenses that maximize shareholder wealth'. *Business Horizons*, 47/5: 15–24.

Porter, M. (1979). 'How competitive forces shape strategy'. *Harvard Business Review*, March–April: 137–45.

Porter, M. (1980). *Competitive Strategy*. New York: Free Press.

Porter, M. (1996). 'What is strategy?' *Harvard Business Review*, November–December: 61–78.

Quinn, J. M. (1989). 'Strategic change: "logical incrementalism"'. *Sloan Management Review*, Summer: 45–60.

Quinn, D. and Jones, T. (1995). 'An agent morality view of business policy'. *Academy of Management Review*, 20/1: 22–42.

Rajgopal, S., Shevlin, T., and Zamora, V. (2006). 'CEOs' outside employment opportunities and the lack of relative performance evaluation in compensation contracts'. *Journal of Finance*, 61/4: 1813–44.

Reich, R. (1998). 'The new meaning of corporate social responsibility'. *California Management Review*, 40/2: 8–17.

Romanelli, E. and Tushman, M. (1994). 'Organizational transformation as punctuated equilibrium: An empirical test'. *Academy of Management Journal*, 37/5: 1141.

Suchman, M. C. (1995). 'Managing legitimacy: strategic and institutional approaches'. *Academy of Management Review*, 20/3: 571–610.

Tengblad, S. (2006). 'Is there a "New Managerial Work"? A comparison with Henry Mintzberg's classic study 30 years later'. *Journal of Management Studies*, 43/7: 1437–61.

Tushman, M. and Romanelli, E. (1985). 'Organizational evolution: a metamorphosis model of convergence and reorientation'. In

Cummings, L. and Staw, B. (eds), *Research in Organizational Behavior*, 7: 171–222.

Tushman, M., Newman, W., and Romanelli, E. (1986). 'Convergence and upheaval: Managing the unsteady pace of organizational evolution'. *California Management Review*, 29/1: 1–16.

Yermack, D. (2006). 'Flights of fancy: Corporate jets, CEO perquisites, and inferior shareholder returns'. *Journal of Financial Economics*, 80/1: 211–42.

End-of-chapter Case Study 2.1: So who needs a strategy? The case of Semco do Brasil

Semco is a diversified Brazilian corporation that has a range of international businesses which includes marine engineering, facilities management, internet services, and software development. Over the last ten years its turnover has grown from $35m to $212m, and it forecasts sales of $1000m by 2009. Its principal shareholder (he owns 90 per cent of the firm, although he explicitly does not classify himself as its chief executive) is Ricardo Semler. He inherited Semco in 1980 from his father, Antonio Semler, a Viennese engineer who had founded the marine pumps company in 1954, although engineering now accounts for only 30 per cent of sales. It has 3,000 employees, ten times as many as in 1980. It is structured as a federation of around ten companies, 'all of which are premium providers and market leaders in their fields'.[111] Ricardo Semler describes its principal purpose as 'selling intelligence, the capacity to think out service solutions and to look at things from an intellectual standpoint. Our rationale for everything we do is that it's heavily engineered or complex . . . businesses that have high entry barriers, and which people can't get into easily and can't get out of easily.'[112]

Mr Semler is rapidly becoming one of the most famous, and certainly least conventional, businessmen in the world. His reputation rests on a number of books, articles, and seminars that describe his rather unusual approach to doing business.[113] On taking over from his father, Mr Semler quickly started making changes to the firm. He sacked two-thirds of his father's senior managers, dismantled the company's 'very conservative' structure, abandoned the practice of searching employees as they left at the end of each day, and did away with time clocks and controls over working hours. Some have suggested that in the early days his approach caused 'havoc', and he had to spend a considerable proportion of his time trying to keep the company solvent.[114] Since the mid-1980s, though, growth has been impressive.

His shaking up of the company has continued since: 'Semco has no official structure. It has no organizational chart. There's no business plan or company strategy, no two-year or five-year plan, no goal or mission statement, no long-term budget. The company often does not have a fixed CEO. There are no vice presidents or chief officers for information technology or operations. There are no standards or practices. There's no human resources department. There are no career plans, no job descriptions or employee contracts. No one approves reports or expense accounts. Supervision or monitoring of workers is rare indeed. Most important, success is not measured only in profit and growth.'[115] In addition:

- Attendance at all company meetings is voluntary.

- Employees have no set working hours and can decide when to take holidays and how much time off they need.

- Staff can choose from a range of 11 ways that they can get paid—including a fixed salary, royalties on sales or profits, share options, and commission or bonuses. One-third of employees set their own salaries; the rest are negotiated within business units according to performance.

- Employees choose their own training, and Semco's Work 'n' Stop programme allows them to take up to three years off for any purpose.

- Its 'Lost in Space' programme makes its young recruits roam the company for up to a year to discover what they want to do.

- The company holds collective job interviews, in which candidates meet their rivals for the position and are interviewed by a cross-section of employees.

Mr Semler would claim that he did not impose these policies, nor were they directly his ideas—as he is not Semco's chief executive—although it seems clear that he likes to do things differently and encourages his colleagues to do the same. He himself does not work regular hours, sometimes absenting himself for several months at a time, and does not even have a physical office in the company. He comes in a few times a week for meetings and claims to do a lot of work at home—in his hammock! He sees it as his role to be disruptive and to encourage divergent thinking, and claims that this is a bedrock for all the company's practices: ➜

➡ '... ask why. Ask it all the time, ask it any day, every day, and always ask it three times in a row',[116] even though this is something that he recognizes is often very difficult for people to do. However, Mr Semler is adamant that this is necessary to prevent 'calcified thinking'. This ethos also means that the company has few written plans, which he believes encourages people to follow them like 'a Pied Piper—mindlessly'.[117] Sometimes this questioning applies to the owner's own role within the company. Mr Semler tells a story of a strategic committee that he had sat on for some time. He was asked why he was there, and when his answer was simply that he had always been on it, he was told that was not a good enough reason—and he was expelled.

This philosophy means that the company has no written mission statement, or written statements of strategic objectives —although he says the firm does have a mission: 'to find a gratifying way of spending your life doing something you like that is useful and fills a need'. Some of this can be put down to his early years. His upbringing was rich and privileged, and he did not need to work. He also played for many years in a rock band, experiences that he claims shaped his subsequent attitude to work and motivation: 'I was testing some of the things I'd learnt in the rock group, where if the drummer doesn't feel like coming to rehearsals you know something's wrong. You can hassle him as much as you want but the problem remains.... So at Semco, the basic question we work on is, how do you get people to want to come to work on a grey Monday morning?'

By not writing strategic objectives down he claims that employees are forced to constantly re-think what they are doing. Mr Semler even says he resists any attempts by journalists to make him define what the firm does: 'once you say what business you're in, you put your employees into a mental straitjacket',[118] blocking them from thinking opportunistically. So rather than trying to dictate Semco's direction, he encourages employees to shape it themselves through their own interests and initiatives.

Every six months, Semco is 'shut down' and started again. Through a 'rigorous' budgeting and planning process all business units have to justify their continued existence. Executives similarly are forced to resign and be rehired in an anonymous assessment process by subordinates whose results are then made public. Such a ruthless focus leads to some being moved 'sideways, downwards or out'.[119] One manager, who had successfully built up his division over many years from a very small base, was no longer seen to be performing effectively and was forcibly transferred to another part of the company—where, incidentally, he was able to repeat his previous successful performance. He was replaced by a 'twenty-something girl' who restructured the division and achieved growth of 30 per cent p.a.[120] Another example concerned a manager whose wife was diagnosed with a terminal illness and who was depressed, but was still dismissed. As Mr Semler says, 'ultimately, all we care about is performance'. How this is achieved is down to the individual.

This shows that Semco judges its businesses, in quite an orthodox way, on their ability to generate profits—and therefore survive in the long term. But Semco does not set sales targets for its businesses, as long as their profits remain healthy. And if profitability tails off employees are encouraged to start anew. The company makes it 'as easy as possible' for employees to propose new business ideas, and to get fast and clear decisions.[121] Proposals go through an executive board that includes representatives from the major business units and the first two employees that turn up to the board meeting, and which all employees can attend. The company is still not listed on any stock exchange, allowing it to bypass the sorts of short-term thinking that Mr Semler believes characterizes share analysts.

It may be that Semco sometimes exaggerates the extent to which its practices differ from the norm. Mr Semler has a clear view on who the top three to five managers in his firm are, and as he prepares to move to Harvard, where he has recently been appointed a Visiting Scholar, he has put in place a process for choosing his successor. However his move to Harvard will allow him to work on discovering what he describes as 'a framework for negotiated hierarchies in organizations instead of a command-and-control or pyramidal hierarchy',[122] a model of quasi-military operations that he sees in many of the world's major corporations, and which he disdains.

Case study questions

1. Does Semco *really* not have a strategy? If it does—what is it?

2. Why might Mr Semler find it useful to claim not to have a strategy?

3. What modes of strategy-making are apparent at Semco?

4. Who are the salient stakeholders at Semco?

5. What are the advantages and disadvantages of Semco's system of corporate governance? How does it avoid principal–agent problems?

6. On the basis of the evidence in the case, does Semco behave ethically and responsibly?

● NOTES

1 It was Henry Mintzberg and James Waters (1985) who first noted this.

2 Warner, M. (2005). 'The food industry empire strikes back'. *New York Times*, 7 July: 1.

3 See for example Carpenter, D. (2006). 'McDonald's profits drop 14 percent; sales still strong'. *Associated Press Newswires*, 21 April; Hoyle, B. (2006). 'Limp reception for salads as diners vote the burger king'. *The Times*, 9 September: 5.

4 Boston Consulting Group (1975).

5 Pascale (1990).

6 Mair (1999).

7 See, for example, the special edition of the *Journal of Management Studies* in January 2003, and the introduction by Melin, Johnson, and Whittington in particular. See also Jarzabkowski, P. (2004). 'Strategy as practice: recursiveness, adaptation, and practices-in-use'. *Organization Studies*, 25/4: 529–60; Carr, A., Durant, R., and Downs, A. (2004). 'Emergent strategy development, abduction, and pragmatism: new lessons for corporations'. *Human Systems Management*, 23: 79–91; and Matthews, J. A. (2003). 'Strategizing by firms in the presence of markets for resources'. *Industrial and Corporate Change*, 12/6: 1157–93. There is now also a track at the US Academy of Management conference that is dedicated to strategizing. The best papers from this conference are normally available through good academic databases such as Business Source Premier/EBSCO Host.

8 See Hart (1992); Hart and Banbury (1994); Bailey and Johnson (1995); and Brews and Hunt (1999).

9 For an overview of analytical techniques see Hofer, C. W. and Schendel, D. (1978). *Strategy Formulation: Analytical Concepts*. St. Paul, MN: West Publishing. For a comprehensive review of developments in the analysis of strategy over time, see Hoskisson, R. E., Hitt, M. A., Wan, W. P., and Yiu, D. (1999). 'Theory and research in strategic management: swings of a pendulum'. *Journal of Management*, 25/3: 417–57.

10 For an influential critique of strategic planning, see Mintzberg, H. (1990). 'The manager's job: folklore and fact'. *Harvard Business Review*, 68/2: 163–76.

11 Hambrick and Mason (1984) is a particularly influential example.

12 The most famous study of how top managers spend their time (and the source of the 10% estimate) is Mintzberg (1973), who found that managerial work has become less fragmented over time. See Hales (1999, 2001) and Tengblad (2006) for more recent reviews and research.

13 For a carefully documented example of a new leader asserting his way of thinking in a firm, see Hellgren, B. and Melin, L. (1993). 'The role of strategists' ways-of-thinking in strategic change processes'. In Hendry, J. and Johnson, G. (with Newton, J.) (eds), *Strategic Thinking: Leadership and the Management of Change*. Wiley, Chichester, 47–68. For an account of Disney's turnaround under Eisner see Grover, R., Vamos, M., and Mason, T. (1987). 'Disney's magic—a turnaround proves wishes can come true'. *BusinessWeek*, 2998 (9 March): 62.

14 <http://www.mcdonalds.com/corp/values/diversity/mission_vision.html>, accessed 28 May 2005.

15 H&M's mission is rarely labelled specifically as this, but the phrase is found repeatedly in almost every H&M Annual Report—see, for example, 2003, pp. 5, 8, 11, 27, 28, 30. The Corporate Social Responsibility Report and Code of Conduct for their Suppliers are published in separate documents (H&M, 2003).

16 <http://www.easyjet.com/EN/About/index.html>, accessed 28 May 2005.

17 For a review of the factors that influence the way in which organizational members espouse ethical practices, see Anand et al. (2005) and Clegg et al. (2007). For a discussion of how organizations can address this, see Kayes et al. (2007).

18 See, for example, Campbell, A. and Nash, L. (1992). *A Sense of Mission*. Reading, MA: Addison-Wesley; Collins, J. C. and Porras, J. I. (1991). 'Organizational vision and visionary organizations'. *California Management Review*, Fall: 30–41; Collins, J. C. and Porras, J. I. (1995). 'Building a visionary company'. *California Management Review*, 37/2: 80–101; Collins, J. C. and Porras, J. I. (1996). 'Building your company's vision'. *Harvard Business Review*, September–October: 65–77; Collis, D. J. and Montgomery, C. A. (1998). Creating Corporate Advantage. *Harvard Business Review*, May–June: 71–83; Drucker, P. (1973). *Management: Tasks, Responsibilities and Practices*. New York: Harper and Row; Drucker, P. (1994). 'The theory of the business'. *Harvard Business Review*, September–October;

Drucker, P. F. (1997). 'The future that has already happened'. *Harvard Business Review*, 75/5: 20–4; Hamel, G. and Prahalad, C. K. (1989). 'Strategic intent'. *Harvard Business Review*, 67/3: 63–77; Hamel, G. and Prahalad, C. K. (1993). 'Strategy as stretch and leverage'. *Harvard Business Review*, 71/2: 75–84; Hamel, G. and Prahalad, C. K. (1994). *Competing for the Future*. Boston, MA: Harvard Business Press; and Peters, T. and Waterman, R. (1982). *In Search of Excellence*. New York: Harper and Row.

19 See Quinn (1989).

20 The role of operational managers is set out in Chakravarthy, B. and Lorange, P. (1991). *Managing the Strategy Process: A Framework for a Multibusiness Firm*. New York: Prentice Hall. There is a whole raft of research relating to middle management's role in strategy formulation. American researchers Steven Floyd and Bill Wooldridge have specialized in this area and their 1994 article, in the *Academy of Management Executive*, gives a readable summary of their work. The role of middle management is also featured strongly in the writings of Kanter, R. M. (1983). *The Change Masters*. New York: Simon & Schuster; Burgelman, R. A. (1994). 'Fading memories: a process theory of strategic business exit in dynamic environments'. *Administrative Science Quarterly*, 39/1: 24–56; Nonaka, I. and Takeuchi, H. (1995). *The Knowledge-creating Company: How Japanese Companies Create the Dynamics of Innovation*. Oxford: Oxford University Press; and Ghoshal, S. and Bartlett, C. A. (1998). *The Individualized Corporation*. London: Heinemann.

21 For a sample of Mintzberg's thinking see Mintzberg (1994). For evidence that organizations benefit from using both transactive and generative modes of strategizing see Brews and Hunt (1999).

22 Corporate entrepreneurship has attracted a lot of recent attention from some influential researchers. See Dess, G. G. and Lumpkin, G. T. (1997). 'Entrepreneurial strategy making and firm performance: tests of contingency and configurational models'. *Strategic Management Journal*, 18/9: 677–95; Kuratko, D. F., Ireland, R. D., and Hornsby, J. S. (2001). 'Improving firm performance through entrepreneurial actions: Acordia's corporate entrepreneurship strategy'. *Academy of Management Executive*, 15/4: 60–71; and Hitt, M. A., Ireland, R. D., Camp, S. M. and Sexton, D. L. (2001). 'Strategic entrepreneurship: entrepreneurial strategies for wealth creation'. *Strategic Management Journal*, 22/6–7: 479–91.

23 Peters and Waterman (1982) op. cit.

24 The technical term for self-organization is *autopoesis*. For a readable discussion, see Brown, S. and Eisenhardt, K. (1998). *Competing on the Edge: Strategy as Structured Chaos*. Boston, MA: Harvard Business School Press. Other writers who have looked at organizations as emergent or complex adaptive systems include Stacey, R. (2000). 'The emergence of knowledge in organization'. *Emergence*, 2/4: 23–39; Morel, B. and Ramanujam, R. (1999), 'Through the looking glass of complexity: the dynamics of organizations as adaptive and evolving systems'. *Organization Science*, 10/3: 278–93. For a nice introduction to the concept of emergence see Johnson, S. (2001). *Emergence: The Connected Lives of Ants, Brains, Cities and Software*. London: Allen Lane/Penguin.

25 Dahl (1957).

26 The term derives from a classic paper by Lindblom, C. E. (1959). 'The science of muddling through'. *Public Administration Review*, 19/2: 79–88.

27 The source of this example is Maitlis, S. and Lawrence, T. B. (2003). 'Orchestral manoeuvres in the dark: understanding failure in organizational strategizing'. *Journal of Management Studies*, 40/1: 109–40.

28 The term 'triangulation' comes from the field of trigonometric mapping that assesses the placement of a third object by calculating its distance from two or more other objects.

29 See, for example, Watson, I. and Heath, A. (2006). 'Now boarding . . . The great airline takeover is preparing for take-off'. *The Business*, 2 December; Kanter, J. (2006). 'EU moves on airline emissions', *International Herald Tribune*, 16 November: 11; Inman, P. (2006). 'Regulator eases rules on closing pension scheme shortfalls'. *The Guardian*, 5 May: 25.

30 Butler, K. (1998). 'Brussels gets tough on BA/American merger'. *The Independent*, 26 June: 18; Shapinker, M. and Fidler, S. (1999). 'American and BA pull out of global tie-up plan'. *Financial Times*, 29 July: 1.

31 For example: Clark, A. (2003). 'Unions warn BA of summer of misery'. *The Guardian*, 23 July: 7; Done, K. (2006). 'BA unions oppose sweeping reforms'. *Financial Times*, 27 May: 6; Osborne, A. (2007). 'BA unions add toenails to list of grievances in sickness row'. *Daily Telegraph*, 23 January: 6.

32 Lencioni (2002) has some interesting examples.

33 *Economist* (2003). 'The complete home entertainer?—Sony'. 1 March 2003; Levy, S. (2003). 'Sony's new day'. *Newsweek*, 27; Nathan (1999): 304.

34 Levy (2003) op. cit.

35 Miles and Snow's (1978) research project covered more than 80 US firms in three different industries.

36 This idea was proposed by Michael Porter (1979, 1980).

37 See Miller, A. and Dess, G. (1993). 'Assessing Porter's 1980 model in terms of its generalisability, accuracy and simplicity'. *Journal of Management Studies*, 30/4: 553–85, and Cronshaw, M., Davis, E., and Kay, J. (1994). 'On being stuck in the middle or good food costs less at Sainsbury's'. *British Journal of Management*, 5/1: 19–32. For a comprehensive review of the evidence, see Campbell-Hunt, C. (2000). 'What have we learned from generic competitive strategy? A meta-analysis'. *Strategic Management Journal*, 21/2: 127–44.

38 Penttila claims that US family firms on average last 24 year: Penttila, C. (2005). 'It's all relative'. *Entrepreneur*, 33/3: 74–8. Velloor suggests that the average corporate life-span in both Japan and the USA is 30 years: Velloor, R. (1999). 'Samsung for less chip on its shoulder'. *Straits Time*, 4 October.

39 Williams, I. (1987). 'Who dares wins—SAS and British Airways are pitted against each other in the battle for BCal'. *The Sunday Times*, 29 November; Harris, C. (1987). 'Man in the news: high-flyer who puts his trust in the crew—Jan Carlzon'. *Financial Times*, 12 December: 6; Prokesch, S. (1989). 'S.A.S. builds on global alliances'. *New York Times*, 20 November; Lorenz, C. (1990). 'The staying power of visionary leaders'. *Financial Times*, 12 February: 38.

40 *The Times* (1987). 'Outline proposals for the creation of a giant European airline could be arrived at within the next few weeks'. 20 April; Harris, C. (1987). 'Determined to join the big five'. *Financial Times*, 28 November: 10; Reuters News (1989a). 'SAS to take stake in Saison's Inter-Continental', 19 April; Prokesch (1989) op. cit.; Prokesch, S. (1990a). 'S.A.S. stabilizes its American niche'. *New York Times*, 13 August.

41 Prokesch, S. (1990b). 'S.A.S. expects to write off investment in Continental'. *New York Times*, 5 December.

42 Austin, T. (1992). 'SAS will cut losses in Intercontinental hotel stake'. *Reuters News*, 5 March.

43 Huddart, A. (1993). 'SAS airline, after third year of loss, seeks partners'. *Reuters News*, 10 March.

44 Taylor, R. (1990). 'He who dares does not always win: Reasons for the reorganisation plans at SAS'. *Financial Times*, 3 December: 21; Webb, S. and Betts, P. (1992). 'SAS looks for cupid in Europe's open skies'. *Financial Times*, 6 April: 19; *Dagens Naeringsliv* (1993). 'Analysts say Scandinavian Airlines System (SAS) must cut costs by more than Nkr 2.5bn'. 23 November: 4.

45 *Financial Times* (1993). 'Airline merger hopes dashed by rift over US link'. 22 November: 1.

46 Carnegy, H. (1994). 'SAS emerges from the red'. *Financial Times*, 18 August: 18.

47 SAS Group Annual Report, 2006: 30.

48 Lin, X. (2002). 'SAS bogged down by neighborly turbulence'. *Dow Jones International News*, 18 June.

49 Townsend, A. (2004). 'The Lowdown—Snowflake is the SAS chief's hope in long-haul hell'. *Independent on Sunday*, 4 January: 5.

50 Townsend (2004) op. cit.; SAS press releases: 'New offer from SAS Scandinavian Airlines meets changing demands of the market', 23 August 2004 and '60,000 snowflake tickets for sale', 23 September 2004; Economist Intelligence Unit—Viewswire (2007) 'Sweden: transport and communications'. 2 March.

51 SAS Group Annual Report, 2006: 30.

52 Ghemawat (1991).

53 Porter (1996).

54 *Economist* (2006a). 'Testing times'. 30 March.

55 *Economist* (2006b). 'Cabin fever'. *Economist Global Agenda*, 29 May.

56 *Economist* (2006c). 'Time for a new, improved model'. 20 July.

57 Ibid.

58 *Economist* (2006a) op. cit.

59 Ibid.

60 For a stimulating view on how conflicting strategic imperatives can be analysed and confronted, see Hampden-Turner, C. (1990). *Charting the Corporate Mind*. Blackwell, Oxford.

61 There are a number of recent reviews of the work that was originally developed by Ghoshal and Bartlett in 1987 (Ghoshal, S. and Bartlett, C. A. (1987). 'Managing across borders: new organizational responses'. *Sloan Management Review*, Fall: 43–53): for example Harzing, A.-W. (2000). 'An empirical analysis and extension of the Bartlett and Ghoshal typology of multinational companies'. *Journal of International Business Studies*, 31/1: 101–20; Buckley, P. J. and Casson, M. C. (1998). 'Models of the multinational enterprise'. *Journal of International Business Studies*, 29/1; Caves, R. E. (1996). *Multinational Enterprise and Economic Analysis*. 2nd edn. Cambridge: Cambridge University Press; Lovelock, C. H. (1999). 'Developing marketing strategies for transnational service operations'. *Journal of Services Marketing*, 13/4–5: 278–90.

62 See Meyer, J. W. and Rowan, B. (1977). 'Institutional organizations: formal structure as myth and ceremony'. *American Journal of Sociology*, 83: 340–63; DiMaggio, P. J. and Powell, W. W. (1983). 'The iron cage revisited: Institutional isomorphism and collective rationality in organizational fields'. *American Sociological Review*, 48 (April): 147–60; and Abrahamson, E. (1996). 'Management fashion'. *Academy of Management Review*, 21/1: 254–85.

63 Probably the two most influential works in the development of the concept of agency theory and the principal–agent problem, and how publicly owned companies can be controlled, were Berle, A. A. and Means, G. (1932). *The Modern Corporation and Private Property*. New York: Commerce Clearing House, and Jensen, M. and Meckling, W. (1976). 'Theory of the firm: managerial behavior, agency cost and ownership structure'. *Journal of Financial Economics*, 3: 305–60.

64 Collins and Porras (1994).

65 Freeman (1984). For a more recent review see Freeman and McVea (2005).

66 For a discussion of different models of capitalism, see Albert, M. (1993). *Capitalism against Capitalism*. London: Whurr; Hofstede, G. (1991). *Cultures and Organizations*. London: McGraw-Hill; and Hampden-Turner, C. and Trompenaars, F. (1993). *The Seven Cultures of Capitalism*. New York: Doubleday.

67 See, for example, Williams, K. (2000). 'From shareholder value to present-day capitalism'. *Economy and Society*, 29/1: 1–12; and Morin, F. (2000). 'A transformation in the French model of shareholding and management'. *Economy and Society*, 29/1: 36–53.

68 *The Observer* (1999). 'The GM controversy—how seeds of doubt were planted'. 23 May: 12.

69 O'Sullivan, K. (1999). 'EU to bring in moratorium on the approval of new GM foods'. *Irish Times*, 25 June: 5; *Economist* (2004a). 'Another gene genie out of the bottle'. Economist.com, 19 May.

70 Rhodes, T. (1999). 'Bitter harvest. The real story of Monsanto and GM food'. *The Sunday Times*, 22 August; *Economist* (2002). 'Genetically modified company'. 15 August; *Economist* (2006). 'Up from the dead'. 4 May.

71 For reviews of trends in and influences on corporate pay, see Bebchuk and Grinstein (2005), Rajgopal et al. (2006), Yermack (2006), and Brick et al. (2006), who find evidence of cronyism.

72 See Pearce and Robinson (2004), Hebb and MacLean (2006), Danielson and Karpoff (2006), and Heron and Lie (2006).

73 This model is taken from Mitchell et al. (1997).

74 Friedman (1962, 1996).

75 *Economist* (2004).

76 Healey, T. (2004). 'The best safeguard against financial scandal'. FT.com, 11 March; Ibrahim, Y. (2004). 'The collapse of capitalism as we know it: corporate Disneyland'. *International Herald Tribune*, 10 March; Agence France-Presse (2004). 'Another four top executives of PetroVietnam arrested amid new scandal'. 26 August.

77 McLean, B. and Elkind, P. (2004). 'Now it's Skilling's turn: why Enron's ex-CEO will "fight this thing until the day I die"'. *Fortune*, 8 March: 37; Teather, D. (2006). 'Trial in Texas'. *The Guardian*, 26 January: 28; Barrionuuevo, A. (2006). 'Skilling sentenced to 24 years'. *New York Times*, 24 October: 1; Doran, J. (2006). 'Skilling sentenced to 24 years in prison for Enron fraud'. 24 October: 48.

78 *Economist* (2004). 'Beware of Bondi—Parmalat'. 7 August; *Guardian* (2005). 'Parmalat trial gets under way'. *Guardian Unlimited*, 28 September; Reuters (2006a). 'Parmalat fraud hearings open in convention centre'. 5 June; Reuters (2006b). 'Factbox—five facts about Italy's Parmalat trials'. 5 June; Michaels, A. (2007). 'Deloitte settles Parmalat lawsuit'. FT.com, 15 January; Agence France-Presse (2005). 'Parmalat founder Tanzi prepares to face fraud charges'. 26 September; Cova, B. (2005). 'The Parmalat fraud has generated too little reform'. *Financial Times*, 7 November: 17.

79 *Economist* (2004b). 'Not so super consob'. 5 February; Cova (2005) op. cit.

80 Bowen (1953) is widely recognized as the pioneer.

81 The case for businesses having a social responsibility ethos is put in Mintzberg (1983) and in papers by Bruno, Nichols, and Davis in Hoffman, W. M. and Moore, J. M. (eds) (1990). *Business Ethics: Readings and Cases in Corporate Morality*. New York: McGraw-Hill. The case against was put by Henderson (2001) and Friedman (1996).

82 *Economist* (1999). 'Sweatshop wars', 27 February: 78–9.

83 See Useem, J. (2000). 'Welcome to the new company town'. *Fortune*, 10 January: 45–7; Levering, R. and Moskowitz, M. (2000). 'The 100 best companies to work for'. *Fortune*, 10 January: 53–63; *Economist* (1999). 'How green is Browne?' 17 April: 104; *Economist* (1999) 'Corporate hospitality'. 27 November: 100; Porter, M. E. and van der Linde, C. (1995). 'Green and competitive: ending the stalemate'. *Harvard Business Review*, September–October: 120–33; Hutchison, C. (1996). 'Integrating environmental policy and business strategy'. *Long Range Planning*, 29/1: 11–21. For an interesting case study on environmental strategy in the carpet industry, one of the most polluting of all, see Kinkead, G. (1999). 'In the future, people like me will go to jail'. *Fortune*, 24 May: 190–200. Some success factors for environmental strategies are suggested in Chiesa, V., Manzini, R., and Noci, G. (1999). 'Towards a sustainable view of the competitive system'. *Long Range Planning*, 32/5: 519–30.

84 H&M Corporate Social Responsibility Report 2003, p. 5.

85 2003 Annual Report.

86 Rhodes (1999) op. cit.

87 Wigfield, M. (2001). 'A primer on the Microsoft antitrust case settlement'. *Dow Jones Newswires*, 15 November; Warsh, D. (2001). 'Fighting back'. *Boston Globe*, 6 November: D1; Krim, J. (2004). 'Microsoft settlement upheld: appeal for tougher sanctions rejected'. *Washington Post*, 1 July: E01; Clark, D. and Greenberger, R. (2004). 'Microsoft wins approval of pact in antitrust case'. *Wall Street Journal*, 1 July: A3.

88 See Boyd et al. (1997) and Norburn et al. (2000).

89 The European Commission in June 2004 stipulated that European listed companies from 2005 would either have to conform to US GAAP (Generally Accepted Accounting Practices) or IAS (International Accounting Standards) procedures. See for example the International Accounting Standards Board's website, <http://www.iasb.org>.

90 Adapted from Williams, K. (2000), op. cit.

91 This concept orginates from Johnson (1987).

92 For a discussion of punctuated equilibrium, see Tushman et al. (1986), Tushman and Romanelli (1985), and Romanelli and Tushman (1994). Time-paced evolution was identified by Brown and Eisenhardt (1997).

93 See Miller, D. (1990). *The Icarus Paradox*. New York: Harper Business. The term competency trap comes from Levitt, B. and J. G. March (1988). 'Organizational learning'. *Annual Review of Sociology*, 14: 319–40. Leonard-Barton, D. (1992). 'Core capabilities and core rigidities: a paradox in managing new product development'. *Strategic Management Journal*, 13: 111–25 was the first to identify the notion of core rigidity.

94 Cope, N. (1999a). 'What the devil has happened to good old Marks and Spencer'. *The Independent*, 15 January; Foster, G. (1999). 'Marks loses spark on fears over foods'. *Daily Mail*, 2 March: 64; Rushe, D. (1999). 'Heads roll as St Michael halo slips further'. *Sunday Times*, 3 October; Voyle, S. (1999). 'Retail giant faces up to fact that there will not be easy return to former glories'. *Financial Times*, 3 November: 29; *Dow Jones International News* (2000). 'M&S Vandevelde: no less than 2yrs for full recovery'. 23 May; Sampson, A. (2004). 'The trouble with fat cats is they lose touch with their customers'. *The Independent*, 5 June: 39.

95 Marks and Spencer Annual Reviews 1999: 23, 2003: 61. Changes in accounting policies during these periods make it difficult to compare figures between reports, which is why we do not give precise profit figures. Figures are for profits before tax but net of exceptional items.

96 Marks and Spencer Annual Reviews 2003: 61; 2007: 34.

97 *Financial Times* (1999). 'St Michael comes a cropper and tarnishes his halo'. 15 January: 21; Cope, N. (1999a) op. cit.; Bevan (2002); Braid, M. (1999). 'Cool? It has all the verve and style of a Saga holiday'. *The Independent*, 19 May.

98 Jarvis, P. (1999). 'Marks & Spencer's CEO well received despite pft Dive'. *Dow Jones International News*, 18 May; Braid (1999) op. cit.; Cope (1999a) op. cit.; Walters, J. (1999a). 'Giants under threat'. *The Observer*, 16 May: 5; Polan, B. and Turner, L. (2000). 'Has M&S forgotten who shops there?'. *Daily Mail*, 25 September: 24.

99 Walters (1999a) op. cit.; Laurance, B. (1999). 'How the bad guys blew it down Baker Street'. *The Observer*, 17 January: 3.

100 Cope (1999a) op. cit.; Foster, G. (1999). 'Marks loses spark on fears over foods'. *Daily Mail*, 2 March: 64; Walters (1999a) op. cit.

101 Cope, N. (1999b). 'M&S loses market share to Bhs', *The Independent*, 19 July: 17.

102 Hollinger, P. (1999). 'M&S axes 25% of top managers'. *Financial Times*, 25 February: 29; Norris, D. (1999). 'Flagging M&S "plans to shed 200 managers"'. *Daily Mail*, 15 February: 15; Guerrera, F. (1999). 'Dismay at M&S over job cuts'. *The Independent*, 6 April: 13; *Financial Times* (1999) op. cit.

103 This is Peter Salsbury's own admission, as reported in the *Financial Times* (1999) op. cit.

104 Quoted in Steiner, S. (1999). 'How grey cast a shadow over profits at M&S'. *The Times*, 19 May: 7.

105 Braid (1999) op. cit.; Cope (1999a) op. cit.; Polan and Turner (2000) op. cit; Hart-Davis, R. (2000). 'Has Marks found its Sparks again?' *The Mail on Sunday*, 18 June: 32.

106 *The Observer* (2007). 'M&S chief bets on restaurants, revamps and foreign stores'. 20 May: 5; Cartner-Morley, J. (2007). 'Catwalk confidence: buoyant M&S unveils autumn collections'. *The Guardian*, 25 May; Hall, J. (2007). 'How I brought the M&S animal back to life'. *The Sunday Telegraph*, 27 May: 7; Elliott, V. (2007). 'Women's Institute members are the secret weapon behind M&S success'. *The Times*, 6 June: 3; Croft, C. (2007). 'National treasures'. *Sunday Times*, 17 June: *Style* 33.

107 Rushe, D. (1999). 'Shopsoiled'. *Sunday Times*, 28 February.

108 See, for example, Bevan (2002); *Economist* (2000). 'Does M&S have a future?'. 28 October; Voyle, S. (2000). 'Troubleshooter sets out his stall'. *Financial Times*, 4 April 2000: 17; Robinson, E. (1999). 'In search of a fresh spark'. *Financial Times*, 1 October: 4.

109 The quotation is from Walters, J. (1999b). 'The harder they fall'. *The Observer*, 16 May: 5. See also Sampson (2004) op. cit.

110 The quotation is from Brummer, A. (1999). 'M&S hair shirt will prove uncomfortable'. *The Guardian*, 19 May: 23. Simlar observations are made by Finch, J. (1999). 'Desperation time at M&S as profits fall 43%'. *The Guardian*, 3 November: 5; *Financial Times* (1999) op. cit. and 'Lex column—markdown'. 15 January; Walters (1999a) op. cit. Salsbury's own admission is cited by Voyle (1999) op. cit.

111 Vogl, A. J. (2004). 'The Anti-CEO'. *Across the Board*, 41/3.

112 Ibid.

113 Ricardo Semler's books include the autobiographical *Maverick: The Success Story Behind the World's Most Unusual Workplace*, published in 1993 (New York: Warner Books), which was on the bestseller lists in 12 countries and sold more than 1 million copies, and in 2004, *The Seven-day Weekend: Changing the Way Work Works* (New York: Portfolio/Penguin USA). Nearly 2,000 executives and researchers from around the world have travelled to Brazil to study the company.

114 *Financial Times* (1997). 'It's still rock and roll to me—Semco's Chief'. 15 May: 18.

115 Extract from Semler (2004) op. cit.

116 Ibid.

117 Ibid., available online at <http://www.inc.com/articles/2004/03/7dayweekend.html>, accessed 29 May 2005.

118 Semler, R. (2000). 'How we went digital without a strategy'. *Harvard Business Review*, 78/5.

119 Ibid.

120 Vogl (2004) op. cit.

121 Semler (2000) op. cit.

122 Vogl (2004) op. cit.

PART TWO

Assessing Fit and Distinctiveness

In this part of the book, we introduce you to the theory needed to assess whether a strategy fits the environment and gives the organization the distinctiveness it needs if it is to flourish.

We show you how to analyse an organization's environment by identifying the key macro-environmental trends and assessing how they will affect the economic structure of the industries in which the organization is active. This will enable you to assess whether the organization has chosen its industries astutely. You will also be able to identify the success and survival factors for the industry, and so gauge whether the organization will be able meet them.

We show you also how to appraise an organization's choices of markets and customers, and decide if it is offering suitable products and services, and differentiating them appropriately. You will also learn how to analyze its value chain, looking in detail at where it differs from that of its competitors.

We look at the trade-offs involved as an organization expands and diversifies. You will learn how to assess if it is too small or too large to prosper in its industry, and whether it has become too diverse. You will learn of the importance of relatedness and synergy and how to assess whether they exist within a portfolio of products or businesses.

PART TWO

Assessing risk and
protectiveness

CHAPTER THREE

Understanding the Influence of the Environment

LEARNING OUTCOMES

After reading this chapter you should be able to:

➔ Assess the factors that a competitor in an industry needs in order to survive and succeed in it, and how those will change over time

➔ Evaluate significant developments in the broad 'macro-environment' and understand how they might impact upon an industry and the organizations within it

➔ Analyse the nature of competition in an industry, and in particular whether it is benign or fierce

➔ Explain the factors that contribute to industry attractiveness.

INTRODUCTION

If an organization is to be an effective economic unit, its managers must have an understanding of the environment in which it operates. They need to be aware of the needs of its customers and users, so as to be able to design products and services to please them and to market these effectively. If the organization's customers are businesses, they will have customers of their own whose needs will also have to be understood. These will not be constant over time, so managers will have to stay alert to the ways in which customer preferences change.

At the same time, changing technology or economic circumstances may alter the ways in which products and services are made and delivered. It may become necessary to improve economies of scale in purchasing, to cut labour costs in order to respond to new competitors from developing countries, or to increase the organization's access to new skills and technologies. Sometimes, the first organization to notice these possibilities can gain an advantage in the market place, or can get the pick of the people with rare but necessary skills.

Lastly, organizations need to be alert to the activities of competitors, both existing and potential. They must understand the nature of competition in their industry, and how and whether it is likely to change. Organizations that assess and understand the environment better than their competitors tend to outperform them over time.[1]

We are interested both in an organization's past and present environment as well as how it is likely to alter in the future. Above all, we need to understand the nature of the competition that an organization confronts. We need to understand how fierce that competition is, and why. We need to look forward, to understand how competition may evolve as the environment changes. This helps us to understand the new challenges that the organization and its competitors are likely to have to confront, and that they should take into account when they formulate strategies for the future.

An analysis of the past environment can also yield useful information. It tells us what kinds of environment the organization's routines were developed to cope with, and what has shaped the outlook of its principal decision-makers. It tells us how different the present and future are likely to be from the past, and how great a change an organization will need to make to its routines, and other internal features such as its culture and architecture, if it is to adjust successfully to the new circumstances.

3.1 Analysing the environment and the nature of competition

An analysis of the environment and the nature of the competition that an organization faces has four main parts.

On the left hand side of Figure 3.1 are the six groups of factors found in the wider environment which affect a whole population and the organizations that serve it—the PESTLE factors. In analysing the macro-environment, we are trying to identify the things that will influence an organization's supply and demand levels, and its costs.

Another important feature that shapes the nature of competition that an organization faces has to do with the stage that its industry has reached in its life-cycle. The challenges that managers face will typically vary according to the different stages of the life-cycle.

The stage of the industry life-cycle and the wider macro-environment will also affect the relative importance of the forces within an industry. The stronger each of these forces is, the more difficult it is for firms in the industry to make profits, and the more fiercely they are likely to compete with one another. The way in which firms compete are also affected by two other factors in an industry: its *concentration* (how many firms contest a particular

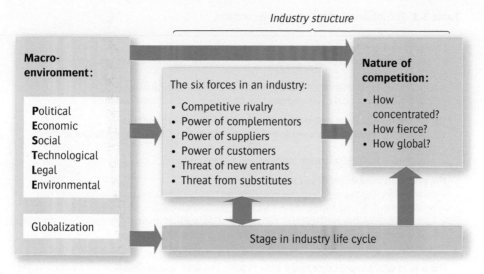

Figure 3.1 Analysing the nature of competition

terrain), and its *scope* (global or local). All these things together determine the key elements in an industry analysis:

- The intensity of competition in an industry—is it fierce or benign?

- What are the ways in which firms compete—for example, on cost and price, or through superior relations with powerful customers or other stakeholders?

- What are the key factors a firm needs to have if it is to survive in the industry, and what further factors must it possess if it is to be among the leaders?

These four environmental features—macro-environment, industry life-cycle, industry structure, and nature of competition—are intimately linked, and analysis of them needs to be undertaken together. We shall look at the analytical frameworks in the order in which they appear from left to right in Figure 3.1. However, you will not necessarily want to use them in that same order—they do not always follow a neat linear flow from left to right.

3.2 The macro-environment: PESTLE analysis

In a macro-environmental analysis we are interested in factors in the wider environment that have the power to alter: demand for the products offered by firms in an industry; the way in which products and services are distributed; the prices that are charged for them; and the ways in which organizations compete with each other in the industry (Table 3.1). These factors can be grouped under six headings:

Political
Economic
Social/cultural
Technological
Legal
Environmental

Some trends transcend these factors, the most important example being globalization, which we examine in Chapter 14.

Macro-environment
The set of factors and influences that are not specific to an organization or the industry in which it operates, but that nonetheless affect them.

Table 3.1 The influence of the macro-environment

Changing demand for products and services
- Changes in the tastes or purchasing power of customers, or *their* customers, and so on down the supply chain
- New technologies that could make products or services more attractive
- Economic and political developments that open up markets in new countries

The way that firms in an industry produce and distribute their outputs
- Changes in the technology used within the product or service, making it cheaper or more powerful.
- New production or distribution methods and technologies.

The price and availability of key inputs
- Factors affecting the supply of raw materials, such as political unrest in the countries that produce them, or new technologies that make production cheaper or more reliable.
- Factors affecting the availability of people and skills, such as improving educational standards in developing countries and rises or falls in the number of young people entering labour markets.

The way in which organizations are able to compete with one another
- New regulations liberalizing international trade and tariff regimes.
- Changes of government which may lead to the liberalization or regulation of particular markets.
- New laws governing pollution standards or minimum wages.

3.2.1 **Political factors**

Political factors encompass actions by local and national administrations and political parties, and by international bodies such as the European Commission, the United Nations, and the World Trade Organization. These affect the stability of an industry's environment, the extent to which firms can take decisions without reference to governments, the costs of operating in a particular area, and the facilities and infrastructure available.

Uncertainty makes it more difficult for managers to develop strategies, so that most organizations find life easier within a stable political system. Wars, revolutions, and governments that change frequently or are unable to assert their authority can disrupt individual markets or whole industrial sectors. The 9/11 terrorist attacks on Washington and New York in 2001, and the subsequent invasion of Iraq, caused global demand for hotel and airline services to plummet, as tourists were deterred from flying. Shortages in the supply of oil, as Iraq was one of the world's largest suppliers, caused petroleum prices to rise worldwide, with a knock-on effect on firms' transport costs. However, other industries benefited. Demand for arms and mercenary services rose, for example.

There may also be direct political intervention in the operation of industries and markets, for example through:

- the use of subsidies or nationalization—to encourage certain industries or to rescue major firms from bankruptcy;

- the building of infrastructure—such as ports, roads, railways, telecommunications links, and of training and education systems that give firms a source of skilled labour.

Political factors often impose costs upon organizations. Apart from the various taxes that firms have to pay, costs are incurred in abiding by government policies. Nationalized firms that have been privatized are usually heavily regulated, and have to conform to strict, and expensive-to-operate, controls over what they can and cannot do. Charities and not-for-profits (NFPs) are subject to regular examinations of their accounts and operations to ensure that they are acting within their remit. And some other industries are heavily regulated because of their importance to national security, or because of concerns over safety (see Real-life Application 3.1).

Real-life Application 3.1 Political factors affecting the airline industry

Both regulations and legislation control what airlines can and cannot do. For example, many airlines are still state-owned and legally prevented from being sold to private investors, a legacy from the days when almost all airlines were part of the strategic defence infrastructure of their countries. This means that they tend to be allowed privileged access to landing slots at their country's major airports—a scarce resource that acts to block competition from other airlines. The proliferation of alliances between many of the world's airlines is one way of bypassing this sort of protectionism: by agreeing to share routes and customers, airlines can exchange access to each others' assets. Even now, in the USA which has mostly deregulated its airline industry and no longer has any state-owned carriers, foreign firms are blocked from owning more than 50 per cent of a US airline.

Political factors also affect airlines in other ways. Because of the need to ensure safety, government agencies exercise strong control over airlines and have agreed worldwide standards over matters such as airline safety and which carriers are allowed to enter a country's airspace.

Governments often try to protect firms in their countries from foreign competition through tariffs and import restrictions, and to encourage their development through cheap loans and large government contracts. These policies can sometimes help domestic producers establish themselves but, in the long term, they risk breeding firms that are made complacent by the easy profits from their home markets. Such organizations are often unable to compete with efficient foreign competitors.

3.2.2 Economic factors

All products and services are either purchased directly by consumers, form inputs into things that are bought by consumers, or are purchased by government departments that are funded by taxes and duties that are paid by consumers. Consumer spending power is thus a major factor in the prosperity of any industry. If an economy booms, it will promote the growth of many industries, particularly those producing highly differentiated or luxury goods. Economic downturns cause difficulties for most industries but may help the growth of sub-sectors that offer exceptional value for money, such as 'no-frills' airlines. Factors such as rates of economic growth, unemployment and interest rates, which affect the spending power of consumers and businesses, also have a major impact on the nature of competition in an industry. Increasingly, strategists are more interested in the state of the global economy than in that of individual countries.

Other important economic factors relate to the supply of and demand for key inputs, such as oil, metals, minerals, and skilled labour. Shortages of these inputs result in prices (or salaries) increasing, which may affect the profitability of industries that need to purchase them.

3.2.3 Social and cultural factors

Just as consumer purchasing power ultimately determines the magnitude of demand for all goods and services, so consumer tastes ultimately determine where that demand is directed. Sometimes these tastes are manifested in what consumers themselves actually buy. In other cases they are expressed through voting, lobbying, and other political processes, which influence the decisions of politicians and civil servants.

Some social trends have a life of only a few years and/or affect few people and societies. Others have a life of several decades and widespread relevance across many developed economies. They may be noticed by sociologists or journalists, and glorified with a name, like 'Generation-X', or 'goths' and 'punks' that are associated with styles of dressing and music genres. Sometimes, these trends are linked to phases of economic boom or bust. A good environmental analysis would need to take all relevant trends into account, including those that do not directly affect the markets or industries in which an organization is currently active, but which may be relevant in the future.

Some examples of social and cultural factors include:

- growing consumer assertiveness and intolerance of poor quality;
- growing acceptance of computers and the internet as tools for education, leisure, information-gathering, and purchasing goods and services;
- increases in average household income, with a corresponding reduction in the time available to spend it, resulting in an increasing demand for childcare services and for products such as ready-prepared meals and fast food;
- the 'greying' of the population in many countries. In Japan, the USA, and Europe, members of the 'baby-boom' generation conceived directly after the Second World War have reached retirement age, while they and their successors have preferred smaller families, so that young people are less numerous. In China, the numbers of single-child families is the result of government policy.

3.2.4 Technological factors

Many major transformations in the ways organizations—and indeed whole societies—operate can be traced to technological change. Intelligent electronics are increasingly incorporated into everyday objects like washing machines and toys. Computers and high-speed internet connections have become more freely available at lower cost, enabling small firms and individuals to afford technologies once limited to large organizations, and to vary their mode and place of work and or purchasing. Bar-coding, RFID radio tags, and EPOS (electronic point of sale) equipment have enabled firms to gather more data than ever before about their operations and customers. Groupware products, intranets, and 'wikis' enable several people in different locations to collaborate in developing a concept or product, while instant messaging, blogs, and social networking software like MySpace transform the ways in which people interact socially and discover music and other media. Marketing technology has benefited from an improved understanding of consumer psychology and the availability of more detailed survey data on consumer habits and preferences.

The 'lean' philosophy that has been so influential in manufacturing has also been incorporated into the technology of logistics, the function that deals with the storage and distribution of inputs and finished products.

Sophisticated sensors have been developed to monitor the condition of items while they are being stored or delivered, reducing wastage. New networking technologies have enabled

➜ We discuss logistics and other supply chain technologies when we look at the manufacturing firm value chain in Section 6.2.1.

producers and retailers to link their ordering systems directly to their suppliers through EDI (electronic data interchange), so that items are ordered automatically and manufacturers/retailers need to carry less stock (Real-life Application 3.2).

Real-life Application 3.2 Information technologies in the retail supply chain

Product life-cycle management (PLM) systems are a type of just-in-time technology that reduces lead times through coordinating each step in the life of a new garment, from initial concept through production, to delivery to the store. These systems allow colours and fabric samples to be shown very realistically on suppliers' computer screens across the world. Designs can therefore be got right at an early stage of the production process, without costly 'hard-copy' mistakes.

At the base of an effective PLM system are good data-capture and management technologies. Part of the process is the capturing in real time, via bar-codes on the clothes which are scanned in to computerized tills, sales and trends from shops across the world. Leading fashion retailers, generally, have invested large sums of money in developing these sorts of systems, which allow them to understand what their customers are buying, and when.

In the past, lack of supplier connections gave some strange supply-chain anomalies in other product categories. Procter & Gamble, a multinational consumer-goods company, noticed that although the number of babies and the demand for nappies remained relatively stable, orders for Pampers, its disposable nappies, fluctuated dramatically.[2] This was because information about consumer demand became increasingly distorted as it moved down the supply chain. If a retailer noticed an increase in demand for nappies, they ordered more from their wholesaler. The wholesaler then increased their own sales' forecasts, and their manufacturer increased production correspondingly. But when the increase in demand turned out not to be sustained, too much stock was left and orders were scaled back—leaving too little stock when demand increased again. A more reliable—and timely—flow of information, as a result of integrating suppliers' systems with the firms', smoothes out these fluctuations.

An extension of the data-capture system is the loyalty card. As well as having potential benefits in making customers feel they are getting a bargain, this also gives retailers valuable information about their customers' habits. This is used to forecast demand for other goods known to be popular with customers in that segment.

Although these technologies are potentially available to everyone, firms may gain competitive advantage from the speed with which they adopt, or the way that they deploy, these technologies. H&M and Zara, its main rival, have exceptionally good PLM systems and can take a design idea from concept to store in less than two weeks. In both cases their competence in the management of this aspect of their value chains is a strategic resource that enables them to differentiate their offerings from their competitors'. How they do this is a trade secret and deeply embedded within their value chains and architectures.

➜ See Chapter 6 for a discussion of the value chain and Chapter 7 for a detailed discussion of strategic resources.

3.2.5 Legal factors

Organizations also have to adjust their products and ways of operating to the different regulatory and legislative frameworks that govern each of the product areas and countries in which they are active. In some areas, such as the countries in the European Union, organizations may be subject to both national and supra-national laws. Recognition of the increasingly global nature of commerce has led to attempts to standardize some aspects of the international legal environment, for example the ways in which companies report financial data.

Other examples of legal or regulatory factors include:

• regulations (known as Basel II) which stipulate that the ratio of reserves to loans on a bank's balance sheet must not be less than 8 per cent.[3] These standards are set by an international body, the Bank for International Settlements, but national governments choose how strictly to enforce them;

- laws that say that employers must pay part of the cost of their employees' health or unemployment insurance, or contribute to insurance schemes designed to ensure that pensions are still paid if the organization goes out of business;

- controls on merger and acquisition activity—most national governments, and the European Union, have set up bodies for this purpose;

- restrictions on monopoly trading—in order to protect consumers; again most developed countries have some sort of system for regulating how firms trade;

- legislation that directs organizations to pay their staff a minimum wage or to install expensive equipment to control pollution;

- regulations that say what prices may be charged for goods, for example in privatized firms.

In some cases the costs of conforming to legal requirements are extremely high. However, this is not always bad for competitiveness. In the USA, organic farmers *asked* the federal government to regulate their industry.[4] They believed that having a clear legal definition of 'organic' produce would help them by preventing competitors who grew food by cheaper methods from passing their produce off as organic. And, paradoxically, costly legal conformance can sometimes enhance firms' competitiveness, if, in order to reduce those costs, firms are forced to develop new routines and technologies. For example, US firms that have been forced to reconfigure their value chains to meet tough new environmental laws have found that they have made gains in terms of reduced wastage and improved efficiency that far outweigh the costs. In Germany, firms have been forced, by that country's exacting legislation, to develop technologies to reduce their own pollution. In compensation, they have been able to establish global leadership positions in the pollution control industry, beating off international competitors who have not been forced to develop such high standards.

3.2.6 **Environmental factors**

A number of factors that affect economic activity derive from the physical environment. For example:

- global warming, believed by most, though not all, people to be due to carbon dioxide and other greenhouse gases produced by industrial activity, cars, and other forms of travel;

- diseases, notably HIV/AIDS, but also avian flu and other potential pandemics;

- the reaction to the development of genetically modified (GM) plants.

These issues are strongly linked to other PESTLE factors—and the significance attached to them by consumers and other stakeholders. General awareness of 'green' environmental issues, which dates back to the early 1970s, appears for example to be increasing, partly driven by pressure groups that can use the internet to spread the word about firms' behaviour.

Awareness of the effects of global warning have led to increased efforts to develop technological solutions to the problem, some of which feeds through to legislation. For example, the awareness that oil is in short supply (an economic factor), and in any case is produced in some of the most unstable regions of the world (a political factor), has led to increased efforts to produce renewable fuels such as bio-ethanol from sugar or bio-diesel from vegetable oil,

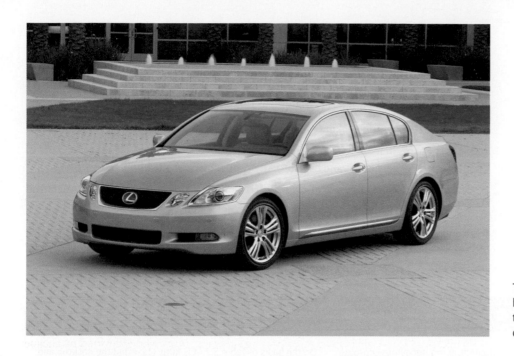

Toyota has developed hybrid petrol/electric cars that use kinetic energy to charge a battery. *Toyota*

and has led to subsidies and other policies to promote emission-free sources of energy, such as wind- and wave-power.[5]

Fear of future legislation on green issues is also concentrating the minds of researchers in those industries most likely to be affected. Toyota is one of the pioneers. It has developed hybrid petrol/electric cars that use kinetic energy to charge a battery which is used as a supplement to the normal engine, thus significantly improving petrol consumption and reducing emissions in built-up areas where traffic speeds are slow.

Although consumers in parts of the world (notably the European Union) have resisted GM technologies, those in other regions appear to be less concerned. Food production in some parts of Asia or Africa, which are regularly blighted by insects, has been boosted significantly by GM techniques, which has led it to be welcomed initially (there appear to be increasing concerns about the technology).[6] And consumers in the USA, where GM was principally developed, also appear to have fewer concerns (although environmental groups are also increasingly active there). It is estimated that 75 per cent of processed foods in the USA contain GM ingredients.[7]

3.3 Analysing the industry

At this stage in this chapter we turn to the problem of deciding which industries a firm is in, and therefore which need to be analysed. For a firm that spans a number of industries, because it is diversified or vertically integrated, a separate analysis is needed for each of the industries involved. An analysis of one of the major mobile telephone manufacturers, such as Nokia or Motorola, would need to take account of their involvement in the manufacture of both handsets and infrastructure. Mobile telephone handsets are small and sold by the million to individual consumers. Mobile telephone infrastructure consists of large items of radio transmission and reception equipment, sold in small quantities to the firms that operate telephony services. Although there are linkages between the two industries, one could certainly not make an industry analysis stretch to both.

This leads to the problem of deciding when two or more related sets of products come from a single industry, or from separate ones. When we defined industries and markets in Chapter 1, we remarked that this is not always simple, but a number of factors can help with the judgement:

- Are the inputs and product technologies similar?
- Are the competitors making each product mostly the same?
- Do the firms in making each of the products look to the same resources as the basis of competitive advantage, and have broadly similar value chains?
- Is there a significant degree of overlap between the different products' customers and end-users?

Real-life Application 3.3 gives some examples of how these factors can be applied.

Real-life Application 3.3 How many industries does Sony's computing business cover?

Sony manufactures laptop computers, computer games consoles, and computer components, some of which are sourced from original equipment manufacturers (OEMs). Does this constitute one industry or three? And do laptop computers qualify as an industry in their own right, or are they a sub-sector of the personal computer industry? (See Table 3.2.)

On the basis of Table 3.2, it is fairly clear that the desktop and laptop sub-sectors are close enough to be considered a single industry, but the components and games consoles businesses each reside in a separate industry, despite a superficial overlap in technology.

Table 3.2 Sony's computer businesses: industries in which they operate

	Inputs	Competitors	Resources and value chain	Suppliers/ collaborators	Customers and end-users
Computer games	Specialized processor and graphics chips, displays, joysticks, DVD drives	Nintendo, Microsoft, Gizmondo	Capabilities in graphics technology. Access to innovative games developers. Sell through non-specialist outlets	Apple, Samsung, Dell, Toshiba	Customers are electrical stores, bookshops, etc. End-users are consumers, mainly young
PCs: desktop sub-sector	Generic components— processors, disc drives, boards, displays, etc.	Lenovo (IBM), Dell, Apple, Toshiba, Hewlett-Packard (Compaq), plus many smaller competitors	Technical capabilities in combining components. Capabilities in low-cost manufacture	ViXS Systems, Microsoft	Customers are distributors, firms and individuals. End-users are consumers of all ages and type
PCs: laptop sub-sector	Modified versions of desktop computer components, LCD displays	Same as desktop sub-sector	Capabilities in designing lightweight machines with low energy consumption	Same as desktop sub-sector	Same as desktop sub-sector
Computer components	Processors, optical discs, wiring, circuit boards, precision optical and mechanical components	Acer, Sharp, Toshiba	Specialist design capabilities, low-cost manufacture	IBM, Toshiba, Nichia, Matsushita, NEC	Most customers and end-users are computer manufacturers. Some sales to hobbyists via distributors

3.3.1 Industry recipes and 'rules of the game'

One defining characteristic of an industry is the way of thinking, or mental model, that participants have come to share. In most industries, firms settle over time into recognizable patterns of competitive behaviour. For example, most clothing retailers will introduce new lines of merchandise twice a year, and hold periodic sales when out-of-date merchandise is sold at heavily discounted prices to make room for the newer lines. These patterns of behaviour often have a basis in the economics of the industry—clothing firms cannot sell the same merchandise in the summer and winter, and have not enough shelf or warehouse space to carry both types of clothing all the year round. Over time, though, they become part of the cultures of many of the organizations in the industry. People learn these routines when they join one organization, and carry them with them as they move from firm to firm. These ingrained routines are known as industry recipes.[8]

Industry recipes can cover a wide variety of routines, such as ways of negotiating with suppliers, manufacturing methods, and the number of days of credit offered to customers. The competitive aspects of these behaviours are sometimes known as the 'rules of the game'. These are accepted and expected pricing and marketing practices that define the boundaries of what firms can do without inciting their competitors to retaliate. No-one will think H&M is starting a price war if it holds an end-of-season sale. Other examples of 'rules of the game' are the unwritten acceptance that certain firms will work closely with particular suppliers and distributors, or will be the leaders in certain markets in which they have historically been strong. Competitors do not challenge these practices, because to do so would probably provoke retaliation and all firms in the industry would lose out.

Acceptance of these kinds of rules of the game rests on the recognition that in most industries competition is a fact of life, and that a manageable degree of competition is actually beneficial in stopping an organization from becoming complacent and stale.

3.3.2 Strategic groups

It is quite rare for there to be just one type of competitive behaviour in an industry. For example, in clothes' retailing, alongside the 'normal' retailers with their twice-yearly collections and sales, there are firms that differentiate on the basis of having very low prices at all times. Others, designer labels such as Armani or Chanel, for example, differentiate on the basis of image, style, and high price, and try to avoid discounting—their out-of-fashion merchandise is sold off discreetly through different outlets.

These different types of behaviour define what are known as strategic groups within an industry. Each group has its own recipe and rules of the game, and there are mobility barriers that make it difficult for firms to move from one group to another— similar to the entry barriers for an industry (Section 3.5.4).

In many industries, there is a strategic group that addresses the top of the market, differentiating on product design or customer service, and another that addresses the lower part of the market by differentiating on price. There will often be survival and success factors that can be identified with the strategies followed by these two groups, and others for firms wishing to steer a course between these two extremes. H&M at present occupies a mid-market group along with firms such as Zara. If it were to want to move to the 'designer label' group, it would need to reposition its reputation and identity, and learn how to work with different fabrics and different customers (Figure 3.2).

Strategic groups may be assessed on a number of attributes, which should include measures of the scope of the firm's activity, such as size and geographical coverage, and of the resource commitment, such as investment in growth or R&D. Figure 3.2 uses breadth of

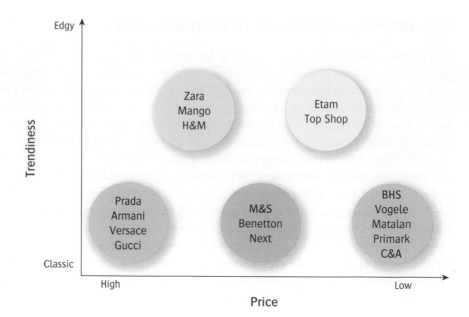

Figure 3.2 Strategic groups in the fasion industry

product trendiness as the scope measure and price levels as a measure of resource commitment. This is a simplified version of the analysis—a more rigorous one would look at several dimensions of both scope and resource commitment, and would look over a number of years to make sure the group structure being examined was stable.[9]

It may, however, sometimes be difficult to tell when a strategic group ends and a new industry begins. For example, although both H&M and Armani are in the clothes manufacturing industry, it could be argued that their value chains, production processes, and customer profiles are so dissimilar that really they operate in two different industries—mass market clothing and luxury clothing.

Understanding the nature of a firm's strategic group is important in a number of ways. First, barriers to entry differ for each strategic group. Second, if a company successfully enters one of the groups, the members of that group become its key competitors. If it hopes to succeed, it needs to have some potential advantage in the specific elements of competition that are important in that group. Third, once in a particular strategic group, it may find itself confined there by mobility barriers—factors such as reputation that make it difficult for a firm to move from, say, a group that differentiates on low prices to one whose members differentiate on luxury. Finally, membership of a strategic group will shape the thinking of the firm's managers—members of a group tend to have similar 'recipes'.[10]

Although competition is most intense within a strategic group, there is also likely to be rivalry between different groups. Firms in neighbouring groups may appeal to overlapping customers. These customers may not perceive much difference in the benefits they receive from one company or another. Companies in different groups might also want to expand the scope of their product range, especially if the firms are fairly equal in size and power and if the mobility barriers between the groups are low.

Industry life-cycle
A model of how a typical industry progresses from its birth, with the creation of a new product type, to its demise, with the sale of its very last product.

3.4 The industry life-cycle

The next focus of our analysis of the environment is the industry life-cycle. If we take the television manufacturing industry as an example, its life-cycle started when the very first television came off the production line and will end when the last one is sold.

The macro-environment, in the form of technological advances or social trends, often triggers changes in an industry's life-cycle through encouraging or enabling the development of new products. The different stages of the industry life-cycle tend to be linked to different types of industry structure, and also variation in the balance between the industry's six forces (see Sections 3.3 and 3.4 below).

A typical industry goes through four phases:

1. An introductory phase when the first products are made, and only just starting to be noticed by potential customers

2. A growth phase when the industry becomes established and the number of firms and sales of the product grow rapidly

3. A mature phase when the industry's sales are stagnant or growing only slowly

4. A decline phase when the industry's sales fall.

Not every industry follows this sequence precisely, and how long each phase lasts varies according to the nature of the product, but the life-cycle model is sufficiently representative to provide some useful generalizations about competitive behaviour.[11]

Figure 3.3 shows a typical industry life-cycle, which maps total sales of the industry's products against time:

In the introductory phase of an industry, new products and their technologies are in their infancy and can be rather unreliable. Customers may be enthusiasts who like and understand the technology well enough to cope with its unreliability, such as the people who bought the first personal computers in kit form and then assembled them. Or they may

→ We return to looking at the effects of life-cycle stages on firm's competitive strategies when we discuss strategic options during the various stages in Chapter 13.

Figure 3.3 The industry life-cycle

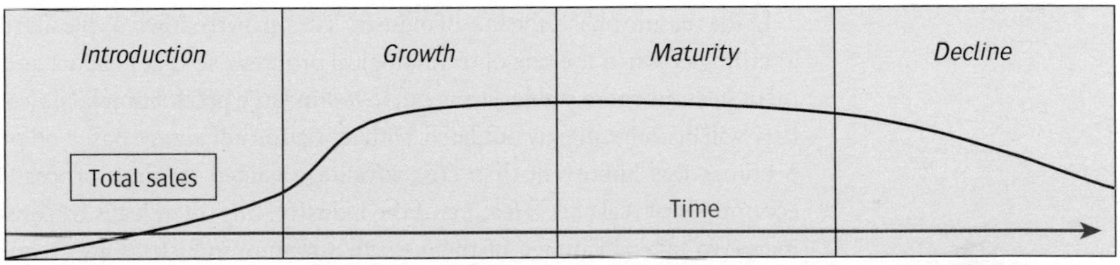

	Introduction	Growth	Maturity	Decline
Competitors	Few to start with, but increasing	Many new entrants, then fight for share/ consolidation/ concentration begins	Stable oligopoly Firms inter-dependent	Declining—exit of firms
Customers	Few and rich	Increasingly discerning	Repeat sales	Moving away
Entry barriers	Technology	Start-up costs Learning curve	Competitors' defensive tactics	Over-capacity
Products	Little choice	Growing availability	Differentiated	Shrinking
	Poor quality	Becoming differentiated	High quality	Reduced choice
Typical pricing	High. Cost-plus	Penetration	Market signalling and occasional price wars	Cut
Profits	Negative	Increasing	High	Declining
Unit costs	High	Declining	Low cost/efficiency focus	Low
Marketing	Information and education	Mass-market persuasion and differentiation	Brand maintenance	Reduced

be people or firms, often wealthy, who like progress for its own sake or want to be seen as progressive. This phase may last a few months or many years.

In the introductory phase of an industry, rivalry between competing firms is likely to be quite mild, since there are few competitors, and those that do exist are concentrating on controlling their own internal processes, and have plenty of potential customers to go for.

In the growth phase, the product starts to become legitimized in the minds of potential buyers; awareness from customers is increasing, and more people consider purchasing it. Demand may be so high that incumbent firms face problems keeping up with it. Awareness also attracts new companies into the industry with 'me-too' products to take advantage of growth opportunities that they see, or because they have some technological innovation that they can use to improve the products and which give them differentiation or cost advantage.

Industries in the introductory or growth phases are sometimes called emerging industries. Quite a high proportion of firms will exit the industry during these phases because of a phenomenon called the liability of newness. New organizations take time to develop the stable routines needed to survive, and during that period there is a high probability that they will collapse.[12]

In the growth phase, as there are still enough customers to go around, competition is not particularly fierce, and is often based on non-price factors such as additional product features or higher standards of service. As the industry matures, competitive rivalry starts to intensify. Competition on the basis of price tends to become more frequent in order to gain market share, as growth can no longer come from finding new customers.

Some variations on the life-cycle model add a fifth 'shake-out' stage between growth and maturity, but research has shown that shake-outs can occur at any stage in an industry's development and are not necessarily more common when the rate of sales growth is falling.[13] However, the number of organizations does fall, as the number of failures rises, later in an industry's life, and some theorists attribute this to inertia.

➤ We introduced the concept of inertia in Section 2.8.1.

In the mature phase, the rate of industry sales growth slows. Typically, this coincides with a settling down in the rate of technological progress, so that product and process development become more stable. Firms can invest in large production facilities with less risk that they will become quickly outdated. Differentiation advantage based on product innovation becomes less important than cost advantage gained through process improvements. If economies of scale are a feature of the industry, this often leads to consolidation as firms merge to take advantage of them, so that mature industries are frequently, though not always, oligopolies.

In the mature phase the behaviour of the main industry participants tends to be predictable and in line with industry recipes. In the most common type of mature industry, these recipes are for steady progress. Firms get feedback from their customers about their requirements and make adjustments to their competitive stance or value chain. Industries such as recorded music, cinema, or pharmaceuticals, however, follow what is termed the creative model—they have to make large investments without knowing whether the product will succeed in the market-place, and fund large numbers of money-losing projects through the successful 'blockbusters'.

➤ We go into greater depth about the different kinds of mature industry in Section 13.4.

Mature industries are not always stable. Some are disrupted by price wars or acquisitions, if one firm spots an opportunity to eliminate one of its weaker rivals, although mergers and monopolies regulators are likely to step in if there is a risk of one firm becoming too dominant. Others are disturbed by the introduction of radically new products, technologies, or business models. The internet revolutionized a number of industries, such as book retailing and travel, in the early years of the twenty-first century, just as the fast fashion business model followed by H&M and its competitors transformed the clothing industry. In such cases, new entrants can gain dominant positions at the expense of established players.[14]

During the decline phase, sales in the industry fall. Eventually, industries start to die when everyone who wants a product has already bought one, so that sales, if any, are largely replacements for broken or worn-out goods. This phenomenon is known as demand (or market) saturation. Because demand is in decline, firms will not normally want to invest a great deal in new product or process technologies. However, it is possible for declining industries to be profitable, as long as there are not too many companies competing for a shrinking customer base.

Competitive rivalry in this stage is often more about who can exit fastest, with the least costs. Mergers are still common, as firms attempt to reduce over-capacity.

Like many strategic models, the industry life-cycle is a simplification of reality that glosses over a lot of exceptions. Not all industries go through all these phases. Some, like housing, will naturally stay in the mature phase, although demand may fluctuate greatly from year to year depending on the state of a country's economy. Some may move to maturity or even decline before being rejuvenated by a change in consumer tastes or by a technological development that moves them back to the growth phase (Real-life Application 3.4). However, there is clear evidence that, for a wide variety of industries, the industry life-cycle is a reasonable approximation of reality: firm numbers do increase and decline over time.

Real-life Application 3.4 Mature industries that rediscover their youth

Bicycles

By the early 1980s, demand for bicycles had reached a low point, as alternative, more comfortable, means of transport such as the car became more affordable. However, some environmental factors such as a renewed interest in healthy lifestyles and the desire to reduce pollution, or fears about the safety of public transport (following the train bombs in London, for example), gave consumers new reasons to buy bicycles. Producers responded with new products, such as the mountain bike and commuter folding bikes, which moved the bicycle industry in many parts of the world into a new phase of growth.

Personal computers

At the end of the 1980s, the personal computer industry appeared to have matured. Technology had stabilized, and new competitors had appeared emphasizing cost rather than quality, supported by new suppliers offering good-quality standard components at low prices. Customers had grown accustomed to specifying and using PCs, and were becoming more discriminating in their purchases. Increasingly, they were reluctant to purchase unnecessary upgrades and were price-selective, partly because a slowing economy was putting pressure on their own margins. However, the incorporation of multimedia technology into PCs opened up new markets in the home, stimulated further by the advent of broadband availability, and a new growth phase began.

When analysing how firms compete over the industry life-cycle, the crucial point to look out for is the changes between the different stages, in particular from growth to maturity. At these points the basis of competition may change; firms may move from seeking differentiation advantage (on the basis of innovation and functionality) and give greater weight to cost advantage.

The two cases in Real-life Application 3.4 illustrate the linkages between the different environmental factors: how changes in PESTLE factors cause industries to move from growth to maturity and back again. The changes in the demand for bicycles and PCs will almost certainly have affected the structure and dynamics of these industries, and so we now move on to the third aspect of our environmental analysis, the 'internal' attributes of the industry itself.

3.5 Industry analysis: the six forces

→ We discuss the relative importance of industry- or firm-level factors on profitability and performance in Theoretical Debate 3.1 on industry attractiveness, and again in Theoretical Debate 7.1 on the resource-based view of the firm.

One of the most powerful conceptual models of the competitive dynamics facing a firm focuses on the forces that affect its industry. These determine the industry's average profitability, and also shape how the firms within it compete. This type of framework is based on an economic theory known as the 'Structure–Conduct–Performance' (SCP) model: the *structure* (numbers of competitors, exit and entry costs, and product homogeneity) of an industry determines organizations' *conduct* (competitive behaviour such as product differentiation, price-setting, relationships between competitors), which in turn determines their *performance* (i.e. individual and collective profitability).

Michael Porter originally identified five such forces, to which Brandenburger and Nalebuff added a sixth (Figure 3.4):[15]

1. The bargaining power of suppliers
2. The bargaining power of customers/buyers[16]
3. The threat of substitution
4. The threat of new entrants
5. The power of complementors (Brandenburger and Nalebuff)
6. The intensity of rivalry between firms in the industry

In this section, we look at these six forces in turn.

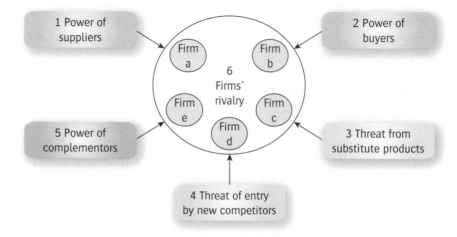

Figure 3.4 The six forces model

3.5.1 Supplier power

Supplier power is the degree to which the suppliers to an industry have the power to dictate prices, quality standards, delivery lead times and other terms and conditions to the firms that they are supplying. If supplier power is strong, they will be able to charge high prices and take for themselves much of the profit that would otherwise have gone to firms in the industry.

In most industries, firms rely upon suppliers to ensure that their goods and services are available on time and at a high enough quality. Fast-food firms like McDonald's need supplies of meat, bread, fuel, and cooking equipment. Airlines need supplies of aeroplanes, fuel, and airport facilities, together with landing 'slots' at airports during which its aircraft are able to take off and land. Service organizations like banks, advertising agencies, or local governments need supplies of office buildings and equipment, as well as skilled people. The balance of power between an industry and its suppliers depends on who needs whom the more.

By and large, if firms in an industry have a wide variety of suppliers to choose from, then those suppliers have little power. Even if the supplier firms are large, they may still not be very powerful—major airlines have power over the oil companies that supply their aviation fuel, which are among the largest corporations in the world. That is because aviation fuel is largely undifferentiated: one supplier is as good as another, and in most locations there are few switching costs—all suppliers offer similar facilities. In all these cases, it is the supplier that needs to win the business, while the firms in the industry can shop around.

On the other hand, suppliers can be powerful if they are relatively few in number and their inputs are vital to the quality of the finished product. Firms that supply major subsystems like braking and fuel injection to the automobile industry are becoming increasingly powerful, even though their customers are themselves large and powerful firms. For each subsystem, there are only two or three firms with the necessary technological competences. The quality of these subsystems makes a major difference to the performance of the vehicle, so it is in the car manufacturer's interest to spend a little extra to be sure of getting these components exactly right.

One reason why the makers of automobile subsystems are becoming powerful is because the technology in their area is increasingly too complex for a non-specialist firm to master. This means that there is little threat of new entrants, for example through backward vertical integration by the automobile manufacturers, whose specialist expertise is in a different area.

Sometimes, even sophisticated suppliers with few competitors may have little power. There are two main suppliers of large passenger airliners: Boeing and Airbus. Airline companies have no prospect of being able to integrate backwards into aircraft manufacturing and their switching costs are high, since a fleet consisting solely of Boeing or Airbus aircraft is far cheaper for airlines to maintain than a mixed fleet. However, the two firms compete strongly on price for every order, partly for reasons of national pride, and partly because of the economics of airliner production: they have to get a high volume of orders if they are to recover the very high costs of developing new aircraft. This gives the airline companies a great deal of power over their suppliers of aircraft.

Supplier power is not stable over time, and both PESTLE and life-cycle developments can affect the relative power dynamics in an industry. Political decisions may give, or remove, a monopoly from particular classes of supplier, as has happened with electricity supply, for example, in the UK, India, and parts of South America. Political or economic instability can also lead to disruption of supply from one country, and this may increase the power of the remaining suppliers. Technological change may make substitutes available for certain kinds

Switching costs
Costs that a firm incurs when it changes from one supplier or type of product to another.

➔ We discuss vertical integration decisions in more depth in Section 6.1.3.

of input. Sometimes this leaves all the suppliers weakened, because firms can play the new producers off against the old. Drinks firms used to be restricted to glass bottles and steel cans, but can now choose PET bottles or aluminium cans. If the new input is clearly superior, on the other hand, its suppliers may start from a position of strength. Entrepreneurs who have switched from bank finance to venture capital find that their new suppliers are very powerful indeed.

It will be clear from these examples that industries may have several types of supplier, some powerful and some not. If the powerful suppliers only account for a small proportion of the cost of the industry's outputs, then supplier power overall can be judged to be low. If, on the other hand, a large proportion of the product's value to the customer is in the hands of powerful suppliers, then overall supplier power will be high.

3.5.2 Buyer power

Buyer power is the extent to which an industry's customers have the power to dictate prices, quality standards and other terms and conditions to the firms that are supplying them. If buyer power is strong, firms in the industry will be limited in how high they can set their prices, and may be forced to incur high costs in order to meet customers' demands.

Many of the same considerations that we looked at in the previous section apply, in reverse, when considering the bargaining power that an industry's buyers have vis-à-vis the firms in the industry. If customers have a wide variety of firms to choose from, and if the industry's products are largely undifferentiated, then buyers will have considerable power.

Switching costs are a particularly important consideration in looking at the relationship between firms and their customers. It can be irksome for an individual to change bank, because of the sheer tedium of notifying all the utilities and other firms that may regularly put money into the account or take payments from it. These constitute switching costs. It is tempting to think that because retailers like H&M and McDonald's are large firms, they are more powerful than their buyers, who are just individuals and families. However, there are very few switching costs for a family when it decides to buy its food or clothing from one retailer or another. A single customer who switches will make little difference to McDonald's, because the proportion that they contribute to the company's turnover will be small. However, if a firm's prices rise or standards fall, there is little to stop customers defecting en masse.

One factor that does reduce buyer power is lack of information on what distinguishes a good product from a bad one, which producers are reliable and which are not. For this reason, one can expect buyer power to be at its lowest during the introductory and growth phases of an industry and to increase as the industry matures. In most established industries, such information is freely available, particularly since the advent of the internet. But usually the relative size of the financial investment is the main determinant of power—or, more accurately, over whether buyers choose to exert their power—especially in business-to-business markets.

Buyer power may be low if a product accounts for a small proportion of their costs, so that they do not notice much if prices rise. However, this will not be the case where this product also makes a major difference to the performance of their own output. The switch that controls the cooling fan in a car costs very little in relation to the whole vehicle, but if it fails the car is unusable, so the car manufacturers will choose to exert a great deal of power over the supplier of that component. Buyers will also choose to use their power more if they are cost-conscious, which is more likely if there is an economic recession, or if their industry is mature.

3.5.3 The threat of substitution

Buyer power is strongly influenced by the availability of substitute products. If customers have a choice, not just between rival products but between competing demands for their spending, then this will increase their power. Confusingly, substitute products are not the same as competitors' products. They are products made in another industry, but which customers may choose to spend their money on instead. If threat of substitution is high, customers will switch to another product if they feel that they are being overcharged, or receiving poor value for money from the industry.

The threat of substitution is probably the most difficult of all the six forces to assess. Not all products have realistic substitutes—there are few for some medical items like blood plasma, for example, or for common necessities like food and underwear. Working out what constitutes a substitute can require a degree of insight. There are three main types:

- things that carry out the same function as the product or service—so audio downloads are substitutes for CDs, and a mobile phone can substitute for a camera, music player, or even a computer;

- dissimilar items that fulfil the same psychological need—for example, chocolates or champagne are substitutes for roses;

- items that compete for the same spending power. These are the most difficult to spot. For example, a holiday is probably a substitute for a car or a new carpet for a young person who has little disposable income and competing social demands.

Like buyer power, the threat of substitution can be moderated if customers incur switching costs when changing between substitute products. In general, the strength of the threat posed by a substitute depends on whether it offers better perceived value than an industry's own products. Technological advances in biotechnology have led to the development of foodstuffs that are genetically modified to repel certain pests. These pose a threat of substitution to firms in the pesticide industry that is likely to grow over time, although, as mentioned in Section 3.2.6, some consumers have reservations about them.

3.5.4 The threat of new entrants

Barriers to entry determine the threat that new entrants—i.e. potential competitors—pose to firms in an industry. If new firms are able to come into the industry, competition will intensify and incumbents' profits will fall. A high entry barrier makes it unlikely that new entrants will want to enter the industry in the first place, or will be forced to close down before they are able to disrupt the way that established producers do business. It also makes it unlikely that they will ever make an acceptable return on their investment, because they are saddled with entry costs that established producers no longer have to bear.

Barrier to entry
Any advantage that firms already operating in an industry hold over other firms that might potentially decide to enter it.

Probably the most obvious barriers to entry are to do with size. Some industries require a great deal of capital to enter. For example, even the smallest manufacturing facility for computer processors or memory chips costs millions of euros or dollars. Even in industries that it is theoretically possible to enter for a modest capital outlay, the production economics may be such that small-scale producers suffer from major cost disadvantages. In industries like this, where economies of scale are important—the automobile industry is one example—a new entrant may be forced to risk considerable amounts of capital on large-scale manufacturing and marketing facilities. However, such a high-profile entry may well provoke established firms to cut prices or step up their marketing efforts to prevent the new competitor from getting a foothold in the market. Fear of such retaliation is also a barrier to entry.

Considerations like these, however, have not prevented new firms from entering both the microchip and automobile industries. The computer memory industry saw large-scale entry by Japanese and Korean firms, who saw it as strategically important, and were able to threaten established American competitors like Intel. In the automobile industry, Malaysia's Proton and Korea's Daewoo have both entered the automobile industry, followed more recently by Indian and Chinese competitors, even though they operate on a far smaller scale than the industry leaders, and the industry itself suffers from chronic overcapacity.

These examples show that if potential entrants have sufficient financial backing, confidence and motivation, then capital requirements and economies of scale do not function as barriers to entry. The Korean and Malaysian firms referred to in the previous paragraph benefited from cheap finance from their national governments, which approved of their ventures into industries they saw as prestigious and strategically important. The newer competitors in automobiles, like those in low-cost airlines, simply believe that their capabilities and large home markets will enable them to succeed in spite of the structural problems in the industry. Some firms accumulate massive financial resources of their own which they can use to enter into almost any industry they wish: Microsoft, the computer software giant has cash reserves measured in the billions, which has enabled it to fund entry into a videogames console business dominated by Sony. It is not deterred by the threat of retaliation—it has the resources to survive a price or advertising war.

Product differentiation is another factor often cited as a barrier to entry. This may be the case in industries where firms have invested strongly in building a reputation, and where reputation is important to customers in making their choices. Here again, though, it is important to be careful. Firms like Zara and Top Shop have had little difficulty in building a reputation that lets them compete with established fashion brands—in some industries, the product seems to speak for itself.

Existing firms may also have strategic assets such as knowledge or core competences, gained through research or experience, which newer entrants can struggle to match. Here again, however, it is sometimes possible to overestimate the advantage that incumbents have. Patents are often easy for competitors to circumvent through minor modifications, and to get one a firm must reveal key technical information. Key staff can be lured away and products can be 'reverse engineered' (i.e. taken apart to see how they work and how they are put together). Sometimes entrepreneurial new entrants just refuse to acknowledge that established firms' competences are better than their own. To be an entry barrier, it really must prevent firms from entering the industry at all.

Nevertheless, there are some factors that genuinely can act as deterrents to entry. If established firms have strong relationships with their distributors, it can be difficult for new entrants to find a place to sell their products—on the supermarket shelves or in the warehouse. Distributors may not want to take the risk of stocking an untried brand, particularly if it involves antagonizing a powerful incumbent firm. If existing firms have taken up all the reasonably priced sources of raw materials, or all the good locations, then it can be difficult for new firms to compete. It is at present difficult for new firms to enter the UK food retailing industry, because most of the good sites for hypermarkets and large supermarkets have been taken.

And quite minor advances in product or production technology can sometimes nullify the benefits of years of experience. Quite small advances in the design of the product's formulation in the semiconductor photolithographic alignment machinery industry led to the replacement of most of the leading firms by new entrants.[17] Recently, the internet has dramatically reduced the cost of entry into retailing by enabling individuals to sell cheaply through their own websites or intermediaries such as eBay.

3.5.5 **The power of complementors**

The fifth force, the power of complementors, is the one that was added later in a 1996 article on Intel by Brandenburger and Nalebuff,[18] who identified the ability of Microsoft to affect the usage of Intel's products, and vice versa, even though the firms were not formally associated. Complementors (please note the spelling: complementary products are not the same as the complimentary products that you find in hotel rooms) are not found in every industry, and so were not really noticed until researchers started investigating new industries like software. Michael Porter[19] himself disputes the power of complementors to directly affect the profitability of an industry—it is not, in his view, a true force.

This force is different from those between collaborating firms within the supply chain who build long-term component-supply relationships, or competitors who agree to jointly develop products. In these cases traditional supplier/buyer or competitive rivalry forces apply. Complementors are businesses that do not themselves compete in the industry and do not supply it or buy from it—although they may be subsidiaries of corporations whose other businesses are buyers, suppliers, or competitors.

Examples of complementors include the following:

- Companies that produce hardware for the reproduction of music or video (CD players, DVD players, VCRs) will not sell many products unless customers can buy music or films in an appropriate format. Sony and Toshiba have therefore both lined up complementors to make movies and hardware available for their competing standards for the next generation of high-density DVDs. Apple, Disney, LG, Panasonic, Philips, and Samsung have backed Sony's Blu-Ray against Toshiba's HD-DVD.[20]

- No computer or videogames console can function without applications software. One reason why Apple remains a minor player in the PC market is because, although its products have a number of excellent design features, fewer applications are written to run under the Mac operating system than under Microsoft Windows, and Apple customers may have to wait months or even years for software houses to produce Mac-compatible versions of their Windows applications.

- Low-cost airlines such as Ryanair, Air Deccan, or Southwest offer extremely cheap fares from one airport to another. But the price-conscious travellers who wish to take advantage of these offers must first find their way to the airport and if the means of getting there are missing, or the fares too high, then the attractiveness of the cheap flight industry will be reduced.

Complementors can pose a threat to the profitability of the industry where there are no effective substitutes for their products. Media companies have a monopoly on the (legal) supply of popular films and music by hit artists. They can also afford skilled lawyers to enforce their copyright. They effectively dictate the price and availability of recorded films and music, and therefore the attractiveness of the products being sold to play them. So firms like Sony, Philips, and Samsung must pay attention to the power of firms like Warner, Disney, and Bertelsmann. On the other hand, train services to airports can be substituted by buses or taxis, and this limits the fares they are likely to charge, since consumers' switching costs from one mode of transport to another are low. This limits the power that train operators exert over British Airways or Ryanair.

Complementors can, in theory, use their power in two main ways: by pushing up the prices of their products, or by limiting their supply. But they need to be careful, since it is not in their interest to kill off an industry that stimulates demand for their own products. Recorded music companies need people to have CD or MP3 players, and oil companies need people to have cars. Although games software houses will want to charge healthy prices for their products, they have no interest in killing the market for the makers of games consoles.

Complementors, however, may sometimes use their power to an industry's detriment:

- if they see the industry's output as a threat to their other revenue streams. The release of copyrights on music for on-line distribution has been delayed for several years because the main recorded music firms wanted to be sure they could retain control of their intellectual property—and make money from it;

- where they have invested in supplying other, substitute, industries and want to make sure that they extract a return on their sunk costs. Recorded music providers have invested large amounts in building distribution networks for CDs and DVDs, and this will limit their willingness to collaborate with suppliers of digital downloads;

- where they would have to make substantial investments in order to adapt their products for the benefit of the industry. Companies running rail services to UK airports may see their core market as travellers paying full price for their tickets and see no reason to lower their prices or standards to suit the no-frills airlines;

- where there are no persuasive reasons why they should see their interests as aligned with those of the industry, perhaps because the industry's users are unimportant to them. Electricity firms in some countries see industry as their main market, and have no reason to structure their prices to encourage the use of consumer electronic devices. In this case, the complementors will set prices at a level which maximizes their overall profits, with little regard for the health of industries supplying non-core users;

- if the complementor industry is concentrated (see Section 3.5.6) so that there are few prospects of playing one complementor firm off against another.

In such cases, the industry may be able to overcome the threat if it can convince complementors that the benefits from collaborating with them outweigh the risks. If they have a credible threat of entering the complementor's industry, this will also improve their bargaining power (and of course the reverse is also true). Otherwise, complementors will drive down demand for the industry's products, restricting profits and leading to intense competition.

Even where firms do not use their power to affect the industry's overall profitability, they may still use it in a way that favours one firm over another. This is one aspect in which complementor power differs from the five forces identified by Porter, which affect all firms in the industry equally. Complementors are likely to use this power if they incur significant costs from making their products compatible with the outputs of many firms or strategic groups, rather than just one. For example, there are significant costs in porting software from a Windows to a Linux or Apple Mac environment, or in writing games for both Xbox and PlayStation consoles. Complementors therefore have the ability to raise barriers to entry if incumbent firms have already developed products that are compatible with the complementors'.

The quality of personal relationships between complementors and individual firms or managers may also come into play: If key complementors have both the power and the incentive to discriminate between vendors in this way, then there is likely to be intensive competition for partnerships with them. This may lead to their being able to negotiate some form of returns, in the form of licence fees or royalties, as the price for their collaboration, which will of course raise costs for those in the industry and reduce its profitability.

It may also stimulate hypercompetition, in which firms that win a critical mass of complementors gain control of the industry and other firms have to exit the industry, or concede control of industry standards to their competitors, as seems likely to happen with DVDs. And if complementors are in a position to limit demand or to extract value from the industry by demanding royalties or licence fees, then survival and success are likely to depend on a firm's cost position, with the most efficient being the most successful.

The ability to establish preferential linkages with key complementors may give individual firms an advantage in such an industry. They may choose to negotiate discounts with complementors on their users' behalf, as Ryanair does with the suppliers of rail services to airports. They may attempt to reduce complementors' costs, as Microsoft did when it made its Xbox games console use the same software protocols as Windows PCs, and offered them free developers' kits and focus group research for their games. It also integrated horizontally into the complementor's industry through the purchase of two small games developers—this is another way of reducing complementor power.[21]

3.5.6 Competitive rivalry between the industry's firms

The sixth force, the competitive rivalry between the firms in the industry, is strongly affected by the other five forces. The stronger the power of buyers, suppliers, and complementors, and the stronger the threats of entry and substitution, the more intense competition is likely to be. And if rivalry is high, firms will compete away (in the form of price wars or other undercutting moves) much of the profit that might have been extracted from the industry.

It is helpful to start with a review of how we might recognize fierce or intense competition. Firms compete in a number of ways, of which the most common are:

- Price, including price wars, where competitors deliberately undercut the prices of their rivals, sometimes to below the amount it costs to produce the goods; fiercely contested competitive tenders; and other forms of price-based competition such as discounting for loyal, repeat-purchase, customers;

- Marketing and advertising. Firms can compete through expensive advertising campaigns sometimes accompanied by endorsements from music and sports stars, by offering promotional gifts to customers and distributors, or by offering inducements to shops and distributors to display and promote their products and services. Sometimes these are inexpensive alternatives to price competition. The free gifts sometimes offered by fast food firms to lure younger customers, for example, are far less expensive than a price cut would be.

- Investment and product development. In some industries, where differentiation on product features is important, firms will compete to bring the latest products to market. In the airline industry, British Airways and Virgin Atlantic have both invested millions of dollars in upgrading their cabins to offer more comfortable sleeping arrangements to long-distance travellers. These decisions represent significant commitments of resources, both financial and reputational. Although they are relatively easy to copy, both airlines are hoping that competitors lack the money and motivation to follow them. An extreme example of this kind of behaviour is an investment war, when every producer makes massive investment commitments in order to gain maximum economies of scale and frighten competitors into quitting the industry. This occurred in the computer memory industry in the 1980s, where a number of Asian producers simultaneously invested in new plant, leading to overcapacity in the industry and a subsequent price war.

- Litigation. Particularly in the USA, but increasingly also elsewhere, organizations may turn to the courts to delay a competitor from launching a new product, to drain its resources or to force open a market. In the pharmaceuticals industry, litigation has become an established part of the armoury for firms seeking to annul the patent protection on established drugs so that they can market cheaper, generic equivalents.

If we can observe one or more of these forms of competitive behaviour and they are making a significant impact on firms' profitability, then competition is fierce. In a fiercely competitive industry, average profit margins are likely to decline over time, or to fluctuate wildly, although the industry leaders may find individual strategies that help them sustain or improve their profitability.

a. The effect of concentration on the intensity of competition

Classical micro-economic theory predicts that the structure of the industry will also have an effect on average profitability and the intensity of competition: Industries may take a number of different forms, according to how many firms there are within it, and their size. Typically, strategists classify industries as concentrated (containing few producers) or fragmented (containing many producers). Concentrated industries fall into two categories:

- Monopolies are industries where there is just one producer and entry barriers are extremely high. In practice this is quite rare, but any industry where one producer dominates with, say 60 per cent or more of the market, and where there are no competitors of comparable size, tends to be considered a monopoly.

- Oligopolies are industries where a small number of firms (say, six or fewer) account for almost all output.

Fragmented industries tend to be examples of what economists (rather confusingly) term 'monopolistic competition', where barriers to entry are low and each of many producers tries to differentiate its products or services from competitors' and/or to control a small market segment. Examples are fashion retailers and restaurants. Thus each firm attempts to carve out a small niche monopoly for itself.

In theory, there is another structure known as 'perfect competition', where the product is a commodity (so no differentiation is possible), barriers to entry are non-existent, and buyers have perfect information—the example that is probably most often cited of this structure is that of crude oil which is sold on a spot market. However, in almost all other products there is nearly always some way in which firms can differentiate themselves (see Real-Life Application 3.5), and we are sure you can think of very many reasons why there are high entry barriers to the crude oil production industry.

Real-life Application 3.5 A 'commodity' product

Salt is often cited as an example of a product that is a pure commodity, i.e. it is the same everywhere, and no differentiation is possible.

However, in fact over one hundred varieties of salt are sold, with different chemical compositions and crystal sizes. Salt sold for de-icing roads is coarser than table salt, while salt for water softeners is purer. Not all producers offer all these varieties of salt, and they also differ in their ability to serve particular customers. Salt is bulky, and costly to ship over long distances. Producers with access to a waterway have an advantage over those without.

Economic theories, such as SCP, predict that competition in fragmented industries is likely to be fierce, as small firms struggle for a place in the market, while competition in concentrated industries is expected to be relatively benign. For example, profit margins in food retailing in the UK, where the five largest firms have almost 80 per cent of the market, are far higher than in other countries where the industry is less concentrated. And the ultimate concentrated industry, the monopoly, is predicted to achieve supernormal profits.

However, monopolies are usually held to operate against the public interest, so, where they arise, government competition or anti-trust authorities tend to step in to break them up or regulate their prices.

But evidence does not always bear SCP predictions out, and many industries do not follow this pattern.[22] The industry life-cycle suggests that in the early, growing, stages there may be many competitors, barriers to entry are low, and yet competition is not intense as firms concentrate on capturing as many new customers as possible and growing the industry. At the later stages, where growth can only come from taking market share from rivals, price wars and heavy discounting are more likely.

Even in mature industries there are anomalies. There are many examples of industries where economies of scale, a key driver of concentration, are not especially important. The restaurant industry is highly fragmented, yet fiercely competitive—often on non-price factors, such as the quality of the cooking and service, and the variety of dishes on the menu. The soft-drinks industry, on the other hand, is very concentrated. In most countries, it is dominated by The Coca-Cola Company, PepsiCo Inc. and perhaps one or two local competitors. Yet Coke and Pepsi compete fiercely through expensive advertising campaigns and constant price promotions. A rational justification for this behaviour is that by broadcasting their reputation as fearsome competitors, the two firms create a barrier to entry to the industry. But the rivalry between the firms has at least as much to do with the firms as social systems as with economic rationality. It dates partly from 1950, when an ex-Coca-Cola executive, Alfred Steele, joined Pepsi as CEO, and made 'Beat Coke' the firm's slogan.[23]

b. The influence of scale on industry concentration

An important influence on an industry's degree of concentration is the extent to which a firm's size and scale are significant. An industry where there are significant economies of scale and scope is likely to become more concentrated over time. One where large firms have no particular advantages over small ones is quite likely to remain fragmented, even when mature. This is even more likely if the minimum economic firm size is a large proportion of the market size, so that there is only room for a few firms.

The extreme case of this is where there is only room for one firm in the market. Such industries are known as 'natural monopolies'. They require such expensive infrastructure that only a monopolist can make sufficient profits to justify the investment involved. Often governments fund the early development of these industries in the public interest. Examples are power, postal services, and telecommunications, which many governments have now privatized. Sometimes governments will set up monopolies on their own account: the Swedish government has a monopoly of the sales of alcoholic drinks, and the Italian government of tobacco sales. Natural monopolies, such as the electricity companies that replaced the former government-run suppliers, are often heavily regulated (not always very successfully) to prevent them abusing their positions.

In most industries that are not natural monopolies, diminishing returns will make it difficult for a monopolist to serve all customers cheaply and effectively. However, if an industry shows increasing returns to scale it might tend towards a monopoly structure.

c. The effects of increasing and diminishing returns on the intensity of competition

Most industries show diminishing returns to scale—the profit per unit decreases after a certain production volume is reached, until eventually the firm's profits would fall if it tried to produce or sell any more goods or services. This is because it gradually becomes more difficult to find good sources of raw materials and appropriately qualified people to run the operations, and because once the 'easy' customers have bought the product, more effort and cost is required to penetrate more difficult markets.

Theorists[24] have claimed that some industries—especially high-technology and know-ledge-based ones—run counter to normal industries and have increasing returns to scale. The more that firms in these industries can produce, the more they can sell and the higher their profits. The products of these industries typically have high up-front R&D costs, which need to be recouped through high sales volumes, and low subsequent unit production costs. There are also network effects—the more people that use a particular product, the more desirable it becomes to all its users, and so the more people are likely to want to buy it.

A good example of increasing returns leading to a market share of 95 per cent[25] comes from the suppliers of PC operating systems. Microsoft spends $6 billion a year on research and development, the majority going into its two dominant software suites, Windows and Office.[26] Retail copies of these programs typically sell for over €100, but the CD-ROM on which the software is distributed will cost less than 5 per cent of the sales price to produce. There are no real limits on production—there are plenty of subcontractors who can repro-duce CD-ROMs at high quality, and on-line downloading has reduced dependence on these physical means of distribution yet further. Nor are there any real limits on demand: everyone who buys a computer needs an operating system and wants a widely used one that runs lots of common applications. As a result, Microsoft's operating system has become the standard for most PC users.

It is unclear whether the industry life-cycle applies to conditions of increasing returns, as the normal life-cycle model appears likely to be distorted by government intervention (as in the case of rulings against Microsoft's dominance by US regulators[27]).

d. Hypercompetitive industries

Increasing returns may give rise to hypercompetitive behaviour,[28] where a firm uses all pos-sible forms of competition to overstretch competitors and force them to quit the industry. Some academics claim that we are seeing a 'hypercompetitive shift',[29] and that will make hypercompetition the norm for competitive behaviour, although not all necessarily agree with this view.[30]

Hypercompetition is characterized by brief periods of stability punctuated by frequent significant disruption, rapid technological change, shortened product life-cycles, high uncertainty about the future, and global competition. Competition in these types of indus-try is intense; firms targeted by hostile competitive initiatives respond to those initiatives with moves of their own, leading to an escalation in instability and competitive rivalry. In hypercompetitive industries, barriers to entry become extremely high once one firm's product is established as a standard. Network effects then make it very difficult for even a technologically superior product to dislodge it—users' switching costs will be too high. Thus, it pays firms to try to establish their products as the industry standard and then reap the benefits.

This form of intensely competitive behaviour is seen especially in the computer industry and telecommunications.[31] Another example is the videogames industry, where successive firms have tried to build commanding market shares through a combination of technolo-gical innovation, aggressive pricing and marketing, and closed software standards that competitors cannot imitate (Real-life Application 3.6).

Real-life Application 3.6 The videogame industry

The first home videogames consoles came onto the market in 1977 and quickly became popular. By 1982, the Californian firm Atari had carved out a market share of over 60 per cent. However, Atari allowed its main competitors to make compatible machines and did not restrict the right of independent developers to make software for its consoles. As a result, the market was flooded with poor quality games, and console sales collapsed.

The next generation of games, using 8-bit processors, was dominated by Nintendo, a Japanese firm. It started a number of practices that went on to become industry standards. It used a character, Mario the plumber, as the lead attraction for its system. It sold the games console relatively cheaply, determined to build volume and make its profits on the sales of games. It made its games' cartridges incompatible with other systems, and restricted the number of software houses that were licensed to produce games, to ensure good quality. Its Famicom and NES systems gained 90 per cent of the market. But Nintendo was late into the market with the next generation of consoles, based on 16-bit processors, and it was outsold by Sega's Mega-Drive system. Aggressive pricing and marketing and a popular character, Sonic the Hedgehog, gave Sega 50 per cent of the market by the mid-1990s.

However, both firms were outmanoeuvred by Sony for command of the next generation of technology. Sony's PlayStation was based on a 32-bit processor and used CD-ROMs in place of cartridges. It ensured a supply of high-quality software, and also benefited from exclusive access to film characters from Sony's cinema business. To keep control of its hardware, it used the courts to stop the distribution of software that would allow PlayStation games to be played on a PC.[32]

Since then, each successive generation of games brought a massive improvement in the quality of sound and graphics. Sega's Dreamcast was launched in Japan in 1998. It offered 3D graphics, and used a version of Microsoft Windows as its operating system. This made it easy for independent houses to develop games for the machine, and also allowed the use of some PC peripherals, such as modems. In March 1999, Sony brought out its PlayStation 2, which promised graphics and animation of similar quality and realism to those found in a top-quality animated film. Its graphics processor was over 20 times as fast as the Dreamcast's and 200 times as quick as the original PlayStation. Sony made a major financial commitment in developing the PlayStation 2. In order to make a good return on its $500 million investment, it needed to sell 50 million units, approximately as many as Nintendo managed during its five-year period of near-monopoly during the 1980s.

By 2004 Sony was in the lead with sales of 70 million consoles, followed by Microsoft with 14 million and Nintendo with 13 million. The fourth generation 'games wars' are now a three-way fight between, Sony's PlayStation 3, Nintendo's Wii, and Microsoft's Xbox 360.[33] Xbox Live, Microsoft's subscription-based online-gaming service, has features such as global player rankings that the PlayStation cannot currently match. Microsoft has also brought out a new software-development platform for games, XNA, which can be used to write games for PCs, Xbox, and the next generation Xbox 2. Sony, in contrast, is focusing on hardware, building in huge microprocessor power into its console along with a player for Blu-Ray DVDs.

The fourth generation: Microsoft's Xbox.
Microsoft Corporation

Since a moderate amount of competition is normally beneficial, most firms are content to live with a few competitors that play by the same rules, and only retaliate strongly against those whose behaviour is unpredictable and potentially disruptive. Michael Porter strongly advocated that firms should choose their competitors carefully.[34] A reputation for hypercompetitive behaviour is therefore a potentially strong factor in creating entry barriers into potentially hypercompetitive industries.

e. Co-opetition, collusion, and game theory

Although high up-front costs may move an industry towards increasing returns and hypercompetition, they may also, paradoxically, encourage firms to collaborate with their competitors in developing new products or markets. This hybrid form of competitive behaviour has been given the name 'co-opetition'.[35] Collaboration may be necessary because the financial risk is too great for one firm to bear alone or because the development needs firms to pool their knowledge assets and capabilities. Firms collaborate to develop new products or services but may compete fiercely to produce and market them.

Some of the best examples of this type of behaviour can be found in knowledge-intensive industries such as recorded music or pharmaceuticals. In the music industry co-opetitive behaviour is common between the independent record companies and the majors, such as Sony, Warner, or EMI, who in other circumstances would be considered to be in direct competition with each other. Each of these company types has what the other needs to succeed, however, and they have to collaborate. The majors bring competence in marketing and financial management, and a global distribution network; the independents are able to find and nurture the creative talent—new artistes—which are the foundation for important new musical trends, and which the rather more bureaucratic majors find harder to attract and develop themselves.

In the pharmaceutical industry, Merck (see Figure 6.2, p. 233) has formal strategic alliances with many of its major competitors such as Johnson & Johnson; Schering-Plough, and Aventis. In some cases co-opetitive relationships are cemented with cross shareholdings; in all cases co-opetition can be an effective method of preventing a firm's competitors from trying to put it out of business. And unlike cartels, which are explicit collaborations between competitors to set prices and share out markets and are illegal in most developed countries, and other forms of collusion, which can be unstable, co-opetitive alliances are legal and usually long-lasting.

→ We examine the reasons for forming strategic alliances in Section 6.1.3, and ways of managing them in Section 9.3.

There are often strong reasons to collaborate, and thereby reduce inter-firm competitive conditions. Prices may be maintained at high levels, efficiencies and expertise can be developed in a narrowly scoped market, and time and resources do not need to be wasted on setting up defensive mechanisms such as distributor tie-in contracts, or patents.

The benefits and risks of collaboration can be investigated using a branch of mathematics known as game theory. This deals with situations in which organizations face choices, and the rewards ('payoffs') from those choices are affected by the actions of another party—a competitor, contractual partner, or even an employee—facing a similar choice. The two parties are playing a 'game' in which their joint moves determine how much money they will make—or lose. For historical reasons, this is called a 'prisoner's dilemma' (Figure 3.5).

Suppose two firms have to choose, in entering a new market, between strategy A (setting its prices high to try to win about half of the market) and strategy B (setting prices lower to try to win almost the whole of the market). If firm X and Y both choose strategy A, they receive a return of £100,000 each, having to share the rewards from the new market. If firm X steals a march and implements strategy B, X receives £500,000 and Y loses £100,000—and vice versa. If both implement strategy B, then the market is flooded with low-price products and both firms end up losing £50,000. What should they do?

	Firm Y enters with low production and a high price	Firm Y enters with high production and a low price
Firm X enters with low production and a high price	Both firms make profits of £100,000	Firm X loses £100,000 Firm Y makes £500,000
Firm X enters with high production and a low price	Firm X makes £500,000 Firm Y loses £100,000	Both firms lose £50,000

Figure 3.5 The prisoner's dilemma

Game theory shows that the 'rational' strategy is for both firms to follow strategy B, since that way they can be sure of avoiding the worst outcome, and have a chance of obtaining the best one—a combination of strategies known as a Nash equilibrium. Of course, they can, where laws permit, try to discuss strategies beforehand, but even then, the rational decision is to assure your competitor that you are going to follow strategy A—and then follow strategy B. This same type of reasoning can be applied to a number of business decisions —do I invest in training staff and risk seeing them poached by competitors? Do I promise my staff a bonus for achieving targets and then refuse to pay it? Do I strike a deal with a supplier and then, when they have invested in capacity to meet the order, renegotiate the price?

If the game were repeated, however, the firms would learn that they do best when they collaborate: if one failed to do so in one game, the other firm could retaliate by not cooperating in the next game and both would lose until they realized that they should cooperate again. And in an experiment carried out in 1980 by the American political scientist Robert Axelrod, 'nice', collaborative, strategies outperformed every other.[36]

And yet, price wars do happen, and firms engage in winner-takes-all behaviours, and there is some evidence that collusion between competitors can be unstable over the long term.[37] Sometimes firms do a small 'test-run,' where they explore their collaborator's resolve to stick to the arrangement—which can have a destabilizing effect as a result of the breakdown in trust between the organizations. Sometimes a price war is enough to destabilize a competitor sufficiently for it to become less of a threat.

g. The effect of exit barriers on competition

The presence of exit barriers may also influence the intensity of competition. Exit barriers are factors that make it difficult or expensive for a firm to leave an industry. If there are high exit barriers, organizations are more likely to compete fiercely in order to try to survive, or at least to get the best return they can on their sunk investment costs.

The most frequent type of exit barrier is when firms have invested in equipment that has no alternative use. For example, when a firm builds a steelworks, it invests huge resources in furnaces and casting and rolling machinery that can only be used for processing steel. However, there may also be legislative and psychological barriers to exit. A steelworks is invariably a major employer, whose closure would be very damaging to the community in which it is located. Governments may forbid it to close, or provide subsidies to keep it open. They may impose expensive conditions about providing training or alternative employment for staff who are made redundant. The organizations themselves may have strong ties to their communities and be reluctant to damage them. Managers may also have strong sentimental ties to the industry that make them unwilling or unable to recognize that exit is needed. They may instead decide to hang in and await the next upturn. All of these exit barriers have been present in the steel industry, which, as a result, suffered overcapacity and periodic price wars for three decades.

h. The effect of globalization on competition

A variety of factors may tend to make firms in an industry compete with global products and utilize a value chain spread across the world, rather than serving customers on a more local basis. We examine these factors in Chapter 14.

Theoretical Debate 3.1 Is a six forces analysis worthwhile?

The six-forces framework (Porter, 1980; Brandenburger and Nalebuff, 1996) and the SCP model from which it emerged (Bain, 1956; Scherer, 1970), were developed as ways of gauging industry attractiveness, originally with the intention of regulators setting measures in place to increase the competitiveness of an industry and protect the consumer from firms that obtained super-normal profits (Barney, 2002 Sheremata, 1998). The thinking went, if firms are making high levels of profits over the long term, they must be engaging in anti-competitive behaviour. Strategy scholars have since turned this model on its head and used its principles to devise ways of allowing firms to reduce, or at least be aware of, the potential barriers to making good profits (Demsetz, 1982).[38] However, Barney (2002), at least, cautions that concepts such as industry attractiveness can be tautological—firms in attractive industries outperform firms in unattractive industries, and at the same time an industry is attractive because of the ability of firms in it to perform well.

He also criticizes Porter and his colleagues for failing to provide the 'theoretical tools for determining when an industry does or does not exist' (the work he cites are Porter, 1990; and Caves and Porter, 1977). Defining an industry poses problems even for seasoned researchers. Relying on the Standard Industrial Classification (SIC) or similar codes used by producers of economic statistics can be problematic. Some have not been updated for many years, making some newer industries virtually invisible, and the codes may not reflect important differences in firms' inputs, operations, and technologies (Markides and Williamson, 1996). The idea that firms can be neatly packaged into discrete strategic groups has also been seriously challenged (Barney and Hoskisson, 1990; Reger and Huff, 1993; Gimeno, 2004).

Ignoring these definitional problems, an industry with low buyer and supplier power, a low threat from substitutes, and high barriers to entry could be expected to have a mild competitive environment and high profits. This should make it an attractive industry— firms already operating in it should consider expanding, and firms not in it should consider entering it. Conversely, if an industry is in decline or is otherwise unattractive, firms should consider exiting. Although broadly sensible, these recommendations have one drawback—that many firms will be undertaking the same analysis and coming to broadly the same conclusions. When the PC industry started to expand, many new firms were formed, and many existing electronics and computing firms tried to enter it. This openness of information means that it is unlikely that any single organization will be able to gain an advantage by spotting

an attractive industry before anyone else. It may also mean that an attractive industry quickly becomes overcrowded and more competitive and so, paradoxically, loses its attractiveness—an example where insights from game theory are helpful. So counter-intuitively a low-profit industry may be better to enter than a high-profit one (Barney, 2002).

Other scholars (e.g. Aktouf et al., 2005) criticize Porter's framework for its hidden messages. Its focus on power relations between industry members, buyers and suppliers might be taken to imply that such relationships are, and should be, antagonistic, rather than collaborative. They go further, suggesting that it contributes towards the concentration of capital and the creation of monopolies and oligopolies. They also suggest that it is unduly deterministic, placing too great an emphasis on the influence of outside 'forces' on profitability, thus diminishing the role of employees.

Other theorists have also questioned the relative importance of industry structure versus the attributes and performance of the firm itself (Beard and Dess, 1984; Rumelt, 1991; Davis and Schul, 1993; Powell, 1996; Roquebert et al., 1996; Ketchen et al., 1997). For example knowledge of trends and culture (Collis, 1991; Kretschmer et al., 1999; Caves, 2000; Reed and DeFillippi, 1990; Fiol, 1991; Camere and Vespalainen, 1988), are often highly context-specific. What may be attractive to one knowledgeable firm, may be in practice deeply hostile to another, whose managers think they understand the conditions and then discovers how wrong they were. This is a mistake which has often been made by firms attempting to integrate vertically: they assume that conditions in an upstream industry are similar to their own, only to discover that many of the critical success factors are very different.

This has led many researchers to focus much more on the attributes of the firm itself. This body of theory is known as the resource-based view (Barney, 1991, 1996b; Grant 2001; Peteraf, 1993; Dierickx and Cool, 1989; Wernerfelt, 1984; Seth and Thomas, 1994), and we discuss it in depth in Chapter 7, and in Theoretical Debate 7.1. However, no-one has demonstrated that the five forces are actually wrong—the addition of the sixth force (still disputed by Porter himself) has been the only change to the framework since 1979, although Mathur and Kenyon (2001) have argued that Porter was looking at the wrong factors—that competition is more fruitfully analysed as being between offerings in market-places, rather than between firms in industries. But their framework has never attained the degree of influence and usage that Porter's still enjoys.

Worked Example 3.1 An analysis of the US fast-food burger restaurant environment

The components of this environmental analysis are two-fold; first, McDonald's wider environment, assessed using PESTLE criteria; and second, the industry itself. For the purposes of this analysis we will ignore McDonald's other businesses, such as Chipotle, and focus simply on the mainstream restaurants.

The wider environment

McDonald's annual report is the starting point for our analysis.[39] There we find that it has five major business segments—United States (35 per cent); Europe (35 per cent, of which France, Germany, and the UK account for over 60 per cent); Asia/Pacific, Middle East, and Africa (15 per cent, of which Australia, China, and Japan account for 50 per cent); Latin America (8 per cent, of which Brazil accounts for over 40 per cent); and Canada. Other competitors such as Yum! Brands are similarly widespread. Thus, if there are any trends which affect the world as a whole, the burger industry is likely to be experiencing them.

➜ We discuss globalization, international positioning and the nature of global brands and products in Chapter 14.

Given its broad range of locations, political instability in some of its markets is a factor that McDonald's needs to consider. In 2003, bombers killed three people at a McDonald's restaurant in Indonesia, as a protest against American policies in Iraq. One of its developing markets is China, which is a country that is rapidly opening up to external influences, but which is not a democracy and not especially responsive to popular opinion. Although the Chinese government has allowed McDonald's to open franchises there, this is a decision that could easily be revoked.

An important economics factor is the variation in international interest rates, which results in profitability levels in McDonald's countries varying relative to the US dollar. Other important economics factors are developments in spending power in the different countries; for example China's economic growth at 10 per cent p.a. is far above most other regions, as is India's, at 8 per cent, another huge potential market for McDonald's.

Social concerns over levels of fat, sugar, and salt in burgers have been held at least partly responsible for the slowing of sales growth in developed countries. But many of the social/cultural factors affecting burger chains are more local in scope. One example is the variation in birth rate between different demographic groups. In the USA, social statistics data[40] tell us that the Hispanic south-west has a higher birth rate and a greater percentage of people under the age of 40 than the rest of the States. They also have less spending power and are more price sensitive than customers elsewhere. And they are increasingly tending to work longer and non-traditional hours.[41]

Technological developments in the form of EPOS links with suppliers and logistics-planning software, and the increasing reliance on cashless means of payment (with corresponding developments in anti-fraud measures), will also have an increasing impact on fast-food operations.

Across a variety of different legal environments, requirements are becoming more stringent regarding food labelling, the employment of minors, and recycling. The UK requires that the industry recycles a proportion of the containers that it sells its meals in, and McDonald's annual report notes that there are 'significant uncertainties, including with respect to the application of legal requirements and the enforceability of laws and contractual obligations' in China.[43]

A pressing environmental concern for restaurant chains is the quality and production of their food. They are under competing pressures from suppliers of GM-based foods and from campaigning organizations who regularly put forward anti-GM motions at many of the large fast-food corporations' annual general meetings. All such firms will have to continue to review policy on whether they will allow GM ingredients to get into their supply chain, whether in the form of GM wheat, or via the foodstuffs that their beef cattle eat.

We can note, in passing, that some firms are more affected by these macro-environmental factors than others. McDonald's, as the most global of the fast-food chains, has to handle a greater variety of regulatory frameworks than its competitors. Its success seems to have made it a target for activists (notably the anti-globalization movement), films such as Morgan Spurlock's *Super Size Me*, or partly anti-American-fuelled sentiment such as the resistance to fast food from elements in 'old Europe'— Italy and France[44]—although paradoxically, McDonald's growth in France has recently been greater than in the US. These firm-specific factors are not handled in this part of the analysis. They result from the firm's competitive stance and from location decisions within its value chain, and are taken into account when we appraise those decisions. The methods for doing this are reviewed in Chapters 4–6.

McDonald's restaurants' industry environment

The second part of our environmental analysis is to look at the industry that McDonald's is in. One problem is whether we limit the definition of a directly competing product to burgers, or pizzas, sandwiches, ethnic foods such as Tex-Mex or curries, or restaurant meals as a whole. A good starting point is to see what industry analysts consider to be the industry. The US *Nation's Restaurant News*, one of the main trade magazines, considers that ➜

→ McDonald's is in the sandwich chain industry. This includes Subway as well as Tex/Mex chains such as Taco Bell, but not KFC or other fried chicken takeaways. In SIC indexes used by databases such as Factiva, McDonald's is in the 'limited-service eating places' category, which includes all genres of fast-food outlets. Industry analysts *Researchandmarkets.com* and *Restaurants and Institutions* also include outlets like Starbucks and Dunkin' Donuts, as well as multi-brand conglomerates such as Compass Group in their lists.

There are also a number of strategic groups in the industry. McDonald's itself, and its major rivals Burger King and Wendy's, are international players using single brands across the world. But most of their competitors are local firms that only operate in individual countries, and there is a further strategic group of much smaller competitors with just one outlet. So do we consider the industry to be global or do we say that the differences in competitive factors are so great that the main markets can be seen as separate industries, with the three largest firms competing in all of them?

So defining the industry in this case is difficult—there are huge areas of overlap and no right answers—it is always a matter of pragmatism and judgement. Here, we shall define the industry as limited service restaurant chains that principally serve burgers in the USA. Similar analyses could be undertaken for other countries or regions.

Supplier power

There are several principal ingredients in a US burger chain's products—meat, buns (which contain wheat and sugar), and soft drinks. In addition there are other supplies that are critical to providing the service element of the product—restaurant premises, including equipment and facilities, and staff.

Some of the industry's suppliers are substantial firms in their own right. Golden State Foods started supplying McDonald's in the 1950s. It is now the largest supplier of liquid products and the third-largest beef supplier to McDonald's in the USA.[45] Its sales are $2.4 billion, 80 per cent of which come from McDonald's. It has recently expanded its customer base to include companies such as Starbucks and KFC, but GSF is very careful not to step on McDonald's toes by, for example, supplying its main competitors.[46] Another major supplier to the industry is Heinz, a giant multinational corporation in its own right, whose strenuous efforts to win a share of McDonald's custom have included frequent visits by one of its senior executives to the company's restaurants to observe customer behaviour.[47]

This is an indication that, although there are few substitutes for a burger chain's inputs, there are many suppliers, and individual supplier power is low. Suppliers have, however, attempted to alleviate that bargaining power through growth, so that size, for a burger chain, can be a success factor—it ensures that the firm retains the upper hand in negotiations. However, environmental factors serve to moderate burger firms' negotiating power. In 2004, wholesale prices of chickens, beef, and 'virtually every major protein, vegetable and grain on which restaurateurs depend' increased by up to 27 per cent,[48] forcing the burger chains to increase their own prices and lose sales. These were the result of a combination of circumstances: hurricanes in Florida, leading to the near extinction of cherry tomatoes, a long-standing drought in the west, discovery of the USA's first case of BSE, a ban on Canadian beef imports, and high transport costs as the result of increasing oil prices.[49] And because of the criticality in maintaining quality (McDonald's share price went down temporarily after 'mad cow disease' (BSE) was identified), many of the burger chains put considerable effort into ensuring that they maintain good relationships with the best suppliers, for example those who can assure traceability of beef cattle.

Similar issues apply to employees and franchisees. They are critical to the effectiveness of restaurants' operations, and although they are mostly not in short supply (though in the late 1990s the industry experienced staffing problems in some parts of the world), they have considerable potential to damage a firm's reputation. Companies like McDonald's therefore spend a lot of time and money making sure that staff are skilled, through heavy expenditure on training and recruitment.

The industry features a large number of franchised outlets. Some 89 per cent of Burger King's restaurants are franchises (McDonald's and Wendy's have about 29 per cent and 22 per cent respectively). Franchisees exercise a degree of power, since their outlets appear to perform better than company-owned restaurants.[50] McDonald's announced in 2006 that it would sell over 100 of its UK-based company-owned restaurants to franchisees. Superior relationships with franchisees may therefore be an industry success factor. Burger King has had limited control over its franchisees and has experienced difficulties in removing them when unhappy with their performance. It is also hard to collect royalties and fees if franchisees get into financial difficulties.[51]

Buyer power

Individual buyer power in the burger industry is very low—each customer spends a miniscule amount relative to the companies' size, and there are no volume purchasers. However, switching costs are low. There are numerous substitute and competing products, so buyer power is increased. Success factors in the →

→ industry relate to increasing those switching costs, by, for example, nabbing the best locations so as to lock customers in through considerations of convenience and travel-time, or through advertising and branding to build brand recognition and loyalty.

Threats of substitution

Burger chains compete for discretionary spending; no-one *has* to eat out. They therefore confront many potential substitutes, such as cinema, TV, full-service restaurant meals and other types of fast food, or microwave dinners to be eaten at home. However, for busy people they provide the benefits of a filling, speedy, and cheap meal, and so convenience for working families may make them a choice destination. But generally threats of substitution are very high, and is another reason why firms attempt to increase the attractiveness of their products through branding, and their convenience through location.

Threat of entry

In some ways entry barriers to the US burger restaurants industry are low. New restaurants start up all the time, and the industry is characterized by a large number of small chains (Table 3.3). But there are some significant barriers to *success*, and the industry is also characterized by high levels of firm exits.

The first is brands. Burger King and McDonald's regularly appear in the lists of the world's most recognized brands, with all their associated benefits of attractiveness to new customers, and repeat business. So unless a firm with an equally recognizable, and relevant, brand decides to enter the industry, new entrants are likely to encounter considerable difficulties, including retaliation from incumbents. The second factor is economies of scale. The size of the major firms gives them huge buying power, and therefore cost advantage, over new entrants, in advertising as well as raw materials. The third is location. The best locations in the most attractive markets have almost all been taken. McDonald's especially has for many years been very astute in →

Table 3.3 US burger chains in 2005

Company name	Sales $m	Increase 04/05%	Market share	Numbers of units
McDonald's	50,120[a]	11.6	64%	30,496[b]
Burger King	11,300	1.8	14%	11,220[c]
Wendy's	8,700	12.3	11%	6,671[d]
Subtotal of top three	**70,120**		**89%**	
The next ten US chains				
Dairy Queen	2,745	N/A	3.5%	5,725
Hardee's	1,804	2.4	2.3%	2,034
Whataburger	794	13.1	1.6%	636
Red Robin	735	31.3	0.9%	255
Friendly's	697	5	0.9%	535
Checker's	575	N/A	0.7%	788
Krystal	415	6.3	0.5%	428
Fuddruckers	325	N/A	0.4%	234
In-n-out	300	N/A	0.4%	187
Max & Erma's	181	−7	0.2%	98
Subtotal of next ten[e]	**8,390**		**11%**	
Total	78,510			

Notes

a McDonald's annual report says that approx. 35% of sales are from North America

b McDonald's annual report states that approx. 50% of its restaurants are located in North America

c About 30% of Burger King's and 10% of Wendy's restaurants are located outside the USA (of which the vast majority are in Canada). The other chains are almost entirely US-based

d This table details only the top 13 burger chains in the USA. There are innumerable smaller restaurants that are not listed here. The proportion of burger chains to the other types of food sellers listed reduces significantly the lower down the table one goes

Source

R&I 400. *Restaurants & Institutions*. 1 July 2005. N.B. In the interests of comparability and consistency we have used the data from this single source. Some of their figures do not tally with those available from, for example, McDonald's own annual reports

→ managing its real-estate: 60 per cent of its sites are freehold, giving it further cost advantages.[52] That leaves new entrants with untapped markets, which in the USA are few, or less attractive spots, both of which offer fewer profits. And the final barrier is a learning curve effect related to the standardization of food production. These, again, have reputational and cost implications for newcomers in their ability to serve low-priced and high-quality burgers reliably. It is significant that the bottom half of the R&I 500 (from which Table 3.3 is taken) contains virtually no burger restaurants.

Power of complementors

It is quite hard to think of examples of complementors in the burger industry. Film or TV companies like Disney or Pixar are complementors in some ways, in that their film character toys that are sold as components of the restaurant meal are part of the attraction for children in going to a Burger King or McDonald's restaurant. The success of the restaurant toy is dependent on the success of the film, *Toy Story* for example. However, they are more accurately counted as suppliers: they license their products to the restaurant chains.

Perhaps a better example of complementary products in the burger industry are retailers and other leisure facilities. Some of the most successful burger outlets in the US are close to Costco (a discount warehouse retailer), major shopping malls, or cinemas. And, perhaps counter-intuitively, some of the biggest complementors are other restaurants, like the food malls in shopping centres. Customers can reduce time, and therefore search costs, by heading to a single, geographically dense, district. Even though each firm competes with the others, they act as an attractor when grouped together. Since such complementors have a vested interest in the burger chains' success, they are unlikely to use any power to the detriment of the industry.

Competitive rivalry

The burger restaurant industry in the USA is highly concentrated and oligopolistic—three firms count for 89 per cent of the market. The next ten count for virtually all of the remaining 11 per cent. This structure of this mature industry has remained broadly stable for many years, as has sales growth, at 3–4 per cent above inflation each year. Even the relative positions of the companies has been stable, although both Wendy's and McDonald's have increased their own share, particularly at Burger King's and the smaller chains' expense, in recent years (Table 3.3).[53]

In a search for differentiation the three main firms emphasize slightly different things: Burger King promotes itself on selling the best-tasting burgers, as it flame-grills them, Wendy's on providing a family-friendly environment, and McDonald's on good value, predictable hot meals in convenient locations.

The oligopolistic structure and attempts at differentiation have not reduced competitive rivalry, which has been hardening to the point that some commentators have described it as →

McDonald's emphasizes its good value and predictable hot meals in convenient locations. *McDonald's Corporation*

→ hypercompetitive. There are signs that McDonald's is gaining at the expense of its two major rivals. McDonald's profit margin in 2005 was 12.7 per cent compared to Wendy's 5.9 per cent and Burger King's 2.4 per cent. The average Burger King outlet gets just over half the sales of an average McDonald's.[54] Burger King has also been faced with high levels of debt and management problems in recent years, and in 2003 was sold by its former owner Diageo to an investment trust, which is making strong efforts to turn the company around.

Price wars, led by the larger firms with superior power over suppliers, are a feature of the industry—Hardee's, for example, has complained of heavy discounting by the majors. Wendy's has tried to avoid them by promoting the quality and value of its products, although as burger chain customers are quite price sensitive, it may be at risk from any discounting by its rivals. High advertising spends to enhance switching costs are another indicator of fierce competition: Burger King spent $268.7 million on advertising in 2005, although this was $54 million less than 2004, and $120 million less than in 2002, the last year that Diageo owned the company.

Social and technological changes are likely to further increase competitive rivalry by increasing demands for investment. Burger chains have had to invest in 'healthy' options such as salads, and lower-fat or size options. However, this has the danger of moving the firms away from their core identity, and some firms are rethinking this policy and returning to traditional high-calorie menus.[55] There are good economic reasons why they should do this, too; there are few marginal costs attached to increasing portion sizes, but considerable potential for increased prices.[56] But the need to provide against the costs of class-action suits by lawyers who claim they are damaging health might reduce industry attractiveness.

Investments in new technology and restaurants will form a further competitive battleground. For example, McDonald's is experimenting with Voice over Internet Protocol (VoIP) ordering systems based in call centres. This is expected to increase speed of throughput in drive-through restaurants, and also reduce staff costs, as ordering will be centralized. The technology also spots when a customer has failed to order a drink with their meal and encourages them to order one, thereby increasing sales. Burger King has tested a restaurant design prototype that is more than 25 per cent cheaper to build than its normal outlets, which would be extended across its estate in due course.[57]

We can conclude that the burger industry in the USA is likely to be an increasingly difficult place to make money. The largest firms, with superior bargaining power and able to afford higher advertising spend, will hold an advantage, although smaller firms able to charge a premium price for a premium product may be able to survive despite their cost and advertising disadvantages. Good relationships with suppliers and franchisees are necessary to survive in the industry, and superior relationships may be a success factor. Scale will help in this area as well.

Practical dos and don'ts

You will notice that this worked example is not a list of bullet points. Whilst it is quite useful to devise a full list of factors that fit into each PESTLE and six-forces category, we would suggest that you think of this as your preliminary homework, which then needs to be condensed considerably. Part of this refining process is to show how, and by how much, the factors that you pick out influence the nature of competition for an organization and its industry or industries. It is this appraisal of the impact of each factor that distinguishes a proper analysis from a mere list. And when you come to write up your analysis, you need not (and in fact probably should not) mention the PESTLE labels at all.

Some of the factors that we have identified above could fit into a number of different PESTLE categories. A PESTLE analysis is better thought of as a set of hooks that can be used to fish for important facts—once these have been 'fished out', it does not matter which hook they were attached to. It is also perfectly legitimate to leave some categories empty. Do not waste time trying to find factors that do not exist. Limit yourself only to important and relevant factors.

When undertaking an industry analysis you should look for *signs* of competitive forces: fierce competition would be indicated by falling margins, price wars and so on. If you do not find these signs, then competition is not fierce, no matter how fragmented the industry, how low the barriers to entry, and how high the barriers to exit may be. One or two firms in an industry may try to differentiate on low prices, but unless this results in consistent price competition that affects most of the competitors, it is not a symptom of fierce competition.

You may also notice that there are some important data that are missing from our analysis—relative profits, or indeed names, of suppliers to the burger industry, for example. This is because they appear not to be available in the public domain. This is a real problem in any analysis of real companies and industries—the data that you want to get hold of may simply not be there. In this case, you have to make inferences, or use alternative sources of data as proxy for the information you really want—and note the limitations of your analysis accordingly.

Creative Strategizing 3.1

Imagine you are the McDonald's manager for the south-west States of the USA. What new restaurant meals or concepts should you be devising? You should pay attention to the types of families—size and scope—that Hispanic and other 'minority' groups have, and their typical behaviour—this may influence the design of your local restaurants. You should also think about the type of food they like to eat, typically spicy and strongly-flavoured. You may also want to consider whether there are any environmental issues that strongly affect this demographic group—to do with diet and food safety perhaps. And you may also want to think about the design and language of your menus.

3.6 The outcomes of environmental and industry analysis

Theorists identify three things an organization needs to know about its environment:[58]

- its munificence—the extent to which resources are freely available to support firms in an industry and enable them to grow;
- its dynamism—the extent to which it is stable or turbulent;
- its complexity—the extent to which it embraces a range of activities that are significantly different from one another.

To a large extent an organization can limit the complexity of its environment by limiting its own degree of diversity, as we discuss in Chapter 6. But the PESTLE, life-cycle, and six-forces analyses enable us to assess munificence and dynamism. If there is, or is likely to be, rapid change or a high degree of uncertainty in important PESTLE factors, then the industry will be highly dynamic, and firms will need to cope with this instability or turbulence.

A high rate of growth in the industry, low buyer, supplier, and complementor power, high barriers to entry, and low threat of substitution are all likely to make the industry more munificent. It may therefore be more attractive (although see our proviso in Theoretical Debate 3.1), because firms have to compete less fiercely for the resources they need. Political and social trends may also affect the extent to which customers, financiers, and other stakeholders are likely to make resources available to the firm.

A crucial stage in the analysis is then to identify the precise factors an organization needs to cope with the degree of munificence and dynamism in the environment, and how this is likely to change over time. The PESTLE, life-cycle, and in particular the six-forces analysis will show what these factors have been in the past, and how they are likely to change in the future. Typically, an industry will feature a number of survival factors—*every* firm hoping to compete in the industry will need to possess *all* of these in order to be viable. In addition, there will be a number of refinements or additions to these survival factors. In order to *succeed*, a firm will have at least *one* of these success factors (Table 3.4).

In an industry where competition is relaxed, and based on non-price factors, what a firm needs to survive may be quite straightforward: an adequate command of the latest technology, a production capability that is adequate to serve existing or emerging markets, and a reasonable reputation, for example. In an industry where competition is fierce, survival factors will be more exacting. Where competition is based upon price, firms' cost structures

Table 3.4 Examples of industry survival and success factors

If industry has/is/ suffers from . . .	Indicative survival factors	Indicative success factors
Powerful buyers with low switching costs	Meeting minimum buyer requirements	Strong differentiation; negotiation skills; strong relationships with buyers (i.e. good architecture)
Powerful suppliers	Negotiation skills	Scale to improve bargaining power; vertical integration or innovation to develop substitute supplies (if possible); co-development
Low barriers to entry and/or high threat of substitution	(Survival difficult without success)	Strong differentiation; low costs
Powerful complementors	Compliance with dominant standards	Strong complementor relationships; dominant technological position
Fast-growing	Technology; cash for growth	Advanced technology
Mature	Minimum economic scale, viable cost structure	Scale or other cost advantage; buyer relationships
Declining	(If success not possible, withdrawal may be best option)	Strong reputation, low costs
Unstable political environment	Understanding of political risks	Ability to influence political outcomes (due to scale, relationships)
Economic recession	Cash reserves to ride out downturn; viable cost structure	Reputation for value for money; superior value proposition; strong non-price differentiation
Fast-changing technology	Innovation to keep up	Disruptive innovation

will need to be competitive. This may in turn mean that firms will need to be of a certain minimum size in order to take advantage of economies of scale or scope. Where competition is based upon marketing or investment, firms will need adequate sources of finance. The resources needed for survival are termed threshold resources.

To succeed in a competitive industry—that is, to make above average returns on investment on a consistent basis—something over and above the success factors will be required. The resources needed for sustained success are called strategic resources. If buyer power is high, then close relationships with customers and the capability to meet their needs better than competitors may yield success. If competition is based upon technological leadership, then the ability to innovate faster than competitors may be a success factor. If cost is all-important, then being the market leader and having maximum economies of scale may be crucial, which may imply having a substantial distribution network.

→ We return to the concept of threshold and strategic resources in Section 7.2.

In an increasing returns industry, success comes from establishing and then controlling the industry standard. Survival may come from being a collaborator of the industry leader, or by having a secondary, alternative, standard—the kind of strategy historically followed by Apple in competing with Microsoft (see Real-life Application 4.5 for details).

Using Evidence 3.1

One way of working out where the balance of power in an industry lies is to look at profit margins and returns on capital. If the suppliers are more profitable than the firms in the industry, then that *may* be a sign that they are powerful enough to take a share of the industry's profits. However, you will always need to make a judgment about this—there may be short-term reasons behind relative performance.

Switching costs may be assessed by looking at how mobile customers are—do they always go to the same firm again and again? If so, it may indicate that it is too difficult to swap. Branding is another indicator—expensive attempts to build a brand may indicate the absence of other switching costs, and an attempt to create them in the form of brand loyalty.

Barriers to entry can be assessed by looking at how many new firms are entering the industry—compared to, for example, other industries. This can be calculated using SIC-code-based data such as FAME or industry reports such as those published by Mintel.

Evidence of decline in an industry takes the form of price competition, redundancies, and other signs of overcapacity such as declining profit margins.

While success and survival factors can be deduced from PESTLE, life-cycle, or six-forces analysis, the attributes of firms that have survived or succeeded can give some useful clues. But be careful to look at the attributes of all the competitors. Do not take one firm and assume that what it does well is a success factor.

What Can Go Wrong 3.1 Mistaking industry attractiveness: Marconi's foray into the telecoms industry

One of the UK's largest and most famous conglomerate's, GEC, began life in 1886, but really took off during the 1980s and 1990s, when Lord Arnold Weinstock built it into one of the world's most formidable defence and electrical manufacturing companies. When he retired in 1996 it had an annual turnover of £11bn, and £1bn in profits.

Lord Simpson, himself one of the UK's most respected industrialists of the time, took over from Lord Weinstock as GEC's chief executive and soon afterwards set about transforming the company from a 'stodgy' conglomerate, to a 'fast-moving' organization focused on the telecoms industry. In the process it was renamed 'Marconi'. Since 2001, however, the story of the company has been one of almost terminal decline. In 2000 (at what appears in retrospect to have been the height of the 'dotcom madness'),[59] Marconi had a market capitalization of nearly £35bn. By 2002, however this had declined to £100m. In 2005 most of the remnants were sold to Ericsson for £1.2bn, with the remainder (now called 'Telent') continuing as a 'small telecoms services company with sales of £300m'.[60] The company, which at its height employed over 160,000 people, now employs 2,000.

At the beginning things had looked promising. In 1999, Lord Simpson embarked on a $9bn programme of acquisitions, buying US telecoms companies such as Reltec (for $2.1bn, including $361m of debt), and Fore Systems, a broadband internet switching company (for $4.5bn). Both were among the market leaders in their field. He also acquired many others—some of which were not profitable at the time of acquisition. The intention was to bring good management practices to companies that had been badly managed and improve their profits as a consequence. The other intention was to gain access to exciting, profitable, industry sectors, particularly parts of the dotcom expansion—the internet infrastructure market in the USA. Technologies such as broadband, wireless, optical networking, data-switching, and routing were the key to accessing the fast-growing broadband and internet markets. Marconi's strategy was to provide a comprehensive range of products and services covering the transmission process, from origination to the home.

In the process Lord Simpson used Marconi's £2.6bn cash, explicitly saying that having it sitting in the bank was an ineffective use of the money and did not 'say much about being a dynamic company . . . I spent the cash as fast as I could'.[61] Many analysts and investors agreed strongly—in 1999, shares rose to £12.50, compared with £3.09p when Lord Simpson took over.

Opinions are divided as to what went wrong. Many other companies were also badly hit by the downturn in internet-related businesses, but few experienced quite such a catastrophic →

➜ decline. In the first place, Marconi had incurred nearly £4bn in debt paying for the acquisitions in cash rather than with GEC shares. This was partly a legacy of the previous management; GEC's accounting procedures were apparently not compliant with US regulations and shares could not be issued. Its debt meant that Marconi had no 'organizational fat' with which to weather the lean times, and also integrate a number of complicated acquisitions. Nortel and Cisco had also announced large write-downs on dotcom acquisitions ($12.3bn and $2.5bn respectively) and inventory, but they had typically paid for the companies with their own shares rather than cash. In time Marconi had problems in meeting interest payments. Its credit rating fell to its lowest ever.

Second, there was a mis-reading of market conditions. In 2002, Marconi wrote down to zero all the goodwill relating to its purchase of Fore Systems, in effect admitting that the acquisition was an 'expensive flop', or in the opinion of another commentator being among 'the most disastrous overseas forays by a British company'.[62] It also wrote off £518m related to excess inventory, suggesting a 'significant misreading of demand'.[63] Fore's problem came from a steep fall in demand from private households, which accounted for about 85 per cent of its turnover, and faster than expected migration away from the company's products to 'gigabyte ethernet' applications. Elsewhere, Marconi experienced what it described as 'unprecedented declines' in spending on network infrastructure in most of its regions. Telecoms companies were themselves debt-laden, and had cut back on capital spending. Mobile networks firms had made what turned out to be an ill-judged assessment of future demand, hoping that new data services based around 'third generation' (3G) networks would provide growth. But consumers were much slower to embrace these new services than expected. And in Europe, operators had incurred huge debts buying the necessary 3G licences from governments.

According to the *Economist*, the 'carnage' in the telecoms industry is partly structural, and unlikely to be solved soon. There is considerable overcapacity, resulting from the need for firms to anticipate demand, because telecoms is an 'infrastructure-intensive business, and infrastructure takes a long time to build'.[64] During the dotcom boom, firms assumed that demand would grow by 100 per cent p.a., as it had done previously. A huge construction programme ensued, aided by cheap capital. The result was that telecoms operators built seven years' worth of capacity in a single year, to be followed by a collapse in demand.

Other problems came from Marconi's lack of size and brand awareness. It was entering markets dominated by international giants of conventional telecommunications manufacturing, such as Lucent, Nortel Networks, Alcatel, Ericsson, and Siemens, as well as the market leaders of the new telecoms world, Cisco, Tellabs, and Nokia. Although most of its competitors were also struggling (Nortel and Cisco had cut around 50,000 jobs each), some gained market share at Marconi's expense, partly because they were larger and better established, with superior linkages to the established telecoms firms that were the main customers. Some commentators applauded the acquisitions of Fore and Relent, because they felt that Marconi needed to increase its scale to be competitive. Marconi itself was aware of the problem, but claimed that being nimble was more important than being large—and believed that it was fastest. However, during the downturn, a number of other analysts[65] were arguing that Marconi's position as a mid-sized company would be a problem: survivors would be large integrated suppliers or niche, leading-edge technology suppliers. Marconi, it was argued, fell into the 'challenging middle ground'.[66]

Eventually Marconi started to sell off its businesses at give-away prices in an attempt to reduce debt. Its medical systems business was sold to Philips, accompanied by 'a sense of shock at the price'.[67] It also reduced its research budget by 40 per cent. This, in an innovation-hungry industry, meant that Marconi 'cut the lifeblood of its existence just to stay alive'.[68] The final nail in Marconi's coffin was its failure to secure a contract from BT (which accounted for 25 per cent of its turnover) to upgrade its communications network. Marconi had incurred huge costs in developing a new generation of equipment that it hoped to sell to BT; its failure to do so also raised questions about the company's ability to win other contracts. Its share price fell sharply.

Since then, opinion appears to be fairly evenly divided about whether blame should be laid at the door of the Marconi senior management team's lack of judgement, or at impossible to anticipate market conditions. Both Lord Simpson and John Mayo, his deputy, left their positions.[69] Those that lay the blame squarely at their door, suggest, variously, that the case was 'one of the swiftest ever exercises in value destruction . . . and one of the great corporate governance fiascos of all time',[70] and the most badly mismanaged company that the analyst had ever seen.[71] Others thought they were guilty of following fashion without the means to acquire a defensible position.[72]

However, other more sympathetic commentators suggested that Marconi's directors' hands had been tied 'because they were doing what the shareholder base wanted them to do', and because no-one could anticipate how much the tech market would implode.[73] Whatever the reason, it is clear that Marconi entered an industry expecting high growth and a successful outcome in terms of profits and shareholder value. In both cases its hopes were sadly dashed.

● CHAPTER SUMMARY

In this chapter we have discussed how to assess the impact of the environment on an organization. We have examined macro-environmental factors:

- political activity by governments at local, national or regional levels. Examples include policies on tariffs or restrictions on trade, national governmental stability, or instability;

- economic developments, locally and worldwide, which affect the purchasing power of customers and end-users, and the availability of raw materials and human resources. Examples include global and national macro-economic booms, recessions, and inflation;

- social and cultural changes, which affect the behaviour and desires of customers and end-users. Examples include broad social and cultural developments such as the emergence of a middle class with significant spending power in Asia and increasing assertiveness on the part of consumers in the developed economies;

- technological developments, which affect the technologies used in products and services, as well as the way in which they are produced, marketed, distributed, and accounted for. Examples include new technologies such as the internet and fuel cells, new product development systems, and biotechnologies such as genetically modified foods;

- legal factors such as laws or regulations which determine how organizations can go about their business;

- environmental factors which influence organizational strategies as well as the preferences of customers and consumers, such as the advent of global warming.

We have also examined the nature of competition in an industry, including industry recipes and rules of the game, and analysed how this develops over time. Specifically we looked at:

- an industry's progress through its life-cycle, through growth and maturity to eventual decline. Changes from one stage in the life-cycle are often triggered by macro-environmental change;

- the six forces relating to the structure of the industry itself, which are shaped by changes in the macro-environment and the industry's stage within its life-cycle. These forces are:

  - the power of buyers and suppliers—if these groups are powerful, they will be able to negotiate deals that reduce the profits of firms in the industry;

  - the threat of substitution—if this is high, firms will be unable to make high profits, because customers will turn to alternative products or services. Organizations need to be alert to social-cultural or technological changes that may make substitutes more attractive and push an industry into the maturity or decline phase of the life-cycle;

  - the threat of entry—if this is high, new firms will enter as soon as the industry starts making decent profits, and make competition more intense;

  - the power of complementors—the existence of complementors can raise profits for all concerned, but they have a great deal of power and if they choose to exercise it, they may set their prices at levels that undermine the attractiveness of the industry's products, or may favour one competitor over another;

  - the nature of rivalry in the industry including the extent to which the industry is concentrated or fragmented—this is in turn affected by the degree to which economies of scale are important to competitive advantage, and whether the industry shows increasing or decreasing returns to scale.

All these factors combine to determine:

- whether the competition in the industry is mild, fierce or hypercompetitive;

- how attractive the industry is—a fiercely competitive industry is likely to be less attractive than a less competitive one;

- the nature of survival and success factors in the industry.

Online Resource Centre
www.oxfordtextbooks.co.uk/orc/haberberg_rieple/

Visit the Online Resource Centre that accompanies this book to read more information relating to the influence of the environment.

● KEY SKILLS

The key skills you should have developed after reading this chapter are:

- the ability to assess the impact of environmental factors on an organization's strategic performance, in the past, present, and also the future, through an assessment of trends and how these factors are changing over time;

- the skills to evaluate how industry-specific factors, such as the stage that an industry is at in its life-cycle, will influence the nature of competition, industry structure, and the strategies available to a firm;

- the ability to assess the strength of the six forces that act on an industry and determine how they are likely to shape the performance and behaviour of organizations;

- the ability to identify the factors required to survive in an industry, and those further ones that are required to succeed in it.

● REVIEW QUESTIONS

1. What are the main PESTLE factors affecting the movie industry? The fashion industry? The European banking industry? How are these likely to change in the next three years, and what are the implications for survival and success in the industry?

2. How will firms in each of these industries need to change in order to counter the effects of global warming?

3. Is McDonald's in the food industry, the restaurant industry, the fast-food industry, or the hamburger industry?

4. The six-forces framework is sometimes criticized as being static in that it only gives a snapshot of an industry at a particular moment in time. Do you agree with this criticism? How big a problem do you think it is?

5. What are the weaknesses of PESTLE analysis?

6. How many industries can you think of, apart from those mentioned in the chapter, that feature increasing returns?

7. 'Unattractive industries are more attractive than attractive ones.' Discuss.

● FURTHER READING

- The classic works that have influenced almost all other discussions on industry analysis are: Porter, M. E. (1980). *Competitive Strategy*. New York: Free Press, and Porter, M. E. (1985). *Competitive Advantage*. New York: Free Press.

- For an exposition of the new industrial world order see the collection of articles in Ilinitch, A. Y., Lewin, A. Y., and D'Aveni, R. (eds) (1998). *Managing in Times of Disorder: Hypercompetitive Organizational Responses*. Thousand Oaks: Sage.

- For a good introduction to the benefits of intra-industry collaboration see **Brandenburger, A. M. and Nalebuff, B. J. (1997)**. *Co-opetition*. London: Harper-Collins.
- For a good alternative textbook that covers industry analysis very well see **Barney, J. (2002)**. *Gaining and Sustaining Competitive Advantage*. 2nd edn. Harlow: Prentice Hall.
- For an alternative view on the industry life-cycle, see **McGahan, A. (2004)**. 'How industries change'. *Harvard Business Review*, July/August: 94–104.

● REFERENCES

Aktouf, O., Chenoufi, M., and Holford, W. David (2005). 'The false expectations of Michael Porter's strategic management framework'. *Problems and Perspectives in Management*, 4: 181–200.

Amburgey, T., Kelly, D., and Barnett, W. (1993). 'Resetting the clock: the dynamics of organisational change and failure'. *Administrative Science Quarterly*, 38: 58–73.

Arthur, W. (1996). 'Increasing returns and the new world of business'. *Harvard Business Review*, July–August: 101–109.

Bain, J. S. (1956). *Barriers to New Competition: Their Character and Consequences in Manufacturing Industries*. Cambridge MA: Harvard University Press.

Barney, J. (1986a). 'Strategic factor markets expectations, luck, and business strategy'. *Management Science*, 32/10: 1231–41.

Barney, J. (1986b). 'Organizational culture: can it be a source of sustained competitive advantage?' *Academy of Management Review*, 11/3: 656–65.

Barney, J. (1991). 'Firm resources and sustained competitive advantage'. *Journal of Management*, 17/1: 99–120.

Barney, J. (2002). *Gaining and Sustaining Competitive Advantage*. 2nd edn. Harlow: Prentice Hall.

Barney, J. B. and Hoskisson, R. E. (1990). 'Strategic groups: untested assertions and research proposals'. *Managerial and Decision Economics*, 11/3: 187–198.

Beard, G., and Dess, D. (1984). 'Dimensions of organizational task environments'. *Administrative Science Quarterly*, 29: 52–73.

Brandenburger, A. M. and Nalebuff, B. J. (1996). 'Inside Intel'. *Harvard Business Review*, 74/6: 168–75.

Brandenburger, A. M. and Nalebuff, B. J. (1997). *Co-opetition*. London: Harper-Collins.

Brown, S. and Eisenhardt, K. (1997). 'The art of continuous change: linking complexity theory and time-paced evolution in relentlessly shifting organizations'. *Administrative Science Quarterly*, 42, 1 March: 1–34.

Burton, J. (1995). 'Composite strategy: the combination of collaboration and competition'. *Journal of General Management*, 21/1: 1–23.

Camerer, C. and Vepsalainen, A. (1988). 'The economic efficiency of corporate culture'. *Strategic Management Journal*, 9: 115–26.

Caves, R. (2000). *Creative Industries: Contracts between Commerce and Creativity*. Cambridge, MA: Harvard University Press.

Caves, R. E. and Porter, M. E. (1977). 'From entry barriers to mobility barriers: conjectural decisions and contrived deterrence to new competition'. *Quarterly Journal of Economics*, 91: 241–62.

Christensen, C. (1993). 'The rigid disk drive industry: a history of commercial and technological turbulence'. *Business History Review*, 67: 531–8.

Collis, D. J. (1991). 'A resource-based analysis of global competition: the case of the bearings industry'. *Strategic Management Journal*, 12: 49–68.

Cool, K., and Schendel, D. (1988). 'Performance differences among strategic group members'. *Strategic Management Journal*, 9: 207–223.

D'Aveni, R. A. (1994). *Hypercompetition: Managing the Dynamics of Strategic Maneuvering*. New York: Free Press.

D'Aveni, R. A. (1995). 'Coping with hypercompetition: utilizing the new 7-S's framework'. *Academy of Management Executive*, 9/3: 45–57.

Davis, P. S. and Schul, P. L. (1993). 'Addressing the contingent effects of business unit strategic orientation on relationships between organizational context and business unit performance'. *Journal of Business Research*, 27: 183–200.

Demsetz, H. (1982). 'Barriers to entry'. *American Economic Review*, 72/1: 47–57.

Derajtys, J. M., Chrisman, J. J., and Bauerschmidt, A. (1993). 'The shakeout in microcomputers: causes and consequences'. *Long Range Planning*, 26/1: 86–97.

Dess, G. G. and Beard, D. W. (1984). 'Dimensions of organizational task environments'. *Administrative Science Quarterly*, 29: 52–73.

Dierickx, I. and Cool, K. (1989). 'Asset stock accumulation and sustainability of competitive advantage'. *Management Science*, 35/12: 1504–11.

Dooley, R. S., Fowler, D. M., and Miller, A. (1996). 'The benefits of strategic homogeneity and strategic heterogeneity: theoretical and empirical evidence resolving past differences'. *Strategic Management Journal*, 17/4: 293–305.

Eisenhardt, K. and Brown, S. (1998). 'Time pacing: competing in markets that won't stand still'. *Harvard Business Review*, March–April: 59–69.

Eisenhardt, K. and Tabrizi, B. (1995). 'Accelerating adaptive processes: Product innovation in the global computer industry'. *Administrative Science Quarterly*, 40/1: 84–110.

Feigenbaum, A., McGee, J., and Thomas, H. (1988). 'Exploring the linkage between strategic groups and competitive strategy'. *International Studies of Management and Organization*, 18/1: 6–25.

Fiol, C. M. (1991). 'Managing culture as a competitive resource: an identity-based view of sustainable competitive advantage'. *Journal of Management*, 17.

Flaviàn, C., Haberberg, A., and Polo, Y. (1999). 'Subtle strategic insights from strategic groups analysis'. *Journal of Strategic Marketing*, June: 89–106.

Gardner, T. M. (2005). 'Interfirm competition for human resources: evidence from the software industry'. *Academy of Management Journal*, 48/2: 237–57.

Gimeno, J. (2004). 'Competition within and between networks: the contingent effect of competitive embeddedness on alliance formation'. *Academy of Management Journal*, 47/6: 820–42.

Gimeno, J. and Woo, C. (1996). 'Hypercompetition in a multimarket environment: the role of strategic similarity and multimarket contact in competitive de-escalation'. *Organization Science*, 7: 322–41.

Grant, R. M. (1991). 'The resource-based theory of competitive advantage: implications for strategy formulation'. *California Management Review*, 33/3: 114–35.

Greene, J., Kerstetter, J., Burrows, P., Hamm, S., and Ante, S. E. (2004). 'Microsoft's midlife crisis: threats abound: Linux. European trustbusters. Key product delays. Can Gates and Co. restore growth?' *BusinessWeek*, 88, 19 April.

Hannan, M. and Carrol, G. (1992). *Dynamics of Organizational Populations: Density, Legitimation and Competition*. New York: Oxford University Press.

Hannan, M. and Freeman, J. (1977). 'The population ecology of organisations'. *American Journal of Sociology*, 82/5: 929–64.

Hannan, M. and Freeman, J. (1984). 'Structural inertia and organizational change'. *American Sociological Review*, 49: 149–64.

Hannan, M. and Freeman, J. (1989). *Organizational Ecology*. Cambridge, MA: Harvard University Press.

Hannan, M., Carroll, G., Dundon, E., and Torres, J. (1995). 'Organizational evolution in a multinational context: entries of automobile manufacturers in Belgium, Britain, France, Germany, and Italy'. *American Sociological Review*, 60: 509–28.

Hatten, K. J. and Schendel, D. E. (1977). 'Heterogeneity within an industry: firm conduct in the US brewing industry 1952–1971'. *Journal of Industrial Economics*, 26/2: 97–113.

Henderson, R. and Mitchell, W. (1997). 'The interactions of organizational and competitive influences on strategy and performance'. *Strategic Management Journal*, 18 (Special Summer Issue): 5–14.

Henderson, R. M. and Clark, K. B. (1990). 'Architectural innovation: the reconfiguration of existing product technologies and the failure of established firms'. *Administrative Science Quarterly*, 35: 9–30.

Hofer, C. (1975). 'Toward a contingency theory of business strategy'. *Academy of Management Journal*, 18: 784–810.

Ilinitch, A. Y. and Lewin, A. Y. (1995). 'New organizational forms and strategies for managing in hypercompetitive environments'. *Organization Science*, 3: 211–20.

Ilinitch, A. Y., Lewin, A. Y., and D'Aveni, R. (eds) (1998). *Managing in Times of Disorder:*

Hypercompetitive Organizational Responses. Thousand Oaks, CA: Sage.

Katobe, M. and Duhan, D. F. (1993). 'Strategy clusters in Japanese markets: firm performance implications'. *Journal of the Academy of Marketing Science*, 21/1: 21–31.

Ketchen, D. J., Combs, J. G., and Russell, C. J. et al. (1997). 'Organizational configurations and performance: a meta-analysis'. *Academy of Management Journal*, 40/1: 223–40.

Klepper, S. and Simons, K. (1996). 'Innovation and industry shakeouts'. *Business and Economic History*, 25/1: 81–9.

Kretschmer, M., Klimis, G., and Choi, C. (1999). 'Increasing returns and social contagion in cultural industries'. *British Journal of Management*, 10: S61–S72.

Lash, J. and Wellington, F. (2007). 'Competitive advantage on a warming planet'. *Harvard Business Review*, 85/3: 94–102.

Lawless, M. W., Bergh, D. D., and Wilstead, W. D. (1989). 'Performance variations among strategic group members: an examination of individual firm capability'. *Journal of Management*, 15/4: 649–61.

Lenox, M., Rockart, S., and Lewin, A. (2007). 'Interdependency, competition, and industry dynamics'. *Management Science*, 53/4: 599–615.

McGahan, A. M. (1999). 'The performance of US corporations: 1981–1994'. *The Journal of Industrial Economics*, 47/4: 373–98.

McGahan, A. (2000). 'How industries evolve'. *Business Strategy Review*, 11/3: 1–16.

McGahan, A. (2004). 'How industries change'. *Harvard Business Review*, 82/10: 86–94.

McGahan, A. M. and Porter, M. E. (1997). 'How much does industry matter, really?' *Strategic Management Journal*, 18 (Summer Special Issue): 15–30.

McGee, J., Thomas, H., and Pruett, M. (1995). 'Strategic groups and the analysis of market structure and industry dynamics'. *British Journal of Management*, 6/4: 257–70.

McKinley, W. and Scherer, A. G. (2000). 'Some unanticipated consequences of organizational restructuring'. *Academy of Management Review*, 25/4: 735–53.

McNamara, G., Vaaler, P., and Devers, C. (2003). 'Same as it ever was: the search for evidence of increasing hypercompetition'. *Strategic Management Journal*, 24/3: 261–78.

Markides, C. and Williamson, P. (1996). 'Corporate diversification and organizational structure: A resource-based view'. *Academy of Management Journal*, 39/2: 340.

Mathur, S. and Kenyon, A. (2001). *Creating Value: Successful Business Strategies*. 2nd edn. Oxford: Butterworth Heinemann.

Mauri, A. J. and Michaels, M. P. (1998). 'Firm and industry effects within strategic management: an empirical examination'. *Strategic Management Review*, 19/3: 211–19.

Miles, G., Snow, C. C., and Sharfman, P. (1993). 'Industry variety and performance'. *Strategic Management Journal*, 14/3: 163–77.

Nelson, R. (1995). 'Recent evolutionary theorizing about economic change'. *Journal of Economic Literature*, 33/1: 48–91.

Peteraf, M. A. (1993). 'The cornerstones of competitive advantage: a resource-based view'. *Strategic Management Journal*, 14/3: 179–91.

Pettigrew, A. M. and Whipp, R. (1991). *Managing Change for Competitive Success*. Oxford: Blackwell.

Porac, J. F., Thomas, H., and Baden-Fuller, C. (1989). 'Competitive groups as cognitive communities: the case of Scottish knitwear manufacturers'. *Journal of Management Studies*, 26: 397–416.

Porter, M. E. (1979). 'How competitive forces shape strategy'. *Harvard Business Review*, 2: 137–45.

Porter, M. E. (1980). *Competitive Strategy*. New York: Free Press.

Porter, M. E. (1981). 'The contributions of industrial organization to strategic management'. *Academy of Management Review*, 6/4: 609–20.

Porter, M. E. (1985). *Competitive Advantage*. New York: Free Press.

Porter, M. E. (2001). 'Strategy and the internet'. *Harvard Business Review*, 79/3: 62–78.

Powell, T. C. (1996). 'How much does industry matter? An alternative empirical test'. *Strategic Management Journal*, 17/4: 323–34.

Reed, R. and DeFillippi, R. J. (1990). 'Causal ambiguity: barriers to imitation, and sustainable competitive advantage'. *Academy of Management Review*, 15/1: 88–102.

Reger, R. and Huff, A. (1993). 'Strategic groups: a cognitive perspective', *Strategic Management Journal*, 14: 103–24.

Rindova, V. P., Becerra, M., and Contardo, I. (2004). 'Enacting competitive wars: competitive activity, language games, and market consequences'. *Academy of Management Review*, 29/4: 670–87.

Roquebert, J. A., Phillips, R. L., and Westfall, P. A. (1996). 'Markets vs. management: What "drives" profitability?' *Strategic Management Journal*, 17/8: 653–64.

Rumelt, R. (1991). 'How much does industry matter?' *Strategic Management Journal*, 12/3: 167–85.

Scherer, F. M. (1970). *Industrial Market Structure and Economic Performance*. Chicago: Rand McNally.

Seth, A. and Thomas, H. (1994). 'Theories of the firm: implications for strategy research'. *Journal of Management Studies*, 31: 165–91.

Sheremata, W. (1998). ' "New" issues in competition policy raised by information technology industries'. *Antitrust Bulletin*, 43: 547–82.

Smith, A. and Zeithaml, C. (1996). 'Garbage cans and advancing hypercompetition: the creation and exploitation of new capabilities and strategic flexibility in two regional Bell operating companies'. *Organization Science*, 7/4: 388–99.

Spender, J.-C. (1989). *Industry Recipes — The Nature and Sources of Managerial Judgement*. Oxford: Blackwell.

Thomas, L. G. (1996). 'The two faces of competition: dynamic resourcefulness and hypercompetitive shift'. *Organization Science*, 7: 221–42.

Vandermerwe, S. (1997). 'Increasing returns: competing for customers in the global market'. *Journal of World Business*, 32/4: 333–50.

Volberda, H. W. (1996). 'Toward the flexible form: how to remain vital in hypercompetitive environments'. *Organization Science*, 7: 359–74.

Wernerfelt, B. (1984). 'A resource-based theory of the firm'. *Strategic Management Journal*, 5/2: 171–80.

Young, G., Smith, K., and Grimm, C. (1997). 'Multimarket contact, resource heterogeneity, and rivalrous firm behavior'. *Academy of Management Proceedings*: 55–9.

Zohar, A. and Morgan, G. (1998). 'Refining our understanding of hypercompetition and hyperturbulence'. In Ilinitch, A. Y., Lewin, A. Y., and R. D'Aveni (eds), *Managing in Times of Disorder: Hypercompetitive Organizational Responses*. Thousand Oaks, CA: Sage, 519–26.

 End-of-chapter Case Study 3.1 The mobile phone industry

Industry origins

The wireless, hand-held phone had been a dream and the stuff of science fiction long before the launch of the first commercial mobile networks in the 1980s. Various types of radio-based phones had appeared in the early years of the twentieth century for industrial and military uses, and since the 1960s there had been experiments and attempts at mobile telephony in Sweden, Finland, and elsewhere. However, these early networks were limited by the technology available at the time and by the beginning of the 1980s most of them had ceased operating.[74]

In the US, AT&T Bell Laboratories had begun developing the cellular phone technology on which today's mobile systems are based in the 1940s. However, it was to be almost another four decades before the first hand-held mobile, the Motorola DynaTAC 8000X, was marketed commercially in 1983 in North America.[75] Motorola's history was closely tied to radio; it had manufactured police and military communications systems for the government as well as consumer car radios and its brand was well known in the US. The first mobiles, or cellphones as they were more com-

monly known in America, worked on networks that used a version of first-generation, or 1G, analogue technology developed by AT&T and Motorola. As mobile telephony spread, different technical standards were adopted throughout the world, which meant that phones designed for use in one country would not normally work in another. Although the 1G technology was a breakthrough, it suffered from reliability problems in its early days and was also susceptible to eavesdropping. The first mobile phones were large and heavy—handsets were the size of small briefcases and often installed in cars, which meant that they were often known as carphones. Handsets and calls were also expensive, but despite this sales began to take off rapidly as buyers, particularly business users, saw the benefits and advantages of mobiles in comparison with traditional 'landline' phones.

Mobile phones: two industries in one

Two separate but interdependent and complementary industries form the most visible parts of the mobile phone industry: network service providers and handset manufacturers.   ➜

The mobile phones we use today (right) look very different from those we used in the early 1990s (left). *iStock*

→ The first of these, network operators, provide the system of base station transmitters and other infrastructure on which a cellular phone network operates. The radio bandwidth spectrum available to mobile networks is controlled and regulated by governments, which grant operators licences to use it. Network operators bid for the rights to use bandwidth, and pay the government fees for doing so for a period of time until their licence comes up for renewal.

In most countries, such as the UK, which is typical, the network industry is comprised of a small number of operators, the owners of which are often consortia of companies which already have, or have had, interests in landline telephony or other media, such as AT&T in the US, BT in the UK, and NTT in Japan. Many networks have expanded internationally, such as the UK's Vodafone, which has equity interests in 27 countries and 33 international partner networks.[76] There are also competitors in this sector, such as Virgin and the supermarket chain Tesco in the UK, which are not network owners themselves, but which buy airtime from the main networks and resell it to consumers under their own brand names and with their own pricing structure, see Table 3.5.

The second complementary industry is handset manufacturers. These are mainly major international companies with consumer electronics divisions (see Table 3.6). A third, less obvious, but important component of the mobile industry is the large phone retailers, such as Carphone Warehouse and The Link in the UK, which have a significant share of the consumer mobile phone market in their respective countries and which often sell handsets combined with network contracts under their own brand.

These retailers are usually national in scope, although some have international operations: for example, the UK's DSG group which owns The Link chain in the UK but also has a growing presence throughout Europe.[77] Although handsets and network airtime can be bought by consumers directly or through various other distributors, these retail chains are an important channel for both handset manufacturers and network providers. Pricing in the mobile phone industry is complex and dynamic, both between sellers and various intermediaries in the supply chain, and at the retail level. Networks and retailers typically offer a range of packages, targeted at different market segments and types of user, which combine a handset bundled together with a monthly allowance of calls and other services.

The development of the mobile phone industry (1): networks

Second-generation or 2G digital phone technology replaced first-generation (1G) analogue throughout the early 1990s. GSM was the most common 2G international standard and was adopted throughout Europe and much of the world, except for in the US, which retained its analogue system before adopting a rival digital technology called AMPS digital. 2G was less susceptible to eavesdropping and therefore offered more secure and private communication than 1G. As they used less power, 2G phones and batteries were also smaller and lighter. For most consumers, however, the main advantage of 2G was that it enabled phones to transmit and receive much more data, and therefore provide new

→ Table 3.5 UK mobile phone network operators and resellers market shares

	UK Market Share
Vodafone UK-based network group	24%
O2 Originally owned by British Telecom but later spun off in 2001	23%
Orange Owned by French telecoms group France Telecom	23%
T-Mobile Owned by German telecoms group Deutsche Telekom	17%
'3' 3G network wholly owned by Hong Kong based group, Hutchinson Whampoa	4%
Virgin Mobile (T-Mobile reseller) Acquired by NTL from the Virgin Group in 2007	8%
Tesco (O2 reseller) UK-based supermarket group	**1%**

Notes
Market shares 2004

Source
Compiled from Mintel, 'Mobile phones and network providers', UK, April 2005

services such as limited connection to the internet and, in particular, SMS text messaging, which rapidly become an increasingly popular form of personal communication. As 2G systems developed, the speed and quality of these services improved.

At the beginning of the 2000s, early versions of third-generation (3G) technology followed, offering higher speed and volumes of data transmission, and the promise of new applications including faster internet connection, email, downloads of software, such as music and games, and video telephony.[78] Japan was the first country fully to invest in and roll out 3G technology; by 2005 around 40 per cent of Japanese consumers had adopted it and it was well on the way to replacing 2G. However, the introduction of 3G was held up in other countries by the enormous investment needed by networks to build new infrastructure, the high costs of licences that resulted from governments' desire to gain revenues from what was seen as a booming, profitable industry, and bidding wars between network operators to acquire licences. Although the services it offered improved rapidly, the introduction of early 3G by new operators, such as '3' in the UK, was received with only moderate enthusiasm by consumers, who were at first disappointed by its high price, restricted geographical coverage, and the limitations of its service, which did not always live up to expectations.[79]

The development of the mobile phone industry (2): handsets

Alongside networks, handsets also evolved since the 1980s. After the success of the first cellphone in 1983, Motorola, AT&T, and other American firms were at the forefront of mobile technology. However, other international major consumer electronics manufacturers had also entered this fast growth industry, including Sony and Matsushita (Panasonic) of Japan, Nokia of Finland, Ericsson of Sweden, European giants Philips and Siemens, and South Korean firms LG and Samsung. Although investment in research and development in 1G had given Motorola an early lead, the company failed to innovate and keep pace with the rapid developments in network technology. It was unprepared for the switch to 2G digital and, as a result, between 1995 and 1997, its market share in the US fell sharply and its lead in the world handset market was overtaken by Nokia, which had collaborated in the development of the new standard in Europe.[80]

Throughout the 1980s, advances in high-tech manufacturing meant that many consumer electronics products, including phones, became smaller and lighter. Older 'brick'-style handsets were replaced by slimmer models so that by the early 1990s, mobile phones had become pocket-sized and truly mobile. There →

→ **Table 3.6** Mobile handset manufacturers' global market shares

Nokia	Motorola	Samsung	LG	SonyEricsson	Siemens	Others
32%	18%	12%	7%	7%	4%	20%

Notes
Market shares 2006

Source
Compiled from the following sources: Farhoomand, A. (2006). Case study: 'Motorola in China: Failure of Success?' Industry reports and data from Gartner Dataquest and IDC quoted in case study, Asia Case Research Centre; Gohring, N. (2006). 'Mobile phone sales grow—except in Japan', *Info World*, 22 January 2006 <http://www.infoworld.com>, accessed 11 May 2007

was rapid innovation as the range of choices widened and successive models became ever more sophisticated. Phone design was also driven by the possibilities offered by new technology—it was important for handset manufacturers to innovate in line with the latest developments in networks. Throughout the 1990s, phones evolved to become multifunctional devices offering users more facilities such as the sending of texts, sound and picture files, email, connection to the internet, streaming sound and vision, and built-in features such as cameras and mp3 players. At the same time, hybrid products that combined the functions of an internet-linked handheld computer and a phone also appeared, aimed mainly at business users.

The handset industry is mainly global and driven by continuous, rapid innovation and short life-cycles for individual models against a background of increasingly sophisticated and fickle consumer tastes and falling prices. Competition is fierce. Some major European players such as Philips and Siemens entered the market only to languish with low market shares. In 2001, Sony and Ericsson merged their phone businesses into a joint venture, Sony Ericsson. In emerging markets such as China and India, where the penetration of mobiles was also growing rapidly, competition also came from local handset manufacturers who could copy existing technology and produce models which were less sophisticated, but at much lower prices.

In more developed countries, as technical sophistication and multifunctionality was taken more and more for granted, the focus of competition often became design, styling, and a fashionable brand. Although Nokia had assumed world market leadership, its position was constantly under threat from rivals. These included LG, which was aggressively pursuing a growth strategy worldwide, and, in particular, Samsung, which had made great efforts to reposition its image away from being a manufacturer of low-end electrical goods towards being a stylish, high-tech, upscale global brand. After substantial investment in R&D and product development, Motorola also regained share to again become a contender for leadership in the world market.[81]

Since their introduction, the number of mobile phones sold and their usage worldwide had shown almost constant and rapid growth. As handset prices and call charges continued to fall, mobiles became commonplace and, for many, their main means of personal communication. Business users and young people, for whom a mobile was now an indispensable part of their lifestyle, had been early adopters, but by the early 2000s, what had once been a high-price, high-tech business tool had become a low-price, multifunctional device and fashion accessory used by most people in developed countries every day.

Market maturity and the future

In 2001, world sales of mobiles suffered a fall for the first time. One possible reason for this was that a severe recession in the US and Europe meant that consumers were reluctant to replace their existing handsets. In 2002, sales recovered and continued to rise again (see Table 3.7). But while it seemed that sales in emerging economies, especially those where there was little existing landline infrastructure, were still growing fast, in more developed countries the market for mobiles was showing signs of reaching saturation: according to one report, by the early 2000s several countries, including the UK, had more mobile phones than people.[82]

It was generally expected however, that the market for mobiles would continue to grow as networks, whose revenues from voice calls were levelling off in mature markets, would promote new value-added applications that would encourage consumers to replace and upgrade their phones.[83] Although no-one could predict the future with certainty, there were several broad trends that seemed clear. The first was increasing competition between landlines and mobiles, as landline owners fought to hold on to a declining market share of telephony. Paradoxically, allied to this was the fact that several operators, such as Virgin Mobile in the UK, which had been acquired by cable operator NTL, had interests in both industries and offered consumers combined mobile and →

→ **Table 3.7** Worldwide mobile phone sales (units × 1000), 1998–2006

1998	1999	2000	2001	2002	2003	2004	2005	2006
162,850	283,580	412,730	399,580	431,630	519,980	674,000	805,100	986,500
change %	+74	+46	–	+8	+20	+29	+19	+23

Source
Complied from the following sources: Farhoomand, A. (2006). Case study: 'Motorola in China: Failure of Success?' Industry reports and data from Gartner Dataquest and IDC quoted in case study, Asia Case Research Centre; Gohring, N. (2006). 'Mobile phone sales grow—except in Japan', *Info World*, 22 January 2006 <http://www.infoworld.com>, accessed 11 May 2007; Gohring, N. (2006). 'Mobile phone sales topped 800m in 2005 says IDC', 27 January, <http://www.infoworld.com/article/06/01/27/74861_HNmobilephonesales_1.html>, accessed 11 May 2007

landline deals, so that further integration of the two sectors was also possible.

A second issue was the rapid rise in popularity of VoIP technology, which had appeared in the early 2000s and enabled international phone calls to be made between computers over the internet anywhere in the world for free. Calls could also be routed to landline or mobile phones for an extra charge. The best-known brand in VoIP was Skype which was launched by two engineers in 2003, sold to eBay for US$2.6 billion in 2006, and in 2007 claimed 171 million users and rising, although other rival systems also existed and were gaining in popularity. Some personal computers were now sold with VoIP software already installed.

As a background to all this, there was already an ongoing, overarching trend for the blurring of boundaries between three areas of communications media—television, the internet, and telecoms—as a consequence of the convergence of the technologies behind them. Mobile phones, as well as being a means of personal communication, were rapidly becoming a platform for all kinds of paid-for and advertising-driven streaming and downloadable content, and network providers were increasingly becoming suppliers of integrated multimedia material. Deals between networks and content providers such as web-based companies, TV channels, and music and games publishers were proliferating. New developments in 3G technology and the advent of 4G, promising further integration of broadband wi-fi with existing mobile networks, would also probably accelerate this trend and expand even more the range of services and information that mobiles could offer.

Case study questions

1. How many industries do mobile phone companies belong to?

2. How well does the industry life-cycle model fit the mobile phone industry?

3. How has the nature of competition in mobile phones changed over time. What factors have led to those changes?

4. Why did Sony and Ericsson enter into an alliance to compete in the mobile phone industry? Are they likely to be more or less successful in the future?

● NOTES

1 Pettigrew and Whipp (1991) being two key academics who have demonstrated this. Others have found similarly.

2 *Economist* (2006). 'A survey of logistics: shining examples'. 17 June.

3 At the time of writing these regulations are being rewritten.

4 *Economist* (1999). 'Let's keep it clean'. 17 April: 70–71.

5 For a review of how global warming affects businesses, see Lash and Wellington (2007).

6 Tsiko, S. (2006). 'Africa must resist pressure over GMOs'. *All Africa*. 24 July.

7 Toner, M. (2006). 'Modified crops' usage grows'. *The Atlanta Journal*, Constitution, 14 May.

8 Spender (1989).

9 The importance of the scope and resource dimension to this analysis was established by Cool and Schendel (1988). For a discussion of the problems associated with strategic groups analysis, and the insights it can offer, see Feigenbaum et al. (1988), Flaviàn et al. (1999), Katobe and Duhan (1993), Lawless et al. (1989) and McGee et al. (1995).

10 This was pointed out by Porac et al. (1989) and Reger and Huff (1993).

11 Hofer (1975) went so far as to propose the life-cycle as a fundamental framework for predicting how firms would behave.

12 The importance of legitimation and the liability of newness was identified by Hannan and Freeman (1977, 1984, 1989) and other members of the organizational ecology school of sociology, such as Hannan and Carroll (1992); Amburgey et al. (1993), and Hannan et al. (1995). These same theorists emphasize the role of inertia later in the life-cycle.

13 See Derajtys et al. (1993) Klepper and Simons (1996). Lenox et al. (2007) have shown that different industries are likely to have different rates of shakeout, depending upon the complexity of decision-making within them.

14 This addition to the theory of the industry life-cycle comes from Anita McGahan (2000, 2004).

15 For a more general discussion of the contribution of industrial economies to strategic management theory, see Porter (1979, 1980); Brandenburger and Nalebuff (1996).

16 In his 2001 article Porter differentiates between channels and end users, which together make up buyer power.

17 See Henderson and Clark (1990). See also Nelson (1995) and Christensen (1993).

18 Brandenburger and Nalebuff (1996).

19 Porter (2001). He says that complementors (or as he terms it, 'complements') affect industry profitability indirectly through their influence on the five competitive forces, rather than directly, as for example substitutes do. 'If a complement raises switching costs for the combined product offering, it can raise profitability. But if a complement works to standardize the industry's product offering, as Microsoft's operating system has done in personal computers, it will increase rivalry and depress profitability.' He further claims that alliances with complementors may exacerbate an industry's structural problems. Instead of focusing on their own strategic goals, firms have to balance their own goals with the potentially conflicting objectives of their partners while also educating them about the business. As a result, rivalry increases and becomes more unstable, and as complementors learn about the business, the threat of entry increases.

20 Prospero, M. (2006). 'The PS3 economy'. *Fast Company*, 110 (November): 28.

21 Tran, K. (2001). 'How Microsoft hopes to win with Xbox'. *Wall Street Journal*, 31 January: B1.

22 See, for example, Rindova et al. (2004).

23 Yoffie, D. (2004). 'Cola wars continue: Coke and Pepsi in the twenty-first century'. *Harvard Business School*, case no. 9-702-442.

24 See for example Arthur (1996), D'Aveni (1994), and Vandemerwe (1997).

25 Miller, M. J. (2005). 'Twenty years of Windows'. *PC Magazine*, 24/19–20.

26 Greene et al. (2004).

27 Wigfield, M. (2001). 'A primer on the Microsoft antitrust case settlement'. *Dow Jones Newswires*, 15 November; Warsh, D. (2001). 'Fighting back'. *Boston Globe*, 6 November: D.1; Krim, J. (2004). 'Microsoft settlement upheld: appeal for tougher sanctions rejected'. *Washington Post*, 1 July: E01; Clark, D. and Greenberger, R. (2004). 'Microsoft wins approval of pact in antitrust case'. *Wall Street Journal*, 1 July: A3.

28 The term 'hypercompetition' appears to have been created by Richard D'Aveni (1994, 1995) with a very specific meaning in mind, although it has since gone into common parlance to indicate a settings where there are very competitive conditions. See also Volberda (1996); Smith and Zeithaml (1996); Gimeno and Woo (1996); Ilinitch and Lewin (1995); Ilinitch et al. (1998); Young et al. (1997); and Zohar and Morgan (1998).

29 Thomas (1996).

30 See McNamara et al. (2003). For another viewpoint see McKinley (2000), who suggests that hypercompetition may be, at least partly, a management 'fad' whose proponents are management consultants with an interest in persuading their clients of the need for change.

31 McKinley (2000); Brown and Eisenhardt (1997); Eisenhardt and Brown (1998); Eisenhardt and Tabrizi (1995). Particularly interesting is the competition between IT firms for human resources (Gardner, 2005).

32 Reuters (2001). 'Company that made PlayStation emulator shuts down'. 19 November.

33 Economist (2004). 'A serious contest—video games'. 8 May.

34 Porter (1985), ch. 6.

35 Brandenberger and Nalebuff (1997); Burton (1995).

36 This example is quoted in the *Encyclopaedia Britannica* (2000).

37 See Barney (2002), ch. 10, for a good discussion of the economics of cooperation and collusion.

38 See also Barney (1986a); Henderson and Mitchell (1997); McGahan and Porter (1997); Mauri and Michaels (1998); McGahan (1999).

39 McDonald's Corporation 2005 Financial Report.

40 See <http://usgovinfo.about.com/od/censusandstatistics/>. The USA's Department of Commerce Census Bureau produces federal statistics on a wide variety of cultural and economic issues. See <http://www.aaas.org/spp/rd/04pch22.htm> for a summary of the various agencies. The equivalent source in the UK is the Office of National Statistics which publishes reports through the Department of Trade and Industry (DTI). *Social Trends*, published by the Policy Studies Institute, also details major social and economic trends in the UK. To carry out a PESTLE analysis properly you will have to use multiple sources, including government data as well as the company's own publications, competitors' publications, and newspaper articles.

41 Steven Gray (2004). 'Midnight snack: fast-food spots serve all night'. *The Wall Street Journal*, 15 July.

42 Defining Hispanic and other non-white groups as minorities is rather inaccurate; in some states they are the majority population.

43 McDonald's Corporation 2005 Financial Report, p. 23.

44 Benoit, B., Roberts, D., Silverman, D., and Thornhill, J. (2004). 'US brand giants suffer a sales slump in "old Europe"'. *Financial Times*, 25 October.

45 Nancy Luna (2006). 'Handshake helped seal supplier's future'. *Orange County Register*, 14 July.

46 Ibid.

47 Adamy, J. (2006). 'Giant woos McDonald's to serve its ketchup again'. *The Wall Street Journal*, 28 June.

48 Prewitt, M. (2004). 'Top 10 restaurant trends. (2004 the Year in Review)'. *Nation's Restaurant News*, 20 December.

49 Prewitt (2004), op. cit.

50 McClary, S. (2006). 'Don't think Big Mac, think McProperty'. *Estates Gazette*, 11 March.

51 'Fitch Initiates Burger King Corporation IDR at "B+"; outlook positive'. *Business Wire*, 21 June 2006.

52 McClary (2006) op. cit.

53 'Major chains post biggest market share increases in 2005'. *Nation's Restaurant News*, 19 December 2005: 18.

54 Foust, D., Grow, B., Cowan, C., and Arndt, M. (2006). 'Where's the beef? Burger King's upcoming IPO looks lucrative . . . for the private-equity firms doing the deal'. *BusinessWeek*, 3979, 10 April: 30.

55 Arlidge, J. and Rogers, L. (2006). 'Big Mac bites back as salad drive wilts'. *Sunday Times*, 21 May: News 5; *Economist* (2005). 'Junior fat—obesity and advertising'. 17 December.

56 Jeitschko, T. D.; Pecchenino, R. A. (2006). 'Do you want fries with that? An exploration of serving size, social welfare, and our waistlines'. *Economic Inquiry*, 44/3: 442.

57 Foust et al. (2006) op. cit.

58 This dates back to Dess and Beard (1984). For discussion of the effects of industry complexity on profitability, see Dooley et al. (1996); Hatten and Schendel (1977); and Miles et al. (1993).

59 *Economist* (2005). 'Business past, business future—takeover of Marconi'. 29 October.

60 *Economist* (2005) op. cit.

61 Barker, T., Daniel, C., and French, P. (2001a). 'Marching the shares to the top of the hill'. *Financial Times*, 23 June.

62 Daniel, C. (2001a). 'Marconi writes off $4.5bn for goodwill'. *Financial Times*, 14 November.

63 Daniel, C. (2001). 'Downbeat Marconi lays its bad news on the line'. *Financial Times*, 14 November.

64 *Economist* (2002). 'No end in sight—the telecoms slump'. 4 May.

65 See, for example, 'The race to gather a digital arsenal'. *Financial Times*, 28 April 1999; Hunt, B. (2002). 'British patient in poor health'. *Financial Times*. 28 August; Barker et al. (2001a) op. cit.

66 Daniel, C. (2001). 'The wisdom of gatecrashing the US when the bullish party is over'. *Financial Times*, 7 April.

67 Barker, T., Bickerton, I., and Hunt, B. (2001b). 'Buyer's market makes Philips the winner'. *Financial Times*, 5 July.

68 Hunt (2002) op. cit.

69 Hunt, B. (2004). 'Dream team's error that led to Marconi's fall'. *Financial Times*, 1 November.

70 Plender, J. (2002). 'Mayo's handy guide to Marconi's road to ruin—no accounting for lost shirts'. *Financial Times*, 19 January.

71 O'Brien, L. (2001). 'Desperate Marconi fights to survive after £5bn loss'. *The Engineer*, 16 November.

72 Barker et al. (2001b) op. cit.; Burt, T., Hunt, B., and Ratner, J. (2002). 'Marconi talks stalled over holders' stake'. *Financial Times*, 17 August.

73 Barker et al. (2001a) and Wilson, R. (2001). 'Games in the boardroom'. *Electronic News*, 47/39: 8.

74 SRI Policy Division (1998). 'The Cellular Telephone'. In *The Role of NSF's Support of Engineering in Enabling Technological Innovation, Phase 2*. <http://www.sri.com>, accessed 11 May 2007.

75 Alcatel Lucent. 'Bell Labs historical timeline', Alcatel Lucent website <http://www.alcatel-lucent.com>, accessed 11 May 2007; AT&T website <http://www.corp.att.com/attlabs>, accessed 11 May 2007.

76 Vodafone website <http://online.vodafone.co.uk/dispatch/Portal/appmanager/vodafone/wrp; wrpsessionid=GW1BTxwbBhw3JPTP0ms1mnJx1GtJD9mm0pmmBYmb2hMQ>, accessed 14 May 2007.

77 DSG Group website <http://www.dsgiplc.com/layout.aspx?ID=4a617bad-1028-486a-a799-b6a045b5e6c5&CatID=8bda4c13-0c51-4a78-aa94-827b1d8350b0>, accessed 24 May 2007.

78 Ali, F. and Sethi, K. (2006). Case study: 'Motorola in China: failure of success?'. Appendix A, Asia Case Research Centre.

79 Ward, M. (2003). 'Mixed messages for mobiles'. <http://news.bbc.co.uk/1/hi/technology/2587247.stm>, accessed 11.5.2007.

80 Ali and Sethi (2006) op. cit.

81 Leydon, J. (2006). 'Big six dominate expanding mobile phone market'. *The Register*, 28 February, <http://www.theregister.co.uk/2006/02/28/gartner_mobile_market_2006/>, accessed 11 May 2007.

82 14 CIA World Factbook, April 2007, <http://www.cia.gov>, accessed 11 May 2007.

83 Jacques, R. (2007). 'Global phone sales top $115bn'. *IT Week*, 25 January, <http://www.vnunet.com/vnunet/news/2173442/global-mobile-phone-sales-top>, accessed 24 May 2007.

CHAPTER FOUR

Distinctiveness (1)
Competitive Stance

After reading this chapter you should be able to:

→ Explain the concept of customer segmentation and why it is important

→ Appraise an organization's distinctive choices of customer segment and product, and their contribution to the success and failure of its individual businesses

→ Explain the concept of a generic strategy, summarize the different classifications of generic strategy that have been proposed, and discuss their limitations.

INTRODUCTION

In Chapter 2, we noted how important it was that an organization's strategy was distinctive in some way. We also saw that distinctiveness can be recognized at two levels: in its competitive stance— the elements of strategy that are visible to customers—and in its value chain and architecture, the elements of strategy that are apparent only to people inside the organization, and to outside observers who know the company very well.

In this chapter we start to consider the effect of some of the basic strategic choices available to firms. We begin by looking at how organizations decide which customer groupings they wish to target. We then show how a firm can seek to gain advantage by developing products to satisfy the requirements of its target segments, and by positioning those products successfully, in the eyes of those customers, in terms of price and quality. We go on to look at ways in which it can position itself relative to its competitors.

4.1 Competitive stance: the right market for the right product

One of the classic questions that managers are supposed to ask themselves about their organization's strategy is 'Which business are we in?' The answer to this question—and to the related question, '*How many* businesses are we in, and how do they connect to one another?'—is what we term the organization's competitive stance. Companies cannot do everything: their value chains, cultures, architectures, and resources are not infinitely versatile, and will be more suited to one type of operation or market than another. This makes an organization's choices of competitive stance—which customers to serve and which products or services to offer them—the most fundamental of its strategic decisions.[1]

These decisions can be visualized, as in Figure 4.1, as an arrow being directed towards a target. The target comprises the organization's customers: markets that are attractive and that the organization can service effectively. The organization tries to 'hit' that target with its products and services by making them attractive to those markets. To do this it uses its value chain (see Chapter 6), the shaft of the arrow that conveys the arrowhead towards the target, of which the resources (Chapter 7) are a crucial element. The feathered part of the arrow, the

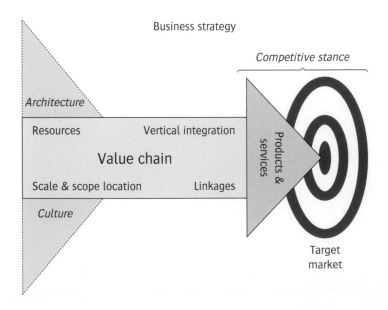

Figure 4.1 Business-level strategy

flight, is the organization's architecture and culture, which give it direction and shapes what it can or cannot do. We discuss these in Chapter 8.

Marketing theorists typically recommend that firms should be market-driven:[2] they should begin by defining their target market and the needs of the customer, and then work out which products and services should be offered to satisfy those needs. Quite often, however, and quite legitimately, businesses start the other way around, with an idea for a product, and their managers then work out whom to sell it to. It is indeed vital that the organization arrives at a fit between the products it offers and the needs of the customers it is serving—but, as Real-life Application 4.1 shows, there may be quite a long period of trial and error before it gets to that point. Once it has done so, and has experience of who its customers are and what preferences they display, it becomes much easier for a firm to become market-driven.

Real-life Application 4.1 How Sony built its competitive advantage[3]

The company that is now Sony Corporation was founded in 1946 by Akio Morita and Masura Ibuka, who had worked together researching weapons' systems during the Second World War. From the beginning, their aims stressed innovation and the common good, including:

- establishing an ideal factory, emphasizing a spirit of freedom and open-mindedness, where engineers with sincere motivation could exercize their technological skills to the highest level;
- reconstructing Japan and elevating the nation's culture through dynamic technological and manufacturing activities;
- giving Japan's civilian population speedy access to advanced technologies developed during the war.

Morita's father helped with funds derived from the family saké business, but components were in short supply, so the two engineers had to rely on their own ingenuity. The tape in the firm's first successful product, Japan's first tape recorder, was originally made of paper, because of a shortage of plastic.

Because there was no obvious market for Ibuka's rather expensive tape recorder, it fell to Morita to find one. One of the first markets turned out to be Japan's courts of justice, which were suffering from a shortage of people to take notes of proceedings.

On a trip to research the US tape-recorder industry Morita and Ibuka came across a new concept, the transistor, for which they were able to obtain a licence, though Bell Labs, its inventor, famously believed its only commercial application was in hearing aids.

The firm had originally aimed to produce radio and communications devices and measuring equipment. However, its initial successes with tape recorders and its good fortune in getting access to transistor technology led to further developments in audio-visual products. It introduced Japan's first transistor radio in 1955, its first pocket-sized radio (the world's smallest) in 1957, and the world's first transistor television in 1960. Other innovations in video-cassette recorders and colour television manufacture followed during the 1960s and 1970s. In 1979 it launched one of its most famous innovations, the Walkman.

Sony decided early on that it would benefit from an international presence. Sony Corporation of America was founded in 1960 and Sony Overseas SA the following year. During the early 1970s it opened a TV-manufacturing facility in the USA and the UK. Overseas subsidiaries were usually run by managers from the countries in question, who were given a lot of autonomy. It was felt that this was the best way to ensure sensitivity to local market and employment practices. This policy seemed to work well, and by the early 1980s, over 75 per cent of Sony's turnover derived from outside Japan. Morita himself lived in the USA for 11 years to enhance his understanding of this key market, and overseas experience became the norm for rising Sony executives.

In some cases, the starting point is an idea of how the value chain will be distinctive; the organization then works out which kinds of product and market will fit it. For example, Amazon, the world's leading internet retailer, began in 1995 when its founder Jeff Bezos, realized that the World Wide Web, then in its early days, presented commercial opportunities. He concluded that books, which people did not need to touch or see before they bought them, would be the ideal product to sell via the internet, and would appeal to the affluent, educated people who were the early users of the Web. Later, Amazon was able to expand its product range to include CDs, electronic goods, and a large range of other items, while the numbers of potential customers expanded as more people acquired internet connections at work and at home.

Regardless of the route that a firm takes to arriving at a viable competitive stance, if we want to understand the basis of its competitive success or failure, an important starting point is to analyse the characteristics of its customers and the precise ways in which its products fulfil their requirements. In the next section, we look at segmentation, an important step in identifying suitable customers and their needs.

4.2 Understanding customers: segmentation

In Section 1.3.7 we introduced the concept of a customer segment—a group of customers with common characteristics. The classification of markets into segments—segmentation —has been a well-known aspect of marketing and strategy theory and practice for many years.[4] It can be applied to individuals, businesses, countries, or any other type of targeting which might underpin a firm's business strategies. When we analyse an organization's past strategy, we can learn a lot about the source, and the strength, of its competitive advantage through an examination of:

- the segments to which it has paid particular attention;
- the precision with which it has tailored its products to the needs of those target segments.

But we start by investigating the concept of segmentation in greater depth.

4.2.1 What do we mean by a segment?

Segments can be groups of individuals, for business to consumer ('B2C') markets, or groups of organizations in business to business ('B2B') markets. The most common characteristics used to distinguish segments in each case are shown in Table 4.1.[5]

Table 4.1 Segmentation variables for consumer and business markets

Consumer characteristic	Examples	Business characteristic	Examples
Geographic	Country of residence; region, district, or town; rural or urban; government housing or privately owned	Geographic	Country or region of operation; location of unit placing the order
Demographic	Age; gender; race; religion; nationality; marital status; family size; educational level; employment type; income	Demographic	Industry; firm size; ownership (private, quoted, public sector)
Psychographic	Social class; life-style; personality; ethical stance	Operations	Technology used; number of services required; technological sophistication
Behavioural	Purchasing pattern; brand loyalty; attitude towards novelty (early adopters, laggards, or main-streamers); taste preferences; product benefits required	Purchasing approach	Preference for: leasing or rental; sealed bidding; service contracts
			Degree of loyalty shown to suppliers. Price sensitivity; requirements regarding quality and service
		Situation	Profitability; cash strength; degree of urgency of requirement
		Cultural	Power structure: engineering, finance or marketing-led Similarity with 'our' firm

Real-life Application 4.2 gives an example of a psychographic and behavioural segmentation of food consumers in Europe. Typically, data like these are combined with geographic and demographic information (much of which is publicly available from government statistics) to give a rounded picture of the numbers, location, spending power, product preferences, and buying and distribution channel preferences of individuals in a segment. The basis of segmentation theory is the assumption that these individuals have some psychological characteristics in common and therefore behave in predictable ways.

The research described in Real-life Application 4.2 has discovered which behavioural patterns are most prevalent amongst which countries' food consumers. This helps us judge whether, for example, a supermarket chain like Carrefour, originally French but with a presence in Italy, Spain, and several other countries, is pursuing the right strategy to attract consumers in each of those places. Equally, it enables us to assess whether a firm like Germany's Aldi, which targets 'price-led' shoppers, has chosen to enter the most appropriate geographic markets.

Real-life Application 4.2 Consumer segments for food retailers in Europe[6]

'**Eat to Live**' place a low priority on food. Do little planning for food shopping, do not look out for special offers or the cheapest price, have little time to prepare and cook fresh food, tend not to try new recipes or products.

'**Open Mouthed**' are open to trying new products, enjoy eating foreign or takeaway food and snacking; like to treat themselves to food that is not good for them.

'**Traditionalists**' do not enjoy foreign food or takeaway meals. Not tempted by new products.

'**Price Led**' always look for the lowest prices or special offers and are very organized in planning their shopping, but are quite adventurous in trying out new products.

'**Quality Seekers**' like to buy free-range products whenever they can, avoid genetically modified food, and will pay a premium for organic food. Like trying new recipes and enjoy eating foreign food.

France has the most demanding consumers, with above-average proportions of Price Led and Quality Seekers.

German consumers show the least interest in food and shopping for groceries, and the Spanish are the most traditional in their attitudes. The combined Eat to Live and Traditionalist segments constitute a large majority of consumers in both countries.

The British are the most adventurous in terms of trying new food products, giving themselves treats and responding to advertising, and have the highest proportion of Open-Mouthed consumers.

Through a similar process, involving a review of the numbers, sizes, profitability, and other characteristics of businesses in the relevant segments, it is possible to appraise the strategy of a firm operating in B2B markets.

Not all segments cross national borders, because cultural differences, and disparities in countries' levels of economic or social development, may lead to large variations in consumer preferences and firm buying behaviours. However, there appears to be a convergence in the types of product that consumers in different countries demand as their income levels increase. Some of the most expensive products, Gucci clothing or Rolex watches for example, are not modified to cater for country differences. Consumers who regularly purchase these types of branded items have more in common with each other, across national boundaries, than they do with other groups of people in their own countries.

4.2.2 Why the right segmentation is important

Segmentation is a compromise between two ideals: customization and mass marketing. If firms were able to produce exactly the right product for each customer's unique needs, they could, in theory, attract everyone. The use of the internet for order-taking, combined with modern, flexible manufacturing systems, has made this 'mass customization' much easier to manage than previously, and in certain industries, such as PC manufacture, knowledgeable customers are able to specify a product pretty well according to their needs and budget.[7] However, complete customization of products is generally very expensive, so that the prices of fully customized items, such as bespoke clothing and shoes, are unaffordable for most consumers.

The alternative ideal is to find a single, uniform, product that would please every conceivable customer. As we discuss in Chapter 5, there are dangers involved in trying to do this—a product designed to be acceptable to everyone may end up pleasing no-one completely. Nevertheless, in the industries that come closest to this ideal, such as microprocessors, soft drinks, or fast food, very similar products—Intel processors or McDonald's hamburgers—are sold to customers with a wide variety of demographic and geographic characteristics. However, both Intel and McDonald's find that there are firms or people that simply will not or cannot buy their products. In Intel's case this may be because they need processors with particular characteristics, whilst in the case of McDonald's they may have specific dietary preferences, needs, or allergies. And there are some people who may avoid both firms because, for emotional or philosophical reasons, they feel uncomfortable about giving money to large US corporations.

So even the broadest-based of firms arrives at a point where it satisfies only a certain proportion of the population—a particular segment, or set of segments—with its existing products. If the firm understands the characteristics of those segments, and can refine its products so that they match the needs of the people or firms within them, then it will be better able to attract and retain customers. A successful product or service—the McDonald's Happy Meal, the Sony PlayStation, an item of H&M clothing or BA Business Class—is invariably conceived with the needs of a particular type of buyer in mind. Other people may buy it, and in doing so open up new markets for the firm that supplies it, but if it is not designed specifically for somebody, then there is a strong danger it will not be bought by anybody.

Understanding the needs of customers in different segments, and their readiness to pay to have those needs satisfied, can also enhance profits for an airline such as British Airways (Real-life Application 4.3).[8] In the early days of their industry, airlines did not have a

Real-life Application 4.3 Segmentation and profitability: a fictional example based on the airline industry

Without segmentation

A long-haul plane bound for China has space for 260 passengers, each of whom pays the same price, €1,500. If the airline achieved an 80 per cent load factor at this price, the profit from this trip would be €147,440.

However, a price of €1,500 is already too much for some travellers with limited budgets, whilst corporate or wealthy travellers might be prepared to pay much more to achieve the quality levels they desire, thus ...

With segmentation

If customers are segmented into four categories, wealthy and top managers (first class), corporate customers (business class),

price-sensitive business (premium economy), and tourists (economy class), profits can be increased by nearly one quarter to €182,420, even though the number of places on the plane must be reduced to allow for sleeper seats and extra leg-room for premium passengers. Price-insensitive first-class passengers will now be prepared to pay €4,500 for their tickets—three times the undifferentiated price. On the other hand, the price for budget travellers can be reduced to €1,200, which boosts the load factor on the flight, particularly if seats that are unfilled shortly before the departure date are sold off at further discounted prices. Table 4.2 summarizes these calculations. The needs of each different customer group are better achieved, increasing their levels of satisfaction, and making it more likely that the flight will be filled and that passengers will fly again with the airline in the future.

Table 4.2 Effects of segmentation on profits

Class	Tickets sold (Capacity)	Price	Variable unit cost	Revenue	Total variable cost	Gross margin
Without segmentation	208 (260)	1,500	70	312,000	14,560	297,440
With segmentation						
Economy	(126)					
Full price	88	1,200	70	105,600	6,160	99,440
Discounted and standby	25	800	70	20,000	1,750	18,250
Premium Economy	35 (35)	1,500	90	52,500	3,150	49,350
Business	43 (48)	2,800	140	120,400	6,020	114,380
First	12 (14)	4,500	250	54,000	3,000	51,000
Total	203 (223)			352,500	20,080	332,420

Total profit after deducting fixed costs of 150,000:

without segmentation: 147,440

with segmentation: 182,420

Note
All prices in €

sophisticated understanding of the needs of their passengers. Over time they became aware that some people were prepared to pay much more than others; thus first-class and economy class seats were born. Subsequently this classification was divided yet further to add a business class, although initially only on some routes. Business travellers valued convenience, comfort, and space to work; they seldom paid for their own tickets, so the price was of less importance. In contrast, leisure travellers wanted cheap tickets, and because they did not fly often were prepared to suffer the loss of comfort on the relatively rare occasions that they travelled. Using differential price/quality mixes allowed airlines to increase profits.

Nowadays, airlines use sophisticated 'yield management systems' to refine their segmentation strategies further. By adjusting the prices at which seats are sold, according to number of seats available on the flight and the length of time left before take-off, they are able to profit from sub-segments with particular behavioural characteristics. Those who prefer to plan ahead may pay a slightly higher price for the security of an advanced booking—or, if they are lucky, get a good price for being the first bookers on an empty flight. Highly price-sensitive customers may be prepared to wait until the last minute in order to get a cheap seat, and to take the risk of not being able to find a place on their preferred flight.

In so doing, the airlines are able to maximize the revenue generated on each flight. But it also enables them to combat, in part, the threat from new airlines, such as Ryanair and EasyJet, which have entered the industry targeting price-sensitive customers. Their rise demonstrates the risk inherent in any segmentation strategy: that competitors may target, and grow strong in, the segments to which a firm chooses to give little attention. McDonald's strategy leaves room for competitors that target vegetarians or people who are allergic to the gluten in burger buns.

An organization that has done well in one segment thus faces difficult choices about how to deal with others. Does it enter those segments, and risk losing its focus on existing customers, or does it leave them open to other firms, and risk allowing a potential competitor to flourish? We investigate the risks and trade-offs attached to these choices in more detail in

Chapter 5, but Real-life Application 4.3 illustrates two things an organization needs to bear in mind when deciding whether to target a segment:

- It must be possible to tailor the products and services offered to the demands of the segment. There would have been no point in identifying the three segments if the company had not been able to adapt its offer to the demands of the three different types of customer. No-one would pay a first-class fare if the service was little different from that in economy or business class. In fact, several airlines stopped offering first-class travel because they were not able to differentiate it from business class, or did not think that it was worthwhile to do so.

 We look at the concept of differentiation in more detail in Section 4.2.4.

- The segments chosen must be in some way attractive—it must be possible to serve them at a profit. The customers for first class are attractive because of their spending power, those for business class because their particular needs for comfort make them price-insensitive, and those for tourist class because there are lots of them. There are a number of attributes like this that might make a segment attractive (see Table 4.3); in the next section we examine them in more detail.

4.2.3 Segment choice and competitive advantage

As we noted in Section 4.1, although we talk about organizations 'choosing' a segment, in fact it may discover its markets through trial and error, as with Sony in Real-life Application 4.1. Sometimes, however, such choices are deliberate (Real-Life Application 4.4).

Real-life Application 4.4 Choices of segment

Holiday Inn was the first chain of hotels designed for families. They offered features such as swimming pools and air conditioning which, when the firm was founded in the USA in 1951, were only available in expensive, upmarket establishments. They were cleaner, more luxurious, but also more affordable than the motels of the day, which made a surcharge for children sharing their parents' rooms. Kemmons Wilson, the company's founder, had a clear idea of what made his segment attractive. 'You can cater to rich people and I'll take the rest. The good Lord made more of them', he is reported to have said.[9]

The Body Shop, a British manufacturer and retailer of toiletries based on natural ingredients, targets the environmentally concerned consumer. This was a segment which no-one believed existed when the firm was started in 1971. Anita Roddick, the company's founder, started the business while her husband was away on a lengthy trip across South America.[10] She sold natural beauty products that she had encountered on her own travels, reasoning that if she liked them, some other people would too. This can be seen as having some elements of an emergent choice of segment, since no-one had any real idea of how large and attractive the segment would turn out to be, or what were the demographic or other characteristics of the customers within it.

From their different beginnings, both The Body Shop and Holiday Inn became substantial multinational concerns with a presence in around fifty countries.

A useful feature of a strategic analysis is an examination of why an organization's choices of market segment were effective, and how they contributed to its success. The characteristics that make a market segment desirable, and potentially profitable, are shown in Table 4.3.

Kemmons Wilson chose for Holiday Inn a broad segment, containing a lot of customers, because it offered the promise of substantial profits. Firms in industries such as automobiles, toiletries, and pharmaceuticals, have decided to target the Chinese and Indian markets for this reason, even though the people and firms there have limited spending power at present. By developing low-priced offerings specifically for these segments, companies aim to tap into the 'fortune at the bottom of the pyramid'.[11] Intel and McDonald's, in very different ways, have settled upon global market segments containing large numbers of customers

Table 4.3 What makes a segment attractive

If a segment is . . .	. . . then it is attractive because
Broad and homogeneous	It offers a large market that can be served at low cost
Easily accessible	Firms can gain competitive advantage by offering customers in that segment more responsive service or better tailored products
Easily served through existing value chain	Firms can serve the market without incurring large extra costs, and gain economies of scope
Affluent	There is the potential for substantial sales if customer needs can be met precisely
Not price-sensitive	It offers the potential for high margins
Potentially brand loyal	Customers can be retained once they have been won
Overlooked by competitors	Barriers to entry are lower and there may be willing customers waiting

and end-users. A broad segment like this is only truly attractive, however, if it is homogeneous—the customers within it all have similar tastes and preferences. This means that they can be satisfied with a limited product range, or using a single value chain, which means that a company can look forward to potential economies of scale. (We look at this type of strategy, and the risks involved, more closely in Chapter 5.)

Not all segments are equally desirable to all firms. Some may be particularly attractive to firms that find them easily accessible. One way in which new firms can get started, and may be able to defend their position afterwards, is by targeting segments to which they have ready access, for example because they are located close by or because their staff have good contacts with potential customers. This enables them to understand the needs of those customers more precisely, and respond to them more quickly, than their more distant competitors. The Body Shop started by targeting people who thought like Anita Roddick—which turned out to be a far larger segment than anyone suspected.

An established firm, on the other hand, may decide to target a segment because it can be easily served through the existing value chain—for example, because the distribution channels are already in place. If organizations can use existing resources to serve the new segment, they will have low start-up costs and will be able to use those resources more intensively, improving the return on the capital invested in them, and generating economies of scope. For example, in its 2000 Annual Report, H&M defined its core customers as 'fashion-conscious women from 18 to 45 years of age—or who feel that they belong in that age range'. By 2003, it had broadened the overall target to 'fashion-conscious and fashion-aware women of all ages' with mention of a range of sub-segments within this broad category: those who want to wear the most up-to-date international fashions; those who prefer classic fashion; pregnant women; and 'plus-sized' women. It also offers ranges of products for male and teenage customers. There is a great deal of commonality between the value chains used to serve these different markets. H&M can use the same network of suppliers of finished garments, the same distribution systems and, at least to begin with, some of the same shops, although it is now starting to roll out specialist stores for teenagers and other specific markets. Only at the design stage is it likely to need separate resources for the different markets. This is not to say that the strategy is risk-free. Sales space that is being used for plus-sized women or teenagers is space that cannot be used for classic women's fashion. H&M has to be careful that sales into the new markets do not squeeze out more profitable products aimed at the traditional core customer.

If the people or firms in a segment are affluent, with a lot of spending power, then this is likely to make the segment a desirable target, and may compensate for it being small in terms of numbers of customers. Mercedes and Gucci both have target segments of this kind. However, not all affluent segments are small. Marketing theorists have identified the emergence in the developed economies, in particular the US, of what has been termed the 'mass affluent': a large proportion of the population with substantial disposable income, who are happy to pay substantial price premiums for products that offer significant user benefits over and above standard products, without being as expensive as out-and-out luxury items.[12]

Any segment becomes still more attractive if, as well as being wealthy, the target customers are, like the mass affluent, not price-sensitive, so that they are willing to pay the price premiums that a firm must charge if it is to offer a differentiated service and still make a decent return. But this is not always the case: one of the ways in which affluent firms and individuals can become rich is by being tough negotiators on price. On the other hand, customers with relatively low incomes can, in countries like the UK or Japan, be willing to pay quite high prices for items they think are essential, such as 'cool' brands of designer clothing or sportswear, or for satellite dishes offering access to extra TV channels.

Brand loyal customers also make a segment particularly attractive, since firms that can rely upon repeat business from existing customers are able to economize on marketing costs and are also likely to have a lower risk of failure when introducing new products.[13] It is not always possible to anticipate this in advance of market entry but it is possible for an analyst, looking back, to see how this attribute of a segment becomes part of a firm's competitive advantage. A company with established brands may also be able to target its existing, brand-loyal customers when it enters a new industry. The UK's Virgin Group targets many of its varied products, such as cosmetics, cola, contraceptives, and financial services, at a youngish customer group that it believes is loyal to its brand values.

 Using Evidence 4.1 Indicators of market segment attractiveness

There are a variety of quantitative indicators you can look for to measure the attractiveness of a market that an organization has entered, or is thinking of entering:

- The profit margins of existing competitors in the segment. Clearly, if the majority of existing players have been able to enjoy high operating profit margins, then it is probable that new entrants with the right resources can do likewise, as long as the segment does not become overcrowded.

- The population of a segment, and the spending power of the individuals or firms in it. This may be crudely measured by GDP or, in B2B markets, by the total turnover (or better the total 'cost of goods sold', which shows how much is spent with suppliers) of the potential target businesses. In many cases, there will be more precise data available from national statistics or company accounts, showing, for example, what proportion of household expenditure is on food, or how much firms are spending on sales and general expenses.

- The rate of growth, actual and/or projected, of a market segment.

Remember, however, that not all market opportunities are equally accessible to every firm. Beware, then, of an apparently attractive market where one or two players are enjoying good profits while the others are struggling, since this may indicate that unusual and rare resources, or customer linkages, are needed to succeed. It can be difficult to work what these are—and whether your firm possesses them—until you actually begin trying to sell in the market-place in question. Beware also of a situation where profit margins are high but sales volumes are so low that it is difficult to earn a good return on the capital invested in a market place.

A segment may be attractive simply because it has been ignored or overlooked by competitors. Holiday Inn and The Body Shop both found segments like these, as we discuss in Real-life Application 4.4. Ryanair, a leading low-cost rival of British Airways, was able to penetrate the airline industry in the early 1990s by focusing on the needs of Irish people living in the UK who wanted to visit their friends and relatives in Ireland. These people tended not to be particularly affluent and were highly price-sensitive. They were not well catered for by mainstream airlines, since the conventional wisdom in the airline industry at that time was that profits came from serving the needs of business travellers. Ryanair developed a highly efficient value chain that enabled it to offer very low fares to these price-sensitive Irish customers, and still operate profitably. It was then able to extend its operations into other market segments, such as young international holidaymakers, and was at the time of writing the most profitable airline in Europe.

4.2.4 Targeting a segment: product choices

In our discussion of segmentation, we have frequently referred to the idea of 'serving' or 'targeting' a segment. This, in practice, involves offering products or services that appeal to the firms or individuals in those segments, developing marketing activities to convince the customer of the products' attractions, and finding a sales channel that is appropriate to the segment. In this section, we examine the various ways in which an organization can distinguish its products or services from those of other firms that are targeting the same group of customers. This involves positioning the product, or the firm, so that the customer can see a benefit from it over a competitor, which in turn implies some form of differentiation.[14]

a. Forms of differentiation[15]

Customers can be persuaded to buy a product if they find the product itself attractive, and/or if they find reasons for wishing to be associated with the organization that is providing it. Table 4.4 summarizes the different types of differentiation relating to the product and the firm:

- Functionality—a product or service has superior functionality if it offers things that few others do. British Airways attempts to attract business and first-class passengers on its long-haul flights by offering seats that fold down to make a flat bed and scheduling its London-bound flights so as to offer travellers an extra hour's sleep. Google, a leading on-line search service, launched a free email service, G-mail, that was differentiated by offering users so much storage in their on-line mailbox that they need never again worry about deleting messages to save space. However, at the time of writing, Virgin and United Airlines, for example, both claim to offer wider or longer sleeper seats than BA's, while Yahoo and other competitors now offer free email services with as much storage as G-mail. This illustrates how difficult it can be to sustain differentiation based on functionality alone.

- Compatibility and interoperability—one reason why Sony's PlayStation has kept its appeal is because a broader range of games software is available for it than for competing products. The range of compatible hardware and software available can be a differentiating factor for certain types of technologically advanced product. A superior ability to inter-operate with a variety of other systems and standards can also be an attractive feature in some cases; it is one of the ways in which competitors seek to differentiate their music players from Apple's iPod, for example.

- Richness of information[16]—retailers, especially on-line businesses, frequently compete on the quantity and quality of the information that they provide regarding the product that is on sale. For example, Amazon and many other internet retailers offer detailed product specifications and reviews of the product by previous purchasers. Real estate

Positioning
The building of an image of a product, service, or brand in the mind of the customer as to what it promises and what values are associated with it.

Differentiation
Distinguishing a product, service, or brand from its competitors in ways that customers find valuable, so that they will pay a price premium or show greater loyalty.

Table 4.4 Types of differentiation

Attributes of the product or service	Examples	Attributes of the firm	Examples
Functionality	Graphics capabilities of a video console; fully reclining seats in BA upper class cabins; storage space available on email service	Reach of the network	Numbers of outlets for a bank or courier; coverage of remote areas by a mobile phone service; number of subscribers to an instant messaging service
Compatibility and interoperability	Number of games available for Sony PlayStation; degree of interoperability of instant messaging service with competing services	Levels of support	Helpful and knowledgeable helpline service from PC manufacturer, mobile phone service, or bank
Richness of information	Information lender provides about 'true cost' of a loan; information Amazon provides about a product, including the opinions of previous buyers	Reputation/brand image	Sony's reputation for reliable, innovative products; prestige from being seen wearing designer clothes or driving an upmarket car
Appearance	Design of H&M clothing	Affiliation	The promise by a retailer such as Tesco, Wal-Mart, or Amazon to take the consumer's side, and negotiate good deals from producers
Build quality, reliability	Low number of faults on a car on delivery, and low incidence of breakdowns during use; McDonald's consistent taste, hygiene and service levels		
Price (high or low)	Low price deals on selected McDonald's products; price as a signal of value of perfume, clothing, legal services		

agents and financial advisors may also differentiate themselves from competitors in this fashion. For a complicated and expensive product or service, the availability of detailed information can help reassure the buyer that both the product and the seller are dependable. Buyers can also be reassured by transparency—where an intermediary, such as broker of insurance or financial products, discloses how much commission it will take from a given sale—although this may come about more because of regulations than through competition between firms.

- Appearance—some products, such as clothes, cars, or furniture, may be bought simply because they look good. H&M, like many other firms in its industry, competes on the cut and appearance of its clothes, and the extent to which they meet the fashion expectations of its various target segments.

- Build quality and reliability—products or services that reach the customer with fewer faults than competitors and/or perform more reliably in use may be deemed more attractive. Volkswagen and Toyota attempt to differentiate their cars in this fashion, and McDonald's hamburgers are consistent in their taste, presentation, and hygiene.

- Price—products can be differentiated on price in two ways:
  - By making their products or services more expensive than competitors', firms hope to signal the superior value of what they offer. This type of differentiation frequently

goes together with differentiation based on the firm's reputation and brand image (see below) and is employed by suppliers of up-market fragrances, designer clothing, and top-range legal and management consultancy services.

- By selling their products more cheaply than their rivals, firms hope to signal that they offer value for money and expect to make up in higher sales volumes what they lose in low profit margins. Clothing chains like the Spanish firm Zara, and airlines such as Ryanair, pursue this form of differentiation.

Customers' purchasing decisions are not always made on the basis of the product alone. The qualities of the organization that is providing it may also play a major role.[17] Organizations can mark themselves out from their competitors through:

- The reach of the network[18]—some organizations can be considered not just as producers of goods and services but also as networks of sales or service outlets, or as networks of subscribers that the firm links together. The 'reach' of the network—essentially its size, in terms of numbers of outlets and/or members—can be a source of differentiation for the firm. Courier firms such as Federal Express, UPS, and DHL attract customers because they have a worldwide network of pick-up and distribution points. Instant messaging services only have value if lots of people can be reached on them, so that as long as the different providers continue to erect barriers to intercommunication between their subscribers, the largest network will have an advantage.

- Support—the quality of sales and after-sales service may be a valuable feature. BMW differentiates itself through the quality of its dealer and service agent network.

- Reputation and brand image—these factors offer value to customers in two ways. First, by buying a prestigious brand of equipment or clothing, buyers hope to acquire some of that prestige for themselves, and so be recognized as possessing wealth or good taste. In the corporate world, by hiring highly regarded firms as auditors or investment bankers, organizations may expect to gain legitimacy in the eyes of investors and other stakeholders. Second, by purchasing from a supplier, such as Sony, with an established reputation, they hope to save themselves search costs: the time and effort needed to evaluate competing products and make an informed choice between them.

→ Reputation and brands are examined in Section 7.3.5. The concept of legitimacy was introduced in Section 2.6.1.

Sony, with its emphasis on innovation, reliable but highly featured products and above-average prices, has pursued a differentiated strategy for much of its history in televisions, audio equipment, and most recently with its PlayStation games consoles and its Vaio portable computers. The Vaio, which featured striking good looks and facilities for video editing never before seen on a laptop, is an excellent example of a differentiation strategy succeeding in an already crowded industry.

However, radical differentiation is not always effective—there are cases, like computers and video machines, where it is more important for a product to be compatible with industry standards, and those that are too different may not succeed. The attractiveness of different types of differentiation is likely to vary as the environment changes: differentiation on reliability may be easier in emerging industries, where products can vary widely in quality, than in mature ones, where product reliability is taken for granted. It is no longer possible, for example, for Sony to differentiate its TVs on the basis of reliability, since the faults in TV components used by all manufacturers have become increasingly rare over the years. And not all attempts to differentiate work equally well in every market, as Vodafone found in Japan (see What Can Go Wrong 4.1, below). Apple (Real-life Application 4.5) offers another example of how the success of differentiation strategies can vary.

Real-life Application 4.5 Differentiation at Apple

The American electronics firm, Apple, has long emphasized product differentiation as a major plank in its strategy. Its Macintosh range of computers was originally differentiated from the IBM PC and similar machines through a superior and easy-to-use interface, but also through price, which was considerably higher than that charged for IBM-compatible machines.[19] Despite this (or perhaps because of it) the Macintosh attracted a fiercely loyal following, particularly in the design, publishing, and education markets that Apple targeted, where its functionality was particularly valuable.[20]

However, successive versions of Microsoft's Windows software gave buyers of other PCs most of the features that were previously only available to Apple users. It became increasingly difficult to justify the Macintosh's price premium over Windows PCs,[21] particularly since many software houses did not feel it worth the expense of producing special versions of their products for Apple's smaller user base.

In 1998, Apple went some way towards reviving its flagging fortunes with the introduction of the iMac, which it targeted at a different segment, the consumer market. The company successfully differentiated this range of computers on the basis of the iMac's colourful appearance and functionality—particularly its networking capabilities. It was also easy to set up and use, and priced at a similar level to a Windows PC of comparable power. Successor products retained differentiation on the basis of their appearance, and were also differentiated through their multimedia functionality: the ease with which they could create and manage audio and video files. However, these were less well received in the market-place, and Apple's sales and profits fell; in 2001 it recorded an operating loss of US$344m on sales of $2.9bn.[22]

In October 2001, Apple unexpectedly introduced a new style of product, the iPod digital music player. The iPod was differentiated from existing MP3 players in a number of ways. It offered functionality benefits: higher than average quality of music reproduction, using Apple's proprietary AAC format, and enough storage, on a miniature hard disk drive, for most people's entire collection of recorded music—most competing products could store only a few dozen tracks. It was also differentiated on appearance—a sleek white box with a clever scroll wheel with which users could easily control the device.

Many observers cautioned that Apple would have a tough time in the consumer electronics industry, where it had no experience, with a product priced at $400, significantly higher than most competing products, and which was only compatible with Apple's own brand of computers.[23] However, the loyal community of Apple computer users was enthusiastic about the product, and early sales were respectable, with some 125,000 being sold in the first three months. Apple persisted with the product; in 2003, it announced a newer, slimmer but higher capacity range of iPods, compatible with Windows PCs as well as Apple Macs, and offering seamless downloading from Apple's iTunes Music Store, the first legal music download site to offer a substantial range of tracks from all major labels. This combination of functionality, compatibility, and reach, together with the iPod's appearance—it became a 'must-have' style icon—led to an explosion in sales of both iPod hardware and downloads from the iTunes site. The iPod mini, a smaller and cheaper version of the product in a variety of 'cool' colours, was launched in 2004 and quickly sold out in several markets.[24]

By early 2005, Apple had sold 16 million iPods, giving it an estimated 76 per cent of the market for digital music players, and iTunes had 82 per cent of the market for digital music downloads. The two products had transformed Apple's financial position—2004 operating profits were $344m on sales of $4.9bn—and there were indications that the iPod was boosting sales of Apple's original core product: sales of Macintosh computers in the third quarter of 2005 were 35 per cent above those in the corresponding period the previous year.[25]

An early iPod developed by Apple. *Corbis*

b. Making effective product choices

In order to effectively tailor its products to its chosen segments—or, alternatively, to choose the right segments to target with a particular product—an organization needs a clear understanding of the needs of its markets, actual and potential. However, it is sometimes difficult to assess what it is exactly that customers want. There is a famous saying in marketing, that customers are 'irreducibly human'—in other words, unpredictable, unmanageable and inconsistent. They often do not know what they want until they have it, and then realize that they really wanted something else.

Thus, even if a firm invests in expensive market research to investigate customer needs, it needs to be careful about interpreting the results—and to bear in mind that other firms can do the same research, which is likely to come up with similar answers. In order to be able to identify and target market segments more effectively than its competitors, an organization needs a deeper understanding of how their customers or potential customers think.[26] This should enable them to interpret market research findings more sensitively—or even to do without them altogether.

A small start-up company will quite often achieve this by targeting buyers with similar backgrounds to its own managers—an 'accessible' segment, in the terminology of Section 4.2.3—so that it intuitively knows what will please them. Anita Roddick was able to do this with The Body Shop's early, mostly female, customers. As they grow, many firms keep this understanding fresh by engaging in a regular dialogue with their most valuable customers. This can be supplemented with careful analysis, or 'mining' of sales data to pick up new trends in customer buying habits. Careful use of test products and test marketing, to try out buyer reactions to different product features before committing too many resources to their production, can help avoid expensive errors.

However, in order to sustain a differentiated position, one also needs to know what the competitors' products are, and how they are different. This is not likely to be a static picture; the basis of differentiated competition may change regularly. Competitors may imitate the firm's products and the firm in its turn may adopt some aspects of those competitors' products or service. So competitive information is an important input into a firm's product positioning strategies.

Finally, not all competitive positions are appropriate for every organization—the firm needs to possess the resources to support its competitive positioning. Differentiation on low price requires capabilities in low-cost production, differentiation on reputation requires a strong brand along with strong relationships with customers.[27]

Using Evidence 4.2 Assessing the effectiveness of a differentiation strategy

Many firms claim to be differentiating themselves from the competitors; how can we tell if those claims are valid? Bearing in mind the warnings we have just given about market research, it may nonetheless tell us which particular elements of a product or service customers currently find most valuable, and how highly they rate 'our' firm's performance in these key areas.

Whether or not such market research is available, it is a good idea to check whether a firm's differentiation is paying off in terms of results. The aim of a differentiation strategy is to attain one or both of the following:

- higher prices than competitors. Customers are expected to be prepared to pay extra for differentiated product or service features, so if the firm's prices are only average, this may be

evidence that the features it is offering are not really valued in the market-place. If you do not have access to price lists, you may still be able to get some insights into this by looking at revenue per unit of output: for example, revenue per passenger seat kilometre in the airline industry, average revenue per customer order in the fast food industry;

- greater customer loyalty than competitors. Some firms are able to quote figures about the proportion of business that derives from established customers, for example as the result of repeat orders or word-of-mouth recommendations. You may also see quotes from customers demonstrating how much they value their association with an organization or its employees.

Theoretical Debate 4.1 What do we really mean by differentiation?

Differentiation is sometimes seen as a way of setting a product strongly apart from competition. Since the early 1960s, the conventional wisdom in marketing has been that every brand requires a 'Unique Selling Proposition' or USP. It should promise a benefit, offered by no-one else in the market, that constitutes such a strong proposition to consumers that they are excited into purchasing the product (Bungey, 1997). Often (e.g. Porter, 1980) it is seen as a way to justify a premium price that more than offsets any extra advertising or production costs.

The term USP was invented by Rosser Reeves, co-founder of US advertising agency Ted Bates (now Bates Worldwide), and some people continue to believe that advertising is a crucial factor in differentiating one product from another. Economists often measure the extent of differentiation in an industry through the proportion of sales that firms spend on advertising. There is even evidence that consumers can be persuaded to buy products on the basis of 'USPs' that have no real meaning—for example, plausible-sounding ingredients in a shampoo that in fact have no effect on the hair (Carpenter and Glazer, 1994).

However, not all marketing theorists are convinced that consumers pay much attention to USPs. Ehrenberg et al. (1997) found that buyers of popular brands and those of lower-selling brands typically believed that they would derive precisely the same benefits from their purchases, and that advertising had little effect on this. For example, around 50 per cent of people buying the best-selling UK toothpaste brand thought it 'promoted strong and healthy teeth'. A very similar proportion of the purchasers of the eighth-best-selling brand believed the same thing about that product—which in fact was promoted more for its tooth-whitening properties. Any difference in sales between two brands was not attributable to differentiation on product features. Rather, it was because the buyers of the best-selling brand were more frequent, and more loyal, purchasers, since the brand was better known, or more widely available. In most cases, any really distinctive product features that a firm used for differentiation were quickly copied.

Observations like this have led Patrick Barwise and Sean Meehan (2004, 2005) to conclude that competitive advantage comes from being 'simply better': providing similar products to competitors', but in a way that meets common customer needs slightly more reliably or conveniently. They believe that differen-

tiation on factors such as reliability, support, or network reach is more effective than USPs based on product functionality. In a similar vein, Sharpe and Dawes (2001) concluded that differentiation is not simply a means of justifying a price premium. Any persuasive reason to purchase a product that enables an organization to overcome disadvantages in another area can be considered as differentiation. A USP, for example, is a product feature that allows a firm to overcome a price disadvantage. But Sharpe and Dawes quote the example of an Australian supermarket chain where the differentiation feature is low prices, which enable the supermarket to overcome disadvantages such as lack of car-parking space, narrow aisles, and limited range of goods stocked. The crucial point here is that a price-sensitive customer segment exists for which these 'disadvantages' are not that important.

These differences are not just theoretical; they matter both for marketing tactics and organizational strategy. Tactically, if your main aim is to make people aware of your brand and give them a good impression of it, then it makes sense to use humour in your advertising rather than try to 'hard sell' product virtues and features. However, advocates of USP-style differentiation, such as Kim Clancy and Jack Trout (2002), protest that such advertising, which has become increasingly common, has eroded differences between consumer brands. Strategically, if you do not believe that product features are crucial to consumer choice, then you would limit the resources given over to marketing and product development. It makes little sense to invest huge sums in breakthrough innovations if consumers do not value them more than incremental improvements to existing offerings, or would rather have existing technology at lower prices. On the other hand, there are sometimes genuine innovations, like the Walkman or the internet browser, that meet needs that no-one knew existed until the product appeared on the market.

To some extent, how you conceive of differentiation will depend on how far you think that firms and their advertising agencies are able to influence consumer requirements. If you believe that their influence is strong, then the USP view will appeal to you. If you believe that buying decisions are influenced more by what buyers experience when they do business with a firm, and use its products and services, then you are more likely to sympathize with the 'simply better' school.

Worked Example 4.1 Analysing McDonald's competitive stance

What segments are being targeted?

The first step in analysing a firm's competitive stance is to identify what its target market segments are, and what products it is using to serve them. Interestingly, although McDonald's 2005 Annual Report and its 2006 Facts brochure are very explicit about most parts of the marketing mix, they do not mention the customer segments the company is targeting. This is not necessarily a criticism—its competitors are no more informative on this point. It may be that detailed segmentation data is too important to make public, or that firms are genuinely targeting a broad segment, and do not want to risk alienating some customers by labelling them as 'non-core'. A March 2006 report by Mintel, a leading market research firm, confirms that, in the UK at least, this kind of fast food is bought by a very wide range of age and income groups, with McDonald's having a particularly broad spread of customers. However, people aged under 35 are significantly more frequent users of chicken and burger bars than those above that age. The proportion of people who never use chicken or burger bars is significantly higher amongst retired people and those whose children have left home than it is amongst families and amongst people who have yet to start a family.

We can also get an insight into the markets that firms are targeting by examining their products and services. The impression that families with children are a key target market for McDonald's is reinforced by the presence on its menu of Happy Meals targeted at children, and by the provision of birthday party services. The breakfast menu is clearly targeted at working people, while the offering of a range of low-priced items indicates that people with limited spending power are a target.

Pulling these various pieces of evidence together, we can see that although McDonald's has genuine aspirations to serve a large proportion of the population, the following three segments appear to be particularly important:

- single people under the age of 35;
- parents whose children have yet to leave home;
- working people on a tight budget.

Of course, these segments overlap: working people on a tight budget may be parents, or single and under 35. And it may well be that McDonald's has access to private research that enables it to characterize these segments in greater detail, or to identify others. But for the purposes of this worked example, this rough segmentation is good enough, and we can move on to the next stage of seeing how attractive the three segments are. To simplify the discussion, we shall limit it to the 25 EU countries for which data were available at the time of writing,[28] but a similar analysis could be undertaken for all the main geographic markets where McDonald's has a presence, or indeed for each major country or group of countries in the EU, since each has its own singular characteristics.

Assessing segment attractiveness

In terms of size, each of these segments in the EU is large. Of the about 460 million people in the European Union, about 126 million are under 35. There are around 170 million households, of which about 72 million include children. There are approximately 170 million people in employment in the EU, and while it is not immediately clear how many of these are on a tight budget, that market, too, is likely to be sizeable. Around one-fifth of them, for example, are on temporary and short-term contracts.

However, only the third of the three segments shows much sign of growth. The annual rate of EU population growth, only 0.3 per cent between 1994 and 2004, is predicted to slow to 0.1 per cent per annum between 2005 and 2015. The proportion of young people in the population has fallen by around 3 per cent between 1994 and 2004, and the number of children per family has been in long-term decline throughout the EU. The number of families is likely to diminish as the population ages. The proportion of people aged 15–64 who are in employment has risen, however, from around 60 per cent in 1995 to 64 per cent in 2005, and there are some large countries (e.g. Italy and Poland) whose employment rates are substantially less, and therefore offer potential for growth. Although economic recovery may stimulate wages and increase the spending power of people already in work, it is also likely to draw in more people in part-time and low-paid jobs.

None of these segments appears to be more easily accessible to McDonald's than to any of its competitors. Fast-food customers in general appear to be price-sensitive and not particularly brand loyal—KFC's same-store sales in the US declined in 2003 and 2004, for example, and it was only when the company introduced new, cheaper meal packages that its sales rebounded. Affluence is also not really a feature of these segments. While young people in employment will have a degree of disposable income for as long as they are living with their parents and not having to support families, people aged 30 and under earn around 25 per cent less than the EU average. People with families may earn more, but also have higher outgoings.

The last criterion to examine is homogeneity. Single people under 35 are probably not that homogeneous in their tastes: there will be large numbers that look for new tastes and experiences, such as ethnic food. In short, while young people will have been an attractive segment for McDonald's for much of the last half of the twentieth century, because of their growing numbers and spending power, they now look to be rather a difficult segment →

→ to serve profitably if you are a fast-food producer. Environmental developments that have already been discussed, such as a growing awareness of the need to eat less fat, and a decline in some young people's enthusiasm for American culture, will contribute to these difficulties.

Families may be more homogeneous in their requirements: children from many cultures seem to be alike in their preferences for certain flavours and for familiarity in their diets and surroundings—and they have a lot of persuasive power with their parents. Parents may, moreover, show a degree of loyalty to a firm that consistently satisfies their children. This segment appears to be an attractive one, but not growing strongly.

Finally, working people on a tight budget, although not affluent, may also be an attractive segment. They are likely to show a degree of homogeneity in wanting cheap food at low prices, and be willing to compromise on variety in order to be sure of fast service and reliable standards of hygiene and comfort.

Identifying bases of differentiation

The next stage in the analysis is to identify the ways in which McDonald's is attempting to differentiate itself to these different types of customer.

Product functionality: McDonald's has since 2002 introduced a number of products, such as salads and toasted sandwiches, to address concerns about the fat, salt and sugar content of its traditional menu items. At the other end of the scale, it launched in 2006 the 'Bigger Big Mac' for unreconstructed burger lovers. However, differentiation in this manner is difficult to sustain, and the menus of competitors such as Burger King feature similar offerings. Some of McDonald's innovative meals in other countries, such as the burger on a rice patty developed for some Asian markets, are also unlikely to be too difficult to copy.

However, service functionality is clearly a battleground in this industry. Burger King is presenting its ability to tailor its products ('Have It Your Way') as a unique selling proposition. Yum! Brands (owner of KFC and several other restaurant chains) devotes several pages of its 2005 Annual Report to its CHAMPS formula (Cleanliness, Hospitality, Accuracy, Maintenance, Product Quality and Speed with Service). McDonald's has a goal of delivering 'great customer experiences', but is placing less explicit emphasis on this than Yum! However, in some restaurants it is extending opening hours, which may be attractive to single customers under 35, and accepting debit and credit cards, which may interest working people on tight budgets. It is also remodelling some of its restaurants to give them a more upmarket feel and installing wireless internet facilities. It is unclear if this is designed to appeal to any of the three segments we have identified.

Richness of information: McDonald's has made extensive nutritional information relating to its products available to the public. However, its main competitors have taken similar steps.

Reliability: McDonald's differentiates itself from smaller competitors through the reliability of its experience. A McDonald's offers consistent standards of taste, speed of service, freshness, hygiene, and comfort in all its restaurants worldwide, and this is likely to be valued by all three of the segments we have identified. However, all major fast-food chains aspire to similar standards of reliability, and Yum! Brands, through its CHAMPS programme, is attempting to outdo all competitors on this dimension.

However, consistent reliability over the years has given McDonald's a clear reputation and brand image. Customers are spared search costs: knowing exactly what to expect, they can quickly opt for a McDonald's meal if that is what they require. Other major restaurant chains offer similar benefits, however.

Price: although McDonald's offers a range of what it terms premium-priced items, it is making a clear attempt to differentiate on low price through its everyday low price menus—$1 in the USA, 99p in the UK, €1 in Germany. This style of differentiation is clearly likely to be valued by all three segments we have identified.

The reach of the network: McDonald's has the largest single-brand restaurant network in the world, with around 32,000 restaurants at the end of 2005. Only Yum! Brands has more restaurants, but these are split between four brands. This complements the company's differentiation on reliability by giving customers a degree of assurance that there is likely to be a McDonald's close by if needed. This may be attractive to parents, and to workers under time pressure.

Final assessment of competitive stance

By proceeding systematically through the different aspects of segmentation and differentiation, we have been able to identify some factors that might then be used in an appraisal of McDonald's competitive stance. Among the questions that might be asked are:

- Are McDonald's chosen segments appropriate, despite their limited growth prospects, or should the company be shifting its emphasis towards more attractive ones? (Remember—even if a segment does not look glamorous, it may still be possible to make good profits by serving it efficiently.)

- Does the firm need a clearer USP, such as Burger King or Yum! Brands are trying to establish? Or is the current differentiation on price, service functionality and (perhaps) network reach adequate in the circumstances?

- Is the move to upgrade the restaurants an appropriate way of keeping old customers from drifting away, a necessary move to attract new types of customer, or a dilution of the brand image that is unlikely to pay off?

4.3　Generic competitive strategies

Certain writers have identified configurations of competitive stance that they believe are particularly important for understanding, and comparing, firms' strategies. These configurations are known as generic strategies. The best-known categorization of generic strategies (discussed in Section 4.3.1) was put forward by Michael Porter in his 1980 book, *Competitive Strategy*. Cliff Bowman's attempt to build and improve on Porter's framework is discussed in Section 4.3.2. Both Porter's and Bowman's frameworks make use of three dimensions: product price, the breadth of the target customer segment, and the degree of value added to the consumer. Treacy and Wiersema (1993), on the other hand, focus more simply on different ways that firms may attempt to add value.

All these frameworks, in particular the first two, have drawbacks that we discuss in Theoretical Debate 4.2. In our view, generic strategy frameworks are probably most useful for:

- charting changes in one firm's strategies over time;
- comparing the strategies being followed by different competitors in an industry. It may be that all members of particular strategic group (see Section 3.3.2), or all the most (or least) successful players in an industry, can be seen to be following a particular generic strategy.

4.3.1　Porter's generic strategies

Michael Porter[29] held that firms can only achieve high returns if their costs are lower than those of competitors', or if they can differentiate their products effectively. He identified three bases for competitive advantage (Figure 4.2):

- A differentiation strategy, which Porter defines as offering a broad range of customers (in many geographic markets, and/or across a broad range of customer segments) something unique and valuable, for which they are ready to pay more. The price premium they pay must more than outweigh the extra costs of providing the unique aspects of the product or service;
- A cost leadership strategy, which involves one firm setting out to be 'the lowest cost producer in the industry' by maximizing economies of scale and other sources of cost advantage. This strategy also involves targeting a broad segment. Porter's theory

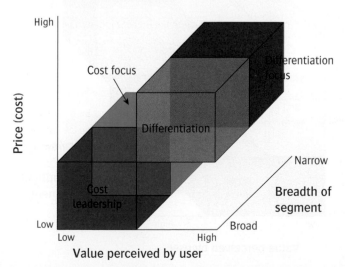

Figure 4.2 Porter's generic strategies. *Reproduced with the kind permission of Free Press*

assumes that the cost leader in an industry will also have the lowest prices. He holds that there is room for only one cost leader in any industry, and that if several firms compete for that position, the result is cut-throat competition.

- A focus strategy involves a firm concentrating on a narrow customer segment. It can be further subdivided into cost focus and differentiation focus strategies, depending on whether the firm tries to achieve cost or differentiation advantage in that particular segment.

- A focus strategy depends on there being significant differences between the focuser's target segment and the rest of the industry. If these differences are not pronounced enough, then a broadly based competitor can serve the segment as well, and probably more cheaply.

The implementation of the different generic strategies requires different resources and skills, different organizational processes, and different styles of leadership, and will mean very different cultures. This, according to Porter, meant that his categories were alternatives: firms could concentrate on *either* minimizing costs *or* creating expensive sources of differentiation. Porter believed that if they did not, they were 'stuck in the middle' and ultimately doomed to fail, although empirical research has now shown that this belief was incorrect.

Because of its simplicity, Porter's framework has been widely adopted by writers on strategy and marketing. However, it is no longer much used in academic circles.[30] If you choose to use it, you should be aware of the danger that you are oversimplifying your analysis. The reasons for this are discussed in Theoretical Debate 4.2.

4.3.2 **Bowman's generic strategies**[31]

Cliff Bowman places less emphasis than Porter on the difference between broad and narrow scope, and analyses a business' competitive stance along two main dimensions: the *prices* of its products, and the amount of value its customers, existing or potential, perceive that those products give them. Figure 4.3 summarizes the generic strategies that arise from different combinations of these factors.

A no-frills strategy provides usable, basic products with very few features, at a low price. A number of low-cost air carriers, such as Ryanair, offer a cheap, basic point-to-point air

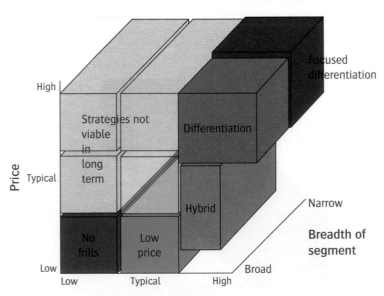

Figure 4.3 Bowman's generic strategies

travel service, with no meals on their flights and no facilities for people who want to transfer to a connecting flight on arrival at their destination. Ryanair, in fact, actively discourages people from booking connecting flights, even on its own services.

Organizations using a low-price strategy charge less than competitors for similar levels of functionality and service. This makes it a risky and difficult strategy, which requires the firm to have lower costs than its competitors, or to be able to block imitation of its prices and survive price wars. It is likely that this strategy will have a short lifespan and will change over time to a stance based either on no frills or on clearer differentiation.

A hybrid strategy offers some form of differentiation without demanding premium prices. Firms following this route include H&M, with its emphasis on fashionable goods at affordable prices. Such firms have made it their business to cut costs in areas that are not important to the customer through manufacturing competences, so as to be able to afford lower prices while still offering distinctive features.

A differentiation strategy in this model involves offerings that are distinctive from those of competitors in ways which are valued by consumers in a broad market segment. This distinguishes it from a focused differentiation strategy, which seeks to achieve high prices for a highly specialized product, targeted at a narrow customer segment where there are few competitors—the kind of strategy pursued by makers of luxury goods such as France's LVMH. Firms following this strategy are likely to have strong competences in areas of particular importance to the customers in that segment, and build strong relationships of trust with them.

Strategies involving high prices for low or unexceptional value, or standard prices for poorly featured products or services, are only likely to be viable for a short period. Even this will depend, for example, on customers not having access to information on where to obtain better value or on legal or historical factors giving the firm an effective monopoly of a particular segment. It is likely that competitors offering better value for money will take market share in the longer term.

If you are considering using Bowman's generic strategies in your analysis, you need to be aware that the framework does not appear to have been empirically tested. In other words, there is no evidence that the differences between his various generic strategies are genuinely important in practice—but also no evidence that they are not.

4.3.3 Treacy and Wiersema's framework

Treacy and Wiersema[32] identify three ways in which a firm may get competitive advantage:

- Operational excellence involves structuring the value chain so as to be the industry leader on price and convenience. Firms with this strategy go to great lengths to minimize overheads and eliminate any activities that are not absolutely necessary. Their culture and belief system emphasize the value of discipline in keeping costs low. Dell, the PC maker, is a firm that has used this strategy to build a market-leading position.

- Customer intimacy involves investing time and effort in tailoring products and services very closely to the needs of each individual customer, or customer segment, with a view to building loyalty and relationships. Firms follow this strategy in the expectation of recouping the investment from customers that make repeat purchases, and for whom low prices are not the main factor in choosing a supplier. This strategy has become increasingly common in financial services and for firms selling to business customers.

- Product leadership involves constantly striving to keep ahead of competition with a stream of new and innovative products. Sony and Apple both pursue this strategy.

The three strategies imply different customer choices and value chains. Some rare companies are able to master two of them simultaneously—Toyota, for example, has successfully blended operational excellence and product leadership, having both the lowest cost base in its industry and innovative products like the Prius hybrid-engined car. However, Treacy and Wiersema suggest that firms do better to focus their efforts on mastering one of them, and there is limited empirical evidence that supports this contention.[33]

Theoretical Debate 4.2   How useful are generic strategies?

Porter's and Bowman's generic strategies are interesting examples of plausible ideas that have taken on a life of their own. Both are widely cited in textbooks, even though the empirical evidence for them is not very strong. In fact we have found no studies at all relating to Bowman's framework, but Colin Campbell-Hunt (2000) pulled together the results of 17 studies of Porter's generic strategies. In this Theoretical Debate we look at the possible drawbacks of all three frameworks, and refer to Campbell-Hunt's work, along with some other research results he was not able to take into account.

The first question to ask about categorizations like Porter's and Bowman's is how complete they are. There is a lot of white space in Figure 4.2. (i.e. a lot of potential generic strategies that he is excluding). There is a square in the middle of Figure 4.3 that represents the 'standard value at a standard price' strategy, which represents a benchmark for all the others—but which does not have a name. Porter believes that the 'breadth of segment' dimension is of fundamental importance; Bowman only takes it into account when looking at differentiation strategies. Are these gaps important?

Campbell-Hunt found that Porter's framework was indeed incomplete: there were six distinct varieties of differentiation apparent from the 17 studies he had analysed, and the differences between them were as important as the difference between differentiation and cost leadership. Bowman's framework, while more detailed than Porter's, is no better from this point of view, and also contains one item, no frills, that does not qualify as an independent strategy—it is almost always combined with one of the others. Treacy and Wiersema's list does not include strategies based upon richness or reach, which have had considerable success in e-commerce (Evans and Wurster, 1999).

A second key question is whether, in practice, it is possible to classify a firm's strategy precisely under one of the generic headings. There are two reasons to doubt if this is possible:

- It is rare to find a cost leader that does not attempt to differentiate as well. Dell in PC manufacture and Nokia in mobile phone production are clearly the cost leaders in their respective industries. In both cases, however, they also offer differentiation: Dell on the basis of fast delivery and good after-sales service; Nokia on the basis of product appearance and functionality. Even in industries, such as metal refining, where the product is highly commoditized and cost leadership is a sensible objective to strive for, firms will try to differentiate by, for example, offering shorter lead times on delivery. It can similarly be difficult to find a firm for which operational excellence is the sole focus of the strategy.

- It is far from clear where the dividing line lies between broad targeting and narrow focus. McDonald's, for example, clearly strives to reach a very broad market-place, operating in over a hundred countries and attracting a wide range of customers. It faces local competitors in India which clearly have no ambitions outside their home market, and so are more focused than McDonald's—but can a focus on a country of 1 billion people be regarded as narrow? And what of Nando's, a South African chain of chicken restaurants that has now expanded into 30 countries, many of them in Africa and the Middle East but also including Australia, the UK, Canada, and the USA? How does one classify the fish restaurant chain Nordsee, with its main focus on Germany and Austria, but with a presence also in Switzerland and Slovenia?

Campbell-Hunt's research supports these doubts. He did find a number of clusters of business strategic behaviour that seemed to occur frequently together, though these did not coincide with either Porter's or Bowman's classifications. However, each of them had some characteristics that also cropped up in other types of strategy—there were no indicators that could be used reliably to assign a firm to one generic strategy rather than another.

A third test of the value of generic strategy theories is whether their predictions are valid. Bowman, for example, predicts that certain types of generic strategy are doomed to ultimate failure; this is plausible, but has never been tested. Porter's hypothesis about the danger of being 'stuck in the middle' has, however, been subjected to a lot of careful empirical testing, which shows the risk to be much less than Porter supposed. Campbell-Hunt found no significant difference between profitability and growth in firms following hybrid, 'stuck in the middle' strategies and those following purer cost- or differentiation-led ones. Studies ➔

→ by Miller and Dess (1993) and Cronshaw et al. (1994) found that firms pursuing clear differentiation strategies tended to be more profitable than those following cost leadership strategies, but that firms that combined cost and differentiation strategies were the most profitable of all. Their research confirms that the concepts of cost and differentiation advantage explain something meaningful about an organization's strategy, but fails to confirm that they cannot co-exist.

This supports the view of Charles Baden-Fuller and John Stopford (1992) that Porter's generic strategies are 'a fallacy' as the best firms are at all times trying to be low cost *and* high quality. As a result, they suggest that no generic strategies, by themselves, can be enduring sources of competitive advantage. Instead, strategic resources and architecture are more important bases of strategic effectiveness. This may, however, be a specific weakness of Porter's framework. Thornhill and White (2007) found that firms following the pure generic strategies suggested by Treacy and Wiersema (1993) did at least as well as, and typically better than, firms that attempted to mix them.

Generic strategy frameworks have other limitations:

- They present quite a static view of a firm and its strategy. Calling a firm a focused differentiator rather implies that this will be the way it chooses to act in all the segments it confronts. Some firms, like LVMH, do indeed make a habit of acting in this fashion for all their products and all their markets. Others start out with what appear to be focused differentiation strategies, but quickly progress towards other strategies as they acquire the financial and reputational resources needed to service larger market segments. Their 'focus' was just a brief phase they passed through on their way to their 'real' strategy.

- It is not clear whether *firms* can be said to have generic strategies at all; it may be that these frameworks work best when applied to the brand or the individual product. While Sony does have a clear strategy of differentiation across its entire product range, H&M's strategy varies. With most of its products, it appears to be following what Bowman would call a hybrid strategy but the fruits of its collaboration with the high fashion designer Karl Lagerfeld can arguably be classed as differentiation, or even focused differentiation. By contrast, a study of strategies for individual products in a major multinational found that most could be clearly identified as either cost leadership or differentiation (Nayyar, 1993).

- Generic strategies are classifications that are of limited use in *evaluating* whether a strategy is strong or weak—which is the point of most strategic analysis. Neither Porter nor Treacy and Wiersema, for example, suggested that any one of their generic strategies was fundamentally better than the others. No-one has found any reason to believe that any one of Bowman's generic strategies, apart from those that he identified as 'destined for failure', is superior to the others under particular circumstances. So, once you have identified a firm as following a cost leadership strategy, or being a global luxury niche player, what do you do next?

 What Can Go Wrong 4.1 Vodafone in Japan

Managers at Vodafone, a UK-based supplier of mobile telephone services, had formulated a clear strategy to achieve pre-eminence in its industry. Vodafone would expand globally by acquisition, building a reputation as a world leader that would attract customers. It would use its size to negotiate volume discounts with handset suppliers such as Nokia, so that it could attract potential users with lower prices than its competitors could afford to offer. At the same time, it would get operating economies from using standardized technology across the world. This would help it make a good return on the massive investment needed for the latest generation of mobile technology, '3G'. This promised users the ability to send and receive music, video, and other large files, for which Vodafone and its competitors were hopeful of charging high prices.

One major step in implementing this strategy was Vodafone's entry into Japan with the acquisition, in 2001, of that country's third-biggest operator, J-Phone. The Japanese market was important because of its size and growth potential: mobile phone penetration there was below that in most large European markets. But it also featured some highly innovative competitors, notably NTT DoCoMo, whose i-Mode system, launched in 1999, offered many of the benefits of 3G using older technology. Not content with this, DoCoMo had launched a 3G service in 2001. Japanese customers had learned to expect a large range of advanced features from light and compact handsets that their network operators had arranged to be manufactured to their own requirements.

The company's efforts to satisfy the high expectations of mainstream Japanese consumers were hindered by problems in the development of 3G technology in Europe. Vodafone's strategy for Japan involved European equipment, which worked to a different technical standard from that employed by its Japanese competitors. The equipment manufacturers experienced →

One of the UK Vodaphone shops. *Vodaphone*

→ teething problems with this technology, so that when handsets became available in Japan, in 2004, it was only in limited quantities, and they were larger and clunkier than competitors' offerings.[34] By mid-2005 J-Phone, by then renamed Vodafone KK, had only 1.1 million 3G subscribers, whilst its two leading competitors had over 30 million between them.[35]

Vodafone's share of the Japanese market began to decline in late 2003, and for five consecutive months in 2005 the firm lost more subscribers than it gained.[36] A journalist described how, in May 2005, shoppers in a large Tokyo electronics store were lining the walls to view the brash displays of phones from Vodafone's rivals, while Vodafone's 'smaller and scruffier' stands were almost ignored.[37] Bill Murrow, the respected head of Vodafone's UK

business was transferred to Japan to help turn the business around, and the firm's results began to improve, aided by the arrival of more attractive handsets.[38] But Murrow's move, too, had an opportunity cost—the CEO of one of Vodafone's UK rivals commented: 'We were thrilled. We would have paid his airfare.'[39]

In March 2006, Vodafone announced the sale of its interest in Vodafone Japan to Softbank, a Japanese IT group that had just been granted its own licence to offer mobile phone services. The £8.6bn purchase price was approximately £5bn below the Japanese operation's value in Vodafone's books. At the time of writing, Vodafone retains an interest in Japan through a joint venture with Softbank to develop handsets and software, and source content.[40]

● CHAPTER SUMMARY

An organization's competitive stance—which products to sell and which markets to sell them to—is of fundamental importance to its strategy. An organization with a successful business strategy will have a clear idea of which market segments it is targeting and of the needs of the customers in those segments. It will also have developed products and services that meet those needs, along with a value chain that delivers them effectively to the customer.

This chapter has introduced the concept of segmentation and the main characteristics used to distinguish one segment from another. A market segment will be attractive to a firm if it is one or more of the following:

- broad and homogeneous;
- easily accessible to the firm;
- easily served through the firm's existing value chain;
- affluent;
- not price-sensitive;
- potentially brand loyal;
- overlooked by competitors.

We have also identified the main ways in which organizations can differentiate themselves and their offerings to make them desirable to customers in a given segment. Products and services can be differentiated on the basis of:

- functionality;
- compatibility and interoperability;
- richness of information;
- appearance;
- build quality, reliability;
- price (high or low).

In addition, the following attributes of the firm itself may attract customers:

- reach of the firm's network;
- levels of support offered to customers;
- reputation/brand image;
- affiliation.

The extent to which the organization's chosen forms of differentiation match the requirements of the customers in its target market segments will determine the success or failure of its business strategy.

The chapter contains summaries of three commonly cited sets of generic business strategies: Porter's generic strategies, Bowman's strategy clock and Treacy and Wiersema's operational excellence/customer intimacy/product leadership framework. You are warned to use these with caution.

 Online Resource Centre
www.oxfordtextbooks.co.uk/orc/haberberg_rieple/

Visit the Online Resource Centre that accompanies this book to read more information relating to distinctiveness.

● KEY SKILLS

The key skills you should have developed after reading this chapter are:

- the ability to identify the key segments in a market;
- the ability to appraise a business' choice of target market and understand how that contributed to its success or failure;
- the ability to analyse the ways in which a firm differentiates itself and its products, and appraise how well this matches the requirements of customers in its chosen market segments.

● REVIEW QUESTIONS

1. Is it more important to identify the market before you develop the product, or to develop a good product that you can be sure someone will want to buy?

2. How attractive would you assess the following market segments to be? What kind of organization might be interested in serving these segments? What kinds or products or services might it offer and how might it differentiate them?

   - fans of 'hip-hop' music (or another genre of your own choice)
   - businesses employing less than 50 people
   - lovers of Indian food
   - video rental firms

3. 'Once you have identified the right segment, the appropriate positioning is normally obvious.' Would you agree?

4. What is the difference between the organization's competitive stance and the functional strategy of the marketing activity? How do the two concepts fit together in a well-designed strategy?

5. Was the Apple iPod (Real-Life Application 4.5) a breakthrough innovation with a clear USP, or a product that represented a 'simply better' way of fulfilling an existing need?

● FURTHER READING

- West, D., Ford, J., and Ibrahim, E. (2006). *Strategic Marketing: Creating Competitive Advantage*. Oxford: Oxford University Press. Provides a comprehensive review of how the marketing activity contributes to strategy, including areas such as segmentation and positioning.

- Ohmae, K. (1982). *The Mind of the Strategist*. New York, NY: McGraw Hill. A classic work that repays reading on many levels, but gives a particularly penetrating account of the fundamental importance of targeting the right products at the right people.

- Aaker, D. (2003). 'The power of the branded differentiator'. *MIT Sloan Management Review*, 45/1: 83–7. Argues passionately for the importance of USP-style differentiation.

- Christensen, C., Cook, S., and Hall, T. (2005). 'Marketing malpractice'. *Harvard Business Review*, 83/12: 74–83. And Yankelovich, D. and Meer, D. (2006). 'Rediscovering market segmentation'. *Harvard Business Review*, 84/2: 122–31. Two recent articles, with lots of examples, about how an obsession with the technical aspects of segmentation can lead organizations to lose touch with the key part of competitive strategy, understanding and fulfilling customer needs.

- Barwise, P. and Meehan, S. (2004). 'Six rules to become simply better'. *Business Strategy Review*, 15/3: 24–31. A useful summary of the 'Simply better' theory and how managers can put it into practice.

- The Fall 2005 issue of *Marketing Research* contains a number of short articles critiquing Barwise and Meehan's theory, along with those authors' response. These give an interesting insight into the nature of the debate.

- Prahalad, C. K. (2005). *The Fortune at the Bottom of the Pyramid: Eradicating Poverty through Profits*. Upper Saddle River, NJ: Wharton School Publishing. Makes a convincing case for developing products and services for the world's huge numbers of poor people. It shows how, by designing business models that take account of people's limited spending power and their communal values, firms can not only generate profits, but also raise the standards of living amongst the poor, and stimulate new thinking and products that may attract affluent customers in the future.

● REFERENCES

Aaker, D. (2004). 'Leveraging the corporate brand'. *California Management Review*, 46/3: 6–18.

Attia, S. and Hooley, G. (2007). 'The role of resources in achieving target competitive positions'. *Journal of Strategic Marketing*, 15/2–3: 91–119.

Baden-Fuller, C. and Stopford, J. (1992). *Rejuvenating the Mature Business: The Competitive Challenge.* Cambridge, MA: Harvard Business School Press.

Barwise, P. and Meehan, S. (2004). 'Six rules to become simply better'. *Business Strategy Review*, 15/3: 24–31.

Barwise, P. and Meehan, S. (2005). 'Simply better'. *Marketing Research*, 17/2: 9–14.

Bonoma, T. and Shapiro, B. (1984). 'Evaluating market segmentation approaches'. *Industrial Marketing Management*, 13: 257–68.

Bungey, M. (1997). 'USP's benefit still stands tall in noisy 1990s'. *Advertising Age*, 68/9: 18.

Campbell-Hunt, C. (2000). 'What have we learned about generic competitive strategy? A meta-analysis'. *Strategic Management Journal*, 21/2: 127–54.

Cardozo, R. (1980). 'Situational segmentation of industrial markets'. *European Journal of Marketing*, 14/5–6: 264–76.

Carpenter, G. and Glazer, R. (1994). 'Meaningful brands from meaningless differentiation: the dependence on irrelevant attributes'. *Journal of Marketing Research*, 31/3: 339–50.

Christensen, C., Cook, S., and Hall, T. (2005). 'Marketing malpractice'. *Harvard Business Review*, 83/12: 74–83.

Clancy, K. and Trout, J. (2002). 'Brand Confusion'. *Harvard Business Review*, 80/3: 22–23.

Cronshaw, M., Davis, E., and Kay, J. (1994). 'On being stuck in the middle or good food costs less at Sainsbury's'. *British Journal of Management*, 5/1: 19–32.

Day, G. (1969). 'A two-dimensional concept of brand loyalty'. *Journal of Advertising Research*, 9: 29–35.

Day, G. (1994). 'The capabilities of market-driven organizations'. *Journal of Marketing*, 58, October: 37–51.

Dick, A. and Basu, K. (1994). 'Customer loyalty: Towards an integrated framework'. *Journal of the Academy of Marketing Science*, 22: 99–113.

Ehrenberg, A., Barnard, N., and Scriven, J. (1997). 'Differentiation or salience'. *Journal of Advertising Research*, 37/6: 7–14.

Evans, P. and Wurster, T. S. (1999). 'Getting real about virtual commerce'. *Harvard Business Review*, November–December: 84–94.

Faulkner, D. and Bowman, C. (1995). *The Essence of Corporate Strategy*. Hemel Hempstead: Prentice-Hall.

Garland, R. (2005). 'Segmenting retail banking customers'. *Journal of Financial Services Marketing*, 10/2: 179–91.

Gilmore, J. and Pine, B., II (1997). 'The four faces of mass customization'. *Harvard Business Review*, 75/1: 91–101.

Gilmore, J. and Pine, B., II (2000). *Markets of One: Creating Customer-unique Value through Mass Customization*. Boston: Harvard Business School Press Books.

Hooley, G. and Greenley, G. (2005). 'The resource underpinnings of competitive positions'. *Journal of Strategic Marketing*, 13/2: 93–116.

Hooley, G., Saunders, J., Piercy, N., and Nicolaud, B. (2007). *Marketing Strategy and Competitive Positioning*. 4th edn. Harlow: FT Prentice Hall.

Kim, W. and Mauborgne, R. (1999). 'Creating new market space'. *Harvard Business Review*, 77/1: 83–93.

Kim, W. and Mauborgne, R. (2004). 'Blue ocean strategy'. *Harvard Business Review*, 82/10: 76–84.

Kim, W. and Mauborgne, R. (2005). 'Blue ocean strategy: From theory to practice'. *California Management Review*, 47/3: 105–21.

Kotha, S. (1995). 'Mass customization: implementing the emerging paradigm for competitive advantage'. *Strategic Management Journal*, 16/5: 21–42.

Kotha, S. and Vadlamani, B. (1995). 'Assessing generic strategies: an empirical investigation of two competing typologies in discrete manufacturing industries'. *Strategic Management Journal*, 16/1: 75–83.

Lam, D. (2007). 'Cultural influence on proneness to brand loyalty'. *Journal of International Consumer Marketing*, 19/3: 7–21.

Mathur, S. and Kenyon, A. (2001). *Creating Value: Successful Business Strategies*. 2nd edn. Oxford: Butterworth Heinemann.

Miles, R. and Snow, C. (1978). *Organizational Structure, Strategy, Process*. New York: McGraw Hill.

Miller, A. and Dess, G. (1993). 'Assessing Porter's 1980 model in terms of its generalisability, accuracy and simplicity'. *Journal of Management Studies*, 30/4: 553–85.

Mintzberg, H. (1991). 'Generic strategies'. In Mintzberg, H. and Quinn, J. B. (eds), *The Strategy Process*. 2nd edn. Englewood Cliffs, NJ: Prentice-Hall.

Nathan, J. (1999). *Sony: The Private Life*. London: HarperCollins.

Nayyar, P. (1993). 'On the measurement of competitive strategy: evidence from a large multiproduct US firm'. *Academy of Management Journal*, 36/6: 1652–69.

Nunes, P., Johnson, B., and Breene, R. (2004). 'Selling to the moneyed masses'. *Harvard Business Review*, 82/7–8: 94–104.

Olsen, S. (2007). 'Repurchase loyalty: the role of involvement and satisfaction'. *Psychology & Marketing*, 24/4: 315–41.

Pine II, B., Victor, B., and Boynton, A. (1993). 'Making mass customization work'. *Harvard Business Review*, 71/5: 108–18.

Porter, M. (1980). *Competitive Strategy*. New York: Free Press.

Porter, M. (1985). *Competitive Advantage*. New York: Free Press.

Reinartz, W. and Kumar, V. (2002). 'The mismanagement of customer loyalty'. *Harvard Business Review*, 80/7: 86–94.

Ries, A. and Trout, J. (1982). *Positioning: The Battle for your Mind*. New York: Warner Books.

Sharpe, B. and Dawes, J. (2001). 'What is differentiation and how does it work?' *Journal of Marketing Management*, 17: 739–59.

Smit, E., Bronner, F., and Tolboom, M. (2007). 'Brand relationship quality and its value for personal contact'. *Journal of Business Research*, 60/6: 627–33.

Thornhill, S. and White, R. (2007). 'Strategic purity: A multi-industry evaluation of pure vs. hybrid business strategies'. *Strategic Management Journal*, 28/5: 553–61.

Treacy, M. and Wiersema, F. (1993). 'Customer intimacy and other value disciplines'. *Harvard Business Review*, 71/1: 84–93.

Vorhies, D., Harker, M., and Rao, C. (1999). 'The capabilities and performance advantages of market-driven firms', *European Journal of Marketing*, 33/11–12: 1171–202.

Wind, Y. (1978). 'Issues and advances in segmentation research'. *Journal of Marketing Research*, 15/3: 317–37.

Yankelovich, D. and Meer, D. (2006). 'Rediscovering market segmentation'. *Harvard Business Review*, 84/2: 122–31.

Zeithaml, V., Rust, R., and Lemon, K. (2001). 'The customer pyramid: creating and serving profitable customers'. *California Management Review*, 43/4: 118–42.

 ### End-of-chapter Case Study 4.1   eBay (a)[41]

A talented public relations man is probably responsible for the story of how computer professional Pierre Omidyar set up Auctionweb, to track down rare Pez[a] containers for his wife's collection. But the truth of how Auctionweb, founded in September 1995, grew into eBay, source of Omidyar's $10.4bn fortune, requires no such embellishment. From one person's hobby, eBay has grown into an institution with 8,100 full-time employees and nearly 150 million registered users, over 150,000 of whom earn their living trading on the site. The number of users grew at an average rate of 99 per cent per year in the period 1998–2004, the volume of merchandise traded at 78 per cent p.a. and the firm's own revenues at 70 per cent. In its 2005 presentation to shareholders, the company claimed that, on an average day, its platform was used to trade one comic book in France, one mobile phone in China, and one car in the USA per minute, whilst a tractor in Germany was sold every seven minutes and a watch in India every five.[42] Omidyar handed over day-to-day control of the company to Meg Whitman in 1998. Though he retains the title of Chairman of the Board, he can afford, at the age of 38, to list his occupation as 'full-time philanthropist'.[43]

What eBay sells

eBay's vision is the provision of 'a global trading platform where practically anyone can trade practically anything'.[44] Almost anything legal, new and old, can indeed be bought and sold on ➜

→ eBay—around 50 million items are available for sale on eBay at any given time—but used goods are very much the core business, including of course the collectible items which form the company's mythical roots. Another staple business is the sale of obsolescent goods—although most traders are individuals and small firms, major companies like IBM, Dell, and Vodafone have woken up to the possibilities that eBay offers for selling off excess inventory.

The firm's auction websites boast 35 major categories of merchandise, from 'Antiques and Art', through 'Automotive'— eBay now hosts the largest used car market (by revenue) in the US—to 'Toys', 'Travel', 'Video Games' and 'Everything Else'. There are over 50,000 sub-categories. Goods worth over $34bn were sold on eBay during 2004, representing 14 per cent by value of global e-commerce transactions.[45]

Revenues from listing fees and commissions (the firm's websites carry next to no advertisements other than for items listed for sale) came to over $3 billion in 2004—a target set by Whitman in 2000[46] had been met with a year to spare. As Table 4.5 shows, this growth has not come at the expense of profitability: operating profit margins are of the order of 30 per cent. The firm has 27 websites, each of which is tailored to the demands of a particular country. Nearly two-thirds of its net transaction revenues derive from the USA, but in its 2004 Annual Report it identified Germany, the UK, Canada, and South Korea as important sources of revenue and profit.[47]

Competition

In many markets, eBay has little direct competition. Although Amazon, the most successful internet retailer, and internet portals Yahoo and Excite (the latter in partnership with Microsoft) all tried to build auction businesses, none has attracted anything like the 11 per cent of Internet users worldwide that have enlisted with eBay. Excite, despite Microsoft's backing, ceased operations as an independent company in December 2001, and its successor site no longer offers auctions.

This is not to say that eBay is unstoppable. Yahoo, which entered the Japanese market first, dominates the auction business there to the extent that eBay closed its operations in Japan in 2002. In the USA, there are successful specialist websites for the sale of used cars (AutoTrader.com) and tickets for concerts and sporting events (StubHub.com). AutoTrader has around 80 times as many cars listed for sale as there are on eBay's US site, although its revenues are estimated to be below those of eBay's US automobile business, because eBay handles the complete transaction, whilst AutoTrader acts mainly as a listings service and does not in most cases play a part in the sale. Similarly StubHub, which, unlike eBay, guarantees delivery of the ticket prior to the event, claims double eBay's number of listings, but actual trading volume appears to be higher on eBay.[48]

Amazon, a major force in online retailing, now offers its website, for a price, as a platform for others to sell all kinds of goods, which are advertised alongside Amazon's own offerings. There are many product categories, such as books, music, videos, and electronics, where Amazon has a strong reputation as a reliable supplier with a broad range. This makes it an attractive alternative to eBay for buyers and sellers of new or used items in those categories, the more so since some 30 per cent of eBay transactions are now at fixed prices rather than at auction.

However, for most transactions, the main alternatives to eBay are classified advertisements in local newspapers or specialist small-ads papers (*Exchange and Mart* and *Loot* in the UK), or specialist intermediaries. There are dealers that buy and sell secondhand goods such as cars, domestic appliances, coins, or furniture. They have considerable knowledge and experience of what an item is worth in the marketplace, how much they will need to spend on repairing it and, perhaps, where they are most likely to find a buyer. They thus know exactly how much they can afford to pay for an item in order to cover their overheads and sell at a profit but, of course, have an interest in keeping the price to the seller as low as possible. However, they typically will offer the seller instant payment upon delivery of the item, or will take it in part-exchange for other goods. Traditional auction houses, by contrast, take a commission from both buyer and seller, and therefore have an interest in maximizing the sellers' revenues. They may also be able to offer advice on how much an item is likely to be worth. However, their commission rates are quite steep, since they need to cover their overheads—the cost of auctioneers, valuers, and warehouses—and they may only hold auctions for a particular class of item (e.g. mid-twentieth-century furniture) every few months.

Buying and selling on eBay

Auctions on eBay, by contrast, can start at any time and typically last seven days, though vendors can opt for a shorter duration or to sell to the first person that offers a fixed 'BuyItNow' price. They receive cash or cheque payments shortly after the auction finishes, or, if their trading record is good enough, they can set up an account with PayPal, a subsidiary of eBay, which enables them to accept credit card payments. eBay charges vendors a commission based on the price at which the item was sold.[b]

Along with information about the item and the progress of the auction, eBay gives buyers and sellers the opportunity to view information about one another simply by following web links attached to each participant's user ID. They can see how many items that person has bought and sold and the feedback that other eBay users have left about him or her, and thus judge their reliability as a buyer or seller. Bidders can assess the risk involved in sending the seller their money, and can also email →

➜ the seller for supplementary information during the auction. Sellers can decide whether a bidder is likely to be serious, and have the option to block bids from buyers whom they reckon to be unacceptable.

How an eBay auction functions

Both buyers and sellers must register with eBay in order to participate in an auction. They must provide email addresses, postal addresses, and in the case of the seller, details of a credit or debit card to which eBay can charge its commission once the sale has been completed. Once registered, a vendor has only a simple form to complete in order to get a basic listing for their item on eBay. Extra features, such as images of the item for sale, can be added to the listing with reasonable ease, although for some, such as headings in large or bold typefaces, a basic knowledge of HTML[c] is needed. The seller pays eBay a small fee for each listing, depending on the value of the item for sale—in the UK, in 2005, these ranged from £0.15 to £2.00 for most items, £6 for a car and £35 for real estate. Multiple items of the same type can be listed for much the same price as a single item, but sellers can opt to pay extra to include extra pictures or have their item given greater prominence—for example, in a highlighted section at the top of their category or even on the eBay home page.

The vendor may have an idea of what the item is worth, and for a small fee (2 per cent of the value between £50 and £5,000 in the UK in 2005) set a reserve price below which they are not prepared to sell it. Bidders will not be aware of this reserve price, but only the starting price for the auction, which typically will be set lower than the reserve price, to stimulate interest and get the auction going. A buyer, once signed into the site, can bid for any item by entering their own maximum valuation in a dialogue box. The eBay software then bids on their behalf in predetermined increments of, say, £5, until the bidding ends or goes above what they are prepared to pay.

Once the auction is over, eBay's proprietary software automatically notifies the winning bidder and the seller of one another's identities, email, and postal addresses. It is then down to the people in question to arrange delivery and payment. Unless the seller notifies eBay of any problems with the buyer, he or she will be debited with eBay's commission charge for the transaction.

Watching an auction develop, either as seller or buyer, can be tremendous fun. Most start slowly, with a few low bids from bargain seekers; serious buyers tend to wait until the last 48 hours, and bidding can get quite fast and furious as they compete to land the knock-out blow as the auction reaches its climax— 30 per cent of eBay bids take place in the final two hours of the auction.

Managing eBay

An unusual organization like eBay poses a number of management challenges. On a day to day basis, there is the need to ensure that users get a fast, reliable and error-free service. In the medium term, there is the challenge of driving the company forward in the absence of the natural spur provided by competition. And alongside this, there is the need to maintain the trust of the broader community that is centred on eBay.

On a busy day in 2004, the company had to support about 890 million page views and process about 7.7 Gb of data during each second of peak usage.[49] It is clearly not acceptable if response times slow down or the system freezes during the crucial minutes towards the end of an auction. So the company has invested substantial sums in information technology—computer hardware and software were valued at over $670 million on its balance sheet at the end of 2004, and the company's IT spending had exceeded $200 million per annum during 2003 and 2004. (By way of comparison, Amazon.com's balance sheet at the end of 2004 showed $246 million of total fixed assets.[50])

All of this is overseen by a team of highly qualified professionals. Meg Whitman herself is a graduate of Harvard Business School and has held high-profile positions at firms including Procter & Gamble, the Walt Disney Company, strategy consultant Bain and Company, and toymaker Hasbro. Many of her senior colleagues have, like her, a background with major strategy consulting firms and a dedication to measuring progress in sophisticated ways, so that performance can be enhanced. 'If it moves, measure it' is a company slogan: the firm knows not only how long users stay on the site (eBay has one of the web's highest 'stickiness' ratios) but which days are busiest and what is the ratio of firms' revenues to the value of goods traded. The category managers (a job title borrowed from Procter & Gamble) develop ways in which lots for sale can be better presented and merchandised. They circulate sophisticated presentations to justify their intended moves to their superiors and win the necessary resources, for which there is fierce competition, even though the company generated $1.3bn of cash from its 2004 operations and has a policy of paying no dividends to shareholders.

Every proposal is subject to detailed scrutiny by specialists in functions such as technology and marketing, which naturally takes time. It took two months for the category management team for clothing to get permission to give women's shoes their own subcategory. To enhance the site's search engine to make it easier to locate shoes in a given colour and size took a further ten months.

Nonetheless, this does not appear to have an adverse effect upon eBay's relationship with its users. As Omidyar and Whitman circulated at eBay's 2003 convention in Florida, signing collectible cards featuring their cartoon images,[d] they were warmly received by the 10,000 assembled members, who had come to ➜

→ socialize with their peers, but also to learn how to improve their sales. The company makes great efforts to stay in touch with these users, emailing them with special offers and inviting feedback. Members who do not feel that they can get their views across using eBay's discussion boards and user forums can—and do—email Meg Whitman directly; she receives 500 emails a day.[51]

The users, in their turn, appear to set great store by their status within the eBay community: their ratings by other users or their designation as 'power sellers' (there are five levels of power seller, ranging from 'bronze' to 'titanium'—the latter sell at least $150,000-worth of goods each month). But the community appears to be more than just a source of personal self-esteem. The eBay website tells of members meeting up for picnics and holidays, doing home repairs for fellow members in need, and policing one another to ensure that etiquette is followed and trust is maintained.

Challenges

Trust is, of course, vital if eBay transactions are to take place. Apart from the rating system, eBay has a customer support team called SafeHarbor to promote a safe, fraud-free, trading environment. Small abuses abound—people contacting members who have bid for an item, offering similar goods at lower prices, or contacting sellers to persuade them to sell outside the auction and avoid the commission. These, although annoying for the majority of members who abide by the community's rules, will not undermine the company's business model. However a small, but increasing, number of professional criminals are using eBay as a platform for fraud. Some auction goods at apparent bargain prices which, once paid for, are never delivered, and may never have existed, while others cancel their payments after the goods have been dispatched.[52]   →

Table 4.5 eBay financial performance 1998–2004

Year ending 31 December	1998	1999	2000	2001	2002	2003	2004
Net revenues	86.1	224.7	431.4	748.8	1,214.1	2,165.1	3,271.3
Cost of net revenues	16.1	57.6	95.5	134.8	213.9	416.1	614.4
Gross profit	70.0	167.1	336.0	614.1	1,000.2	1,749.0	2,656.9
Operating expenses							
Sales and marketing	36.0	96.2	166.8	253.5	349.7	567.6	857.9
Product development	4.6	24.8	55.9	75.3	104.6	159.3	240.6
General and administrative	15.8	43.9	73.0	105.8	171.8	302.7	415.7
Patent litigation expense						30.0	
Payroll taxes on stock options	—	—	2.3	2.4	4.0	9.6	17.5
Amortization of acquired intangible assets	0.8	1.1	1.4	36.6	15.9	50.7	65.9
Merger related costs	—	4.4	1.6	—	—		
Total operating expenses	57.3	170.5	301.0	473.6	646.0	1,119.8	1,597.7
Income from operations	12.8	(3.4)	35.0	140.4	354.2	629.2	1,059.2
Net income	7.3	9.6	48.3	90.4	249.9	441.8	778.2
Registered users (M)	2.2	10.0	22.5	42.4	61.7	94.9	135.5
Number of items listed (M)	33.7	129.6	264.7	423.1	638.3	971.0	1,412.6
Gross merchandise sales	745	2,805	5,422	9,319	14,868	23,779	34,168
Balance sheet data							
Cash and cash equivalents	37.3	221.8	201.9	524.0	1,109.3	1,381.5	1,330.0
Short-term investments	40.4	181.1	354.2	199.5	89.7	340.6	682.0
Long-term investments	—	374.0	218.2	287.0	470.2	934.2	1,266.3
Working capital	72.9	372.3	538.0	703.7	1,082.2	1,498.6	1,826.3
Total assets	149.5	969.8	1,182.4	1,678.5	4,040.2	5,820.1	7,991.1
Short-term debt	n/r	n/r	15.3	16.1	3.0	2.8	124.3
Long-term debt	18.4	15.0	11.4	12.1	13.8	124.5	—
Total stockholders' equity	100.5	854.1	1,013.8	1,429.1	3,556.5	4,896.2	6,728.3

Notes

All figures in $ million except where stated

n/r = not reported

Source

2002 and 2004 Annual Reports

→ EBay spends millions of dollars on preventing and prosecuting such activity. It also has a clear policy against the listing of any items that are illegal, and will step in and cancel any auctions that it believes are inappropriate. Some of these, such as a University of Washington student who offered his soul for sale in 2001, simply show questionable taste.[53] Others, such as the Bristol University student who in 2004 auctioned her virginity to reduce her debts, are on the fringes of illegality.[54] But the sheer number of listings on eBay—5 million new ones each day—makes it difficult for the firm to intercept all suspicious transactions. A *Sunday Times* journalist in 2005 found pornographic material and throwing-knives—illegal in the UK—on sale, and there have also been complaints—strongly rebutted by eBay—that guns are being sold illegally on the site.[55] Employees of the subsidiaries in India and Korea have been prosecuted in connection with listings on eBay's sites there.[56]

Meanwhile of course, eBay is as affected as any other internet-based business by the increased hazards presented by worms and viruses, and by the overloading of the World Wide Web with unsolicited email traffic. And the headlong pace of eBay's growth is posing other kinds of challenge. It faces an exacting task in continuously upgrading its hardware and software to keep pace with demand. During 2004, an upgrade to the billing system led a number of customers being overcharged, while an upgrade to the PayPal payment system disrupted access to that site.[57] The firm has also had to hire around 2,000 new employees each year since 2002 and train them in the eBay ethos of customer service.

Case study questions

1. Who are eBay's customers for its auction business, and to what extent do they constitute an attractive target market?

2. What forms of differentiation does eBay use with those customers? How appropriate is this positioning to the segments it is targeting?

3. How good is the match between eBay's resources and its positioning? How sustainable is its differentiation?

Notes

a Pez is a brand of US sugar confectionery. The spring-loaded dispensers it sells for its sweets, featuring the heads of figures like Donald Duck, Miss Piggy, or Garfield, have become collector's items.

b For vehicles there is a fixed commission of £18. There is no commission charge for real estate.

c HTML, the Hypertext Mark-up Language, is the standard coding used for pages on the World Wide Web.

d An autographed set of these cards was subsequently sold on eBay for $22.

● NOTES

1   The term 'competitive stance' is our own, but forceful arguments for the importance of product and market selection in strategy can be found in Ohmae (1982) and Kim and Mauborgne (1999, 2004, 2005).

2   See, for example, Day (1994). Vorhies et al. (1999) have found empirical evidence of the benefits of being market-driven.

3   Source: Nathan (1999) and numerous public sources.

4   For a good review of segmentation techniques, see Chapter 7 of Porter (1985).

5   The definitive work on this was by Wind (1978). Cardozo (1980) and Bonoma and Shapiro (1984) extended this for B2B markets.

6   Source: Mintel International Group Limited: Food Retailing—Europe—November 2004.

7   The idea of mass customization was introduced in the early 1990s, and has gained momentum with the spread of the internet. See Pine et al. (1993), Kotha (1995), and Gilmore and Pine (1997, 2000).

8   Zeithaml et al. (2001) give some interesting advice on how firms should segment their customers.

9   Quoted in his obituary in the *Economist*, 1 March 2003: 91.

10 Steiner, R. (1999). 'Pinstripes put Roddick on the right scent—My first break—Interview—Anita Roddick'. *Sunday Times*, 24 October; Billen, A. (2001). '"If your husband has an affair you end up being kinder to each other . . . more caring"'. *Evening Standard*, 28 March.

11 This is discussed in depth by C. K. Prahalad (2005).

12 See Nunes et al. (2004).

13 In fact, the relationship between brand loyalty and profitability is rather more complicated than this—not all loyal customers are profitable (Reinartz and Kumar, 2002), and not all brands are equally likely to engender loyalty (Smit et al., 2007). See Lam (2007) and Olsen (2007) for analyses of the cultural and other factors that make customers loyal; Day (1969) and Dick and Basu (1994) for early conceptual papers in the area; and Garland (2005) for a readable review.

14 The classic work on positioning theory is Ries and Trout (1982). For a more recent review, see Hooley et al. (2007).

15 The following analysis is a development of a framework set out by Henry Mintzberg (1991); see Kotha and Vadlamani (1995) for an empirical test.

16 The importance of richness was identified by Evans and Wurster (1999).

17 For a discussion of the importance of the organization versus the product in positioning, and in strategy more generally, see Aaker (2004) and Mathur and Kenyon (2001).

18 This is another concept of Evans and Wurster (1999).

19 Kehoe, L. (1990). 'Window of opportunity: the latest challenge to Apple's pioneering place in the personal computer market'. *Financial Times*, 24 May: 25; Mossberg, W. (1992). 'Personal technology'. *Wall Street Journal*, 6 August: B1; Weber, T. (1992). 'Apple's PC Price Cuts Fall Within Expected Range'. *Dow Jones News Service*, 28 September.

20 Corcoran, E. (1995). 'Putting muscle into Apple's marketing'. *The Washington Post*, 30 July: H01; Hick, V. (1996). 'Cutting to the core', *St Louis Post Despatch*. 24 March: 01E.

21 Kehoe (1990) op. cit.; Mossberg (1992) op. cit.

22 Apple form 10K405, pp. 15 and 38, filed with SEC on 21 December 2001. Downloaded from <http://www.apple.com/investor> on 11 June 2007.

23 *Dow Jones Business News* (2001). 'Apple plans digital music player, moving beyond computer buyers'. 24 October; Schlender, B. (2001). 'Apple's 21st-century Walkman'. *Fortune*, 144/9: 213; Salkever, A. (2002). 'Finally, a chance for Apple to flourish'. *BusinessWeek Online*, 23 January.

24 <http://osviews.com/modules.php?op=modload&name=News&file=article&sid=4259>, accessed 17 June 2005.

25 Schlender, B. (2005), 'How big can Apple get?', *Fortune*, 21 February: 39–45; Teather, D. (2005) 'iPod sales get Apple Computer dancing'. *Guardian*, 14 July: 19; Vaughan, A. (2005). 'Not so safe and sound'. *Guardian*, Online section, 16 June 2005: 19.

26 For further evidence on the importance of a precise understanding of customer needs, see Christensen et al. (2005) and Yankelovich and Meer (2006).

27 See Attia and Hooley (2007) and Hooley and Greenley (2005).

28 The figures cited in the coming discussion are all taken from the Eurostat database at <http://epp.eurostat.cec.eu.int/>, accessed 17 July 2007.

29 Porter (1980).

30 When academics refer to generic strategies, they normally use the 'prospector/defender/analyzer' typology proposed by Miles and Snow (1978), which does not relate to competitive stance.

31 Because of the shape of the two-dimensional diagram that Faulkner and Bowman (1995) originally used to illustrate this framework, it is often known as the 'strategy clock'.

32 Treacy and Wiersema (1993) derived this framework from their work as consultants.

33 Thornhill and White (2007).

34 *Daily Mail* (2005). 'Does Japan offer the shoots of recovery?' 16 November: 16; Lewis, L. (2006). 'Vodafone licks its wounds after five years of failure in Japan'. *The Times*, 4 March, 62; White, D. (2004). 'Japanese customers hang up on Vodafone'. *Daily Telegraph*, 7 August: 25. Nakamoto, M. (2003). 'J-Phone rings changes to keep callers engaged'. *Financial Times*, 30 September: 32.

35 Durman, P. (2005). 'Vodafone's tough call to succeed in Japan', *Sunday Times*, Business Section, 19 June: 12.

36 *Economist* (2004). 'Not so big in Japan', 30 September; Judge, E. and Lewis, L. (2005). 'Vodafone accused of desperation over Japan relaunch'. *The Times*, 16 June.

37 Durman, P. (2005) op cit.

38 Wray, R. (2005) 'Vodafone makes gains in Japan', *Guardian*, 8 September, 21.

39 Davidson, A. (2006). 'Telefonica stops O2 boss flying off into the sunset: the Andrew Davidson interview: Peter Erskine'. *The Sunday Times*, Business Section, 29 January: 9.

40 *Citywire* (2006). 'Vodafone sells Japanese interests to SoftBank'. 17 March; *Economist* (2006). 'Calling for a rethink', 26 January; *Economist* (2006). 'Not-so-big is beautiful', 9 March; Turner, D. (2006). 'Softbank and Vodafone form mobile joint venture', *Financial Times*, 19 May: 28.

41 Apart from the other sources directly cited, this case study has drawn from: <http://www.ebay.com>, accessed 12 September 2003 and 16 October 2005; Rushe, D. (2003). 'Net profit'. *Sunday Times*, Business Section, 6 July: 3.5; *Economist* (2005). 'Meg and the power of many'. 11 June: 71–4; *Economist* (2005). 'Happy e-birthdays'. 23 July: 62–3.

42 Microsoft Powerpoint—Shareholder Presentation FINAL, downloaded from <http://investor. ebay.com> on 16 October 2005.

43 <http://pages.ebay.com/aboutebay/thecompany/executiveteam.html#Omidyar>, accessed 12 June 2007.

44 Microsoft Powerpoint—Shareholder Presentation FINAL, p. 4.

45 Ibid.: 9 and 2004 Annual Report: 1.

46 Lashinsky, A. (2003). 'Meg and the machine'. *Fortune*, Europe Edition, 8 September: 48–54.

47 2004 Annual Report: 44.

48 Wingfield, N. (2004). 'Taking on eBay'. *Wall Street Journal*, September 13: R10.

49 eBay 2004 Annual Report: 11.

50 Amazon.com Investor Relations <http://phx.corporate-ir.net/phoenix.zhtml?c=97664&p=irol-reportsHistorical>, accessed 19 October 2005.

51 Lashinsky (2003) op. cit.

52 Bowcott, O. (2004). 'Cheated take on the cheats in battle of internet sales site'. *Guardian*, 22 March: 3.

53 Rahner, M. (2001). 'Woodinville man sells soul for $400. eBay ousts listing from online auction site'. *The Seattle Times*, 9 February: B2.

54 Cave, F. (2004). 'Virginity auction girl faces legal action'. *Financial Times*, 11 February: 6; Bowcott (2004) op. cit.

55 Rowan. D. (2005). 'It offers everything—including the dream of success and financial independence'. *Sunday Times Magazine*, 20 February: 42–8.

56 eBay 2004 Annual Report: 54.

57 Ibid.: 53.

CHAPTER FIVE

Distinctiveness (2) Scope, Scale, and Diversity

LEARNING OUTCOMES

After reading this chapter you should be able to:

→ Discuss why organizations may choose to be either broad or narrow in the number of markets they address and the products that they offer

→ Explain the reasons why organizations diversify, and the risks involved and evaluate the arguments for and against diversification

→ Explain the factors that have been shown to make for effective, as against ineffective, diversification

→ Assess an organization's diversification strategy in terms of the trade-offs between risks and benefits

→ Evaluate an organization's portfolio of offerings and businesses, particularly in terms of the degree of relatedness, and the potential for synergies, between them.

INTRODUCTION

In the previous chapter we discussed competitive stance in terms of organizations' choices of which segments to serve and how to target their products at those segments. But the concept of competitive stance also embraces decisions as to *how many* segments to serve and *how many* products to put on the market, and at corporate level, how many businesses to be in. Should an organization concentrate on one product in one market, or spread itself more broadly across a number of different products, markets or even industries?

There are clear attractions to being bigger, and more diverse. By offering a broader range of choices to its customers, an organization can make itself attractive to them. If it can make the different parts of the company work well together, then it may become a more formidable competitor in other ways as well: more efficient, and with a broader range of skills to call upon. Less obvious, however, are the very real risks that the sales from the new products or markets will not be profitable, or that any profits will not justify the extra investments involved. In this chapter we explore the benefits and risks of diversity, and the trade-offs between them.

So this chapter examines the implications of organizations' choices in respect of the scope and diversity of their markets and 'offerings'—the products and services they offer in those markets. Organizations also have important choices to make about whether, for example, they should design or manufacture these products and services themselves, or get other firms to do so. Such decisions, about vertical integration in the value chain, are examined in Chapter 6.

5.1 Expansion and diversification

Most organizations start out with limited resources, which means that they are constrained in the numbers of different types of customer they can look after and the range of products and services they can develop. This forces them to focus their efforts, so that the different elements of a firm's value chain are set up to cater specifically for the needs of a particular segment and for any specialized technologies.

But there are potent forces, which we discuss in more detail in Section 5.2, that drive organizations, particularly successful ones, to consider broadening the scope of their activities. One force is the fear of being dependent upon one small set of customers or technologies. Probably more important is the fact that good entrepreneurs will, once they have found customers and developed the value chain to serve them, spot other ways that they can use their resources to generate profits.[1] They may find that their customers have other, unfulfilled, needs which their organization is in a position to meet. Or, they may encounter new customers, who require a modified version of the product or service, or who have other needs that can be met using the resources that the organization has developed. Meeting these needs may lead a firm into completely different industries from those in which it started (see Real-life Application 5.1). As a result, over time, ambitious companies, like Sony, expand so that they have many different divisions, with their own differently configured value chains, which provide a wide variety of products tailored for specific segments.

Real-life Application 5.1 SonyCierge: how a mass market electronics conglomerate got into personal services for the rich and famous

When Jacqueline Krueger was hired to develop a business-to-business service team at Sony Corporation seven years ago,[2] the company's newly appointed chairman, Howard Stringer, asked her over to his house. Her task was to analyse his technological needs and install the most up-to-date, top-of-the-line products that Sony makes for the home. She did, and he was delighted.

Soon, she was providing the same service for other executives at the company, artists associated with Sony's music and film businesses, and Stringer's friends. 'It kept growing and growing', she says. 'So I wrote a business plan for creating a personal shopping group.'

SonyCierge, as the unit is now called, was launched in the US in 2001 and has offices in New York, Los Angeles and Miami, employing 20 'cierges' and 20 installers. Membership is by invitation only; Sony has its own list of worthy entrants and partners with outside organizations, such as Sotheby's, which invites some private clients, or Manhattan developments One Beacon Court and Trump Park Avenue, which offer the service to residents. Annual dues are $1,500, not including any equipment purchased or installation costs incurred.

An outside observer might conclude that SonyCierge is getting paid to sell its own company's products. But Krueger, the unit's director, contends that it is also providing a unique service: experts in home electronics who oversee the selection and installation of gadgets and who are then available to meet your technology demands and answer your questions—or find someone who can—24 hours a day. [. . .]

Although SonyCierge has been successful, the group plans to cap membership at 10,000 for now. 'It's not a programme that appeals to everyone (and) we need to maintain a certain level of customer service', Krueger says. 'Once we hit that we can talk about opening another satellite office.'

Reproduced with kind permission of the *Financial Times*

Business development is not always a good thing. It is surprisingly easy for a firm to be lured into pursuing opportunities that appear attractive, but in fact are unprofitable, because the firm does not have the resources to manage them efficiently or effectively.[3] On the other hand, being too focused may also have disadvantages. A firm that has too limited a range of products can lose out to firms with products that meet the range of a customer's needs more closely. In Section 5.2, we shall look in more detail at the trade-offs a company makes in deciding how diverse it wants, or needs, to be, and at how to assess the resulting strategies.

5.1.1 Diversity and diversification at business level

There are a number of ways, summarized in Figure 5.1, in which a firm can increase its diversity. The simplest is by developing *slightly* different offerings, perhaps to target *slightly* different markets from those it serves at the moment, or to meet more precisely the needs a sub-segment of existing customers. Examples include:

- McDonald's introduction of the Bigger Big Mac, targeted at existing customers with above-average appetites, in order to increase their spend at McDonald's;

- H&M's development of a line of clothing for pregnant women. Women who are pregnant can and do buy clothes marketed for women who are not—but they are likely to feel more at home in a store where some of the clothes are designed especially for them. H&M can increase its chances of retaining existing customers who become pregnant, and also make it more likely that those same women will buy clothes from its children's ranges in due course;

- Sony's introduction of a range of LCD TVs.

These extensions to a firm's offerings typically do not involve any radical changes to the way the firm does business. However, taken to extremes, they can make a firm difficult to manage. Unilever, the Anglo-Dutch consumer goods conglomerate, found itself in 1999

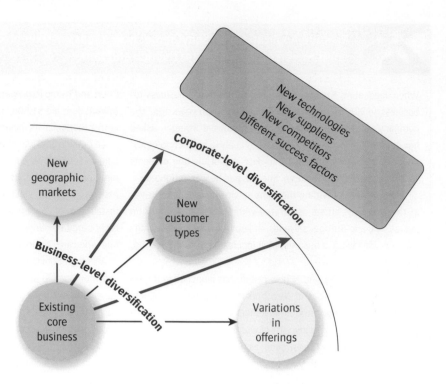

Figure 5.1

with 1,600 brands, (products, or variants of products), of which just 400 'power brands' accounted for 90 per cent of sales. It decided that, by disposing of some of these and focusing its marketing, research and personnel, it could raise its profit margins closer to those of its leading competitors.[4]

Firms may also become more diverse by extending the range of customers and markets that they are consciously targeting. Typically, this involves an addition to the range of offerings as well, since customer segments differ in their tastes and requirements. For example, the camcorders that Sony makes for consumers have a limited range of features so that they can be compact and easy to set up and use. The camcorders offered to corporate markets are bulkier, but offer a choice of formats in which to record, a higher resolution microphone and greater variety of video and audio inputs and outputs—they are designed for experienced, demanding professionals. Such differences can become even more pronounced when firms extend themselves geographically, into different regions of countries where they already do business, or into entirely new countries or continents. Firms may try to keep things simple and avoid adding new product variants for each new market, but this policy involves risks that we discuss in Section 5.2.

Substantial changes to the range of offerings, or to the markets served, or both, are known as diversification. This term was originally reserved for moves involving both new offerings and new markets.[5] It has come, however, to denote any extension of an organization's activities into new areas. It is now regarded as perfectly correct to speak of 'product' or 'geographic' diversification even if there is some overlap between the organization's new customer bases and offerings and its existing ones.

There is a third path an organization's managers can take towards greater diversity. They may extend its range of offerings in ways that do not necessarily follow from the requirements they have identified for existing customers. Maybe an enterprising employee has developed an innovative product or service, or an innovative improvement to an existing one, as was the case with Apple and the iPod. Perhaps they have unused capacity that they believe can be used to generate profits. This was the logic that led airlines such as BA to offer cargo services—to capitalize on underutilized space in the holds of their aircraft.

Diversification

A substantial extension of an organization's activities through the introduction of new varieties of product or service and/or moves into markets which the organization has not penetrated to any great extent.

5.1.2 Business-level versus corporate-level diversification

Whatever the path an organization takes to increase its diversity, at some stage it is likely to cross the boundary between business-level and corporate-level diversification. Corporate-level diversification comes about when a firm finds itself involved in two or more separate industries with different success factors. For example, SonyCierge (Real-life Application 5.1), which is a technology-based service, has very different success factors and different competitors from those its parent confronts in the manufacturing of consumer electronics, or even in its established service businesses—insurance and banking. Sony, in fact, is a highly diversified corporation that we analyse in detail in Worked Example 5.1.

Real-life Application 5.2 Corporate-level diversification

BA, like many airlines, offers a cargo service, which is a logical way of gaining economies of scope by utilizing spare hold space on its passenger aircraft. Maintenance facilities and timetabling competences can also be shared between the two businesses. The corporate clients that purchase freight services may well be the same firms that purchase business-class tickets for travelling executives. So this could be conceived as a business-level expansion. However, it is highly unlikely that the people in a firm who purchase cargo services will be exactly the same as those that organize executive travel, so that the two product lines will need separate sales channels.

When BA launched this service, most of the major competitors in freight were other passenger airlines, some of which, like Germany's Lufthansa, remain very active in that business. Nowadays, however, key competitors like FedEx and DHL are dedicated freight carriers that do not tie their delivery schedules to the times of passenger flights. They also offer their customers a range of other logistical services, and competing with them requires dedicated delivery fleets and expensive warehouses, such as BA's at Heathrow. Success in this industry comes from ensuring that every item is delivered precisely when promised, and giving the customer precise information on the status of their delivery, which in turn requires sophisticated IT capabilities. So while at the beginning BA's cargo business might have appeared a simple, business-level product extension, it is now too dissimilar from the core business to be regarded as such.

As we noted in Chapter 3, the boundaries of an industry can be difficult to define, so that it is often difficult to judge at what stage a firm makes this transition between business-level and corporate-level diversification (Real-life Application 5.2). The distinction between the two is not the same as the difference between minor and major strategic moves. SonyCierge is, as yet, too small to be considered vital to Sony Corporation, but is a corporate-level diversification. On the other hand, when Airbus managers decided to develop a 'jumbo' aircraft, the A380, to compete with Boeing's 747, this was clearly a major strategic decision. They committed Airbus to massive investments of cash and other resources, in an attempt to tackle Boeing in a product area that it had dominated since 1967. But this did not move the company away from its existing business of airline manufacture.

As we shall see in the following sections, there is a great deal of overlap between the challenges of managing a business with a broad portfolio of offerings and the challenges of managing a corporation with a broad portfolio of businesses. However, there are also important differences in emphasis, with the degree of relatedness between businesses, and the extent to which synergies are possible between them, being particularly important at corporate level. That is why it is important to recognize whether an organization has made the transition from single business to corporation.

Portfolio

The range of products, services, or brands offered by a business. Also, the range of strategic business units (SBUs) controlled by a diversified corporation.

**Strategic business
unit (SBU)**

A part of a firm that operates
in a distinct industry, or
sometimes a substantial
sub-sector within an
industry: an independent
subsidiary company, an
operating division, or
part of a division.

5.1.3 Assessing an organization's scope

Both at business and corporate level, managers face important choices about the scope of their organization. At business level, these choices relate to the numbers of markets to be targeted and the breadth of their portfolio of offerings (Real-life Application 5.3). At corporate level, the choices relate to the breadth of the portfolio of strategic business units (SBUs).

Real-life Application 5.3 Different firms' scope decisions

British Airways offers a full range of passenger travel classes—first, club (business), premier economy, and economy. It markets a comprehensive range of cargo and logistics services, through its World Cargo subsidiary, including courier services and specialist handling for fresh produce. Both passenger and cargo services have an extensive international network, augmented in the case of passengers through flights provided by BA's partners in the oneworld alliance. BA offers three further B2B services: aircraft maintenance, flight training, and AirMiles, a leading UK provider of staff and customer loyalty rewards. It also markets package holidays directly to consumers. Lufthansa's portfolio, similarly contains equivalents to all of BA's business, along with businesses offering catering and IT services to other airlines, and travel management and insurance services to corporate clients. By contrast, Ryanair is entirely focused upon the passenger airline business, having withdrawn from the cargo business in 1997. Within that business, it has a narrower range of offerings than BA, with a single class of travel that is available only in Europe.

In order to assess whether, for example, BA, Ryanair, or Lufthansa has made better choices regarding their portfolio of businesses, we need to understand the impact of scope decisions on a range of factors summarized in Table 5.1. Increasing its degree of product, business or market diversity gives an organization benefits in certain of these areas, which must be traded off against disadvantages in others. In the following Section 5.2 we discuss each of these factors in turn.

5.2 Factors affecting expansion and diversification decisions

The range of choices open to a firm as it expands can be encapsulated in three extreme examples. One is provided by the Ford Motor Company, which from 1908 to 1927 offered one sole product on the world market, the Model T. Between 1914 and 1925 this, famously, was available in just a single colour, black. In total, some 15 million model Ts were sold, making it one of the most successful cars of all time.

A second extreme is the bespoke tailor, furniture-maker, or software author, operating in a single business but customizing every one of its offerings so that each is uniquely adapted to the requirements of each client. And the third extreme is represented by highly diverse corporations such as Sony, Samsung, or General Electric, active across the world in a wide variety of businesses, each of which may offer, not an infinite variety, but certainly a broad range of products or services.

In choosing how close to each of these extremes they wish their organization to be, managers have a number of judgements to make. The first relates to the extent to which the organization benefits from diversity by capturing profitable opportunities, enhancing its service to its customers, frustrating its competitors, and gaining access to crucial resources.

Table 5.1 Considerations in expansion and diversification

Market and competitive factors	
Growth potential	The extent of market opportunity for a business' offering
Control	The extent to which an organization needs a presence in a sector to control its operating environment—a factor in vertical diversification
Competition	The impact on competitors of contesting a given industry or market
Legitimation	The extent to which increased scope, scale or diversity gives the organization greater legitimacy and therefore easier or cheaper access to resources
Differentiation	The impact on customer responsiveness—the extent to which a firm can respond quickly and appropriately to new and changing customer needs—network reach and richness
Dependency and risk	The extent to which a firm is dependent for its success on a particular product, technology, customer, or market, and is therefore exposed if demand for the product or in that market turns down sharply

Attention and knowledge factors	
Management attention	The extent to which senior managers can give proper attention to a particular offering, market or industry, understand the relevant success factors and challenges and thus contribute to good, well-informed strategic decisions. Strongly influenced by degree of **relatedness** between parts of the portfolio
Exploration	Learning how to do new things. Inventing new products and processes, and combining existing ones together in innovative ways
Experience/exploitation	Learning how to refine particular processes over time so they are more efficient and/or effective.

Efficiency factors	
Overheads costs	The costs associated with administering and coordinating an organization's activities
Economies of scale	Benefits from the overall size of an organization, and from producing particular outputs in large quantities
Economies of scope and synergies	Benefits from being able to share resources or link activities between different offerings, businesses, and markets

The second is whether the organization can make best use of its knowledge assets by focussing on a narrower set of related markets and offerings, or by broadening its scope to give more opportunities for the harvesting and sharing of knowledge. The third is how best to profit from the potential, which often arises with expansion, to become more efficient, reducing the unit cost of offerings through experience, economies of scale, and economies of scope.

5.2.1 Market and competitive arguments for and against diversity

a. Growth potential

One of the most common reasons for diversification is because firms perceive opportunities for growth that are not available from their core businesses, offerings, or markets. Sometimes, it is an emergent strategy where the organization finds itself expanding because

The Walt Disney Company now owns and operates all the hotels in its theme parks. *Walt Disney*

customers ask it to supply a product or service they cannot find elsewhere, or because entrepreneurial employees seize opportunities in new areas. Equally, it may be part of a deliberate strategy, in which new products are finely tuned to the requirements of specific customers and where the characteristics of any industry into which a firm is diversifying are carefully matched to the organization's resources.[6]

Sometimes, firms see that their suppliers or distributors are making attractive profits, and want to capture some of that value added for themselves. For example, the Walt Disney Company now owns and operates all the hotels on its theme parks, having seen how profitable the independent hotels were that sprang up around the first Disneyland in California.

Diversification for growth can be particularly tempting for successful companies that are producing such large profits that there is a real problem in what to do with the resulting cash. It may be that the structure of their existing industry prevents companies from expanding within it. They may be blocked from achieving a monopoly position, or have entrenched competitors that are too powerful to take on—and yet they may be very profitable. If these firms face investor pressures for steadily increasing returns, their managers may decide that they have little choice but to move into a new business area.

At the opposite end of the spectrum are organizations that have become aware of the likely decline of existing products. Perhaps they have come to the end of their life-cycles, or are threatened by substitute or competing products. There are times when it appears easier to move into a new business area rather than waste resources in attempting to defend or regain a competitive position. This was the route taken by Japanese steelmakers Kobe and NKK, for example, when they faced stagnant demand and increasing competition in their core business.[7]

b. Vertical diversification and control

It is very common for an organization to have a presence in many stages of the value chain—for example, H&M's competitors, Zara and Benetton, both have substantial investments in clothing manufacturing, as well as retailing. However, because both firms only make clothes to sell in their own outlets, and neither sells other firms' garments in their stores, their manufacturing and retailing operations can be considered as part of a single business.

However, if internal demand does not use all this upstream or downstream capacity, the firm may start to sell some of that capacity to other users, as BA does with its maintenance and pilot training. This is vertical diversification, which can also come about if a commercial growth opportunity presents itself. For example, Sony used to manufacture microprocessors only for its own internal use, but now, through Felica Networks, a joint venture with DoCoMo, a leading Japanese mobile phone service provider, it markets specialized chips that enable mobile phones to be used as an electronic wallet, key, or travel ticket.

Vertical diversification is not always just a form of growth, however. It may be conceived as a way of achieving greater control over their firm's operating environment, for example the regularity and quality of supplies of raw materials, or the prices they pay. They may want to control how their products are displayed or promoted or ensure that their firm is not squeezed out of its distribution channels by competitors. The Walt Disney Company bought ABC in 1996 to ensure that it could still have an outlet for its TV productions, other TV networks having been acquired by its competitors.

Vertical moves can prove problematic if the competences needed in the upstream and downstream businesses are very different from those needed in a firm's original business. Under Disney's management, ABC lost money for several years and declined to last place among the four major US TV networks; only since 2005 have hit shows such as *Lost*, *Ugly Betty*, and *Desperate Housewives* returned it to top place in the ratings.[8]

c. Competition

Some moves into different products and markets are defensive and carried out in order to prevent a competitor or potential competitor from gaining or exploiting a foothold in a product or a market. A firm may try to gain first-mover advantage[9] and build reputation and experience before the competitor has time to do so. If large competitors are already well-established in a business, a firm may contest it simply to limit their profits and cash flow. The returns on investment, measured in standard accounting terms, may be low, but these investments are justified because they prevent damage to the firm as a whole. Competitors may also be discouraged from hostile moves against a diversified firm, such as market entry and price wars, because of the threat of reprisals in other markets, and may be encouraged to find ways of co-operating with it.[10]

Other defensive strategies include launching products in areas where competitors are strong, in order to make it more difficult for them to charge high prices and generate cash that they can use to compete with you in *your* areas of strength. Slightly more subtle is the idea of launching a product, or entering a market, to lure a competitor into following you there. You may know from the outset that neither firm will make money, but believe that you can afford the wasted resources, whilst your competitor will be weakened.

If, on the other hand, the competitors are smaller specialists with limited resources, a large conglomerate, which is likely to have considerable reserves of capital and management strength, as well as a productivity advantage from its higher investments, may be able to squeeze them out, for example through engaging in long-term price reductions.

d. Legitimation

There is some evidence that managers are influenced in their product and market decisions by what they believe key stakeholders expect of them and their organizations. If they fail to meet those expectations then they may suffer competitively because it will be more difficult to raise funds or find good suppliers. Customers may avoid them, not because the product is poor, but because they do not want to risk being associated with an unorthodox operator. If, as sometimes happens, it becomes a mark of 'professionalism' in an industry to have a diversified product range, then managers may be inclined to pursue diversification in order

First-mover advantage
The advantages the first major entrant to a new industry/market can obtain, e.g. by appropriating locations, obtaining patents and reputational resources, and moulding customers' processes to suit its value chain.

→ The concept of
legitimation and its
importance in strategy
development was introduced
in Chapter 2.

to win legitimacy, for their organizations and themselves. If competitors get favourable press coverage and a rise in their share prices when they diversify, then managers will be tempted to follow suit.

A pattern has certainly been observed in a number of industries—accountancy, financial services, and radio—where the moves by successful and prestigious firms into new products and markets are widely imitated.[11] Many theorists believe that the desire for legitimation plays a role in this. Toyota's success with its Prius hybrid-engined vehicle has pushed its competitors to offer similar products, even though some are said to believe that there are better technologies for improving cars' energy efficiency and lowering emissions.[12] Variations from country to country in the extent to which large corporations pursue diversification[13] have also been ascribed to differences in the attitudes of governments and other key stakeholders to large, diversified conglomerates. The French government, for example, has been quite open in encouraging its largest firms to become involved in new sectors.

Views on what is legitimate in strategy often change over time. For example, until the 1980s, diversification was seen as such a natural and important part of the strategic management of large corporations that many important books referred to little else. However, it then fell out of favour as popular writers urged their readers to 'stick to the knitting'—to focus on areas of existing strength.[14] This means that strategic decisions may sometimes be dictated by fashion. This does not mean that they are mistaken—at the time they are taken, they may genuinely help the firm remain competitive. However it is important that they be reviewed periodically, to make sure that the original benefits from legitimation are not being outweighed by some of the factors we examine elsewhere in this section.

e. Expansion, diversification, and differentiation

Small, focused firms are likely to be the most responsive to the particular needs of their target customers compared to firms serving a broad set of segments. They can devote all their attention to understanding what those customers require and to tailoring their value chain to deliver those precise requirements. In industries where it is important to differentiate on support, these are important advantages. Once an organization expands beyond its original customer and product base, it is almost inevitable that it will lose some of that focus. It may also appear unresponsive if it tries to limit its range of offerings to maximize economies of scale.

→ Architecture was defined
in Section 1.3.4 and culture
in Section 1.6.4. Both are
considered at length in
Chapter 8.

A larger firm may be able to overcome this disadvantage if it has a culture and architecture that give its employees the flexibility and motivation to adapt to specific customer needs, and good information systems to tell it what those needs are. It may also be able to afford to forgo some economies of scale to offer a broader range of products, each of which is targeted a particular customer segment.

Moreover, size and diversity may allow the firm to differentiate in other ways. If a large firm can harness the efficiency benefits we discuss in Section 5.2.3, then it may be able to differentiate on price. A diverse organization may, as we discussed in Section 4.2.4, be able to differentiate on network reach and on the richness of its offerings. Chris Anderson of *Wired* magazine has described how some firms profit from offering a 'long tail' of products with low, but steady volumes of sales.[15] He quotes the example of Amazon, which derives half its book sales from titles outside the range of around 130,000 stocked by a large bookstore.

f. Avoiding dependency and spreading risk

→ The relative power of
suppliers and buyers is
covered in the discussion of
the six forces in an industry
in Section 3.5.

Increasing diversity also lessens the organization's degree of dependency on any particular product or market. This means that if a particular market experiences an economic downturn, an important customer gets into financial difficulties, or a product falls out of fashion or is discovered to be flawed in some way, the company has other sources of income to turn to. Too great a degree of dependency on any one customer can also disadvantage a firm in negotiations over price or delivery conditions.

Diversification should also, in theory, help shareholders such as pension funds, investment trusts, or banks achieve stable returns on their investments. If one SBU is in a high-risk business area, perhaps because it is new or in an unstable environment, profits from another in a different area will compensate if it fails. Firms may also look to 'balance' a business that generates most of its sales in the winter, such as ski wear, with a product line that is bought in the summer, such as barbeques.

However, it is now generally agreed that spreading risk is, of itself, an inadequate reason for a corporation to diversify. Investors can achieve their desired spread of investment risks by diversifying their own shareholdings, at less cost than a corporation incurs in entering and leaving businesses and markets. There are exceptions to this where corporations are involved in businesses or geographical locations (the former Soviet Union, or China, for example) that have less well-developed capital or stock markets, and where the opportunities for buying a spread of shares are limited or risky because of a lack of information. In these circumstances, a corporation's management can add value by diversifying on their shareholders' behalf—but they would still be advised, for reasons set out in the next section, to look for businesses that are related to ones they already manage.

5.2.2 Management attention and organizational knowledge

Whatever the reasons for expansion into new areas, the benefits may come at a price. Organizations that do not focus adequately on the needs of particular customers or segments risk losing business to firms that do. Senior managers in firms which diversify too much (how much is too much is difficult to say—see Theoretical Debate 5.1 later in this chapter) appear to lose the ability to oversee the different products or businesses in their portfolio. Their attention and expertise are diluted, allowing competitors who are specialists (and therefore more likely to have deep knowledge which is unique and inimitable) gain advantage—a process which happens individually in each product or market in which the diversified firm competes.

→ We examine the problems of managing complex, diverse organizations in Chapter 9.

One reason for this is that a diversified firm is quite likely to retain a foothold in its original business—perhaps it still offers decent returns on investment, or there may be large exit costs. The personal interests of powerful stakeholders in the organization and managers' sentimental attachment to old products are other factors that may lead firms to retain old core businesses after it has moved into new ones.

This, however, will heighten the difficulties that managers immersed in the paradigms of one industry can experience in understanding the success factors in new and less familiar ones. This can lead them to position their products incorrectly, or to choose the wrong technologies in which to invest. Robert Grant[16] points out that history is 'littered with companies that overpaid in order to gain a position in a seemingly attractive industry', and attractive industries may not necessarily yield the desired growth. Many other firms may spot those attractions, and enter the industries in question, alongside completely new start-ups. They will come with a variety of managerial mindsets and cultures which may make the competitive rules of the game in the new industry very different from those in any pre-existing one.

a. Relatedness

The risk of dilution of management attention can be reduced, and the chances of success in diversification increased, if the elements in a portfolio are strategically related: that is, if the industry success factors are similar. This is particularly important in the case of corporate-level diversification.

Table 5.2 Potential sources of relatedness between businesses in a portfolio

Category of success factor (and examples)	Assets giving short term advantage if scarce	Competences offering possible longer term advantage
Customer factors Brand recognition; customer loyalty; large installed base of products	Brands and reputation	Brand-building; customer relationship management
Channel factors Established access to distribution channels; distributor loyalty	Reputation with dealers; logistics assets	Dealer recruitment; negotiation with dealers and retailers
Input factors Supplier loyalty; or preferential access to scarce skills or raw materials	Knowledge of where to find inputs at the right price or quality; reputation; finance for purchases	Supplier negotiation and management
Process factors Proprietary technology; product or market-specific experience; organizational systems	Patents and proprietary systems	Technological and innovation competences
Market knowledge factors Understanding of the industry and the market	Accumulated information on: the goals and behaviour of competitors or customers, the price-sensitivity of products	Data gathering; customer psychology

There are five sets of factors[17] that may form the basis of competitive advantage in an industry, and so be the source of inter-SBU relatedness: customer factors, channel factors, input factors, process factors, and market knowledge factors. A firm may be able to use assets, such as knowledge or reputation, that have contributed to success in one business to build advantage in another—*if* they are relevant—although such advantages may be short-lived as competitors learn how to replicate them. More importantly, however, the competences needed to build these success factors can also be transferred from one business to another where the basis of success is similar. These are likely to be less easy to copy, and so are potential sources of longer-term advantage. The five types of success factor are summarized in Table 5.2, along with examples of the associated assets and competences.

This makes the judgement of relatedness a very subtle affair. Businesses may be superficially unrelated, but actually similar in ways which are not immediately apparent to an outside observer; equally, superficial similarities can conceal important differences (Real-life Application 5.4). Two businesses that share the need to develop effective teams of skilled employees will have quite a high degree of strategic relatedness, even if they provide different services in different markets. A pair of businesses, one of which requires highly skilled staff and the other a base of cost-effective, low-skill workers, may in fact be less related, even though the first business' products may be 'just' up-market versions of the second's. And relatedness along a single dimension may not be enough to generate competitive advantage. The clearest benefits from diversification arise when businesses share three areas of relatedness: product knowledge, customer knowledge, and industry success factors.[18]

Real-life Application 5.4 Relatedness

Watches and computer printers superficially look very different, but Citizen Watch Company saw them as related businesses, because of similarities in process and channel factors. Citizen claimed that its diversified products, which include watches, printers for personal computers, floppy disk drives, small portable PCs, liquid crystal colour TVs, quartz oscillators, and precision machine tools and robots, shared a common set of advanced, precision technologies that the company developed in the course of manufacturing watches. Citizen's president recalled how the company learned from its failures after venturing into what it now considers unrelated, non-precision businesses.[19]

To the untrained eye, a motor scooter or a small motorcycle might appear to be little more than a cut-down version of one of the glamorous, large-capacity machines offered by firms like BMW or Harley Davidson. In fact, however, their degree of relatedness is not high: the larger machines are far more technologically sophisticated, and associated with significantly different product design architectures, manufacturing processes, and marketing challenges. Manufacturers of high-powered motorcycles that have extended their range down to small- or medium-sized ones have experienced problems, because it devalued their brand in the eyes of their core customers, and have returned to the top end of the market.[20]

The larger motorcycle machines are technologically sophisticated. *Harley Davidson*

Creative Strategizing 5.1

Develop a shortlist of industries into which a successful maker of large motor cycles might diversify. Do the same for a manufacturer of motor scooters. In both cases, you should start by listing the strategic knowledge and other resources that you would expect to be able to use as the basis of your diversification strategy.

If a company has shown the ability to develop brands with prestige or youth appeal in one market and then diversifies into another where building brands is equally important, the company can transfer its brand-building competences into the second market. Diversified luxury goods conglomerates like LVMH work very much in this way, and have built structures that enable managers of struggling brands to learn from others that oversee market leaders. But this will probably only work if the target markets for the different brands are the same, or share a similar psychology. Competences in how to recruit dealers and negotiate for shelf-space with retailers will be valuable across businesses—provided that they share similar levels of dependence on similar types of dealers, distributors or retailers.

So it is important to be very specific in identifying the competences in each business, and demonstrate exactly how they can contribute to competitive advantage in another. Worked Example 5.1 shows how this can be done using a 'relatedness matrix'. Beware of superficial relatedness, based on apparent similarities in products and markets.[21] For the same reason, one should be wary of vertical diversification, since it is actually quite rare for two vertically related businesses to share significant assets and competences, although there may, as we discuss in the next section, be some scope for synergies between them. Another consideration is whether the assets or competences that underpin the relatedness between SBUs are readily available on the open market; if they are, then they will not contribute to competitive advantage.

Finally, it should be emphasized that the benefits from relatedness in a portfolio are not automatic. They will only come to fruition if the organization's architecture and culture encourage managers to share knowledge and experience to their mutual benefit, or if the parent's staff are allowed to use their knowledge to help product or SBU managers with their own challenges.[22]

b. Exploration and exploitation

Relatedness between parts of a portfolio can help an organization profit from the knowledge that it has built up in specific areas where its managers already have experience. Diversity also influences an organization's capacity for deepening and broadening that knowledge.

One path to doing this is through exploration, where it tries out and learns about new and different things.[23] Diversity in an organization tends to encourage this. The more market influences and product technologies that employees are exposed to, the more ideas they will encounter that can be used to enhance the way the firm develops, makes and markets its offerings. They may just copy other firms' concepts, or they may combine and adapt them into something genuinely innovative. Some theorists also believe that exposure to a broad range of influences opens the minds of employees and makes them more responsive to novel ideas from outside their immediate circle of colleagues. This means that the firm's absorptive capacity—its ability to absorb, spread and utilize new knowledge—is enhanced.[24]

Increasing its diversity can, however, make it more difficult for an organization to benefit fully from another kind of learning, known as experience or exploitation, where it refines what it already does. It is when an organization limits itself to a small range of products that it maximizes the opportunity to become expert, over time, in marketing them and effectively making them efficiently. In the extreme case of the Model T, Ford was able to bring the price down over time from $850 to $300 as it became more proficient at learning how to make it. The car was offered only in black once Ford's managers realized that the black enamel dried so much more quickly than other colours, increasing the number of cars that could be built in a day.[25]

The benefits of exploitation have the most opportunities to emerge if the organization produces large volumes of an output over time; although available in some degree to small, focused firms, the potential advantages are greatest for businesses targeting many broad, perhaps even global, segments. Note, however, that these benefits are not automatic—the organization needs the right architecture and learning culture if it is to profit from them.

It is possible to overdo both exploration and exploitation. Too much emphasis on exploration may lead to a situation where a firm learns many things, but never implements any of them properly. Managers in organizations that target broad market niches appear to become particularly prone to overstretching in this way.[26] Too great a focus on exploitation may make an organization very efficient and effective, but unable to adapt to a changing environment. However, it is difficult to combine the two to gain an effective balance—in

Exploration
The search for new possibilities through activities such as experimentation, risk-taking, and innovation.

Absorptive capacity
An organization's capacity to absorb new knowledge, disseminate it, and implement it in new products or practices.

Exploitation
Utilizing and refining existing knowledge and capabilities, in order, for example, to increase the efficiency or effectiveness of existing activities.

what is termed an 'ambidextrous organization'—indeed, some theorists see exploration and exploitation as polar opposites.[27]

→ Organizational learning and ambidextrous organizations are discussed in greater detail in Chapter 10.

5.2.3 Efficiency

One argument for expansion is the potential a larger firm enjoys for enhancing efficiency and lowering unit costs. Along with the experience benefits discussed in the previous section, size brings in some industries the potential for economies of scale at the business level, while diversity brings the possibility of economies of scope. We discuss these below.

The efficiency argument does not entirely favour larger more diversified organizations; smaller and more focused firms are likely to enjoy proportionally lower overhead costs. Organizations' structures and administrative processes necessarily become more complex as the size and scope of their business increase. Firms that have large ranges of products and/or address many markets find themselves needing managers, departments or even whole divisions to look after each group of products or each major market segment. This in turn leads to the acquisition of extra staff and sophisticated information systems to coordinate and monitor these varied activities. If not controlled, the costs of these administrative systems can outweigh the benefits that large firms get from their scale and experience.

a. Economies of scale

One way in which an organization may gain efficiency is through economies of scale, which can be obtained in a number of ways:[28]

Economies of scale
When for each 1% increase in production volume, the total cost of production increases by less than 1%, and the organization's average cost per unit of output falls.

- Purchasing discounts. The sheer size of an enterprise may enable it to get bulk discounts on all the main inputs that it uses, as with the major UK supermarket chains,[29] or on selected items, such as energy or office furniture, that may be shared across a variety of products and markets. It may be a very large user of a single, important input, as McDonald's is with soft drinks. Supplier power may, however, limit the extent to which firms can negotiate these discounts.

- Spreading of overheads and other fixed costs over a large sales volume. This is particularly important in industries with high fixed manufacturing costs like aircraft and car manufacturing, high development costs, such as pharmaceuticals, or high advertising costs, such as fast-moving consumer goods. To gain maximum scale benefits, these products need to be sold to broad market segments and to as many of them as possible, probably spanning several countries and perhaps even the entire globe.

- Division of labour into discrete activities so that instead of having a few people multi-tasking, there are many people, each with a specialist role. In a manufacturing environment, this specialization of tasks tends to improve productivity, and is the basis of the production line. Major accountants and other professional services firms also gain scale advantages over their medium-sized rivals by having people dedicated to administration and winning new business, something that only makes economic sense if sales are above a certain minimum. This kind of specialization also makes it easier to become more efficient in performing a task, which can bring costs down still further.

- Use of expensive technologies that bring costs down radically, and may be more effective as well as more efficient. In pharmaceuticals, the largest firms have been able to invest in new, IT-based, technologies that have radically improved the economics of research into new drugs, while also speeding up the process.[30]

The most extreme economies of scale are available only to firms that limit their range of offerings, as did Ford with the Model T, to very few items supplied in large quantities. This enables them to simplify the supply chain and production process so that little time and cost is spent on changeovers between product types. It may take time for a firm to work out how best to optimize their production processes, so that experience effects (Section 5.2.2) are an important complement to economies of scale.

Some industries, however, may not offer many economies of scale to firms beyond a certain size (see Real-life Application 5.5), so it is important to understand the economics of the industry in assessing whether these are an important factor in a business strategy. Beyond a certain point, most organizations will start to show diseconomies of scale, as increasing size makes them more difficult to manage. These can take the form of high overheads costs, of poor decisions as managers struggle to get to grips with the problems of an increasingly complex organization, or of increased agency costs as senior managers become increasingly insulated from their lower-level colleagues and begin to take decisions for their own benefit, rather than those of their organization.[31]

Real-life Application 5.5 Does British Airways enjoy economies of scale?

British Airways is much larger than Ryanair—but this does not mean it gains economies of scale:

- The more routes that BA offers, the more aircraft and staff, and the more infrastructure—booking, passenger handing, refuelling, and maintenance facilities—it needs. This means that, although BA's size and global scope raises its revenues, its costs rise more or less in the same proportion.

- BA's size makes it a sought-after customer when it purchases aircraft from Boeing or Airbus—but Ryanair, too, has been able to negotiate hefty discounts from those same manufacturers, helped by an ability to time its orders to coincide with periods of low demand for aircraft. Smaller airlines can procure their aircraft through leasing companies that purchase in bulk, and then pass on to their clients some of the discounts they obtain.

- Personnel costs are a substantial proportion of airline costs—and BA cannot pay skilled people less because it recruits lots of them.

- Airport charges in the main airports are set according to a published tariff that may vary according to the time and day of take-off and landing, but otherwise is the same for everyone. BA obtains no discounts for being the largest user at Heathrow, for example.

- Prices for aviation fuel are largely dependent on those set on the main commodity exchanges. There are local variations, but little scope for airlines, however large, to negotiate preferential rates. It is more important for an airline to use financial markets to hedge against major rises in oil prices—and small airlines have proven to be as good at this as large ones.

b. Economies of scope and synergies

Synergy
'[T]he ability of two or more units or companies to generate greater value working together than they could working apart' (Goold and Campbell, 1998).

As a firm's degree of product and market diversity increases, it loses some economies of scale, but may be compensated by what are known at the business level as economies of scope, and at corporate level as synergies. These take six main forms:[32]

- Sharing tangible resources, such as manufacturing, research or head office, or IT facilities. Having such facilities fully utilized across a range of products makes more economic sense than having them specialized but half-used.

- Pooling negotiating power, primarily vis-à-vis suppliers, to obtain lower prices, better quality, or more responsive service, but also to obtain better treatment from retailers (more prominent displays of the firm's products) customers, regulators, or even investors.

- Coordinating SBU strategies, such as market entries, new product launches or pricing moves, so as to avoid wasteful duplication of effort and improve the effectiveness of the company's response to competitors' moves. Large conglomerates involved in multiple market places, where some of their products may even be substitutes for each other, can benefit from a coordinated approach to product pricing across the divisions.[33] Margins across all their divisions are likely to increase—something known as the *efficiency effect*. Divisions can also cross-sell one another's products.

- Vertically coordinating the provision of goods and services across SBUs can help to minimize inventories, improve asset utilization, and speed up product development.

- Creating combined businesses. Corporations can link the expertise from different SBUs to produce new products or businesses or can pull particular activities out of individual SBUs and combine them into a new business.

- Sharing intangible resources. Hamel and Prahalad[34] showed how a number of, mostly Japanese, corporations discovered that knowledge about particular technologies or markets could profitably be applied to businesses or products that, to an outsider, often appeared completely unrelated to the firm's original sphere of operations. Nonetheless, the genuine similarities in terms of market needs, technological characteristics, or manufacturing processes justified a move into them. Businesses may also exchange information on customers—their details and preferences for cross-selling of products, for example. When intangible resources are shared in this way, they are sometimes said to be leveraged across businesses—their power is multiplied by being shared, in the same way that a lever multiplies the force applied by a person or machine. Virgin, a London-based conglomerate, has a brand name and corporate identity that is distinctive and recognizable to a specific group of its potential target customers, mainly younger people. It attaches that brand to around fifty businesses, including airlines, mobile phone services, financial services, cosmetics, saucy underwear, and space travel, whose products might be attractive to those target customers. Virgin's understanding of those customers' needs is an intangible resource that it leverages across all those businesses. The brand is similarly leveraged. Every time the group's charismatic founder, Richard Branson, generates favourable press coverage—as he has a gift for doing—he boosts the brand image of every single one of those businesses, at no greater cost than if Virgin were a small firm with just a single product.

The main difference between corporate-level synergies and the business-level economies of scope is the ease with which they can be achieved. Let us take pooled negotiating power as an example, as something that can help a multi-product business as much as it does a multi-business corporation. In order to *obtain* the benefit of pooled negotiating power, managers must be persuaded to design similar inputs into their products or processes, and then to order them from the same supplier, probably quoting the same part number or order code. This is *relatively* easy to achieve when the products are all being specified by the same design team and ordered through a single purchasing department, which can monitor what is going on—although even then, it can be difficult to persuade designers to re-use parts or subassemblies from existing products. This becomes more difficult to enforce and monitor if the business is operating from a number of sites worldwide, perhaps in different languages. It becomes more difficult still when there are several design teams and several purchasing departments, each reporting to the powerful head of an independent business unit.

This is why there have been some important writers (notably Goold and Campbell, 1998) who claim that it is easy to overestimate the potential for synergy between different parts of a business. Some diversified conglomerates such as Hanson Industries were famous in their heyday in the 1980s for deliberately refusing to attempt to achieve synergies between the firms in their portfolio—they thought there were more potential risks than benefits.

Where synergies are available, relatedness between businesses and markets can be important in extracting them. The sharing of tangible resources, knowledge and brands is easier if

➜ We review different approaches to managing synergies across business units in Section 9.2.

the sharers have markets or technologies in common. On the other hand, competences in some 'back office' processes, such as order processing or credit control, may be transferable between businesses that have little in common other than that they periodically take orders and win new customers. However, although it can be beneficial for the business with the best-run back office to share its skills with the rest of the corporation, they are rarely going to be the source of competitive advantage for any part of the firm. The coordination of prices and other strategies is only likely to be effective if the businesses share customers, and probably if their positioning in their markets is similar enough for the customers to be able to view the products as an integrated package.

The other types of synergy are less dependent upon relatedness. Vertical coordination (Real-life Application 5.6) and the pooling of negotiating power on items like office supplies or advertising are not dependent on strategic relatedness—although the firm must be careful that, by centralizing purchasing, it does not disrupt operational relationships with key suppliers and introduce bureaucracy into the purchasing process that costs more in delay than it saves through bulk discounts. Combined businesses can come from unexpected quarters: there was little relationship between Oral B toothbrushes and Braun electric shavers until the parent company, Gillette (now merged with Procter & Gamble), made them cooperate to develop an electric toothbrush.[35] Similar technology has now been incorporated in Gillette's newest lines of wet shavers. The possibility of combining existing businesses in this way to take advantage of 'white space opportunities'[36]—businesses that simply did not exist before—is one argument in favour of a diversified portfolio.

Real-life Application 5.6 Synergies from vertical coordination

When Nouvelles Frontières, a French travel firm and resort operator, bought a controlling share in Corsair, a charter airline, in 1990, it did not necessarily possess any of the assets or competences needed for success in the airline business. However, it was able to coordinate activities vertically, so that Corsair could ensure the availability of transport for people flying to one of Nouvelles Frontières' holiday destinations, and the holiday business could ensure that over 90 per cent of the seats were occupied on an average Corsair flight. It also helped that Nouvelles Frontières ran, as a long-standing part of its core business, a very efficient and popular chain of retail travel agents, which many airlines used, in the days before the internet, to sell off spare seats on their aircraft. High utilization of aircraft assets is very important to profitability in the airline industry, so preferential access to these other subsidiaries helped Corsair to be the only French airline to remain profitable right through the 1990s.[37] There was, of course, a risk that these synergistic benefits could have been offset if Nouvelles Frontières' managers had interfered unproductively in the operation of the airline—but they were wise enough to avoid that trap.

➔ We look more closely at the architectures needed to foster synergies in complex organizations in Section 9.2.

Real-life Application 5.5 illustrates an important point: that achieving synergy requires a finely balanced architecture and culture, where the search for synergies does not take away too much of the autonomy that unit managers require to run their businesses effectively. Even if the architecture is set up favourably, synergies can still be difficult to realize in practice, and the costs of searching for them may outweigh the benefits. There is also a danger that, if SBU P tweaks its strategy so as to achieve synergies with SBU Q, it may erode its own competitive advantage (see What Can Go Wrong 5.1 for an example). This is why there is a debate (see Theoretical Debate 9.1) amongst theorists as to whether managers at the centre of large organizations should actively press SBU managers into synergistic cooperation, or simply help them identify promising opportunities and offer help and encouragement.

The existence of synergies does not imply an automatic need for a firm to diversify into other businesses in order to take advantage of them. Licensing deals or partnerships may be much more effective methods of maximizing value from proprietary technologies or brands than attempting to manage their exploitation within a corporate umbrella. Sony, for example, does not always attempt to promote or develop its music products itself, but enters into partnerships with companies who can provide expertise on local geographical or market characteristics and have knowledge about specialized musical tastes.

5.3 The international dimension

The decisions about how many products a business should deploy, and the breadth and scope of the markets it should serve with them, acquire an added level of complexity when they involve doing business in more than one country. We examine these issues in Chapter 14.

5.4 Assessing an expansion and diversification strategy

In Section 5.2 we discussed a number of reasons for expansion and diversification. When managers explain their expansion decisions in interviews or annual reports, they will frequently invoke concepts like synergy, globalization, and market opportunity. There are a number of reasons why, when we review these decisions, we should do so in a sceptical frame of mind.

The first is that many expansions and diversifications can be seen, in retrospect, as having been motivated by the personal ambition of the decision-maker—even though that is probably not what he or she said at the time. In the past, managers were often rewarded for the size of their empires, with less emphasis given to financial performance. This emphasis has changed in recent years, as profitability and shareholder value have become much more important. It is, of course, possible that decisions taken for these personal reasons can still be good business moves—but it is important to check how they have turned out.

→ The achievement of personal goals through the growth of the firm is one aspect of the principal–agent problem that we discussed in Chapter 2.

The other two reasons for scepticism relate specifically to diversification. One is that there is a clear and consistent message from research on this topic (see Theoretical Debate 5.1). Whether diversity is viewed in terms of product variety, geographic spread, or breadth of a business, a little of it can be helpful, particularly if it takes the company into areas related to its original business, but too much impedes performance. Some companies, however, appear to be immune to the problems associated with broad diversification. Large Asian corporations like Sony and Samsung have shown little desire to cut back to 'core' businesses, or had any apparent need to. Some Western companies such as Virgin and Indian ones such as Tata and Reliance are still diversifying into new products and markets. One of America's most admired and, measured by total returns to shareholders, most successful corporations is General Electric, whose interests span fields as diverse as light bulbs, jet engines, power stations, and credit cards. There is, in short, no evidence regarding precisely how much diversification constitutes 'too much'—so that is an assessment that we need to make individually for each organization we look at.

Third, although there are a number of potential benefits from diversification, there are also very real costs. The most obvious of these is the corporate head office—which after all has no direct customers from whom costs can be recouped, and so represents a potential 'dead weight' on the businesses. The owner or parent company will have administrative staff and a management team who are responsible for controlling the interactions between the business units and overseeing their individual contacts with the parent company. There are also hidden transaction costs, such as the cost to the business units of responding to head office requests for information. Referring decisions to corporate headquarters for approval

→ We examine the challenges of parenting in diversified organizations in Section 9.2.

can introduce delays that can, in some cases, lead to a loss of business to more agile competitors. Therefore the existence of a parent company can only be justified if it is able to cover these costs and add more value than the subsidiaries would be able to achieve themselves as independent units.

Theoretical Debate 5.1 Is diversification a good idea?

A great deal of research has gone into whether firms, and their shareholders, benefit from diversification or not. The consensus now appears to be that they do—but *only* as long as the diversification is into areas related to the firm's core business, and the organization has the architecture in place to manage the resulting complexity. If a firm diversifies too far, into unrelated businesses or in an unplanned fashion, then its performance is likely to suffer.

Diversification has been subject to fashion. In the 1960s and 1970s, the writings of Alfred Chandler (1962), Igor Ansoff (1965), and Richard Rumelt (1974) suggested that the decentralized, multi-divisional, corporation was the ideal. The success of conglomerates like Textron (with interests in activities as diverse as military helicopters, gold bracelets, chain saws, writing paper, and fine china) or Pearson (with interests in china, leisure facilities, oil, and publishing) seemed to epitomise this (Leavy, 1998; Bettis and Hall, 1983). The Boston Consulting Group's growth-share matrix (which we review in Section 5.4.3) was in common use to help companies decide what type of product or business to be in, and how to allocate resources among them. The recommended task for corporate management was to balance their portfolio of businesses and set in place appropriate control and capital appraisal systems.

In the 1980s the tide seemed to turn against diversification. Michael Porter (1987) pointed out that the 33 largest US corporations had retained fewer than 50 per cent of the operations they had diversified into between 1950 and 1986, and that for unrelated diversification the figure was only 26 per cent. He characterized this performance as 'dismal'.

Other empirical studies established that, on average, diversified firms performed worse than focused ones. If performance was measured in terms of accounting returns on investment or equity, diversified firms' results were no better than single-business ones—some studies found that they were worse.[38] A diversified firm's stock market valuation typically suffered from a diversification or conglomerate discount: it was lower, on average, than that of an undiversified firm of similar size (Wernerfelt and Montgomery, 1988) and lower than that of a portfolio of undiversified firms that covered the same range of industries (Berger and Ofek, 1995).[39] And diversification by manufacturing firms tends to lead to a reduction in productivity (Schoar, 2002).

However, the picture is more complicated than that. Although diversified firms perform relatively badly, it does not appear to be the diversification that is causing the poor results. If one looks at

what happens to firms over time, there is no evidence of a decline in stock market value following a diversification (Villalonga, 2004a). The 'diversification discount' appears to arise because firms diversify after their core businesses have passed their peak in terms of profitability (Gomes and Lidvan, 2004) and then choose businesses that are themselves poorly rated by the stock markets (Graham et al., 2002). Indeed, it is not clear that, if the correct data are used to determine how diversified firms are, there is a diversification discount at all. Belen Villalonga, of Harvard University, drew on data showing precisely what firms did at different locations (most studies draw upon firms' less detailed reporting of their own activities) and also included service firms—the older studies had looked only at manufacturers. She found (Villalonga, 2004b) that there was actually a premium, rather than a discount, in the valuation of diversified firms.

Her explanation for this was that the majority of diversifying firms followed a strategy of related diversification, which attracted a premium valuation. The shares of firms that diversified into unrelated businesses did indeed trade at a discount. Her findings agreed with that of another stream of research, initiated by Richard Rumelt (1974, 1982) that organizations that build their diversification strategy around a particular capability, and limit themselves to industries that make use of it, were more profitable than single-line businesses and firms that favoured unrelated diversification. Other studies have established that the relationship between financial performance and degree of diversification has an inverted U-shape: moderately diversified firms perform better than undiversified ones, but widely diversified ones perform worse than either (Wernerfelt and Montgomery, 1988; Palich et al., 2000). Since it seems quite plausible that a moderately diversified portfolio will consist mostly of related businesses, these sets of findings fit together well.

It seems to be important that firms pursue the right kind of relatedness. Markides and Williamson (1996) emphasize the importance of being able to transfer strategic resources between businesses; this is far more significant than relatedness based on similarities between products or markets, which can turn out to be superficial. Relatedness based on technological knowledge boosts profitability (Miller, 2006) and involvement in businesses with common inputs or common customers increases the value of widely diversified firms (Fan and Lang, 2000). Firms that diversify vertically suffer from a diversification discount unless their portfolio is limited to three or fewer businesses. And firms do →

→ not get the full benefit of diversification unless they have the right architecture in place to take advantage of the particular relationships between the businesses in their portfolio (Hill and Hoskisson, 1987; Markides and Williamson, 1996). Having the right parenting skills at the corporate centre also appears to be important (Goold et al., 1994).

→ We look in detail at parenting skills and at the architecture needed to manage complex organizations in Chapter 9.

Even so, it is not completely clear that the superior performance and valuation of related diversifiers is due solely to the quality of their corporate-level strategy. There is evidence that they are simply better at everything they do. Even before they diversify, they tend to be more profitable performers in their chosen industries than firms that later choose unrelated diversification, and they are also better than unrelated diversifiers at selecting profitable industries to enter (Park, 2003; Wernerfelt and Montgomery, 1988).

Most of the studies cited above have been carried out on US corporations, but recent research has shown how the benefits or penalties from diversification can vary from country to country. The shares of diversified corporations appear to suffer from a diversification discount in the UK and Japan, but not in Germany or Korea (Fauver et al., 2004; Hall and Lee, 1999; Servaes and Lins, 1999). The overall impact of diversification on a firm's return on assets (ROA) also varies from country to country. In countries, such as France, Sweden, and the UK, with well-developed capital and labour markets, product diversification reduces ROA; where these markets are less well developed (e.g. in Italy or Portugal)

diversification improves it (Wan and Hoskisson, 2003). The extent to which related diversification outperforms other strategies varies from country to country, and also over time (Mayer and Whittington, 2003). Part of the problem in the US and UK in the past may have been that much diversification—70 per cent of the cases in Porter's (1987) sample—has been through acquisition, which itself is a very difficult process to manage, and frequently leads to problems.

→ The management of mergers and acquisitions is reviewed in section 17.5.

The extent of diversification by US and UK companies appears to have declined substantially since the 1970s (Carroll, 1994; Leavy, 1994, 1998; Peters, 1992; Verity, 1992). ITT, a prototypical American conglomerate of the 1970s and 1980s, and Hanson Industries, one of the most successful conglomerates of the 1980s, both voluntarily split into three or four more companies. More recently, Sumner Redstone, an American billionaire who built Viacom into a media conglomerate spanning cable TV (MTV), film-making (Paramount), video rental (Blockbuster), billboard advertising, and the CBS TV and radio networks, has voluntarily broken up his empire. His verdict: 'The world of the conglomerate is over. Divorce is better than marriage.'[40]

This trend was visible, not just in the USA, but also in Europe, Japan, and Korea, which have in the past looked kindly on conglomerates. According to Franko (2004), for a variety of global industries, the proportion of highly diversified firms featuring in the top 12 competitors fell dramatically between 1980 and 2000, while the proportion of focused firms—with 95 per cent or more of their sales in their core business—rose (Figure 5.2).

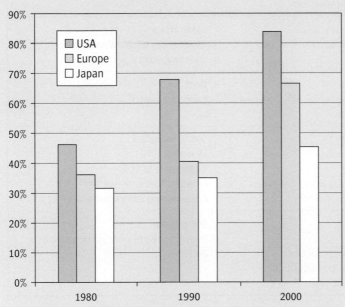

Percent of firms among world's top industrial companies with 95% or more of sales in main industry

Figure 5.2 The rise of focused firms (Franko, 2004: 44)

In this section we review, in turn, the assessment of strategies at business and corporate level. The difference between them lies in the prominence given to relatedness and synergy, which are crucially important at corporate level, but less so at business level. We also look briefly at some older, and somewhat discredited, models which assess an organization's portfolio in terms of the attractiveness of the industries in which it is involved and the strength of the businesses or products within them.

5.4.1 Assessing business level scope decisions

Section 5.2 sets out 12 factors that need to be considered when an organization expands. Of these, growth opportunities are a prerequisite for business development, vertical diversification decisions are dictated by the particular needs of a business to control its environment, and relatedness tends not to be an issue until a firm makes the transition to corporate-level strategy. However, in opting for a greater or lesser degree of focus or diversity in a business, managers are making a complex set of trade-offs between the other nine factors. These are summarized in Figure 5.3. Organizations do not need to operate in the same way for all elements of their value chain. It is possible, for example, to opt for a large-scale manufacturing plant but have small, localized subsidiaries or partner firms to handle after-sales service. We discuss these choices in Chapters 6 and 14.

Markets	*Many/broad*	**Best for:** Economies of scale Experience/exploitation	**Best for:** Economies of scope Exploration Avoiding dependency Pre-empting competition
		Some potential benefits Avoiding dependency Exploration Economies of scope Pre-empting competition	**Some potential benefits** Economies of scale Responsiveness
		Main risks Responsiveness	**Main risks** Experience/exploitation Overhead costs
	Few/narrow	**Best for:** Low overheads Responsiveness	**Best for:** Responsiveness
		Some benefits Experience	**Some benefits** Learning Economies of scope Avoiding dependency Pre-empting competition
		Main risks Dependency Pre-emption by competition Lack of exploration opportunities No economies of scale or scope	**Main risks** Few economies of scale or experience benefits
		Few	*Many*
		Products	

Figure 5.3 Benefits and risks of different degrees of diversity

Given the complexity of these decisions, a crucial influence over firms' strategies is likely to be the desires of specific stakeholders. Shareholders may encourage firms into new markets to sustain growth in profits and hence in share prices. Owners or influential managers may be attracted by the idea of managing a global enterprise—or they may be discouraged by the complexity involved. Culturally, organizations can be divided into 'prospectors', constantly seeking innovation and new worlds to conquer, 'defenders', content to make themselves secure in their existing industries and markets, or 'analysers', which act as prospectors in some areas of their business and defenders in others. None of these three cultural orientations offers any performance advantage over the others.[41] There is no clear 'right place' on Figure 5.3 for a business to occupy, or a 'wrong place' for it to avoid, which makes the assessment of a business strategy a matter of complex judgement.

This judgement needs to be conditioned by the demands of industry in which it operates, as we discussed in Chapter 3. In industries such as clothing manufacture and fast food, small and medium-sized firms can hold their own with large, global organizations. In contrast, the economics of the videogames industry make it imperative for firms to target a large market segment—preferably more than one. Sony would never have recovered the development costs on its PlayStation games console if it had sold the product only to Japanese teenagers. It needed to sell the product in large quantities, which meant launching it in Europe and, crucially, the USA—so that the hardware and software needed to be designed accordingly. Broadening the market for videogames to include young (and not-so-young) adults further enhances the viability of the product. And there are also arguments for using the sophisticated technology developed for videogames consoles in other products as well, or for making the console part of a suite of products that work well together and which consumers can be tempted to buy as a package. Sony has indeed been following precisely such a strategy, marketing TVs, audio equipment, PCs, and game consoles that can be used together as part of a home entertainment package.

Using Evidence 5.1 Assessing a business strategy

The complex judgments needed to assess a business strategy can be assisted by careful use of evidence. First, look at the strategies being followed by firms in the industry as a whole, and match them to the financial results, in particular return on capital employed and profit margins. Are the highest financial returns being made by the largest firms? If so, this may be evidence for the existence of economies of scale in the industry—you can then look closely into the value chains of those firms to discover exactly where—production? marketing?—those economies reside. If all firms below a certain size are clearly less profitable than those above it, then this can be seen as evidence for a minimum economic size for an enterprise in this industry. You can look for similar patterns for other elements of the strategy—are the most profitable, or fastest growing firms the most focused, the most diverse, or the most international? You can then combine this with qualitative reasoning on *why* these patterns are coming about.

5.4.2 Assessing corporate-level diversification decisions

Corporate-level diversity is in some ways easier to assess than business-level diversity, since there are clear criteria that can be used to discriminate between an effective and an ineffective portfolio—even if applying these criteria is far from simple in practice.

The crucial question managers have to answer before diversifying into a new business was set out by Michael Porter (1987) as the 'better off test': will a particular business be better off—that is, better able to compete—under the ownership of the corporation than it would be if it stayed independent? If the answer to this question is 'no', then the business should not be diversified into—and if the organization already owns it, it should be divested. This view of corporate strategy—that it is the parent's job to add value to the subsidiary—has largely replaced earlier theories that emphasized the value that the businesses would add to the parent. This is because an SBU can only benefit the parent if the parent, in its turn, is able to manage it successfully. Only then will it be in a position to profit from the subsidiary's brands, distribution channels, or other resources.

There are two basic ways in which a business is better off residing within a larger portfolio under a controlling parent:

- It can tap into the knowledge, competences, or other resources held at the centre of the organization. In order for this to be possible, it must be sufficiently related to other important businesses in the portfolio, so that the parenting skills at the centre can add value.

- It can draw upon synergistic relationships with other businesses in the corporation. It is not necessary for the corporate centre to involve itself in stimulating these relationships, though in some firms it does. Although some synergies, such as knowledge sharing, are simpler to spot and extract if the businesses are strongly related, it is possible for synergies to occur between businesses that on the surface have very little obvious relationship.

To sum up, relatedness dictates the extent to which the centre can add value to the subsidiary businesses, whilst synergies allow businesses to add value to one another—although, to complicate this distinction slightly, some synergies may depend upon the businesses being related. In the worked example that follows, we show how to assess how related the businesses in a portfolio really are. We then offer some advice on how to extend that analysis to assess the scope for synergies.

Worked Example 5.1 Analysing relatedness at Sony

Sony in March 2005 had organized its businesses into the segments shown in Table 5.3. The breakdown of businesses in this table gives some idea of Sony's breadth and complexity. If we are to make sense of this portfolio, we must start by breaking the company's activities down into SBUs. It is important to note that these are *not* likely to be the same as the units shown in the corporate organization chart or annual report. Those are often collections of SBUs that may be grouped under one heading for administrative or presentational purposes. We must therefore take our own view of what the SBUs really are, based upon the extent to which they are in the same industry, with similar competitors and success factors. If in doubt, it usually pays to treat a reported business as several SBUs rather than one. That way you are more likely to pick up on important details relating to their competitiveness—and it is always easier to amalgamate

two SBUs if detailed scrutiny reveals them to be the same, than it is to break the analysis into more detail when you are half-way through. To take some specific examples:

- In the Games segment, hardware and software have radically different production processes. Although there are clear reasons why one might want the two under the same management, they should be treated as different SBUs.

- In the Music segment, recorded music and music publishing are different SBUs, with different customers and production processes. Classical music is arguably a different SBU from popular music: the success factors are different, and so are the customers, though there is the potential for synergies (the classical music business can learn from the popular side how to promote its photogenic young musicians, for example). →

Table 5.3 Sony's revenue and profit by business segment in 2004

Business segment	Proportion of revenues	Proportion of profits
Electronics:	66.9%	(25.8%)
Audio (portable stereos, home and car audio systems)	8.0%	
Video (DVD recorders/players, still digital cameras, video cameras)	14.5%	
Televisions and computer monitors	13.4%	
Information and communications (notebook and desktop PCs, PDAs, broadcast/professional use products)	10.9%	
Semiconductors	3.4%	
Components (CD & DVD drives, batteries)	8.7%	
Other (manufacture of CDs/DVDs and mobile phone handsets)	8.1%	
Games (PlayStation consoles & software)	9.8%	32.5%
Music (recorded music businesses)	3.0%	6.6%
Pictures (motion pictures and TV programming)	10.2%	48.0%
Financial services (life assurance, general insurance, banking, credit cards, leasing and credit assurance)	7.5%	41.7%
Other	2.6%	(3.1%)

Reproduced with the kind permission of Sony Corporation

- Although the Pictures segment looks pretty homogeneous, we should at least start by analysing motion picture production and TV programming as if they were separate SBUs.

- In the Financial Services segment, banking and insurance are different businesses with different competitors and success factors. Actuarial assessment of risks, for example, is of marginal importance in banking but absolutely vital in life assurance and general insurance. And the leasing and credit assurance businesses, with their corporate customers, have different requirements from the individuals that buy credit cards.

- The Electronics segment is clearly too broad to be considered as a single business, and Sony reports some figures for the businesses within it. But even those businesses are mostly too broad to be treated as individual SBUs. In the Video business, digital cameras are not self-evidently the same SBU as DVD recorders, although the target customers may be the same. Broadcast and professional use products may differ radically from PCs, though both are grouped under Information and Communications. The processes, and the competitors, involved in the production of CDs and DVDs are different from those involved in manufacturing mobile phones for Sony-Ericsson. Even in the Components business, one could ask the question (at a level of detail not

shown in the table) about whether Charge Coupled Devices (the sensors used in digital cameras) belong in the same SBU as LCD panels used in mobile phone and PDA displays.

- The Other segment contains SBUs as disparate as: an advertising agency; Sonet, an internet service provider; DeNa, which marketed e-commerce solutions; and a company that imports and sells general merchandise. Some of these had grown out of existing businesses, others, such as SonyCierge (Real-life Application 5.1) were the result of staff spotting new opportunities for utilizing the firm's assets.

So, depending on the view we take, we could easily end up with a list of between 25 and 40 SBUs for Sony, rather than the 12 segments and sub-segments shown in the table. Analysis at this level of detail can be intimidating—but less so than the consequences of getting it wrong, through over-simplification.

An exhaustive analysis of all these SBUs would be rather long and complex for the purposes of a worked example of this kind, so we examine just seven SBUs: PlayStation hardware, PlayStation software, cameras, video recorders, motion pictures, life assurance, and SonyCierge. In Table 5.4 we set out an example of a relatedness matrix, which analyses the key points of each business under the main categories defined by Markides and Williamson.

By inspecting this matrix we can pick out the extent of the similarities and differences between the businesses. For example: ➡

→ Table 5.4 A relatedness matrix for selected Sony business units

	PlayStation hardware	PlayStation software	Cameras	Video recorders	Motion pictures	Life assurance	SonyCierge
Customers/markets	Children and young adults, globally	Children and young adults, globally	General consumers, professionals and hobbyists, globally	General consumers and professionals, globally	General consumers, globally	Adults, Japan	Selected affluent individuals, USA
Brands	Sony Computer Entertainment, PS2, PSP	Sony Computer Entertainment—but the game title is the real brand	Sony	Sony	Sony Pictures, but the powerful brands are attached to actors and directors, sometimes to book or play from which movie adapted	Sony	Sony
Channels	Specialist electronics and games retailers	Specialist games retailers, music retailers, general retailers. Specialist video outlets	Specialist electronics and camera retailers, general retailers	Electronics and general retailers	Cinemas. Music retailers. General retailers. Specialist video outlets	Direct salesforce. Selected agents	Invitation + word of mouth
Inputs	CPU. Graphics processors. DVD players. LCD screens. General electronics components	Computers for coding. Programmers. Sometimes actors and directors	Lenses. Charge coupled devices or CMOS sensors. Imaging software. LCDs. Flash memory. General electronics components	Lasers. TV tuners. Graphics processors. Hard disk drives. General electronics components	Scripts. Actors, cinematographers, directors, etc. Studio space. Editing suites. Film processing	Actuarial expertise. Investment expertise	Consumer electronics. Specialist knowledge
Processes	Surface mounting of components. Mass assembly.	Programming. Project management. Direction of live footage. Marketing	Surface mounting of components. Mass assembly	Surface mounting of components. Mass assembly	Script development. Actor recruitment. Project management. Marketing. Intellectual property management	Customer need assessment. Risk assessment. Quotation. Account management. Claims management	Customer need assessment. Project management of installation
Industry success factors	Superior graphics rendition. Ease of use. Relationships with software producers. Creation of dominant standard	Realistic graphics. Creativity: strong stories, characters, gameplay. Empathy with target audience	Superior image resolution. Ease of use. Low cost	Picture quality. Ease of use. Compatibility with multiple record and playback standards	Risk management (avoiding expensive failures). Empathy with target audiences. Superior marketing and distribution. Superior linkages to key actors/directors	Risk management. Investment expertise. CRM. Reputation for reliability	Access to state-of-art technology and expertise. Customer responsiveness. Project management. Discretion

→

- Most of the seven businesses are targeted at broad, global consumer markets, though cameras and video recorders have professional users as well. The life assurance and SonyCierge businesses are more targeted and require different sales channels.

- The Sony brand is used across all the businesses, so that there is the opportunity for synergies. It may be vital for the life insurance business, giving it a visibility and reputation that it would have taken much longer to develop without a well-regarded parent. However, the brand is of less importance for the PlayStation software and Motion Pictures businesses.

- PlayStation hardware, cameras and video recorders show a great deal of commonality in terms of target markets, channels, inputs, and processes. It is clear why they might belong in the same portfolio. In fact, there is also a vertical relationship—the DVD hardware from the video recorders business is used in the PlayStation. There are, however, differences in the success factors involved, but ease of use is common to all three. It would be reasonable to expect Sony to have found ways in which these three businesses, and others with the same success factors, can share knowledge on what makes hardware easy to use.

- SonyCierge is also vertically related to the consumer electronics businesses, but it is debatable whether it needs to be part of the same corporation in order to profit from them. It also offers other companies' hardware where there is no Sony product that fills the customer need.

- There are potential synergies between Motion pictures and PlayStation software—they can share characters and storylines, as well as distribution and marketing channels and competences and expertise on what consumers are looking for.

- The motion pictures business calls upon a number of channels, inputs, and processes that are not used in any of the other six businesses in the relatedness matrix (though it does have many features in common with the recorded music business).

- Although SonyCierge and the life insurance businesses operate in very different industries and markets, they share the need to make very precise assessments of customer requirements and win customer trust. It is possible that they could usefully share experience in these areas. It is a matter of judgement whether opportunities like this outweigh the risk that top management attention may be too thinly spread if called upon to understand two businesses that are so very different from one another, and from most of Sony's other businesses. It takes very able managers to understand this level of diversity.

To summarize, at the end of this kind of analysis, we are able to assess:

- what are the common assets and competences that define the organization's core businesses—in the case of the Sony example, these would be the consumer electronics businesses;

- whether there are any businesses that are clearly unrelated to the others, and so may be candidates for divestment—although they may also be seen as the seeds of future core businesses. We can also see, as in the case of SonyCierge and the insurance business, what linkages and learning opportunities would be sacrificed if these SBUs were divested;

- to what extent there are opportunities for synergies between the businesses. By further looking at the extent to which these opportunities are being pursued within the organization, we can assess how well the style of management being used at corporate level fits the organization's portfolio—we look at this topic in Chapter 9.

Practical dos and don'ts

It is important to be precise in this analysis. It may be helpful to use internet sources to get an idea of the inputs and processes involved in a product or service. You can also use a search engine to locate product reviews (often available on-line) to give you an idea of exactly what makes the difference between success and failure in the industry.

Beware of vague or superficial similarities. General assertions that two businesses are related, or have potential synergies because they make intensive use of IT, or high-technology, are not sufficiently exact: almost any two businesses could be said to be related in such ways. In the example here, it might appear at first glance that the motion pictures business and the life assurance business could share expertise on risk management. But the risks to be managed in the movie business—essentially, the risk of investing large sums of money in films that no-one wants to watch—are very different from the risks of underpricing life insurance or pension contributions and then finding yourself with large payouts that are not covered through income from premiums and investments. So this too is a superficial synergy, and probably not valid.

Using Evidence 5.2 Assessing synergies

When assessing synergistic benefits within a portfolio, you should first compile a relatedness matrix (see Worked Example 5.1) and use the evidence from this to assess whether there really are any potential synergies between any of the businesses. For example, you could identify which, precisely, are the tangible or intangible resources that might be combined, and how this combination might improve the competitiveness of the SBUs in question. You can then look for specific examples of whether any of those synergies are actually being realized. Are tangible and intangible resources being effectively shared, is negotiating power being pooled, are strategies actually being coordinated, and have any combined businesses been created?

The next, very tough, question to ask is whether benefits from the synergies outweigh the costs. If a firm has combined its salesforce across product areas, has this led to increased sales, because of cross-selling, or decreased sales, because the salesforce has lost its focus and is trying to sell products it does not understand very well?

Finally, you will need to reach a judgement, for which hard evidence will not be easy to find. If synergies have failed to happen, or to succeed, why is this? It may be that the SBU managers are hampered by an inappropriate culture or architecture—but perhaps they are right, and the costs of potential synergies outweigh the benefits. Perhaps the firm does not need to own, or control, all the businesses in order to profit from the synergy, but would be equally well off fostering an alliance or partnership with an independent firm.

5.4.3 Portfolio models and balance

Many strategy writers, particularly in the 1970s, felt that it was important for a portfolio to be 'balanced'—displaying a mixture of different characteristics. Balance might be achieved across a number of dimensions:

- size—a mix of small and large businesses;
- the age or the life-cycle stage of the industry—a mix of young, fast-growing businesses and more mature ones;
- the extent to which the businesses are net producers or consumers of cash.

One theoretical benefit of a balanced portfolio is a reduction of risk, since it would minimize the likelihood of all the businesses facing severe problems at the same time. A second potential benefit is that resources can be redistributed from the businesses that have them to those that need them—for example, a mature business can become a source of cash and of marketing and production expertise for a younger one. However, there is absolutely no evidence that firms that have balanced portfolios perform any better (or worse) than those that have not.[42]

The main tools used to assess balance in a portfolio are the well-known matrices developed by the Boston Consulting Group (the BCG growth-share matrix) and General Electric (the Business Attractiveness Screen). Both matrices attempt to plot businesses on two scales:

- industry attractiveness (measured in terms of growth rate on the BCG matrix);
- business strength (measured in the BCG matrix in terms of market share relative to that of the competitor with the highest share).

Both frameworks suggest that a firm should invest in, hold, or divest a business, depending on where it appears when plotted in the respective matrix. However, empirical studies have not found any systematic differences in the way in which businesses appearing in different parts of these matrices need to be managed. This implies that it may not be valid to make investment decisions on the basis of such a simple piece of two-dimensional analysis, without, for example, taking account of an SBU's or product's relationship with the others in the portfolio. Moreover, certain of the assumptions behind the frameworks are false, notably the assumption that 'dogs'—low-growth, low-share products or businesses—are likely to consume rather than generate cash.[43]

In fact, the limited amount of testing that has been conducted on these frameworks suggests that managers who employ them make *worse* investment decisions than those who do not.[44] You are therefore advised not to use portfolio matrices in your analysis.

What Can Go Wrong 5.1 Helpful and unhelpful synergies at Sony

In any organization as diverse as Sony, there will be scope for the businesses to collaborate, sometimes in unexpected ways. For example, Sony's credit card services unit, Sony Finance International, has launched a new card containing a sophisticated embedded chip that offers cardholders a range of secure electronic payment options, both in-store and over the internet. It is highly likely that the electronics businesses will have played a role in the development of these products, even if they only stimulated thinking about the way in which technology could be used in credit card transactions and helped Sony Finance understand its potential and its limitations.

Sony's Music Entertainment business (now part of Sony BMG, a joint venture with Bertelsmann) was acquired, along with the motion pictures business Sony Pictures Entertainment, to make sure that the firm could be assured of a supply of software content to place on any new recording medium that the electronics businesses might develop. A scarcity of compatible films was believed to be one of the reasons why Sony's Betamax video recording format lost out in the market-place to Matsushita's VHS in the 1970s.[45] Sony could now be sure this would never happen again. There was also the potential for the music and the pictures businesses to coordinate their strategies, so that the release of an album by an artist could be synchronized with the release of a film where that artist appeared, or sang in the soundtrack.

The downside of this synergistic relationship became apparent when, at the end of the 1990s, Sony started to develop its response to the increasing trend for music fans to rip tracks from their CDs and listen to them in MP3 format. Sony Music, fearful of loss of control of its intellectual property and of music revenues, worked to discourage the development of a portable music player that could play these ripped files and facilitate the downloading of music from the internet. '[B]ecause we had music [as a business], Sony was reluctant to introduce an iPod type product', Ken Kutaragi, then Sony's deputy president, admitted in January 2005.[46] The company concedes that it has been hurt[47] by the success of Apple's iPod (Real-life Application 4.4). Its long-standing lead in portable music, dating back to its launch of the first, cassette-tape-based, Walkmans in 1979, is under threat.

Sony's initial response to the iPod may have been hampered by its preference for using its own MiniDisc technology rather than flash memory or hard disk devices. Its latest generation of Network Walkman players have had enthusiastic reviews and enjoyed strong sales.[48] But the firm's strongest riposte to the iPod may come from another part of the corporation—the games business. As more and more establishment figures, including the British Queen, become known as iPod owners, some fashion conscious people may be looking for a new emblem of 'cool'. One of the products they seem to be turning to is the PlayStation Portable (PSP), launched in December 2004, which has enjoyed strong sales, and whose European launch was so eagerly awaited that the company had to take legal action to prevent it from being imported in advance.

● CHAPTER SUMMARY

A successful organization is likely to find avenues for expansion and diversification into new products and market segments. An organization may eventually expand to the point where it ceases to be simply a multi-product business and becomes a conglomerate with multiple businesses spanning different industries with different success factors. Diversification brings a number of potential risks along with the potential benefits, and involves trade-offs between the following factors:

● Do the new offerings or markets offer the firm growth potential? If not, does the firm need to be present in a particular market, or offer a particular product, in order to control its operating environment or to prevent competitors from gaining a foothold or making easy profits?

● Does growth or diversification improve the organization's legitimacy in the eyes of key stake-holders, and help it gain access to important resources?

● Do customers require a broad range of products and services to respond to their precise needs? If not, will the firm's loss of focus affect its differentiation?

● Can the organization afford to be dependent on its existing products or markets?

● Will top management attention be dissipated if it is spread across too many products or markets? Are the elements of the portfolio sufficiently related to reduce that risk?

● Will the organization, if it diversifies, learn anything new and important from exposure to multiple markets and technologies?

● Will overheads costs proliferate if the organization becomes too broad and complex?

● Can the organization derive economies of scale and experience (exploitation) benefits from using a narrow product range across a number of markets, or a few broad segments, with homogeneous needs?

● Will economies of scope and synergies between different parts of the portfolio compensate for any lost economies of scale?

Research indicates that a moderate degree of diversification enhances profitability and market value, but that too much often destroys them. Related diversification is more likely to succeed than unrelated.

Relatedness may come from:

● similarities in the success factors in the industries where the different SBUs operate. These may be: customer factors, channel factors, input factors, process factors, or market knowledge factors;

● similar strategic assets, such as knowledge or reputation, that are used within the businesses to achieve industry success factors. These may only give temporary advantage;

● competences, needed to build strategic assets, which can be usefully transferred between the businesses, and are more likely to confer sustainable advantage.

In addition, there may be synergies between the businesses, which may come from:

● sharing tangible resources;

● pooling negotiating power;

● coordinating SBU strategies;

● vertically coordinating the provision of goods and services across SBUs;

● creating combined businesses;

● sharing intangible resources.

The chapter concludes with a review of how to appraise the expansion and diversification strategy of a business, and the degree of relatedness and synergies between the SBUs in a corporation's portfolio.

Online Resource Centre
www.oxfordtextbooks.co.uk/orc/haberberg_rieple/

Visit the Online Resource Centre that accompanies this book to read more information relating to distinctiveness.

● KEY SKILLS

The key skills you should have developed after reading this chapter are:

- the ability to appraise the trade-offs an organization has taken in its choices of how far to diversify and critique its diversification strategy;

- the ability to conduct a systematic and thorough analysis of an organization's portfolio and to identify where the different elements are related, and where there are potential synergies;

- the ability to appraise an organization's portfolio and determine which businesses do and do not belong in it.

● REVIEW QUESTIONS

1. Why do many people find it difficult to distinguish between economies of scale and economies of scope?

2. It has been known for many years that the returns from diversification are often poor. Why do managers persist with it as a strategy?

3. How can organizations try to manage the risks that come with increased diversification?

4. When might it be right to defy Porter's better-off test and diversify into businesses that are *not* better off under this particular parent?

5. Unrelated diversification can sometimes work well. Find some examples and find *why* the firms in question succeeded. Does this mean the theorists are wrong?

6. In Worked Example 5.1, the PlayStation Software, Motion Pictures, and SonyCierge businesses all use forms of project management as part of their processes. To what extent would this be the basis for synergies between them?

● FURTHER READING

- Franko, L. G. (2004). 'The death of diversification? The focusing of the world's industrial firms, 1980–2000'. *Business Horizons*, 47/4: 41–50. A useful summary of global trends and the underlying reasons.

- Goold, M. and Campbell, A. (1998). 'Desperately seeking synergy'. *Harvard Business Review*, 76/5, September–October: 131–43. A readable review of the concept of synergy and the difficulties firms encounter in obtaining synergies in practice.

- Gottfredson, M. and Aspinall, K. (2005) 'Innovation versus complexity: what is too much of a good thing?' *Harvard Business Review*, 83/11, November: 62–71. This contains many useful, though largely American, examples of how product proliferation can harm profitability, and what managers have done, and can do, to address the problem.

- Tanriverdi, H. and Venkatraman, N. (2005). 'Knowledge relatedness and the performance of multibusiness firms'. *Strategic Management Journal*, 26/2: 97–119. A more scholarly review of the theory of diversification.

● REFERENCES

Abrahamson, E. (1996). 'Management fashion'. *Academy of Management Review*, 21/1: 254–85.

Amit, R. (1986). 'Cost leadership strategy and experience curves'. *Strategic Management Journal*, 7/3: 281–92.

Anderson, C. (2007). *The Long Tail: How Endless Choice is Creating Unlimited Demand*. London: Random House Business Books.

Ansoff, H. I. (1965). *Corporate Strategy*. New York: McGraw-Hill.

Armstrong, J. and Brodie, R. (1994). 'Effects of portfolio planning methods on decision making: experimental results'. *International Journal of Research in Marketing*, 11/1: 73–84.

Auh, S. and Menguc, B. (2005). 'Balancing exploration and exploitation: the moderating role of competitive intensity'. *Journal of Business Research*, 58/12: 1652–61.

Bayus B. and Putsis W. (1999). 'Product proliferation: an empirical analysis of product line determinants and market outcomes'. *Marketing Science*, 18: 137–53.

Berger, P. and Ofek, E. (1995). 'Diversification's effect on firm value'. *Journal of Financial Economics*, 37/1: 39–65.

Bernheim, B. and Whinston, M. (1990). 'Multi-market contact and collusive behaviour'. *Rand Journal of Economics*, 21/1: 1–26.

Besanko, D., Dranove, D., and Shanley, M. (1996). *The Economics of Strategy*. Wiley, New York.

Bettis, R. and Hall, W. (1983). 'The business portfolio approach—where it falls down in practice'. *Long Range Planning*, April: 95–104.

Capon, N., Farley, J., and Hulbert, J. (1987). 'A comparative analysis of the strategy and structure of United States and Australian corporations'. *Journal of International Business Studies*, 8/1: 51–74.

Carroll, G. R. (1994). 'Organizations: the smaller they get'. *California Management Review*, 37/1: 28–41.

Chandler, A. (1962). *Strategy and Structure*. Cambridge, MA: MIT Press (2nd edn, 1969; 3rd edn, 1990).

Cohen, W. and Levinthal, D. (1990). 'Absorptive capacity: a new perspective on learning and innovation'. *Administrative Science Quarterly*, 35/1: 128–52.

Combs, J. and Ketchen, D. (1999). 'Explaining interfirm cooperation and performance: Toward a reconciliation of predictions'. *Strategic Management Journal*, 20/9: 867–88.

Day, G. and Montgomery, D. (1983). 'Diagnosing the experience curve'. *Journal of Marketing*, 47: 44–58.

Fan, J. and Lang, L. (2000). 'The measurement of relatedness: An application to corporate diversification'. *Journal of Business*, 73/4: 629–59.

Farjoun, M. and Starbuck, W. (2007). 'Organizing at and beyond the limits'. *Organization Studies*, 28/4: 541–66.

Fauver, L., Houston, J., and Naranjo, A. (2004). 'Cross-country evidence on the value of corporate industrial and international diversification'. *Journal of Corporate Finance*, 10/5: 729–52.

Franko, L. G. (2004). 'The death of diversification? The focusing of the world's industrial firms, 1980–2000'. *Business Horizons*, 47/4: 41–50.

Graham, J., Lemmon, M., and Wolf, J. (2002). 'Does corporate diversification destroy value?' *Journal of Finance*, 57/2: 695–720.

Gomes, J. and Lidvan, D. (2004). 'Optimal diversification: reconciling theory and evidence'. *Journal of Finance*, 59/2: 507–35.

Goold, M. and Campbell, A. (1998). 'Desperately seeking synergy'. *Harvard Business Review*, 76/5, September–October: 131–43.

Goold, M., Campbell, A., and Alexander, M. (1994). *Corporate-level Strategy: Creating Value in the Multi-Business Company*. New York: Wiley.

Grant, R. (1998). *Contemporary Strategy Analysis*. 3rd edn. Oxford: Blackwell.

Greenwood, R., Suddaby, R., and Hinings, C. (2002). 'Theorizing change: the role of professional associations in the transformation of institutionalised fields'. *Academy of Management Journal*, 45/1: 58–80.

Greve, H. R. (1998). 'Managerial cognition and the mimetic adoption of market positions: what you see is what you do'. *Strategic Management Journal*, 19: 967–88.

Gupta, A., Smith, K., and Shalley, C. (2006). 'The interplay between exploration and exploitation'. *Academy of Management Journal*, 49/4: 693–706.

Hall, E. Jr and Lee, J. (1999). 'Broadening the view of corporate diversification: An international perspective'. *International Journal of Organizational Analysis*, 7/1: 25–53.

Hambrick, D. and MacMillan, I. (1982). 'The product portfolio and man's best friend'. *California Management Review*, 25/1: 84–95.

Hamel, G. and Prahalad, C. K. (1994). *Competing for the Future*. Boston, MA: Harvard Business Press.

Haveman, H. A. (1993). 'Follow the leader: mimetic isomorphism and entry into new markets'. *Administrative Science Quarterly*, 38: 593–627.

Henderson, B. (1984). 'The application and misapplication of the experience curve'. *Journal of Business Strategy*, 4: 3–9.

Hill, C. W. L. and Hoskisson, R. E. (1987). 'Strategy and structure in the multi-product firm'. *Academy of Management Review*, 2: 331–41.

Hoskisson, R. and Hitt, M. (1990). 'Antecedents and performance outcomes of diversification: A review and critique of theoretical performance'. *Journal of Management*, 16: 461 509.

Jennings, D., Rajatmaram, D., and Lawrence, F. (2003). 'Strategy-performance relationships in service firms: a test for equifinality'. *Journal of Managerial Issues*, 15/2: 208–20.

Kekre S. and Srinivasan K. (1990). 'Broader product lines: a necessity to achieve success?' *Management Science*, 36: 1216–31.

Kogut, B., Walker, G., and Anand, J. (2002). 'Agency and institutions: national divergences in diversification behavior'. *Organization Science*, 13/2: 162–78.

Leavy, B. (1994). 'Two strategic perspectives on the buyer–supplier relationship'. *Production and Inventory Management Journal*, 35/2: 47–51.

Leavy, B. (1998). 'The concept of learning in the strategy field: review and outlook'. *Management Learning*, 29/4: 447–66.

Levitt, T. (1983). 'The globalization of markets'. *Harvard Business Review*, May–June: 90–102.

Li, S. and Greenwood, R. (2004). 'The effect of within-industry diversification on firm performance: synergy creation, multi-market contact and market structuration'. *Strategic Management Journal*, 25/12: 1131–53.

Lieberman, M. and Montgomery, D. (1988). 'First-mover advantages'. *Strategic Management Journal*, Summer Special Issue, 9: 41–58.

Lieberman, M. and Montgomery, D. (1998). 'First-mover (dis)advantages: retrospective and link with the resource-based view'. *Strategic Management Journal*, 19/12: 1111.

Lounsbury, M. and Leblici, H. (2004). 'The origins of strategic practice: product diversification in the American mutual fund industry'. *Strategic Organization*, 2/1: 65–90.

McGee, J. (2005). 'Economies of scale'. *Blackwell Encyclopedic Dictionary of Strategic Management*. Oxford: Blackwell, 1–113.

MacMillan, I., Hambrick, D., and Day, D. (1982). 'The product portfolio and profitability—a PIMS-based analysis of industrial-product businesses'. *Academy of Management Journal*, 25/4: 733–55.

March, J. (1991). 'Exploration and exploitation in organizational learning', *Organization Science*, 2: 71–87.

March, J. and Levinthal, D. (1993). 'The myopia of learning', *Strategic Management Journal*, 14: 95–112.

Markides, C. and Williamson, P. (1996). 'Corporate diversification and organizational structure: A resource-based view'. *Academy of Management Journal*, 39/2: 340–67.

Martin, J. and Sayrak, A. (2003). 'Corporate diversification and shareholder value: a survey of recent literature'. *Journal of Corporate Finance*, 9/1: 37–57.

Mayer, M. and Whittington, R. (2003). 'Diversification in context: a cross-national and cross-temporal extension'. *Strategic Management Journal*, 24: 773–81.

Miles, R. E. and Snow, C. C. (1978). *Organizational Structure, Strategy, Process*. New York: McGraw-Hill.

Miller, D. (2006). 'Technological diversity, related diversification, and firm performance'. *Strategic Management Journal*, 27/7: 601–19.

Montgomery, C. (1994). 'Corporate diversification'. *Journal of Economic Perspectives*, 8/3: 163–78.

Nathan, J. (1999) *Sony: The Private Life*. London: HarperCollins.

Nightingale, P. (2000). 'Economies of scale in experimentation: knowledge and technology in pharmaceutical R&D'. *Industrial & Corporate Change*, 9/2: 315.

Palich, L., Cardinal, L., and Miller, C. (2000). 'Curvilinearity in the diversification-performance linkage: an examination of over three decades of research'. *Strategic Management Journal*, 21: 155–74.

Park, C. (2003). 'Prior performance characteristics of related and unrelated acquirers'. *Strategic Management Journal*, 24: 471–80.

Penrose, E. (1959). *The Theory of the Growth of the Firm*. Oxford: Oxford University Press. 2nd edn (1995).

Peters, T. (1992). 'Rethinking scale'. *California Management Review*, Fall: 7–29.

Peters, T. and Waterman, R. (1982). *In Search of Excellence*. New York: Harper & Row.

Porter, M. E. (1987). 'From competitive advantage to corporate strategy'. *Harvard Business Review*, May–June: 43–59.

Prahalad, C. K. and Hamel, G. (1990). 'The core competence of the corporation'. *Harvard Business Review*, 68/3: 79–91.

Rumelt, R. P. (1974). *Strategy, Structure and Economic Performance*. Boston, MA: Harvard University Press.

Rumelt, R. P. (1982). 'Diversification strategy and profitability'. *Strategic Management Journal*, 3: 359–69.

Schoar, A. (2002). 'Effects of corporate diversification on productivity'. *Journal of Finance*, 57/6: 2379–403.

Schmalensee, R. (1978). 'Entry deterrence in the ready-to-eat breakfast cereal market'. *Bell Journal of Economics*, 9: 305–27.

Servaes, H. and Lins, K. (1999). 'International evidence on the value of corporate diversification'. *Journal of Finance*, 54: 2215–40.

Sidhu, J., Commandeur, H., and Volberda, H. (2007). 'The multifaceted nature of exploration and exploitation: value of supply, demand, and spatial search for innovation'. *Organization Science*, 18/1: 20–38.

Slater, S. and Zwirlein. T. (1992). 'Shareholder value and investment strategy using the general portfolio model'. *Journal of Management*, 18/4: 717–32.

Sorenson, O., Mcevily, S., Ren, C., and Roy, R. (2006). 'Niche width revisited: organizational scope, behavior and performance'. *Strategic Management Journal*, 27/10: 915–36.

St. John, C. and Harrison, J. (1999). 'Manufacturing-based relatedness, synergy, and coordination'. *Strategic Management Journal*, 20/2: 129–45.

Tanriverdi, H. and Venkatraman, N. (2005). 'Knowledge relatedness and the performance of multibusiness firms'. *Strategic Management Journal*, 26/2: 97–119.

Villalonga, B. (2004a). 'Does diversification cause the "diversification discount"?' *Financial Management*, 33/2: 5–27.

Villalonga, B. (2004b). 'Diversification discount or premium? New evidence from the Business Information Tracking Series'. *Journal of Finance*, 59/2: 479–506.

Verity, J. (1992). 'Deconstructing the computer industry'. *Business Week*, 23 November: 44–52.

Wan, W. and Hoskisson, R. (2003). 'Home country environments, corporate diversification strategies, and firm performance'. *Academy of Management Journal*, 46/1: 27–45.

Wernerfelt, B. and Montgomery, C. (1988). 'Tobin's q and the importance of focus in firm performance'. *American Economic Review*, 78: 246–50.

Wezel, F. and van Witteloostuijn, A. (2006). 'From scooters to choppers: Product portfolio change and organizational failure'. *Long Range Planning*, 39/1: 11–28.

Williamson, O. (1975). *Markets and Hierarchies: Analysis and Antitrust Implications*. New York: Free Press.

Zahra, S. and George, G. (2002). 'Absorptive capacity: a review, reconceptualization and extension'. *Academy of Management Review*, 27/2: 185–203.

End-of-chapter Case Study 5.1 eBay (b)

By 2005, eBay had built itself a formidable position as a leading internet auction house and trading platform (see eBay (a) at the end of Chapter 4). Its speedy growth and growing prominence had left it facing a number of challenges, but these have not held eBay back from diversifying its activities.

Expansion and diversification

Early attempts to move into real estate and into fine arts and antiques (the latter in a joint venture with Sotheby's, a leading traditional auctioneer) have had to be scaled back. A traditional San Francisco auction house bought in 1999 was sold off in 2002 when it became apparent that there were no real synergies between on-line and off-line auctions.[49]

The next move related to payments processing, which eBay has identified as a key factor in generating more business through the auction site. If potential sellers have confidence that they will receive payment, the logic ran, they are more likely to list their goods, particularly if the item in question is valuable. Once it became known that sellers preferred a given payment clearer, buyers would acquire accounts with it too. So, in 2001, eBay introduced its own payments processing system, only to be met with vehement protests from sellers who were used to using PayPal, the market leader.[50] eBay ended up paying $1.5 billion for PayPal in 2002, effectively writing off the many millions of dollars invested in its own loss-making payments processing operation.[51]

Having got over this initial misstep, however, eBay claims considerable success in growing PayPal's business. Part of this growth has come on the back of eBay's own increasing sales volume, but the proportion of eBay transactions cleared through PayPal has increased in the USA from just over one-half at the time of the takeover to just under three-quarters at the end of 2004. Dedicated PayPal sites have also been set up for Australia and eight key European markets. The quarterly value of eBay payments cleared through PayPal increased steadily from around $150m at the time of the acquisition to around $950m in the final quarter of 2004. Benefits have been felt in the opposite direction, too, with the rate of growth of eBay in the UK, for example, having increased perceptibly since the dedicated PayPal site for the UK opened for business.[52]

Its owner sees plenty of potential for growing the payments business further, in the first instance by simply increasing the proportion of eBay transactions settled through PayPal outside North America to closer to the levels found in the USA and Canada. But eBay represents less than one-tenth of the total volume of transactions cleared on-line. The advantages of PayPal (see Exhibit 5.1—How Paypal Works) have also led to its increasing acceptance outside the eBay community, and the parent in 2005 saw clear opportunities in expanding there, particularly for cross-border transactions.[53]

Meanwhile, eBay's own geographical scope continued to expand. The company acquired 38 per cent of Eachnet, China's leading auction site, in 2002, and the rest of the firm's equity in 2003. India's Baazee.com followed for $50m in 2004, which also saw eBay launches in Malaysia and the Philippines. The company had also taken steps to learn about classified listings, an activity which it saw as complementary to auctions. In 2004, it acquired a minority interest in craigslist.com, a quirky but hugely popular free listings site, based originally in the USA but with offshoots around the world. It also acquired listings sites in Germany and the Netherlands. In March 2005 it launched a clutch of city-based listing sites in various countries under the Kijiji brand (Kijiji is Swahili for 'village') then made acquisitions in Spain and the UK.[54]

The Skype acquisition

All of these deals were, however, dwarfed by the acquisition, announced on 12 September 2005, of Skype. Skype's business was the provision of voice telephony over the internet (VoIP). Skype was founded in 2003 by Niklas Zennström and Janus Friis, two Swedes with a history of disruption of established industries. Their first venture was Kazaa, a piece of software which, once downloaded, enabled any user to find and swap files with any other without going through a central server. Phenomenally popular—by one estimate, 90 per cent of all files swapped over the internet went via Kazaa—it was nonetheless hugely controversial, since many of those files were music tracks for which the copyright owners received no payment.[55] Although Zennström and Friis sold their interest in Kazaa in 2002, they still fought shy of entering the USA for fear of lawsuits from vengeful recorded music firms.[56] Skype was developed in Estonia, where it maintained a team of around 100 programmers—including the four that wrote much of the code for Kazaa—and administered from Luxembourg and London.[57] It thus kept its operations beyond the reach of American lawyers, even though many Americans, not least the group of venture capital funds that injected $18.8m into the firm in 2004,[58] were enthusiastic supporters.

Skype followed the Kazaa model of providing users with a small piece of free software, easily downloaded and installed, which enabled users to communicate between themselves, in this case using microphones attached to their PC, without going through a central server. Its legality, unlike that of Kazaa, was not in question, but its implications for established competitors were no less radical than those of Zennström and Friis' previous ➜

→ brainchild. Computer-to-computer calls via VoIP were free, and it was generally agreed that by 2005 the software had become reliable and offered perfectly acceptable sound quality if used over a good broadband connection.[59]

Some users paid subscriptions that enabled them to make calls to or receive them from traditional telephones. Users of such services could choose the country or area code in which their VoIP telephone appeared to be located, so that people in that area could phone them at local call rates, even if the computer was located thousands of kilometres away.

By undercutting established telephony providers in this way, Skype had become, largely by word-of-mouth, one of the fastest-growing internet start-ups ever, which encouraged its founders to search for internet partners to expand its distribution. They are said to have held discussions with Yahoo!, Google and Microsoft, and conducted negotiations with News Corporation regarding the sale of a 20 per cent stake in Skype, before they began talking to eBay.[60] Zennström, Friis, Omidyar, and Whitman began talking with no great expectations on either side, but as they progressed, they arrived at what Zennström later described as an 'Aha! moment' when he and Whitman 'both kind of went crazy on the whiteboard, mapping out ideas'.[61]

As later presented to investors, those ideas appeared to revolve around the incorporation into eBay, Paypal, and the firm's classified listings sites of 'Skype Me' links (for which the lister would pay a fee) enabling the potential buyer to telephone the seller or advertiser there and then, via a Skype number which might, if the seller chose, be forwarded to a normal phone. Such a call would generate revenue for both eBay and Skype. The two parties could then exchange detailed information, discuss options and build a relationship in a way which was not always easy using email, the only communication option offered by eBay up to that point. eBay believed that this extra dimension would be attractive to buyers and sellers of expensive, complex, and high-involvement goods, such as cars, collectibles, musical instruments, jewellery, and real estate, and services such as travel. It would thus improve their penetration of these business categories, and also help them in large emerging markets—China, Russia, Poland, Brazil, and India—where they believed people were more comfortable with the telephone than with the internet, and where there was a tradition of haggling.[62]

eBay's presentation to stock analysts also made much of the quality of Skype as a standalone business. Demand for VoIP was expected to grow 20-fold by 2009 as traditional telephony providers were undercut on price. Skype was the clear market leader measured by numbers of subscribers, of which it had 54 million. Although its revenues in 2004 were a mere $7m, they were expected to amount to $60m in 2005 (ten times eBay's turnover at a similar stage in its existence) and surpass $200m in 2006, by which point the company was expected to be breaking even.[63] eBay also highlighted the quality of Skype's management (Zennström and Friis were both committed to stay with the corporation) and its technology, which was claimed to be more secure and allow a higher proportion of completed calls than its competitors'.[64]

Skype nonetheless faced a number of competitors, both new and established. Some, like Vonage, which specialized in handsets that plugged into a computer but could then be used to communicate with traditional telephones, were new ventures in the same vein as Skype. But others, like Google, the market leader in internet search, Microsoft, and AOL, were established firms with considerable financial resources, though their services only linked people who subscribed to their own instant messaging networks.[65] In the UK, Dixons, an electronics retailer which had been an early entrant to internet service provision with its Freeserve service (later sold to Wanadoo), launched its own VoIP service shortly after the announcement of the eBay/Skype merger.[66]

Many observers therefore felt that the agreed price was high for a firm with modest revenues that had yet to turn a profit.[67] That price was $1.3bn in cash and $1.3bn in shares, plus a further $1.5bn if Skype met certain targets by the end of 2009.[68] One analyst suggested that, if eBay wanted to incorporate VoIP technology into its sites, it could have built its own software at far lower cost.[69] A poll showed that Skype's user community, whose word-of-mouth recommendation had been a major factor in the firm's expansion, was also sceptical as to the merger benefits, and fearful of losing their free calls.[70]

Such fears might be groundless, since Skype's business model was unusual—because it did not have to pay for servers, and because marketing was largely by word-of-mouth, the marginal cost of a user was extremely small. It therefore did not mind sustaining a large base of users, many of whom generated little or no revenue, if that gave it the opportunity to sell profitable add-on services to a small proportion of them.[71] And in any case, not all the comments from the Skype community were so negative. One of the firm's software developers wrote approvingly, in the *Financial Times*, of the clarity that eBay was already bringing to Skype's strategy, in particular the near-certainty that an enterprise version of the software would now be quick to arrive. He also believed that eBay's entrepreneurial members were likely to find novel ways to extract profit from this untried form of telephony.[72]

(Sources: <http://www.ebay.com>, accessed on 12 September 2003 and 16 October 2005; *Economist* (2005). 'Happy e-birthdays'. July 23: 62–3.) →

→ Exhibit 5.1 How PayPal works

Any seller with a PayPal account is able to receive money from any buyer that also has one. If there are funds in the buyer's account, the payment is taken directly from them; otherwise, PayPal takes the money from the buyer's credit card. The commission that PayPal charges the seller still works out cheaper than the cost of accepting credit cards through a normal merchant account; it is also far simpler to set up and administer. Since PayPal vets both parties before opening the account, whilst the seller never sees the buyer's credit card details, the rate of fraudulent transactions on PayPal is far lower than on other types of electronic payment. This enables eBay to offer buyers a guarantee of repayment up to a limited sum (approximately £170 in the UK) if the seller fails to deliver.

One problem, however, is that unless the seller is resident in selected countries, withdrawing funds from a PayPal account can be awkward, particularly if the sums involved are small, although such funds can easily be used for PayPal purchases, on eBay or elsewhere. This is one reason why the opening of a dedicated PayPal site for a country can make a difference to the rate of usage of both PayPal and eBay.

Case study questions

1. Assess eBay's expansion and diversification strategy before the addition of Skype. How great was the degree of relatedness between the different businesses? How strong was the potential for synergies between them? Were there any businesses in the portfolio that eBay should not have entered?

2. Evaluate the strategic arguments in favour and against the Skype acquisition (Porter's better-off test in section 5.4.2 may help). Do you agree with the people who say that eBay paid too much for Skype?

● NOTES

1   See Penrose (1959) for a discussion.
2   This Real-life Application is extracted from Beard, A. (2004). 'WiFi please, Jeeves'. *Financial Times*, Surveys RES1, 6 October: 14. 'Seven years ago' relates to 1997, when Howard Stringer, now CEO of Sony, had just been nominated head of Sony Corporation, the US subsidiary.
3   These sources of these dangers are analysed in depth by Gottfredson and Aspinall (2005).
4   Smith, A. (1999). 'Unilever steps up brand sales'. *Financial Times*, 5 May: 28; Willman, J. (1999a). 'Unilever to focus on core "power brands"'. *Financial Times*, 22 September: 25; Willman, J. (1999b). 'Unilever thinks the unthinkable to accelerate its growth'. *Financial Times*, 24 September: 27; Willman, J. (1999c). 'Unilever takes Radion off the shelves'. *Financial Times*, 11 December: 15.
5   Diversification was conceptualized in this way by Igor Ansoff (1965), one of the pioneers of strategic management.
6   Kekre and Srinivasan (1990) and Bayus and Putsis (1999) show that organizations generally profit from having broader product lines. Farjoun and Starbuck (2007) look at the risks and rewards if organizations move *beyond* what their existing resources can accommodate.
7   This was reported by Franko (2004).
8   *Dow Jones Business News* (2004). 'Disney weighs timng of ABC restructuring'. 24 April: B10; *Financial Times* (2004). 'The ABC of making profitable television'. US edition, 12 April; Grover, R. (2004). 'An Eisner exit strategy?' *BusinessWeek Online*, 22 April; Burt, T. (2004). 'The mountains facing Iger', *Financial Times*, Surveys CRE 5 October: 8; *Economist* (2004). 'A new king for the Magic Kingdom'. 19 February; Mcdonald, M. (2007). 'The most powerful woman in television—that you've never seen'. *Observer*, 10 June: 30.
9   First mover advantage is discussed in detail by Lieberman and Montgomery (1988, 1998).
10 Bernheim and Whinston (1990) and Schmalensee (1978) have studied the deterrent effects of diversification. Combs and Ketchen (1999) and Li and Greenwood (2004) have shown that diversification increases opportunities for collaboration between firms.
11 Haveman (1993) and Lounsbury and Leblici (2004) have studied this phenomenon in financial services in the US. Greenwood et al. (2002) observed it in Canadian accountants, and Greve (1998) in the way in which US radio stations adopted and abandoned new broadcasting formats.

12 *Economist* (2005). 'Battery assault'. 22 September: 79.

13 Kogut et al. (2002).

14 The phrase 'stick to the knitting' comes from Peters and Waterman (1982). For a review of fashion in management, see Abrahamson (1996).

15 See Anderson (2007). The original *Wired* article can be found at <http://www.wired.com/wired/archive/12.10/tail_pr.html>, accessed 17 July 2007.

16 Grant (1998: 372).

17 These factors come from Markides and Williamson (1996), who actually call them 'strategic assets'. Since they use the term slightly differently from the way in which we do elsewhere in this book, we have changed it to avoid confusion.

18 See Tanriverdi and Venkatraman (2005).

19 This example is taken from Markides and Williamson (1996).

20 This case is described in Wezel and van Witteloostuijn (2006).

21 St John and Harrison (1999) have shown, for example, that sharing similar manufacturing processes does not by itself lead to synergies between businesses.

22 See Hill and Hoskisson (1987) and Markides and Williamson (1996).

23 This definition is adapted from that given by March (1991), who brought the ideas of exploration and exploitation into the mainstream.

24 The term was coined by Cohen and Levinthal (1990). See Zahra and George (2002) for a review, and Sidhu et al. (2007) for an alternative conception.

25 These facts come from 'The Henry Ford' <http://www.hfmgv.org/exhibits/showroom/1908/specs.html>, accessed on 17 July 2007. Cost advantages from experience effects were for many years believed, as the result of influential work by the Boston Consulting Group, to be a crucial element of a winning strategy; see Amit (1986), Day and Montgomery (1986), and Henderson (1984). This idea has fallen from favour.

26 See Sorenson et al. (2006).

27 March (1991) and March and Levinthal (1993) emphasized the incompatibility between the two philosophies. Writers such as Auh and Menguc (2005) believe that balance is possible. See Gupta et al. (2006) for a summary of the debate, along with the other articles in the same special issue of the *Academy of Management Journal*.

28 For a very thorough definition and discussion of the concept of economies of scale, see McGee (2005).

29 The main UK supermarkets are reportedly able to sell goods more cheaply than small retailers can buy them from their wholesalers. See Davey, J. (2007). 'Small shops rap watchdog'. *Sunday Times*, Business section, 6 May: 2.

30 See Nightingale (2000) for an account of this.

31 See Williamson (1975).

32 Goold and Campbell (1998).

33 Besanko et al. (1996).

34 The key readings are Prahalad and Hamel (1990), one of the most requested articles of all time, and Hamel and Prahalad (1994).

35 Kahn, J. (1999). 'Gillette loses face'. *Fortune*, 140/9: 147–52.

36 The term 'white space opportunities' comes from Hamel and Prahalad (1994). Although not strictly speaking an efficiency issue, we include it here along with the other types of synergy identified by Goold and Campbell.

37 These facts are extracted from Dussauge, P. (2001). *Nouvelles Frontières in 2000*. HEC, Paris.

38 For reviews of the research in this area see Hoskisson and Hitt (1990) and Montgomery (1994).

39 Martin and Sayrak (2003) give a good review.

40 Gunther, M. (2006). 'Viacom unbound'. *Fortune*, Europe Edition, 153/7: 73.

41 Prospectors, defenders, and analysers were identified by Miles and Snow (1978)—and when academics use the term generic strategies, it is this categorization that they tend to refer to. Jennings et al. (2003) confirmed that there were no significant differences in the way the three types of organization performed.

42 Although the concept received a lot of attention during the 1970s and 1980s, we have been unable to find even one empirical study of its validity.

43 The empirical findings in this paragraph come from Hambrick and MacMillan (1982) and MacMillan et al. (1982).

44 See Armstrong and Brodie (1994); Capon et al. (1987); and Slater and Zwirlein (1992).

45 Nathan (1999): 175 and 183.

46 The quotation is from Lashinsky, A. (2005). 'Saving face at Sony'. *Fortune*: 49. See also Nakamoto, M. (2005). 'Sony battles to make headway in networked world'. FT.com, 26 January; Woods, G. (2006). 'Sony cracks open new book with Reader'. *The Toronto Star*, 20 February: C05.

47 Nakamoto (2005) op. cit.

48 Sony Annual Report 2005.

49 Lashinsky, A. (2003). 'Meg and the machine'. *Fortune*, Europe Edition, 8 September 8: 48–54; *Dow Jones News Service* (2002). 'Dynamic buys U.S. fine art auctioneers Butterfields from eBay'. 1 August; Kopytoff, V. (2002). 'EBay CEO applauded for cutting Butterfields'. *San Francisco Chronicle*, 2 August: B.3.

50 Lashinsky (2003) op. cit.

51 Richtel, M. (2002). 'EBay to buy PayPal, a rival in online payments'. *New York Times*, 9 July: 1; Fuscaldo, D. (2002). 'EBay acquisition of PayPal seen as strategic in long term'. *Dow Jones News Service*, 8 July; Financial Disclosure Wire (2002). 'eBay to Acquire PayPal Conference Call—Final'. 8 July.

52 All facts in this paragraph from eBay presentation to CSFB Global Services conference, 15 March 2005. Downloaded from <http:// investor.ebay.com> on 16 October 2005.

53 Ibid.

54 *Economist* (2005a). 'Meg and the power of many'. June 11: 71–4; *Wall Street Journal* (2005). 'EBay Inc.: sites offering classified ads launched in cities outside U.S.' 9 March. Lashinsky, A. (2005). 'Burning sensation'. *Fortune*, 12 December: 55.

55 *Economist* (2004). 'The quiet iconoclast'. 1 July.

56 Roth, D. (2004). 'Catch us if you can'. *Fortune*, 9 February: 64; Salkever, A. (2004). 'Skype gives telcos a wake-up call'. *BusinessWeek Online*, 11 August; *Economist* (2005b). 'The meaning of free speech'. 17 September; Evans, M. (2005). 'Skype founder's Kazaa connection keeps him out of the U.S.'. *Financial Post*, 27 September: FP9.

57 Klapper, J. (2005). 'How to make a million connections'. *Financial Times*, 8 July: 12; Roth (2004) op. cit.

58 Nutall, C. (2004). 'Skype secures $18.8m funding'. FT.com, 14 March.

59 Roth (2004) op. cit.

60 Hibbard, J., Reinhardt, A., and Lowry, T. (2005). 'Skype: how a startup harnessed the hoopla'. *BusinessWeek*, 26 September: 35. Economist (2005b). 'The meaning of free speech'. 17 September.

61 *BusinessWeek Online* (2005). 'Skype's "Aha!"' cxpcrience'. 19 September; *Economist* (2005c). 'How the internet killed the phone business'. 17 September; Hibbard et al. (2005) op. cit.

62 Levy, S. (2005). 'eBay's bet: the Skype's the limit'. *Newsweek*, 3 October: 15; <eBaySkype2005Sep14-NewYorkLunch.pdf> downloaded from investor.ebay.com on 16 October 2005.

63 Hibbard et al. (2005) op. cit.; Wray, R. (2005). 'Dotcom boom returns as eBay spends $4bn on loss-maker'. *Guardian*, 13 September: 22; <eBaySkype2005Sep14-NewYorkLunch.pdf> op. cit.; Waters, R. and Politi, J. (2005). 'EBay to pay $4.1 billion for Skype'. FT.com: 12 September.

64 <eBaySkype2005Sep14-NewYorkLunch.pdf> op. cit.

65 Waters, R. (2005). 'Google to move beyond search business'. FT.com. 24 August.

66 Naughton, J. (2005). 'Dixons' tipping point—or the end of telephony as we know it'. *The Observer*, 2 October: 8.

67 Waters and Politi (2005), op. cit.; *Economist* (2005c) op. cit.; Wray (2005) op. cit.

68 <eBaySkype2005Sep14-NewYorkLunch.pdf> op. cit.

69 Wray (2005) op. cit.

70 Extremetech.com (2005). 'Gripes from Skype users after eBay buy-out'. Reprinted by Reuters, 13 September.

71 <eBaySkype2005Sep14-NewYorkLunch.pdf> op. cit.; *Economist* (2005b) op. cit.

72 Henshall, S. (2005). 'Skype plus eBay equals conversational markets'. *Financial Times*, 21 September: 2.

CHAPTER SIX

Distinctiveness (3)
The Value Chain

LEARNING OUTCOMES

After reading this chapter you should be able to:

→ Critically evaluate an organization's degree of vertical integration, the scale, the scope and the location of its different activities, the resources deployed within these activities and the linkages between them, and show how these may lead to competitive advantage

→ Differentiate between manufacturing, professional service, and network types of organizations

→ Classify value chain activities for the different types of organization and explain how they contribute to its cost or differentiation advantage.

INTRODUCTION

This is the third chapter in which we examine the factors that contribute to organizational distinctiveness. Here we look at how a business's activities and resources may be configured to serve its target market segments through the choice of where and how it makes its products, how it connects with its suppliers in order to obtain the inputs it needs, and how it connects with its customers and end-users. The value chain[1] is a way of assessing how and where an organization adds value to the inputs that make up its products, and how it achieves cost and/or differentiation advantage in its industry. This involves several elements of strategy:

- choosing the right resources to fulfil the needs of a particular customer group;
- combining them, where appropriate, with resources brought in from other organizations—suppliers, distributors and customers;
- deciding what scale and location of operations will allow the organization to make the most profitable use of all of these resources;
- finding ways of linking different types of activities and resources to serve the customer better and/or at lower cost.

In the value chain, the emphasis is mainly on what gives individual businesses a distinctive position in their chosen market places, although as we shall see in Chapters 7, 8 and 9, there are close links between an organization's value chain and the way it is able to build and develop a *sustainable* strategic position.

6.1 **Value chain analysis**

The basic idea of the value chain is quite simple, and is based on the chain of events that every product must go through from its inception to its eventual sale (this includes services, although there are some differences between these and tangible products that we shall return to later). First of all, someone has to invent it, and develop the processes that will allow it to be produced. Then the raw materials and parts need to be brought together to make it, after which it must be distributed to customers and eventually to the end users. At some point, customers must be persuaded to buy the product. Finally, once it is delivered, the firm needs to take care of any problems that arise, and sometimes offer spare parts and maintenance or other forms of after-sales' service.

Value chain analysis is a way of seeing where in this chain or network of activities an organization is successfully adding value. It lets us pinpoint the particular capabilities and resources that are important to an organization and show precisely where and how they are being applied.

A number of frameworks have been developed to help map firms' activities and compare them between different organizations. Most of these frameworks, following the lead given by Michael Porter in his 1985 book, *Competitive Advantage*, set up checklists of the different activities that occur in a firm, under two broad headings: primary and support activities.

6.1.1 **Primary and support activities**

Primary activities

Primary activities are those *directly* involved with delivering products or services to a user. The primary activities in a value chain include manufacturing operations, sales and marketing, and after-sales service for a manufactured product like a car; journalism and advertising sales

Table 6.1 Strategic decisions in the value chain

Deployment of resources	Which assets and capabilities an organization chooses to use in connection with specific activities
Vertical integration	Whether the organization decides to carry out an activity itself, or to outsource it to a specialist supplier or a franchisee
Scale of operations	Whether an organization tries to gain economies of scale, or other types of advantage, from the scale of its operations in a particular activity
Scope of operations	Whether an organization tries to share one or more activities across different products and markets
Location of operations	In which country or region an organization chooses to locate particular activities
Linkages	Whether the organization tries to gain advantage by linking its activities together in a new and different way

for a magazine; till service and cheque handling for a bank. Different types of organizations' value chains have different types of primary activity. We will discuss these differences later in Section 6.2.

Support activities

Support activities contribute indirectly to the adding of value, through supporting one or more of the primary activities. Support activities include purchasing, process development, human resource management, planning, and financial control.

Activities in a value chain are not the same as the functions in an organization structure, even if they may, confusingly, sometimes have the same names. The sales and marketing activity, for example, includes all marketing that goes on anywhere in the organization—whether it be sales people on their rounds, marketing executives developing promotional campaigns, senior managers lunching with prospective clients, or the finance department helping to calculate price levels.

Table 6.1 lists the types of strategic decision that determine how well each primary and support activity adds value. We now look at each of these in more detail.

6.1.2 **Deployment of resources**

➜ We have a detailed discussion, with examples, of assets, capabilities, and other types of firms' resources in Chapter 7.

If an activity utilizes distinctive assets or capabilities then it may enable the organization to be differentiated from its competitors in the levels of quality it provides customers, or the benefits that it incorporates into its products. Capabilities can be deployed in production or in after-sales service. Strong brands and reputations can be deployed to attract good staff, to give differentiation in marketing and sales, or to target a different market.

6.1.3 **Vertical integration and outsourcing**

A key issue in a value chain is how much of the organization's activities should be carried out in-house and how much undertaken by a partner. Vertical integration (sometimes known as 'make or buy') decisions involve important trade-offs between keeping control of important activities and profiting from other firms' specialist resources.

Broadly, there are three ways in which a firm can obtain the products or services that it needs in order to produce and sell its own products or services:[2]

1. It can buy them from third-party suppliers on the open market. This is sometimes known as outsourcing, and can be a short-term or a long-term commitment. A more recent term is insourcing, where a firm is contracted to carry out a role but undertakes it within the organization rather than on its own premises. Some firms make it clear to their suppliers that they will always purchase at the lowest price. Other firms look for longer-term relationships that are close to being a strategic alliance or partnership. These suppliers may be located far away, usually in a foreign country, in which case the terms are offshoring[3] (if in a distant country) or nearshoring (if closer by). For example, American firms locating in Canada or Mexico would be nearshoring; operations in China or India would be offshoring.

2. It can produce them within its hierarchy, so that the people providing the product or service are under direct management control and have (in theory) to do what they are told.

3. It can use other hybrid forms of organization that are intermediate between markets and hierarchies, such as networks, joint ventures, strategic alliances, and franchising arrangements. In these cases, although the supplier is not under the direct control of its clients, there is a continuing relationship between them that is likely to make each more sensitive to the needs of the other. These types of structure allow the partners to, for example, develop specialist component parts jointly, or reach agreements about just-in-time deliveries. They are particularly common in industries that have high needs for innovation and creativity, such as pharmaceuticals, music, and biotechnology, where they can allow the very different types of organizational culture and structure to be kept separate but their outputs combined when necessary.[4]

In manufacturing companies, the issue of which components to make in-house and which to buy in from outside suppliers has always been important. Similarly, the question of whether a firm should sell directly to customers—through a direct salesforce, over the telephone or through the internet—or sell its products through franchisees, distributors, or retailers, has long been an important element of most firms' marketing strategy. Some support functions, like cleaning and catering, are nowadays outsourced almost as a matter of course.

But companies have been known to use third-party suppliers for almost any activity in the value chain, including advertising, product and packaging design, brand development, manufacturing, distribution, sales, and after-sales product maintenance. Crucial support activities, such as the IT function, may also be carried out by external firms, and some organizations have experimented with third-party suppliers in areas like human resource management and accounting.

Organizations may choose to join a network or web of a large number of firms, each of which specializes in a different aspect of the value chain—i.e. the value system or value stream[5]—a technology or geographic region, for example. Each firm is dependent on some or all of the other firms in the network to a greater or lesser extent. A network allows one firm to concentrate on what it does best, whilst allowing others to develop their own areas of expertise. This is known as co-specialization. Such networks are often cemented by cross-shareholdings, or other long-term contractual arrangements. One example of a networked value system is shown in Figure 6.1.

Networks like this enable small firms to appear to clients as if they are large corporations, with access to a wide range of resources. If one firm in the network receives an enquiry for some business that it cannot handle itself, it calls in one of its partners, or passes the enquiry

Outsourcing
The contracting out of part of an organization's operations to a separate company.

Insourcing
When a separate firm carries out part of the organization's operations, but undertakes them in the organization itself, rather than on its own premises.

Offshoring
The outsourcing of value chain activities to companies in another country, distant from the home organization, and usually one that offers lower costs or other benefits.

Nearshoring
The outsourcing of value chain activities to companies located in a foreign country, but one that is closer geographically to the home organization.

→ We discuss the management of strategic alliances in more detail in Chapter 9. We discuss offshoring and other international location decisions in more detail in Chapter 14.

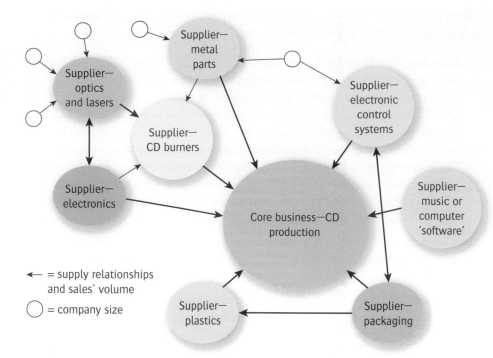

Figure 6.1 A networked value system

on to them. Sometimes a single firm acts as the 'server' at the centre of the network, taking in the work and allocating it to the other partners. In other types of network, firms are part of a confederation of more equal alliance partners—some of whom will have alliances with only one firm in the network; others with several. Each partner may specialize in a certain part of the value chain (product development, marketing), have a particular expertise (website maintenance, computer network installation), or specialize in particular market segments (retailers or local governments).[6]

But it is not just small firms that feel the need to build such networks. For complex or technologically sophisticated products, it is very unlikely that one firm can contain all the necessary resources in-house. Figure 6.2 shows some of the network of alliances involving Merck, a major pharmaceutical company. The development and distribution of drugs requires a wide range of knowledge and competences, not all of which Merck has or wishes to have itself.

Companies which, like Merck and H&M, sit at the centre of networks of suppliers specifying the outputs and determining which supplier should do what, are called orchestrators or servers. There are even companies, like Hong Kong's Li & Fung, whose only role is as orchestrators: they specialize in finding and managing suppliers for whatever product their client may choose to offer, but have no product brands of their own.

Whatever the form of outsourcing network an organization may consider joining, it has to arrive at a trade-off between five factors:

1. Production and set-up costs;
2. Transaction costs;
3. Flexibility and incentive;
4. Quality;
5. Control and the risk of loss of key resources.

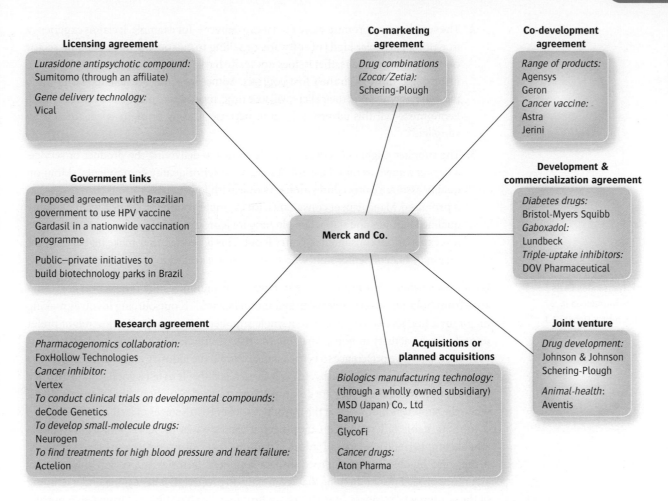

Figure 6.2 Merck's network of strategic alliances in 2006. In 2005 the firm signed 44 agreements for external alliances (according to its 2005 Annual Report). Source: numerous industry reports

Production and set-up costs

By using an outside supplier, an organization can take advantage of that firm's economies of scale and its learning. This is particularly true when the potential suppliers have core capabilities that a firm would have difficulty in matching. The value of these economies or competences sometimes outweigh any margin that the supplier charges for its services. This means that sourcing from an experienced third-party supplier may be cheaper than in-house production.[7]

Transaction costs

The downside of buying goods and services on the open market is that there is a danger that the supplier may try to exploit the situation for extra profit. There are three main ways in which this may happen:[8]

1. A supplier may increase the amount it charges for its services, because it believes that the client has become dependent upon it, a practice sometimes known as hold-up. It may believe that the client has invested so much in the relationship, for example by changing its information systems or changing its factory layout to make space for the supplier's personnel, that it cannot afford to pull out. Or it may have control of an important resource, such as a firm's customer database.

2. The supplier may promise more than it can deliver—for example, it claims experience in writing particular kinds of software, or selling to customers in the banking sector or in emerging markets, that it does not really have. There are many stories of young firms doing this to win their first contract. Sometimes they are able to learn on the job, but if they cannot, their client will lose time, money, and maybe customers as well. Economists call this adverse selection, because it leads firms to select the wrong supplier.[9]

3. The supplier might cut corners when it comes to delivering the product or service, a danger known as moral hazard. It may use inferior quality components, skimp on quality assurance procedures, or use people with lower qualifications than those that it promised. Management consultants, for example, routinely parade a team of highly qualified partners and staff when pitching for a project, but try as far as possible to use less experienced consultants to carry it out. This is because they make higher margins on junior than on senior staff, who in any case are needed to sell the next project.

→ Transaction costs were introduced in Theoretical Debate 1.1 and in Section 1.3.3.

Economists believe that firms behave in a way that minimizes the transaction costs that arise from hold-up, adverse selection, and moral hazard.[10] If outsourcing involves making major investments that commits it to a single supplier, then an organization might prefer to perform the activity in-house, to avoid the risk of suppliers exploiting its vulnerability. Firms may also give preference to vertical integration if the industry is complex and reliable information is difficult to come by. In such cases it is difficult to tell a good supplier from a bad one, or to work out if they are doing as they promised. Situations like these may occur when the supplier's industry is at the introductory or growth stages of its life-cycle.

In more stable or less complex industries, it can be easier for an organization to find a reliable supplier, and to write and enforce a contract that will protect it from being exploited. It may also be able, for example, to inspect suppliers' factories and review their quality assurance procedures, something that it can only do properly if it has a good understanding of those suppliers' business. In such cases, a firm may be able to benefit from using outside suppliers.

Some people believe that transaction cost economics places too much emphasis on the negative aspects of human behaviour,[11] and argue that it is possible to build relationships of trust between firms and their suppliers. These relationships reduce the likelihood of exploitation, so that organizations can take advantage of savings on production costs with less fear of incurring high transaction costs.

Flexibility and incentives

Not all suppliers are crooks, and the profit motive does not necessarily make them try to exploit their clients in the ways described in the previous section. It also gives them an incentive to do things that the customer probably welcomes, such as keeping down production and delivery costs and inventory levels low. Third-party suppliers may well feel these incentives more keenly than people within the firm's hierarchy. This is one of the reasons why H&M's outsourcing of its manufacturing to independent suppliers is so effective (Real-life Application 6.1).

H&M illustrates one of the other benefits of outsourcing—flexibility. If demand turns up or down, a firm can increase or decrease the number of suppliers or the quantity of products it buys from them, without having to worry about new investment or redundancy costs. The supplier is in effect taking away some of the client's risk. However, this sort of policy has its downsides: the supplier may be heavily dependent on orders from the buying firm, and may think about developing alternative customers if it is regularly used as a convenient means of protecting the firm's own profits without regards for its own.

The control of key resources

There are other grounds, apart from quality, why a firm may decide that an activity is too strategically important to allow a supplier to take it over. It may fear that the supplier may exploit control of an important resource, or it may want its knowledge of the activity to remain proprietary. For example, H&M, although it outsources much of the fabrication of its clothes, keeps most of the design and product development activities in-house (see Real-life Application 6.1).

Real-life Application 6.1 The control of key resources in H&M[12]

H&M outsources all of its clothes manufacturing, a structure that is not unusual within the fashion retailing industry. The key drivers shaping competitiveness in this industry are the speed and flexibility of the supply chain. According to Mintel,[13] this means that life is becoming increasingly difficult for retailers with traditional supply chains. And yet, two of H&M's major, and highly successful, competitors, Zara/Inditex and Mango, have in-house production facilities. Many commentators have claimed that Zara/Inditex's vertically integrated structure has been a major source of competitive advantage through the ability it confers to respond quickly to trends.

H&M in contrast, has chosen to work with a network of 750 or so carefully selected and managed independent suppliers. The trade-off choice that H&M has made is exchanging speed and control for the ability to reduce costs through switching suppliers, by purchasing large volumes directly from their suppliers without middlemen, and manufacturing clothes in the cheapest location at any given time.

Under this structure, H&M's buyers act like product/brand managers working with both fashion designers and suppliers and specifying the requirements of both. This activity is located in the firm's head office in Stockholm, along with the main design departments which employ up to 100 designers. On top of this, H&M has 13 country offices that are responsible for the various functions in each of its major retail locations. It also has 21 production offices worldwide (ten in Europe, ten in Asia, and ➔

H&M keeps most of its design and product development activities in-house. *H&M AB*

➜ one in Africa). The role of these offices is to assist the buyers in finding the right markets and the right suppliers, planning and following up on-site production, and inspecting working conditions and quality. This allows them to oversee the quality of their products early on in the production chain and shorten lead times. New goods are delivered to the stores daily, and a particularly popular item can be sourced and supplied to all the stores within weeks.

In June 2004, H&M restructured its buying department into two different functions: a buying division (focusing on customers, fashion, and product range) and a production division. This was part of a drive to reduce lead times; time from production to stores in 2004 was about 20 per cent less than in 2001.

According to Larsson et al. (2003), H&M, along with other Swedish companies like IKEA, Ericsson, and Skandia, has been able to develop a peculiarly 'Swedish cocktail', which combines the branding and control advantages of internal growth with the resource-saving and risk-minimizing advantages of alliances with suppliers, and which companies from other countries find hard to replicate.

Quality

Considerations of quality may influence a firm either away from or towards outsourcing activities. A dedicated supplier may have capabilities superior to those a firm could develop on its own. In the motor industry, firms such as Bosch have better innovative capabilities for specialist products like brakes and fuel injection systems than even the largest car-maker.

However, particularly in a young industry, a firm may be unable to locate a supplier or distributor with the right expertise. It may also decide that an activity is so important to its overall cost or differentiation advantage that it has to control the quality directly, and if necessary learn how to do it well. British Airways during the 1980s believed that the process of getting to and from a plane, quickly and comfortably, was important in shaping passengers' attitudes to an airline. To keep control of the quality of this activity, it ran the bus service that ferried passengers around its Heathrow airport hub, making it, for a time, the UK's second largest bus operator.

 Theoretical Debate 6.1 Outsourcing: good or bad?

There has been considerable debate on whether outsourcing is a good or bad thing. Many writers (for example Bettis et al., 1992; Quinn and Hilmer, 1995; Chesborough and Teece, 1996; Mazur, 1999) have argued that it is a fundamental mistake for firms to outsource key activities:

- Outsourcing may give away important commercial information to suppliers who may then extend the scope of their own activities and become competitors (Quinn and Hilmer, 1995; Steensma and Corley, 2000).

- It may erode their ability to develop distinctive capabilities. In the consumer electronics industry, US companies that outsourced much of their manufacturing found that their competences in research and development withered as well as their ability to commercialize new products (Rasheed and Gilley, 2005).

- Although outsourcing may be undertaken because it appears, for reasons discussed in Section 6.1.3, to be cheaper, firms often find that the costs of managing the relationship are higher than expected. High transaction costs, such as travel to partners located across the globe, may be incurred to protect against opportunistic behaviour and the risk of hold-up. Currency translations between international partners can cancel out cost savings. And as Rasheed and Gilley (2005) say, by the time these problems are discovered it may be too late to bring the outsourced activities back in-house, because the 'required physical, financial, and human assets are no longer there'.

On the other hand there may be very good reasons to outsource some activities, even those that are critical to the firm's success.

- Firms may be able to focus on developing stronger competences in core areas, because they are not being distracted by trying to manage something that they are not particularly good at—even if it is critical to the firm's success.

- There are benefits to tapping into suppliers' own distinctive capabilities (Kiely, 1997; Quinn, 1999). As well as having greater expertise and assuming some of the risk involved ➜

→ in an activity, an outside contractor may offer better coordination of an activity across a large organization. This is especially true of unglamorous but important activities like tax reporting or energy management, which may not otherwise get a lot of senior management attention.

- Although transaction costs may be high, there are almost certainly some cost savings to be had from outsourcing an activity to a firm that is able to pool that activity with other firms, thereby developing economies of scale, scope, and learning. Airlines are increasingly outsourcing key activities such as aircraft maintenance to outside contractors. Even though it might be imagined that this is a critically important activity underpinning the reputation and credibility of an airline, it is different from their other main activities of providing a high standard of travel service.

Consultants such as the Boston Consulting Group (BCG) now advocate the outsourcing of any activity in which the organization does not have world-class capabilities. They argue that it is no longer possible for a firm to survive, as it once could, with a value chain that is excellent in a few areas but merely adequate in others. Such a firm is in danger of being out-manoeuvred by a rival that focuses on only a few strategically important activities where it can develop distinctive capabilities. If this rival picks the right outside suppliers for its other activities, it will have a value chain that will outperform any other.

Baden-Fuller et al. (2000) propose that the outsourcing of what seems to be core activities makes sense when the firm is threatened under four circumstances:

1. Catch-up; where, in a slow moving environment, the firm has fallen behind its competitors
2. Changing value chains; where the firm must respond to changing customer needs
3. Technology shifts; when the firm's core is outdated because of new technology
4. In emerging markets; where new markets are available to the firm because of rapid changes in technology and customer demand.

Virtual value chains

The logical outcome of an outsourcing strategy is a virtual value chain,[14] where almost all linkages are electronic. Value chains that might once have been contained within a single organization are increasingly being split up across networks of specialist suppliers connected by EDI systems—potentially located across the globe. A linked effect of this is that purchasing is increasingly taking place through websites that also may be located anywhere in the world.

Such virtual ways of organizing have a number of profound effects on the way that customers behave, and the workplace itself, including changes to:[15]

- when we work;
- where we work;
- work group membership;
- the ways that projects/tasks are carried out;
- the cultural backgrounds of personnel;
- organizational affiliations and loyalties.

A virtual value chain is a hyperarchy,[16] where structures are constantly responding to changes in customer demands and competitor behaviour. This requires an ability to reconfigure contacts and projects on a much more short-term basis than has hitherto been required—something that has been given the wonderfully graphic name of Velcro hooking.[17]

Virtual value chains therefore require different competences and capabilities from the 'traditional' hierarchy, not least of which is the ability to develop and use websites to transact business. Travel agencies, retailing, and other services such as banks are good examples of industries whose value chains are changing fast. Disintermediation—the cutting out of the middleman—has reduced the need for intermediate agents (or at least has forced them to

→ We discuss hierarchies, projects, and other types of organization structure in more detail in Sections 8.1 and 9.1.

change their roles), as customers are searching on-line for the services and information they need.

Where once upon a time a customer would visit a store to select goods, now they are using the internet to find the best deals and compare availability. For example, retailers now not only have to deal with providing a store presence, increasingly they are having to provide a seamless interaction between store, website, and in the case of many fashion retailers, a book catalogue as well—something known as multi-channel retailing. Customers are increasingly demanding the ability to view goods in store, buy on-line, have the goods delivered to their home, and then return them to the store if they are not satisfied. For most companies this requires a complete change of culture, let alone the implementation of IT systems that are powerful and flexible enough to cope with such a complex set of interactions.[18]

Real-life Application 6.2 Virtual value chains

Cisco systems, the manufacturer of internet hardware, and at one point in 2000 the largest company (by market capitalization) in the world, outsources manufacturing of almost all of its core industrial products. It exercises what it describes as 'strong centralized control' over its partners, but what matters for Cisco is having an 'agile, adaptable and speedy supply chain'.[19] Although Cisco's manufacturing director does not think that this model would necessarily translate to its consumer products, and indeed it has grown in other parts of the company through acquisition, many commentators put down Cisco's stunning growth to this policy.

Boeing began development of the 787 aircraft by seeking the advice of its suppliers, who are located at over 130 sites worldwide. They are linked to Boeing's development teams through regular face-to-face meetings, known as 'partner councils'.[20] Urgent items are dealt with using video conferencing. The sharing of information between Boeing and its suppliers allows everyone in the supply chain to take a longer-term view of how the market for the new aircraft will develop, and allows suppliers to prepare for future demand.

Strategic alliances

A partnership between two or more firms is commonly known as a strategic alliance. Sometimes companies' managers will reach a friendly agreement as to, say, which of them will set up retail outlets in a particular geographical area. Such informal arrangements are common in areas where there are long-standing friendships and relationships between firms, such as in the Italian clothes manufacturing industry or the Japanese system of Keiretsu. However, alliances, including almost all outsourcing agreements, normally involve a legal contract which defines the areas of cooperation:

- Licensing is the allocation of specific rights by one 'parent' firm to a partner. The partner may be given local manufacturing rights for a patented product, or licensed to market locally produced items under the parent firm's brand name. In exchange, the parent company receives a royalty payment for each item made or sold. This arrangement is common in media-based industries, where licences are issued for the manufacture of toys based on the characters in a TV programme. In the music industry it is common for the owner of a music copyright to license another firm to broadcast or perform it, or incorporate it on a compilation CD. Licensing means that the parent firm does not have to bear the development costs involved in setting up in a foreign market.

- Franchising involves the sharing of profits and ownership between the parent and a franchisee, who agrees to sell the company's products in a defined format. Typically, franchises, for example shops, are owned by independent firms but their owners agree a certain layout and colour scheme for the premises, and undertake to sell only goods and services specified by the franchisor. Franchising is particularly common in service industries, including fast-food restaurants, hotels, print-shops, and household repairs. Franchisees may be small businesses, but it is also quite common for them to be large companies that manage several outlets within the same franchise. Pizza Hut's and TGI Friday's UK franchisee, for example, is Whitbread PLC, a major leisure firm and restaurateur in its own right.

- Distribution rights: agents with local geographical knowledge will be given rights to sell a company's products in return for a commission. This type of arrangement is common in international businesses. Agents, unlike franchisees, are rarely bound by an exclusivity deal and often sell many firms' products.

- Development agreements: a firm will enter into a memorandum of understanding with another firm. This sets out what each partner will do to develop a new area of business—without the alliance being specific about precise outcomes, or it being set up as an entirely separate joint venture.

- Manufacturing agreements are contracts, stipulating that a particular element of a completed product will be provided by a specific partner organization. They are common in many industries. Contracts typically specify time-scales for delivery, and expected standards of cost and quality.

Contractual arrangements may be combined with equity exchanges, which involve the taking of a share stake in one company by another, and often by both partner companies in each other. They are frequently used as a way of indicating long-term commitment to the relationship: the higher the proportion of shares that are cross-owned, the greater the involvement. Sony Music Japan, along with two other Japanese record companies, Nippon Crown and Toshiba-EMI, bought 5.5 per cent stakes in a leading Japanese independent music label, Avex DD, in order to develop the Japanese music market. Many of the airlines in the worldwide alliances of airlines, such as BA's oneworld, SkyTeam, or the Star Alliance have taken equity stakes in their partners.[21]

Another way of formalizing an alliance is as a joint venture, where two or more firms agree to set up a third, legally separate, company which is then jointly owned by the partners. They are usually set up with a specific purpose in mind, for example the joint development of a product or the introduction of a product into a new international market. Sony came into the music business in 1968 when it entered into a joint venture with CBS Records, a relationship that was cemented in 1988 when it purchased CBS for $2 billion.[22] It now has a number of joint ventures with companies across the world, for example cable operators in Asia, Latin America, and India. In 2004, it set up a joint venture, Sony-BMG, with one of its major music industry competitors, Bertelsmann, and another with Samsung to supply it with LCD panels. It has many others. One of the best known is probably Sony Ericsson Mobile Communications AB, established in October 2001 as a fifty-fifty joint venture between Sony and Ericsson to make mobile phones.[23]

There are many examples of this type of alliance in manufacturing, especially for complex new products. Some industry experts suggest that Boeing, nor any other aircraft manufacturer, is likely to ever launch a major aircraft project alone again.[24] Boeing's major competitor, Airbus Industrie, is itself a joint venture, although one of an unusual nature (see Real-life Application 6.3).

Real-life Application 6.3 Airbus Industrie[25]

Airbus began life in 1970 as a partnership between France's Aerospatiale and Deutsche Airbus, a group of German aircraft manufacturing firms. The companies had come together to build the A300, the first twin-engine wide-bodied airliner. Soon afterwards, Spain's CASA joined the consortium, and in 1974 the Airbus Industrie GIE (Groupe d'Intérêt Economique, an EU legal structure which makes no profits or losses in its own right, though they accrue to their ultimate owners) was formed and set up its headquarters in Toulouse. In 1979, British Aerospace joined Airbus Industrie.

Each of the four partners, Airbus France, Airbus Deutschland, Airbus UK, and Airbus España, operated as national companies with special responsibilities for producing parts of the aircraft, which were then transported to Toulouse for final assembly. The GIE provided a single face for sales, marketing, and customer support. In 2001, Airbus became a single integrated company, incorporated under French law as a simplified joint stock company or SAS (Société par Actions Simplifiée). The European Aeronautic Defence and Space Company (EADS), a merger of the French, German and Spanish interests, acquired 80 per cent of the shares in the new company, and BAe Systems (formerly British Aerospace), 20 per cent.

Although it was not without its problems, for many years Airbus proved a model for how effective inter-country collaboration could be. Airbus out-competed its main competitor Boeing on sales' growth, and also, arguably, on manufacturing efficiency and technological innovation.[26] In 2005, it became the world's largest commercial aircraft manufacturer. However, in 2006 evidence emerged of some difficulties in the partnership. We return to these in What Can Go Wrong 6.1.

The benefits of alliances

In addition to the benefits of outsourcing that we discussed above, alliances can offer a firm a number of benefits:

- Learning from organizations with complementary competences. Some of the most important alliances span different industries, bringing together different types of knowledge in order to develop new products which no partner firm could have achieved on its own. For example, Siemens, IBM, and Toshiba set up a joint venture to build on IBM's existing 64-mbit DRAM design and semiconductor technologies. According to an IBM manager, his company had 'plenty of depth in research and development, in physics, integrated circuits, materials science, reliability and engineering'. But IBM would rely on 'Toshiba for designs for manufacturability and Siemens for process expertise'.[27]

- Being able to penetrate countries that restrict access to part or all of their economy —for example, giving their national airline control over key routes. The oneworld alliance between, for instance, BA, American Airlines, and their other partners allows each firm access to some, if not all, of the partners' protected positions, thereby making life more difficult for their joint competitors. The firms in such protected markets also benefit from bringing in knowledge and contacts from elsewhere, if not immediately, then perhaps at some point in the future.

- Accessing a local partner who knows the accepted ways of doing business, has the necessary contacts, or understands the particular requirements of local customers in newly opened markets about which there is little external knowledge.

- Access to organizations with cultures and architectures that promote creativity and innovation.[28] Such cultures may be squashed within a large hierarchical organization.

Management challenges

The management of external linkages with alliance partners can pose challenges. Trust has to be maintained between the organizations, which may be difficult to do at times when these same firms are potentially in competition with one another for scarce resources, and may even be selling products which are substitutes for their collaborators'. There is the risk of hold-up and possible logistical problems.

If physical inputs are being supplied, then partners have to be close enough to each other for essential supplies to be delivered to the right place at the right time, and quality has to be consistently high for the buyer to be able to use the suppliers without constantly checking for faults. Communication between the firms has to be very good. This may be through personal contact, or more often through the use of good IT systems.

→ We discuss the management of complex organizational structures, including networks, in Chapter 10.

Hold-up
One partner's potential to blackmail the other, e.g. by raising prices or demanding other concessions. This is more likely to happen when the victim is irrevocably committed to the project.

6.1.4 Scale of operations

Organizations face important trade-offs in choosing whether to maximize the scale of an activity, in order to try to get a cost advantage or opt for a smaller, but more expensive, scale of operation. In the latter case it would hope to gain a differentiation advantage by offering a high level of service to a limited set of users. Organizations can operate at different scales at different stages in their value chain, and for different market segments. IKEA, the Swedish furniture retailer, centralizes its product design and procurement for the entire globe in its home country. It serves most markets from a few, very large out-of-town stores, strategically placed on major roads so as to be accessible to a large population. Its UK sister company, Habitat,[29] serves a more affluent market segment. It has a larger network of smaller stores located more centrally in towns and cities.

To get the maximum benefit from a large-scale operation, it must be intensively utilized. Manufacturing firms will try to use their factories and expensive equipment for two or three shifts every day, stopping only for retooling and maintenance. Organizations therefore must decide between a small operation, where capacity may more easily be fully utilized, or a larger one which may not be. Lower capacity may offer higher profits and lower risk in the short term, but this must be balanced against the danger that the company will be unable to respond quickly if the market starts to grow strongly.

→ Economies of scale and scope were defined in Section 5.2.3. We also discussed scope and scale in relation to the organization's competitive stance and its choice of international markets and location in Chapter 4.

6.1.5 Scope of operations

A firm may opt for broad or narrow scope within an activity. An activity can serve a distinct market segment and or set of products and value chain. Sony has specialized marketing and distribution channels for different classes of electronics products—mature and strategic—each managed in a slightly different way to target different customers. It hopes that, by tailoring the value chain precisely to the needs of the target market, it will satisfy customers better and avoid wasting resources where they are not needed or useful.

Alternatively, a firm can try to share activities across compatible products and markets. Amazon and eBay, for example, both leverage a single IT infrastructure across a wide variety of products.

6.1.6 Location decisions

By choosing the right country or region to locate a particular part of the value chain, a company can get access to local expertise or to low-cost resources. We review these issues in detail in Chapter 14, where we discuss the internationalization of organizations' value chains.

6.1.7 **Linkages**

One of the most subtle and difficult parts of value chain analysis is the identification of how linkages between different activities can generate value. There are several ways that this can happen:[30]

- One activity can partially substitute for another. For example, an investment in systems to screen potential clients may improve sales productivity (because it reduces the amount of time salespeople waste with individuals who are unlikely to buy the service) and reduce debt collection costs—although it may also screen out some marginal leads that a good salesperson might have converted into orders. Increasing the amount of training in quality procedures offered to factory workers can lead to a reduction in the amount of finished goods inspection and after-sales service that is needed.

- One activity can improve the performance of another. For a train or bus operator, more frequent maintenance keeps vehicles in better order and improves the reliability of operations.

- One activity can generate information that can be used by another. A firm with its own service operation can keep track of customers' problems and suggestions, and feed them back to the product development activity. A sales system can take details of customer orders that can be used for factory scheduling.

Firms can alter their activities to fit in with the value chains of suppliers, distributors, retailers, and end-users. These vertical linkages between different organizations' value chains generate benefits on both sides that can be shared. By investing in new vehicles with improved temperature controls, a food distribution firm can reduce the amount of wastage suffered by its customers, for example. Similarly, horizontal linkages with competitors/collaborators can lead to synergistic benefits for both firms in technology or new product development.

An organization's capability in managing internal and external linkages better than its competitors can be an important part of its competitive advantage. Such a capability depends on the firm's architecture, which we discuss in Chapter 8.

6.1.8 **Decisions and trade-offs in the value chain**

The previous sections have shown that an organization faces a variety of trade-offs when configuring each activity in the value chain. These are summarized in Table 6.2.

6.2 **Types of value chain**

Value chain analysis uses as a framework a set of 'generic' value chains which vary across different types of organization, and which are based on the activities that are emphasized within the different organizational settings. In this section, we look at generic value chains that have been developed for three different types of organization.[31]

- Manufacturing-style organizations—these are the kinds of organization where a set of inputs is translated into a set of outputs using a classic path, from product development through to after-sales service, that we sketched in the introduction to Section 6.1.

- Service-manufacturers—organizations like fast-food providers and hotels, which produce a standardized product that happens to have a strong service component to it—also use a manufacturing-style value chain. One way to judge whether an organization falls into this category is to look at the way it measures its outputs and judges

By investing in new vehicles with improved temperature controls, food distribution firms can reduce the amount of wastage for customers.
Spar

Table 6.2 Trade-offs in the value chain

Type of decision	Different alternatives and their potential advantages	
Resources deployed	*Proprietary* Potential source of distinctiveness	*Generic* Cheap, quick and easy to acquire and update
Vertical integration	*Make (hierarchy)* High degree of control of resources and quality, no risk of exploitation, potential for developing distinctive capabilities	*Buy (market)* Set-up costs may be lower, flexibility likely to be greater, can profit from suppliers' distinctive capabilities and economies of scale
Scale and scope	*Large scale, broad scope* Economies of scale and scope, leverage resources across many products and groups of users	*Small scale, narrow niche* Achieve specialist excellence in narrow field, avoid wasting resources in places where they are not appropriate
Location	*Everything in one place* Economies of scale, relatively easy to control activities and share information and learning	*Distributed* Tap into local knowledge and expertise, stay responsive to user requirements, cost advantages
Linkages	Enable activities to collaborate to meet customer needs in coherent way Possible source of sustainable advantage	

its success. Service manufacturing firms' outputs, like traditional manufacturers, are measured in volume terms (numbers of hamburgers or hotel room nights produced and sold, just like a computer manufacturer would measure the number of computers sold), and unit costs are an important measure of efficiency.

• Professional services—these organizations exist to solve difficult problems for individual clients, each of which is likely to require a customized service. Examples are consultancies, educational and scientific research institutions, oil exploration firms, and government departments. Professional services add value by solving their clients' problems in a creative and effective manner. They measure themselves more by the size, prestige, and value of the projects they win than the volume of outputs that they produce.

- Networks—these are organizations whose main function is the linking of people together. The bigger they are, the more people they link together and the more attractive they become. Sometimes the linkages are obvious—a telephone operator or on-line auctioneer adds value by being able to link more people together, to talk to or buy things from one another. However, other types of organization also fit into this category. A retail bank like LloydsTSB or Deutsche Bank is a network, not because it exists to bring its customers together, but because the larger the pool of deposits that it has, the more secure it becomes and the better able to make profitable loans. A newspaper is a network partly because many readers like to feel part of an influential 'club', but mainly because a large readership makes it more attractive to advertisers. For some newspapers, this works the other way around—the more small advertisers there are, the more readers are likely to buy the paper. These organizations will measure themselves by the size of their customer or asset base.

By this stage in the book, you should not be surprised to read that it is not always clear into which of these categories an organization falls, and that different parts of an organization may have different types of value chain. Some professional services may have standardized or 'manufactured' elements such as a training manual or programme, although these are not likely to be the most important part of the overall service. A newspaper is a network, but its printing arm has a manufacturing function (and possibly external customers) and will assess its performance like a manufacturer, using measures like 'cost per copy'. A retail bank is a network, but its corporate finance division, which advises commercial clients on how to fund major transactions, is a professional service organization.

6.2.1 **Manufacturing-style organizations**

The generic value chain for a manufacturing-style organization (although a customized version is suitable for most firms) is shown in Figure 6.3.[32] It includes six primary activities:

Figure 6.3 The value chain for manufacturing-style organizations

- Product design and development—this includes pure and applied research in areas like materials science and electronics, as well as product design, development, and testing.

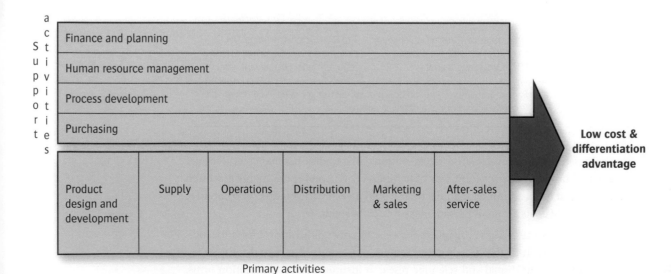

Primary activities

- Supply—the processes that bring inputs into the organization: ordering and delivery procedures, the inspection of components to make sure that they meet quality requirements, and so on.

- Operations—the transformation of inputs into the finished product or service. In a factory it embraces all the functions related to production, including scheduling, production engineering, quality assurance, and maintenance. In a restaurant it includes the cooking and serving of food and the washing of dishes, cutlery and linen. A retailer's operations include the stacking of shelves and serving of customers at the counter or checkout.

- Distribution—the physical transportation of products from the point of production to the point of sale, and then on to the end-user. It also includes the process of managing relationships with distributors, wholesalers or retailers to ensure that they have adequate stocks of the products they require. For some retailers, the distribution activity covers the process of getting goods from centralized depots to the stores.

- Marketing and sales—locating customers, identifying their requirements, making them aware of the organization through promotional activity, and setting the prices at which the product is to be sold. This activity has responsibility for the selection and management of salespeople, distributors, and retailers to make sure that they have the knowledge and motivation to 'push' the organization's products and services.

- After-sales service—everything that an organization provides to customers after the goods or service has been delivered. It includes repair and maintenance services, complaints handling, customer training, and telephone help-lines.

Table 6.3 summarizes the main alternative ways in which organizations might try to gain competitive advantage through these primary activities.

The manufacturing-style value chain includes four support activities, which also appear in the generic value chains for professional service and network organizations:

- purchasing—the identification of potential suppliers and negotiation of prices and delivery terms;

- process development[33]—all activities to do with enhancing the routines and technologies that the organization uses;

- human resource management—the recruitment and training of employees and the design of appraisal, payment, and employee welfare systems;

- finance and planning—invoicing, treasury, accounting, budgeting, planning, and related activities.[34]

Table 6.4 summarizes the main ways in which these support activities can contribute to competitive advantage. See also Worked Example 6.1. The detailed example on the website also give further details.

 Online Resource Centre
www.oxfordtextbooks.co.uk/orc/haberberg_rieple/

Visit the Online Resource Centre that accompanies this book to read more information relating to value chains.

The purchasing activity is sometimes grouped together with the supply and distribution activities and called supply chain management. In this book, we consider the three as separate activities.

Table 6.3 Possible sources of competitive advantage in the primary activities of a manufacturing-style value chain

	Resources	Vertical integration	Scale and scope	Location	Linkages
Product design and development	Capabilities in: • innovation • customer responsiveness • risk management Laboratories IT facilities Designers	Use alliances and partnerships (May be dangerous to outsource activity fully)	Large scale and broad scope to allow cross-fertilization of ideas: • between people • across products and markets	Close to customers and competitors to allow exposure to latest ideas	Operations Distribution Marketing and sales After-sales service
Supply	IT systems (EDI and extranets)	Activity devolved to suppliers		Suppliers located nearby for speedy response	Operations Purchasing *Vertical linkage:* suppliers
Operations	Proprietary equipment Capabilities in: innovation, reliability, customer responsiveness, speed of response	Retain *core* activities and develop capabilities Outsource other activities to world-class suppliers	Economies of scale and scope, plant utilization	Low-cost locations Close to customer to gain responsiveness	Product design and development Supply Marketing and sales Distribution Human resource management
Distribution	Specialized vehicles, depots, and handling equipment Capabilities in reliability, customer responsiveness, speed of response	Keep in-house to ensure customer satisfaction Use top-class wholesalers, retailers	Economies of scale and scope	Many distribution points for speedy customer response Few, strategically located points for economies of scale	Distribution Sales *Vertical linkage:* wholesalers and retailers
Marketing and sales	Reputational assets Customer databases Knowledge of consumer preferences Capabilities in communication	In-house sales to retain control of customer service and information Agents and distributors for local knowledge and contacts	Economies of scope in branding and sales Economies of scale in advertising Large scale to maximize exposure to customers	Close to customer for local sensitivity Clustered near competitors' outlets	All other internal activities *Vertical linkage:* distributors and retailers
After-sales service	Trained human resources Testing and diagnostic equipment and software	In-house to capture product and customer data Outsource to gain benefits of third parties' scale, scope, local availability	Scale to offer customers local service Economies of scope	Close to customer for local sensitivity Call centre for cost advantage	Product design and development Marketing and sales Human resource management

Table 6.4 Possible sources of competitive advantage in the support activities of a value chain

	Resources	Vertical integration	Scale and scope	Location	Linkages
Purchasing	Supplier databases Capabilities in negotiation		Economies of scale and scope: discounts and spreading of overheads	Centralize to maximize scale and scope economies Devolve to maximize flexibility and responsiveness	All primary activities *Vertical linkage*: suppliers
Process development	Substantial human and financial resources	Keep in-house to give tailored solutions and preserve expertise Outsource to specialist system suppliers and consultants	Larger scale and scope bring exposure to more technologies and markets	Central management to transfer best practices around organization	Most other activities *Vertical linkage*: suppliers and researchers in other firms
Human resource management	Communications and training systems				Most other activities
Finance and planning	IT and financial control systems Planning systems (rarely)		Small, low-cost and non-intrusive		Most other activities *Vertical linkage*: financial institutions, governments

Using Evidence 6.1 Assessing how value is created in the different activities

Primary activities

a. Product design and development

The design and development activity often is focused on creating products that are differentiated from their competitors, but it also can reduce costs through designing products that are cheaper to manufacture, transport, or service, and that link effectively with the operations, distribution, or after-sales service activities. Cars are now manufactured in ways that allow economies of scale or scope across different products. Volkswagen and Toyota, for example, both design their cars so that core elements—or platforms—are shared across different models. In-company data would allow costs to be calculated, although this level of detail may not be available in public sources.

Often, parts of the design and development activity are outsourced, especially where differentiation is looked for. Automobile manufacturers often commission specialist design houses like the Italian firm Pininfarina and its star designer, Lowie Vermeersch, to give their cars distinctive looks. Companies are increasingly building customer feedback into their product design decisions.[35] And in some industries, like microprocessors and aircraft, the expertise needed to develop new generations of products is so diverse that firms like Airbus or Boeing have to seek joint ventures.

In this case you will need to assess as far as possible the nature of the links between the firms—is there a long-term relationship? Is this relationship formal or informal—in the form of detailed contracts or more vague? Is it a risky relationship, or one that appears solid and stable? How much does this relationship cost—and what is the downside if the relationship sours? For example, core knowledge may leak to outsiders who could then develop competences in these products, and become competitors. H&M outsources almost all of its manufacturing, but all its designers are based at its head office in Sweden. In other cases, firms like Honda or Ford may choose to maintain their design hubs in centres of design and innovation excellence, even if their main product development effort is elsewhere.

One of the ways in which the effectiveness of this activity may be assessed is by using qualitative data from press reports. Other suitable data include the sales, and profits, figures relating to the various product groups that you will often find in companies' annual reports. And if you have access to internal company →

→ accounts, then the costs of R&D as a percentage of sales that come from new products may be used, remembering that R&D may have a very long lead time before it returns a profit.

b. Supply

The supply activity, or 'inbound logistics', is particularly important in retailing and some manufacturing organizations. Here it is common for considerable investment to be made in information technology resources, such as MRP (materials requirements planning), JIT (just-in-time), or EDI (electronic date interchange) systems, to link firms with their suppliers. These allow firms to place orders with suppliers quickly and reliably, resulting in both differentiation and cost advantage.

Because of such 'just-in-time requirements', the firm's location relative to its suppliers is an important consideration. Fashion companies like Zara or H&M, which require new designs and new stock to be in their shops on almost a weekly basis, have to be able to transport their clothes from their manufacturing locations (often a long distance away from their shops and chosen because of their low costs), quickly and reliably. There is sometimes a trade-off here between transport costs and speed. Some automobile firms, such as General Motors and Fiat, build their assembly plants on large sites and insist that their suppliers build their own factories on the same complex.

As well as links with manufacturing, the supply activity often needs to work closely with the firm's purchasing function. Costs may be minimized if raw materials are bought in bulk and then distributed across a range of products.

Assessing the effectiveness of this activity depends on being able to evaluate the costs of poor quality supplies on either customer satisfaction (measured through sales' volumes or surveys), or in causing problems further down the manufacturing process. These data are sometimes to be found in industry reports or press articles.

c. Operations

Because they are so central to an organization's competitiveness, firms may spend a lot of resources seeking to reduce unit production costs, reduce wastage, maximize the utilization of key assets, and improve output quality.

The operations activity is one where economies of scale and scope are often important. The organization may be able to share overheads between operational activities and reduce unit costs. Differentiation is less of an issue, except perhaps where complex additional features make a product difficult to manufacture.

The location of operations can be a major influence on both an organization's costs, and its ability to meet customer needs promptly. For example, low wage levels coupled with high education standards give some Asian countries cost advantages over western Europe or the USA, but these countries are a long distance away. The availability of key resources, such as skilled staff, is also an issue, and hence the link with the human resource management activity is an important one. This is even more important in service businesses or service manufacturers like McDonald's, where operational staff are in direct contact with customers and help to shape their view of the organization. Where organizations are seeking to develop innovative products or differentiate on the basis of customer responsiveness, linkages with process development, marketing and sales, product design, and development activities are likely to be important.

Assessing the operations activity is through evaluating financial data; the costs of goods sold, costs of defects, or wastage costs[36] will give an indication of manufacturing effectiveness. Other quantitative indicators of the operation activity's effectiveness are measures like sales per square metre (for a retailer) or passenger load factor (for an airline—see Section 11.2).

d. Distribution

In restaurants and service manufacturers, where production and delivery are more or less the same thing, distribution, or 'outbound logistics', does not have a distinct identity—it can all be regarded as part of operations. In other manufacturers an efficient distribution system can give differentiation advantage by making sure that customers can get the products they need when they need them. It may also give cost advantage through reducing waste or breakages, or by minimizing transportation costs.

Because of its potential importance to customer satisfaction, some producers and retailers prefer to keep the distribution activity in-house, although there are an increasing number of specialist logistics firms to whom it may be outsourced. Firms also need to decide whether to maintain their own chain of depots, or to distribute through intermediaries. It may be able to achieve economies of scope, if the different products can use the same distribution systems and resources. It also faces trade-offs in its location decisions. Having a large number of small distribution points may be best if the firm is seeking to differentiate through offering a prompt response to customer orders, particularly if the distribution depots are also the locations for the after-sales service activity.

Assessing the distribution activity can be achieved by calculating its overall costs, relative to sales, as well as through qualitative means such as surveys of customer satisfaction.

e. Marketing and sales

Marketing and sales has prime responsibility for generating sales in the present, and building reputational assets such as brands for the future. The activity may have physical assets at its disposal, such as sales offices, or, increasingly, a presence on the internet. In the case of services and service manufacturers it is difficult to →

→ separate out the sales and marketing activity from that of operations—McDonald's serving staff are also their sales staff.

A firm can gain differentiation advantage by building customer databases to analyse buyer preferences, allowing it to respond quickly to trends. This is a function which is rarely outsourced in its entirety. Marketing and sales also has important linkages with most of the other activities, and also with external bodies. Sony sells its products through department stores and other outlets that it regards as compatible with its market positioning. Both retailer and Sony then use their own reputation to complement the other's. Although distributors may be difficult to motivate and discipline, since they will also be selling competitors' products, they may offer the customer a more attractive range of complementary products than the firm can by itself. Also, because they focus on a particular locality and may also offer after-sales service, they may be able to build deeper knowledge of local conditions and better relationships with the community than a firm's own salesforce could. Firms usually have a sales representative located near their important customers, however far away the other value chain activities may be. Increasingly, the sales and marketing activity is being carried out on-line, proximity to customers being achieved 'virtually'.

Marketing offers some potential for economies of scale and scope. Provided that the organization's products complement one another well and appeal to the same target markets, then they can benefit from a shared brand and corporate reputation, and be sold through the same channels. A large advertising campaign may benefit from bulk discounts. Economies of scale are less likely in the sales activity, since an organization will find it needs to increase the size of its salesforce or distributor network as sales increase.

Assessing the effectiveness of the sales activity is relatively easy: at a local level, depots, restaurants, or shops can be judged on their turnover, although local conditions will always need to be taken into account. Making quantitative assessments of the marketing activity is harder, because it is diffused through the organization and across products, although advertising campaigns can be costed and there are trade organizations that report on the effectiveness of campaigns in increased sales. The value of a brand and goodwill are published in industry surveys.[37] But you may need to use qualitative data, for example articles that discuss the effects of a corporate identity programme such as BA's controversial multicultural tail-fins.[38]

f. After-sales service

For services, there is not really any such thing as after-sales service—the product is 'consumed' at the time it is sold. But in other types of firms, good after-sales service can be an important element in an organization's differentiation strategy. It can be particularly important for new entrants; by offering extended warranties, a firm may be able to reassure customers that their products are reliable, and offset some of the advantages that established firms get from their reputation.

The after-sales service is important in generating vital information about what customers like and dislike about products, and the number and type of product defects. It needs therefore to link with the product design, operations and marketing activities.

As with marketing and sales, firms will usually have some local representation close to important customers. For some firms, like those manufacturing specialized equipment, for example, it may be that only a few people have the necessary expertise to service the products. In such a case, the after-sales service activity has to be centralized. Sony, for instance, collects its broken Vaio computers from customers' homes and couriers them to dedicated repair centres, often located half way across the world.

After-sales service costs will usually be relatively easy to calculate, although often not available in the public domain. Included in these will be the fixed costs of providing a unit that can undertake repairs, and variable costs on each piece of faulty equipment that is repaired. What is more difficult to value is the loss of reputation or customer goodwill when an organization supplies faulty goods. Sometimes the effects of this are very long lasting.

Support activities

Unlike the primary activities, support activities are often spread through a firm in ways that vary from company to company and may need some digging to identify. Major decisions and programmes may be initiated and managed centrally, while small purchasing, hiring and training decisions may be taken by individual managers. When we assess a value chain, we therefore have to look at all these activities together wherever they are found.

g. Purchasing

Because the raw materials, components and services that an organization buys in may represent over 50 per cent of a product's sale value, the purchasing activity has the potential to reduce the organization's costs significantly. Purchasing can benefit from economies of scale and scope. Large firms are likely to attract better discounts from suppliers than smaller ones, and large quantities if bought centrally, may be spread across many products. Global firms which centralize their purchasing decisions have to have links with the finance activity, to offset the effects of fluctuating prices. Locally responsive firms are likely to prefer to allow managers to negotiate their own deals with local suppliers.

Purchasing covers not only operational inputs, like raw materials, energy and advertising time, but also fixed inputs like land, →

Table 6.5 Examples of linkages between purchasing and primary activities

Activity	Operational purchases	Fixed asset purchases
Product design and development	Computer-aided design (CAD) software	Laboratories, testing equipment, CAD equipment
Supply		Materials handling and testing equipment
Operations	Fuel, raw materials, components and sub-assemblies, goods for resale, third-party services: maintenance, laundry, etc.	Plant, machinery, land in prime locations, buildings, office equipment, bar-code scanners
Distribution	Fuel, third-party services	Depots in key locations, materials handling equipment, vehicles
Marketing and sales	Fuel, vehicle, and office maintenance, advertising space, brochures and catalogues, hotel rooms	Offices and equipment, computer hardware and software, customer databases, market research
After-sales service	Fuel, parts, telephone services	Offices, vehicles, call-centres

→ buildings and equipment. Firms such as Tesco, Wal-Mart, McDonalds, and Novotel build their outlets to a common specification, with similar decor, furnishings and, for hotels, room sizes across the world, thus achieving economies of scale in interior and architectural design.

Some of the main links between purchasing and other organizational activities are shown in Table 6.5. Internal financial data on the discounts obtained through bulk purchase, or details of supply contracts, will give strong indications as to the effectiveness of the purchasing activity. Otherwise it may have to be inferred from costs of sales' figures, or press articles.

h. Process development

Large, mature, firms are more likely to be concerned with implementing process improvements than newer companies. Process development in manufacturing firms is almost always carried out by local in-house experts, sometimes with the assistance of outside consultants. However, some global manufacturers employ small teams of head-office-based experts whose role is to improve the manufacturing process worldwide. Unilever, the Anglo-Dutch foods and detergents conglomerate, holds regular meetings to enable managers from similar countries and similar product groups to share experiences.

The process development activity may benefit from external linkages to suppliers of technology and advice, and, via professional associations, to people developing and using similar processes in other organizations. In recent years there has been a move towards firms passing responsibility for some of the firm's processes (such as payroll, personnel, and database management) to suppliers of integrated systems, such as the German software company SAP.

Consultants are also frequently employed for IT system development, an activity whose competences are usually some way away from the core activities of the firm.

Process development has linkages to most of the other activities such as product testing methods in product design and development; scheduling, inspection, and unloading procedures in the supply activity; and manufacturing procedures in operations.

Assessing the effectiveness of the process development activity is likely to use comparable quantitative data such as efficiency ratios.

i. Human resource management

Human resource (HR) management ensures that an organization has available the skills it needs to compete effectively in all aspects of its operations. It is the support activity that is most clearly involved in all of an organization's other activities. Most firms employ specialist HR personnel in central and divisional human resources or personnel departments, but they are invariably outnumbered by local supervisors and managers who carry out HR management activities every working day.

An interesting question is whether it is possible to gain economies of scale or scope in human resource management. Jack Welch of GE claimed that there was no point in being the largest company in the world (as it was at the time) unless it used the huge amount of expertise within it by transferring good practice from one unit to another.[39]

One of the biggest measures of HRM effectiveness is profits per employee. However, the best levels will vary widely from industry to industry, and so here it is necessary to compare the firm's performance with industry benchmarks as well as with its own past. →

→ Measuring employee motivation is best done through looking for staff turnover rates, days lost through strikes, and staff satisfaction surveys.

j. Finance and planning

Finance and planning is another support activity that is connected to all others. An important part of the planning and finance activities is carried out centrally at corporate or divisional headquarters. However, most local managers will retain some control over their own budgets and financial information. The effective flow of information to where it is most useful is dependent on good IT systems. Internet hardware manufacturer Cisco Systems has configured its internal financial systems so that within 24 hours it can do a 'virtual close'—get a complete picture of its profit and loss situation and balance sheet. This extremely rare ability allows Cisco to take far better-informed pricing decisions than its competitors and reduces its risk of taking on unprofitable business.[40]

Some firms choose to locate their finance activities close to financial centres, or to place their headquarters in a country with a favourable tax regime. Linkages to governments may also be important.

Assessing the effectiveness of the finance and planning activity is dependent on the type of industry the firm is in. For an international company that is dependent on currency risks being minimized, and costs being taken in the most tax-friendly way, then measures of profits after tax and currency write-downs are important indicators. The share price and P/E ratio are other indicators of how well the finance function is managing its relationships with key investors. Local data on profit margins and costs will indicate performance at an individual unit or manager's level. The planning activity is less easy to assess—partly because it is likely to have very long lead times before its effectiveness can be judged. A strategic plan set in place by a chief executive now, is unlikely to show results for many months, or probably years.

In Worked Example 6.1 we apply these principles to undertaking a value chain analysis of one of our four running case studies—H&M.

Worked Example 6.1 A value chain analysis of H&M

The distinguishing feature of a good value chain analysis is thoroughness. To make sure of locating *all* the distinctive features in the chain, we must work systematically through all the primary and support activities, applying to each the checklist of where the activity contributes to cost and/or differentiation advantage in relation to the six aspects that we discuss in this chapter: resources, vertical integration, scope, scale, location, and linkages.

The first step is to work out what form of value chain we use for H&M. It clearly is in the business of transforming inputs to outputs, so the manufacturing-style value chain is appropriate. But do we treat it as a retailer, or a manufacturer? H&M owns no factories, so does not fit the classical manufacturing mould—but equally, it is not the kind of retailer, like Wal-Mart or Carrefour, that operates mainly as an outlet for products that are manufactured and branded by other firms. H&M designs its own offerings and oversees their production, and competes directly with firms like Zara/Inditex and Mango that do much of their own manufacturing. So, slightly paradoxically, it makes most sense to treat it as a manufacturer. If it were 'just' a retailer, H&M's operations would be the stores that it owns and runs, and the three 'middle' primary activities—operations, distribution, and sales of a retailer's goods—would have been treated as one because they are carried out synchronously. Here, we separate them.

Whilst H&M owns no factories, it remains closely involved in the production of its designs.   →

→ Primary activities

a. Product design and development

Product design and development	Supply	Operations	Distribution	Marketing & sales	After-sales service

Figure 6.4a Product design and development

The positive reaction to its fashion collections by its customers is (according to recent annual reports) 'the single most important factor in H&M's success'. Hence the design activity is critically important, and there is evidence that it adds considerable value to the firm's differentiation advantage. There is plentiful qualitative evidence (in the form of articles on the company, as well as through visiting their stores)[41] that H&M's product ranges are regularly updated, and they also add new concepts or ranges (e.g. menswear or clothes for pregnant women) on average once every couple of years. And there is quantitative evidence to support this too. Three hundred million garments were sold in 2000; by 2004, this had increased to 600 million.[42] Until very recently there has been a corresponding increase in turnover—indicating that customers like the products that they find in the shops. And for some years, until 2005, when it was overtaken by Zara, it was the largest European fashion retailer.

In this section of the analysis, our aim is to pinpoint, as best we can, *how* this happens. H&M's product design is almost all vertically integrated and carried out within its large design department in its head office in Sweden—it has a hundred designers based there. Its major competitors are similarly vertically integrated, and there is little that is obviously distinctive about the tangible resources devoted to this activity. There is no evidence that Zara or TopShop employ designers that are less talented than H&M's, or have inferior IT or other facilities. Any scale or scope benefits that H&M gets from centralizing the design activity in this way are also likely to be shared with its competitors.

There are no obvious benefits from H&M's choice to base its design activity in Sweden. Other companies' design centres are located in Milan or Paris where they can be close to a community of fashion-related firms, although H&M's designers do not simply just sit in splendid isolation in Sweden—they get out and about. As well as attending the major fashion shows in Paris, Milan, etc., they visit other countries around the world regularly for inspiration; they also watch films and note music trends. Other firms, for example TopShop, have similar policies, and are also successful, and so this does not appear to be an area of particular distinctiveness. However, there is evidence that someone in the design area is well connected with other designers. Karl Lagerfeld and Stella McCartney have both produced ranges for H&M in recent years.

Fashion shows in Paris and Milan provide H&M with inspiration for new trends.

But in terms of internal linkages, the location at head office means that there is likely to be close contact between designers and H&M's senior management team. The design manager also has close links with merchandisers and the buying director, who liaises with the twenty or so production offices around the world and suppliers.

H&M's designers and merchandisers sometimes get it wrong—the company is quite open when it makes mistakes in its ranges. Occasionally this is due to factors beyond its control, like unpredictable weather. But more worryingly H&M in 2006 lost its place as the largest European clothing retailer after Inditex's Zara increased sales faster than H&M over eight consecutive quarters. Inditex's revenue rose to €6.74 billion, 1.6 per cent more than H&M's.[43] However, at least part of this increase was down to more new Zara stores being opened. In order to assess the relative effectiveness of the product design activity, indicators like footfall within the stores, and sales per square metre would give a better (albeit not perfect) indicator than comparisons of raw sales. It does not appear that these data are in the public domain.

b. Supply

Product design and development	Supply	Operations	Distribution	Marketing & sales	After-sales service

Figure 6.4b Supply

→ There is no indication that there is anything especially distinctive about the resources that H&M uses to schedule or transport deliveries of cloth or other raw materials, or the degree of vertical integration or location of this activity. The chances are that it uses the same logistics partners as many of its competitors. The scope or scale of its activities may give it preferential transportation rates, but it is unlikely that these are much different from those obtained by its main competitors.

Because H&M are concerned to protect their reputation as a socially responsible company, it gets involved with the growers and producers of cotton and dyes and other components that go into their cloth, and requires them to conform to H&M's standards. This does not directly affect the performance of the supply activity, but there is a linkage to the marketing and sales activity—it manages its suppliers so as to maintain the value of its own reputation and brand.

c. Operations

Figure 6.4c Operations

H&M uses 700 or so manufacturers across the world. Around 60 per cent of its clothes are produced in various countries in Asia and the remaining 40 per cent in Europe. As we have already discussed in Real-life Application 6.1, the company has opted for a low level of vertical integration in this activity: it does not own any factories and therefore has a huge task to coordinate its suppliers. Its resources are its 22 production offices around the world, nine in Europe, ten in Asia, and one each in Africa and Central America, which coordinate the buying and ordering of stock and monitor the quality and costs of the manufacturing process.

So how successful are H&M in this activity? The large number of suppliers, and their location around the world, allows H&M to differentiate its offering from other fashion retailers by updating its ranges much more frequently than most of its competitors, and by its fast response to fashion trends. It can capitalize on the specialist production knowledge of some of its suppliers and give more or fewer orders to, for example, cotton manufacturers rather than those working principally in viscose, as circumstances demand. It can also tailor lead times according to product type.

But its supply activity confers most advantage in reducing its costs. Unlike its major competitor Zara, whose manufacturing is carried out in-house and near its Spanish head office, H&M has chosen to outsource much of its manufacturing to suppliers in countries that have significant cost advantages. This requires strong competences in managing relationships between people with very different cultures and languages; it requires equally strong competences in electronic stock control and ordering systems; and it requires considerable expertise in setting up and managing contracts across different international legal and financial regimes. All of these require strong linkages with HR management, planning and finance, and process development support activities.

Data are not available on the specific costs of the supply chain, but sales for the H&M Group for the six months in May 2006 were SEK 32,134m, an increase of 14 per cent on the comparable period in 2005. Profits after financial items were SEK 6,600m, an increase of 11 per cent. Some commentators have suggested that H&M's product positioning is towards the less expensive end of the market, where there has been much stronger competition recently. But the relatively poor increase in profits suggest that there are some concerns about the company's costs relative to sales—in which the supply activity may play some role. These results were also worse than those of Inditex, whose most recent comparable figures for the three months to April 2006 show both sales and profits up 20 per cent.

d. Distribution

Figure 6.4d Distribution

There is little evidence of anything particularly distinctive in H&M's distribution activity—the physical transportation of the finished garments from factory to retail outlets.

e. Sales and marketing

Figure 6.4e Marketing and sales

H&M has three main resources in its sales and marketing activity —the intangible brand, the tangible network of sales outlets, and the human resources that sell the products. →

The location of H&M stores plays a key role in attracting customers.

→ H&M has a strong brand—it typically spends a high proportion —4 per cent—of its revenue on marketing,[44] and has used some extremely well-known names, for example Madonna and Richard Avedon, to promote itself—both in front of and behind the camera. This is a probable source of differentiation advantage, although it should be noted that its main competitors also have invested in building strong brands.

The physical resources are high-quality, the scope is broad to ensure proximity to the target customer, and store locations are carefully chosen, in the best shopping areas in any town—thereby ensuring high visibility and footfall, and therefore sales. There seems to be little wrong with this policy, although we would want to know how expensive these locations are, whether they are freehold, and therefore how vulnerable the company would be to rises in lease prices. It should also be noted that this policy is not truly distinctive—in many countries, H&M's main competitors will be located close by.

A distinctive feature of H&M's sales and marketing activity is the high degree of vertical integration. All its stores are wholly owned, unlike those of their main competitors, most of which operate through franchisees or licensees in some markets. It is not entirely clear what benefits it gets from the greater degree of control this gives it.

H&M spends a lot of time making sure that the key players in the sales and marketing activity—its sales staff—promote the H&M brand. There are strong links with the HR management activity to ensure that selection and training of staff means that they share the core values of what appears to be a strongly value-driven company. As it opens new stores around the world, a particular problem for H&M is finding suitable skilled staff in places that are not yet familiar with its culture and ways of doing business. One way that it overcomes some of these problems is by asking managers from neighbouring countries to 'hold the hand' of staff in new countries that it enters—until they are sufficiently familiar with how they are expected to behave.[45]

f. After-sales service

Figure 6.4f After-sales service

It has proved impossible to find anything particularly distinctive to say about H&M's after-sales service. It appears neither to be a subject of concern in the press nor a matter for especial commendation, and we have been unable to find any data about the costs of returned goods. As a result, we propose saying no more about it!

Support activities

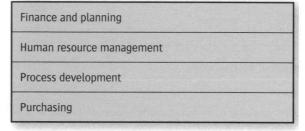

Figure 6.4g Support activities

Of the support activities, two appear to have significant distinctive elements: HR management and purchasing. H&M is a company that appears to be very strongly ethical. This is an aspect that forms part of its brand and its reputational assets. It allows it to differentiate itself from some of its competitors both in terms of attracting customers and in recruiting high-quality staff and suppliers. The HR management activity therefore has an important role in first recruiting and then socializing staff. No information appears to be publicly available about staff turnover rates or motivation, except that H&M claims that its socially responsible support of suppliers gives it lower staff turnover and higher productivity.[46]

The purchasing activity in H&M is also a potentially important one. H&M recently restructured some of its head office functions to separate out the buying and production activities. Each is now under the control of a separate director. It also took steps to improve its stock control process—in the case of a retailer with fast-moving stock turnover, two strongly linked activities. It has moved away from a twice-yearly buying cycle to one that →

→ happens on an ongoing basis throughout the season. H&M claims that this has led to higher levels of full-price sales as it can respond faster to customer preferences, and more cost-effective stock management. It is not clear whether in this case H&M is distinctive.

Practical dos and don'ts

- The value chain that we have carried out on H&M has a number of flaws. There are large gaps in our understanding of H&M's situation that in an ideal world we would like to fill—comparison data on sales per square metre for example. But

the reasons for undertaking a value chain analysis are to illustrate areas of strength or weakness, or places where there are poor linkages between critically important activities. If a value chain model is less than perfect, it doesn't matter as long as it forces consideration of the most important of these issues.

- There are always likely to be gaps where the data is missing, or has to be inferred from indirect sources. Fill in as many boxes as you have data for, draw as many linkages as you can—and acknowledge the limitations in any report you write.
- Where possible, quantify the cost of the activities.

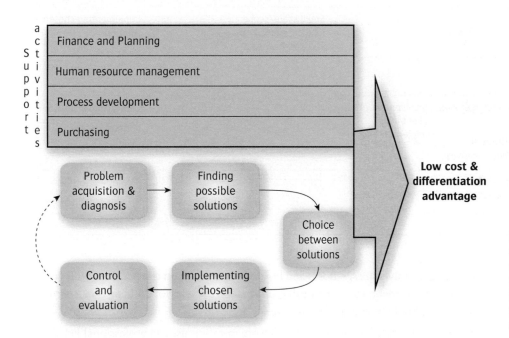

Figure 6.5 Generic value chain for a professional services organization. From Stabell and Fjeldstad (1998: 425). *Reproduced with the kind permission of John Wiley*

6.2.2 **Professional services organizations**

A professional services value chain is illustrated in Figure 6.5. The support activities are very similar to those in the manufacturing-style value chain, but the primary activities are different. They comprise:

- Problem acquisition and diagnosis—persuading clients to bring their problem to the organization, making and recording an initial assessment of the problem and then choosing an overall approach. For example, a dentist will conduct an initial examination of a patient, determine if there are any problems with their teeth, and then map out a plan of treatment. For organizations like management consultancies and architecture practices, problem acquisition and diagnosis may involve a number of marketing activities, including advertising and making presentations to clients. In less commercial situations, it will involve liaising with funding and administrative bodies that control the flow of 'problems' and allocate them to one organization rather than another. For

Table 6.6 Possible sources of competitive advantage in the primary activities of a professional services value chain

	Resources	Vertical integration	Scale and scope	Location	Linkages
Problem acquisition and diagnosis	Reputation Capabilities in communication, negotiation, and management of expectations	Development of in-house expertise Astute use of out-sourced specialist professionals			Finding possible solutions Control and monitoring (of previous projects) *Vertical linkage*: customer networks, professional networks
Finding possible solutions	Knowledge assets Capabilities in innovation		Large scale/scope offers customer 'one-stop shop' and access to genuine specialists		
Choice between solutions	Ability to manage interactions between professions		Small scale/scope for focused expertise and low overheads		Implementing chosen solutions *Vertical linkage*: Professionals in other firms
Implementing chosen solutions	Project management systems Capabilities in customer sensitivity	Involvement of client in implementation			Control and evaluation *Vertical linkage*: Customers
Control and evaluation	Monitoring systems				Problem acquisition Finding and choosing solutions

example, universities, schools and hospitals will maintain relationships with government departments to make sure they understand the rules for deciding how a particular person should be educated or treated.

- Finding possible solutions—where the organization uses its professional knowledge to develop a set of alternative answers to a problem. A doctor may be able to treat a patient through drugs or surgery. An architect may have several possible designs to fit a house or a hospital to the topography of the chosen site.

- Choice between solutions—choosing between the various alternatives proposed. It may be quite a brief phase in each project, and involve few resources, but it is crucial to obtaining a workable solution to the problem.

- Implementing chosen solutions—communicating the proposed solution to the client and putting it into effect.

- Control and evaluation—monitoring the extent to which the implementation process is actually solving the problem. It includes activities like the monitoring of patient progress in a hospital, client feedback meetings for an architect or consultant, and safety testing in a new building by a construction firm.

The ways in which the organization can try to seek competitive advantage from each of these primary activities are summarized in Table 6.6. See also Real-life Application 6.4 and the worked example on the website.

Online Resource Centre
www.oxfordtextbooks.co.uk/orc/haberberg_rieple/

Visit the Online Resource Centre that accompanies this book to read more information relating to competitive advantage in the worked example.

Professional services organizations differ from manufacturing organizations in a number of important ways:

- There is far less division of labour between activities. The people who bring work in to the organization are frequently the same people that work on the problem-solving and implementation. In fact the most important inputs everywhere in this value chain are specialized human resources.

- The activities are frequently more like a cycle than a chain. Successful solution of one problem may lead to the identification of more problems, leading to more work for the same client. In an accountancy firm, the discovery and resolution of a problem with a client's accounts may throw up other, smaller, irregularities. Alternatively, it may lead to a contract to design a system to prevent the problem from recurring. In a research institute, one research programme invariably highlights unanswered questions that form the starting point for the next one.

- The value chain is configured to deal with unique cases. Although organizations will frequently develop standard routines to handle many simple problems such as audit procedures in accountancy, modular programmes in education, and methods for open-heart surgery in medicine, the professional normally needs to look out for unusual problems: accounting irregularities, failing students, and surgical complications.

Real-life Application 6.4 SonyCierge: a professional services value chain

SonyCierge, which we introduced in Real-life Application 5.1, is a professional services business. Its objective is to win complex projects involving the installation of state-of-the-art consumer electronics into wealthy people's homes, and it differentiates on the quality of the advice it offers and the speed and discretion with which it can diagnose and meet the requirements of demanding customers.

Linkages with Sony Corporation are clearly very important to SonyCierge. For problem acquisition, the reputation of the parent and its linkages with the rich and famous, via the music and film businesses, are clearly advantageous, and shared by few other businesses. Being able to call upon the technological competences of the Consumer Electronics business is also an advantage for diagnosis of client needs and finding possible technological solutions to meet those needs. That same expertise will be helpful in choosing which equipment to install and working out how to put it in place.

But SonyCierge has developed competences of its own in choosing between solutions, including those that do not involve Sony equipment, and in project management to ensure prompt delivery and installation of equipment.

Creative Strategizing 6.1

You have recently acquired SonyCierge from Sony Corporation. Where, with whom, and why, would you now wish to form strategic alliances.

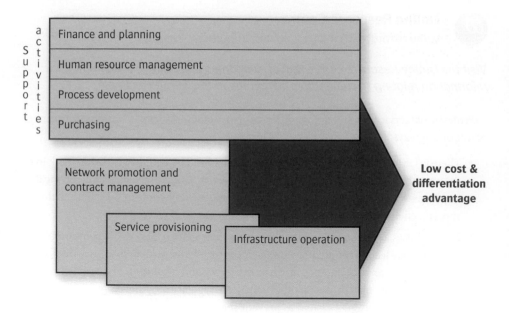

Figure 6.6 Generic value chain for a network organization. From Stabell and Fjeldstad (1998: 430). *Reproduced with the kind permission of John Wiley*

- There is no strong correlation between the cost of an activity and its importance. The process of finding possible solutions, for example, may take far fewer resources than their implementation, but be equally as vital to the success of a project.

6.2.3 **Network organizations**

Network organizations exist to bring people together and act as intermediaries between them. A newspaper links journalists with readers, and advertisers with potential customers. A bank links depositors who have money with people who want to borrow it. A social network provider such as MySpace links people who want to interact with one another, and also aspiring musicians with potential listeners.

Having a network value chain is not the same as being part of a network of alliances (discussed in Section 6.1.3). A firm with a networked value chain may choose to be vertically integrated in most of its activities, and form few alliances, while many firms within a network of alliances have manufacturing-style or professional services value chains.

In network organizations, it can sometimes be difficult to distinguish between a supplier and a customer. The people who advertise in newspapers or offer goods for sale on eBay are suppliers in one sense, since they provide part of the content that attracts people to the site. However, they are also charged for the space or bandwidth they consume. It is simpler to think of them as customers.

The generic value chain for this kind of organization is shown in Figure 6.6. Again, the support activities are similar to those for manufacturing-style organizations, but there are different primary activities. The primary activities are shown overlapping, rather than as a sequence (like the manufacturing value chain) or a cycle (the professional services one). This is because they all have to happen simultaneously if the network is to function. They are:

1. Network promotion and contract management—this involves four basic classes of activity:
   - marketing the network to potential users. For a newspaper or magazine this would involve finding distributors and arranging subscriptions. For a retail bank, it means finding credit-worthy individuals or companies and persuading them to take out

a loan. For many on-line activities, such as MySpace, it means creating a 'buzz' that enables the site to gather users 'virally'—by word of mouth, which then makes it attractive to advertisers;

- marketing the network to potential providers. For a newspaper this involves selling advertising, for a retail bank, persuading people to open accounts and deposit money. An on-line service provider has to find providers of information and advice, and persuade them to make some part of their service exclusive to that particular network;

- setting up and terminating contracts: opening and closing customer accounts or subscriptions;

- screening potential members, for example assessing their credit-worthiness.

2. Service provisioning—the day-to-day operation of the network: initiating, maintaining and ending contacts through the network, keeping track of customers' use of it, billing them and handling complaints. It includes activities like writing and printing a newspaper, the operation of the servers and modems for an on-line network, and the processing of deposits, withdrawals, and interest payments in a bank.

3. Infrastructure operation—keeping the network ready to service customers. It involves the specification and maintenance of physical resources, including buildings, and the IT and telecommunications infrastructure. It has a strong linkage with the procurement activity. For a newspaper, this activity might include the maintenance of delivery vehicles and the operation of telecommunications links between the editorial office and printing plants in other cities or countries. For a bank, it includes the operation of branch offices and ATMs, maintaining relations with the central bank and with correspondent banks in other countries, and the management of the bank's funds to ensure that it has adequate ready cash to service its customers.

The ways in which these primary activities may deliver competitive advantage to a network organization are summarized in Table 6.7 with details in Real-life Application 6.5 and the worked example on the website.

Table 6.7 Possible sources of competitive advantage in the primary activities of a network value chain

	Resources	Vertical integration	Scale and scope	Location	Linkages
Network promotion and contract management	Brand and reputation Capabilities in communication, negotiation, risk management	Outsource to top-grade supplier	Economies of scale or increasing returns to scale	Centralized for economies of scale Close to customer for personal service	Service provisioning Infrastructure operation *Vertical linkage:* customers
Service provisioning	Computers and other physical resources Capabilities in reliability, customer sensitivity, speed of response	Retention in-house of activities crucial to competitive advantage Choice of world-class supplier		Centralized, possibly in low-cost country with skilled human resources	Other primary activities Purchasing Process development *Vertical linkage:* suppliers
Infrastructure operation	Technological competences: e.g. IT, building maintenance				

Online Resource Centre
www.oxfordtextbooks.co.uk/orc/haberberg_rieple/

Visit the Online Resource Centre that accompanies this book to read a fuller worked example of a network value chain.

Real-life Application 6.5 eBay: a network value chain

We introduced eBay, the on-line auction provider, in the case studies at the end of Chapters 4 and 5. It is a network organization, linking people who wish to sell goods with those that wish to buy them.

A great deal of effort goes into network promotion, and this is largely done through word-of-mouth and internet marketing, avoiding expensive newspaper and TV advertising. Reputation is thus a key asset in drawing in new subscribers, and there are important linkages to the user community. There are linkages to the service provisioning activity, which is responsible for ensuring that the reputation is not undermined. Considerable effort is expended on nurturing linkages with the sellers, through conferences and email contact, making them feel part of the community and giving them an emotional interest in making eBay thrive.

While eBay has people charged with service provisioning on a day-to-day basis, substantial elements, like marketing, are in effect outsourced to the user community. A lot of reliance is placed on eBay's user community to police the network, exert peer group pressure to keep members honest, and report poor behaviour to eBay. The auction software was originally bought in, though much time, money, and effort has been expended into tailoring it to eBay's precise needs, so that it may now constitute a distinctive resource.

The key resource in infrastructure operation appears to be IT hardware, on which eBay has invested substantially more than other internet trading houses. This enables eBay to differentiate on speed and reliability. The accumulated information on purchasing patterns is another distinctive resource that helps the organization plan capacity and also assists with process development—the expansion of the network to new areas.

6.2.4 How many value chains do you need?

Normally, value chain analysis is used on the strategies of a single business unit in a single firm. A value chain tracks how a firm adds value to a particular set of customers. If it is attacking more than one target market, then it might be helpful to draw more than one value chain within the business unit or firm as a whole. The way in which Sony adds value to individuals purchasing its consumer electronics will be different from the way in which it adds value to corporate purchasers of its audio-visual equipment. Its innovation capability in the product design activity is important to both sets of customers. However, its reputation is more of an asset in the consumer market than in the corporate market. Corporate buyers will have more expertise and, because they purchase these items more frequently, will have been able to form their own opinions about whose products work best—they do not need reputation as a guide. The sales and after-sales service channels are also different for the two markets.

It can sometimes be useful to use it in a more general way, to show what distinguishes the firms in an industry from those marketing substitute products and services, or to work out what makes one strategic group different from another. For example, in understanding McDonald's competitive advantage, it might be helpful to do a single value chain for all global fast-food firms, to show how they gain advantage over smaller local competitors.

6.2.5 What you should include in a value chain analysis

Value chain analysis is potentially a very powerful tool for understanding an organization's strategy. It brings together a number of different aspects of the organization—decisions about scale and scope and vertical integration, strategic resources—and shows how they combine to generate competitive advantage. However, as you will have seen, it can get quite complex and difficult, particularly if you try to incorporate every single detail about every single activity. Here, we look at how to simplify the analysis to make it less daunting and more useful.

In *Competitive Advantage*, Porter proposed using the value chain as a framework for the financial analysis of a firm. He suggested assessing the costs and assets associated with each activity, to see whether the amount the firm is investing in an activity is in line with its strategic value. However, it is very difficult to do this in practice, especially using secondary data. There may also be a strong temptation, when confronted with a value chain diagram for the first time, to try to fill in every square in meticulous detail. The problem with this approach is that, although your list would include the important aspects of a firm's strategy, they will be obscured by a lot of mundane and unimportant ones. So we suggest you are selective in your approach, and only pick out the *important* elements of a firm's strategy and operations.

If you identify an activity as an important part of an organization's value chain, be sure that it is exceptional, and identify how it leads to advantage. Scope, location, and structural decisions such as vertical integration or alliances with other firms should only feature in your analysis if they are genuinely unusual in the industry in question. You need to show in your analysis, using quantitative and qualitative evidence, *how* it leads to cost and/or differentiation advantage.

You may also want to highlight in your analysis why some elements of an organization's strategy do *not* feature in its value chain.

Finally, although in this chapter we have focused on how the value chain can lead to cost or differentiation advantage for a firm, it is also possible to undertake a value chain of an industry. Kristina Dahlström and Paul Ekins[47] have undertaken an excellent analysis of how value is gained (and lost) in a whole sector—the UK iron and steel processing industry. We summarize their analysis on the website.

Online Resource Centre

www.oxfordtextbooks.co.uk/orc/haberberg_rieple/

Visit the Online Resource Centre that accompanies this book to read more information relating to value chain analysis of an industry.

What Can Go Wrong 6.1 The Airbus consortium

For most of its life since its start in 1970, Airbus has been one of the most successful international consortia, producing world-beating aircraft such as the A320 and A350 and implementing innovative fly-by-wire technologies in its aircraft long before its main rival Boeing. By 2005, it had overtaken Boeing as the largest civilian aircraft maker in the world.

But despite its success, for a long time there have been those who expressed concern about the consortium's structure and operations. Questions have been raised about national governments' involvement in the consortium's constituent firms, areas of inefficiency inherently built into the value chain, and the potential problems of coordinating companies from very ➜

→ different national cultures and legal regimes.[48] Others have suggested that Airbus' apparently superior performance was in fact boosted by government subsidies that allowed it to undercut Boeing in order to achieve market share—not just through price-cutting, but by offering extensive performance guarantees and warranties.[49] Because of the consortium's opaque structure, none of this could be easily judged.[50] And in 2005/2006, attempts to change the organization's multi-national management and control structure, from one in which the German and French shareholders had the right to appoint two co-chairmen and two co-chief executives to one with a more normal single line of command, apparently degenerated into in-fighting.[51]

By 2006, evidence of considerable operational problems had become apparent. Although the new A380 super-jumbo made its maiden flight during the spring of 2005 and flew to New York in March 2007, Airbus' parent company, EADS, announced that the aircraft's development programme was likely to be €1.45bn overspent, on a budget of approx €8bn, figures that apparently started to become 'alarming' during 2004.[52] In addition, Airbus had not launched its promised newest product—the A350 mid-sized jet. Qantas, Air France, and Singapore Airlines all announced that they were likely to demand compensation totalling hundreds of millions of euros as a result of the delays.[53] And FedEx and UPS 'walked, which killed the cargo version of the plane'.[54] As a result, Airbus announced that it had had to reduce its forecast operating profits for the A380 programme by about €500m a year from 2007 to 2010.

And Airbus was also said to be losing orders to Boeing since the row over the firm's new structure and managerial appointments became public.[55] Goldman Sachs, the American investment bank, said 'We are concerned that several businesses and programmes, especially A380 development, appear to be encountering problems and fear this could in part be evidence of management distraction due to recent management conflict within the company'.[56] They also suggested that the manner in which the cost overruns on the A380 had been disclosed implied that it had been used 'at least as much as a weapon within the current senior management battle as it was intended as a means to inform investors'.[57]

Many of Airbus' current problems go back a long way. Under its original GIE legal structure (see Real-life Application 6.3), Airbus simply undertook the design, production, and marketing of aircraft. It had no obligation to publish annual accounts and was therefore not exposed to the same public scrutiny as a listed company.[58] Its finances were known only to its four international corporate shareholders—the Dasa aerospace division of German company Daimler (which later merged with Chrysler), France's Aerospatiale Matra, BAE Systems from the UK, and Spain's Construcciones Aeronauticas, or Casa. These four independent but allied companies were also Airbus' main suppliers, and because of this, even if Airbus itself made a loss (which it probably did[59]), the parent companies could claim a profit by selling components to the consortium. Even the partners may not have known the true state of Airbus' costs; as one analyst said, 'central management does not know how much it costs each company to make its components. And without a clear idea of costs, it has no way of reducing them.'[60]

As far back as 1993, it was recognized that this structure was too unwieldy and inefficient if Airbus was to develop and manage such a complex project as the A380 super-jumbo.[61] Critics of the consortium structure focused on:

- the allocating of contracts to the partners in proportion to their investment, rather than to the best supplier (or even to a supplier outside the consortium);
- the inefficiencies of having ten manufacturing plants scattered around Europe;
- decisions being taken by shareholder committees rather than on-the-spot managers;
- the bureaucratic and long-winded decision-making process;
- duplication in R&D and in many production tasks;
- political pressures reflecting different national priorities of some partners and their governments;
- difficulties in rationalizing the overall process because of differing labour and social regulations in the partner countries;
- the lack of financial flexibility to raise funds,

Eventually, in July 2001, Airbus was consolidated into a single SAS, or 'Société par Action Simplifiée', a move that was forecast to achieve €350m p.a. savings through synergies (e.g. in purchasing, having a single-management structure, and R&D optimization).[62] The Airbus company was to be owned 80 per cent by EADS (which was formed from a merger of Aerospatiale, Dasa, and Casa, but which still reflected the previous shareholding structure, which included DaimlerChrysler, a French conglomerate, Lagardère, and the French and Spanish governments) and 20 per cent by the British PLC, BAE Systems. A further planned step was eventually to fully integrate Airbus into EADS, after BAE Systems sold its stake. This happened in 2006, and was another complication in Airbus' problems: BAe and EADS failed to agree a price which had had to be decided by an independent arbitrator.[63] The stake was eventually sold for €2,750m in October 2006.[64]

Since then, a further restructuring was attempted in 2006, to make EADS/Airbus into a proper corporation with a unified, →

→ single-management structure and public accountability, and a corresponding selling-off of government stakes in the various partners, thereby reducing their meddling in operational matters.[65] Countless articles have suggested that relations between the different partners in Airbus, particularly the French and Germans, have not always been smooth; and doubts have been raised about whether either side could trust each other,[66] although these difficulties have previously been overcome. The first two years under Philippe Camus and Rainer Hertrich (the first Franco-German co-chief executives) were allegedly 'very, very difficult . . . but after that it worked',[67] although, it has been suggested, only because of the personal chemistry between the two.[68]

Problems then centred around who should manage the new unified company. If a German was appointed to the single CEO position, there would be fears from the French, and vice versa; and if the new appointment came from another country, then the French and German governments would be concerned because of EADS' importance to the countries' air and defence interests.[69] The compromise was to appoint Airbus' COO Gustav Humbert (a German, and the first non-French CEO) to succeed Noel Forgeard as president and CEO, while Forgeard was appointed chairman of the Airbus Shareholder Committee and co-CEO of EADS with Thomas Enders (a German). Humbert as a German CEO had to report to a hierarchically-higher French EADS CEO, and vice versa.[70] Mr Humbert's accession at Airbus was accompanied by a major top management reshuffle, which included the 'surprise departure' of executive vice president of operations, Gerard Blanc.[71]

Things did not get any better. In a major shuffle in July 2006, Humbert and Forgeard left, and Christian Streiff was appointed as the new co-CEO to work alongside Louis Gallois, the new co-CEO of EADS and the former head of France's state railway SNCF, and Thomas Enders. Mr Streiff is now at Peugeot, where he moved after 'three disastrous months' trying to run Airbus,[72] a move that has led to him being described as the smartest CEO Airbus ever had—getting out while the getting was good.[73] And in June 2007, the 'last of the old guard' who had been involved in the setting up of EADS in 1999, Jean-Paul Gut, resigned in a 'disagreement over strategy'.[74]

Difficulties apparently extended to lower-level staff too. Just as management minds needed to be focused on Airbus' challenges, not least a resurgent Boeing, executives apparently had to fight their own internal battles for survival or promotion[75]—'the right people are not in the right jobs and the wrong people are in the wrong jobs'.[76] And employees were said to be increasingly demoralized by the 'debacle'.[77]

Aside from any internal problems, the delays to the A380 are partly due to struggles to keep the aircraft's weight down, and implement a complicated cabin wiring system that connects to the entertainment systems in the aircraft's seat backs.[78] Ironically this is not a high-tech aspect of aircraft manufacturing. Previously, the French state-controlled group Aerospatiale had been responsible for this. But when Aerospatiale merged with Lagardère's Matra—with Lagardère subsequently becoming the main French partner in EADS—the decision was taken to opt for a new cable management system. This is now said to be at the heart of the A380's technical woes.[79] Assembled planes have to be flown from the Toulouse factory to Hamburg, where ill-fitting wiring is ripped out and painstakingly replaced. It will be 2008 before new software systems will allow engineers in Toulouse and Hamburg to work together and avoid any rewiring.[80]

The first passenger-carrying plane, for Singapore Airlines, is now expected to be delivered in October 2007 with total production delays estimated to cost up to $6bn.[81]

● CHAPTER SUMMARY

In this chapter we have looked at how organizations configure themselves to achieve cost and differentiation advantage: Value chain analysis lets us pinpoint the *particular* capabilities and assets that are important to an organization and show *precisely* where and how they are being applied to add value.

The value chain consists of a number of primary and support activities. Each activity can contribute to cost and/or differentiation advantage by virtue of:

- the resources deployed in the activity;
- the extent to which it is vertically integrated or outsourced;
- its scale and scope;
- its location;
- its linkages with other activities.

Different types of generic value chain can be used for the analysis of an organization, depending on whether it is a manufacturing-style organization, a professional services organization, or a network.

Value chain analysis is most valuable if used to identify the distinctive elements that give an organization cost and differentiation advantage, rather than as a framework for cataloguing every aspect of every activity.

Online Resource Centre

www.oxfordtextbooks.co.uk/orc/haberberg_rieple/

Visit the Online Resource Centre that accompanies this book to read more information relating to distinctiveness.

● KEY SKILLS

The key skills you should have developed after reading this chapter are:

- the ability to construct a value chain analysis for a number of different types of organization, showing where in each activity the organization is able to add value to its cost or differentiation advantage, and where not. In some cases this will be assessed through the use of qualitative data, in other, more rare examples where suitable quantitative data are available you will also be able to calculate the precise contribution that each activity makes to the organization's profits and/or costs;
- the ability to select the appropriate model of a value chain to use according to the organization's business type.

● REVIEW QUESTIONS

1. Are the following types of organization manufacturing-style, professional services or network organizations?

    (a) a firm of painters and decorators

    (b) an insurance company

    (c) an insurance broker

    (d) the rubbish collection department of a local authority

    (e) an up-market clothing firm, such as Versace or Ralph Lauren

2. Draw value chains for:

    (a) Bertelsmann (End-of-chapter Case Study 1.1)

    (b) eBay (End-of-chapter Case Study 4.1)

    (c) the university or college where you are studying

    (d) another organization where you have worked or with which you are familiar

3. How great is the coherence between competitive stance, value chain, culture, and architecture in each of these organizations?

4. For each of your organizations, identify specific areas where costs could be reduced; linkages improved, or differentiation achieved. Be precise, and estimate costs and benefits if you can.

5. Caterpillar, the US manufacturer of earth-moving equipment, extended its 'CAT' brand into a line of jeans and hard-wearing leisure clothing. Why was it not afraid that Levi-Strauss would retaliate by entering Caterpillar's core business? (Try using the value chain to structure your answer.)

6. In ten years time, do you think that all organizations will have virtual value chains? What may make this more likely? What would make it less so?

● FURTHER READING

Value chain

● A collection of some of the classic articles that have appeared in *Harvard Business Review* on the topic of value chain management has been collated into a book: *Harvard Business Review on Managing the Value Chain* (2000). Boston, MA: Harvard Business School Press.

● Some other useful books on various aspects of value chains of value and supply chain management are: Bruhn, M. (2005). *Services Marketing: Managing the Service Value Chain*. Harlow: FT Prentice Hall; Tapscott, D. (2000). *Digital Capital: Harnessing the Power of Business Webs*. London: Nicholas Brealey.

Logistics and supply chain management

● Christopher, M. (2004). *Logistics and Supply Chain Management: Creating Value—Adding Networks*. Harlow: FT Prentice Hall—probably the best known European author on the topic.

● Holweg, M. and Pil, F. K. (2005). *Second Century: Reconnecting Customer and Value Chain Through Build-to-Order*. Cambridge, MA: MIT Press, which discusses the strategic implications of just-in-time systems, and the increasing requirement for mass-customized products.

Vertical integration and outsourcing

● Greaver, M. (1999). *Strategic Outsourcing: A Structured Approach to Outsourcing Decisions and Initiatives*. New York: Amacom.

● Doz, Y. and Hamel, G. (1998). *Alliance Advantage: The Art of Creating Value Through Partnering*. Boston, MA: Harvard Business School Press.

● And the classic author, from whom much of the theory on outsourcing and vertical disintegration stems: Williamson, O. (1985). *The Economic Institutions of Capitalism*. New York: Free Press, and Williamson, O. (1975). *Markets and Hierarchies: Analysis and Antitrust Implications*. New York: Free Press.

● REFERENCES

Alexander, M. (1997). 'Getting to grips with the virtual organization'. *Long Range Planning*, 30/1: 122–4.

Baden-Fuller, C., Targett, D., and Hunt, B. (2000). 'Outsourcing to outmanoeuvre: outsourcing re-defines competitive strategy and structure'. *European Management Journal*, 18/3: 285–95.

Barney, J. (1999). 'How a firm's capabilities affect boundary decisions'. *Sloan Management Review*, 40/3: 137–45.

Barney, J. (2002). *Gaining and Sustaining Competitive Advantage*. 2nd edn. Harlow: Prentice Hall.

Benjamin, R. and Wigand, R. (1995). 'Electronic markets and virtual value chains on the information superhighway'. *Sloan Management Review*, 36/2: 62–72.

Bettis, R. A., Bradley, S., and Hamel, G. (1992). 'Outsourcing and industrial decline'. *Academy of Management Executive*, 6: 7–22.

Brouthers, K. D. and Brouthers, L. E. (2003). 'Why service and manufacturing entry mode choices differ: the influence of transaction cost factors, risk and trust'. *Journal of Management Studies*, 40/5: 1179–204.

Bunyaratavej, K., Hahn, E. D., and Doh, J. P. (2007). 'International offshoring of services: A parity study'. *Journal of International Management*, 13/1: 7–21.

Chesbrough, H. W. and Teece, D. J. (1996). 'When is virtual virtuous? Organizing for innovation'. *Harvard Business Review*, 74: 65–73.

Chiles, T. and McMackin, J. F. (1996). 'Integrating variable risk preferences, trust and transaction cost economics'. *Academy of Management Review*, 21/1: 73–99.

Dahlström, K. and Ekins, P. (2006). 'Combining economic and environmental dimensions: value chain analysis of UK iron and steel flows'. *Ecological Economics*, 58/3: 507–19.

Das, T. K. and Teng, B.-S. (2002). 'Alliance constellations: A social exchange perspective'. *Academy of Management Review*, 27: 445–56.

DeFillippi, R. and Arthur, M. (1998). 'Paradox in project-based enterprise: the case of film making'. *California Management Review*, 40/2: 125–39.

Donaldson, L. (1995). *American Anti-management Theories of Organization*. Cambridge: Cambridge University Press.

Doz, Y. and Hamel, G. (1997). 'The use of technology alliances in implementing technology strategies'. In Tushman, M. L. and Anderson, P. (eds), *Managing Strategic Innovation and Change*. New York: Oxford University Press.

Doz, Y. L. and Hamel, G. (1998). *Alliance Advantage; The Art of Creating Value Through Partnering*. Cambridge: Harvard Business School Press.

Evans, P. B. and Wurster, T. S. (1997). 'Strategy and the new economics of information'. *Harvard Business Review*, September–October: 70–82.

Faulkner, R. R. and Anderson, A. B. (1987). 'Short-term projects; emergent careers: evidence from Hollywood'. *American Journal of Sociology*, 92: 879–909.

Gander, J. and Rieple, P. A. (2002). 'Inter-organisational relationships in the worldwide popular recorded music industry'. *Creativity and Innovation Management*, 11: 248–54.

Gander, J. and Rieple, P. A. (2004). 'How relevant is transaction cost economics to inter-firm relationships in the music industry?' *Journal of Cultural Economics*, 28: 57–79.

Gander, J., Haberberg, A. B., and Rieple, P. A. (2005). 'Hybrid organizations as a strategy for supporting new product development'. *Design Management Review*, 16/1: 48–56.

Gander, J., Haberberg, A. B., and Rieple, P. A. (2007). 'A paradox of alliance management: resource contamination in the recorded music industry'. *Journal of Organizational Behavior*, 28: 1–18.

Gibson, C. and Gibbs J. (2006). 'Unpacking the concept of virtuality: the effects of geographic dispersion, electronic dependence, dynamic structure, and national diversity on team innovation'. *Administrative Science Quarterly*, 51/3: 451–95.

Gibson, P. R. (2004). 'The strategic importance of e-commerce in modern supply chains'. *Journal of Electronic Commerce in Organizations*, 2/3: 59–76.

Gilley, M. and Rasheed, A. (2000). 'Making more by doing less: an analysis of outsourcing and its effects on firm performance'. *Journal of Management*, 26/4: 763–90.

Gosain, S., Malhotra, A., and El Sawy, O. (2004). 'Coordinating for flexibility in e-business supply chains'. *Journal of Management Information Systems*, 21/3: 7–45.

Gosain, S. and Palmer, J. W. (2004). 'Exploring strategic choices in marketplace positioning'. *Electronic Markets*, 14/4: 308–21.

Grant, R. (1998). *Contemporary Strategy Analysis*. 3rd edn. Blackwell, Oxford.

Handfield, R. B. and Nichols, E. L. (2002). *Supply Chain Redesign: Transforming Supply Chains into Integrated Value Systems*. Upper Saddle River, NJ: Prentice-Hall.

Harrison, A. E. and McMillan, M. S. (2006). 'Dispelling some myths about offshoring'. *Academy of Management Perspectives*, 20/4: 6–22.

Hendry, C., Brown, J., and DeFillippi, R. (2000). 'Regional clustering of high-technology-based firms: opto-electronics in three countries'. *Regional Studies*, 34/2: 129–44.

Hill, C. and Jones, G. (1998) *Strategic Management—An Integrated Approach*. 4th edn. Boston: Houghton Mifflin.

Husted, B. W. and Folger, R. (2004). 'Fairness and transaction costs: the contribution of organizational justice theory to an integrative model of economic organization'. *Organization Science*, 15/6: 719–29.

Johnsson, T. and Hägg, I. (1987). 'Extrapreneurs: between markets and hierarchies'. *International Studies of Management and Organization*, 17/1: 64–74.

Kauffman, R. J. and Walden, E. A. (2001). 'Economics and electronic commerce: survey and directions for research'. *International Journal of Electronic Commerce*, 5/4: 5–116.

Khan, M. N. and Azmi, F. T. (2005). 'Reinventing business organisations: the information culture framework'. *Singapore Management Review*, 27/2: 37–62.

Kiely, T. (1997). 'Business processes: consider outsourcing'. *Harvard Business Review*, 75/3: 11–12.

Kling, R. and Wigand, R. T. (1997). 'Electronic commerce: definition, theory, and context'. *Information Society*, 13/1: 1–16.

Kotabe, M., Martin, X., and Domoto, H. (2003). 'Gaining from vertical partnerships: Knowledge transfer, relationship duration, and supplier performance improvement in the U.S. and Japanese automotive industries'. *Strategic Management Journal*, 24: 293–316.

Larsson, R., Brousseau, K. R., Driver, M. J., Holmqvist, M., and Tarnovskaya, V. (2003). 'International growth through cooperation: brand-driven strategies, leadership, and career development in Sweden'. *Academy of Management Executive*, 17/1: 7–24.

Lawton, T. C. and Michaels, K. P. (2001). 'Advancing to the virtual value chain: learning from the Dell model'. *Irish Journal of Management*, 22/1: 91.

McCubbrey, D. J. and Taylor, R. G. (2005). 'Disintermediation and reintermediation in the U.S. air travel distribution industry: a Delphi reprise'. *Communications of AIS*, 15: 464–77.

Mahnke, V. (2005). 'Strategic outsourcing of it services: theoretical stocktaking and empirical challenges'. *Industry and Innovation*, 12/2: 205–53.

Mayer, K. J. and Salomon, R. M. (2006). 'Capabilities, contractual hazards, and governance: integrating resource-based and transaction cost perspectives'. *Academy of Management Journal*, 49/5: 942–59.

Mazur, L. (1999). 'Why marketing is too important for outsourcing'. *Marketing*, 8 July: 16.

Miller, D. and Shamsie, J. (1996). 'The resource-based view of the firm in two environments: the Hollywood film studios from 1936 to 1965'. *Academy of Management Journal*, 39/3: 519–43.

Mol, J., Wijnberg, N., and Carrol, C. (2005). 'Value chain envy: explaining new entry and vertical integration in popular music'. *Journal of Management Studies*, 42/2: 251–76.

Murray, J. Y. and Kotabe, M. (1999). 'Sourcing strategies of US service companies: A modified transaction-cost analysis'. *Strategic Management Journal*, 20/9: 791–809.

Murray, J. Y. and Kotabe, M. (2005). 'Performance implications of strategic fit between alliance attributes and alliance forms'. *Journal of Business Research*, 58/11: 1525–33.

Nassimbeni, G. (1998). 'Network structures and co-ordination mechanisms'. *International Journal of Operations & Production Management*, 18: 538–55.

Nathan, John (1999). *Sony: The Private Life*. New York: Houghton Mifflin.

Poppo, L. and Zenger, T. (1998). 'Testing alternative theories of the firm: transaction cost, knowledge-based and measurement explanations for make-or-buy decisions in information services'. *Strategic Management Journal*, 19: 853–77.

Porter, M. (1985). *Competitive Advantage*. New York: Free Press.

Porter, M. E. (1990). *The Competitive Advantage of Nations*. New York: Free Press.

Porter, M. E. and Stern, S. (2001). 'Innovation: location matters'. *Sloan Management Review*, 42/4.

Prahalad, C. K. and Ramaswamy, V. (2000). 'Co-opting customer competence'. *Harvard Business Review*, 78/1: 79–88.

Prahalad, C. K. and Ramaswamy, V. (2003). 'The new frontier, of experience innovation'. *Sloan Management Review*, 44/4: 12–18.

Prahalad, C. K. and Ramaswamy, V. (2004). *The Future of Competition: Co-creating Unique Value with Customers*. Boston, MA: Harvard Business School Press.

Quinn, J. B. (1999). 'Strategic outsourcing: leveraging knowledge capabilities'. *Sloan Management Review*, 40/4: 9–21.

Quinn, J. B. and Hilmer, F. G. (1995). 'Strategic outsourcing'. *McKinsey Quarterly*, 1: 48–70.

Rasheed, A. A. and Gilley, K. M. (2005). 'Outsourcing: national and firm level implications'. *Thunderbird International Business Review*, 47/5: 513–28.

Rayport, J. F. and Sviokla, J. J. (1995). 'Exploiting the virtual value chain'. *Harvard Business Review*, 73/6: 75–85.

Robins, J. A. (1993). 'Organization as strategy: restructuring production in the film industry'. *Strategic Management Journal*, 14: 103–18.

Shamis, G. S., Green, M. C., Sorensen, S. M., and Kyle, D. L. (2005). 'Outsourcing, offshoring, nearshoring: what to do?' *Journal of Accountancy*, 199/6: 57–61.

Sobek, D. K., Liker, J. K., and Ward. A. (1998). 'Another look at how Toyota integrates product development'. *Harvard Business Review*, 76/4: 36–50.

Sobek, D. K., Ward, A., and Liker, J. (1999). 'Principles from Toyota's set-based concurrent engineering process'. *Sloan Management Review*, 40/2: 67–83.

Spekman, R., Forbes, T., Isabella, L., and MacAvoy, T. (1998). 'Alliance management: a view from the past and a look to the future'. *Journal of Management Studies*, 35/6: 747–72.

Stabell, C. B. and Fjeldstad, Ø. D. (1998). 'Configuring value for competitive advantage: on chains, shops, and networks'. *Strategic Management Journal*, 19: 413–37.

Steensma, H. K. and Corley, K. G. (2000). 'On the performance of technology-sourcing partnerships: the interaction between partner interdependence and technology attributes'. *Academy of Management Journal*, 43/6: 1045–67.

Steensma, H. K. and Corley, K. G. (2001). 'Organizational context as a moderator of theories on firm boundaries for technology sourcing'. *Academy of Management Journal*, 44/2: 271–91.

Steensma, H. K., Marino, L., Weaver, K. M., and Dickson, P. H. (2000). 'The influence of national culture on the formation of technology alliances by entrepreneurial firms'. *Academy of Management Journal*, 43: 951–73.

Strebinger, A. and Treiblmaier, H. (2006). 'The impact of business to consumer e-commerce on organizational structure, brand architecture, IT structure, and their interrelations'. *Schmalenbach Business Review*, 58/1: 81–113.

Turnipseed, D., Rassuli, A., Sardessai, R., and Duns, C. P. (1999). 'A history and evaluation of Boeing's coalition strategy with Japan in aircraft development and production'. *International Journal of Commerce & Management*, 9/1–2: 59–83.

Urbaczewski, A. and Jessup, L. M. (1998).
'A manager's primer in electronic commerce'.
Business Horizons, 41/5: 5.

Urbaczewski, A., Jessup, L. M., and Wheeler, B.
(2002). 'Electronic commerce research: a
taxonomy and synthesis'. *Journal of
Organizational Computing & Electronic
Commerce*, 12/4: 263–305.

Uzzi, B. (1997). 'Social structure; competition
in interfirm networks: the paradox of
embeddedness'. *Administrative Science
Quarterly*, 42: 35–67.

Venkatraman, N. and Henderson, J. C. (1998).
'Real strategies for virtual organizing'.
Sloan Management Review, 40/1: 33–48.

Williamson, O. (1975). *Markets and Hierarchies*.
New York: Free Press.

Williamson, O. E. (1991). 'Comparative economic
organization: the analysis of discrete structural
alternatives'. *Administrative Science Quarterly*,
36/2: 269–96.

Womack, J. and Jones, D. (1996). *Lean Thinking:
Banish Waste and Create Wealth in Your
Corporation*. New York: Simon and Schuster.

End-of-chapter Case Study 6.1 CEMEX S.A.B. de C.V.

A Mexican company, CEMEX is the world's third largest cement company. *CEMEX*

CEMEX is the largest building solutions firm in Mexico, the world's third largest cement company, and the largest producer of concrete mix. Its turnover is close to that of Switzerland's Holcim, the world's second largest cement company behind the world leader, France's Lafarge. In 2004, CEMEX employed 26,000 people, and had a turnover of $8bn (Figure 6.7, page 270). Its turnover has more than trebled over the last decade and it has doubled profits in the same period. In 1998 CEMEX was voted Latin America's most respected company, along with Petrobras of Brazil and YPF of Argentina, and was the only Latin American company to feature in the list of the world's most respected property/construction companies, in fifth place.[82]

Its current CEO, 61-year-old Lorenzo Zambrano, worked for the company for 18 years before being appointed CEO in 1985. He is the grandson of one of the founders. Under Mr Zambrano, CEMEX has developed from a firm that was principally based in Mexico to one that is global, both in its geographic scale (with operations in more than fifty countries) and its product characteristics. This has been achieved through a combination of innovation in logistics, fuel supply and IT, and acquisitions.

CEMEX operates out of Mexico, a country that neighbours the USA, but which has many of the characteristics of third-world countries—currency crises, economic instability, high inflation and costs of capital, corruption, poor institutional and transport infrastructure, and 'chaotic' legal systems.[83] Some commentators have argued that CEMEX's success is down to its having been forced to cope with this environment, resulting in innovative capabilities that have become world-beating.[84]

Mexico is also a country with a young and growing population, and a shortage of good-quality housing. In 2001, Mexico's ➤

	2004	2003	change
Net sales	8,149	7,164	14%
Operating income	1,852	1,455	27%
EBITDA	2,538	2,108	20%
Consolidated net income	1,328	659	101%
Earnings per ADR[2]	3.93	1.99	97%
Free cash flow	1,478	1,143	29%
Total assets	17,381	16,016	9%
Net debt[3]	5,588	5,641	(1%)
Stockholders' equity, majority interest	7,831	6,234	26%

Figure 6.7 CEMEX financials. Source: 2004 Annual Report. *Reproduced with the kind permission of CEMEX*

→ newly elected president promised that every peasant shack in the country would have its mud floor cemented by the time he left office.[85] For many years this location provided a growth market for CEMEX, which mainly sold its cement to individual house-owners who bought small quantities from their local hardware shop. About half of CEMEX' Mexican sales are still made to people building their own houses. It uses a strong branding strategy to sell to this group, and has seven regional brands throughout Mexico, many of which it obtained through acquisition. In fact CEMEX models itself on fast-moving consumer goods (FMCG) companies like Procter & Gamble rather than western cement companies, which generally sell in bulk.[86] As such, it competes for a share of a relatively small disposable income with entertainment or clothes.

There are few large public-works building projects in Mexico. This feature makes it uneconomic for the large bulk-suppliers of cement that are the norm in the developed world to import their cement to Mexico, a factor exacerbated by the poor transport infrastructure. Cement is difficult to transport overland cheaply —its economic limit is about 400km—so plants need to be near construction sites. Although cement can be shipped by sea, some of the biggest population centres in Mexico, like its capital Mexico City, lie inland. Foreign competitors would have had to develop costly distribution networks to compete with local manufacturers, although the saturation of the market in Europe, for example, has meant that there has been some attempt to break into the developing world's markets. CEMEX is the largest

manufacturer of cement and concrete in Mexico, with approximately 45 per cent market share, second is Holcim's local division Apasco. The three main producers have something like 80 per cent of the market between them.[87]

Entry of the international companies has commonly been through the acquisition of a local producer whose cement can profitably be exported by sea. As the major firms already have big shipping operations, they can use cement produced in the developing world to smooth out supplies, allowing them to maintain stable prices.

International expansion

Over the years, CEMEX has engaged in an ambitious series of international acquisitions, part of a global trend towards consolidation in the still relatively fragmented cement industry.[89] In 2004, the top-five cement makers world-wide had just over 20 per cent of the market, and most of the remaining manufacturers in Europe, for example, are relatively small and family owned.

CEMEX began its international expansion in the mid-1980s when Mexico started to dismantle its protectionist trade barriers and the country was opened to foreign competitors. CEMEX found itself competing with large international companies at a time of increasing consolidation in the world cement industry. Its response was to sell its other businesses to focus on its core product, and to embark on a series of acquisitions. It first →

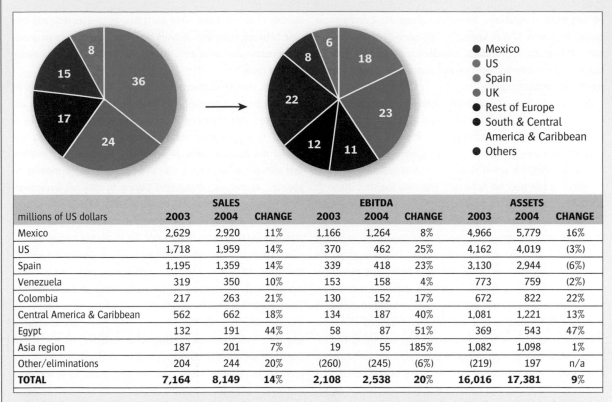

millions of US dollars	SALES 2003	SALES 2004	CHANGE	EBITDA 2003	EBITDA 2004	CHANGE	ASSETS 2003	ASSETS 2004	CHANGE
Mexico	2,629	2,920	11%	1,166	1,264	8%	4,966	5,779	16%
US	1,718	1,959	14%	370	462	25%	4,162	4,019	(3%)
Spain	1,195	1,359	14%	339	418	23%	3,130	2,944	(6%)
Venezuela	319	350	10%	153	158	4%	773	759	(2%)
Colombia	217	263	21%	130	152	17%	672	822	22%
Central America & Caribbean	562	662	18%	134	187	40%	1,081	1,221	13%
Egypt	132	191	44%	58	87	51%	369	543	47%
Asia region	187	201	7%	19	55	185%	1,082	1,098	1%
Other/eliminations	204	244	20%	(260)	(245)	(6%)	(219)	197	n/a
TOTAL	**7,164**	**8,149**	**14%**	**2,108**	**2,538**	**20%**	**16,016**	**17,381**	**9%**

Figure 6.8 CEMEX international operations. Source: 2004 Annual Report. *Reproduced with the kind permission of CEMEX*

→ bought its two main domestic rivals, Cementos Anahuac and Cementos Tolteca. Between 1992 and 1996, CEMEX acquired cement plants in Venezuela, the USA, Panama, Colombia, and the Dominican Republic, markets where sales of cement also tend to be in individual bags, and in Spain. At the time, the $1.85bn purchase of Spain's Sanson and Valenciana was Mexico's largest ever international acquisition.

Since then CEMEX has acquired other major cement firms in South America and the USA. In 2000 it acquired Houston-based Southdown, America's second biggest cement manufacturer, for $2.8bn, making it the number one in terms of market share in the USA. Southdown had twelve cement plants and 45 distribution centres in the American south-west and Florida. This acquisition allowed it to overcome high import tariffs, brought about by domestic producers who had argued that CEMEX sold at below-market prices.

In the late 1990s and early 2000s, CEMEX also expanded into Asia, taking over operations in Thailand, the Philippines, Taiwan, Bangladesh, and Indonesia. In 1999, CEMEX bought 90 per cent of Assiut, Egypt's largest cement producer. By 2004, two-thirds of its operations were outside Mexico (Figure 6.8). It has said it is considering expanding into China and India, especially when opportunities that meet CEMEX's investment criteria are found.

Its most recent, and perhaps most ambitious, move was the 2005 takeover of RMC, Britain's biggest cement company and the world's biggest ready-mixed concrete maker, for £2.3bn ($4bn), the largest acquisition ever by a Mexican company. This deal doubled CEMEX's turnover and number of employees.

CEMEX claimed that the motivation for the RMC acquisition was 1) to enhance its position as one of the world's largest building materials companies, with a global presence in cement and aggregates and a leading position in ready mix concrete; 2) to enhance its growth platform and to diversify its geographic base by strengthening its presence in the US; and 3) to give it an important position in mature markets in Western Europe and exposure to high-growth markets in Eastern Europe. CEMEX managers thought that these areas would grow quickly after joining the EU. RMC also has operations in the UK, Germany, and Malaysia. However, some analysts criticized the move for taking CEMEX away from its core strength of selling cement in developing economies; instead it has become a developed-market company with a different risk/return profile as a consequence.[90]

Although the integration of RMC would be a daunting task, Southdown had already shown how CEMEX could release value from acquisitions, making it more profitable than either of its →

→ two major competitors, Holcim or Lafarge. Mr Zambrano expected to achieve $200m savings by 2007 through 'standardizing some management processes, capitalizing on trading network benefits, consolidating logistics and improving global procurement and energy efficiency'.[91]

To turn around its acquisitions, CEMEX is disciplined in reducing costs. It dispatches a hit squad of company experts to new plants to negotiate with suppliers, increase efficiency, and improve marketing strategies. It also implements its proprietary centralized logistics and IT systems on its acquisitions, systems for which it has become famous.[92] Improved logistics alone at Southdown were said to have saved $15m a year, 5 per cent of the company's pre-tax profits. In each case, 'post-merger integration teams' armed with laptops are dispatched to deploy the 'CEMEX Way' on the acquired firm.[93] This is a corporate philosophy that involves 'wholeheartedly embracing new technology and imposing tightly controlled standards worldwide, for both its technology and in-house management techniques'.[94] It does this because it is a consciously globalized company, selling one identical product the world over and using English as its lingua franca, even though most executives are Mexican. The CEMEX Way specifies even the make of computers that employees must use, and ensures that post-acquisition organizational communication is smooth. CEMEX has now become expert at this process. Some commentators estimated that turning its two Spanish acquisitions into true subsidiaries took 18 months, whereas the more recent and much bigger Southdown took four.[95]

IT and logistics

Its experience in selling cement as a type of FMCG, as well as integration of acquisitions, means that CEMEX's competence in managing complex logistics is also exceptional. The need to regularly communicate with its thousands of retailers and make sure they had an adequate inventory, gave the company a powerful incentive to computerize its logistics and carry out most of its transactions online. Ready-mix concrete is just as much of a problem, as it needs to be poured within 90 minutes of mixing.

It has developed a logistics system that uses 'dazzlingly complex computer systems'.[96] This is based on the same GPS technology as the emergency systems of major US cities,[97] FedEx's model of coordinating aeroplanes and lorries, and an algorithmic tool based on chaos theory. A computer and a GPS receiver are placed in every lorry, and then matched with the output at the plants and orders from customers, whilst an algorithm calculates the most efficient routes for the delivery lorries. As a result CEMEX has been able to substantially increase the

number of orders it can meet each day, as well as reducing the time between order and delivery time from three hours to under 20 minutes—the same sort of promise as that made by pizza delivery firms.

CEMEX uses IT in many other aspects of its operations. The company began automating its manufacturing operations at an early stage. This allows each large cement plant to be run by a handful of people. Even some aspects of quality checking are carried out automatically. It developed a proprietary program that allows it to plan each month's purchases three months in advance, as well as centralizing buying to take full advantage of the company's global nature. As a result CEMEX can obtain better prices and reduce working capital. It has also implemented standardized IT systems that enable the sharing of market intelligence amongst divisions as well as suppliers. Before the end of the 1980s, CEMEX had set up a satellite network that allowed management information to be transmitted to headquarters. This meant that senior executives could check sales figures or kiln temperatures on the network, and then 'ask managers why their units were not keeping up to scratch'.[98] As staff knew that they were under observation, their performance began to improve. In addition, some data are distributed to lower-level employees allowing 'a healthy degree of competition' between different units.

In 2000, the company spun off its internal IT unit, Cemtec, and along with four other Spanish and Latin American firms with a total turnover of about $100m, created an IT consultancy subsidiary Neoris, based in Miami. Neoris was regarded as a means of expanding into e-business but also had other aims. One was to set up a construction-industry on-line market-place, with the intention of improving the efficiency of the process in Latin America and cutting out some of the sometimes shady middlemen. Over time it was also expected to provide other services, such as a discussion forum for everyone involved in a specific construction project, where, for example, updated blueprints could be put online, or as a site where insurance, financing, or other linked services could be bought.[99]

In time Neoris is expected to steer the company towards all its operations becoming web-based, including employees' own files, financial data, and outside information, allowing staff worldwide access to the same information.

Fuel

CEMEX is a pioneer of alternative fuels too. Energy efficiency is another reason that CEMEX has higher profit margins than its two major competitors. In 2004/2005, a period when energy prices rose considerably, CEMEX's energy cost increased by only 3 per cent.[100] And it had already cut its energy bills by 17 per cent →

➜ over the previous four years.[101] Not surprisingly, CEMEX uses IT to maximize its use of cheaper off-peak electricity.

Each one of CEMEX' 54 cement plants consumes the same amount of energy as a small town. Energy accounts for up to 40 per cent of operating costs in the cement industry. Most companies use coal; however, over the previous ten years, CEMEX spent $150m refitting its plants so they could use cheaper fuels such as pet (petroleum) coke, a residue from the oil-refining industry, and industrial waste like oily rags.

A strong motivation for this development was the need to guarantee long-term access to a plentiful fuel source with stable prices. This was a problem that was not helped by Mexico's poor infrastructure; the country's ports were too shallow for the big tankers that carry coal. Another motivation for this move was the fear that electricity shortages would worsen as Mexico's economy expanded. Although other alternative fuels were considered, such as old tyres and plastic bottles, which are used in some European plants, these could not be obtained in sufficient quantities or reliably enough.

Pet coke has been used occasionally by cement manufacturers for many years. It burns hotter than coal, and is much cheaper. But supply problems had previously prevented it from becoming a primary fuel source, and it tended to clog kilns when burned. CEMEX managed to overcome these problems, using knowledge gained from one of its Spanish acquisitions who were using the fuel, and pet coke now accounts for between one-quarter and one-half of its fuel needs. CEMEX's plants in Mexico, Spain, and Latin America now run mostly on pet coke. In addition to pet coke, some plants use other alternative fuels. Industrial waste supplies a further 5 per cent to 10 per cent of the Mexican plants' fuel needs, and in Spain, they use ground bonemeal, which burns nearly as hot as coal. In CEMEX's 13 US plants, pet coke supplies up to half CEMEX's fuel needs, the rest coming from coal.

To acquire pet coke, CEMEX set up a subsidiary in Houston which negotiates directly with oil refineries, and which supplies the company worldwide. This allows CEMEX to sign for large-scale, long-term contracts. It also guarantees the 'removal of every bit of pet coke at an entire refinery'[102]—thereby helping the refineries to dispose of their waste, for which they would otherwise have to pay. This latter service means that CEMEX is, in effect, being paid to collect some of its energy supply. The pet coke is then shipped to all the company's plants around the world, an innovation for an industry where individual plants have traditionally ordered their own fuel supplies. Any surplus is sold elsewhere, also making profits for the company.

CEMEX has also diversified into other power-related businesses. In 2004, it opened its own 230-megawatt power plant fuelled by pet coke. This guarantees electricity for the company during the frequent power shortages in Mexico. It also makes CEMEX money, as its output is cheaper than Mexico's own state-owned generator. After 6 pm, when electricity prices increase, CEMEX cuts back on its own usage and starts selling every watt it can to the government. Sometimes this means they are more profitable as a power company than a cement manufacturer.[103]

Financing

Another supply challenge concerns CEMEX's ability to raise funds for expansion. In common with other major firms from developing economies, the national financing infrastructure cannot supply the company with the capital it needs.[104] As a result, CEMEX was listed on European stock exchanges via Valenciana, its Spanish subsidiary, to centre its operations in Europe. Already, with CEMEX's debt financing largely carried out by Valenciana, and with an investment grade credit rating its borrowing costs were very competitive.

CSR

Because of its leadership of the Mexican market, and the desire to create sustainable value for all its stakeholders, CEMEX has strong corporate social responsibility programmes. These include large-scale environmental and conservation projects. But they also extend to providing additional benefits for the company's customers and their friends and relations. Most of CEMEX's Mexican clientele are small family-owned hardware stores—4,000 or so in Mexico City alone—whose owners want to build a business that they can pass on to their children. In order to respond to this, CEMEX created the 'Construrama' network in Mexico, whose members typically sell only CEMEX cement, although the company cannot legally require them to do so. Retailers receive consulting advice into the running of their business and also on building and construction, so that their members can in turn train their employees and families. Shop owners join for free and receive a new computer from CEMEX, which also pays half the cost of Construrama signage and store painting. CEMEX uses its buying power to help its distributors buy other hardware products at lower prices.

And in 2001, CEMEX opened a chain of shops in the US for Mexican immigrants seeking to build houses back home. It has been estimated that up to 20 per cent of the $9bn sent home to their families by the 15 million Mexicans living in the USA goes into house building.[105] A service provided by CEMEX' shops, called Construmex, allows low-income, US-based Mexicans to buy building materials, which is then delivered to their families in Mexico.[106] CEMEX decided to provide this ➜

→ service to deal with the high currency commission charges that transactions between the two countries accrued (sometimes as high as 12 per cent; in contrast, CEMEX charges 1 per cent), but also in response to the frustration felt by some emigrants who saw the money they sent being spent on parties and weddings rather than on re-modelling their homes. However, lest it be thought that CEMEX is a party-pooper—when one of CEMEX's Mexican house-builder customers finishes their home, the company has been known to participate in the neighbourhood get-together!

Case study questions

1. Draw a value chain for CEMEX identifying key linkages and areas where the company has distinctive competences.

2. Given the recent developments in the cement and concrete industry, where in the value chain should CEMEX now concentrate its strategic resources?

3. Is CEMEX a manufacturing company, a service manufacturer, a professional service, or a network-style organization? Explain your answer.

● NOTES

1 We are following conventional practice here in using the term 'value chain', although it is rather misleading. A chain implies a nice linear sequence of links and, as you will see later in this chapter, value chains in practice are far less tidy. A more accurate term would be 'value web' or 'value network'.

2 As we suggested in Chapter 1, a large and influential body of theory deals with these issues, broadly under the heading of transaction cost economics. This field was started off by Oliver Williamson (see Williamson, 1975, 1991). His work has since been taken up by a wide variety of writers (the present authors included) who are interested in, for example, the recent increase in networked organizational forms and the need to protect critical competences within specialist units. See for example Steensma and Corley (2005); Gilley and Rasheed (2000). See Mahnke (2005) for a recent discussion of the outsourcing of the special case of services.

3 See, for example, Bunyaratavej et al. (2007); Harrison and McMillan (2006); Shamis et al. (2005).

4 See, for example, Johnsson and Hägg (1987).

5 The term 'value stream' is used by Womack and Jones (1996); other authors (for example Handfield and Nichols (2002). Mol et al. (2005); Nassimbeni (1998); Steensma et al. (2000) tend to use the term supply chain or value system—they mean much the same thing.

6 A large number of writers have discussed the increasing prevalence of strategic alliances. See, for example, Doz and Hamel (1998); Spekman et al. (1998).

7 For recent discussions on transaction costs see Barney (1999), Das and Teng (2002); Mayer and Salomon (2006); and Gander and Rieple (2004).

8 For more detail see Barney (2002).

9 It also happens in the job market, when applicants 'embroider' their CV to make themselves more attractive to potential employers.

10 Particularly in service industries, empirical research does not always support the idea that transaction costs *alone* can explain firms' vertical integration decisions. See Poppo and Zenger (1998); Kotabe et al. (2003); and Murray and Kotabe (1999 and 2005). This also applies to industries where creativity is a key resource (see Gander and Rieple, 2004, on the music industry; Robins, 1993 and Faulkner and Anderson, 1987, on film, and Uzzi, 1997, on fashion).

11 See, for example, Donaldson (1995: ch. 6); Chiles and McMackin (1996); Brouthers and Brouthers (2003); and Husted and Folger (2004).

12 Based principally on: H&M's annual reports 2003–2006, and Christopher Brown-Humes. *Financial Times*. 16 April 2004: 24.

13 UK clothing retailing industry. *Mintel*, August 2003.

14 See for example Benjamin and Wigand (1995); Rayport and Sviokla (1995); Alexander (1997); Lawton and Michaels (2001); Venkatraman and Henderson (1998); Gibson and Gibbs (2006); Gibson (2004); Gosain et al. (2004); Gosain and Palmer (2004); Strebinger and Treiblmaier (2006); Kauffman and Walden (2001); Urbaczewski et al. (2002); Kling and Wigand (1997); Urbaczewski and Jessup (1998).

15 Khan and Azmi (2005).

16 The term appears to have been coined by Evans and Wurster (1997).

17 Prahalad and Ramaswamy (2000). See also McCubbrey and Taylor (2005) for a discussion of disintermediation.

18 Rome, J. (2007). 'Multi-channel retailing in the UK fashion industry, case study'. CEPLW, University of Westminster.

19 *Economist* (2006). A survey of logistics: manufacturing complexity. 17 June.

20 *Economist* (2006) op. cit.

21 BA's partners in the oneworld alliance include Aer Lingus, American Airlines, Cathay Pacific, Finnair, Iberia, LANChile, and Qantas. SkyTeam includes Aeroflot, Aeromexico, Air France, Alitalia, Continental Airlines, CSA Czech Airlines, Delta Air Lines, KLM, Korean Air, and Northwest Airlines. The Star Alliance includes Air Canada, Air New Zealand, ANA, Asian Airlines, Austrian Airlines, bmi, LOT Polish Airlines, Lufthansa, SAS Scandinavian Airlines, Singapore Airlines, Spanair, TAP Air Portugal, Thai Airways International, United Airlines, US Airways, and VARIG.

22 Nathan (1999).

23 Sony Corporation Annual Reports, 2002–2007.

24 Turnipseed et al. (1999).

25 Sources: <http://www.airbus.com/en/corporate/people/Airbus_short_history.html> accessed 4 July 2006; Cochennec, Y. (2005). 'Genesis of a giant'. *Interavia Business and Technology*, 679: 14–19; Rossant, J. (2000). 'Birth of a giant'. *Business Week*, 3689.

26 See, for example, Braddorn, D. and Hartley, K. (2007). 'The competitiveness of the UK aerospace industry'. *Applied Economics*, 39/6: 715–26; Lawrence, P. K. and Thornton, D. W. D. (2005). *Deep Stall: The Turbulent Story Of Boeing Commercial Airplanes*. Aldershot: Ashgate Publishing; and Varga, L. and Allen, P. M. (2006). 'A case-study of the three largest aerospace manufacturing organizations: an exploration of organizational strategy, innovation and evolution'. *Emergence: Complexity and Organization*, 8/2: 48–64.

27 See Wallace, R. (1992). 'IBM, Siemens, Toshiba tie up for 0.25-Micron Tech—Dram Dream Team'. *Electronic Engineering Times*. 20 July. The alliance is also described in Doz and Hamel (1997).

28 We have written on this topic elsewhere: see Gander et al. (2005, 2007); Gander and Rieple (2002, 2004). See also DeFillippi and Arthur (1998); Hendry et al. (2000); Porter (1990); Porter and Stearn (2001).

29 Both are now owned by the Netherlands-registered Ingka Holdings: see Warnaby, G. (1999). 'Strategic consequences of retail acquisition: IKEA and Habitat'. *International Marketing Review*, 16/4–5: 406–17.

30 Porter (1985): 48–53.

31 Much of the analysis in this section comes from Stabell and Fjeldstad (1998). We have altered their terminology a little to make it easier to understand.

32 The value chain presented here combines elements of Michael Porter's value chain (Porter, 1985: 37), The McKinsey Business System (Grant, 1998: 121), and the version proposed by Hill and Jones (1998).

33 Porter calls this 'technology development' and uses it to encompass both product and process development. We prefer to separate out product development from process development. It is actually quite difficult to find a logical place to analyse a firm's basic research activities within Porter's framework.

34 Porter calls this activity 'Firm Infrastructure' and includes quality control within it.

35 For a description of how Toyota involves suppliers in its design processes, and also for a very detailed description of the competences and architecture that enable Toyota to be one of

the motor industry's leaders in product development lead times while using fewer engineers than its American counterparts, see Sobek et al. (1998, 1999). See also Prahalad and Ramaswamy (2000, 2003, 2004) for a discussion of co-creation of products by customers and firms.

36 See the Worked Example on the UK iron and steel industry at <http://www.oxfordtextbooks. co.uk/orc/haberberg_rieple/>.

37 See, for example, reports from Mintel Interbrand and specialist industry consultancies such as A. T. Kearney or Forrester Research; and surveys that report on the companies that have the highest levels of balance-sheet intangibles.

38 This was a project which many of the UK design community rather disdained, as did Margaret Thatcher and many of BA's customers, although we rather liked them! See Beattie, J. (1999). 'Flagging profits, so you're all right, Jack'. *Birmingham Post*, 7 June; *Design Week* (2005). 'Branding: identity crises'. April: 17; Bray, R. (2005). 'Why companies get in a tailspin over tailfins'. *Financial Times*. 15 March; and *Design Week*, 21 April: 17.

39 See, for example, *Economist* (1999). 'The house that Jack built', 18 September: 23–6; and Byrne, J. A. (1998). 'JACK'. *Business Week*, 8 June, 3581: 90–111.

40 See Nee, E. (2001). 'Cisco how it aims to keep right on growing never mind the slowdown'. *Fortune*, 143/3; and *Economist* (2006). 'A survey of logistics: manufacturing complexity'. 17th June.

41 See, for example, *BusinessWeek* (2006). 'H&M: it's the latest thing—really; the lesson: spot shifts in demand and tune your company so you can deliver to the market in weeks, not months'. 27 March, 3977: 70; Murphy, R. (2003). 'France fights back—fast-fashion retailers get nimble and quick'. *Women's Wear Daily*, 19 June; Capell, K. and Khermouch, G. (2002). 'Hip H&M: the Swedish retailer is reinventing the business of affordable fashion'. *BusinessWeek*, 11 November, 3807: 58.

42 Source: H&M press release 27 May 2004, 'H&M strengthens the buying organisation'.

43 Bloomberg.com 29 March 2006.

44 Capell and Khermouch (2002) op. cit.

45 See, for example, H&M Annual Report 2005: 39.

46 H&M Annual Report 2005: 32.

47 Dahlström and Ekins (2006).

48 See, for example, Edmondson, G., Browder, S., and Reinhardt, A. (1998). 'Up, up, and away at last for Airbus?' *Business Week*, 9 February: 58; *Financial Times* (1993). 'Penalties for excess baggage— the airbus consortium'. 1 December; and *Economist* (1991). 'Airbus flies into trouble'. 16 February: 79.

49 The reverse is of course also claimed: see Ford, J. and Nicoll, A. (1998). 'The sum of its parts'. *Financial Times*, 27 August; *Economist* (2005). 'Air war—Boeing and Airbus'. 25 June; Done, K. (2007). 'WTO to hear of "lavish" Boeing aid'. *Financial Times*, 22 March; and Done, K. (2007). 'Brussels rejects claims of "illegal Airbus subsidies" '. *Financial Times*, 10 February.

50 *Financial Times* (1998a). 'Forget Toulouse', 3 September; and *Financial Times* (1998b). 'The sum of its parts'. 27 August, 1998.

51 Peggy Hollinger (2006). 'EADS turmoil'. *Financial Times*, 3 July; *Economist* (2006). 'Forgeard's forward defence: the mess at EADS'. 24 June; Done, K. (2004). 'Competing by the seat of their pants'. *Financial Times*, 17 December.

52 Done, K. (2004) op. cit.

53 Betts, P., Done, K., Hollinger, P., and Spiegel, P. (2005). 'EADS board reshuffle delayed'. *Financial Times*, 2 June.

54 Gumbel, P. (2007). 'Airbus' tangled wires'. *Time*. 2 April: 169 (14).

55 Hollinger, P. (2005). 'Question of trust will haunt EADS: despite reconciliation, bitter discord has left its mark on the Franco-German defence group'. *Financial Times*. 30 May.

56 Done (2004) op. cit.

57 Done (2004) op. cit.

58 *Financial Times* (1993). 'Penalties for excess baggage: the airbus consortium'. 1 December.

59 Skapinker, M. (1999). 'On guard against complacency: Airbus Industrie'. *Financial Times*, 14 June.

60 *Financial Times*. (1998). 'The sum of its parts'. 27 August 1998.

61 Michaels, D. (2000). 'It's official: Airbus will become a company and market A3XX Jet: EADS kicks off IPO roadshow'. *The Wall Street Journal*, Europe, 26 June.

62 *Airclaims Airline News* (2001). 'Airbus to take integrated form in February'. no. 2, 12 January.

63 Betts, P. (2006). 'EADS needs new model and pilots to fly again'. *Financial Time*. 20 June.

64 BAe 2007 Annual Report.

65 Done, K. and Mackintosh, J. (2006). 'Daimler and Lagardere cut EADS stakes'. *Financial Times*, 5 April.

66 Hollinger (2005) op. cit.

67 *Ibid*.

68 Done, K. (2005). 'EADS chiefs look to ease tensions'. *Financial Times*, 28 June.

69 Betts, P. (2001). 'Take-off delayed by squabbles in the cockpit'. *Financial Times*, 16 November.

70 *Air Transport World* (2005). 'Boeing, Airbus name CEOs'. 42/8: 7.

71 Op. cit.

72 *Economist* (2007). 'Giants forced to dance: European companies'. 26 May.

73 *Aviation Week and Space Technology* (2007). 'Cross-border stall warning'. 26 February, 166/9: 74.

74 *Agence France-Presse* (2007). 'EADS strategy chief resigns after disagreement'. 11 June.

75 Done (2004) op. cit.

76 Betts, P. (2006). 'EADS needs new model and pilots to fly again'. *Financial Times*. 20 June.

77 Ibid.

78 Schwartz, N. D. (2007). 'Big plane, big problems'. *Fortune*, 5 March; *Economist* (2006). 'In place of Streiff: Airbus'. 14 October; Done, K. (2004). 'Airbus seeks Euros 1bn launch aid for new airliner'. *Financial Times*, 16 October.

79 Hollinger, P. (2006). 'Forgeard under fire over crisis at EADS'. *Financial Times*. 20 June.

80 Gumbel (2007) op. cit.

81 Gumbel (2007) op. cit.

82 Tricks, H. (1998). 'Survey: world's most respected company: deliveries in pizza-style: CEMEX'. *Financial Times*, 30 November.

83 Lyons, J. (2004). 'Power play: expensive energy?' *The Wall Street Journal*, 1 September.

84 For example, Santos, J. (2007). 'Strategy lessons from left field'. *Harvard Business Review*, 85/4; and Dawar, N. and Frost, T. (1999). 'Competing with giants'. *Harvard Business Review*, 77/2.

85 *Economist* (2001). 'The CEMEX way'. 16 June.

86 Authers, J. (2004). 'Why Mexicans mix cement with football: brand names'. *Financial Times*, 8 July: 13.

87 Orta, A. (2006). 'Mexico's cement industry overview', 12 July <http://66.102.9.104/search?q=cache:fzVFM2pj62MJ:commercecan.ic.gc.ca/scdt/bizmap/interface2.nsf/vDownload/ISA_5297/%24file/X_7825291.DOC+mexico+cement+market+share+2006+Apasco&hl=en&ct=clnk&cd=3&gl=uk>, accessed 28 June 2007, and <http://www.canacem.org.mx/la_industria_del_cemento.htm>, accessed 28 June 2007.

88 Fritsch, P. (2002). 'Hard profits: a cement titan in Mexico thrives by selling to poor'. *The Wall Street Journal*, 22 April.

89 Lyons, J. (2004). 'Ship endures troubled waters in Mexico'. *The Wall Street Journal*, 14 December 2004.

90 *Economist* (2004). 'One giant leap for Mexico: cement'. *2 October 2004*: 373; Silver, S. (2004). 'CEMEX waits to cement its gains'. *Financial Times*, 18 November.

91 Authers, J. (2005). 'CEMEX seals RMC Group acquisition'. *Financial Times*, 2 March: 32.

92 See, for example, *Financial Times* (1997). 'Long reach opens new sources of finance'. 7 November.

93 *Economist* (2001) op. cit.

94 Ibid.

95 Ibid.

96 Tricks (1998) op. cit.

97 Fritsch (2002) op. cit.

98 *Economist* (2001) op. cit.

99 *Economist* (2001) op. cit.

100　CEMEX 2004 annual report.

101　Lyons (2004) op. cit.

102　Ibid.

103　Ibid.

104　Tricks, H. (2000). 'High-tech strengthens the mix: CEMEX'. *Financial Times*, 16 November 2000.

105　Emmott, R. (2001). 'CEMEX opens stores in the US'. *Financial Times*, 27 July.

106　Hanrath, A. and Authers, J. (2002). 'Cement brands struggle to set their prices'. *Financial Times*, 23 May 2002: 29.

PART THREE

Assessing the Sustainability of Advantage

In this part, we show you how to assess whether the attributes of the organization are sufficient to give it a sustainable advantage. Having learnt how to identify distinctive features such as the resources that are used in the organization's value chain in Part Two, you will learn how to appraise the extent to which these features meet the defining criteria for sustainability. We give particular attention to knowledge, learning, and the capacity to innovate, which many theorists believe to be of particular importance in sustaining competitive advantage.

Sustainable advantage derives from the idiosyncratic features of an organization, those that cannot easily be replicated elsewhere. These form its architecture and its culture, which determine the degree to which its members are appropriately motivated and able to carry out their work effectively. In this part, we develop methods for assessing them. We also examine contemporary trends in structuring and controlling organizations of all sizes, and also networks of organizations, such as supply chains.

CHAPTER SEVEN

The Resource-based View of the Firm

LEARNING OUTCOMES

After reading this chapter you should be able to:

→ Discriminate between strategic and threshold resources using the VIRUS criteria

→ Discuss the advantage given by different kinds of resource—strategic assets, capabilities and competences—and identify those that an organization possesses

→ Assess the extent to which an organization's resources give it sustainable advantage

→ Discuss the risks that arise through the development of specialized resources and evaluate those risks within a given organization.

INTRODUCTION

In the previous chapter we discussed how to evaluate an organization's value chain and learnt how its configuration enables the organization to serve its target markets. A key aspect of value chain effectiveness is the way in which it allows the organization to first acquire or develop suitable, resources, and then deploy them effectively.

In this chapter we look at the kinds of resources that organizations may possess, and what it is that makes a resource valuable. Differences in resources are now widely believed to be the most important factor in explaining why some organizations do better over time than others, and this chapter will summarize the theory that underpins that belief.

But we also consider the cost and risk for organizations of investing time and effort in building excellent resources, and how over-investment in some resources may lead the organization to develop 'competency traps' and 'core rigidities'.

7.1 The resource-based view of the firm

Organizations cannot achieve sustainable competitive advantage *just* by selecting the right combination of products and services, and positioning them to appeal to attractive target market segments. Although these decisions are a vital part of strategy, and may lead to desirable economies of scale and scope, they are not sufficient in themselves, because they are too easy for competitors to notice and copy. The munificence, dynamism, and complexity of an industry environment (see Section 3.6) are also not enough to explain the very real differences in profitability between firms in the same industry. After all, if the industry was the only factor, then all firms in an industry would have similar levels of profits—and they do not.

The 'resource-based view of the firm' (RBV), which emerged towards the end of the twentieth century, focuses on organizational features—resources—that are the basis of competitive strength if exploited properly. Edith Penrose[1] showed how over time firms built up human and physical resources and the capability to use them to provide different kinds of services, some of which could be used in different products and markets from the ones for which they were developed. Subsequent developments of this theory[2] focused on the importance of the unique, often hidden, aspects of an organization, such as tacit knowledge, or the things that it has learnt to do, in understanding differences between firms. Because tacit knowledge is unknown, it is hard to codify or write down, and therefore almost impossible for competitors to acquire or replicate. It can be knowledge that an individual has (e.g. how to pilot a racing car at high speeds), but is particularly powerful when it is common to a group of people (e.g. a team's routines for developing a new product).

These differences in resources arise because two firms can start from a common base, yet end up over time with very different sets of routines, capabilities, and knowledge, something now known as path dependence. Moreover, if a firm starts earlier than competitors, it may be able to build up advantages that they will have difficulty in overcoming.

Time also means that competitors find it difficult to copy a firm's resources, because they may not be able to understand precisely how and when they were developed—in other words there is causal ambiguity. These resources may also be part of a complex interaction with a number of other, complementary, resources within the firm that make them more effective than they would be if used on their own.

Competitive advantage can be defined as the ability to generate higher economic rents than another firm could achieve, given the same investment. In order for a resource to

Tacit knowledge
Tacit (literally, 'silent') knowledge is knowledge that exists within an organization, but about which its members are unconscious or unaware.

Economic rents
The returns from a given investment that an organization is able to achieve, over and above those expected by stockholders for a given level of risk.[3]

generate value for customers and rents for the firm, it must be significantly different from the resources held by other organizations. So the resource-based view focuses on the *differences* between organizations as much as it focuses on the inherent properties of a resource.

It also assumes that these differences will need to be maintained and somehow protected from competitors if the position of the firm is not to be eroded. Since the environment is likely to change over time, organizations, in order to sustain their competitiveness, have to renew their resource base in order to maintain its value.[4]

7.2 Strategic and threshold resources

Organizations use a wide variety of resources—physical, financial, human, intellectual, and reputational, and most will have some of each of these categories. However, not all will qualify as a source of *sustainable* competitive advantage—in other words be strategically important.

A resource is anything that a firm has or has learned to do which enables it to conceive and implement strategies that improve its efficiency and effectiveness. It is something that an organization owns, controls, or has access to on a semi-permanent basis. Resources include tangible assets, competences, capabilities, organizational processes, firm attributes, information, and knowledge.[5] A *strategic* resource is one that provides a *significant* benefit to a firm's strategic position. Resources that are not strategic, but are still important because they help the firm meet the criteria for *survival* in an industry are called *threshold* resources.

In order to count as strategic, a resource needs to meet four 'VIRUS' criteria:[6]

1. It must be **V**aluable. A resource is only strategic if it makes an appreciable difference to a firm's cost and/or differentiation advantage, or its capacity to adapt and innovate. It will also need to correspond to one or more of the success factors identified for the industry. Retailers that were early pioneers in the use of electronic point of sale (EPOS) systems were able to develop both cost and customer-service advantages, as their shelves could be re-stocked regularly and efficiently, and stock-holding costs were lessened. These were important success factors in that particular industry, even though the early EPOS systems were expensive to develop and difficult to implement.

2. It must be **I**nimitable—difficult for other firms in the industry to copy or acquire. This may be because the resources are prohibitively expensive, difficult to learn how to use effectively, or because considerable time has gone into building them up. Architects who were the early users of CAD systems invested large amounts of money in buying them and training staff to use them. Few firms could afford to do this, and the use of the software was so specialized that it could not be emulated by cheaper or simpler systems.

3. It must be **R**are—or, to use our terminology from earlier in the book, distinctive. If every firm in an industry has the same resource, then it is likely to be a threshold resource, rather than a strategic one. Sometimes, a resource will start out being strategic, and then become a threshold resource as competitors work out how to copy it, or it becomes available on the open market. In the early 1980s, CAD systems cost tens of thousands of euros and were difficult to use, so very few architecture practices could afford them. They were a strategic resource for the firms that had invested time and money in acquiring them and training people to use them. Once cheaper,

user-friendly systems became available for the PC, they ceased to be rare and turned into a threshold resource—very few architects could look credible to their customers if they did not have a CAD system.

4. It should be **UnS**ubstitutable. Substitutability occurs when a competitor can implement the same strategy through finding alternative resources to do the job. For an architect, the alternative to a CAD system would be to employ large numbers of people to make the drawings. Given the presence of countries such as India or China, with large numbers of skilled employees and low wage costs, this may well be a reasonable option—although there would be a question as to how long this would remain viable, if wages were to increase.

The four tests we have described above are very exacting. Not many resources can be expected to pass them, and a firm may have only one or two. Not all firms develop strategic resources; even apparently successful organizations may flourish for a while, in a favourable environment, and then find that they cannot stand up to a strong competitor. Those firms that possess truly strategic resources are likely to be more profitable than their competitors; remain profitable as competition intensifies, whereas newer or weaker competitors may struggle; and be more resilient in the face of changes in the environment.

And for a resource to be considered truly strategic, it is important that all four of these criteria are met:

- A resource that has taken a lot of time and effort to develop, but is not valuable, represents nothing more than wasted effort.

- A valuable resource that is rare, but not inimitable, will not stay rare for long—competitors will buy it or develop their own version.

- Similarly, a valuable resource will not retain its value if substitutes are freely available, since competitors will be able to use the substitute resource to gain the same cost or differentiation advantages.

- Resources that are inimitable, but not rare, will not give any one company in the industry an advantage over its competitors. These resources may constitute barriers to entry to the industry for firms that do not have them, and enable *all* the companies in the industry to make reasonable profits. However, they will not make the difference between being an industry leader and one of the also-rans, and they will not protect a small firm in the industry from a larger competitor that wants to invade its markets.

7.2.1 **What makes a resource difficult to acquire or copy?**

One important factor that can prevent resources being copied is because they have a high tacit knowledge content—the people who develop the products or operate the service may not have documented what they do, or may be unconscious of the importance of their role. In extreme cases, perhaps in a very new firm or industry, people may genuinely not understand the difference between success and failure. It took the makers of microchips a long time to work out why some batches of silicon wafers would result in usable products, while others would not. Without a conscious recognition of what goes into making a successful product, there is nothing to imitate—even if competitors could get access to the processes.

Tacit knowledge content is one example of how inimitable resources result from the way that they are built up over time. Sony's capabilities have been strongly shaped by its origins in post-war Japan, and the vision of its founders as well as its subsequent experience in learning about new markets and product technologies. Research and development, and advertising that leads to brand recognition, are two examples of investments that can take a long time to take effect. Because of these 'time compression diseconomies', competitors will be unable to replicate the resource, even if they devote a long time or considerable sums of money in the effort.

Even where time is not a factor, there are cases where firms' sunk costs—their investments in an existing base of resources—may confer an enduring advantage. Consider the case of two competing mobile telephone operators, one an established firm that already serves one-third of the country, the other a new start-up. If they both invest €20 million in new equipment, the first firm will end up with an appreciably larger network than the second, and will be more attractive to both new and existing customers as a result. This is an example of asset mass efficiencies, where an investment that adds to a strong base makes a greater improvement to an organization's position than one that reinforces a weak one. The new competitor may still be able to catch up, by making larger investments or offering a more reliable service, but in principle the entrenched competitor has the advantage.

Another instance of sunk costs conferring advantage is where other, complementary assets are needed in order to make a resource work to its best advantage. For example, a firm may successfully invest in the knowledge needed to develop an innovative new product, but may still lose out to a firm with an inferior product but a superior sales network. An extreme example is the case of a natural monopoly, such as electricity distribution, where there is simply no point in one firm investing to duplicate an existing network of assets.

7.2.2 **What makes a resource rare?**

Sometimes resources cannot be obtained because they are in genuinely short supply, not just within the industry but throughout the world. For example, deposits of metal ores that are close to the surface (and so cheap to mine) with a high metal content and low in bothersome impurities (and so cheap to process) are rare.

Similarly, if a firm has managed to attract the world's leading experts in a particular technology or area of expertise, it will have a competitive advantage for as long as they stay with the firm. A famous recent example of this is Steve Jobs who left Apple, the company he co-founded in 1976, in 1985 and returned in 1997. In the opinion of many, it was his return to the company that provided the spark that triggered the substantial improvement in the company's performance and the development of the iPod and iTunes (see Real-life Application 4.5).[7] And when he announced in August 2004 that he had been diagnosed with pancreatic cancer, the company's shares fell 2 per cent in one day.

7.2.3 **What makes a resource valuable?**

Perhaps the most obvious way in which a resource may be judged strategic is if it adds to the profitability of a firm. It will therefore need to fulfil one or more of the industry's success factors. This will make customers choose the firm over its competitors, or perhaps allow it to develop relationships with key suppliers which will give it advantages over competitors in the quality and prices that it is able to obtain from them. This shows up as superior organizational performance over the long term—*relative* to its competitors.

McDonald's has for many years now been no. 1 in the fast-food industry. As we mentioned in Worked Example 3.1, it has recently increased its market share at the expense, particularly, of smaller firms, and has for years now shown superior profitability to almost all its competitors.[8] One of McDonald's most important strategic resources is its brand name and logo. This is an important reason behind people choosing it over its competitors—it regularly appears in the top ten of the Interbrand list of the world's most recognized brands, with a value ascribable to the brand alone of more than $1bn. When it enters a new market it is quite usual for queues to form round the block when a restaurant opens, particularly in developing countries, and the 'pester power' of children who want their parents to take them to a McDonald's knows no bounds. But the brand would not sustain the company's performance on its own, and this resource is supported by other strategic resources such as capabilities in service manufacturing, that allow McDonald's to produce predictably good-value, tasty, meals in any of its restaurants—features that fast-food customers value highly.

7.2.4 What makes a resource hard to substitute?

In some cases, in business-to-business markets especially, some resources are difficult to substitute because they involve long-standing relationships between people. If people work well together, and these relationships lead to the development of a capability in innovation, for example, then it is difficult to replace that with an alternative way of developing new products. Sometimes a firm may be able to substitute a competitor's strategic resources—its internal new product development processes—by acquiring another firm that has already created a similar product, but these sorts of opportunities are rare, especially if the technology involved is leading-edge.

The passage of time can make resources difficult to substitute, just as it can make them rare and inimitable. Individual relationships within and between firms are difficult to substitute for this reason, and so are reputations, or strong brands, which are psychological, relational contracts between a firm and its various stakeholders.[9] They build up over time and are person- and time-specific.

→ We examine relational contracts in Section 8.3.1.

7.3 The different types of resources

The previous section describes a large number of different features that can be included under the umbrella of the resource-based view of the firm. In addition to its large scope, the resource-based view is also a mass of conflicting and confusing terminology. Some scholars use the term 'capabilities'; others use 'competences' to mean very similar things. Sometimes these are further refined to become 'distinctive capabilities', 'core capabilities', or 'core competences'. Some authors use 'assets' where others use 'resources', or 'strategic assets' instead of 'strategic resources'. To complicate matters further, some theorists include all kinds of resource under the heading of 'assets' or 'capabilities', while others give these words specialized meanings. In this book, we use 'resources' as the umbrella term and 'assets', 'capabilities', and 'competences' for particular types of resource.

Things that a firm *has*, like a reputation, a distribution infrastructure, or a customer database, are assets. If they are important and fulfill the VIRUS test, we call them strategic assets.

Things that a firm *does* with its assets—the skills that it deploys—are competences or capabilities. Capabilities contribute to an organization's competitiveness by, for example, enabling it to cut costs, or serve customers quickly and responsively. A competence is deeper-seated, for example a profound understanding of a specialized field of information technology, human psychology, engineering, or chemistry.

Competences and capabilities usually incorporate routines that have been built up over time. If they meet the criteria for being considered strategic resources, they are termed core competences or distinctive capabilities.[10]

Competences or capabilities make a difference to an organization's cost or differentiation position at a specific point in time. *Dynamic* capabilities are resources that also help an organization to develop that position over time and as the environment changes.

In this section, we look in turn at different categories of resource and the extent to which they are likely to qualify as strategic.

7.3.1 **Physical assets**

It is quite unusual for physical assets to be the basis of sustainable competitive advantage. Exceptionally cheap or pure sources of raw materials, such as the mineral deposits discussed in Section 7.1.1, may count as strategic assets if they are genuinely rare and valuable. The South African minerals corporation, De Beers, for decades owned or controlled 90 per cent of the world's sources of diamonds. This undoubtedly qualifies as a strategic asset, since diamonds are valuable and there are few ready substitutes for them.

Most common types of physical assets, such as factories, offices, computer systems, and retail outlets, can be bought on the open market. However new and up-to-date they may be, they are also available to competitors, who may even be able to buy cheaper and more powerful facilities. These kinds of assets are normally only strategic if:

- They incorporate a firm's proprietary technology. For example, some Japanese firms insist on making their own machine tools rather than purchasing them off the shelf. If they genuinely deliver lower wastage or higher throughputs than commercially available products, they can be considered strategic assets.

- They have been bought cheaply, before other firms woke up to their value. McDonald's has for many years now bought prime sites for its restaurants. This means that it blocks competitors from gaining access to locations which are convenient for customers, but also means that they are not affected by the pricing whims of landlords. The UK supermarket chain, Tesco, has similarly been building up a 'bank' of sites for future development that is widely regarded as a strategic asset—to the point where other retailers have complained about its behaviour to the regulator.[11]

7.3.2 **Financial assets**

Financial assets are rarely strategic, because money is available from banks, stock markets, and venture capitalists. There are however, exceptions to this general rule.

Sometimes a company has access to funds in such quantity that it can use them to strike deals from which poorer firms are excluded. But these need to be substantial—probably in the billions of dollars or euros—to count as strategic. In 1999, the US conglomerate General Electric was able to win an exclusive contract to supply jet engines for the long-range version of Boeing's 777 aircraft, by promising to fund one-half of the aircraft's $1bn development cost. Competitors were only able to offer a contribution of $200m.[12] However, it is possible for organizations to have too much money. Berkshire Hathaway, an American conglomerate headed by a legendary investor, Warren Buffett, found its return on capital depressed because it had a lot of capital and, in a stock market that it regarded as overpriced, too few places to invest it.

'Deep pockets'—large cash reserves or borrowing capacity—can offer an advantage in other ways, by giving a company a superior ability to survive a price war or a recession. Deep-pocketed organizations may also be better able to attract key personnel, particularly in industries like sport, entertainment, and banking, where a few 'star' individuals may have a disproportionately large impact on organizational performance.

Real-life Application 7.1 Financial assets and the performance of soccer clubs

For many years, there has been a clear relationship in soccer between financial performance and competitive success. The richer teams are able to pay for the most talented players, and also to build larger squads so that, if a star player is injured, a good-quality substitute is immediately available. This enables them to win trophies, so attracting new supporters and commercial sponsors, and boost sales of branded merchandise. The televising of soccer has emphasized this phenomenon by weakening the traditional link between soccer fans and their home-town team, and enabling top clubs like Chelsea and Real Madrid to build support around the world. As a result, in most European countries, only the members of a small elite of wealthy clubs, often funded by a rich sponsor, are realistic contenders for the top trophies.[13]

7.3.3 **Human assets**[14]

Human assets are more heterogeneous than physical or financial assets—there are considerable differences in the skills that human beings have. They are therefore much more likely to give rise to advantages that are rare and difficult to copy. This is particularly true in 'people businesses' such as advertising, consultancy, and financial services.

Some human assets are rare because they require the brain to be 'wired' in a particular and unusual way, so as to make split-second judgements about whether to shoot, pass, or run with a football, or to buy or sell a share. Football clubs and merchant banks pay a great deal to attract individuals with these rare skills. Sometimes a large part of a firm's competitive advantage may seem to rest with a single individual, because of their industry knowledge, technological abilities, or ability to inspire the people around them. Someone like Steve Jobs (see Section 7.2.2), Richard Branson, or Bill Gates is undoubtedly a strategic asset.

Organizations may offer money or share options, a pleasant working environment, or the opportunity for people to be creative and to mix with stimulating people in an attempt to retain these individuals. However, they must be on their guard that these people are not lured away to other firms. This is a particular danger during acquisitions, when culture clashes and conflict in expectations can lead to the departure of some of the most knowledgeable staff. Sometimes firms attempt to persuade key employees to stay by providing 'golden handcuffs', pay and compensation that is strongly weighted, to staff who remain. Unfortunately these are rarely effective for the most marketable staff, as competing firms can entice them with equally attractive 'golden hellos'.[15] So quality of life, attractive working conditions, and other intangibles are more likely to be important (see Real-Life Application 7.2).

Real-life Application 7.2 Google's strategies for recruiting and retaining key staff

Google employs more than 4,000 people across the world and is one of the fastest-growing internet firms. One of its priorities is to attract the best new recruits. In 2006, it came second in a survey of where US undergraduates most wanted to work. It does this partly through selling its culture and ethos as a fun place to work. It also promotes its meritocratic culture. Employees worldwide can e-talk to Sergey Brin and Larry Page, Google's co-presidents and founders, part of its deliberate attempt to maintain a 'flat' organization where every employee has a direct line to the most senior managers. To attract the most motivated and innovative staff it encourages every Google employee to spend 20 per cent of her/his time developing a new project. In the past this has contributed to new products like Google News and Froogle.

In addition, Google offers many perks. It provides an on-site doctor and dentist and massage chairs, and puts on Friday afternoon get-togethers with subsidized beer. It offers free lunches, →

Google encourages every employee to spend 20% of his/her time developing a new project such as Google News. *Google*

→ soft drinks, and frozen yogurt, that help to contribute to its offices feeling 'like a college campus'. It also promotes a good work–life balance, providing subsidized gym membership, allowing employees to bring their dogs to work and wear what clothes they find most comfortable—whether this is shorts and flip-flops, or suits. Staff are provided with laptops and BlackBerries, that allow them to work when and where they wish.[16]

7.3.4 Intellectual assets

Intellectual assets such as databases, patents, and research programmes often have the capacity to be a source of competitive advantage. If a firm's customer database is larger and more detailed than its competitors' or if it has patents or other forms of technological knowledge, then these may be strategically important. However, they really must be *significantly* better than other firms' assets, and be *genuinely* difficult to copy, in order to be considered strategic.

Intellectual assets that have a high tacit knowledge content are particularly valuable. Because the knowledge is not written down, it cannot be copied or stolen. It may be possible for a competitor to lure away individual personnel, but this may not give them access to the shared knowledge those people have acquired over time. There have been examples in the UK of whole research teams being lured to competing universities because of this precise problem. However, research in cognitive psychology has shown that people's ability to use knowledge is influenced by the setting in which they are asked to employ it, potentially reducing its effectiveness if moved to a new setting.[17] It may also depend on complementary assets, such as proprietary software, to be employed effectively.

→ The problems of diversification and the management of complex organizations are discussed in Sections 5.2 and 9.2.

Management attention is a particularly important class of intellectual asset.[18] Top managers are often (though not always) the people in an organization with the greatest ability to solve business problems. Either they have seen a similar problem in the past, or they have deep, tacit knowledge of the firm's operations and customers that tells them where to look for a workable solution. However, organizations have only a few of these people, and they can only give proper attention to a limited number of issues at a time. Diluting their focus is one of the issues identified as causing problems in unrelatedly diversified corporations.

7.3.5 Reputational assets

Reputational assets covers two main types of resource: firms' brands—the names they use in the market-place—and their reputation—the degree of esteem in which they are held by current or potential customers.[19] The two are not quite the same—brands tend to be associated with products, or families of products, for example Sony's Vaio computer brand, while reputation tends to belong to an organization, although there are overlaps in the case of company brands such as McDonald's.

a. Brands

When a firm builds a brand, it wants it to symbolize certain things to prospective purchasers.[20] It hopes that, when buyers choose between products, its brand will be strong enough to make its product a more or less automatic choice as customers' search costs are reduced. It hopes that this will allow it to charge premium prices. If a brand is linked to a particular market segment it allows the firms to tailor their marketing effort to this group, reducing costs by not wasting money trying to sell to customers who are unlikely to be interested in what they offer. Brand-building strategies aim to get customers to buy a particular product because they aspire to the brand values embodied in, say, a BMW car, a Gucci bag, or a Budweiser beer. And over time—long enough to benefit from time compression diseconomies (see Section 7.2.1)—the investments made in advertising and brand design, and strong efforts to ensure coherence between product and brand values, can result in a sustainable source of competitive advantage and count as a strategic asset.

In industrial markets, brands have traditionally been seen as having limited value, because customers were thought to use price and performance as the main criteria for choosing which product to buy. Industrial advertising has therefore tended to give detailed product information rather than trying to establish brand personalities. However, some theorists[21] now believe that industrial products are becoming so similar that it is increasingly difficult to differentiate on the basis of price and functionality alone. They say that, increasingly, brands are becoming important for industrial buyers as well.

In consumer goods industries, on the other hand, brands have traditionally been regarded as strategic resources par excellence. The French conglomerate LVMH has built its entire corporate-level strategy around the acquisition of prestigious brands such as Moët et Chandon (champagne), Louis Vuitton (luggage), Tag Heuer (watches), Dior and Kenzo (fashion). Firms like Diageo, the world's largest drinks company, specialize in managing a portfolio of brands like Guinness, Smirnoff, and Johnnie Walker (all market leaders), whose customers are unlikely to know, or care, who owns them, but whose loyalty gives their owner a considerable advantage over most of its competitors. Diageo, for its part, also has strategic resources in the way that it manages these brands—it has core competences in this area (see Section 7.4 below).

Consultancies such as Interbrand have developed a whole industry around assigning a value to brands, which now appear on company balance sheets as intangible assets. In 2005, the value of Diageo's intangible assets on its balance sheet was £4,252m, more than twice its tangible assets (£2,097m).[22] Because of the need for considerable financial prudence when valuing such an intangible thing as a brand, which in contrast to physical assets, requires complementary resources such as competences to extract its full value, Diageo's balance sheet is filled with caveats about how they assess the value. And even though they cannot be touched, brands can be traded—just like property. Diageo sold two of the brands that it felt did not fit especially well into its portfolio (Burger King and Pillsbury) for nearly £5bn. Although some of this value could be ascribed to the physical assets, much was due to their brands.

b. Reputation

Branding and advertising may establish an organization's reputation; many companies *are* their brands (BA, McDonald's, H&M); others are subsidiaries of a larger corporation (Pizza Hut, Kookai), whose own reputation may be affected by that of their parent company. A company's reputation may arise from word-of-mouth, and not just from customers. Suppliers may tell one another about good or bad experiences, analysts can discuss the company at conferences or trade associations, and industry gossip can emerge from the trade or financial press. A firm may have a reputation for reliable, well-designed, or innovative products, for good customer service, for financial soundness, and paying its bills promptly, or for being a good employer. All of these may, in different ways, lead to an organization being effective and successful.

A good reputation, like a brand, can reduce customers' search costs. In industries like clothes or fresh fruit, where consumers will typically look at a number of possible suppliers before buying, reputation can help a supplier become one of the places where they will look for good quality or good value. If customers are pressed for time, they may head straight for a retailer which has a reputation for offering reasonable prices, rather than laboriously compare prices in different shops.

For larger items like hi-fi equipment, washing machines, or cars, or for services like consultancy or accountancy, reputation can be a key factor in consumers' choice. Buying a product or service like this represents a major commitment for most people, and yet they cannot tell, at the time of purchase, how good it will be. Suppliers with good reputations take some of the risk away, and for this they often charge a premium.

A good reputation can be valuable to an organization in its relationship with a variety of stakeholders. It can give employees a positive image of themselves, help motivate them to give of their best, and help the firm attract talented staff. It can help persuade suppliers to deal with a firm and grant favourable credit terms. It can help the firm persuade bankers to make loans on risky projects and help to keep its stock price high. A reputation as a tough competitor may help a company deter other firms from entering its markets.[23]

Sometimes a reputation can buy a firm time to get itself out of trouble. IBM's products long enjoyed a strong reputation for durability and reliability. This was important in sustaining the company's recovery from its record losses of $7.8bn in 1991 and 1992, which would have threatened the survival and credibility of a lesser firm.

A corporate reputation, unless mismanaged, can be an exceptionally durable thing, rated by chief executives as their most important intangible asset.[24] And this is why, when things sometimes go wrong, managers will make the utmost effort to undo any damage done by rogue products. In 2006, Dell took great pains to deal with the potential damage to its own reputation when batteries in its laptop began spontaneously to catch fire. Sony, which made the batteries and which has already, it is said, lost orders to its rivals Sanyo and Matsushita, faced similar problems.[25]

BP (see Real-life Application 7.3) offers another illustration of the importance of corporate brands and reputations.

Real-life Application 7.3 What's in a name?

British Petroleum changed its name to BP with an advertising campaign to emphasize that it now looked 'Beyond Petroleum'.
British Petroleum

In 1999 British Petroleum changed its name to BP, accompanied by an advertising campaign that emphasized that it was no longer just a petroleum company but now looked 'Beyond Petroleum'. It wished to indicate its global reach, as well as its involvement in alternative energy sources. In July 2006, the company's oil pipelines in Alaska leaked as a result of corrosion, and were shut down, thereby reducing the supply to the US market by 8 per cent and causing the world oil price to rise by 3 per cent in a day.[26] When allegations (which the company denies) surfaced that BP had failed to inspect this pipeline properly for many years,[27] American TV newscasters, who had started off by naming the company as BP, soon decided that it was 'British Petroleum' that was responsible for the problems. As this took place soon after BP had been involved in two other serious incidents, some other commentators decided that BP stood for 'Big Problems'.[28]

At the time of writing in August 2007, it is not known what BP can do to remedy the damage done to its reputation, although some suggest that its decisive action (which included a new head of safety) has minimized it.[29]

Creative Strategizing 7.1

BP had many years of a virtually unblemished reputation—unlike many of its major oil company competitors. What would you do to restore it, in the aftermath of the problems highlighted here?

7.3.6 **Relational assets**

The importance of relational assets has only been appreciated fairly recently, mainly because inter-organizational relationships only became commonplace in the 1990s. This triggered an interest in the factors that made them happen, and made them successful. An appreciation by marketing theorists of the importance of customer relationships began to emerge at about the same time.[30] Because the RBV originally focused on resources that were specific to one firm, it has taken a while to extend it to relationships, which are not 'owned' by one party or the other (see Theoretical Debate 7.1 for a more detailed discussion).

Relational resources fall into two broad categories:

- Relational capital is the term used for the value derived from a relationship between two or more firms (or individuals) that is highly important to them (Dyer and Singh, 1998). This can include relationships with customers and suppliers, or with alliance partners. Relationships of this kind can be difficult to build and make effective, because they require many of the same socialization processes that we described in Chapter 1 for the building of individual organizations. People in each organization need to acquire an understanding of how the other one operates, and then develop shared routines and cultural norms. Once they are effective, they therefore become difficult to copy, and this makes them a strong potential source of competitive advantage, particularly as the costs and risks of building relationships can be high.[31]

→ We outlined the ways in which routines and cultural norms develop in Sections 1.4.and 1.6.

- Institutional capital deals more specifically with relationships with key institutions, such as governments, local administrations, regulators, and religious bodies. These are all stakeholders that can influence a firm's access to resources, either directly or by affecting its legitimacy with other stakeholders. Institutional capital differs from relational capital in that the relationships are more one-sided—a firm may benefit from building unusually good relationships with an institution, but the institution does not expect direct benefits in return. BA, like many other airlines, enjoys good relationships with its national administration, which can help it in an industry where regulations are decided by negotiations between governments. However, the government does not expect anything directly in return for supporting BA—it acts because it believes that BA's prosperity is good for the country. A good relationship, however, sharpens the government's desire to help the airline, and helps it get the knowledge it needs in order to do so.

→ We describe the challenges of building and managing alliances in Section 8.3.

→ We introduced the concept of legitimacy in Section 2.6.1.

Institutional capital has been found to be an important influence on the birth and mortality rates of certain kinds of organization.[32] Firms that make efforts to build relational capital have been shown to obtain a number of benefits:

- They are better able to build alliances and transfer crucial, tacit knowledge to their partners, and are less likely to experience problems with partners that try to keep all alliance benefits for themselves.[33]

- They enjoy better relationships with other firms in their supply chain. This is particularly important given that competition is increasingly between different supply chains, rather than individual companies—but one supplier may participate in the supply chains of several competing firms, so that the firm that strikes up the best relationship may gain an advantage.[34]

- They gain access to local business networks that make them more competitive and more innovative—particularly important for small enterprises.[35]

→ We examine strategy for small businesses in Section 15.1.

An important corollary to both types of relational assets is social capital, which relates to the benefits that *individuals* get from their *personal* relationships. One of the crucial ways in which firms build relational and institutional capital is by encouraging the employees to build personal relationships with their counterparts in other organizations. This can lead to difficulties in assessing whether a particular relationship is between two organizations (i.e. a relational asset) or a part of the individual's personal social capital. In some industries, such as investment banking, it is common for individuals to be head-hunted on the strength of their personal client network.[36]

7.4 Capabilities and competences

The difference between capabilities and competences is a subtle one and, as we noted earlier, many authors do not distinguish between them. However, when trying to get a deep understanding of an organization's competitive advantage, we believe it is useful to distinguish between competences, which are routines that have potential uses in many places in an organization, and capabilities, which are specific, useful, things that organizations do in specific situations.

Capabilities are things that customers and other stakeholders notice when they are dealing with an organization. They notice whether orders are met quickly, whether they talk to a real person rather than a disembodied automated phone system, whether bills are paid on time. On the basis of these observations, they decide whether they want to do business with a firm, and, if so, whether they are willing to pay any kind of price premium. Capabilities like these have a direct impact on a firm's differentiation advantage; others have a similar impact on its cost advantage, such as a firm's logistics and supply chain processes.

Customers care whether their orders are met accurately and quickly. They do not necessarily care whether that is because an organization has a state-of-the-art computer system, or an army of well-trained, well-motivated employees—that is the firm's problem. However we, as analysts trying to work out whether the firm will be around and profitable in five years' time, will care quite a lot about whether the firm has underlying competences in IT or in staff training. We may hold the view that, in future, the IT competence is likely to be more valuable, because of the way the environment is going to change.

From this discussion, it should be clear that capabilities and competences are both important. Without underlying general competences, there can be no capabilities. Unless competences can be translated into useful capabilities, they are of no advantage to the organization (Table 7.1).

7.4.1 Core and distributed competences

Many organizations possess a large number of competences. Some of these qualify as *core competences*—they meet the VIRUS criteria,[37] and they underpin an organization's critically important capabilities in its core business.

However, core competences are not the whole story. A study of US patents has shown that successful large organizations undertake research, and develop competences, in many areas, not all of which are directly related to its core business. These are distributed competences. Some of these, like production machinery, have an obvious link to their main activity, and so represent a potential source of advantage there. However, others may be a long way away from the core, in fields where firms might logically be expected to get their specialist knowledge from subcontractors (Table 7.2). Ford, for example, has patents not just in vehicle engineering, but in fields like instrumentation, chemical processes, semiconductors, power plants and textiles.[38]

→ We discuss the role of distributed competences in knowledge management and innovation in Chapter 10.

In fact some scholars would suggest that focusing exclusively on core competences, which tend to concentrate expertise in a narrow field, is a bad idea.[39] Distributed competences are an important way in which an organization can retain a toehold in important areas that may become core in the future, or gain knowledge in order to apply the learning to other areas of its business—particularly important in innovation development. It is also an important way in which organizations can retain sufficient diversity to respond to uncertain environments.

Table 7.1 Examples of capabilities and competences

Types of capability	Examples	Types of competence	
Product innovation	Sony, Apple, and Canon all have multiple capabilities in innovation development	**Technological**	Apple's iPod and iTunes depend on competences in design—but also in designing robust, easy-to-use software
			Sony's Bravia TVs were based on deep-seated competences in picture display technology
Process innovation	Dell and Ryanair are both strong at finding ways to refine their operating processes to minimize cost and delays		
Reliability	McDonald's has a distinctive capability in reliability—it has learned how to reproduce and control its processes so that its burgers taste similar, and are of equivalent quality, in Frankfurt or Moscow	**Control**	McDonald's capabilities in reliability are built upon competences in implementing control systems—of suppliers as well as staff
	Many international hotel chains have mastered the challenge of achieving similar standards of hospitality across the world		
Sensitivity to customer requirements	Cisco Systems, which dominates the market for internet routers, is renowned for the way in which it stays close to its customers' developing technological needs and satisfies them with the next generation of its hardware	**Detecting and assessing environmental change**	H&M relies on its store managers and designers to stay abreast of changes in popular taste
Speed of reaction to customers	H&M's distinctive capability lies in its supply chain management, and its ability to get fashionable items into its stores more quickly than most of its competitors	**Ability to learn**	Microsoft has shown itself able to adapt quickly to radical changes in the way in which people use computers and software
Communication brand- and reputation-building	McDonald's has a capability in building awareness of the firm and its products through its advertising and other PR initiatives such as product placement in films and TV	**Understanding of people**	McDonald's competences in communication depend on the strength of its competences in consumer psychology
			H&M's capabilities in supply chain management depend on the interpersonal competences needed to manage relationships with suppliers
Risk management	In the airline industry risk management has become even more critical since 9/11. BA now has to deal with the risk of terrorism as well as weigh up the potential consequences of unpredictable weather, fuel price changes, unstable political regions, or a major accident	**Financial technologies**	BA's capability in risk management rests on its competences in applied financial economics that help it judge, for example, when or whether to hedge its oil purchases
	For banks and insurers, the ability to manage risk in their financial portfolios can be crucial, and the absence of such a capability can lead to huge losses, or even bankruptcy		Banks use of sophisticated economic and financial models in developing new forms of derivatives and other financial instruments

Table 7.2 The distributed competences of large corporations

Core business of firm	Proportion of patents related to			Examples of other fields
	Core business	Machinery	Other fields	
Electrical/electronic	66%	20%	16%	Telecoms, materials, photography, chemical applications
Chemicals	67%	16%	17%	Plastics, bleaching and dyeing, photography
Automobiles	30%	46%	24%	Metallurgy, computers, textiles, cloth and wood, semiconductors

Source
Granstrand et al. (1997: 10)

Using Evidence 7.1 Assessing capabilities and competences

It is important when evaluating an organization's capabilities and competences to show precisely how and why they lead to competitive advantage. Most successful organizations are likely to have a small number of core competences, a larger number of threshold competences, and a much larger number of capabilities. If you discover what you believe to be a large number of core competences, then it is quite likely that you have not been rigorous enough in applying the tests for 'strategicness'.

In order to judge whether a competence or capability counts as a strategic resource, you first of all have to look at the organization's profitability or other performance indicators, in comparison with its competitors over the long term. If these are significantly better then others you are likely to be able to claim that it has core competences in some area. But this is simply the first stage; then you have to use qualitative indicators such as analyst's reports, or press articles. If the organization appears to be doing something well, but these activities are also being done well by other firms in the same industry, then it is a threshold resource. If it appears to be doing something different—*and* this is attracting favourable comment from industry experts—then it may be strategic.

Telling the difference between competences and capabilities is harder. The main point is to identify things that the organization does well; if these appear to be being used across a range of activities, they are likely to be core competences; if only found in one or two areas of the business, they are more likely to be capabilities.

You should also be aware that not all firms develop strategic competences or capabilities. Even apparently successful organizations may flourish for a while in a favourable environment, and then find that they cannot stand up to a strong competitor.

Theoretical Debate 7.1 Competing theories of performance: which of the resource-based or industry views best explains superior profits?

The resource-based view of the firm now represents the mainstream of orthodox strategic management theory. However, the fact that everyone believes something does not mean that it is true. The resource-based view is based upon a great deal of careful reasoning, but there is little empirical evidence to support it.

A key point in the development of the resource-based view was a 1991 study by Richard Rumelt (summarized in Table 7.3). This used a statistical analysis of American manufacturing companies between 1974 and 1977 to estimate the proportion of the variance in their profits that could be explained by different factors, ➜

Table 7.3 Rumelt's findings: variation in the profits of US manufacturing firms, 1974–7, attributable to different causes

Corporate parent effects—differences in ownership	0.8%
Industry in which a firm operates	8.3%
Differences in conditions from year to year	7.8%
Business-unit specific effects	46.4%
Unexplained factors	36.7%

→ such as firm-level decisions, or the industry they were in. Rumelt's data showed that decisions that firms took at business level (line 4 in Table 7.3) were much more significant than corporate level decisions, their choice of industry (line 2), or the cyclicality of the industry.

This was taken to contradict the, at that time dominant, views of economists (dating back to Mason, 1939 and Bain, 1956) who favoured the Industrial-Organization (I-O), or Structure-Conduct-Performance (S-C-P), view of the source of firms' profits. A number of writers, for example, Kay (1993), Baden-Fuller and Stopford (1992), and Levinthal (1995), used the findings of Rumelt's study to claim that it was the businesses' unique resources that were responsible for performance, although Rumelt himself did not link his findings to any particular theory.

One problem with the data that Rumelt used is that it did not allow him to be specific about what was included under the different factors. In particular, the business unit effect could as easily have been due to market position as resources—let alone specific resources.

Since then a number of other scholars have sought to replicate Rumelt's findings. McGahan and Porter (1997), using data that covered a longer and more recent time period (1982–94), found that the company effect was smaller than Rumelt's. They calculated

(Table 7.4) that firms' choice of industry accounted for a much greater proportion of the variation in profits than Rumelt's study suggested—19 per cent as against 8 per cent (a finding borne out by others, e.g. Powell, 1996). The difference appeared to be largely due to the inclusion of data from non-manufacturing firms. In service sectors (transport, retailing, lodging and entertainment, and other services), industry choice was the largest single influence on profitability, accounting for 40–65 per cent of the variance.

McGahan and Porter agreed that, across all industry sectors, business segment factors account for more of the variation in profits than industry ones. However, looking more deeply into the data, they found variations across sectors. Except in the manufacturing and services sectors, business segment effects were quite small. Their data suggested that a firm's choice of industry, or the impact of a corporate parent, played a greater role than Rumelt had found, and a more significant one than business-level decisions. In a separate study, McGahan (1999) discovered that industry effects seemed to be more persistent over time than business-unit effects, which were less stable and less predictable, rather undermining the resource-based view's claims that resources lead to sustainable performance. Her results also suggested that the links between organizational factors and performance were 'particularly difficult to understand'. →

Table 7.4 McGahan and Porter's findings: factors explaining the variation in US company profits, 1982–94

	All sectors	Agriculture and mining	Manufacturing	Transport	Wholesale and retail	Lodging and entertainment	Services
Corporate parent effects	4.3%	22.4%	N/A	28.3%	44.1%	14.7%	N/A
Industry	18.7%	29.4%	10.8%	39.5%	41.8%	64.3%	47.4%
Less overlap between parent and industry[a]	−5.5%	−9.5%	−2.3%	−16.5%	−20.2%	−29.8%	−23.0%
Year-to-year differences	2.4%	2.3%	2.3%	3.3%	2.6%	N/A	4.2%
Business segment effects	31.7%	5.0%	35.5%	9.7%	2.0%	19.4%	33.5%
Unexplained factors	48.4%	50.5%	53.7%	35.7%	29.7%	31.4%	39.0%

Note
a This item takes account of the fact that certain corporate parents are more likely to have subsidiaries in particular industries

→ Since then, a further contribution has come from Hawawini et al. (2003), who used economic value added, rather than accounting returns, as a measure of success. Their findings indicated that for the few firms that performed exceptionally well or badly in each industry, firm-level effects were more important than industry ones. However, for the majority of firms, which delivered average performance, the choice of industry had a greater effect on returns than any inter-firm differences. There is, however, a debate about whether it is methodologically justifiable to treat the 'outliers' separately in this way (McNamara et al., 2005; Hawawini et al., 2005). Another study of exceptional performers (McGhahan and Porter, 2003) reached different conclusions regarding firm and industry effects.

In fact methodological problems make the identification of resource-specific effects tricky, if not impossible. Given that part of the claimed strength of many resources is that they are tacit and intangible, how can they be identified, let alone measured (Parnell and Hershey, 2005; Barney, 2001b)? Indeed, claiming that resources are the cause of firms' performance has the danger of being tautological—because a firm makes profits that cannot otherwise be explained, this must therefore be due to the possession of strategic resources (Priem and Butler, 2001a, 2001b; Priem, 2001).

And some of the basic premises of the RBV also turn out to be problematic (Lavie, 2006; Priem, 2001; Harrison et al., 2001; Gulati, 1999). Amongst them is the idea that resources have to be imperfectly mobile to be valuable (Parnell, 2002; Peteraf, 1993; Barney, 1991). Firms have, in fact, been shown, by, for example, Hardy et al. (2003), to benefit from accessing resources *across* organizational boundaries, from their strategic partners':

- reputation (Saxton, 1997);

- technological and commercial status (Stuart, Hoang, and Hybels, 1999);

- strong relationships with venture capital firms (Lee et al., 2001);

- complementary new technologies (Rothaermel, 2001; Stuart, 2000).

Despite the definitional or methodological problems, a number of scholars have attempted to calculate the effects of resources on performance. An empirical study by Richard Makadok (1998) of the US money-market fund industry, where products can easily be copied, found that the first firms to introduce a product appeared to be able to develop resources that gave them an advantage over later imitators. Sustained advantage in the US pharmaceutical industry has been linked to firm resources in the marketing and R&D functions (Yeoh and Roth, 1999). And Russo and Fouts (1997) controlled for a number of potentially competing strategy variables, such as product market position, in their study which established links between reputation and performance.

None of these studies offers conclusive proof of the relative importance of firms' resources over the effects due to the industry. Indeed, it is unlikely that either industry effects or the resource-based view *can* be proved or disproved conclusively; in the end, the popularity of these approaches rests on the strength of their underlying economic logic—and the absence of a more precise or persuasive theory of performance. Calculating the relative impact of resources and industry on a firm's performance may in any case be fruitless. On the one hand, it is probably impossible to disentangle the effects of industry structure from those of interactions between a firm and its rivals' (Miles et al., 1993; Henderson and Mitchell, 1997). One of the biggest problems is how to take account of a firm's ability to redefine an industry or change its structure to its advantage, 'even to the extent that it has no direct competitors' (Parnell, 2002). And on the other hand, defining the boundaries of an industry is, as we discussed in Theoretical Debate 3.1, very tricky (Stimpert and Duhaime, 1997).

Worked Example 7.1   Assessing strategic resources in Sony's games business

The questions we are seeking to answer, are, first, to what extent, and how, do resources contribute to the cost or differentiation advantage of Sony's games business, and second, whether these resources will offer sustainable advantage over the long term.

For the moment we are interested in the resources that one of Sony's subsidiaries has; we shall look at corporate-level resources when we discuss parenting competences and portfolio and network management in Chapter 10. But despite this focus, one question we need to address is how important Sony Corporation's resources are to the games segment. And here, because of the

role of some of the technology, we discover some interesting effects, which we will return to below.

First, in assessing resources we need to know what the key success factors are in the videogames industry both now and in the future. Only then will we be able to assess whether Sony's games business will survive or thrive. These include the ability to:

- provide interesting, stimulating, and popular games, which young people, especially, will want to play. This has two components: →

→

- Being able to access specialist skills in software development in order to produce the games' software;
- Being able to provide popular content, particularly that can link to current music, film, and TV trends;
- provide hardware that is both technically reliable and sophisticated enough to satisfy the needs of games players. It is a matter of speculation whether consumers will want high levels of technological sophistication, or lower, but cheaper, specifications;
- make available complementary assets such as broadband internet access.

Sony has now been a player in the computer games industry since 1993. For almost all of this time there have been two or three other competitors—Atari, Sega and Nintendo to begin with, and now Nintendo and Microsoft. Both Atari and Sega withdrew, after finding conditions too hostile. Sony's PlayStation by 2005 had more than 60 per cent[40] of the console market with sales of over 90 million units, Microsoft's Xbox had 22 million units, and Nintendo's GameCube, 19 million units.[41] In the hand-held segment, in which Microsoft does not compete, in 2006, Nintendo's Game Boy had approximately 90 per cent share of the US market, and the PSP (PlayStation Portable) 10 per cent.[42]

So Sony has a strong market position which may confer some advantages (brand loyalty and distributor tie-in for example), but really this market share says more about what Sony did right in the past—we have to look beyond this to see if it has the resources to be equally successful in the future.

All three competitors had new versions of their consoles out in 2006; all have slightly different views of the future market, and all are positioning their products accordingly. In the past, the move to new generations of technology have often been marked by major shifts in industry leadership. At the moment the jury is out as to whether the market will want a cheaper machine with less sophisticated graphics but an innovative way of interacting with the user (Nintendo's 'Wii', $250, launched in Autumn 2006), one slightly more expensive one with full network connectivity but without an expensive HD disc (Microsoft's Xbox 360, $400), or one with highly sophisticated graphics functionality and additional features, but which is much more expensive ($499–$599, Sony) and whose launch was delayed until November.

In 2005, games accounted for 10 per cent of Sony's sales but 40 per cent of its profits. Although it had shown a decline in revenue over the past few years, this is at least partly because consumers are waiting for the new-generation consoles to be released. The games segment is forecast to contribute 30 per cent of Sony's profits in the next few years. So a great deal of hope rests on the PlayStation 3 (PS3).

Sony itself (in several annual reports) assesses its environment as 'highly competitive', characterized by 'continual new product introductions, rapid development in technology and subjective and changing consumer preferences'. It is betting that consumers want fast, realistic graphics, and raw computing power that will enable the development of high-quality interactive, real-time, virtual reality games. And so it has focused all its efforts on bringing out a console (PS3) with an extremely fast 'Cell' processor and a new format, Blu-ray, high-definition (HD) disc. Its console also has ethernet and wireless features that will allow on-line gaming. As it happens, both Microsoft and Sony appear to believe that the networking and graphics issues are converging, so are likely to be competing head to head with one another.

Another key market factor is the availability of games for the consoles, whose technologies are not compatible with one another. Much of the console manufacturers' profits come from the games, on royalties of 10 per cent to 20 per cent per game sold. The consoles themselves typically sell at a loss initially, given the huge development costs, to be followed by high overall profitability later.

So given this industry and market context, does Sony have the resources to compete? We assess this using the framework outlined in Section 7 (Table 7.5).

Practical dos and don'ts

Neither you, nor we (nor, indeed, Sony), know what consumers will want in future. The point of this analysis is not to assess the demand for sophisticated and expensive technology. The aim is to determine whether, assuming that demand materializes, a firm's resources appear to be a basis for both distinctive and sustained advantage in a given industry and market. If not, then there are questions about whether it is in fact caught in a competency trap (see Section 7.7).

In identifying strategic resources, remember that you are looking for something that clearly is a source of strength *in the particular industry context* of the organization you are analysing. The capacity to produce radical technological innovations is clearly a strategic resource for Sony in the games industry, but for a firm in a mature industry, it may be nothing more than an expensive distraction. Be sure to relate your analysis of resources to what you have found out about success and survival in the industry (see Chapter 3).

It is helpful to use the classes of resource we have listed here—physical assets, human assets, capabilities, competences, etc.—as a framework to catalogue a firm's resources. The value chain framework (Chapter 6) can also provide a useful checklist to ensure that you do not miss out any aspects of the organization from your review. But remember—strategic resources are rare, so do not expect to find one in every category, and do not be surprised if you find none at all.   →

→ **Table 7.5** An assessment of Sony's games segment resources

Resource category	Sony	Competitor/market issues	VIRUS
Physical assets	Sony already has high-quality manufacturing plants across the world, and development labs near its Japanese HQ Perhaps more of an issue in this industry is access to the internet and the bandwidth needed to download and play the new generation of games on-line. Sony does not yet own any of these infrastructure assets, and is therefore dependent on broadband providers	Both Nintendo or Microsoft are similarly dependent on broadband availability, and also lack ownership of broadband supply	It is hard to see Sony's physical resources as strategic. Although they are important, its competitors have similar assets, in similar locations and they appear neither rare nor inimitable
Financial assets	Much of the development costs for the PS3 have already gone through Sony's books (the Cell alone cost approximately $400 million to develop[a]). Sony has explicitly stated that it expects low levels of initial profits from the PS3. However, some analysts estimate that Sony could lose close to $1bn on the hardware alone in 2006, in addition to substantial marketing costs.[b] Deep pockets are therefore needed to compete in this industry Sony's 2006 value of $45 billion is much smaller than Microsoft's $272bn. It is also smaller than Samsung's ($98 billion), Apple's ($54 billion), or Matsushita's ($53 billion),[c] none of whom are currently engaged in the games market, but who may conceivably choose to participate in the future. Nintendo, at $29bn, is much smaller than any of its competitors, but is also more focused on one business area, and its shares have been on a steady upward curve recently, unlike its two larger rivals Some estimates suggest that nearly 50% of Sony's market capitalization is due to the games business. This is an indicator that it would probably be able to obtain external funds for investment if needed	The first Xbox was a 'consistent money-loser' and according to some estimates, Microsoft's losses from videogames have been greater, at about $1.2 billion a year, than Sony's profits. This was 'the cost to get into the game that is about to begin'.[e] It can be taken as a sign that Microsoft is in the industry long-term and will play extremely competitively. Although Microsoft has said that it would cut the price of its console to boost demand and would not see it as a 'strategic move', 'since Sony can immediately match Microsoft's price', this comment could be interpreted in a number of ways; Microsoft would probably win a price war, although both players would be weakened by it Financial assets may be more of a concern for the smaller Nintendo, although its competitive stance means its development costs are not as high	Sony's current financial situation compared to that of its actual and potential competitors, suggests that its financial assets are neither rare, nor valuable, and indeed could be insufficient if market conditions become particularly hostile
Human assets	One question is whether two of the company's senior managers, Sir Howard Stringer and Ken Kutaragi,[d] count as strategic assets. Both are quite clearly brilliant men; both are, as yet, relatively unknown quantities in their present roles Sir Howard is Sony's new CEO, appointed in 2004. He is the first non-Japanese to be appointed to the role, and his background was in Sony's American media business—i.e. he is not an engineer. This gives him some advantages; many commentators have focused on the CEO's need to bridge Sony's 'warring' divisions, and achieve the synergies between content and hardware that has long been the stated aim of the company. Many analysts seem to think that he has started well. But he faces many problems, not least the fact that he is in his mid-60s, and spends much of his life on aeroplanes between Japan, the USA, and the UK, where his family lives	Microsoft is in something of a transition phase with the gradual withdrawing of Bill Gates from day to day operations.	It is certainly arguable that Sir Howard Stringer and Ken Kutaragi are strategic assets—but this is dependent on whether their visions for the company (consumer demand for high levels of processing power, and across-media synergies) are correct

→

→ **Table 7.5** (cont'd)

Resource category	Sony	Competitor/market issues	VIRUS
	Ken Kutaragi, 'the official Sony bad boy',[f] was passed over for Sir Howard's job because it is said he has a more abrasive personality than Sony's consensual culture could tolerate.[g] As a result he was removed from the main board and returned to head the games division, a role he had held before. By all accounts he is a brilliant visionary and 'one of Sony's most creative dynamos'.[h] His PlayStation and PlayStation 2 were the two best-selling game consoles ever, with sales of over 100 million units each. He was also responsible for initiating the development of the Cell processor. He approached IBM in 2000 with the hope that they could develop a computer that would 'let gamers experience a world like the Matrix movies',[i] and make the PS3 the 'Ferrari of games consoles'[j] However, there are a number of analysts who criticize the Cell as being too high-powered and too expensive (we return to this issue below), and therefore there are unresolved questions over the value of his judgement. There is also the issue of whether Mr Kutaragi will be demotivated at being returned to his former job		
Intellectual assets	Mr Kutaragi is also an intellectual asset—but is symptomatic of a problem Sony has, which is how to access and use the knowledge that is located in 'silos' in the company.[k] Sony has been described as a 'dysfunctional empire'.[l] Many of the company's divisions and product groups have pursued independent agendas, resulting in duplication and poor coordination. Given the need to achieve synergies, how Mr Kutaragi's knowledge and strengths may be brought together with the other divisions, and vice versa, is a key issue Another intellectual asset issue is the location of the knowledge that went into the development of the PS2's technologies. The Cell was jointly developed with, amongst others, IBM and Toshiba (two of Sony's potential rivals, and in Toshiba's case, also the developer of the rival HD-DVD disc format. As Sir Howard Stringer said 'One day my enemy is my enemy, the next day the enemy is my friend.'[m] Press reports are clear that the PS3 uses breakthrough technologies, and is the Trojan Horse to ensure that the Blu-ray is adopted as the future standard for DVDs. Sony also intends to build TVs using the Cell chip, although as Toshiba plans to do the same, it is by no means certain how much advantage this configures In fact, how valuable this superior technology is, is unknown. Blu-ray has gained the backing of Matsushita, News Corp., Walt Disney, Warner Bros, and Paramount Pictures, despite some of	The rival HD DVD disc format is championed by Toshiba and has recently been backed by Microsoft. However, analysts appear to give Sony's format the edge, as 60 per cent of consumer electronics makers are coming out with Blu-ray disc products, they have a better chance of getting shelf space'.[o] Not everyone thinks Sony is doing the right thing in investing in such high-level technologies. Some go so far as to suggest that Sony should quit Cell. 'It has so many advanced features that they don't know how to use it . . . it will make the PS3 too expensive to compete with Microsoft's Xbox 360 and will not repay Sony's investment.' A potential problem is Samsung. Despite the 'deepening alliances' between the companies, Samsung recently agreed to supply Disney with its 'MovieBeam' set-top film player, which allows free access to video-on-demand services. Some interpret this as Samsung branching out into the content sector, which means it is on a path for direct competition with Sony in its digital content business.	Because of the need to share content between, e.g. films and games, and because of the intended links between the games technology and other hardware, the issue of relationships between the games division and the rest of the corporation is a relevant one. The knowledge within the company is best thought of as a *potential* strategic resource. If it can be successfully accessed, it is likely to be a source of huge advantage The ability to use its large content archive across its various hardware platforms provides another potentially large source of profits for Sony. Sony also recently acquired a stake in MGM, the holder of the largest library of colour films in Hollywood Although there are issues about the commercial value of both the PS3's and PSP technologies, the →

→ **Table 7.5** (*cont'd*)

Resource category	Sony	Competitor/market issues	VIRUS
	these initially backing the rival HD-DVD format. The HD-DVD format is easier to manufacture and is cheaper, and is backed by Toshiba, Microsoft, and General Electric/NBC Universal. It appears that Sony is headed for another standards war (it lost the previous one between Betamax and VHS for video recorders). If Sony can create a market for the Blu-ray disc 'the synergies between the games, entertainment and Blu-ray could be significant' . . . but if PS3 flops, it will be a problem. As two-thirds of Sony's semiconductor production will be channelled to PS3, if it does not sell, it will affect not only Sony's games business but its chip business as well.'[n] The PSP also represents Sony's attack on the market for portable media players; Sony is active in the spaces where Apple wants to go with the video iPod. Sales of PSPs are growing fast, marking the 'fastest penetration of any PlayStation model ever', according to Sony's annual report		knowledge that Sony has gained, and the fact that none of the other console manufacturers has managed to bring such a sophisticated machine to fruition, suggests that the intellectual assets enshrined in Sony's games segment must also count as a strategic asset. It is rare, and apparently both inimitable and unsubstitutable The knowledge gained from developing the Blu-ray disc is arguably a strategic asset—although, given its development with alliance partners, where it is located is an interesting issue
Reputational assets	Sony is one of the most recognized brands in the world, appearing at number 26 (number 3 in Japan, behind Toyota and Honda) on the Interbrand list of global brands with a 9% increase in its brand value in 2005/2006 to $11.695bn. And there are plenty of industry analysts that still believe that Sony Corporation, as a whole, after sixty years of solid performance retains a reputation for innovation, miniaturization and product quality. Sony insiders point to the LCD turnaround as evidence of the residual power and strength of the Sony brand[p] However, it faces reputational problems in some of its game segment's key markets. Its music division's attempts to deal with the piracy of its records backfired dramatically, causing damage to its reputation with young people. It bundled some anti piracy software onto its CDs, which secretly installed itself on to consumers' computers and in the process introduced a security breach. There are also potential reputational problems with young, new-generation gamers because of the console's price and expectations about software[q]	Microsoft is also perceived by some young people as a corporate fat-cat, although there appears to be less hostility to its game console than its operating system Nintendo appears to have a committed support base, and has attracted less opprobrium than its rivals. The Wii is also attracting considerable accolades—boosting sales and Nintendo's share price as a result	Sony has probably retained a lot of goodwill from gamers who loved their previous PlayStations, and also who are strong believers in its innovative capabilities. Notwithstanding the problems in the music division, we assess Sony's brand as a considerable resource—the only problem is that its major competitors also appear in the list of the world's best-known brands—Microsoft at no. 2, Nintendo at no. 51, and Samsung at no. 20. Sony's brand could therefore be considered to be a threshold resource, as it is not rare
Capabilities & competences	a. Software/hardware technologies Sony clearly has competences in developing innovative technologies, both itself and with partners Its consoles have become increasingly sophisticated over time. This has had a corresponding impact on the complexity of the games, many of which are developed by independent games developers and often tied in to major film or music themes	Microsoft has been assessed as 'way behind' Sony, being a decade later with 'the tricky blend of manufacturing, marketing, pricing and partnerships needed to field a hit game machine'[u] The cost of developing games has 'skyrocketed' in the past 10 years, now averaging $5 million to $10 million, and this is expected	Even though it is clear that Sony has many extremely strong competences in a number of critically important areas, it is also clear that it is not alone in this. Both Microsoft and Nintendo have worked with IBM to build their next-generation gaming chips, →

→ **Table 7.5** (cont'd)

Resource category	Sony	Competitor/market issues	VIRUS
	b. Relationship management Part of the success of the PlayStations' development process has been Sony's competences in managing relationships with some of its potentially most bitter rivals. However, relationships with other technology developers are not the only ones critical to the PS3's success. Others are internal ones—with the music and film divisions—and also with games developers. Although Sony has some capabilities in software, there is evidence that it recognizes that it has not involved its software developers in the process as early as they probably should be[r] **c. Consumer understanding** In an interesting statement of perceived strengths Samsung assesses their alliance as bringing together Sony's marketing strengths with Samsung's digital technologies.[s] Marketing has certainly been traditionally perceived to be one of Sony's strengths. Akio Morita, was famed for his ability to judge what consumers needed—well before they themselves realized this **d. Manufacturing** Manufacturing its own key components allows the company to utilize its distinctive R&D and mass-production technologies. Sony will make its own Blu-ray chips, the drive and the blue laser optical pick-up, which has been assessed as very difficult to produce and unable to be copied immediately, especially by low-end manufacturers[t]	to double or treble for the new consoles which have much more processing power: 'Games that used to be 100,000 lines of code —are now 3m lines'[v] Microsoft has been attempting to attract games developers to its own console with better programming languages and software tools that automate some of the process and therefore make it easier to create the far more complicated new games. This is expected to give Microsoft an advantage, if in the process it can 'reduce the pain' for developers[w] Some analysts have suggested that Sony is less sophisticated than its rivals in enticing customers. Microsoft is using new tactics, such as a co-marketing deal with Samsung. Nintendo is using innovative controllers and simpler games to attract non-gamers, like elderly people 'who want to sharpen their mental faculties'[x]	and there is evidence that Toshiba and Samsung also have extremely strong competences in managing alliances. Although this is perhaps overly churlish, we assess Sony's relationship-management competences as threshold resources Its technology is another matter—it has produced the most technically sophisticated consoles, and appears to have production and manufacturing competences that its rivals appear likely to have problems in matching

Notes

a David Kirkpatrick (2005). 'The 9-in-1 wonder chip built for games, IBM's mighty Cell chip could help reshape all of computing'. *Fortune*, 5 September.

b Gunther, M. and Lewis, P. (2006). 'The Welshman, the Walkman, and the salarymen'. *Fortune*, 12 June.

c Gunther and Lewis (2006) op. cit.

d After this worked example went to press, in April 2007 it was announced that Ken Kutaragi would retire from his position and take up a role as Honorary Chairman.

e Guth, R. A., Wingfield, N., and Dvorak, P. (2005). 'It's Xbox 360 vs. PlayStation 3, and war is about to begin'. *Wall Street Journal*, 9 May.

f Bremner, B., Edwards, C., and Grover, R. (2005). 'Sony's sudden Samurai'. *BusinessWeek*, 21 March.

g BusinessWeek Online (2006). 'Can Sony's Kutaragi score big? Once pegged as CEO material, the outspoken exec was bounced back to the games unit. Now his fortunes are tied to PlayStation 3'. 9 February.

h Bremner et al. (2005) op. cit.

i Kirkpatrick (2005) op. cit.

j Nakamoto, M. (2005). 'Stringer's strategy for Sony'. FT.com, 20 September.

k Goldsmith, J. (2006). 'Traveling man: turning Sony around puts Stringer through the ringer'. *Daily Variety*, 5 March.

l Bremner et al. (2005) op. cit.

m Goldsmith (2006) op. cit.

n Nakamoto, M. (2006). 'Scrutinising Stringer: a year of candour and resolve has started to energise Sony'. *Financial Times*, 22 June.

o Nakamoto (2005) op. cit.

p Goldsmith (2006) op. cit.

q Zuckerman, G. (2006). 'Sony's big hopes for PlayStation 3 may fall short'. *Wall Street Journal*, 19 July.

r Nakamoto (2006) op. cit.

s *Electronic Gaming Business* (2004). 'Integration now: making games safe for other media'. 2/3, 11 February.

t Nakamoto (2005) op. cit.

u Guth et al. (2005) op. cit.

v Ibid.

w Ibid.

x *Economist* (2005). 'Stringing along'. 10 January: 58.

Reproduced with the kind permission of John Wiley

7.5 Assets, capabilities, and competences

The relationship between assets and competences/capabilities is a close one. Just as an asset is useless without the capability to apply it, so a capability is pointless without the assets to deploy it (Real-life Application 7.5).

Real-life Application 7.5 Assets and capabilities in the automobile industry

In the 1980s, General Motors (GM) committed billions of dollars of investment to fit its brand new Hamtramck factory in Detroit, Michigan with state-of-the-art robots, automated guided vehicles, laser measurement, and computing equipment. Its aim was to overcome the cost advantage that Japanese competitors Toyota and Honda had gained through their application of lean manufacturing techniques. By applying sophisticated American information technology, GM hoped to save heavily on labour costs and improve reliability.

However, software bugs led to quality problems—in some cases robots painted each other, rather than the cars they were meant to be building. GM also needed time to develop the skills to use the new technology to its best advantage—for example, ways of presenting the mass of information produced by the laser measurement systems in an accessible format, so that workers could act upon them. In the end, some of the automated equipment was removed. Its Japanese rivals, in the mean time, opted for cheaper plants with less technology and more people—whom they managed very carefully to obtain high productivity.[43]

Often the way in which a firm acquires its assets is by applying its capabilities.

- McDonald's brand and reputational assets are the result of many years developing and applying competences in marketing and capabilities in the consistent production of edible hamburgers. Microsoft's $37 billion cash and readily available assets[44] are the result of a raft of competences in areas like software and applications development, marketing, and relationship management.

- Cisco Systems' more than 80 per cent share of the global router market, and its profit margin of 39 per cent, by far the highest of the large computer hardware manufacturers, comes from competences in lean manufacturing and supply-chain management.[45]

- Procter & Gamble's position as the world's top corporate brand[46] is the result of competences in portfolio management, capabilities in customer segmentation, and competences in product brand-building.

A really strong strategic asset can confer easier advantages than competences and capabilities, often over a long period. Low-cost mineral reserves will confer cost advantage as long as the mineral is in demand, and large cash reserves will retain their value for as long as inflation or managerial inertia does not dilute them.

Competences and capabilities, on the other hand, require constant attention to ensure that they do not become outdated, or do not freeze the organization into a rigid way of behaving. However, it is more common for a capability or competence to conform to the four VIRUS criteria than for an asset to do so. This is because capabilities are 'home-grown' within each organization and time-dependent, whereas physical assets can often be bought by competitors from the same suppliers and recruit their human resources from the same pool of talent.

7.6 Dynamic capabilities

The previous sections have discussed how resources contribute to an organization's competitive advantage in the present. But we are also interested in whether these will lead to sustainable advantage, in other words competitive success in the future. This requires a view on how the environment is likely to change.

Some strategic assets, as we have already said, retain their value well even if the PESTLE factors trigger changes in the industry structure. Factors like a strong reputation, access to low cost inputs, and extremely large financial reserves are likely to help to sustain a firm's advantage, no matter what happens to the environment. But sometimes, a firm's resources can be devalued by environmental change. The value of some firms' high-street retail property portfolios, accumulated over many years, has been diminished by changes in preferences. Shoppers have gravitated towards larger and more spacious stores, enclosed in malls with plentiful parking space.

So we are also interested in how an organization is able to adapt to changes in its environment—whether it has dynamic capabilities—its capacity to learn, adapt, and innovate. Dynamic capabilities include:[47]

- the ability to detect and assess environmental change, since this gives the organization the data from which to learn constructively;
- the ability to innovate, which demonstrates that the organization can use its learning to good effect. This can be in the form of new product development, which can lead to differentiation advantage, or in process or system innovations, which can lead to cost advantage;
- the ability to manage across multiple product development schedules;
- the ability to transcend technology cycles and integrate technologies across disparate units.

Dynamic capabilities involve the ability to learn, to exploit knowledge, and to innovate—all of which are sufficiently important to warrant a chapter of their own—Chapter 10.

7.7 Core rigidities and competency traps

In order to sustain its advantage, an organization has to balance two conflicting priorities: exploitation and exploration. It must make sure that its core competences and distinctive capabilities are kept up-to-date and efficient. However, it must also make sure that attention is not focused upon them to the extent that they squeeze out innovation and learning in other areas.

→ We introduced the concepts of exploitation and exploration in Section 5.2.2.

Like any other commitment made by a firm, the development of strategic resources has an opportunity cost. The investment of time and assets in developing competences and capabilities, in particular, carries with it the risk that the organization will be caught in a competency trap. Once managers recognize that a particular competence or capability is strategically important, they will be tempted to invest in refining it. The organization will want to keep its head start over competition, and may see that they will get a better return on investment in existing resources than in newer, riskier ones. This is an example of a strategy that seems rational in the short term, but may turn out badly in the longer term since, generally speaking, organizations need a spread of competences in order to be successful.

If economic reasons may tempt an organization to over-invest in their competences, socio-cultural factors may tempt it to over-use them. When a group of people has a routine that has worked well, they will tend to use it again. And a similar problem happens with knowledge. Tacit knowledge within teams is known to lose its usefulness as a result of 'knowledge ossification' if not renewed through new inputs.[48]

Such core rigidities[49] in routines or relationships can somehow 'take over' the organization. Its users may not stop to look at subtle differences between the way a routine or resource has operated in the past and the way they want to use it now. They may even reject new and better routines because they have developed experience and efficiencies that can confer some short-term competitive advantage, in operating an inferior one. However, even small differences in the technology that is being used or the needs of the target market that is being addressed may call for a different way of working, rendering the old routine unsuitable.

What Can Go Wrong 7.1 Core rigidities and competency traps at Novotel[50]

The international hotel chain, Novotel, is an example of a firm that found itself in a competency trap. Novotel was founded by two French entrepreneurs in 1967. Its steady expansion during the 1970s and 1980s owed much to distinctive capabilities in reliability. It developed a standard format for hotel room designs, for furnishing, and for standards of service that enabled it to offer business travellers, in particular, a uniform standard of comfort throughout Europe and, later, the world. This capability was backed up with competences in control that enabled the firm to make sure standards were maintained.

In 1987, Novotel began to extend the use of this competence in control. It developed a rigid set of rules and procedures, the '95 Bolts' that governed every aspect of the operation of their hotels in minute detail. For example, the words used to greet guests were standardized worldwide.

Even though it made the guests' experience even more reliably uniform, this strategy was not a success. The new systems made it difficult for staff to show personal warmth towards their guests and react spontaneously to their requirements, making Novotel seem less hospitable. New competitors appeared, but Novotel's procedures prevented managers from matching their prices or from offering priority to regular guests. The hotels started losing business, and Novotel recorded a sharp decline in profits.

By basing its entire strategy around its competence in control, Novotel transformed that core competence into a core rigidity. In 1992, and after widespread consultation within Novotel, a new management team scrapped the '95 Bolts' system and adopted a new strategy, which improved hotel occupancy rates and financial results. Hotel general managers were given greater autonomy to respond to guests' needs and competitors' moves. New systems and structures were put in place to help hotel managers to learn from one another—for example, an interest group was set up where managers of all airport hotels could share their experiences.

● CHAPTER SUMMARY

This chapter has introduced you to some of the key themes in the resource-based view of the firms. In this view strategic resources are:

- rare (distinctive)—only a few firms in the industry have them;
- valuable, making a genuine difference to a firm's cost and/or differentiation advantage, and corresponding to success factors within the industry;
- difficult to acquire or copy, because they are in genuinely short supply, because they have a high tacit knowledge content or because the way they have developed over time makes them impossible to copy;
- difficult to substitute with other resources.

Threshold resources are those which many firms in an industry possess, and which are necessary to compete, but which are not likely to sustain the firm's position if competition becomes more intense, or the environment changes to a more hostile one. Physical and financial assets are not usually rare enough or difficult enough to copy to be considered strategic. Human, intellectual and reputational assets are more often difficult to imitate, and so can be the source of advantage.

An organization's competitive position at any given point in time depends on its having assets and capabilities that generate cost and/or differentiation advantage. Resources that are valuable in one industry or market segment may not be valuable in another. Whether or not an organization has a sustainable advantage depends on whether it has assets and capabilities that will remain valuable as the environment changes.

Strategic resources are rare; few organizations have more than two or three. Hardly any organization has strategic resources in every one of the categories listed in this chapter.

Online Resource Centre
www.oxfordtextbooks.co.uk/orc/haberberg_rieple/

Visit the Online Resource Centre that accompanies this book to read more information relating to the resource-based view of the firm.

● KEY SKILLS

The key skills you should have developed after reading this chapter are:

- the ability to use the VIRUS tests to assess whether a resource is strategic or not;
- the ability to identify a business' core competences and other strategic resources and how they interrelate;
- the ability to evaluate the extent to which resources give an organization a sustainable advantage;
- the ability to identify core rigidities and competency traps and assess the dangers they pose.

● REVIEW QUESTIONS

1. Take an organization you know well. What is the basis of its competitive advantage? Is that advantage sustainable?

2. Does H&M have any strategic assets?

3. Does BA have any distributed competences? If BA has core competences, but few distributed competences, is this a good thing?

4. Do McDonald's human assets constitute a strategic resource? Why (or why not)?

5. What impact might the recall of Dell computer batteries have on Sony's reputation? Does this matter?

6. What steps can an organization take to guard against core rigidities and competency traps? What problems would it risk if it did take those steps?

● FURTHER READING

The resource-based view has an abundance of writings to choose from. For good summaries of the key aspects of the RBV see:

- Barney, J. B. (2001). 'Resource-based theories of competitive advantage: A ten-year retrospective on the resource-based view'. *Journal of Management*, 27/6: 643–50.

- Barney, J. (2001). 'Is the resource based view a useful perspective for strategic management research? Yes'. *Academy of Management Review*, 26/1: 41–56.

- Conner, K. (1991). 'A historical comparison of resource-based theory and five schools of thought within industrial organization economics: Do we have a new theory of the firm?' *Journal of Management*, 17/1: 121–54.

- A special edition of the *Strategic Management Journal* (2003, 24/10) focused on resource-based theory. Another special issue (2000, 21/10–11) focuses on the evolution of firm capabilities.

- Gulati, R. and Kletter, D. (2005). 'Shrinking core, expanding periphery: The relational architecture of high-performing organizations'. *California Management Review*, 47/3: 77–104 is an excellent review of current practice in building and managing relational capital.

On corporate reputation and branding

- Fombrun, C. J. and Riel, C. B. M. v. (2003). *Fame and Fortune: How Successful Companies Build Winning Reputations*. Upper Saddle River, NJ: Prentice Hall/Financial Times.

- De Chernatony, L. and McDonald, M. H. B. (2003). *Creating Powerful Brands in Consumer, Service and Industrial Markets*. 3rd edn. Oxford: Butterworth Heinemann.

- Feldwick, P. (2002). 'What is brand equity, anyway?' Henley. World Advertising Research Center/NTC Publications.

On the value of intangibles

- Low, J. and Kalafut, P. C. (2002). *Invisible Advantage: How Intangibles Are Driving Business Performance*. Cambridge, MA: Perseus Publishing.

● REFERENCES

Amit, R. and Schoemaker, P. J. H. (1993). 'Strategic assets and organizational rent'. *Strategic Management Journal*, 14: 33–46.

Ancona, D. G., Goodman, P. S., Lawrence, B. S., and Tushman, M. L. (2001). 'Time: a new research lens'. *Academy of Management Review*, 26/4: 645–63.

Andrews, K. (1971). *The Concept of Corporate Strategy*. Homewood, IL: Irwin.

Baden-Fuller, C. and Stopford, J. M. (1992). *Rejuvenating the Mature Business: The Competitive Challenge*. Cambridge, MA: Harvard Business School Press.

Bain, J. S. (1956). *Barriers to New Competition*. Cambridge, MA: Harvard University Press.

Barney, J. (1991). 'Firm resources and sustained competitive advantage'. *Journal of Management*, 17, 99–121.

Barney, J. (1995). 'Looking inside for competitive advantage'. *Academy of Management Executive*, 9/4: 49–65.

Barney, J. (2001a). *Gaining and Sustaining Competitive Advantage*. Upper Saddle River, NJ: Prentice Hall.

Barney, J. (2001b). 'Is the resource based view a useful perspective for strategic management research? Yes'. *Academy of Management Review*, 26/1: 41–56.

Barney, J. B. (2001c). 'Resource-based theories of competitive advantage: A ten year retrospective on the resource-based view'. *Journal of Management*, 27: 643–50.

Baum, J. and Oliver, C. (1991). 'Institutional linkages and organizational mortality'. *Administrative Science Quarterly*, 36: 187–218.

Baum, J. and Oliver, C. (1992). 'Institutional embeddedness and the dynamics of organizational populations'. *American Sociological Review*, 57/4: 540–59.

Benner, M. J. and Tushman, M. L. (2003). 'Exploitation, exploration, and process management: the productivity dilemma revisited'. *Academy of Management Review*, 28/2: 238–56.

Berman, S. L., Down, J., and Hill, C. W. L. (2002). 'Tacit knowledge as a source of competitive advantage in the National Basketball Association'. *Academy of Management Journal*, 45: 13–31.

Berthon, P., Hulbert, J., and Pitt, L. (1999). 'Brand management prognostications'. *Sloan Management Review*, 40/12: 53–65.

Brown, S. L. and Eisenhardt, K. M. (1997). 'The art of continuous change: linking complexity theory and time-paced evolution in relentlessly shifting organizations'. *Administrative Science Quarterly*, 42/1: 1–34.

Cappelli, P. (2000). 'A market-driven approach to retaining talent'. *Harvard Business Review*, 78/1.

Capello, R. and Faggian, A. (2005). 'Collective learning and relational capital in local innovation processes'. *Regional Studies*, 39/1: 75–87.

Collins, J. and Hitt, M. (2006). 'Leveraging tacit knowledge in alliances: the importance of using relational capabilities to build and leverage relational capital'. *Journal of Engineering & Technology Management*, 23/3: 147–67.

Conner, K. (1991). 'A historical comparison of resource-based theory and five schools of thought within industrial organization economics: do we have a new theory of the firm?' *Journal of Management*, 17/1: 121–54.

Cousins, P., Handfield, R., Lawson, B., and Petersen, K. (2006). 'Creating supply chain relational capital: the impact of formal and informal socialization processes'. *Journal of Operations Management*, 24/6: 851–63.

Day, G. (1994). 'The capabilities of market-driven organizations'. *Journal of Marketing*, 58: 37–52.

De Chernatony, L. and McDonald, M. H. B. (2003). *Creating Powerful Brands in Consumer, Service and Industrial Markets*. 3rd edn. Oxford: Butterworth Heinemann.

Del Canto, J. G. and Gonzalez, I. S. (1999). 'A resource-based analysis of the factors determining a firm's RandD activities'. *Research Policy*, 28/8: 891–905.

Delerue-Vidot, H. (2006). 'Opportunism and unilateral commitment: the moderating effect of relational capital'. *Management Decision*, 44/6: 737–51.

Dierickx, I. and Cool, K. (1989). 'Asset accumulation and sustainability of competitive advantage'. *Management Science*, 35: 554–71.

Dyer, J. and Singh, H. (1998). 'The relational view: cooperative strategy and sources of interorganizational competitive advantage'. *Academy of Management Review*, 23/4: 660–79.

Eisenhardt, K. M. and Brown, S. L. (1998). 'Time pacing: competing in markets that won't stand still'. *Harvard Business Review*, March–April: 59–69.

Eisenhardt, K. M. and Martin, J. A. (2000). 'Dynamic capabilities: what are they?' *Strategic Management Journal*, 21/10–11: 1105–21.

Fluke, C. and Badenhausen, K. (2004). 'Power brands'. *Forbes*, 173/8: 59–62.

Foster, R. and Kaplan, S. (2001a). 'Creative destruction'. *McKinsey Quarterly*, 3: 40–51.

Foster, R. and Kaplan, S. (2001b). *Creative Destruction: Why Companies that are Built to Last Underperform the Market—and How to Successfully Transform them*. New York: Currency.

Granovetter, M. (2005). 'The impact of social structure on economic outcomes'. *Journal of Economic Perspectives*, 19/1: 33–50.

Granstrand, O., Patel, P., and Pavitt, K. (1997). 'Multi-technology corporations: Why they have distributed rather than core competencies'. *California Management Review*, 39/4: 8–25.

Grant, R. (1991). 'The resource-based theory of competitive advantage: implications for strategy formulation'. *California Management Review*, 33: 114–22.

Grunert, K. G. (1996). 'Automatic and strategic processes in advertising effects'. *Journal of Marketing*, 60/4: 88–101.

Gulati, R. (1999). 'Network location and learning: the influence of network resources and firm capabilities on alliance formation'. *Strategic Management Journal*, 20: 397–420.

Gulati, R. and Kletter, D. (2005). 'Shrinking core, expanding periphery: the relational architecture of high-performing organizations'. *California Management Review*, 47/3: 77–104.

Hall, R. (1992). 'The strategic analysis of intangible resources'. *Strategic Management Journal*, 13: 135–44.

Hamel, G. and Prahalad, C. K. (1994). *Competing for the Future*. Boston, MA: Harvard Business Press.

Hardy, C., Phillips, N., and Lawrence, T. B. (2003). 'Resources, knowledge and influence: the organizational effects of interorganizational collaboration'. *Journal of Management Studies*, 40/2: 321–47.

Harrison, J. S., Hitt, M. A., Hoskisson, R. E., and Ireland, R. D. (2001). 'Resource complementarity in business combinations: extending the logic to organizational alliances'. *Journal of Management*, 27: 679–90.

Hart, M. (2002). *Diamond: The History of a Cold-blooded Love Affair*. London: Fourth Estate.

Hawawini, G., Subramanian, V., and Verdin, P. (2003). 'Is performance driven by industry- or firm-specific factors? A new look at the evidence'. *Strategic Management Journal*, 24/1: 1–16.

Hawawini, G., Subramanian, V., and Verdin, P. (2005). 'Is performance driven by industry- or firm-specific factors? A reply to McNamara, Aime, and Vaaler'. *Strategic Management Journal*, 26/11: 1083–6.

Helfat, C. and Peteraf, M. (2003). 'The dynamic resource-based view: capability lifecycles'. *Strategic Management Journal*, 24/10: 997–1010.

Henderson, R. and Mitchell, W. (1997). 'The interactions of organizational and competitive influences on strategy and performance'. *Strategic Management Journal*, 18 (Special Issue), 5–14.

Hitt, M. A. and Ireland, R. D. (1985). 'Corporate distinctive competence, strategy, industry, and performance'. *Strategic Management Journal*, 6/3: 273–93.

Hoang, H. and Rothaermel, F. T. (2005). 'The effect of general and partner-specific alliance experience on joint RandD project performance'. *Academy of Management Journal*, 48/2: 332–46.

Hoopes, D. G., Madsen, T. L., and Walker, G. (2003). 'Why is there a resource-based view? Toward a theory of competitive heterogeneity'. *Strategic Management Journal*, 24/10: 889–902.

Kakabadse, A., Kakabadse, N., and Lake, A. (2007). 'Investment dealers' ways of working: integrating compensation with relational capital'. *Thunderbird International Business Review*, 49/1: 103–21.

Kale, P. and Singh, H. (2000). 'Learning and protection of proprietary assets in strategic alliances: building relational capital'. *Strategic Management Journal*, 21/3: 217–37.

Kay, J. (1993). *Foundations of Corporate Success: How Business Strategies Add Value*. Oxford: Oxford University Press.

Lave, J. (1988). *Cognition in Practice: Mind, Mathematics and Culture in Everyday Life*. Cambridge: Cambridge University Press.

Lavie, D. (2006). 'The competitive advantage of interconnected firms: an extension of the resource-based view'. *Academy Of Management Review*, 31/3: 638–58.

Lee, C., Lee, K., and Pennings, J. M. (2001). 'Internal capabilities, external networks, and performance: a study of technology-based ventures'. *Strategic Management Journal*, 22: 615–40.

Leonard-Barton, D. (1992). 'Core capabilities and core rigidities: a paradox in managing new product development'. *Strategic Management Journal*, 13: 111–25.

Levinthal, D. A. (1995). 'Strategic management and the exploration of diversity'. In Montgomery, C. A. (ed.), *Resource-based and Evolutionary Theories of the Firm*. Boston, MA: Kluwer.

McGahan, A. M. (1999). 'The performance of US corporations: 1981–1994'. *The Journal of Industrial Economics*, 47/4: 373–98.

McGahan, A. M. and Porter, M. E. (1997). 'How much does industry matter, really?' *Strategic Management Journal*, 18 (Summer Special Issue): 15–30.

McGahan, A. and Porter, M. (2003). 'The emergence and sustainability of abnormal profits'. *Strategic Organization*, 1/1: 79–108.

McNamara, G., Aime, F., and Vaaler, P. (2005). 'Is performance driven by industry or firm-specific factors? A response to Hawawini, Subramanian, and Verdin'. *Strategic Management Journal*, 26/11: 1075–81.

Makadok, R. (1998). 'Can first-mover and early-mover advantages be sustained in an industry with low barriers to entry/imitation?' *Strategic Management Journal*, 19: 683–96.

Makadok, R. (2001). 'Towards a synthesis of the resource-based and dynamic capability views of rent creation'. *Strategic Management Journal*, 22: 387–401.

Markides, C. C. and Williamson, P. J. (1996). 'Corporate diversification and organizational structure: A resource-based view'. *Academy of Management Journal*, 39/2: 340.

Mason, E. S. (1939). 'Price and production policies of large-scale enterprises'. *American Economic Review*, 29/1: 61–74.

Miles, G., Snow, C. C., and Sharfman, P. (1993). 'Industry variety and performance'. *Strategic Management Journal*, 14: 163–77.

Milgrom, P. and Roberts, J. (1982). 'Predation, reputation and entry deterrence'. *Journal of Economic Theory*, 27: 280–312.

Molina-Morales, F. and Martínez-Fernández, M. (2006). 'Industrial districts: something more than a neighbourhood'. *Entrepreneurship & Regional Development*, 18/6: 503–24.

Morash, E. A. and Lynch, D. F. (2002). 'Public policy and global supply chain capabilities and performance: a resource-based view'. *Journal of International Marketing*, 10/1: 25.

Nahapiet, J. and Ghoshal, S. (1998). 'Social capital, intellectual capital, and the organizational advantage'. *Academy of Management Review*, 23: 242–66.

Nelson, R. S. and Winter, S. (1982). *An Evolutionary Theory of Economic Change.* Cambridge, MA: Harvard University Press.

Ocasio, W. (1997). 'Towards an attention-based view of the firm'. *Strategic Management Journal*, 187–206.

Oliver, C. (1997). 'Sustainable competitive advantage: combining institutional and resource-based views'. *Strategic Management Journal*, 18: 697–713.

Parnell, J. A. (2002). 'Competitive Strategy Research: Current Challenges and New Directions'. *Journal of Management Research*, 2(1): 1–12.

Parnell, J. A. and Hershey, L. (2005). 'The strategy-performance relationship revisited: the blessing and curse of the combination strategy'. *International Journal of Commerce and Management*, 15/1: 17–33.

Patel, P. and Pavitt, K. (1997). 'The technological competencies of the world's largest firms: complex and path-dependent, but not much variety'. *Research Policy*, 26: 141–56.

Pavitt, K. (1998). 'Technologies, products and organization in the innovating firm: what Adam Smith tells us and Joseph Schumpeter doesn't'. *Industrial and Corporate Change*, 7: 433–57.

Pavitt, K. (2002). 'Innovating routines in the business firm: what corporate tasks should they be accomplishing?' *Industrial and Corporate Change*, 11: 117–33.

Penrose, E. (1959). *The Theory of the Growth of the Firm*. Oxford: Oxford University Press (2nd edn, 1995).

Peteraf, M. A. (1993). 'The cornerstones of competitive advantage: a resource-based view'. *Strategic Management Journal*, 14: 179–91.

Phillips, N., Lawrence, T. B., and Hardy, C. (2000). 'Interorganizational collaboration and the dynamics of institutional fields'. *Journal of Management Studies*, 37: 23–45.

Pitt, M. and Clarke, K. (1999). 'Competing on competence: a knowledge perspective on the management of strategic innovation'. *Technology Analysis and Strategic Management*, 11/3: 301–16.

Powell, T. C. (1996). 'How much does industry matter? An alternative empirical test'. *Strategic Management Journal*, 17: 323–34.

Prahalad, C. K. and Hamel, G. (1990). 'The core competence of the corporation'. *Harvard Business Review*, 68/3: 79–91.

Priem, R. (2001). 'The business level RBV: Great wall or Berlin wall?' *Academy of Management Review*, 26/4: 499–501.

Priem, R. and Butler, J. (2001a). 'Is the resource based view a useful perspective for strategic management research?' *Academy of Management Review*, 26/1: 22–40.

Priem, R. and Butler, J. (2001b). 'Tautology in the resource-based view and the implications of externally determined resource value: further comments'. *Academy of Management Review*, 26/1: 57–66.

Rice, J. and Hoppe, R. (2001). 'Supply chain vs. supply chain'. *Supply Chain Management Review*, 5/5: 46–52.

Rothaermel, F. T. (2001). 'Incumbent's advantage through exploiting complementary assets via interfirm cooperation'. *Strategic Management Journal*, 22, Special issue: 687–99.

Rumelt, R. (1991). 'How much does industry matter?' *Strategic Management Journal*, 12: 167–85.

Russo, M. V. and Fouts, P. A. (1997). 'A resource-based perspective on corporate environmental performance and profitability'. *Academy of Management Journal*, 40: 534–59.

Sapsed, J. D. (2005). 'How should "knowledge bases" be organised in multi-technology corporations?' *International Journal of Innovation Management*, 9/1: 75–102.

Saxton, T. (1997). 'The effects of partner and relationship characteristics on alliance outcomes'. *Academy of Management Journal*, 40: 443–61.

Shenkar, O. and Yuchtman-Yaar, E. (1997). 'Reputation, image, prestige and goodwill: An interdisciplinary approach to organizational standing'. *Human Relations*, 50/11: 1361–81.

Stalk, G., Evans, P., and Shulman, E. (1992). 'Competing on capabilities: the new rules of corporate strategy'. *Harvard Business Review*, 70/2: 57–69.

Stimpert, J. L. and Duhaime, I. M. (1997). 'Seeing the big picture: the influence of industry, diversification, and business strategy on performance'. *Academy of Management Journal*, 40: 560–83.

Stuart, T. (2000). 'Interorganizational alliances and the performance of firms: a study of growth and innovation'. *Strategic Management Journal*, 21/8: 791–811.

Stuart, T., Hoang, H., and Hybels, R. (1999). 'Interorganizational endorsements and the performance of entrepreneurial ventures'. *Administrative Science Quarterly*, 44: 315–49.

Szymanski, S. and Kuypers, T. (1999). *Winners and Losers: the Business Strategy of Football*. London: Viking,

Teece, Pisano, G. and Shuen, A. (1997). 'Dynamic capabilities and strategic management'. *Strategic Management Journal*, 18: 509–34.

Tripsas, M. and Gavetti, G. (2000). 'Capabilities, cognition, and inertia: evidence from digital imaging'. *Strategic Management Journal*, 21/10–11: 1147–61.

Tushman, M. L. and O'Reilly, C. A. (1996). 'Ambidextrous organizations: managing evolutionary and revolutionary change'. *California Management Review*, 38/4: 8–30.

Tushman, M. L. and O'Reilly, C. A. (1997). *Winning through Innovation*. Boston, MA: Harvard Business School Press.

Tushman, M. L. and O'Reilly, C. A. (2004). 'The ambidextrous organization'. *Harvard Business Review*, 82/4: 74–81.

Vergin, R. and Qoronfleh, M. (1998). 'Corporate reputation and the stock market'. *Business Horizons*, 41/1: 19–26.

Ward, S., Light, L., and Goldstine, J. (1999). 'What high-tech managers need to know about brands'. *Harvard Business Review*, 77: 85–95.

West, D., Ford, J., and Ibrahim, E. (2006). *Strategic Marketing: Creating Competitive Advantage*. Oxford: Oxford University Press.

Yeoh, P.-L and Roth, K. (1999). 'An empirical analysis of sustained advantage in the U.S. pharmaceutical industry: impact of firm resources and capabilities'. *Strategic Management Journal*, 20: 637–53.

 End-of-chapter Case Study 7.1   De Beers: are strategic resources forever?

Company History

Take some wood from prehistoric trees, subject it to intense volcanic heat and pressure under the surface of the earth for thousands of years, and the result is the formation of crystals called diamonds which, when cut and polished, are among the most valuable and sought after of gemstones and the hardest known material that exists in nature—the word 'diamond' derives from the ancient Greek *adamas* meaning 'invincible'.

Of the 26,000kg of diamonds mined annually around the world, roughly half come from central and southern Africa, with other important sources being Canada, Australia, and, increasingly,

Russia. Until the late nineteenth century, total global output was only a few pounds in weight each year. However, in the 1870s, large deposits were found in southern Africa near the Orange River. A diamond rush followed as speculators and entrepreneurs stampeded to open mines as quickly as possible, and the supply of the stones increased rapidly.

Since then, one company whose name is synonymous with diamonds has dominated the world trade in them: De Beers. Based in Johannesburg, South Africa, the firm was founded in 1888 by British businessman Cecil John Rhodes, after whom the African state formerly called Rhodesia, now Zimbabwe, was also named. Originally a cotton farmer, Rhodes and his partner, Charles ➜

De Beers diamond mining: are strategic resources for ever? *Corbis*

➜ Dunell Rudd, bought a farm on which diamonds had been found from two Afrikaner brothers, Nicholas and Dierderik Arnoldus de Beer, for £6,300. The first two mines which formed the foundation of the company's fortunes were dug on this site. Although no longer owned by the brothers, one kept the de Beers name, the other was known as the 'Big Hole' or 'Premier Mine'. Subsequently, Rhodes and Rudd began buying out or investing in many of the other rival mines in the region, until within a few years De Beers was a major force in diamond production in Africa. In one transaction, a competitor's mining interests were reportedly bought with the handing over of a cheque for £5,338,650, then the largest cheque ever written.[51]

The diamond industry and the De Beers company have played a significant role in South Africa's economy ever since. Rhodes himself was also an active politician and legislator. As well as contributing to the founding of the state of Rhodesia, he was a member of the Cape Parliament and in 1890 became prime minister of the Cape Colony, as that part of southern Africa was then known.

The Diamond Supply Chain

There are two main types of diamonds: those of high grade, gemstone quality that will eventually become expensive jewellery, and lower grade stones that are used for industrial purposes such as in drilling and cutting tools. Diamonds can also be made synthetically, although the quality of these has traditionally made them suitable only for industrial use. Unlike gold and other precious commodities, gemstone diamonds are not sold and traded on world markets but marketed and distributed through a system of controlled channels. Gem quality stones go through various stages of production, processing and distribution between being mined from the ground and appearing in the windows of up-market jewellery stores, and De Beers has interests to a greater or lesser extent in several of them.

Diamonds are rare. There are few locations around the world where they occur naturally, and the diamond mining industry, particularly in Africa, is highly concentrated in terms of ownership and control by a small group of major players, of which De Beers is a leading member. The company owns or has a stake in almost all diamond mining operations in Africa and its mining interests produce around 60 per cent of the world's output.[52]

In the mining and first stages of processing, ore is extracted from the ground and crushed to reveal raw stones of different sizes. A large proportion of the rough diamonds produced globally are then sold to and marketed through the Diamond Trading Company or DTC, a De Beers subsidiary, which has branches around the world and handles stones from mines owned by ➜

➜ both De Beers and other producers. The share of the world rough diamond trade that is handled by the DTC has been estimated at around 70–80 per cent.[53] DTC sorts rough diamonds into different categories by weight and density. It then releases these for sale in controlled amounts of bulk lots to a limited number of specially chosen and authorized distributors called 'sightholders' several times a year. In 2006, DTC's turnover was reported to be approximately US$5.7bn.[54]

After being bought by sightholders, the stones are sent to be cut and polished. This transforms raw stones, which are naturally dull in colour, into the glittering gemstones that consumers prize so highly. The final value of a diamond can be significantly affected by the skill with which it is cut and finished, and the cutting process relies on a set of highly specialized skills that are concentrated in only a few locations around the world, traditionally Antwerp, Amsterdam, Johannesburg, New York, and Tel Aviv. More recently however, newer cutting centres offering the same quality of work but at lower cost have appeared in India, China, and Thailand.[55]

Distribution after cutting and polishing is also limited and controlled. Cut stones are marketed through 26 registered diamond exchanges or 'bourses', where wholesalers buy small lots which will either be incorporated into manufactured jewellery or sold on to final consumers through retailers.[56]

Finished diamonds and jewellery are usually sold through up-market stores, and De Beers also has a presence in retailing. In 2001, it formed a joint venture with LVMH, a French luxury goods company, to open a number of De Beers branded stores in upscale locations in major cities including London, Paris Tokyo, Dubai, and Beverly Hills.[57]

'Diamonds are Forever'

Although diamonds are rare and De Beers exerts a strong degree of control over their production and distribution, it is still necessary to position them in consumers' minds as objects of desire.

Historically, diamonds have always competed for jewellery buyers' affections with other types of gemstones. In 1938, however, when the world was in recession and, despite De Beers's efforts, diamond prices had fallen, the company appointed US advertising agency N W Ayer to try and revive its fortunes and those of the diamond industry. As Europe was moving towards war, attention was focused on the US. The goal was to change the image of diamonds from being unattainable trinkets and investments available only to the very rich, to being aspirational and more affordable purchases for those at the more affluent end of the mass market.

Ayer defined the target market for diamonds as 'some 70 million people, 15 years of age or over whose opinion we seek to influence in support of our objectives'. The advertising and publicity campaign, which was supported by extensive market research, was spectacularly successful and the slogan that an Ayer copywriter created, 'A Diamond is Forever', became synonymous with the company, and is still used today. Ayer's campaign focused on making De Beers indelibly associated with diamonds, but some later advertisements did not even feature the company's name, simply the slogan, the aim being to make the diamond a brand in itself. Successive campaigns used a skilful blend of advertising and public relations to position diamonds as being not only unique and superior to other stones, but also precious works of art signifying eternity and romance, and therefore the first choice of gemstone for wedding and engagement rings. As well as being an inseparable part of courtship and marriage, diamonds were also promoted as symbols of prestige and status that, as gifts, could commemorate life's great occasions. The idea that diamonds were for a lifetime and 'forever' also deterred customers from reselling them, discouraging the growth of a second-hand market.

Spectacular stones were also donated to and worn by Hollywood stars and celebrities including Queen Elizabeth of England. By 1941, sales in the US had increased by a reported 55 per cent. Further successful moves into international markets were made in the 1960s, particularly into Brazil, Germany, and Japan, where large numbers of young Japanese, for whom diamonds held no traditional significance, were persuaded that they were an indispensable part of modern courtship and marriage rituals. For De Beers, Japan became, from virtually nothing, a US$1 billion a year market, exceeding the firm's most optimistic expectations.[58]

New Challenges in the Diamond Trade

De Beers has long played a dominant role in the world diamond trade, especially through its large share of upstream mining operations and the control that DTC exerts over the distribution of stones. In response to concerns that its strong position was anti-competitive, there have historically been long-term restrictions imposed on the company by American trade authorities which meant that it could not deal directly with companies in the US but only through intermediaries. In 1994, the company was also charged by the US Justice Department with violations of antitrust (competition) laws for conspiring to fix prices of industrial diamonds. However, after pleading guilty and agreeing to pay a US$10 million fine in 2004, these trade restrictions were lifted and De Beers was again allowed to trade directly with the US after many years.[59]

De Beers has also faced regulatory forces in Europe. To stop what were seen as anti-competitive practices which restricted ➜

➔ the flow of rough diamonds onto the market, the European Commission ordered De Beers to stop buying stones from a rival Russian producer, Alrosa, in a settlement which allows the firm to make commitments to cease what the Commission describes as 'abusive practices' or face a fine of 10 per cent of global turnover.[60] Similarly, before its retail joint venture with LMVH was allowed to launch, the European Commission carried out an investigation into whether this move into retailing was anti-competitive. Eventually, it was decided that the joint venture could go ahead.[61]

There have also been criticisms of the detrimental effects to the environment of diamond mining and the poor conditions experienced by workers in some parts of the diamond mining industry. De Beers and other industry members have responded by emphasizing its attempts to adopt an ethical approach to production and the benefits to some African economies and communities that come from the diamond trade.[62]

The diamond business is changing as new sources of diamonds have been discovered in different parts of the world. As well as exploring for new sources in Africa, De Beers has developed a joint venture mining operation in Canada, but other supplies originating outside the company's ownership and control from both Canada and a newly liberalized Russia, have appeared on world markets.[63] As a result, company chairman Nicky Oppenheimer announced in 2003 that De Beers was 'certainly moving away from being the ultimate controller of the diamond business'.[64]

As they improve in quality with advances in technology, synthesized or 'cultured' diamonds, which have the same composition as real stones but are produced in a laboratory, may also encroach more into the markets for traditional gems. It is now possible to produce synthetic diamonds which are flawless and increasingly difficult to tell apart from those that are mined from the ground, but which are considerably cheaper. Producers of synthesized stones also claim that their production process is more environmentally friendly and ethical.

In response, De Beers is lobbying for synthetic diamonds to be labelled as such and is promoting the idea that only natural diamonds are 'real'.[65] It has also begun to register and imprint a unique serial number onto each mined gemstone to try to prevent synthetic diamonds being sold as natural gems. Diamonds may well be forever, but can the same be said of De Beers's long-standing hold over the world diamond trade?

Case study questions

1. What are De Beers's key strategic resources.

2. How do these strategic resources link with the company's history and heritage?

3. To what extent do you think these strategic resources are sustainable in the twenty-first century. What factors may pose a threat to their sustainability?

4. What competency traps might De Beers encounter?

● NOTES

1 Penrose (1959).

2 See Nelson and Winter (1982); Amit and Schoemaker (1993); Peteraf (1993). See Barney (2001c) for a review.

3 This definition is based on the one in Barney (2001a).

4 See, for example, Hitt and Ireland (1985); Dierickx and Cool (1989); Prahalad and Hamel (1990); Conner (1991); Grant (1991); Hamel and Prahalad (1994); Pitt and Clarke (1999); Makadok (2001); Morash and Lynch (2002); Del Canto and Gonzalez (1999); Hoopes et al. (2003). A special edition of the *Strategic Management Journal* (2003), volume 24, also focuses on resource-based theory.

5 The definition of resource is adapted from Barney (1991: 101) and Helfat and Peteraf (2003). Our definition of strategic resource is based on Amit and Schoemaker's (1993) definition of strategic *assets*. As we mention later in this section, the whole area is a minefield of conflicting terminology.

6 These criteria were first laid down by Barney (1991, 1995), who uses the acronyms VRIN or VRIO.

7 See, for example, *Canberra Times* (2006). 'The genius behind'. 29 January: 20; *The Australian* (2006). 'Without Jobs, Apple just wouldn't compute'. 3 April: 30; Lunlin, J. and White, E. (2007). 'Can Dell succeed in an encore?' *Wall Street Journal*, 5 February: B4.

8 McDonald's profit margin in 2005 was 12.7% compared to Burger King's 2.4% and Wendy's 5.9%.

9 This insight into reputation comes from Barney (1991).

10 The term 'capability or 'distinctive capability' dates back at least to Kenneth Andrews' 1971 book, *The Concept of Corporate Strategy*, although it is also used by John Kay (1993). Core competences were first introduced by Prahalad and Hamel (1990). The distinction we draw between capabilities and

competences is similar to that in Stalk et al. (1992: 57–69), Day (1994: 37–52) and Pitt and Clarke (1999). Day defines distinctive capabilities as 'complex bundles of skills and accumulated knowledge, exercised through organizational processes, that enable firms to make use of their assets' (Day, 1994: 38). Core competences as 'higher second-level aggregations of capabilities'.

11 Fletcher, R. (2005). 'Secret Tesco plan to grab 45% of market'. *The Sunday Times*, Business Section, 18 September: 1; Butler, S. (2006). 'We won't be forced to sell off land, says chief'. *The Times*, 26 April: 49; Power, H. (2007). 'Tesco faces threat to land bank'. *Sunday Telegraph*, 7 January: 1.

12 Lorenz, A. (1999). 'Rolls Royce fuels industrial power deals', *Sunday Times*, Business Section, 1 August 1999.

13 Szymanski and Kuypers (1999).

14 We are using the term 'asset' here in order to be consistent with the rest of our discussion. The terminology that is more commonly used is 'human resources'—they refer to the same thing.

15 See, for example, Cappelli (2000).

16 Based on Lovewell, D. (2005). 'Searching for talent'. *Employee Benefits*, October: 66–70; *Business Week Online* (2006), 'Googling for a gig'. 21 July; BusinessWeek Online (2006). 'They love it here, and here and here'. 5 June 2006.

17 Lave (1988). Lave's most-quoted example is of people doing their shopping, who were capable of quite sophisticated calculations and feats of memory while in the supermarket working out which products to buy, but could not reproduce those calculations in another context—for example, seated at a desk.

18 See Ocasio (1997).

19 'Reputation' is the term we use, but others, such as 'goodwill' in accounting terminology, tend to refer to the same thing. Shenkar and Yuchtman-Yaar (1997) offer a useful overview.

20 See Berthon et al. (1999), Grunert (1996), and De Chernatony and McDonald (2003).

21 See, for example, Ward et al. (1999).

22 Source: Diageo's 2005 annual report and accounts.

23 Shenkar and Yuchtman-Yaar (1997) showed that US firms' share-price performance is related to their standing in *Fortune* magazine's annual survey of America's most respected corporations. Vergin and Qoronfleh (1998), showed a relationship between corporate reputation and stock market valuations. Milgrom and Roberts (1982) showed the value of reputation on deterring competition.

24 Hall (1992).

25 See, for example, Cole, R. (2006). 'Dell in the line of fire'. *The Australian*, 17 August; *Guardian* (2006). 'Viewpoint: Dell drags its feet and burns its fingers'. 16 August 2006; *The Wall Street* Journal, Asia (2006). 'Sony's computer-battery recall likely won't unplug its revival'. 22 August 2006.

26 AFX International Focus (2006). 'Oil prices climb on oil field shutdown'. 7 August 2006.

27 Schwartz, N. D. (2006). 'Can BP bounce back?' *Fortune*, Europe, 154/7: 39–43.

28 AFX International Focus (2006). 'Oil prices spike by $2 a barrel'. *AFX International Focus*, 7 August.

29 *Financial Times* (2006). 'BP's failure of execution, not strategy'. *FT.com*, 8 August 2006.

30 For a review of the relevant marketing theory see West et al. (2006), ch. 6.

31 See Dyer and Singh (1998) for a theoretical discussion of the importance of relational capital, and Gulati and Kletter (2005) for a more recent review of current business practice. Granovetter (2005) and Phillips et al. (2000) discuss the issues of building social norms and shared understanding between organizations.

32 See Baum and Oliver (1991, 1992). Oliver (1997) discusses how institutional factors interact with organizational resources.

33 See Delerue-Vidot (2006), Collins and Hitt (2006), and Kale and Singh (2000).

34 Rice and Hoppe (2001) discuss the nature of competition between supply chains, while Cousins et al. (2006) investigate how firms build relational capital within them.

35 Capello and Faggian (2005) and Molina-Morales and Martínez-Fernández, M. (2006).

36 Nahapiet and Ghoshal (1998) is a seminal article on social capital, while Gulati and Kletter (2005) and Kakabadse et al. (2007) give some examples of how it is used in practice and how it relates to relational capital.

37 Hamel and Prahalad's definition stipulates that a core competence should provide the basis for expansion into new businesses. This stipulation does not appear to have been taken up by the many writers who use the terminology in a much less restricted way (as we do) to indicate a competence that fulfills the criteria to be a strategic resource.

38 See Granstrand et al. (1997). See also Patel and Pavitt (1997), Pavitt (1998, 2002), although we cover these authors' discussions of knowledge and innovation in more detail in the next chapter.

39 See Sapsed (2005).

40 Some estimates suggest that this had increased to 70% by 2006, although the asynchronous launch of the three new consoles makes an accurate comparison hard to make.

41 Some estimates forecast that Sony's share in the next year or so will drop to about 50%. Total revenue worldwide from machines, games, and online game playing reached $29 billion in 2006, of which Sony took $8 billion. See Kilby, Nathalie. (2005). 'The future in your hands'. *Marketing Week*. 25 August, 28/34, p20–21.

42 Bulik, B. S. (2006). 'Next leap coming for Nintendo, Sony'. *Advertising Age*, 77/26.

43 Nag, A. (1986). 'Tricky auto makers discover "factory of the future" is headache just now'. *Wall Street Journal*, 13 May; Ingrassia, P. (1987). 'Who makes technology work: the grades are in for nine major industries: Autos'. *Wall Street Journal*, 12 June; *Economist* (1991). 'When General Motors' robots ran amok'. 10 August.

44 Source: Microsoft's 2005 annual report.

45 Fluke and Badenhausen (2004).

46 Ibid.

47 This avenue for discussion was started by Teece et al. (1997). Eisenhardt and Martin (2000) provide a good overview, but see also Brown and Eisenhardt (1997); Markides and Williamson (1996); Foster and Kaplan (2001a, 2001b); Tushman and O'Reilly (1996); Eisenhardt and Brown (1998); Tripsas and Gavetti (2000); Benner and Tushman (2003); and Ancona et al. (2001). A special issue of the *Strategic Management Journal* (2000, 21/10–11) focused on 'The evolution of firm capabilities'. Much of the discussion on dynamic capabilities has focused on the need for organizations to be able to focus concurrently on its existing business and future ones—what has been described as an ambidextrous organization (Tushman and O'Reilly, 1996, 1997, 2004).

48 Hoang and Rothaermel (2005); Berman et al. (2002).

49 Leonard-Barton (1992).

50 The facts in this example are all taken from field research by Baden-Fuller, C., Calori, R., and Hunt, B. (1995). '395-113-1; Novotel'. *European Case Clearing House*. See also Segal-Horn, S. and McGee, J. (1997). 'Global competencies in service multinationals'. In Thomas, H. and O'Neal, D. (eds). *Strategic Discovery: Competing in New Arenas*. Chichester: Wiley.

51 Campbell, Colin (1988). 'De Beers puts a sparkle into 100 years'. *The Times* 7 March. See also Millin, S. G. (1993). *Cecil Rhodes*. New York, Harper and Brothers Publishers.

52 'Diamond business faces tough year', <http://news.bbc.co.uk/1/hi/business/2732097.stm>, accessed 10 May 2007.

53 <http://www.debeersgroup.com/debeersweb/About+De+Beers+World+Wide/INTRODUCTIONhtm>, accessed 10.5.2007.

54 The Diamond Trading Company Factsheet <http://www.hoovers.com/dtc/--ID__105809--/free-co-factsheet.xhtml>, accessed 8 May 2007.

55 <http://dendritics.com/scales/diamond-lore.asp>, accessed 8 May 2007.

56 <http://www.worldfed.com/website/>, accessed 3 May 2007.

57 'De Beers ties up with luxury goods firm', 16 January 2001 <news.bbc.co.uk/1/hi/business/1120075.stm>, accessed 8 May 2007.

58 The information in this section is derived from Epstein, E. J. 'Have you ever tried to sell a diamond?' <http://www.edwardjayepstein.com.diamond.htm>, accessed 27 April 2007.

59 'De Beers settles price fixing charge', 14 June 2004 <http://news.bbc.co.uk/1/hi/business/3892333.stm>, accessed 8 May 2007.

60 'De Beers in EU competition deal', 22 February 2007 <http://news.bbc.co.uk/1/hi/business/4739574.stm>, accessed 3 May 2007.

61 'Diamonds are not forever', <http://news.bbc.co.uk/1/hi/business/1456877.stm>, accessed 8 May 2007.

62 <http://www.debeersgroup.com/debeersweb/Investing+in+the+Future/Ethics/>; <http://www.diamondfacts.org/index.aspx>, both accessed 9 May 2007.

63 Hart (2002).

64 'Diamond market faces a tough year', 6 February 2003 <http://news.bbc.co.uk/1/hi/business/2732097.stm>, accessed 10 February 2007.

65 Rowan, D. (2006). 'Trendsurfing: the next big thing—synthetic diamonds', *Sunday Times*, 16 December.

CHAPTER EIGHT

Architecture, Structure, and Culture

LEARNING OUTCOMES

After reading this chapter you should be able to:

→ Discuss the concepts of architecture, culture, and belief systems, identify their main elements, and explain how they interact

→ Analyse how an organization's architecture and culture have contributed to its competitive advantage, and in particular to the sustainability of that advantage

→ Assess the degree of fit between the organization's architecture and its environment, and between its architecture and strategy

→ Analyse an organization's culture, and its underlying belief systems, and evaluate the extent to which they fit its strategic situation.

INTRODUCTION

A crucial question in strategic management is why certain groups of people—organizations—perform better than others, with similar aims, confronting similar competitive challenges. Some organizations, we have already seen, arrive at better decisions than others regarding their competitive stance and value chain, so they thrive while others struggle or even die out. Moreover, as we saw in the previous chapter, some are able to build routines—competences and capabilities—and accumulate assets that can be the basis of lasting competitive advantage.

But this leads on to more questions. Why do some organizations seem consistently to make better decisions than others? Why do some build more effective routines than others with a very similar competitive stance and value chain? If one firm decides to outsource the management of its IT infrastructure, any of its competitors can easily follow suit. They can hire the same consultants as advisers, and perhaps outsource to the same service provider. So why are some able to use outsourcing and partnering as the basis of a successful strategies, while others try and fail? Similarly, why, in some organizations, are groups of people with complementary but diverse skills able to forge productive and harmonious linkages, whilst in others this diversity breaks down into factional squabbling?

The differences arise from the way in which organizations set up and manage their internal and external linkages—their architecture. The degree of autonomy people are given and the systems used to control and reward their behaviour affect their degree of motivation, and what they are motivated to do. The extent to which information systems can gather and distribute timely information influences the effectiveness of those control and reward systems, while the organization's structure helps determine whether that information reaches people who have the skills and the time to make good use of it.

The way that architecture evolves is in turn influenced by the organization's culture, particularly the belief systems that develop over time and determine which information is given priority and which behaviours are valued.

In this and the following chapter, we set out the theory that enables you to analyse and evaluate an organization's architecture and culture. This chapter focuses on the underlying theory that is relevant for all organizations, while Chapter 9 expands this for complex organizations.

8.1 Architecture and culture: an overview

Architecture and culture both deal with the ways in which people in an organization relate, on a day-to-day basis, to one another, and to other stakeholders such as suppliers, distributors, franchisees, and customers.

8.1.1 Evaluating architecture and culture

We use several key criteria, summarized in Table 8.1, to evaluate an organization's architecture and culture.

First, they must stimulate the organization to perform effectively in meeting industry survival and success factors. They must allow, and even stimulate, the transfer of information and the sharing of knowledge and learning around the organization, which may involve the coordination of different nationalities and specialist groups, each with their own subculture and language. The speed with which decisions are taken must allow the organization to remain competitive. Effective use must be made of a key resource, top management attention.[1] Top managers often represent a reservoir of experience and high-level, industry-specific skills that can be invaluable in helping people resolve problems. It is

Table 8.1 Key questions in the evaluation of architecture and culture

Do they promote the effective transfer of information and the sharing of knowledge and learning?
Do they allow decisions to be taken with sufficient speed?
Do they make effective use of top management attention?
Do they promote congruence between the goals of the organization and those of its members?
Do they minimize administration, agency, and transaction costs?
Do they fit the organization's environment and strategy?

beneficial if their attention is brought to bear on all important problems, but is not wasted on trivial ones. An effective architecture and culture must foster the right degree of independence in employees, so that they feel empowered to take decisions for themselves where appropriate, but should also feel able to seek help from senior managers when they are confronted with important and difficult decisions.

Effective decision-making is also made easier if the people in the organization are motivated in a way that helps it achieve its aims, so architecture and culture should ideally achieve goal congruence. This can be achieved through well-designed control and reward systems, so that people benefit financially, or advance their careers if they help the organization meet its objectives. More subtly, relationships with employees, or with suppliers, customers, and other stakeholders, can be structured in such a way that they believe it is in their long-term interests for the organization to succeed. This may mean setting up relational contracts (a term we define in Section 8.3.1) or establishing a set of organizational values that appeal strongly to stakeholders and stimulate them to work for the firm's benefit.

An appropriate architecture and culture can make the organization more efficient as well as more effective, by minimizing coordination, agency and transaction costs. Goal congruence may help reduce agency and transaction costs: if people trust the organization and have signed up to its values, then they are less likely to exploit it, and it can spend less on preventing them from doing so. Cultural norms that discourage people from inappropriate behaviour—fiddling their expenses or overstating their performance—can also assist in this.

Coordination and other costs cannot be avoided altogether—every organization needs to devote some effort to gathering information on its performance and making sure that all its cash is properly accounted for. The more complex and diverse the organization becomes, the more complex—and costly—the structures and systems it will need in order to give the right degree of management attention to each product or market. In general, the organization's architecture should fit with its environment and strategy. An influential school of theory—contingency theory—holds that organizations' structures and behaviour are determined in predictable ways by their circumstances, and performance will suffer if structures differ from those norms.[2]

8.1.2 The elements of architecture and culture

The main elements of architecture are shown in the right-hand hexagon in Figure 8.1:

- The structural **hierarchy** affects the speed with which information and knowledge are shared—if they have to travel up and down a tall hierarchy, they travel more slowly, but may benefit from a higher degree of scrutiny along the way. Motivation is also affected: some people get frustrated if they have to work through many layers of management, others find comfort in the extra degree of oversight. It also determines how management attention is allocated between different types of decision.

Goal congruence
Compatibility ('congruence') between the goals of the organization and the personal goals of the individuals that work for it or with it.

➜ Transaction and agency costs were introduced in Section 1.3.3.

Contingency
A feature of an organization or its environment that influences something else. E.g. an organization's size and environment appear to influence the structure that its managers are likely to choose.

Hierarchy
The shape or format of reporting and decision-making relationships in an organization. Hierarchies may be *tall* with many layers of management, or *flat*, with few.

- Control and reward systems may directly affect people's incentives to perform well in their everyday work and to share information and learning. Control systems also affect the way in which information is presented within the organization, which influences the way in which issues are prioritized and decisions are taken. The amount of information that is requested and speed with which it is processed affect the speed of the organization's response to its environment, and also affect employee motivation—quite a lot of people dislike spending time on elaborate reporting procedures.

- Information infrastructure can be thought of as the 'hard wiring' that underpins linkages between activities in the value chain. It allows managers to 'see' and monitor their teams and partner organizations over long distances, without needing to be physically present. The potential span of control of a manager (the number of people he or she can effectively manage) has therefore increased substantially, although at some risk of information overload. Information technology has become so widespread that it is rarely a source of competitive advantage. Implementation of appropriately structured databases, of extranets, intranets, and instant messaging (IM) for external and internal communications, and of enterprise resource planning (ERP) systems for the management of order processing, supply chains, and salesforces has, rather, become a survival factor in many industries. However, Tesco in retailing and Dell in computing have still managed to gain advantage from being able to gather and interpret customer data more efficiently than their competitors.

- Values and belief systems and the manner in which contracts and relationships are structured to encourage a long-term commitment can affect goal congruence and motivation in an organization, in ways that we have already hinted at, and shall explore more fully in Section 8.3.

As Figure 8.1 shows, values and belief systems, as well as being important elements of an organization's architecture, are central to its culture. However belief systems are not often easy to examine directly, since they are held unconsciously, or regarded by insiders as so obvious that they may never come up for discussion or review. So, when trying to analyse what an organization's members really believe, we have to look for clues elsewhere.

Some important pointers lie in the architecture. For example, things that are most prominent in control systems, such as product quality or particular types of cost, are typically the ones that people in the organization believe to be most important. This is an instance of reification: culture and beliefs being reflected in organizational characteristics like structures and the way that relationships are managed, or in tangible features like buildings and

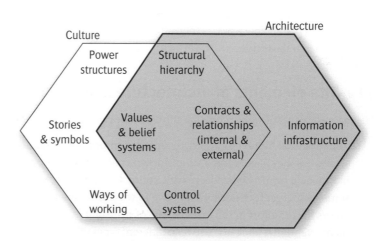

Figure 8.1 Components of culture and architecture

equipment. Reification (the term comes from the Latin for 'to make into a thing') explains the overlap between architecture and culture in Figure 8.1. This means that architecture is not only an object of interest in its own right, whose effectiveness we wish to assess; but also a source of evidence about the organization's belief system.

Other important reifications of culture, that are not part of the architecture, include:

- power holders—who is granted power in the organization, and how they exercise it;
- what kinds of stories people in the organization tell about it and about their working lives, and what kinds of symbols are prominent within it;
- what ways of working people have developed—work routines and social habits.

These are examined in greater detail in Section 8.4.

8.1.3 Ownership, organizations, and architecture

Much of the theory and vocabulary of organizations was introduced in a world where organizational boundaries were largely defined by ownership structures. An organization had owners, who appointed a board of directors, who in turn appointed a CEO and senior management team, which put in place a hierarchy of people who reported to them. Those hierarchies had recognizable forms—functional or divisionalized—that we shall discuss in Section 8.2. Organizations which did not follow this model, but acted mainly as orchestrators of the efforts of smaller firms, were regarded as exceptions and were said to have a 'network' structure.

Several things have changed that make this way of thinking outdated. First, as we saw in Chapter 6, the outsourcing of non-core value chain activities is now commonplace. Many large firms, and some small ones (see Real-life Application 8.2 for an example), have structures that, at least in part, look like 'networks'. As a result of this, competition in many industries, particularly in manufacturing but also in sectors like computer services, involves not just individual organizations but their entire supply chain. This means that organizations need to share knowledge with, and motivate, people in independent firms, not just their own employees. Many organizations, therefore, have a 'vertical architecture'[3] that extends beyond the boundaries defined by legal ownership.

Finally, the developments in information infrastructure that we discuss in Section 8.1.2 have made working across organizational boundaries much more like working within a single hierarchy (see Real-life Application 8.1). If a customer has a window into its supplier's information system and routinely monitors its progress hour by hour, then the supplier effectively becomes part of its customer's hierarchy, even if the organization chart and legal formulations may say something different.[4]

Real-life Application 8.1 Networks and hierarchies in the pharmaceuticals industry

A number of firms offer specialized services to the major pharmaceuticals corporations. One type of service involves running clinical trials of new treatments: finding doctors who will offer the treatment to their patients, making sure that the results are properly reported, and carrying out some of the analysis. Outsourcing the building and running of networks of medical practitioners, a time-consuming and tricky task, is attractive to pharmaceuticals firms that would prefer to focus on core competences in research and marketing.   →

> ➜ The firms offering these clinical trials are legally independent entities. But the interim results of these trials may be posted on intranets that are also accessible to their clients, and the people managing the trials may find themselves fielding detailed queries about data they have barely had time to read themselves.
>
> The pharmaceuticals firms, on the other hand, have teams of researchers looking for new treatments. Although practices vary between firms, typically these researchers will be given a budget, a defined area within which to direct their research, and a set of reporting milestones. They will enjoy a great deal of operational autonomy, and not have managers monitoring them closely on a daily basis.
>
> Although the R&D unit is formally part of the pharmaceutical firm's hierarchy, it is likely to enjoy almost as much autonomy as the small biotechnology start-ups with which most pharmaceuticals firms also have collaborative R&D relationships. On the other hand, the clinical trial providers and their employees are bound quite tightly into the big pharmaceutical corporations' hierarchies.

The relevance of ownership to architecture then becomes more a question of motivation. Just as there are arguments for giving employees shares or stock options as a form of motivation, there are arguments for giving entrepreneurs legal ownership of, and the right to profit from, parts of a value chain. However, just as some organizations will manage and motivate their employees better than their competitors do, others may develop superior ways of managing and motivating suppliers or franchisees.

8.2 Hierarchical structures and control systems

Structures and control systems allow managers to coordinate the activities of various parts of the organization in order to maximize their joint skills and capabilities. Most organizations feature a figurehead—the CEO, chairman, or managing partner—at the top, with a hierarchy of managers and employees below. Shareholders and other key stakeholders typically prefer there to be a single person who can be held accountable for the performance and spending of the organization. And the existence of a clear hierarchy appears to help people cope with everyday existence in a complex world.[5]

The shape of that hierarchy and the nature of the systems used to operate it can have a major impact on an organization's effectiveness. They can encourage innovation and exploration or promote efficiency and exploitation. On the other hand, they can inhibit information flows, destroy motivation and leave decision-making and supervisory power in the hands of people who are ill-qualified to use it.

8.2.1 Key dimensions of structure and systems

In assessing a structure and systems, we need to judge if the organization has reached an appropriate balance on five ABCDE dimensions:

- **A**utonomy
- **B**ureaucracy
- **C**ultural control
- **D**ecentralization
- **E**conomic incentives.

The appropriate point of balance will vary according to several contingencies, some external, such as the degree of maturity of the industry, some internal, such as the organization's size, diversity, culture, and the potential for synergy between different businesses.

a. Autonomy

Giving day-to-day operational autonomy to individuals or to teams of employees has a number of benefits. It enables the organization to harness creativity, entrepreneurialism, and problem-solving skills, qualities that tend to be suppressed if people are constrained to use routines that are strictly defined by someone else. It makes jobs more varied and responsible, with a higher knowledge content, and hence more rewarding for the individual. It allows the organization to manage with a flat hierarchy, since less supervision, and therefore fewer supervisors, are required.

Autonomy speeds up decision-making, since fewer issues are referred upwards for resolution. When decisions are referred upwards, information can get distorted, or even lost, by middle managers who misunderstand the problem, underestimate its importance, or add in concerns of their own. Decisions are taken by those individuals who have most contact with customers and operational reality, and this may use top management attention more effectively.

Not all people enjoy autonomy; some may find it intimidating, or may derive comfort from working in a tall hierarchy where responsibilities are clearly delimited and which offer a promise of regular increases in salary and status. Moreover, if people are given too much autonomy, there is a danger that they may lose their sense of belonging to the organization, becoming reluctant to share information and incurring agency costs as they act in their own interests rather than those of the firm. They may also, in good faith, undertake actions, such as offering excessive discounts to win a big order, that make sense from their operational viewpoint, but do not fit the overall positioning or strategy of the firm. The most extreme examples of the dangers of autonomy tend to arise in firms trading commodities or financial securities, where unsupervised and enterprising dealers have been known to take risks that jeopardize the future of their firm.

Autonomy also works against standardization of procedures and rules by the head office. Uniformity in these areas can help organizations to avoid wasting resources on systems that overlap, or even conflict, and gives people in different parts of the organization a common language. This makes it easier to transfer information and practices between different locations and business units, and for top management attention to be effectively used across them all. The benefits from standardization are greatest when products are uniform and customers have similar requirements across all businesses and markets. Organizations with a more diverse competitive stance may require a degree of autonomy and decentralization to make them responsive to local conditions.

b. Bureaucracy

Bureaucracy is an important tool in enforcing standardization in an organization, and also in monitoring progress even where standardization is not required. Formal procedures for recruitment and the authorization of expenditure, and systems for reporting on performance, are common instances of bureaucracy that are found in most organizations.

Bureaucracy is often regarded in a negative light. Bureaucratic procedures are rarely enjoyable, divert time and resources from other activities and tend to be resented by the most entrepreneurial employees. They slow down decision-making, since following any formal procedure in advance of a decision is likely to delay it, and tend to force decisions into a fixed mould, reducing organizational flexibility. However, they also may be beneficial, in reducing the incidence of errors and forcing decision-makers to consider the implications of their intended actions. By making data available in a common format, bureaucracy can make it easier for knowledge to be shared. It also helps ensure that employees and other stakeholders are treated consistently and fairly, which can improve goal congruence in environments such as the public and not-for-profit sectors.

c. Cultural controls

Cultural controls are controls over people's behaviour that arise from other people's expectations. Commonly, they are exerted through peer group pressure, where employees adapt their behaviour to match the norms of, and gain acceptance into, the group with whom they share their workplace. Training and socialization show newcomers what kinds of behaviour are expected and valued. People hear 'stories' that illustrate desirable activities, observe the things that established colleagues do, and listen to their views of what is expected. If they find that they do not fit in, they leave.

Another type of cultural control is self-control, where people undertake their work willingly, without direction or supervision, and without requiring very much from the owners or directors except fair play and a reasonable salary. They may do this because of a high degree of congruence between their personal goals and those of the organization—because they are inspired by the mission, for example—or because they gain personal legitimation from association with it. Also, they may be intrinsically motivated by the work itself, as is the case with researchers and many other professionals.

Organizations that have particularly powerful cultural control systems are known as clans or missionary organizations.[6] Often they are family-run or have a family-like ethos that strongly shapes behaviour, are dominated by the owner/founder even after he or she has left, and are hugely resistant to change or deviant views.

The benefits of cultural control come in two forms. It can lower agency costs or, in the case of suppliers and other external stakeholders, transaction costs. Cultural controls can make it less likely that people will try to cheat the organization, and also reduce the costs of preventing such cheating, allowing for less bureaucracy and fewer supervisory staff. It can also enhance the speed of decision-making, since people have less need to seek guidance further up the hierarchy. Instead, they can draw on what they have learnt about the organization's norms to guide their behaviour in unfamiliar situations. As a result, cultural control is particularly effective in environments which are uncertain, fast-changing, or unstable.

However, there are costs incurred in making sure that the organization finds, and retains, people who are susceptible to its cultural controls. Most people are quite selective about whom they will oblige, so that if peer-group pressure is to operate, firms must recruit like-minded people, who will get on with one another. Similarly, not all people are disposed towards self-control, and those that are may need financial incentives ('golden handcuffs') to remain with their employer.

Another problem lies in ensuring that the 'right' cultural norms prevail. People tend to become particularly like-minded when they work in the same types of jobs and share similar experiences—for example, when they work in the same functions or the same part of the world. Different sub-units develop their own routines, objectives, and subcultures, and employees may develop loyalty to the sub-unit rather than to the organization as a whole. This can make managers and staff in those units reluctant to share information and learning with colleagues elsewhere in the organization. They may even adopt a specialized language that those colleagues cannot understand. These splits can occur between functions or value-chain activities in quite small organizations. They become increasingly likely in a larger and more diverse corporation in which different divisions may be both physically and culturally distant from one another, and see one another as competitors for attention and funds from the centre. Where knowledge sharing and synergies are important to the strategy, a strong overarching culture or some form of incentives, may be needed to induce collaboration between subcultures.

The final drawback of reliance upon cultural controls is that, while it enhances flexibility in the short term, it can increase long-term vulnerability to strategic drift. Cultural norms established over a long period are notoriously difficult to change. If the environment develops in an unexpected way, that runs counter to an organization's or sub-unit's belief system, then it may be difficult to persuade people that their behaviour must change, or even to recognize the true nature of the changes in the environment.

An example is Leica, a German firm with strong family values that achieved an iconic reputation among professional photographers for the quality of its cameras. But Leica seemed to find it hugely difficult to adjust to the arrival of digital photography, partly because its main external contacts were with a loyal base of fans of its traditional, film-based products. The firm came close to liquidation before it hired an American chief executive, a seasoned businessman with no experience of the camera industry, who was able to guide it to the launch, in 2006, of the first digital version of its classic cameras.[7]

d. Devolution

A fundamental issue in any sizeable organization, particularly one that has diversified, is how centralized it should be—to what extent decision-making and control should be undertaken by the head office. The alternative to centralization is the devolution or decentralization of authority to local managers to deal with their specific markets and operational requirements. Decentralized organizations may have lower coordination costs than centralized organizations, because corporate overheads are lower, although these savings can be offset by the cost of duplicating some functions at business or local level. They also allow for decisions to be taken more quickly, and by managers who are close to the customers and understand their needs.

Decentralization, however, may encourage the proliferation of subcultures and inhibit knowledge sharing. There is also the danger of 'empire building'–directors building up the size of their unit in order to increase their self-esteem, their salary or their power within the organization. Within limits, of course, such behaviour benefits the organization as well as the director concerned—a degree of creative conflict and personal ambition can be beneficial for everyone. However, there is always the danger that powerful directors may start to dictate, ignore or even subvert corporate policy as the congruence between corporate and divisional goals is lost.

It is a challenge for many organizations to find the right balance, and it is quite usual, as we discuss in Section 8.2.2, for them to go through one or more cycles of centralization and decentralization before arriving at a solution.

Highly centralized structures are found most often, and work best, in firms with standardized products, predictable demand, and a stable and relatively simple environment.[8] However, goal congruence at lower levels in centralized architectures may be difficult to achieve, since managers may feel they have little responsibility, opportunity for achievement, or recognition of their worth. There is also a lot of pressure on the attention of the few people who are able to take important decisions. Organizations will want to be decentralized enough to enable them to innovate and respond quickly if the environment is dynamic and turbulent, or if speedy customer responsiveness is a success factor. In such cases, decisions need to be taken, and there may be little time for top management to be consulted. At the same time they may want to maintain control over financial performance and take advantage of any economies of scale in activities such as R&D and human resource management.

e. Economic incentives

It is common practice to link rewards for employees at various levels, or for suppliers or franchisees, to the attainment of certain goals. Common examples are bonuses, performance-related pay, profit-sharing agreements, or allocations of shares or share options. The owners of independent firms in a larger firm's supply chain share, through dividends, in the profits earned from meeting their client's needs.

While incentives are typically given to individuals, they may sometimes take the form of resources made available to the organization as a whole. This is common in the UK public sector, where schools or hospitals may have funding expanded or withdrawn according to their performance against targets set by the government.

Financial ambition, or even greed, can be a powerful motivating factor, which it is sensible to harness for the good of the organization. Even people who are not particularly materialistic may find that their self-esteem is enhanced by a bonus or other tangible sign of appreciation. Well-designed economic incentives can thus enhance goal congruence, and also speed up decision-making by clarifying to people what is expected of them.

However, once rewards become linked to a particular target, agency and transaction costs can arise as people find ways of meeting the target that do not help the organization meet its strategic aims. Managers may meet short-term profit targets by cutting expenditure on advertising, maintenance, or training, thus harming their firms' longer-term effectiveness. It was found that some UK hospitals had responded to a government target that demanded that newly admitted patients be seen by a doctor within a certain period by delaying their admission and leaving them waiting in ambulances.

→ The balanced scorecard and other issues in the design and application of control and reward systems are examined in depth in Chapter 17.

Systems such as the 'balanced scorecard' have been developed as a means of ensuring that managers do not focus on one target to the detriment of other parts of the business. Cultural controls may also help in restraining unwanted responses to economic incentives.

Worked Example 8.1 McDonald's structure and systems in 2006

McDonald's is an international company with branches of its restaurants as far apart as China and South America. Despite the diverse environments in which it operates, it aims to give customers a predictable meal which shows little variation across the world. This implies a high degree of uniformity in the routines for preparing and serving food, so that although many of its restaurants in 2006 were managed by franchisees, staff there had little autonomy, and there was limited scope for devolution in management practices. Most outlets used the same reward systems and the same hierarchical management structure, and there was a global system—ROIP (restaurant operation improvement process) for enhancing performance. McDonald's was also imposing increasing degrees of standardization on its IT procurement and supplier management systems in order to maximize purchasing economies of scale. These standardized systems necessarily entailed a degree of bureaucracy, as did the quality management systems implemented to ensure that the product met required standards.

McDonald's had a strong culture at the top. Many directors and restaurant managers, whether company employees or franchisees, stayed with the company for many years. Ray Kroc's core

values of QSCV—quality, service, cleanliness, and value—were still widely cited. The company used its in-house 'Hamburger Universities' to pass those values to new generations of employees and managers. However, with a high rate of turnover amongst restaurant staff (a problem common to most quick-service restaurants), the company could not rely upon people at lower levels staying long enough to become thoroughly socialized into the McDonald's way of thinking, and so supplemented cultural controls with more direct methods of supervision.

In 1997, McDonald's restructured itself into five geographical divisions, which have since been set up as separately registered companies. Since then there has been increasing variation in the products offered, to meet local tastes. But although decisions regarding menu design have been devolved to regional or country management, the company allowed little variation within a country except to test-market products approved at the centre.

The company's extensive and increasing use of franchisees (in 2006 it announced its intention to re-franchise around 50 company-owned outlets in the UK, for example) shows an awareness of the importance of economic incentives.

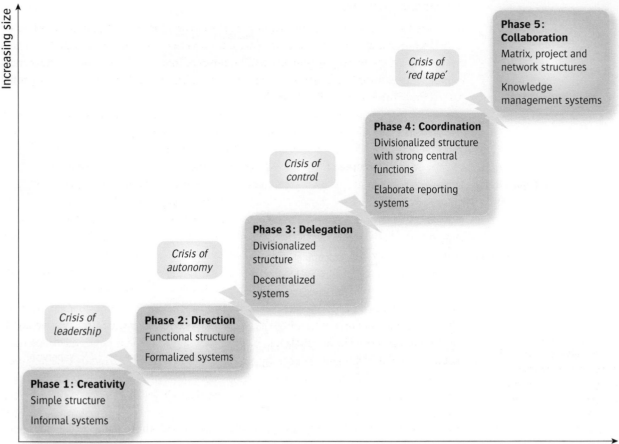

Increasing size

Phase 5: Collaboration
Matrix, project and network structures

Knowledge management systems

Crisis of 'red tape'

Phase 4: Coordination
Divisionalized structure with strong central functions

Elaborate reporting systems

Crisis of control

Phase 3: Delegation
Divisionalized structure

Decentralized systems

Crisis of autonomy

Phase 2: Direction
Functional structure

Formalized systems

Crisis of leadership

Phase 1: Creativity
Simple structure

Informal systems

Increasing age

8.2.2 **Common types of structure**

Organization structures are ways of grouping together people who need to collaborate on a regular basis, under the supervision of someone who can guide them in their work, ensure their activity is well-directed, and take decisions on complex or important issues. How best to do this in order to achieve the organization's strategic objectives is a key decision. There are a number of ways in which these groupings can take place, which tend to vary with the age and size of the organization.[9]

a. Early stages—simple and functional structures

In a young or small firm, such as a small printer or a design consultancy, it is not always necessary to put groupings in place. These entrepreneurial organizations[10] would be expected to feature a simple structure (Figure 8.3), where there is little specialization of roles and few formal rules and procedures. Decision-making is centralized and flexible. One person, often the founder, is in charge, and the organization is small enough for him or her to be able to know what is going on and have input into most decisions. He or she may deliberately keep the organization small for this reason.

However, the virtue of the simple structure—that the top people are close to everything —is also its limitation. There seems to be a need for an organization's structure to become more complex in order to reflect the complexity of its environment—this is sometimes known as 'the law of requisite variety'.[11] Simple structures can only be sustained for as long as the range of activities is small enough to be accommodated within the attention span of one or two people. If the organization moves beyond this point, the need for professional management and formal systems becomes critical.[12]

Figure 8.2 Typical phases in the development of an organization (after Greiner, 1972). *Reproduced with the kind permission of Harvard Business School Publications*

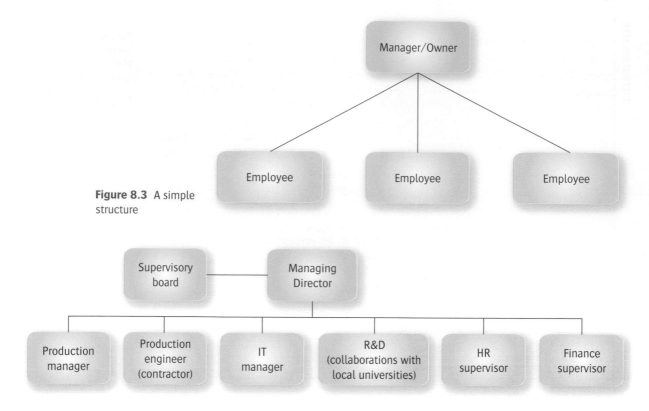

Figure 8.3 A simple structure

Figure 8.4 A functional structure. *Reproduced with the kind permission of Si.Sac*

A common option then is to group people together with those with similar skills—for example, all sales consultants together under a sales manager, all IT staff together under an IT director. A structure which gives priority to these skill-based functions is known as a functional structure (or U-form structure) (Figure 8.4). Its introduction typically coincides with the formalization of systems for accounting, budgeting, control, and communication.

A functional structure allows finer tuning of control and reward systems to achieve goal congruence within the different functions. For example, the finance function might be rewarded for maximizing returns on the firm's investments and the personnel function for achieving high levels of staff motivation. Most of all, it allows specialists to develop their skills and perform more efficiently, learning from fellow specialists without being distracted by tasks for which they have no aptitude, under the supervision of a manager with the same professional background. It makes sense in mid-sized (say 100–500 employees) organizations, as long as they have a relatively narrow range of products or services and are not aiming to diversify beyond a limited set of markets (Real-life Application 8.2).

Real-life Application 8.2 Si.Sac SpA: a functional structure in a stable environment

Si.Sac is a company with some 50 employees and a turnover of approximately €25 million located in Ragusa, a predominantly agricultural region in south-eastern Sicily. The mainstay of the local economy is the cultivation of tomatoes, aubergines, and courgettes in greenhouses which are made of plastic sheeting spread over frames made of wood or, increasingly, steel. This method of cultivation was developed in the region at around the time that Si.Sac was founded in 1967. It is particularly well-suited to the region's soil and climate, though it has since spread around the Mediterranean, and as far afield as California and China. Si.Sac specializes in the conversion of polyethylene pellets into the plastic film used in these greenhouses. Different types of film have differing degrees of durability, and specific uses. They regulate the temperature in the greenhouse to a given level—to ➜

→ diffuse the sunlight to lower the risk of burning certain types of plant, to allow or inhibit certain frequencies of radiation. Multi-layered films may be used on the floor of the greenhouse—black underneath to inhibit plant growth, while the top layer reflects sunlight back upwards to encourage plant growth.

Si.Sac's main markets are in Italy, where it has approximately 7 per cent of the market, and more specifically in the local area, where it has built up long-term relationships with its key customers. Although price may vary considerably—the key inputs are petroleum derivatives and energy, whose costs fluctuate with the market price of oil—demand is quite stable, since from the customers' point of view the film is an essential production input.

The firm's organization structure is shown in Figure 8.4. The managing director, Elio Guastella, was appointed thirty years ago by the three entrepreneurs who set up the company, but play little active role in its management. The firm has managers in charge of production, where most of the staff are employed, and IT, which is crucial for operations. The entire production operation is computer-controlled in order to ensure that sheeting is produced at the correct thickness (a fraction of a millimetre) and with the correct formulation to give it the properties required for a specific application. There are also functional supervisors for accounting and personnel, while Sg. Guastella himself takes charge of marketing and sales.

Even a firm this small has elements of the network within its functional structure. It does not need a full-time production engineer—once set up, the production process does not need frequent adjustments—so it relies upon a long-term collaborator for that function. The firm cannot afford its own R&D facilities, but has relationships with the universities of Catania and Bari, some of which have resulted in patented products.

Creative Strategizing 8.1

Suppose that the entrepreneurs that control Si.Sac have decided upon a major expansion to serve the global market. How would the structure need to change?

As organizations grow they frequently (as we noted in Chapter 5) become more diverse in the range of products offered and market sectors served. A functional structure can only cope with a limited degree of diversity before the attention of senior functional managers becomes spread across too many problems. Above a certain natural boundary, the need to give adequate management attention to each set of products or each market segment may become more pressing than the need to keep all functional specialists together in the same department. That boundary typically seems to lie between 400 and 800 employees, though functional structures can be found in much larger organizations, such as British Airways.

Meanwhile, employees' specialist knowledge of their markets or technologies may have developed to the point where they are better placed than top managers to take certain decisions. Not only is top management attention being used inefficiently, but key employees may become frustrated at being unable to act on their own initiative. If senior managers are unwilling to devolve responsibility, the organization reaches another transition point.[13] If it does not want to risk losing its more independently-minded staff it needs to arrive at some more decentralized structure.

b. Divisionalized structures

The natural next stage for organizations is the divisionalized structure (also known as multi-divisional or M-form structure) (Figure 8.5). Divisions concentrate on a particular dimension of the business. In the case of the Sony structure in Figure 8.5, these are product groups, while in McDonald's the main divisions represent geographical areas, although there is also a separate divisional grouping for the various non-hamburger businesses. But divisions might be structured around customer segments or any other grouping that

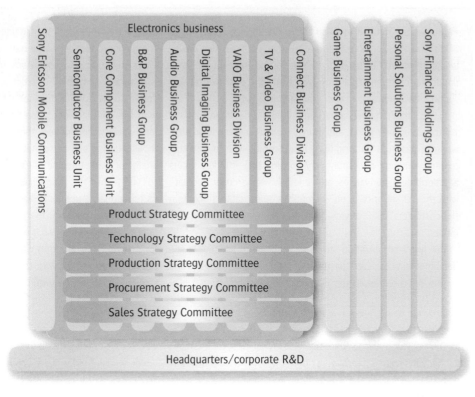

Figure 8.5 Sony's divisionalized structure in April 2006. Source: <http://www.sony/net/SonyInfo/CorporateInfo/Data/organization.htm>, accessed 1 October 2006. *Reproduced with the kind permission of Sony Corporation*

makes commercial or operational sense. Each division can be responsive to the particular needs of its environment, and can be measured and controlled separately using appropriate criteria.

The introduction of a highly decentralized divisional structure, sometimes leads to further problems[14] where divisional subcultures put their local objectives above those of the firm as a whole, and their initiatives run out of control, perhaps undercutting the corporation's reputation (see What Can Go Wrong 8.1). Perhaps opportunities valuable to the firm as a whole are also being overlooked because local managers see no benefit in pursuing them.[15] The organization then moves to the next phase, coordination, where the planning and control systems are changed to give central functions such as IT, HR, and especially finance more power over divisional activity. The structure remains divisionalized, and divisions retain devolved responsibility for their day-to-day operations, but reward systems give divisional managers more incentive to act in the interest of the firm as a whole, rather than just their own section of it.

The aim is to allow senior managers to impose some degree of organizational coherence and ensure that values are being adhered to. The staff at the centre may be able to improve the quality of some decisions and lessen the risk of expensive errors. On the other hand, conflicts frequently arise between the central staff and divisional 'line' managers who find that centrally imposed policies do not fit their local needs (Real-life Application 8.3). Most importantly, the centre's demands for data and for an input into divisional policies may increase the degree of bureaucracy to a disabling extent.[16]

Powerful political forces may make it difficult for the organization to move beyond this phase, with the specialists at the centre reluctant to relinquish power or believe that the firm can survive without bureaucratic controls. Organizations that have accumulated substantial financial and reputational assets may survive for years without fully overcoming the problems of excessive bureaucracy.

Real-life Application 8.3 The double shuffle

The following, true story illustrates the tensions that can arise between corporate policy and market needs in large corporations, and the lengths to which people will sometimes go in order to get around centrally imposed policies that they think are inappropriate.

The corporation in question exercised a strong central control over the prices of its products. This was partly because of cultural conflict between the centre and the operating divisions. The headquarters staff, predominantly from an accounting background, distrusted the divisional managers, many of whom had risen up through the salesforce, and were trying to assert control over them. However, there were other reasons why price controls were thought to be necessary. The corporation had a very high share of its markets, and there was a genuine danger that the authorities in the USA and Europe might take action if the firm was seen to be abusing its monopoly position. It could not afford to appear to discourage competition by setting its prices too low. In addition, some large customers were becoming increasingly unhappy if they found they were being charged different prices in different markets, or that other firms were being offered lower prices than they were.

In one subsidiary, located a long way from headquarters, the management grew frustrated by this. They felt that, because staff at headquarters were preventing them from offering discounts on the list price of their equipment, they were unable to compete effectively in their local markets. Almost the only time they were allowed to offer a substantial discount was as a loyalty bonus to customers who, after renting the equipment for a while, decided to buy it. So they hatched the following scheme, known as 'the double shuffle'.

Every time a rental contract came to an end, the customer was offered the option of buying the equipment. If they chose not to take up that option, then the equipment, instead of being returned to the company's warehouse, was stored in a salesperson's home or garage until a buyer was found for it. The new buyer would be offered the machine at a discount that was equivalent to the loyalty bonus to which the previous renter was entitled. Once the deal was concluded, it would be entered in the accounts as if the machine had been sold to the earlier rental customer.

Eventually, the arrangement was uncovered during a routine audit by headquarters staff. Although there was no suggestion that people were attempting to defraud the company, every senior manager who knew about the double shuffle was fired. Headquarters staff believed this action was justified because of the potential consequences if regulators or major customers had found out about the illicit discounts. They also wanted to send out a warning to other subsidiary managers who might be tempted to excesses of entrepreneurship.

c. Collaboration

In order to overcome excessive bureaucracy, an organization's top managers must find a way to get divisional managers to recognize the needs of other divisions or functions alongside those of their own. There are a number of ways of doing this:

- giving top managers overarching responsibility for activities that are seen as crucial for competitiveness. These managers have titles such as 'Chief Technology Officer' or 'Chief Knowledge Officer';

- implementing coordinating structures, such as the strategy committees shown spanning Sony's electronic business in Figure 8.5;

- formalizing the links between areas in a matrix structure, where an employee may have two or more bosses, each in charge of a different dimension of the organization. For example, they may have a country manager who determines their pay and to whom they report on a day-to-day basis, a functional manager who looks after their training and professional development, and another director in charge of the particular market segment at which their efforts are targeted;

→ Matrix structures and their drawbacks are reviewed in more detail in Section 9.1, along with other ways of structuring complex organizations.

- making the different units buy and sell from one another, in the hope that market mechanisms will improve the internal service that they offer;

- replacing formal control systems with informal ones, based around culture and self-discipline, designed to encourage teamwork and collaboration. The reward systems may also be rebased around team performance, and IT systems developed to facilitate the sharing and management of knowledge across the organization.

→ Knowledge management systems are examined in detail in Chapter 10.

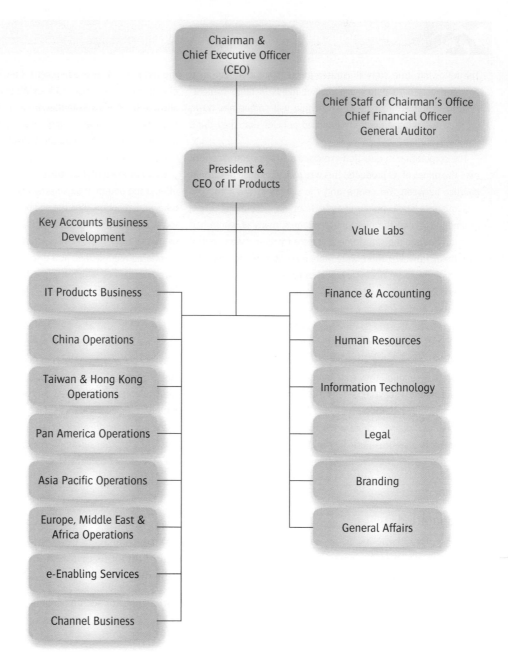

Figure 8.6 Acer Inc.'s network structure. Source: <http://global.acer.com/about/organization01.htm>, accessed 1 October 2006. *Reproduced with the kind permission of Acer Inc.*

d. Network structures

The main alternative to the divisionalized form is the network structure (or 'N-form' structure), in which the organization is divided into a large number of essentially autonomous units. This is suitable for tasks and environments that demand flexibility and adaptability. Unlike most other structures, which tend to be fixed relationships suitable for processing standardized, repetitive problems, the network organization allows responses to individual issues.[17] Unlike the units in divisionalized structure, those in a network may show no particular logic in the way in which they are defined. Moreover, they are normally 'loosely coupled' —the organization's hierarchy and bureaucratic procedures do not compel them to interact in any predefined or regular way (although, see Real-life Application 8.1 for an exception).

Also sometimes known as a virtual, cellular, or shamrock organization,[18] the network structure has been portrayed as novel, but is actually quite ancient: organizations such as Lloyd's, the London insurance exchange, and the markets ('souks') of the Middle East have used it for centuries. More recently, it has become a feature of the virtual value chains discussed in Chapter 6.

The classic network consists of independently owned firms, perhaps with an orchestrator firm at the centre. However, as we mentioned in Section 8.1.3, some groupings of independent firms are best conceived as having a divisionalized structure, while some corporations choose to give their wholly owned business units such a high degree of operational independence that they function as a network. One example is Acer, a Taiwanese IT firm (Figure 8.6), which operates using a highly decentralized management style. Its network embraces not just the wholly owned business units shown in Figure 8.6, but a dealer network and several manufacturing units. Acer retains shareholdings in the manufacturing firms, some of which were formerly wholly owned business units.

Organizations may move to the network structure straight away from the simple structure, or may implement it as a way of reducing red tape. The N-form structure has all the advantages and disadvantages discussed in Section 8.2.1 of a high degree of decentralization and a low degree of bureaucracy, which are its main distinguishing characteristics. Instilling a common purpose and avoiding anarchy in this kind of organization pose particular kinds of management challenges, which we return to in Section 8.3.

➡ The advantages and disadvantages of network structures in complex firms are discussed in Section 9.1.

 Theoretical Debate 8.1 How predictable are choices of structure

There are definite patterns in the relationship between strategy, environment, and certain organizational structures. This was first noticed by Alfred Chandler (1962), who suggested that the strategy adopted by an organization at various stages of its development led to particular structural forms: a centralized functional form for vertically integrated organizations, and a divisionalized structure for those that had pursued strategies of related diversification through internal growth.

His work was extended considerably by writers such as Danny Miller (1987), Lawrence and Lorsch (1967), Burns and Stalker (1961), Derek Pugh and his associates of the Aston school (1963, 1968, 1969) and John Child (1974, 1997), who noted links between particular features of an organization, such as the degree of functional specialization, and different environmental factors, such as uncertainty. Some also investigated whether organizations with a particular set of features performed better than others. Certain combinations of structure and context have been researched across many types of organization and many national environments, so that we know, for example, with considerable certainty from the work of the Aston school that diversified firms tend to have divisionalized rather than functional structures, and those that follow this pattern tend, on average, to perform better than those that do not.

These contingency theories can therefore offer some measure of useful guidance as to how managers can achieve fit between structure and strategy, and between structure and environment.

They do not conclusively demonstrate that firms' strategy is driving managers' choices of structure rather than the other way around. There have been periodic attempts (e.g. Hall and Saias, 1980) to argue that the structure drives the strategy, as well as vice versa. Once a structure is in place, these theorists argue, it starts to shape information flows and cognitive processes, and to involve incentives to encourage certain types of behaviour. The result is to make certain types of strategic decision more likely than others. One large-scale study (Amburgey and Dacin, 1994) indeed found that the relationship between strategy and structure was a reciprocal one—that diversified firms tended to implement divisional structures, but also that after firms set up divisional structures they tended to diversify. Over time, however, the influence of strategy on structure appeared to be about twice as strong as the influence of structure on strategy.

These theories also do not show how the strategy–structure fit comes about in practice. One view, from writers such as Hannan and Freeman (1989) is that it is an ecological mechanism: firms that are unsuited to their environment go out of business, leaving those with a suitable strategy–structure mix to thrive. However, a major study (Fligstein, 1985) of the adoption of the M-form structure by major US corporations did not support this hypothesis: it found that along with the firm's product strategy, the factors that were most closely associated with the adoption of the new organizational form were the background of the CEO and the behaviour of similar firms. ➡

→ Other studies of the spread of new structural forms tend to support the idea that firms copy one another to a greater degree than can be explained by their simply reacting in a similar way to a common environment. Some theorists, such as DiMaggio and Powell (1983) and Abrahamson (1996), put this down to managers pursuing 'fashions' in organizational structure, spread by outside influences, such as management consultants and gurus, perhaps to win the approval of stock analysts and their own peer group outside the firm. Others, such as Child (1972, 1997) place more emphasis on the role of managers' own strategic choices— though these may of course be influenced by seeing what has worked in other organizations.

It pays to remember that mimicking the strategy–structure mix found in the average firm is not necessarily the best way to achieve exceptional results. British Airways and Canon are two successful firms that have retained a functional structure even though they are large and diverse enough to justify a divisional-ized form. In addition, the structure is not the whole story—it is just one factor in shaping the routines that determine if a firm is effective. Oxman and Smith go so far as to contend that: 'Although most companies obsess about it, the structure of an organization is increasingly irrelevant to how its work is actually done' (2003: 77).

A word of caution is also in order: contingency theories of organizational structure may appear more seductively logical on paper than they do to a practising manager. A review using modern statistical techniques (Acar et al., 2003) of a sample of the firms originally analysed by Chandler indicated that the strat-egy–structure relationships that he believed he had found were actually only present in around one-third of the cases. And a more intricate framework developed by Henry Mintzberg (1979), a no less eminent scholar, was later found (Doty et al., 1993) to be wanting—there was no evidence that a significant number of firms adopted the structures he proposed under the circum-stances indicated by his theories, and the ones that did adopt them performed no better than the ones that did not.

8.2.3 International trends in architecture

As we noted in Section 2.6.2, different nations differ in their interpretations of the nature of capitalism and their views of the relative importance of different stakeholders. There is nonetheless a high degree of similarity in the kinds of architecture that are chosen in differ-ent countries. The divisionalized form, for example, is the one most commonly used by large firms in all the largest European states, although firms are likely to operate within that structure in different ways, depending upon their nation's legal framework and cultural values. There are, for example, different norms in terms of the degree to which decision-making rests centrally with the CEO, and large Japanese firms tend to have one more layer of management than their European equivalents.[19]

From the 1980s onwards, there has been a clear tendency for management writers and theorists to advocate network structures, along with architectures that promote autonomy, minimize bureaucracy, favour cultural over other kinds of controls and devolve authority to a considerable degree (there is less consensus on the need for economic incentives).[20] It is argued that only these kinds of architecture give the organization the flexibility and respons-iveness they require to remain competitive, along with the ability to build the kinds of linkages they need, both internally and with their partner firms, to run an international organization effectively. These authors have supported their conclusions mainly with case studies of outstandingly successful firms—not all of which have sustained that performance (see What Can Go Wrong 9.1 for an example).

There have been very few studies of how widely, and with what degree of success, these newer forms of organizing have been adopted outside the pioneering firms in those case studies. The consensus from these few studies is that, in Europe and Japan, adoption has been steady rather than sudden. There are some sectors, such as auto components, where most firms have taken these practices on board to some degree. In newly industrializing countries, on the other hand, old-style formal systems are still quite common, although some of the leading firms in such countries, such as the Indian IT services firm Infosys, have highly innovative structures.[21]

Nissan's plant in Sunderland (UK): large Japanese firms often have one more layer of management than their European counterparts.
Nissan

There is evidence that these architectures lead to performance benefits, but only if adopted as a package. Network structures, outsourcing, autonomy, and devolved decision-making do not, separately or together, appear to lead to improved performance. This is only realized if a firm also implements structures, IT systems, and HR practices that encourage teamwork and communication inside and outside the firm.[22]

Using Evidence 8.1 Assessing organizational form

The model of organizational development over time, which we presented in Section 8.2.2, is not followed rigidly by every organization—some never arrive at the collaboration phase, preferring the greater informality of the earlier phases, while others, like Virgin Group, a UK conglomerate, appear to skip directly from an informal structure to a network and avoid all the traumas in between.

If you see an organization whose structure appears to be more appropriate to a larger or small firm, or to a different stage in its development, then it is worth querying whether it has made the right decisions. However, the important thing about a structure is whether it works. If there is clear evidence of goal congruence and if knowledge and learning are flowing well around the organization, then the structure is probably appropriate. Such evidence might include accounts of:

- people making extra efforts to meet tight deadlines or satisfy unusual or difficult requests from customers or colleagues;
- voluntary and enthusiastic participation in training events or other company rituals;
- contributions to suggestions schemes;
- knowledge that has actually been shared.

Be careful, however, to look at outcomes rather than inputs; structures and routines that are *intended* to encourage participation and sharing may not actually be working!

It is also helpful to look at how sales, administration, and general costs are building up over time as a percentage of sales or of total costs. A comparison with key competitors, especially those with a similar competitive stance, may show if the organization is efficiently run, or is imposing too high an administrative burden on itself.

8.3 Informal influences on relationships and motivation

Formal hierarchies and control systems can be deliberately designed to encourage particular groups of people to work closely together, and to motivate people to achieve specific objectives. The elements of architecture we review in this section are less specific in the way they influence and motivate people, but for this very reason, they may be more powerful.

8.3.1 Contracts and relationships

The architectural relationships the organization maintains internally, with the people that work for it, and externally, with the other organizations with which it does business, can be viewed as contracts, of which there are two kinds (Table 8.2):

- Transactional contracts are short-term in nature. They may be formal documents setting out terms and conditions of employment, or delivery terms for a supplier. Alternatively, they may be unwritten understandings that an employee or firm will get a certain type of reward for carrying out a particular task.

- Relational contracts, on the other hand, are long-term agreements that are hardly ever put in writing. They may involve an understanding that an organization will offer stable employment, and look after employees who experience personal misfortune. Externally, a firm may continue to use a supplier over the long term even though there is no formal contract to say that it will do so, and will work with it to improve quality and bring down costs. Relational contracts promote the building of trust between the parties in the relationship.[23]

Real-life Application 8.4 Internal and external relational contracts at Sony and HCL Technologies

Sony[24]

We shall guide and foster subcontracting factories in ways that will help them become independent, and we shall strive to expand and strengthen mutual cooperation with such factories.

We shall carefully select employees, and our firm shall be comprised of minimal number of employees. We shall avoid to have formal positions for the mere sake of having them, and shall place emphasis on a person's ability, performance and character, so that each individual can fully exercise his or her abilities and skills.

We shall distribute the company's surplus earnings to all employees in an appropriate manner, and we shall assist them in practical manner to secure a stable life. In return, all employees shall exert their utmost effort into their job.

(Text reproduced with the kind permission of Sony Corporation)

HCL Technologies[25]

HCL Technologies was the first, and remains one of the largest, of the large Indian information technology firms. Beginning as a

hardware manufacturer in the 1970s, it claims, with some justification, to have created the business process outsourcing (BPO) industry, in which it is a world leader. In a 2006 interview, the CEO, Shiv Nadar, said:

> HCL has to become a partner, a strategic partner, to our clients. We can't remain just a vendor. Frankly, out of 500 organizations for whom we work, we are bound to be vendors to some 450. If we don't work for them, somebody else will. But to the other 50, we make a real difference. Those 50 firms cannot do without us because we are their strategic partners. That's not a very comfortable statement, but it is true—they cannot do without us. Does it mean that they are prisoners of HCL? They are not prisoners, but they have stopped doing the work that we do. There's a huge amount of trust. Annual contracts are no longer necessary or even relevant.

(Text reproduced with the kind permission of the Wharton School, University of Pennsylvania.)

Table 8.2 Examples of internal and external transactional and relational contracts

	Transactional contract	Relational contract
Internal	Terms and conditions of employment Bonus scheme	Paying for medical care if an employee's family falls ill Implicit promise of lifetime employment Employees expected to work evenings and weekends at the close of the financial year – but allowed to take Friday afternoons off for the following month
External	Detailed written contracts Negotiated prices valid for single transaction only Dispute resolution mechanisms	Deals done on a handshake Long term agreement to do business on assumption that price will be set at levels both parties find reasonable Commitment to collaborate to reduce costs and improve quality

A transactional contract may be an adequate framework for a relationship that is not expected to continue for very long. Game theorists call this a finite game—both participants know that it will end after a few periods. In such cases, game theory shows that it is not rational for either player to offer anything more than the minimum required by the contract. So, when McDonald's takes on students to serve in one of its restaurants, it gives them a formal contract that specifies the desired behaviour very tightly, because it knows that many of them will move on after a few months. This transactional contract is reinforced by very specific training and close supervision.

→ We introduced game theory in Section 3.5.6.

When, however, an organization and an employee or a supplier embark on a relationship that both hope will continue indefinitely, the nature of the game changes. In a repeated game, it becomes more rational for the players to experiment with policies that may cost them a certain amount in the short term, but will bring them benefits as long as the other player eventually collaborates. Moreover, if the game has no fixed end, then there is no obvious stage at which it becomes rational for the players to stop collaborating and revert to doing the contractual minimum.

So when Sony takes on some new engineers, it makes sense for the firm to offer them an implicit promise of long-term employment and an opportunity to exercise their skills creatively. On the other side of this relational contract, the engineers are expected to devote more time and energy to the job than is required by the formal contract. If the relationship lasts long enough, the company and the engineers will both benefit.

It is possible to prove, using the mathematics of game theory, that there are certain situations under which relational contracts give better outcomes for both parties than transactional ones, and that this is true both for internal contracts (employer–employee) and external ones (buyer–supplier).[26] There is also a substantial body of theory that suggests that people naturally gravitate towards relationships built on trust and fairness, and that relational contracts are better than transactional ones at motivating both sides to contribute their best efforts under certain circumstances.[27] This explains why relational contracts, far from being an idealized form of relationship, are actually extremely common.

Many factors have been found to affect the extent to which a particular relationship tends to fall into a relational rather than a transactional pattern. Relational contracts appear to increase in importance as the relationship becomes more complex (which raises the costs of drafting a comprehensive transactional contract or makes it impossible to write) and the degree of mutual commitment between the parties increases. In many regular commercial relationships, formal contracts are infrequently referred to—bringing them out may be an unwelcome sign of lack of trust. But in general relational contracts typically co-exist with and complement transactional contracts.[28]

Getting the right relational contracts in place is not simple, since it involves managers throughout the organization behaving consistently over time, and in a way that makes it clear to employees and other stakeholders what the relational contract really is. In the case of Sony, it would ruin the relational contract if engineers were frequently redirected to mundane duties because their manager had overspent on his research budget. Structure and systems also shape relational contracts and need to be made compatible with them. For example, rigid control systems imply a relational contract in which people are discouraged from taking risks and from taking actions that are not in accordance with the organization's formal policies.

Trust is an important element of a relational contract, and if that trust is broken at any stage, the contract is broken too. It can be difficult to achieve an appropriate balance between formal and relational contracts, and to change a relational contract once it is established. When Sony announced it was to make thousands of staff redundant in 1999, and again in 2006, it was signalling that the part of its relational contract that had previously offered lifetime employment was only valid if the staff could deliver commercial success—but it was unclear what was on offer to replace the old relational contract.

Because relational contracts are so difficult to manage, they are a possible source of competitive advantage.[29] They are not a direct form of advantage—people do not buy a Sony PlayStation because they like the way the firm treats its engineers. However, strong and appropriate relational contracts with employees can form the basis of competences and capabilities in areas like customer responsiveness and innovation. For a company that has opted for a virtual value chain, or one with a very low degree of vertical integration, the nature of relational contracts with the partner firms is likely to be vitally important.[30] They may represent the only way that it can obtain advantage over competing firms that are tapping into the same supplier/distributor network.

8.3.2 Mission, vision, and values

Part of the relational contract between a firm and its other stakeholders—staff, suppliers, distributors and so on—is bound up with the organization's values. If people feel that an organization stands for something that they can subscribe to, they are more likely to trust it, and will be happier with the idea of a long-term relationship.

→ Mission, vision, and values were defined in Section 2.2.3.

Frequently, an organization's values are manifested through its mission and vision, which are regarded as important by many influential writers.[31] They may be expressed formally in mission and vision statements (we gave some examples in Chapter 2). They may be displayed indirectly, through an organization's ethical stance (a refusal to behave in unethical ways itself, or to own the shares of unethical companies), or its creativity (the designs of offices or websites). The target audience for these messages consists of both external stakeholders, such as customers and suppliers, and internal ones, such as employees. Displaying the organization's identity in this way can also help reinforce cultural controls by attracting compatible staff and discouraging those who might not fit in.

There is no reason in theory why an organization's mission, vision, and values should not focus on financial performance and shareholder value, if it aims to create a mercenary culture, and to attract staff who are motivated by wealth and its creation. One study has found that stockmarket returns are higher in service firms whose mission statements make mention of shareholders.[32] However, this is an isolated result: most writers in this area advocate that mission, vision, and values should have an uplifting and ethical content, and other research has found that superior performance tends to be found in firms whose mission statements emphasize core values and concern for employees and other stakeholders.[33] A good mission should contain a number of elements:[34]

1. A clear ideology, or set of values—these may relate to the company's policies towards its employees and customers, to the quality of its products or to its beliefs about what constitutes good business practice. For example: 'The H&M spirit of today is based on the same we had from the very beginning—open doors, unambiguous communication, short decision paths and common sense. We work according to values rather than manuals. Continuous improvement, teamwork and cost-consciousness are a few of our core values.'[35]

2. A core purpose—the organization's reason for being. Many theorists advocate that a firm's purpose should be more than just a broad statement of what it does ('We make computers for knowledge workers'). Rather, it should embrace a wider set of ideals that can inspire employees and enlist their loyalty. Sony's core purpose is 'to experience the joy of advancing and applying technology for the benefit of the public'.[36]

3. An envisioned future—an idea of what the company hopes to become in the future, and what it will be like to work there. Some theorists advocate that it should be very ambitious—perhaps even unrealistically so. Highly ambitious aims, referred to as stretch targets or as BHAGs ('big, hairy, audacious goals')[37] have one main benefit. They force people in the organization to think beyond the constraints of its current resources and environment, and look more broadly and creatively at what might be possible. The idea of the future may be expressed through:

   - Targets—'Achieve sales of €1 billion in four years' time' or 'Become the world leader in our industry by 2010';

   - focus on a common enemy—Komatsu, a Japanese manufacturer of earthmoving equipment, adopted the slogan 'Maru-C' ('encircle Caterpillar'—a US company that was the long-standing industry leader, with a high reputation for product quality);[38]

   - a role model—to be 'the Microsoft' or 'the Mercedes' of a particular industry;

   - internal targets—ABB, the Swedish Swiss heavy engineering group, coined the slogan 'Think global, act local' to encapsulate the transnational strategy and architecture towards which it was striving.[39]

A clear mission, vision, and set of values represent certainties that the organization can cling to as the world around it alters, and have three main theoretical advantages. First, they can speed up decision-making in organizations, by providing clear guidelines for behaviour and decisions that are instilled into people's everyday routines. People at all levels can thus take quick, intuitive decisions without needing to waste time consulting a manager at a higher level. Second, they can reduce agency costs, since if everyone believes in the mission and values, they are less likely to try to cheat the organization, and require less supervision. Third, they can enhance an organization's reputation, particularly if the values are close to those that are espoused by important customers or other stakeholders. Firms that enjoy enduring success (measured by stock market performance) over a number of decades have been found to have clearer missions and stronger core values than similarly sized firms in the same industry.[40]

If a mission is to be meaningful, however, then the organization's strategy, and the way that its members behave in practice, should be compatible with it; if they are, then this can lead to superior motivation and financial performance, while if they are not, it can lead to disenchantment.[41] Merely having a mission statement does not make a difference to a firm's performance, particularly as there tend to be many similarities between the mission statements of firms competing in the same industry.[42] An organization may have a clear purpose and set of values without needing a written mission statement.

8.4 Organizational culture

There are two types of model of organizational culture. The first classifies cultures according to what can be observed regarding the organization's ways of working: its work routines and the ways employees interact. These models are contingency theories: they postulate that certain cultures work better in specific contexts. The second type of model offers ways of analysing an organization's belief system, or paradigm, but does not classify those belief systems or claim that there is systematic link between belief system and performance. We deal with each type of model in turn.

8.4.1 Culture as ways of working

a. Burns and Stalker's mechanistic/organic model

Burns and Stalker identified two types of organizational culture:

- mechanistic cultures, in which relationships are very formalized and there are extensive, bureaucratic control systems;
- organic cultures, in which relationships and control systems are much less formal.

They found that innovative organizations tend to develop organic cultures. This seems to be because the highly qualified and creative people that are needed for successful innovation become frustrated if their working life is burdened with too much bureaucracy and control. Mechanistic cultures, on the other hand, are suited to organizations in which conditions are stable and control of costs is more important than innovation. If you encounter a mechanistic culture in an industry where innovation is a success or survival factor, then the firm in question is likely to experience problems. More recent research, however, suggests that in high-technology firms facing very dynamic environments, a degree of formalization in the architecture helps with survival.[43]

b. Goffee and Jones' sociability/solidarity model

Rob Goffee and Gareth Jones[44] proposed a more detailed classification of corporate cultures using two dimensions of behaviour:

- sociability—the degree of sincere friendliness among an organization's members, as evidenced by people frequently stopping to talk and joke together in the office, lunching in groups, socializing after work and celebrating fellow workers' birthdays, long service, or retirement;
- solidarity—the extent to which people are able to 'pursue shared objectives quickly and effectively, regardless of personal ties', evidenced by a clear sense of shared objectives, often enhanced by an idea of a common enemy, and intolerance of behaviour that does not further those objectives.

The Goffee–Jones model identifies four types of culture (Figure 8.7), each featuring a different combination of low and high sociability and solidarity. None of these four cultures—networked, mercenary, fragmented, and communal—is consistently superior to any of the others, but each has strengths and weaknesses that make it appropriate for particular types of environment.

Networked cultures[45] feature a lot of social interaction within close-knit work groups and cliques. This can stimulate creativity, flexibility, and commitment in employees. However, people tend to show more loyalty to their social groups than to the organization, making networked organizations very political. People fight for their groups' interests and may be reluctant to collaborate with other groups. Managers may also be reluctant to take strong action against a loyal member of their work group who is underperforming, so productivity can be low.

The benefits of networked cultures tend to show under two sets of circumstances. The first is when employees are required to put up with a long period of risk, discomfort or frustration before seeing much by way of reward—for example, when entering an emerging market or launching an untried technology. People's loyalty to their colleagues may be crucial in holding an organization together in these circumstances. The second is when specialized local market knowledge is crucial for success, and the sharing of knowledge between business units is of minor importance. In these circumstances, the lack of collaboration between work groups will not be a problem, and close-knit local teams will perform well.

Mercenary cultures, by contrast, place little value on social ties between employees, who tend to keep their work and social lives separate. Managers encourage competition between employees and rarely hesitate to discipline underperforming individuals, so productivity is often high. Employees who meet expectations are, on the other hand, fairly, even generously, treated, which increases their affection towards the organization and their commitment to beating the competition. This makes mercenary organizations very responsive to competitive challenges and opportunities, and effective in fast-moving but well-established industries, such as investment banking and consumer goods. They perform less well in ambiguous situations—for example, when there is no clearly dominant technological standard, or when relevant government policies have not yet been determined. These make it difficult to reach a clear consensus regarding the way forward, establish clear goals, or define who the main enemy might be.

There are, moreover, limits to the degree of commitment this kind of organization is able to gain from its staff. People will leave if they see a better opportunity elsewhere, and may be reluctant to allow distractions from their personal performance. This may inhibit them from taking the time to share information or ideas with colleagues or other business units.

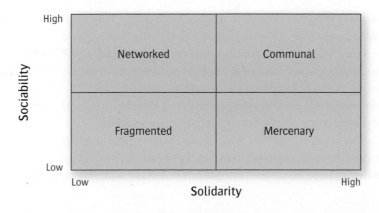

Figure 8.7 The Goffee–Jones culture matrix.
Source: Goffee and Jones (1996: 134)

The mercenary culture works well where it is advantageous for routines to be standardized, without much discussion or negotiation, across the organization, but less so when sharing is important.

Ambiguity, and the need for sharing, are handled better under the communal culture, which is sometimes seen as a form of ideal,[46] where managers get the benefits of both high sociability and high solidarity. People in this type of organic culture work readily in teams, share the firm's strong mission and values and identify strongly with the firm and its leaders. As in mercenary cultures, people have a clear view of who their competitors are, but in communal cultures people see the competitive battle as a clash of competing values, which further sharpens their hunger for victory. Internally, they value fairness and justice and the even-handed sharing of risks and rewards.

This type of culture has, like the networked culture, advantages when it is difficult for the organization to achieve its goals quickly: sociability is important to hold people together for the long term, in the face of short-term disappointments. This may explain why it is found very frequently—though not exclusively—in newly formed entrepreneurial firms. It is particularly appropriate in situations where genuine sharing and teamwork are vital for competitive advantage. This may occur in industries such as pharmaceuticals, where different groups of specialists must collaborate closely to bring products to market, or in firms where there are real and important benefits to be gained from synergies, in particular knowledge sharing, between business units. It also has the edge over the mercenary culture in dynamic and complex environments, since high sociability assists the organization in pulling together information from multiple sources on technology, markets, public policy, and stakeholder requirements.

Goffee and Jones nonetheless conclude that the communal culture works best in religious or political organizations driven by a strong underlying mission, and may be 'an inappropriate and unattainable ideal' for most commercial enterprises. This is because it may be naturally unstable, particularly once the founder has departed. To quote Goffee and Jones: 'The sincere geniality of sociability doesn't usually coexist—it can't—with solidarity's dispassionate, sometimes ruthless focus on achievement of goals' (1996: 145). In particular, when organizations face upheaval while growing or diversifying, they may migrate to a mercenary culture, whose ruthless focus may yield better and faster performance.

Even when a communal culture is appropriate, the levels of commitment it extracts from its members may lead to a risk that they will 'burn out'—exhaust their reserves of energy, or find that their personal lives have suffered to such an extent that they no longer have anything left to give in the workplace. Avoiding these problems may require expensive investments by the firm in crèches, and counselling and concierge services.

Fragmented cultures, by contrast, are much easier and cheaper to maintain, but would seem at first glance to be naturally dysfunctional, since members do not care very much about either the firm or their colleagues. Hospitals, newspapers, and universities can all exhibit this culture and may indeed be difficult to manage, since people have little commitment to the organization's objectives. They may identify more with their professional peer groups—doctor, researcher—and see their duty in terms of caring for patients, or advancing mankind's store of knowledge, rather than enhancing the performance of their employer. They may work secretively, behind closed doors or at home, on their own projects, telling no one what they are doing unless asked and avoiding social events linked to their employment. There may sometimes be unhealthy levels of malicious gossip and rumour.

These cultures can nonetheless function well where there is little interdependence between departments, and the most important factor in organizational success is recruiting self-motivated staff who can be relied upon to operate professionally, and who can achieve

→ We examined the concept of synergies, and the analysis that is needed to establish whether there is genuine potential for them, in Section 5.2.3.

worthwhile innovation when working alone or in teams they have selected themselves. Such people may in turn be attracted by the independence, and the tolerance of individual quirks, that the fragmented culture offers.

Some consultancy and law firms and research-led organizations therefore exhibit this kind of culture. Virtual organizations, and other firms that outsource a lot of work to freelance contractors, may similarly find little need to incur the costs that come with trying to keep one of the other cultures operating smoothly.

8.4.2 Culture as belief systems

An organization's belief system, often referred to as its paradigm, or less frequently as its 'dominant logic', 'theory-in-use' or 'organizational code' is, as you have already seen, the 'glue' that guides behaviour and shapes organizational decision-making.[47] It is different from the organization's mission, which is the conscious message the organization broadcasts to its stakeholders, or from its deliberate strategies, which often incorporate a measure of conscious analysis. The belief system consists of unconscious behaviours and decision rules, built up over time. It is rare for an organization to be able to articulate what its paradigm is—it can only be observed and inferred from the other elements ('cultural artefacts') shown around the border of the hexagon in Figure 8.8.

Each of these elements has a two-way relationship with each of the others—for example, the power structures give rise to stories within the organization about the deeds (sometimes misdeeds) of powerful people, which in turn reinforce the impression that these people are capable of (or can get away with) unusual actions, which serves to reinforce their power. More importantly, for the purposes of our analysis of organizational culture, each of the cultural artefacts has a two-way relationship with the belief system:

- On the one hand, as we discussed in Section 8.1.2, each is a representation or reification of the belief system.

- On the other hand, each of them serves to constantly reinforce the belief system, by constraining the kinds of information processed by people in the organization, and the decisions that people are ready to consider on the basis of that information. Information that challenges the paradigm is rarely acknowledged, and information

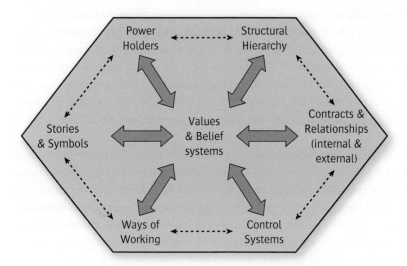

Figure 8.8 Analysing belief systems

that supports it is given greater weight.[48] For example, people working in a tall hierarchy with pervasive bureaucratic control systems will adapt their thinking and ways of working to that environment. They are unlikely to put forward the kind of bold suggestions that might persuade senior managers to question the decision not to grant employees more autonomy—and if such initiatives were forthcoming, middle managers might well suppress them, or pass them off as their own.

Together or separately, the various cultural artefacts give us insights into the underlying beliefs in an organization (or in one of its subcultures). These beliefs and assumptions may relate, for example, to:

- what constitutes normal and acceptable behaviour in a firm or an industry—how one can or should treat individuals or other organizations;

- what kinds of people the organization needs to recruit, and how to get acceptable, or excellent performance—whether the organization needs steady, reliable people who want clear instructions and a predictable wage packet, or more entrepreneurial people who respond to financial incentives, or creative ones that desire autonomy and the chance to produce something original;

- what customers expect—low prices, friendliness, or luxurious surroundings—and how the environment is developing;

- what the organization's role is in society or in the industry—a respected opinion leader or an operator in the niches that are neglected by more prestigious firms;

- what kinds of behaviours allow organizations to survive or succeed, and which aspects of the business are most important.

These beliefs are accumulated over time and are conditioned by the words and past actions of the organization's leaders and by the history of the industry, of the organization's home nation,[49] and of the organization itself. There is a danger that, over time, an organization's internal belief system may fall out of tune with reality—it may become fixated with delivering services to customers that they no longer require, or overlook changes in industry survival or success factors. The point of understanding a belief system, therefore, is to identify any gaps between the paradigm and reality; this can then be used as the basis for future change.

Separately and together, the formal organizational structure, control systems and types of contract and relationship are likely to provide indications of beliefs in a number of ways. If the organization is tall, with extensive bureaucratic controls, this is evidence of a belief that people cannot really be trusted, or that the kinds of people the organization recruit respond to clear objectives and firm supervision. A flatter structure with greater use of relational contracts and cultural controls may indicate a belief that trust and autonomy bring about the best in people. Extensive use of transactional contracts with bonus payments may show a cynical belief that people are dispensable and only motivated by greed, or a belief that the organization does best by employing entrepreneurs who are hungry for success.

The titles of the people who report to the CEO in a divisionalized structure give clues about whether the organization believes that success comes from product technology or an understanding of the needs of particular market segments. BA's functional structure, in a global business, could signify a belief that, deep down, customers and airlines operations are the same the world over—though we would need to look at the ways of working in the different countries, and the amount of power exercised by the people in charge of marketing in different parts of the world, before finalizing that conclusion.

Control systems give strong indications about which behaviours the organization believes should be rewarded and encouraged, or vice versa. Also, the things a company measures are powerful clues as to what it really thinks is important. British Airways, like almost all other airlines, measures the punctuality of its services and even reports it in its annual report—strong evidence of a belief in its importance. PC-maker Dell reports regularly on how low its inventories are—and this item is given as much prominence on its website as its sales and profits. The amount that a firm invests in measuring certain factors, and the frequency with which controls take place, are also useful clues.

Sometimes the *absence* of control systems can be an indication that the organization believes deeply that certain things are *unimportant*. For example, if an organization has no effective systems for measuring quality or customer satisfaction, this is powerful evidence that it does not care deeply about either of those things, however loudly it may claim otherwise.

Ways of working may be routines that are built up to meet some operational purpose within the value chain or purely social rituals, such as joining and leaving ceremonies, regular get-togethers and celebrations of birthdays or promotions. By looking at which of these attracts investments of time, effort, and money by the organization's managers and employees we can see what—cost control, innovation, employee welfare—is seen as important in that culture. The nature of the rituals and routines, formalized or ad hoc, can also give useful clues. Executives of Yum! Brands, a fast-food firm, have, for example, developed the habit of 'rewarding' good performance with gifts of rubber chickens or cheese-shaped hats delivered to the accompaniment of an in-house kazoo 'orchestra'. This demonstrates a belief that people are motivated by being valued, and also that they will respond to humour.[50]

Stories and symbols play a central role in showing what the organization holds to be important. Stories are the tales told by organizational members to each other and to outsiders about what has gone on in the organization (these are not stories that *outsiders* tell *about* the organization, which are indicative of its reputation, but not of its belief system). They may relate to the history and exploits of leaders, past and present, or of successes and failures in the history of the organization. A story they choose to tell about difficulties the founder experienced in the firm's early days, for example, will be told because it contains some lessons that are believed still to be valid for the organization. It therefore gives clues about what kinds of behaviour people believe will bring success to the organization, and which kinds should be avoided. Company reports and accounts, biographical books, websites, and press articles are a good source of officially sponsored stories—the ones the senior managers want to promote. Worked Example 8.2 contains some examples.

The term 'symbol' incorporates anything or anybody that transmits a message about the culture and belief system. Many of the other cultural artefacts—control systems, organization charts, and rituals—also have a symbolic value. Headquarters buildings, if large and located in an expensive financial city district, symbolize beliefs in the need to be close to high-powered clients and to appear to be their equal. A shabby building in a remote suburb may symbolize a belief that cost control is important and that appearances are not. Logos, advertising slogans, and important people and events from the company's history can all be seen as symbols. The way they are evoked by people working in the organization today can give important evidence about the belief system.

Mission and vision statements are symbols too, although before accepting them as evidence of the belief system it would be advisable to check to what extent they are commonly understood and reflected in actual ways of working. Some are, such as Sony's Founding

Prospectus, written in 1946, in which Ibuka, one of Sony's two founders, set out his vision of the future company as being designed by and for engineers, 'establishing a stable workplace where engineers could work to their hearts' content . . . creating an ideal workplace, free, dynamic and joyous where dedicated engineers will be able to realize their craft and skills at the highest possible level'. For a while this document was only available to be seen by special request, although it apparently could be recited verbatim by many employees. It is now on the company's website.[51]

Power holders are the people that actually exercise power in an organization. The people at the top of the structural hierarchy—the top management team—are typically amongst the main power holders, but this is not always the case. It sometimes happens that decision-making authority is taken over by one board member who is not the CEO, or is concentrated in one function or one head-office unit. In any case, there will be groups further down the organization, such as the franchisees at McDonald's or the cabin crew at BA, who have a degree of day-to-day power because they control key resources or are the company's face towards the customer. In some organizations power may reside with union representatives or outside stakeholders.

→ We discuss the concept of power, and ways of identifying who has it, in detail in Section 16.2.

If power is concentrated at the centre, this may demonstrate a belief in the need for uniformity and control, whereas if local managers retain a lot of autonomy, it may symbolize the opposite. Recognizing what kinds of people get to the top in the organization—engineers, accountants, sales executives—and which functions are most influential also offers important clues about what types of competence the organization believes to be key to its success. In British Airways, in the times just after privatization when marketing and customer care were seen as key differentiators, power moved from people with an engineering or aircrew background, as was the case in its early days, to people with a marketing background. The most recent CEOs have a background in airline operations, reflecting the need to enhance efficiency to compete with low-cost operators, without compromising safety and other operating standards.

Worked Example 8.2 Analysing the belief system at McDonald's

The easiest way into an analysis of a belief system is to pick out anything about the organization that is strikingly unusual. This may be an unusual ritual or a prevalence of family members in the power structures, but most often it is found among the stories and symbols.

McDonald's has a number of prominent brand marks. One is the Golden Arches logo, a stylized letter M, but famous though this is, it does not appear to symbolize anything in the firm's belief system. On the other hand Ronald McDonald, the equally famous clown figure, can be said to symbolize the importance of appearing friendly to children and families. If we now look at the rest of the cultural artefacts, we can find support for the idea that this belief is very deep in the organization's paradigm. The firm's long-standing collaboration with the Walt Disney Company, another family-friendly corporation, is a symbol of this. There are

stories on the website regarding the move towards offering more family-friendly menus. There are rituals and routines in every restaurant relating to holding children's parties, and ensuring that sexual offenders are not employed in its restaurants.[52]

This last routine is indicative of another belief: in the need to control the environment very carefully in order to avoid damage to the firm's reputation. The limited degree of individual autonomy and of managerial delegation below the regional level, to which we referred when talking about structure and control systems in Section 8.2.1, also reflect this belief. They also appear to show a belief, widely shared in the industry, that relationships with operational staff will typically be short-lived.

However, McDonald's clearly hopes that some of those relationships may last longer. Its website contains the following proud story: →

➜ In our restaurants, people can learn what it takes to succeed. Many move on to careers in other fields, taking with them essential workplace skills and values. Others move up within the System. More than *forty percent* of our worldwide top management team started as crew members, including:

- Vice Chairman and CEO Jim Skinner.
- Chief Restaurant Officer Jeff Stratton.
- The President of McDonald's Asia, Pacific, Middle East and Africa.
- The Executive Vice President/COO of our U.S. business and two of our three U.S. Division Presidents.[53]

This shows that McDonald's paradigm includes the belief that its success comes from taking under-achieving or poorly qualified people and transforming them. The training rituals that are part of the everyday experience of arriving and working also show how deeply ingrained this belief is—some of the UK restaurants now have facilities for studying for and taking public examinations. The company's famous 'Hamburger Universities', the bases for its corporate training programmes, are symbols of this belief.

These are not the only elements of the firm's paradigm: there is also evidence, from the hierarchical structure and the new menus, of a new belief in the importance of being locally responsive, and if we dug further we could probably find more. The results can be summarized in a matrix similar to that in Table 8.3.

The remaining step is to assess whether the belief system is in tune with the environment which is analysed in Worked Example 3.1—and that is a judgement we can leave to you. There is clearly a logic to all of these beliefs, but it is worth mentioning that they are not all shared by all of its competitors. Yum! Brands, for example, has taken steps to increase the level of loyalty of its restaurant staff, and has succeeded in reducing the rate of staff turnover quite substantially.

Table 8.3 An analysis of McDonald's belief system

Element of belief system	Supporting evidence					
	Structural hierarchy	Contracts	Control systems	Ways of working	Stories & symbols	Power structures
We must embrace the family				Children's parties	'No sex pests' Ronald McDonald Disney alliance	
We must control our environment and guard our reputation	Limited autonomy	Transactional for lower-level staff	Detailed operational prescriptions			Central & regional management
Most of our people are only interested in short-term relationships						
Success comes from taking under-achieving or poorly qualified people and transforming them				Training	Hamburger University Crew members who have worked their way up	Ex-crew members
We must make allowances for cultural differences	Regional divisions				New menu items for specific countries	

Creative Strategizing 8.2

Which elements of McDonald's belief system would you alter in order to enhance its competitiveness? Which new elements need to be added?

Using Evidence 8.1 Analysing organizational culture

Cultural analysis requires a different style of reasoning from that which we have encountered elsewhere in this book. It requires a degree of intuition and a willingness to 'read between the lines' of a case study or other documentary evidence, to look at what is going on.

The Goffee–Jones model is conceptually quite simple,[54] but it can be difficult to apply in practice. This is because it requires evidence on both solidarity and sociability—if either is missing, then the model cannot be used. Evidence on solidarity can be seen by looking at the control systems to see the extent to which they are linked to performance, and by looking for statements by staff of commitment to the organization's goals. Evidence of sociability is more difficult to come by unless you know the organization well—few case studies include data of this kind. If, however, you have detailed information on all other aspects of the organization, and can see no signs of regular social activity, then it may be legitimate to conclude that there is none, and that sociability is low.

The analysis of belief systems is more complex and subtle, but is easier to carry out with incomplete evidence. You only need a couple of stories or symbols, or a little information about the architecture, to be able to start drawing some conclusions regarding the paradigm. In doing so, it is not necessary to be too fussy about which category a particular phenomenon falls under. Some are unclear: Sony's Founding Prospectus could be a symbol or a story, and McDonald's 'Hamburger University' could be seen as a symbol, a way of working or even a control system. The important thing is to make sure that the important phenomena are captured and that logical conclusions are drawn.

What Can Go Wrong 8.1 Structural and cultural issues in BP's United States operations

British based oil company BP (formerly British Petroleum) expanded rapidly in the 1900s, acquiring Arco and Amoco, two major American oil producers. It gained widespread plaudits for the way it was able to improve the efficiency of these firms' operations, and also for the manner in which it seemed able to share knowledge and learning throughout its worldwide operations.

However, a sequence of unfortunate events led observers to reconsider these favourable judgements. In March 2005, 15 people were killed and over 170 injured as the result of an accident at BP's Texas City refinery. Safety mechanisms at the refinery had failed to function as intended. And in March 2006, corrosion in a pipeline at BP's Prudhoe Bay oilfield in Alaska leaked 5,000 barrels of crude oil, triggering a prolonged shutdown of the field, the largest in the USA.[55]

Then, in June 2006, the US's Commodity Futures Trading Commission started an enquiry into possible manipulation of the propane market by BP traders. This was followed in August 2006 by revelations of enquiries into possible manipulation of crude oil and petrol markets in 2003 and 2004.[56] Finally, in September 2006, the company announced that the start of production at Thunder Horse, a large new field in the Gulf of Mexico, would be delayed at least two years beyond the projected starting date.[57]

The delays at Thunder Horse stemmed in part from the exceptionally severe hurricanes of 2005, but observers attributed the remaining problems to BP's culture and structure. First, the company's core belief in the importance of being the industry's most efficient cost-cutter was judged to have overridden other factors. US federal officials in charge of pipeline safety noted that most other operators applied a higher standard of care. In the words of veteran oilman T. Boone Pickens, 'BP is a tightfisted operator, and they pushed too far. A culture of being too tightfisted can develop in an organization . . . When it does, it starts to show up in your maintenance.'[58]

BP was not blind to safety issues, and employees were free to raise safety and maintenance concerns with management. However, managers at Prudhoe Bay attempted to manage the risk in a way that avoided unnecessary expenditure—and this may have led to the postponement of necessary measures. It emerged that, in some of the smaller pipelines, inspections for corrosion had been limited to spot checks. More thorough procedures, involving sending mechanical 'pigs' down the pipe to clean it and check it for flaws, had not been carried out since 1998 or even earlier, although on the bigger pipelines it was done every 14 days. The President of BP North America, Bob Malone, ➜

→ admitted at a Congressional hearing that his company had fallen short of the standards it set itself.[59]

Some observers also felt that BP's structure, with large numbers of business units, allowed too great a degree of autonomy to local managers. BP's divisionalized structure was compared unfavourably to the more centralized functional structure of ExxonMobile, its partner at Thunder Horse, which some believed to be more appropriate to the massive and technologically challenging projects that were becoming the norm in the industry.[60] It did seem that, although the managers in charge of safety reported to BP's headquarters rather than to local management in the USA, BP's structure had allowed the development of strong local subcultures that did not fully reflect the company's ethical stance. Rather than imposing safety systems from the centre, BP allowed plants to continue with locally developed practices.[61] The new British managers installed to run the Texas City plant have spoken of the need to change the safety culture there.[62] Tapes of the propane traders' conversations produced evidence of behaviour that Malone admitted 'may not have broken the law, but ... broke our values'.[63]

BP's safety record prior to the Texas City incident was strong, and the company has clearly moved to address the problems, installing Malone to run BP North America, giving him direct access to CEO Browne (his predecessor reported to Browne's chief-of-staff), and direct authority over two new 'czars' appointed to oversee safety and compliance in the USA.[64] Some see evidence, in the delays at Thunder Horse, of an enhanced emphasis on safety at BP. But, as we mentioned in Real-life Application 7.3, the damage to the company's reputation has been substantial.

Creative Strategizing 8.3

What additional changes would you advocate to BP's architecture to resolve the problems in the USA? How would they help? What risks would they entail?

● CHAPTER SUMMARY

This chapter has built upon the basic definitions of architecture and culture that we gave in Chapter 1, establishing the components of each concept and the relationship between them, summarized in Figure 8.1. The criteria against which to evaluate the effectiveness of an architecture and culture are the degree to which they promote:

1. The transfer of information and the sharing of knowledge and learning

2. Speedy decision-making

3. Effective use of top management attention

4. Goal congruence

5. Efficiency, through the minimization of coordination, agency, and transaction costs

6. Fit with the organization's environment and strategy.

There are five main factors which vary between organizations' structure and control systems, and influence their effectiveness:

● autonomy;

● bureaucracy;

● cultural controls;

● devolution;

● economic incentives.

Organizations typically start with a simple structure and move, as they get older and larger, to first a functional and then a divisionalized hierarchical structure. The degree of centralization in the structure may fluctuate over time. Each of these structures has its advantages and disadvantages, which need to be matched to the organization's circumstances.

Organizations have a choice as to how they can structure their relationships with employees and with other stakeholders such as suppliers. They can use formal, short-term transactional contracts, but there is evidence that less formal relational contracts lead to better long-term outcomes on both sides. A firm's mission, vision and values are important contributors to these relational contracts and may speed up decision-making, reduce agency costs and enhance reputation.

A number of different classifications of culture have been developed, which identify various benefits and disadvantages, for example, organic cultures appear to be better than mechanistic ones at stimulating innovation. The four cultures identified by Goffee and Jones—networked, mercenary, communal and fragmented—display different combinations of sociability and solidarity and are appropriate to different environments.

Further insights can be achieved by analysing an organization's paradigm. This is done by examining the clues provided by the various reifications of the belief system: hierarchical structure; internal and external relationships; control systems; ways of working; stories and symbols; and power structures.

Online Resource Centre
www.oxfordtextbooks.co.uk/orc/haberberg_rieple/

Visit the Online Resource Centre that accompanies this book to read more information relating to architecture, structure, and culture.

● KEY SKILLS

The key skills you should have developed after reading this chapter are:

- the ability to appraise how well an organization's hierarchical structure corresponds to what might be expected, given its age and stage of development;
- the ability to evaluate an organization's existing structure, control systems, and other elements of the architecture against the ABCDE criteria set out in the chapter;
- the ability to recognize the relational contracts at work within an organization and appraise their appropriateness;
- the ability to categorize the culture of an organization and appraise its appropriateness;
- the ability to deduce an organization's belief system from its visible manifestations, such as the organization's structure, control systems, and ways of working.

● REVIEW QUESTIONS

1. Why is it likely that a successful firm will have a structure similar to that of other successful firms in the same industry? Which aspects of its architecture and culture are likely to be different?

2. How might some of the differences of opinion that develop between different functions or divisions in an organization be minimized, or made useful?

3. If a firm offers strong financial incentives clearly linked to performance, does this take away the need for cultural controls? What role might bureaucracy play in such an organization?

4. What are the possible problems that might arise over time in a supply chain in which there are strong relational contracts between the various firms?

5. How do people know what the mission is if the firm does not have a mission statement?

6. Look back to Chapter 3, Real-life Application 3.6 and End-of-chapter Case Study 3.1. Which of the four cultures identified by Goffee and Jones would be appropriate to firms in the videogames and mobile telephone industries, and why? What culture would be appropriate for Si.Sac (Real-life Application 8.2)?

7. What would you deduce about the belief system in a firm where:

- all new joiners are given a door and instructed to use it to make themselves a desk, like the founder did 12 years ago?

- no one has an allocated desk—workstations are allocated each morning on a first-come, first-served basis?

- people have to submit a timesheet each week detailing how their time has been allocated between clients and various activities that do not earn revenue for the company?

- everyone goes to lunch together at the same time every day?

● FURTHER READING

- Organization theory is a mature field and much of the key research dates back several decades. Pugh D. S. (ed.) (1997). *Organization Theory*. London: Penguin, is an inexpensive compendium containing a number of seminal articles relating to the structure of organizations.

- Leavitt, H. J. (2003). 'Why hierarchies thrive'. *Harvard Business Review*, 81/3: 96–102 explains why so much of this theory remains valid today.

- Oxman, J. and Smith, B. (2003). 'The limits of structural change'. *MIT Sloan Management Review*, 45/1: 77–82 argues equally cogently that structure no longer matters that much!

- Jacobides, M. and Billinger, S. (2006) 'Designing the boundaries of the firm: from "make, buy, or ally" to the dynamic benefits of vertical architecture'. *Organization Science*, 17/2: 249–61 is a more learned article that gives an overview of how some of the classical concepts on architecture have to be rethought in the light of the increasing prevalence of outsourcing and virtual value chains.

- Kay, J. (1993). *Foundations of Corporate Success*. Oxford: Oxford University Press can claim credit for introducing the concepts of architecture and relational contracts into the mainstream and Chapters 3 to 5 contain good explanations of these concepts along with a thorough explanation of the underlying game theory.

- Gibbons, R. (2005). 'Incentives between firms (and within)'. *Management Science*, 51/1: 2–17 is a more learned and more recent article that summarizes the state of play regarding the economic theory of incentives and relational contracts.

- Bart, C. (1997). 'Sex, lies, and mission statements'. *Business Horizons*, 40/6: 9–18 is a résumé of what can go wrong with mission statements, written by one of the few serious researchers in that field.

- Edgar Schein's (2004). *Organizational Culture and Leadership*. 3rd edn. San Francisco: Pfeiffer Wiley is a readable and academically sound book on organizational culture. As an organizational psychologist, he takes a deep look at how culture develops over time, and how it influences individual behaviour.

- Goffee, R. and Jones, G. (1996). 'What holds the modern company together?' *Harvard Business Review*, 74/6: 133–48 is the source of one of the frameworks presented in this chapter and contains useful examples of life within the different types of culture.

- Welch, D. and Welch, L. (2006). 'Commitment for hire? The viability of corporate culture as a MNC control mechanism'. *International Business Review*, 15/1: 14–28 is a comprehensive academic review article that looks critically at a variety of strands of thinking on culture and cultural control.

- Morris, J. (2004). 'The future of work: organizational and international perspectives'. *International Journal of Human Resource Management*, 15/2: 263–75 gives an interesting overview on the extent to which new forms of organization and working practices are actually being adopted.

● REFERENCES

Abrahamson, E. (1996). 'Management fashion'. *Academy of Management Review*, 21/1: 254–85.

Acar, W., Keating, R., Aupperle, K., Hall, J., and Engdahl, R. (2003). 'Peering at the past century's corporate strategy through the looking glass of time-series analysis: Extrapolating from Chandler's classic mid-century American firms?' *Journal of Management Studies*, 40/5: 1225–54.

Agthe, K. (1990). 'Managing the mixed marriage'. *Business Horizons*, 33/1: 37–43.

Ahuja, M. and Carley, K. (1999). 'Network structure in virtual organizations'. *Organization Science*, 10/6: 741–57.

Amburgey, T. and Dacin, T. (1994). 'As the left foot follows the right? The dynamics of strategic and structural change'. *Academy of Management Journal*, 37/6: 1427–52.

Andreoni, J. A. and Miller, J. H. (1993). 'Rational cooperation in the finitely repeated prisoner's dilemma: experimental evidence'. *Economic Journal*, 103/418: 570–85.

Argyris, C. and Schön, D. (1978). *Organizational Learning: A Theory of Action Perspective*. Reading, MA: Addison Wesley.

Ashby, W. (1958). 'Requisite variety and its implications for the control of complex systems'. *Cybernetica*, 1/2: 1–17.

Atrill, P., Omran, M., and Pointon, J. (2005). 'Company mission statements and financial performance', *Corporate Ownership & Control*, 2/3: 28–35.

Baker, G., Gibbons, R., and Murphy, K. (1994). 'Subjective performance measures in optimal incentive contracts'. *Quarterly Journal of Economics*, 109: 1125–56.

Baker, G., Gibbons, R., and Murphy, K. (2002). 'Relational contracts and the theory of the firm'. *Quarterly Journal of Economics*, 111: 39–84.

Baker, W. (1992). 'The network organization in theory and practice'. In Nohria, N. and Eccles, R.

G. (eds), *Networks and Organizations*. Boston, MA: Harvard Business School Press.

Bart, C. and Baetz, M. (1998). 'The relationship between mission statements and firm performance: an exploratory study'. *Journal of Management Studies*, 35: 823–53.

Bart, C., Bontis, M., and Taggar, S. (2001). 'A model of the impact of mission statements on firm performance'. *Management Decision*, 39/1: 19–35.

Bartkus, B., Glassman, M., and McAfee, R. (2000). 'Mission statements: are they smoke and mirrors?' *Business Horizons*, 43/6: 23–8.

Bartkus, B., Glassman, M., and McAfee, R. (2006). 'Mission statement quality and financial performance'. *European Management Journal*, 24/1: 86–94.

Barton, H. and Delbridge, R. (2004). 'HRM in support of the learning factory: evidence from the US and UK automotive components industries'. *International Journal of Human Resource Management*, 15/2: 331–45.

Bower, J. L. (2003). 'Building the Velcro organization: creating value through integration and maintaining organization-wide efficiency'. *Ivey Business Journal*, 68/2: 1–10.

Budhwar, P. and Boyne, G. (2004). 'Human resource management in the Indian public and private sectors: an empirical comparison'. *International Journal of Human Resource Management*, 15/2: 346–70.

Bull, C. (1987). 'The existence of self-enforcing implicit contracts'. *Quarterly Journal of Economics*, 102/1: 147–59.

Burns, T. and Stalker, G. (1961). *The Management of Innovation*. London: Tavistock.

Campbell, A. and Nash, L. (1992). *A Sense of Mission*. Reading, MA: Addison-Wesley.

Campbell, A. and Yeung, S. (1991). 'Creating a sense of mission'. *Long Range Planning*, 24/4: 10–20.

Castells, M. 1996. *The Rise of the Network Society*. Oxford: Blackwell.

Chandler, A. (1962). *Strategy and Structure*. Cambridge, MA: MIT Press. 2nd edn (1969); 3rd edn (1990).

Child, J. (1972). 'Organization structure, environment and performance: the role of strategic choice'. *Sociology*, 6: 1–22.

Child, J. (1974). 'Managerial and organisational factors associated with company performance'. *Journal of Management Studies*, 11/3: 175–89.

Child, J. (1997). 'Strategic choice in the analysis of action, structure, organizations and environment; retrospect and prospect'. *Organization Studies*, 18/1: 43–76.

Collins, C. and Smith, K. (2006). 'Knowledge exchange and combination: the role of human resource practices in the performance of high-technology firms'. *Academy of Management Journal*, 49/3: 544–60.

Collins, J. and Porras, J. (1991). 'Organizational vision and visionary organizations'. *California Management Review*, 34: 30–41.

Collins, J. and Porras, J. (1995). 'Building a visionary company'. *California Management Review*, 37/2: 80–101.

Collins, J. and Porras, J. (1996). 'Building your company's vision'. *Harvard Business Review*, 74/5: 65–77.

Davidow, W. H. and Malone, M. S. (1992). *The Virtual Corporation*. New York: Burlingame/Harper Business.

Deeds, D. and Hill, C. (1999). 'An examination of opportunistic action within research alliances: Evidence from the biotechnology industry'. *Journal of Business Venturing*, 14/2: 141–63.

DiMaggio, P. and Powell, W. (1983). 'The iron cage revisited: institutional isomorphism and collective rationality in organizational fields'. *American Sociological Review*, 48: 147–60.

Doty, H., Glick, W., and Huber, G. (1993). 'Fit, equifinality, and organizational effectiveness: a test of two configurational theories'. *Academy of Management Journal*, 36: 1196–250.

Drucker, P. (1973). *Management: Tasks, Responsibilities and Practices*. New York: Harper and Row.

Drucker, P. (1994). 'The theory of the business'. *Harvard Business Review*, 72/5: 95–104.

Fehr, E. and Gächter, S. (2000). 'Fairness and retaliation: the economics of reciprocity'. *Journal of Economic Perspectives*, 14/3: 159–81.

Fehr, E. and Schmidt, K. (1999). 'A theory of fairness, competition, and cooperation'. *Quarterly Journal of Economics*, 114: 817–68.

Fligstein, N. (1985). 'The spread of the multidivisional form amongst large firms, 1919–1979'. *American Sociological Review*, 50: 377–91.

Gamble, J., Morris, J., and Wilkinson, B. (2004). 'Mass production is alive and well: the future of work and organization in east Asia'. *International Journal of Human Resource Management*, 15/2: 397–409.

Garud, R., Kumaraswamy, A., and Sambamurthy, V. (2006). 'Emergent by design: performance and transformation at Infosys Technologies'. *Organization Science*, 17/2: 277–86.

Ghoshal, S. and Bartlett, C. (1998). *The Individualized Corporation*. London: Heinemann.

Gibbons, R. (2005). 'Incentives between firms (and within)'. *Management Science*, 51/1: 2–17.

Goffee, R. and Jones, G. (1996). 'What holds the modern company together?' *Harvard Business Review*, 74/6: 133–48.

Greenwood, R. and Hinings, C. (1988). 'Organizational design types, tracks and the dynamics of strategic change'. *Organization Studies*, 9/3: 293–316.

Greiner, L. (1972). 'Evolution and revolution as organizations grow'. *Harvard Business Review*, 50/4: 37–46.

Gupta, A. (1984). 'Contingency linkages between strategy and general manager characteristics: a conceptual examination'. *Academy of Management Review*, 9/3: 399–412.

Guthrie, J. and Olian, J. (1991). 'Does context affect staffing decisions? The case of general managers'. *Personnel Psychology*, 263–92.

Hall, D. and Saias, M. (1980). 'Strategy follows structure!' *Strategic Management Journal*, 1/2: 149–63.

Hamel, G. and Prahalad, C. (1989) 'Strategic intent'. *Harvard Business Review*, 67/3: 63–77.

Hamel, G. and Prahalad, C. (1993). 'Strategy as stretch and leverage'. *Harvard Business Review*, 71/2: 75–84.

Hannan, M. and Freeman, J. (1989). *Organizational Ecology*. Cambridge, MA: Harvard University Press.

Handy, C. (1989). *The Age of Unreason*. London: Penguin.

Handy, C. (1992). 'Balancing corporate power: a new Federalist Paper'. *Harvard Business Review*, 70/6: 59–72.

Hedlund, G. (1994). 'A model of knowledge management and the N-Form corporation'. *Strategic Management Journal*, 15: 73–90.

Hickson, D., Hinings, C., Lee, C., Schenk, R., and Pennings, J. (1971). 'A strategic contingencies theory of intraorganizational power'. *Administrative Science Quarterly*, 16/2: 216–29.

Hofstede, G. (1980). *Culture's Consequences: International Differences in Work-related Values*. London: Sage.

Hofstede, G. (1991). *Cultures and Organizations*. London: McGraw-Hill.

Jacobides, M. and Billinger, S. (2006). 'Designing the boundaries of the firm: From "make, buy, or ally" to the dynamic benefits of vertical architecture'. *Organization Science*, 17/2: 249–61.

Johnson, G. (1987). *Strategic Change and the Management Process*. Oxford: Blackwell.

Kay, J. (1993). *Foundations of Corporate Success*. Oxford: Oxford University Press.

Kiesler, S. and Sproull, L. (1982). 'Managerial responses to changing environments: perspectives on problem sensing from social cognition'. *Administrative Science Quarterly*, 27/4: 548–70.

Lawrence, P. and Lorsch, J. (1967) *Organization and Environment. Managing Differentiation and Integration*. Cambridge, MA: Harvard University Press.

Leavitt, H. J. (2003). 'Why hierarchies thrive'. *Harvard Business Review*, 81/3: 96–102.

McIlroy, R., Marginson, P., and Ida, R. (2004). 'Regulating external and internal forms of flexibility at local level: five European regions compared'. *International Journal of Human Resource Management*, 15/2: 295–313.

Macaulay, S. (1963). 'Non-contractual relation in business: a preliminary study'. *American Sociological Review*, 28: 55–67.

Macneil, I. R. (1978). 'Contracts: adjustment of long-term economic relations under classical, neoclassical, and relational contract law'. *Northwestern University Law Review*, 72/6: 854–905.

March, J. (1991). 'Exploration and exploitation in organizational learning'. *Organization Science*, 2: 71–87.

Mike B. and Slocum, J. (2003). 'Slice of reality: Changing culture at Pizza Hut and Yum! Brands, Inc.', *Organizational Dynamics*, 32/4: 319–30.

Miles, R., Snow, C., Mathews, J., Miles, G., and Coleman, H. (1997). 'Organizing in the knowledge age: anticipating the cellular form'. *Academy of Management Executive*, 11/4: 7–20.

Miller, D. (1987). 'The genesis of configuration'. *Academy of Management Review*, 12/4: 686–701.

Mintzberg, H. (1979). *The Structuring of Organisations: A Synthesis of the Research*. Englewood Cliffs, NJ: Prentice Hall.

Morris, J. (2004). 'The future of work: organizational and international perspectives'. *International Journal of Human Resource Management*, 15/2: 263–75.

Nathan, J. (1999). *Sony—The Private Life*. London: HarperCollins.

Nohria, N. and Eccles, R. G. (eds) (1992). *Networks and Organizations*. Boston, MA: Harvard Business School Press.

Ocasio, W. (1997). 'Towards an attention-based view of the firm'. *Strategic Management Journal*, 18, Summer special issue: 187–206.

Omran, M., Atrill, P., and Pointon, J. (2002). 'Shareholders versus stakeholders: corporate mission statements and investor returns'. *Business Ethics: A European Review*, 11/4: 318–26, Towards an attention-based view of the firm.

Ouchi, W. (1978). *Theory Z*. Reading, MA: Addison-Wesley.

Ouchi, W. (1981). 'Organisational paradigms: a commentary on Japanese management and theory of organisations'. *Organisational Dynamics*, 9/4: 36–43.

Oxman, J. and Smith, B. (2003). 'The Limits of Structural Change'. *MIT Sloan Management Review*, 45/1: 77–82.

Peters, T. and Waterman, R. (1982). *In Search of Excellence.* New York: Harper & Row.

Pettigrew, A., Massini, S., and Numagami, T. (2000). 'Innovative forms of organising in Europe and Japan'. *European Management Journal*, 18/3: 259–73.

Peyrefitte, J. and David, F. (2006). 'A content analysis of the mission statements of United States firms in four industries'. *International Journal of Management*, 23/2: 296–301.

Poppo, L. and Zenger, T. (2002). 'Do formal contracts and relational governance function as substitutes or complements?' *Strategic Management Journal*, 23: 707–25.

Prahalad, C. and Bettis, R. (1986). 'The dominant logic: a new linkage between diversity and performance'. *Strategic Management Journal*, 7/6: 485–501.

Provan, K. and Gassenheimer, J. (1994). 'Supplier commitment in relational contract exchanges with buyers: a study of interorganizational dependence and exercised power'. *Journal of Management Studies*, 31/1: 55–68.

Pugh, D. and Hickson, D. (1976). *Organization Structure in its Context: The Aston Programme, I*. Farnborough: Gower.

Pugh, D., Hickson, D. J., Hinings, C., and Turner, C. (1968). 'Dimensions of organisational structure'. *Administrative Science Quarterly*, 13, June: 65–105.

Pugh, D., Hickson, D. J., Hinings, C., and Turner, C. (1969). 'The context of organization structures'. *Administrative Science Quarterly*, 14/1: 91–114.

Pugh, D., Hickson, D., MacDonald, K., Hinings, C., Turner, C., and Lupton, T. (1963). 'A conceptual scheme for organisational analysis'. *Administrative Science Quarterly*, 8: 289–315.

Ranson, S., Hinings, B., and Greenwood, R. (1980). 'The structuring of organizational structures'. *Administrative Science Quarterly*, 25/1: 470–4.

Roxenhall, T. and Ghauri, P. (2004). 'Use of the written contract in long-lasting business relationships'. *Industrial Marketing Management*, 33/3: 261–8.

Saunders, C. (1990). 'The strategic contingencies theory of power: multiple perspectives'. *Journal of Management Studies*, 27/1: 1–18.

Schein, E. (1997). 'What holds the modern company together?' *Harvard Business Review*, 75/6: 174–6.

Schein, E. (2004). *Organizational Culture and Leadership*. 3rd edn. San Francisco: Jossey-Bass.

Schilling, M. and Steensma, H. (2001). 'The use of modular organization forms: AN industry-level analysis'. *Academy of Management Journal*, 44: 1148–67.

Sine, W. D., Mitsuhashi, H., and Kirsch, D. A. (2006). 'Revisiting Burns and Stalker: formal structure and new venture performance in emerging economic sectors'. *Academy of Management Journal*, 49/1: 121–32.

Trompenaars, F. and Hampden-Turner, C. (1997). *Riding the Waves of Culture*. London: Nicholas Brealey.

Van Witteloostuijn, A. and Boone, C. (2006). 'A resource-based theory of market structure and organizational form'. *Academy of Management Review*, 31/2: 409–26.

Whittington, R., Pettigrew, A., Peck, S., Fenton, E., and Conyon, M. (1999). 'Change and complementarities in the new competitive landscape: a European panel study, 1992–1996'. *Organization Science*, 10/5: 583–94.

Zahra, S. and Pearce, J. (1990). 'Research evidence on the Miles-Snow typology'. *Journal of Management*, 16/4: 751–68.

End-of-chapter Case Study 8.1 The importance of being Googley

Few firms can have risen quite as quickly as Google from total obscurity to being part of many people's lives and also their vocabulary. The company's search engine has become the prime tool for most people seeking information on any topic. In July 2006, over 49 per cent of all internet searches were conducted on Google, compared with under 25 per cent for its nearest rival, Yahoo.[66]

Google's foundation

Google Inc. only came into being in 1998, the fruits of a project by two computer science PhD students at Stanford University, Sergei Brin and Lawrence Page. The search engines in use at the time were not good at understanding user queries and the answers they delivered typically included many irrelevant links. Users ➤

Google Inc. is the fruit of a project by two PhD students at Stanford University, Sergei Brin and Lawrence Page. *Google*

→ either had to sift through pages of results to find what they really wanted, or be skilled in putting together sophisticated queries to limit the volume of responses. Brin and Page's PageRank™ algorithm, however, prioritized the results of an enquiry according to how many other sites linked to them—in essence, allowing web users to vote for sites that had the most useful content. As Google's website proudly proclaims, 'Democracy on the web works': Google users are typically able to locate what they want amongst the first few results of a search.

Google distinguished itself in another way: by keeping its home page free of the advertisements with which competitors filled theirs in an attempt to generate revenue. Advertisements on Google were confined to the pages which showed the results, and were designed to be relevant to the search—an aid to the user, not a distraction. This ease of use and effectiveness quickly gave Google a prime position among search engines that it has retained ever since.

Google's founders had also figured out a way of conquering another disadvantage of the early search engines: slow delivery of results. Sheer computing power was the answer: making sure that the IT architecture allowed for the easy addition of new servers as the volume of queries increased, and also for the storage of copies of the entire web to allow for ease of indexing. Such massive computing power required funding, of course, but the clarity of Brin and Page's vision was such that they were able, relatively easily, to find funding from the venture capitalists and business angels that clustered in the area of California where they were studying. Brin has described how they convinced one investor, a well-known computing industry veteran: 'We met him very early one morning on the porch of a Stanford faculty member's home in Palo Alto. We gave him a quick demo. He had

to run off somewhere, so he said, instead of us discussing all the details, why don't I just write you a cheque? It was made out to Google Inc., and was for $100,000.'[67] Google (the name is a play on the mathematical name for 1 followed by 100 zeroes) was incorporated shortly afterwards. Brin and Page suspended their studies and, according to the company's website, are still 'on leave' from the Stanford PhD programme.

Development and diversification

Selling space for relevant advertisements on their own site, and licensing the search engine for use on other peoples', generated modest revenues for Google. In 2000, however, the firm launched AdWords™, a system whereby advertisers bid to have links to their sites appear at the top of and alongside the results of searches containing particular words or phrases, such as 'Vaio' or 'Chinese restaurant'. Sites that bid the most initially appear highest amongst these 'sponsored links', which Google is careful to distinguish from its normal search results. However, if a link further down the list of sponsored links attracts a lot of hits, it will be moved closer to the top. This method of giving advertisers targeted access to people interested in their product has proved extremely lucrative. In 2005, advertising generated 99 per cent of Google's revenues of $6.1bn and its growth rate in the first half of 2006 was well above 70 per cent per annum. The company's operating profit margin was 33 per cent and its return on total assets 20 per cent.[68]

Larry Page stepped aside as CEO in 2001 when he and Brin recruited Eric Schmidt, who had held senior posts at Novell and Sun Microsystems, both prestigious names in IT. They recognized that a more experienced executive was needed to guide →

➡ Google's growth from its then 200 employees. Since then, the company's substantial financial resources (nearly $10bn of cash reserves at the end of Q2 2006) have allowed it to launch a raft of new initiatives. These include an online word processor and spreadsheet, Calendar (a personal organizer), Google Maps and its more sophisticated 3D cousin, Google Earth (which offer detailed map and satellite data of most places in the world), Froogle (a shopping site), Google Scholar (enabling searches of scholarly articles), and Picasa (for sharing photos). Some of these have managed to stir up the industry—the free email site, Gmail, offered users much more online storage than competitors had offered, and more than most would ever need. Competitors like Yahoo! and Hotmail were forced to match Google's offering. However, neither Gmail nor its stablemates have come close to matching the popularity of the original search product.

Working life at Google

These products are justified as being 'Googley'—helping the company pursue its vision of organizing the world's information and making it universally accessible and useful. The company goes to great lengths to stimulate the creation and sharing of new Googley ideas. Although there is a management team with defined roles (see Table 8.4), employees are lightly supervised. ➡

Table 8.4 Google's Management Team in 2006

Executive Management Group
Dr. Eric Schmidt†*#, Chairman of the Executive Committee and Chief Executive Officer
Larry Page*, Co-Founder & President, Products
Sergey Brin#, Co-Founder & President, Technology
Shona Brown†, Senior Vice President, Business Operations
W. M. Coughran, Jr.†#, Vice President, Engineering
David C. Drummond†, Senior Vice President, Corporate Development
Alan Eustace†#, Senior Vice President, Engineering & Research
Urs Hölzle†#, Senior Vice President, Operations & Google Fellow
Jeff Huber*, Vice President, Engineering
Omid Kordestani*μ, Senior Vice President, Global Sales & Business Development
George Reyesμ, Senior Vice President & Chief Financial Officer
Jonathan Rosenbergμ, Senior Vice President, Product Management
Elliot Schrage†, Vice President, Global Communications & Public Affairs

Google Management Group
Tim Armstrong, Vice President, Advertising Sales
Nikesh Arora*μ, Vice President, European Operations
Laszlo Bockμ, Vice President, People Operations
Sukhinder Singh Cassidy, Vice President, Asia-Pacific & Latin America Operations
Vinton G. Cerf†#, Vice President & Chief Internet Evangelist
Johnny Chou*†, Vice President, Sales and Business Development & President, Greater China
David Eun, Vice President, Content Partnerships
Dave Girouard*μ, Vice President & General Manager, Enterprise
Salar Kamangar, Vice President, Product Management
Kai-Fu Lee†*#, Vice President, Engineering, Product, and Public Affairs & President, Greater China
Udi Manber†#, Vice President, Engineering
Marissa Mayer#, Vice President, Search Products & User Experience
Douglas Merrill†, Vice President, Engineering
Norio Murakami*, Vice President & General Manager, Google Japan
David Radcliffe*μ, Vice President, Real Estate
Miriam Rivera†μ, Vice President & Deputy General Counsel
Sheryl Sandbergμ, Vice President, Global Online Sales & Operations
Susan Wojcickiμ, Vice President, Product Management

Notes
† holds a PhD or other doctoral qualification
* holds a qualification in engineering
# holds a qualification in computer science
μ holds an MBA
(Honorary qualifications not included)

Source
<http://www.google.com>

→ They work in clusters of three or four, but often congregate to discuss solutions to IT problems in the corridors or in the many free cafés and snack rooms. The result has been called 'structured chaos'—and if it results, as it sometimes does, in expensive mistakes, these are regarded as preferable to a predictable or safety-first mentality.[69]

Reminders of the company's core advertising and search business, on which employees are meant to spend 70 per cent of their time, are easy to find. Current search queries from around the world are projected on a screen in the lobby, and one office features a 3D rotating image of the world, on which can be seen traffic patterns for the internet and representations of real-time searches, rising into space from their point of origin and colour-coded according to the language. The latter is an example of the 'wild fun' on which Sergei Brin encourages employees to spend 10 per cent of their time. The remaining 20 per cent is expected to be spent on non-core products, and there are many small teams working on over a hundred of these.

A great deal of effort goes into recruiting staff members with the Googley mindset. One example is a billboard that directed readers to a website whose address was the solution to a complex mathematical puzzle. Solvers of that puzzle who accessed the site found another, tougher puzzle, whose solution led to a page where they could submit their CV to Google. The firm has a liking for puzzles—they left one on the seat for each attendee at a 2006 conference presentation—and for mathematical references, both of which are also seen as Googley. The amount of money it raised in its 2004 stockmarket flotation ($2,718,281,828) is related to e—the root of natural logarithms.

Another element of being Googley is expressed in a phrase that captured much attention—and not a little ridicule—when it appeared in the flotation prospectus: 'Don't be evil.' The firm believes that its targeted advertising adds value to both advertiser and reader. Simple text links avoid distracting the reader, while the company also offers tools to help advertisers improve their click-through rates—the proportion of readers that click on a link.

Setbacks and criticisms

Despite its profitability and high-mindedness, the company has encountered criticism. First, the proliferation of products, not all profitable, is said to dilute the simplicity and focus that characterized Google in its early days.[70] Second, many products are released unfinished. While some are explicitly under the Google Labs umbrella, as new ideas that users are invited to help the company develop, more mature ones, such as Froogle, may spend three or more years as 'beta' products—the industry's term for unfinished software that users are helping to refine for final release.[71]

The company has not always anticipated how others might view its projects. A plan, announced in 2004 but conceived much earlier, to digitize books in the collections of major libraries encountered strenuous opposition from publishers and authors concerned about infringement of copyright. Although some librarians and users share Google's view of the benefits, and although publishers can limit how much of a book is downloadable, lawsuits have been launched in France and the USA to halt the project.[72]

And finally, not all products match those on offer elsewhere. Some are released without some features that many would regard as obvious and essential: the launch version of the spreadsheet lacked a print facility, and business users cannot synchronize their Google Calendar with the Microsoft Outlook calendars that many use at work.[73] Except in South America, Google's social networking site, Orkut, has not matched the success of FaceBook and MySpace—its share of the US market in mid-2006 was under 0.4 per cent—while Google Video has also fallen behind the leader in video sharing, YouTube.[74] On 9 October 2006, Google agreed to purchase YouTube for $1.65bn.[75]

Case study questions

1. Appraise Google's architecture. How well suited is it to the company's present competitive situation?

2. In which sector of the Goffee–Jones matrix would you place Google? How appropriate is that culture for the challenges confronting the company?

3. Analyse Google's belief system. Are any parts of its paradigm outdated?

● NOTES

1 The importance of management attention was discussed by Ocasio (1997).

2 Influential writers who have worked in a contingencies tradition include: Greenwood and Hinings (1988); Saunders (1990); Guthrie and Olian (1991); Zahra and Pearce (1990); Gupta (1984); Ranson et al. (1980); and Hickson et al. (1971). For a more recent example see Van Witteloostuijn and Boone (2006).

3 See Jacobides and Billinger (2006) for discussion of vertical architecture.

4   See Ahuja and Carley (1999), who found evidence of hierarchy in a virtual organization.

5   See Leavitt (2003) for a very clear discussion of the reasons for the existence of hierarchies.

6   The term 'clan' was introduced by Ouchi (1978, 1981), while Mintzberg (1979) prefers 'missionary'.

7   Woodhead, M. (2006). 'New boy Lee focuses on a labour of love at Leica'. *Sunday Times*, 1 October: 3.8.

8   See, for example, Mintzberg (1979) and also the writers from the influential Aston Group who wrote about the relationship between context and structure in the 1960s and 1970s, for example Pugh and Hickson (1976), Pugh et al. (1969).

9   This relationship was first pointed out by Greiner (1972).

10 This term is used by Mintzberg (1979).

11 This 'law' (Ashby, 1958) derives from cybernetics. It is advisable to be careful when taking theory developed for one discipline and applying it in another, but in this case, it appears to be valid to do so.

12 Greiner (1972) describes this as a 'crisis of leadership'.

13 Greiner (1972) termed this a 'crisis of autonomy'.

14 Greiner's (1972) 'crisis of control'.

15 See Bower (2003) for some examples of how the divisionalized structure can malfunction in this way.

16 Greiner's (1972) 'crisis of red-tape'.

17 Baker (1992).

18 The network organization is discussed in Nohria and Eccles (1992). The terms 'federalist' and 'shamrock' come from Charles Handy (1989, 1992), the 'virtual corporation' from Davidow and Malone (1992), and the cellular organization from Miles et al. (1997). See Schilling and Steensma (2001) for a review.

19 For comparisons of practices across countries, see Pettigrew et al. (2000), Morris (2004), and McIlroy et al. (2004).

20 See, for example, Castells (1996); Ghoshal and Bartlett (1998); Handy (1992); Hedlund (1994); Miles et al. (1997); and Peters and Waterman (1982).

21 See Pettigrew et al. (2000), Morris (2004); Barton and Delbridge (2004); Budhwar and Boyne (2004); and Gamble et al. (2004). Infosys' architecture is reviewed by Garud et al. (2006).

22 Whittington et al. (1999).

23 The distinction between transactional and relational contracts is usually attributed to Macneil (1978).

24 Extracted from the 'Management Policies' section of the 1946 Founding Prospectus of the Tokyo Telecommunications Engineering Corporation—later to become the Sony Corporation <http://www.sony.net/SonyInfo/CorporateInfo/History/prospectus.html> accessed 11 May 2007.

25 Aron, R. (2006). 'HCL's Shiv Nadar: "When someone brings China and India together, it will be a big story"'. *Knowledge@Wharton*, September 27 <http://knowledge.wharton.upenn.edu/article.cfm?articleid=1563>, accessed 21 July 2007.

26 See, for example, Bull (1987), Baker et al. (2002) and Gibbons (2005).

27 Andreoni and Miller (1993); Fehr and Gächter (2000); Fehr and Schmidt (1999).

28 Macauley (1963) is a classic study of how little formal contracts are actually used. For theory and evidence regarding the complementarity between formal and relational contracts, and how this varies according to context, see Baker et al. (1994), Provan and Gassenheimer (1994), Poppo and Zenger (2002), and Roxenhall and Ghauri (2004).

29 Kay's (1993) research identified the use of relational contracts within the architecture as a source of competitive advantage. For more recent evidence, see Collins and Smith (2006).

30 Deeds and Hill (1999) observed this effect in R&D alliances.

31 See for example Drucker (1973, 1994) along with the other writers cited in this section.

32 Atrill et al. (2005).

33 Bartkus et al. (2006).

34 Campbell and Yeung (1991); Collins and Porras (1991, 1996).

35 H&M Annual Report, 1999: 16.

36 Cited in Collins and Porras (1996: 69).

37 The phrase 'stretch targets' is used by Hamel and Prahalad (1993); the notion of BHAG comes from Collins and Porras (1996).

38 Goffee and Jones (1996); Hamel and Prahalad (1989).

39 Agthe (1990).

40 Collins and Porras (1991, 1995, 1996). Peters and Waterman (1982) also found that strong values were one of the characteristics of excellent companies—but have been criticized for not checking whether those characteristics were also present in less successful firms.

41 Bart et al. (2001); Bartkus et al. (2000); Campbell and Nash (1992); Campbell and Yeung (1991).

42 Bart and Baetz (1998); Omran et al. (2002); Peyrefitte and David (2006).

43 For the original findings see Burns and Stalker (1961); the updated research comes from Sine et al. (2006).

44 Goffee and Jones (1996).

45 Please note that networked cultures are not necessarily associated with network value chains or network structures. Different theorists may, confusingly, use the same terms to denote very different things.

46 Peters and Waterman (1982) wrote enthusiastically about this kind of culture.

47 Writers on the paradigm include Johnson (1987) and Schein (2004). The phrase 'dominant logic' is used by Prahalad and Bettis (1986), 'theory-in-use' by Argyris and Schön (1978), and 'organizational code' by March (1991).

48 See Kiesler and Sproull (1982) for a discussion.

49 For research into how national culture shapes managerial thinking, see Hofstede (1980, 1991) and Trompenaars and Hampden-Turner (1997).

50 See Mike and Slocum (2003).

51 Nathan (1999) and <http://www.sony.net/SonyInfo/CorporateInfo/History/prospectus.html>, accessed 7 October 2006.

52 Nation's Restaurant New (2006). 'McD beefs up its hiring policy after sex offender news reports'. 40/22: 1–6.

53 <http://www.mcdonalds.com/corp/values/people/opportunity.html>, accessed 5 October 2006. Italics are reproduced from the original. Similar stories have appeared in annual reports for earlier years.

54 In fact, it has been criticized as over-simplified by one of the most eminent cultural theorists, Edgar Schein (1997).

55 Schwartz, N. D. (2006). 'Can BP bounce back?' Fortune, Europe, 154/7: 39–43.

56 Hope, C. (2006). 'Browne's annus miserabilis at BP is not over. The Texas explosion investigation, allegations of market rigging and huge oil leaks are making life tough'. Daily Telegraph, 31 August: 4.

57 Macnulty, S. (2006). 'BP and ExxonMobil are at odds', Financial Times, 21 September: 22.

58 Bartiromo, M. (2006). 'Boone Pickens follows the oil'. BusinessWeek, 25 September: 142.

59 Grant, J. (2006). 'BP officials admit "unacceptable" failures'. Financial Times Ft.com, 8 September.

60 Hoyos, C. (2006). 'BP battles to clear its Augean stables'. Financial Times, Ft.com, 19 September.

61 Hoyos (2006) op. cit.

62 Schwartz (2006) op. cit.

63 Lustgarten, A. (2006). 'Beyond Prudhoe'. Fortune, 154/5: 24.

64 Schwartz (2006) op. cit.

65 Main sources: Economist (2004). 'How Google works'. Technology Quarterly supplement, 18 September: 28–32; Economist (2006). 'Fuzzy maths'. 11 May; Lashinsky, A. (2006). 'Chaos by design'. Fortune, Europe, 154/6: 34–42; <http://www.google.com/corporate>, accessed 9 October 2006.

66 Source: Nielsen Netratings, cited by 22 August 2006, cited by <http://www.searchenginewatch.com>, accessed 14 October 2006.

67 Burkeman, O. (2002). 'Engine trouble', Guardian, 5 September.

68 <http://investor.google.com/fin_data.html>, accessed 14 October 2006.

69 Lashinsky (2006) op. cit.

70 Economist (2006). 'Fuzzy maths'. 11 May.

71 Lashinksy (2006) op.cit. and Kesmodel, D. (2005). 'For some tech cos, "beta" becomes long-term label'. Wall Street Journal Online, 29 November.

72 Nuttal, C. (2005). 'Publishers try to halt Google library plan'. *Financial Times*, 20 October: 31. Thompson, B. (2006). 'Search me?: Google wants to digitize every book. Publishers say read the fine print first'. *The Washington Post*, 13 August. Guardian Unlimited (2006). 'Google has offered the first glimpse at the results of their controversial Book Search project, releasing the top 10 most-viewed texts in English for one week in September'. 5 October.

73 Lashinsky (2006) op.cit.

74 *Wall Street Journal Europe* (2007). 'Breakingviews: Google still searching for hit'. *Dow Jones News Service*, 10 April; Wallenstein, A. (2006). 'YouTube may be good fit'. *Hollywood Reporter*, 9 October; Lashinsky (2006) op. cit. Market share figures are from Hitwise and cited in *Business Wire* (2006). 'MySpace is the number one website in the U.S. according to Hitwise'. 11 July.

75 *Economist* (2006). 'Two kings get together—Google and YouTube'. 14 October: 81.

CHAPTER NINE

The Management of Complex Organizations

LEARNING OUTCOMES

After reading this chapter you should be able to:

→ Explain the advantages and drawbacks of holding company, matrix, hybrid and flexible structures, for complex organizations in particular situations

→ Assess whether a given complex organization has made an appropriate choice between divisionalized, network, matrix, and hybrid forms

→ Discuss the concept of a parenting proposition and its importance in assessing how a parent adds value to its different businessses

→ Explain the different parenting styles that have been identified and the types of portfolio to which each is most appropriate

→ Identify the parenting propositions that a corporation's management is offering, and the style that it is using, and assess their appropriateness for its portfolio

→ Explain the principal challenges involved in managing alliances and portfolios of alliances

→ Assess whether a firm is structuring its alliances appropriately and using good practice in their management.

INTRODUCTION

As organizations become larger and more diverse, they acquire a degree of complexity that poses extra challenges for their managers. As we saw in Chapter 5, relatedness between different businesses in a diversified company is key to gaining the benefits from diversity, but to profit from relatedness, a firm must have a culture and architecture that promote knowledge sharing between the businesses. Other key challenges including using management attention and corporate-level resources to best advantage, when there are so many businesses competing for them, and sustaining goal congruence across a variety of subcultures, some internal to the organization and some within its network partners. Because this is so difficult to do effectively, it is possible for organizations to gain competitive advantage from getting it right. Firms like General Electric (GE), whose track record in this area is exceptional, are highly rated by the capital markets and have an enviable record of profitability.

In this chapter, we examine the options that organizations have at their disposal for managing this complexity. In Chapter 8, we saw how organizations' choices of structure and their degree of decentralization tend to change as they grow; here, we look in more detail at the specific structural options at their disposal. We then review the various styles of management that are available at the corporate level, ranging from hands-off management to intensive participation in business unit strategy development. Finally, we examine the particular challenges of developing and managing the networks of alliances and partnerships that have become an important part of the value chains of many successful firms.

9.1 Structural choices for complex organizations

Most diversified organizations need, in their structure, to take account of five dimensions:

- functions;
- products—grouped so that commonalities in technology can be exploited;
- geographic markets;
- vertical markets and customer segments;
- projects, which may include products or services for an external client or for internal use within the organization—for example, a new financial control system.

The main challenge in devising an organizational structure is to allocate these responsibilities for different elements of each of these dimensions to particular units. Each unit must be allocated a charter: a set of responsibilities for a particular combination of functions, product, market, and projects—examples might be 'the design of clothing for teenagers in Europe' or 'the development and maintenance of customer relationship management software for our global operations'. As we saw in Section 6.1.3, firms increasingly make use of regular collaborators who fill a defined role in a business' value chain, and who may be located in a different continent (see Real-life Application 9.4 for an example), so that some important charters may belong to units that the organization does not formally own. In Section 8.2.2 we set out three of the main options for handling these dimensions:

- giving priority to integration within each function, in a functional structure;
- giving priority to one out of the middle three dimensions in a divisional structure. In commercial organizations, divisions are often set up as completely different companies,

Project
The commitment of resources over a defined time-scale to produce a one-off output: a product such as a new airliner, or a service such as a major consultancy investigation and report.

→ We examined the relationship between ownership and participation in an organization's structure in Section 8.1.3.

with functional or even multi-divisional structures of their own, and even may be in partial public ownership themselves. The M-form is also frequently found in the public sector: a local administration will have different divisions dealing with, say, housing, education, and waste disposal;

• dividing the organization in an ad hoc fashion in a network structure.

The advantages and disadvantages of those three structural forms, which can be used in organizations of any size, were discussed in the previous chapter. In the rest of this section, we set out the main alternatives for larger and more complex organizations: holding company, matrix, project-based, and hybrid structures.

9.1.1 **The holding company**

The holding company is, in essence, an extremely decentralized form of multi-divisional structure, with all the advantages and disadvantages of highly devolved architectures (see Section 8.2.1). A small head office simply acts as the overall owner of a range of separate companies whose finances are closely monitored, although they are allowed a high degree of operational and strategic autonomy. Outside shareholders may be permitted for some of the divisions. This structure does not contribute much to synergies between the divisions, but is quite common in developing countries, where highly diversified conglomerates can add value simply by offering their subsidiaries financing options that are not necessarily available through financial markets and institutions (Real-life Application 9.1).

 Real-life Application 9.1 **Orascom**[1]

OHD designs and builds leisure complexes and hotels in the Middle East. *Orascom*   →

→ Orascom is a firm, founded over 50 years ago by Onsi Sawiris, that in 2005 accounted, in total, for 40 per cent of the capitalization of Egypt's stock market. It has three main divisions (a fourth, smaller division provides IT and telecoms solutions):

- Orascom Telecom Holdings (OTH) operates mobile telecoms services in Algeria, Pakistan, Egypt, Tunisia, Iraq, Bangladesh, and Zimbabwe. Its chief executive is Naguib Sawiris, Onsi's eldest son.

- Orascom Construction Industries (OCI) is a construction contractor active in emerging markets and also one of the world's 15 largest cement producers. Its CEO is Nassef Sawiris, Onsi's youngest son.

- Orascom Hotels and Development (OHD) designs and builds leisure complexes and hotels in the Middle East. Its CEO is Sawih, the middle of the three Sawiris brothers.

OTH, OHD, and OCI are all publicly quoted companies in which the Sawiris family retains a stake of at least 50 per cent, over half of which is vested in the brother who is the CEO. The three companies each have different strategies, said to reflect the characters of the brother that heads them. OTH is structured into geographic divisions with strong central functions, OCI's executive board members are heads of its main product groupings, while OHD appears to have a functional structure.

Although family members have been known to help one another out with loans from time to time, business dealings between their companies are minimal. Although both OCD and OTH have need of construction services, less than 1 per cent of OCI's revenues comes from sales to them. The brothers believe that outside investors in the three firms would be unhappy if their businesses were too strongly linked.

9.1.2 Matrix and project-based structures

Although there are theoretical differences between matrix and project-based structures, it makes sense to consider them together. On the one hand, many firms that deploy their staff mainly in project teams, such as consultancies, use a matrix for their formal structure. On the other hand, projects frequently figure as one dimension in a matrix.

In a matrix structure the hierarchy is not linear, up and down the organization. In a structure like the one shown in Figure 9.1, an employee might at any given moment be reporting to:

- the managers in charge of one or more projects using his or her specialist skills, such as project management, cost estimation, or marketing;

- the manager in charge of that specialist skill area across the organization. That manager would keep track of which employees have shown aptitude for specific kinds of project, and would also lay on professional training to make sure that skills are kept up to date;

- a local manager who would hire employees, ensure that their time was being effectively utilized, and maybe allocate them marketing or after-sales service duties for their region.

Companies following a transnational strategy are likely to use a form of matrix structure. Leading insurance company AXA does so in its Asian operations, to allow its local operating companies to respond autonomously to their local market, while getting input from their colleagues in other countries; however, the centre is able to retain tight control of the corporate brand and the way it is used. This structure is particularly common in professional service and research environments. Samsung Group, the Korean technology conglomerate, uses a matrix structure for SAIT, its central R&D unit, which has ten laboratories spanning five core technologies. For another example, see Real-life Application 9.2.[2]

→ We defined transnational strategies in Section 1.3.8, and discuss them in greater detail in Chapter 14.

Real-life Application 9.2[3] Cementation Foundations Skanska

Cementation Foundations Skanska is a leading UK piling and ground engineering company. *Skanska*

Cementation Foundations Skanska is a leading UK piling and ground engineering company, a subsidiary of the Swedish Skanska Group. It operates globally, offering services to firms engaged in construction projects, such as dams, which require specialist advice to ensure that the foundations are secure. The firm prides itself on its innovative design skills, the cost-effectiveness of the alternative solutions it offers and its reputation for quality and performance.

Its matrix structure has three dimensions, of which two are illustrated in Figure 9.1. On one there are the principal operating units, some of which are geographical (e.g. South of England), and some of which are oriented to a particular type of service (rail,

ground engineering). The depot at Bentley, the firm's historic headquarters, which serves as a resource centre for the entire organization, is a unit in its own right. The second dimension, shown down the left-hand side of the figure, comprises the main value chain activities of proposal-writing (which requires a great deal of technical expertise), operations, and commercial (e.g. purchasing and legal expertise). The hidden dimension is the project, each of which calls upon resources from the other two dimensions.

The executives in charge of the operating units all report to the operations director, but the manager in charge of ground engineering has, in addition, a direct reporting line to the Managing Director for overseas projects.

→ We examine decisions about which activities in its value chain a firm might outsource to partners in Section 6.1.3.

→ We review organizational issues to do with network structures in Section 8.2.2.

A project will often involve significant input from independent service providers who offer a particular competence. Some of these may be major firms in their own right (Cementation Foundations Skanska works in this way on large construction projects), others independent programmers or consultants. The accompanying matrix structure must incorporate mechanisms for managing these inputs, and the relationships with the partners. We return to this in Section 9.3.

A successfully implemented matrix structure achieves balance between the different dimensions. It promotes economies of scale across similar elements of each business, by unifying the people involved in those parts of the value chain under one dimension of the matrix, while allowing for flexibility across other dimensions. This helps knowledge and information to flow freely and allows employees' expertise to be applied flexibly to the most

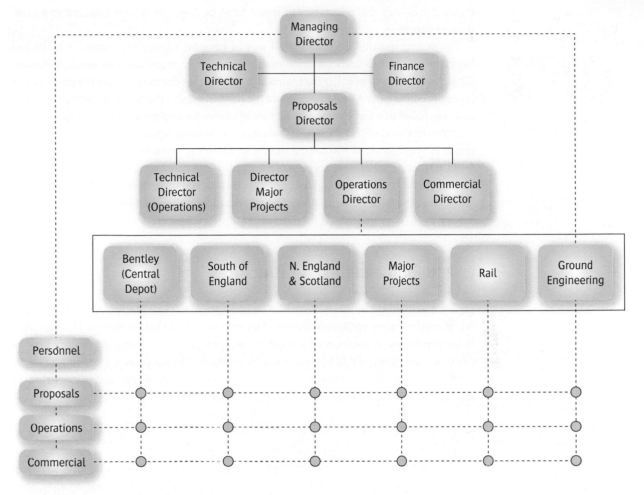

Figure 9.1 Cementation Foundations Skanska's matrix management structure in May 2007. Source: <http://www.skanska.co.uk/index.asp?id=2849>, accessed 11 May 2007. N.B. some elements omitted for clarity. *Reproduced with the kind permission of Cementation Foundations Skanska*

appropriate outputs at a given time, rather than being tied exclusively to what is going on in a particular locality or division. As a result, the organization can pursue a variety of business objectives without needless duplication of resources.

It is not, however, easy to implement, or work within, a matrix structure. Problems can arise because accountability and responsibility—whom to blame, whom to praise, who takes action when things go wrong or right—are confused; see Real-life Application 9.3 for an example. If conflicts arise between the requirements of the project manager, the local manager, and the disciplinary specialists, then it is not clear whose orders take priority. Resolving such conflicts may slow the organization down, or lead to expensive compromise solutions in order to meet the demands of all the different parties.[4] Employees may need to make sophisticated judgements as to who the real power-holders are. In a matrix structure where one of the authors worked, the executives nominally leading the various dimensions of the global matrix actually exercised very little power—day-to-day authority rested firmly with the managers in charge of the 'nodes' (equivalent to the circles in the matrix in

Figure 9.1, though this relates to a different firm), each of which corresponded to a small team of people.

The project remains the only logical way of bringing together resources from several organizations or sub-units to tackle major customer or organizational needs. Opinions differ, however, as to whether the matrix is a structure for the future or for the past. A 2002 report by consultants AT Kearney praised the performance of the best-run matrix structures and concluded that they were the structure of choice for dealing with the complexity that characterizes modern businesses. However, some leading academics disagree, suggesting that it is better to avoid formalized matrix structures in favour of encouraging a state of mind in managers that takes account of the needs of the entire firm, not only their part of it. This might be achieved through cultural controls backed up with financial incentives that are tied to the performance of the entire organization, rather than just the manager's own sub-unit.[5]

9.1.3 Hybrid and flexible structures

Traditional multi-divisional structures essentially break an organization down into a number of similar pieces, each with control of its own key value chain activities. This sacrifices either production economies of scale, if the organization is divisionalized by markets, or customer sensitivity, if it is broken down by products. Moreover, as we saw in Chapter 8, conflicts between the divisions may inhibit the transfer of knowledge and information. In this section, we discuss ways that have been tried to overcome these drawbacks, without the complexity and ambiguity that arise in matrix structures.

One relatively simple variation to the M-form entails allowing different divisions to have different structures. An organization may have some divisions that operate in stable, predictable conditions, like the retail part of a high street bank. These can operate perfectly well using a functional structure. Others, like a bank's corporate finance division, may need to be faster moving, more innovative, and combine different types of expertise in a single team. It might be better off with a matrix structure. The challenge then is to manage the cultural differences between the two types of division to avoid conflicts, but also contamination. The stable divisions should not acquire too much of a risk-taking culture and the growing ones should not become too risk-averse, as a result of corporate-level contacts.

A subtler variation on this theme is where the whole organization adopts what looks like a functional or simple divisional structure to run its day-to-day operations, but some parts of the business set up project teams to work on critical problems or important innovations. This kind of hybrid between a functional and a matrix structure has been called a 'hypertext organisation'.[6] The challenge in this case is to manage any conflicts of loyalty that employees feel between the task force and their home division.

A rather more radical move away from the divisionalized form involves separating the value chain activities into two. Those which benefit from economies of scale or scope at the level of the product, such as R&D or operations, are grouped in product-based units. Those that need to be tuned to the needs of particular customer segments (or even individual major clients), such as sales and after-sales service, are placed in market-based units. This 'front-back' structure has been observed in computing (e.g. IBM's structure in Figure 9.2), the automotive industry, financial services, and ebusinesses (Real-life Application 9.3). Each of the market-based units can source and sell products from all over the organization and its alliance partners. It is not tied to one set of products from its own factories

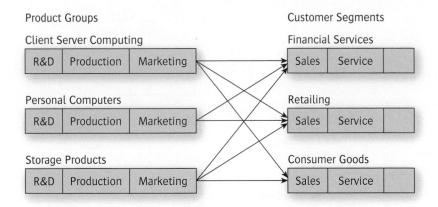

Product Groups

Client Server Computing

| R&D | Production | Marketing |

Personal Computers

| R&D | Production | Marketing |

Storage Products

| R&D | Production | Marketing |

Customer Segments

Financial Services

| Sales | Service | |

Retailing

| Sales | Service | |

Consumer Goods

| Sales | Service | |

Figure 9.2 IBM's customer product structure. Source: Galbraith (1998: 53)

or service units, as it would be under a 'normal' divisional structure. Some of these units may be managed directly from the centre, as occurs at Infineum (Figure 9.3), a joint venture between Exxon and Royal Dutch-Shell that sells additives used in oil and petrochemicals production.

Real-life Application 9.3 Peanut butter and structural change at Yahoo!

Yahoo! Inc is a prominent internet company—its email and internet portal sites are market leaders in the USA, and its search engine ranks second to Google.[7] It also offers many other products including instant messaging, problem-solving through Yahoo! Answers, and Flickr, a leading photo sharing site.

For many years, Yahoo! had a structure based largely around its products, but with a matrix element that gave marketing, engineering, and corporate strategy staff a significant decision-making input.[8] As it expanded into new product areas, often by acquisition, the number of product units proliferated. This meant that development efforts were not always coordinated among the different products, some of which, for example, Yahoo! Photos and Flickr, overlapped.[9] Some critics were reported as describing the firm as 'unwieldy and bureaucratic'.[10] One senior vice-president went so far as to make his doubts public in what was became known as the 'Peanut Butter Manifesto'. In a memo, he suggested that Yahoo!'s strategy had become reactive, that people in the firm lacked passion and clear accountability, and that the company showed indecisiveness, spreading its investments thinly and smoothly, like peanut butter, across a multitude of opportunities.[11]

On 5 December 2006, Yahoo! announced a restructuring that it said would 'increase accountability [and] speed decision-making'.[12] The new architecture was a front-back structure with two customer-facing divisions, Audience Group and Advertiser & Publisher Group, and a third division focused on the underlying technology:

- The Audience Group was to build on Yahoo's success as an internet destination and extend its relationships with its users. Its internet search service, communities such as Flickr and communications services such as instant messaging, would all come under this group. The group's charter included developing further 'unique, tailored and engaging experiences' for users, expanding Yahoo!'s international scope, and embracing opportunities away from the existing network, for example those using mobile devices

- The Advertiser & Publisher Group's charter was to position Yahoo! as the leader in creating value for advertisers and publishers of internet content. For Yahoo!, as for many internet companies, such as Google (see End-of chapter Case Study 8.1), advertisements were the key generator of revenue.

- The Technology Group was to furnish the hardware and software infrastructure needed by the other groups, and build on existing investments to 'create the technology platforms for new social media environments' and support the company's expansion.

Each of these groups would require an internal structure that would meet its particular challenges. The Technology Group would need to manage major software design and hardware implementation projects, while the Advertiser and Publisher Group would need to manage relationships with many thousands of partner firms.

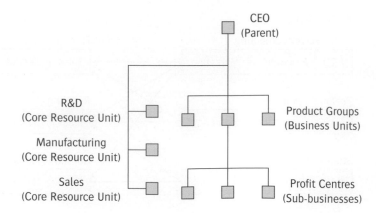

Figure 9.3 Infineum's organization structure.
Source: Goold and Campbell (2002b: 223).
Reproduced with the kind permission of
Reed Elsevier

The front-back structure is well suited to the management of situations where a firm is extensively involved in outsourcing and other partnerships. Key suppliers or supplier networks can be managed as part of a product-based unit, or the entire activity can be outsourced—specialists like Li & Fung develop and manage supplier networks for clothing manufacturers, for example. These structures also assist firms in identifying diversification opportunities: Amazon.com's web services unit, which provides the infrastructure that its parent uses to manage its website, has become an income generator in its own right, running on-line shopping services for retailers like Marks & Spencer in the UK or Target in the USA, and renting processing and storage capacity.[13]

A further development in organizational structures has been a move away from the idea that structures are fixed for periods of years. Stability in structures has the advantage that it enables people to develop and refine their work routines, which assists in the exploitation of established competences. However, theorists are increasingly advocating that managers should be prepared to 'patch' their structures—update them every year or two to take account of changes in the environment and the organization itself. The financial services firm in Figure 9.4 moved from a holding company structure, to a product-based divisionalized structure and then to a front-back structure, all in the space of five years.[14] In other firms, the structure of business units remains quite stable, but the product and market responsibilities, or 'charters', allocated to them changes on a regular basis. Charters that do not fit the capabilities of unit A might be given to unit B, and a new business area allocated to unit A by way of compensation.[15]

This can be taken further, to the creation of 'virtual' groupings of business units that have particular issues in common, such as managing particular sets of suppliers or customers (Figure 9.5). These can be initiated at the centre, or by the business units themselves in a mode of working that has been termed 'federalism'. Collaborations can last as long as the issues remain important, and new groupings created as needed. They can also draw on the expertise of outsourcing partners and other strategic allies as appropriate. Structures of this kind are a kind of half-way house between divisional and network forms. They can be effective in exploiting synergies between units, and between the organization and its strategic partners, but require strong cultural controls, and perhaps economic incentives, if they are to operate effectively.[16]

9.1.4 **Assessing complex structures**[17]

In Section 8.1.1 we set out a number of criteria that can be used to assess the appropriateness of a culture and architecture in any organization. For complex organizations, there are a

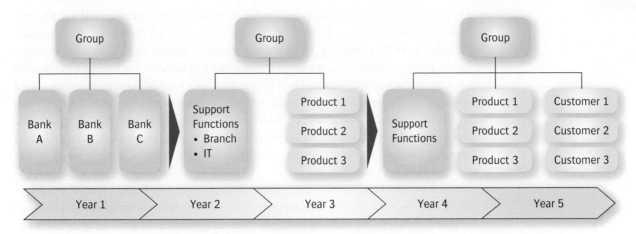

Figure 9.4 Patching the organization structure of a financial services company. Source: Marakon Associates (Kibble and Kissel, 1999). *Reproduced with the kind permission of Richard Kibble*

number of further attributes that have been identified as marks of good design. Flexibility, of the kind discussed in the previous section, is one of these. Ensuring that there is a unit with clear responsibility for each key market segment is another—the structure should not take management attention away from serving customers and users. An appropriate choice of outside partners for selected activities can contribute to both flexibility and the conservation of management attention.

The architecture should include mechanisms for managing situations where responsibilities are shared. Managers or employees should not waste time and energy on conflicts as to who is accountable for a particular customer or value chain activity, or neglect shared areas of the business in favour of those for which they themselves have sole jurisdiction. This does not mean that shared responsibilities should be avoided entirely. Research in the airline industry has shown that there can be a case for making teams responsible for entire areas of customer service, rather than breaking it down into smaller tasks which are allocated to individuals. The same research has shown the value of putting in extra layers of supervision in such cases, to sort out any problems between functions.[18]

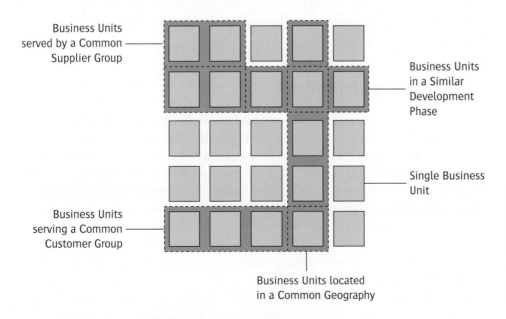

Figure 9.5 Flexible structure in a natural resources firm. Source: Marakon Associates (Kibble and Kissel, 1999). *Reproduced with the kind permission of Richard Kibble*

In general, however, to conserve cost and avoid slowing down decision-making, a hierarchy should boast no more levels than is truly necessary, and each level should clearly add value to decision-making. However, the structure should also fit the organization's culture. In one company that we know, a hierarchy that featured ten levels from the chief executive to the field staff was replaced by one with only four. Although there were sound business reasons for this change, it made staff accustomed to a higher level of supervision uncomfortable, and about 18 months later, one of the layers was reinstated. Similarly, the structure should fit the talents and personalities of its key people. It should not call upon them, for example, to exercise financial skills they do not possess, or to be more or less assertive than they naturally are.

A well-designed architecture also allows the organization to respect specialist cultures that need to be nurtured, and insulate them from possibly harmful interference. They may be R&D laboratories, project teams for new business initiatives or units set up to serve key clients, which may need to be as steeped in the customer's culture as they are in that of the parent firm. If they are put together with mainstream business units and asked to report to the same director, using the same reporting systems, then their cultures may be affected in ways that undermine their effectiveness. (A similar problem has been observed in strategic alliances—see Section 9.3 below).

Last but not least, an effective architecture for a complex organization must handle two challenges: making effective use of parenting skills held at the corporate centre; and enabling the business units to collaborate so as to benefit from any available synergies. These are the subject of the next section.

Parenting skills
Corporate-level competences that add value to individual businesses, and/or to the company overall.

➜ Synergies are defined and discussed in Section 5.2.3.

9.2 Parenting: adding value to units from the centre

In Chapters 6 and 7, we examined how individual businesses and their resources can be potential sources of value. In a corporation, the corporate headquarters or parent is another. Research has suggested that the success of a portfolio may be dependent, not just on whether the businesses are related, but on whether the management style of the parent is appropriate for them.[19] According to these theories, some of the problems of unsuccessful diversification are due to corporations moving into businesses that are not responsive to their parenting approach and skills.

9.2.1 Parenting propositions

Corporations have to add something beyond and above what they could achieve by simply holding a diversified portfolio of shares. A head office that simply provides finance has little justification for its existence except, as mentioned in Section 9.1.1, in countries where efficient capital markets do not exist. Moreover, the head office represents extra costs over and above what would be required if the subsidiaries were independent. Some of these are financial: the head office's buildings, equipment, and payroll, and the resources needed to gather the data it requires. The delay while the corporate centre makes its input to business unit decisions represents a further, hidden cost. In order to justify these costs, the corporate centre must be able to offer 'parenting propositions' for adding value to its subsidiaries. These may be:[20]

- Build propositions: the parent can help its units expand and diversify more effectively than they would on their own. Sony's headquarters, for example, understands how to stimulate innovation, launch new products, and internationalize businesses. InBev, an international brewer based in Belgium, understands how to globalize the beer brands that it acquires on a regular basis. Electrolux (a Swedish manufacturer of domestic appliances) and Intel are companies that have expertise at the centre in mergers, acquisitions, and alliances, which they are able to place at the disposal of business units wanting to expand. Pre-merger planning and post-merger integration are highly skilled activities that businesses would not expect to carry out very frequently for themselves.

➡ We examine pre-merger activities and post-merger integration in Chapter 17.

- Stretch propositions: the parent can help units improve profitability through improvements in cost or quality. One way of doing this is through imparting valuable knowledge, competences, or capabilities, such as H&M's in logistics. Another is through an architecture that stimulates a greater awareness of the need for high performance than business units would have if they were subject only to the discipline of open markets, with less appropriate or up-to-date information. In the 1980s, both Hanson and GEC (two UK conglomerates that no longer exist in the same form) were famous for the fierceness of the review process to which strategic business units' (SBUs') annual plans were subjected. This was intended to make sure that those plans were watertight, and to discourage wasteful spending. Other corporations, such as GE, use management information systems to let SBU managers know how their performance compares with that of other units on certain critical dimensions. They also foster a culture that encourages informal competition between businesses to be 'top of the league'.[21]

- Link propositions: the parent can identify areas where synergy can be achieved (but see Theoretical Debate 9.1) or resources may be centralized. It can also stimulate a culture and architecture that encourage exchanges of competences and learning that would not be possible in an open market. This is often achieved by staff rotation, joint management initiatives, or through cross-business teams. GE is famed for its ability to groom top managers across its businesses; those that do not reach the top in its own hierarchy are much sought after by other large corporations.[22]

- Leverage propositions: the parent finds ways to leverage resources that reside at corporate level in products or markets where they have not yet been utilized. These may be brands and technologies as with Sony, or relationships with other firms or with governments, as is the case with many conglomerates in countries such as Korea, India, or Malaysia.

- Select propositions: the parent has skills in valuing businesses and in detecting what kinds of businesses it can add value to. This enables it to acquire businesses that are a good fit at a favourable price. Similar skills may enable it to acquire talented people that are undervalued elsewhere. No less importantly, it will recognize businesses for which it is not an appropriate parent, and sell them on to a corporation that will place a higher value on them. Diversification sometimes happens in an opportunistic and emergent fashion, so it may be some time before the head office realizes what its parenting skills are, and the businesses it accumulates in the meantime may not be related to them or to each other. It takes a clear mind and a strong will to admit to past mistakes and set about rationalizing the portfolio.

Theoretical Debate 9.1 Whose role is it to manage synergies?

In Chapter 5, we outlined the ways in which synergies could be obtained across a diversified organization. There is nonetheless a considerable debate about the role that headquarters should play in ensuring that potential synergies are exploited. In essence, some theorists argue that corporate staff should leave it to unit managers to decide which synergistic opportunities they should grasp, and how to implement them. Others argue that it is quite proper for headquarters staff to set up potentially synergistic linkages and dictate to SBU management regarding how they should be used. These differences can be traced to two rather different conceptions of what a corporation is.

The first regards the corporation as a portfolio of competences and resources and not just businesses. Prahalad and Hamel (1990) claimed that the distinguishing feature of companies with long track records of successful diversification, like Honda and Canon, was that they thought of their companies in this way. They suggested that the most successful companies will be those that see SBUs as a reservoir of competences, skills, and people that can be transferred between different businesses as needed, to share the knowledge gained.

There is empirical evidence that supports this view. Robins and Wiersema (1995), who examined technology flows between businesses in diversified firms, found that performance improved as 'dynamic relatedness' (when a competence accumulated by one division is used to build new strategic assets elsewhere in the firm) increased. Other research (Gambardella and Torrisi, 1998; Miller, 2006) has shown that high corporate performance comes from having a small portfolio of products and a larger and diversified portfolio of competences and technologies.

The alternative, more traditional conception of the corporation focuses on the business unit, rather than the resource, as the key component. Each of the businesses in a portfolio is regarded as an independent unit that 'owns' its own resources. The modern version of this view, championed by Michael Goold and Andrew Campbell (1987, 1998; also Goold et al., 1994) downplays the need for sharing resources between businesses and suggests that with the right parenting skills, superior performance can be extracted from quite unrelated portfolios.

In the first view, linkages between the businesses are the reason for the corporation's existence, and business units need to be managed as a synergistic whole. Raynor and Bower (2001; Bower, 2003) have emphasized the dangers that can occur if SBU managers are allowed to maximize the performance of their own unit without taking account of broader corporate needs. They provide examples to suggest that corporate intervention is needed to ensure business unit managers do not make decisions that spoil opportunities for other, growing SBUs, or ignore promising new business areas that might benefit the corporation but would lower their unit's profits in the short term.

The second view admits that synergies are possible, but suggests that it is the business unit managers who are best equipped to spot and evaluate them. Since corporate staff are, almost inevitably, less expert in the businesses they oversee than their local colleagues, there is always a danger that they may use their power to force local managers into collaborations decisions that anyone with detailed market knowledge would know are unlikely to bear fruit. The central managers, under pressure to justify their existence, may also be tempted into overestimating the benefits from such collaborations, and underestimating the costs involved and the skills needed in extracting the synergies. Goold and Campbell (1998) provide a number of cautionary examples. Under this view, supported by Eisenhardt and Galunic (2000), the corporate centre should provide encouragement for synergistic activities, and an architecture that allows SBU managers to discuss joint opportunities, but not force the issue.

The gap between the two views is not unbridgeable; both agree that synergies are possible and desirable. Raynor and Bower recognize the key role played by business units in sustaining corporate profitability, while Goold and Campbell have admitted (2002a) that there may be occasions when corporate managers might need to intervene to impose synergies. Ghoshal and Bartlett (1998) have proposed an ideal type of architecture—the 'individualized corporation' (see Section 9.2.3)—for managing an organization's twin portfolios of competences and SBUs. However, the question of who is the best custodian of the organization's resources, under which circumstances, remains unresolved.

9.2.2 Parenting styles

In theory, there is a very large number of combinations of parenting propositions, and of architectures that can be used to apply them across the organization. The architectures that have actually been observed in practice, however, tend to fall into one of a small number of styles[23] (Figure 9.6), depending on the degree to which the centre decides to intervene in:

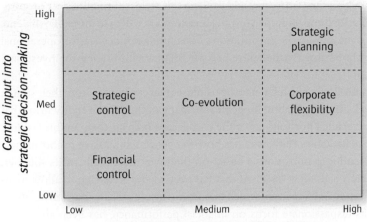

Central influence on inter-SBU relations   **Figure 9.6** Parenting styles

- strategic decision-making by the business units;
- relations between the business units, in particular the extent to which they collaborate amongst themselves to obtain synergies.

Each of these styles represents a way of allocating top management attention across a range of businesses. Each tends to be best suited to a particular type of portfolio or to a particular business context (Table 9.1).

a. Financial control

When headquarters seeks neither to influence strategy or to influence inter-SBU relations, the style is termed financial control. In this case, the corporate centre adds value principally through stretch propositions, implemented typically through the procedure used in setting short-term financial targets. The target setting process may, for example, involve SBU managers in strenuous reviews and negotiations with headquarters. The relational contract with the subsidiaries' managers may involve handsome bonuses for exceeding targets and near-certain dismissal for failure to meet them.

These stretch propositions may be underpinned by a degree of central expertise in managing businesses with certain success factors. For example, BTR, a British conglomerate that is now part of Siebe plc, was legendary in the 1980s and 1990s for its ability to help its SBUs, all mature businesses, to boost their profit margins.[24] However, it is typically left to SBU managers to find ways of achieving their targets as they see fit. There is little attempt to stimulate synergies between units, although it is quite common to use the smaller businesses as nurseries of management talent for the larger ones.

Table 9.1 Matching the style to the portfolio and context

Style	Appropriate portfolio/context
Financial control:	Stable businesses, low investment needs (portfolio can be very diverse)
Strategic planning:	Narrow portfolio of closely related businesses
Strategic control:	Broad portfolio of fast-growing businesses
Corporate flexibility:	Rapidly changing business environments
Co-evolution:	(no context specified)

The other way in which the centre may add value in this style is through select propositions, spotting undervalued and underperforming businesses in which to invest. To this end, it will often keep a tight rein on the corporation's cash: funds not needed for operational purposes will usually be returned to the centre, and subsidiaries will bid anew for investment capital where needed.

Some financial controllers give preference to businesses that can benefit from their stretch competences, and sell off those that no longer do so. Many of the private equity firms that have accumulated diversified portfolios over the past decade manage them in this fashion. The US conglomerate Berkshire Hathaway has however generated massive profits using a gentler style. Its parenting proposition is based on the investment skills of its founder, Warren Buffett. It rarely sells an investment that has been made, preferring to allow managers of underperforming units space in which to nurture their businesses back to health.

This style, with its dispassionate focus on financial performance, has been applied to very broad portfolios with little relatedness between their resources and competences (see Real-life Application 9.4). However, some relatedness between industry success factors is needed; specifically, the businesses need to be mature and have low investment needs. If the headquarters needs to appraise detailed investment proposals from the subsidiaries, then it will need to acquire a degree of strategic knowledge of SBU affairs and move to one of the other styles. The centre must also guard against the portfolio growing to the point where it may find it difficult to add any value at all. However, since the degree of intervention from the centre is strictly limited, it is possible to keep the headquarters small—Berkshire Hathaway's contains fewer than 20 people—and the cost burden it imposes on the subsidiaries low.

Real-life Application 9.4 Hanson plc[25]

As a matter of policy, we use modern companies, that most readers will have heard of, for our Real-life Applications. There are two reasons for making an exception for Hanson. First, more than any other company, in its heyday in the 1980s and early 1990s, it typified the financial control style. And second, the reasons why it no longer exists in that form are themselves extremely instructive.

Hanson plc (Hanson Trust until 1987) grew by acquisition over thirty years from a small fertilizer firm to a highly diversified conglomerate with a 1996 turnover of £12bn. It successfully bid for over forty firms and took major stakes in 22 further companies.

The two founders, James Hanson and Gordon White, had strong capabilities in selecting firms for acquisition. They also timed their bids well, spending a great deal of time gathering information on prospective acquisitions and then bidding at a time when the share price was temporarily depressed. Their most successful bids were for conglomerates whose constituent parts were worth more than the entire firm.

In 1986, they bought Imperial Group for £2.5bn, and sold off its brewing and crisp-making businesses (both household names at the time). This, along with some smaller divestments recouped £2.3bn, leaving Hanson with Imperial's highly profitable core business, tobacco, at a cost equivalent to one year's profits from that business. From its acquisition the same year of US conglomerate SCM, it recouped over 120 per cent of the purchase price from divestments and was left with profitable businesses which had essentially cost it nothing.

Along with the businesses that it deemed not to fit its style, Hanson would sell off assets such as headquarters buildings and corporate jets, which did not fit its austere culture. This gained it, unfairly, a reputation as an 'asset stripper'. In fact, however, it proved able to add considerable value to the businesses it retained. It had well-honed routines for integrating them into the corporation, involving replacement of their top managers and of their financial systems. However, it frequently promoted middle managers to run those businesses after Hanson's own integration team had done its work—another aspect of its select proposition.

It would then set about using its stretch propositions to boost profitability in those businesses, imposing stringent financial targets and rigorous control systems. Any expenditure of over £100, famously, had to be approved by Hanson's head office. Performance against budget was closely controlled, and a team of accountants would be sent in to any business where headquarters was not satisfied as to the reasons for any shortfall. Failure to meet targets would result in the sack, but performance related →

→ bonuses could double a manager's pay, and there was also a generous stock option scheme.

This formula allowed Hanson to manage a portfolio that included, at one time or another (it made as many disposals as acquisitions) coal, electricity generation, construction materials, chemicals, batteries, vitamins, golf clubs, cookware, and tobacco businesses in Europe and the US. However, in 1996, after the death of Lord White and the retirement of Lord Hanson (both founders having by this time been awarded British peerages as a result of the firm's performance), it announced that it was to split itself into four smaller firms covering energy, chemicals, tobacco, and construction materials. It is the last of these that bears the Hanson name today.

There were several reasons for this change of direction. First, the capital markets became attuned to the Hanson formula and would bid up the share price of any firm that appeared likely to be one of its acquisition targets. This made it more difficult for the firm to add value through its select propositions. In addition, a bid target would often set about making any necessary improvements itself, so that Hanson's stretch propositions also became less valuable.

Another fundamental reason for the change was that investment decisions for the electricity and chemicals businesses required a degree of expert knowledge of the advantages and disadvantages of different processes. Hanson's tradition of hands-off strategic management did not fit well with this need. On the other hand, Lord Hanson's successor, Derek Bonham, appeared enthusiastic about a greater degree of involvement in such decisions. The financial control style had ceased to fit the key people in the business.

b. Strategic planning

Diametrically opposed to financial control is strategic planning, when corporate headquarters takes a very close and active interest in the setting of strategy by all its SBUs. This style blurs the distinction between SBU and centre, regarding the corporation as a co-ordinated whole. Typically, headquarters is staffed by experienced ex-SBU managers who are qualified to offer specific advice, and who provide detailed strategic plans for each of their businesses. The targets set tend to be long-term and strategic in nature, looking for penetration of particular market segments, for example. The SBU's financial performance is reviewed within the context of long-term strategic objectives for the group as a whole.

The centre under this style has the expertise to offer very clear stretch, build, and leverage propositions. With its deep knowledge of each of the businesses, it is also equipped to offer link propositions, and will typically be very active in seeking synergies. It may also offer select propositions, although, since the style requires a lot of management attention to be given to each business, the portfolio is typically kept small and closely strategically related. An example of a firm using this style is Cadbury-Schweppes, a UK firm whose three businesses, chocolate, sugar confectionery, and soft drinks, share common channels, customers, and success factors.

c. Strategic control

Strategic control represents a compromise whereby corporate staff set an overall strategy for the corporation. They monitor business-level strategies to ensure they fit the corporate-level direction, and seek to improve them through advice and comment, but not to dictate them. They offer a mixture of build, stretch, and select propositions, and set SBU managers a mixture of financial targets to sharpen short-term performance, and strategic targets to foster long-term sustainable advantage.

The strategic control style can cope with more businesses than the strategic planning style, and with more strategic complexity than financial control. It therefore represents the natural choice for firms that seek to add value to a wide portfolio of high-technology or other fast-growing businesses. It attempts to focus the attention of corporate top management on the most urgent and important issues, trusting SBU management to resolve the less pressing ones.

However, during the 1980s, firms using this style appeared to underperform relative to those using strategic planning or financial control.[26] Some were acquired and broken up by firms like Hanson (Real-life Application 9.4). And other firms with broad portfolios developed strategic styles that offered clearer link and leverage propositions.

d. Corporate flexibility

The corporate flexibility style involves a strongly proactive role from the corporate centre in ensuring that new and long-term opportunities are not missed. SBU managers are expected to be able to formulate viable strategies to take their own businesses forward. However, they are seen as being narrowly focused upon the resources in their units and on opportunities in existing and neighbouring markets. In this case, the centre is better equipped to scan the environment for developing trends, and to spot how the corporation's resources might be used to take advantage of them. This is especially the case for 'white space' opportunities[27]— those that fall outside current business unit charters or might logically be claimed by several units at once.

The underlying assumption is that SBU managers will normally be reluctant to collaborate. The centre will therefore need to take the lead in encouraging, indeed enforcing, collaboration, unless the short-term payoffs to the business units are so clear that they will collaborate of their own accord. The parent is therefore offering strong link and leverage propositions, of which a major part lies in the design of an appropriate architecture. This involves designing financial control and compensation systems that measure and reward collaborative behaviour, while at the same time maintaining strong incentives linked to business unit profitability.

The structure should also facilitate collaboration. WPP, the world's leading advertising and marketing services company, has virtual companies with just one or two employees, which meet the needs of clients in specific sectors, such as health care, by pulling in resources from the corporation's various agencies. These can be set up quickly, with low additional overhead costs.

The value added by this style is greatest when the portfolio is diverse, and the environment is too fast-moving for business unit managers to keep up with all relevant developments.

e. Co-evolution

The final style, co-evolution, has a great deal in common with corporate flexibility. Under both styles, the compensation of business unit managers is closely tied to their own units' performance. Indeed, a degree of competition between businesses is allowed and even encouraged. For example, HP, the American IT firm, allowed its inkjet printer business to grow in competition with its established laser printer business. Eventually, each became a leader in its own target market segments, in a way that was not predictable at the time. If corporate managers had intervened to prevent the two businesses from cannibalizing each other's sales, then highly profitable opportunities would have been lost.

Under co-evolution, however, SBU managers, rather than the centre, also have responsibility for spotting potential synergies and for making them work. Corporate headquarters does offer link propositions, but these are limited to the creation of an architecture that assists collaboration, such as regular meetings to bring managers from different businesses together to exchange experiences, or 'fairs' where they can show off new developments to interested executives from across the corporation.

Alongside this architecture, the centre fosters a culture in which collaboration is expected, but is not expected to be permanent. Links last as long as they are useful, and are then cut in favour of new ones. Managers are discouraged from spreading their attention too thinly across too many linkages.

Individual Ink

The HP Inkjet 2800. HP allowed its inkjet printer business to grow in competition with its established laserjet business.

Co-evolution has been observed mainly in fast-moving technological sectors, but its advocates do not limit its applicability to any single context or type of portfolio.

Using Evidence 9.1 Identifying a firm's parenting style

It can sometimes be difficult to identify precisely what a firm's parenting style might be. For example, strong financial control systems, which might be thought of as an indicator of the financial control style, are important to the corporate flexibility and co-evolution styles as well, and also play a role in strategic control. Strong cash management from the centre is perhaps a more reliable indicator of the financial control style in operation.

One important indicator is what the top managers actually do, and how often. Annual, set-piece reviews are likely to indicate either a financial control style, if the discussion revolves around short-term financial performance, or strategic control, if the discussion is longer-term in scope. On the other hand, if top management are frequently seen in discussions with SBU managers, then it is unlikely that the style is financial control. If they are discussing current business unit strategy, then the style may well be strategic planning, while if they appear to be focusing more on corporate-level issues, then corporate flexibility is more likely to be the style.

It is important to use evidence, not just of the structures that appear to be in place, but of the practical outcomes. As the desirability of synergies has become more widely understood, quite a number of corporations introduced forums, such as coordinating committees and corporate universities, where ideas can in theory be shared and collaborative networks fostered. In judging the parenting style, we need to look for evidence of whether synergies are actually occurring, and if so, whether the centre appears to be playing any role in them.

9.2.3 Management roles in parenting complex organizations

It will be clear from the previous sections that it can be difficult to reconcile the needs of a diversified corporation for synergistic management of its resource base with the operational requirements of the business units. In order to overcome this problem, not just the form of the organization but also the roles of managers at different levels need to be carefully thought through.

Sumantra Ghoshal and Christopher Bartlett (1998) in their book *The Individualized Corporation* mapped out a potential set of roles, based on what they observed in a number of major multinational corporations (Figure 9.7).

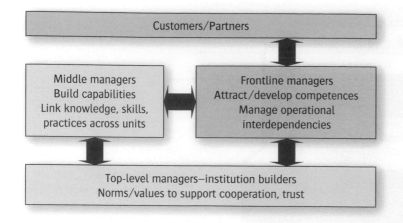

Figure 9.7 The individualized corporation (after Ghoshal and Bartlett, 1998). *Reproduced with the kind permission of Heinemann*

Their model of individualized corporations uses cultural control, in particular self-control (see Section 8.2.1) to instil a sense of discipline and direction in employees. The role of their top-level managers is to put in place the norms and values that underpin these cultural controls. These should support co-operation, trust, and self-discipline. Middle managers act as a form of glue that holds the organization together, and spread capabilities, knowledge, skills and best practices from one unit to another. They are thus crucial to successful link and leverage propositions. Frontline managers look after the day-to-day operations and liaise with customers. They develop competences and capabilities, and manage the day-to-day linkages between their units and other businesses in the corporation.

The theory of parenting was largely developed before outsourcing and virtual value chains became a common feature in organizational strategies. It does not, therefore, cover relationships with partner organizations, something that we examine in the following section. However, it seems plausible that many parenting propositions, in particular stretch, link, and select propositions, should prove valuable in building and managing networks of suppliers and collaborators, and that they should also be a factor in attracting the right partners to a corporation.

Worked Example 9.1 Analysing and appraising Sony's architecture and parenting style

In Worked Example 5.1, we analysed Sony's portfolio, and saw that it was highly diverse, with clear scope for synergies between some of the business units. In this Worked Example, we look at how to analyse how well-suited Sony's architecture and parenting style have been to the management of this portfolio.

Although Howard Stringer maintains a retinue of planners and accountants next to his office, Sony's parenting style is not financial control. Stringer is not a 'numbers man' by training and, like his predecessors, prefers a degree of personal involvement in strategic discussions that is incompatible with that style. Financial control, in any case, would be inappropriate given the size of the investments required in new generations of semiconductors or games consoles, or new movie projects. On the other hand, Sony's various businesses have a long tradition of independence, so the style is not one of strategic planning, which again would be inappropriate given the diversity of the firm's portfolio.

The businesses have in the past been highly resistant to efforts to amend their strategies to achieve synergistic benefits across the corporation. Stringer has frequently criticized what he calls the 'silo mentality' whereby the various product divisions are focused almost exclusively upon their own products.[28] There is, however, an apparent strategic control mechanism in the form of Stringer himself. He is a frequent visitor to the main business units, clocking up many airline miles each week. This style is seen as appropriate for diverse portfolios of high-technology businesses. However, the fact that fruitful synergies have been missed (see What Can Go Wrong 5.1 for an example on digital music players) implies that co-evolution or corporate flexibility might be more appropriate. Since the tradition of independence for the business units is so deeply entrenched, co-evolution is unlikely to be attained without a major cultural change that would take many years to implement. This leaves corporate flexibility as the most appropriate style. →

→ The organization chart of April 2006 (Figure 8.5) shows that, for the electronics businesses at least, a need for structures to enhance collaboration and synergy has been recognized. Several overarching committees are shown, whose role it is to coordinate strategy across the divisions, as well as ensuring that the customer's voice is heard in engineers' deliberations about new products. The Bravia TV, a hit product based on an alliance with Samsung (see below), is attributed to this system.[29] The question is whether these committees are necessary to overcome the culture of independent working, or whether they are a redundant level within the hierarchy. Interestingly, they were not shown on a revised organization chart issued in November the same year. It may be, for example, that appropriate cultural controls, if they could be introduced, would do the job better.

The parenting propositions offered by Sony's centre can also be evaluated:

- Build propositions: The firm has been successful in building its game and Vaio units into viable international businesses. The evidence is, therefore, that the centre is able to add value in this area. However, it rarely makes acquisitions and there is little evidence that it has built strong competences in pre-merger planning or post-merger implementation. It was widely regarded as having overpaid for its 1989 acquisition of Columbia Pictures Entertainment, and eventually wrote off $2.7bn of the $4.8bn purchase price,[30] though more recent, smaller acquisitions have not been criticized in the same way.

- Stretch propositions: In September 2005, Sony was forced to announce a $2bn cost-reduction exercise involving 11,000 redundancies and the closure of 14 plants. This followed earlier restructuring in 1996, 1999, and 2001. The need for these periodic, radical restructurings might be seen as evidence that there is scope for the centre to review the cost structure of the subsidiaries more closely and more frequently.

- Link propositions: As has already been mentioned, Sony, and in particular its electronics businesses, has been making efforts to improve these.

- Leverage propositions: Sony Corporation seems to add some value in this area. It has been able to leverage its brand into computers and financial services, and its graphics and other electronic capabilities into computer gaming. The PlayStation is an example of a product that was not originally wanted by any of the businesses but which found a champion at the top of the organization.[31]

- Select propositions: Sony has a mixed track record in this area. Its moves into games consoles, computers, and banking have proved successful. Its entry into the recorded music and movies businesses eventually became profitable, but only after considerable initial problems. It also accumulated a number of peripheral businesses, such as a restaurant chain, cosmetics, health spas, and a mail order company; a majority stake in these was sold off to a Japanese private equity group in February 2006.[32] However, it has not always been able to exit easily from businesses. A 2002 plan to sell 50 per cent of Sony Life Insurance stalled in the face of opposition from the unit's staff.[33]

Practical dos and don'ts

It is helpful to take careful note of the background of the top managers in a firm, as that will yield clues regarding their preferred style.

It is quite common to find that an organization shows elements of more than one of the parenting styles—that they have prominent financial control systems alongside an attempt to foster synergies, for example. This could be interpreted in one of two ways: either the organization is practising a variant of strategic control (which is the most common compromise style); or there is a predominant style which the organization is not implementing in a thorough fashion—which may mean that it will suffer in the long term.

Remember, however, that the object of this exercise is not just to classify an organization's parenting style, but to appraise it. It is very important, therefore, to review what you have found out about the parenting style in the light of your analysis of the portfolio, to see if the two fit together.

9.3 Managing alliances and other forms of collaboration

We noted in Chapter 6 and again in Section 8.1.3 how competition is no longer just between firms, but also between extended networks of firms, such as supply chains. This means that the management of strategic alliances—formal and informal collaborations across organizational boundaries—has become crucial to many complex organizations. Around 1,000

→ We discuss the forms that alliances can take and some of the possible transaction and other costs involved in Section 6.1.3.

joint ventures, and many more formal alliances of other kinds, are launched in an average year. The typical corporation relies on alliances for 15–20 per cent of its turnover.[34]

The term 'alliance' is a broad one that spans a wide variety of relationships, from informal agreements between two firms to formal joint ventures incorporating a dozen or more. They are a way of deriving synergies from several organizations' resources. Some of those resources may be financial; sometimes alliances are used to share the risk of major investments in markets or technologies, as with Sony's alliance with Samsung to manufacture flat-panel TVs.[35]

Other resources commonly exchanged through alliances are market knowledge and technological competences. In their flat-panel TV alliance, Samsung is contributing competences in LCD manufacturing, and Sony in TV picture rendition.[36] Organizations may use alliances to penetrate new markets or to improve their competitiveness in established ones where competition is becoming fiercer.[37] Thus, British Airways franchises small airlines like LoganAir to run BA branded services to some small airports, and combines with ten other major airlines to extend its global reach in the oneworld alliance. Relational capital can also be a factor: Sony/BMG, and other major music labels, use alliances with small independent record labels to gain access to emerging talent who can build comfortable relationships with the independents, but might feel put off by the idea of dealing directly with the more formal corporate executives.

→ We introduced the concept of absorptive capacity in Section 5.2.2.

Another attraction of alliances is the ability to learn from one's partners; being part of a network of alliances can improve an organization's absorptive capacity.[38]

In this section, we review the risks inherent in alliances. We then draw out the implications for the selection of alliance partners and the management of the alliance once it has been initiated.

9.3.1 Risk factors in alliances

Two major types of problem might stop an organization from successfully accessing the resources of its alliance partners. One is that the resources in question might not perform as hoped, because of difficulties in adapting them to the product or market in question, which might in turn be due to unforeseen environmental developments. These 'performance risks', although not just found in alliances, need attention when one is set up. The second type of problem, only found in an alliance context, is 'relational risk'—that the alliance may fail to meet its objectives because it proves impossible to get the partners to work effectively together.[39]

There are two sources for relational risk: social and economic. Socially, even with good intentions on both sides, it can be difficult for two distinct organizational cultures to 'gel'

The Sony Bravia LCD TV (2007).
Sony Corporation

to the extent that they can establish compatible goals and develop routines for effective collaboration. If the firms involved are drawn from different nationalities or different industries, or if there are more than just two partners to accommodate, then the chances for misunderstanding are magnified.[40] The individuals involved may also feel conflicting loyalties, particularly if the alliance takes the form of a separate joint venture entity. They may feel a genuine commitment to the alliance, and to the people working in it. However, their ultimate career prospects may lie in a return to the parent company—and this may have separate objectives of its own.

Economically, alliances are a classic example of the prisoner's dilemma from game theory. Alliances will only work if both parties deliver the quantity and quality of resources that they promise, and allow their partner access to them. However, there are clear temptations for organizations to try to profit from the partner's resources while committing fewer of their own than they originally promised. For example, the people they send to work in the alliance may be second-rate, and they may exaggerate the quality of the resources that they can bring to the alliance, and the degree of their commitment, in order to tempt a partner to give freely of its people and knowledge. Alliances sometimes turn into 'learning races', where firms contribute limited resources to the alliance for long enough to master key elements of their partner's knowledge, with the intention of breaking free of it as soon as they no longer have need of the partner.[41]

> → We introduced the concept of the prisoner's dilemma in Chapter 3.

These tensions can contribute to disappointing performance and a short lifespan for alliances. Seventy per cent of respondents in one survey were involved in partnerships that were underperforming. Other researchers have estimated that a quarter of joint ventures last less than three years and the median lifespan for alliances is only about seven years. It is worth noting, however, that some short-lived alliances are dissolved because their objectives have been successfully attained, and in 75 per cent of cases end with the acquisition of one party by the other—by no means an indicator of failure.[42]

9.3.2 Selection of alliance partners

A number of factors have been identified as important in selecting a potential alliance partner:[43]

- The partners' resources should be complementary, as with the Sony/Samsung and BA examples given earlier. Care should be taken to avoid needless overlap, or situations where a resource that is critical to the success of the venture is possessed by neither partner.

- The objectives, expectations, and cultures of the two partners should be compatible; there have been instances where a company has planned a diversification in the expectation that its alliance partner would contribute resources, only to discover that the other firm had no interest in expanding into the area in question.[44]

- Both sides should have something to lose if the alliance fails: the perceptions of the partners need to be that there is an equal exchange. If this is not the case, then the more committed partner will be fearful of hold-up by the less committed one, particularly if that is a larger organization.[45]

> → The concept of hold-up is explained in Section 6.1.3.

Establishing the degree of compatibility requires careful investigation and negotiation to establish precisely what the partners' aims and expectations are—making allowance for differences in language, which may lead to particular terms being interpreted differently by the two partners. It is also likely to require a period in which the partners' top management, and the people who will be managing the alliance in the partner firms, get to know one another. This ritual, which has been likened to a courtship before a marriage, assists in building trust, as a basis for the relational contracts that are likely to be needed to sustain a lasting relationship. Spending substantial amounts of management time in this way also serves as a signal to the partners that the organization is committed to sustaining the alliance.

A firm contemplating an alliance needs to consider any potential downside, such as the costs of exit, potential damage to a competitive position as a result of a breakdown in a previously successful relationship, or the leakage of important knowledge to competitors. It has to select its partners carefully so as to minimize such risks. This can involve the use of option theory to compute the probabilities of success or failure, and identification of the main factors to which those estimates are sensitive. The firm can than select its partners with those factors in mind.[46]

9.3.3 Structuring and administering the alliance

No less important than finding the right partner is putting appropriate governance structures in place for the alliance. These include:[47]

- a clear agreement as to which resources are going to be committed to the alliance on either side, and how access to them will be regulated;[48]

- The appropriate legal form—licence, informal alliance, separate jointly owned organization—for the alliance.[49] Each form tends to have its own needs and suitable management styles, depending on the number of partners involved. The management of a complex consortium, which brings together multiple partners to work on multi-stranded problems in order to develop a complicated new product, for example, is likely to be more difficult to manage than a simple collaboration between two partners with a specific focus, such as a distribution agreement;

- what performance goals should be set for the alliance and how precisely they are to be measured. This can be particularly important to specify when the alliance embraces a variety of cultures and accounting conventions. It may be desirable to appoint outside auditors;

- how often, and through which medium, the various parties should communicate. These may be a combination of informal norms established during the 'courtship' phase and formal meetings. This may be particularly important if partners come from different countries and are located thousands of miles apart;

- how any disputes—and there are likely to be some—will be resolved; for example, which legal or arbitration regime should apply. In the case of a joint-venture, it may be desirable to appoint outside directors to oversee fair dealing between the parties;

- what will happen at the end of an alliance, which may be set up with specific time frames and goals in mind. Toshiba attempts to minimize the risk of any problems by setting up what are in effect prenuptial agreements which detail what each partner would do in the case of the alliance not working out;

- how the alliance can be restructured during its life if performance falls short of expectations, or if the environment changes. Research has found that alliances that are periodically restructured are twice as likely to be considered successful as those that are not.[50]

Organizations are also being increasingly advised to put in place internal mechanisms to ensure that alliances are meeting the objectives set for them and that their expenditure is under control. In particular, firms are advised to develop appropriate financial and other performance measures ('metrics') for their alliances.[51] Attention should also be given to the structures that are used to manage alliances. Some Japanese firms have specialist departments at corporate or regional level to manage alliances, while others set up task forces to manage individual partnerships.[52]

Many firms also have individuals whose responsibility it is to manage the relationship with specific partners. In some alliances these boundary spanners play an important role in helping the partners understand each other's ways of working so that, for example, if an investment proposal must be presented, it arrives in a format that looks professional to the other partner. No less importantly, they need to make sure that the distinctive cultures of the alliance partners are preserved, since in some cases, if one partner becomes too much like the other, it will lose the distinctiveness that made it a valuable ally. It can be a significant challenge to find the right people, able to command respect in both organizations, to act as relationship managers.[53]

Boundary spanners can be useful inside diversified organizations as well. A Japanese executive, Masyuki Nozoe, is credited with having shown Sony's US-based Pictures division how to communicate effectively with the corporation's Tokyo head office during the late 1990s, describing to them the format that business plans should take and the statistics they should contain.[54]

Real-life Application 9.5 The oneworld™ alliance[55]

Most of the world's major airlines are now part of one of the alliance groupings—Star, SkyTeam, and oneworld—whose member airlines between them account for over 80 per cent of world passenger airline capacity. These alliances are a response to the perceived need to respond to the globalization of world travel by offering passengers a seamless experience. Cross-border mergers between airlines, although they are becoming more common, are made very difficult by regulations in many countries, so alliances are clearly the best alternative.

Airline alliances aim to offer passengers a single point of booking for their journey worldwide. Airlines typically share codes on key flights—so that a connecting flight in Europe might carry an American Airlines code alongside its British Airways or Iberia one. Business- and first-class travellers on one of the airlines also have access to the passenger lounges of its alliance partners, and can earn frequent flyer miles on their flights. Airports such as Heathrow are now starting to relocate the check-in desks of member airlines to be close to one another.

British Airways is part of oneworld along with, at the time of writing, American Airlines, British Airways, Qantas, Cathay Pacific Airways, Iberia, LAN, Finnair, and Aer Lingus. Malev, Royal Jordanian, and Japan Airlines are reported to be on schedule with preparations to join the alliance by the time you read this. oneworld claims to be better integrated than its competitors, being the only alliance to enable passengers to fly throughout its network, on any combination of carriers, using just electronic tickets. It also claims to offer a greater variety of alliance fares and products, such as round-the-world tickets.

oneworld quotes a number of other metrics in claiming to be successful. Almost two-thirds of this was incremental revenue that would not have been earned had oneworld not existed. Interlining—single tickets for journeys involving flights with two or more member airlines—accounted for around 3 per cent of the airlines' 2005 turnover, and was rising significantly faster than their overall revenues. This represented a useful boost in a low-margin business with high fixed costs, so that each extra ticket sold on a scheduled flight fed through as extra profit.

There is a clear coherence in the objectives and positioning of the alliance members, whose target market is 'the multi-sector, premium, frequent international traveller'.[56] It was named the World's Leading Airline Alliance for the fourth year running in the 2006 World Travel Awards, based on votes cast by travel professionals across the world. Member airlines often figure in first place in the global and regional rankings in the same survey. On the other hand, Aer Lingus, which has changed its strategy since joining to compete head-on with low-cost carriers such as Ryanair, announced in May 2006 that it would leave the alliance in March 2007.

The alliance has its own management structure. The oneworld Management Company (oMC) was established in Vancouver, Canada, in May 2000, under a Managing Partner who reports to a governing board of the chief executives of each of the member airlines. The board, chaired by the chief executive of one of the members, meets regularly to set strategic direction and review progress. The chairmanship changes periodically.

Reporting to the Managing Partner are function heads for Commercial, IT, Public Relations, Airports, and Customer Service, and a Global Project Director. They liaise with working groups drawn from all the member airlines, using dedicated IT facilities such as eRooms and an intranet to facilitate communication across firms and time zones.

Creative Strategizing 9.1

If you were a manager of Star or SkyTeam, how would you position your alliance to compete with oneworld?

9.3.4 Managing portfolios of alliances

As alliances and outsourcing partnerships have become a more common and more important element of strategy, large firms find themselves in the situation where they need to manage not just single relationships but broad portfolios of alliances. A typical large European firm can be involved in more than a hundred alliances; a diversified, high-technology corporation such as Philips or Siemens in over a thousand.[57] Yahoo!, as already noted (Real-life Application 9.3), reports having thousands of distribution partners.

In these circumstances, it can be difficult to avoid duplication, or even conflict, between alliances and alliance partners. Each individual alliance should respond to a specific business need, and therefore needs to be set up and managed by the relevant business unit. However, at both business and corporate level, it is desirable to ensure that the objectives of the various alliances are aligned with the organization's strategies. At the same time, there are opportunities for managers to profit from experience built up elsewhere in the organization as to how to manage alliances effectively and avoid predictable pitfalls. There may also be synergies between different alliances, from which the organization can profit—for example, by bringing different partners together to share knowledge and build new, joint competences.

At the very least, therefore, a firm needs to be able to track which alliances have been formed, with whom, and with what scope and objectives. However, experienced practitioners may go beyond this minimum in a number of ways:[58]

- putting processes in place for capturing learning about effective alliance management, including formal reviews and evaluations of particular alliances or self-assessment procedures. The resulting knowledge is made available in the form of checklists or manuals;

- establishing centres of competence for alliance management whose role is two-fold:

  - to establish general principles for managers to abide by when initiating and operating alliances, along with sets of rules and procedures about the activities and business situations when alliances are or are not encouraged, and on how to set them up;

  - to ensure that business unit managers have specialist advice available to them when they embark upon an alliance. There may also be specialist alliance managers in business units, and internal consultants.

- setting up interest groups or formal seminars or workshops where people can share their experiences and problems;

- formalizing systems for measuring the performance, not just of individual alliances, but also of each business unit's portfolio of alliances, and of the corporate portfolio;

- developing processes at corporate level for managing relationships with the most important partners.

The importance of these different initiatives can vary over time, with central coordination becoming less necessary over time, as alliances and partnerships become increasingly part of the normal way of operating, and the necessary skills are more widespread in the company (Real-life Application 9.6).

Real-life Application 9.6 Learning to manage multiple alliances at Siemens[59]

In the course of the 1990s, Siemens, the German engineering combine, moved from a situation where it had just a few alliances of minor importance to one where it had over a thousand, with a major impact on strategic performance. Its first step towards managing this came in the form of a central department that provided support for business unit managers in areas such as the selection of alliance partners and the negotiation of contracts. This department also coordinated a less formal 'community of practice' in which Siemens' alliance practitioners could share experience and knowledge.

As the decade progressed, procedures for alliance management became progressively more formalized. The central department wrote case studies and checklists, and set up databases and systems for benchmarking alliances against others in the Siemens portfolio.

By the end of the decade, learning about alliances in the company had reached a stage where less central supervision was needed. The centre still provided support for the largest alliances and maintained the monitoring systems: the company evaluated the financial and strategic contributions made by its alliances as part of its annual planning cycle. The main alliance management task had been devolved to the business units; however, a member of the board of directors oversaw relationships with Siemens' key alliance partners, which had strategic collaborations with several business units.

What Can Go Wrong 9.1 ABB

Engineering conglomerate ABB was formed in 1988 from the merger of the Swedish firm Asea, strong in northern Europe and the USA, with the Swiss firm Brown Boveri, strong in the rest of Europe. Percy Barnevik, from Asea, was nominated CEO and he put in place an acquisition-led growth strategy and a novel structure designed to equip ABB for competition in globalizing markets.

The structure implemented was a matrix with two dimensions: products (power generation, power transmission and distribution, industrial and building systems and transportation) and regions (Europe, the Americas, and Asia Pacific). However, within that formal structure, bureaucracy was pared to a minimum and managers were given a great deal of autonomy to follow Barnevik's famous maxim 'think global, act local'. In 1998, two respected management scholars were able to write in the *Financial Times* that Barnevik should be recognized as 'the creator of a new corporate form, a fundamentally different model of how a large company can be organised and managed', in which resources and authority had been devolved to the heads of '1,100 little companies'.[60]

The results were spectacular: by the time that Barnevik handed over to Göran Lindahl in 1997, ABB's turnover ($34bn) had nearly doubled from its 1988 levels, its profits ($2.2bn) were nearly four times as high, and its return on capital employed had increased from just under 12 per cent to nearly 20 per cent. However, five years later, the company was reporting a loss of $691m and it had

debt of over $4bn, much of it short-term. Its corporate bonds had been downgraded to junk status by Moody's, a major credit-rating agency, and commentators were seriously querying whether it could find the liquidity to survive.[61]

Some of the problems stemmed from a downturn in key Asian markets, notably Japan, where ABB had expanded. But a major factor lay in the select and build propositions offered at the centre. Under Barnevik, the company had spent $5bn in purchasing some two hundred companies. Some, such as the 1989 purchase of Westinghouse's power-transmission and distribution business, were spectacularly successful and formed the basis of global leadership positions. However, others proved to be problematic, including a number of firms in eastern Europe, and Widmer and Ernst, a garbage-burning firm in the USA whose former owners were eventually sued by ABB for misrepresentation. The most fateful decision of all was to buy Combustion Engineering, an American industrial boiler manufacturer, in the knowledge that it had used asbestos to insulate its products. The division was declared bankrupt in 2003 in the wake of litigation from people claiming to have suffered from exposure to this asbestos. Settlement of these claims was finally agreed in December 2005 at a cost to ABB of $1.43bn. Barnevik has since admitted that the Combustion Engineering and Widmer and Ernst deals were 'bad purchases'.[62]

➜

→ Moreover, the firm took the decision to use the access to cheap short-term credit, derived from its earlier success, to expand into financial services, as GE had done successfully. At its high point this new venture accounted for 40 per cent of ABB's operating profits, but by 2001 it too was making substantial losses, and the firm's cost of borrowing had increased substantially.[63]

The company's innovative structure also played a role in its problems. Minimal bureaucracy led to lack of standardization and by some accounts 'a culture of waste and duplication'. There were four separate headquarters buildings, and some 600 different spreadsheet programs were found to be in use around the company, leading to difficulties in sharing files. Independence was taken to extremes: one factory continued manufacture of one product for nearly a year after being told by HQ to stop, and another exported transformers to Africa, although this was not within its charter. There were stories of plants in one country poaching orders from their colleagues in another, leading managers to be reluctant to use internal databases designed to keep track of major bids.[64]

Shortly after Lindahl took over as CEO, he simplified the structure to one with eight product-based divisions, dissolving the regional dimension from the matrix. As well as saving costs (the regional layer employed 100 people), this was welcomed as increasing focus and flexibility. One ex-employee said that the matrix had led to lengthy political debate and compromise solutions as managers strove to reconcile the demands of regional and product bosses. His other major decisions involved exiting from the transportation and power-generation businesses, expanding financial services and automation, and closing 11 factories in Europe, with the loss of 10,000 jobs, to take advantage of lower production costs in Asia.[65]

Although these decisions had increased profitability, Lindahl was replaced as CEO in October 2000 by Jörgen Centermann, head of the automation business. He quickly restructured the firm along customer segment lines, although he retained two product-based divisions and set up a new one to manage the transformation of the company to make greater use of knowledge and the internet.[66] However, in September 2002, as the size of the group's problems became apparent and losses mounted, he was replaced as CEO by Jürgen Dormann, ex-head of chemicals firm Hoechst, who had joined the board as chairman when Barnevik had relinquished that role.

He quickly saw deficiencies in ABB's control systems. Despite having one year's prior experience as chairman, Dormann did not, on taking over as CEO, have full information as to the extent of the group's liquidity problems. The board had also been surprised to discover, in February 2002, that the former co-chairmen had agreed to set up pension funds for Barnevik and Lindahl containing $85m and $51m respectively. More than half of this money was later returned.[67] An audit commissioned by Dormann unearthed a number of assets including jet planes, armoured limousines, and a 50 per cent stake in a South African airport.[68]

Dormann successfully negotiated lines of credit and later a bond issue to tide the firm over while it sold assets worth $3bn, including its petrochemicals division and its leasing business. The company that he handed over to Fred Kindle in January 2005 is now focused on two core businesses, power transmission and automation, and has fewer employees than in 1988. But the restructuring, together with the capping of the asbestos liabilities, allowed ABB in 2006 to retire early some of the bonds issued at the time of its liquidity crisis.[69]

 Creative Strategizing 9.2

With the benefit of hindsight, how would you have modified the changes that Barnevik made to ABB's architecture and culture to avoid the problems that the company later experienced? What possible disadvantages would your suggestions have entailed?

● CHAPTER SUMMARY

This chapter has examined the particular difficulties that are encountered in managing diverse, complex organizations, and the solutions that have been proposed over time.

In structuring a complex organization, managers can opt for one of the structures—functional, divisional, or networked—reviewed in Chapter 8. They may also opt for:

● a holding company structure—a highly decentralized divisional structure with a small head office monitoring the finances. This is appropriate when there are few synergies between the businesses, and head office can add value through the provision of finance at advantageous rates;

- a project-based structure that makes extensive use of teams for specific, temporary assignments. This is appropriate when such assignments are a constant element of the business;

- a matrix structure that gives equal formal status to a number of structural dimensions. Matrix organizations frequently make extensive use of project teams. Matrix structures may help organizations reconcile tensions between the strategic priorities of geographic markets, vertical customer segments, and the product and other business dimensions. However, they can be complex and reduce accountability in decision-making;

- one of a number of hybrid structures, including the hypertext and front-back organization, which may help give a balance between economies of scale in production and product development and sensitivity to different market needs;

- a flexible or virtual structure, which helps the organization to 'patch' its structure quickly to respond to changing circumstances.

A well-designed architecture for a complex organization is one that passes a number of tests:

- It allows for flexibility.
- It gives high visibility to key markets, so they get top management attention.
- It has mechanisms for managing situations where responsibilities are shared.
- It contains no more levels of hierarchy than are strictly needed.
- It fits with the organization's culture and the skills of its key people.
- It gives protection to specialist cultures, such as those in R&D.
- It helps the corporate parent add value.

The corporate headquarters of a diversified corporation must add value in order to justify its existence —otherwise, there is no virtue in the subsidiaries being part of the corporation, rather than independent. It can do so through:

- build propositions—helping the business units expand;
- stretch propositions—helping them run their businesses more effectively or efficiently;
- link propositions—helping them establish synergistic collaborations;
- leverage propositions—helping them leverage brands or other corporate assets;
- select propositions—making profitable decisions about which businesses should join or leave the portfolio.

Five styles have been identified which parents use in practice, distinguished by the degree of corporate input into business unit strategy and the degree to which the parent seeks to influence relationships between the SBUs, and each applicable to a different type of portfolio:

- financial control, appropriate for a very diverse portfolio of businesses with low investment needs;
- strategic planning, appropriate for a narrow portfolio of strongly related businesses;
- strategic control, appropriate for a broad portfolio of fast-growing businesses;
- corporate flexibility, appropriate for a diverse portfolio in a fast-changing environment;
- co-evolution, which has been mostly observed in high-technology organizations, but whose proponents believe it to be more widely applicable.

Alliances are a major part of most modern complex organizations since they offer ways of allowing organizations to share or access one another's resources. Their management is a key parenting skill.

There are two main sources of risk in alliances: performance risk (the resources may not work as desired) and relational risk (the partners may not be able to work together). Cultural differences between firms are one source of relational risk, particularly if they have different national backgrounds. There are also economic incentives for firms to exploit one another in alliance situations, which may lead to their treating the alliance as a learning race.

In selecting alliance partners managers should look to ensure that:

- the partners' resources are complementary;
- their objectives and cultures are compatible;
- both sides have something to lose if the alliance fails.

Ensuring compatibility and building trust between partners involves significant commitments of management time. In addition, attention needs to be given to a number of factors in setting up the alliance, including governance structures, how performance is to be measured, how disputes should be resolved, and what happens when the alliance ends. Most alliances have a finite life.

Firms also need to give attention to what metrics they will use internally to measure alliance performance.

 Online Resource Centre
www.oxfordtextbooks.co.uk/orc/haberberg_rieple/

Visit the Online Resource Centre that accompanies this book to read more information relating to the management of complex organizations.

● KEY SKILLS

The key skills you should have developed after reading this chapter are:

- the ability to determine the most appropriate of the different ways of structuring complex organizations for an organization's circumstances and to diagnose the basis of problems in existing architectures;
- the ability to evaluate the parenting propositions offered by the headquarters of a diversified organization;
- the ability to critique the architecture and parenting style chosen by a firm in the light of the type of portfolio it possesses;
- an understanding of the risks inherent in alliances and the ability to critically appraise an organization's management of its partnerships.

● REVIEW QUESTIONS

1. Under what circumstances is a matrix likely to work better than a divisionalized structure, and why?

2. What might be the disadvantages of the virtual structures described in Section 9.1.3, from the point of view of people working in the organization, for its suppliers and for its customers?

3. Do the problems at ABB show that there really is no lasting alternative to traditional hierarchical structures?

4. Which of the five types of parenting proposition is the most important, and why?

5. Four of the cells in Figure 9.6 (showing the different parenting styles) are empty. Under what circumstances, if any, might an organization's management want to try one of these unnamed styles?

6. What kind of performance metrics might be used:

- by Sony to assess the performance of its joint-venture with Samsung?
- by BA to assess the performance of its agreement with one of its franchisees?
- by an American investment bank to assess the performance of its alliance with a state-owned bank in China?

Now look at these three alliances the other way around and suggest metrics that the other party might use to assess the performance of the partnership.

● FURTHER READING

- Goold, M. and Campbell, A. (2002). 'Do you have a well-designed organization?' *Harvard Business Review*, 80/3: 117–24. This gives an excellent overview of the difficulties that can be encountered in structuring large organizations, as well as a resumé of the skills of the parent.

- Raynor, M. and Bower, J. (2001). 'Lead from the center'. *Harvard Business Review*, 79/5: 92–100 and Eisenhardt, K. and Galunic, D. (2000). 'Coevolving'. *Harvard Business Review*, 78/1: 91–101 give interesting and contrasting views on how best to obtain synergies in complex organizations.

- Ghoshal, S. and Bartlett, C. (1998). *The Individualized Corporation*. London: Heinemann is still worth reading as a reminder of the virtues of decentralization and empowerment, even though some of it looks a little idealistic in the light of what happened at ABB.

- Bamford, J., Ernst, D., and Fubini, D. (2004). 'Launching a world-class joint venture'. *Harvard Business Review*, 82/2: 90–100. Gives a number of tips for the setting up and management of joint ventures and examples of what can go wrong.

- Goerzen, A. (2005). 'Managing alliance networks: emerging practices of multinational corporations'. *Academy of Management Executive*, 19/2: 94–107. Focuses on the running of large networks of firms, rather than individual alliances. Based upon interviews with Japanese executives participating in such networks.

- Grant, R. and Baden-Fuller, C. (2004). 'A knowledge accessing theory of strategic alliances'. *Journal of Management Studies*, 41/1: 61–84. A more learned paper summarizing and extending current theory on why alliances happen.

- Hoffman, W. (2005). 'How to manage a portfolio of alliances'. *Long Range Planning*, 38/2: 121–43 is a very thorough pioneering study of how large European firms actually go about the challenge of managing multiple alliances.

● REFERENCES

Bacharach, S. and Lawler, E. (1980). *Power and Politics in Organizations*. San Francisco: Jossey Bass.

Balakrishnan, S. and Koza, M. (1993). 'Information asymmetry, adverse selection and joint ventures: theory and evidence'. *Journal of Economic Behavior and Organization*, 20: 99–117.

Bamford, J. and Ernst, D. (2002). 'Tracking the real pay-offs from alliances'. *Mergers and Acquisitions: The Dealermaker's Journal*, 37/12: 33–7.

Bamford, J. and Ernst, D. (2005). 'Governing joint ventures'. *McKinsey Quarterly*, 2005 Special Edition: 62–9.

Bamford, J., Ernst, D., and Fubini, D. (2004). 'Launching a world-class joint venture'. *Harvard Business Review*, 82/2: 90–100.

Bartlett, C. and Ghoshal, S. (1990). 'Matrix management: not a structure, a frame of mind'. *Harvard Business Review*, 68/4: 138–45.

Bleeke, J. and Ernst, D. (1991). 'The way to win in cross border alliances'. *Harvard Business Review*, 69/6: 127–37.

Bleeke, J. and Ernst, D. (1995). 'Is your strategic alliance really a sale?' *Harvard Business Review*, 73/1: 97–108.

Blodgett, L. (1992). 'Factors in the instability of international joint ventures: an event history analysis'. *Strategic Management Journal*, 13/6: 475–81.

Borys, B. and Jemison, D. (1989). 'Hybrid arrangements as strategic alliances: Theoretical issues in organizational combinations'. *Academy of Management Review*, 14/2: 234–49.

Bower, J. L. (2003). 'Building the Velcro organization: creating value through integration and maintaining organization-wide efficiency'. *Ivey Business Journal*, 68/2: 1–10.

Brouthers, K., Brouthers, L., and Wilkinson, T. (1995). 'Strategic alliances: Choose your partners'. *Long Range Planning*, 28/3: 18–25.

Cartwright, S. and Cooper, C. (1996). *Managing Mergers, Acquisitions and Strategic Alliances*. 2nd edn. Oxford: Butterworth Heinemann.

Cohen, W. and Levinthal, S. (1990). 'Absorptive capacity: a new perspective on learning and innovation'. *Administrative Science Quarterly*, 35/1: 128–52.

Das, T. (2006). 'Strategic alliance temporalities and partner opportunism'. *British Journal of Management*, 17/1: 1–21.

Das, T. and Teng, B-S. (1999). 'Managing risks in strategic alliances'. *Academy of Management Executive*, 13/4: 50–62.

Das, T. and Teng, B-S. (2000a). 'A resource-based theory of strategic alliances'. *Journal of Management*, 26/1: 31–61.

Das, T. and Teng, B-S. (2000b). 'Instabilities of strategic alliances: An internal tensions perspective'. *Organization Science*, 11/1: 77–101.

Dyer, J., Kale, P., and Singh, H. (2001). 'How to make strategic alliances work'. *Sloan Management Review*, 42/4: 37–43.

Dyer, J., Kale, P., and Singh, H. (2004). 'When to ally & when to acquire'. *Harvard Business Review*, 82/7–8: 108–15.

Eisenhardt, K. and Brown, S. (1999). 'Patching—restitching business portfolios in dynamic markets'. *Harvard Business Review*, 77/3: 72–82.

Eisenhardt, K. and Galunic, D. (2000). 'Coevolving: at last, a way to make synergies work'. *Harvard Business Review*, 78/1: 91–101.

Ernst, D. and Bamford, J. (2005). 'Your alliances are too stable'. *Harvard Business Review*, 83/6: 133–41.

Faulkner, D. (1995). *International Strategic Alliances*. London: McGraw-Hill.

Galbraith, J. R. (1998). 'Linking customers and products'. In Mohrman, S. A., Galbraith, J. R. and Lawler III, E. E. and Associates (eds), *Tomorrow's Organization*. San Francisco: Jossey-Bass.

Galunic, D. and Eisenhardt, K. (2001). 'Architectural innovation and modular organizational forms'. *Academy of Management Journal*, 44: 1227–47.

Gambardella, A. and Torrisi, S. (1998). 'Does technological convergence imply convergence in markets? Evidence from the electronics industry'. *Research Policy*, 27/5: 445–63.

Gander, J. Haberberg, A., and Rieple, A. (2007). 'A paradox of alliance management: resource contamination in the recorded music industry'. *Journal of Organization Behaviour*, 28: 1–18.

Ghoshal, S. and Bartlett, C. (1998). *The Individualized Corporation*. London: Heinemann.

Gill, J. and Butler, R. (2003). 'Managing instability in cross-cultural alliances'. *Long Range Planning*, 36/6: 543–48.

Gittel, J. (2000). 'Paradox of coordination and control'. *California Management Review*, 42/3: 101–17.

Goerzen, A. (2005). 'Managing alliance networks: Emerging practices of multinational corporations'. *Academy of Management Executive*, 19/2: 94–107.

Goold, M. and Campbell, A. (1987). *Strategies and Styles: The Role of the Centre in Managing Diversified Corporations*. Oxford: Blackwell.

Goold, M. and Campbell, A. (1998). 'Desperately seeking synergy'. *Harvard Business Review*, 76/5: 131–43.

Goold, M. and Campbell, A. (2002a). 'Do you have a well-designed organization?' *Harvard Business Review*, 80/3: 117–24.

Goold, M. and Campbell, A. (2002b). 'Parenting in complex structures'. *Long Range Planning*, 35/3: 219–43.

Goold, M., Campbell, A., and Alexander, M. (1994). *Corporate-Level Strategy: Creating*

Value in the Multi-Business Company. New York: Wiley.

Goold, M., Campbell, A., and Luchs, K. (1993). 'Strategies and styles revisited: strategic planning and financial control'. *Long Range Planning*, October: 49–60.

Grant, R. and Baden-Fuller, C. (2004). 'A knowledge accessing theory of strategic alliances'. *Journal of Management Studies*, 41/1: 61–84.

Hamel, G. (1991). 'Competition for competence and inter-partner learning within international strategic alliances'. *Strategic Management Journal*, 12/12: 83–103.

Hamel, G. and Prahalad, C. (1994). *Competing for the Future*. Boston, MA: Harvard Business Press.

Handy, C. (1995). *Beyond Certainty*. London: Hutchinson.

Harrigan, K. and Newman, W. (1990). 'Bases of inter-organizational co-operation: propensity, power and persistence'. *Journal of Management Studies*, 27/4: 417–34.

Helfat, C. and Eisenhardt, K. (2004). 'Inter-temporal economies of scope, organizational modularity, and the dynamics of diversification'. *Strategic Management Journal*, 25/13: 1217–32.

Hoffman, W. (2005). 'How to manage a portfolio of alliances'. *Long Range Planning*, 38: 121–43.

Inkpen, A. and Beamish, P. (1997). 'Knowledge, bargaining power and the instability of international joint ventures'. *Academy of Management Review*, 22/1: 177–202.

Kale, P., Singh, H., and Perlmutter, H. (2000). 'Learning and protection of proprietary assets in strategic alliances: Building relational capital'. *Strategic Management Journal*, 21/3: 217–38.

Kanter, R. (1994). 'Collaborative advantage: the art of alliances'. *Harvard Business Review*, 72/4: 96–109.

Kibble, R. and Kissel, N. (1999). 'Structure is strategy: gaining strategic advantage through organizational design'. *Marakon Commentary*, 5/4: 1–10.

KPMG International (2006). *Globalizing the Risk Business*. KPMG International.

Lei, D. and Slocum, J. (1992). 'Global strategy, competence-building and strategic alliances'. *California Management Review*, 35/1: 81–97.

Miller, D. J. (2006). 'Technological diversity, related diversification, and firm performance'. *Strategic Management Journal*, 27/7: 601–19.

Mjoen, H. and Tallman, S. (1997). 'Control and performance in international joint ventures'. *Organization Science*, 8/3: 257–74.

Mohr, A. and Puck, J. (2005). 'Managing functional diversity to improve the performance of international joint ventures'. *Long Range Planning*, 38: 163–82.

Mowery, D., Oxley, J., and Silverman, B. (1996). 'Strategic alliances and interim knowledge transfer'. *Strategic Management Journal*, 17: 77–91.

Nathan, J. (1999). *Sony—The Private Life*. London: HarperCollins.

Nonaka, I. and Takeuchi, H. (1995). *The Knowledge-creating Company: How Japanese Companies Create the Dynamics of Innovation*. Oxford: Oxford University Press.

Porter, M. and Fuller, M. (1986). 'Coalitions and global strategy'. In Porter, M. (ed.), *Competition in Global Industries*. Cambridge, MA: Harvard University Press, 315–44.

Powell, W. (1987). 'Hybrid organizational arrangements: new form or transitional development?' *California Management Review*, 30/1: 67–87.

Prahalad, C. and Hamel, G. (1990). 'The core competence of the corporation'. *Harvard Business Review*, 68/3: 79–91.

Raynor, M. and Bower, J. (2001). 'Lead from the center'. *Harvard Business Review*, 79/5: 92–100.

Robins, J. and Wiersema, M. F. (1995). 'A resource-based approach to the multibusiness firm: empirical analysis of portfolio interrelationships and corporate financial performance'. *Strategic Management Journal*, 16/4: 277–99.

Segil, L. (2005). 'Metrics to successfully manage alliances'. *Strategy & Leadership*, 33/5: 46–52.

Senge, P. (1992). 'Building learning organizations'. *Journal for Quality and Participation*, 15/2: 30–8.

Shaughnessy, H. (1995). 'International joint ventures: managing successful collaborations'. *Long Range Planning*, 28/3: 10–17.

Spekman, R., Forbes, T., Isabella, L., and Macavoy, T. (1998). 'Alliance management: a view from the past and a look to the future'. *Journal of Management Studies*, 35/6: 747–72.

Suh, W., Sohn, J., and Kwak, J. (2004). 'Knowledge management as enabling R&D innovation in high tech industry: the case of SAIT'. *Journal of Knowledge Management*, 8/6: 5–15.

Tanriverdi, H. and Venkatraman, N. (2005). 'Knowledge relatedness and performance of multibusiness firms'. *Strategic Management Journal*, 26: 97–119.

Varadarajan, P. R. and Ramanujam, V. (1987). 'Diversification and performance: a re-examination using a new two-dimensional conceptualisation of diversity in firms'. *Academy of Management Journal*, 30/2: 380–93.

End-of-chapter Case Study 9.1 The three pillars of Bayer AG

Foundation and expansion

Bayer AG, one of Germany's largest diversified chemicals and healthcare groups, traces its foundation, as a producer of dyestuffs, back to 1863. By the early 1880s, it had operations in the USA (its first acquisition), Russia, and France. In 1888, it set up its pharmaceuticals division, which in 1897 synthesized the compound that was to become famous as Aspirin (Table 9.2). The company moved its headquarters to the present location, Leverkusen, in 1912; the local football team, Bayer Leverkusen, remains a wholly owned subsidiary. In 1925, the company merged with a number of competitors as I.G. Farbenindustrie AG. Its assets were confiscated and the conglomerate broken up by the Allies after the Second World War. Bayer reemerged as a separate entity in 1951 and it took its present name, Bayer AG, in 1972.

While continuing to make significant scientific breakthroughs, including the first high-performance polycarbonate plastic, the company diversified its geographical and product scope through the 1970s and 1980s. It made major pushes into agricultural science and diagnostics systems, the latter through a major acquisition, Cooper Technicon, in the USA. America was a major source of growth for the firm, but its rights to its trademark there had been ceded to Sterling Drug Inc. as part of Germany's First World War settlement with the Allies. It bought back those trademark rights for industrial products in 1986, and full rights were regained with the 1994 acquisition of the North American self-medication business of what had become Sterling Winthrop.

Setbacks in 2001

By the start of the twenty-first century, Bayer's strategy had converged around four 'pillars': pharmaceuticals, polymers (the raw material for plastics and many man-made textiles), agrochemicals such as pesticides, and chemicals such as dyes, pigments, and basic compounds used in the manufacture of more complex products. But in 2001, the firm was hit severely when its cholesterol treatment, marketed under the names Baycol and Lipobay, was found to be connected with the deaths of over 50 people The withdrawal of the drug, which had been expected to generate annual sales of €2bn, together with manufacturing problems in

Bayer's treatment for haemophilia, led to three profit warnings in 2001 and gave force to a major rethink within the firm.[70]

Some investors and analysts were calling for the company to put its pharmaceuticals business, which a senior Bayer executive had admitted was 'second-tier',[71] under the umbrella of a larger player. Bayer's management, under the newly appointed Chairman Werner Wenning, had indicated that it was open to finding a partner for its pharmaceuticals arm, particularly one that was strong in the USA, but was intent on retaining majority control. In their view, the root of the company's problems lay in what one correspondent called a 'top-down, finger-in-every-pie management structure' that lacked transparency. This structure was also seen as inhibiting the formation of effective partnerships.[72]

They embarked upon a radical restructuring, where Bayer would become a holding company, and the four pillars would become independent legal entities with considerable operational autonomy. However, their chiefs would no longer sit upon Bayer's Board of Management—the body in charge of formulating strategy for the group as a whole, with the power to define which businesses counted as 'core'.[73] That committee was to shrink from seven members to just four.

From four pillars to three

Wenning and his three Board of Management colleagues, Klaus Kühn, Wolfgang Plischke, and Richard Pott, moved decisively in a number of areas. The agrochemicals business was strengthened by the acquisition in 2002 of Aventis CropScience, which made it one of the two largest players in that sector, with a market share of around 30 per cent. They were able to limit the cost of litigation resulting from the Baycol problems to around €5bn—expensive, certainly, but at the lower end of what had been forecast in 2001. However, they were unable to find a partner for their pharmaceuticals business that met their criteria, and in November 2003 announced that they had opted instead to retain that business as a 'mid-sized European' player.[74]

At the same time they announced the proposal, highly controversial within Germany, to reduce the number of pillars by spinning off a new entity combining most of the chemicals and around one-third of the polymers businesses. This entity, which ➔

→ **Table 9.2** Milestones in Bayer research

1899 Aspirin®
The world's best-known painkiller, based on the active ingredient acetylsalicylic acid

1937 Invention of polyurethanes
Plastics made from isocyanates and polyols; may take the form of elastomeric materials, adhesives, foams, fibres or coating raw materials

1953 Invention of Makrolon®
The first high-performance thermoplastic based on polycarbonate

1971 Sencor®
Selective herbicide for soybean and potato crops

1975 Adalat®
Medicine for the treatment of coronary heart disease

1976 Bayleton®
Systemic fungicide for use in cereal, vegetable, coffee, and fruit crops

1985 Nimotop®
Medicine to combat age-related loss of cognitive function

1987 Ciprobay®/Cipro®
Antibiotic for the treatment of bacterial infections

1990 Glucobay®/Precose®
Medicine with a new principle of action for the treatment of diabetes

1990 Bayhydrol®/Bayhydur®
Raw materials for waterborne coating systems

1991 Confidor®/Gaucho®
Systemic insecticide with long-term effectiveness

1993 Kogenate®
Bayer's first genetically engineered medicine, for the treatment of haemophilia

1995 Baytron®
Electrically conductive polymer

1996 Advantage®
Flea control product with long-term effectiveness for cats and dogs

1997 Glucometer Dex®/Esprit®
User-friendly blood glucose monitoring system, now available as Ascencia DEX® 2

1998 ADVIA®
Umbrella brand for fully automated large-laboratory systems used to diagnose cardiovascular disease, infections, metabolic disorders, and other conditions

1998 Bayrepel®
Novel active ingredient with very good skin compatibility, for insect repellents

1998 Axiom®
Selective grass herbicide

1999 Avelox®/Avalox®
Respiratory antibiotic

2000 Melt-polycarbonate process
New process for the production of ultra-pure Makrolon®

2001 Calypso®
Effective, environmentally friendly, broad-spectrum insecticide

2002 Atlantis®
Selective herbicide for cereals

2002 MaisTer®
Herbicide for corn

→

→ Table 9.2 (cont'd)

2003 Levitra®
Erectile dysfunction treatment

2003 Gamunex®/Gamimune®
Treatment for immune deficiency

2003 Advantix®
Flea, tick and mosquito control product for dogs

2003 Levasil®
Brand name for silica sols (aqueous colloidal solutions of silicic acid)

2003 Dispercoll® S
Raw materials for waterborne one-component adhesives with a nanoscale additive

2003 Poncho®
Insecticide for seed treatment in corn, canola, sugar beets, and cereals

2003 Ascencia®
Blood glucose monitoring systems

2003 Envidor®
Insecticide (acaricide) for citrus, pome fruits, nuts and grapes

2004 Oxygen depolarized cathode
New hydrochloric acid electrolysis process that saves up to 30 per cent energy

2004 Multitec®
Fast-curing, multi-component polyurethane system for spray application to manufacture moulded plastic parts

2004 Fandango®
Fungicide for cereals

2004 Proline®
Fungicide for cereals and canola

2005 Oberon®
Insecticide for fruit, vegetables, cotton, and ornamental plants

2005 Curbix®
Rice insecticide

2005 Nexavar®
Trade name for the active substance sorafenib

2005 Allectus®
Insecticide for lawn care

2005 Armada®
Fungicide for lawn care

2005 k-o Tab® 1-2-3
Insecticide for impregnating mosquito nets

Source
Bayer Names_Figures_Facts 2006_2007: 34–7, <http://www.bayer.com/en/Names-Figures-Facts-06-07.pdfx>, accessed 29 July 2007

incorporated the original dyestuff products, was to have 20,000 employees and accounted for some 20 per cent of Bayer's turnover. It became a fully independent company, Lanxess AG, in 2004 and gained its own listing on the Frankfurt stock exchange in 2005. Bayer was following a path already taken by a number of its peers, including ICI, Ciba, and Hoechst, which had separated their commodity chemicals from their riskier but higher-yielding pharmaceuticals operations.

The move was nonetheless controversial in the context of the company and of German industry. Most of the employees destined for Lanxess were reported to prefer to remain under the familiar Bayer umbrella. Like all German companies of any size, Bayer had a Supervisory Board whose approval was required for any major changes to the group's structure. The chairman of that board was Manfred Schneider, Wenning's predecessor as chairman of the Board of Management, who like many longstanding →

→ Bayer executives was strongly committed to the four-pillar concept. The Supervisory Board eventually approved the proposals unanimously, but not before, according to one participant, Wenning had threatened to close some factories.[75]

While some observers welcomed this move as reducing the degree of complexity within Bayer, it was not enough for some of the firm's critics. They noted that, unlike its competitors, Bayer had not made a clean break with either its chemicals or its polymer operations. The heavily cyclical parts had been placed within Lanxess, but selected, higher margin elements of both, such as polycarbonates and cellulose products, remained within the corporation as part of a new materials science division. Wemmer and his colleagues contended that the products remaining in Bayer's portfolio had important features in common: a high growth rate and innovation as a key success factor. However, some shareholders were of the opinion that the synergies between the two life sciences divisions—pharmaceuticals and agrochemicals—were far greater than between those divisions and materials science.[76]

Success factors

It was certainly true that there are considerable similarities between pharmaceuticals and agrochemicals. Both were industries that had seen a great deal of consolidation through mergers since the 1980s, and were dominated by large players with global marketing clout. In both industries, a new strategic group of producers of generic products had arisen to challenge the supremacy of the established players, who tended to be research-led. In both, the pattern was of large investments in a search for the next breakthrough product, with a small number of big hits paying for the larger number of compounds that failed to get through many tests needed for regulatory approval. This search was becoming increasingly difficult, with the rate of introduction of new molecules falling over time. And both were looking increasingly to bioscience and genetics as a source of new inspiration.

However, there were also differences. The marketing and distribution of pharmaceuticals, via medical practitioners, hospitals, and government health agencies, was very different from that for agrochemicals, where marketing might be direct to the end-user, albeit involving distributors in some countries. Although some drugs might lose their effectiveness over time as the target organism developed immunity to them, others, such as Aspirin, remained effective, and indeed might develop new uses. The agrochemicals industry, on the other hand, faced the challenge of retiring whole classes of products, such as organophosphates, that fail to meet modern health and environmental standards.[77]

The main thing that the polymer industry had in common with the other two was that advanced, proprietary compounds could yield higher margin products. This meant that productivity in R&D

and careful management of the resulting intellectual property were as important for polymers as for life sciences. However, demand in polymers was highly sensitive to the economic cycle, and costs were sensitive to the price of raw materials—typically derived from petroleum—and energy. Production costs and efficiencies were far more important to success in polymers than in life sciences, and Asian producers with low labour costs and ready access to feedstocks were making inroads in many products.

Bayer in 2006

The structure into which Bayer had settled in 2006 (Figure 9.8) was distinctive in two ways. The first was the separation between strategic and operational decision-making; it is quite unusual, in a business of this kind, for the heads of the main operating subgroups not to sit on the main executive decision-making body. The second was the presence, alongside the three subgroups, of three service companies, which sold services principally to the operating subgroups and to Lanxess, but also marketed services to other firms.

Bayer HealthCare had five global divisions: Animal Health, Consumer Care, Diabetes Care, Diagnostics, and Pharmaceuticals. It had some 34,000 employees and 2005 earnings of €1.1bn on sales of €9.4bn. The Animal Health and Pharmaceuticals divisions were based in Germany, and Consumer Care, Diabetes Care, and Diagnostics in the USA. Bayer HealthCare's Animal Health, Consumer Care, and Diagnostics divisions had leading positions in their global markets. HealthCare's emphasis was increasingly on marketing directly to consumers, using the strength of the Bayer brand. It had been bolstered by the acquisition of Roche Consumer Health, in 2005, which made it a leader in over-the-counter medicines (i.e. those that can be dispensed without a doctor's prescription). In the same year, it had sold off its plasma business and withdrawn from research in urology and infectious diseases.[78] In 2006, Bayer acquired Germany's Schering AG, which like HealthCare was an exploiter of specialized niches, and sold off its Diagnostics Division to Siemens.

Bayer CropScience had its headquarters in Monheim, Germany and vied with Switzerland's Syngenta for global leadership in crop protection and non-agricultural pest control. It had some 18,500 employees and 2005 earnings of €690m on sales of €5.9bn. Following a 2006 reorganization to bring its business structure more closely into alignment with the strategic market segments, it had six divisions: four regional crop protection businesses, Environmental Science, and BioScience. Alongside this the subgroup featured a Business and Global Marketing Platform with global responsibility for Portfolio Management, Industrial Operations, Research, Development, Business Planning and Administration, Human Resources, and Communication. The heads →

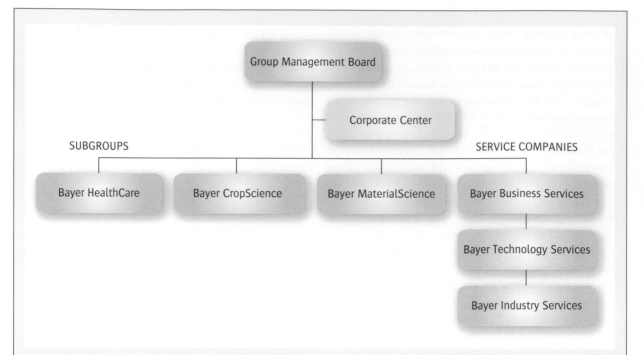

Figure 9.8 Bayer AG's structure in November 2006. Source: <http://www. bayer.com/bayer-group/profile-and-organization/page2351.htm>, accessed 11 November 2006.

➜ of Portfolio Management, Industrial Operations, and Business Planning and Administration sat on the Board of Management of Bayer CropScience AG alongside the subgroup head.[79]

Bayer MaterialScience supplied high-performance materials to the automotive and construction industries, the electrical/electronics sector and to manufacturers of sports and leisure articles, packaging, and medical equipment. It had five business units: Polycarbonates; Polyurethanes; Coatings, Adhesives and Sealants; Thermoplastic Polyurethanes; and Inorganic Basic Chemicals. Two other, independent, companies within the subgroup, H. C. Starck and Wolff Walsrode, were reported to be earmarked for sale to finance the Schering acquisition.[80] Bayer MaterialScience had about 19,300 employees at 40 production sites worldwide and 2005 profits of €1.4bn on sales of €10.7bn.

There were three service companies:

- Bayer Business Services offered services in IT, telecommunications, procurement, logistics, human resources, executive personnel services, finance and accounting.

- Bayer Technology Services offered design and consultancy services in process development, and in the engineering, construction, and optimization of plants and processes.

- Bayer Industry Services managed the firm's network of chemical parks in Germany and also offered facilities management services. It marketed fully developed facilities on those parks to outside customers.

In addition, there was a Corporate Centre that handled functions such as investor relations, finance, auditing, and corporate HR.

The performance of the subgroups was measured using an innovative system introduced in 1997, known as cash value management. Each division was given a target for cash value added (CVA)—the extent to which its cash flow for the year exceeded the economic cost of its debt and equity. Since each subgroup embodied different levels of risk, their 2005 cost of capital varied from 8.0 per cent for HealthCare, to 6.5 per cent for CropScience and 6.0 per cent for MaterialScience. Each group was also measured on its cashflow return on investment (CFROI), the ratio of CVA to invested capital. In 2005, Healthcare reported a CFROI of 14.9 per cent, CropScience of 11.2 per cent and MaterialScience of 16.4 per cent.[81] No less unusual than this method of measuring performance was the openness with which the company displayed the methodology, and the results, to its stakeholders—including its competitors.

Each division had met its financial targets for the year, and Bayer reported earnings before interest and tax of €2.8bn, the highest since 2000, and a return on assets of 9 per cent. The comparison with the dark days of 2001, which had culminated in a reported operating loss of €1.1bn, was plain. But the management team was clearly not complacent. Along with the flurry of acquisitions and disposals in HealthCare, the firm announced the launch, in April 2006, of a 'Triple-I' initiative, 'Inspiration, Ideas, Innovation', to encourage employees throughout the ➜

→ group to develop new business ideas. This is an addition to the century-old 'Bayer Idea Pool', which offers cash bonuses for ideas to improve existing businesses.

Case study questions

1. How appropriate is Bayer's architecture to the contexts in which it operates? How well does it meet the tests set out in Section 9.1.4?

2. What are the parenting propositions offered by Bayer's corporate centre? Which parenting style is it using? How good a parent is it for the businesses in its portfolio?

3. Some analysts have suggested that Bayer should simplify its portfolio. Do you agree?

NB: You may find it helpful to re-read Chapter 5 and to draw up a relatedness matrix for Bayer's SBUs.

● NOTES

1 Sources: *Economist* (2005). 'The new Pharaohs'. 12 March: 80–1; <http://www.orascom.com> accessed 15 October 2006.

2 The AXA example is quoted by KPMG International (2006): 17. The SAIT example is the subject of Suh et al. (2004).

3 All data from <http://www.skanska.co.uk/>.

4 See, for example the situation in the 1970s at the Swiss pharmaceuticals and chemicals firm Ciba-Geigy, described on the opening page of Collis, D. (1995). 'Smashing the cube: corporate transformation at Ciba-Geigy Ltd', Harvard Business School Case 9-795-041.

5 The case for matrix structures is put in A. T. Kearney (2002). 'Waging war on complexity: how to master the matrix organizational structure' <http://jobfunctions.bnet.com/whitepaper.aspx?docid=59138>, accessed 21 July 2007. For the opposing view, see Bartlett and Ghoshal (1990) and Bower (2003).

6 The hypertext organization was advocated by Nonaka and Takeuchi (1995), who quoted Honda as an example.

7 <http://www.hitwise.com/datacenter/rankings.php>, accessed 18 July 2006 and *Business Wire* (2006). 'MySpace is the number one website in the U.S. according to Hitwise'. 11 July.

8 Delaney, K. (2006). 'Spreading change: as Yahoo falters, executive's memo calls for overhaul'. *New York Times*, 18 November.

9 Mills, E. (2006). 'A revamped Yahoo turning to users'. CNET News.com, 6 December; Hof, R. (2007). 'Even Yahoo! gets the blues'. *BusinessWeek*, 28 May: 37; Helft, M. (2006). 'Yahoo, aiming for agility, shuffles executives'. *New York Times*, 6 December: 1.

10 The quotation is from Dow Jones News Service (2006). 'Yahoo reorganizing, COO Rosensweig to leave.' 6 December. See also Hof (2007) op. cit.

11 The manifesto is reprinted on the Wall Street Journal website with a copy date of 18 November 2006: <http://online.wsj.com/public/article/SB116379821933826657-0mbjXoHnQwDMFH_PVeb_jqe3Chk_20061125.html>, accessed 18 June 2007. See also Dow Jones News Service (2006) op. cit.; Caplan, J. (2006). 'How Yahoo! aims to reboot'. *Time*, 12 February: 52; Helft (2006) op. cit.

12 <http://yhoo.client.shareholder.com/press/ReleaseDetail.cfm?ReleaseID=220987>, downloaded on 17 June 2007. All direct quotes in the following paragraphs are from this source.

13 Richmond, R. (2007). 'Tales of the tape: Amazon sells golf balls—and gigabytes'. Dow Jones News Service, 19 June; Birchall, J. (2007). 'Amazon's pursuit of innovation pays off'. *Financial Times*, 28 April: 21.

14 The concept of patching is drawn from Eisenhardt and Brown (1999), who cite Dell as an example. The (unnamed) financial services example is quoted by Kibble and Kissel (1999).

15 This process is described by Galunic and Eisenhardt (2001) and Helfat and Eisenhardt (2004).

16 Charles Handy (1995) has been a strong advocate of self-organizing federalist models of organization. The example of virtual groupings shown here was described by Kibble and Kissel (1999).

17 This section draws heavily on the work of Goold and Campbell (2002a), two prolific British researchers in this field.

18 Gittel (2000).

19 See, for example, Goold et al. (1994), Varadarajan and Ramanujam (1987) and Tanriverdi and Venkatraman (2005).

20 Goold and Campbell (1998, 2002a).

21 This is reported by Ghoshal and Bartlett (1998).

22 *Economist* (2006). 'Everybody's doing it'. 5 October.

23 The groundwork on these styles was undertaken by Goold and Campbell (1987) and extended by them and their associates (Goold et al. 1993; Goold et al. 1994). They identified the financial control, strategic control, and strategic planning styles. Two new styles have since been observed: corporate flexibility (Raynor and Bower, 2001) and co-evolution (Eisenhardt and Galunic, 2000).

24 Goold et al. (1994).

25 Sources: *Economist* (1991). 'On the shop floor'. 13 July: 78–9; *Economist* (1996). 'Widow Hanson's children leave home'. 3 February: 51–2; Lynn, M. (1996). 'The Hanson inheritance'. *Management Today*, June: 30–33.

26 Goold et al. (1993).

27 This term comes from Hamel and Prahalad (1994).

28 See, for example Edgecliffe-Johnson, A. and Nakamoto, M. (2006). 'Year of candour and resolve starts to energise Sony'. *Ft.com*, 21 June, and Singer, M. (2006). 'Stringer's way'. *New Yorker*, 5 June.

29 Edgecliffe-Johnson and Nakamoto (2006) op. cit.

30 Nathan (1999: 180 and 238). The $4.8 billion purchase price included $1.6 billion of debt taken over by the acquirer.

31 See Nathan (1999: 304).

32 Pilling, D. (2006). 'Sony takes first step towards leaner structure'. *Ft.com*, 27 February.

33 Economist Intelligence Unit (2002). 'Sony, Softbank hit snags with divestment plans'. *EIU Viewswire*, 10 September.

34 These figures are drawn from 2004 data gathered by consultants McKinsey and Co. and quoted by Bamford et al. (2004) and Ernst and Bamford (2005).

35 For discussion of the purposes of alliances see Das and Teng (2000a); Grant and Baden-Fuller (2004); Porter and Fuller (1986); and Powell (1987).

36 Edgecliffe-Johnson and Nakamoto (2006) op. cit.

37 See Lei and Slocum (1992) and Faulkner (1995).

38 See Cohen and Levinthal (1990). See Hamel (1991) and Senge (1992) for discussion of the learning implications of alliances.

39 The distinction between performance and relational risk comes from Das and Teng (1999).

40 The difficulties involved in transferring resources across organizational boundaries are discussed by Cohen and Levinthal (1990) and Mowery et al. (1996). The instabilities resulting from divergent cultures are examined by Das and Teng (2000b) and Gill and Butler (2003). The national cultural dimension is reviewed by Brouthers et al. (1995), Mohr and Puck (2005), and Mjoen and Tallman (1997).

41 These kinds of behaviours in alliances are discussed by Balakrishnan and Koza (1993) and Inkpen and Beamish (1997). Learning races are described by Hamel (1991) and Kale et al. (2000).

42 See Bleeke and Ernst (1991, 1995), Cartwright and Cooper (1996) and Ernst and Bamford (2005). For a theoretical exploration of why different alliances have different time horizons, see Das (2006).

43 For good explanations of these criteria see Brouthers et al. (1995) and Kanter (1994), who is the source of the 'courtship' analogy we quote below.

44 See Kanter (1994) for an example.

45 Unequal commitments can arise because partners contribute unequal shares of equity to joint ventures (Blodgett, 1992) or uneven amounts of resource (Bacharach and Lawler, 1980; Hamel, 1991), or because the alliance is relatively more important to one partner than the other (Harrigan and Newman, 1990).

46 See Bamford and Ernst (2002) for examples.

47 Bamford and Ernst (2005); Shaughnessy (1995).

48 See Borys and Jemison (1989) and Spekman et al. (1998).

49 Dyer et al. (2004) suggest that where the main assets to be exchanged are 'soft'—human or know-ledge-based—then it is advisable for some exchange of equity to take place in order to allow both sides a measure of control. See also Faulkner (1995).

50 Ernst and Bamford (2005).

51 See Bamford and Ernst (2002), Bamford et al. (2004), and Segil (2005).

52 See Dyer et al. (2001) and Goerzen (2005).

53 See Gander et al. (2007).

54 Nathan (1999: 312).

55 Source: oneworld press releases, 4 June 2006, 29 September 2006, 11 October 2006; oneworld Fact sheet, 'An introduction to oneworld—the alliance that revolves around you', 12 January 2006.

56 'Aer Lingus' withdrawal date set as 1 April 2007', oneworld press release, 29 September 2006.

57 These figures are from Hoffman (2005).

58 Hoffman (2005).

59 Source: Hoffman (2005).

60 Ghoshal S. and Bartlett, C. (1998). 'Fired into the firmament—personal view'. *Financial Times*, 5 February: 15.

61 *Economist* (2002). 'Neither lender nor borrower be'. 28 May; *Economist* (2002). 'All over?—Europe's second biggest engineering group is dangerously close to collapse', 26 October; Hall, W. and Roberts, D. (2002). 'How a toxic mixture of asbestos liabilities and plummeting demand poisoned an industrial powerhouse'. *Financial Times*, 23 October: 17; Bream, R. and Hall, W. (2002). 'Downgrade adds to the gloom for ABB'. *Ft.com*, 31 October.

62 Simonian, H. (2005). 'Court backs ABB asbestos settlement'. *Financial Times*, 21 December: 17; Bilefsky, D. and Raghavan, A. (2003). 'Blown fuse: how "Europe's GE" and its star CEO tumbled to earth'. *Wall Street Journal*, 23 January: A1.

63 *Economist* (2002). 'Neither lender nor borrower be', op. cit.

64 Bilefsky and Raghavan (2003) op. cit; Bilefsky (2004). 'Risks and rewards: Chief Dormann shakes up ABB corporate culture'. *Wall Street Journal*, 22 January: A6.

65 Kabel, M. (1998). 'ABB overhauls management to boost growth'. *Reuters*, 12 August; Hall, W. (1998). 'ABB shakes up top management', *Financial Times*, 13 August: 21; Hall, W. (1998). 'All the power but none of the glory—PROFILE—Göran Lindahl, ABB'. 24 August: 8.

66 *Economist* (2001). 'A great leap, preferably forward'. 18 January.

67 Bilefsky and Raghavan (2003) op. cit.; *Economist* (2002). 'Neither lender nor borrower be', op. cit.

68 Bilefsky and Raghavan (2003) op. cit.

69 Simonian, H. (2004). 'Dormann to leave ABB lights on'. *Financial Times*, 12 July: 8; Bilefsky (2004) op. cit. Mitchell, L. (2006). 'ABB retiring bonds early'. *Financial Times*, 10 May: 43.

70 Silber, S. (2001). 'Bayer set to approve plan to split group into four units'. Reuters, 5 December; Dow Jones (2001). 'German press: Tweedy Browne criticizes new Bayer structure'. 12 December; Michaels, A. and Firn, D. (2002). 'Bayer dealt blow as pharma chief Ebsworth quits'. *Ft.com*, 8 January.

71 Michaels and Firn (2002) op. cit.

72 Silber (2001) op. cit.; Wassener, B. (2003). 'Bayer to float parts of chemicals business'. *Ft.com*, 7 November. The quote is from *Economist* (2002). 'Making up for lost time: face value—Bayer's Werner Wenning'. 27 April.

73 *Dow Jones International* (2002). 'Bayer to propose new exec structure at next bd mtg-report'. 28 February.

74 Firn, D., and Wassener, B. (2003). 'Bayer to refocus as it moves out of chemicals'. *Financial Times*, 8 November: 6; Milner, M. (2003). 'Bayer to distil its corporate structure'. *Guardian*, 8 November: 27. Le Masson, T. (2004). 'Bayer n'est pas encore tiré d'affaire'. *Les Echos*, 16 February: 44.

75 *Financial Times Deutschland* (2004). 'Der Durchmarshierer'. 30 April: 46.

76 Wassener, B. (2004). 'Bayer faces challenges despite rise in demand'. *Financial Times*, 10 May: 27; Smolka, K. (2004). 'Bayer-Aktionäre kritisieren Mischstruktur des Konzerns'. *Financial Times Deutschland*, 3 May: 27.

77 Boswell, C. (2006). 'Sunnier days for agrochemicals'. *ICIS Chemical Business*, 1/23: 20; Jung, R. (2006). 'The challenge facing agrochemistry sector'. *ICIS Chemical Business*, 1/38: 18.

78 *Le Monde* (2006). 'Pour l'industrie du médicament, la taille n'est pas un gage de succès'. 13 April: 13.

79 *Dow Jones News Service* (2006). 'Bayer to change Cropscience Ops' corp structure'. 17 February.

80 Madelin, T. (2006). 'Avec Bayer-Schering, l'Allemagne retrouve un champion dans la santé'. *Les Echos*, 27 March: 30.

81 Bayer Annual Report 2005: 27–8.

CHAPTER TEN

Knowledge, Learning, and Innovation

LEARNING OUTCOMES

At the end of this chapter you should be able to:

→ Describe the different types of knowledge that are useful to organizations

→ Explain how knowledge is developed or acquired, and how organizations learn

→ Summarize the characteristics of a learning organization, and assess the extent to which an organization possesses those characteristics

→ Explain how organizations manage knowledge, and the ways that it can be protected, and evaluate an organization's policies and processes for knowledge management

→ Define innovation, describe different forms of innovation, and discuss its perils alongside its benefits

→ Explain how organizations develop innovation

→ Describe the organizational and environmental features that are known to encourage innovation, and assess the extent to which they are present in a particular organization.

INTRODUCTION

As we saw in Chapters 6 and 7, resources are a major source of sustained competitive advantage. Those with a high knowledge content, or which have been learnt over time, such as capabilities and competences, are particularly useful because they tend to be difficult to imitate. But not all organizations seem to be able to use the knowledge that they gain to best advantage, or learn from their mistakes. Some of the factors affecting this relate to architecture and culture, and were discussed in Chapters 8 and 9. In this chapter we look in more detail at the ways in which knowledge and learning can be encouraged and enhanced in an organization, and how best to manage the development of innovative new products and processes.

10.1 Knowledge and knowledge management

There has been an increasing recognition over the last twenty or so years of the value of knowledge, in parallel with our understanding of what makes resources strategic. In the early 1990s, two Japanese academics, Ikujiro Nonaka and Hirotaka Takeuchi, wrote a pioneering work on how organizational knowledge was created and developed in Japanese companies.[1] Another stimulus came from Sweden, where researchers recognized that the physical assets that feature on firms' balance sheets accounted for a very low proportion of their true value, as measured by their stock market valuations and the price that acquirers would pay for them.[2] Firms in Europe began to value their 'intellectual capital' and to feature it in supplements to their annual reports.[3] Knowledge and other forms of intellectual assets are crucial elements of intellectual capital, along with human resources and reputational assets.

Knowledge is more than just data or information, the raw 'flow of messages' into and around an organization. Personal involvement and judgement turn data into information and then knowledge. So knowledge is the application of information—in a specific context.[4] It also provides a framework for evaluating new information. Suppose, for example, that I have in front of me last month's sales figures for my company in four areas (call them North, South, East and West). These are data—they tell me very little, apart from which has the largest and which the smallest sales. If I then compare the figures with those from earlier months, I may discover that sales in the North are growing at 2 per cent per month and those in the East at 1 per cent per month, while those in the South are stagnant and those in the West are declining sharply. These growth patterns are information. I might combine that with other information that I already have about my most dangerous competitor, who is:

- not very active in the North or East;
- competing strongly on price in the West, where my manager has kept prices high;
- also competing strongly on price in the South, where my manager has reduced her prices to just 2 per cent above competitors'.

Now that I see recurring patterns in the information, I have knowledge. I know that our products are good enough to stand a 2 per cent price premium, but not much more, and that other competitors are not dangerous to me. I may also decide that I know that the sales manager in the South is more competent than the one in the West.

Although knowledge originates in the minds of individuals, in organizations it often becomes embedded 'not only in documents or repositories but also in organizational routines, processes, practices, and norms'.[5] These shape what people in a group or organization collectively do—and are therefore closely influenced by the organization's culture and architecture.

Sometimes this knowledge can be codified—written down or related in a form of explicit, or narrative, knowledge. It is this that goes into academic papers, handbooks, or instruction manuals. And it is this codified form that has led to most of the practical application of knowledge management systems in organizations—IT-based systems that allow employees to access other employees' learning.

But knowledge can also be practical and not based on information at all—if you learn to ride a bicycle you just *know* how to do it, and it is unlikely that this could be written down in a form that could be shared with anyone else. In fact it may be impossible to write down this knowledge—it is something that you have learned to do by practising it. This is embodied knowledge.

Practical knowledge equally can apply to tasks that groups of people have learned to do together. As we suggested in Chapter 7, this type of knowledge is an important component of tacit knowledge, which is often a considerable source of competitive advantage because it cannot be imitated or understood by anyone outside the immediate group—indeed, the group itself, by definition, may not be aware that it has it.

➔ We introduced tacit knowledge in Section 1.4.1 and Section 7.1.

And a final type of knowledge is symbolic—communicated by symbols that are only understood by a specific group of people who are already sensitized to them. For example, the lyrics of many rap artists contain references that are not easily understood by people who are not used to listening to them. Any knowledge that they are trying to convey is lost to people who do not understand the code. The same is true of many academic articles. For insiders, however, these symbols are an efficient way of communication—and help build a sense of exclusivity and of group identity.

All these types of knowledge have different characteristics and are transmitted in different ways—embodied knowledge is slowest as it requires personal contact and transmission by example. Narrative knowledge can be transmitted faster and to a more widespread group of people. All are potentially very important to organizations; many major corporations now have knowledge management systems and knowledge officers, and there is a whole industry of management consultants that focus on this topic.

There are three major issues to do with the management of organizational knowledge:

- how to attain new knowledge;
- how to deploy knowledge in the most appropriate place in the organization;
- how to protect important knowledge from being acquired by competitors, or used in an inappropriate way, for example through harming existing organizational routines.[6]

In the following sections, we review each of these in turn, but it is worth noting that achieving all these different aims can cause real problems. For example, innovation often comes about because two or more companies join together to combine what they individually know to develop a new technology; but strategic alliances of this nature can also result in learning races and the loss of important proprietary knowledge.[7] Telling potential customers about a new product, which may help build demand for it, also allows competitors to know that you are bringing it out. And in order to stop it from being appropriated or stolen, you need to be able to clearly identify what you consider to be *your* knowledge. This is not easy.[8]

10.2 Knowledge development and organizational learning

Knowledge is always available within the organization itself; if it meets the VIRUS criteria, it will count as a strategic asset. An organization that is especially adept at developing and applying knowledge is likely to have a sustainable source of competitive advantage through

➔ The VIRUS test for a strategic resource was set out in Section 7.2.

its ability to develop relevant capabilities and competences, respond to changing customer requirements, and develop innovative products that fulfil their needs. Those organizations that are the best at this process have been categorized as learning organizations,[9] and the body of academic work that has identified the particular attributes of such firms is organizational learning theory.

10.2.1 Incremental knowledge development

How knowledge is developed depends on the type of knowledge involved, and its degree of 'tacitness'. Researchers[10] have identified a number of stages during which knowledge is developed and shared with others:

1. Knowledge acquisition by individuals
2. Knowledge sharing
3. Knowledge utilization.

a. Knowledge acquisition by individuals

People learn by making sense of their individual concrete experiences. They observe what happens to them and reflect upon it. This process may be instant and intuitive—'I told you when we launched this product that the packaging is wrong'—or may involve a longer period of reflection—'I hate this type of packaging, but all the other products using it are selling fine. However, this is the first time we've tried to sell through department stores rather than pharmacies.' The upshot is some theory or generalization about what is going on, which can then be tested—we change the packaging, or the distribution strategy—and which then leads to a new experience. After that, the learning process starts all over again, as people refine their knowledge further.[11] This process is called internalization.

b. Knowledge sharing

The fact that certain people in an organization have learned something does not signify that the organization has done so, so their knowledge needs to be shared if it is to be used on a wider scale. Knowledge passes most easily between members of the same work group, or community of practice,[12] although knowledge is also shared with people that are part of the same strategic group or industry. They learn a particular way of doing things, which may spread outside an organization to become part of the industry recipe.

➜ We discuss industry recipes in Section 3.3.1.

Knowledge sharing is very much a social activity, with tacit knowledge especially being shared through a socialization process: people exchange experiences and tips, or brainstorm problems together, and they watch one another at work. Tacit knowledge can also be developed by mingling with customers and watching how they use a firm's products or services.

People find a way of putting this tacit knowledge into words, often using some kind of striking image to help others understand it. This part of the process, which makes tacit knowledge more widely available, is called externalization. And this type of narrative, explicit knowledge can be shared through the writing down of experiences in formal documentation and procedures, or through training seminars and conferences. This sort of knowledge can be shared with a much wider group of people, but requires an active reading or listening process—and also needs to be made available to the right people (collaborators), and not to others (competitors, for example).

Often explicit knowledge is combined with tacit knowledge from different sources to create a new understanding about something. For example, a designer's tacit knowledge of a product's characteristics may be combined with market research data, to come up with a new product. The mingling of tacit and narrative knowledge is why face-to-face communication in organization-wide conferences is valuable, even though these may be very expensive to put on.

c. Knowledge utilization

The final stage is where knowledge is broadly available and can be generalized to new situations. The outcome of this process is often a new organizational competence.

These stages can be repeated in a 'spiral of knowledge creation'.[13] What we have just described is a learning process, in which routines are developed and enhanced over time. For an organization to do this exceptionally, and predictably, well, organizations have to set in place processes and structures that systematically allow individual experiences to be translated into new, shared work practices. In most organizations this is done in a form of single-loop learning; learning organizations on the other hand use a more complex set of processes known as double-loop learning.

10.2.2 **Single- and double-loop learning**

Most organizations use single-loop learning (Loop 1 in Figure 10.1) as a matter of routine if there is a problem, or if they simply feel that there is scope for improving something. For example, if McDonald's profits were to be out of line with expectations, they would be most likely to look at their pricing, their advertising, at new products that Pizza Hut or Burger King might have launched, and see if this explains what is going on. They might then experiment with lower prices or new products; if sales recovered, they would have learned how to fix that particular problem. If they did not, McDonald's might look at other parts of the way it does business, to see if the quality of its ingredients or of its customer service had somehow been allowed to deteriorate.

All these lines of enquiry would be formed from within McDonald's existing belief system, which (as it appears to us) includes a belief that if the burgers are good enough and served with a smile at an attractive price, then people will want them. Because assumptions like these become so deeply ingrained in organizations, they can be difficult to challenge. McDonald's, we suggest, would take a lot of convincing that the world had fallen out of love with the hamburger, although in the 1980s it eventually took that possibility seriously enough to introduce McDonald's pizza to counter the threat from Pizza Hut. And more recently it experimented with 'healthier' options such as salads and fruit.[14]

→ The factors that inhibit double-loop learning are similar to those that make it difficult for organizations to change: see Chapter 16.

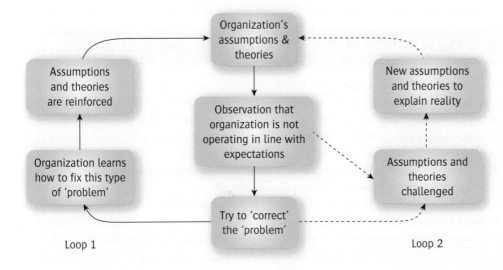

Loop 1   Loop 2

Figure 10.1 Single- and double-loop learning

These are examples of double-loop learning (Loop 2 in Figure 10.1)—someone in McDonald's has been able to challenge and change some of its deeply held assumptions and theories. Because of the psychological wrench involved, few organizations seem to be consistently capable of double-loop learning, and even fewer are able to challenge their assumptions unless confronted by an insoluble problem, or even a crisis.

It is important to strike a balance between the two types of learning. Single-loop learning is necessary to build core competences, since routines are rarely perfect the first time they are put into practice. Double-loop learning is important if an organization is to adapt to major changes in its environment. Evidence that a firm is capable of double-loop learning is thus a useful indicator that it may have a sustainable advantage.

10.2.3 The learning organization

Those organizations that appear to learn more consistently and easily than others are learning organizations, and as we hint above, they are relatively rare. They can be defined as:

> an organization *skilled* at creating, acquiring and transferring knowledge, and at *modifying its behaviour* to reflect new knowledge and insights.
>
> (Garvin, 1993: 80, our italics)

The key words that we have highlighted in the above definition are that the organization is *skilled* at learning—that is, it does so consistently and well—and that it *modifies* its behaviour as a result of what it has learnt; in other words, they exhibit high levels of double-loop as well as single-loop learning. An organization's ability to do this well is sometimes referred to as its absorptive capacity. Practice, in the form of previous experience of learning and the development of new products, makes it more likely that an organization will develop absorptive capacity, and is a reason why some recommend that firms invest in undertaking their own R&D instead of simply acquiring the results of someone else's.[15]

Just because a firm has learnt one or two important things over a long period of time does not make it a learning organization. Similarly, a firm that takes in lots of information, but does not change its behaviour as a result, does not qualify. Learning organizations are those that are open to information from the outside and react quickly to it. They may be innovators in their own right, such as Sony or 3M, or they may make sure that they catch up quickly with other people's innovations. They are able to recognize when they have made a mistake, and take swift action to put it right (Real-life Application 10.1).

Real-life Application 10.1 Microsoft: a learning organization?

Although Microsoft, the US software giant, is a firm many people like to hate, it has many of the features of a learning organization. It has a hunger for information from all sources. This sometimes creates controversy, as when it built features into its Windows 98 operating system to help it track how people were using the software. Users reacted strongly against what they saw as an invasion of privacy. But it has also created an enormous database of problems, and solutions, that users have encountered in dealing with its software. The Microsoft Knowledge-Base provides on-line searchable access to both customers and developers, and the on-line reporting of errors allows Microsoft to understand what has caused problems. Often these are not even the fault of Microsoft, but are the result of other companies' products. Microsoft, in many cases, works closely with these companies to develop combined solutions.

One of the most impressive aspects of Microsoft is its ability to recover from its mistakes. It built a number of features into its Office 97 suite of applications to try to help inexperienced users, but has taken them out of its successors, because users found them bothersome. In 1994, it underestimated the importance →

Microsoft offers a wide range of products. *Microsoft*

➜ of the World Wide Web, and tried to set up its own proprietary computer network, MSN. However, once it realized its error, it redirected its resources. It reconfigured MSN to use the World Wide Web, and within a year had launched its own browser software, Explorer, to compete with the market leader, Netscape. Internet Explorer is now the dominant browser, although the open source software update of Netscape, Firefox, has managed to reclaim as much as 15 per cent of the market.[16] Microsoft responded in 2006 by updating Explorer to include features pioneered by Firefox.[17]

Recently, Microsoft has recognized that it needs to collaborate with other firms in its industry,[18] including some with which it has had disputes in the past, perhaps to prevent the unwelcome attentions of regulators, but also perhaps because better products are likely to be the outcome—and there is no doubt that Microsoft wants to make world-beating products.

Some of the most important attributes of learning organizations are:

- Top managers are committed to the learning process and set an example by becoming 'star learners'.

- People have a strong understanding of the assumptions they make about their organization and the world in which it operates.

- The culture encourages openness, so that people own up to not performing as well as they might and experiment to find new solutions.

- There is systematic use of quantitative measurement and logical tools for analysing and solving problems and monitoring the results of actions taken.

- The organization already has some prior knowledge in fields related to those where it is trying to learn, and people routinely take part in research and learning activities, even though it may be in other areas.

- The organization has high levels of absorptive capacity—its ability to absorb information, recognize when it has found something important, and make practical use of it.

Using Evidence Assessing organizational learning

There are two types of evidence that can be used in assessing organizational learning: inputs and outcomes. Inputs include the amount the organization spends on training and staff development, both in absolute terms and as a proportion of revenues, and can be helpful quantitative indicators of commitment to learning. Training spend per employee and training hours per employee are particularly useful ratios to calculate.

There are also more qualitative indicators of commitment to learning, including structures designed to encourage socialization and externalization, such as inter-departmental meetings, conferences, and wikis. Signs of top management commitment to learning and an open culture —specific examples of senior executives listening to more junior staff, for example—are helpful indicators if you want evidence of a learning organization.

But effort is not the same as achievement, and in order to be sure that you are looking at a true learning organization, you will need to be able to produce *specific* examples of things that the organization—and not just a few individuals—has actually *learnt*. If you do not discover any, or if the only instances are from several years in the past, it means that this is not a true learning organization. Do not be surprised at this—remember, learning organizations are rare.

10.2.4 The paradoxes of organizational learning

→ These are forms of the Icarus paradox we met in Section 2.8.4.

→ We looked at competency traps in Section 7.7.

From the more passionate advocates of organizational learning, it is easy to get the impression that no organization can learn too much, or too fast. However, there are a number of traps into which organizations can fall:[19]

- Too much single-loop learning: Some single-loop learning is essential. There is a danger, however, that if an organization gets too good at it, it will cease to see the need for double-loop learning, which offers less certain returns. The result can be competency traps that make the organization vulnerable to long-term environmental change.

- Too much double-loop learning: Sometimes organizations are so intent upon innovation and change, and so afraid of bureaucracy and formalization, that they neglect the basics of running an efficient business. This can be a particular problem where an organization is locked into a cycle of failure, and tries ever riskier ways of getting out of it.

- Learning too fast: This is the organizational equivalent of a person's jumping to conclusions, and can happen if everyone in an organization has a very similar mindset. Simulation exercises have shown that organizations that take their time learning arrive at a better understanding of their environment than those that learn faster.[20] A creative tension between people who want to move forward quickly and those who want to preserve the old values can actually help an organization to learn more effectively.

- Misinterpreting success or failure: Sometimes an organization can be misled by good results into thinking it has strong capabilities, when it may just have benefited from, say, an economic boom. This leads it to use its assets to develop those capabilities further, when in fact they are not sources of enduring strength. Failure can be equally misleading—sometimes an organization strives desperately for a solution, when in fact it has just been unlucky, or has set itself unrealistic goals. This kind of misreading of success or failure is called superstitious learning.

For example, when the UK water companies were privatized in the 1980s, many of them felt that their high profits showed that they had strong management skills. Some tried to capitalize on this 'strength' by diversifying into other businesses, such as plumbing services, and lost a lot of money thereby. In fact, their initial success was in large part due to the regulatory regime under which they were privatized: they were given a local monopoly, allowed to charge generous prices and not forced to upgrade their infrastructure as quickly as many observers thought they should. Many of the companies were eventually taken over by foreign water firms, such as France's Lyonnaise des Eaux and Vivendi, which had long-standing experience in running a commercial operation. However, the largest, Thames Water, has remained independent and successfully expanded overseas in water supply, where its core competences truly lie.

10.2.5 Attaining knowledge through acquisitions and alliances

Clearly, incremental learning is an important way for an organization to build the stocks of knowledge that it needs to sustain competitive advantage. But sometimes firms are not able to do this; they may lack the time needed to learn about a new technology before competitors gain a dominant position. Or perhaps they need to acquire knowledge that will be complementary to their own, and which they hope may lead to the development of new products. And so organizations also sometimes enter into relationships of one sort or another with external partners in order to acquire the knowledge they need.

For example, knowledge may need to be obtained about:

- the legal and social characteristics of a new market;
- how a new technology works;
- the culture of a new business area;
- the competitive forces in a new industry.

Sometimes this knowledge is obtained through acquiring a firm. In the IT industries, the major players will often acquire smaller, newer companies in order to obtain access to the hardware technologies or software that they have developed. Cisco (which is probably the industry benchmark in this activity) has made this type of acquisition a major plank in its strategy—so much so that new firms in the industry are reported to have set out with the specific intentions of developing something that they believe Cisco will want to acquire.[21]

A risk in an acquisition strategy such as this, is that knowledgeable employees—the reason why an acquisition is made in the first place—have legs, and can walk out the door. Successful acquirers have to be able to retain staff in order to benefit from their knowledge (again Cisco is one of the most successful in this respect[22]).

But often alliances are the chosen method of supplementing internally developed knowledge with that from outside the organization (Real-life Application 10.2).

→ We discuss the challenges of executing mergers and acquisitions in Section 17.5.

10.3 Deploying and protecting knowledge

The development of knowledge that we have described is often a time-consuming (incremental) or costly (alliance/acquisition) process. And the same principles that make knowledge hard to acquire or develop also make it hard subsequently to manage and allocate it. For example, important knowledge may be lost:

Real-life Application 10.2[23] Building knowledge through alliances at Kodak

The 1980s Apple Quicktake digital camera: developed through an alliance between Apple Computer and Kodak.
Kodak/Apple

Kodak, for many years, focused on producing chemical imaging equipment and materials. Since the late 1980s Kodak has had to move swiftly into digital imaging technologies such as electronic sensing and file compression (not entirely successfully—see What Can Go Wrong 13.1). Most of the knowledge and routines that Kodak had previously used were too slow for the new environment in which it found itself: the company's traditional system of product development phases and 'stage-gates' through which all new products had to pass typically took three years. Through an alliance with Apple Computer, the development of a digital camera—the Apple Quicktake—was reduced to seven months.

Kodak has used alliances with many other firms to obtain the specialist knowledge that they hold, and which Kodak itself lacks. Much of this knowledge has widespread potential application and can benefit from economies of scope. Internalizing this knowledge would 'inevitably result in substantial underutilization'.

Kodak's knowledge-accessing alliance partners include:

- Intel for expertise in data storage;

- Microsoft for document and image management know-how;

- AT&T and Cisco Systems for internet protocols and digital networking knowledge;

- Hewlett-Packard for thermal inkjet technologies;

- Lockheed Martin for know-how in integrating massive information systems;

- Motorola for semiconductor manufacturing expertise.

But Kodak also uses alliances to exploit its own spare knowledge assets. Through selling these to partners, it is able to benefit from economies of scope—but outside its own borders—thus obtaining income for assets that would otherwise go to waste. Its knowledge-exploiting alliance partners included:

- manufacturers of telescopes and high-resolution cameras in satellite imaging systems, who used Kodak's knowledge of optics and lens design;

- Heidelberger Druckmaschinen AG, who accessed Kodak's digital scanning and colour management software technology;

- Hewlett-Packard, Lexmark, Canon, and Heidelberger for whom Kodak provided data compression, image storage, and colour management technologies;

- manufacturers of cameras and digital imaging equipment who accessed Kodak's knowledge of CCD and CMOS image sensors.

- through not being recorded or documented;
- because people do not recognize its value;
- thorough attrition and lack of use;
- because it is too difficult or expensive to manage knowledge sharing or transfer;
- because an organization does not have an architecture which encourages sharing.

Valuable knowledge may also get into the wrong hands through theft or simple carelessness and loose talk—this is more likely to happen to explicit knowledge.

Because organizations have recognized how valuable knowledge can be, two related bodies of theory and practice have emerged to deal with the issue. The first is that of knowledge management; the second that of knowledge protection.

10.3.1 **Knowledge management**

Organizations typically have a lot of knowledge scattered around—in a variety of databases, in people's heads, and in their filing cabinets (Real-life Application 10.3). The aim of knowledge management is to make it more widely available. Theorists and practising managers have come up with a number of ideas about how to manage their firms' knowledge:[24]

> **Knowledge management**
> The process of turning unrecognized or inaccessible knowledge into recognized and accessible knowledge through mechanisms that facilitate the emergence, storage, and transfer of knowledge within an organization.

1. Create knowledge repositories: Organizations can set up central libraries and databases containing scientific and market research reports, copies of marketing materials and technical and sales manuals. The aim is to prevent people from needlessly having to rediscover or reinvent something that already exists. Some firms, including most major management consultancies, have set up 'discussion databases', often using 'groupware' software. After a major project, staff summarize the lessons they have learned and put it on the database for the benefit of anyone who might need to do a similar job.

2. Improve knowledge access: One way of giving people better access to knowledge is by having a readily accessible directory that sets out who knows what in the organization. British Petroleum/Amoco (BP), one of the world's largest oil companies, and Bain and McKinsey, two of the world's most prestigious and successful management consultancies, all established 'Yellow Pages'-style directories to help their staff locate employees with the right expertise. No less important is the communications infrastructure that enables people to 'talk' to one another. For a large, international organization, this might include e-mail chat rooms, intranets, and video-conferencing facilities. BP has invested heavily in these, and encourages any employee to set up a home page on the intranet.

3. Enhance the knowledge environment. Busy consultants and sales staff will not always welcome sitting down at the end of a hard day to type their experiences into a database. Organizations can try and give them incentives to share knowledge, and to use knowledge from elsewhere. Quite often, knowledge sharing is underpinned by strong cultural norms. At McKinsey, the norm is that consultants will respond quickly to queries from colleagues. An Australian consultant could leave voice-mail messages for colleagues in the USA or Europe at the end of a working day, and confidently expect to have most of their replies the following morning.

Real-life Application 10.3 A knowledge-sharing culture and architecture at GE

General Electric Co (GE) in its heyday was the largest company in the world, and was regularly voted the 'most admired company' in the world. Accolades poured on to its CEO, Jack Welch, who was widely perceived to have transformed GE from a stodgy corporation to a world-beater.

Mr Welch was (and still is, although he retired from GE in 2001) a passionate advocate of proactively managing the knowledge that is within an organization.[25] As he has said, it is pointless having an organization as large as GE, unless you can exploit the knowledge that is held within it. He was responsible for initiating a widespread knowledge-sharing architecture. These included:[26]

- modifying the organization's structure, including flattening the hierarchy so that communication between employees and decision-making could be speeded up;
- job rotation, cross-functional teams, and the use of taskforces that often involved one or more senior managers;
- large investments in training and development throughout the corporation. This included what became the world-famous 'Six-Sigma' skills development and productivity improvement methodology;
- information technology, including an e-business initiative, EPOS (electronic terminals in stores), and a database that collected all customer complaints in a database along with potential solutions. These were accessible by customer service staff, and could be used to advise customers who called with similar problems;
- external benchmarking;
- internal best practice transfer, again with heavy involvement of the company's Executive Council. This included a deliberate policy of 'walking the job'. Jack Welch himself was famed for the regular visits he made to all parts of the company. If he found an example of good practice he was on the phone immediately to his executives, telling them to use it themselves.

The way in which an organization manages its knowledge needs to take account of the kind of problems that it faces. A firm that confronts similar problems all the time, like McDonald's or an information systems consultancy, should consider a codification strategy. This would involve having staff document their knowledge and experience, and investing heavily in IT systems to make the narratives available to others. For an organization that never encounters quite the same problem twice, like McKinsey or Sony's product designers, that kind of investment would probably be wasteful. They might be better off following a personalization strategy,[27] which involves bringing people together as needed to discuss problems and exchange experiences.

10.3.2 Protecting knowledge

The other side of the knowledge management process is to protect the knowledge that organizations have from appropriation by competitors. Tacit knowledge is usually harder to obtain than explicit knowledge, although sometimes firms poach key personnel from competitors in the hope that they will bring their knowledge with them. To some extent they will, but it is easy to underestimate the importance of context in making knowledge useful: tacit knowledge that is group based is even harder to transfer. Some universities have managed to recruit whole teams of researchers from rival institutions; this may be an effective policy, as the tasks that they are likely to be working on are relatively self-contained. In a commercial firm, knowledge has to be applied within a much more complicated and inter-connected setting, severely limiting the potential benefits, in the short term at least, of a newly recruited team.

Explicit knowledge is a different matter. In theory, anything that is written down or expressed in some way (even in the form of a tangible product or artefact) may be copied or used by a rival. Organizations can do much to prevent this happening themselves through encouraging staff to be careful who they talk to and what they say, and through keeping data safely locked up and allowing it to be accessed by legitimate users only.

But for many organizations legislation provides an added layer of security. Most countries have laws that protect inventions from being copied and brand marks and designs from being imitated, or that protect authors from other people passing off their words as their own.

a. Patents, copyright, and IPR (intellectual property rights)

The generic term for protectable knowledge is intellectual property. Companies usually go to great lengths to protect their intellectual property, using legislation and the courts in order to do so. Legislation relating to intellectual property includes:

- Copyright: This protects the rights of publishers of written materials such as articles or music from copying. It includes works that are printed on paper or other tangible materials, as well as anything that is published on the internet. Copyright generally lasts automatically for up to 70 years after the author's death.

- Patents: A patent is a set of rights granted by a government to an individual or group of individuals, or a company, who want(s) to protect their ideas from being copied and exploited by others, perhaps because they themselves are not yet able to make the most of them, or often, because they want others to pay to use them. A patent is awarded for a limited period of time (usually 20 years, though this can vary across different countries).[28]

- Design rights: In the UK these may be registered or unregistered—with different legal rights attached to them in each case. Design rights are especially relevant in the case of aesthetic products such as fashionable clothing and household items.

- Trade or Brand Marks: These have to be able to be represented on paper. They are typically a firm's logo or product name, represented in colours and patterns, but can include sounds such as Intel's 'Intel inside' jingle, or even, potentially, smells!

Intellectual property
The product of intellectual endeavour. It includes written material (words or music), designs, works of art, trade marks and logos, and databases.

Although some countries are less proactive in protecting intellectual property than others, most parts of the developed world have long been signed up to international agreements on IPR, such as the World Trade Organization's Agreement on Trade Related Aspects of Intellectual Property Rights (TRIPs).

IPR management is one of the fastest-changing and most complex areas that a firm has to deal with—and access to specialist lawyers can be important. Recent developments in some industries means that regulation and its application have a hard time keeping up. For example:

- Animal and plant varieties: The selective breeding of animals or plants, using in some case genetic modification techniques, is a major area for IPR protection, as is the patenting of the genetic blueprints of plant and animal varieties.

- In pharmaceuticals, there have been many successful challenges against the legality of some of the pharmaceutical companies' patents by manufacturers of generic versions of their medicines. They are also under considerable pressure to give up their hold on patents in order to allow affordable generic versions of some pharmaceuticals to be made available in the developing world, for example AIDS drugs.

- Biotechnological research generates data that potentially has great value for the prevention and treatment of diseases. However, some private firms researching in the area have sought to keep their discoveries private, or to patent genes for which they have discovered the code.

- Open-source software (OSS), for example Linux, has a very strict legal status, and operates under the terms of an American licence (the GPL) which grants users the rights to change or add to the initial software program, and to distribute it—with strict conditions. Software is automatically protected by copyright, even so called 'free-source' or 'open' software, and those who infringe it can be, and have been, sued.[29] Nonetheless, open-source principles are now being applied to innovation and new product development (see Section 10.4 below).

- Digital music and film: the rise of the internet and sites which allow digitized content to be downloaded has generated a number of copyright protection issues. US companies such as Napster have been sued by record and film companies. This has driven peer-to-peer file-sharing sites to, for example, China, Russia, and even Canada, where legislation is imperfectly implemented or even permits downloading.

Trademarks or brand names are an important component of an organization's reputation, and these are normally legally registered to prevent their misuse. But if the firm's trademark becomes so recognizable that people simply refer to the brand rather than the activity it represents the company can lose its rights to that name. Some very well known trade marks that have now become generic words are bikini, heroin, cellophane, brassiere, escalator, gramophone, and aspirin. And Sony has lost its control over the term 'Walkman' in some parts of the world.[30]

The increasing globalization of both maketing and production has added to the difficulties of protecting intellectual property, particularly in countries where legal protection for intellectual property is weak, or weakly enforced. China, although it has become more rigorous in protecting intellectual property since its entry into the World Trade Organization, is seen as a particular challenge. But because of its enormous economic potential, many western firms feel that they cannot avoid doing business there: 'There's hardly an economic arena of the scale of China that is simultaneously as big an opportunity and as potential a threat for companies.'[31] Starbucks has sued two Chinese competitors for using logos similar to its green and white one, and names that closely resembled the transliteration of Starbucks into Chinese.[32] And a three-year lawsuit by Italian chocolate maker Ferrero against a local rival, which it alleges has copied its Ferrero-Rocher confectionery, has gone as far as China's Supreme Court and has been raised in diplomatic exchanges between China and the EU.[33] International strategic alliances pose particular challenges, since partners may need to be given access to proprietary knowledge, designs, and technology in order for the alliance to function. There may be little by way of mutual respect or shared cultural norms to prevent a partner from making use of that intellectual property for purposes outside the scope of the alliance.[34]

→ We look at the problems of managing alliances in Section 9.3.1 and the international dimension of alliance management in Chapter 14.

10.4 Innovation

Invention
The first occurrence of an idea for a new product or process.[35]

There are probably hundreds of definitions of innovation—as there are of creativity and invention, with which it is often confused. Here we define invention as the first occurrence of a new idea, creativity as the expression of an original idea, and innovation as the implementation of a *significantly* new idea in a specific context.

In some industries it is almost impossible to separate out invention from innovation—in biotechnology, for example, where the development of, say, a new gene modification technique happens through practical, applied, development in the laboratory. And in some other industries, such as fashion, creativity and innovation are often used synonymously, although one company (Real-life Application 10.4) makes a distinction between the two concepts.

Real-life Application 10.4 Creative and innovative products in Swarovski Crystals[38]

The Swarovski Group is an Austrian firm that manufactures fine crystals which are used in a number of fashion-related products such as clothing, handbags, and jewellery. It also manufactures crystals that are used in interior design applications (in ceramic tiles, for example) and lighting—in chandeliers as well as fibre-optic light systems. They have a division that focuses on precision optical equipment and another that produces jewellery manufacturing equipment. In all of these areas it undertakes research and development. But within the company a distinction is made between creative products and innovative products—both are equally important to the firm, but the way they are managed is very different.

Swarovski's creative products are designed to express ideas, to make something beautiful, or to signify something, for example to 'lend a touch of poetry'[39] to a setting. Most of the crystals that are used in the fashion industry or in their jewellery are creative—they come out of the designer's imagination, and may well be novel in the ideas that they express. But they require no adjustments to the company's value chain, or the way that it manufactures or distributes its products.

Swarovski's innovative products, on the other hand, may well be creative—but they are also significantly different in fundamental ways from the products that the company has previously made. They may require it to re-tool its manufacturing processes, find new applications for them, and convince its distributors and retailers that they will be able to find customers for them.

Innovation implies that there is a step change, or discontinuity,[40] in the normal pace of development within an industry:

- Technological discontinuities result in advances so significant that 'no increase in scale, efficiency, or design can make older technologies competitive with the new technology'.[41] Technological innovations such as this alter the industry's success factors and recipes.[42] Sometimes, perhaps counter-intuitively, the most forceful technological innovations make products that are less sophisticated than existing products. These may be unattractive to core customers for the established product, but, because they are also much cheaper, make life simpler and/or more affordable for consumers who have previously been forced to buy products with features that they do not need. These innovations have been termed disruptive technologies;[43] often, they later develop the functionality of traditional products, while retaining their cost and price advantage.

  No-frills air travel is a classic example: it lacked the inflight meals and other comforts that business travellers were used to, and typically flew to airports that did not offer convenient access to major population centres. Traditional airline passengers would not have been interested in such a product, and would have found it difficult to understand why anyone else might be. But customers—people wanting to visit faraway friends and relatives—existed, who were prepared to put up with the relative inconvenience of no-frills travel in return for its ultra-low prices. Gradually, the no-frills model was extended to major airports and became an accepted—perhaps even the dominant —model for short-haul air travel in the US, Europe, and elsewhere.

Creativity

The production of novel or original ideas in a domain. Some authorities regard creativity as a necessary precursor to innovation.[36]

Innovation

The implementation of a significantly new idea in a specific context. This may apply to products, technologies, or processes. Some further subdivide it into radical (or transformational) and incremental innovation.[37]

- Product discontinuities show up in the form of new product classes, or in radical product improvements, and a corresponding change in consumer behaviour.
- Process discontinuities show up in either process substitution or in improvements that have the potential to fundamentally challenge the way that an industry operates.

Many writers appear to assume that innovation is inherently a good thing, and something that all organizations should aspire to.[44] Perhaps this is partly because innovation may be classified in so many different ways, but if we use our definition of innovation as being a *significant* change from what has gone before, it is by no means automatic that innovation will lead to success, or indeed, that it should be a priority for all firms. Innovation is certainly linked with high economic returns in certain industries. However, whether innovation is necessary for all firms, and how it should best be managed, has been the subject of considerable debate (see Theoretical Debate 10.1 later in this chapter).

Nevertheless, great wealth can accrue to successful innovators who transform the rules of competition in their industries.[45] First-mover firms can take their time to build up defensible positions before competitors have become aware of the need to copy them. But innovation can be a high-risk strategy. It involves significant change to existing systems, structures, and beliefs. Innovation can also be hugely expensive, has a high failure rate, and sometimes can take much longer to show benefits or a financial return than firms hope for at the outset. It is also something that not all firms can do well; implementing the process effectively appears to be a competence in its own right (see Real-life Application 10.5, and also What Can Go Wrong 10.1).

→ We discuss effecting change in organizations in Chapter 16.

Real-life Application 10.5 Innovation winners and losers[46]

An organization may invest considerable time and resources in developing a breakthrough technology, only to have an imitator reap the benefits (Figure 10.2). Sometimes, this is because the product is launched prematurely. Apple launched a handheld computer, the Newton, with several innovative features. Unfortunately, the handwriting recognition software was unreliable, and the Newton was an expensive flop. Another firm, Palm, learnt from Apple's mistakes, realizing that most users wanted a simpler

machine that could exchange information with a PC. They gained market leadership in handhelds with a well-designed device that carried out this key function simply and reliably.

EMI, a major British firm, had successfully diversified away from its original base of music recording (it was originally known as Electrical Musical Industries) into advanced electronics. EMI had pioneered high resolution TVs and also developed the UK's first all solid-state computers in 1952. By the late 1960s, EMI →

	Technology leaders	Technology followers
Competitive winners	Pilkington (float glass)	GE Medical Systems (CAT scanner) Matsushita VHS (video recorder) Compaq (PC) Palm Pilot (hand-held computer)
Competitive losers	EMI (CAT scanner) Sony Betamax (video recorder) Xerox (PC) Apple Newton (hand-held computer)	Kodak (instant photos) DEC (PC)

Figure 10.2 Innovation winners and losers. Adapted from Teece (1986).

→ engineers had developed a technology that allowed 'pictures' to be taken of the human body—the CAT scanner. This was an innovation that transformed medical assessments, and was the biggest advance in radiology since the discovery of X-rays in 1895. Although initially successful, within six years of its launch in the US in 1973, it had lost market leadership and two years later had withdrawn from the CAT business altogether.

Commentators suggest that it ceded position to the technology follower, GE Medical Systems, because of a lack of specialized complementary assets.[47] These include capabilities in marketing, competitive manufacturing, and after-sales support.[48] The scanner was a much more technologically sophisticated product than hospital staff were familiar with, requiring a high level of training, support, and servicing, none of which EMI was able to provide.[49] It also apparently failed to make full use of the intellectual property laws in order to protect its innovation. This allowed two competitors, GE and Technicare, both of whom were experienced providers of medical equipment and also had the required complementary capabilities in manufacturing and marketing, to step in and gain market share at EMI's expense.

On the other hand incremental improvements to existing products, systems, or processes are normal activities for organizations, and indeed are essential to their survival. Often an initially discontinuous product is followed by many subsequent incremental iterations that improve its functionality or reliability. Sometimes these will be undertaken by the innovator itself, but often they will be carried out by imitators (such as Compaq in Real-life Application 10.5), who make adaptations to the extent that later iterations may be barely recognizable as the same product as the original (the motor car being a good example).

10.4.1 The risks of innovation

Innovation can be unpredictable and expensive. Although there is a methodology, 'real options', for assessing and calculating risks, eventually a commitment has to be made to the innovation and resources directed towards it. The risks of innovation fall into four major categories:

→ We discuss real options in Chapter 12.

- costs of development;
- time-scales for success;
- unpredictability of take-up;
- disruption to existing products and organizational routines.

a. Costs of development

Most writers agree that innovation is expensive, with frequent failures, and difficult to predict. Simply investing cash in R&D is no guarantee of success. Some research even suggests that increasing R&D spend has, on average, a negative effect on the frequency of new product introductions and profitability.[50] Another study has suggested that 46 per cent of the resources devoted to product development go to unsuccessful projects and 35 per cent of new products fail commercially.[51] In pharmaceuticals, one of the most R&D-intensive industries, in the late 1990s, only one-eighth of all new potential drug discoveries made it through to patients; in a more recent five-year period, this proportion has nearly halved, to one in every 15[52] (Figures 10.3a and 10.3b).

However, in pharmaceuticals, as in other 'creative' industries such as music, film, and biotechnology, the huge amounts spent on new product development may be recouped a hundred-fold by one success. Worldwide sales between the early 1980s and 1996 from Glaxo's drug Zantac, which cost less than £40m to develop, were about $27bn. At times it alone was responsible for about 50 per cent of the firm's turnover, and 30 per cent of profits.[53] But for those firms that do not find success, innovation costs have the potential to bring down the whole company.

→ We introduced 'creative' industries as a category of mature industry in Section 3.4 and examine it more closely in section 13.4.2.

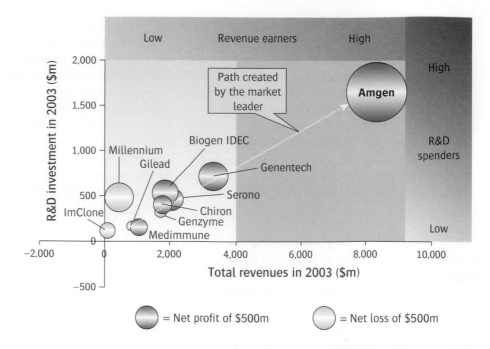

Figure 10.3a
Biotechnology R&D spend and profitability. Positioning of the top ten biotech companies in terms of revenues, R&D investment and net profit or loss recorded in fiscal year 2003. Note: bubble size indicates net profit or loss. Source: Datamonitor, company reports, Reuters and EDGAR on-line, cited in Pavlou and Belsey (2005: 172)

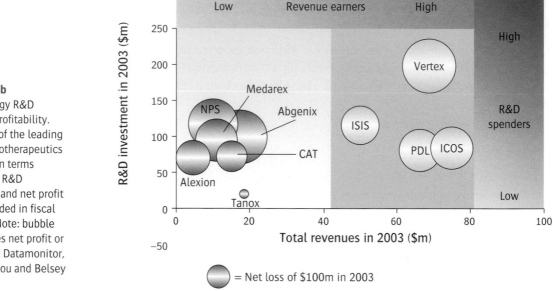

Figure 10.3b
Biotechnology R&D spend and profitability. Positioning of the leading emerging biotherapeutics companies in terms of revenues, R&D investment, and net profit or loss recorded in fiscal year 2003. Note: bubble size indicates net profit or loss. Source: Datamonitor, cited in Pavlou and Belsey (2005: 174)

b. Time-scales for success

Figure 10.4 shows some of the costs of development in the pharmaceutical industry—and also shows why innovation can be a high-risk business. The time-scales before an innovation is likely to become a commercial success can also be very long—more than 15 years in this industry, and the drop-out rate is very high. A large-scale study carried out in the late 1970s[54] also found that it took an average of eight years before a new venture reached profitability, and eight to ten years before its return on investment equalled that of mainstream activities. Building market awareness and demand for a new product, even if it is fundamentally a good one, may take further time. Many companies do not have the finance or the ability to take such risks or such a long-term view.

Stage	Pre-Clinical	Clinical Trials Phase I	Clinical Trials Phase II	Clinical Trials Phase III	Regulatory Approval and Market Launch	PIV Testing
Purpose	Synthesis and screening of compounds. Toxicology safety and dosage testing. Involves pre-clinical trials using animals.	Establish safety in human volunteers.	Establish safety and efficacy in human patients, therapies on the market.	Establish efficacy relative to other therapies.	Submit results of clinical trials to gain regulatory approval. Process development, distribution and marketing.	On-going monitoring of drug in market to ensure safety and efficacy.
Time[1] (15 years in total)	6 years	←——— 27% of time	6.7 years ——— 27% of time	——→ 46% of time	2.2 years	on-going
Cost[2] ($300 to $500 million in total)	40.6%	11% of cost	26.5% 27% of cost	62% of cost	27%	5.8%
Number of Compounds entering stage[3]	5 to 10,000 screened 250 enter pre-clinical trials.	5 compounds enter clinical trials				
Probability of compound making it to market[4]	3–5%	10%	30%	60%	90%	N/A
Regulatory Success	Only 23.3% of drugs that entered clinical trials between 1980 and 1984 were expected to gain regulatory approval to be marketed (DiMasi, 1995).					
Financial Success	The Net Present Value of drugs introduced onto the US market between 1980 to 1984 was $22 million in 1990 dollars. Only 30% of drugs launched on the market generated enough revenues to recoup R&D and other associated costs (Grabowski and Vernon, 1994).					

[1] Average number of years obtained from PhARMA (1999) annual survey of the US pharmaceuticals sector.
Percentage of time for Phase I, II and III trials from Pharmaceutical Education and Research Institute, 1996.

[2] Percentage total costs from PhARMA, 1999 annual survey of US pharmaceuticals sector.
Percentage of cost attributable to Phase I, II and III clinical trials from Pharmaceutical Education and Research Institute, 1996.

[3] Source: PhARMA, 1999.

[4] Source: Zeneca/Lehman Brothers, as quoted in Brown and Srikanthan. 1999.

Figure 10.4 Time-scales in pharmaceuticals R&D. Source: Mc Namara (2000). *Reproduced with the kind permission of City Business School*

c. Unpredictability of take-up

Building market awareness is made more problematic for innovators because gaining buy-in to a significantly new idea often requires customers to change their behaviour. If customers are companies, they may have to alter their own value chains and production processes as a consequence, which can contribute to resistance.

There are other reasons why take-up can be unpredictable. For some products, such as music or fashion-driven consumer electronics, there may be a bandwagon effect, where consumers will only buy a product if they see someone else buying it. Companies can experience a form of bandwagon effect too: if complementary products are available, they may help to increase the uptake of an innovation. Innovations, once launched and visible, may quickly spawn imitations that may be superior or have access to a better distribution network, and so eat into the market for the new product.

Predicting international market acceptance is a special problem. Products which are developed for one country do not necessarily sell well elsewhere. The length of time that new products take to reach 'take-off' varies widely even within western Europe; the Scandinavian countries have the shortest time—four years, nearly half that for Mediterranean countries.[55] National culture partly explains these differences,[56] although economic factors also appear to be important—take-off is faster in wealthier countries and the more open economies.

As the managers of an innovative product are often under great pressure to kill it off if it does not take off quickly; introducing it in a country that is more likely to show early sales can help to convince critics, both inside the company and in other countries, of its potential and prevent its premature withdrawal. And, an early take-off in one country can generate profits, which the innovator can use to improve the product, and promote it more aggressively in other markets.

c. Lack of competence in some aspects of the innovation-development process

Companies whose cultural preference is for exploitation—to gain maximum returns from existing investments—are often much less competent at exploration even if there are good strategic reasons why they should do this.

➜ We introduced the concepts of exploration and exploitation in Section 5.2.2.

These differences apply on an individual level, too. People tend to be predisposed to either do something new and different—'innovators', or do something better—'adaptors'.[57] Innovators are more likely to be common in explorative organizations; adaptors in exploitative organizations. 'Adaptor' firms are likely to encounter difficulties if they attempt to recruit innovators—who will be regarded with some suspicion as they attempt to change the status quo.

The different stages of innovation—from invention to full commercialization—require both these types of organization (and personality) at different times, but even firms that are strong at exploration are often better at some aspects of the innovation process than others. For example, even though some of the major pharmaceuticals, biotechnology, or software firms have innovation strategies, and are hugely dependent on new products for their success, many use independent companies to undertake the initial phases of the new product development process, or what in some sectors is known as the 'fuzzy front-end'.[58] Qualcomm, for example, has developed expertise in carrying out early-stage research in telecommunications, which it licenses to many of the major mobile phone manufacturers.[59]

d. Disruption to existing products and organizational routines

Innovation is often disruptive to an organization's existing operations—and this is a risk that many firms cannot afford to take. Because they have to set up dedicated processes and systems to exploit existing products, changes to these in order to accommodate new products are likely to be expensive and distract management attention. Routines have to be adjusted to take in the needs of the new product, plant and machinery may have to be re-dedicated, and distribution and supplier chains adjusted.

Moreover, as we shall see when we discuss organizational change in Chapter 16, deeply held beliefs and values may have to be abandoned. This is not easy. The need to focus on one type of operation is one of the reasons why highly innovative industries are characterized by many partnerships between firms, especially between larger multinationals and smaller specialist companies, which focus, like Qualcomm, on a relatively narrow aspect of the new product development process.[60]

Therefore firms face a problem—either to focus exclusively on exploiting their existing products, and risk losing out to competitors who develop new technologies or substitute products, or to embrace innovation and risk losing out to more rivals who can focus on producing existing products and services more efficiently.

Because of the need to reconcile what can seem like these irreconcilable forces, some scholars have proposed that firms try to become 'ambidextrous'[61]—develop the capability of moving between the different modes. Some recommend that innovation should take place in separate corporate venturing units,[62] where everything can be dedicated to new product development. However, this model has been criticized because it does not easily allow knowledge gained during the development process to be shared with other parts of the organization, and the new product may find it hard to be taken up by the mainstream's managers without a passionate advocate—or 'champion'—for it in the main part of the organization. Others argue that new product development should take place within the mainstream organization, encouraging serial innovations and benefiting existing products at the same time.[63] Others have suggested that innovation which fits the existing culture and belief system—which is likely to favour either exploration or exploitation—can be managed within the existing organization, while the other kind of innovation should be set up in different units.[64]

It is because of these risks that companies sometimes prefer not to undertake innovation on their own. Alliances are set up with co-developers who bring knowledge but also share the risks (and of course also the rewards). And often funding is provided by specialist suppliers of venture capital, who may however want a large share of the business in exchange.

10.4.2 Creating the conditions for innovation

For those organizations that *do* want to confront these risks in order to benefit from the potential rewards from successful innovation, certain features, both within and outside the organization, appear to be beneficial.

a. Innovation-supporting environments

Research suggests that there are benefits for firms if they locate their innovation-developing arms within a region that has a supportive infrastructure.[65] For example, California's Silicon Valley[66] offers a whole range of innovation-supporting elements, including:[67]

➜ We discuss location decisions of this kind in Chapter 14, and discuss Silicon Valley in Section 14.5.

- a culture of risk-taking and Californian-style enthusiasm for new ideas;
- favourable tax policies that act as incentives to the development of a venture capital market;
- government-supported R&D funding programmes;

- a liquid stock market and strong 'business angel' venture capital network;

- considerable information sharing between competing firms;

- cooperation between firms, research institutions, and universities;

- numerous sophisticated local customers, for example in the California electronics industry;

- easy access to extremely high concentrations of the resources needed to bring an innovation to fruition, including chip designers, specialist software writers, patent lawyers, high-tech marketeers, headhunters, and PR experts.

b. The innovative organization

Along with factors in the environment, scholars have identified a number of features within the organization that tend to encourage innovation:[68]

- Top management commitment to innovation, and capabilities in managing it.[69]

- Organizational mechanisms for recognizing and developing new ideas: These may be as simple as an employee suggestion box, but it would also include committees that meet regularly to review product prototypes or the results of experiments, discussion forums on the company's intranet, or new conferences where presentations may be made about new developments. Consistently innovative companies are often learning organizations (see Section 10.2 above), which have routines that allow knowledge to be developed and deployed across the organization.

- The availability of resources: These include development funding (or the ability to access it), and the presence of technical or market experts who can be brought in to the new product development team as needed. Another important element is organizational slack—time and facilities that are not fully committed to existing projects.[70] Although slack could be thought of as waste,[71] it frees time for imagination and experimentation, and allows failures to be absorbed. Slack can sometimes take the form of official 'skunk works'—small units where staff can spend time experimenting on their own projects, such as in 3M—an American conglomerate that manufactures industrial coatings and adhesives. 3M invented the 'Post-It Note', and was, for many years, the benchmark example of a serially innovative company.[72]

- Reward systems that are directed towards encouraging new ideas. Thus pay or bonuses would be paid for the numbers of new products developed, rather than for a reduction in the numbers of faulty products, for example, and targets set for the percentage of turnover to be derived from products developed during, say, the previous three years. In innovative companies staff are often promoted and/or appointed to membership of prestigious internal societies if they are successful in bringing about innovation.

- Control systems and culture that allow independent-minded thinkers their head, and in which tolerance of experimentation and 'failure' is embedded in corporate values. Any managerial attempt to impose strict bureaucratic controls on innovators is likely to meet with hostility and quite possibly the departure of the staff concerned. Tolerance of individualism and independence is sometimes formally sanctioned, as in 3M above and Google, where key engineers are allowed—even expected—to be 'doing their own thing' on their own projects one day a week.

Real-life Application 10.6 The development of innovative products: the iPod

Apple's iPod changed the way that music was acquired, stored, and played. *iStock*

Apple's portable music player, the iPod, changed the way that music (and now other digital content) was acquired, stored, and played. It was a step up from both tape- and CD-based players and from earlier MP3 (digital music) players, which were bulky and had less storage size or downloading functionality. It was instrumental in changing the rules of the portable music player industry, as well as supplier industries such as music distribution.

Apple was able to do this through combining knowledge from a number of different sources, and exploiting innovations that had already changed competition in other industries. These included:

- digital technologies that allowed music and other content to be stored on a computer;
- music compression technologies, such as MP3 or WMA, which are the encoding algorithms that convert music into data files and which allowed it to be transferred between

machines through, for example, Apple's 'firewire' protocol— an innovation in its own right;

- hard drive and battery miniaturization technologies, which respectively allowed large media files to be stored in physically small spaces and meant that the iPod could play for a reasonable length of time without needing to be recharged;
- power consumption technologies, which reduced the amount of power the device used and thereby increased the play life of the now smaller batteries. The iPod stores the music in its memory chips, allowing the hard drive to shut down during playback;
- DRM (digital rights management) technologies which made content copyright holders, such as EMI and Universal Music, willing to make their products available for download;
- display technologies that allowed the iPod to have a scroll-wheel controller which facilitated sophisticated searches and management of content.

Jon Rubinstein, the senior vice-president for hardware development, was asked by Apple's CEO Steve Jobs to put together a product-development team that could produce the device in a very short time—less than a year. Rubinstein recruited a group of about fifty hardware and software engineers, including some from outside the company, without any of them knowing exactly what they were working on. But eventually they knew 'they were designing what was in effect a computer platform that could be improved with software upgrades and adapted to other uses'.[73] The iPod was part of Apple's 'Digital Hub' strategy for the Macintosh, which brought together a number of different applications that could link together, for example video and music editing, digital photo management, as well as downloading and transferring of content. To this end a development division was set up which focused on such cross-functional applications.

But an important innovative element was the holistic design of the iPod itself, which was the outcome of the bringing together of the capabilities of Apple's chief designer, Jonathan Ive, and the perfectionism of Steve Jobs. This resulted in the combination of must-have looks and functionality that Apple, almost uniquely, appears able to achieve.

Since the iPod was first launched it has gone through a number of incremental improvements (see Real-life Application 4.5) resulting in models of smaller size and greater capacity. It has also clearly influenced a more recent Apple product, the iPhone.

In 2005 Apple announced that it was setting up a separate division centred on the iPod, which was intended to create a developer community around the product.

Worked Example 10.1   Assessing innovation structures at Sony

There are question marks over the costs of the development of two of Sony's newest products, the Blu-ray disc and the PS3. These are arguably examples of products that are ripe for being brought down by competitors' technologies and products, such as Nintendo's Wii.

Sony's CEO, Sir Howard Stringer, has gone on record as saying that Sony had become 'so decentralized—so not interconnected'[74] that its knowledge was located in silos that needed to be broken down if it was to continue to develop world-beating new products. Sony had developed the 'Network Walkman', a digital music player two years before the iPod was launched. In theory it should have had the same functionality as the iPod, but, 'because the engineers and the software developers apparently were never introduced, getting the music into the player was laughably cumbersome',[75] and it was withdrawn. And Sir Howard has also made a concerted effort to cut back the number of products and technologies that the company has—'you have a hundred and sixty thousand employees and a thousand products and you're pulled every which way'.[76] He is said to look enviously at Apple with its lone 'six products'. So Sony recently has cut back on the number of areas in which it undertakes R&D.

However Sony's annual reports consistently report on the firm's desire to create novel and unique products, and innovation still appears to be a core element in its corporate DNA. Sony mixes regular reinvention of their main businesses (recent developments are based around the Cell processor, digital camera sensors, and digitization and networking technologies), incremental improvements to existing products within the local divisions, and radical new product development. Business units focus on a small number of core technologies, which fuel product development in each of these areas. However, radically new technological and knowledge development—'blue sky' projects—are carried out in units that report directly to the CEO.

Sony also appears to be becoming less insular. Like Apple, it is embracing a model of innovation development that is becoming increasingly prevalent: collaborative partnerships with other specialists—innovation networks. These bring together expertise from many different organizations, sometimes across international boundaries, although they are often located within a narrow geographical area. In Sony's case, the Blu-ray DVD format and the Cell processor which is a key component of the PS3, were developed with partners that included IBM and Toshiba.

c. Open innovation

The use of extra-organizational communities to develop innovation in an 'open' model[77] has emerged as a variant of the open-source software model, where products such as Linux have been developed using a wide net of participants, many of whom have no affiliation to any single organization and can be located in any part of the world. Open-source software development can take place because of the nature of software—and because of an infrastructure, the internet, which allows its swift and easy transfer. The development of innovative tangible products using the same principles is harder, yet many industries are beginning to embrace a similar model. They include film and TV, IT and telecommunications hardware, pharmaceuticals, military weapons and communications systems, financial services, and consumer packaged goods.[78]

The reasons behind the move are simple: it is believed that many of today's innovations require knowledge and inputs from a wider variety of people and technologies than can be found within a single organization, or even nation. Some estimates suggest that 80 per cent of large companies across different industries now use external sources of innovation.[79]

An open innovation model also recognizes that companies may develop innovations that they are unable to exploit, and which therefore represent a wasted resource. In some cases, this may be used to benefit the public good. Sony has made available software from its Aibo robot 'pet' dog project in order to aid the development of knowledge in robotics, a research area that it has pulled back from.

Consumer goods firm Procter & Gamble now has a 'director of external innovation' and has set a goal of sourcing 50 per cent of its innovations from outside the company in five years. The company has also instituted a policy of offering ideas from its labs to outside firms if these ideas are not used internally within three years.[80] Another example is DSM, which

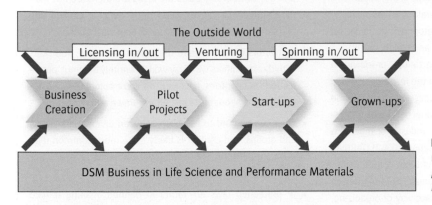

Figure 10.5 DSM's open innovation model. *Reproduced with the kind permission of the Industrial Research Institute Inc.*

was founded in 1902 as the coal mining company Dutch State Mines but has since been transformed into a multinational life sciences and performance materials company with sales of €8bn. This has come about as a result of a stream of innovations in its competences and technologies. It embraces an open innovation model in which various contact points are set up with the 'outside world' in order to gain access to knowledge, but also to exploit new ideas (Figure 10.5).[81]

Open innovation also allows companies to experiment with new ideas without damaging their brand or reputation. Google has a separate Web page, mashedup.com, where it tries things out under another name to see how customers react, although it also has experimental ideas on its home page under the Google Labs section.[82]

However, open innovation is not for all companies, and there are some real problems to be overcome in managing the process (see Theoretical Debate 10.1). As with innovative architectures, some companies are better at it than others. Those that succeed are likely to have developed core competences in managing alliances and networks of innovators, ensuring that the separate parts of the innovation process fit together coherently. Boeing and Airbus, for example, create the overall design of an aircraft and coordinate its manufacture, but let other companies, or other parts of the consortium in Airbus' case, develop its constituent parts. They have strong competences in relationship management—although Airbus' recent experiences (see What Can Go Wrong 6.1) show how difficult this can be, especially in an international context.

 Theoretical Debate 10.1 Whither innovation?

Historically, there have been many scholars who have attempted to identify the best way for innovation to be developed. Schumpeter (1950) suggested that large firms operating within largely oligopolistic industries were more likely to pursue a radical innovation strategy. Subsequently many others have recognized the important role that large organizations have played in the development of radical innovations (Acs and Audretsch, 1987; Pavitt, 1991; Rothaermel, 2001). Those advocating this model suggest that it is only large organizations that have the resources to fund large R&D budgets and provide the necessary innovation-enabling infrastructure. The company can also control each step of the process, and ensure coordination and collaboration.

Scholars working in the core competence and strategic resource-based tradition also implicitly support this approach.

Any innovations that firms develop are kept a closely guarded—imitable—secret, protected if necessary by patents or other forms of IPR protection mechanisms. Such innovations form the basis of new core products, and the learning and knowledge that went into their development form core competences and capabilities that can be used to develop further new products and services.

A contradictory view has been taken by scholars such as Tripsas and Gavetti (2000), and Hannan and Freeman (1984), who suggest that larger firms are less likely to develop radical innovations, preferring an incremental approach. Instead, they suggest that new entrants and smaller firms are more likely to develop radical innovations. This is a way of combating the market power and production efficiency advantages of the incumbents (Henderson and Clark, 1990; Hill and Rothaermel, 2003), but is also because ➜

→ the inertial forces associated with large-scale operations, established revenue streams, and supplier relationships are likely to block the consideration or effective development of radical, i.e. deviant, ideas (Kirton, 1984; Sadler-Smith and Badger, 1998).

So firms have a dilemma: smaller organizations, or individual inventors, unlike larger firms, do not have the resources needed to commercialize radical innovations successfully, but they do have the ideas and the culture that may allow new ideas to blossom. Clusters such as the UK's racing car industry or high-tech firms in California's Silicon Valley (see Section 10.4.2) (Tallman et al., 1999; Jenkins et al., 2004; Pinch and Henry, 1999; Porter, 1998; Romanelli and Khessina, 2005; Saxenian, 1994; Audretsch and Feldman, 1996) provide an intermediate way of organizing, bringing together the necessary innovation-development resources in a concentrated area whilst allowing smaller companies the ability to retain their independence and diverse cultures.

Now another 'third way' has been proposed—open innovation, in which individuals and smaller communities of idea generators and developers (sometimes located in firms, but sometimes not) can come together to develop new products. Their development involves the drawing together and building upon of a range of ideas, knowledge and resources dispersed across organization and territory (Storper, 1996; von Hippel, 1998; Lundvall, 1992, 1998; Dewar and Dutton, 1986).

At its most extreme, collaborative partnerships in an open innovation model can include anyone that wishes to participate in the new product development process—a firm's competitors and customers as well as non-aligned individuals. 'Creation networks' or 'creation nets', use internet portals or discussion sites, as well as other physical methods such as workshops, to bring together perhaps thousands of people to work on the development of a new product. This is most obviously seen in the development of new software products, but has also been used to develop motorcycles in China and consumer electronics products in Taiwan, as well as in the development of surfboards (Brown and Hagel, 2006).

Open innovation's proponents focus on the many major firms of the recent past that have encountered strong competition from 'upstarts'. Cisco Systems, which at the beginning lacked the strong internal R&D capabilities of Bell Labs, nevertheless managed to compete successfully with it through acquiring technology from the outside, in the form of partnerships or investing in promising start-ups. They argue that the 'open' and 'closed' models of innovation can both weed out 'false positives'—products that look promising but fail in the market-place. However, open innovation also has the ability to identify and recover 'false negatives': projects that seem to lack promise but subsequently turn out to be enormously rewarding—for someone else. A prime example of this is Xerox's PC—see What Can Go Wrong 10.1.[83]

However, open innovation is not without its difficulties—and its critics:

- Although the concept of a 'market-place for ideas' is attractive in theory, it is 'devilishly tricky to accomplish' in practice (Chesbrough, 2003b). Ideas are plentiful, but their very abundance makes good ones difficult to find and extract from the many irrelevant or poor-quality ones.

- Innovators must integrate their ideas, expertise, and skills with those of others who may work in entirely different organizations or countries, have very different objectives, and different ideas about costs and effort (Brown and Hagel, 2006).

- Trust can be hard to establish between diverse individuals and groups, and conflict is likely to be more common than in an organization where employees, at some level at least, share common values.

- IP protection laws are rather ill defined, making it hard for open innovators to define responsibility and allocate rewards. Firms are unlikely to want to spend money on R&D if the results are also available to rival firms (West and Gallagher, 2006; Jacobides and Billinger, 2006).

- Some of the principles of open innovation seem paradoxical, such as not taking legal action against owners of pirated copies of software in certain markets (China for example, which has under-developed IP laws) or patent 'trolls'[84] (Abril and Plant, 2007). It is therefore likely to encounter resistance from managers in established—conventional—companies.

- A coordinator, or orchestrator, is needed—along with a 'precise set of institutional mechanisms to make clear who assembles the network, who can participate in it, how disputes will be resolved, and how performance will be measured' (Brown and Hagel, 2006).

- Companies that wish to coordinate an open innovation network have to find a way of making themselves more attractive to network participants, against the competing entreaties of other companies. These attractors may take the forms of better manufacturing capacity, distribution channels, marketing muscle, reputation, and synergies with existing competencies, technologies, or products (Fetterhoff and Voelkel, 2006).

- Somebody still has to undertake the 'arduous work necessary to convert promising research results into products and services that satisfy customers' needs' (Chesbrough, 2003b) and assemble the resources and complementary assets that are needed to commercialize an innovation successfully.

Perhaps for these reasons, open innovation, despite the apparent increase in popularity claimed by its proponents, is by no means yet a mainstream model of innovation development. And one interesting move is from Apple, which in 2006 set up an iPod open-forum developer community. It had already used a group of developers under the organization of a company called PortalPlayer to solve the problems of delivering inexpensive high-quality audio for small spaces. But at the time of writing there are indications that it has had second thoughts, and has backed off from working with an open developer community (Segan, 2007).

10.4.3 Innovation in processes and systems

Up to now, we have mostly talked about product innovation. But some organizations have innovated in other ways and introduced new business models,[85] for example introducing a value chain that is radically different from competitors'. In doing this they can change the rules of competition in their industries. This is sometimes known as 'strategic innovation', and examples include:

- Dell, which pioneered the online ordering and customization of computers;

- PEOPLExpress, which pioneered the no-frills airline model later refined by Southwest Airlines in the USA and Ryanair in Europe. This innovative value chain was designed for high asset utilization: flying to little-used airports so that planes could be turned around quickly, using just one type of aircraft in the fleet to keep maintenance costs down, and not serving meals on board so that time was not wasted readying the plane between landing and take-off;

- Amazon.com, which was the first major internet bookseller (set up in 1995), and a pioneer of the online ordering and postal delivery of books. Along with the new concept of internet selling, the value chain that it set up in order to fulfil its orders was also highly innovative.

The most likely reaction from competitors is to wait and see if the new value chain succeeds. If it does, then they can start to build a similar value chain. In the mean time, however, the originator has a breathing space in which it can accumulate financial resources and build a reputation and distinctive capabilities in operating its innovative value chain. Even if the value chain is eventually copied, its inventor will probably retain first mover advantage.

However, as with other innovations there are risks. For many years Amazon.com was unprofitable, and could, if it had not had sympathetic investors, have gone out of business. Indeed, for years, many commentators were questioning its viability. As it has turned out, Amazon has been successful, and will probably reap the rewards of its risk-taking for many years to come.

 Using Evidence 10.1 **Assessing innovation**

As with learning (see earlier this chapter) innovation needs to be assessed in the light of both inputs and outcomes.

In the case of inputs, R&D spend as a percentage of revenue is a well-accepted measure of how much effort an organization is investing in innovation. The actual size of the R&D activity in terms of people employed there can also give some clues. More qualitative measures, such as the existence of websites, communities of practice, reward schemes, and other elements of architecture designed to stimulate innovation, will also be of interest.

When it comes to outcomes, on the other hand, researchers in the field of innovation tend to use measures such as the number of patents a company produces. Innovative companies have been known to set themselves targets relating to the proportion of profits (or sometimes revenues) generated by products introduced in, say, the last two years (the number of years can vary to suit the innovation cycle of the industry). But one simple measure is to count the number of genuine innovations a company produces, and how frequently they arrive.

What Can Go Wrong 10.1 Xerox and the Palo Alto Research Center

One of the companies whose brand name would be close to being genericized (see Section 10.3 above) if it was not proactive in protecting it, is Xerox, which is almost synonymous with paper copying. It also appears regularly in the 'most admired' lists, as do its personnel, and its Palo Alto Research Center (PARC) is legendary as the base of some of the brightest and best innovators in the IT industry. It was created in 1970 to carry out research in computing and electronics and to study 'the architecture of information'—how complex organizations use information.[86] It is located close to Stanford University near San Francisco in California, and is one of the key institutions that make up 'Silicon Valley'.

Yet PARC is also famous for what has gone wrong. It has long been held up as 'a prime example of how hard it is to translate cutting edge research into product improvements'.[87] Although Xerox invented the laser printer, and made billions from it, it is also notorious for having failed to capitalize on many of the other innovations that it developed at PARC in the 1970s and 1980s. These include:[88]

- the personal computer (the 'Star' model);
- bit-map display technologies that underpin graphic user interfaces (GUI);
- overlapping screen windows;
- the computer mouse;
- Smalltalk, the first object-oriented programming language;
- the first non-expert word processing program;
- the ethernet (then known as the Arpanet, which was developed to allow staff in Xerox' two facilities, El Segundo and Palo Alto, to 'talk' to one another).

Most of these innovations are now fundamental elements in other companies' computers and information-processing technologies. Thus Xerox also has the reputation of having made fortunes for others, but little for its parent: 'Xerox's unused technology has spilled all over Silicon Valley, feeding start-up firms from Apple to Sun Microsystems to Novell'.[89] Silicon Valley lore has it that Apple's founder CE, Steve Jobs, visited PARC in the early days and realized the value of those applications, which were then incorporated into the design of Apple computers.[90]

So one of the criticisms focuses on Xerox' failure to protect its own intellectual property, through patenting its inventions. However, some commentators point out that Xerox was prevented from doing this at the time by a government anti-trust action that placed restrictions on what the company was able to patent,[91] as well as being distracted by developing patents in other new, complicated and untested areas.

But the main body of criticisms focus on Xerox' inability to exploit its own innovations. A number of reasons are put forward

to explain this; most appear to agree that it was the parent company's fault rather than PARC's:

- In 1969 Xerox bought a computer maker, Scientific Data Systems, that quickly became a financial millstone,[92] meaning that management attention was almost certainly distracted at a time that Xerox could have been focusing on marketing its new products.

- Xerox saw itself solely as a company that made copiers when rivals were transforming themselves into broader-based information-handling companies. This meant that there were few supporters in the mainstream company who were interested enough in what PARC was doing to overcome the very real hurdles that would have got in the way of commercializing what they did. There were said to be internal jealousies between the copier divisions and the 'upstart' computer division, meaning that marketing efforts were less than wholehearted. And the reward systems, which paid large bonuses to sales staff on the sale of leases of printers that cost up to $500m, did not promote the selling of stand-alone computers.

- The researchers at PARC were 'treated like inmates of a zoo—admired and fed but rarely let loose'.[93] The one time that a PARC innovation, laser imaging, became a successful multi-billion dollar business for its parent, it was because it had a champion in the laboratory, Robert Adams, who moved with it to Xerox and pushed the commercialization hard.

- The researchers at PARC worked on young, and therefore *pre*mature, ideas, that needed to be supported by incorporation into wider commercial applications. They also worked independently on digital technologies without a great deal of parental control or coordination of their efforts into a coherent 'whole'.

Some of the most trenchant criticisms are reserved for Xerox' early computers. The first real PC, the Alto, was a workstation initially developed for internal use at Xerox, and also distributed to a few universities. The Alto had many of the advanced features described above. But as a commercial product, it was a failure. Every application required sophisticated knowledge on the part of users, and, crucially, the Alto did not offer any spreadsheet or database programs. It was followed in 1981 by the Star computer, which was not developed by PARC, but in Xerox' Systems Development Department (SDD) in El Segundo, 200 miles from Palo Alto. Ethernet technologies helped communications between the two sites, but having a development organization that was split between Palo Alto and El Segundo was 'probably a mistake', not only because of distance but because of SDD's lack of shared background in 'PARC-style' computing.[94] →

→ The Star was not a stand-alone computer, but formed part of an integrated 'personal office system', in which the Star was networked to other computers and printers. A single unit sold for $16,000; however, a typical office would have to purchase at least two or three machines along with a file server and a print server, which cost a total of $50,000 to $100,000. This was not easy to sell, and only 25,000 or so units were sold.[95] Partly driven by excitement over what they were doing, Star's developers 'didn't pay enough attention to the "other" personal computer revolution that was occurring outside of Xerox'. Blinded by its own powerful technical tradition, Star's designers failed to notice customers' needs for cheap, stand-alone PCs.[96] Xerox also chose to keep the Star's technologies proprietary for fear of losing its competitive advantage,[97] but doing so prevented them from being taken up by complementors and from becoming industry standards.

There were also applications problems—the complexity of the software overwhelmed the Star's limited hardware capabilities. At one point, it would take more than half an hour to reboot the system. Saving a large file could take minutes, and crashes could be followed by an hours-long process called 'scavenging'.[98] It also didn't have the functionality customers wanted. Like the Alto it initially lacked a spreadsheet program, which, given its intended use as an office-based system, was a critical problem.

A book that outlined some of the difficulties that Xerox had encountered, *Fumbling the Future*, was published in 1988, and the impact of this book 'reverberated throughout Xerox'.[99] In response to the problems outlined by its authors, Xerox decided to improve its ability to profit from technology that was not utilized in its core businesses and Xerox Technology Ventures (XTV) was set up in 1989, under the leadership of Robert Adams, the original champion of the laser printer. It was given $30m to nurture projects that didn't fit within the parent firm and turn them into commercial ventures, much like an internal venture capital firm. If turned down by Xerox, engineers with a bright idea could take their project to Mr Adams's 'intrapreneurs' at XTV.[100] PARC also became 'more tightly coupled' with the mainstream company.[101]

● CHAPTER SUMMARY

This chapter has introduced you to some of the issues to do with the acquisition and use of knowledge in an organization, how organizations learn, and the management of innovation.

Knowledge, which is distinct from data or information, is embedded in organizational routines and practices as well as in knowledge repositories. It comes in different forms:

- codified—narrative or explicit—knowledge goes into documents and instruction manuals;
- embodied knowledge is physical and developed through experience and practical learning;
- tacit knowledge is unconsciously held. Because its 'owners' are often unaware of what they know, it can often be a source of competitive advantage;
- symbolic knowledge is communicated only between people that are already sensitized to its meaning.

These different types of knowledge are transmitted in different ways. Knowledge can be developed through internal development and also through alliances and acquisitions. Organizations that are especially skilled at developing, disseminating, and utilizing knowledge can be characterized as learning organizations. Not only do such organizations learn how to solve problems, they are also skilled at examining the underlying causes of problems and amending what they do accordingly—in a form of 'double-loop learning'. Learning organizations have a number of characteristics such as an open and self-critical culture, high levels of absorptive capacity, and systems and processes that encourage learning.

However it is possible to fall into learning 'traps'. A firm may focus too much on learning and experimentation, and neglect to exploit its existing products. Or it may misinterpret the causes of good performance—superstitious learning.

One important way in which knowledge is obtained is through alliances and acquisitions. However, this may lead to 'learning races', in which one company gains more knowledge than its partner.

Because knowledge is a source of competitive advantage, firms need to protect it. This may be done by means of IPR mechanisms such as brands, patents, and copyright. Firms also need to deploy knowledge effectively; this can be done through knowledge management systems such as knowledge repositories, and a culture and architecture that encourages the sharing of knowledge.

One of the most important benefits of organizational knowledge is when it is used to develop innovative products or business models. Innovation may be categorized as radical or incremental, continuous or discontinuous, and may relate to products, processes, or technologies. For successful innovators, there can be significant benefits. But not all innovations succeed, and there are considerable costs and risks in developing radically new products or ways of doing business. These include the costs and time-scales for development, which are often greater than expected, the unpredictability of take-up, and the disruption to existing products and services.

For those organizations who do wish to innovate, there are some features—both inside the organization and external to it—that are known to be supportive of innovation development. An innovative-supportive environment, such as the one in Silicon Valley in California, can help. So can relationships with external partners which allow each partner to specialize in a particular technology or product, and maintain a dedicated culture and value chain. A recent extension of this model is the concept of open innovation, in which outside individuals and firms contribute to the development of a new product, and its exploitation is shared.

But for firms that wish to develop innovation 'in-house', a number of features appear beneficial, including the availability of resources, a supportive culture, systems that allow new ideas to be recognized and developed, and most important of all, top management commitment to innovation.

Online Resource Centre

www.oxfordtextbooks.co.uk/orc/haberberg_rieple/

Visit the Online Resource Centre that accompanies this book to read more information relating to knowledge, learning, and innovation.

● KEY SKILLS

The key skills you should have developed after reading this chapter are:

- the ability to assess whether an organization has the attributes of a learning organization, and know-how that impacts on its ability to acquire and deploy knowledge;
- the ability to identify the different types of innovation at work in an industry;
- the ability to propose ways in which an organization can configure itself so as to become more innovative.

● REVIEW QUESTIONS

1. Consider the importance of collaborating knowledge, learning and innovation. For instance, could the Apple iPod (Real-life Application 10.6 and also Real-life Application 4.5) have been developed by Apple alone? What might have stopped this happening?

2. How important is location of resources? Consider whether Google could have become the dominant search engine if it had not been based in Silicon Valley.

3. Discuss why a company might cut back on the number and scope of its products and technologies. What would the advantages and disadvantages be? How might a company generate value from its redundant products and technologies?

4. Which companies would you consider to be innovative and why? For instance, how far are Amazon, IBM, McDonald's, or H&M innovative companies?

5. Pick an organization that you know well. How could it improve the way that it develops and deploys its knowledge?

FURTHER READING

- Dierkes, M., Antal, A., Child, J., and Nonaka, I. (eds) (2001). *Handbook of Organizational Learning and Knowledge*. Oxford, Oxford University Press provides a comprehensive series of articles by some of the major theorists in the field.

- For a concise recent summary of the state of the field of organizational learning and knowledge management see Argyris, C. (2004). 'Reflection and beyond in research on organizational learning'. *Management Learning*, 35/4: 507–9.

- Adams, R., Bessant, J., and Phelps, R. (2006). 'Innovation management measurement: a review'. *International Journal of Management Reviews*, 8/1: 21–47 provides an excellent review of the management and measurement of innovation.

- Christensen, C. M. (1997). *The Innovator's Dilemma*. Boston, MA: Harvard Business School Press and Christensen, C. M. and Raynor, M. E. (2003). *Innovator's Solution*. Boston, MA: Harvard Business School Press discuss the power of disruptive innovations.

- As an example of openness in the practice of publishing about innovation see von Hippel, E. (1998). *Sources of Innovation*. Oxford, Oxford University Press and von Hippel, E. (2005). *Democratizing Innovation*. Cambridge, MA: MIT Press. Both are available in full text from <http://web.mit.edu/evhippel/www/books.htm>, accessed 5 March 2007.

- Chesbrough, H. W. (2003). *Open Innovation: The New Imperative for Creating and Profiting from Technology*. Cambridge, MA: Harvard Business School Press is the book that introduced the idea of open innovation and open business models to the world. Chesbrough, H., Vanhaverbeke, W., and West, J. (eds) (2006). *Open Innovation: Researching a New Paradigm*. Oxford: Oxford University Press brings together many of the main writers on the topic of open innovation.

REFERENCES

Abril, P. S. and Plant, R. (2007). 'The patent holder's dilemma: buy, sell, or troll?' *Communications of the ACM*, 50/1: 37–44.

Acs, Z. and Audretsch, D. B. (1987). 'Innovation, market structure and firm size'. *The Review of Economics and Statistics*, 69/4: 567–74.

Adams, R., Bessant, J., and Phelps, R. (2006). 'Innovation management measurement: a review'. *International Journal of Management Reviews*, 8/1: 21–47.

Adner, R. (2002). 'When are technologies disruptive: a demand-based view of the emergence of competition'. *Strategic Management Journal*, 23/8: 667.

Adner, R. and Zemsky, P. (2005). 'Disruptive technologies and the emergence of competition'. *RAND Journal of Economics*, 36/2: 229–54.

Amabile, T. M. (1983). *The Social Psychology of Creativity*. New York: Springer-Verlag.

Amabile, T. M. (1988). 'A model of creativity and innovation in organizations'. In Staw, B. M. and Cummings, L. L. (eds), *Research in Organizational Behavior*. Greenwich, CT: JAI Press, vol. 10, 123–67.

Amabile, T. M., Hill, K. G., Hennessey, B. A., and Tighe, E. M. (1994). 'The work preference inventory: assessing intrinsic and extrinsic motivation orientations'. *Journal of Personality and Social Psychology*, 66: 950–67.

Archibugi, D. and Coco, A. (2005). 'Is Europe becoming the most dynamic knowledge economy in the world?' *Journal of Common Market Studies*, 43/3: 433–59.

Argyris, C. (1976). 'Single-loop and double-loop models in research on decision making'. *Administrative Science Quarterly*, 21/3: 363.

Argyris, C. (2004). 'Reflection and beyond in research on organizational learning'. *Management Learning*, 35/4: 507–9.

Argyris, C. and Schön, D. A. (1978). *Organizational Learning: A Theory of Action Perspective*. Reading, MA: Addison Wesley.

Argyris, C. and Schön, D. A. (1996). *Organizational Learning II: Theory, Method and Practice*. Reading, MA: Addison Wesley.

Asheim, B. T. and Gertler, M. S. (2005). 'The geography of innovation; regional innovation systems'. In Fagerberg, J., Mowery, D. C., Nelson, R. R. (eds), *The Oxford Handbook of Innovation*. Oxford: Oxford University Press, 291–317.

Audia, P. G. and Goncalo, J. A. (2007). 'Past success and creativity over time: a study of inventors in the hard disk drive industry'. *Management Science*, 53/1: 1–15.

Audretsch, D. B. and Feldman M. P. (1996). 'R&D spillovers and the geography of innovation and production'. *American Economic Review*, 86: 630–40.

Benner, M. J. and Tushman, M. L. (2003). 'Exploitation, exploration, and process management: the productivity dilemma revisited'. *Academy of Management Review*, 28/2: 238–56.

Berkhout, A. J., Hartmann, D., van der Duin, P., and Ortt, R. (2006). 'Innovating the innovation process'. *International Journal of Technology Management*, 34/3–4: 390–404.

Biggadike, R. (1979). 'The risky business of diversification'. *Harvard Business Review*, May/June: 103–11.

Boersma, A. (2006). 'Protecting intellectual assets in China'. *KM Review*, 9/31: 22–5.

Boisot, M. (2006). 'How much knowledge should a business give away?' *European Business Forum*, 24, Spring.

Brown, J. S. and Duguid, P. (1991). 'Organizational learning and communities of practice: toward a unified view of working, learning and innovation'. *Organization Science*, 2/1: 40–57.

Brown, J. S. and Hagel, J. (2006). 'Creation nets: getting the most from open innovation'. *McKinsey Quarterly*, 2: 40–51.

Brown, S. L. and Eisenhardt, K. M. (1997). 'The art of continuous change: linking complexity theory and time-paced evolution in relentlessly shifting organizations'. *Administrative Science Quarterly*, 42/1: 1–34.

Brown, T. and Srikanthan, S. (1999). 'Building commercial viability into pharmaceuticals in research and development, and increasing their value to shareholders'. *European Pharmaceutical Contractor*, November: 96–101.

Burgelman, R. (1983). 'A process model of internal corporate venturing in the diversified major firm'. *Administrative Science Quarterly*, 28/2: 223–44.

Burgelman, R. (1984). 'Managing the internal corporate venturing process'. *Sloan Management Review*, 25/2: 33–48.

Burgelman, R. A. and Sayles, L. R. (1986). *Inside Corporate Innovation: Strategy, Structure and Managerial Skills*. New York: Free Press.

Chesbrough, H. W. (2003a). *Open Innovation: The New Imperative for Creating and Profiting from Technology*. Cambridge, MA: Harvard Business School Press Books.

Chesbrough, H. W. (2003b). 'The era of open innovation'. *MIT Sloan Management Review*, 44/3: 35–41.

Chesbrough, H. W. (2003c). 'The logic of open innovation: managing intellectual property'. *California Management Review*, 45/3: 33–58.

Chesbrough, H. W. (2004). 'Managing open innovation'. *Research Technology Management*, 47/1: 23–6.

Chesbrough, H. W. (2007). 'Why companies should have open business models'. *MIT Sloan Management Review*, 48/2: 22–8.

Chesbrough, H. W. and Socolof, S. J. (2000). 'Creating new ventures from Bell Labs technologies'. *Research Technology Management*, 43/2: 13.

Chesborough, H. W. and Teece, D. J. (1996). 'When is virtual virtuous? Organizing for innovation'. *Harvard Business Review*, 74/1: 65–73.

Chesbrough, H. and Crowther, A. K. (2006). 'Beyond high tech: early adopters of open innovation in other industries'. *R&D Management*, 36/3: 229–36.

Chesbrough, H. and Schwartz, K. (2007). 'Innovating business models with co-development partnerships'. *Research Technology Management*, 50/1: 55–9.

Chesbrough, H., Vanhaverbeke, W., and West, J. (eds) (2006). *Open Innovation: Researching a New Paradigm*. Oxford: Oxford University Press.

Chong Siong, C., Wong Kuan, Y., and Binshan, L. (2006). 'Criteria for measuring KM performance outcomes in organisations'. *Industrial Management & Data Systems*, 106/7: 917–36.

Christensen, C. M. (1997). *The Innovator's Dilemma*. Boston, MA: Harvard Business School Press.

Christensen, C. M. and Overdorf, M. (2000). 'Meeting the challenge of disruptive change'. *Harvard Business Review*, 78/1: 67–76.

Christensen, C. M. and Raynor, M. E. (2003). *The Innovator's Solution*. Boston: Harvard Business School Press.

Christensen, J. F., Olesen, M. H., and Kjær, J. S. (2005). 'The industrial dynamics of open innovation: evidence from the transformation of consumer electronics'. *Research Policy*, 34/10: 1533–49.

Cohen, W. and Levinthal, D. (1990). 'Absorptive capacity: a new perspective on learning and innovation'. *Administrative Science Quarterly*, 35/1: 128–52.

Cooke, P. (2005). 'Regionally asymmetric knowledge capabilities and open innovation: exploring globalisation: a new model of industry organisation'. *Research Policy*, 34/8: 1128–49.

Covin, J. G. and Miles, M. P. (2007). 'Strategic use of corporate venturing'. *Entrepreneurship: Theory & Practice*, 31/2: 183–207.

Cox, J. (2007). 'Qualcomm races to retool the mobile phone'. *Network World*, 24/8: 26.

Crawford, C. (1979). 'New product failure rates: facts and fallacies'. *Research Management*, September: 9–13.

Crossan, M. M., Lane, H. W., and White, R. E. (1999). 'An organizational learning framework: From intuition to institution'. *Academy of Management Review*, 24: 522–37.

Danneels, E. (2002). 'The dynamics of product innovation and firm competences'. *Strategic Management Journal*, 23, 1095–121.

Danneels, E. (2004). 'Disruptive technology reconsidered: a critique and research agenda'. *Journal of Product Innovation Management*, 21/4: 246–58.

Das, T. K. and Teng, B.-S. (2000). 'Instabilities of strategic alliances: an internal tensions perspective'. *Organization Science*, 11/1: 77.

Davenport, T., De Long, D., and Beers, M. (1998). 'Successful knowledge management projects'. *Sloan Management Review*, Winter: 43–57.

Dewar, R. and Dutton, J. (1986). 'The adoption of radical and incremental innovations: an empirical analysis'. *Management Science*, 32/11: 1422–33.

Dierkes, M., Antal, A., Child, J., and Nonaka, I. (eds) (2001). *Handbook of Organizational Learning and Knowledge*. Oxford: Oxford University Press.

DiMasi, J. (1995). 'Success Rates for New Drugs Entering Clinical Testing in the United States'.

Clinical Pharmacology and Therapeutics. Vol. 8(1).

DMSTI (2003a). *Analysing Intellectual Capital Statements*. Copenhagen: Danish Ministry of Science, Technology and Innovation.

DMSTI (2003b). *Intellectual Capital Statements: The New Guideline*. Copenhagen: Denmark. Danish Ministry of Science, Technology and Innovation.

Dodgson, M., Gann, D., and Salter, A. (2006). 'The role of technology in the shift towards open innovation: the case of Procter & Gamble'. *R&D Management*, 36/3: 333–346.

Drazin, R. and Schoonhoven, C. (1996). 'Community, population, and organization effects on innovation: a multilevel perspective'. *Academy of Management Journal*, 39: 1065–83.

Drazin, R., Glynn, M., and Kazanjian, R. (1999). 'Multilevel theorizing about creativity in organizations: A sensemaking perspective'. *Academy of Management Review*, 24/2: 286–307.

Easingwood, C., Moxey, S., and Capleton, H. (2006). 'Bringing high technology to market: successful strategies employed in the worldwide software industry'. *Journal of Product Innovation Management*, 23/6: 498–511.

Economist, The (1997). 'In-line skating in the 4x4'. 22 March.

Economist, The (1999). 'Silicon envy'. 20 February.

Economist Intelligence Unit (2004). 'Scattering the seeds of invention: the globalisation of research and development', available from <http://graphics.eiu.com/files/ad_pdfs/RnD_GLOBILISATION_WHITEPAPER.pdf>, accessed 14 February 2007.

Edvinsson, L. (1994). *Intellectual Capital*. Skandia, Stockholm, Sweden.

Edvinsson, L. (1997). 'Developing intellectual capital at Skandia'. *Long Range Planning*, 30/3: 366–73.

Edvinsson, L. and Malone, M. (1997). *Intellectual Capital*, London: Piatkus.

Enkel, E., Perez-Freije, J., and Gassmann, O. (2005). 'Minimizing market risks through customer integration in new product development: learning from bad practice'. *Creativity and Innovation Management*, 14/4: 425–437.

Fagerberg, J., Mowery, D. C., Nelson, R. R. (eds) (2005). *The Oxford Handbook of Innovation*. Oxford: Oxford University Press.

Fetterhoff, T. J. and Voelkel, D. (2006). 'Managing open innovation in biotechnology'. *Research Technology Management*, 49/3: 14–18.

Freiberg, K. and Freiberg, J. (1998). *Nuts! Southwest Airlines' Crazy Recipe for Business and Personal Success*. London: Orion Business Books.

Gander, J., Haberberg, A., and Rieple, A. (2007). 'A paradox of alliance management: resource contamination in the recorded music industry'. *Journal of Organization Behaviour*, 28: 1–18.

Garvin, D. A. (1993). 'Building a learning organization'. *Harvard Business Review*, July–August: 78–91.

Gassmann, O. (2006). 'Opening up the innovation process: towards an agenda'. *R&D Management*, 36/3: 223–228.

Geiger, S. W. and Makri, M. (2006). 'Exploration and exploitation innovation processes: the role of organizational slack in R & D intensive firms'. *Journal of High Technology Management Research*, 17/1: 97–108.

Ghoshal, S. and Bartlett, C. A. (1998). *The Individualized Corporation*. London: Heinemann.

Gilbert, C. G. (2006). 'Change in the presence of residual fit: can competing frames coexist?' *Organization Science*, 17/1: 150–67.

Govindarajan, V. and Kopalle, P. K. (2006). 'The usefulness of measuring disruptiveness of innovations ex post in making ex ante predictions'. *Journal of Product Innovation Management*, 23/1: 12–18.

Govindarajan, V. and Trimble, C. (2005). 'Organizational DNA for strategic innovation'. *California Management Review*, 47/3: 47–76.

Grabowski, H., Vernon, J. (1994). 'Returns to R&D on new drug introductions in the 1980s'. *Journal of Health Economics*, 13: 383–406.

Grant, R. M. (2004). *Contemporary Strategy Analysis*, 5th edn. Oxford: Blackwell.

Grant, R. M. and Baden-Fuller, C. (2004). 'A knowledge accessing theory of strategic alliances'. *Journal of Management Studies*, 41: 61–84.

Grant, R. M. and Neupert, K. E. (2003). 'Eastman Kodak: meeting the digital challenge'. In *Cases in Contemporary Strategy Analysis*, 3rd edn. Oxford: Blackwell Publishers, 98–121.

Groenewegen, J. and Van der Steen, M. (2006). 'The evolution of national innovation systems'. *Journal of Economic Issues*, 40/2: 277–85.

Gulati, R. (1995). 'Does familiarity breed trust? The implications of repeated ties for contractual choice in alliances'. *Academy of Management Journal*, 38/1: 85–112.

Hall, J. K. and Martin, M. J. C. (2005). 'Disruptive technologies, stakeholders and the innovation value-added chain: a framework for evaluating radical technology development'. *R&D Management*, 35/3: 273–84.

Hamel, G. (1991). 'Competition for competence and inter-partner learning within international strategic alliances'. *Strategic Management Journal*, 12 (Special Issue): 83–103.

Hannan, M. T. and Freeman, J. (1984). 'Structural inertia and organisational change'. *American Sociological Review*, 49: 149–64.

Hansen, M., Nohria, N., and Tierney, T. (1999). 'What's your strategy for managing knowledge?' *Harvard Business Review*, 77/2: 106–16.

Henderson, K. and Clark, R. (1990). 'Architectural innovation: the reconfiguration of existing product technologies and the failure of established firms'. *Administrative Science Quarterly*, 35/1: 9–30.

Henderson, R. (2006). 'The innovator's dilemma as a problem of organizational competence'. *Journal of Product Innovation Management*, 23/1: 5–11.

Hennart, J.-F., Roehl, T., and Zietlow, D. S. (1999). '"Trojan horse" or "workhorse"? The evolution of US–Japanese joint ventures in the United States'. *Strategic Management Journal*, 20: 15–29.

Higgins, J. M. and McAllaster, C. (2002). 'Want innovation? Then use cultural artifacts that support it'. *Organizational Dynamics*, 31/1: 74–84.

Hill, C. and Rothaermel, F. (2003). 'The performance of incumbent firms in the face of radical technological innovation'. *Academy of Management Review*, 28/2: 257–74.

von Hippel, E. (1998). *Sources of Innovation*. Oxford: Oxford University Press.

von Hippel, E. (2005). *Democratizing Innovation*. Cambridge, MA: MIT Press.

Hofstede, G. (1980). *Culture's Consequences*. London: Sage. 2nd edn (2001).

Inkpen, A. C., Sundaram, A. K., and Rockwood, K. (2000). 'Cross-border acquisitions of US technology assets'. *California Management Review*, 2/3: 50–71.

Jacobides, M. G. and Billinger, S. (2006). 'Designing the boundaries of the firm: from "make, buy, or ally" to the dynamic benefits of vertical architecture'. *Organization Science*, 17/2: 249–61.

Julian, S. D. and Keller, R. T. (1991). 'Multinational R&D siting'. *Columbia Journal of World Business*, 26/3: 46–57.

Kale, P., Singh, H., and Perlmutter, H. (2000). 'Learning and protection of proprietary assets in strategic alliances: building relational capital'. *Strategic Management Journal*, 21: 217–37.

Kanter, R. M. (1985). 'Supporting innovation and venture development in established companies'. *Journal of Business Venturing*, 1: 47–60.

Kanter, R. M. (1989). 'Swimming in Newstreams: Mastering Innovation Dilemmas'. *California Management Review*, 31/4: 45–69.

Kanter, R., Richardson, L., North, J., and Zolner, J. (1991). 'Engines of progress: designing and running entrepreneurial vehicles in established companies'. *Journal of Business Venturing*, 6/3: 145–63.

Kaplan, R. S. and Norton, D. P. (1996). 'Using the balanced scorecard as a strategic management system'. *Harvard Business Review*, 74/1: 75–85.

Kaplan, R. S. and Norton, D. P. (1992). The balanced scorecard: Measures that drive performance. *Harvard Business Review*, January–February: 71–79.

Kelly, D. and Talley, M. R. (2004). 'The high price of popularity'. *Managing Intellectual Property*, 136: 57–61.

Khanna, T., Gulati, R., and Nohria, N. (1994). Alliances as learning races. *Academy of Management Proceedings*, 42–46.

Kirschbaum, R. (2005). 'Open innovation in practice'. *Research Technology Management*, 48/4: 24–8.

Kirton, M. J. (1976). 'Adaptors and innovators: a description and measure'. *Journal of Applied Psychology*, 61: 622–9.

Kirton, M. J. (1984). 'Adaptors and innovators: why new initiatives get blocked'. *Long Range Planning*, 17: 137–43.

Kirton, M. J. (1989). 'Adaptors and innovators at work'. In Kirton, M. J. (ed.), *Adaptors and Innovators: Styles of Creativity and Problem Solving*. New York: Routledge, 1–36.

Kline, S. J. and Rosenberg, N. (1986). 'An overview of innovation'. In Landau, R. and Rosenberg N. (eds), *The Positive Sum Strategy*. Washington, DC: National Academy Press.

Knibb, D. (2006). 'upGrowing'. *Airline Business*, 1 August.

Kolb, D. A. (1984). *Experiential Learning: Experience as the Source of Learning and Development*. Englewood Cliffs, NJ: Prentice-Hall.

Lakshman, C. (2005). 'Top executive knowledge leadership: managing knowledge to lead change at general electric'. *Journal of Change Management*, 5/4: 429–46.

Lavie, D. (2006). 'The competitive advantage of interconnected firms: an extension of the resource-based view'. *Academy of Management Review*, 31/3: 638–58.

Levinthal, D. A. and March, J. G. (1993). 'The myopia of learning'. *Strategic Management Journal*, 14: 95–112.

Levitt, B. and March, J. G. (1988). 'Organizational learning'. *Annual Review of Sociology*, 14: 319–40.

Lundvall, B.-A. (ed.) (1992). *National Systems of Innovation: Toward a Theory of Innovation and Interactive Learning*. New York: Pinter.

Lundvall, B.-A. (1998). 'Why study national systems and national styles of innovation?' *Technological Analysis & Strategic Management*, 10/4: 407–21.

MacMillan, I. C. and McGrath, R. G. (2004). 'Nine new roles for technology managers'. *Research Technology Management*, 47/3: 16–26.

Mc Namara, P. (2000). 'Managing the tension between knowledge exploration and exploitation: the case of UK biotechnology'. Ph.D thesis, City University Business School Library, London.

March, J. (1991). 'Exploration and exploitation in organisational learning'. *Organisational Science*, 2/1: 71–87.

Markides, C. (1997). 'Strategic Innovation'. *Sloan Management Review*, 38/3: 9–23.

Markides, C. (1998). 'Strategic innovation in established companies'. *Sloan Management Review*, 39/3: 31–42.

Markides, C. (2006). 'Disruptive innovation: in need of better theory'. *Journal of Product Innovation Management*, 23/1: 19–25.

Martin, M. J. C. (1984). *Managing Technological Innovation and Entrepreneurship*. Reston, VA: Reston Publishing.

Martin, R. and Sunley, P. (2003). 'Deconstructing clusters: chaotic concept or policy panacea?' *Journal of Economic Geography*, 3: 5–35.

Mittal, S. and Swami, S. (2004). 'What factors influence pioneering advantage of companies?' *Vikalpa*, 29/3: 15–33.

Moreno, R., Paci, R., and Usai, S. (2006). 'Innovation clusters in the European regions'. *European Planning Studies*, 14/9: 1235–63.

Mowery, D. C. and Sampat, B. N. (2005). 'Universities in national innovation systems'. In Fagerberg, J., Mowery, D. C., Nelson, R. R. (eds), *The Oxford Handbook of Innovation*. Oxford: Oxford University Press, 209–39.

Nevis, E. C., DiBella, A. J., and Gould, G. M. (1995). 'Understanding organizations as learning systems'. *Sloan Management Review*, 36/2: 73–85.

Nohria, N. and Gulati, R. (1997). 'What is the optimum amount of organizational slack?' *European Management Journal*, 15/6: 603.

Nonaka, I. (1991). 'The knowledge-creating company'. *Harvard Business Review*, 69/6: 96–104.

Nonaka, I. (1994). 'A dynamic theory of organizational knowledge creation'. *Organization Science*, 5/1: 14–37.

Nonaka, I. (1988). 'Toward middle-up-down management: Accelerating information creation'. *Sloan Management Review*, 9–18.

Nonaka, I. (1990). 'Redundant, overlapping organization: a Japanese approach to managing the innovation process'. *California Management Review*, 32/3: 27.

Nonaka, I. and Konno, N. (1998). 'The concept of "Ba": building a foundation for knowledge creation'. *California Management Review*, 40/3: 40–54.

Nonaka, I. and Takeuchi, H. (1995). *The Knowledge-Creating Company: How Japanese Companies Create the Dynamics of Innovation*. Oxford: Oxford University Press.

Nurton, J. (2002). 'How to avoid genericization'. *Managing Intellectual Property*, 123: 14.

O'Connor, G. C. and Rice, M. P. (2001). 'Opportunity recognition and breakthrough innovation in large established firms'. *California Management Review*, 43/2: 95–116.

Olleros, F. X. (2007). 'The power of non-contractual innovation'. *International Journal of Innovation Management*, 11/1: 93–113.

Pavitt, K. (1991). 'Key characteristics of the large innovating firm'. *British Journal of Management*, 2/1: 41–50.

Pavlou, A. K. and Belsey, M. (2005). 'Key financial trends that shape biotech business growth'. *Journal of Commercial Biotechnology*, 11/2: 171–5.

Peters, T. (1988). *Thriving on Chaos*. London: Macmillan.

Peters, T. and Waterman, R. (1982). *In Search of Excellence*. New York: Harper and Row.

PhARMA (1999). *Pharmaceutical Industry Profile 1999*. Washington DC: Pharmaceutical Research and Manufacturers America.

Piller, F. T. and Walcher, D. (2006). 'Toolkits for idea competitions: a novel method to integrate users in new product development'. *R&D Management*, 36/3: 307–18.

Pinch, S. and Henry, N. (1999). 'Paul Krugman's geographical economics, industrial clustering and the British motor sport industry'. *Regional Studies*, 33: 815–27.

Porter, M. (1998). 'Clusters and the new economics of competition'. *Harvard Business Review*, 76/6: 77–90.

Prokesch, S. E. (1997). 'The management of intellectual capital'. *Long Range Planning*, 30/3 (June special issue).

Quintas, P., Lefrere, P., and Jones, G. (1997). 'Knowledge management: a strategic agenda'. *Long Range Planning*, 30/3: 385–91.

Romanelli, E. and Khessina, O. (2005). 'Regional industrial identity'. *Organization Science*, 16/4: 344–58.

Roos, G. and Roos, J. (1997). 'Measuring your company's intellectual performance'. *Long Range Planning*, 30/3: 413–26.

Rothaermel, F. (2001). 'Incumbent's advantage through exploiting complementary assets via interfirm cooperation'. *Strategic Management Journal*, 22: 687–99.

Rothaermel, F. T. and Hill, C. W. L. (2005). 'Technological discontinuities and complementary assets: a longitudinal study of industry and firm performance'. *Organization Science*, 16/1: 52–70.

Sadler-Smith, E. and Badger, B. (1998). 'Cognitive style, learning and innovation'. *Technology Analysis & Strategic Management*, 10/2: 247–65.

Saxenian, A. (1994). *Regional Advantage, Culture and Competition in Silicon Valley and Route 128*. Cambridge, MA: Harvard University Press.

Schumpeter, J. (1950). *Capitalism, Socialism and Democracy*. 3rd edn. New York: Harper Perennial.

Schwartz, E. S. (2004). 'Patents and R&D as real options'. *Economic Notes*, 33/1: 23–54.

Segan, S. (2007). 'The iPhone: Mac or iPod?' *PC Magazine*, 14 February: 72.

Senge, P. (1990). *The Fifth Discipline: The Art and Practice of the Learning Organisation*. New York: Doubleday.

Shaikh, J. M. (2004). 'Measuring and reporting of intellectual capital performance analysis'. *Journal of American Academy of Business*, 4/1–2: 439–48.

Smith, D. K. and Alexander, R. C. (1988). *Fumbling the future: How Xerox Invented, Then Ignored, the First Personal Computer*. New York: W. Morrow.

Smith P. G. and Reinertsen D. G. (1991). *Developing Products in Half the Time: New Rules, New Tools*. New York: Wiley.

Storper, M. (1996). 'Innovation as collective action; conventions, products and technologies'. *Industrial and Corporate Change*, 5/3: 761–90.

Tallman, S., Jenkins, M., Henry, N., and Pinch, S. (2004). 'Knowledge, clusters, and competitive advantage'. *Academy of Management Review*, 29/2: 258–271.

Talukdar, D., Sudhir, K., and Ainslie, A. (2002). 'Investigating new product diffusion across products and countries'. *Marketing Science*, 21/1: 97–114.

Teece, D. J. (1986). 'Profiting from technological innovation: implications for integration, collaboration, licensing and public policy'. *Research Policy*, 15: 285–305.

Tellis, G. J., Stremersch, S., and Yin, E. (2003). 'The international takeoff of new products: the role of economics, culture, and country innovativeness'. *Marketing Science*, 22/2: 188–208.

Teresko, J. (2003). 'Innovating Innovation'. *Industry Week*, 252/7: 12.

Tidd, J., Bessant, J., and Pavitt, K. (1997). *Managing Innovation: Integrating Technological, Market and Organizational Change*. Chichester: Wiley.

Tripsas, M. and Gavetti, G. (2000). 'Capabilities, cognition and inertia: evidence from digital imaging'. *Strategic Management Journal*, 21: 1147–61.

Tsoukas, H. and Vladimirou, E. (2001). 'What is organizational knowledge?' *Journal of Management Studies*, 38/7: 973.

Tushman, M. L. and Anderson, P. (1986). 'Technological discontinuities and organizational environments'. *Administrative Science Quarterly*, 31: 439–65.

Tushman, M. L. and O'Reilly, C. A. (1996). 'Ambidextrous organizations: managing evolutionary and revolutionary change'. *California Management Review*, 38/4: 8–30.

Tushman, M. L. and Romanelli, E. (1985). 'Organizational evolution: a metamorphosis model of convergence and reorientation'. In Cummings, L. L. and Staw, B. M. (eds), *Research in Organizational Behavior*. Greenwich, CT: JAI Press, ch. 7, 171–222.

Utterback, J. M. and Acee, H. J. (2005). 'Disruptive technologies: an expanded view'. *International Journal of Innovation Management*, 9/1: 1–17.

Van De Ven, A. H. and Johnson, P. E. (2006). 'Knowledge for theory and practice'. *Academy of Management Review*, 31/4: 802–21.

Van Looy, B., Martens, T., and Debackere, K. (2005). 'Organizing for continuous innovation: on the sustainability of ambidextrous organizations'. *Creativity and Innovation Management*, 14/3: 208–21.

Verspagen, B. (2005). 'Innovation and economic growth'. In Fagerberg, J., Mowery, D. C., and Nelson, R. R. (eds), *The Oxford Handbook of Innovation*. Oxford: Oxford University Press.

Von Stamm, B. (2003). *The Innovation Wave*. West Sussex: John Wiley & Sons.

Welch, J. and Byrne, J. A. (2003). *Jack: Straight from the Gut*. New York: Warner Business Books.

West, J. and Gallagher, S. (2006). 'Challenges of open innovation: the paradox of firm investment in open-source software'. *R&D Management*, 36/3: 319–331.

Westerman, G., McFarlan, F. W., and Iansiti, M. (2006). 'Organization design and effectiveness over the innovation life cycle'. *Organization Science*, 17/2: 230–8.

Wiig, K. M. (1997). 'Integrating intellectual capital and knowledge management'. *Long Range Planning*, 30/3: 399–405.

Wonglimpiyarat, J. (2006). 'The dynamic economic engine at Silicon Valley and US Government programmes in financing innovations'. *Technovation*, 26: 1081–9.

Yaveroglu, I. S. and Donthu, N. (2002). 'Cultural influences on the diffusion of new products. *Journal of International Consumer Marketing*, 14/4: 49.

Zi-Lin, H., and Poh-Kam, W. (2004). 'Exploration vs. exploitation: an empirical test of the ambidexterity hypothesis'. *Organization Science*, 15/4: 481–94.

End-of-chapter Case Study 10.1 Samsung Electronics

Samsung is South Korea's largest Chaebol (conglomerate). Interbrand's 'Top Global 100 Brands' in 2006 ranked Samsung, 20th, up from 25th in 2003, and 42nd in 2001, and ahead of brands such as Siemens, Philips, Apple, Nintendo and even Sony, which was 26th, down from 21st.[102] By 2006, sales had reached 57,457,670 million Won (about US$56,720m), with profits of 7,640,213 Won.

Samsung had been founded in 1936 as a rice mill, and subsequently diversified into transportation, chemicals, and real estate. Samsung Electronics was established as a division in 1969 to manufacture cheap 12-inch black-and-white televisions under the Sanyo label. By the 1980s, it had become the fourth largest chaebol in Korea after Hyundai, Daewoo, and Lucky Goldstar (now LG). But as recently as 1987, Samsung was, by some accounts, a 'bit player', years behind its Japanese rivals, and apparently content to make 'me-too' products that it sold at low prices.[103] However by 2003, the Samsung Group had the second largest net profit of any electronics company outside the USA, and was the global leader in both sales and profits in the production of DRAM chips.

In 2006, Samsung Electronics had five business divisions: Semiconductors; Digital Appliances (refrigerators, air conditioners, and washing machines); Digital Media, (TVs, AV equipment, and computers); Telecommunications (mobile phones and network equipment); and LCDs (LCD panels for laptop computers, desktop monitors, and HDTVs). Some of these businesses were described as 'not very related'.[104] The semiconductor business was historically the biggest, and was certainly the one on which the recent success of the company was founded, although things were changing.

Samsung had moved into semiconductors when Lee Kun Hee (the current chairman and major shareholder, and the third son of Samsung's founder and chairman Lee Byung Chull) bought the Korea Semiconductor Company using his own personal savings. He felt that semiconductors offered high growth rates and the chance to move into the design and marketing of advanced technologies.[105] In the early 1980s, the semiconductor industry went into recession and many firms, including Intel, exited the business. Samsung instead allocated millions to DRAM development, believing in the long-term future of the technology, even though it accrued high losses in the early years. But the risk paid off: Samsung gained number one market share in the DRAM industry in 1992, and maintained it thereafter.

In 2004, Samsung moved into Flash memory. DRAM sales followed those of the maturing PC market. Flash memory was instead linked to sales of digital cameras and camera phones, which were expected to grow.

The move into consumer products

In recent years, Samsung has moved increasingly into consumer products. By 1992, it had recognized that it was overly dependent on US and Japanese technologies and was incurring losses on its 'me-too models' of television sets and microwave ovens.[106] This appears to have been a spur to an organizational restructuring, and changes to its competitive stance.[107] The ambition was to be 'the Mercedes of home electronics' according to Yun Jong Yong, Samsung's chief executive, although given the pace of change, one commentator thought an analogy with Ferrari was more appropriate.[108]

By 2000, the company had launched a number of new products, such as mobile phones, internet music players, ultra-thin laptops, and flat-panel displays, which competed head-on with products from Sony and Nokia. By 2001, Samsung was ranked fifth in patents—behind IBM, NEC, Canon, and Micron Technology, but ahead of Matsushita, Sony, Hitachi, Mitsubishi Electric and Fujitsu.[109]

Lee Kun Hee was strongly commited to R&D, even though this might hurt short-term profits. In 2005 Samsung spent 206bn Won on R&D (up from 190bn Won in 2004), from sales of 5.61 trillion Won. By the end of 2005, more than 12,000 Samsung employees had a master's degree or a doctorate and over 25 per cent of the workforce were involved in R&D.[110] Mr Lee's advice is to 'always demand superiority in product design and process efficiency'. He has promised to 'richly reward individuals for their accomplishments, while at the same time not firing people for failure', only those who 'lack ethics, are unfair, tell lies, hold others back or stand in the way of our unified march'.[111]

Lee Kun Hee also counsels against complacency in the company, suggesting that most of Samsung's success has come from the 'leading companies' negligence, pure luck, and our predecessors' sacrifice. He is now encouraging the company to be worried about the threat from Chinese companies, and the development of, for example, nanotechnology, which is likely to replace Flash and DRAM memory in the future.

The role of design

Design has been a critical element in Samsung's recent innovation push. Koo Ki Seol, who heads Samsung's Design Institute, wants the company to be remembered as the designer of iconic products.[112] In 1994, Samsung Electronics moved its design centre from Suwon, a small 'sleepy' town near Seoul, to Seoul itself, marking the beginning of its focus on product design over cost.[113] In the first four years of the twenty-first century, Samsung ➜

→ doubled its design staff to 470, adding 120 of those in 2003 alone. At the same time its design budget increased 20 per cent to 30 per cent annually.[114]

In 2004, Samsung created the post of chief design officer. Choi Gee Sung, former head of Samsung's TV, computer, and audio businesses, was appointed to the post. It also holds quarterly design meetings where the heads of all the business units review new products and evaluate their designs, encouraging communication between the heads of the various units. Between 2000 and 2004, it won 19 Industrial Design Excellence Awards, tying with Apple, and in 2004, was the first Asian company to win more awards than any of its European or American rivals.[115]

Samsung now gives designers greater power to influence what gets built, including totally new product categories. Mr Choi ensures that designers have good access to the top of the company. Previously, they had to go through the marketing department and mid-level executives before reaching top management. A recent example is where designers came up with an idea for a rear-projection TV, which they were not sure could be built. The head of design went to the head of engineering, who said that if he could be given some time and resources, he'd try to do it.[116] They succeeded.

Hundreds of millions of Won have been spent improving the look, feel, and function of Samsung's products. The 'Swan' TV monitor, which can be folded after use, was the result of designers focusing on appearance, as one would expect, but also on costs: the foldable design significantly cut distribution costs, which could be passed on in reduced prices.[117] The so-called 'Lee Kun Hee Phone' helped create a new product category of 'colour phones', which has since spawned numerous imitators, when designers adopted TFT LCD.[118] Samsung Electronics also operates a design bank system. Designs which are difficult to commercialize now are stored in a database for the future—ten years from now.[119]

Since 2000, Samsung has opened or expanded design centres in San Francisco, London, Tokyo, Los Angeles, and Shanghai. Here, designers spend time studying the needs of the consumer in depth—Americans in particular. Samsung has, for example, a 'usability laboratory' that resembles a typical kitchen/living room to provide a lifelike forum for product testing. In 1995, the company set up the Innovative Design Lab of Samsung, an in-house school where designers could study under experts from one of the top US design schools. It has long-term relationships with some of the world's most famous design consultancies and encourages designers to spend time abroad at fashion and cosmetics companies, and visit galleries and museums to keep up to date with trends in other industries and cultures. One design manager, who works on colours and finishes, spent an autumn in residence at a furniture designer in Italy. Not only was she able to obtain inspiration, she was brought face to face with a very different culture, in which 'a 23-year-old novice could interrupt the 60-year-old master'. Since returning, she has tried to be more open to ideas percolating up from the bottom of her own department.[120]

Samsung is, as a result, shedding its traditional Confucian hierarchy. Although this still prevails in Samsung as a whole, the design centre is different. It is physically located a few minutes away from the HQ building, and everyone is encouraged to speak up and challenge their superiors. The designers, who have an average age of 33, clutter their desks with toys, often work in blue jeans and sneakers, and dye their hair pink, green, or blue. They work in three- to five-person teams, with members from various specialisms and levels of seniority—all working as equals.[121]

Samsung is challenging Korean norms about employment elsewhere in the company as well. Korean firms often hire employees because they came from the right high school or the right region, but Samsung has now made it taboo to ask a colleague about his or her background. It has also tried to break the mould of traditional seniority-based promotion. Employees are now promoted on merit. As a result younger managers in their early 40s are now reaching high positions in the organization's hierarchy. Many of these managers were placed in a foreign country for one year to learn the local language and culture, or are the MBA and PhD graduates that Samsung sponsored in foreign countries. It has also actively recruited foreigners.

Samsung's innovation architecture

Samsung sees advantages in having diversified product lines and in achieving cross-product sharing and support. As products such as mobile phones, computers, and monitors are converging on to a few product platforms, which requires the convergence of different technologies, Samsung feels that it can achieve such cooperation internally. This avoids 'the difficulties and delays of seeking and working with external partners', enabling the company to make fast product decisions and reduce time to market.[122]

The company has a corporate lab where engineers work on long-term R&D assignments or on projects that benefit multiple divisions. Product divisions can send engineers or engineer teams to work on important projects there, but also have their own labs that work on medium-to-short-term projects. They sometimes also engage in multiple competing development projects. At one point, for example, Samsung's handset division had five groups working on a similar new product.[123] This competition helps the company to hedge the risks of R&D activities and assess the market potential of each product. As a result the company is able to select a few high potential products from a pool of candidates.

However, managing the diverse business lines is 'challenging'. The aim is to achieve consensus through discussion, but →

→ sometimes HQ staff have to intervene to prevent conflict between the independent and autonomous divisions.[124]

Case study questions

1. By 2010, China is expected to become the world's second largest purchaser of semiconductors, after the USA. How should Samsung respond to this?

2. What are the advantages of locating the design department away from the main HQ building? Are there any disadvantages? If so, how may these be overcome?

3. Is Samsung an innovative-enabling company? If so, what are the aspects of Samsung's culture, management style, and architecture that make it so?

● NOTES

1 Nonaka (1991); and Nonaka and Takeuchi (1995).

2 Corporations that acquired US software firms between 1981 and 1993 typically paid up to nine times their book value, according to Edvinsson (1997).

3 See for example Chong et al. (2006); Shaikh (2004); Roos and Roos (1997); Edvinsson (1994); and Edvinsson and Malone (1997). The Danish government has also published a widely cited guide to reporting and measuring intellectual capital available from <http://videnskabsministeriet.dk/site/forside/publikationer/2003/intellectual-capital-statements---the-new-guideline>, accessed 16 February 2007. Many of today's methodologies for measuring intellectual capital refer to the balanced scorecard, so it is worth also referring to Kaplan and Norton (1992, 1996). See also DMSTI (2003a, 2003b).

4 Tsoukas and Vladimirou (2001).

5 Ibid.

6 See Gander et al. (2007).

7 The term 'race to learn' or 'learning race' appears to have been first applied to strategic alliances by Gary Hamel (1991). It has since been taken up by many theorists, including Khanna et al. (1994); Kale et al. (2000); Das and Teng (2000); and Lavie (2006). Hennart et al. (1999) called such cases of knowledge appropriation 'Trojan Horses'.

8 Boisot (2006).

9 This concept was popularized hugely by Senge (1990) but academic work in the area has a long and solid history, notably by Chris Argyris (1976) and Donald Schön (Argyris and Schön 1978, 1996), but see also Nonaka (1991, 1994), Garvin (1993), and Nevis et al. (1995). For a recent summary of the state of the field see Argyris (2004).

10 For example, Nonaka and Takeuchi (1995), Nevis et al. (1995). For a definitive summary see Crossan et al. (1999).

11 This is called 'experiential learning', and was described by the psychologist Kurt Lewin. For details see Kolb (1984).

12 The term community of practice was popularized by Brown and Duguid (1991).

13 This term comes from Nonaka (1991), and is very close to what other researchers call 'learning'. See also Nonaka and Konno (1998).

14 Henckoff, R. (1990). 'Big Mac attacks with pizza'. *Fortune*. 26 February: 87; Buss, D. (2005). 'McDonald's salad days'. *Chief Executive*, 1 November: 16.

15 See Cohen and Levinthal (1990).

16 <http://marketshare.hitslink.com/report.aspx?qprid=3>, accessed 28 June 2007.

17 Taylor, P. (2006). 'The leading windows on the web receive a fresh polish'. *Financial Times*, 7 July: 9.

18 See, for example: Waters, R. (2006). 'Microsoft links up with Nortel Telecommunications'. *Financial Times*, 19 July: 28; Reuters News (2007). 'Dell joins Microsoft, Novell in Linux pact'. 7 May; Bishop, T. (2007). 'Microsoft and Linspire find peace in patents; Linux vendor strikes a deal with former court opponent'. *Seattle Post-Intelligencer*, 14 June: E1.

19 See Levitt and March (1988) and Levinthal and March (1993).

20 See March (1991).

21 Kehoe, L. and Price, C. (1999). 'The race to gather a digital arsenal'. *Financial Times*, 28 April; *Economist* (2007). 'Out of the dusty labs: the rise and fall of corporate R&D'. 3 March.

22 See Inkpen et al. (2000).

23 This section is based principally on Grant and Neupert (2003), and Grant and Baden-Fuller (2004).

24 This framework comes from Davenport et al. (1998). See also Prokesch (1997), in particular the articles by Quintas, P. et al., (1997), and Wiig, K. M., (1997), Ghoshal and Bartlett (1998) have some very interesting examples of knowledge sharing, including the McKinsey example we use in this section. See also Van de Ven and Johnson (2006).

25 See his autobiography for a fascinating account of what makes him tick (Welch and Byrne, 2003).

26 Lakshman (2005) provides a good summary of these practices.

27 Hansen et al. (1999).

28 Wikipedia provides a good summary of some of the complexity, see <http://en.wikipedia.org/wiki/European_patent_law#Types_of_patent_protection_in_Europe>, accessed 21 February 2007.

29 Joshi, P. (2006). 'Patents may block open source growth'. *Business Standard*, 29 August.

30 There are many articles on the internet discussing these issues. See also Kelly and Talley (2004); *Economist*, 22 March 1997; Nurton (2002).

31 Boersma (2006). In a survey by the Economist Intelligence Unit in 2004 (Economist Intelligence Unit, 2004), 39% of the western executives surveyed said that China was where they were going to spend most of their international R&D investments in the next three years. And in the same survey 38% cited intellectual property protection as their most critical challenge.

32 At the time of writing both Chinese companies are appealing against the decision.

33 Xinhua Financial Network (XFN) News (2006). 'Italian chocolate-maker Ferrero Rocher wins China lawsuit—report'. 12 January; Yeh, A. and Bounds, A. (2006). 'Ferrero Rocher dispute calls for diplomacy'. FT.com, 16 December; Fatiguso, R. (2007). 'Ferrero Rocher dispute rumbles on in China (I cinesi: no alla pace sui Rocher)'. *Il Sole 24 Ore*, 11 January: 17.

34 Hamel (1991) See also Julian and Keller (1991); Gulati (1995).

35 Fagerberg et al. (2005): 4.

36 For example Amabile (1983, 1988). Amabile also brings in the notion of *usefulness* to her definition of creativity.

37 For example Verspagen (2005). However, there are writers who regard this as an artificial distinction (see Kline and Rosenberg, 1986 for example), and see innovation as a continuum of interactive and iterative development.

38 Case example based on personal communication with Swarovski's head of design.

39 <http://www.swarovski.com/SVK_Relaunch/GLOBAL/globalShowBinary/0,3210,26585,00.pdf>, accessed 29 July 2007.

40 This is another example of the 'punctuated equilibrium' (Tushman and Romanelli, 1985) phenomenon we noted in Section 2.8.3. See also Brown and Eisenhardt (1997).

41 Tushman and Anderson (1986): 441.

42 See Govindarajan and Kopalle (2006). There is also a special edition of the *Journal of Product Innovation Management* devoted to the issue (vol. 23, 2006).

43 Disruptive technologies were discussed by Adner (2002); Adner and Zemsky (2005); Christensen (1997); Christensen and Overdorf (2000); Christensen and Raynor (2003); Danneels (2004); Hall and Martin (2005); Henderson (2006); and Utterback and Acee (2005).

44 Two of the most powerful early proponents of the importance of innovation were Peters and Waterman (1982). There have been many since then, however, including Burgelman (1983, 1984); Kanter (1989); Peters (1988); Nonaka (1988, 1990); Nonaka and Takeuchi 1995); and Tushman and O'Reilly (1996).

45 Easingwood et al. (2006); Mittal and Swami (2004); Rothaermel and Hill (2005); Tidd et al. (1997).

46 The EMI story is summarized in Martin (1984).

47 Rothaermel and Hill (2005).

48 Teece (1986).

49 Schwartz (2004).

50 Grant (2004).

51 Crawford (1979).

52 Shaw, G. (2005). 'Costs, controversies frame 2005'. *Drug Discovery & Development*, 8/12: 16–20.

53 Peter Mc Namara, Charles Baden-Fuller, and John Howe (2000). *Biotechnology Industry Note: Strategy and Performance of Some UK Biotech Independents 1995 to 1997*. London: City University Business School; 'Glaxo has launched a new ulcer treatment, Zantac (ranitidine)'. *Textline Multiple Source Collection (1980–1994)*, 14 October 1981.

54 Biggadike (1979).

55 See Tellis et al. (2003), who incidentally describe how difficult it is to obtain good data on the measurement of innovation success. See also Talukdar et al. (2002); Yaveroglu and Donthu (2002).

56 Based around Hofstede's categories of national cultural differences (Hofstede, 1980). Take-off speed increased with higher need for achievement, industriousness, and lower uncertainty avoidance.

57 See, for example, Kirton (1976, 1989).

58 The term 'fuzzy front end' appears to have been first used by industrial designers, but has now entered common usage in the new product development literature. See Smith and Reinertsen (1991).

59 See Cox (2007).

60 See Govindarajan and Kopalle (2006); Audia and Goncalo (2007); Benner and Tushman (2003); O'Connor and Rice (2001).

61 The term was first used by Tushman and O'Reilly (1996), but has since been discussed by many others: for example, Adams et al. (2006); Van Looy et al. (2005); Zi-Lin and Poh-Kam (2004).

62 New Venture Division is another term used to describe this structure: see Covin and Miles (2007), and Chesbrough and Socolof (2000). Historically, some of the authors to discuss new venture divisions are Burgelman and Sayles (1986); Burgelman (1983, 1984); Kanter (1985, 1989); and Kanter et al. (1991).

63 See, for example, Brown and Eisenhardt (1997). Also included in this camp would be most of the learning organization and knowledge management theorists.

64 Westerman et al. (2006); Chesbrough and Teece (1996); Govindarajan and Trimble (2005); Gilbert (2006).

65 See Asheim and Gertler (2005); for a rather sceptical view of Porter's 'diamond' and the current fashion for clusters, see Martin and Sunley (2003); Archibugi and Coco (2005); Groenewegen and Van der Steen (2006); Moreno et al. (2006); Mowery and Sampat (2005).

66 *Economist* (1999). 'Silicon envy'. 20 February.

67 The details in this example are based on Wonglimpiyarat (2006).

68 See Amabile (1983, 1988); Amabile et al. (1994); Higgins and McAllaster (2002); and Adams et al. (2006).

69 See, for example, MacMillan and McGrath (2004).

70 Geiger and Makri (2006).

71 Nohria and Gulati (1997) identified a curvilinear relationship between slack and innovation. Moderate levels of organizational slack were found to help innovation development, but too much had a negative effect.

72 See Drazin et al. (1999); also Drazin and Schoonhoven (1996).

73 Brent Schlender (2001). 'Apple's 21st-century Walkman: CEO Steve Jobs thinks he has something pretty nifty. And if he's right, he might even spook Sony and Matsushita'. *Fortune*, 12 November.

74 Singer, M. (2006). 'Stringer's way', *New Yorker*, 5 June.

75 Singer (2006) op. cit.

76 Singer (2006) op. cit.

77 The most passionate advocate of this model is probably Henry Chesbrough. See Chesbrough and Teece (1996); Chesbrough (2003a, 2003c, 2004, 2007); Chesbrough and Crowther (2006); Chesbrough and Schwartz, (2007). See also Chesbrough et al. (2006); Christensen et al. (2005); Berkhout et al. (2006); Brown and Hagel (2006); Cooke (2005); Dodgson et al. (2006); Enkel et al. (2005); Gassmann (2006); Jacobides and Billinger (2006); Jana (2006); Olleros (2007); Piller and Walcher (2006); Teresko (2003); West and Gallagher (2006).

78 Chesbrough (2003b).

79 Fetterhoff and Voelkel (2006).

80 Chesbrough (2003b).

81 See Kirschbaum (2005).

82 Jana, R. (2006). 'Thriving in the new innovation landscape'. *Business Week Online*, 28 November: 20.

83 As a footnote, PARC became a separate, independent entity—albert a wholly-owned subsidiary of Xerox—in 2002.

84 A patent 'troll' is a person or firm that undertakes no research or development, but who seeks to make profits by suing infringers of an existing patent.

85 Freiberg and Freiberg (1998); Knibb (2006); Markides (1997, 1998, 2006).

86 Howard, R. (1991). 'PARC: seedbed of the computer revolution'. *Harvard Business Review*, 69/1.

87 Holusha, J. (1994). 'Xerox's new strategy will not copy the past'. *New York Times*, 18 December.

88 For a comprehensive list, see <http://64.233.183.104/search?q=cache:LV_cv-UnLXIJ:www.parc.xerox.com/about/history/default.html+xerox+parc+star+alto&hl=en&ct=clnk&cd=1&gl=uk>, accessed 29 July 2007.

89 *Economist* (1993). 'The Xerox lesson'. 10 July.

90 Ibid.

91 According to Wikipedia, see <http://en.wikipedia.org/wiki/Xerox_Star>, accessed 24 February 2007.

92 Holusha (1994) op. cit. Also see <http://www.answers.com/topic/scientific-data-systems>, accessed 24 February 2007.

93 Holusha (1994) op. cit.

94 Johnson, J., Roberts, T. L., Verplank, W. et al. 'The Xerox "star": a retrospective', available from <http://members.dcn.org/dwnelson/XeroxStarRetrospective.html> accessed 24 February 2007.

95 Wikipedia <http://en.wikipedia.org/wiki/Xerox_Star>, accessed 24 February 2007.

96 Johnson et al. op. cit.

97 Ibid.

98 Wikipedia, see <http://en.wikipedia.org/wiki/Xerox_Star>, accessed 24 February 2007.

99 Smith and Alexander (1988). See also Chesbrough, H. (2003). 'XTV: Xerox's attempted recovery from "Fumbling the Future"', Harvard Business School, Working Knowledge, 7 April.

100 *Economist* (1993) op. cit. See also *Harvard Management Update* (2003). 'Managing your false negatives'. *Harvard Management Update*, 8/8.

101 Holusha. (1994) op. cit.; see also Howard (1991) op. cit.

102 <http://www.interbrand.com/best_brands_2006.asp>, accessed 8 July 2007.

103 Siegel, J. and Chang, J. J. (2006). 'Samsung Electronics'. Harvard Business School Publishing case study.

104 *Journal of Asia Business Studies*, Spring 2007: 77.

105 Siegel and Chang (2006) op. cit.

106 Sireesha, M. (2005). 'Samsung vs LG: similar goals, dissimilar strategies'. ICFAI Business School Case Development Centre.

107 Breen, B. (2005). 'The Seoul of design. Fast Company'. *Research-Technology Management*, 1 December.

108 Rocks, D. and Ihlwan, M. (2004). 'Samsung design'. *Business Week*, 29 November: 88–96.

109 Sireesha (2005) op. cit.

110 Samsung 2005 Annual Report, p. 8.

111 Ibid.

112 Ihlwan, M. (2003). 'Pink-haired designers, red cell phones—Ka-Ching!' *Business Week*, 16 June.

113 Sireesha (2005) op. cit.

114 Rocks and Ihlwan (2004) op. cit.

115 Ibid.

116 Ibid.

117 *Electronic Times* (2007). 'Design change leading to a new growth engine'. 4 July 2007.

118 Ibid.

119 Ibid.

120 Rocks and Ihlwan (2004) op. cit.

121 Ihlwan (2003) op. cit.; Rocks and Ihlwan (2004) op. cit.

122 Chen, R. and Li, Z. (2007). 'A synthesis of interviews with executives of Samsung Electronics'. *Journal of Asia Business Studies*, 1/2.

123 Ibid.

124 Ibid.

PART FOUR

From Strategic Analysis to Strategy Formulation

In Parts Two and Three, you have learned how to analyse and assess an organization's strategy. In Part Four we show you how to turn that analysis into concrete and robust strategic proposals.

The first step in this process is to distil the outcomes of this analysis into a number of strategic issues on which the organization should focus attention. We then show you how to develop a range of alternative options that the organization's managers might realistically consider to address those issues. You then learn how to use the RACES criteria to assess which of those options is the best—or least worst!

To assist you in developing and selecting options, we review what has been discovered about best practice in strategy in particular circumstances: for profit-making firms confronting different types of industry and global competition; for small firms; and for public sector and not-for-profit organizations.

CHAPTER ELEVEN

Assessing Organizational Performance and Setting Strategic Priorities

LEARNING OUTCOMES

After reading this chapter, you should be able to:

→ Explain the key measures used to assess an organization's strategic performance

→ Analyse an organization's performance, both financial and non-financial

→ Assess the extent to which a firm can be said to be successful

→ Identify areas in which the organization is performing strongly or weakly; and how a review of an organization's performance leads to the identification of key issues and priorities that can be used to evaluate and shape its choice of future strategy.

INTRODUCTION

In earlier chapters we examined the ways in which organizations compete. We discussed the environmental forces that can shape the organization's choice of customers and products, and the forces that limit the amount of money that a firm in a specific industry may make. We have discussed some of the competitive strategies that allow firms to differentiate themselves successfully from others, or that allow performance to be sustained over time, through the organization's ability to adapt and learn. All these factors govern whether the organization succeeds or fails.

If we are to assess a firm's current competitive position and develop strategies that will enhance its chances of success in the future, we need to evaluate how effective the organization has been in the past at using its resources to deal with the challenges posed by its environment. We need to assess its performance.[1] This will help us to identify areas of weakness that have to be addressed. Some of these may be critical to the organization's short-term survival and have to be tackled urgently. Others may require longer-term actions that, for example, would allow it to develop the structure and culture to respond to changes in its future competitive environment.

Evaluating performance may also highlight extremely successful areas, perhaps indicating core competences that are under-exploited or a value chain that could process a wider range or greater number of products than it is currently doing.

The ways in which an organization's executives may choose to respond to this performance are the strategic options that we discuss in much more detail in the following chapters of this book. But the first part of this process is the topic of this chapter—assessing how well the organization is doing now.

11.1 Evaluating an organization's financial performance

In other chapters we have sections on using evidence, where we show specific examples of the sorts of data you need to examine in order to reach conclusions about what you are examining. This chapter is a bit different; almost all of it is about using evidence—in order to assess the performance of a firm, in absolute terms, and in relationship to key competitors.

One part of the assessment of whether an organization is succeeding or failing will be qualitative. Do the firm's current strategies 'feel' right? Do they fit in with strategies that have succeeded or failed for other organizations in similar circumstances? Are they the kinds of choices that theory would recommend for this kind of industry?

→ We looked at organizational objectives in Chapter 2.

But there is another, equally important way to answer the question. This comes from quantitative analysis of an organization's financial and operational performance. Quantitative analysis also offers the answer to another question: To what extent is the organization achieving its purpose? This is important in two ways. First, if an organization is not achieving the aims it sets itself, then we are entitled to question the quality of its management, and its viability. But there is a subtler angle to this type of analysis. Sometimes, it is only by looking at what a company measures, and seeing what *precisely* it does well, that you can work out what its strategy really is.

Of course, many firms say what their strategy is supposed to be, and you will see these declarations—mission statements and lists of objectives—reproduced in annual reports and case studies. But even in a successful company, these statements are not always true (see Real-life Application 11.1). Sometimes a firm may deliberately try to mislead its competitors, or even its shareholders and regulators. In other cases, its managers may paint an optimistic picture of its strategic prospects to win time from creditors or shareholders, and stave off the prospect of being sacked. Sometimes a firm chooses to keep its strategy deliberately flexible and vague. And there are times when a firm may be genuinely confused about what its strategy really is, or why people buy (or decline to buy) its services, perhaps because it is in the process of changing direction.

Real-life Application 11.1 Actions and words

Some years ago, one of the authors was consulting with a small subsidiary of a medium-sized UK engineering firm. This subsidiary's managers prided themselves on the lengths to which they would go to meet customer requirements on quality and delivery. They believed that customers purchased their products because of this dedication to customer service. Customers indeed had a high opinion of the firm, but in interviews they all said that the main reason why they bought its products was because of its very competitive prices. The firm was highly profitable, and its staff's dedication to customer service was completely sincere, but the emergent low-price strategy turned out to be far more important than the deliberate strategy of differentiation on quality.

To get a full picture of a firm's strategies and how well they are succeeding thus demands a very hard-headed kind of analysis, which looks at actions rather than words, and at results rather than intentions or opinions. This is equally true for a student preparing a case study for an assessment, or a practising manager trying to come to grips with real-life strategic problems.

11.1.1 Key steps in assessing performance

In assessing an organization's success or failure, there are three stages: working out what to observe and measure, establishing the standards against which to measure performance, and drawing conclusions.

a. Working out what to observe and measure

Since almost all organizations have an economic purpose, part of their success will be measured in financial and economic terms, using a financial performance measure like return on capital employed or profits.

➜ We summarize the most common accounting terms and ratios in Appendix 11.1.

Usually we are also interested in how fast the organization is growing relative to competitors. We also need see how well the organization is succeeding in meeting key stakeholder requirements, particularly in public sector and non-profit organizations. A school, for example, may be evaluated more against its pupils' examination results than against its success in keeping within the budget.

These will give us general measures of an organization's overall success or failure. However, if we are to make useful proposals for its future strategy, we need to be able to diagnose the strength or weakness of specific elements of its strategy. We want to know whether it is performing better in some competitive arenas than in others—so we should try, where possible, to compare the performance of different business units. We want to know which particular elements of the value chain, or which specific strategic resources, are important to the organization's success or failure. This requires the use of ratios that assess particular elements of strategic performance, such as inventory control or quality.

There are a number of operational performance measures that are applicable to a wide variety of organizations. As well as helping us assess the efficiency and effectiveness of particular parts of the strategy, these also give us insights into how well the organization is managed. However, further insights can be gained by assessing how well the organization is performing by the standards of its own industry, and also by the standards that it has set itself. For example, Sony competes in industries where innovation is important to sustaining competitive advantage, and part of its corporate mission relates to being a leader in product innovation. We shall therefore want to measure how innovative it really is. This kind of analysis requires the use of performance measures that are tailored to the organization and its industry.

b. Choosing the standards against which to measure performance

Most organizations have internal measures of success. Owners and other major stake-holders will set goals for the organization, which will typically be expressed in financial terms. The organization's managers (who are not always its owners) will often set operational targets against which they assess their own progress. In theory, by achieving these targets the organization should also satisfy the requirements of the major stakeholders.

However, an organization that is meeting, or even surpassing, its internal goals may still be performing poorly when compared against other measures. Performance needs, if at all possible, to be gauged externally—against that of competitors or other comparable firms, against industry norms and even against how the organization itself has performed in the past.

c. Drawing conclusions about how strong or weak is the performance

Analysis of the organization's results gives us a relatively *objective* way of assessing whether the organization's performance is good, mediocre, or poor, and whether or not it is improving relative to its competitors. The analysis can also give clues about which particular functions or business units give rise to this good or poor performance, and whether the organization can claim to have any particular competences.

In drawing these conclusions, the quantitative analysis needs to be brought together with qualitative evidence. An organization may be making losses, but are these because it is poorly managed or because it is a new venture that is investing in building its new market aggressively? Poor performance may be due to economic conditions that are beyond managers' short-term control. One also has to understand how good and objective the evidence is. Does it all come from the organization's managers, who might normally be expected to give an optimistic point of view, or from customers or outside experts?

11.1.2 **Overall measures of financial performance**

Strategy is about using resources to give value to customers and users, and the first stage in any assessment of strategic performance is to try to measure, in broad terms, how effectively the organization is doing so. These broad measures of performance are also the only ones that can be used to compare organizations with radically different business models. The only way to know if the strategy of a low-cost carrier, such as Ryanair, is better than that of a traditional airline, such as BA, or if H&M's strategy is better than The Gap's, is to compare these overall measures.

In Real-life Application 11.2 British Airways starts with presenting its profits, and for any commercial organization, the logical starting point for the analyst is to look at profitability. BA quotes both pre-tax profits and profit attributable to shareholders (net of tax and interest charges). From the strategist's point of view, the most appropriate measure of profit is before interest and tax, since the management of tax and interest by the treasury function, while valuable to shareholders, does not normally add value to users of the company's products. (There are some types of business, such as financial services firms, where the treasury function *is* crucial to adding value. In cases like these, which we discuss below, profit is best measured after interest and tax.)

However, the *absolute* level of profit does not help us to assess BA's strategic performance in comparison with that of other airlines, or with its own past results. This is because it does not take account of the quantity or value of the resources that are needed to produce that profit. The starting point for a strategic analysis is therefore a ratio that expresses profits as a percentage of the resources invested in the business. This is an illustration of a very basic rule that:

> a well-chosen ratio generates more useful information than a raw number such as revenue or profit.

For a firm that has an extensive fixed-asset base, such as a manufacturing firm or a retailer, look at the ratio of profit before interest and tax to assets. In the UK, the most commonly employed ratio is return on capital employed (ROCE), while US analysts often prefer return on (total) assets (ROA). Which you use will depend upon the data available and on personal taste, although it is of course important to use the same ratio for each company and each year of data that you analyse.[2]

For a firm where the management of financial assets is a crucial part of the business, look at the ratio of profits *after* interest and tax to assets. Firms in this category will include banks, insurers, and other financial service providers, but also property companies (which typically take on a lot of debt to finance the purchase and development of land). For these companies, the management of debt and taxation *is* crucial to competitiveness, so performance measures need to take account of profits (or losses) from these areas of operations. Typically, you will look at return on equity (ROE), but sometimes you will see commentators talk about post-tax returns on total assets. ROE will also be of interest for firms engaged in long-term projects, such as power station development, because they get large payments in advance that need to be carefully invested.

For a firm whose main assets are highly trained professionals, such as consultancies and advertising agencies, classic accounting measures of return on assets are deceptive, since they take no account of human capital. This kind of business may have few balance sheet assets beyond some office equipment and a small amount of working capital, so their ROCE may seem absurdly high. There is no perfect overall measure for this kind of business; profit per employee is perhaps the best available.

British Airways in fact straddles all these categories. Like many companies it uses a basket of financial measures to assess its performance and does not just rely on one. It has a large investment in buildings and aircraft, but many of the aircraft are leased (putting a premium on financial management). It also has a major investment in highly trained pilots, engineers, and cabin crew. Accordingly, in assessing BA's performance, we would look at all three measures.

Real-life Application 11.2 British Airways' position in 2007[3]

British Airways is one of the most successful airlines in the world. In 2006 it was in the top ten in terms of sales and was the world's most profitable passenger airline—and one of the very few that has been regularly profitable in recent years.[4] Its base is London's Heathrow Airport, which is one of the world's busiest international airport hubs.

Unlike many of the world's other airlines, British Airways is owned entirely by private investors. In 1987, its former owner, the British government, sold the company to the public. In 2007, it had almost 220,000 shareholders. Many of its employees own shares, and there is a share option scheme as part of many staff's remuneration package.   ➜

The 1999 alliance between BA and American Airlines became the oneworld alliance of eight airlines across the world. *oneworld*

→ For many years BA described itself as the 'world's favourite airline', based on the fact that it flew more international passengers to more destinations than any other carrier. Other airlines always flew more passengers, but most of these were domestic. In the last few years it has been overtaken on this measure by the merged AirFrance/KLM.[5] Nevertheless, in 2006/2007 BA flew to nearly 150 destinations in 75 countries and carried more than 33 million passengers.[6] In 1999, British Airways entered into an alliance with American Airlines. This became the oneworld alliance, which now includes eight other airlines from across the world, whose members collectively serve more than 570 destinations in 135 territories. Despite this, BA's own home base remains resolutely British; the vast majority of its managers and employees are based in the UK.

The first page of BA's 2007 report and the chief executive's and chairman's statements contains the following summary of its performance:

- BA won the OAG (Official Airline Guide) 'Airline of the Year' award—an accolade it found 'surprising', as it had experienced a year marked by disruptions to services and inconvenience to passengers created by government-led security initiatives.
- Revenue performance it assessed as 'good'—sales were up 3.4 per cent to £8,492m.
- Group pre-tax profit for the year was £611m, compared to £616m in 2006. Operating profit, at £602m, was down 13.3 per cent on the previous year. The operating margin of 7.1 per cent was 1.4 points down from 2006. However, it was also pointed out that this margin 'would be the envy of many other airlines', especially as it had had to cancel 1,400 flights at one point as a result of government-imposed security measures, which it estimated cost it £231m.
- Net assets were up 16.2 per cent to £2,411m.

- Passenger yields (pence/RPK) for the year were up 2.1 per cent, although passenger load factor was 'flat' at 76.1 per cent. Cargo volumes and revenue were up slightly.
- Net debt fell by 15.1 points to 29.1 per cent (from 44.2 per cent). Earnings per share were 25.5 pence, down 37 per cent. As in previous years, no dividend was to be paid.
- It also discussed a number of efficiency measures it had taken, such as taking steps towards achieving its goal of a 10 per cent margin by March 2008. These included retiring Boeing planes and replacing them with Airbus aircraft, thereby moving towards a single-aircraft short-haul fleet.
- High fuel costs, which had affected BA's profits significantly, were highlighted, and there were few signs of these easing off. Other potential impact on costs included the increasing public awareness of the impact of air travel on climate change, and increases in air passenger duty.
- BA also reported that it had set aside an amount of money that it expected to have to pay in fines to the US, European, and UK competition authorities for staff breaches of competition law—and their own internal compliance procedures.
- Changes made to its UK operations included the sale of BA Connect, its regional airline. It also discussed some possible future actions concerning the Spanish carrier Iberia, in which it already had a 10 per cent stake.
- BA reported that it had pretty much solved the £2.1bn pension deficit that had bedevilled the company for many years, to the extent that BA's chairman was forecasting resuming dividend payments from 2008.
- In terms of its industry environment, BA's chairman made some rather critical remarks about the way in which the US/European air routes had been unevenly deregulated (in favour of US airlines) by US and European trade negotiators, although he did see some positives from these moves: →

Table 11.1 BA's key financial indicators

Group results

			12 months to March 31 2007	2006
Turnover	£m	Up 3.4%	8,492	82,138
Operating profit	£m	Down 13.3%	602	694
Profit before tax	£m	Down 08%	611	616
Attributable profit for the year	£m	Down 35.7%	290	451
Net assets	£m	Up 16.2%	2,411	2,074
Basic earnings per share	p	Down 36.9%	25.5	40.4
Key financial statistics				
Passenger yield	p/RPK	Up 2.1%	6.44	6.31
Operating margin	%	Down 1.4 points	7.1	8.5
Net debt/total capital ratio	%	Down 15.1 points	29.1	44.2
Group operating statistics				
Passengers carried	'000	Up 2.0%	33,068	32,432
Revenue passenger kilometres (RPK) (*the number of passengers carried, multiplied by the distance they flew in kilometres*)	m	Up 2.9%	112,851	109,713
Revenue tonne kilometres (RTKs) (*the revenue load in tonnes multiplied by the distance flown*)	m	Up 1.3%	16,112	15,909
Available tonne kilometres (ATKs) (*the number of tonnes of capacity available for the carriage of revenue load (passenger and cargo together) multiplied by the distance flown*)	m	Up 0.7%	22,882	22,719
Passenger load factor (*the percentage of seats available that were actually purchased*)	%	flat	76.1	76.1
Aircraft in service		−42	242	284
Employees—MPE (*Manpower Equivalent i.e. full-time equivalent*)		−3.5%	43,501	45,072
Productivity (*in terms of ATKs per MPE*)	(000)	+4.3%	526	504.1

Source
BA's Annual Report 2007. *Reproduced with the kind permission of British Airways*

→ some of BA's major US routes could now be moved from Gatwick (London's second largest airport) to Heathrow.

- And also on a positive note, BA's chairman was looking forward to moving in to the purpose-built 'magnificent' fifth terminal at Heathrow Airport, with facilities that would make the travel experience 'effortless' and give BA a 'truly competitive advantage' over their rivals.

Table 11.1 shows a selection of BA's financial indicators.

Practical dos and don'ts

For a commercial organization, we suggest that you start your analysis, as we have done, by examining the organization's published accounts. These often contain, already calculated for you, some of the most important indicators of financial performance. If these are not readily available (and they sometimes are not), then a good way of trying to understand the situation is to compute one or more of the ratios described in Appendix 11.1. In →

→ some cases you may have to dig a little deeper to try to understand what is going on. Perhaps the company uses different types of accounting standards and presentations of its data; international firms, although they are increasingly conforming to international standards may be based in a country that has not yet adopted them formally. In these cases you are likely to have to make a judgement about what you can legitimately use to compare this organization with one that uses different accounting conventions.

In some rare cases, an organization may be deliberately trying to mislead (see, for example, What Can Go Wrong 1.1). But in all cases, it is worth bearing in mind that few companies are going to flaunt bad news. To uncover this, you will have to be alert to potentially conflicting data, and use your own calculations and judgement to assess the situation. It is never a good idea to take a company's pronouncements entirely at face value.

Perhaps even more important than profit is the organization's cash flow, which is now reported in the accounts of most large firms. An organization that is generating cash can pay its bills, and invest in new equipment, products, or markets. On the other hand, a profitable firm that is not generating cash—perhaps because it is young and is not yet making sufficient sales to cover its initial investments in production facilities and marketing—is vulnerable. The cash burn—the number of months for which the company has sufficient cash in the bank to cover its cash outflow—is an important performance measure for this kind of firm.

There is also an increasing tendency for firms to report EBITDA (earnings before interest, tax, depreciation, and amortization) as a measure of how much profit they would be making if they were not making provision for the replacement of their assets. In firms where the next generation of assets is likely to be much less, or more, expensive than the current one— for example, because the production technology is not yet mature—this can be a helpful measure to put alongside more traditional measures of profit.

It is also important to gauge an organization's financial strength. The most important strategic indicator of this is the debt/equity ratio (also known as gearing or leverage). If this is persistently growing and reaches abnormal levels (50 per cent is a 'normal' rule of thumb) then it may indicate that the firm has expanded beyond the limits its cash flow permits. Interest cover (the number of times interest payments can be covered from profits) is also a useful check, to see if interest charges are manageable. If the debt/equity ratio is low then the organization has spare financial resources that might be used for expansion. However, short-term measures of liquidity are not of great interest in strategic analysis, except where they show that a firm is in imminent danger of bankruptcy.

For a public sector or not-for-profit organization, there will be few financial measures of this kind. Instead you might want to review whether the organization is meeting its budgetary targets. However, unless it is competing in commercial markets with private sector firms, like a publicly owned airline or broadcaster, a public sector unit will not normally be expected to generate commercial-style financial returns.

d. Measures of size and growth

Size and growth are important to British Airways. In Real-life Application 11.2 the company emphasizes the number of passengers, routes, and destinations served, the size of its fleet, and the extent of its route network. It also gives great weight to its profits, and to revenue passenger kilometres7 (although not to the slower growing cargo tonne kilometres, information which is only to be found later in the 2007 Annual Report).

It is quite usual in a strategic analysis to look at the size of an organization and the rate at which it is growing. Typically, this analysis will examine sales and profits and, if the data are available, non-financial measures of volume such as numbers of product units produced and sold, numbers of customers, of contracts and of outlets. Such figures need to be put in the context of what is happening in the industry as a whole, so the organization's market share will also be of interest.

The assumptions underlying this type of analysis are that successful organizations are able to grow, perhaps at the expense of unsuccessful ones, and that large organizations are better able to compete than small ones, partly because they may be able to achieve economies of scale or scope.

11.1.3 Specific stakeholder requirements

A firm is successful only if its key stakeholders are happy to keep it in existence. The requirements of these stakeholders may not always be expressed in terms of the straightforward accounting measures reviewed in the previous sections. The owners and shareholders of commercial organizations are looking for financial returns on their investments, measured by indicators like share prices and earnings per share. Different kinds of measure are needed for public sector and not-for-profit organizations.

a. Shareholding institutions and stock markets

As we saw in Section 2.6.1, individuals and institutions hold shares as financial investments that are required to generate a return, through dividends, share price increases, or both. They are interested in ROCE, ROE, and similar measures of overall performance, together with the firm's profit and growth record, which has a strong influence on its share price. Measures like earnings per share (EPS) and economic value added (EVA) have also often been used, as have measures such as dividend per share and net asset value per share.

Theoretical Debate 11.1 Financial engineering and shareholder value

A variety of measures have been proposed as ways of assessing the extent to which a firm is delivering value to its shareholders (Drongelen et al., 2000; Marco and Umit (2006); Garengo et al., 2005; Kit Fai and White, 2005; Bititci et al. (2001, 2005); Chun (2005); Neeley (1999); Bourne and Neely, 2002; Casson and McKenzie, 2007; Kanji and Moura, 2002; Kelleher and MacCormack, 2005; Kaplan and Norton, 1992, 1996a, 1996b, 2001). The simplest of these are subject to manipulation, the more complex ones are difficult for anyone bar experts to calculate accurately. Here, we discuss some of the various thoughts on their respective advantages and disadvantages.

Earnings per share

For many years, earnings per share was an important measure of firms' performance (Casson and McKenzie, 2007). Entire corporate strategies, often involving acquisitions, have been built around the sole aim of improving the earnings per share of the acquiring company. Such acquisitions are technically called 'earnings enhancing'. Suppose that a company with a high price/earnings (p/e) ratio acquires a firm with a lower p/e ratio. It pays for the acquisition with shares of its own, whose value is the same as

the market value of the acquired company's shares. Then, as if by magic, the EPS of the combined company becomes higher than that of the high p/e company before the acquisition.

However, such 'financial engineering' has become less fashionable in recent years, although you will still find earnings per share used to evaluate acquisitions in the financial press. This is likely to be because of what psychologists call the 'availability bias'—or the tendency to base assessments on widely available, rather than relevant, information (Mauboussin, 2006). From the strategic point of view, earnings enhancing acquisitions may be questionable unless the acquiring company has the skills and resources to manage its new subsidiary effectively (Financial Management Association, 2006; Dobbs et al., 2005).

EPS can also be manipulated through managing the timing at which discretionary accruals, which includes things like charges for work that has been done but not yet billed for, or a liability to do something that has already been paid, but not yet done, are put through a company's accounts (Bergstresser and Philippon, 2006; Ball and Shivakumar, 2006). This is termed 'smoothing' and is used as a way of stabilizing earnings—an important factor in share price management. However, it can also be used to increase the firm's earnings—'coincidentally' just as a chief ➜

➔ executive's salary and bonuses are decided on the basis of the company's EPS performance (Bartov and Mohanram, 2004). This obviously has the potential to lead to rather less than ethical behaviour (Heflin et al., 2002) and has meant that tying executive pay to EPS has become rather discredited.

Although measures like EPS can tell how likely it is that shareholders will sell a firm's stock, allow a firm to be taken over, or try to change its top management, many finance theorists now suggest that using EPS, or indeed any other measure based solely on share price, has little strategic significance. It is difficult to see any real link between the ratio of profits to the number of shares in issue and an organization's ability to add value to its customers. At best, EPS constitutes a substitute for ROE in cases where detailed accounting data are unavailable.

Sometimes the firm's share price on its own may be cited as a performance measure. In evaluating what share prices say about a firm's success or failure, it is important to bear in mind the imperfections of stock markets. Share prices are, in essence, an expression of a number of people's (shareholders or stockbrokers) estimates of what a firm's profits will be in the future. Some of these people may never have gone near the firm or sampled its products or services, but their bonuses often depend upon their ability to sell its shares at high prices. The more professional analysts will have evaluated the firm's financial data, and may have been able to visit the company and assess the quality of its strategy and its managers. However, even they are fallible human beings who may make errors of judgement. They may even have been given misleading or incorrect information.[8]

Share price movements are, therefore, only indirect evidence of how well a firm is performing. They tell you whether stock market analysts believe that firms will generate the kind of profits that they expect, as quickly as they would like. In order to evaluate this evidence, you need to know whether the markets are well informed, their judgement is strategically sound and their expectations are realistic.

Share price and shareholder value

A more complex use of the share price to assess a firm's performance is as an element in measures of shareholder value. This term became fashionable after a 1981 *Harvard Business Review* article by Alfred Rappaport (Rappaport, 1981; Rappaport and Sirower, 1999).[9] Shareholder value combines any capital gains from the firm's stock market value and the dividends paid out in a given period. The share price represents the net present value of the firm's resources and all future profits likely to flow from them, and dividends are the proportion of profits that the firm returns to shareholders, usually twice a year.

➔ We define net present value in Section 12.3.4.

Shareholder value can be lost or gained depending on how many shares are in issue. It can be destroyed if companies issue new shares when the market undervalues their stock, or vice-versa—if they buy in their company's shares when they are expensive. But share prices and numbers in issue must be considered alongside dividend yields to achieve a complete picture.

Dividend payments on their own cannot really be used to assess the firm's underlying performance, unless so much cash is paid out in dividends that it leads to liquidity problems, in which case the judgement of the firm's managers may be called into question.

The percentage of a firm's profits that is returned in the form of dividends is first of all based on the company's ability to fund them (which indicates success). However, this percentage may also, paradoxically, be increased if managers fear that shareholders could obtain more from their money by investing it elsewhere, and are therefore in danger of selling the shares. Or it may be very bullish, and feel that it is better able to generate overall returns by investing the money in its own activities. Thus assessing a firm's strength only by the size of its dividends could result in very different interpretations. British Airways, for example, has chosen not to pay dividends since 2001, yet it is one of the world's most profitable airlines. You would need to dig deep into the company's activities to find out why they might have done this; in BA's case it appears to be because of a pensions shortfall—a problem that they now judge is nearly solved.[10]

This type of approach at least focuses managers' minds on the need to provide a return to the owners of their company—their shareholders. But it has its critics. In 2000, Allan Kennedy published a book, *The End of Shareholder Value*, in which he critiqued the short-termism that measures like shareholder value encourage. Because of this, he argues, firms have cut costs, pruned workforces, and reduced customer choice. Another criticism (which Kennedy also discusses) focuses on over how long a period shareholder-value creation should be judged. As Kerin (2004) says, it is difficult to say who are good chief executives while they are still 'in the saddle' because their task is to build long-term value, beyond their own tenure (a point which Rappaport, 2004, also makes). Kerin also criticizes the fact that good, value-creating chief executives often do not use formal 'value-creation' processes such as those 'peddled by the value-based management industry that sprang up post-Rappaport'. Indeed, he argues that a focus on shareholder value tools bogs executives down in a focus on process and distracts them from strategy fundamentals, such as getting the right products to customers who want them.

And we agree. As we mentioned in Section 2.6.2, some studies have shown that firms that focus on increasing shareholder value rather than on developing 'real' strategies that generate ➔

→ long-term benefits for customers, are actually likely to lose value for shareholders. So, in our view the strategic situation of the firm is best assessed using measures of strategic performance that we discuss elsewhere in this chapter. Over the long term, if the firm can generate competitive advantage, it will also generate shareholder value and its share price should rise.

Economic value added

A newer measure is economic value added (EVA). This was developed by a US accounting consultancy firm, Stern Stewart, and comprises operating profit, less taxes and a charge for the economic cost of the capital tied up in the firm's assets. Because of the introduction of a calculation for the cost of capital (in other words its opportunity cost), EVA is believed by some theorists to hold more promise as a valid strategic performance measure (Tully, 1999). Policies aimed at increasing EVA should, in theory, increase a firm's value to its shareholders. Tully (albeit reporting on a 1999 study by Stern Stewart themselves) suggested that firms using EVA methods did increase their returns to share-holders compared with similar firms. Griffith (2004) and Kleiman (1999) similarly suggested that firms using EVA achieved better stock market returns than their immediate competitors.

Other research has shown more equivocal results (Malmi and Ikäheimo, 2003; De Wet and Du Toit, 2007; Kyriazis and Anastassis, 2007). Bhalla (2004), for example, found that many of the companies that have tried to implement EVA have not been able to do it, as it is a 'complex jumble of metrics, methods and messages that managers find very difficult to understand'. And therefore firms attempting to implement EVA have not been able to obtain commitment from senior managers, nor from other staff to collaborate in applying a consistent measure of EVA throughout the organization.

However, there are no indications as yet that EVA has led to the kind of strategically questionable policies observed in firms that targeted their strategies on the basis of EPS. On the other hand, a company's EVA is difficult to compute from a firm's published accounts. Adjustments are needed to items such as depreciation before EVA can be calculated, and it is not always clear what a firm's cost of capital might be.

b. Other stakeholder requirements

Other stakeholders will measure the organization's performance in ways that correspond to their particular requirements, and you will need to take account of those requirements in assessing the organization's success. Private owners may measure the firm on its ability to generate cash for their retirement. Governments want to know whether their investments are achieving their political ends, such as providing housing services cost-effectively. Donors are interested in whether a medical charity is using their money productively to fight disease.

→ The specific requirements of stakeholder groups were reviewed in Section 2.6.

An organization's stakeholders may change in the future—small firms grow and are floated on the stock exchange, and government bodies are privatized. This means that you need to be alert for changes over time in the way in which an organization's success will be judged. Its strategy may need to change to satisfy the new criteria—for example, by shedding surplus staff that government or private owners were happy to retain.

11.2 **Measures of operational performance**

Measures of overall performance only indicate whether the firm is performing well or badly. For clues as to why this good or bad performance is occurring, there are operational measures that can be brought into play.

11.2.1 **Standard measures of operating performance**

There are several measures of different aspects of efficiency and effectiveness that are more or less standard for all types of firm, although the precise definition of the performance measure may vary slightly from industry to industry.

First, there are three types of measure that together give insights into why the company's overall financial returns might be rising or falling. Sales and profits may rise (or fall) because the organization's assets are generating more (or fewer) orders, because the value of the average order is increasing (or decreasing), or because the profit margin on the average order is changing. Each of these three elements can be assessed by the following:

- Measures of how productively assets are being utilized: The classic accounting measures are net asset turnover or fixed asset turnover, but in many cases you will find that particular industries have their own, specific measures. Airlines measure passenger load factors, retailers measure sales per square metre (or square foot) of shopping area, and consultants measure staff utilization (the proportion of staff time spent on fee-earning work).

- Measures of unit sales value: BA uses sales per revenue passenger kilometer (RPK), while most other organizations measure the value of the order or transaction.

- Measures of profitability: Typically gross profit margin or operating profit as a percentage of sales.

Improvements in margins might be due to improved effectiveness in product quality (enabling the firm to command higher prices), to improvements in cost efficiency, or to better market conditions. BA has recently highlighted many of the measures it has taken to save costs, notably through reduction in staff numbers and better use of technology. Although its overall profits are the highest in the passenger airline industry, BA's profit margin is not—that distinction is held by Ryanair and other 'no-frills' carriers.[11] There is no doubt that worries about the increasing dominance of the no-frills sector is focusing BA and other 'full-service' airlines' attention on controlling costs.

There are two other useful general indicators of the effectiveness of a firm's management, which also measure particular aspects of a firm's strategy:

- Debtors (measured in days of sales): When the average number of days it takes an organization to obtain payment rises, it can indicate one of a number of problems. The firm may be overtrading, and so choosing its customers without fully checking their creditworthiness. It may be selling customers products that they do not really want, and so are reluctant to pay for. Goods may be being delivered broken or in the wrong quantities, the invoicing systems may be faulty, or there may simply be weak management in the finance area, so that outstanding invoices are not properly followed up.

- Stock turnover: When inventory (measured in relation to total sales or cost of sales) rises, it can be a sign of emerging problems with sales, of poor production or purchasing controls, or of general slackness in management.

11.2.2 Tailored measures of performance

One of the most difficult aspects of strategic analysis is to work out *specific* ways of measuring how well an organization is performing. These specific measures can, however, be very useful. First, they give more precise insights into the nature of an organization's competitive advantage than the more general indicators we have reviewed earlier in the chapter. Second, they can show whether there is a mismatch between what the organization says it is doing and what it really is doing. You will often get a better indication of an organization's true strategy from observing what it measures and does than from its declared goals or what it says it does.

Finally, the process of developing these measures can offer insights into the strategies that are being pursued by the organization and its competitors. This last sort of insight comes from looking at what the organization and its competitors measure (Worked Example 11.1).

Worked Example 11.1 Assessing BA's actions and strategies

If we look at Real-life Application 11.2 again, there are strong indications of some of BA's key goals and aspirations. It is clear that the management of costs is important. The emphasis placed in previous reports on being perceived as a global airline and market leader in world travel are nowhere to be seen. Instead almost all its focus is on how profitable and efficient it is. On this occasion what BA claims its goals to be and the measures it adopts appear to be closely aligned.

In 2007, it quotes figures relating to passenger load factors (broadly, an indicator of how full the average passenger aircraft is when it takes off) and yields (a measure of how much revenue each passenger generates). Passenger revenue was up 4.9 per cent primarily from long-haul premium passengers. Passenger yields were up 2.1 per cent per RPK. But these are not the best in its industry (see Table 11.3 later in this chapter). Time will tell whether it actually addresses these issues, as it claims to want to do.

There are some issues that we might want to think about further. BA talks about continuing to 'lead the way' in product innovation (its new Club World service, for example, and its website). These are the kinds of statement that trigger questions in the mind of a suspicious analyst. For example what *precisely* does product innovation mean in this industry? And is it really that important—does it correspond to one of the industry success or survival factors? Previous annual reports (an important source of comparative data) placed much more emphasis on this indicator than the 2007 report does. Is this an indication of a change of strategy, or simply an attempt to make the annual report less aspirational and more accurately reflect the organization's activities?

Other companies are not so consistent, and BA itself has not always been so. In 1999, it introduced a new mission, 'To be the undisputed leader in world travel', and also changed its corporate goals and values. The new goals were to be the 'Customers' Choice', to have 'Inspired People', 'Strong Profitability', and to be 'Truly Global'. The new values were to be 'Safe and Secure', 'Honest and Responsible', 'Innovative and Team Spirited', 'Global and Caring', and a 'Good Neighbour'. Of these, only 'strong profitability', and to a lesser extent 'to be truly global', were obviously linked to the measures that the company used to evaluate its performance, or at least the ones that it discussed in public. This is an illustration of an important principle of strategic analysis: in the words of an old management saying, 'What gets measured, gets done.'

Other industries also have their standard measures of efficiency and effectiveness. Steel firms measure the number of person-hours required to produce a tonne of steel, and automobile manufacturers measure the number of cars per staff-year—both of which are examples of labour-intensive industries measuring labour productivity. Retailers and many other service businesses measure sales per employee for similar reasons. The measures that firms in an industry employ to monitor their own operational performance provide a useful starting point for our analysis.

Sometimes, however, it will be necessary to invent our own measures of the organization's progress towards its declared goals. For example, if an organization like Sony has set itself up to be a leader in product innovation, then we shall want to measure its innovativeness. This can be done in a number of quite simple ways, as we noted in Chapter 10. For example we could review Sony's R&D expenditure as a proportion of sales. This is an input measure—it shows how seriously Sony is trying to be innovative. We could also count the number of new products that Sony has launched, or the number of patents that it has filed, over the last three years. This is an outcome measure—it shows how effective this innovation process really is.

One goal emphasized in BA's Annual Report is to have strong profitability, and the firm's success in achieving it can be assessed using standard accounting measures of output—profit margins, overall profits, and efficiency measures such as passenger load factors. The company also talks about cost-saving tactics, such as simplifying its operations by selling off its regional airline, and a move towards a single-aircraft fleet, which will save on maintenance and fitting-out costs. Measuring the inputs—numbers of people, fare levels—will provide evidence that the company is taking concrete steps in pursuit of its goal. But we would also want to measure relevant outcomes—sales per employee, passenger load factors—to see if it is bringing about the desired results.

→ We cover strategic control systems in Sections 8.2 and 9.2, and again in 17.2 when we discuss strategy implementation.

→ We examine the balanced
scorecard in more depth, in
Section 17.2.3 and in Worked
Example 17.1.

Some writers have focused on the need to take a more holistic picture of measures used to assess strategic performance, and to control it subsequently. Kaplan and Norton's balanced scorecard[12] was developed as an explicit response to organizations only focusing on financial performance measures to assess strategic performance. The balanced scorecard includes financial measures that measure past performance, but it also includes operational measures that are the drivers of future financial performance. A key aspect of this model is that it explicitly *links* the various performance measures.

11.3 Making comparisons

Quite understandably, the message conveyed by BA's chairman and chief executive (Real-life Application 11.2) is confident and upbeat. Improvements are highlighted and plausible reasons given for any downturns. They have faced some difficult circumstances and have taken whatever actions are needed to maintain the health and effectiveness of their company. It would, however, be a mistake to accept this message unchallenged. We need to place these results in some kind of context to evaluate how well BA really has performed.

11.3.1 Trend analysis

Trend analysis is an important strategic evaluation tool and can be used on both internal and external data. Trends in raw figures can be used to assess the path of a firm's sales and profits over time—growth or decline—and trends in ratios and tailored performance measures can also be used to assess whether performance is improving or getting worse, all of which BA has done (Table 11.2).

Other performance trends, such as growth in share price, which may be important to major stakeholders, can also be calculated. This shows whether stakeholders are likely to demand action. BA, for example, provides five-year trends on how fuel efficient its aircraft are, and also employee safety indicators—both of which are likely to help it establish a reputation as a responsible, caring, and 'green' company.

However, trend analysis is not always straightforward. For example, over how long a period should trends be assessed? The answer here depends on the industry and environmental factors. In a fast-changing industry (computer hardware or consumer electronics, for example) in a dynamic environment, using ten-year trends is likely to be pretty pointless; three years may be long enough—or 12 quarters if detailed data are available. In ten years, so many changes will have occurred in the characteristics of the industry and environment that performance comparisons are likely to be meaningless. On the other hand, for a less dynamic industry in a relatively stable environment (food or cement production for example), ten years may be an appropriate time-span. Five years is probably a good average period for most industries, and indeed, is the period that BA typically uses (for example, Table 11.2), although it sometimes uses shorter periods (Table 11.3). One might want to dig a little deeper in these cases.

The second problem is to eliminate 'noise' from trends. Financial reports are full of one-off events. These include:

- charges for organizational restructuring, such as redundancy payments;
- exceptionally large expenditure on new investments, such as an acquisition or a new factory, or expansion into new markets, or exceptional income items, such as the sale of a business unit or large building;
- provision against future legal action, as BA has made in its most recent financial year;
- provision for exceptional items, for example BA's pension shortfall;

Table 11.2 BA's five-year financial trends

OPERATING AND FINANCIAL STATISTICS
For the five years ended March 31, 2007

Total group operations		2007	2006*	2005	2004	2003
Traffic and capacity						
Revenue passenger km (RPK)	m	112,851	109,713	107,892	103,092	100,112
Available sex km (ASK)	m	148,321	144,194	144,189	141,273	139,172
Passenger load factor	%	76.1	76.1	74.8	73.0	71.9
Cargo tonne km (CTK)	m	4,695	4,929	4,954	4,461	4,210
Total revenue tonne km (RTK)	m	16,112	15,909	15,731	14,771	14,213
Total available tonne km (ATK)	m	22,882	22,719	22,565	21,859	21,328
Overall load factor	%	70.4	70.0	69.7	67.6	66.6
Passengers carried	'000	33,068	32,432	35,717	36,103	33,019
Tonnes of cargo carried	'000	762	795	877	796	764
Frequent flyer RPKs as a percentage of total RPKs	%	2.6	2.8	3.2	4.0	4.4
Revenue aircraft km	m	637	614	661	644	635
Revenue flights	'000	276	280	378	391	413
Break-even overall load factor	%	65.0	63.6	64.3	63.6	63.9
Financial						
Passenger revenue per RPK	P	6.44	6.31	6.02	6.30	6.58
Passenger revenue per ASK	P	4.90	4.80	4.51	4.59	4.74
Cargo revenue per CTK	P	13.16	12.94	9.73	10.38	11.50
Average fuel price (US cents/US gallon)		209.60	188.22	136.44	94.49	36.01
Operations						
Average manpower equivalent (MPE)		43,501	45,072	47,472	49,072	53,440
RTKs per MPE		370.4	353.0	331.4	301.0	266.0
ATKs per MFE		526.0	504.1	475.3	445.4	399.1
Aircraft in service at year end		242	284	290	291	330
Aircraft utilization (average hours per aircraft per day)		10.82	10.29	9.83	9.21	8.91
Unduplicated route km	'000	589	574	623	657	693
Punctuality—within 15 minutes	%	67	75	76	81	76
Regularity	%	98.5	98.8	98.8	98.8	98.2

		2007	2006	2005	2004**	2003**
Financial**						
Interact cover	times	16.7	6.0	3.8		
Dividend cover	times	n/a	n/a	n/a		
Operating margin	%	7.1	8.5	7.2		
Earnings before interest, tax, depreciation, amortization and rentals (EBITDAR)	m	1,549	1,666	1,552		
Net date/total capital ratio	%	29.1	44.2	67.7		
Net date/total capital ratio including operating leases	%	39.6	53.0	72.4		
Total traffic revenue per RTK	P	48.91	47.53	44.4		
Total traffic revenue per ATK	P	34.44	33.28	30.94		
Total expenditure on operations per RTK	P	49.26	47.26	40.85		
Total expenditure on operations per ATK	P	34.68	33.10	28.43		

* Restated for the disposal of the regional business of BA Connect
** Financial ratios are only available under comparative IFRSs from the Group's transition date of April 1, 2004
n/a = not applicable

Source
BA's Annual Report 2007, p. 33. *Reproduced with the kind permission of British Airways*

Table 11.3 British Airways' turnover by destination, 2006–2007

By area of destination	Turnover £m	
	2007	2006
Europe	5,316	5,117
The Americas	1,731	1,602
Africa, Middle East, and Indian subcontinent	649	825
Far East and Australasia	796	669
Total	8,492	8,213

Source
British Airways Annual Report 2007, p. 62. *Reproduced with the kind permission of British Airways*

Share buy-back
When a company buys
back its own shares from
shareholders.

Share split
Issuing new shares to each
shareholder, and reducing
each share's nominal value.
For example, a company may
issue 10 shares of nominal
10p value to replace each
£1 share.

- share buy-backs, or share splits. A firm can buy back its shares to use up surplus cash, when it has it, and at the same time reduce the number of shares in circulation—therefore increasing its EPS ratio. Because of this, the share price may also rise. Share splits do the opposite—they increase the total number of shares in existence, and therefore reduce EPS. But companies sometimes need to do this in order to reduce the quoted value of the shares, and thereby make them more tradable. For example, when Coca Cola was first floated, its shares were worth $40. If it had not split these along the way, each share would now be worth $4m—and virtually un-sellable.[13]

Any trend analysis needs, therefore, to strip out rare and exceptional items such as these, and look at the underlying trends. If we return to Table 11.2 we can see that BA has 'adjusted' (i.e. removed the effect for us) the sale of its BA Connect unit.

Nevertheless trend data is a very useful tool to help us question the claims that you will see made about organizations in case studies and their annual reports. An improvement in BA's profitability over time would justify the claims of its senior managers to have successfully dealt with some of the company's external problems, while a decline in some of the key indicators would cast doubt upon them—and, by implication, on their judgement. This questioning process is another very important element of strategic analysis.

11.3.2 **Making comparisons with other organizations**

Even if profits or sales' trends show that an organization is performing worse than it did in the past, this does not mean that it is weak, just as improvement in performance is not the same as strength. Confusing the two is a common error. Strength and weakness both need to be measured relative to an organization's competitors. An improvement in performance may appear impressive, until one learns that competitors are improving at double the rate. Equally, a seemingly catastrophic decline in profits may be the result of a sudden collapse in the firm's main markets. The firm may actually have sound strategies that have helped it survive these problems better than its competitors.

➔ We discussed strategic
groups in Chapter 3.

It is therefore important to assess an organization's performance against its closest competitors—especially those in its strategic group (Table 11.4). In BA's case these are the full-service airlines that specialize in carrying Business (Club) class passengers on medium- and long-distance flights—companies like American Airlines and United Airlines in the USA, Lufthansa/Swiss and France/KLM in Europe, and Singapore Airlines in Asia.

However, although it may make little sense to compare British Airways with low-cost carriers like Ireland's Ryanair or America's Southwest Airlines, or with charter operators

Table 11.4 BA's financial performance compared with some of its competitors

Airline	Airline type LC = low cost; IFC = International full service;	Operating profit margin %	Operating revenue $(000)	% chg.	Operating expense $(000)	% chg.	Operating Profit $(000) current year	Operating Profit $(000) previous year	Net profit $(000) current year	Net profit $(000) previous year	Load factor	FTK	% chg.	Passengers	% chg.	RPK	% chg.
Air Asia	Domestic/regional	12.7	231,287	28.4	201,995	38.4	29,291	34,086	34,313	30,175	74.8	N/A	–	4,414	55.5	4,881	76.1
Air France/KLM[1]	IFS	4.4	25,901,248	13	24,770,906	11.3	1,130,342	664,197	1,112,227	2,048,140	80.6	10,606,000	2.3	69,159	6.1	185,709	8.3
All Nippon	IFS	6.5	11,643,010	5.9	10,887,700	5.4	755,310	661,553	227,300	229,409	N/A	14,776	–				
American	IFS	–1.7	20,657,147	11	21,007,890	10.4	–350,743	–421,012	–891,719	–820,981	78.6	2,915,290	1.7	98,098	7.1	222,634	6.3
American Eagle	US Domestic	12.5	1,795,067	24.2	1,570,132	28	224,935	219,186	46,190	48,804	71.3	210	–19.1	17,534	17.9	12,070	29
Bmi	LC/IFS	0.6	1,495,367	4.7	1,435,903	4.7	9,464	–5,506	17,208	4,474	68.4	109,413	42.8	6,016	–16.1	5,746	–8.5
British Airways	IFS	8.3	14,814,227	9.6	13,587,682	8.3	1,226,545	967,318	784,644	655,897	75.6	4,928,000	–0.5	35,634	–0.2	111,859	3.7
Cathay Pacific	IFS	8.1	6,527,000	19.1	5,996,000	24.7	531,000	673,000	423,000	566,000	78.7	6,618,000	10.2	15,438	13	65,110	13.7
China Airlines	IFS	3.1	3,380,000	17.9	3,276,000	21.4	104,000	168,000	20	125,000	76.5	6,078,000	5.4	9,731	9.1	32,047	8.4
Continental	IFS	–8.3	1,108,038	16.6	11,199,880	14.2	–91,842	–280,730	–65,617	–362,965	79.8	1,234,417	–2.9	42,822	5.1	110,003	7.9
Delta	IFS	–7.4	16,111,713	6.3	17,308,865	3.2	–1,197,152	–1,612,738	–3,797,551	–3,362,180	77.5	1,760,240	–0.6	86,104	–0.9	166,918	5.6
easyJet	LC	7.3	3,045,036	20.7	2,823,572	14.8	221,464	62,416	176,908	110,920	85.2	–	–	29,600	21.4	27,448	27.3
Emirates	IFS	12.1	6,597,400	27.2	5,797,000	31.5	800,400	777,800	761,400	725,600	75.9	4,191,931	19.5	13,976	16.2	59,299	21.6
EVA	IFS	0.5	2,735,964	10.6	2,723,160	16.7	12,804	141,178	41,220	97,094	78.7	5,285,329	–3.6	5,904	8.6	23,099	6.2
FedEx	Freight	8.2	21,446,000	10.1	19,679,000	8.9	1,767,000	1,414,000	–	–	–	14,577,425	0.5	–	–	–	–

Table 11.4 *(cont'd)*

Airline	Airline type LC = low cost; IFC = International full service;	Operating profit margin %	Operating revenue $(000)	% chg.	Operating expense $(000)	% chg.	Operating Profit $(000) current year	Operating Profit $(000) previous year	Net profit $(000) current year	Net profit $(000) previous year	Load factor	FTK	% chg.	Passengers	% chg.	RPK	% chg.
Gol	LC	23.3	1,140,296	36.1	874,840	48.2	265,456	247,558	219,263	165,258	73.5	–	–	13,000	41.1	9,736	54.8
Iberia	IFS	2.4	5,838,272	2.8	5,700,403	4.3	137,869	214,523	468,568	234,860	77.1	973,495	–5.8	27,436	2.8	48,975	6.6
Japan Airlines	IFS	–1.2	18,713,200	3.3	18,941,161	7.4	–227,961	477,187	–401,483	255,180	67.5	4,929,736	–2.9	58,036	–2.4	100,345	–2
JetBlue	LC	3.6	1,703,181	34.5	1,641,355	42.4	61,826	113,129	–20,592	47,467	84.6	1,825	14.6	14,681	25.1	32,482	28.4
Kalitta Air	Freight	12.4	494,191	30.1	433,146	40.6	61,045	71,881	62,194	71,804	–	2,093,935	38.5	–	–	–	–
Kenya Airways	IFS	14.6	738,200	25	630,512	26.5	107,688	92,114	67,509	54,270	75.4	253,133	30.9	2,351	21.3	6,511	23.2
Korean	IFS	5.7	7,486,900	–1.3	7,060,000	–1.3	426,900	432,500	197,000	200,400	73.8	6,146,841	2.8	22,966	7.4	52,534	12.4
Lufthansa Group	IFS	3.2	21,397,000	6.5	20,713,663	5.5	683,337	453,644	536,555	478,518	75	7,829,000	–1.7	51,255	0.7	108,185	4
Omni Air	Charter	16.5	370,449	25.6	309,477	32.2	60,972	60,935	66,904	62,128	62.9	502,316	32.8	622	0.2	4,150	6.6
Qantas	IFS	5.3	9,962,091	8.6	9,432,257	11.9	529,834	740,220	350,400	503,189	76.3	2,371,328	31.4	32,658	8.6	86,986	7
Ryanair	LC	22.2	2,042,884	28.3	1,590,203	34.7	452,681	411,271	370,201	338,012	85.2	–	–	33,384	25.6	31,205	38.4
Singapore	IFS	9.1	8,236,128	11.1	7,487,097	13.4	749,031	813,112	765,946	834,904	74.5	7,555,356	3	16,628	4.3	80,906	4.3
Southwest	US Domestic	10.8	7,583,837	16.1	6,763,757	13.2	820,080	553,581	548,383	313,369	70.7	195,501	4.06	88,474	9	97,097	12.7
United	IFS	–1.4	17,304,154	10.2	17,545,500	4	–241,346	–1,166,406	–21,036,384	–2,002,147	81.5	2,415,071	2.6	66,801	–5.8	183,862	–0.8
UPS	Freight	7.2	4,105,212	1		20.3	293,889	224,263	108,998	–6,573	–	8,507,711	10.4	–	–	–	–

Notes

Based on 2006 data—the most recent complete results for all airlines; therefore the figures for BA apply to one year earlier than those shown in Table 11.1

Source

World Airline Financial Results. Air Transport World, 1 January 2007: 40: and authors' calculations. Reproduced with the kind permission of Air Transport World

like America's Omni Air, which have set up their value chains in a different way to deliver a low-cost, low-priced service, leaving them out of the equation altogether may be dangerous. One of the very real problems that managers have is that they tend to limit their attention to familiar issues and competitors, and don't gather data outside those areas.

→ We discussed the limitations in managers' thinking in Section 1.6.4.

BA's strategic group competitors are not the most profitable airlines, or even arguably its biggest threat. What if FedEx, a leading global provider of air courier, freight and logistics services, decided to diversify into carrying passengers? It has considerable financial resources.

Creative Strategizing 11.1

What would you do if you were BA's CEO and FedEx *did* decide to diversify into carrying passengers?

In fact, the airline industry provides a wonderful example of a setting in which the rules of the game appear to be changing. Although many people (including us, in our previous book) predicted that the low-cost carriers would have low margins and would not pose a threat to the full-service carriers, it is very clear from the figures in Table 11.4 that this is not how things have turned out.

a. Benchmarking

So BA may well be advised to keep an eye on a wider group of competitors than simply those in its own strategic group, and benchmark its return on capital employed or return on assets against the best of these other types of airline. It may even be able to copy some elements of their operations to make its own business model more efficient or effective.

In most industries, there are a few leading firms that set the standards for the rest. They are more profitable, more innovative, faster growing, can respond faster to orders or produce their outputs more cheaply than their competitors. Trade magazines or management journals often publish rankings. In the auto industry, Toyota has long been the standard against which other manufacturers assess their efficiency; it regularly makes the list of *Fortune* magazine's most admired companies world-wide.

It is important to benchmark a firm against such industry leaders. This is true even if factors like trade barriers or a different market focus stop them competing directly with the organization you are analysing. The difference in performance between the leader and the rest gives some measure of the opportunities available if performance can be improved. Benchmarking is used to establish stretch goals, as well as helping an organization to identify potential problem areas.

Benchmarking
Measuring products or practices against those of top-ranking competitors or of organizations seen as industry leaders. Sometimes undertaken on best practices in unrelated sectors to make comparisons with world-best performers.

b. Provisos in making comparisons with other organizations

For most firms, use can be made of industry norms and averages, but you may need to be careful if you use external sources such as industry trade bodies or financial analysts. The various data providers often use different ways of calculating their figures. For example, whilst writing this chapter, the authors came across three different sets of numbers for British Airways' passengers. These were quite similar to one another, admittedly, but, nevertheless, none agreed absolutely with BA's own figures.

We also need to be alert to any possible inconsistencies between different data sources. For example, any ROE figures from China Airlines or other international carriers may well not be strictly comparable to BA's, since they are likely to have been prepared under different accounting conventions. Although there has been an attempt to develop a comparable set of international accounting standards, tax regimes or definitions of terms may still vary from country to country. The way that ratios are calculated and presented in annual reports can also vary from company to company, for example by including short-term as well as long-term debt in calculations of gearing—another reason why you should make the calculations using raw data yourself. Data in different exhibits, or from different sources, may span slightly different time periods.

McDonald's (Real-life Application 11.3), for example, chooses not to include sales figures from franchisees within its turnover figures. This is an entirely legitimate choice—franchisees are not wholly owned subsidiaries whose accounts *would* need to be included in McDonald's overall sales' figures. However, it also has the effect of making any ratios which use sales figures as the denominator higher than they otherwise would be (and of course has the opposite effect where sales are the numerator). McDonald's also has its problems in attempting to reconcile the income from a very international business and its large number of semi-independent franchisees. It explicitly says that it makes no attempt to calculate earnings ratios, although it does point out some of the problems that those attempting to do so might encounter.

Real-life Application 11.3 Accounting for McDonald's franchisees and international sales

McDonald's international and franchise sales play an important part in its financial performance. *iStock*

Sales by franchisees or affiliates are not recorded within the company's total revenues in McDonald's' 2004 Annual Report. Instead, the rent and service fees that franchisees pay are included in the overall revenue figures. In 2004, worldwide sales totalled $19,065m of which $4,841m was the income from franchisees and affiliates. At the bottom of their summary figures, however, is a separate amount of $37,065m, which are the sales that have been made by McDonald's 22,349 franchised or affiliated restaurants (from a total of more than 30,000 restaurants worldwide). McDonald's management believes that this information is important in understanding the company's financial performance because 'it is the basis on which the Company calculates and records franchised and affiliated revenues and is indicative of the financial health of their franchisee base'.

Another problem in presenting their accounts concerns the international nature of the McDonald's business. As the 2004 Annual Report states:

> While the Company does not provide specific guidance on earnings per share, the following information is provided to assist in analyzing the Company's results.   ➜

→ • The Company does not provide specific guidance on changes in comparable sales. However, as a perspective, assuming no change in cost structure, a 1 percentage point increase in U.S. comparable sales would increase annual earnings per share by about 2 cents. Similarly, an increase of 1 percentage point in Europe's comparable sales would increase annual earnings per share by about 1.5 cents.

• A significant part of the Company's operating income is from outside the U.S., and about 70% of its total debt is denominated in foreign currencies. Accordingly, earnings are affected by changes in foreign currency exchange rates, particularly the Euro and the British Pound. If the Euro and the British Pound both move 10% in the same direction (compared with 2004 average rates), the Company's annual earnings per share would change about 6 cents to 7 cents. In 2004, foreign currency translation benefited earnings per share by 6 cents due primarily to the Euro and the British Pound.

Most strategy case studies will adjust their data to compensate for differences in accounting practices between firms and countries. However, the data is likely to be incomplete, and you may find examples of apparent inconsistencies. This is not just a way of making sure that the reader is awake; it reflects the incomplete and sometimes contradictory information with which managers and case writers have to make do in real life.

11.3.3 **Internal comparisons**

Another source of comparison is between different parts of the same organization. This can help us to identify whether good or bad performance comes especially from one part of the organization, or whether all divisions or functions are performing at more or less the same level. The managing director or CEO might ask, for example, why every part of an organization is not performing at the level of its most profitable division.

At the strategic business unit (SBU) level, there is a strong emphasis on performance relative to competitors. We will want to look for evidence of success or failure in the marketplace, comparing growth and profitability with that of competitors, and look at market share and the results of independent quality assessments to see how customers perceive the business unit or firm.

This type of analysis is also where we start to get an insight into possible operational problems. It is important, if the data are available, to look at operational performance measures such as unit production costs and inventory turnover. The attitudes of employee stakeholders, as expressed through absenteeism and staff turnover statistics, may also be revealing (Worked Example 11.2).

Worked Example 11.2 Assessing Sony's divisions' performance

If we look now at Sony, it has very helpfully provided detailed—and graphically clear—information about the performance of its five divisions in its annual report (Figure 11.1).

Sony's divisions' performance

From this we can see that only one division, the financial services unit, appears to be doing extremely well—both in terms of sales and

turnover growth—albeit partly as a result of favourable external conditions. However, this is one of Sony's smaller divisions, accounting for less than 10 per cent of the company's sales. In the largest division, electronics, profits are declining, and sales are also declining in real terms.

Sony, once again, is very open about some of these problems: elsewhere in its Annual Report it says 'strengthening Sony's Electronics business is our top priority given the significant →

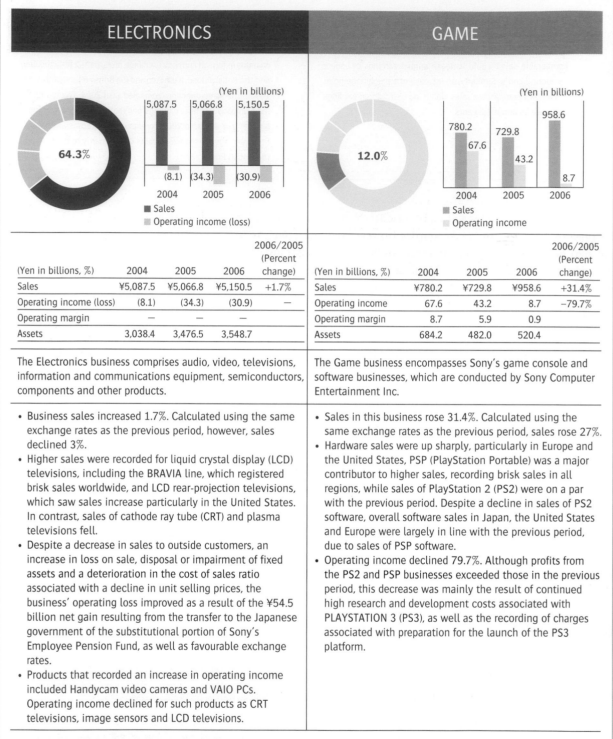

(Yen in billions, %)	2004	2005	2006	2006/2005 (Percent change)
Sales	¥5,087.5	¥5,066.8	¥5,150.5	+1.7%
Operating income (loss)	(8.1)	(34.3)	(30.9)	—
Operating margin	—	—	—	
Assets	3,038.4	3,476.5	3,548.7	

The Electronics business comprises audio, video, televisions, information and communications equipment, semiconductors, components and other products.

- Business sales increased 1.7%. Calculated using the same exchange rates as the previous period, however, sales declined 3%.
- Higher sales were recorded for liquid crystal display (LCD) televisions, including the BRAVIA line, which registered brisk sales worldwide, and LCD rear-projection televisions, which saw sales increase particularly in the United States. In contrast, sales of cathode ray tube (CRT) and plasma televisions fell.
- Despite a decrease in sales to outside customers, an increase in loss on sale, disposal or impairment of fixed assets and a deterioration in the cost of sales ratio associated with a decline in unit selling prices, the business' operating loss improved as a result of the ¥54.5 billion net gain resulting from the transfer to the Japanese government of the substitutional portion of Sony's Employee Pension Fund, as well as favourable exchange rates.
- Products that recorded an increase in operating income included Handycam video cameras and VAIO PCs. Operating income declined for such products as CRT televisions, image sensors and LCD televisions.

(Yen in billions, %)	2004	2005	2006	2006/2005 (Percent change)
Sales	¥780.2	¥729.8	¥958.6	+31.4%
Operating income	67.6	43.2	8.7	−79.7%
Operating margin	8.7	5.9	0.9	
Assets	684.2	482.0	520.4	

The Game business encompasses Sony's game console and software businesses, which are conducted by Sony Computer Entertainment Inc.

- Sales in this business rose 31.4%. Calculated using the same exchange rates as the previous period, sales rose 27%.
- Hardware sales were up sharply, particularly in Europe and the United States, PSP (PlayStation Portable) was a major contributor to higher sales, recording brisk sales in all regions, while sales of PlayStation 2 (PS2) were on a par with the previous period. Despite a decline in sales of PS2 software, overall software sales in Japan, the United States and Europe were largely in line with the previous period, due to sales of PSP software.
- Operating income declined 79.7%. Although profits from the PS2 and PSP businesses exceeded those in the previous period, this decrease was mainly the result of continued high research and development costs associated with PLAYSTATION 3 (PS3), as well as the recording of charges associated with preparation for the launch of the PS3 platform.

Figure 11.1 Sony's divisions' performance   ➔

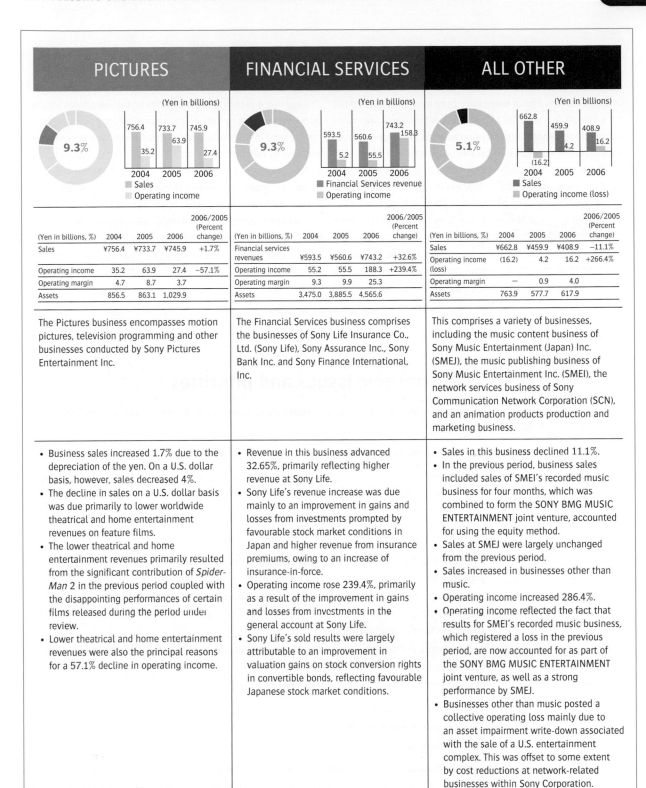

PICTURES	FINANCIAL SERVICES	ALL OTHER
(Yen in billions)	(Yen in billions)	(Yen in billions)

PICTURES

(Yen in billions, %)	2004	2005	2006	2006/2005 (Percent change)
Sales	¥756.4	¥733.7	¥745.9	+1.7%
Operating income	35.2	63.9	27.4	−57.1%
Operating margin	4.7	8.7	3.7	
Assets	856.5	863.1	1,029.9	

FINANCIAL SERVICES

(Yen in billions, %)	2004	2005	2006	2006/2005 (Percent change)
Financial services revenues	¥593.5	¥560.6	¥743.2	+32.6%
Operating income	55.2	55.5	188.3	+239.4%
Operating margin	9.3	9.9	25.3	
Assets	3,475.0	3,885.5	4,565.6	

ALL OTHER

(Yen in billions, %)	2004	2005	2006	2006/2005 (Percent change)
Sales	¥662.8	¥459.9	¥408.9	−11.1%
Operating income (loss)	(16.2)	4.2	16.2	+266.4%
Operating margin	—	0.9	4.0	
Assets	763.9	577.7	617.9	

PICTURES

The Pictures business encompasses motion pictures, television programming and other businesses conducted by Sony Pictures Entertainment Inc.

FINANCIAL SERVICES

The Financial Services business comprises the businesses of Sony Life Insurance Co., Ltd. (Sony Life), Sony Assurance Inc., Sony Bank Inc. and Sony Finance International, Inc.

ALL OTHER

This comprises a variety of businesses, including the music content business of Sony Music Entertainment (Japan) Inc. (SMEJ), the music publishing business of Sony Music Entertainment Inc. (SMEI), the network services business of Sony Communication Network Corporation (SCN), and an animation products production and marketing business.

PICTURES

- Business sales increased 1.7% due to the depreciation of the yen. On a U.S. dollar basis, however, sales decreased 4%.
- The decline in sales on a U.S. dollar basis was due primarily to lower worldwide theatrical and home entertainment revenues on feature films.
- The lower theatrical and home entertainment revenues primarily resulted from the significant contribution of *Spider-Man* 2 in the previous period coupled with the disappointing performances of certain films released during the period under review.
- Lower theatrical and home entertainment revenues were also the principal reasons for a 57.1% decline in operating income.

FINANCIAL SERVICES

- Revenue in this business advanced 32.65%, primarily reflecting higher revenue at Sony Life.
- Sony Life's revenue increase was due mainly to an improvement in gains and losses from investments prompted by favourable stock market conditions in Japan and higher revenue from insurance premiums, owing to an increase of insurance-in-force.
- Operating income rose 239.4%, primarily as a result of the improvement in gains and losses from investments in the general account at Sony Life.
- Sony Life's sold results were largely attributable to an improvement in valuation gains on stock conversion rights in convertible bonds, reflecting favourable Japanese stock market conditions.

ALL OTHER

- Sales in this business declined 11.1%.
- In the previous period, business sales included sales of SMEI's recorded music business for four months, which was combined to form the SONY BMG MUSIC ENTERTAINMENT joint venture, accounted for using the equity method.
- Sales at SMEJ were largely unchanged from the previous period.
- Sales increased in businesses other than music.
- Operating income increased 286.4%.
- Operating income reflected the fact that results for SMEI's recorded music business, which registered a loss in the previous period, are now accounted for as part of the SONY BMG MUSIC ENTERTAINMENT joint venture, as well as a strong performance by SMEJ.
- Businesses other than music posted a collective operating loss mainly due to an asset impairment write-down associated with the sale of a U.S. entertainment complex. This was offset to some extent by cost reductions at network-related businesses within Sony Corporation.

Figure 11.1 *(cont'd)*

→ impact a turnaround would have on our consolidated performance'.[14] Cathode ray and plasma television sales fell (although we are not told by how much), as did their profits—the result of lower unit sales' prices. Profits would have been even lower were it not for a one-off deal with the Japanese government and favourable exchange rates. In fact, the television business in general appeared to be experiencing setbacks—operating income for LCD TVs also fell.

So the division for which Sony is probably least well known, at least outside Japan, and which has less in common with the rest of the company than any other, is doing best. In theory, the obvious answer would be to suggest that Sony transfers best practice and learning from this division to the others, but that does not seem especially plausible in this case. And in fact, we don't really know whether this is a successful division or not—for that we would have to look to the division's outside competitors.

A more useful comparison is probably to be made between the plasma section of the Electronics division and the LCD one. And Sony is with us here—the division has a new CEO and a new strategy that is planning to concentrate on turning around Sony's television business by 'rationalizing manufacturing sites, increasing the ratio of internally sourced components and centralizing engineering functions'.[15] In addition it reports that action plans have already been implemented for nine of 15 selected business categories, including plasma televisions, actions which were anticipated to lead to ¥50.0 billion in improved profits.

It also comments on the relatively high demand for its LCD-based products. We would have to go elsewhere to find out if this is because of generally lower demand for plasma TVs, or because Sony's products are simply not as well received as those of its competitors.

11.4 Strategic issues and priorities

In assessing an organization's performance, we are trying to answer a number of basic questions:

- Are we dealing with a successful organization/SBU, or an unsuccessful one?

- Is the organization's performance improving relative to its competitors, or getting worse?

- Are there any particular parts of the organization or businesses that are significantly more or less successful than the others?

These analyses will give us a good baseline from which to make judgements, enough possibly to encourage us to invest in the firm, or alternatively sell our shares. But this is not enough; it is simply the first stage in a comprehensive, systematic process of assessing the organization's situation. Only when this is done can we develop the most appropriate strategies for the organization.

So as well as knowing the financial position of the organization, we also need to review the topics discussed in Chapters 3 to 10. For a multi-business corporation this analysis will need to be undertaken on each of its major SBUs. As a reminder, these topics are:

- the environment: how it is changing, and how this may impact on the competitiveness of the organization, given any developments in the survival and success factors in its industry(ies) (Chapter 3);

- the sources of the organization's distinctiveness—features that allow it to achieve differentiation and/or cost advantage, and which make it different from its competitors, such as its competitive stance (Chapter 4), scope, scale and diversity (Chapter 5), and value chain (Chapter 6);

- the organization's sources of sustainability—features that allow it to maintain competitive advantage over time, for example its resources (Chapter 7), architecture, and culture (Chapter 8), ability to manage complexity (Chapter 9), and knowledge, learning, and innovativeness (Chapter 10).

This review will raise a number of concerns, which can be expressed as strategic issues. These can then be prioritized according to their importance to the organization, given its specific environmental conditions. Strategies can then be developed to respond to the highest priority issues, noting that each issue may be solved by a range of different strategic options. We discuss the process of developing and evaluating strategic options in Chapter 12. But for now we look at the processes of identifying strategic issues and then prioritizing them.

Scenario planning

Sometimes executives use techniques such as scenario planning to forecast a range of different futures and likely issues and priorities, and devise strategies that would be able to cope with them. That way they are not faced with a nasty surprise if events turn out differently from predictions. Real-option thinking is another way of coping with such uncertainty.

→ We discuss strategy formulation in turbulent environments further in Section 13.4.3, and real-option thinking in Section 12.1.1.

Scenario planning is about thinking the unthinkable, and as such overlaps with contingency planning, which is about the development of specific plans to cope with an exceptional event—a stock market collapse, or catastrophic weather, for example. However, recent developments have seen the technique being used much more to develop creative and imaginative strategies to cope with opportunities as well as threats; it helps to break down managers' cognitive processes, and thereby lead to greater creativity in strategic decision-making[16] (Real-life Application 11.4). It is also a useful tool to assess in depth the underlying components of the various strategic issues, in order to get a full picture of resource implications, risks and potential benefits.

Scenario planning involves a number of elements:[17]

- Key managers and staff set down their ideas about what they think the future might hold, and what could be most exciting or frightening about a world ten years from now.

- Data about current trends are gathered, from as wide a range of sources as is practicable —including all the PESTLE categories.

- Stories are developed to sketch out the potential futures, using metaphors and detailed outlines of 'what-if' situations. Most writers appear to think that three or four possible scenarios are enough—one case which will challenge current sources of advantage, one which will challenge the organization's ability to manage growth, and one or two intermediate examples. However, even extreme cases should represent plausible conditions of the business environment. Such stories contain as much background information as possible, for example the technological and social conditions necessary to make the mass production of hybrid cars possible.

- The implications of each scenario, local as well as global, are assessed.

- Indicators, such as new regulations, competitors' behaviour, or demographic trends that would imply that the scenario is happening, are assessed.

Real-life Application 11.4 Scenario planning at UPS[18]

Scenario planning's most famous exponent was Royal Dutch Shell, the oil company, whose managers used it in the 1970s to imagine a future in which the oil producers held the upper hand. As a result Shell was able to deal with the subsequent OPEC embargo much better than many of its competitors.

More recently United Parcels Service (UPS), one of the USA's major courier and postal services companies, undertook two rounds of scenario planning workshops in which managers representing a wide range of functions devised four scenarios for UPS. The first took place in 1997. Benefits had been noted in the process' subtle and informal influences on strategic decision making. For example, senior managers became aware of the need to establish a retail presence to satisfy more proactive customers, leading eventually to the acquisition of Mail Boxes →

→ Etc, a franchised network of stores providing shipping and business services. Some also noticed a change in managers' 'mind sets'.

The process was repeated in 2004. Participants once again defined two axes of uncertainty: the horizontal axis was 'the range of possible business models and demand characteristics, moving from traditional, proprietary business models and focused, incremental demand to a more proactive, open, and collaborative world of commerce'.[19] The vertical axis addressed the global and regional business environments, which ranged from bordered, chaotic, restricted, and fragmented to borderless, harmonious, free, and holistic.

These two axes produced four scenarios that were named:

1. Company city
2. Networks without borders
3. Bordered disorder
4. Connected chaos.

Key themes and causes were mapped on to the axes (Figure 11.2), and story lines developed, and then managerial implications were drawn out (Figure 11.3)[20] for the following ten years up to 2017. Participants met in regional teams to define implications for technology and infrastructure initiatives, growth strategies and options, and workforce development at both the global and regional levels, and also identified 'loose' early warning signals to indicate movement towards one scenario or another.   →

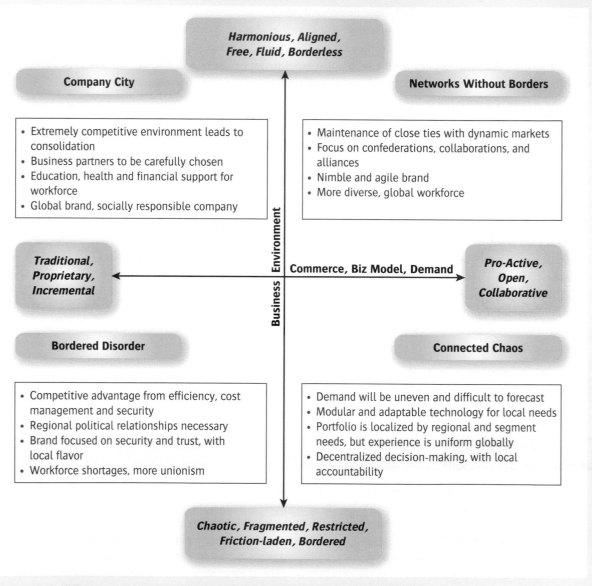

Figure 11.2 UPS scenarios' key themes and implications (Garvin and Levesque, 2006: 23)

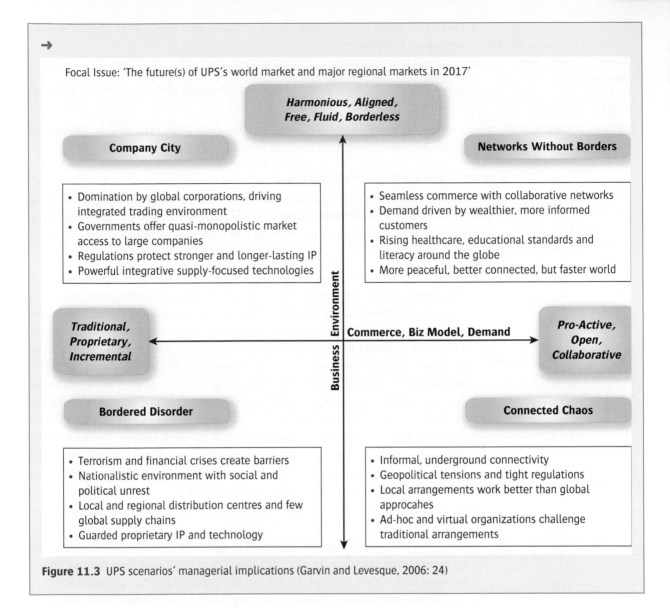

Focal Issue: 'The future(s) of UPS's world market and major regional markets in 2017'

Harmonious, Aligned, Free, Fluid, Borderless

Company City

- Domination by global corporations, driving integrated trading environment
- Governments offer quasi-monopolistic market access to large companies
- Regulations protect stronger and longer-lasting IP
- Powerful integrative supply-focused technologies

Networks Without Borders

- Seamless commerce with collaborative networks
- Demand driven by wealthier, more informed customers
- Rising healthcare, educational standards and literacy around the globe
- More peaceful, better connected, but faster world

Business Environment

Commerce, Biz Model, Demand

Traditional, Proprietary, Incremental

Pro-Active, Open, Collaborative

Bordered Disorder

- Terrorism and financial crises create barriers
- Nationalistic environment with social and political unrest
- Local and regional distribution centres and few global supply chains
- Guarded proprietary IP and technology

Connected Chaos

- Informal, underground connectivity
- Geopolitical tensions and tight regulations
- Local arrangements work better than global approcahes
- Ad-hoc and virtual organizations challenge traditional arrangements

Figure 11.3 UPS scenarios' managerial implications (Garvin and Levesque, 2006: 24)

11.4.1 **Strategic issues**

The result of a comprehensive analysis of the organization is likely to be a list of strategic issues that the organization needs to do something about. Issues may be internal or external in nature, and may have a positive or negative impact on the organization. It is helpful to conceive of a strategic issue as an important question to which the organization must find an answer, for example:

- How should it react to the emergence of new technologies?
- What should it do about emerging or disappearing markets?
- How should it respond to changing customer requirements?
- How should it deal with newly emerging competitors or respond to changes in strategy by existing competitors?
- How should it react in businesses where it is competitively disadvantaged in terms of differentiation or cost?

- How can it utilize its strategic resources to consolidate its lead over its existing competitors, or to expand?
- What should it do with business units that do not fit well with its parenting skills?
- What should it do about synergies between businesses that are not working, or that have not yet been fully exploited?

Issues will be different for a successful firm than for a failing one. They will be different for firms in a stable environment than for those operating in a fast-changing one.

a. Issues relating to the environment

An important element in a firm's performance is its environment. So we need to know about *future* trends and how survival and success factors in the future are likely to differ from those in the past and the present. The types of issues that relate to environmental developments include:

- How should the business respond to new markets or the decline of existing markets? These might result, for example, from political or economic developments in regions such as Indo-China or eastern Europe, or from socio-economic trends that increase the spending power of groups such as older people and pre-teen children. Social trends may make a product no longer desirable or fashionable. Alternatively, the industries in which customer firms operate may be maturing or declining—something that is particularly problematic if the firm's fortunes are intertwined with those of a single customer. H&M, for example, has clearly identified the potential for expansion further afield than its traditional heartland of the European Union. In former Soviet Union countries and the USA (where many European retailers, incidentally, have come unstuck), it has been very successful in using its tried and tested methods. But in the Middle East, where legal and social conditions are different, it is experimenting with a new expansion method—franchising—for the first time.
- How should the business respond to changes in the competitive environment? New competitors may have entered the market, existing ones may have altered their strategy with apparent success, while other, formerly powerful, competitors may be experiencing management problems. Barriers to entry may have become higher or lower as the result of social, legal, or technological changes. Customer industries may be maturing and consolidating, meaning that the business has fewer—but more powerful and price-sensitive—customers. BA currently faces threats, not only from competitors with different business models, but also from the mergers between Air France and KLM, and Lufthansa and Swiss Airlines. These have increased their market share and the benefits that come from size accordingly. BA is also likely to face stiff competition from one or two large US airlines, once local competition in the American market becomes less intense.

b. Issues relating to competitive stance

The review of the organization's competitive stance aims to establish whether it is addressing the right target markets, and whether its positioning in each of those markets is appropriate. It raises the following sorts of issues:

- How should the business react to markets where the firm is making particularly high or low profits? If the market is promising, the firm may need to consider diverting resources to it. If declining, then it has to decide whether it should withdraw, or whether making increased investment in, for example, advertising or product improvements will stimulate the market into growth.

- What should the firm do about cases where its positioning is particularly strong or weak? If the positioning is strong, as evidenced by strong sales, good margins, and positive customer feedback, then the firm may be building reputational assets that can be 'leveraged'—used for other products, in other markets or businesses. Alternatively, the firm's positioning may be weak. It may be offering services or products that have too few features, or features that customers do not want, or products that are of inappropriate quality. It then may need to recover its reputation, especially if it wants to expand into new markets or business areas.

c. Issues relating to scope, scale and diversity

A review of the organization's scope, scale, and diversity aims to establish whether it should focus on a narrow range of products and markets or whether there is scope for profitable further diversification. It also asks whether managers have the competences to manage a diverse portfolio of businesses. This is likely to overlap with a review of the environment, which will highlight instances of markets or technologies which the firm might benefit from entering or leaving. It will also interact with the analysis of the organization's value chain, resources, architecture, and management of complex organizations, since many of the issues arising within diversified organizations relate to executives' ability to manage the diversity and exploit synergies properly. Issues include:

- What should the firm do about situations where competitors are reaping benefits from scale or scope that the organization cannot currently match? This may imply, for example, limiting the product range or expanding into new markets to enhance economies of scale, enhancing the product range to increase the richness of the offering, or retreating into niche markets where the organization's reputation, competences, or relational assets mean that opponents' scope and scale are not decisive factors. Alternatively, the organization may look at reconfiguring its value chain so that its costs are low even if it is not the largest firm in the industry, as firms like Ryanair and (in its early days) Dell did.

- What should the organization do with businesses that do not appear to fit within its portfolio? A unit may not share any important resources with the other businesses in the portfolio, and the parent may not have any skills that help it develop. The corporation may be better off selling such a unit, even if it is profitable, to an owner that can extract more value from it, and investing the sale proceeds in businesses it understands better. Alternatively, it may need to enhance its parenting skills in order to be able to manage the business effectively. BA's withdrawal from its BA Connect low-cost business, which was not profitable, is an example of a company choosing to redeploy its assets where they are more likely to be effective—in BA's case in its long-haul and full service routes.

d. Issues related to the value chain

Issues arising from a review of a business unit's value chain looks at whether an organization is able to compete efficiently and effectively in its chosen market segments. They include:

- What should the organization do about poorly functioning value chain elements, or particularly effective ones? For example are an organization's operations located in the best place, bearing in mind:
  - the characteristics of its products and services;
  - the location of suppliers and customers, and whether proximity to them will lead to lower costs or better supplies;

- factors such as the relative stability of a particular location such as newly industrializing economies.

H&M's creation of a single major distribution centre in Hamburg, and the aggregation of its buying offices into larger units close to its main suppliers, is an example of its response to value chain elements that appear not to have been functioning as effici-ently as they could be. The Hamburg warehouse also allows it to transport many of its clothes by sea or rail, thereby reinforcing its explicit stance as an ethical organization.

- How should the organization respond to the availability of new suppliers and com-munication mechanisms? Competitors may have reduced their degree of vertical integration and developed an innovative value chain—which is likely to have become apparent from a review of the environment and innovation, knowledge, and learning. The question, then, is: Does the organization have the necessary capabilities and resources to manage a network of external relationships—something which will also emerge from the review of managing complex organizations—or alternatively, does it have the competences, time, and resources to develop and manage everything in-house? Airlines are increasingly outsourcing many non-core activities, including aircraft maintenance and catering, which are critically important functions for the airlines. In this industry, it appears that the costs to be saved, and the standards that can be achieved by specialists, outweigh any risks of losing control. On the other hand, some firms have prospered by adopting a 'contrarian strategy'—doing the opposite of what most competitors are doing. For example, Eastern Airways, a small British airline, maintains its own aircraft and engines, and keeps a large stock of spares, something that almost all competitors have outsourced.[21]

e. Issues relating to resources

We are especially interested in whether an organization has strategic resources. A successful organization will face the issue of how to build on, or leverage, them. An unsuccessful organ-ization confronts the challenge of how to acquire some. A crucial step in this assessment is to identify resources that may lose or gain in value as the environment changes. Thus for an already successful organization some issues to emerge from an analysis of resources would be:

- what to do with specific resource advantages over weaker competitors. This may mean engaging in a price war, but is more likely to involve moves that will take market share away from weaker rivals. Technological and innovation competences can be used to stretch any lead in product features or to generate a cost advantage which may be then passed on to customers in the form of lower prices;

- how to use its strategic resources in other businesses or markets (Real-life Application 11.5). Many large firms, such as Sony and Marks & Spencer, have used their strong reputations and their know-how in managing customers' financial transactions as the basis of diversification into financial services. Successful firms may be able to undertake R&D programmes and develop new technologies around which innovative products may be built. Other companies, for example GE, have used their expertise in delivering products to their own customers to set up successful logistics firms.

For a less successful firm, a review of resources is likely to highlight different issues, relating to what to do about the absence of strategic resources in a particular business. For an unsuccessful organization, a concern is likely to be how can it develop resources that will be strategic in a future environment before deteriorating financial results persuade its owners to close it down or sell it off. It may be able to do this through development of existing,

Real-life Application 11.5 Leveraging spare resources in McDonald's

> I think that, over time, we owe it to our shareholders, our owner operators, our employees and our suppliers to see how we can take advantage of our skills and competencies . . . We know how to run a multi-unit restaurant at a high quality standard. We know how to train people, how to buy real estate and construct buildings, and how to market products. And together with our suppliers, we have a unique global supply infrastructure. If we can find a way to leverage this for the long run, then we must try.
>
> (Jack Greenberg, CEO of McDonald's, interviewed for the company's 1999 Annual Report, p. 11)

McDonald's sought to use its strategic resources through actively investing in Chipotle, a chain of Mexican-style restaurants, Pret-a-Manger and Aroma, British sandwich chains, and by buying the Donato's pizza business in Ohio.

non-strategic resources, perhaps allying with a partner with complementary assets, which would increase the strategic strength of both companies. Alternatively the firm may be able to obtain sufficient funds to invest in, for example, a brand-building programme. In the days shortly after it was privatized, British Airways decided that it would need high levels of staff skills in customer service if it were to compete successfully in its newly deregulated environment. It then spent a large amount on a staff training programme, one of the objectives of which was to change staff's values and attitude towards their customers.

Managers might also consider whether any of the organizations' resources might be more valuable in other businesses. An unsuccessful firm is likely, in the end, to need to give priority to restoring the competitiveness of its existing business, but occasionally salvation can come from diversification.

f. Issues relating to architecture and culture

An organization's culture and architecture underpin many other aspects of its effectiveness, for example the value chain and whether it is able to deploy its competences and capabilities. They also affect the organization's ability to learn and respond to changes in its environment. Examples of issues that emerge from an analysis of culture and architecture are:

- How should the organization respond to any lack of fit between its architecture and its future environment? A divisional structure may be needed as the organization expands into new services and markets. Or an existing divisional structure may need to move from, say, a focus on geographic regions to products, as the organization chooses to emphasize global economies of scale over local responsiveness. Control and reward systems may need to alter to reflect changes in the organization's strategic priorities—for example, to a new emphasis on reducing waste and pollution.

- How should the organization respond to problems in motivating its employees, and those of other firms in its supply and distribution network? It may be desirable for the organization's culture to exhibit more sociability or solidarity, as the nature of competitive advantage in its industry changes over time. Formal or relational contracts between the firm and other stakeholders, which may be motivating people inappropriately, may need to be modified.

g. Issues relating to the management of complex organizations

For a complex organization that is involved in many business areas and managing a network of partners and suppliers, a review of corporate and network-level strategy looks not only at whether it has appropriate alliance partners, but also at whether it has the skills to manage these relationships. From this review the following types of issue are likely to emerge:

- How might the corporation's parenting skills be best used? If a firm has parenting styles and skills that are appropriate for a business area in which it currently does not operate, then it may wish to acquire a firm in this area. It may well be able to buy one from another corporation cheaply, if that corporation has been unable to add value to the business. In this case, a subsidiary question might be: How should the parent respond to unexploited synergies between its businesses? Corporate managers need to decide to what extent they wish to intervene in the management of individual businesses to compel their managers, or give them incentives, to cooperate. They will need to judge if potential synergies justify the resources that will be diverted from the individual businesses.

- How is it best to respond to problems in alliance management, such as the devaluation or leakage of proprietary knowledge? Companies may need to look again at the legal structure and governance of their partnerships, or at the skills they bring to bear in controlling and motivating their partners.

h. Issues relating to innovation, learning and change

Three times in recent years, at the beginning of the 1980s and the 1990s, and in the mid-2000s, Sony has appeared to be in trouble, with profits falling and competition increasing. Twice a combination of product innovation and changes to its architecture and value chain have enabled it to rebound. At the time of writing—in 2007—whether Sony will rebound again is not yet known, but its culture of innovativeness and long-standing and deeply-held competences in new product development suggest that it may.[22]

Firms with that kind of dynamic capability confront the strategic issue of how to utilize their capacity for innovation and learning to maintain or improve their competitive position. After reviewing the firm's environment and competitive stance, it may be clear that product innovation is desirable in certain areas. Sony, for example, might benefit from product development in its audio and television businesses, or from reducing its production costs in those same businesses to levels closer to those of its Korean competitors.

Firms that are less successful in this area face the issue of how to respond to their inability to innovate or their low learning capacity. Developing such a capacity may involve a large investment in a company-wide training programme, or the recruitment of 'star' learners', who can act as change agents, to senior management positions. This type of option is likely to be accompanied by changes to the organization's structure, architecture, and culture, otherwise any symbolic value attached to the new appointment will get swamped by existing structures and systems. Alternatively, the organization might decide to adopt a defender strategy, restricting its activities to certain areas, perhaps declining industries, where innovation is unlikely to become a source of advantage.

11.4.2 Establishing strategic priorities

The list of issues identified in the previous section is by no means comprehensive, nor are they the ones that you should necessarily be looking out for. Any organization will have a set of issues that are unique to itself and its industry, and its time and place. From this unique list of, possibly many, issues (particularly for a large and diverse organization), some will be more important than others. The next task is to prioritize these. And, like the issues themselves, priorities are likely to be different for a successful firm than those for an unsuccessful one. In this section we outline some ways of establishing those issues that should have the highest priority and the greatest senior management attention.

Strategic priority measures the importance of an issue to the organization's survival or success, and also the urgency with which it must be addressed. The highest priority belongs to issues that, if not resolved immediately, will lead to the disappearance of the organization, for example, a severe shortage of cash or the departure of staff with key skills.

At the other end of this scale are the strategic issues faced by a successful firm in deciding what to do with the reserves of cash that it has accumulated. Unless its shareholders are pressing for the cash to be distributed to them, the organization can afford to take its time in responding to this issue, important though it is.

Real-life Application 11.6 Survival factors at Delta Airlines?

The Atlanta-based Delta Airlines has been in Chapter 11—a procedure under which firms in the USA can use to gain respite from their creditors and avoid bankruptcy—since September 2005. Its performance has suffered as a result of overcapacity in the US airline industry, too many employees in proportion to its sales and especially in comparison to the low-cost carriers, a route/hub network that was less effective than its competitors, and a culture which was, some said, rather too gentle for its new cut-throat environment.[23] As a result, and despite its management team apparently going some way to successfully turn around the firm, in November 2006 it found itself at the end of an unwelcome take-over bid by US Airways.[24]

Issues can be grouped under the following six categories, in descending order of priority:

1. Survival factors and threshold resources that the organization will no longer possess: These issues are clearly the most urgent of all, in that they may threaten the entire survival of the organization (Real-life Application 11.6). They will become particularly apparent from the reviews of the environment, resources, and the value chain.

2. Strategic advantages that are missing, being eroded by environmental change, imitated/substituted by competitors, or dissipated through internal problems: A high priority also attaches to issues that suggest that the organization may have lost, or be losing, its basis of competitive advantage. Its positioning may not be distinctive, or its existing sources of advantage within the value chain may be being eroded and it may lack evident replacements. Inappropriate parenting skills may be eroding the competitiveness of one or more businesses. The less successful the business is, and the more important it is as a source of profit, the higher the priority that will need to be given to replacing its remaining sources of competitive advantage.

3. Time-constrained issues: These are issues that, because of external pressures, need to be resolved within a limited time frame. Governments may set deadlines for the expression of interest in a certain opportunity, or for meeting particular pollution standards. Management will not always want to place these issues high on their internal agenda, but may be forced to make a commitment. In 2000–2001, British mobile phone service operators were forced to decide whether to participate in a government auction of licences to operate 3G networks, although the technology was still under development and the extent of demand was unclear. Prices paid in the auction far exceeded expectations, and unexpected delays with the technology, and slow take-up of services, have made it difficult to recoup the investment. However, few of the phone companies felt they could risk withdrawing and allowing their competitors freedom to exploit the new technology.[25]

4. Proven resources, value chain attributes and parenting skills that can be made strategic and/or leveraged into other businesses or markets: For a successful business with few issues to consider in categories 1 and 2, these issues will have a high priority, since they represent the bases for future expansion and sustainable advantage in a new arena. Diversifications, such as those pursued by Sony when it moved into the games business or H&M when it moved into perfumes, may result. For an unsuccessful firm these expansion opportunities normally take lower priority than repairing the competitiveness of the core business.

5. Speculative opportunities: new markets and products with long-term potential, undeveloped or unproved resources: These are a less certain source of potential advantage than the better-proven opportunities in category 4. They should therefore be given a lower priority, unless they represent a much larger source of potential profit, in which case the rewards may outweigh the greater risk. A firm may be able to generate a number of these opportunities if it is strong in learning and innovation. Virgin's original move into the airline business in 1984 may be considered an example of this type of strategy; at the time, it was involved in music, retailing, and little else. It certainly had no experience in managing a travel business.

6. Spare resources: As long as they do not represent a drain on the organization's finances or management, there may be no pressing strategic need to use spare resources. However, shareholders or owners will want to see their invested capital being put to efficient use, or press for spare resources to be turned into cash that they can reinvest in another firm. Acquisitions sometimes appear to be undertaken because a firm has too much money and does not know what to do with it—although this is not usually a good reason for them. On the other hand, if spare cash is put towards acquisitions, joint ventures, or R&D with a view to experimenting with potential new developments, as Sony does in its laboratories, and Kodak and Cisco do in their joint ventures with numerous technology partners,[26] then that is a much more rational use of spare resources.

Within each category, the highest priority will clearly go to the issues with the greatest implications in terms of future profits (or losses).

Worked Example 11.3 BA's strategic issues and priorities

In order to begin our assessment of BA's strategic issues and priorities we will follow the structured analysis described above. As always, the opinions expressed here are our own: you, and indeed BA's managers, may assess the situation differently.

Returning to the data in Tables 11.1, 11.2, and 11.4 we can begin to summarize BA's performance:

- turnover up 3.4 per cent (85.5 per cent of which came from passengers, 7.3 per cent from cargo, and 7.2 per cent from other activities);

- operating margin of 6.9 per cent, down 13.3 per cent, and attributable profit down nearly 36 per cent;

- EPS down 37 per cent;

- passenger yields (pence/RPK) up 2 per cent;

- cargo volumes down 4.7 per cent;

- productivity up 4.3 per cent;

- passenger load factor was flat;

- no dividend was to be paid, but the chairman signalled that it would return to paying a dividend next year as the BA pension deficit is finally dealt with;

- we are not provided with information about the relative profitability of BA's various regions (unlike in previous years' annual reports); we know, however, that the great majority of BA's revenue continues to come from Europe and the USA, although sales volume from the east Asian and Australasian routes is increasing strongly. ➔

→ From this initial scan we might conclude that BA is not doing very well. On some key performance measures it appears to be struggling: its profit margin has declined, although we do not yet know if this is less than the industry benchmark. It talks about conditions having been challenging, indicating that there may have been external factors that are responsible for its worsening figures.

But at this point we need to dig deeper in to the company's accounts, and, most importantly, those of its competitors (Table 11.4), to find out if the company should be really worried. Here we find that there is less cause for concern. BA is profitable (and an industry prize winner to boot), unlike many of its competitors. However, its profit margin, while superior to that of Lufthansa and Air France, is lower than that of the best performers—many of which are budget operators with low-cost business models. One issue is how BA should respond to the threat that these airlines pose, as more routes come within their grasp, given that, according to Table 11.3, European routes account for over 60 per cent of its revenues. Low-cost carriers increased their share of the European market substantially in 2006[27] and, with Ryanair leading the way, are gearing up to tackle long-haul routes.[28] Single-class airlines, providing business-class services at economy prices, are starting to compete against BA on its key transatlantic routes.[29]

Comparisons with its competitors indicate that BA is not the largest airline in the world by revenue, nor indeed the largest European passenger airline—that place is held by Air France/ KLM, and Lufthansa/Swiss. This is indicative of a trend towards mergers in the industry also manifested in US Airways' bid for Delta in the US, and Ryanair's bid for Aer Lingus.[30] If we believed that size matters in this industry, we would want to flag BA's lack of market share as an issue. However, we have seen (Real-life Application 5.4) that economies of scale appear not to be a determining influence on competitive advantage in this industry; the fact that BA's profit margins are superior to theirs only reinforces this conclusion.

This increased acquisitiveness on the part of competitors might be worrying, however, if it began to undermine the oneworld alliance that is a cornerstone of BA's strategy. If its partners in the alliance were to be acquired by members of rival alliances, BA could find itself stranded, and forced either to go it alone or to seek membership of another alliance, possibly on unfavourable terms.

This is not the only worrying aspect of the environment from BA's point of view. In March 2007, EU ministers approved an 'Open Skies' accord with the USA, which gave rights to any EU or American airline to fly from any airport in the USA to any in Europe, and vice versa, with effect from March 2008. US airlines were, in addition, to be able to fly between European destinations.[31]

Not only does this add force to the previous issue, by indicating that current restrictions on airlines operation and ownership are likely gradually to be lifted,[32] in theory, it will also open up competition for BA at its Heathrow hub, on the key transatlantic routes hitherto open only to BA, Virgin Atlantic, American Airlines, and United Airlines.[33] Heathrow is one of the world's major—and best connected—international airports, and is owned by BAA (and now ultimately the Spanish company Ferrovial). BA has recently had several altercations with BAA,[34] which controls most of the UK's major airports. The issues, therefore, relate to what BA should do about threats to what is arguably its most valuable strategic asset, the Heathrow slots, and one of its key revenue generators, the transatlantic routes.

There are other issues related to sustainability and distinctiveness that we might want to consider. Turning to BA's geographical scope shown in Table 11.3, we can speculate how the airline might deal with a downturn in demand on its European routes. However, there is no reason to suppose that those routes are especially likely to suffer such a downturn—intensifying competition is, as we have noted, more of a threat. Threats to demand are more universal, and come from an increased awareness of climate change and the high level of greenhouse gas emissions that result from air travel. While demand up until 2007 had continued unabated, BA would be advised to be thinking about strategies in case it suddenly turns down. Air travel is considerably less 'green' than rail on short-haul routes, and Europe's major rail firms have announced a formal alliance designed to increase their competitiveness on cross-border routes.[35] Improving IT will make video-conferencing an increasingly viable substitute for long-haul travel. Issues like this are prime candidates for scenario planning, since the range of potential outcomes is vast and forecasting on the basis of past trends is not possible.

A review of the value chain and industry power structures points us to the importance of BA's relationship with key suppliers. However, there is little reason to see issues here. BAA is a monopoly supplier, but its power is constrained by a powerful regulator.[36] Boeing and Airbus are duopoly suppliers of aircraft but, as we noted in Section 3.5.1, fierce competition keeps their power low.

More worrying issues emanate from BA's ground-handling and catering functions, some of which are contracted out to independent firms. Both have recently suffered disruption through industrial action.[37] Looking internally at BA, we note that industrial relations with its own employees are currently a concern—in 2007, staff threatened to strike.[38] Industrial action from any quarter has the potential to impact on the company's critically important customer service standards and/or profits if its wage bill increases.

From this review, we assess the main strategic issues facing BA, and their priority as shown in Table 11.5.

In Worked Example 12.1 we will return to these to develop a range of strategic options for the highest priority issues. →

→ **Table 11.5** BA's strategic issues and priorities

Strategic issue	Priority
How to respond to the Open Skies agreement	Since Open Skies will affect all the competitors in BA's strategic group, this is unlikely to be a threat to the company's survival. However, only three other airlines apart from BA are similarly threatened by the opening up of Heathrow–US routes to direct competition, so a strategic resource is under threat. The issue is also time limited, since an initial response is called for before Open Skies takes effect in March 2008. **Level 2 with a time constraint**
How to deal with increasingly acquisitive competitors	Size is not the main determinant of airline profitability, and BA clearly has sufficient scale to give itself bargaining power with key suppliers. If other airlines match or surpass that scale, this is unlikely to affect BA significantly. In fact, acquisitive competitors may suffer, at least in the short term, from poor performance, since few have experience in handling large acquisitions. What makes this a potential **Level 1** threat to survival is the latent threat to the integrity of the oneworld alliance. This may make it advisable for BA to become an active consolidator rather than a spectator
How to respond to the threat from airlines with more profitable business models	The manner in which BA has managed to fight off competition from low-cost carriers in Europe can be taken as evidence that its survival is not threatened by them. However, their expansion into BA's long-haul heartland, which will be aided by the Open Skies agreement, poses a significant threat to the airline's competitive advantage. **Level 2**
How to respond to increased public awareness of climate change and greenhouse emissions	This could be seen as threatening the survival of the entire industry, since it is unlikely that air travel could ever be made as 'green' as rail for short-haul routes. The survival of the industry might therefore hinge upon continued demand for long-haul travel, and BA would want, above all, to look at how it can build the resources that will make it one of the survivors if the market were reduced just to long-haul. **Level 1**
How to respond to persistent industrial relations problems	The fact that BA managed to win an industry award and sustain profitability despite service disruptions in 2006 indicates a degree of public tolerance and perhaps a strong reputation. In the longer term, as competitors grow stronger, this will become a more significant issue. As it is, the other issues on this list appear more pressing. **Level 2, but without a clear time constraint for resolution**

What Can Go Wrong 11.1 Performance management in the UK rail industry

The UK's nationalized state-owned railway, known as British Railways or BR, was returned to private ownership during 1995–97 as part of a programme of privatizations carried out by the then Conservative government. The privatization of BR took an unusual form. It was broken up into over a hundred units, each of which focused on a different aspect of the railways' operations. Amongst others, the main changes were:

- The track and infrastructure (stations, signalling, etc.) were to be taken on by a new company, Railtrack, which remained initially in government hands but which in 1996 was floated and shares issued. It continued to receive large subsidies from the government thereafter.

- BR's trains and rolling stock were allocated to three leasing companies (ROSCOs).

- The passenger train services were franchised to 25 private train companies. These companies were not in competition with one another initially, although it was intended that this would change over time. They rented track time and station access from Railtrack.

- Similar arrangements were made for six freight operating companies.

- Two regulatory bodies were created, one to monitor Railtrack, and the other to allocate franchise and monitor the performance of the train operating companies. →

➔ The new structure was subject to some pretty trenchant criticism, not just for its complexity, but also for the ways in which the targets were set and the way in which performance was measured.[39] All of these appear to have affected the behaviour of the new rail companies in ways that were not intended. Criticisms have focused on train delays, poor quality service, and, during one particularly bleak period between 1997 and 2002 when some major crashes resulted in a number of serious injuries and deaths, safety.

Government subsidies to the rail network declined (although not by as much as the government hoped) in anticipation of the efficiency benefits that were expected to come from privatization; the new structure focused the new companies' attention very firmly on costs. One effect was that the train operators were said to be rather too keen to reduce staff numbers, resulting in driver shortages and therefore train cancellations and delays.[40] In addition, there was little incentive (because of the short-term nature of the contracts that the franchisees had been awarded) for the train operators to invest large sums of money to make improvements to their rolling stock. Instead they had incentives to boost short-term passenger numbers and fare income.

The contracts between the different rail companies, and between them and the regulator, did not foster cooperative working arrangements amongst the various players. Previously there was a single line of hierarchy, with clear accountability and areas of responsibility. Since privatization, with a 'labyrinthine' structure and over a hundred different organizations where once there was one, and several regulators as well, no one knew who should do what.[41] Sometimes this led to conflict between the different types of company, with passenger operators accusing Railtrack of unfairly allocating more track time to the freight companies and vice versa. Now if a train was late and Railtrack could be blamed for inadequate maintenance of the track (50 per cent of delays were said to be its fault), the train operators claimed compensation, making lots of work for lawyers, and of course increasing costs substantially.[42] A large body of people were employed by various firms in the industry to ensure that they were not held responsible for delays—these people contributed little, if anything, to improved service on the network.

The need to provide a return for shareholders was also alleged to have distorted firms' attitude to maintenance and safety. Some of the most serious concerns were expressed about Railtrack, whose emphasis was said to be very much concerned with short-term financial targets, rather than a focus on the whole-life, efficient management and development of its assets. A major crash, at Hatfield, was blamed on a broken track, which was clearly, at least in part, Railtrack's responsibility.[43] However, because of the new structure, even here there was scope for a different interpretation. One question that was raised was how much inadequate maintenance of the trains' wheels had damaged the track—in which case some of the blame could be laid at the train operators' doors.

The entire board of Railtrack, including the director of safety, received share options—something which came in for considerable criticism after the crashes. Public disquiet was expressed about the sort of mixed messages that were coming out of Railtrack, about its problems being due to lack of funding, at the same time as its managers were receiving bonuses and a 7 per cent increase in dividend payments was being made to shareholders.[44]

In 2001, Railtrack went into administration with debts of more than £3bn, and in October 2002, a new company, Network Rail, took its place. In the process the government paid £500m in compensation to Railtrack's shareholders. However a group of 48,000 individual shareholders took legal action, claiming that this compensation was not enough; the British High Court ruled against them in October 2005.[45]

● CHAPTER SUMMARY

This chapter has taken you through the process of using both qualitative and quantitative data to broaden your understanding of an organization's strategy, how well it is succeeding and what specific areas seem to be performing well or badly. And specifically we have advised you to be cautious when examining an organization's own data:

- It is important not to rely upon what organizations say about their strategy, but to examine actions and events, and measure results.

- A complete analysis starts with general measures of strategic effectiveness (like return on capital employed and growth rate).

- Good strategic analyses make use of measures of operational performance (like debtor turnover) and combine them with tailored indicators designed to show how well the organization is performing by the specific criteria for its industry.

- Tailored indicators are also used to show how well an organization is meeting its specific strategic objectives. It is desirable to measure both how hard the organization is trying (inputs) and how effectively it is succeeding (outcomes).

- In most cases, a well-chosen ratio generates the most valuable information, although useful insights can be gained simply by counting things like numbers of alliances and new product launches.

We then identified some of the strategic issues that may confront an organization—both challenges and opportunities. Strategic issues are phrased as questions: 'What should the organization do about X?' 'How should it respond to Y?' Strategic issues are identified from a thorough analysis of the organization's performance, its future environment, its competitive stance, value chain, resources, culture and architecture, management of complexity, and how it manages innovation, learning, and knowledge.

The next stage is to prioritize these issues and reduce them to a more manageable size. Issues relating to threats to an organization's survival take the highest priority, followed by issues relating to how an organization can obtain or protect sources of sustainable advantage. If these issues do not consume all available resources, then the organization can turn its attention to how to use them in new ways, how to develop new resources and what to do with spare ones. Some issues require a quick decision, and they take priority over those that do not.

Online Resource Centre

www.oxfordtextbooks.co.uk/orc/haberberg_rieple/

Visit the Online Resource Centre that accompanies this book to read more information relating to assessing organizational performance and setting strategic priorities.

● KEY SKILLS

The key skills you should have developed after this chapter are:

- the ability to analyse an organization's results, both financial and non-financial; specifically, an understanding of the different purposes of ratio analyses, calculating absolute figures, and comparison data;

- a heightened awareness of how organizations can sometimes represent their performance in a more favourable light than its absolute performance would justify;

- skills in identifying where an organization is performing strongly or weakly;

- an ability to assess the key strategic issues facing the organization and prioritize these.

● REVIEW QUESTIONS

1. What input and output measures would be appropriate for organizations whose major strategic objectives were:

   (a) to be the lowest-cost producer in its industry?

   (b) to demonstrate to US industry that environmentally friendly practices were not just feasible, but also profitable?

   (c) to allow its 25-year-old founder and chief executive to retire by the age of 32?

   (d) to bring opera to the people?

2. Companies sometimes use hidden reserves, restructuring charges and other accounting devices to 'massage' their earnings figures, normally to give the appearance of steady, unbroken growth in profits. Why would they do this? What kinds of data would you look for to give you clues about the true situation?

3. Is our focus on quantifiable results a mistaken attempt to bring scientific precision to the inexact art of strategic management?

4. What types of strategic issues would lead you to recommend:

   - an acquisition of a major competitor

   - a relocation of manufacturing to eastern Asia

   - an organization restructuring

   - a major R&D programme

● FURTHER READING

- A UK classic that makes accountancy and financial principles accessible for non-accountants is Reid, W. and Myddleton, D. R. (2005). *The Meaning of Company Accounts*. 8th edn. Aldershot: Gower.

- For international financial management issues, there are a number of good books, each focusing on different aspects of international finance:

  - Buckley, A. (2003). *Multinational Finance*. 5th edn. Harlow: FT Prentice Hall.

  - Alexander, D., Britton, A., and Jorissen, A. (2005). *International Financial Reporting and Analysis*. London: Thomson Learning.

  - Eiteman, D., Stonehill, A., and Muffet, M. (2003). *Multinational Business Finance*. 10th edn. Reading, MA: Addison-Wesley.

  - Stolowy, H. and Lebas, M. (2002). *Corporate Financial Reporting: A Global Perspective*. London: Thomson Learning.

- In order to hone your propaganda-detection skills, you may like to read one or two of the books that describe some of the tricks that corporate financiers use to try to pull the wool over our eyes. One of the best is **Terry Smith's** *Accounting for Growth*. London: Century Business. The second edition was published in 1996, so it is now getting rather out of date, but many of his examples are still relevant and it is written in an accessible style. An American book that also exposes some of the tricks that unscrupulous accountants can get up to, and which uses Enron as an example, is **Mulford, C. W. and Comiskey, E. E.** (2002). *The Financial Numbers Game: Detecting Creative Accounting Practices*. New York: Wiley.

● REFERENCES

Antill, N. and Lee, K. (2005). *Company Valuation under IFRS: Interpreting and Forecasting Accounts Using International Financial Reporting Standards*. Petersfield, Harriman House.

Ball, R. and Shivakumar, L. (2006). 'The role of accruals in asymmetrically timely gain and loss recognition'. *Journal of Accounting Research*, 44/2: 207–42.

Bartov, E. and Mohanram, P. (2004). 'Private information, earnings manipulations, and executive stock-option exercises'. *Accounting Review*, 79/4: 889–920.

Beebe, P. (2005). 'Delta's tailspin'. *The Salt Lake Tribune*, 25 September.

Bergstresser, D. and Philippon, T. (2006). 'CEO incentives and earnings management'. *Journal of Financial Economics*, 80/3: 511–29.

Bhalla, V. K. (2004). 'Creating wealth: corporate financial strategy and decision making'. *Journal of Management Research*, 4/1: 13–34.

Bititci, U. S., Suwignjo, P., and Carrie, A. S. (2001). 'Strategy management through quantitative modelling of performance measurement systems'. *International Journal of Production Economics*, 69/1: 15–22.

Bititci, U. S., Mendibil, K., Martinez, V., and Aibores, P. (2005). 'Measuring and managing performance in extended enterprises'. *International Journal of Operations & Production Management*, 25/4: 333–53.

Bourne, M. and Neely, A. (2002). 'Cause and effect'. *Financial Management*, September: 30–1.

Boyer, R. (2005). 'From Shareholder Value to CEO Power: the Paradox of the 1990s'. *Competition & Change*, 9/1: 7–47.

Casson, P. and McKenzie, G. (2007). 'A comparison of measures of earnings per share'. *European Journal of Finance*, 13/3: 283–98.

Chun, R. (2005). 'Corporate reputation: meaning and measurement'. *International Journal of Management Reviews*, 7/2: 91–109.

De Wet, J. H. v. H. and Du Toit, E. (2007). 'Return on equity: A popular, but flawed measure of corporate financial performance'. *South African Journal of Business Management*, 38/1: 59–69.

Dobbs, R., Nand, B., and Rehm, W. (2005). 'Merger valuation: time to jettison EPS'. *McKinsey Quarterly*, 15: 82–8.

Drongelen, I. K.-v., Nixon, B., and Pearson, A. (2000). 'Performance measurement in industrial R&D'. *International Journal of Management Reviews*, 2/2: 111.

Financial Management Association (2006). 'Roundtable on Stock Market Pricing and Value-Based Management'. *Journal of Applied Corporate Finance*, 18: 56–81.

Foust, D. (2006). 'Flight plan: inside Gerald Grinstein's struggle to save Delta'. *Business Week*, 4 December.

Garengo, P., Biazzo, S., and Bititci, U. S. (2005). 'Performance measurement systems in SMEs: a review for a research agenda'. *International Journal of Management Reviews*, 7/1: 25–47.

Grant, R. (2004). *Contemporary Strategy Analysis*. 5th edn. Oxford: Blackwell.

Griffith, J. (2004). 'The true value of EVA'. *Journal of Applied Finance*, 14/2: 25–30.

Heflin, F., Kwon, S. S., and Wild, J. J. (2002). 'Accounting choices: variation in managerial opportunism'. *Journal of Business Finance & Accounting*, 29/7–8: 1047–78.

Jacobs, C. D. and Statler, M. (2006). 'Toward a technology of foolishness'. *International Studies of Management & Organization*, 36/3: 77–92.

Kanji, G. K. and Moura, E. Sá. (2002). 'Kanji's business scorecard'. *Total Quality Management*, 13/1: 13–27.

Kaplan, R. S. and Norton, D. P. (1992). 'The balanced scorecard—measures that drive performance'. *Harvard Business Review*, 70/1: 71–9.

Kaplan, R. S. and Norton, D. P. (1993). 'Putting the balanced scorecard to work'. *Harvard Business Review*, 71/5: 134–47.

Kaplan, R. S. and Norton, D. P. (1996a). *The Balanced Scorecard: Translating Strategy into Action*. Boston, MA: Harvard Business School Press.

Kaplan, R. S. and Norton, D. P. (1996b). 'Using the balanced scorecard as a strategic management system'. *Harvard Business Review*, 74/1: 75–85; repr. (2007). *Harvard Business Review*, July–August: 150–61.

Kaplan, R. S. and Norton, D. P. (2001). 'Transforming the balanced scorecard from performance measurement to strategic management: part I'. *Accounting Horizons*, 15/1: 87–104.

Kaplan, R. S. and Norton, D. P. (2004). 'How strategy maps frame an organization's objectives'. *Financial Executive*, 20/2: 40–5.

Kelleher, J. C. and MacCormack, J. J. (2005). 'Internal rate of return: a cautionary tale'. *McKinsey Quarterly*, August: 70–5.

Kennedy, A. A. (2000). *The End of Shareholder Value: Corporations at the Crossroads*. Cambridge, MA: Perseus Publishing.

Kennerley, M. and Neely, A. (2003). 'Measuring performance in a changing business environment'. *International Journal of Operations & Production Management*, 23/2: 213–29.

Kerin, P. (2004). 'Create value'. *Business Review Weekly*, 19 August.

Kit Fai, P. and White, A. S. (2005). 'A performance measurement paradigm for integrating strategy formulation: a review of systems and frameworks'. *International Journal of Management Reviews*, 7/1: 49–71.

Kleiman, R. (1999). 'Some evidence on EVA companies'. *Journal of Applied Corporate Finance*, 12: 80–91.

Kyriazis, D. and Anastassis, C. (2007). 'The validity of the economic value added approach: an empirical application'. *European Financial Management*, 13/1: 71–100.

Malmi, T. and Ikäheimo, S. (2003). 'Value based management practices—some evidence from the field'. *Management Accounting Research*, 14/3: 235–54.

Marco, B. and Umit, S. B. (2006). 'Collaborative performance management: present gaps and future research'. *International Journal of Productivity & Performance Management*, 55/1: 7–25.

Mauboussin, M. (2006). 'Michael Mauboussin on strategy. Long-term investing in a short-term world: how psychology and incentives shape the investment industry'. 18 May. Legg Mason Capital Management. Available on-line <http://www.leggmasoncapmgmt.com/pdf/Long-TermInvesting.pdf>, accessed 6 June 2006.

Mulford, C. W. and Comiskey, E. E. (2002). *The Financial Numbers Game: Detecting Creative Accounting Practices*. New York: Wiley.

Neely, A. (1999). 'The performance measurement revolution: why now and what next?'

International Journal of Operations & Production Management, 19/2: 205–28.

Pun, K. and White, A. (2005). 'A performance measurement paradigm for integrating strategy formulation: a review of systems and frameworks'. *International Journal of Management Reviews*, 7/1: 49–71.

Rappaport, A. (1981). 'Selecting strategies that create shareholder value'. *Harvard Business Review*, 59/3: 139–49.

Rappaport, A. (1987). 'Linking competitive strategy and shareholder value analysis'. *Journal of Business Strategy*, 7/4: 58–68.

Rappaport, A. (2002). 'Why competitive advantage and shareholder value dovetail'. *Business Times Singapore*, 9 November.

Rappaport, A. (2004). 'Shareholder scoreboard'. *The Wall Street Journal*, 8 March.

Rappaport, A. (2005). 'Shareholder scoreboard'. *The Wall Street Journal*, 28 February.

Rappaport, A. and Sirower, M. L. (1999). 'Stock or cash?' *Harvard Business Review*, 77/6: 147–59.

Reid, W. and Myddelton, D. (2005). *The Meaning of Company Accounts*. 8th edn. London: Gower.

Smith, T. (1996). *Accounting for Growth*. 2nd edn. London: Century Business.

Tully, S. (1999). 'The EVA advantage'. *Fortune*, 139/6: 210.

End-of-chapter Case Study 11.1 British Airways

This case study follows on from Real-life Application 11.2 ('British Airways' position in 2007') and Worked Example 11.1 ('Assessing BA's actions and strategies'). Tables 11.2 and 11.3 earlier in this chapter show five years' selected performance data for British Airways, and Table 11.4 shows selected comparative performance data.

Table 11.6 and Figure 11.4 provide additional information about BA's financial performance, and Tables 11.7a and 11.7b provide some data on various international air travel indicators.

Case study questions

1. Use the data in Tables 11.2, 11.3, 11.4, 11.6, and Figure 11.4, together with the other information given about BA and its com-

petitors in this chapter, to appraise BA's strategic performance. (Look hard. As in many case studies, some relevant information is buried in obscure places.) Use these data to evaluate whether BA has (a) sustainable (b) distinctive sources of competitive advantage.

2. The fastest growing sector in the airline industry is the low-cost/value sector. BA moved into this sector in 1998 with its low-price brand Go. However BA sold Go to its management team for £110m in 2001, and it was subsequently resold to easyJet for £375m in 2002. Was this a good strategic move on BA's part? Give reasons for your answer in terms of your understanding of theory on strategic resources, management attention, and industry forces, as well as the financial data found in this chapter.

3. Tables 11.7a and 11.7b give some data on various international air travel indicators. What do these tables imply for BA? ➜

BA uses a basket of measures to assess its financial performance. British Airways plc.

Table 11.6 British Airways' ranking on selected criteria

Criterion	Global ranking
Numbers of international passengers carried (RPKs)	3rd
System traffic (RPKs)	7th
Airlinequality.com star ranking	4*
Cargo carried (freight tonne kilometre)	13th
Sales revenue	8th
Operating profits	2nd
Net profits	3rd
European sales	2nd
Profit margin	57th
Number of aircraft	14th

Notes
These figures may not agree precisely with the data in Table 11.2—different ends of financial years, and different methods of calculating the figures may lead to some slight anomalies

Sources
Air Transport World, May 2005: 60–4; 1 February 2005: 64; and January 2005: 43–5; *Airline Business*, May 2005, 21/5: 60–4; <http://www.airlinequality.com/StarRanking/4star.htm>, accessed 15 May 2005; and authors' own calculations

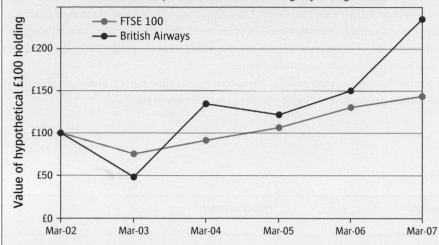

Figure 11.4 Shareholder value in British Airways (BA Annual Report 2006–2007, p. 42). *Reproduced with kind permission of British Airways*

Table 11.7a IATA international industry data

	January–September 2004 vs. 2003					January–September 2004 vs. 2000				
	RPK growth (%)	ASK growth (%)	PLF (%)	FTK growth (%)	ATK growth (%)	RPK growth (%)	ASK growth (%)	PLF (%)	FTK growth (%)	ATK growth (%)
Africa	10.7	9.4	67.1	17.2	10.4	17.0	13.6	1.9	11.5	4.0
Asia/Pacific	25.3	18.0	72.6	15.4	16.5	11.7	14.9	−2.1	25.3	21.8
Europe	11.3	8.7	75.6	11.2	9.2	1.8	−0.2	2.6	6.9	3.0
Middle East	29.1	24.3	72.3	28.4	28.0	48.4	43.2	2.6	53.5	51.2
North America	16.6	11.3	79.6	11.7	9.6	4.1	−0.5	3.4	2.0	3.2
South America	11.1	6.9	74.0	12.3	9.4	11.7	7.6	2.7	13.9	18.8
Industry	17.7	13.1	74.6	14.1	13.1	8.1	7.2	0.6	15.9	11.8

Source
Reproduced with the kind permission of Air Transport World

Table 11.7b Regional world airline traffic, January–October 2006

	Latin America			Asia/Pacific			Europe			US		
	2006	2005	change (%)	2006	2005	change (%)	2006	2005	change (%)	2006	2005	change (%)
RPKs (millions)	105,746	105,767	0.0	457,834	441,971	3.6	621,390	590,675	5.2	936,560	925,785	1.2
ASKs (millions)	148,504	148,738	−0.2	607,126	601,889	0.9	806,796	773,534	4.3	1,166,755	1,175,307	−0.7
Passengers (000)	76,771	73,629	4.3	110,637	106,471	3.9	290,887	278,361	4.5	460,937	465,845	−1.1
PLFs (%)	71.2	71.1	0.1	75.4	73.4	2.0	77.0	76.3	0.7	80.3	78.8	1.5
FTKs (millions)	2828	2896	−2.3	44,387	42,333	4.9	29,992	29,204	2.7	30,558	28,991	5.4

Source
Reproduced with the kind permission of Air Transport World

Appendix 11.1 Measures used in assessing an organization's strategic performance

Tables 11.8a and 11.8b summarize the most frequently used accounting terms and ratios, and the way in which they are calculated. They also give a brief review of the significance of each item in a strategic analysis. Please bear in mind that there is no universally agreed definition of some of these terms. There is a possibility that they may differ slightly from those you have read or been taught elsewhere.

For a more detailed account of what these terms and ratios signify, and a description of basic accounting theory, you should consult a specialist textbook.[46]

Table 11.8a Standard accounting terms

Term or ratio and their alternatives	Definition	Points to watch
Profit and loss (income statement) items		
Sales; revenue; turnover	The money brought in from selling goods and services	Some firms include sales tax or value added tax in their turnover figures, others do not
Cost of goods sold; cost of sales	The cost of the inputs needed to produce the goods—raw materials, labour costs and depreciation of equipment	Cost of goods sold refers only to those costs attributable to a single product. The total costs of the organization will also include, for example, mortgage repayments and interest charges
Gross profit (income; earnings—international firms tend to use different terms; all mean the same thing)	Sales turnover less cost of goods sold	Measures whether production process is profitable
Operating profit Trading profit Profit/earnings before interest and tax (PBIT; EBIT)	Gross profit less selling, administrative and general expenses	The terminology here can be very confusing—international firms, especially US ones, use different terms from those we are used to in the UK
Earnings before interest, tax, depreciation, and amortization (EBITDA)	Operating profit with depreciation and amortization charges added back	Measures the profits a firm has available for re-investment. Increasingly commonly used. Sometimes incorrectly used as if it measured a firm's cash flow
Profit before tax	Operating profit plus interest earned less interest charges	Measures the profits of the firm as well as indicating how well it has financed its operations
Net profit (sometimes known as the bottom line)	Profit before tax	Measures profit accruing to shareholders and effectiveness of entire firm (including the treasury function)
Retained profits Balance sheet items	Net profits less dividends paid	Measures money left in firm for reinvestment
Current assets	Stocks (inventories), plus debtors (accounts receivable), plus cash, plus marketable securities	Measures the amount of ready assets that could be easily realized if, for example, the firm faced a sudden demand for money
Current liabilities	Creditors plus short-term loans (borrowings)	Measures the amount of money that a firm may need to pay out at short notice
Net current assets; working capital	Current assets less current liabilities	Measures the amount of money available to finance operations. If working capital is a negative figure (i.e. current liabilities exceeds current assets), this indicates a funding gap that will need to be met, normally through obtaining new debt or equity

Table 11.8a (cont'd)

Term or ratio and their alternatives	Definition	Points to watch
Stocks; inventory	Value of raw materials held awaiting processing, materials being processed (work-in-progress—WIP), and finished items awaiting sale or shipment	Aim is normally to keep stocks to the minimum level needed to ensure continuity of supply of goods to customers
Debtors; accounts receivable (often shortened to just receivables)	Value of goods/services invoiced but as yet unpaid	
Creditors, payables	Value of inputs received but not paid for. Sometimes also includes loans repayable within 12 months	This is money that suppliers effectively lend a firm. If this number rises, a firm gets extra free money, at the risk of antagonizing suppliers
Fixed assets	Long-term investments made by the firm, include tangible assets (land, buildings, equipment) and intangible assets such as financial investments that are not easily converted into cash	
Net assets; net worth	Working capital plus fixed assets	Measures the amount of funds available to finance the business in total. Mathematically the same as capital employed
Capital employed	Shareholders' funds plus long-term debt	The total money invested in the firm. Some people believe this should also include short-term bank loans, if the firm is in the habit of rolling them over from year to year
Shareholders' equity; shareholders' funds	Total assets less total liabilities	The money invested in the firm by its shareholders, plus retained profits accumulated over time. Sometimes also includes various reserves against future liabilities
Intangibles	Non-material assets, that nevertheless have a monetary value. They include things like patents, software, music copyrights, and other intellectual property	Many innovative companies have large intangibles values on their balance sheet
Goodwill	The difference between an asset's nominal book value and the value placed on it by the market	Goodwill is often valued during a merger or acquisition, and is the additional amount that the acquirer is prepared to pay over and above the balance sheet amount. Brands and intangibles such as competences are particularly important sources of goodwill in services and knowledge-intensive businesses

Table 11.8b Ratios and other measures that can be used to assess an organization's strategic performance

Measures of product or service effectiveness		
Turnover (sales)	Total value of goods sold in a particular period	Used to compare performance of a unit or firm over multiple periods, and between firms
Unit sales	Total numbers of units sold in a particular period	An alternative way of measuring sales
Overall profitability ratios		
Return on capital employed (ROCE); return on net assets (RONA)	Operating profit (PBIT) × 100/capital employed (net worth). Capital employed is sometimes, confusingly, called equity in international reports	Probably the best overall measure of most firms' financial performance. Used especially to assess the earnings generated by operations. Particularly useful for assessing businesses with a large fixed asset base. ROCE can be improved by either increasing profits or by reducing the amount of capital in the firm. If this is redundant this would be a good move, but beware firms that improve ROCE in the short term at the expense of long term investment
Return on (total) assets (ROA)	Operating profit (PBIT) × 100/total assets	An alternative to ROCE. Sometimes computed using profit after tax instead of operating profit, as alternative to ROE
Economic value added (EVA)	Net profit after tax/(capital employed × cost of capital)	EVA assesses income compared to the return that investors could get in other securities of comparable risk
Profit/employee	Operating profit (PBIT)/no. of employees (full-time equivalents)	Useful for businesses where people are the main resource, and there are few fixed assets
Yield	Operating profit per unit (e.g. airline seat, hotel room)	Useful in companies where specific indicators of operational effectiveness are important
Profit margins		
Gross margin (or percentage)	Gross profit × 100/sales	Measures extent to which production costs are covered
Operating profit margin (percentage); return on sales (ROS)	Operating profit × 100/sales	Measures extent to which overall costs are covered. Indicator of strength of competition in industry. Varies widely according to type of firm; 8–10% is typical for manufacturing but will be much less in high volume businesses such as retailing. Need to look at trends over time; a low profit margin may indicate poor performance, but may also reflect short-term spending on investments
Net profit margin (percentage)	Net profit × 100/sales	Alternative to ROS for financial and similar firms
Asset utilization		
Net asset turnover	Sales/net assets	Measures intensity with which asset base being used. Higher is better
Fixed asset turnover	Sales/fixed assets	Measures intensity with which fixed assets are being used
Sales/employee	Sales/no. of employees	Measures intensity of staff utilization; especially important in firms with high staff costs
Sales/square metre	Sales/total floor space in sq metres	Used especially in retailing, although could also be used to assess space utilization effectiveness in other firms
Debtor turnover	365 × debtors/sales (gives result measured in days)	Measures time taken to collect payment—lower is better. In most industries there are standard payment terms—30, 60, and 90 days are typical. An efficient firm will have debtors around this norm
Liquidity		
Current ratio	Current assets/current liabilities	These measures show how easily a company could repay its short-term liabilities if the need arose. Important if you are planning to lend the company money or offer it credit. Of little significance in a strategic analysis

Table 11.8b (cont'd)

Measures of product or service effectiveness		
Acid test (quick ratio)	Cash and easily sellable securities plus debtors/current liabilities	The acid test is a measure of how easily a company could repay its short-term liabilities if called upon to do so. Normally should be more than 1.
Indebtedness		
Debt/equity ratio, gearing	Long-term debt (sometimes includes short-term debt as well)/ shareholders' funds	Rule of thumb says that should be no greater than 50% in many industries, although some industries with high levels of leasing will have much higher levels
Interest cover	Operating profit/interest charge	Number of times interest can be paid out of profits. Measures sensitivity of firm to fluctuations in profits or interest rates, and so soundness of its funding strategy
Stock market ratios		
Dividend cover	Net profit/dividend expense	Shows to what extent dividends are justified by current profits. A consistently low figure may mean that the firm is dipping into reserves to maintain its dividend in order to keep its share price high
Earnings per share (EPS)	Net profit/no. of shares in issue	Imperfect substitute for ROE that has the virtue of being easy to calculate
Net assets/share	Net assets/no. of shares in issue	Indicates extent to which the company's share price reflects the value of its 'hard' assets. Sometimes used by analysts to assess how over- or under-valued a share is
Price/earnings (p/e) ratio	Quoted share price × no. of shares in issue/net profit	Can be calculated using last reported profits ('historic p/e') or forecast profits ('projected p/e'). Shows how many years of profits are built into the share price—a high number shows optimism about future profits growth
Dividend yield	Dividend per share/share price (normally expressed as a percentage)	Indicates annual income that investor gets from investment in the share. Can be compared to the interest rate on a loan or the yield on a bond

● NOTES

1 For a review of how companies themselves assess performance see Kennerley and Neely (2003).

2 The difference between ROCE and ROA is rarely important when interpreting trends and comparisons. It hangs on whether you see the resources invested in the business as being the *total* asset base (ROA), or whether you deduct the part of the organization's working capital that is financed by credit from suppliers (ROCE).

3 Based on BA's annual reports from 2005–2007 unless otherwise specified.

4 Source: World Airline Financial Results 2005. *Air Transport World*, <http://www.atwonline.com/ channels/dataAirlineEconomics/World_Airline_Report_2005.pdf> and <http://www.iata.org/NR/ rdonlyres/FCD02107-B81D-4064-AF58-2B42CA9196D7/0/Profits_and_Size_Briefing_ June2006.pdf>, both accessed 10 June 2007.

5 <http://www.atwonline.com/channels/dataAirlineEconomics/f&f_page2_0507.pdf> and British Airways Plc Hoover's Company Profiles, 27 April 2005, Hoover's, Inc., Austin, Texas.

6 BA 2007 Annual Report.

7 Revenue passenger kilometres (RPK) and cargo tonne kilometres are combined measures of the quantity of passengers or cargo carried and the distances they were conveyed. An airline notches up one RPK for each kilometre it carries a fare-paying passenger, so a 200-kilometre flight with 120 passengers on board would generate 24,000 RPK. Cargo tonne kilometres are calculated similarly.

8 Boyer (2005) provides an interesting evaluation of the psychological, sociological, and economic environment that influenced some of the choices of valuation methods during the 1990s.

9   See also Rappaport's many other articles, for example Rappaport (1987, 2002, 2005).

10 See BA's annual reports over the last several years.

11 The airline industry is unusual in that there appear to be few links between firm size and profitability. See <http://www.iata.org/NR/rdonlyres/FCD02107-B81D-4064-AF58-2B42CA9196D7/0/Profits_and_Size_Briefing_June2006.pdf>, accessed 10 June 2007.

12 A whole consultancy industry has arisen around the balanced scorecard. The original article on which it is based is Kaplan and Norton (1992). See also Kaplan and Norton (1993, 1996a, 1996b, 2001, 2004). Other writers who have developed or applied the idea include Bourne and Neely (2002), and Kanji and Moura (2002). Also see Pun and White (2005) for a review.

13 This example comes from The Motley Fool <http://www.fool.co.uk/school/2005/sch050808.htm>, accessed 13 June 2007.

14 Sony Annual Report 2006, p. 6.

15 Ibid.

16 Jacobs and Statler (2006).

17 These examples are taken from Harvard Management Update (2006). 'Scenario planning reconsidered'. 11/5: 3–4.

18 Garvin, D. A. and Levesque, L. C. (2006). 'Strategic planning at United Parcel Service'. Harvard Business School Case Study, 19 June.

19 Ibid.: 11.

20 Ibid.: 23–4.

21 O'Connell, D. (2007). 'Airline boss goes back to basics'. Sunday Times, Business Section, 10 June: 12.

22 Singer, M. (2006). 'Stringer's way', New Yorker, 5 June; Nathan, J. (1999). Sony: The Private Life. London: HarperCollins; Wray, R. (2007). 'Game over for creator of Sony's PlayStation', Guardian, 27 April.

23 See, for example, Foust (2006) and Beebe (2005).

24 Lengell, S. (2006). 'Preparing for takeoff'. The Washington Times, 13 December: C08.

25 Baker, S. and Clifford, M. (2002). 'Tale of a bubble: how the 3G fiasco came close to wrecking Europe'. BusinessWeek, 3 June: 46.

26 See Grant (2004).

27 Business Wire (2007). 'The market share of low-cost carriers in Europe reached 16.3% in May 2006 — a full 2.4% higher than at the same point 12 months prior'. 16 January.

28 Reiter, C. (2006). 'Ryanair Aer Lingus bid may serve as industry model'. Reuters News, 6 October; Financial Times (2007). 'Sceptics not ready for take-off'. 14 May, Surveys GTC1: 9.

29 See, for example, Wilen, J. (2007). 'New low-cost airline Zooms into JFK with $199 London fare'. Associated Press Newswires, 21 June.

30 Lengell (2006) op. cit.; Smith, M. (2006). 'Irish flag carrier rejects Ryanair's takeover offer'. The Herald, 6 October: 22.

31 Agence France-Presse (2007). 'EU agrees transatlantic "open skies" agreement'. 22 March.

32 Economist (2007). 'The battle of the North Atlantic'. 16 June.

33 O'Connell, D. (2007). 'Scramble for Heathrow slots'. Sunday Times, 1 July.

34 Beattie, J. and Prynn, J. (2007). 'Airlines and business leaders attack BAA over mismanagement'. Evening Standard, 15 June; Harrison, M. (2007). 'BA in Heathrow dogfight with BAA'. Independent, 6 February; Air Transport World (2006). 'Airlines call for BAA breakup'. 1 October.

35 Economist (2007a). 'A high-speed revolution'. 7 July: 65–6.

36 Economist (2007b). 'The man who bought trouble'. 7 July: 71.

37 Russell, J. (2007). 'BA puts catering out to tender'. Sunday Telegraph, 17 June; Farmer, B. and Massey, R. (2007). 'BA baggage fiasco leaves 6,000 cases in the rain'. Daily Mail, 19 June; Financial Times (2007). 'BA completes labour talks for move to Heathrow T5'. 30 May.

38 Warner, J. (2007). 'British Airways averts strike threat'. Independent, 30 January: 37; Evans, G. (2007). 'Strike threat likely to cost BA £80 million'. Press Association National Newswire, 2 February; Ashworth, J. (2007). 'BA faces new strike threat over £2bn pension hole'. The Business, 3 February.

39 Pollitt, M. G. and Smith, A. S. J. (2002). 'The restructuring and privatisation of British rail: was it really that bad?' Fiscal Studies, 23: 4; Wright, R. (2004). 'Crossed lines: railway review ambitions curbed by industry size and complexity'. Financial Times, 3 July; Economist (2005). 'Railroaded? Railtrack'. 2 July.

40 Nifield, P. (2002). 'Wales on the edge of nowhere'. *South Wales Echo*. 5 April; Pollitt and Smith (2002) op. cit.; they quote Affuso, L., Angeriz, A., and Pollitt, M. G. (2002), 'Measuring the efficiency of Britain's privatised train operating companies'. London Business School, Regulation Initiative Discussion Paper Series, no. 48.

41 See, for example, Knill, C. and Lehmkuhl, D. (2000). 'An alternative route of European integration: the Community's railways policy'. *West European Politics*, 1 January; Elliott, L. and Smithers, R. (1999). 'Successful sell-off or cynical sell-out?' *Guardian*, 7 October.

42 Nifield (2002) op. cit.; Hirst, C. (2004). 'The interview: Chris Bolt: "The rail reorganisation now arriving at platform one cannot be allowed to fail"'. *Independent On Sunday*, 31 October.

43 Martin, B. (2002). 'Derailed: the UK's disastrous experience with railway privatization'. *Multinational Monitor*, 1 January; Webster, B. (2005). 'The far-reaching legacy of a crash waiting to happen'. *The Times*, 7 September; *Daily Mail* (2006). 'Anger at cut in £10m rail crash fine'. 6 July.

44 Leathley, A. (2001). 'Railtrack set to stand firm on £100m in dividends'. *The Times*, 17 May; Batchelor, C. (1997). 'Rage over Railtrack: company in the news: big profits spark fresh attacks'. *Financial Times*, 7 June; Reuters News (2001). 'British business'. 17 May.

45 Milner, M. (2005). 'Railtrack shareholders lose court battle for compensation'. *Guardian*, 15 October: 12.

46 See, for example, Reid and Myddelton (2005) or Antill and Lee (2005).

CHAPTER TWELVE

Options and Strategic Methods

LEARNING OUTCOMES

After reading this chapter you should be able to:

➜ Develop a range of strategic options to address priority issues, as identified using the frameworks set out in Chapter 11

➜ Discuss the trade-offs between different modes of development:

    ➜ expansion using the organization's existing value chain and resources

    ➜ mergers with or acquisitions of existing players

    ➜ strategic alliances

    ➜ outsourcing some elements of the value chain to a specialist provider

➜ Explain the different elements of the RACES framework for the assessment of strategic options

➜ Evaluate a set of strategic proposals or options and select those that the organization should adopt and implement.

INTRODUCTION

INTRODUCTION

This chapter is concerned with the development of future strategies for an organization. It builds on (and should be read in conjunction with) Chapter 11, where we outlined the means of assessing the financial performance of an organization, its overall situation, and the strategic issues facing it. This assessment will form the basis on which future strategies will be developed.

There will always be a variety of strategic options available to any organization. These are alternative ways of dealing with issues such as weaknesses in the organization or the potential actions of competitors, or capitalizing on any areas of strength that are currently being under-exploited. In this chapter we discuss the various types of strategic option and the different methods that may be used to implement them. Finally, we introduce the RACES framework, which is a tool to help decide which are the best options for an organization.

This process is mapped in Figure 12.1.

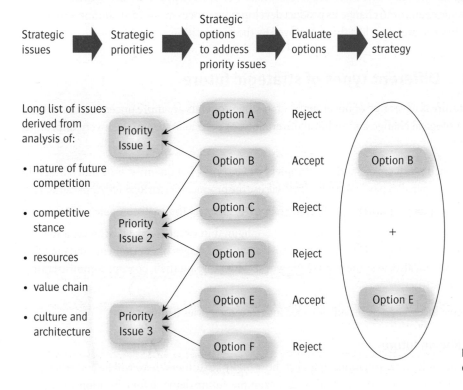

Figure 12.1 The option development and evaluation process

12.1 Strategic options

After assessing the performance of an organization and identifying the main strategic issues facing it, the next stage in the analysis is to develop a range of strategic options that will address the highest-priority issues. For each issue, it is a good discipline to seek out a number of different alternative strategic options. This is to stimulate the creative reasoning that is a vital part of top-level strategic thinking. It also helps to avoid automatically gravitating towards 'obvious' strategies that may give no advantage, because competitors are following identical paths.

One option that is always available, in theory, is for the organization to carry on with its present strategy. This is sometimes referred to as the 'do nothing option', although in competitive markets most organizations have to 'run to stand still': doing nothing is rarely an option.[1] However, a broad continuation of the present strategy may be quite a reasonable way forward where there is no obvious way of resolving an issue, or where the present strategy is obviously successful. Nevertheless, even highly successful organizations need to change their strategy to cope with potential new developments in the environment. Sticking too rigidly to the same strategy for too long may lead the organization into competency traps.

The options an organization's managers consider needs to be conditioned by the type of future that it is confronting: some types of strategy make sense in very dynamic or uncertain environments, but not where demand for a product and the features that will be required are predictable. In coping with that future, alternative strategic options may differ from one another along two dimensions. Organizations can try to do different things: one option may be to match competitors' products and service, while another may be to try to raise levels of service beyond what customers receive at present. And they can try to achieve the same things in different ways: when copying a competitor's product, a firm can opt to use its existing value chain, or to change its product development processes and distribution systems so that they too are more like those deployed by the competition.

→ Competency traps were discussed in Section 7.7.

12.1.1 Different types of strategic future

The future is never free of uncertainty—but some contexts are more uncertain than others. Technological change and political uncertainty, in particular, can make it very difficult to predict:

- which products or services customers will buy, in what quantity, how much they will be prepared to pay—and what they will use the product for (see Real-life Application 1.3);
- how many competitors will emerge, and how fiercely they will compete;
- how the value chain will need to be configured in order to give customers a reliable source of supply; firms may need to deal with shortages of components and qualified staff, but also, in some parts of the world, with rampant theft, corrupt administrations, or violence.

Strategic futures can be broadly divided into four categories (Figure 12.2).[2]

a. A known future

In some, quite rare, situations, it is clear how many customers there will be and what they will require—or be persuaded to buy. For example, future demand for education services or for care for the elderly can be predicted on the basis of freely available demographic statistics. What people will want or need to learn, or how older people will want to spend their time, can also be extrapolated with reasonable confidence by looking at the behaviour of similar customers in the past.

Some allowance must be made for differences between generations, and there is still the possibility of surprises—the take-up of the internet by older people, the so-called 'silver surfers', has exceeded some expectations. But managers are able to make informed and confident decisions about how much capacity to build, where, and with what features.

Managers need to be cautious in deciding whether they have a known or a limited-option future. A manager running a power utility could at one stage look back at past patterns of usage in order to predict demand for the future. However, changing consumer concerns, and climate patterns may mean increased use of air-conditioners or solar panels, which may affect demand in unprecedented ways.

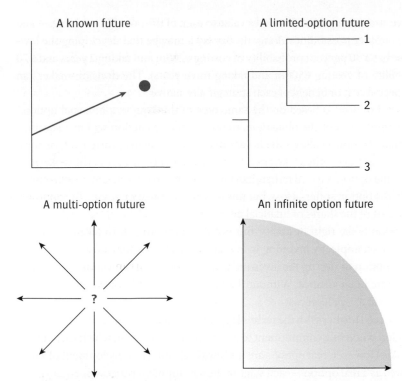

A known future

A limited-option future

A multi-option future

An infinite option future

Figure 12.2 A number of potential strategic futures. *Reproduced with the kind permission of* Harvard Business Review

b. A limited-option future

In this, more common, situation, it is possible to identify a small number of potential outcomes from a strategic decision, some of which may be more favourable than others. The final outcome may depend on a number of factors—whether overall demand for a product gets beyond a certain threshold, for example, or whether certain competitors enter the market with competing products.

Take, for example, a car manufacturer's decision as to whether to invest in developing its own, low-emissions engine technology. It is conceivable that, in future, a combination of consumer pressure and new laws will mean that practically all cars will have to incorporate such an engine. In that case, having the best-performing engine may be a vital source of competitive advantage (outcome 3 in Figure 12.2). It may be, on the other hand, that public concerns over climate change will abate, and that demand for low-emissions automobiles will be limited to a segment of environmentally concerned consumers. That segment may be quite small (outcome 1 in Figure 12.2) or around, say, 40 per cent of the market (outcome 2).

The car manufacturer is likely to have a number of choices. It can invest immediately in the new technology, or it can postpone major investment for a year or two until it becomes clearer how the market will pan out. It can join an alliance with some of its competitors to develop such an engine—or it can decide that it will only ever make petrol-engined cars (a possibility if it is a niche manufacturer of sports cars, for example). These decisions will depend on how probable it believes each outcome to be, and what the costs and benefits will be.

Decision structures like this can be found, in particular, in mature industries, where technological options, and the number of competitors, tend to be few. For example, decisions as to whether to roll out a new supermarket format, launch a new type of beer, or alter the way in which an accountant approaches an audit would all fit this pattern. Tools such as decision trees, real options, and game theory can all help inform them.

→ We examine strategic options in mature industries in Section 13.4.

A decision tree attaches a probability and a value to each of the possible outcomes—and indeed, to some of other possibilities along the way (so it may be that developing the low-emissions engine has a 30 per cent probability of costing €200m and taking 2 years and a 70 per cent probablility of costing €500m and taking three years). The decision-maker can compare the expected cost or benefit of each strategic alternative.[3]

The strategic real option[4] is based on the same type of thinking as a financial option.[5] An option is the right, but not the obligation, to take a specified action within a specified time-frame. A financial option allows the holder to buy or sell shares, currencies, or commodities at a particular price—the strike price. If the price does not rise above the strike price (or fall below it, if the option is to sell rather than buy), the option is not taken up (exercised). The purchaser of the option suffers a loss, but this is simply the cost of buying the option—and not the total cost of the shares or financial instrument.

Thus a real option is the right or ability, but not the commitment, to take a particular strategic action. For example, by investing in low-emissions technology now, a car manufacturer gains the option to step up the investment later, if the technology looks promising, or to negotiate a role in an alliance. Without the investment, neither of those alternatives may be open except at a very high cost.

If it does not proceed further with the technology, the firm has lost some money—but far less than if it made a wholesale commitment to a new strategic direction which then turned out to be a mistake. However, real options are not always cheap. The development of a new drug can be viewed as a real option—each stage in the development process opens up more options along the lengthy path (see Figure 10.4) of bringing the product to market. But the initial investment can be large. Viewing an investment as a real option makes it easier to value it effectively, particularly if the potential benefits are large but may not be realized for a number of years. For some theorists, it also signifies a different way of looking at an investment, with decisions being reviewed periodically, to take account of market growth and unexpected developments.[6]

→ We introduced game theory in Section 3.5.6.

Game theory is particularly relevant to the timing of a strategic option that competitors are also likely to be considering. By investing early in a new market or technology, a firm may bear extra costs, and take extra risks that the opportunity will turn out to be less profitable than it first appears to be. However, it also sends a signal to other companies that, if they go into the same competitive space, they will face opposition. They may decide to direct their resources elsewhere, so the early mover may end up with a larger share of the market, and much higher profits, than if it had waited.

To be able to make decisions in this way, a manager clearly needs some insights into its competitors' strategies, and their cultures. An opponent with a fiercely competitive culture, for example, may be provoked into matching the firm's investment, rather than being deterred from doing so.

c. A multi-option future

In emerging or growing markets or industries, the situation is much less clear than in situations considered in sections a and b above. It is possible to draw some conclusions based on experience elsewhere, but not enough to limit the possible outcomes to just a few.

For example, it is by now clear that there are opportunities for selling western-style luxury goods to the increasingly affluent population of India.[7] However, the size of the market, and the speed at which it will grow, are not yet known. Demand may be limited to the most affluent, or it may spread throughout the emerging middle class. Some may want the same products that are available in the USA and Europe, others may want colours and styling that have a particularly Indian flavour. Some may see European brands as prestigious and desirable, others may promote the emergence of Indian brands that reflect their country's increasing confidence and prosperity. The types of retail outlets they will prefer for purchases are also unknown.

A supplier doing business in such an environment faces a number of choices, therefore, about competitive stance, about whether to go it alone or to seek an Indian partner—and which partner that should be. It can use focus groups and other types of market research to get some idea of underlying consumer attitudes—or even send its employees to live with potential consumers, as Procter & Gamble has done in China and Latin America.[8] But flexibility is a virtue in such circumstances: a firm may decide to hedge its bets by pursuing a number of paths, in an extension of the real options thinking mentioned in section b. French luxury goods conglomerate LVMH is opening its own stores in India alongside its franchised outlets and has also bought a majority stake in its Indian partner.[9]

d. An infinite option future

The last, and least predictable, of the four categories of future relates to situations where there are no useful points of reference because they are entirely unlike anything that has been encountered before. The developers of MySpace or YouTube, for example, and their early investors, could have no real idea as to who was going to use their product, and how it was going to generate revenue.[10] They were making up the whole idea of social networking and video sharing as they went along. In such circumstances, the best tools available are often intuition based upon personal experience and the way that buyers have reacted to similar innovations in the past.

12.1.2 Doing different things

In confronting a strategic issue, an organization has a number of alternatives to consider, each of which may involve differing degrees of internal change, and change to the competitive dynamic within the industry. It can attempt to:

- catch up with or match competitors' products or methods;
- use advantages in one area to compensate for disadvantages elsewhere;
- seek new businesses or markets;
- go beyond competitors with a 'breakthrough strategy';
- withdraw from, or outsource, the relevant business or activity;
- make experimental moves into new technologies, products, or markets;
- make a minimum investment so as to 'reserve the right to play' later;
- engage in feints and spoiling actions;
- neutralize competition.

a. Catching up with or matching competitors' offerings

This 'copycat' strategy may involve introducing products that compete directly with a competitor's, in the way that Burger King developed its 'Big King', which competes against McDonald's 'Big Mac'. It can also involve emulating their processes, as McDonald's did when it launched 'Made for You' to compete with both Burger King's and Wendy's product customization. This kind of strategy is basically defensive, with the apparent aim of fixing a weakness rather than building on strength. It involves a tacit admission by a firm that, in this area of its operations, it cannot do any better than its competitors. However, it might be right for an organization to conduct a 'holding operation' to build survival factors in one part of its business, while it tries to build advantages elsewhere.

b. Using advantages in one resource area or part of a value chain to offset disadvantages elsewhere

Strategy is about trade-offs, and businesses frequently take judgements about where they can use strategic resources to offset areas where they may possess only the bare minimum requirements for survival (Real-life Application 12.1). A common example is where an established firm uses its cash reserves to fund price reductions in order to combat a new entrant with a superior product. We have also encountered situations (e.g. Real-life Application 10.5) where incumbent firms use complementary assets, such as sales and maintenance networks, to fight off new entrants with innovative product technologies.

In its TV business, Sony is trying to use its reputation and its strength in innovation to sell television sets with advanced features, and offset the competences of Samsung in low-cost production of generic products. Samsung is fighting back by developing its own reputational assets and design competences, essentially taking the battle to Sony on its home turf (see end-of-chapter 10 Case Study).

A strategic option like this may involve changing a product's positioning—its price or advertising—to emphasize the organization's particular areas of advantage. It may also require the organization to enhance those particular resources and value chain activities, to make sure that they form the basis of a genuine differentiation or cost advantage.

c. Seek new competitive arenas

Good products, strategic resources, and value chain activities may give an organization the basis for diversifying into new businesses, markets, or product areas. Sony and Marks & Spencer have used their strong reputations and their know-how in managing customers' financial transactions as the basis of diversification into financial services. GE has similarly used its expertise in delivering products to its own customers to set up a successful logistics firm. Vertical integration into the businesses of suppliers or distributors is one type of diversification that might be considered.

A move of this kind may need to be accompanied by a withdrawal from another business or market in order to free up necessary resources.

> ➡ Diversification was discussed in Chapter 5, and the arguments for and against vertical integration in Chapter 6.

d. Breakthrough strategies

Some of the most thrilling stories in strategic management are of breakthrough strategies: product or service innovations that transform the nature of competition in an industry. Another word for this is outpacing. In the 1970s and 1980s, Toyota was able, through its manufacturing systems, to cut the delivery lead time on its cars to levels unimaginable by its competitors.

There are more mundane 'leapfrog' strategies that also come into this category, where firms try to outdo one another with successive product offerings (Real-life Application 12.2).

A breakthrough strategy almost always consists of more than a product innovation. Often, as in the Toyota example, the value chain as well as product development and production processes will themselves be innovative, and new distribution channels pioneered. Typically, changes to the architecture and culture will be needed to make all this possible. Unless this happens any product innovation may be imitated.

e. Withdrawal

Sometimes organizations need to end their involvement with an activity. Withdrawal from a business, segment, or activity may not mean closing it down. Sometimes the activity will be spun off as an independent unit or sold to a third party, or the people and assets

Real-life Application 12.1 Outpacing strategies in consumer electronics

Microsoft, Nintendo, and Sony are currently each attempting to gain advantage over one another with successive generations of computer games consoles. Nintendo's Wii has a 'wand' held by the player which translates their movements into screen movements, making action games such as tennis or football more exciting. Sony has developed what it hopes will be a breakthrough technology in the form of its Blu-ray disc format.

But perhaps the most outstanding exponent of breakthrough strategies is Apple. Almost all of its major product launches have changed the rules of the game in their respective industries. In its time Apple has created:

- the personal computer (in 1977), and subsequently the personal computer industry based around a windows-type GUI and operating system. Before the first Apple models appeared,[11] computers were minis or main-frames, huge beasts. The launch of that first Apple moved society towards the point where most of us has their own computer on their desk, or their lap, which has radically changed the way that each of us works;

- the iPod portable digital music player (in 2001—see Real-life Application 5.4). Apple not only virtually created the downloadable music industry, but as a consequence has hugely disrupted the established recorded music industry (and film and TV industries since), and the way that they produce, sell, and distribute their products;

- its reconception of the retail store as a place where people can try out and connect with the company and its products, rather than just buy them. As well as being unusually attractively designed, they feature a 'genius bar' where people can get answers to technical questions, a theatre running demonstrations of new products, and exceptionally well-

trained and enthusiastic staff who can show off Apple's sophisticated software;[12]

- the iPhone (launched in 2007), which Apple's chief executive does not regard as a computer, but a 'reinvention' of the phone.[13] It goes some way to achieving the convergence of the PDA (personal digital assistant), digital music player, camera, and phone that has been forecast for some time. If successful it is likely to shake up the handheld computer, mobile email, camera, digital music, and phone industries.[14]

The 2007 iPhone: regarded as a reinvention of the phone

redeployed in other areas. In 1997, BA sold its kitchens and catering operations to Gate Gourmet, the Swiss–American principal supplier of meals to the worldwide airline industry, now owned by the Texas Pacific Group investment trust.[15]

A corporation may decide to withdraw from a business because it does not believe that it has appropriate parenting skills or doubts its ability to compete effectively, or because it believes that there are more attractive opportunities elsewhere. A business may also decide to withdraw from particular activities in the value chain, such as distribution or maintenance, and outsource them.

→ We discussed outsourcing in Section 6.1.3.

It is becoming increasingly difficult for firms to sustain their position if they have weaknesses at any point in the value chain. A firm may therefore do best to focus its own resources in the activities in which the firm has a sustainable advantage, and buy other activities in from specialists who will bring it at least a threshold capability.

→ The benefits of buying back shares were discussed in Section 11.3.1.

Finally, where an organization has spare or under-utilized resources, it may decide simply to cut them back rather than seek an alternative use for them. Superfluous cash reserves can be returned to shareholders as a special dividend or through a repurchase of some of the firm's shares.

f. Experimental moves

Most organizations experiment with new ideas. These experiments may take the form of large-scale R&D labs, like Sony's, or moves into new business areas, like BA's low-cost Go subsidiary. H&M experiments with new clothes ranges all the time.

Sometimes these experiments lead to a completely new basis for competition, as Sony's development of the Blu-ray technology has done. Sometimes the experiment does not become part of the future strategy of the organization, although this should not necessarily be considered a failure and waste of resources. Although BA did not persist with its experiment with Go, selling it off because it had become a distraction from running its main airline business, it learnt a lot about the low-cost carriers' business model, and how to minimize costs, along the way.

g. Reserving the right to play

Sometimes a firm does not want to be drawn into the kind of commitment needed to match or surpass competitors, but does not want to withdraw completely from an activity. In that case, it can 'reserve the right to play'[16]—make the minimum investment needed for it to maintain the necessary threshold resources whilst it waits to see how the market or economic situation develops. The firm is buying a real option (see 12.1.1b) to participate in the business later.

This investment can be in people and research facilities or take the form of a stake in, or a joint venture with, another firm. If the business or activity starts to show greater promise, then the investment can be increased. If not, then the firm will not have wasted too much money, and may have gained knowledge that it can use elsewhere. This is a particularly common strategy in emerging industries or markets, where it is not yet clear which technologies will prevail, or indeed whether there is any profit potential at all.

Firms also adopt this kind of option for new technologies, which they judge will be profitable in the future but which are a long way from generating profitable products. Japanese firms such as Sharp followed this strategy with liquid-crystal diodes (LCDs). They started by allocating a few scientists to the technology, and gradually developed core competences in it. When laptop PCs came to the market, Sharp and Toshiba were able to gain a lucrative, dominant position in the supply of LCD displays for them.

One attraction of this strategy is that it enables firms to learn from the mistakes made by any competitors that have decided to make a greater early commitment. The drawback is that if these other firms make a successful breakthrough, they may gain early-mover advantages in market position, reputation, and distinctive capabilities that will be difficult for their followers to match.

h. Feints and spoiling actions

On occasions companies will want to attempt to disrupt competitors' activities. One tactic is to pretend to be developing something, a new product or market for example, in order to stimulate competitors into wasting money and resources developing a response to it. This can also disrupt the smooth functioning of the competitors' value chains. This is an especially effective tactic for a dominant firm in an unstable environment, which wishes to prevent a weaker rival from developing its own capabilities and rival products.

A commonplace strategy in the computer software industry is to announce details of a new program well in advance of its launch. When the product finally arrives some of the announced details are not present. In the meantime its competitors have potentially built in expensive features that customers do not want. This type of announcement is known as vapourware (or vaporware).[17]

Quite similar to a feint is a spoiling action, where products are launched, or markets entered, purely to make it more difficult for competitors to make money. Examples would be the Japanese operations of some large western computing and electronics firms, and the small-car arms of some American car companies. These product or market entries may do no better than break even, but they make it more difficult for the Japanese firms to extract high profits from markets where they are dominant—profits that could be used to expand into the western firms' profitable markets.

A variation on this theme occurred during the development of what became the DVD, where two rival alliances, one led by Toshiba and the other by Sony and Philips, were promoting competing and incompatible technologies. The two camps traded claims about the superiority of their technology and who had adopted it.[18] One commentator believed that announcements from the Toshiba alliance had led to the Sony/Philips camp bringing forward the development of a key element of the technology, which it had earlier indicated it would leave till a later stage.[19] The two camps eventually agreed on a common standard, in response to computer industry pressure.[20]

i. Neutralize competition

An extension of a spoiling action is when the organization takes steps to eliminate or neutralize competitors, rather than to out-compete them. This typically involves the use of financial assets and sometimes capabilities in negotiation. Strategic options that come under this heading include:

- Acquisition of bothersome competitors: Microsoft was frustrated by the dominance of Quicken, the US market leader in PC software for managing personal finances, which was seen as an important gateway to competing in financial services on the internet. Microsoft tried to acquire Quicken, but withdrew from the deal after the US Department of Justice sued to block it.[21] In a declining industry plagued by over-capacity, stronger firms will buy up weaker competitors and then take them out of commission. This brings supply in line with demand and allows the remaining assets to make an adequate financial return.

→ We deal with strategies in declining industries in Section 13.5.

- Blocking acquisitions: A variation on the acquisition theme is when one firm acquires another, or takes a large share in it, to block its acquisition by another rival (Real-life Application 12.2).

- Litigation and lobbying to erect or penetrate barriers to entry: A firm may use, or threaten, a lawsuit alleging patent infringement to discourage firms from launching competing products. It is also possible for new entrants to use legal proceedings alleging anti-competitive behaviour as a lever to prevent incumbents from retaliation. easyJet, a low-priced UK airline, went to the courts to try to prevent British Airways from launching Go, which competed directly with easyJet. Although BA won that legal battle, easyJet gained a great deal of favourable publicity (and, incidentally, subsequently bought Go).[22] Firms may also lodge anti-dumping suits, and lobby parliaments and governments to win protection from foreign competitors—the US steel industry has used this tactic consistently over several decades.

Real-life Application 12.2 News Corporation's blocking acquisition

Britain's biggest commercial broadcaster, BSkyB, a satellite broadcasting company that is part of Rupert Murdoch's News Corporation, in 2006 bought a 17.9 per cent stake in the main commercial terrestrial broadcaster, ITV. This has been interpreted as an attempt to block NTL, the main UK cable company (where Sir Richard Branson is the major shareholder) from acquiring ITV. Had it done so, it might have posed a threat to BSkyB in its own core markets. Sir Richard called on regulators to intervene in what he termed BSkyB's 'blatant attempt to distort competition'.[23]

12.1.3 Doing things in different ways

In addition to developing new business areas, a firm may elect to change the way it operates. Typically these will involve changes to corporate-level strategy or competitive stance, for example:

- Moving resources from one business to another: This may involve the transfer of finances from a mature, profitable business to one that is developing and requires an injection of capital, or perhaps the relocation of key managers from one business unit to another. This can encourage the transfer of knowledge between the businesses. It may also be a means of implementing a turnaround in an under-performing division.

- Moving a product's positioning up- or down-market: Toyota has gradually moved its cars from a low-priced position to a much higher-priced position differentiating on reliability and build quality.

→ We discuss the management of change in Chapter 16.

An organization may also alter its value chain to improve the cost effectiveness or reliability of different processes. These kinds of change are often difficult to implement, because they involve disruptive change to established routines, and the development of new ones. However, they are a vital part of an organization's strategic repertoire.

An organization's culture and architecture can also be the basis of strategic options aimed at improving ways in which information is gathered and communicated, and the motivation of people in and around the organization. Changes in this area may be aimed at improving levels of innovation or customer service.

New capabilities and competences may also be required in order for the organization to cope with a changing environment. This may mean recruiting new human resources to bring in additional skills, or implementing training programmes for existing staff.

However, it would be wrong to restrict strategic thinking to any single part of the strategic mix—strategic moves frequently combine several different elements in a holistic package. Moving a product to a more up-market positioning, for example, is not normally just a simple matter of changing the pricing and advertising. The value chain may need to be changed to deliver higher levels of service and support. The physical assets used to manufacture the product may need to be upgraded so that new features can be incorporated and the proportion of defective products reduced. The culture and architecture will also need to be addressed: the structure and control systems may need to change to empower staff to respond more directly to customer needs, reward systems will need to reflect the emphasis on quality, and the management information systems will need to gather and monitor customer satisfaction data. Smart, a subsidiary of DaimlerChrysler which makes a small city car, uses design and manufacturing techniques and distribution channels that differ from its parent's.[24]

12.2 **Strategic methods**

For every strategic option there are likely to be a number of alternative ways of achieving it. In this section we briefly summarize some of the major strategic methods available to organizations. These include:

- mergers and acquisitions (M&As);
- strategic alliances;
- sub-contracting (usually known as outsourcing);
- internal development.

In addition to these expansive methods, there are a number which are concerned with reducing the size of the organization. These include methods such as divestment, float-offs, and management buy-outs (MBOs).

12.2.1 **Advantages and disadvantages of different methods**

It is important to realize that the methods discussed in this section *are not strategies* in their own right.[25] They are means to an end: alternative ways of implementing particular strategic options, such as entering a new market, developing a new product, or reducing the level of competition in a declining industry. Nevertheless, when deciding upon a particular strategic option, how it will be implemented has to form an important part of an assessment of its suitability. It is no use recommending a major push into a new technology if a firm does not itself have competences in it, and no means of developing a sustainable market position before competitors catch up with it. In this situation an acquisition may be the best method, in which case we would want to know whether the firm has experience of, or capabilities in, managing the acquisition process.

Table 12.1 summarizes the respective advantages and disadvantages of the various strategic methods. In choosing between them, managers are trading-off three different types of risk (see Figure 12.3):

→ The challenges of implementing mergers and acquisitions are discussed in Section 17.5.

→ Outsourcing and alliances were discussed in Section 6.1.3 and issues in managing alliances in Section 9.3.

→ Internal development, and innovative strategies, were discussed in Sections 10.3 and 10.4.

Merger
The creation of a new legal entity by the bringing together of two or more previously independent companies.

Acquisition or takeover
The buying of one company (the 'target') by another.

Table 12.1 Relative merits and drawbacks of internal development, mergers and acquisitions, alliances, and outsourcing

	Advantages	Disadvantages
Internal Development	Keep control Retain all benefits	Limited to own resources Take all risks May be slow
Mergers and Acquisitions	Ready-made products, markets, know-how, organization	Acquisitions are: • difficult to value • difficult to integrate
Alliances	Pool resources and know-how Spread risk, capital commitment	Partners' goals may conflict Organizational confusion Lose control of knowledge
Contracting-out/ outsourcing	Activity undertaken by specialist Low cost Predictable price	Some contracts difficult to value accurately Loss of control Lose know-how in managing the activity

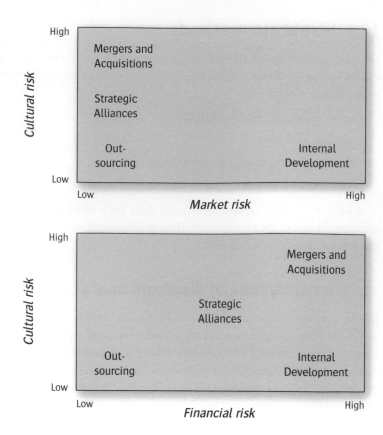

Figure 12.3 (a) Risk of market failure versus cultural risk. (b) Financial versus cultural risk

- Financial risk is the risk that money will be invested for insufficient return. Because of the sums involved, this is highest in the case of a major acquisition which, if it goes wrong, can bring down an entire corporation. It can be quite high with internal development, since one firm is bearing all the risks of a new venture or the costs of developing an innovative technology. This risk can, however, be reduced by keeping initial investments in new technologies small at the beginning (what we termed 'reserving the right to play' in Section 12.1.1), and gradually committing more resources once the potential becomes clearer.[26] A well-structured alliance agreement, in which cost and risk are shared between partners, may be one way of reducing financial risk—but then, of course, the rewards must also be shared. Outsourcing has low financial risk, in that all the costs are known at the outset when the contract is written, and also low cultural risk, in that there is no attempt to bring the two organizations together, but is dependent on the activity being available on the open market at an acceptable price and quality. It also cedes control to an outside organization, with all of the attendant transaction costs and risks that that entails.

➜ Transaction costs were defined in Section 1.3.3 and discussed in Section 6.1.3.

- Market risk is the risk that a venture will fail because the organization lacks the knowledge and skills to penetrate the market effectively, or because it arrives in the market too late, or because there is no market for it at all. This risk is highest for internal development, where a firm may be venturing into markets and technologies where it has no experience. It is lowest for outsourcing and acquisitions, where a firm typically obtains a package of products and resources that have already proved their value in the market-place. Alliances represent an intermediate position—the overall package is unproven, but the partners in the alliance should be able, between them, to provide all the necessary resources.

- Cultural risk is the risk that a venture will fail because it cannot develop a viable working culture. This risk is lowest for internal development, since the venture will build a homogeneous culture of its own. On the other hand, cultural risk is very high for alliances, mergers, and acquisitions, particularly those that involve firms from different nations. For international alliances, for example, one question is: do the benefits outweigh the coordination costs involved in interacting with a firm that may have very different ways of doing business? The partners may have different systems and languages, and operate under very different legal regimes.

  In an alliance, there is the problem of establishing mutual understanding and consistent objectives between the different partners, and mergers and acquisitions are notoriously difficult to integrate. However, there appear to be benefits from experience in managing alliances and acquisitions, and firms can develop capabilities in post-merger integration that can reduce cultural risk. Outsourcing poses lower cultural risk because there is no attempt to combine the two partner organizations, although they may work very closely together.

- Learning risk is the risk that an organization will become locked into its own routines and worldview unless it periodically refreshes itself through contact with other organizations. This can be done through participation in alliances and networks.[27] Successful acquisitions can also give an organization an infusion of new vitality, and firms have been seen to go through cycles of internal development and acquisition-based expansion.[28]

There is no one method, out of internal development, strategic alliances, mergers and acquisitions, or outsourcing, that is clearly best in all circumstances. Which approach is most suitable depends on the industry and environment in which an organization is operating, and its particular capabilities.

12.2.2 Reasons why firms seek mergers and acquisitions

The most common method by which firms in the USA and UK diversify is through mergers and acquisitions (M&As). M&A is also a preferred strategic method in a number of other contexts. One common context is in a mature industry where competition is intensifying and there are strong pressures to reduce costs. Horizontal mergers between companies in the same industry are a natural response, reducing the number of competitors and so the intensity of competition, and improving the competitiveness of the organizations that remain.

→ Competition in mature industries is examined in Section 13.4.

Firms can take advantage of synergies between their different operations and product lines. When Tata Steel bought Corus in 2007, it gained access to Corus' rolling mills and distribution channels in Europe, while Corus gained access to Tata Steel's in-house sources of iron ore. Mergers can also give the resulting organization greater legitimacy, and improve its negotiating power with lenders, suppliers, and customers. One rationale that many observers invoked for the 2005 merger between Procter & Gamble and Gillette was to increase their joint bargaining power vis-à-vis Wal-Mart and other powerful retail chains.[29] If the industry is confronting radical or intermediating change, then mergers between incumbent firms can buy them time to develop their response.

→ Sources of synergies were detailed in Section 5.2.3.

Not all such mergers are defensive. In a fragmented industry, one firm may choose to play the role of consolidator, acquiring a series of small players in order to build an entity that has superior economies of scale, reach, and reputational assets. Firms such as Countrywide have achieved this in the UK estate agency industry, and Mittal Steel in the global steel industry. In other industries, the consolidator may aim to achieve pricing power—the ability to resist customer demands for discounts, and to signal to its smaller competitors the price levels to which they can aspire—with a view to improving margins.

Similar acquisition patterns can be observed in firms whose aim is simply to expand, rather than consolidate an industry (see Real-life Application 12.3). Firms may choose to use geographic roll-up acquisitions to roll out their business model across a single country or region. M&As may present a relatively cheap and quick route into new markets or new product areas, offering the acquirer a functioning value chain along with knowledge about customers, technologies, and market characteristics. UK retailer Tesco has used acquisitions to speed its expansion into the convenience stores sector in its home market in the UK, but deals of this type can be particularly helpful to companies expanding abroad, although an alliance may be a viable alternative.

→ International expansion strategies are discussed in Chapter 14.

An extreme case of the new product/new market M&A is one which leads to industry convergence. This is where two established firms merge in the expectation that their fields of activity are about to converge, and that they need to join forces in order to take advantage of this. The most prominent example was the acquisition of Time-Warner, a film, TV, and publishing conglomerate, by AOL, a provider of internet services and content, in 2000. The deal gave Time Warner access to AOL's expertise in internet distribution, which was expected to grow in importance, while AOL gained proprietary access to all the media in Time-Warner's stable, and to its cable networks.[30] However, the newly merged combined AOL-Time Warner recorded a loss of $99 billion in 2002.[31] AOL's ability to charge subscriptions for its content and services was eroded as users bought broadband connections from other providers, content of all kinds became freely available on the web while advertising revenues also fell, and its assets had to be written down in the accounts.[32] The company is now known as Time Warner.[33]

Real-life Application 12.3 Mergers and acquisitions: the building of Grupo Santander[34]

Spanish banking group Grupo Santander has used acquisitions in a variety of ways to aid its expansion since its foundation in 1857. Its original core business was the financing of trade between the northern Spanish port of Santander and Latin America, and for the first hundred years of its existence it grew mainly through internal development, building a small branch network in its home province and opening regional offices in several Latin American countries and in London.

Santander's first use of M&As was for geographic roll-up, starting with an acquisition of a small Madrid bank in 1942, to gain a presence in the national capital. During the 1960s, it expanded nationwide by acquiring a large number of local Spanish banks. It also used acquisitions to expand its Latin American base, starting with Banco del Hogar Argentino in 1960. The use of M&As to penetrate new markets in Latin America continued with the

purchases of the First Nacional Bank of Puerto Rico in 1976 and of Banco Español-Chile in 1982. Further Latin American acquisitions followed from 1995 onwards, with a major push, starting in 2000, that led to mergers with Banespa, a leading Brazilian Bank, and with major players in Mexico and Chile.

Expansion in Europe initially utilized a mixture of acquisitions and alliances. CC-Bank, a German concern specializing in vehicle finance, was acquired towards the end of the 1980s, around the same time the group forged an alliance with Royal Bank of Scotland and took a stake in Portugal's Banco de Comercio e Industria. As Group Santander's knowledge of European banking practices increased, it took on greater commitments, culminating in its 2004 acquisition of Abbey (then known as Abbey National), the sixth-largest UK bank. In 2007, it had subsidiaries in 12 European countries.   →

→ Meanwhile, Grupo Santander has led to the consolidation of the Spanish banking industry, through its 1994 acquisition of Banco Español de Crédito (Banesto) and its 1999 merger with Banco Central Hispano (BCH). This latter also brought together the two banks' extensive Latin American networks. Although expansion has clearly been the main driver for Grupo Santander's mergers and acquisitions, there is some evidence of other motives as well. BCH had been able to extract higher returns from its overseas operations than had Santander, and learning might have been one motive for the merger.

On the other hand, the Abbey acquisition was seen by many observers as a turnaround opportunity. Abbey National had suffered problems in the wake of unsuccessful diversifications. Grupo Santander's had identified a number of opportunities to reduce costs and improve sales, including some from the extension to Abbey of Partenon, Santander's cutting-edge IT system. Whereas its normal practice had been to leave its foreign subsidiaries managed by nationals of the country in question, the CEO it appointed for Abbey was a Spaniard, who had overseen the implementation of Partenon at Banesto.[35]

Some acquisitions are less directly connected to immediate expansion. Their intention is to give the acquirer control of specific strategic resources, such as raw materials, particular technological competences, or even a particular top executive (see Real-life Application 17.1 for an example). M&As can represent the quickest and most certain way of getting hold of such resources. However, it may be possible to access the same resources at lower cost and with less commitment through a strategic alliance. Acquisitions represent the better method where:[36]

- the resources in question are physical or financial. There is a danger that people in the acquired firm will leave after the acquisition, taking vital knowledge with them, or that they will simply function less well if their firm's culture is changed by the merger. Alliances may be a better way to access human and intellectual assets, since they call for less change in the partners' cultures;

- all the resources can be fully utilized in the combined business, as is likely to be the case with, for example, Tata Steel's iron deposits and Corus' rolling mills. It makes less sense to pay a premium to acquire full control of resources that are only of marginal importance;

- there is a risk that a potential alliance partner might be acquired by a rival—in such cases, a merger may be the only secure way of accessing its resources;

- there is not too much uncertainty as to market requirements or technological standards. In such cases, it is possible to predict with greater confidence if a good return can be earned on the investment required for an acquisition.

However, some firms use small acquisitions to gain knowledge-based resources in evolving, high-technology sectors, even when theory might suggest that alliances are a better proposition. The US firm Cisco, a leading supplier of data networking hardware is, as we noted in Section 10.2.5, renowned for this. In such a fast-moving technological environment, time to market is a crucial consideration, and the risk of being outpaced by a competitor outweighs the risk that a particular acquisition might not bear fruit.[37] By limiting the size of the acquisition, the acquirer also limits the potential damage if it does not work out.

Some takeovers are driven by the acquirer's conviction that it can generate higher profits and cash flow from the target's assets than are being achieved at present. This can be through a combination of:

- improved management. The new parent may have competences that enable efficiency to be improved or revenues increased, as Grupo Santander is attempting with Abbey

(Real-life Application 12.3). Private equity firms typically make sure that the target's top managers have strong incentives, through bonuses and shares, to find ways to enhance profitability;

- asset sales. An acquirer may sell off assets that it feels are not needed: corporate jets or superfluous headquarters buildings are common examples. In its extreme form, where a target's operations are shut down and its fixed assets, in particular its land, are sold off, this is termed 'asset stripping'. More commonly, buildings and land may be sold to, and then leased back from, a financial institution, liberating cash that can be used to repay debt taken on for the acquisition, or simply returned to shareholders;

- improved working capital management, to liberate cash tied up in inventories and tighten up on errors and fraud in payments to suppliers. Debtors can sometimes be collateralized—the company gets a lump sum from a lender, repaid from, and secured against, future customer payments.

Private equity funds such as Blackstone, Kohlberg Kravis Roberts, and Carlyle are prominent users of this type of financially driven acquisition, which has become increasingly common since 2000.[38] These firms have access to very substantial financial resources, so that even large corporations can be a target, as long as it generates the cash or has the property assets needed to repay the debt that is typically taken on to finance the takeover. Retailers are common targets for these reasons.

The personal desires and ambitions of executives may also play a role in mergers and acquisitions. In some cases managers opt to merge with another organization that they feel comfortable working with—sometimes known as a 'white knight'. They hope to avoid being taken over by a firm that might impose uncomfortable changes in their ways of working, or simply sack them. Proposed mergers of this kind have been known, however, to act as a signal to competitors, and to the financial markets, that the two participants are 'in play'—potential candidates for takeover. A third party then gatecrashes the deal, purchasing one or both of the firms involved.

Some other deals appear to stem from a different human weakness: top managers' desire for power, status, and recognition as leaders of substance who can beat the odds (see Section 17.5.2) against making a success of a major merger. Investment bankers and other professionals, who may stand to earn large fees from deals in which they act as advisers, have been known to play upon their clients' egos when encouraging them to proceed with a high-profile acquisition.

12.2.3 Divestment options

Divestment

The selling off or closing of parts of a business in order to concentrate on core business areas, or to raise the funds to invest in expansion.

Organizations also have a different type of option that is often overlooked: divestment.

Even if they do not form particularly satisfying strategic recommendations on their own, divestments may well form an essential part of a package of both expansive and consolidating options that would make an organization more focused, more efficient, and more effective.

Divestment options include:

- liquidation;
- sale to an external buyer;
- float-offs;
- management buy-outs and management buy-ins.

a. Liquidation

Liquidation is the straightforward (in theory) shutting down of a business or business area. The main consideration in the case of liquidation is the costs of withdrawing from the business; redundancy costs and legal fees may be high.

→ We examined exit costs and exit barriers in Section 3.5.6. We look at exit costs again in Section 13.5.

b. Sale to an external buyer

Just like selling a house or a car, selling part of a company is relatively straightforward: a price is negotiated and the business transferred. A key issue is the price, which is often based on historical price/earnings ratios. However, this is hugely subjective and is dependent on the perceptions of strategic value that both the seller and purchaser believe could accrue from the business, for example if the purchaser thinks they may be able to achieve synergies between the new and existing businesses.

→ We examine the negotiation process for acquisitions in Section 17.5.3.

This method is appropriate where the existing parent believes that it does not have the skills needed to manage a particular business unit, even though the unit may be sound and profitable. It can exchange the business for cash which it can reinvest into other areas that suit its capabilities better. If both parties have a good understanding of their relative skills, then both will benefit from the transaction.

In other cases a complete business will be sold by its owners. This is a common path for 'serial entrepreneurs'—people who have no interest in managing mature, stable businesses, but instead enjoy the challenge of creating new firms again and again.

→ We give an example of a serial entrepreneur in Section 13.3.

c. Float-offs

Float-offs, which are sometimes known as spin-offs or de-mergers, involve part of an organization being set up as an independent company. This usually happens in big, publicly owned corporations that have got too large and unwieldy, and where the break-up value of the company appears to be greater than the value placed on it by stock markets as a single entity. A business unit is formed into a separate public company with its own equity issue, which is offered to shareholders on the open market. The parent often, but not always, retains a large stake in the floated company. These happen more often when the floated unit is profitable and when stock markets are buoyant.

d. Management buy-outs

A form of float-off is to sell the business to its managers—this is known as a management buy-out, or MBO. In an MBO, managers acquire full financial control of the business unit that they are already running. Often this involves them in taking a substantial equity stake while they provide only a small proportion of the total funding involved; the rest comes from venture capitalists, an issue of shares, a bank loan, or some combination of these. Financiers are attracted to these because MBOs offer the potential to earn higher financial returns than by investing in larger companies or in traditional start-up businesses.

MBOs are a well-established option in the UK, which sees around 700 a year, and are becoming increasingly common in the rest of the EU, where the number of transactions nearly doubled between 1996 and 2005, when nearly 200 MBOs were recorded.[39] The value of the deals trebled in the UK in this period, and increased nine-fold in the rest of Europe, with a total 2005 value of €125 billion.[40] Some of the advantages and disadvantages to the various participants in an MBO are summarized in Table 12.2. There are, however, some other concerns with MBOs:

- The vendor has to obtain the best price for its own shareholders. The managers may not be the only bidders and because of their knowledge of the business may offer a lower price than competing bids (although if this becomes public knowledge, that could depress the offers from elsewhere).

Table 12.2 Advantages and disadvantages of management buy-outs

Advantages to the vendor	• It allows the firm to concentrate on its core businesses
	• The vendor can reduce debt levels, and perhaps allow it to get rid of a loss-making activity
	• Relationships between the parent's and MBO's managers are likely to be good, allowing any desired interdependencies of activities to continue
Advantages to the managers	• The management team is likely to be highly committed to the future success of the unit because of their personal financial involvement and likely financial gain
	• The unit is bought by a management team who know the business. This is likely to help the corporate image of both the newly floated firm and the parent, and should help the firm to retain customers and enable it to obtain future finance
	• There is a continuity of both employment for staff and trading relationships with suppliers and customers

- If the unit is loss-making, are the members of the current management team the best people to carry on with the job?
- Does the unit's recent financial performance give a true indication of its future performance and thus its value?
- The vendor is unlikely to be particularly happy at seeing the unit's performance improve post-sale, thereby exposing its own management failings.

A variation on the MBO theme is a management buy-in (MBI), in which a group of managers or entrepreneurs is brought in to manage a unit, financed in the same ways as if the existing management team were doing it. However, there is some evidence that MBIs have a much higher failure rate than MBOs.[41]

Another variation which has grown in importance recently is the institutional buy-out (IBO). Here financiers, such as investment trusts or private equity firms, set up the deal and own the majority of the company, normally offering managers a smaller stake (perhaps 10 per cent rather than the 30 per cent they would get in an MBO), and involving them in negotiations at a relatively late stage. IBOs often happen when a business under-performs (Real-life Application 12.4).

Real-life Application 12.4 The institutional buy-out of Burger King

Following a period of poor performance, and a fierce price war with McDonald's, in 2002 Burger King was sold off by its owner Diageo, the UK drinks conglomerate, to a consortium of three private equity financiers from Texas Pacific Group, Bain Capital Partners, and Goldman Sachs. These took ownership of approximately 28 per cent, 24 per cent, and 24 per cent of the company respectively.

Diageo had finally only been able to sell Burger King after reducing the price by more than one-third, to $1.5 billion.[42] Yet the consortium of financiers believed that they could improve Miami-based Burger King's performance, where Diageo had not, citing the improved performance of the number three burger firm, Wendy's, as evidence for its potential. They believed that they could achieve better efficiencies in the value chain, improve the marketing, and introduce innovations to the menu. Although some of the existing management were retained, a new chief executive and international director were appointed soon after the consortium took over.

→

→ By 2006, the consortium had already achieved a positive return on their investment. They are forecast to withdraw from the company in a few years' time (private equity firms such as these typically work on a five to seven year time horizon, turning around the company if necessary, and then selling off their share to the public or on to other financiers), when $600m-worth of shares is likely to be offered to the public in an initial public offering (IPO) while they retain a majority stake in Burger King. If the IPO is successful, *Business Week* assesses the financiers' performance as 'not bad for about three years' work'.[43]

12.3 Evaluating strategic options: the RACES framework

Once a number of strategic options and potential methods have been determined, these elements have to be assessed and prioritized, and formed into a coherent strategy. It is unlikely that an organization will either wish to or be able to implement all the options available to it.

The strategy and method that are eventually chosen will have to address all the high priority issues identified, give the organization the factors required for survival in its chosen industries, and ideally provide the basis for successful competition over the longer term.

This is the stage in our analysis at which creativity must be tempered by practical realities. There is no point in recommending a strategy, however imaginative, that the organization cannot put into practice. So, the successful strategic option *must* meet the first four of the following five RACES criteria, and it is highly desirable that it meets the fifth:

- **R**esources needed to implement the option must be available, or the organization must be able to obtain them quickly.

- It must be **A**cceptable to powerful internal and external stakeholders, for example the firm's owners, regulatory bodies, and key managers and staff.

- It must be **C**oherent with other proposals and existing strategies.

- It must be **E**ffective in resolving the issues that it is intended to address.

- The chosen strategy should also contribute to the **S**ustainability of the organization's competitive advantage.

12.3.1 Resources

The first consideration in determining whether a strategic option should be accepted or rejected is the practical one of whether the organization has, or can obtain quickly enough, the resources needed to put it into effect.

a. Physical assets

The land, buildings, equipment, and software needed to implement a strategic option can usually be purchased if the organization needs them, so it is often more important to ensure that it has the financial resources to buy them and the competences to use them. There are cases, however, when the lack of physical assets may be a reason to reject an option. This happens when the resources concerned are difficult to buy on the open market, perhaps because supply is controlled by a competitor or because they are in short supply. For example, McDonald's has already taken possession of many of the best positions in the prime locations in the USA; this means that new competitors have to locate where it is harder to make profits.

b. Financial assets

Most strategic moves cost money. There will be up-front costs of market research and R&D. If an organization needs to relocate part of its operations elsewhere, it must take account of exit costs such as redundancy payments or political recriminations that may result from the large-scale loss of jobs in its original location. Cash may be needed for additions or improvements to production facilities or sales outlets, for recruiting new staff and making existing people redundant, for training and advertising. If sales volumes increase, then the firm is likely to need extra working capital to finance inventories and debtors. If the funds for all this are not available then the option will need to be rejected in favour of something more affordable.

→ Ways of raising funds are examined in more detail in Section 17.3.

Using Evidence 12.1 Assessing an organization's financial resources

After preparing an estimate, however crude, of the likely cost of an option, it is important to analyse an organization's cash flows and balance sheet for possible sources of cash:

- Cash generated by existing operations: Remember that cash is not the same as profit. If the firm is already investing heavily in its existing operations, then it may have no funds available from this source, even if it is profitable.

- Loans: An organization's borrowing capacity is normally determined by its gearing and interest cover. If gearing is already high and/or interest cover low, a firm is likely to have difficulty in obtaining new loans, unless they can be secured against existing assets.

- Share or bond issues: If the firm's prospects are good, or its managers have built a following among investors, then it may be able to raise new funds in the capital markets or from private shareholders. If it can make a sufficiently strong case, it may be able to ask the market to fund a specific strategic option, such as an acquisition, expansion into a major new market, or the development of a completely new range of products. Young firms in fast-growing industries may find that venture capital is available, at a price, even if they have no track record in their current firm.

- Asset disposals: If there are surplus plant, buildings, or parts of the business, firms may raise cash to reinvest elsewhere. It may be possible to liberate cash from operational assets by selling them to a finance house and then leasing them back.

- Improved use of working capital: If levels of working capital are above those needed by competitors then, by reorganizing its operations to cut the amount of inventory or reduce the level of debtors, a company can release capital for investment.

c. Capabilities and intellectual resources

We have already shown in Chapter 7 the importance of competences and intellectual resources. Therefore, two important judgements need to be made:

- Does the organization already have the capabilities or knowledge needed to put the option into practice?

- If not, can the organization acquire the intellectual resources it needs quickly enough? If the organization has a good track record in learning, then the answer to this question may be 'yes'. Otherwise, the organization will need to buy in or borrow these resources, if they are available. They may, however, be obtainable from consultants or from other businesses that belong to the same corporation or strategic network, or may be obtained through outsourcing some elements of the option to specialist firms.

The competences and knowledge that are needed may go beyond product and process technology. A strategic option may imply substantial changes in structure, systems, or culture, and the management of these changes requires specialist skills. The management of a merger or acquisition, if this forms part of the proposed strategy, also calls for particular competences.

➜ The skills of the change agent are discussed in Section 16.4 and the challenges of post-merger integration are discussed in Chapter 17.

d. Human resources

Even if the organization does not need to acquire new knowledge or competences, a strategic option may require it to increase the number of people with a particular skill, such as software engineers or salespeople. It may also need to strengthen its management with people with experience in, for example, electronic commerce, running overseas sales operations, or managing the implementation of large-scale IT systems. In determining whether to accept or reject an option, we need to decide:

- whether the organization's existing staff can implement the option, with relevant training if necessary. This requires a judgement about whether those people have the right level of education, and the right attitude and motivation, to take on board any new skills;
- whether new employees can be recruited to supplement the existing staff. This involves ascertaining whether there is an adequate supply of people with the relevant education and training who will come for the pay offered. It also requires a judgement on how easy the organization will find it to attract people with the right degree of motivation. Organizations with a poor reputation or with a strong and unusual culture may find it difficult to recruit enough of these people.

e. Reputational assets

The importance of an organization's reputational assets will depend on the nature of the strategic option and the industry at which it is aimed. For options aimed at improving internal processes, they may not be relevant, although a strong corporate reputation may help in recruiting people with key skills, and motivating staff to renewed efforts. In emerging industries, or in new segments of established industries, the lack of an established brand need or reputation may not be a problem. In the airline industry, firms like Virgin Atlantic and Emirates have been able to establish themselves in competition with established airlines with strong reputations. Options aimed at entering or expanding in a brand-sensitive market, on the other hand, will be hard to achieve if the firm does not have a strong brand.

➜ We discussed reputational assets in Section 7.3.5.

A firm does not necessarily need reputational assets in the precise segment that the strategic option is targeting. Reputation can be transferred from one business to another, as Richard Branson did when he used the Virgin brand built in the music industry to move, first into airlines, and then railways and a range of other businesses. Honda has done the same in moving into the aircraft production business (Real-life Application 12.5).

Reputational assets can be bought by acquiring another company or can sometimes be built quickly (albeit expensively) through advertising and sales promotion.

f. Relational assets

An important consideration in the assessment of some types of strategic option is whether the organization has the relationships and relational capital with those individuals and firms that it depends upon in order to implement the option. A firm expanding into a new

Real-life Aplication 12. 5 Honda's move into aircraft manufacturing[44]

Honda has partnered with General Electric and Piper Airlines to produce, sell, and service the HondaJet plane. *Honda*

For many years Honda has had a ambition to provide airplanes for the masses—a 'flying car'—ever since the company's founder Soichiro Honda talked of it in the early 1960s. For some decades Honda has spent an unknown proportion of its $400m research budget on aviation. Finally, Honda has built an aeroplane that can compete in the light business jet market. The HondaJet had its first flight on 3 December 2003. Production was planned to start in 2007, and the plane expected to be priced at $300,000.

The HondaJet is being developed in a partnership with General Electric, the manufacturer of jet engines, and Piper Aircraft Inc., which will sell and service the planes. Building on its reputation for efficiency in its cars and motorcycles, the HondaJet is planned to have considerably better fuel economy than competitors'.

The expense and complexity of making new jet engines are extremely high, but in Honda's case it has had a number of benefits. For example, it has used experimental projects like its aircraft engine to attract and train bright young engineers whose

capabilities could be transferred elsewhere. And though as recently as in 2004 Honda claimed that its plane was a development project, and that it had no plans to enter the commercial market, at least one commentator suggested that it was not so long ago that Honda, 'originally a motorcycle company, couldn't envision making cars either'.[45] It is now clear that the jet is a commercial project. And even if the aircraft only sells in small numbers, some think that it will add extra polish to the Honda brand.

Honda's reputation for its engineering design is also attracting favourable comment. Some writers expect that Honda will bring about 'continual, radical improvements to small aircraft flight ... Honda has prodigious resources that enable its engineers to examine airflow around the airframe',[46] amongst other relevant capabilities. Their research into road-tracking sensors, radar systems, and crash-prevention technology is predicted to be able to minimize the risk of novice pilots crashing!

location may find it important to have, or build, good relationships with the local adminis-tration, and opinion formers may help avoid misunderstandings and with recruitment. If the firm does not have this institutional capital, it may be advised to find a partner that does.

If the chosen strategic method involves alliances or outsourcing, then it may be important for the organization to have established relational capital with the right partners—who may themselves be in short supply, and have a number of other firms seeking a similar relation-ship. If the organization does not have relational assets, then it is likely to need to configure its architecture in order to build it. This may involve putting 'boundary-spanning' staff[47] in place—people who can move comfortably between different organizations.

→ We reviewed issues in managing alliances in Section 9.3.

g. Time

Finally, it is important to assess whether the organization has sufficient time to make a success of the option in question.

As we noted in Chapter 11, some strategic issues have a very obvious time constraint attached to them, but for any strategic option it is worth asking if the organization can implement it before competitors do something that destroys its benefits. If competitors are going to be clearly first to market with a new product, or will have made further advances before a catch-up strategy has time to take effect, then maybe the option should be discarded.

For an unsuccessful organization, the owners or controlling stakeholders will be another source of time constraints. Any proposed changes in the strategy will need to take effect before stakeholders lose patience and shut the organization down.

12.3.2 Acceptability

Organizations, as we have seen, contain various groups of stakeholders who typically differ in what they want from the organization, and in the power they have to achieve their own desires and/or frustrate those of other people.

→ The concept of stakeholders was introduced in Section 1.1.4.

In order for an option to be acceptable it must first meet the objectives of the *controlling* stakeholders. It should help the organization to achieve the financial returns and growth that those stakeholders are seeking. It should not involve more (or less) risk than they are prepared to accept, and be compatible with any requirements they have regarding ethics, social responsibility, and so on.

The second requirement, if an option is to be judged acceptable, is that any objections from powerful stakeholders can be overcome. Most significant shifts in strategy will upset some people, who fear that they will lose power or status, or that they will end up doing more work for the same, or less, reward. If those people have the power, and the desire to use it, then they can block an option through political manoeuvring, strike action, or simple refusal to do as they are asked.

→ Obstacles to change are discussed in Chapter 16.

The resulting conflict may alienate customers, or take management attention away from everyday operations, so that the organization becomes less effective. For an option to be acceptable, therefore, it must clearly be possible to execute the change process in such a way as to limit the damage from such conflict, or to avoid alienating powerful stakeholders.

→ Relational contracts are defined in Section 8.3.1.

The assessment of acceptability will draw upon an analysis of the organization's culture and architecture. In particular, it will be important to understand the nature of the relational contracts between the organization and its different internal and external stakeholders. It is by upsetting these relational contracts that an organization can trigger damaging resistance to change.

There is rarely a simple 'yes' or 'no' answer to the question 'Is this option acceptable?' Most proposals, however radical, can become acceptable if the management is prepared to spend enough effort and money on winning over the key stakeholders, or if the organization is so obviously on the brink of disaster that radical solutions need to be tried. However, acceptability can be used as a criterion on which to *rank* proposals, and a decision can then be made as to whether the most acceptable proposal is also the best overall. We return to this point in Section 12.3.6 below.

12.3.3 Coherence

We have already mentioned the need for a strategy to be implemented coherently—for value chain, culture, and architecture to be configured to deliver the chosen combination of cost and differentiation advantage in the chosen markets, and to sustain advantage for the future. Therefore the new strategy of which they will form part should also be coherent. That means that any combination of strategic options must work with one another, and with any parts of the existing strategy that are being maintained (see What Can Go Wrong 12.1). Particular points to look out for include:

- Brand values and reputation: A strategic option should not undermine the organization's reputational assets. For example, it would be difficult for H&M to launch a line of expensive, classic clothes for older women without confusing consumers who are used to its products being fashionable, youthful, and reasonably priced. If it wanted to extend its products in this direction, it might need to launch a new brand, as Toyota did with Lexus.

- Culture and architecture: A new option should not undermine the values and relational contracts that are important for sustaining motivation and innovativeness elsewhere in the organization, or that will alienate consumers who expect a particular type of product or service from the organization.

- Value chain: An organization should beware of overloading its value chain or stretching it in too many potentially conflicting ways. Careful judgements are required as to whether a new product or new form of positioning will force people to do mutually contradictory things—for example, produce custom-designed and mass-produced items at the same time, using the same equipment.

Note that this criterion does not prevent unrelated diversifications. A strategic option can be radically different from the existing strategy, but may still be coherent with it, as long as it does not undermine it. British Airways' move into tourist attractions, with the London Eye, was a world away from its core business, but still coherent with its brand values, and did not consume enough resources to interfere with the smooth running of the airline.

Lack of coherence with the existing strategy is not always a reason to reject an option. In a poorly performing organization, or one that is threatened by a changing environment, a clean break with the past strategy may be needed. A firm that is attempting to develop a breakthrough technology will almost always find that some elements of this may be incompatible with its current operations, but the disruption may be worth the risk. However, when appraising an option, we need to be alert to any difficulties that this incoherence may entail.

12.3.4 Effectiveness

An effective option is one that resolves the strategic issue that it is intended to address, as discussed in Section 12.2. Some options, however, may be more effective than others. Effectiveness, like acceptability, is a criterion on which alternative options can be ranked.

Certain types of strategy are likely to be more or less effective according to the context in which they will be used. For example, effective strategies in mature industries are those which address the key issues of a declining growth in sales and an increasingly large and powerful competitor group, and respond to the needs of a sophisticated, and potentially bored, customer base. In newer industries, an effective strategy is one that makes the most of rising market demand and builds a strong competitive position for the future.

→ We look at strategies in different contexts in Chapters 13 and 15.

a. Financial appraisal of strategic options

One important step towards assessing the effectiveness of an option is to calculate its likely future economic value. However, this is not necessarily straightforward and can be done in a number of different ways that generate different answers. The main methods are:

- Payback: The number of months or years it will take for the profits from an option to repay the initial investment. A payback of under one year is very attractive—and some cost-saving projects are able to achieve this. A more normal rule of thumb is to expect a payback of between two and three years. Payback is easy to calculate and to understand, but does not take account of the opportunity cost of having money tied up in an investment that could be put to other uses, or the value of any profits made after the payback date. This makes it unsuitable for dealing with options with a long time horizon.

- Discounted cash flow (DCF) gives a more accurate picture of the economic costs and benefits of an investment. Cash inflows and outflows (rather than profits) are the raw data for the calculation, and each period's cash flows are 'discounted' at a rate of interest that reflects the company's cost of capital—whether borrowed or obtained from shareholders. The sum of these discounted cash flows is the net present value (NPV) of the option. (The precise details of the calculation of the cost of capital (also known as the discount rate) and of NPV are beyond the scope of this book, but can be found in any good corporate finance textbook.) If the NPV is positive, then the option is economically viable—if negative, then it should be rejected.

- Internal rate of return (IRR) is a variation on the discounted cash flow method. The IRR is the discount rate which, if applied to the option cash flows, gives them an NPV of zero. If the IRR is greater than or equal to the firm's cost of capital, then the option is economically viable. The IRR and NPV tests of viability are essentially equivalent, but IRR is tricky to calculate and can give misleading answers if the option has alternating periods of positive and negative cash flow, so that NPV is generally reckoned to be the more reliable method.

- Real options are a concept we introduced in Section 12.1.1b. They are evaluated using what is known as the Black-Scholes formula, using the value of the initial investment, the forecast returns from the investment, the forecast time before those benefits arrive, the rate of interest on a risk-free investment (such as government bonds), and the degree of variability in the returns.[48] The virtue of this method is that it takes account of the possibility of fine-tuning a project as it goes along, or abandoning it before it has cost too much, thus limiting the downside.[49] It also takes account of the value of an early investment in enabling subsequent options.

NPV and real options methods both have drawbacks that we discuss in Theoretical Debate 12.1.

Theoretical Debate 12.1 Discounted cash flow methodologies versus real options reasoning

There are broadly two approaches that companies can use in attempting to deal with an uncertain environment: predictive approaches and adaptive approaches (Wiltbank et al., 2006). Predictive approaches lock organizations into planned strategies, while adaptive approaches place a premium on rapid adaptation rather than strategic intentions (Schoemaker, 2002).

Traditionally, potential investments have been assessed through a combination of managerial judgement and predictive techniques such as payback and DCF. However, there are a number of problems with these techniques in respect of some types of options, particularly those with long lives and those more speculative ones where the outcome is uncertain. In DCF-based financial evaluations, these will appear unattractive, because the costs are immediate and certain, while the benefits are far away (so have a low value once discounted) and may have a low probability of coming to fruition. But in fact, they may be the options that will produce the greatest strategic benefit and the highest overall long-term value for a company's shareholders. Other problems with DCF methods include:

- The future environment needs to be predictable and precisely definable for DCF techniques to calculate an accurate assessment of value (Courtney et al., 1997).

- Any risks subsumed under the discount rate's beta are assumed to be exogenous to the firm and not amenable to control by knowledgeable managers as the project develops over time. Thus NPV methods tend to undervalue investments because of their inability to incorporate a firm's capacity to adapt to unexpected market developments. Such flexibility can limit downside losses while preserving the upside potential (Trigeorgis, 1996; Copeland and Antikarov, 2005).

- Because long-term projects have to use a higher discount rate to account for the greater likelihood of problems developing in the future, investors require higher returns. As a result, the risk that real cash flows may be lower than predicted are captured in the valuation, but not the possibility that cash flows may be much higher than forecast. Consequently managers may be dissuaded from investing in uncertain but highly promising opportunities (van Putten and MacMillan, 2004).

- If managers focus exclusively on projects that have a probability of success, they restrict the number of options that are pursued.

- DCF methods ignore any potential strategic, but non financial, value of a project, such as the opening up of future options without any current cash flows. A better type of analysis requires explicit consideration of an investment's subsequent commercial effects (Smit and Trigeorgis, 2006b).

Adaptive approaches appear to be becoming more common (Grant, 2003), particularly in dynamic industries. Real options (Myers, 1977) are a way of allowing organizations to both plan and adapt through encouraging the development of systems that facilitate innovation and change, and establishing formal rules that guide the evaluation and pursuit of emerging opportunities, and which would otherwise not be considered (McGrath and Boisot, 2005; MacMillan et al. (2006); Miller and O'Leary (2005); Ashby, 1956). They also encourage the ruthless abandonment of floundering projects before they eat up too much money (van Putten and MacMillan, 2004).

Its inherent flexibility is the main benefit of real options reasoning, so that some have suggested it will soon replace NPV as the paradigm for investment decisions (Copeland and Antikarov, 2005). Some go so far as to suggest that strategy is now focusing on firms as a portfolio of opportunities rather than as a portfolio of businesses or capabilities (Venkatraman and Subramaniam, 2002).

Critics of real-option evaluation, however, point out that it can lead managers to overestimate the value of uncertain projects, encouraging companies to over-invest in them (van Putten and MacMillan, 2004). Some critics (Adner and Levinthal, 2004; McGrath et al., 2004), doubt that it is as precisely developed as it needs to be to gain popular acceptance—there is no clear definition of what a real option actually is.

Further problems relate to the assumptions underlying real-options calculations. For example (van Putten and MacMillan, 2004), it is hard to find good proxies for the input variables the model requires. Financial options theory assumes that the option and the underlying asset can be bought and sold in an open market, which is not true for strategic investments that are specific to an organization.

The real-options philosophy of flexibility also has its critics, who argue that firms should invest strongly in those resources and competences that they know will give them advantage, that they should aim to shape their environment, rather than wait to see what it does, and that they should commit early in some cases to signal strength and credibility to competitors (Smit and Trigeorgis, 2006b). And the flexibility involved in real options may imply considerable disruption for the real people involved—who may not be accommodating (McGrath et al., 2004).

12.3.5 Sustainability

Within the options that are accepted for incorporation into the overall strategy, there should be some that give the organization a reasonable expectation of sustainable advantage. Other strategies may be needed in order to keep the organization viable in the short term, allowing time for the development of other longer-term benefits. But long-term options cannot be ignored altogether.

A major focus for long-term sustained success is therefore the development of valuable strategic resources. In fast-changing environments, this is likely to involve the development of dynamic capabilities.

→ Strategic resources, including dynamic capabilities, that lead to sustainable competitive advantage were examined in Chapter 7.

12.3.6 Balancing the different criteria

At the end of your RACES analysis you will end up with a number of potential strategic options, each of which should be given a ranking as to how well it meets each of the five criteria. It may be helpful to summarize the analysis in a matrix (see Worked Example 12.1). The final task is to decide which options to accept and which to reject.

Sometimes an option will rank low on several of the criteria, and can obviously be rejected. Sometimes there will be a clear winning option that ranks highest on most of the criteria and scores acceptably on all of them. More frequently, however, you will be confronted with one of the following two situations:

- Several options perform adequately on all the criteria, but there is no clear winner. The option that scores highest on effectiveness, for example, is not the one that scores highest on acceptability. You are forced to judge which criterion is the most important.

- Every one of the available options fails on at least one criterion, and you are forced to judge which of them is, on balance, the least bad.

These are precisely the kinds of compromises and trade-offs that confront practising managers, and there is no easy formula for judging them. It may be comforting to realize that once you have got this far in the analysis, and eliminated the truly ridiculous options, there are no right or wrong answers. It is, however, important to understand the trade-offs that would have to be made, and the precise reasons why, in the end, one option may be preferable to another. The following guidelines may help:

- Options for which the resources clearly are not available or obtainable should normally be rejected. However, if the option represents a very valuable opportunity, and other criteria are met, it may be worth looking again to see if there are creative ways of finding the resources needed. If the organization is in deep trouble, then it may seriously be worth considering the gamble of taking resources from a failing operation to fund a speculative opportunity.

- Low effectiveness will also normally be a reason for rejecting an option, although the entire analytical process we have mapped out here and in the previous chapter, tying options to specific issues, is designed to minimize the number of ineffective options that are considered.

- A trade-off will frequently be necessary between acceptability and effectiveness. The options that enable the organization to make radical advances in the market-place, or in reducing costs, can often imply substantial changes to people's working practices and involve giving power to people who understand new markets or new technologies. People who are wedded to established practices, or who hold power under the existing structure, can be expected to resist these changes. In the end, effectiveness must win out over acceptability, since an organization that is not effective in meeting the needs of customers will not be able to afford to keep its other stakeholders happy for very long.

- Not every option will need to meet the sustainability criterion, but those that do may merit preference over those that do not.

We now apply these principles to the assessment of strategic options for British Airways.

Worked Example 12.1 Developing strategic options for British Airways

In this Worked Example we are going to go through the process of option development for British Airways, continuing from the worked examples we undertook in Chapter 11 in which we evaluated BA's performance and assessed the major strategic issues facing the company.

In this Worked Example we will follow the structure of Chapter 12 in order to recommend strategic options and methods for the company. But before we can assess these, we need to understand whether its performance is good or bad. So the first task is to remind ourselves of the strategic issues that it faces using the structure outlined in Chapter 11.

Issues confronting BA

In Worked Example 11.3, we reviewed BA's performance, environment, sources of distinctiveness, and sources of sustainable advantage. Our analysis there (Table 11.5) indicated that there were five main strategic issues facing BA:

1. How to respond to the Open Skies agreement
2. How to deal with increasingly acquisitive competitors
3. How to respond to the threat from airlines with more profitable business models
4. How to respond to increased public awareness of climate change and greenhouse emissions
5. How to respond to persistent industrial relations problems

We can now develop a range of options to respond to these issues. In the interests of space we will only focus on two of the five issues, and for each we will develop three options and methods. There are many more. Our suggestions are shown in Tables 12.3 and 12.4.

It is important to say at this point that the evaluation of problems and suggestions for options discussed here, are ours and ours alone. You—and indeed the company itself—may well come to different conclusions. As long as those conclusions are well argued, and based on sound evidence, it will be difficult to disagree with you. As we have said before, there are few absolute right or wrong answers in strategic analysis—simply more or less plausible solutions.

Summary

None of the six options examined here stands out as a clear winner:

- Option 1(a)—going carbon neutral—stands out from the others in terms of effectiveness and sustainability. It promises a degree of sustainable competitive advantage that none of the other options match—if it works. It is also emotionally attractive to urge a company to 'do the right thing' by the environment. However, it also represents a substantial commitment of resources, with a real risk that there will be no return on the investment. If the efforts to go carbon neutral were to fail, then BA—its managers, employees, and shareholders—would be worse off and the environment would not have benefited.
- Option 1(b)—pretending to go carbon neutral—can, on our analysis, clearly be rejected. It offers no sustainable advantage and a significant degree of reputational risk.
- Option 1(c)—purchasing Eurostar—has attractions. It is highly coherent and offers some promise of effectiveness and sustainable advantage. A great deal would depend upon the price that Eurostar's shareholders exacted. There is also a substantial risk that a buyer from outside the rail industry, such as BA, would have difficulties in adapting to a new technological and regulatory environment.
- Both options 1(a) and 1(c) win extra points because they address two issues, and not just one.
- Option 2(a)—emulating the low-cost model—may be the way in which the entire shorthaul airline industry is moving. However, it offers no sustainable advantage, and as such would need to be partnered with another option that did. There are also question-marks as to its coherence with BA's strategy.
- Option 2(b)—boosting the cargo business—is a fine example of a plausible and apparently low-risk option that loses its attractiveness once we take a closer look at the competitive environment. There may be an angle that BA could exploit against FedEx or Lufthansa, but on the information available to us here, it is not at all clear what it might be. ➔

→ **Table 12.3** BA's issues, options, and methods

Strategic issue	Strategic options	Methods
How to respond to increased public awareness of climate change and greenhouse emissions[a]	1(a) Go 'carbon neutral'. Reduce emissions to lowest degree possible (for example through reconfiguring routes, reducing baggage allowances, changing the fleet to fuel-efficient aircraft, and working with aircraft manufacturers to develop alternative-fuel aircraft) and develop carbon offset programme for remainder	Internal development + alliance for value chain changes; alliance (probably with not-for-profit organization) for carbon offset
	1(b) Pretend to go carbon neutral. Purchase carbon offsets on open market.	Outsourcing
	1(c) Diversify into rail business through acquisition of Eurostar	Acquisition
How to respond to the threat from airlines with more profitable business models	2(a) Change short-haul value chain to emulate low-cost model	Internal development, probably involving hiring in of key staff from a low-cost carrier
	2(b) Increase sales from cargo to offset threatened passenger revenue stream	Internal development
	2(c) Develop a regional hub airport in Mumbai to develop a revenue stream not threatened by Ryanair	Alliance/joint venture—the necessary relational resources to do business in India could not be developed internally in a realistic time-scale, and acquisition in India might hit regulatory hurdles

But note—options 1(a) and 1(c) will address this issue as well. 1(a) will, if properly implemented, reduce fuel costs significantly and render BA more competitive. Option 1(c) will take BA into an industry which offers a close, and more environmentally friendly, substitute for short-haul low-cost air travel

a For an interesting discussion of these issues see *The Economist*, 'Travelling green tonight'. 16 June 2007

- Option 2(c)—opening a hub in Mumbai—has some attractions, but the amount of investment involved, and the fiercely competitive nature of the Indian airline industry, would make one think twice before recommending it.

It may be that the answer for BA is a combination of these options, or perhaps others that you might be able to think of for yourself.

Practical dos and don'ts

Option development

- Do not restrict yourself to options that have been mentioned by the firm's management or by outside observers such as journalists or case-writers. There is no guarantee that they have correctly identified all the issues, or all the possible ways of addressing them.
- Remember that there is almost always more than one way of addressing a particular issue. Try to look at each issue from a number of the different angles set out in Section 12.1.1. What would the strategy be if we tried just to copy the most successful competitor? What would it be if we tried for a breakthrough innovation? If we withdrew from the business or market affected by the issue, could the resources be put to good use elsewhere?

- It may also be fruitful to try to think of different ways of achieving a given outcome. If an organization has a weakness in after-sales service, should it fix the problem by improving the organization of its own service department, or by outsourcing the activity? Or should it decide to ignore that problem and compensate through superior product innovation, or by repositioning its product further down-market and trying for extra sales volume? Do not focus exclusively on product/market changes and diversification. Enhancements to the value chain, culture, and architecture can be equally important strategically.

- Try to be creative. There is no harm, at this stage in the process, in putting forward ideas that at first sight are slightly impractical—they may trigger other, more sensible ideas. Brainstorming the issues in groups can be helpful. Any truly mad suggestions can be eliminated at the evaluation stage (Section 12.3). →

→ **Table 12.4** Evaluating BA's options

RACES criteria	Resources	Acceptable	Coherent	Effective	Sustainable
1(a) Go 'carbon neutral'. Reduce emissions to lowest degree possible (for example through reconfiguring routes, reducing baggage allowances, changing the fleet to fuel-efficient aircraft, and working with aircraft manufacturers to develop alternative-fuel aircraft) and develop carbon offset programme for remainder	This is uncharted territory—and not just for BA. The competences and technologies required for low emissions operation are at a very early stage of development and would require substantial investment of people and money—and not just BA's. In March 2007 BA had approximately £2.3bn in cash, cash equivalents, and interest bearing deposits, gearing of around 40% (a rule of thumb would indicate that it was close to its comfortable borrowing capacity). It generated operating cash flow of around £750m in 2006/2007. This indicates that it could manage an investment of several hundred million pounds in this option

Expertise to develop forestry schemes and other genuine forms of carbon offset are in development and could be bought in. Similarly, R&D is being undertaken on sustainable fuels, not least by car manufacturers. BA could seek a co-development alliance with one of these companies or a research institute | This option would be likely to split investors—some would applaud the vision and also the social responsibility shown, others might deplore the risk

If presented to staff in a way that demonstrated sincerity, this might prove highly acceptable, even if it implied significant change in working practices. Staff and customers alike will see climate change as a significant issue, let alone regulators and legislators | Assuming that this did not disrupt the route structure unduly (see the evaluation of 2(a) below for an analysis of the implication of that), this option is perfectly coherent with BA's strategy and brand values. It might be a way to renew the 'World's favourite airline' tag | Experience in other industries indicates that there is a possibility that moves in this direction would generate ideas that would lead to significant cost savings. However, it is less clear that these would repay the investment involved | If this worked, the sustainability benefits would be high. BA would develop competences and reputational assets that would keep it at the forefront of its industry |

Option					
1(b) Pretend to go carbon neutral. Purchase carbon offsets on open market	This is a low commitment option requiring financial resources, which are available (see option 1(a)) and marketing expertise, which BA possesses	This option poses significant acceptability risks. A cynical attempt to manipulate this issue for commercial advantage will be quickly seen through, and doubts made public by bloggers. Staff and customers may be alienated	The reputational risk involved (see under Acceptability) means that this option would not be coherent with BA's brand positioning	This might bring short-term marketing benefits but risks long-term damage to the brand	No competences or knowledge will be developed through this option
1(c) Diversify into rail business through acquisition of Eurostar	The experience of Virgin indicates that, while some competences in airline travel management do transfer between the businesses, it is not easy to transfer operational expertise. There might well be a learning curve as BA came to terms with the new environment. BA lacks experience in planning and integrating large mergers, although its earlier experience of change management might help	Eurostar has been improving its revenues but is not yet believed to have become consistently profitable.[a] This will limit the acceptability of the deal to BA shareholders. Eurostar's shareholders and staff may be persuaded by the right price if they believe that their long-term investment and patience is about to bear fruit BA staff on short-haul routes might feel threatened by the move, though some might also see it as a way of safeguarding their jobs against the threat of climate change	There have been plans for a rail line that would link Heathrow with the European rail network, and this option would therefore be coherent with BA's long-haul provision. Eurostar's brand values are sufficiently similar to BA's for there to be coherence on that dimension	The effectiveness depends upon the rate at which rail travel develops in competition with air. BA might need to shoulder several years of rail losses before any profits emerged	Eurostar has a unique set of assets, and if BA can help it to improve profitability, then it would become a strategic resource

→ **Table 12.4** *(cont'd)*

RACES criteria	Resources	Acceptable	Coherent	Effective	Sustainable
2(a) Change short-haul value chain to emulate low-cost model	Although BA will have learnt from its past experience with Go and Deutsche BA, and at least one commentator[b] believes that its strategy is moving in that direction in any case, but that the cost base has some way to go before matching that of Ryanair and easyJet. However, it may be that, after competing with low-cost carriers for ten years, BA has gone as far down this road as its competences and architecture will allow. There are likely to be some exit costs from this option, in the form of redundancy payments and renegotiating of contracts, but these should be achievable from within existing financial resources	If this option improves BA's profitability, then it is likely to be acceptable to the majority of institutional stakeholders. Employees may object. Even if profitability improves, staff jobs are likely to be lost or altered and employees may not be happy. Industrial relations at BA have a troubled history, as shown in Worked Example 11.3 The oneworld alliance is based around full-service offerings and its members might object if BA went too far down this route	As a reconfiguration of existing operations this is coherent with BA's current strategy. However, BA will have to be careful about disturbing its network of connections—making life inconvenient for its high-paying business travellers. Loss of these will have an impact on BA's ability to differentiate its long-haul services	One of the biggest problems facing airlines is profitability. The best-run low-cost carriers are the most profitable airlines. However, the low-cost, direct-flight model will sacrifice the (unquantifiable) economies of scope from being able to use route combinations to their highest capacity. Route density is an industry success factor for the full-service carriers	This option has little impact on sustainability, in that no new strategic resources are likely to emerge from it. BA would be emulating business models perfected by others
2(b) Increase sales from cargo to offset threatened passenger revenue stream	As this is a reconfiguration of current strategy, other resources such as capabilities in cargo operations are likely to be already present within the company, or obtainable through training redeployed staff	Related diversification is likely to be acceptable to most stakeholders, especially as it is an expansion of existing services rather than a contraction	Many airlines, notably Lufthansa, run profitable freight services alongside high-class passenger provision. There do not appear to be any clashes between the two businesses	Competition in cargo is stiff, with a number of dedicated carriers, such as FedEx and UPS, alongside the freight arms of other established airlines. It is not immediately clear how BA would differentiate its offering, or develop a business model that would enable it to compete on price	It is unclear how sustainable advantage would result in the face of entrenched and dedicated competitors

2(c) Develop a regional hub airport in India (for example, Mumbai)	Developing an airport hub is likely to involve considerable expense—to acquire or extend the existing airport, or the land to set up a new one, as well as develop the subsequent infrastructure. The new Terminal 5 at Heathrow is estimated to have cost over £4bn, and although Indian costs would be lower, this would not be a cheap option. This would stretch BA's financial resources

The competence and capabilities to own and run an airport would also need to be acquired—they are likely to be very different from running an airline. However, any lack of resources could be lessened by undertaking this option with a local partner, or one who understands the management of airports | Key stakeholders influencing the acceptance of this strategy are likely to be the Indian government, Mumbai City authorities, Indian airport operators, and the other Indian airlines. All are likely to view this option with interest and BA will have its work cut out to overcome some of the objections from, e.g. competitor airport operators that have superior relationships with the Indian regulatory authorities | Developing an airport is not obviously coherent with BA's current strategy, particularly in a country so far away—both culturally and geographically—from BA's UK base. However there is no reason to think it would undermine the current strategy, except in as much as management attention may be diluted | A new hub would provide BA with a solid base from which to expand into newly opening markets in south and east Asia. However, those markets, although fast-growing, are also fiercely competitive[c]

It would provide a convenient place for passenger interchanges, and its relatively central location should allow BA to reduce maintenance costs and improve fuel efficiencies as aircraft would not need to constantly return to a distant base

India is famous for the congestion at its major airports. Mumbai airport (which services one of the largest cities in the world) has a 'pathetic infrastructure'[d] and is ripe for development (in fact improvements are already planned). In 2006, Mumbai airport was sold to a private consortium by the Indian government

Delays at the airport add hugely to all its airline customers' fuel costs. Any firm that is able to improve this situation is likely to have a winning business on its hands | If successful, a new Asian hub would provide BA with a platform for considerable expansion into new markets, as well as new airports. It may also provide a means of shutting out competitors from the same routes |

a Wright, R. (2007). 'Eurostar expect passenger increase'. *Financial Times*, 12 January: 23
b Williams, T. (2006). 'BA tilts towards no-frills'. *Travel Trade Gazette UK*, 4 August: 16
c Lakshman, N. (2007). 'Merger mania reshapes Indian airlines'. *BusinessWeek Online*, 12 June
d Ibid. and Ranganathan, A. (2006). 'Chaos in air and on the ground'. *Business Line (The Hindu)*, 7 November: 9

→ Option evaluation

- Try to resist the temptation to jump straight to what seems to be the 'obvious' right answer, and use the RACES criteria, for that option only, to show that it works. Your arguments and your proposals will be improved if you can look at a range of alternatives, evaluate each of them, and demonstrate why your proposal is the best and why you have rejected the others.

- Make sure that your proposals, taken together, add up to a complete and coherent whole. Together, they must address all the high-priority issues that you have identified. In addition, it should be clear from your proposals:

  - why anyone should want to buy the organization's products or services in future;

  - how the organization will earn an acceptable return while serving its users;

  - how it will *sustain* its position in a changing world.

- Do not forget the financial evaluation of options. Putting forward sets of proposals without checking whether the organization has enough money to implement them is not a sensible idea.

- Do not underestimate the problems that employees may have in accepting ideas that may (you think) be for the good of the organization as a whole. Try to imagine yourself in the situation of each set of stakeholders—senior management, junior management, operational staff, suppliers, and so on—and thinking 'Would I really like it if this were happening to me?'

- Competitors are also stakeholders. When considering acceptability, do not neglect the possibility that they may retaliate, or call in regulators or lawyers to block, or at least delay, a proposal.

- When assessing the effectiveness of an option, remember to think of the downside—the things that may go wrong, and their cost.

What Can Go Wrong 12.1 Problems and solutions at Nokia

The Nokia 6230 phone led Nokia's recovery.
Nokia   →

→ Nokia, the world's biggest mobile phone manufacturer, had a bad year in 2004. Its shares lost over half their value between March and August—from a high of $23 to a low of $11 on 13 August—its sales declined, and its market share, having stabilized around 35 per cent for many years, fell to a low of 28.9 per cent.[50] And in April 2004, one of its main rivals, Samsung, overtook Nokia in market capitalization. However, some commentators thought that Nokia's decline began even earlier than this.[51] Sales peaked at €30.4bn in 2000 when 128m phones were sold. In 2003, despite selling 179m handsets, revenue was €29.5bn. Samsung, in contrast, was able to achieve much higher average selling prices for its phones, even though its volumes were lower.

Although some thought that Nokia's problems were partly because it had reached saturation in many of its main markets as well as facing increased competition,[52] others laid the blame for Nokia's problems at the company's strategy of focusing on high-volume, lower price sales, and ignoring design. The needs of increasingly fashion-conscious young mobile phone owners were ignored, and Nokia was accused of missing the change 'from brand to style'.[53] This is surprising given that Nokia had previously been the pioneer of the handset as a fashion item, with choices of colours and styles. But in 2003/2004 Nokia was sticking to its traditional 'monobloc' or 'candy bar' format for its handsets; meanwhile rivals were bringing out more innovative models.

A particular problem was the demand for folding 'clam-shell' phones, especially in Asia and North America. Motorola's RAZR V3 model, a slim-line design with a stylish aluminium shell, was a particular hit with consumers. Nokia has admitted that it failed to anticipate how successful clamshells would be.[54] But other design features were also missing. Cameras, high-quality colour screens, and user interfaces, that had formerly been 'streets ahead' of the competition, were all less well developed than they needed to be. This meant that previously loyal customers were forced to turn to competitors' models. As one said, 'Nokia just does not seem to have changed its look much over the last 10 years.'[55]

Nokia's design problems happened at the same time as mobile phone service providers were wanting customized handsets as a means of increasing their own brand differentiation. Operator-specific handsets are normally locked to prevent them being used on another operator's network, thereby attempting to boost customer loyalty as well as security. Operators in Europe and America were contracting with smaller Asian 'original design manufacturers' (ODMs), to provide handsets to their own design specifications. And Vodafone, the world's largest mobile services provider, chose to provide its 'Vodafone live!' data service on handsets supplied by Sharp.

Similar problems affected the development of 3G services. Japanese and South Korean companies were some years' ahead in this technology;[56] Vodafone, for one, chose Samsung and Sony Ericsson to supply its 3G handsets as a result. And Hutchison Whampoa's Three, a new entrant to the 3G market in Europe, declined to sell Nokia's handset because it lacked video-calling capabilities.[57]

Some have suggested that Nokia, as the leading handset-maker with the strongest brand, displayed a certain unwillingness to yield to the demands of service operators.[58] This was said to be partly because it had not properly recognized their power; it still regarded end-users as its customers, even though they usually bought their handsets through service operators. The service companies were apparently not surprised; one suggested that given its size, Nokia 'didn't need to listen to us'.[59] Some, though, suggested that Nokia's attitude was understandable.[60] In Europe, switching between operators is easy. Therefore consumers have traditionally been more loyal to handset-makers. However other manufacturers were prepared to concede to the operators' wishes in return for a boost in their own market share.

Nokia executives said that the company's apparent reluctance to embrace customized handsets was actually the result of technical factors.[61] Given Nokia's reliance on volume and scale, it could not make different handsets for individual operators without a reorganization of its value chain. Until 2005, this was oriented towards large-scale production runs of relatively undifferentiated handsets. It preferred to hold off adding new features, such as high-quality colour screens or higher-resolution cameras, until the components were available in large volumes.[62] It also preferred to customize handsets through software. Its Series 60 software, which is run on high-end phones, is especially configurable, allowing the same hardware to support providers' various services.

However, the shock appeared to stimulate Nokia into making the necessary changes. It has since moved into operator-focused hardware customization despite its preference for software customization, and made the changes to its logistics system. Nokia's new modular hardware designs made it easier for the company to customize products faster, and it set a target for 50 per cent of its products to have alternative designs, such as clamshells, sliders, and swivels, by the end of 2005. One of its products, the Nokia 6230, was so popular that Nokia was at times unable to meet demand.

And, according to one commentator, Nokia became a 'beehive of experiments'.[63] It launched a range of innovative handsets, the N-series, which had additional features as well as being phones. And its 770 Internet Tablet, is a hand-held computer that does not contain a phone at all but supports web-browsing, e-mail, and voice-over-internet calls using Google Talk software and Wi-Fi technology. Nokia's then CEO Jorma Ollila (who has since retired) directed R&D to areas where Nokia had particular strengths, for example radio technology and mobile-phone software, not wasting it on technologies that the company could buy in. In 2004, it spent more than $4.8 billion on R&D, of which 60 per cent went on software. At 12.8 per cent of sales, Nokia's R&D ratio was 3 per cent higher than Motorola's and about twice that of Sony.[64]

Nokia is now the largest camera company in the world. And convergence means that its phones provide music-playing, video-recording, and computing facilities so that its competitors include Apple, Sony, Canon, and other consumer-electronics firms.

By May 2006, Nokia was described as having a renewed spring in its step.[65] Its market share has recovered to 35 per cent.

● CHAPTER SUMMARY

In this chapter we have set out a framework for developing strategies that are tailored to the particular challenges and opportunities confronting an organization. This framework has four stages:

1. The identification of a range of strategic options for an organization. These are the possible alternative answers to the questions posed by a strategic issue. Different options will vary in the extent to which they call on the firm to match, outdo, or neutralize competition, to expand into new competitive arenas, and withdraw from old ones. Options will also make use of different combinations of changes to the organization's competitive stance, resources, value chain, culture, and architecture.

2. An assessment of the potential methods that may be adopted to implement the chosen strategy. These may include the acquisition of a bothersome competitor, an alliance with a specialist firm, the disposal of a business unit, or any combination thereof.

3. The evaluation of each of the options to determine which to accept and which to reject. For this, we suggest the use of the RACES criteria: resources, acceptability, consistency, effectiveness, and sustainability.

4. The combining of the options that have been accepted into a coherent strategy that addresses all the high-priority issues.

 Online Resource Centre
www.oxfordtextbooks.co.uk/orc/haberberg_rieple/

Visit the Online Resource Centre that accompanies this book to read more information relating to options and strategic methods.

● KEY SKILLS

The key skills you should have developed after reading this chapter are:

- the ability to develop a range of alternative strategic options for the organization to address the specific key issues identified. This will build upon the techniques discussed in Chapter 11 to assess:
  - the major strategic issues facing an organization;
  - the importance and urgency of the various issues;
- the ability to recommend appropriate alternative methods that may be used to implement the chosen strategic option;
- the ability to evaluate strategic options, using the RACES framework and select the options that best meet the organization's strategic needs;
- the ability to develop a coherent strategy for an organization, which may combine a number of different options, and which addresses all the high-priority issues that the organization faces.

● REVIEW QUESTIONS

1. What is the difference between a strategic issue and a strategic option?
2. What is the difference between a real option and a strategic option?

3. Which types of strategic option are particularly appropriate when there is a multi-option future? Or an infinite option future?

4. When might you expect an organization to give serious consideration to strategic options that:

   (a) require resources that will be very difficult to obtain?

   (b) will be unacceptable to significant parts of the management or workforce?

   (c) will be inconsistent with large parts of the existing strategy?

   (d) have a high risk of being ineffective—of failing to achieve their aim?

   (e) do not give sustainable advantage, even if effectively implemented?

● FURTHER READING

- There are few articles or books that discuss the evaluation of strategic options apart from other strategic management textbooks. Perhaps the originator of this type of thinking was **Rumelt R.** (1980). 'Corporate strategy'. *Journal of Business Strategy*, 1/2: 63.

- Bryson, J. M. (2004). *Strategic Planning for Publication and Nonprofit Organizations*. San Francisco: Jossey Bass, **chaps 6 and 7** discusses the development of strategic issues and options in a public sector context, although many of the principles he uses are the same as for the private sector.

- In contrast, for readings on the management of mergers and acquisitions we are spoilt for choice (for a more comprehensive list of references on M&As see Chapter 17).

  - Bower, J. (2001). 'Not all M&As are alike—and that matters'. *Harvard Business Review*, 79/3: 93–101.

  - Hitt, M. A., Harrison, J. S., and Ireland, R. D. (2001). *Mergers and Acquisitions: A Guide for Creating Value for Stakeholders*. New York: Oxford University Press.

  - A series of collected papers edited by **Cary Cooper and Stanley Finkelstein** (*Advances in Mergers and Acquisitions*. Amsterdam: JAI Press/Elsevier—now up to volume 5, 2006), brings together key academic writers on the topic of M&As.

- For an enlightening read on what can go wrong in strategic alliances see **Suen, W.** (2005). *Non-Cooperation—the Dark Side of Strategic Alliances*. New York: Palgrave Macmillan. Huxham, C. and Vangen, S. (2005). *Managing to Collaborate: The Theory and Practice of Collaborative Advantage*. London: Routledge is another comprehensive book on the various types of inter-firm collaborative arrangements based around some of the most influential theoretical papers in the field over the years.

- Real options are discussed comprehensively in **Boer, P.** (2002). *The Real Options Solution: Finding Total Value in a High-risk World*. New York: Wiley Finance. Real options in strategy are also the subject of a special issue of the *Journal of Applied Corporate Finance*, 17/2, Spring 2005. They are also discussed as part of a wider discussion of corporate finance by the creator of real option theory, Stewart Myers in **Brealey, R. and Myers, S.** (2005). *Principles of Corporate Finance*. 8th edn. Boston, MA: Irwin McGraw-Hill.

● REFERENCES

Adner, R. and Levinthal, D. A. (2004). 'What is not a real option: considering boundaries for the application of real options to business strategy'. *Academy of Management Review*, 29/1: 74–85.

Ashby, W. R. (1956). *An Introduction to Cybernetics*. London: Methuen.

Automotive News. (2006). 'Look, up in the sky, it's a Honda'. 80/6214.

Baker, S., Shinal, J., and Kunii, I. M. (2001). 'Is Nokia's star dimming?' *Business Week*, 22 January.

Barnett, W. P. and Hansen, M. T. (1996). 'The red queen in organizational evolution'. *Strategic Management Journal*, 17/7: 139–57.

Barnett, W. P. and Pontikes, E. G. (2005). 'The red queen: history-dependent competition among organizations'. *Research in Organizational Behavior*, 26: 351–71.

Bawden, T. (2005). 'Drinking to a growing market'. *The Times*, 6 December.

Bayus, B. L., Jain, S., Rao, A. G. (2001). 'Truth or consequences: an analysis of vaporware and new product announcements'. *Journal of Marketing Research*, 38/1: 3–13.

Blackwell, D. (2006). 'Cobra strikes out for market expansion with £27.5m fundraising'. *Financial Times*, 17 July.

Boer, P. (2002). *The Real Options Solution: Finding Total Value in a High-risk World*. New York: Wiley Finance.

Borison, A. (2005). 'Real options analysis: where are the emperor's clothes?' *Journal of Applied Corporate Finance*, 17(2), 17–31.

Bower, J. (2001). 'Not all M&As are alike—and that matters'. *Harvard Business Review*, 79/3: 93–101.

Bowman, E. H. and Hurry, D. (1993). 'Strategy through the option lens: an integrated view of resource investments and the incremental-choice process'. *Academy of Management Review*, 18/4: 760.

Brealey, R. and Myers, S. (2005). *Principles of Corporate Finance*: 8th edn. Boston, MA: Irwin McGraw-Hill.

Brown, S. F. (2004). 'Honda gets its wings'. *Fortune*, 149/3.

Brown-Humes, C. (2002). 'Nokia faces a fight to stay ahead of the game'. *Financial Times*, 4 June: 19.

Brown-Humes, C. (2004). 'Battles for market force bold strategy'. *Financial Times*, 5 February 2004: 10.

Brown-Humes, C. and Budden, R. (2004). 'The Finnish company has dominated mobile telecoms but has been slow to recognize recent challenges to its market share'. *Financial Times*, 7 May: 17.

Business Wire (2006). 'Fitch initiates Burger King Corporation IDR at 'B+': outlook positive'. 21 June 2006.

Carey, D. (2000). 'Making mergers succeed'. *Harvard Business Review*, 78/3: 145–54.

Cohen, W. M. and Levinthal, D. A. (1990). 'Absorptive capacity: a new perspective on learning and innovation'. *Administrative Science Quarterly*, 35: 128–52.

Colvin, C. and Charan, R. (2006). 'Private lives'. *Fortune*, European Edition, 27 November: 80–8.

Coomber, S. (2006). 'Snake bite'. *Business Strategy Review*, Winter: 32–7.

Copeland, T. and Antikarov, V. (2001). *Real Options: A Practitioner's Guide*. New York: Texere LLC.

Copeland, T. E. and Antikarov, V. (2005). 'Real options: meeting the Georgetown challenge'. *Journal of Applied Corporate Finance*, 17/2: 32–51.

Courtney, H., Kirkland, J., and Viguerie, P. (1997). 'Strategy under uncertainty'. *Harvard Business Review*, 75/6: 67–79.

Cuypers, I. and Martin, X. (2006). 'What makes and what does not make a real option? A study of international joint ventures'. *Academy of Management Proceedings*, QQ1–QQ6.

Daily Telegraph (2005). 'Change and you beat the rest'. 22 September.

Dao, F. (2005). 'Lessons from the red queen'. *Across the Board*, 42/3: 53–5.

DiGeorgio, R. (2002). 'Making mergers and acquisitions work: what we know and don't know—Part I'. *Journal of Change Management*, 3/2: 134–48.

Dyer, J., Kale, P., and Singh, H. (2004). 'When to ally & when to acquire'. *Harvard Business Review*, 82/7–8: 108–15.

Economist, The (2005). 'The giant in the palm of your hand'. 12 February: 67–9.

Economist, The (2006a). 'Face value: more, more, more'. 27 May.

Economist, The (2006b). 'The Murdoch factor—the battle for ITV'. 25 November: 381.

Ernst, D. and Halevy, T. (2004). 'Not by M&A alone'. *McKinsey Quarterly*, 1: 68–9.

Express on Sunday (2004). 'Cobra strikes success with curry coup'. 14 March.

Faherty, C. (2006). 'Cobra Beer vies for Premium American Lager Crown'. *New York Sun*, 14 November.

Foust, D. et al. (2006). 'Where's the beef?' *Business Week*, 10 April.

Frick, K. and Torres, A. (2002). 'Learning from high-tech deals'. *McKinsey Quarterly*, 1: 113–23.

Fulford, B. and Huang, P. (2004). 'Honda takes to the Skies'. *Forbes*, 174/10.

Gander, J., Haberberg, A., and Rieple, A. (2007). 'Managing alliances: the paradoxes of resource transfer, protection and contamination within the recorded music industry'. *Journal of Organizational Behavior*, 28: 607–24.

George, F. (2005). 'Oskosh debutantes: the VLJs'. *Business & Commercial Aviation*, 97/3: 54–64.

Gumbel, P. (2005). 'Small wasn't smart'. *Time*, 166/16: A6.

Haan, M. A. (2003). 'Vaporware as a means of entry deterrence'. *Journal of Industrial Economics*, 51/3: 345–58.

Hamel, G. and Prahalad, C. K. (1994). *Competing for the Future*. Boston, MA: Harvard Business Press.

Hindustan Times (2005). 'Cobra Beer's European "Grand Canyon Plan"'. 9 February.

Jardine, A. (2003a). 'Cobra aims "history" redesign at bars'. *Marketing*, 7 August 2003: 10.

Jardine, A. (2003b). 'King Cobra'. *Marketing*, 10 July: 18–20.

Kellogg, K. C., Orlikowski, W. J., and Yates, J. (2006). 'Life in the trading zone: structuring coordination across boundaries in post-bureaucratic organizations'. *Organization Science*, 17/1: 22–44.

Kirkland, R., Burke, D., and Demos, T. (2007). 'Private money'. *Fortune*, 155/4: 50–60.

Leung, S. (2002). 'Leading the news: McDonald's to serve up first loss: reeling from price wars, fast-food chain warns charges could increase'. *Wall Street Journal*, 18 December.

McGrath, R. G. and Boisot, M. (2005). 'Options complexes: going beyond real options reasoning'. *Emergence: Complexity & Organization*, 7/2: 2–13.

McGrath, R. G., Ferrier, W. J., and Mendelow, A. L. (2004). 'Real options as engines of choice and heterogeneity'. *Academy of Management Review*, 29/1: 86–101.

MacMillan, I. C., Van Putten, A. B., McGrath, R. G., and Thompson, J. D. (2006). 'Using real options discipline for highly uncertain technology investments'. *Research Technology Management*, 49/1: 29–37.

Marketing (2006). 'Cobra Beer'. 26 July: 83.

Markoff, J. (2007). 'Steve Jobs walks the tightrope again'. *New York Times*, 12 January: 3.

Miller, P. and O'Leary, T. (2005). 'Managing operational flexibility in investment decisions: the case of Intel'. *Journal of Applied Corporate Finance*, 17/2: 87–93.

Morrow Jr, J., Sirmon, D., Hitt, M., and Holcomb, T. (2007). 'Creating value in the face of declining performance: firm strategies and organizational recovery'. *Strategic Management Journal*, 28: 271–83.

Myers, S. C. (1977). 'Determinants of corporate borrowing'. *Journal of Financial Economics*, 5/2: 147–75.

Myers, S. C. and Turnbull, S. M. (1977). 'Capital budgeting and the capital asset pricing model: good news and bad news'. *Journal of Finance*, 32/2: 321.

Palter, R. and Srinivasan, D. (2006). 'Habits of the busiest acquirers'. *McKinsey Quarterly*, 4: 18–27.

Perrin, S. (1998). 'The buy-out is back'. *Management Today*, May: 78–82.

Press Trust of India Limited (2004). 'Cobra beer wins Grand Gold medal at Monde selection again'. 7 July.

van Putten, A. B. and MacMillan, I. C. (2004). 'Making real options really work'. *Harvard Business Review*, 82/12: 134–41.

Reinhardt, A. (2004). 'Looking beyond Nokia's bad news'. *Business Week Online*, 8 April.

Reinhardt, A. (2005). 'Is Nokia's battery recharged?' *Business Week Online*, 3 January.

Reinhardt, A. and Ihlwan, M. (2005). 'Will rewiring Nokia spark growth?' *BusinessWeek*, 14 February 2005: 46.

Richter, A. W., West, M. A., van Dick, R., and Dawson, J. F. (2006). 'Boundary spanners' identification, intergroup contact, and effective intergroup relations'. *Academy of Management Journal*, 49/6: 1252–69.

Rigby, R. (2001). 'Coming up fast: the Cobra man bottles up his own dream'. *Management Today*, 18 October: 89.

Sagner, J. (2007). 'Why working capital drives M&A today'. *Journal of Corporate Accounting and Finance*, January/February: 41–5.

Sanchez-Peinado, E. (2003). 'Internationalisation process of Spanish banks: strategic orientation after the mergers'. *European Business Review*, 15/4: 245–61.

Schoemaker, P. J. H. (2002). *Profiting From Uncertainty: Strategies for Succeeding No Matter What the Future Brings*. New York: Free Press.

Smit, H. T. J. and Trigeorgis, L. (2006a). 'Real options and games: competition, alliances and other applications of valuation and strategy'. *Review of Financial Economics*, 15: 95–112.

Smit, H. T. J. and Trigeorgis, L. (2006b). 'Strategic planning: valuing and managing portfolios of real options'. *R&D Management*, 36/4: 403–19.

Trigeorgis, L. (1993). 'The nature of option interactions and the valuation of investments with multiple real options'. *Journal of Financial and Quantitative Analysis*, 28/1: 1–20.

Trigeorgis, L. (1996). *Real Options: Managerial Flexibility and Strategy in Resource Allocation*. Cambridge, MA: MIT Press.

Tushman, M. L. and Scanlan, T. J. (1981). 'Boundary spanning individuals: their role in information transfer and their antecedents'. *Academy of Management Journal*, 24: 289–305.

Venkatraman, N. and Subramanian, M. (2002). 'Theorising the future of strategy: questions for shaping strategy research in the knowledge economy'. In *Handbook of Strategy and Management*. London: Sage.

Vermeulen, F. (2005). 'How acquisitions can revitalize companies'. *Strategic Management Review*, 46/2: 45–51.

Vermeulen, F. and Barkema, H. (2001). 'Learning through acquisitions'. *Academy of Management Journal*, 44/3: 457–76.

Walsh, D. (2006). 'Cobra Beer shelves its float plans after finance deal raises £27.5m'. *The Times*, 17 July.

Williamson, C. (2006). 'Refreshing investment: Och-Ziff Capital taps into Indian beer'. *Pensions & Investments*, 34/16: 8.

Wiltbank, R., Dew, N., Read, S., and Sarasvathy, S. D. (2006). 'What to do next? The case for non-predictive strategy'. *Strategic Management Journal*, 27/10: 981–98.

Womack, S. (2004). 'My Bombay dream'. *Mail on Sunday*, 7 November.

Cobra Beer Ltd is one of the fastest growing bottled beer companies in the UK. *Cobra Beer Ltd*

Cobra Beer Ltd is one of the fastest growing bottled beer companies in the UK. It was founded in 1989 by Lord Karan Bilimoria, a 45-year-old Indian-born British entrepreneur who, along with a partner, had spotted a gap in the market for a lager that could be drunk easily with meals in Indian restaurants. The idea was simple; they would produce a high-quality lager-type beer that was less gassy than those normally sold by restaurateurs, and would therefore not bloat diners.

Early days

Lord Bilimoria, who was born in Hyderabad, came to the UK in 1981 to further his education, obtaining a law degree from Cambridge University as well as accountancy qualifications. After a short while working as an accountant, and in the face of opposition from his highly respectable family,[66] he along with his partner, Arjun Reddy, started up a business importing from India such varied things as polo sticks, leather goods, jackets, towels, and pearls. These were sold with varying degrees of success, but as Lord Bilimoria says, his 'big idea' was always beer. And so in

1989 the partners founded Cobra Beer Ltd. Their mission from the beginning was to brew the finest Indian beer, and make it into a global brand.

Lord Bilimoria claims that they owed some of their subsequent success to luck, for example a chance contact with staff from Mysore Brewery, which supplies beer to the Indian army, in which his father had been a general. Lord Bilimoria discussed his idea for the new beer with the brewery's master brewer, who had, also by chance, a PhD in brewing from the Czech Republic, a country famous for its brewing technology: 'To him it was a challenge but I was very clear about the product, its taste and texture, and we worked with him to create it from scratch',[67] adding maize and rice to the usual lager mix.

By now Lord Bilimoria's family had decided he was 'nuts'! He was planning to enter one of the most competitive beer markets in the world. The main brand, Carlsberg was firmly entrenched, a new competitor, Kingfisher, had already entered eight years earlier, and numerous other beer brands were also trying to break into the market. The partners also knew nothing about the industry, and they had no money.[68] Their timing could not have been worse—it was the recession of the early 1990s. But Lord Bilimoria was determined to succeed and clearly had a passionate belief in the product.

However, early production was not straightforward; Lord Bilimoria, who had returned to the UK, kept on receiving telexes from India which told of insurmountable difficulties.[69] Customs and Excise were a constant problem, and there were also issues with the size of the bottle. While most beer in the UK was sold in 330 ml bottles, the standard size in India was 650ml, and this could not be changed. The beer was two weeks away from bottling when it was subjected to a 'haze test', which tests the beer's clarity. Unfortunately the result was marginal and one of the two UK distributors that had been signed up pulled out. This left 'half a container of beer with no one to get it to market'.[70]

Initially Cobra Beer was run out of Lord Bilimoria's flat—up three flights of stairs—and deliveries were made from his decrepit old Citroen 2CV which held exactly fifteen cases. The road could be seen through the floor of the car, and most days it required a push start. It was so tatty that the partners would park it out of sight of the restaurants to which they were delivering. Competitors' beer, meanwhile, was distributed in vans 'furnished with smart corporate livery'.[71]

Given that Cobra beer was £1 more expensive (typically 10 to 15 per cent more than competitors beers), and deliberately positioned up-market, this could have been a problem. But Lord Bilimoria and his partner had vision and determination—and a sales pitch. Forced to do the selling themselves, the partners went for the best restaurants first, on the basis that others ➜

➔ would follow their lead. Their pitch pointed out that the restaurants were missing a trick. If they could supply diners with a beer that did not make them feel so full, because it was less gassy and of better quality—i.e. Cobra—they could sell more food and drink. Within two years, Lord Bilimoria and Reddy were delivering over a thousand cases of Cobra a month to over a hundred restaurants with a large number of repeat orders from regular customers.

For ten years, Cobra Beer sales in Europe averaged annual growth of over 40 per cent. For the three years up to 2005, it increased to 48 per cent. By 2005, Cobra Beer's turnover was £80.3m. It sold over 44 million bottles in more than 40 countries, which were served in 90 per cent of the 6,000 licensed Indian restaurants in the UK, and was one of the fastest growing beer brands in Britain. It was also available in virtually all the major supermarkets and off-licence chains, as well as 6,000 mainstream bars, pubs, and clubs.[72]

Growth

By way of contrast, the world's leading brewer, Anheuser Busch (AB), producer of Budweiser and Michelob, produces nearly 150m barrels of beer per year, yielding net sales of $15bn and income before taxes of $2.6bn.[73] In the UK alone, sales of Budweiser total nearly £0.5bn (650,000 barrels), still well behind the leaders Carling (sales of £1.8bn/3.7m barrels) and Stella Artois (£1.8bn/2.7m barrels).

Cobra's history reveals much about Lord Bilimoria's business philosophy, such as a focus on innovation, never giving in, being disciplined, perfecting the product, and turning setbacks into opportunities; as well as 'being different, being better, and changing the marketplace forever'.[74] As he says, 'it's practically impossible to patent a beer. The only way you can win is by staying ahead, and you do this through constant innovation.'[75]

Cobra Beer has regularly won Grand Gold Medals at the prestigious Monde Selection Awards in Brussels (the brewing industry's 'Oscars'), and created history in 2004 by winning the medal for the fourth time in a row with its UK brewery partner Charles Wells. Its Polish brewery Browar Belgia went further, winning four gold medals in 2004—the first year it had brewed Cobra—an 'astonishing achievement'.[76] And in 2006, for the second year running, Cobra was awarded more gold medals than any other company in the world: it won twelve.

Cobra, the company, appeared on the 1999 Virgin Fast Track 100 list of the fastest growing, privately owned companies in the UK. On many of the indicators it has appeared repeatedly in the top 10 of the top 100 best small firms to work for in the UK, and its chief executive has been personally honoured in many ways. Lord Bilimoria has been awarded the title of entrepreneur of the year more than once, and London businessman of the year in

2004, beating retail billionaire Philip Green into second place. He was appointed a Commander of the British Empire by the Queen in 2004, and appointed to the House of Lords in the British legislature in May 2006, sitting on the 'cross benches' (i.e. not affiliated to any political party). In addition, he supports numerous charities and lists over 32 appointments and memberships on his CV, including Deputy Lieutenant of Greater London, membership of many government bodies, as well as founding UK president of the faith-based Zoroastrian Chamber of Commerce.[77]

Financing

The way that Cobra has been financed also says a lot about Lord Bilimoria's innovativeness and resourcefulness. Funding has come from a variety of unusual sources, including government-guaranteed loans, factoring, and invoice discounting as well as cash flow, and various types of shares.[78] An early example of innovative financing concerns one of their UK distributors, who wanted 60 days' credit, which was almost impossible given Cobra's cash flow. Lord Bilimoria used a financial instrument called a 'bill of exchange' on the distributor's unused overdraft facilities enabling Cobra to get what was effectively cash on delivery for a relatively low fee.

In 1995, Arjun Reddy left the company, and Lord Bilimoria had to find £250,000 to buy him out. Venture capitalists wanted 30 per cent, but as Lord Bilimoria did not want to cede ownership he managed to get a £190,000 small-firms loan from the government and £50,000 from an 'angel' for just 5 per cent of the business. Lord Bilimoria's stake stood at 72 per cent with the remainder held mainly by university friends and City contacts who invested through an enterprise investment scheme share issue in 1995.[79] Since then further external financing has been obtained to fund expansion, most recently £25m in the form of payment in kind (PIK) notes issued by Och-Ziff Capital Management, a US hedge fund. The deal means that Cobra will not pay any interest until the repayment date.[80] In addition, it has raised £2.5m through the placing of new ordinary shares to private and institutional investors.[81] This valued the group's equity at £80m, or about £100m including debt. Lord Bilimoria still retains 67 per cent of the equity.

Future funding is likely to come from a full floatation on the stock market in 2009.

Cobra in the twenty-first century

Although principally focused on Cobra beer, the company has engaged in some product diversification. In 1999, the company set up the General Lord Bilimoria wine brand, in honour of Karan's father. Like the beer, it was designed to accompany Indian food, and to replace the often mediocre house wines that were served ➔

→ in Indian restaurants. By 2006, it had nine vintages available. It is produced in France and Spain, and sells about 350,000 bottles a year.

In 2005–2006, Cobra launched an alcohol-free beer, and a low-calorie beer aimed at women aged between 25 and 35, promoted as an alternative to both full-calorie lagers and bland low-calorie brands. It also launched King Cobra, the world's first méthode champenoise, bottle-conditioned, strong (8 per cent) lager, which is sold in 750 ml champagne-style bottles.

It has also expanded geographically. Although Cobra exported beer to continental Europe soon after being founded in 1990, this was only in a small way. However in 1996, export sales began to take off. Even though there are fewer than a hundred Indian restaurants in the country, the Italians have apparently taken to Cobra. 'They find it exotic.'[82] However, Britain still accounts for over 90 per cent of Cobra's sales, with the largest export market to the Irish Republic, and after 9/11, Lord Bilimoria realized that the company was too reliant on the UK and needed to spread market risk. As a result Cobra opened subsidiaries in South Africa, India, and the United States. The company has also now expanded into Russia and eastern Europe. Its taste is a selling point, as consumer preferences there are for beers that are halfway between lager and British bitter.

Cobra is now available in 11 states in the USA, although they were unable to use the Cobra name there, and so call it 'Krait', a snake from the same family as the cobra. Krait Prestige is the equivalent of the King Cobra brand. Lord Bilimoria's cousin, Hoshang Chenoy, has responsibility for Cobra Beer in America. He has ambitions to achieve a 3 per cent share of the US beer market, and is already experiencing double-digit growth.[83] China is another country where Cobra plans to establish operations soon.

However, the main push now is into India, the world's second most populous country with over 1bn inhabitants, with a market estimated to be about 100m cases of beer a year and growing at around 7 per cent p.a. Cobra entered the Indian market in 2003, and according to Lord Bilimoria by 2010 half of the company's sales may come from there. It is not alone in this ambition, however. One of the world's largest brewers, the American/South African drinks company SABMiller, has committed $125m to expand and to protect its position in the Indian market. It currently has 31 per cent share, behind the leader United Breweries Ltd, which has approximately 48 per cent.

Consumer tastes are changing fast in India. Despite religious intolerance of alcohol consumption, it is becoming increasingly acceptable for Indians, especially women, to be seen drinking. And since the country began to deregulate and open its economy to foreign investment in 1992, an increasingly affluent middle class of about 300 million people has emerged. Much of their newly disposable income is being spent on food and drink.[84] Beer accounts for 19 per cent of alcohol consumption in India, compared with more than 50 per cent in the west, and 15 per cent of alcohol sales five years ago. However, beer consumption rates there are still very low (Table 12.5).

The Indian beer market, however, is heavily regulated as well as taxed. To side-step the government regulations which prevent alcohol from being advertised, Cobra plans to promote its non-alcoholic beer instead.[85] Distribution is equally heavily regulated. Hyderabad, in the south-eastern state of Andhra Pradesh, recently dropped prohibition, although it is still an issue in Gujarat, where only 28 stores in nine cities are permitted to sell alcoholic drinks. At this stage Lord Bilimoria's strategy is to build awareness of the company, so that when the market opens up Cobra will be ready and waiting. →

Table 12.5 International beer consumption

Beer—litres consumed per capita	2004	Per cent growth since 1999
Russia	60	100.0
China	22	37.5
India	1	0.0
UK	99	−3.9
USA	79	−4.8
Germany	117	−10.0
France	34	−12.8
Czech Republic	160	n/k

Source
Bawden (2005). 'Drinking to a growing market'. *The Times*, 6 December.

→ Currently, the import duty on beer in India is around 400 per cent, and hence brewing locally makes rather more sense than importing the beer from Poland or the UK. Recently Cobra licensed Mount Shivalik Group, the largest independent brewing company in India, to brew Cobra in their Behror brewery in Rajasthan. In 2006, Perses Bilimoria, the regional director of Cobra Beer in India, set up production agreements with three more Indian breweries, including one worth £5.5m on a green field site near Lord Bilimoria's home town of Hyderabad.

The return to Indian production is a recent development. Paradoxically, although Cobra is marketed as an Indian beer, for most of its life its production has been carried out in Europe. Although the beer was produced in Mysore's brewery in Bangalore for the first seven years of the company's life, quality and supply problems meant that production was later transferred to Charles Wells' brewery in Bedford, the UK's largest independent brewer.[86] Subsequently another brewery was added: the Belgian brewer Palm's Browar Belgia brewery, in Kielce, Poland. It began producing Cobra beer in 2003, to service continental Europe.

Cobra is also negotiating with two major wine producers in India to produce a wine for its General Lord Bilimoria range. This is the same format the company has used elsewhere—it sets up a relationship with particular wine-makers, who make wine to their specification, and bottle on location.

Branding and design

Cobra, although brewed in Britain for much of its history, has always been promoted as an Indian beer. From the outset the bottle featured an outline of India, and it used Indian script. Despite initially causing some worry because it was larger than normal beer bottles, by making a sales feature of its sharing potential, the Cobra bottle's size was turned to the company's advantage. Instead of ordering a bottle each, customers were encouraged to share the larger-sized bottle, as food was also typically shared in Indian restaurants. Customers ended up drinking more, the atmosphere was livelier as a result, and the restaurants were happy. Over half of the company's sales still come from the 660ml bottles.

In 2002, Lord Bilimoria decided that, since the bottle had not been redesigned for a few years, a change was needed. Lord Bilimoria has been a long-standing advocate of design, and was on the Design Effectiveness Awards judging panel in 2004. The new design tells the story of Cobra in embossed icons on the bottle—inspiration came from those Indian, Persian, and Roman columns that tell a story in sculpture. Palm trees next to a build-ing marked 'B' signify its journey from Bangalore to Bedford; a pair of scales reflects that the brand has succeeded 'against all odds'; and a boat laden with kegs illustrates its global avail-ability.[87] The result was the most embossed beer bottle ever developed, unlike anything else.[88] The bottle won several design awards. Point-of-sale items such as coasters explained the icons to consumers, and they could also look them up on the company's website.

The firm's website and other promotional material expand further on the Indian motif. The theme of its much-praised 2003 TV advertising campaign, a collaboration between UK advertising agency Team Saatchi and renowned Indian film director Shamin Desai, was 'Indian ingenuity', such as a car wash powered by elephants. Promotional activity, such as sponsorship of the hit musical *Bombay Dreams*, retains this link, although the firm also supports a number of charities with no connection to India or to the restaurant business, and Bilimoria sits on a large number of committees and boards, including the UK government's National Employment Panel.

The striking images and inventive humour in Cobra's advertising are helpful in compensating for the limitations in its marketing budget compared with its competitors. Although sales are growing, Cobra still does not figure in the UK's top ten beer brands and the awareness of its brand is far ahead of its actual size; the company has a mere 95 UK employees; 19 of whom are marketers.[89]

Future plans

Lord Bilimoria is nothing if not ambitious for his company—he has said he wants to increase sales to $1bn a year by 2010—a ten-fold compound growth rate. International sales will form most of that, and his aim is to 'cement Cobra as a truly global brand'.[90]

Case study questions

1. Analyse the source of Cobra's competitive advantage at the end of the case in 2006. How sustainable is it?

2. What are the major strategic issues facing Cobra Beer in 2006? Prioritize these.

3. Devise at least three strategic options for Cobra. Assess these using the RACES criteria.

4. What strategic methods should Lord Bilimoria use to achieve your chosen options?

● NOTES

1 Articles on the 'red queen problem' discuss some of these issues, for example Barnett and Hansen (1996); Barnett and Pontikes (2005); and Dao (2005).

2 Courtney et al. (1997).

3 For the details of how to carry out decision tree analysis, you are referred to any good textbook on quantitative methods in business.

4 Real options is an example of a concept that has been developed in another field—financial management—and transferred into strategy theory. The first use of the term appears to have been made by Myers (1977) but has been extensively developed since by Myers as well as by, for example, Lenos Trigeorgis and Rita Gunther McGrath and her colleagues. See also Borison (2005); Bowman and Hurry (1993).

5 Myers and Turnbull (1977); Trigeorgis (1993).

6 Smit and Trigeorgis (2006b).

7 See, for example, Bellman, E. (2007). 'Name game: as economy grows, India goes for designer goods'. *Wall Street Journal*, 27 March: A1.

8 Teather, D. (2005). 'Profile of a giant'. *Guardian*, 27 October: 28.

9 Ibid. and *Times of India* (2006). 'Retail mania: LVMH to set up boutique chain in India'. Indian Business Insight, 4 December.

10 Petkovic, J. (2006). 'Can corporations tame unruly Internet frontier?' *Grand Rapids Press*, 29 October: D4; Brandle, L. and Sutherland, S. (2007). 'Cash from clicks'. *Billboard*, 3 February; Creamer, M. (2006). 'How to win Web 2.0; want to survive? Find a way to monetize video'. *Advertising Age*: 13 November: 3.

11 To be strictly fair, the first 'proper' PC with a graphical user interface, was the Xerox Alto, in 1973. However, this was never properly released as it was believed to be far too expensive for individuals to buy one. In the meantime Apple entered the market.

12 *Display and Design Ideas* (2005). 'Retailer of the Year: Apple Computer Inc.'. 1 September.

13 Markoff (2007).

14 Hoffman, A. (2007). 'Dose of iExistence delights buyers'. *The Star-Ledger*, 1 July: 3.

15 Ashworth, J. (1997). 'SAirGroup pays £65m for BA's in-flight catering'. *The Times*, 9 October: 30.

16 The term 'reserving the right to play' comes from Courtney et al. (1997).

17 See Haan (2003) and Wee, E. (2004). 'High-tech dreams vanish into vapourware'. *Straits Times*, 15 February. See also Bayus et al. (2001) for a games theory analysis of such pre-announcements.

18 Smit and Trigeorgis (2006a); *Audio Week* (1995). 'Toshiba DVD pushes high density CD "a stage too far"—Philips'. 6 March; *Electronics Weekly* (1995). 'A vision of the future for CDs—Philips, Sony'. 22 March: 16; *Consumer Electronics* (1995). 'DVD camps promoting computer industry support'. 22 May; Schofield, J. (1995). 'Battle of the super discs'. *Guardian*, 8 June.

19 *Electronics Weekly* (1995) op. cit.

20 Consumer Multimedia Report (1995). 'DVD compromise pact wins unanimous praise'.

21 Bloomberg Business News (1994). 'Microsoft merger may tap future'. *Austin American-Statesman*, 15 October: C2; Wright, C. (1994). 'Gates opens Quicken'. *The Age*, 18 October; 18; *The Times* (1995). 'Microsoft quits merger'. 22 May.

22 Associated Press Newswires (1998). 'Cut-price carrier takes legal action agains BA'. 26 February; Harper, K. (1998). 'EasyJet issues writ against BA'. *Guardian*, 27 February: 21; *Financial Times* (1998). 'EasyJet get go-ahead to continue BA court case'. 14 May:12; *Accountancy* (2000). 'Interview—Stelios Haji-Ionannou chairman easyEverything'. 1 April: 39; Addley, A. (2002). 'The easy life'. *Guardian*, 5 August: 6.

23 *Economist* (2006b); Grover, R. and Capell, K. (2007). 'The battle of Britain'. *BusinessWeek*, 23 April: 40; Hodgson, J. (2007). 'BskyB's move on ITV to get stepped-up scrutiny'. *Dow Jones International News*, 26 February.

24 See, for example, Gumbel (2005).

25 The point that mergers and acquisitions, in particular, are not strategies in their own right is well appreciated by practitioners—see Carey (2000), and Palter and Srinivasan (2006). Different reasons for mergers are discussed in Bower (2001), Carey (2000), and, for deals in high-technology industries, Frick and Torres (2002).

26 This policy was also described by Hamel and Prahalad (1994), who identified it in the Japanese firms that formed their sample.

27 See Cohen and Levinthal (1990).

28 Vermeulen and Barkema (2001); Vermeulen (2005).

29 Lynn, B. (2006). 'Breaking the chain'. *Harper's Magazine*, 1 July: 29; AFX International Focus (2005). 'European regulators clear P&G's acquisition of Gillette'. 15 July; Teather, D. (2005). 'Profile of a giant'. *Guardian*, 27 October: 28.

30 Oestricher, D. (2000). 'AOL, Time Warner merger shows future of entertainment'. *Dow Jones News Service*, 10 January; Waters, R. (2000). 'A new media world'. 11 January: 22; Murphy, P. and Cassy, J. (2000). '$350bn media merger heralds net revolution'. *Guardian*, 11 January: 1.

31 Teather, D. (2003). 'Turner quits AOL after $99bn loss'. *Guardian*, 30 January: 2; Larsen, P. (2003). 'AOL's $98bn loss is largest in US history'. *Financial Times*, 30 January: 1; Kapadia, R. (2003). 'AOL Time Warner posts 2002 loss of nearly $100bln'. *Reuters News*, 30 January.

32 Ibid. and Mehta, S. (2003). 'Signs of intelligent life at AOL'. *Fortune*, 15 September: 89; *Financial Times*, 11 December: 23. Waters, R. (2003). 'Surfing alone'. *Financial Times*, 27 April: 10; Loomis, C. (2002). 'AOL Time Warner's new math'. *Fortune*, 4 February: 98.

33 Burt, T., Parsons, D., and Larsen, P. (2003). 'It has been four years since the troubled merger with AOL'.

34 Source: Sanchez-Peinado (2003) and <http://www.santander.com/csgs/Satellite?accesibilidad=3&canal=CAccionistas&cid=1146205899430&empr=SANCorporativo&leng=en_GB&pagename=SANCorporativo/Page/SC_ContenedorGeneral>, accessed 29 March 2007.

35 Kollewe, J. (2004). 'Santander names its finance director as new Abbey chief'. *Independent*, 22 October: 42; Waples, J. (2004). 'Banco Abbey'. *Sunday Times*, 19 September: Business 5.

36 See Morrow et al. (2007); Ernst and Halevy (2004); and Dyer et al. (2004).

37 See DiGeorgio (2002) for a case of Cisco's approach to M&A in the late 1990s.

38 See Colvin and Charan (2006) and Kirkland et al. (2007)—other articles in the same issue of *Fortune International* are also instructive regarding the private equity industry—and Sagner (2007).

39 These figures are data gathered by Nottingham University's Centre for Management Buyout Research (CMBOR) in collaboration with Barclays Private Equity and Deloitte. <http://www.nottingham.ac.uk/business/cmbor/cmbor20.pdf>, accessed 7 July 2007.

40 Ibid.

41 Study carried out by CMBOR quoted in Sarah Perrin, 'The buy-out is back', *Management Today*, May 1998, pp. 78–82.

42 Leung (2002).

43 See *Business Wire* (2006); also Foust et al. (2006).

44 Based on Fulford and Huang (2004); George (2005); and *Automotive News* (2006).

45 Brown (2004).

46 Fulford and Huang (2004).

47 The role of boundary spanners has been discussed extensively in relation to sales staff and inter-group communication and motivation by, for example, Richter et al. (2006); Tushman and Scanlan (1981), and more recently in respect of knowledge and alliance management by, for example, Gander et al. (2007) and Kellogg et al. (2006).

48 Black-Scholes is the classic method for evaluating options but there are alternatives. For details of the Black-Scholes method see Brealey and Myers (2005) or any other good finance textbook. For more on the valuation of real options, see Cuypers and Martin (2006).

49 Trigeorgis (1993); van Putten and MacMillan (2004).

50 *Economist* (2005) and Reinhardt (2005).

51 Brown-Humes and Budden (2004) and Reinhardt (2004).

52 Brown-Humes (2004).

53 Brown-Humes and Budden (2004).

54 Ibid.

55 Ibid.

56 Baker et al. (2001); and Brown-Humes (2002).

57 Brown-Humes and Budden (2004).

58 *Economist* (2005).

59 Reinhardt and Ihlwan (2005).

60 *Economist* (2005).

61 Ibid.

62 Reinhardt and Ihlwan (2005).

63 Ibid.

64 Ibid.

65 *Economist* (2006a).

66 Rigby (2001).

67 *Express on Sunday* (2004).

68 Rigby (2001).

69 Coomber (2006).

70 Ibid.

71 Ibid.

72 *Hindustan Times* (2005).

73 Source: Anheuser-Busch 2005 Annual Report. Although the company has other interests, in packaging and theme parks as well as other alcoholic beverages, beer represents the overwhelming majority of its sales and profits.

74 Coomber (2006).

75 *Daily Telegraph* (2005). Also Rigby (2001).

76 Press Trust of India Limited (2004).

77 Womack (2004).

78 Rigby (2001).

79 Walsh (2006).

80 Williamson (2006).

81 Blackwell (2006).

82 Ibid.

83 Faherty (2006).

84 Bawden (2005).

85 Ibid.

86 Rigby (2001).

87 Jardine (2003a).

88 Jardine (2003b).

89 *Marketing* (2006).

90 Womack (2004).

CHAPTER THIRTEEN
Strategies in Profit-making Contexts

LEARNING OUTCOMES

After reading this chapter you should be able to:

➜ Explain the industry life-cycle and discuss its impact on industry survival and success factors

➜ Describe the strategic options that theorists have identified as most appropriate at each stage of the life-cycle, and discuss the implications of using options not recommended by this theory

➜ Identify situations that do not fit the classic industry life-cycle, including industries where returns to scale increase rather than decrease

➜ Assess an organization's existing competitive stance, value chain, architecture, and innovation strategy, and its strategic proposals, to determine the degree of fit with industry survival and success factors

➜ Apply the theory to identify the types of strategy that are most likely to be appropriate for an organization

➜ Discuss the limitations of the life-cycle model and of the conventional wisdom that it represents.

INTRODUCTION

Effectiveness is one of the five RACES factors by which a strategic option should be judged. The effectiveness of an option, however, depends upon the context in which it is to be implemented. Options that might make perfect sense if you are selling oil may not be valid if your business produces wind turbines or biofuels, even though these are just different sources of energy. The oil industry is well established, with many large, rich, and experienced competitors, which however in 2006 were under growing threat from the nationalized oil companies of Russia and the countries of the Middle East. The biofuels industry is growing, on the back of popular concerns about issues such as global warming, which have led to some governments subsidizing its development. Some oil companies such as BP are active in this industry, but firms with no track record in energy, such as the Virgin Group, have also entered. The wind power industry features some of these same players, alongside giant conglomerates such as GE and new start-ups.

The economics and technology of oil extraction are well understood by producers, consumers, and investors. The technology for converting maize or sugar into fuel is also well understood, thanks to experience in countries like Brazil, but needs to be scaled up if it is to meet anything more than a small fraction of oil demand. New technologies for making fuel from other raw materials, such as plant waste, are still under development. Wind power technology is developing fast, but making the economic case to investors remains difficult. And no one knows if popular pressure for alternatives to oil will last if oil prices decline.

In short, each of these industries operates in a different context: each shows differing degrees of maturity and of turbulence and uncertainty. In this chapter, we build on some of the theory that we introduced in Chapter 3 to discuss the strategies that have been found to be appropriate in specific industry contexts.

13.1 The impact of the industry life-cycle[1]

In Figure 13.1 we give examples of industries at the different stages of their life-cycle, remembering that the life-cycle is a generalized model of how a typical industry develops over an indeterminate period of time. The stages can vary substantially in length:

→ We looked at different types of environmental conditions and the industry life-cycle in Chapter 3.

- The digital music download industry passed from introductory to growth stage in just a couple of years.

- The first patent for an RFID tag was granted in 1973, but the industry's growth phase started in 2002.

- The first working fuel cells appeared in 1843, but the industry is still in its introductory phase, with a few, low-volume, applications such as portable electricity supplies. The industry is confidently expected to enter the growth phase once the product's unit cost and weight have fallen enough to make it viable as a low-emissions power source for something widely used, such as cars or laptop PCs.

An industry's developmental stage may also vary significantly in different parts of the world. In much of Europe and Asia, mobile telephony is a mature industry, with a saturated market —most people who want a mobile phone already have one. In Africa and the less-developed countries in Asia, there is still a great deal of untapped demand. The market grows as economic development allows more and more people to afford phones, and as users work out ways to make them affordable, for example by sharing them between people in the same village. The fact that the infrastructure for the main substitute, fixed-line telephony, is sparse in these countries encourages the development of mobile phones.

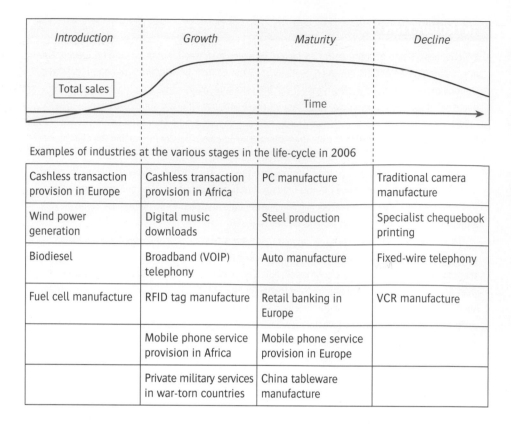

Figure 13.1 The industry life-cycle.

Expansion is also promoted by people's ingenuity in finding new uses for mobiles—for example, as a way of making cashless payments in countries with a low level of banking infrastructure. The cashless payment industry in Africa is further down its life-cycle than in Europe, where banking networks make it easier for people to get cash when they need it and to keep it safe.

Industries can also mature in very different ways. Some move from growth into slow, steady decline in demand. But some products, such as cars, clothing, or travel, become so much part of daily life that underlying demand for them does not really decline: there is always a requirement to replace the products that have worn out. The crucial determinant of demand is therefore the state of the economy: when times are good, people will spend freely, when they are bad, they will wait an extra year before replacing their coat or their car, or taking an expensive holiday. Demand in such industries will therefore be cyclical, and it is important to be careful not to confuse a cyclical downswing or upswing with a move out of maturity to decline or to renewed growth.

Already at the growth phase, larger firms have better survival prospects, since their greater resource base helps them survive the frequent technological and other changes that occur at this point. In many industries—chemicals, cars—the logical response to the price pressures that come with maturity is for firms to become still larger, so that they can use economies of scale to sustain their profitability. However, mature industries may follow a number of patterns (see Section 13.4), in many of which smaller firms compete as niche players alongside the dominant ones.[2]

Whatever the pattern that the industry follows through the life-cycle, moves from one phase to another are likely to have profound effects on the strength of the forces that determine industry structure (Table 13.1). This in turn influences survival and success factors for

Table 13.1 Industry structure through the life-cycle

	Introduction	Growth	Maturity	Decline
Threat of substitution	Low—the industry's products will typically be substituting for others	Low	May increase	High
Threat of entry	Moderate—few barriers to those with appropriate knowledge, but this, and funding, may be rare	High as industry is legitimized with investors and attractiveness becomes clear	Low in most industries as tends to become oligopoly with scale, reputation, and threat of competitive retaliation as barriers to new entrants Remains high in fragmented industries	Low: poor growth prospects and threat of retaliation by incumbents will deter entrants
Supplier power	May be high if established firms control key inputs	Lessening as firms in industry grow and input technologies become more widespread	Varies according to the extent to which supplier industries consolidate	
Buyer power	Low	Low—demand outstrips supply and buyers lack knowledge to use in negotiations	High—buyers more knowledgeable and fewer differences between products	High except for those for whom substitutes are unacceptable
Power of complementors	May be very high—complementors can make or break product or firm	Low—have vested interest in helping industry grow	Typically low—industry can integrate into complementors' industry	May become high as determinant of residual demand for product
Nature of competition	Unlikely to be fierce. Common interest in legitimizing and growing industry	Benign. There are enough customers to go around	Fierce—often price-driven	Can be cut-throat if over-capacity persists. Otherwise benign

the industry, and the strategies likely to be followed by firms in it. In the following sections, we discuss the typical environment at each stage of the life-cycle and the strategic challenges that result. We examine the main options for competitive stance, value chain, and architecture in order to meet such challenges. We do this also for industries that offer increasing returns to scale, which do not follow the usual life-cycle pattern.

Using Evidence 13.1 How can you tell where an industry is in its life-cycle?

The ideal situation for life-cycle analysis is where you have access to annual sales figures for an industry and can use them to plot a curve like the one in Figure 13.1. For physical and software products, these figures should ideally be for numbers of units shipped. Sales figures by value can be used instead, but they can give a slightly misleading picture, because the unit price of a product often falls quite sharply as the volume of production increases over the life-cycle.

Hopefully, the sales curve will look sufficiently similar to the classic S-curve in Figure 13.1 for it to be clear whether the industry is growing, mature, or declining. However, it is not always so straightforward. If an industry's sales fall unexpectedly, this may be due to the onset of industry decline, which can come very suddenly (see What Can Go Wrong 13.1). But the drop may have an external cause, such as a dip in the economic cycle, or a one-off event—a terrorist attack that makes people too frightened to ➡

→ spend on an item, or a fire that curtails supplies of a key input—from which the industry may well recover in a year or two. Sudden surges in demand may similarly be the signal that the industry has entered, or re-entered, the growth phase—or they may be due to cyclical or temporary phenomena.

This means that it is important to look at recent changes in PESTLE factors, to see if any of them have changed in a way that will irreversibly alter people's attitudes to the industry and its products. Recent legislation in Europe and the USA, for example, seems to signal the decline of the tobacco industry in those regions, as people appear to be observing smoking bans, rather than subverting or ignoring them. It is also important to look at the behaviour of important customers and end-users, such as governments and major corporations. The adoption of RFID tags by Wal-Mart, the world's largest retailer, was a signal that that industry has been legitimized, and was likely to be entering its growth phase.

In the absence of figures on sales, it is legitimate to look at numbers of firms in the industry, and the numbers that are entering and leaving it. Academic researchers actually use these measures to differentiate between a growing industry, where there are large numbers of firms and the rate of entry and exit are high, and the mature phase, where all three statistics are typically lower.

What you should avoid, however, is the assumption that, because the industry shows one of the characteristics that we outline in Figure 3.3, it is automatically in that phase of the life-cycle. For example, many mature industries have high-quality products and high profits, but the fact that quality and profits are high does not necessarily mean that the industry is mature. Some industries develop high product quality and profitability during the growth, or even the introductory, phase.

13.2 Strategies for the introductory phase of an industry

a. The strategic environment at the introductory stage

→ We look at the ways in which mature companies create the conditions for innovation in Section 10.4.2.

The introductory phase begins with the creation and sale of a single new product. The firm responsible for this, and its immediate future competitors, will quite often be small, offering only a single product or service. Where a large company is involved, it may well be through an independent new venture division, with many of the characteristics of a small firm, or through collaborations with smaller companies.

Dominant design
A configuration for a product or service that becomes accepted and expected by producers and customers. It may embrace the appearance, functionality, basic features, and sometimes also the production technology.

At this stage products and their technologies are undeveloped, with no clear dominant design[3]—different products or services may be configured in very different ways. The customers who buy them are termed innovators or early adopters, and are prepared to put up with unreliable technology and service for the sake of being at the forefront of new things, or because they have an especially strong need for what the industry offers. The early users of mobile phones tolerated heavy handsets and poor and unreliable reception—not to mention the disapproval of the people who were unused to hearing those kinds of conversations in public. They did so because they had the money (or wanted to appear as if they had) and felt a strong need to be contactable when on the move. The early buyers of renewable energy either have no easy access to other power sources, or are prepared to pay extra in the hope of alleviating global warming.

→ We examine different bases for differentiation in Section 4.2.4.

This conventional wisdom about the poor reliability of early products is less applicable to software offerings, such as internet telephony (e.g. Skype and Vonage) and social networking (MySpace). In these cases, even early versions of the product work quite well, although they lack some of the features that appear in later versions. Differentiation in these industries is still the norm, based upon ease of installation and use and, sometimes, on compatibility and interoperability with hardware and other software.

b. Strategic challenges at the introductory stage

The main strategic challenges faced by the innovator firm and its competitors during the introductory phase of an industry are:

- to build legitimacy, not just for themselves, but also for the industry as a whole. Once the industry becomes 'respectable', people will be readier to invest in it and to consider buying its products;

- to develop the product or service, and the associated supply and distribution chain, to the point where they are robust enough to serve a mass market. The industry will then be ready to move into its growth phase;

- to avoid cash flow problems as start-up costs mount while customers remain few. The firm will need to reinvest any income in building market positions and in developing the product. This means that, although prices charged for the new product are high, profits are likely to be low and cash flow negative. Cash burn—the number of weeks or months for which the firm can continue to trade before its cash reserves are exhausted—is a key performance measure.

In new industries there are no set rules of the game, which can make it difficult for stakeholders to agree upon what strategies and objectives are realistic. In particular, there is no shared idea of the industry's 'clockspeed'—the pace of external change. This can make it difficult for people to develop the shared rhythm that enables them to work effectively together.[4] In addition, because there is no settled technological standard or customer base, the firms may experience many of the challenges typical of turbulent industries (Section 13.6).

c. Strategic options at the introductory stage

Because companies in industries at this stage are typically small, the degree of diversity they can handle is limited. Firms that are seeking to build a mass market may focus on their home market, where they can rely upon the goodwill of local customers and are in a position to respond quickly to problems with the product or its service. Nokia, in the early days of the mobile telephone industry, built a secure base in Scandinavia before it expanded into the rest of Europe. This is a traditional route for many manufacturers, and may be adopted even by large firms in a new industry (see Real-Life Application 13.1).

However, the internet has made it possible for firms selling some products like software or fine foods, which do not require a service network, to bypass this local phase before they internationalize. The availability of reliable commercial distributors and delivery services, and of sales platforms such as eBay, has made an integrated distribution network unnecessary. Such sales and distribution channels may help firms build to a viable scale more quickly than if they were restricted to their home country. The internet, similarly, can help them find, and manage, a network of suppliers and collaborators that spans the globe.[5]

It is natural at this stage to differentiate on functionality and, to a lesser extent, reliability. Early adopters are rarely price-sensitive, and are more interested in advanced features and the availability of after-sales service. Product and production technology are unstable, so that, even if funds are available, it is quite risky to build lots of capacity and sophisticated systems in an attempt to obtain economies of scale and experience. Investments of this kind could be wasted if the next generation of new technology is radically different.

For a small company at this stage, it will be natural to restrict the scope of operations to a few products and to outsource many value chain activities. It may, for example, outsource manufacturing to other firms, use agents and distributors for sales and service, and work out of serviced office accommodation. Amazon.com, in its early days in the book trade, relied upon a nearby book wholesaler to manage its inventory.

However, if the product and the associated technology are very new, then a firm may find itself forced to integrate vertically, simply because it cannot find suppliers, distributors, or service agents with the necessary expertise. In the 1960s, an early UK entrant into the super-conducting magnets industry, Oxford Instruments, found that it could not obtain sufficient supplies of liquid helium. Although it had little expertise in gas production, it had to form its own subsidiary to supply this vital ingredient, needed to maintain the magnets at the near-absolute-zero temperatures at which they operate.

Elsewhere in the value chain, strategic priorities are likely to be:

- R&D: developing genuine capabilities in product innovation, to keep offerings at the leading edge of development. At this stage of the life-cycle firms often aim for break-throughs that will set their product or service apart from competitors.

- Production: building capabilities that increase product reliability, and improve the firm's ability to handle increasing scale of production.

- Marketing: although a firm will want to build its own brand and reputation, it will often be as concerned with building the reputation of the industry. A firm may help to found an industry association to establish guidelines for product safety and design (see Real-Life Application 13.1) or for good practice. It may also practise some odd-seeming competitive behaviours, such as publicly praising competitors that have behaved in a 'responsible' fashion. When the financial derivatives industry found itself with a poor public profile, after several firms had taken heavy losses on futures and options in the early 1990s, one major player, J. P. Morgan, acted to try to reassure customers. It made its proprietary risk management methodology, developed at great expense, freely available on the internet, so that customers and regulators could see that, with the right tools, financial derivatives were a respectable part of an investment portfolio.[6]

 We discuss communal cultures in Section 8.4.1 and simple structures in Section 8.2.2.

The culture and architecture of the firm will also be developed at this time. Internally, a communal culture and informal structure are typical at this stage in a firm's development, as people work long hours together to solve challenging problems. It is important for the organization to develop its own time-pacing—a self-imposed rhythm, such as the introduction of a new generation of products every nine months—to enable people to coor-dinate their actions effectively. Firms that do this typically outperform those that do not.[7]

Externally, management time needs to be invested in educating, and building relationships with, banks and venture capitalists or other sources of financial capital. Once these people have understood the nature of the industry, they can be of great assistance in helping the firm and the industry to develop to maturity. The expertise and network of contacts of venture capital firms such as Sequoia Capital and Kleiner Perkins Caufield & Byers makes them valuable and sought-after partners for technology start-ups.[8]

Real-life Application 13.1 Sony FeliCa and the contactless payment industry

It may seem strange to talk of an industry as being in the introductory stage when one of the two main players boasted in October 2005 of shipping its 100 millionth unit, and where there were estimated to be 10 million active users in Japan alone at the end of 2005.[9]

However, the contactless payment industry is unusual. Its products seek to replace something that has been in use, in the form of coins and, later, banknotes, for 27 centuries—cash. It

takes the form of a card that can be 'topped up' with credit, that can then be spent by waving the card close to a reader. The card contains a specialized microchip that comprises a tiny, low-power radio transmitter and also stores a few pieces of information about the user. When placed close to a reader, it is switched on so that it can transmit information about how much credit is left, and can be debited for the cost of a new transaction.   →

→ The potential advantages are plain: users' pockets are not weighed down with heavy or bulky currency, and there is no more need for agonising searches for the right money or waits to be given change. The first trials of 'electronic wallets' were run in the early 1990s, by Mondex, a consortium involving BT and several banks, and later by Visa, the credit card issuer. But people in the 20 countries covered by these trials preferred good old-fashioned currency.[10]

The early adopters for contactless payment were therefore transport authorities, which had an urgent need to speed the flow of travellers on and off trains and buses. In order to persuade people to use electronic cards in place of cash and paper tickets, schemes such as Octopus in Hong Kong and Oyster in London used a variety of methods: advertising stressing the convenience, combined with discounted fares and other incentives. Over 200 cities now have such schemes, and boast millions of users. However, this represents just a small fraction of the number of cities, and of potential users, worldwide.

Moreover, the potential for exploiting these systems for a greater range of transactions has hardly been tapped. At one extreme, Octopus is so widely employed for purchases other than bus and train tickets that it has been claimed that Hong Kong is on its way to becoming a cashless society. MasterCard has introduced its PayPass contactless credit cards in the USA and many Asian countries. In the USA, some fast-food chains and filling stations accept contactless payment. However, a project to allow London's Oyster card to be used in the same way was axed in May 2006; it proved impossible to make a good financial case for putting its technology into shops that had already invested heavily in other payment systems.[11]

One way of expanding use has been to build the specialized chip into devices that people are used to carrying with them, such as watches or, in particular, mobile phone handsets. These then can be waved in front of readers and used to pay for rail travel, a coffee, or a parking space—or to unlock a door. Japan is famously open to new technology, and early deployment of 3G mobile technology (see What Can Go Wrong 4.1) has made people open to innovative uses for their mobile phone. But only 31,000 stores there accept Edy, the most widespread of the cashless payment systems, although some 3 million people have registered to use it. Even in Hong Kong, Octopus accounts for no more than 1 per cent of retail transactions.[12]

The relative success of Octopus came about because the various Hong Kong transport authorities agreed a common standard and worked hard to get Octopus cards to 50 per cent of the population within three months of launch. This meant that retailers could see a clear benefit from putting in card readers that all those people could use. Elsewhere, there is less uniformity, not only because the chips from the two main producers, Sony and Philips, employ different wireless technologies and software. The East Japan Railway Co. and Edy both have systems based on Sony's FeliCa chip, but cannot read one another's cards, so that retailers that want to accept both have needed to double up on the technology they install.[13]

To judge from their recent actions, Sony and Philips have come to appreciate that greater compatibility would assist the development of their business. They have agreed a joint standard, NFC (short for near field communication), intended to integrate Sony's FeliCa and Philips Mifare technology. In 2004, they, along with Nokia, the market leader in mobile phones, formed the →

The early adopters of contactless payment were transport providers, including Oyster in London. *Oyster*

➜ NFC Forum to promote its use. The other major mobile phone producers have since joined, along with the main credit card issuers. Meanwhile, independent firms have begun to offer readers that will support all the different cards available in Japan.[14]

Partnerships are clearly seen by Sony as important to building up FeliCa, whose strategic importance is becoming plain—it appeared as a separate business unit on the main organization chart for the first time in November 2006. Its partnership with DoCoMo, Japan's leading mobile phone operator, has proved vital in expanding usage of the chips and has been formalized in a jointly owned subsidiary, FeliCa Networks. Both firms are also members of the consortium that owns Edy.

The company has taken other steps to prepare the ground for its wider adoption in its crucial home market (in 2005, Japan accounted for half of the FeliCa cards in circulation[15]). In 2004, it made low-cost card-reader technology available that would be affordable for small firms, including the family-owned retailers that are extremely common in Japan. DoCoMo, for its part, is providing loans to help these key stakeholders purchase the equipment.[16]

13.3 Strategies for the growth phase of an industry

a. The strategic environment in growth-stage industries

By the time the growth phase starts, the product or service is becoming established in the minds of buyers and users. The early competitors are beginning to learn how to make improvements to the product and to production and sales processes, so that quality is generally higher than at the introductory stage. Consumers are becoming increasingly sophisticated and able to make choices about the levels of service or product differentiation that they require. Numbers of new entrants, who see money to be made in copying or improving the original product, are likely to increase.

The growth phase resembles the introductory phase in some important regards. The R&D and marketing strategies used in the earlier phase may still be valid. Technology may not yet have stabilized, so that it will still be risky to invest in physical assets with the sole aim of acquiring cost advantage. Some firms may find that they have achieved cost advantages through routines that they have developed incrementally over time. However, the enhancement of these advantages is likely to take second place to the challenge of meeting demand.

The increasing level of demand for products at this stage means that some firms can survive for a considerable period even though they are inherently weak and unlikely to endure more competitive conditions. In order to survive, they may need to do no more than provide a usable product, and basic levels of service.

b. Strategic challenges at the growth stage

When demand is increasing at this pace, the main challenge for firms lies in keeping up with it, and in establishing a viable position in the market-place (Real-life Application 13.2). This implies keeping abreast of technological developments and ensuring that products are compatible with any emerging standards. New uses may be appearing for the product or service, and so firms may also need to attend to new customer groups and new geographic markets, or take the risk of conceding those markets to competitors or new entrants.

At the same time, firms need to give attention to achieving a viable size. Larger organizations benefit from better developed processes and from better access to funding and highly qualified employees, partly because they enjoy more legitimacy with external stakeholders. A number of studies have found that by the end of the growth stage, these advantages offset any disadvantages derived from the greater flexibility of small firms, a situation that persists into the maturity phase.[17]

Production capacity has to be increased rapidly, which in turn means that suitable personnel must be recruited, or new suppliers or collaborators located. Attention must also be given to the location of suppliers, or of new production facilities, to make sure that the logistics of supplying them and getting their output to the distributor or customer are workable. Quality and service levels are at risk if selection, planning, or training is rushed or inadequate. If key staff are redeployed to look after these issues, however, there is a danger that they will be distracted from their operational roles, so that product quality or customer service will suffer in any case. Managing this trade-off between speed of expansion and quality is a key challenge at this stage in the life-cycle.

c. Strategic options at the growth stage

Some firms may choose deliberately to differentiate themselves by offering products with a restricted range of features and low levels of support, at a low price. They may even be instrumental in driving growth in the industry, by introducing its offerings in an affordable form to new customers. Ryanair has followed this strategy in the airline industry, and Dell in PCs. Such firms may continue with this competitive stance as the industry matures, if they possess the relevant strategic resources.

It is more usual, however, for firms to take advantage of abundant demand by keeping prices high, and justifying them through differentiation. This may be on the basis of reliability. During the growth phase of the PC industry in the UK, firms would advertise the number of hours that their products had been tested at the factory. This was intended to show that they were not prone to the frequent hardware crashes that had bedevilled earlier computers. Other areas of differentiation might be better levels of customer service, superior reach (see Real-life Application 13.2), additional features (such as ease of use or storage capacity for a music player), or distinctive designs. If a firm can demonstrate that it is consistently at the cutting edge of innovation, and associate its name with product standards in the industry, this can also be valuable in building reputation.

There are no set patterns for culture and architecture for firms at this stage of the life-cycle. Some firms find it advantageous to formalize their structures and systems to cope with the management problems of increasing size, and to move towards a mercenary culture as a way of driving growth within the firm. Other competitors may find it preferable and effective to stay with the informal structures developed earlier, since the formalization of systems will take management attention away from the main priority, meeting demand.

Acquisitions feature as a way of buying in innovative knowledge that organizations have not had the time or competence to develop themselves, in the form of personnel from smaller, more creative, firms. They are also a way of increasing scale, and acquiring additional distribution channels. Smaller or weaker firms, therefore, can contemplate withdrawal through sale to one of their stronger competitors, the negotiation of a suitable price being a major consideration.

This strategy should not always be considered an admission of failure—it may rather be a recognition that not all owners of small firms can, or should want to, develop their companies into major concerns. They may be better employed as 'serial entrepreneurs' who create something new and, having developed it to a certain stage, move on to develop something else. For example, Raymond Kurzweil, an American entrepreneur who is also a renowned author and futurologist, has founded many companies. His first, in the 1960s, developed software that helped aspiring university students choose a suitable college. The second, in the 1970s, developed reading machines based on path-breaking optical character recognition software. The third, in the 1980s, produced electronic keyboards that could emulate grand pianos. All of these were sold on after periods of between two and twelve years. His most recent firms deal in a variety of new applications of computing technology such as artificial intelligence and virtual reality.[18]

Real-life Application 13.2 Friendster, MySpace, and the social networking industry

Social networking websites—where people can post pictures and information about themselves and exchange messages with their nominated circle of friends—were first launched in the late 1990s. However, the first truly popular site, Friendster, emerged in 2003. Developed by Jonathan Abrams as a way of locating eligible girls in his friends' address books, it attracted 3 million users in its first six months—with no advertising.[19]

Friendster's subsequent decline indicates some of the pitfalls of working in a growing industry. Abrams turned down a $30m offer from Google to develop the firm himself, with the help of money from some of California's best regarded venture capitalists and business angels.[20] They not only joined Friendster's board but also recruited experienced managers and programmers to help drive the company's growth. By some accounts, this saddled the firm with a taller hierarchy than was needed at the time, and led it to focus on expansion abroad and the addition of new features.[21] However, there was a more urgent need to scale up the company's IT infrastructure to cope with the ever-increasing number of users. Access to Friendster's web page became, on the company's own admission, very slow, and new features could not be added to the site without making this problem worse.[22]

Users began to shift their allegiance to new competitors that were differentiating on the basis of features such as blogs and tools to let users make their profiles stand out. Although Friendster retained many registered users, it had only about 1 million visitors in the USA in September 2006, and they stayed for an average of only 7 minutes, compared to over 3 hours when the site's popularity was at its peak.[23]

The dominant competitor in social networking became MySpace, which claimed 100 million registered users and had 56 million unique visitors in the US alone in September 2006. This represented a 150 per cent increase on the previous year; its main competitor, FaceBook, grew US visitor numbers by 50 per cent in the same period, so industry growth remained buoyant.

Competitors have tended to focus on particular user groups. FaceBook limited membership to university and college students before opening up to all internet users in September 2006. Bebo is strong in the UK, while outside the English-speaking countries there are individual sites with a national following, such as Studivz in Germany, Skyblogs in France, and Orkut (owned by Google) in Brazil. Firms have also attempted to differentiate their offerings. MySpace's growth was fuelled by the way it allows people with common musical interests to build networks. It has also become a place where musicians, whether new or established, can nurture a fan base.[24]

This is important because there are few barriers to entry into the industry and many substitutes, including video and picture-sharing sites such as YouTube and Flickr. Users, particularly the younger ones, can easily get bored with a site and move on to another, or be put off a site if they receive unwelcome →

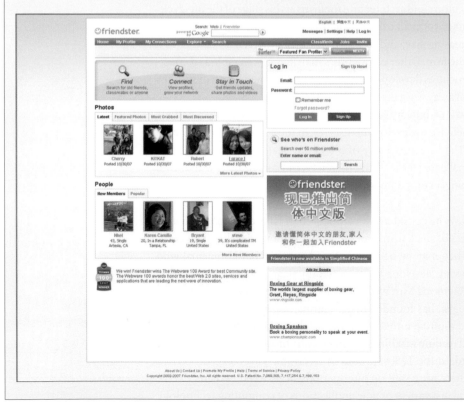

Friendster was the first truly popular social networking site. *Friendster*

→ messages from strangers.[25] All sites are free to the user, so switching costs are negligible. MySpace faced stiff competition in some markets from Bebo, Facebook, and Piczo.[26]

MySpace, meanwhile, is building a broader, global presence that is less dependent upon children and young adults: in September 2006, 41 per cent of its users were over 35, an increase of ten percentage points over the previous year. Its expansion plans are being guided by the media conglomerate News Corporation, which bought the company from its founders in 2005. It has also begun to solve the problem of generating revenue from what is essentially a free service. In August 2006, it struck a $900m deal to allow Google to place targeted advertising on its pages, and in September 2006 it announced plans to sell MP3 music downloads.[27]

Friendster, meanwhile, is not admitting defeat. It retains a loyal user base in places such as the Philippines (where it has established a team of ten engineers) and Malaysia. Its backers have put in a further $10m and it has been granted what may turn out to be lucrative patents on key elements of the social networking concept.[28]

Creative Strategizing 13.1

What are Friendster's strategic resources? How might it position itself against MySpace and other competitors, and which market segments might it target? How might it regenerate its position amongst the global industry leaders?

13.4 Strategies for the mature phase of an industry

In the mature phase of an industry, the rate of growth in sales slows, and the rate of entry by new firms declines. This stage can last for many years, with small increases and decreases in sales growth rates as economies pass through cycles of boom and recession, fashions come and go, or major firms launch marketing campaigns to rekindle sales.

The paths that industries follow through maturity vary significantly, however (Figure 13.2).[29] There are two types of industry where the competences and assets that underlie competitive advantage remain stable over time:

- The progressive model is the most studied, and the most common: in the 1980s and 1990s, over 40 per cent of US industries developed in this way. Firms are able to get quick feedback on new products or markets as they are introduced, and so can move

		Core activities	
		Threatened	**Not Threatened**
Core assets	**Threatened**	**Radical Change** *Everything is up in the air* Examples: makers of landline telephone handsers, overnight letter-delivery carriers, and travel agencies	**Creative Change** *The industry is constantly redeveloping assets and resources* Examples: the motion picture industry, sports team ownership, and investment banking
	Not Threatened	**Intermediating Change** *Relationships are fragile* Examples: automobile dealerships, investment brokerages, and auction houses	**Progressive Change** *Companies implement incremental testing and adapt to feedback* Examples: online auctions, commercial airlines, and long-haul trucking

Figure 13.2 Types of mature industry. Source: McGahan (2004: 90). *Reproduced with the kind permission of* Harvard Business Review

forward by small, progressive steps. This makes product-based competitive advantage difficult to obtain, so firms look to improve their efficiency in order to obtain superior profitability. Many industries in the manufacturing and retail sectors follow this path.

- The creative model is much rarer—only 6 per cent of US industries fitted this pattern. In this kind of industry, firms are forced to make large investments in new products without ever being sure that they will get a return. This may be because it is difficult to gauge consumer reaction in advance, as with recorded music and film-making, or because of technological uncertainties, as is the case with pharmaceuticals and oil exploration.

Not all mature industries, though, are stable. Some may follow the progressive or creative model for a while, and then be disturbed by the introduction of a new approach that fundamentally alters the way the industry works, and which gives new entrants or early movers the possibility of reshaping it to their advantage. This kind of turbulent change can take two forms: intermediating and radical.

Nearly one-third of US industries in the 1980s and 1990s experienced intermediating change, affecting the ways in which firms interact with customers and suppliers.[30] For example, the arrival of the internet, the development of the call centre industry, and the availability of offshore processing facilities in countries like India changed the business models of insurers and retail bankers in much of the developed world. New entrants, firms selling insurance directly rather than through brokers, made significant advances. Incumbent firms' resources—reputations, financial assets, capabilities in assessing the risk associated with particular types of business—did not lose their value, but they had to rethink how they used them.

On the other hand, almost one-fifth of the US industries in the same period experienced radical change, which did affect the value of incumbents' assets and capabilities. For example, providers of traditional telephone systems, such as BT or France Telecom, having had to cope with competition from cable TV providers and substitution from mobile telephony, are now confronted with the threat of internet telephony, led by companies such as Skype and Vonage. Although some have fought back to retain a share of the voice telephony market, their revenue stream, and the value of their fixed-line networks, will be diminished. Similarly, the advent of 'fast fashion' firms like Zara, H&M, and TopShop has upset the business models of established fashion retailers, whose supplier networks and established routines suddenly lost much of their value.

In the following sections, we look at these three types of mature industry—progressive, creative, and turbulent—in more detail.

13.4.1 Competition in progressive mature industries

a. The strategic environment in progressive industries

In a progressive, mature industry, such as soft drinks, passenger aircraft, or accountancy, there are well-defined rules of the game. Brand names and corporate reputation are well developed, and customers will have learnt which firms and which products are suited to their needs. All the major firms know one another and watch each others' actions carefully. Changes in one firm's competitive stance—price changes or new product introductions—are likely to be quickly copied, or offset by some countervailing move. There are few barriers to the imitation of any firm's offerings.

Quite often, product and process technologies have stabilized around a dominant design, so that it becomes more difficult to differentiate the product or service on functionality. This is the problem that British Airways faces with economy-class air travel, or Sony with its TVs or laptop computers. Customers, many of them repeat buyers, have become familiar with the product or service and have developed a clear idea of what constitutes value for money. This makes it more difficult for firms to sustain positions based on premium prices, since few buyers will pay over the odds for something which is little different from what is offered by competitors.

This makes price one of the few ways in which a firm can differentiate, and so firms are driven to invest in finding ways of reducing costs. For two reasons, this is likely to lead, over time, to an increase in the average size of firms and eventual concentration into an oligopoly. First, since the technology has stabilized, economies of scale or scope, where available, will be amongst the easiest sources of cost advantage. Second, it is easier for a large firm to get a return on its investment in process R&D, since the cost is largely the same for a small firm as for a large one, but the benefits are greater if they can be applied to a large production volume.[31]

This effect may not be immediate; these industries may stay fragmented for quite a long time. Even after concentration has taken place, small firms can and do continue in competition with the larger ones, concentrating their efforts on product and market niches. However, as efficiency becomes more and more important, and investment in process efficiency starts to pay off, it becomes increasingly difficult for new entrants to compete with established firms. Their survival rate declines, and the rate of new entry falls away until such a time as the process technology has stabilized, at which point it becomes viable again.[32]

An industry is most likely to remain fragmented when there are many possible sources of advantage, none of which gives a competitor a position of overwhelming strength. Economies of scale and scope may be small, so that there are few returns on an investment in consolidating through merger or acquisition. Firms that are out-competed in some areas are able to retain a viable position because of their strengths in others, so that even where there are worthwhile economies of scale, no firm will naturally grow to a dominant size. For example, in industries like restaurants and fashion, flexibility, inspiration, and ingenuity may allow small firms to compete with a large one.

b. Strategic challenges in progressive mature industries

The prime challenges confronting large firms relate to achieving and sustaining cost advantage whilst avoiding triggering a damaging price war. There are a number of reasons why such a war might develop. Extra capacity, ordered when the industry was still growing in the expectation that growth would continue, may come on stream when the industry has matured. There will be a temptation for firms to cut their prices to try to utilize the extra capacity, and get some return on the sunk investment. Salespeople may press for price reductions to help them make their targets. However, since most of the firms in the industry will be in a similar situation, a round of price cuts will simply lead to a reduction in profits for all competitors. Damaging price wars of this kind occur periodically in industries such as automobiles, air travel, and insurance.

Small firms have less reason to fear that their actions will trigger a price war. However, they face the challenge of establishing and defending a niche against larger competitors that may have national or global reputations and a superior cost structure.

One hazard of working in a progressive mature industry is that of meeting stakeholder expectations conditioned by achievements during the growth phase. Shareholders may expect growth in sales and earnings to continue at its former pace. Employees, in particular salespeople, may have come to expect, or even depend upon, large bonuses for meeting ambitious targets.

→ We explored the Icarus Paradox, competency traps, and core rigidities in Sections 2.8.4 and 7.7.

→ The advantages and disadvantages of diversification are discussed in Chapter 5.

Managers also need to beware of the problems that arise from adapting too well to an environment that changes only slowly: competency traps, core rigidities, and the Icarus Paradox.

c. Strategic options for organizations in progressive mature industries

Firms can respond to these challenges by diversifying into new products and markets, in order to escape from existing competitive pressures, satisfy stakeholders' expectations of continued growth, and gain economies of scale and scope. The larger organizations in a mature industry are likely to be expanding, probably globalizing, the scope of their operations, if they have not already done so at the growth phase. They may take on the role of industry consolidator, buying up competitors and rationalizing shared costs in areas such as marketing and administration. Economies of scale may also be sought in particular value chain activities, for example through investment in large production and distribution facilities.

Firms that can will seek to differentiate on the basis of reputation and image, to reap the kinds of price premiums that BMW and Mercedes, for example, obtain in the automobile industry. Small firms will seek to build a reputation with customers in their particular target market. While the industry remains fragmented, larger competitors will try to capitalize on their brands and financial resources by investing in advertising, and perhaps in networks of branded outlets, either wholly owned or franchised. Both McDonald's and H&M pursue this strategy.

Firms with a well-developed innovation capability may look to product innovation as a path to differentiation advantage, like Sony in consumer electronics and Virgin Atlantic in air travel. However, these are likely to be small, incremental innovations, designed to create demand for repeat purchase and respond to customer requirements for product enhancements, with major breakthroughs being few and far between.

→ We examine outsourcing and offshoring in Chapter 6.

→ Tools for understanding an organization's belief system were introduced in Section 8.4.2. We look at processes of organizational change in Chapter 16.

The main thrust of R&D effort at this stage of the life-cycle typically shifts from product innovation to process innovation—in fact, this shift is a defining aspect of a mature industry. Firms may re-examine their value chain and reconfigure it to reduce costs, by trimming excess overheads and through selective outsourcing and offshoring of activities where the firm has no distinctive capability. For example, car firms have divested themselves of their component subsidiaries. This may involve painful processes of internal change and the re-examination of the organization's belief system and of industry rules of the game.[33] Developing collaborative relationships with, for example, firms in other industries that use similar technologies or address similar customers may help improve absorptive capacity and reduce the risk of being taken by surprise by a radical or intermediating change (see 13.4.3).

Questioning the fundamentals in this way may give managers a new perspective on their firm's resources and how they can be used to generate competitive advantage. Like IBM in the 1990s, they may rethink the purpose of the business as a provider of services (computer systems integration) rather than products. Such 'strategic innovation' can significantly improve the profitability of mature businesses, and may lead to a radical restructuring of the industry, to the firm's advantage.[34]

Less fundamental process innovations may still be enough to give the firm a degree of differentiation on the basis of superior support and on responding faster to customer requests. This involves building personal linkages to customers that are not easy for competitors to copy through, for example, staff secondments and regular visits.

Marketing activities are devoted to maintaining awareness of the brand and building customer loyalty, so that customers do not defect to competitors. Radical price reductions are typically avoided unless a firm believes that it has achieved a significant cost advantage, or to try to 'kill off' a competitor that has cash flow problems. However, cut-throat competition of this kind is rarely appropriate in a mature industry, since it can incite strong competitors to retaliate in kind. It is better to try to retain a stable base of competitors that understand the industry 'rules of the game'.

→ We introduced the concept of industry rules of the game in Chapter 3.3.1.

As the processes and technologies stabilize, the firm's culture and architecture are likely to change to reflect the new circumstances. People's roles within the firm typically become more closely defined and specialized, and firms adopt sophisticated control systems and a formalized hierarchy. A networked or mercenary culture may be appropriate, depending on the competitive situation.

13.4.2 Strategies in creative mature industries

a. The strategic environment in creative industries

Creative industries are characterized by the search for a blockbuster product—a wonder drug, a hit record, or major box-office success in the cinema. Individually, these are massively profitable, but from those profits the firm must support the cost of the development products, that are less successful, or that fall by the wayside during the development process. The producer has no reliable way of predicting in advance which products will succeed and which will flop, so must make many investments to find the few that pay off. Nonetheless, these industries can be very profitable. They justify these profits on the basis of the risks they have to bear, and the high professional standards and levels of service they offer.

As with progressive industries, creative industries tend to have a dominant design. Movies are around 90 minutes long and are distributed on 70mm film, pharmaceuticals are distributed in a number of accepted formats for swallowing or injection. This enables companies to invest in complementary assets, such as sales and distribution networks, which are important if the product is to be sold in sufficient quantity to recover the cost of its development.

They tend to feature a dominant strategic group containing a few major firms, such as Merck and GlaxoSmithKline in pharmaceuticals, and Time Warner and Sony in movies and music, which have built strong complementary assets. There are other strategic groups containing smaller firms—biotechnology start-ups and independent studios and record labels—whose strength is their ability to generate new ideas and their willingness to try them out. Barriers to entry to these latter strategic groups are typically quite low, but the mobility barriers separating them from the dominant group are high, since building the complementary assets requires high investments of time and money.

→ We examined strategic groups and the concept of mobility barriers in Section 3.3.2.

b. Strategic challenges in creative industries

The main strategic challenge in industries of this nature is to manage the risks that come with multiple failures of large projects. There may be other challenges linked to this, such as keeping abreast of the tastes of a fickle public, and retaining access to the talent—top researchers, famous musicians, actors, producers, and directors—that give firms a better-than-average chance of success.

c. Strategic options for firms in creative industries

Quite often, firms reduce some of the risk by avoiding direct competition and specializing in certain areas. Pharmaceuticals companies specialize in specific types of therapy, film and music companies in particular genres. For large firms, the aim is, where possible, to dominate that specialism, whereas smaller firms may specialize in elements of the value chain—developing drugs or movies to a certain point before selling them on to a major, for example.

Another way of managing the risk is by producing 'me-too' versions of commercially successful products, such as marginal improvements on existing blockbuster drugs, or movies in a genre—chick-flick, spoof horror, epic—that appears to have popular appeal at the time. A final way is to invest in innovative ways of diminishing the risk. Software has been produced that appears to be able to analyse a song and determine whether it shares the key characteristics of hit records of the past. Real options theory can be used to assess the financial viability of investing in the next stage of development and testing for a particular drug.[35]

The firm's architecture has to reflect the need to retain access to talent, and also to distribution channels and other complementary assets. This may mean forging alliances that give large firms access to the creativity of smaller ones, or of researchers in universities and specialist institutes, and small firms access to the complementary assets of the majors.[36]

13.4.3 Strategies in mature industries undergoing turbulence

a. The strategic environment in turbulent mature industries

Intermediating or, in particular, radical change in an industry can stimulate firms to enter as early exploiters of different approaches, such as innovative technologies or new communication channels with suppliers or customers. On the one hand, this may help expand the industry by opening it up to customers who have not been able to afford its products, as happened with the entry of low-cost providers of airline travel (a radical change) and with the arrival of internet booking firms, such as Opodo and Lastminute.com, into the travel agency industry.

On the other hand, while not all new entrants will be successful, their arrival may increase the industry's production capacity and will present customers with new choices. The resultant increase in buyer power and the temptation to cut prices to maintain capacity utilization will make the industry less attractive than when it was stable. It may even split into several new industries, as new technologies or information sources make it economic for smaller firms to perform activities that were previously vertically integrated.

For example, the retailing of consumer electronics and electrical goods has been transformed by the internet. In the past, retail outlets functioned as showrooms, as sources of information regarding prices and product specifications, as sources of advice, as order-takers, and as stockage points from which items could be picked up or delivered. However, many people now employ the web as the first source of product and price information, often using dedicated firms whose only function is to allow buyers to make comparisons between providers. The World Wide Web is also a good source of product advice, much of it free and based upon consumers' experiences. Retailers compete in these sub-industries through their own websites; their retail outlets are still valuable as showrooms and pick-up points for items that increasingly are pre-ordered over the internet.

Firms may be drawn into large investments in the new approaches, either because of a belief that they will be profitable, or out of fear of seeming out of touch. This will erode profitability further in the short term, though some firms, which are able to master the new approach quickly or gain favour with customers, can find this period very profitable. Dell, in PCs, and Direct Line, in UK insurance, both profited handsomely from intermediating change in their industries, being amongst the pioneers of direct sales channels.

However, other firms may be vulnerable to the new entrants, because they fail to react to the changed approach. This may be because they want to wait until they have extracted as much value as possible from their past investments and established resources. Or they may

Direct Line was one of the pioneers of direct sales channels in the UK insurance industry. *Direct Line*

simply fail to perceive the threat, if it comes from firms outside the established group of competitors that they are used to monitoring. The most vulnerable organizations will be those that do not have the resources or the architecture needed to fight off the threat, including for example:

- capabilities in low cost production, since new entrants often will have lean cost structures and may aim to compete on price;

- strong reputations and relationships with customers. Firms that have allowed themselves to become complacent or arrogant as a result of having market-leading positions may find that their customers are more likely to experiment with the new providers;

- strong distribution networks and other complementary assets;

- financial resources to withstand a temporary dip in customer numbers, and technological resources to adopt any new technologies involved.

b. Strategic challenges in turbulent industries

Research[37] suggests that the highest performing firms in an industry undergoing turbulent change are the first-movers, who take the risk of introducing new approaches before they can be fully sure that customers will accept them. However, premature or mistaken commitments can lead to significant losses. The challenges a firm confronts in managing this trade-off differ depending on whether it is a new entrant or an incumbent.

For a new entrant, some challenges can be similar to those confronted in a new industry: the need to build legitimacy for themselves and for their new approach. People needed time to adjust to the idea of buying groceries or conducting their financial affairs over the internet. However, it may also be confronted with existing competitors that may have strong reputations and balance sheets, and important complementary assets. In those situations, it has the added challenge of acquiring a reputation and other assets of its own quickly, before the incumbents get to grips with the innovations that are leading to the change.

Incumbents, on the other hand, have two main challenges. First, they may need to overcome the inertia that often comes to a firm that has survived for a long period in a mature industry. This means changing their established routines and architecture so as to adapt to the changing environment. Diversified companies may need firm central management action to deal with conflicts between business units, some of which may see opportunities from the new approach while others may see threats. We have already

(What Can Go Wrong 5.1) seen the example of the conflicting reactions within Sony to the rise of digital music; the consumer electronics division wanted to take advantage of the new medium to sell hardware, while the music division wanted to manage the perceived threat to its intellectual property.[38]

The second challenge is to time the tricky transition from old to new business models correctly. For example, in the long run, it may make sense for established banks to run down their branch networks as customers make more and more transactions via the internet. In the short term, this may antagonize customers, typically but not exclusively older people, who prefer to deal with a person face to face, or who need to do so for a particularly complex transaction. More generally, substantial investments in new supply chains and in reaching new customer groups may be needed, but managers will also want to maximize the returns on existing assets (see What Can Go Wrong 13.1 at the end of this chapter for another example of how difficult it can be to time a response correctly).

A third challenge, specific to intermediating change, is to profit from the increase in the quantity and quality of information that becomes available as change of this kind takes hold. Firms like Dell found themselves with a larger amount of more up-to-date information about their customers than did PC-makers that sold through dealers, and had more control over which data were collected. Similarly, the processes (discussed in Chapter 6) that allow H&M to function as it does are only possible because of the way in which it gathers detailed and timely data right through the supply chain. Properly used, this can give firms the ability to spot problems and trends more quickly than their competitors, and to reduce the costs of transactions with suppliers and customers.

c. Strategic options in turbulent industries

Firms confronting turbulence must choose from three strategic postures:[39]

- Shaping the future: leading the industry towards a new approach, stimulating demand for it, and trying to establish a dominant design. This will often be simpler for new entrants that do not need to protect existing investments and have no emotional commitment to the old approach. They may be able to phase in their investment, testing the market in a low-key fashion, and developing their capabilities, before taking on incumbents in their most important markets (see Real-life Application 13.3). Incumbents, on the other hand, are likely to have any experimental moves closely watched and emulated.

- Adapting to the future: relying upon their ability to respond quickly to moves by pioneering players and the market opportunities they create. Some theorists have strongly advocated an incremental approach in turbulent industries, where firms use low-cost methods to probe what the future may hold, rather than commit themselves to the implementation of detailed plans.[40] These methods might include:

  - frequently launching experimental products to test customer reactions;

  - having one or two 'futurists', employees, or collaborators with exceptional technological knowledge and connections to the market place to picture what the future might hold;

  - holding regular internal meetings to contemplate how the industry might develop;

  - strategic alliances with future-minded customers or potential customers;

  - envisaging 'scenarios'—extreme combinations of outside events that might stretch the resources of the industry, or the organization—so that managers can think through their potential reaction and develop strategies that are robust against them.

- Reserving the right to play through a phased adoption of the new approach to gain experience of running the new processes, and defend their reputations. This can be, for incumbents, a viable alternative to massive early investment in the new-style industry. For example, retailers have run websites and traditional retail in parallel. This may enable incumbents to emerge as the long-term winners against the new entrants. In many forms of retailing, established players such as Wal-Mart, Tesco, and Carrefour have retained leadership against the challenge of purely internet-based firms. Where a new approach takes the form simply of product developments, existing firms with good complementary assets are often able to ride out the storm and come back to dominate the industry, perhaps acquiring the new competitors in the process. Fundamental advances in diagnostic medical imaging technologies in the 1980s were pioneered by new entrants, but the industry ended up with the older firms very much in control.[41]

→ We introduced the concept of 'reserving the right to play' in Section 12.1.2.

Online Resource Centre
www.oxfordtextbooks.co.uk/orc/haberberg_rieple/

Visit the Online Resource Centre that accompanies this book to read more information relating to scenario planning.

Product development can, however, lead to spectacular success where existing competitors have grown complacent, as occurred in the domestic appliance industry when Dyson entered with a new form of vacuum cleaner in 1993. New entrants have two other main avenues that have been shown to lead to successful entry.[42] One is to specialize in particular market segments: new firms such as Eclipse Aviation are entering the aircraft industry with small, low-cost designs aimed at firms that cannot afford current business jets, or for use as jet taxis.[43]

The second avenue applies in industries where the technology is very stable and the advantage to be gained from further process developments is small. This enables new firms to enter with low-cost business models based either on low-cost manufacturing, using efficient, up-to-date technology, or on reselling other firms' excess output. Entry along these lines has been seen in industries as diverse as petrochemicals, disposable nappies, and fixed-line and mobile telephone service provision.

Regardless of their posture in relation to the new approach, existing competitors should aim to take speedy advantage of the profit potential of their established resource base. To this end, they might strike up alliances with old competitors who are facing the same threats to postpone the day when the new approach takes hold, perhaps with a view to future mergers if the industry declines (see Real-life Application 13.3). New investments in the old approach should be avoided unless the payback is short and the level of commitment is low, or unless it is to help blend the two approaches, since firms that are able to do this well can be amongst the highest performers.

These incumbent firms will, however, need to be able to judge when the moment has arrived to get rid of the old approach and go over to the new. They therefore need to consider changing their architecture to help them get closer to suppliers and customers, and judge how they are reacting. They may also re-examine their degree of vertical integration, to see whether some activities can be spun off or outsourced. In order to make these decisions, they may need to invest in new control systems, so that the costs of each transaction are clear and are accurately reflected in internal transfer prices between divisions.

Real-life Application 13.3 The UK package holiday industry[44]

Thomson Travel Group was one of the four largest air-inclusive travel operators in the 1990s. *Thomson Travel Group*

Sunshine has a magnetic attraction for holidaymakers from the UK, whose home climate has offered too little of it. During the industry's introductory phase, 1950–65, air travel was exotic and expensive, and packaged holidays were aimed at affluent and adventurous people in search of glamour. The air-inclusive travel (AIT) industry was small and fragmented. However, as jet airline travel started to become more affordable, and UK workers were given longer paid holidays, the industry started to broaden its customer base. One- or two-week package holidays in the Mediterranean countries, particularly Spain, became the norm for many people, and the industry grew strongly from 1965 onwards, though the rate of growth tailed off slightly in the 1990s.

Along with growth came a change in the industry structure. Managers found that size conferred significant advantages, notably bargaining power in negotiating with resort owners for bedrooms during the high season, and with travel agents, the main distribution channel. The industry consolidated, and by the end of the 1990s the four largest operators, Airtours (since renamed MyTravel), Thomson Travel Group, Thomas Cook, and First Choice, controlled some 55 per cent of industry capacity. Most had links with other European AIT firms to further increase their buying power, with Thomson and Thomas Cook being ultimately owned by German companies (respectively Tui and Lufhansa/Karstadt).

These operators were also highly vertically integrated: in 1999 their in-house airlines, such as Britannia, carried 80 per cent of charter passengers from the UK. The four leading tour operators also had their own chains of retail travel agencies, and either owned large amounts of capacity at the best holiday resorts or had locked it in via long-term contracts. People were booked on fixed 7- or 14-day package holidays, and this predictable rhythm of travel enabled airline and resort schedules to be tightly co-ordinated, so that both sets of assets were used efficiently and intensively.

The 1990s, however, brought radical change in the form of low-cost airlines. The latter deliberately, at first, avoided competing directly with the tour operators' charter airlines. Their initial destinations were places like Dublin or Glasgow, of more interest to Irish or Scottish exiles visiting friends and relatives than to holidaymakers seeking sun and sand. But by 1998 they had started services to places like Palma de Mallorca and Faro. Because they were very efficient and sold direct, avoiding the commission that established operators paid to travel agents, they were able to compete on price, despite the high load factors of the charter airlines. Between 2000 and 2005, the big charter airlines lost over 30 per cent of their share of traffic on major routes to Spain.

The new airlines were assisted by intermediating change, in the shape of the internet, which made it easier for customers to communicate directly with hoteliers and resort owners. Not only did this lessen holidaymakers' need for travel agents to find and book holidays—it also allowed them to determine the length of their stay, since low-cost flights were frequent, and not locked into the AIT firms' rigid cycles. The big holiday companies' vertically integrated business model lost much of its power. Between 1995 and 2005, package holidays' share of UK leisure travel had fallen from nearly 90 per cent to under 50 per cent, although this was offset by a massive increase in the volume of overall demand: the new entrants, along with a strong economy, had expanded the UK travel market by nearly 150 per cent.

The established players retained some important resources, such as their supply of hotel rooms. They attempted to retaliate in a number of ways. Many launched their own low-cost airlines to compete with the new entrants—Britannia, for example, became Thomsonfly.com. And in November 2006, exploratory talks took place between MyTravel and First Choice, with a view to combining their respective AIT operations.

There are many ways of conceptualizing the way that organizations change over time—see Van de Ven and Poole (1995, 2005) for a deep discussion—but life-cycle models are amongst the most common. The industry life-cycle was developed from the product life-cycle in the 1970s, with Utterback and Abernathy (1975) contributing the key insight about the way in which the emphasis of innovation changes from product to process innovation as the industry matures. Hofer (1975) suggested it might become the basis for a comprehensive contingency theory of strategic behaviour, and Porter (1980) made it the organizing framework for his path-breaking book on competitive strategy.

Studies seem to suggest that there is substance to the theory—that there are indeed predictable patterns in firms' behaviour that can be linked, at least in part, to the industry life-cycle. The life-cycle can be related to the form that manufacturing firms choose for their operations—for example, bespoke production, batch processing or mass production (Hayes and Wheelwright, 1979; St John et al., 2003). The way in which firms use alliances changes over the life-cycle of the industry too (Rice and Galvin, 2006).

The most convincing evidence in favour of the existence of some form of industry life-cycle comes from studies that have found consistent patterns, across a wide variety of industries, in organizational entry and mortality rates (Klepper, 1997, 2002; Agarwal et al., 2002). These show that it is possible, in most industries, to distinguish the growth phase, where both entry and mortality rates are substantially higher, from the maturity phase.

The empirical evidence, however, does not offer the same degree of support for every part of the model set out in Figure 13.1. The boundaries between the introductory and growth phases, and between maturity and decline, are less easy to observe empirically. Moreover, as we mentioned in Section 13.4, the maturity phase is less uniform across industries than was thought when the basic theory was drawn up in the 1970s and 1980s. Not all industries develop a dominant design (Porter, 1983) and, as we noted in Section 13.4.3, mature industries differ in the ways that firms specialize. Charles Baden-Fuller and John

Stopford (1992) suggest that the very concept of a mature industry is misleading. They cite a number of case studies of firms that have successfully introduced radical product and marketing innovations in industries, such as steel cutlery, that were widely seen as mature and unexciting.

The toughest critique of the industry life-cycle comes from Anita McGahan (2000, 2004), based upon her own empirical studies. She does not dispute the existence of the industry life-cycle, but she gives several reasons for doubting how useful it is as a practical tool for strategic analysis. First, as we pointed out in Chapter 3, it can be difficult to define the boundaries of an industry—and conclusions as to whether an industry is growing or declining can depend on which products are counted as part of the industry and which as substitutes. Second, patterns of investment, and the length of time that is needed to get a return on that investment, vary significantly between industries in a way that is not apparently linked to whether they are growing or mature.

She even disputes whether there are in fact any significant differences in innovative activity between growing and mature industries. She found (McGahan and Silverman, 2001) no evidence that there was less innovative activity in mature industries, that process innovation was more prevalent there, or that leading firms in such industries were less innovative than those in emerging industries.

This, in McGahan's (2004) view, means that, in developing strategic options, firms need to be guided by different considerations, particularly when their industry is undergoing fundamental change. She suggests that industries pass through one or more cycles of fragmentation, as a new approach begins to take hold, followed by convergence between the new and the existing approach, as incumbent firms evaluate and adopt it. The two approaches co-exist for a period, during which buyers and suppliers familiarize themselves with it, and finally the new approach comes to dominate. She suggests that locating themselves in this cycle (Figure 13.3) will help managers react correctly to their environment.

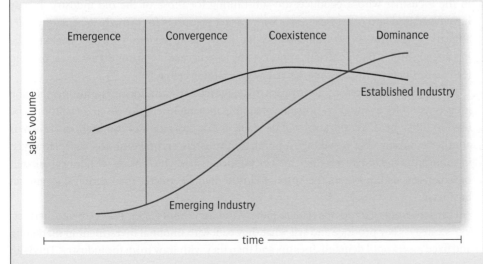

Figure 13.3 Cycles of industry fragmentation and convergence. Source: McGahan (2004: 92). *Reproduced with the kind permission of* Harvard Business Review

13.5 **Strategies for the decline stage of an industry**

a. The strategic environment in declining industries

By the final phase of an industry's life-cycle, sales have begun to decline and substitute products have taken over. However, it is still possible for declining industries such as cigars and fountain pens to be extremely profitable.[45] As long as there are not too many companies competing for a shrinking customer base, profits can be obtained in the decline phase, sometimes for many years. These products have minimal marketing costs and need little investment, since demand is predictable, the remaining customer base is likely to be loyal, and the product and process technologies are stable.

It is not unknown for industries in apparently terminal decline to be rejuvenated. The industry producing nuclear power generation equipment appeared, for much of the 1980s and 1990s, to be in decline because of high capital costs, the long-term problems involved in disposing of radioactive waste products and a general popular reaction against all things nuclear. But with increasing awareness of the risks involved in the production of greenhouse gases, new nuclear power plants, which do not give rise to such gases, are being commissioned once more.

b. Strategic challenges in declining industries

The challenges for a firm in a declining industry are to maximize the profits to be obtained from existing investments, to minimize the new investment needed, and to avoid a destructive price war with its remaining competitors, which may be reluctant to withdraw because of high exit costs.

➜ We examined exit costs and exit barriers in Section 3.5.6.

Exit costs include the costs of dismissing staff who can no longer be employed, such as redundancy or relocation payments, or legal action for unfair dismissal. They also include the costs of dismantling plant and machinery and restoring land to a condition fit for subsequent use. This can be substantial in industries that give rise to waste products that are radioactive, or penetrate into the soil. Exit costs may also be less tangible: for example, the damage to the reputation of a firm, or a group of managers, that is seen to have failed, or to have fallen down on its responsibility to a community.

c. Strategic options at the decline stage

Withdrawal can be an attractive option for a firm which does not believe that it has the reputation or other resources that are needed to profit from the decline, or that has more attractive opportunities elsewhere. If the firm is wise, it will itself have created a strong position in the industries whose products are substituting for those of the old industry. It may have diversified into other businesses with greater prospects for growth. Product diversity appears to help firms survive industry decline. However, diversifying once the decline stage has already begun, paradoxically, appears to be less successful—firms do better to invest in leading the industry into decline, a strategy we examine below.[46]

For many firms, therefore, decisions at this stage relate to winding up the business, selling it or its assets for as much as possible, or simply moving its employees and facilities to be used in other areas. Withdrawal will be viable if exit costs are not too high, or if there is another company that is willing to purchase the assets and take on the staff. However, in some areas and industries there may be political issues which make withdrawal difficult or expensive, and in others the costs of closure may be greater than those of staying in business.

Firms that cannot or do not want to quit the industry immediately may pursue a 'harvesting' strategy. They produce and sell what they can, with minimal investment in marketing and fixed assets, until demand dries up, and then they withdraw from the industry. This is an effective strategy if competition in the industry remains benign, so that the company can enjoy the fruits of its past investment without worrying about aggression from its competitors.

However, firms that believe that they have some form of sustainable advantage may prefer a more proactive strategy. One option is to focus on a profitable niche market where the organization may have built good relationships in the past, or where its resources are particularly valuable.

If a firm believes that it has the basis for competitive advantage over a broad competitive arena, then it may make sense to attempt to lead the industry into an orderly decline, with a view to dominating it for the rest of its life. This is more likely to succeed when the firm has strong financial assets, or good relational assets that give it preferential access to finance for restructuring.[47]

➜ We explained the nature and value of relational assets in Section 7.3.6.

A leadership strategy involves a measure of up-front investment intended to frighten competitors out of the industry, and at the same time make it easy for them to withdraw. For example, a firm might invest aggressively in new, low-cost production facilities and in marketing to build market share. This would demonstrate that the 'leader' was committed to the industry for the long term. At the same time it might make public pronouncements about its belief that the industry's decline was permanent. These would be aimed at competitors whose owners or managers were sentimentally attached to the industry, and who might be tempted to hold on in expectation of a future upturn. Finally, it might ease competitors' path out of the industry by assuming some of their exit costs. It might buy their plant, hire their people, and assume their commitments to fill orders and maintain service and the supply of spare parts for existing users. Sometimes, governments or supra-national bodies such as the European Commission can be persuaded to assist in restructuring an industry.

Once the threat of a price war in a declining industry has been averted, the strategies that the remaining firms should pursue are straightforward. It makes sense to profit from the stability and predictability of the environment by simplifying everything. Product features can be minimized, production schedules optimized by making a limited range of products and aiming for long production runs. Competences can be refined, and systems and structure can be simplified and made extremely efficient.

It may be possible to enhance profitability further by differentiating the product. Brand names in the industry will be very well known and may have grown quite prestigious with age. The dwindling band of users may take pride in their association with an old-fashioned product or service, and be open to marketing campaigns based upon special editions or collectors' items. Dunhill, an English manufacturer of tobacco pipes, has founded a club for pipe smokers, the Fellowship of the White Spot. Members receive a regular newsletter in which they are informed of gatherings of pipe aficionados and are offered limited edition pipes made in special shapes and decorated in silver.[48]

13.6 Strategies in hypercompetitive industries

a. The strategic environment in hypercompetitive industries

There is one form of competitive environment that appears to fall outside the life-cycle model: hypercompetitive industries. These frequently (although not always) arise when there are increasing returns to scale, and the dynamic which drives firms to compete exceptionally fiercely for industry dominance persists over time, whether the industry is growing quickly or slowly. One reason for this, some theorists believe, is that this intensely

→ Hypercompetition and increasing returns were introduced in Section 3.5.6.

competitive behaviour becomes embedded in the belief systems of the firms in the industry. Hypercompetition has been recognized since the 1990s as an important phenomenon, though it does not, as some writers have suggested, appear to be becoming more widespread.[49]

Hypercompetition flares up where one or more significant competitors believes that the rewards from winning the competitive battle are high enough to justify the risks and effort involved. In industries like PC processor chips, computer games consoles, and digital music downloads this is because one competitor can gain an unusual degree of control if its technology is adopted as the industry standard. However, such behaviour can sometimes flare up in previously stable mature industries. In the Japanese beer industry in the 1980s, Asahi, languishing with a market share below 10 per cent, attacked the long-time leader, Kirin, with a new type of beer, Asahi Super Dry. Asahi's market share doubled within two years, and the industry was led into a hypercompetitive cycle of new product introductions.[50]

b. Strategic challenges in hypercompetitive industries

A distinguishing feature of hypercompetitive environments is that competitive advantage is transient—it is very difficult to construct enduring strategic resources.[51] Even companies that dominate their industry, such as Intel, Microsoft, and Apple, still face stiff challenges in staying ahead, while those that are contesting their dominance have to try to establish a credible alternative, or seek calmer niches where they can operate profitably.

A major challenge, therefore, is coming up with products or services that are sufficiently differentiated to achieve at least temporary dominance in the industry. In an industry that depends upon product standards, this implies establishing the next generation of their offering as the industry standard. At the time of writing, as we have already noted, Sony is vying with Toshiba to establish its technology for high-capacity DVDs as the industry standard, and with Microsoft and Nintendo for supremacy in a new generation of videogames consoles.

Firms will therefore at some stage face the challenge of fostering capabilities in product innovation. They may also need to develop capabilities in communication, to help them to persuade an overwhelming mass of customers to adopt their standard. Strong marketing capabilities helped Sony to achieve, and then sustain, leadership in computer games consoles with its 'power of PlayStation' advertising campaign. Intel went further—its 'Intel inside' branding exercise appealed directly to PC end-users, over the heads of its own direct customers.

→ The concept of dynamic capabilities was explored in Section 7.6.

These are both examples of specialized capabilities that may be needed at certain stages in a hypercompetitive battle. Firms may need to alter these as the basis of competition changes from product features, to price, to non-price barriers to entry and then back again. In order to keep these capabilities current, they require dynamic capabilities that enable them quickly to recombine and redeploy their resources.[52]

c. Strategic options in hypercompetitive industries

Both leader and challenger firms are likely to favour strategies, based upon strong product development activity, that will enable them to outpace their competitors (see Real-life Application 13.4). This may on occasion call for them to replace products that are still profitable, simply to make sure that competitors do not get the opportunity to do so.[53]

Dominant firms, in particular, will aim for frequent product upgrades to limit the time and resources that competitors have available for the development of blockbuster products of their own. They may aim to stretch their competitors in other ways, through aggressive pricing and frequent feints, spoiling actions, and experimental moves.

Aggressive pricing, in particular price reductions that coincide with the launch of competing products, serve another purpose—to lock customers in to one firm's offerings.

Companies may also try to do this by signalling their intentions for the next generation of technology several years in advance. Microsoft makes a point of announcing new versions of its software well in advance of the eventual release date. Sony adopted the same tactic when it announced its PlayStation 2 games console over a year ahead of launch. Its promised product was so impressive that Sega was unable to meet its targets for the rival Dreamcast console; despite selling 6 million Dreamcasts, it exited the industry in 2001.[54]

In order to keep up with the pace of change in these industries, firms will need cultures and architectures that foster innovation and responsiveness to market developments. Structures will need to be flexible, and may be patched continuously as the nature of competitive advantage in the industry evolves.[55]

> ➜ We introduced the concept of 'patching' organization structures in Section 9.1.3.

Membership of networks is also important for firms' competitiveness in hypercompetitive industries:

- Firms seeking a dominant position in a hypercompetitive industry typically require a strong network of complementary firms. For example, producers of videogames hardware or computer operating systems have needed to forge relationships with software firms that will write compatible games and other applications. Sony and Toshiba have both assembled powerful alliances to support their competing standards for high-capacity DVDs. Toshiba's includes Intel and Microsoft, which has contributed copy-management software. Sony has reached out to the hardware manufacturers: Apple, Dell, HP, and Philips, which has been a Sony partner since the days when they co-developed the CD. Each alliance embraces about 70 further companies that hope to benefit from royalties on the intellectual property they have made available.[56]

- Firms with the less ambitious objective of survival in a hostile hypercompetitive environment may find that membership of networks of like-minded organizations helps them develop the necessary learning and change management skills.[57] They may also develop less formal relationships with networks of 'open-source' providers, such as the one that develops the Linux operating system that is the main competitor to Microsoft's Windows. Sun Microsystems has Open Office, a version of its Star Office suite, available as an open-source alternative to Microsoft's Office suite.[58] These relationships give organizations access and legitimacy with a broad-based group of highly skilled and motivated people. These may contribute their skills for free, and are also potential customers, since they are often strongly and emotionally antagonistic to the market leader.

- Firms trying to depose a dominant competitor may attempt to attract firms away from their network. When Microsoft was attempting to establish the first generation of its Xbox in competition with the PlayStation, it offered games developers a number of inducements, including programming protocols, familiar from the PC, which would reduce their lead time and investment.[59]

As an alternative to networks, firms sometimes use vertical integration, typically by acquisition, to assure themselves of supplies and distribution outlets. This has the same potential drawbacks as any vertical diversification strategy.

> ➜ We examined issues to do with vertical diversification in Section 5.2.1 and review the challenges of managing acquisitions in Section 17.5.

For a firm that is seeking to compete with an established leader, there are two main possibilities. One is to launch a new product or technology that dramatically outperforms the leader's (Real-life Application 13.4). The second is to focus on a market or segment that the leader has neglected. Nintendo has for many years maintained its presence in the videogames industry by focusing upon hand-held consoles, leaving Sony and Microsoft to contest the larger market for free-standing machines. In 2005, Sony introduced the PlayStation Portable to compete with Nintendo's hand-held, but Nintendo in 2006 launched a full-sized machine, the Wii (see Worked Example 7.1).

Real-life Application 13.4 Competing with an 800 pound gorilla: AMD versus Intel

Intel has had a dominant position in the supply of processors for personal computers that dates back to IBM's adoption of its 8088 processor for the first IBM PC. Its 1999 share of the market was approximately 90 per cent.[60] Demand for PCs induced it to license its processor technology to other chip-makers in the 1980s and this gave them an entrée into the market. Cyrix and Advanced Micro Devices (AMD) went on, in the early 1990s, to produce competitors to Intel's 80386 and 80486 ranges of processors.[61]

Intel fought back, using legal action to try to curtail the two firms' activities.[62] Finally, it launched the Pentium processor, which along with a proprietary brand name, had certain features that its competitors were unable to emulate satisfactorily. It then launched the Pentium II processor, with a new, proprietary standard for the connection between the processor and the motherboard.

This was intended to entrench Intel's advantage, but it left open to AMD and Cyrix a market for users who wanted a faster processor to fit their old-style motherboards. They were able to build on this to establish an alternative standard for motherboards, which they used for a range of processors with expanded capabilities. However, Intel retaliated with its Celeron range of inexpensive processors, designed to compete with Cyrix and AMD for price-sensitive customers. In 1999, AMD's chairman and CEO, W. J. Sanders III, had compared its struggle with Intel to that of a monkey competing with an 800 pound gorilla.[63]

AMD then acquired a small firm which had developed a technology for rendering the three-dimensional images used in computer games that was superior to Intel's. Its Athlon processor,

incorporating this technology, was enthusiastically received.[64] However, Intel's formidable marketing prowess and strong relationships with the leading PC manufacturers meant that its dominance of the PC market remained unchallenged until 2003. Then, it made what was regarded as a misstep with the introduction of a new generation of processors that transferred 64 bits of data with each processor cycle, rather than the previous 32.

Intel's own offering, the Itanium, was expensive and was not fully compatible with 32-bit versions of Microsoft's Windows operating system. AMD, however, produced a more reasonably priced 64-bit product, the Opteron, that also allowed users to run their old 32-bit software.[65] This processor proved particularly attractive to purchasers of network servers, where by late 2006, AMD had won one-quarter of the market. It also won a similar share of the mainstream PC processor market,[66] where its Athlon processors offered a price and performance advantage over Intel's Pentium 4.[67] PC manufacturers, such as Dell and Toshiba, which had previously been exclusively Intel customers began to offer machines with Athlon and Opteron processors.[68]

However, in 2006, Intel hit back. It launched a new generation of processor, the Pentium Core 2 Duo, which industry observers found outperformed Athlon 64s with a similar specification and price.[69] AMD, for its part, had acquired ATI, a leading manufacturer of graphics processors, and was promising a product that combined the processor and graphics chips found in every PC. Such a product would offer many price and performance advantages—if it could be brought to the market.[70] For the time being, experts believed that AMD had achieved technological parity with its larger rival.[71]

Worked Example 13.1 Assessing the effectiveness of possible types of strategic option for H&M

In this Worked Example, we examine how the theory in this chapter can be used to assess the effectiveness of the different types of strategic option set out in Section 12.1 of the previous chapter.

The first stage, of course, is to identify in what type of industry H&M is operating. Although we do not have the statistics to help us plot the graph of sales over time, we know enough about the apparel industry to be sure which phase of the life-cycle it occupies. It clearly passed its introductory phase several centuries ago, when the Industrial Revolution made mass-produced clothing available to all. Equally clearly, this is not the kind of industry

that is likely to suffer decline unless there is an economic or environmental catastrophe—as long as there are people, they will want clothes to keep them warm and flatter their appearance.

In countries such as India and China, the industry may be entering a growth phase as people's spending power enables them to enjoy more and better clothing. However, in the developed countries that are H&M's main markets, the industry is mature, with demand fluctuating largely according to economic factors such as GDP growth, although the introduction into the supply chain of countries with low labour costs may have boosted volume sales as fashionable clothing became more affordable. ➔

→ We must then decide what kind of mature industry this is. Thirty years ago, there would have been a case for classifying it as a creative mature industry, since firms produced only two collections each year, and profitability depended on enough parts of that collection being big-selling hits. However, although creativity remains vitally important in fashion, it no longer meets the particular definition of 'creative industry' used in this chapter. It ceased to do so with the introduction in the 1980s of the technologies that enabled close monitoring of sales, the curtailment of production of unpopular products, and fast introduction of new lines, so that the search for blockbuster hits is no longer so vital.

The introduction of that technology caused turbulence in the industry that has now largely passed. Although competition can be fierce, it is not hypercompetitive: the bases of competition, design and price, remain constant from year to year, and it makes no sense to try to drive a competitor out of the market, since another will soon take its place. There are few barriers to entry to prevent a new player with strong design and retailing competences emulating the recent success of firms like Benetton, Zara, and H&M.

So, this is a progressive mature industry. We can also see that it is likely to remain fragmented, since it is difficult for any one firm, or one source of advantage to prevail. People are likely to want a choice of styles and the ability to show their own style by combining the offerings of different producers. There is likely also to remain a niche open for the quirky designer that caters for the tastes of a particular group of people, and for the astute retailer that can anticipate the tastes of people in her locality.

This means we can already eliminate certain types of strategic option. There is little scope for using one competence, such as clothing design, to compensate for weaknesses in, say, retailing or supply chain management. A big competitor needs to be at least competent in all those areas to remain viable in the era of fast fashion. However, H&M should be striving, as mentioned in 13.4.1, to use its buying power, technological competences and branding to their fullest extent, in order to minimize the danger that small, flexible competitors will outflank it in particular markets.

Neutralizing competitors has little sense when another, unknown quantity is likely to rise up in its place. Feints are unlikely to bring much benefit in an industry where no one player has a sufficient lead in resources to be able to gain from getting others to waste theirs. Reserving the right to play is not really necessary in this industry, which is not turbulent. Even in new and relatively turbulent markets, there is little for a retailer with an established global reputation to gain by establishing an early presence—it should find it simple enough to enter when the turbulence has abated.

Equally, certain classes of option clearly are worth considering. In a mature industry, even one which is too fragmented to be a real oligopoly, it makes sense to be able to match the products and methods of major competitors as quickly as possible. This has implications also for H&M's architecture, which should be attuned to gathering and using information about competitors' moves and customers reactions to them. It may be sensible to consider spoiling actions in markets where a competitor has a runaway success, in order to ensure that it does not have a free hand to build a commanding cash flow advantage. And in order to ensure that it is not taken by surprise by competitors' moves, theory (Section 13.4.1) suggests that H&M would be well advised to make consistent improvements to its own processes.

Experimental moves into new products and markets are the norm for the industry, and are a way of making steady progress without disturbing its equilibrium. And product and market expansion is the classic strategy for sustaining growth in mature industries, and is consistently pursued by H&M and all its major competitors. The choice between, and timing of, such product and market moves is of course a matter of considerable skill, and H&M would need to tailor its moves carefully to the resources at its disposal.

The final class of strategies to be considered is that of outpacing competitors. In a mature industry, this is both difficult and risky—but complacency and stagnation carry their own risks. H&M appears to have no need of a major breakthrough in either product or processes, and the conventional wisdom suggests that it would be unwise to make major investments in seeking one. However, in the course of its continuing efforts to refine its value chain, it may hit upon something that is as revolutionary as fast fashion was in the 1990s. It needs then carefully to weigh up the benefits of destabilizing the industry, and assure itself that the rewards outweigh the risks, before it acts.

Practical dos and don'ts

Life-cycle theory represents conventional wisdom, but certain exceptional (or exceptionally lucky) firms, with particular insights into their industry and how their firm's particular resources can be used to make money there, may flourish using different strategies.

You should not, therefore, entirely rule out creative strategic proposals that go against this conventional wisdom. However, if you make such a proposal, you should show an awareness of why life-cycle theory suggests that the odds are against its succeeding. You should then set out, very clearly and precisely, the reasons why you think your strategy can be successful in spite of this.

What Can Go Wrong 13.1 Kodak and the digital photographic revolution

Often, when one reads about dominant firms that are brought low by new technology, the story is of obstinate leaders that fail to recognize looming threats until it is too late. But Kodak's story is different. The pioneer, in 1900, of affordable mass-market photography, the Eastman Kodak Company was also the inventor, in 1976, of the first digital camera and the developer, in the early 1980s, of the first megapixel digital image sensor—the device that is at the heart of every digital camera and camera-phone.

Kodak had long operated on a business model similar to that used by manufacturers of razors—and now by those of printers and videogames consoles. The most expensive component—the razor, printer, console, or camera—is sold at low margins, or even below cost. The firm makes its profits through high-margin sales of consumables: blades, ink cartridges, games software, or, in Kodak's case, film, photographic paper, and chemicals.

By the mid-1970s, Kodak had already recognized the long-term threat that digital photography posed to these principal sources of profits.[72] Its managers nonetheless found it extremely difficult to arrive at the appropriate way to react and, no less importantly, time its reactions correctly. And, as we shall see, even when they did identify a promising strategy, they found that capricious markets limited the returns that they could reap from it.

First, they appeared to overestimate the speed with which the silver halide film industry would mature. This led them to invest in diversification—into high-end photocopiers, instant cameras, and, most controversially, pharmaceuticals.[73] Although this is a reasonable strategy when expecting an industry to decline, and although their chosen diversifications appeared to have some logic, none worked out well. Although Kodak's photocopier technology was of a high standard, the firm proved unable to market it effectively and lost out to Xerox.[74] A patent infringement in the instant camera technology led to a damaging court settlement in 1991.[75] Kodak's management was unable to add value to Sterling Drug, purchased for $5.1bn in 1988; it was sold off in 1993 and the debt taken on to finance the acquisition, which limited investment in the photography business, was paid down.[76]

Apart from incurring debt, the diversification policy appeared to take management attention away from the core silver halide film business when it was most needed. Kodak's great Japanese rival, Fuji, launched an aggressive expansion strategy in 1983, outbidding Kodak as official film for the 1984 Los Angeles Olympics.[77] It followed this with a price war in the 1990s that almost led to Kodak losing its number one slot in the film market. Kodak also fell behind with important innovations like the disposable camera.[78]

George Fisher, recruited from Motorola to become CEO in 1993, refocused the organization on the photography business. But he had to battle with the paradox that, despite the perception inside Kodak that the future would eventually be digital, people seemed anxious to postpone that future. Although Kodak had a technological lead in digital image technology, people were reluctant to introduce products that would cannibalize the traditional core business. As a result, although Kodak launched its first professional digital camera (with a 1.3 megapixel sensor) in 1991, and its first consumer model in 1994, other firms had greater early success with affordable digital cameras. Kodak was sidetracked by the Photo-CD system introduced in the 1990s, which stored pictures on compact discs for playback on TV screens, but sold poorly.[79]

Under Fisher and his successors there was renewed investment in silver halide photography, an industry which in fact continued to grow during the 1980s and 1990s, fuelled by improved and cheaper film and cameras, disposable cameras and the Advanced Photographic System that Kodak developed jointly with four of its Japanese competitors. This innovation followed Kodak's new strategy of using digital technology to complement the traditional medium, which at that stage still offered superior quality pictures. It invested heavily in websites and photo booths designed to allow people to produce high-quality prints (on Kodak media) of their digital snaps.

The company also hit upon another way to stretch the revenues from its established technologies. Noting that ownership of cameras in China was well below that in western countries, in 1998 it started a $1.2bn programme to acquire or ally with film manufacturers there and set up a network of over 8,000 Kodak Express outlets. It also moved some of its manufacturing to China and developed products, such as a $12 starter kit of a specially designed camera and four films, to stimulate interest in photography. The strategy appeared to pay off handsomely—in 2004 Kodak sold over 4 million film cameras in China, and predicted confidently that it would continue to sell many more even as the more sophisticated buyers moved to digital cameras—which, because PCs were not yet common, would generate business for Kodak's developers.[80]

Meanwhile, the firm had rethought its approach to the consumer market. In 2001, it launched the first of its EasyShare cameras, often sold with docking devices that enabled users to recharge their cameras and connect to printers quickly and easily. Although differentiated on their ease of use, they were aggressively priced, sometimes at 40 per cent below a Japanese camera of similar specification. In 2004, it took over from Sony as market leader in digital camera sales in the USA. With an eye to future revenues, Kodak had also launched a range of paper that it claimed, somewhat controversially, would produce durable and high-quality photographic prints on any manufacturer's printer.[81] ➡

> → Kodak had rediscovered the knack of connecting with consumers. But although the firm had also trimmed its cost base, rolling out the 'Kodak Operating System' (KOS) designed to eliminate all forms of waste,[82] and cutting over 25,000 jobs since 2001,[83] profits remained elusive. When the long-expected collapse of film sales finally started, with a 30 per cent decline in 2005, it occurred amongst China's newly sophisticated consumers as well as in Western markets.[84] The carefully crafted strategy to prolong the life of the silver halide business turned out to have a far shorter life than had been expected even 12 months previously.[85]
>
> Digital cameras, meanwhile, have turned into a commodity industry from which it is difficult to extract high margins, with many people content with relatively low-definition pictures, taken with mobile phones, that are never printed. Even the market for printing and finishing digital snaps has turned out to be far more competitive than the business of processing silver halide photos. So the returns on Kodak's investments in these important growth businesses are likely to be lower than the company had hoped for.
>
> In August 2006, Kodak announced its seventh successive quarterly loss, along with plans to transfer its camera manufacturing facilities to Flextronics, a contract manufacturer.[86]

● CHAPTER SUMMARY

This chapter has reviewed the environmental factors, the strategic challenges, and the strategic options that typically are found or employed in common industry contexts—in particular, those associated with different phases of the industry life-cycle:

- At the introductory stage of the life-cycle, key challenges relate to managing scarce cash and legitimizing both firm and industry in the eyes of customers, finance providers, and other key stakeholders. Firms typically avoid geographic diversification and costly investment in manufacturing to focus upon the needs of core markets. Differentiation on functionality is the norm, so that capabilities in innovation need to be built. Marketing strategies look to build legitimacy for the product as well as sell it.

- During the growth phase, the key challenges relate to gearing up output to meet demand, and achieving viable size, without sacrificing quality and reputation. Some firms may opt to expand the market with low-price offerings that offer reduced functionality and support. However, the norm is for firms to continue to differentiate—on reliability, customer service, reach, or functionality—and to build the necessary capabilities to support the chosen stance. Acquisitions may be used to build scale in production and distribution, while withdrawal is an option for firms whose entrepreneurial owners are not attracted by the task of managing a large organization in a maturing industry.

- In stable, 'progressive' mature industries with well-established rules of the game, the larger firms' primary challenge is to achieve and sustain cost advantage. Smaller firms must find and defend sustainable niches. Both types of organization confront the challenges of managing stakeholder expectations formed during the growth phase, and avoiding the dangers of inflexibility that come with stable environments. Firms may pursue strategies aimed at building reputational assets. Sometimes they will do so through product innovation, though process innovation is more important at this stage of the life-cycle, and most firms are likely to look hard for ways of changing their value chain to eliminate cost and waste.

- Creative mature industries are driven by the need to find blockbuster hit products and to manage the risks involved with funding multiple projects of which only a few will succeed. Firms may seek to reduce risk by specializing in particular segments, by copying successful hit products or by using technology to appraise the risks and benefits of proceeding with a given project. Large firms make use of alliances and networks to retain access to creative talent, and small ones to gain access to distribution and other complementary assets.

- Incumbent firms in mature industries undergoing turbulent change—radical change in product or process technology, or intermediating change in the way in which its members interact with customers and suppliers—face several problems. They are likely to have to cope with new entrants that will destabilize the industry and may introduce excess capacity. They must balance the attractions of investing quickly in the new approach so as to gain first-mover advantage with those of extracting as much value as possible from existing investments in traditional technology. The new entrants, on the other hand, face similar challenges to those found at the introductory phase of the life-cycle. Both types of firm face a choice between 'shaping the future' (taking the initiative in leading the industry forward), 'adapting to the future' (responding quickly to moves by pioneering competitors), and 'reserving the right to play'. New firms can consider attacking niches neglected by incumbents, or using new and efficient technology to undercut incumbents on price.

- Firms in declining industries face the challenge of obtaining the best return possible on their investments there. Allowing their assets to be bought by a firm with stronger commitment and better long-term prospects is one option. Firms may also seek to harvest their assets, to build a niche position or to move aggressively in search of market leadership.

- In hypercompetitive industries, firms confront the challenge that the basis of competitive advantage is constantly changing. They will require specialized capabilities—in product innovation or in marketing—to cope with the competitive position at any given moment, and also dynamic capabilities to keep those specialized capabilities up to date. Dominant firms may seek to build on their superior resources, stretching their competitors through frequent product upgrades, feints and spoiling actions, and aggressive pricing. They may also seek to lock customers in to their products. Other firms may seek to profit from niche markets while preparing to compete for superiority in the next generation of technology. Membership of alliances and networks can be important for both leaders and followers.

 Online Resource Centre
www.oxfordtextbooks.co.uk/orc/haberberg_rieple/

Visit the Online Resource Centre that accompanies this book to read more information relating to strategies in profit-making contexts.

● KEY SKILLS

The key skills you should have developed after reading this chapter are:

- the ability to anticipate the changes that will occur to a firm's environment over the course of the industry life-cycle, or in a hypercompetitive industry;

- the ability to develop strategic proposals that fit with the different stages of the industry life-cycle, including creative industries and mature industries undergoing turbulent change, and with hypercompetitive situations;

- the ability to evaluate the likely effectiveness of a strategic proposal relating to a firm confronting one of these industry contexts.

● REVIEW QUESTIONS

1. Identify the different factors about which firms can become complacent at each stage of the life-cycle, and the dangers that this can pose.

2. Would it be easier to manage a firm in the introductory or in the decline stage of an industry?

3. Price wars and shake-outs can occur even when an industry is growing quickly. Identify some of the factors that lead to them, and how they might be avoided.

4. Under what circumstances might you want to:

   ● advertise your competitors' products?

   ● start a price war?

   ● conceal a world-beating innovation?

   ● launch a product which has no chance of success?

   ● form an alliance with your bitterest competitors?

   ● try to convince people that your industry has no long-term prospects?

5. How important are the differences between creative and progressive mature industries?

● FURTHER READING

● Michael Porter's (1980) classic *Competitive Strategy*. New York: Free Press is the source for much traditional theory of firm behaviour through the life-cycle and of the strategies recommended at the different phases.

● Klepper, S. (1997). 'Industry life cycles'. *Industrial & Corporate Change*, 6/1: 119–43 is a readable and comprehensive summary of the empirical evidence on the life-cycle model.

● McGahan, A. (2004). 'How industries change'. *Harvard Business Review*, 82/10: 86–94 gives a contrasting view of the applicability of that model.

● Wiltbank, R., Dew, N., Read, S., and Sarasvathy, S. (2006). 'What to do next? The case for non-predictive strategy'. *Strategic Management. Journal*, 27/10: 981–98 gives an up-to-date overview of how to develop strategies in turbulent environments. It is also an object lesson in how to make a learned article easy to read.

● D'Aveni, R. (1995). 'Coping with hypercompetition: Utilizing the new 7S framework'. *Academy of Management Executive*, 9/3: 45–57 is an interesting article with some useful strategic suggestions, and illustrates how excited even academics can become when they think they have discovered a new phenomenon.

● McNamara, G., Vaaler, P., and Devers, C. (2003). 'Same as it ever was: The search for evidence of increasing hypercompetition'. *Strategic Management Journal*, 24/3: 261–78 is an example of how good researchers use data to cut through hype.

● REFERENCES

Abernathy, W. and Utterback, J. (1978). 'Patterns of industrial innovation'. *Technology Review*, 80/7: 40–7.

Agarwal, R., Sarkar, M., and Echambadi, R. (2002). 'The conditioning effect of time on firm survival: an industry life cycle approach'. *Academy of Management Journal*, 45/5: 971–94.

Aldrich, H. and Auster, E. (1986). 'Even dwarfs started small: liabilities of size and age and their strategic implications'. In Staw, B. M. and Cummings, L. L. (eds), *Research in Organizational Behavior*. Greenwich, CT: JAI Press, ch. 8: 165–98.

Anand, J. and Singh, H. (1997). 'Asset redeployment, acquisitions and corporate strategy in declining industries'. *Strategic Management Journal*, 18: 99–118.

Audretsch, D. (1997). 'Technical regimes, industrial demography and the evolution of industrial structures'. *Industrial and Corporate Change*, 6/1: 49–82.

Baden-Fuller, C. and Stopford, J. M. (1992). *Rejuvenating the Mature Business: The Competitive Challenge*. Cambridge, MA: Harvard Business School Press.

Baum, J. and Oliver, C. (1991). 'Institutional linkages and organizational mortality'. *Administrative Science Quarterly*, 36: 187–218.

Berthon, P. and Hulbert, J. (2003). 'Marketing in metamorphosis: breaking boundaries'. *Business Horizons*, 46/3: 31–40.

Bogner, W. C. and Barr, P. (2000). 'Making sense in hypercompetitive environment: a cognitive exploration for the persistence of high velocity competition'. *Organization Science*, 11/2: 212–26.

Brown, S. and Eisenhardt, K. (1997). 'The art of continuous change: linking complexity theory and time-paced evolution in relentlessly shifting organizations'. *Administrative Science Quarterly*, 42/1: 1–34.

Caves, R. (2000). *Creative Industries: Contracts between Commerce and Creativity*. Cambridge, MA: Harvard University Press.

Copeland, M. (2006). 'The mighty micro-multinational'. *Business 2.0*, 7/6: 106–14.

Courtney, H., Kirkland, J., and Vigeurie, P. (1997). 'Strategy under uncertainty'. *Harvard Business Review*, 75/6: 67–79.

Craig, T. (1996). 'The Japanese beer wars: Initiating and responding to hypercompetition in new product development'. *Organization Science*, 7/3: 302–21.

D'Aveni, R. (1995a). *Hypercompetitive Rivalries*. New York: Simon & Schuster.

D'Aveni, R. (1995b). 'Coping with hypercompetition: utilizing the new 7S framework'. *Academy of Management Executive*, 9/3: 45–57.

Dunne T., Roberts M., and Samuelson L. (1989). 'Patterns of firm entry and exit in US manufacturing industries'. *RAND Journal of Economics*, 19: 495–515.

Eisenhardt, K. and Brown, S. (1998). 'Time pacing: competing in markets that won't stand still'. *Harvard Business Review*, 76/2: 59–69.

Filatotchev, I. and Toms, S. (2003). 'Corporate governance, strategy and survival in a declining industry: a study of UK cotton textile companies'. *Journal of Management Studies*, 40/4: 895–920.

Fine, C. (1996). 'Industry clockspeed and competency chain design: an introductory essay'. *Proceedings of the 1996 Manufacturing and Service Operations Management Conference*, Dartmouth College, Hanover, NH, June 24–5.

Gersick, C. (1994). 'Pacing strategic change: the case of a new venture'. *Academy of Management Journal*, 37/1: 9–45.

Hammer, M. and Champy, J. (1993). *Re-engineering the Corporation: A Manifesto for Business Revolution*. London: Nicholas Brealey.

Hannan, M. and Freeman, J. (1984). 'Structural inertia and organizational change'. *American Sociological Review*, 49: 149–64.

Hanssen-Bauer, J. and Snow, C. (1996). 'Responding to hypercompetition: the structure and process of a regional learning network organization'. *Organization Science*, 7/4: 413–27.

Harvey, M., Novicevic, M., and Kiessling, T. (2001). 'Hypercompetition and the future of global management in the twenty-first century'. *Thunderbird International Business Review*, 43/5: 599–616.

Hayes, R. (1985). 'Strategic planning: forward in reverse?' *Harvard Business Review*, 63/6: 111–19.

Hayes, R. and Weelwright, S. (1979). 'The dynamics of process-product life cycles'. *Harvard Business Review*, 57/2: 23–32.

Henderson, R. and Clark, K. (1990). 'Architectural innovation: the reconfiguration of existing product technologies and the failure of established firms'. *Administrative Science Quarterly*, 35: 9–30.

Hofer, C. (1975). 'Toward a contingency theory of business strategy'. *Academy of Management Journal*, 18: 784–810.

Kim, W. C. and Mauborgne, R. (1997). 'Value innovation: the strategic logic of high growth'. *Harvard Business Review*, 75/1: 103–12.

Klepper, S. (1996). 'Entry, exit, growth, and innovation over the product life cycle'. *American Economic Review*, 86/3: 562–83.

Klepper, S. (1997). 'Industry life cycles'. *Industrial & Corporate Change*, 6/1: 119–43.

Klepper, S. (2002). 'Firm survival and the evolution of oligopoly'. *RAND Journal of Economics*, 33/1: 37–61.

Klepper, S. and Graddy, E. (1990). 'The evolution of new industries and the determinants of market structure'. *RAND Journal of Economics*, 21/1: 27–44.

Kodama, M. (2003). 'Strategic innovation in traditional big business: case studies of two Japanese companies'. *Organization Studies*, 24/2: 235–68.

McGahan, A. (2000). 'How industries evolve'. *Business Strategy Review*, 11/3: 1–16.

McGahan, A. (2004). 'How industries change'. *Harvard Business Review*, 82/10: 86–94.

McGahan, A. and Silverman, B. (2001). 'How does innovative activity change as industries mature?' *International Journal of Industrial Organization*, 19/7: 1141–60.

McNamara, G., Vaaler, P., and Devers, C. (2003). 'Same as it ever was: The search for evidence of increasing hypercompetition'. *Strategic Management Journal*, 24/3: 261–78.

Nault, B. and Vandenbosch, M. (1996). 'Eating your own lunch: protection through preemption'. *Organization Science*, 7/3: 342.

Nichols, N. (1994). 'Scientific management at Merck: an interview with CFO Judy Lewent'. *Harvard Business Review*, 72/1: 88–98.

Okhuysen, G. and Eisenhardt, K. (2002). 'Integrating knowledge in groups: how formal interventions enable flexibility'. *Organization Science*, 13/4: 370–86.

Okhuysen, G. and Waller, M. (2002). 'Focusing on midpoint transitions: an analysis of boundary conditions'. *Academy of Management Journal*, 45/5: 1056–65.

Porter, M. (1980). *Competitive Strategy*. New York: Free Press.

Porter, M. (1983). 'The technological dimension of competitive strategy'. *Research on Technological Innovation, Management Policy*. Greenwich, CT: JAI Press.

Rice, J. and Galvin, P. (2006). 'Alliance patterns during industry life cycle emergence: the case of Ericsson and Nokia'. *Technovation*, 26/3: 384–95.

Rindova, V. and Kotha, S. (2001). 'Continuous "morphing": competing through dynamic capabilities, form, and function'. *Academy of Management Journal*, 44/6: 1263–80.

St John, C., Pouder, R., and Cannon, A. (2003) 'Environmental uncertainty and product-process life cycles: a multi-level interpretation of change over time'. *Journal of Management Studies*, 40/2: 513–41.

Simons, K. (2003). 'Industry life cycles and their causes'. *Academy of Management Proceedings*, I1–I6.

Souza, G., Bayus, B., and Wagner, H. (2004). 'New-product strategy and industry clockspeed'. *Management Science*, 50/4: 537–49.

Sutton, J. (1997). 'Gibrat's legacy'. *Journal of Economic Literature*, 35: 40–59.

Swaminathan, A. (1995). 'The proliferation of specialist organizations in the American wine industry, 1941–1990'. *Administrative Science Quarterly*, 40/4: 653–80.

Thomas, L. G. (1996). 'The two faces of competition: dynamic resourcefulness and the hypercompetitive shift'. *Organization Science*, 7/3: 221–42.

Utterback, J. and Abernathy, W. (1975). 'A dynamic model of process and product innovation'. *Omega*, 3: 639–56.

Van de Ven, A. and Poole, M. S. (1995). 'Explaining development and change in organizations'. *Academy of Management Review*, 20: 510–40.

Van de Ven, A. and Poole, M. S. (2005). 'Alternative approaches for studying organizational change'. *Organization Studies*, 26/9: 1377–404.

Volberda, H. (1996). 'Toward the flexible form: how to remain vital in hypercompetitive environments'. *Organization Science*, 7/4: 359–74.

Wright, M., Pruthi, S., and Lockett, A. (2005). 'International venture capital research: From cross-country comparisons to crossing borders'. *International Journal of Management Reviews*, 7/3: 135–65.

End-of-chapter Case Study 13.1 **Mittal Steel and the global steel industry**

Mittal Steel's Ostrava steelmaking plant. *Mittal Steel*

Steel is an important component of many of the objects we take for granted: buildings (girders, pipes, and reinforcement for concrete), cars (chassis and bodies), ships, and washing machines. Although it has been partially replaced for some applications by lighter metals, such as aluminium, and modern composite materials, such as carbon fibre, steel remains fundamental to economic activity, and demand fluctuates with the state of the global economy.

Steel production processes

Steel has been made since 200 BC, and the essentials of the process for the mass production of steel from iron ore, coke, and limestone date back to the 1850s. This does not mean that the industry has been stable, however. Metallurgists are constantly seeking new combinations of steel with chromium, nickel, and other metals to produce alloys with greater strength, resistance to corrosion, or other desirable properties. Some 70 per cent of the steels used in automobile manufacture in 2006 had been developed in the previous 10 years.[87] And the process of steel-making has undergone several radical changes.

Traditional methods of making steel involve large, vertically integrated complexes in which iron ore is converted to molten iron, which is then made into steel and cast or rolled into slabs, bars, or sheets, according to the desired end use. Sometimes the coke needed for steel-making is produced at the same site.

The investment required for an integrated steelworks, and the large numbers of people employed, meant that the companies who owned them needed to be large. Size also assisted employers in negotiations with the trades unions that played a prominent role in many countries' steel industries. This meant that the industry consolidated around a few firms in any given country.

These large firms absorbed one major change in steel-making practice, when the 'basic oxygen' process, invented in Austria in 1952, displaced the century-old Bessemer and open-hearth processes. However, they found it more difficult to cope with competitors that produced steel by melting scrap metal in an electric arc furnace. These 'mini-mills' were viable at a much lower scale than integrated steelworks, cost far less to build, and could be located close to the customers. They were operated by smaller, nimbler firms, with flexible labour practices, and as a result their costs were far lower.[88]

Turbulence and consolidation

Initially mini-mills only offered the lowest grades of steel, but they gradually acquired the ability to compete with sophisticated products in the larger firms' traditional markets. By 2005, they accounted for about one-third of steel production. Competition from mini-mills and more modern integrated producers in countries such as South Korea led to a difficult time for large firms in Europe and the USA. They fought back by increasing productivity, ➜

→ but this only increased the degree of over-capacity in an industry where demand stagnated through the 1980s and 1990s. Eighteen American steel firms, including LTV, the third largest, filed for bankruptcy between 1998 and 2001.[89] In Europe there was a wave of cross-border consolidation, involving the formation in 1999 of Corus, a merger of British and Dutch steelmakers, and in 2001 of Arcelor, combining large producers from France, Spain, and Luxembourg.[90]

The industry was transformed by a sudden surge in demand in 2003, driven by strong economic expansion, and a construction boom, in China. China's own steel industry, although the world's largest, could not fulfil that demand. By 2005, the price of steel had trebled from its 2001 level, and steel firms worldwide returned to profit, even though the costs of their major inputs rose sharply. However, it was unlikely that China would continue to import steel in such quantities; while its own domestic capacity continued to increase, many observers doubted that its economy could sustain its current rate of expansion.[91]

Mittal Steel: the early days

If anyone in 1980 had suggested that the leading firm in the steel industry in 2005 would be Indian, they would have been considered mad. The traditional industrial powers of the USA and western Europe (Germany being particularly strong in steelmaking) saw competition as coming from Japan and, increasingly, industrializing countries such as South Korea. It was indeed a Korean firm, POSCO, which had constructed the world's most efficient integrated steelworks, learning from the mistakes of older producers to optimize location and layout.[92]

Mittal Steel had started life in the 1970s as part of Ispat Industries, an Indian industrial group with small-scale steel-making operations in Bangalore and Kolkata. Expansion in India itself was difficult because of that country's strict regulation of the industry, so Ispat had hit upon Indonesia as a country with expansion potential. The market for construction steel—the basic product of early mini-mills—was unregulated there, and Ispat was able to grow quickly. However, when Lakshmi Mittal, son of Ispat's founder, was sent out to run the operation, he found that the Indonesian operation was having problems in acquiring sufficient good-quality scrap to feed its operations.[93]

The only alternative to scrap as a raw material was directly reduced iron (DRI). Although this had a number of advantages over scrap—it contained fewer impurities and required less energy for conversion into steel—it was deeply unfashionable in the industry. This was mainly because it could only be produced economically where there were plentiful supplies of iron ore and natural gas. Mittal located one such source, Iscott (the Iron and Steel Company of Trinidad and Tobago), and signed a long-term deal with it in 1981. Despite having a large customer for one of its main outputs, however, Iscott found it difficult to make profits in the industry climate of the 1980s. Ispat was able to lease the loss-making plant from its government owners—and was then able to make it profitable within 12 months. The plant was acquired for $101m, and renamed Caribbean Ispat, in 1994.[94]

Growth in a mature industry

Ispat's success in turning around Iscott without controversial redundancies made it welcome in several other countries burdened with loss-making steel operations. The first was Mexico, whose government invited Ispat to take on the chronically unprofitable Sibalsa plant, like Iscott a producer of DRI alongside finished steel. Operating at 25 per cent capacity at the time of acquisition, the renamed Ispat Mexicana achieved 110 per cent capacity utilization within four years under Mittal's management. Further successful turnarounds, in places like Canada and New Zealand, followed.[95] One of the most spectacular was the 1995 revival of Ispat Karmet, a Kazakh company that had been the third largest steel plant in the former Soviet Union. This was achieved within one year, without redundancies and while maintaining all the social services (such as a hospital and TV station) that were commonly supplied by former communist enterprises.[96]

In 1994, Ispat's steel businesses were split into two new companies: LNM Holdings, a private firm (LNM are Mittal's initials) that held the operations in central and eastern Europe and Ispat International, which incorporated the other plants.[97] They were formally separated from the parent company, their domicile was moved from Indonesia to London, and in 1997 Ispat International listed on the New York and Amsterdam stock exchanges, raising $776m, a record for a steel company.[98]

Becoming number one

Ispat International and LNM were by now present in the US and European markets. They had started to penetrate the USA and Canada through a deal with the venerable American company Wheeling-Pittsburg, which enabled Ispat to market its excess Mexican output there.[99] The group made further acquisitions throughout Europe and the rest of the world during the 1990s.[100] With its largest deal to date, the $1.4bn acquisition of Inland Steel in 1998, it clearly became a force to be reckoned with.[101]

Two further transforming deals were in the pipeline. The first was the 2004 acquisition of International Steel Group, an American company that had bought up and revived the fortunes of a number of the American plants laid low by competition from mini-mills. This $4.5bn deal was accompanied by a buy-out of LNM by Ispat International. The merged entity, renamed Mittal Steel, was by some distance the largest producer of steel on the planet.[102]
→

→ The second, and perhaps most audacious deal, was the 2005 bid for Arcelor, the second-largest competitor. However, it also fitted with Mittal's vision of a steel industry dominated by around five global competitors with an annual capacity in excess of 100 million tonnes of steel. The benefits of this were not so much production economies of scale, which are found, if at all, at the level of the plant, rather than the firm. They related more to the extra power that large firms had to resist price rises from suppliers of iron ore and other key inputs.[103]

The two companies' geographic spreads and product mixes were highly complementary, and a merger would give Arcelor access to Mittal's considerable reserves of iron ore. The acquisition was nonetheless fiercely contested by Arcelor's management, who favoured a tie-up with Severstal, a Russian competitor, to create a firm larger than Mittal. However, Arcelor's shareholders favoured the Mittal offer which, after several weeks of legal manoeuvring, was accepted. Lakshmi Mittal was named chairman of the new firm, Arcelor Mittal and shortly afterwards took the position of CEO as well.[104]

Inside Mittal Steel

When Mittal acquired the Dabrowa Gornicza steel plant in Poland, it sent in a 15-person team of managers, many Indian, headed by a man involved in two previous acquisitions, which quickly restructured the company's finances.[105] However, the details of what it then did to return that plant to profitability, as it has many others, remain unknown. Invariably, however, Mittal seems to be able to find ways to raise output—thereby reducing unit costs, since a steel plant carries substantial fixed costs—and also increase the proportion of high-margin products in the mix. Lakshmi Mittal is reported to play a significant personal role in defining the right product mix—his knowledge of the world steel market is probably unsurpassed—and in identifying potential leaders amongst the managers in the firms he acquires.[106]

The group has a simple, geographically based, divisionalized structure, that is not noteworthy in any way. It does, however, have a long-standing Knowledge Sharing Programme, which gives its different plants access to one another's managers for problem-solving and dissemination of best practice. A number of its plants around the world have advanced expertise in specific steel-making technologies, and an ex-consultant has been hired to help share these around the corporation. Mittal's management claims that this has been a major factor in the company's success, with one eastern European executive estimating that being part of the Mittal group reduces his operation's costs by 10 per cent. Mittal hosts a conference call each Monday morning for managers worldwide to discuss market and performance issues, which may result in customers being identified for surplus output, or in supplies of coal or iron ore being diverted where they are most needed.[107]

One competence may relate to the ability quickly to identify production bottlenecks and the investment needed to clear them. This was a factor in returning Iscott to profitability, something which teams from the USA and Germany had failed to achieve. The revival of Ispat Karmet was aided by investment, part-funded by the World Bank and European Bank for Reconstruction and Development,[108] in up-to-date technologies that more than halved the production cost of a tonne of steel. It spends its money judiciously on under-performing assets, a cheaper way of buying capacity than building it from scratch. And its expertise in DRI production, built over several decades, may be difficult for any competitor to emulate.[109] As scrap prices rise in line with demand for steel, the value of this expertise is likely to increase.

Case study questions

1. How well does the steel industry fit the life-cycle model? Allocate rough dates to the different life-cycle phases identifiable in the case.

2. How was Ispat/Mittal Steel able to grow so strongly in a mature industry? How well did its strategies fit with those normally recommended for this type of industry?

3. Where in the life-cycle is the steel industry at the end of the case? Appraise Mittal Steel's strategic moves in 2004–2006 in the light of your conclusion.

● NOTES

1 The analysis in Sections 12.4.1–12.4.3 draws heavily on the pioneering work of Michael Porter who discusses strategic options at the various stages of the industry life-cycle in his 1980 book *Competitive Strategy*.

2 The arguments as to why size is important at different life-cycle phases are summarized by Agarwal et al. (2002). The different ways in which industries can mature are discussed by Klepper and Graddy (1990), Klepper (1997), and McGahan (2000, 2004).

3 The importance of the emergence of a dominant design in an industry's evolution was pointed out by Abernathy and Utterback (1978).

4 St John et al. (2003) make some interesting observations about the difficulties of establishing shared objectives at various stages of the life-cycle. The importance of natural rhythm ('time pacing') to an organization was noted by Gersick (1994) and Eisenhardt and Brown (1998), and developed further by Okhuysen and Eisenhardt (2002), Okhuysen and Waller (2002), and Kodama (2003). Hannan and Freeman (1984) also suggest that a degree of inertia is helpful to a firm. The concept of an industry clockspeed appears to originate from Fine (1996).

5 See Copeland (2006) for some interesting examples.

6 Glasserman, P. (2000). 'The quest for precision through Value-at-Risk'. *Financial Times*, 16 January: Survey 6.

7 This observation comes from Eisenhardt and Brown (1998), although research using simulations (Souza et al., 2004) indicates that there may be situations in which alternative ways of organizing may be preferable.

8 For examples of the influence and respect these firms command, see Warner, M. (1998). 'Kleiner Perkins: inside the Silicon Valley money machine', *Fortune*, 26 October: 110–18; Durman, P. (2006). 'The Brit with the Midas internet touch'. *Sunday Times*, 12 November: Business 6; Stone, B. (2006). 'The color of money: how green is their Silicon Valley? The redoubtable venture capitalists of Kleiner Perkins are now betting $200 million on environmentally friendly technology'. *Newsweek*, 13 November: E10. For a more general review of the venture capital industry, see Wright et al. (2005).

9 <http://www.sony.net/Products/felica>, accessed 17 November 2006, reporting on contents of Japanese language press release of 15 October 2005. *Al-Bawaba News* (2006). 'Booz Allen Hamilton: mobile payment, a successful model for the Middle East'. 2 August.

10 *Financial Times* (2005). 'Mobile phone that puts cash out of business'. *Ft.com*, 15 December. *Economist* (2005a). 'In the very near future'. 10 December.

11 Sambandaraksa, D. (2006). 'Cashless society; Hong Kong's Octopus Cards wants to show Thailand how to do smart cards'. *Bangkok Post*, 29 March: D1; Goff, S. (2006). 'TfL drops proposal to expand Oyster card use'. *Financial Times*, 1 May: 4.

12 Tsai, M. (2006). 'Technology (a special report): telecommunications: what's a phone for? In Asia, probably a lot more than you can imagine'. *Wall Street Journal*, 19 June: R12. Shimbun, A. (2006). 'With a wave of a handset, people can use their cellphones to do just about anything they could do with a cash card or credit card, at least in theory'. 28 June; Nakamoto, M. (2005). 'Wireless wallet waits for grand opening'. *Financial Times*, 15 June: Surveys IM11.

13 Nikkei Report (2006). 'USC develops reader module for different contactless smart cards'. 15 February; Nakamoto (2005) op. cit.

14 Economist (2005a) op. cit.; *Financial Times* (2005) op. cit; Nikkei Report (2006) op. cit.

15 <http://www.viamichelin.com/viamichelin/gbr/tpl/mag4/art20050501/htm/tech-puce-felica.htm>, accessed 20 May 2005.

16 Nakamoto (2005) op. cit.; Kyodo News (2004). 'Sony to release low-cost card issuing system using FeliCa tech'. 13 December.

17 For empirical evidence that organizational survival rates improve with size, see Audretsch (1997), Dunne et al. (1989), Hannan and Freeman (1984), and Sutton (1997). For theoretical arguments as to why this shuld be so, see in addition Aldrich and Auster (1986), Baum and Oliver (1991), and Agarwal et al. (2002).

18 *Economist* (2005b). 'The future, just around the bend'. *Economist Technology Quarterly*, 12 March: 33–4.

19 Rivlin, G. (2006). 'Wallflower at the web party'. *New York Times*, 15 October: 1; Fast Company (2007). 'A cautionary tale : rumors of Facebook's refusal to sell to Yahoo set off a chorus of predictions that it would repeat Friendster's fall from grace'. 13 April: 80.

20 Rivlin (2006) op. cit.; Potts, L. (2004). 'Won't you be my Friendster?' *Albequerque Journal*, 15 February: E8.

21 Rivlin (2006) op. cit.

22 Potts (2004) op. cit.; Tedeschi, R. (2004). 'Social networks: will users pay to get friends?' *New York Times*, 9 February: 1; Rivlin (2006) op. cit.; Fast Company (2007) op. cit.; Chow, C. (2005). 'Is Friendster dead?' *Straits Times*, 4 September; Nolan, C. (2006a). 'Friendster showered with $3.1m for makeover'. *Dow Jones Newswires*, 19 May.

23 Rivlin (2006) op. cit.; Noguchi, Y. (2006). 'In teens' web world, MySpace is so last year: social sites find fickle audience'. *Washington Post*, 29 October: A01; Nolan (2006a) op. cit.

24 Levine, R. (2006). 'MySpace aims for a global audience, and finds some stiff competition'. *New York Times*, 7 November: 3.

25 Noguchi (2006) op. cit.

26 Durman, P. (2006). 'Network sites use girl power'. *Sunday Times*, 10 December: 3.7; Levine (2006) op. cit.; Rosmarin, R. (2007). 'TheirSpace'. *Forbes Asia*, 3/3, 12 February: 62b; Vara, V. (2006). 'MySpace has large circle of friends, but rivals' cliques are growing too'. *Wall Street Journal*, 2 October: B1.

27 Foley, S. and Shah, S. (2006). 'Murdoch gamble pays off as MySpace takes over'. *The Independent*, 11 August: 50; Garrity, B. (2006). 'MySpace turns up the volume on MP3; labels leery'. *Reuters News*, 11 September.

28 Nolan, C. (2006b). 'Venture firms help fund social sites'. *Wall Street Journal*, 21 September; B2D; Letzing, J. (2006). 'Something ventured: VCs digesting proposed Patent Act'. *Dow Jones News Service*, 25 October; Fowler, G. (2007). 'Friendster didn't die: the site lives on in Southeast Asia'. *Wall Street Journal*, 6 June: B1.

29 The typology of industries that follows was identified by Anita McGahan (2000, 2004). She is also the source of the estimates of the relative frequency of the different models.

30 For an interesting discussion of the implications of intermediating change, see Berthon and Hulbert (2003).

31 This was noted by Klepper (1996, 2002).

32 These patterns of behaviour among smaller competitors have been observed by Agarwal et al. (2002), McGahan (2000), Simons (2003), and Swaminathan (1995).

33 This style of 'business process re-engineering' was fashionable in the 1990s—see Hammer and Champy (1993).

34 For a number of striking examples, see Baden-Fuller and Stopford (1992).

35 See Nichols (1994).

36 For a detailed analysis of the working of creative industries, see Caves (2000).

37 See Kim and Mauborgne (1997) and McGahan (2000, 2004).

38 Lashinsky, A. (2005). 'Saving face at Sony'. *Fortune*: 49. See also Nakamoto, M. (2005) : Sony battles to make headway in networked world. *Ft.com*, 26 January ; Woods, G. (2006). 'Sony cracks open new book with Reader'. *The Toronto Star*, 20 February: C05.

39 Courtney et al. (1997).

40 See Brown and Eisenhardt (1997) and Hayes (1985).

41 This was noted by Klepper (1997). But see Henderson and Clark (1990) for a well-known counter-example.

42 Klepper (1997).

43 *Economist* (2006a). 'Flight of the bumblebee', 29 June.

44 The facts underlying this Real-life Application are drawn from O'Connell, D. (2006). 'Journey's end for the package tour'. *Sunday Times*, 3 December: 3.7 and Evans, N. (2001). 'The UK air inclusive-tour industry: a reassessment of the competitive positioning of the independent sector'. *International Journal of Tourism Research*, 3/6: 477–91.

45 This insight came from Porter's collaborator Kathryn Rudie Harrigan. See Porter (1980).

46 Filatotchev and Toms (2003) noted the positive effects of diversification in their study of the decline of the UK cotton textile industry, while Anand and Singh (1997) noted its negative aspects while examining the US defence industry.

47 Filatotchev and Toms (2003).

48 See <http://alfreddunhill.net>, accessed 29 July 2007.

49 The concept and basic theory of hypercompetition were developed by Richard D'Aveni (1995a, 1995b). Bogner and Barr (2000) discuss the cognitive reasons why hypercompetitive behaviour persists over time. Harvey et al. (2001) is one example of a paper that claims that it is increasingly becoming the norm, while McNamara et al. (2003) provides evidence it is not.

50 See Craig (1996), and also Wagstyl, S. (1988). 'How Japan went "dry" with more alcohol'. *Financial Times*, 28 July: 12; Miller, K. (1991). 'Can Asahi brew up another blockbuster'. *Business Week*, 4 March: 41; Kilburn, D. (1991). 'Marketing Week reports on the highly competitive beer market'.

Marketing Week, 6 September: 32; *Economist* (1996). 'Japanese beer—how Kirin lost its sparkle'. 14 September.

51 See Craig (1996) and Thomas (1996) for explorations of the defining characteristics of hypercompetition.

52 The cycle of changing competition in hypercompetitive industries is described by D'Aveni (1995a). The distinction between specialized and dynamic capabilities was made by Craig (1996).

53 See Nault and Vandenbosch (1996).

54 Markoff, J. (1999). 'Silicon Valley's awesome look at new Sony toy'. *New York Times,* 19 March: 1; Arthur, C. (1999). 'Sony blinks first in game makers' war of nerves'. *The Independent,* 14 October: 8; *Economist* (2001). 'Cast aside'. 25 January; Guth, R. and Tran, K. (2001). 'Game battle claims a casualty'. *Wall Street Journal,* 31 January: B1.

55 Volberda (1996) established the importance of flexible forms, and Rindova and Kotha (2001) gave an extensively researched example of continuous patching by prominent firms in the internet search industry.

56 *Economist* (1995a). 'Singin' the Blues'. 5 November: 87.

57 See Hanssen-Bauer and Snow (1996) for a Norwegian example.

58 Kirny, K. (2006). 'Open source programs offer alternatives to Microsoft Office'. *San Francisco Chronicle,* 27 February.

59 Tran, K. (2001). 'How Microsoft hopes to win with Xbox'. *Wall Street Journal,* 31 January: B1.

60 *Personal Computer World* (1999). 'AMD K7 and Intel: K7 heaven'. 1 September: 122.

61 *Economist* (1993). 'Special: Intel'. 3 July; Simon, M. (2001). 'Profile/Jerry Sanders/Silicon Valley's tough guy'. *San Francisco Chronicle,* 4 October: E1.

62 *Economist* (1993) op. cit.; Simon (2001) op. cit.; Kehoe, L. (1992). 'Intel files patent suit to block Cyrix challenge'. *Financial Times,* 30 March: 2; Yoder, S. (1992). 'Intel and AMD gear up for showdown'. *Wall Street Journal Europe,* 31 January: 4.

63 Kehoe, L. (1998). 'AMD challenge for chip market'. *Financial Times,* 23 September: 31; Eden, S. (2000). 'AMD battles back, bests bad reputation'. *Dow Jones News Service,* 13 March.

64 Iwata, E, (2001). 'AMD digs in for tough fight with Intel'. *USA Today,* 18 October: B.03.

65 *Economist* (2004a). 'The 64-bit battle: the future of chips'. 28 February.

66 Gardiner, B. (2007). 'AMD gains market share, but not profit'. Extremetech.com, 1 February; *Calgary Herald* (2007). 'Intel loses market share to rival AMD'. 31 January.

67 See, for example, Randazzese, V. (2001). 'Athlon edges past Pentium 4'. *Computer Reseller News,* 12 February: 4; Mclaughlin, L. (2003). 'AMD's latest is a winner'. *PC World,* 1 April; Aklass, C. (2005). 'Athlon thrashes Pentium as Intel moves goalposts'. *Personal Computer World,* 1 August: 16.

68 Clark, D. and Lawton, C. (2006). 'Dell to use AMD chips in some servers'. *Wall Street Journal,* 19 May: A3; *M2 Presswire* (2007). 'Trading alert for Advanced Micro Devices, Inc'. 30 May.

69 Schofield, J. (2006). 'Intel raises the bar as AMD drops prices in chip battle'. *Guardian,* 27 July; Krazit, T. (2006). 'Intel's Core 2 Duo delivers on promises'. *ZDNet UK,* 17 July; Kirkpatrick, D. (2007). 'The joy of blood feuds'. *Fortune,* 19 March.

70 Avery, S. (2006). 'The chips are down'. *The Globe and Mail,* 29 July: B5.

71 Kirkpatrick (2007) op. cit.

72 Chakravarty, S. and Feldman, A. (1993). 'The road not taken (Kay Whitmore's management of Eastman Kodak)'. *Forbes,* 30 August: 40.

73 Jackson, T. (1995). 'Pictured from a new angle: Eastman Kodak'. *Financial Times,* 11 May: 21; Chakravarty and Feldman (1993) op. cit.

74 Chakravarty and Feldman (1993) op. cit.

75 Ibid.

76 Jackson (1995) op. cit.; *Independent on Sunday* (1995). 'Kodak gambles all on its digital vision'. 2 April.

77 Chakravarty and Feldman (1993) op. cit.

78 Dobbin, B. (2003). 'Kodak struggles to find its focus in fast-paced digital photography era'. *Associated Press Newswires,* 25 July; *Financial Times* (1997). 'Kodak sees need for family values'. 15 November: 17; Chakravarty and Feldman (1993) op. cit.

79 Hamm, S. and Symonds, C. (2006). 'Mistakes made on the road to innovation: led by CEO Antonio M. Perez, Kodak is struggling to reinvent its business model. It's not alone'. *BusinessWeek,*

27 November: 26; *Independent On Sunday* (1995) op. cit.; *Economist* (1994). 'Is Kodak still out of focus?' 28 May.

80 Graham, J. (2004). 'Kodak says strategy to shift to digital is working: outsourcing part of plan'. *USA Today*, 23 September: B.06; *Dow Jones International News* (2004). 'Kodak: now specifically designing for China as mkt grows'. 28 October; Collier, A. (2004). 'Kodak snaps up China opportunities: aggressive investment and focus on low-end cameras are paying dividends'. *South China Morning Post*, 1 November: 2; Taylor, S. (2005). 'Kodak sees China film sales offsetting global drop'. *Reuters*, 19 May.

81 Graham (2004) op. cit.; Kher, U. (2005). 'Getting Kodak to focus'. *Time*, 14 February: B10; Bulkeley, W. (2005). 'In digital age, a clash over fading photos'. *Wall Street Journal*, 1 April: B1; Dobbin, B. (2005). 'Kodak surges ahead of Japanese giants in US digital-camera market'. *Associated Press Newswires*, 3 February.

82 Kher (2005) op. cit.

83 Hamm and Symonds (2006) op. cit.; Bulkeley, W. (2006). 'Kodak's loss widens as revenue declines 8.8%'. *Wall Street Journal*, 26 August: B10.

84 Dickie, M. (2006). 'China rejects its role in a corporate escape plan'. *Financial Times*, 26 January: 15; Hamm and Symonds (2006) op. cit.

85 Taylor, S. (2005). 'Kodak sees China film sales offsetting global drop'. *Reuters News*, 19 May; Yee, A. (2006). 'Banishing the negative: how Kodak is developing its blueprint for a digital transformation'. *Financial Times*, 26 January: 15.

86 Bulkeley (2006) op. cit.; China Daily Information Company (2006). 'Kodak shifts digital camera production to Flextronics'. *Industry Updates*, 3 August.

87 <http://www.uksteel.org.uk/>, accessed 1 July 2007.

88 The UK steel industry website <http://www.uksteel.org> has details of steel-making processes. See also <http://www.p2pays.org/ref/01/text/00778/chapter2.htm>, accessed 29 July 2007.

89 *Economist* (2001). 'A tricky business'. 28 June.

90 Gow, D. (1999). 'Steel rebranding corus rolls out'. *Guardian*, 1 October: 27; Alden, E. and Marsh, P. (2001). 'A lot to hammer out'. *Financial Times*, 17 December.

91 *Economist* (2005c). 'Steelmakers on a roll, until the next glut'. *Economist Global Agenda*, 28 November.

92 Baseline (2002). 'POSCO: The next big steel'. 1/7; Bremner, B., Ihlwan, M. and Roberts, D. (2004). 'One sharp steelmaker'. *BusinessWeek*, 30 August: 66.

93 *Economist* (1995b). 'India's Mittal-stand'. 12 August; Jones, B. (2004). 'Lakshmi Mittal's ring of steel'. *Management Today*, 5 February: 38.

94 *Economist* (1995b) op. cit.; Jones (2004) op. cit.; James C. (1988). 'Ispat leases Trinidad State Steel Plant'. *Financial Times*, 27 October : 38.

95 <http://www.mittalsteel.com/Company/History/#>, accessed 1 July 2007.

96 Ibid.; Timmons. H. (2004). 'A financier finds the future in an old industry'. *The Hindu*, 1 November: 17; Reed, S. and Arndt, M. (2004). 'The Raja of steel'. *Businessweek*, 20 December: 50.

97 <http://www.mittalsteel.com/Company/History/#>, accessed 1 July 2007; Jones (2004) op. cit.

98 *Economic Times* (1998). 'Mittals smoke peace pipe, may work under one umbrella'. 24 March; Haflich, F. (1995). 'Sittard named head of burgeoning Ispat'. *American Metal Market*, 14 September: 3; Datamonitor (2004). 'Ispat International N.V.: history'. *Datamonitor Company Profiles*, 23 January.

99 Lambert, J. (1994). 'No layoffs from merger'. *Intelligencer*, 24 September: 1.

100 Associated Press (2006). 'A look at how the Mittal empire was built'. *Associated Press Newswires*, 5 March.

101 Edwards, C. (1998). 'Dutch firm purchases Inland Steel for $888.2 million'. *Associated Press*, 17 March. Ispat also assumed $539 million of Inland's debt.

102 Reed and Arndt (2004) op. cit.; Economist (2004b). 'Big is back'. 28 October.

103 *Economist* (2004b) op. cit.

104 *Economist* (2006b). 'Little love lost'. 29 June; 'Lakshmi's gamble', 31 January.

105 Reed and Arndt (2004) op. cit.

106 Ibid.

107 Ibid.; Jones (2004) op. cit.; <http://www.mittalsteel.com/Company/Our+Philosophy.htm>, accessed 21 December 2006.

108 Russell, B. (2002). 'Mittal fortune is based on complex loan deals'. *The Independent*, 8 March: 4.

109 *Economist* (1998). 'The Carnegie from Calcutta'. 8 January.

CHAPTER FOURTEEN

Strategies in International Contexts

LEARNING OUTCOMES

After reading this chapter you should be able to:

➡ **Discuss some of the push and pull factors contributing to globalization**

➡ **Explain the role and responsibilities of the major international trade organizations**

➡ **Understand the major economic, financial, legal, political, and socio-cultural factors that shape the international environment, and show how these features affect organizations and the way that they do business**

➡ **Describe the economically important features of the major world countries and regions**

➡ **Apply the theoretical concepts that affect an organization's competitive stance, such as product-market decisions, its architecture, and value chain, to specific international location decisions.**

INTRODUCTION

In this chapter we focus especially on the factors that are increasingly making strategy an international issue for all organizations—large and small, new and old, public and private sector.

The position we have taken throughout this book is that competitors (Chapter 3), and the markets that firms target (Chapter 4), may be found anywhere in the world. Similarly, an organization's value chain activities (Chapter 6), elements of its architecture (Chapter 8), and the places where it is able to access, for example, knowledge through alliances (Chapters 9 and 10), can be located in many different regions, not just in its home country. But in none of these have we identified exactly in which country an organization may locate, and why. So in this chapter we fill in some of the gaps and focus on the specific factors that shape international strategic decisions.

First, we briefly discuss the factors that are driving organizations, and countries, worldwide into increased inter-dependency and internationalization. These include factors such as technological developments in communication, logistics, and transportation, but also developments in political and economic ideologies that have been brought about by travel and the understanding of the benefits of cooperation. These changes have been accompanied by the setting up a number of regulatory and developmental bodies such as the World Trade Organization and the International Monetary Fund, which have played an important (and sometimes controversial) role in shaping and controlling international activities.

We then discuss the major financial, economic, political, legal, and socio-cultural factors affecting the world's different regions and countries. These have a profound effect on the ways in which business is conducted in these areas, and which will make them more or less attractive to companies—depending on their strategic priorities. For example, many developing countries that have poor levels of education and low costs of living are very attractive to some manufacturing firms that do not require a particularly skilled workforce but who need to minimize costs. Other countries may be more expensive, but have a highly skilled and educated workforce which knowledge-intensive firms may need. Some countries may even have low costs *and* an educated workforce. These countries provide a major threat to companies located in countries that have neither—but also opportunities for setting up alliances or relocating parts of their value chain there. What is clear is that organizations increasingly need to factor in an assessment of the characteristics of a country or region into their strategic decision-making processes.

We also discuss the major features of the main countries and regions of the world, and their impact on world trade now and in the future. New trading blocs are emerging, and parts of the world, such as China and India, that have previously been economically weak appear likely to become world powers in the next decades. This is likely to correspond to a weakening of the previously dominant 'triad' economies of the USA, Japan, and Europe, with profound effects on the world's political and financial landscape.

Finally, we show how this international environment and the changes that may occur in them, affect organizations. In particular we focus on the international product-market and international structure and location decisions, for example where value chain activities such as manufacturing or after-sales service should be located, according to a match between organizational contingencies and country characteristics, and whether a product has the characteristics to achieve global scale.

14.1 **The drivers of globalization**

First of all we consider what globalization means, and why it is happening.

Globalization
A reduction in market segments, and increasing inter-dependence of national markets worldwide.[1]

Globalization is characterized by an increasing homogenization of markets worldwide, and increasing inter-dependence between nations. Between 1950 and 2001, world exports rose 20-fold. By 2001, international trade accounted for 25 per cent of all the goods and services produced. In the early 1970s, less than $20 billion in national currencies was exchanged daily. By the twenty-first century this had risen to more than $1.5 trillion.[2] It is hard to think of a country that is not affected by globalization, although some choose to embrace it less than others.

This definition of globalization is not the same as the centralizing of organizational decision-making in one location, or the creation of a 'global' product, designed to serve multiple international markets (see Section 14.5). These are organization-level decisions, influenced by global trends in the environment, but specific to a firm or its industry.

→ We discussed value chains, and the location of organizational functions in Chapter 6.

There are a number of principal factors that appear to be contributing to globalization, many of which are interlinked (Real-life Application 14.1). These include:

- greater understanding of the economic and business theories that emphasize the benefits of international trade, and a convergence in economic ideology worldwide as a result;

- technology, including developments in communications and transportation technologies;

- increasing levels of international travel;

- reduction in worldwide conflict and social integration in the form of greater inter-country links;

- the availability of a legal and financial infrastructure that enables international trade.

Real-life Application 14.1 Drivers of globalization in H&M

H&M owns stores in 22 countries, mostly in Europe and north America. In 2007 it expanded into Qatar, Dubai, China, and Kuwait, partly through opening franchised stores for the first time. It manufactures its clothes mainly in Asia and Europe. Although it customizes its store selections according to local demand, all of its clothes are designed in Sweden.

H&M has been able to become an international firm through:

- focusing on customers who are mainly young, well-travelled, and fashion-conscious, and who are sensitized to 'global' fashion styles that are promoted in similarly international magazines and websites;

- transportation. H&M manufactures its products in low-cost regions of the world, and because of the nature of the products, which are not perishable (although some have a shorter fashion life than others) and are easily transportable, it is able to locate manufacturing in regions at a distance from where they are sold. It has been aided by the development of cheaper and more reliable shipping, low levels of piracy on its sea-routes, and also containerization technologies in ports and transporters—the ships and the lorries that

move the goods to H&M's centralized distribution centres. European stores are mainly supplied through a single port, Hamburg, which allows throughput scale economies;

- sophisticated logistics software that allows H&M to track its shipments across the world;

- currency trading and hedging technologies, which allows it to minimize any harmful consequences of currency fluctuations and inflation in the countries in which it does business;

- the development of the European monetary union, and the creation of the euro, which has stabilized currencies in many of its markets and thereby lessened its currency risk;

- improved CAD/CAM technologies which allows H&M to shorten the product development life-cycle—colours and fabrics can be chosen at a distance, on screen;

- the availability of skilled staff in (currently) lesser developed countries (LDCs);

- a legal and regulatory infrastructure that allows inter-country trade.

The last century saw some profound changes in political and economic theory and ideology. There have been successive rounds of trade liberalization agreements, and market-driven regimes in which the country's assets are typically held in private hands, have replaced centrally controlled, or planned, economies where assets are held by the state. In a society where people own and control their own economic wealth, they are naturally concerned to maximize it—and if this is best achieved through international trade, then that is what they will demand. And there is good evidence that international trade increases individual wealth. Two of the oldest and most important trade theories are those of absolute and comparative advantage (Figure 14.1).[3]

Maximum production per day	Chocolate	Bread
Country A	200 units	100 units
Country B	100 units	100 units

Two countries, **A** and **B** produce two goods, **bread** and **chocolate**.
- In 12 hours, A can make 200 bars of chocolate, and 100 loaves of bread.
- In 12 hours, B can make 100 bars of chocolate and 100 loaves of bread.

A has an **absolute advantage** in chocolate—it can make more than B given the same resources. *Neither* has an **absolute advantage** in clothes.

For A, the opportunity cost (i.e. how much of the other product has to be foregone) of producing one unit of chocolate is 0.5 unit of bread, and the opportunity cost of one unit of bread is 2 units of chocolate. So A has a **comparative advantage** in chocolate because of its lower opportunity costs of production compared to B, whose opportunity costs of both bread and chocolate are 1 unit.

But B has **comparative advantage** over A in the production of bread, even though the opportunity cost of producing one unit of chocolate is one unit of bread. This is because of its lower opportunity cost compared to A—which would have to forego 2 units.

Figure 14.1 Absolute and comparative advantage

These underpin models such as Porter's diamond (see Section 14.5.4) on national competitive advantage, and have important implications for firms in choosing where to locate their activities, or for new firms in choosing the type of product to make. Comparative and absolute advantage comes about because there are inherent differences in the factors of production, such as an abundance of raw materials like coal or gold, or through developed—or acquired—advantages, such as high labour productivity rates and technological skills.

The second major driver of globalization is technological. This principally relates to two areas—transportation and communication:

- Transporting goods internationally is now easier and cheaper than it has ever been. Containerization and logistics technologies have resulted in easier tracking of goods, faster throughput through ports, and less wastage in the form of pilferage, lost items, or breakages. Between the early 1980s and 1996 sea freight costs fell 70 per cent in real terms, and air freight costs have fallen 3 to 4 per cent a year over a long period.[4] This makes it feasible for firms to manufacture products in one part of the world, and transport them cheaply and quickly to where they are needed.

- Information and communication technologies (ICT) such as the internet, electronic data interchange, or intranets, use another globalization-encouraging technology, fibre optics. This has enabled near-instantaneous transfer of data across the globe, enabling round-the-clock trading in currencies and other financial assets, and orders to be placed and processed speedily as they travel from supplier to customer. Because ICT costs have declined radically, companies can be located almost anywhere and still be in communication with their employees, customers, or suppliers. The internet has also enabled the sharing of ideas and knowledge, and allowed relationships and understanding to form across previously unbridgeable geographical distances.

- Other technologies have made the world 'smaller' in many other ways. Satellites allow television and radio broadcasters to bring real-time news of far-away events, and make previously unknown countries familiar. The World Wide Web provides a means of accessing vast data stores that are held beyond national boundaries. Newspapers and radio programmes from all over the world can be accessed by anyone with an internet connection.

Technology has made people curious, and allowed them to indulge this curiosity through visiting parts of the world that were previously inaccessible or too expensive to reach. This has a number of effects: first, people who travel internationally learn to be comfortable with people that look or behave differently from those in their home area. Second, international travel brings contact with different goods, or different ways of making things, stimulating demand for imports of both products and people. Migration is a major feature of globalization.

The last fifty years have also seen a significant reduction in international conflict and wars worldwide (quite possibly helped by the increase in international travel and understanding) and much greater social integration in the form of formal inter-country links—the EU and ASEAN agreements being good examples. The result has been increased prosperity as a result of trade, and increasing stability as a result of prosperity—a virtuous circle.

14.2 International trade organizations

A number of bodies have been set up to promote and regulate international trade. Three of the most important of these institutions are the World Bank, the International Monetary Fund (IMF), and the World Trade Organization (WTO) (Real-life Application 14.2). It is beyond the scope of this book to discuss these organizations in detail, but more information is available on the website.

Online Resource Centre
www.oxfordtextbooks.co.uk/orc/haberberg_rieple/

Visit the Online Resource Centre that accompanies this book to read more information relating to international trade and finance, and international trade bodies.

Real-life Application 14.2 The role of the IMF, WTO, and World Bank

The World Bank, WTO, and the IMF all have the role of improving international trade and reducing poverty, not all companies or countries view these three organizations as entirely benevolent. Many hold that they are agents of western (especially US) imperialism, benefiting their own trade at the expense of poorer regions—despite the rhetoric that claims the reverse. Many commentators assume that the US government appoints the head of the World Bank, just as it is assumed that the European Union says who should head the IMF.[5] And the man who invented the IMF's voting formula (based on factors such as a country's economic strength, volatility, and openness) has even said that it was a 'subtle contrivance, carefully designed to deliver a result pre-cooked by the Americans'.[6]   →

→ Criticisms of these organizations include:

- LDCs have faced increased prices on goods they import, yet their exports are subjected to tariffs on agriculture or manufactured goods in order to protect western companies.[7]

- Instead of increasing economic stability, financial liberaization imposed by the IMF has *caused* financial crises in some of the world's poorest economies, because they lacked the sufficiently strong infrastructure (regulatory agencies or know-how) necessary to oversee the financial sector.[8]

- They have used their influence to persuade LDCs to privatize industries such as utilities, banks, and transport, as a result of a 'free-market' conviction that private firms are superior to the public sector.[9]

Some scholars[10] have pointed out that the countries that have benefited most from globalization, such as India, China and Vietnam, are those that have not played by the IMF or WTO's rules. In contrast, many of those that have obeyed the rules, such as many Latin American countries, have performed worse.

As a result, some governments are starting to withdraw their support. Venezuela's president, Hugo Chavez, announced in May 2007 that it would be terminating its membership of both the IMF and the World Bank—agencies that he described as 'mechanisms of imperialism'.[11] This followed a similar move from Ecuador, which had expelled the World Bank's representative in Quito after accusing the organization of 'extortion'.[12] For Chavez, the goal was 'to kill the so-called Washington consensus, the economic prescriptions championed by the International Monetary Fund and the U.S. Treasury'.[13]

14.3 Economic unions

Economic union
Characterized by the free movement of goods between member countries and the integration of economic policies; it implies a common fiscal regime and currency, or at least a fixed exchange rate.

Free-trade area
A free-trade area is not as extreme in terms of integration as an economic union, but involves the agreement of member countries to reduce or eliminate barriers to trade, such as tariffs or quotas.

Common market
A form of free-trade area.

Another type of globalization-encouraging infrastructure is an economic union, and its dose relative, a free-trade area. There are many of these arrangements in the world, with varying degrees of integration of the member countries. They include:

- the Andean Community, an economic union of Bolivia, Colombia, Ecuador, Peru, and Venezuela;

- Mercosur, a free-trade group made up of Argentina, Brazil, Paraguay, and Uruguay with Bolivia and Chile as associate members;

- the Association of Southeast Asian Nations (ASEAN) formed by Indonesia, Malaysia, the Philippines, Singapore, and Thailand;

- the North American Free Trade Agreement (NAFTA) of Mexico, the United States, and Canada;

- the European Union (EU), now comprising 27 countries including France, Germany, Italy, and the UK, and, since 2004, a number of countries from the former Soviet Union.

The EU is one of the best-known economic and political entities in the world, with a population of nearly 500 million and a combined 2006 GDP of €11.5 trillion.[14] It is now the world's largest market. In 1952, six countries (Belgium, France, Italy, Luxembourg, the Netherlands, and West Germany) formed the European Coal and Steel Community (ECSC) for the purpose of creating a common market that would enhance the competitiveness of these industries. This expanded into the European Economic Community (EEC) free trade area in 1957. The EEC's purpose was to eliminate tariffs, quotas, and other trade barriers, allow the free movement of labour, capital, and businesses, and develop common policies and standards across its legal and physical infrastructure. It also created a development fund whereby the richer countries financed projects in the Community's poorer regions.

In 1993, the European Community was renamed the European Union, with corresponding strengthening of the integration of its members. The EU has five key bodies: the

The European Commission in Brussels flies the EU flag. *iStock*

European Council, comprising the heads of all member states; the Council of the European Union, the policy decision-making body, in which the relevant ministers from each country participate; the European Commission, in effect the executive branch, equivalent to the Civil Service; the European Parliament, which comprises elected representatives from the member countries and decides on how EU funds are spent; and the European Court of Justice, the authority on EU law.

In 1999, twelve of the EU's countries agreed to form a monetary union, and created the euro as a trading currency. In 2002, euro banknotes and coins were issued. This has removed the costs of currency transactions for companies selling entirely within the 'euro zone'. The currency is now one of the largest and most stable in the world.

14.3.1 Barriers against trade

Despite all these efforts to increase trade, there are also many instances where countries seek to protect their own trade at the expense of others'. A number of barriers can be erected that prevent or reduce the flow of goods and services in and out of a country. These include:

- financial measures such as exchange controls which limit the flow of currency. Holidays abroad a few years ago, even within Europe, were constrained by the fact that only €90 could be taken out of the home country. Exchange controls still exist—but for much larger amounts than a typical traveller could ever spend;

- international investment controls which limit the amount of foreign direct investment (FDI) in a country;

- tariffs—taxes on goods that are shipped between countries. Tariffs are usually levied on imported goods, although sometimes they are also charged on goods that are exported, or transported through the country;

- quotas that restrict imports to a particular quantity;

- import licences that are necessary to be able to import goods;

- embargoes that forbid the importing of certain goods; for example, Cuban cigars may not be imported into the USA.

The reasons why countries would want to implement such protectionist policies include:

- to protect local jobs or encourage local production by shielding them from stronger international competition. Sometimes this is in order to nurture infant industries that would otherwise never be able to get off the ground;

- to reduce the potential for dependence on foreign suppliers, especially if they are located in unstable parts of the world;

- to deal with balance of payments problems when a country has spent more than it earns (just like individuals do) on goods from external sources.

The USA has a range of 'buy American' policies which, for example, require government departments to give preference to local producers. It also has foreign investment controls that affect US airlines, transport, telecommunications, and energy generation. These are forecast to become even more stringent.[15] Both the USA and the EU regulate trade in some agricultural products by quotas, tariffs, and subsidies or price supports for domestic producers.

Just as there have been criticisms of the international trade organizations (which are perceived to sustain the hegemony of the developed countries), so there have been many criticisms of these policies.[16] Many LDCs, which tend to be dependent on agriculture, are unable to export their goods to the biggest markets. And, although some trade barriers may have short-term benefits for the home country, long term they increase the inefficiency of domestic firms through protecting them from competition.

14.4 Criticisms of globalization

Globalization is not universally popular.[17] There have been concerns about the polluting effect of international trade on the environment, the exploitation of children and low-paid workers in LDCs, and the destabilizing effect on labour markets worldwide, as well as the harmful effect that cultural imperialism has on indigenous populations.[18] McDonald's, the

WTO, and the IMF have been the target of protests against the inequalities that these organizations are perceived to perpetuate, and which protesters believe harm employees and the environment.[19]

Creative Strategizing 14.1

Imagine you are the director of an American multinational that believes it will be the target of anti-globalization protestors. What should you do to counteract this possibility?

And by some measures inequality is growing worse, not better. More than 80 countries had lower per capita income at the end of the 1990s than they had at the end of the 1980s. In 1960, the top 20 per cent had 30 times the income of the poorest 20 per cent. By the end of the twentieth century, top countries earned over 5,000 times the annual income of the lowest earners (Table 14.1).

Table 14.1 Selected countries' GNI per capita 2005 (Atlas method)

Top 20	(US dollars)	Bottom 20	(US dollars)
Luxembourg	65,630	Guinea	370
Norway	59,590	Central African Republic	350
Switzerland	54,930	Togo	350
Denmark	47,390	Tanzania	340
Iceland	46,320	Zimbabwe	340
United States	43,740	Tajikistan	330
Sweden	41,060	Mozambique	310
Ireland	40,150	Gambia	290
Japan	38,980	Madagascar	290
United Kingdom	37,600	Uganda	280
Finland	37,460	Nepal	270
Austria	36,980	Niger	240
Netherlands	36,620	Rwanda	230
Belgium	35,700	Eritrea	220
France	34,810	Sierra Leone	220
Germany	34,580	Guinea-Bissau	180
Canada	32,600	Ethiopia	160
Australia	32,220	Malawi	160
Italy	30,010	Liberia	130
Hong Kong, China	27,670	Congo, Dem.Rep.	120
		Burundi	100

Notes
Some figures are estimates and ranking is approximate.

Source
World Development Indicators database, World Bank, 1 July 2006

Such inequalities in participation in the global economy are a concern for both governments and international organizations. In some poor countries, crime is the only profitable activity, making life difficult for any firm that wants to locate there. In the next section we discuss in more detail some of theses issues, when we examine the characteristics of the different countries and regions of the world.

14.5 The international environment

Although both trade and foreign direct investment have increased substantially in recent years, much of this activity has been carried out by large multinational organizations that trade with other multinationals. Over 50 per cent of all world trade and 80 per cent of FDI is undertaken by the 500 largest firms in the world,[20] most of whom are located in the so-called triad—the USA, Japan, and Europe—or in countries that form part of a triad cluster, like South Korea. A number of countries are becoming increasingly prominent in world trade, notably Australia, Brazil, Canada, China, India, Mexico, the Russian Federation, Singapore, and South Korea. Nevertheless, there are large parts of the world that are still excluded from global trade—or are used (and sometimes abused) only as sources of cheap labour.

In the next section we will examine the country-specific features that are particularly important for international organizations, namely:

- political and legal issues;
- socio-cultural issues;
- infrastructure issues.

14.5.1 Political and legal issues

The legal and regulatory climate in a country strongly influences how easy it is for a firm to do business there. Governments create policies on, for example, privatization and nationalization, and have a strong influence on the country's economic climate—what the tax regime is, and whether it is heavily regulated and centrally controlled, or more flexible. Political decisions determine interest rates, which influence exchange rates and inflation, and in turn economic stability and wealth. Financial factors like interest rates, currency strength, and exchange rates are important issues for managers of international firms, as activities in one currency have to be translated into the head office's when accounts are compiled. Movements in any of these can significantly affect profits—either way. As a result firms have had to develop strong treasury activities, such as currency hedging, options, and currency dealing in order to smooth out any instability in their financial environment.

 Online Resource Centre
www.oxfordtextbooks.co.uk/orc/haberberg_rieple/

Visit the Online Resource Centre that accompanies this book to read more information relating to currencies, interest rates, exchange rates, inflation, and other international financial and economic factors.

International companies have to deal with political and economic regimes that may be very different from the ones they are used to. Political systems may be democratic or authoritarian, and either type of system may co-exist with a deregulated, free market economy or with a degree of central regulations and planning. There are no obvious correlations between economic health and particular political systems. India, for example, has been the world's largest democracy for a long time, but has large elements of centralized planning, as has France. In contrast, Chile, Indonesia, and South Korea have all recently built strong market economies despite the lack of fully democratic systems. China is currently doing the same.[21]

Legal systems are similarly varied, and may be based upon:

- common law—where legislation is the result of years (often centuries) of common practice and past cases, interpreted and ruled on by the judiciary, as in many English-speaking nations;

- civil law—where legislation is based on a legal code: a set of detailed written rules and statutes. This type of legal system is the most common worldwide;

- theocratic law—a legal system that is based on religious doctrine, for example those of the Jewish, Hindu, and Islamic religions.[22]

Legal systems matter to international organizations because of the way that they protect, or fail to protect, their operations. For businesses the most important aspects of a legal regime are:

- intellectual property rights such as patents, trademarks, or copyright;

- standardization—whether the country adopts internationally agreed standards and laws, for example those relating to financial reporting conventions,[23] product standards such as food content and labelling, and productions standards, for example ISO 9000;[24]

- product safety and liability—where the responsibility lies in the case of damage, injury, or death being caused by a faulty product or through negligence. Environmental laws are becoming increasingly important worldwide;

- employees' working rights—legislation that sets down, for example, the working hours that children can work, and the types of jobs they can do. Many LDCs have weak employee legislation;

- anti-trust (anti-monopoly) legislation—laws against market sharing, cartels, price fixing, and monopolies. Some parts of the world condone market sharing, making it hard for international firms to do business there without local partners;

- ownership of assets—some countries prefer to own important national assets. Companies wanting to do business in these countries usually have to have strong relationships with the government or its industry body;

- taxation—legislation regarding tariffs on imports, exports, and transit, as well as taxes that are levied on products and employees.

→ We discussed intellectual property rights in Section 10.3.

Some countries make it hard for international organizations to work there (and their own national organizations too, for that matter) by burdening them with large taxes or extensive bureaucratic controls. Others try to attract inward investment through creating favourable tax and regulatory regimes. Some countries have a special status as tax havens. These are stable territories that have few, if any, regulations and taxes, except, usually, strong privacy laws. International companies sometimes use these—at a cost—in order to minimize their tax payments.

Multinational managers have to assess countries on a 'political risk' scale depending on whether they are stable, or beset with economic or political instability, or high levels of corruption. Sometimes practices that other countries would consider illegal are simply the local rules of the game.[25] Crime is a problem in some poorer countries which have a weak or corrupt police force. These can create a substantial obstacle for international businesses, who have to worry about their reputation back home, apart from putting their staff at risk. Companies in gold- and diamond-producing regions in some cases have taken to employing their own private armies to protect their operations.

14.5.2 Socio-cultural issues

In addition to needing to understand the very different legal and political regimes that operate around the world, international firms have to work in environments where people have different values and beliefs, and divergent approaches to doing business. They also face consumers with equally divergent preferences.

A nation's culture is expressed in the country's institutions (a theocratic or civil legal system, for example), and also in the ways that people approach business issues. Culture is therefore an important consideration in international management. Most managers are steeped in their own culture. When dealing with people of different nationalities, they are presented with extra challenges in understanding:

- the needs and preferences of consumers, their attitudes to different forms of marketing, and the channels they might prefer to use for their purchases;
- what accounting and financial reporting standards are preferred, and how results are measured;
- the way in which other firms—customers, distributors, suppliers and professional advisers—do business, and how things are organized and planned. Some cultures rely upon formal contracts, in others these play a secondary role to personal relationships that may take years to build;
- the expectations of employees regarding work–life balance and job security. Some parts of the world have a tradition of life-time employment; in others, there is much greater employee mobility: workers would expect to be fired or made redundant occasionally, and certainly would have few qualms about leaving one employer for another;
- what are considered to be acceptable leadership behaviours;
- whether or not junior employees are permitted to question decisions made by their superiors;
- the types of rewards and control systems that are used;
- attitudes towards issues like child labour, bribes, human rights, and the environment.

➜ We discuss reward systems and control systems in Chapter 15, and organizational structures in Chapter 7.

National cultures have been the basis of a number of detailed studies. A number of dimensions of national culture have been identified, including the following:[26]

- Power distance is the extent to which the less powerful members of organizations and institutions (like the family) endorse the unequal distribution of power. High power-distance countries tend to have strongly hierarchical structures.
- Uncertainty avoidance measures a society's tolerance for uncertainty and ambiguity, and the extent to which people feel either uncomfortable or comfortable in unstructured situations (defined as novel, unknown, surprising, different from usual). Uncertainty-avoiding cultures try to minimize the possibility of such situations by strict laws and rules.

- Individualism and its opposite, collectivism, measure the degree to which individuals are integrated into groups—whether everyone is expected to look after him/herself and his/her immediate family or integrated from birth into strong, cohesive in-groups, or extended families.

- Masculinity and its opposite, femininity, refer to the distribution of roles between the genders. Masculine values include assertiveness and competitiveness; feminine values include modesty and caring.

- Long-term orientation vs short-term orientation. Values associated with a short-term orientation are respect for tradition, fulfilling social obligations, and protecting one's 'face'. A long-term orientation is characterized by thrift and perseverance.

- Universalism and its opposite, particularism, measures the degree to which universal rules are applied regardless of individual circumstances.

- Neutral vs emotional measure the degree to which emotions are expressed in the workplace.

- Specific vs diffuse measure whether work relationships remain at work or diffuse into socializing outside of the work environment.

- Achievement vs ascription measure the degree to which status, credibility, authority, and power are believed to be the result of achievement, or of class, gender, education, or age (ascription).

- Attitudes toward the environment measures the emphasis a particular culture places on people's relationship with nature and the natural environment.

- Performance orientation reflects the importance that people place on achievement.

- Humane orientation is the emphasis on fairness, altruism, and generosity.

Getting culture wrong can lead to conflict and lack of respect for multinational managers, or at the very least a degree of discomfort with their behaviour. For example, an executive from a masculine/assertive tradition, such as the US, who does not adjust his (or her) behaviour is likely to be viewed by colleagues from other cultures as autocratic and abrasive. Equally, managers from low assertiveness countries risk being seen as weak and 'wishy-washy'.

14.5.3 Infrastructure issues

As well as political/legal and socio-cultural issues, managers of international organizations also have to consider infrastructure factors. These include physical infrastructure such as roads, levels of internet access, and telephony, all of which affect companies' abilities to take and process orders, as well as deliver goods. Many LDCs are held back by their poor telephone cabling, although, in some, mobile phones are providing a good alternative to land-lines (Table 14.2).

Another infrastructure concern (albeit not a physical one) is the education and skills of the workforce. International organizations almost always need to employ local staff, even if they favour home country nationals for key positions. The choice of location is likely to be governed by whether the labour force has at least the minimum skills the organization needs. Countries vary widely in the level of education and standards of literacy of their populations (Table 14.3). And countries similarly vary widely in their cost of labour (Table 14.4).

International companies may need to trade off their need to reduce costs with the likely expense of training poorly educated staff. An ideal is to find a country with both low costs and highly skilled staff—India and China are current examples.

Table 14.2 'Connectedness' infrastructure indicators for selected countries (2005 figures)

Country	Fixed line and mobile phone subscribers (per 1,000 people)	Internet users (per 1,000 people)
Bangladesh	71	3
Brazil	N/A	195
Burundi	N/A	5
Canada	1,080	520
China	570	85
Colombia	648	104
France	1,376	430
Germany	1,628	455
Hong Kong, China	1,798	508
India	128	55
Japan	1,202	668
Kenya	143	32
Malaysia	943	435
Netherlands	1,436	739
Pakistan	116	67
Poland	1,073	262
Russian Federation	1,119	152
South Africa	825	109
United Kingdom	1,616	473
United States	N/A	630[a]
World	523	137

Notes
a 2004 figures

Table 14.3 Literacy and education indicators for selected countries (2005 figures unless otherwise specified)

Country	Literacy rate, adult total (% of people ages 15 and above)	Education enrolment, primary (%)	Education enrolment, secondary (%)	Education enrolment, tertiary (%)
Bangladesh	N/A	N/A	43	6
Brazil	89	N/A	N/A	N/A
Burundi	59	60	N/A	2
Canada	100	N/A	N/A	N/A
China	91	N/A	N/A	19
Colombia	93	87	55[*]	28
France	100	99	96	56
Germany	100	N/A	N/A	N/A
Hong Kong, China	100	93	80	31
India	61	90[*]	N/A	12[*]
Japan	100	100[*]	100[*]	54[*]
Kenya	74	80	42	3[*]
Malaysia	89	N/A	N/A	N/A
Netherlands	100	99[*]	89[*]	59[*]
Pakistan	50	68	21	5
Poland	100	97[*]	90[*]	61[*]
Russian Federation	99	91[*]	N/A	68[*]
South Africa	82	87[*]	N/A	16[*]
United Kingdom	100	99[*]	95[*]	60[*]
United States	100	92[*]	89[*]	82[*]
World	82	N/A	N/A	24[*]

Notes
* 2004 figures

Source
World Bank World Development Indicators data

Table 14.4 Steel-making industry employment cost comparisons

Worldwide hourly compensation costs	
US$/hour	2004
Australia	23.1
Brazil	3.0
Canada	21.4
China	1.0
Czech Republic	5.4
France	23.9
Germany	32.5
India	0.8
Italy	20.5
Japan	21.9
Kazakhstan	0.9
Korea	11.5
Mexico	2.5
Spain	17.1
Sweden	28.4
Taiwan	6.0
Ukraine	0.7
United Kingdom	24.7
United States	23.2

Source
<http://laborsta.ilo.org/ or http://www.steelonthenet.com/labour_cost.html> accessed 19 April 2007

14.5.4 The competitive advantage of nations

These various international political, legal, socio-cultural, and infrastructure issues can be used to develop a profile of each country in the world and assess its attractiveness. Different countries and regions have different qualities, and therefore varying degrees of attractiveness to firms in particular industries. In a manufacturing industry like clothing or shoes, where production costs are important, it makes sense to locate facilities in countries like Indonesia or China, where labour costs are low. The availability of cheap electricity or other inputs may influence location decisions in industries such as aluminium smelting. In other industries, the availability of good transport links or specialized knowledge in information technology, will be more important considerations.

As a result of having a combination of relevant factors, some countries and regions are particularly beneficial locations for certain industries. These factors are modelled in what has come to be known as Porter's diamond (Figure 14.2).

→ Porter's diamond is a variant of cluster theory, applied to nations or regions. See Theoretical Debate 10.1 for a more in-depth discussion of clustering.

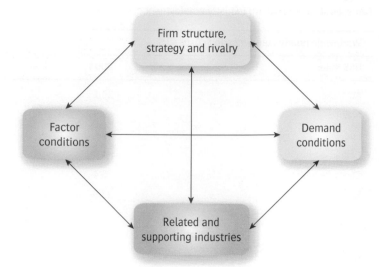

Figure 14.2 Porter's 'diamond' (Porter, 1990: 72)

The four determinants of national competitive advantage are:

- strong factor conditions—the basic ingredients that are needed to make a product: for example land, labour, and finance. These factors may be naturally available, like gold deposits, or develop over time, like workers' skills;

- high, and knowledgeable, local demand for the goods that are being produced. This helps companies to be profitable and therefore to invest in developing products that will be strong enough for a global market;

- related and supporting industries, which help companies obtain low-cost inputs as well as know-how that helps the development of products;

- firms' structure, strategy, and rivalry. The visibility of nearby rivals encourages competitiveness between firms, and therefore stimulates innovation.

Some of the competitiveness indicators and rankings of selected nations are shown in Figure 14.3a–c.[27]

Nationally or regionally competitive environments often have a very long gestation period.[28] If circumstances are favourable, a firm and its competitors and customers become partners in the creation of a strong industry that is based on a deep understanding of customer needs. Knowledge and skills about, for example, manufacturing techniques, do not simply stay the property of a single firm, but spread through the network of organizations in the area as employees move between them. Systems of supplier firms develop to provide what are often specialist inputs, while roads and transportation systems are built to distribute the finished product. These factors shape the types of product firms sell and the type, size, and structure of the companies that arise there, and competitive rivalry between the firms in the region stimulates them to superior performance. Over time, an infrastructure and knowledge base arises which means that firms located in this area have benefits that firms located elsewhere do not.

One example of such a world-beating region is California's Silicon Valley (Figure 14.4). Its 'godfather' was Fred Terman, an engineering professor at Stanford University in Palo Alto who persuaded two of his students, William Hewlett and David Packard, to form a company in a lock-up garage nearby. To encourage his more entrepreneurial students to remain in the

➜ We discuss the factors that have resulted in Silicon Valley being so supportive of high-tech firms in more detail in Section 10.4.2.

The Business Competitiveness Index

Country/Economy	BCI ranking	Quality of the national business environment ranking	Company operations and strategy ranking
United States	1	1	1
Germany	2	2	2
Finland	3	3	8
Switzerland	4	4	4
Denmark	5	6	6
Netherlands	6	5	7
Sweden	7	8	3
United Kingdom	8	7	9
Japan	9	9	5
Hong Kong SAR	10	10	12
Singapore	11	11	21
Austria	12	14	10
Iceland	13	12	19
Norway	14	13	20
Canada	15	16	18
France	16	18	11
Belgium	17	17	13
Australia	18	15	23
Israel	19	19	15
Malaysia	20	20	14
Taiwan, China	21	22	16
Ireland	22	23	17
New Zealand	23	21	24
Estonia	24	24	35
Korea, Rep.	25	28	22
Tunisia	26	25	33
India	27	27	25
Portugal	28	26	40
Chile	29	28	29
Spain	30	31	31
United Arab Emirates	31	30	39
Czech Republic	32	32	28
South Africa	33	34	27
Qatar	34	33	44
Indonesia	35	38	26
Slovenia	36	36	34
Thailand	37	37	30
Italy	38	42	32
Hungary	39	35	43
Slovak Republic	40	39	45
Malta	41	40	63
Barbados	42	41	60
Lithuania	43	45	37
Kuwait	44	44	59
Cyprus	45	43	67
Turkey	46	46	41
Latvia	47	48	47
Mauritius	48	49	46
Greece	49	47	53
Costa Rica	50	52	36
Bahrain*	51	50	64
Jordan	52	51	70
Poland	53	53	49
Jamaica	54	55	52
Brazil	55	58	38
Croatia	56	54	56
Mexico	57	56	42
Panama	58	57	58
Colombia	59	59	54
El Salvador	60	60	61
Guatemala	61	66	50
Uruguay	62	61	71
Trinidad and Tobago	63	64	65

Country/Economy	BCI ranking	Quality of the national business environment ranking	Company operations and strategy ranking
China	64	65	69
Sri Lanka	65	68	68
Morocco*	66	52	80
Pakistan	67	67	72
Kenya	68	72	57
Botswana	69	63	86
Kazakhstan	70	70	74
Peru	71	75	51
Philippines	72	76	48
Tanzania	73	71	75
Romania	74	73	73
Namibia	75	69	83
Egypt	76	74	76
Azerbaijan*	77	78	66
Argentina	78	79	62
Russian Federation	79	77	78
Nigeria*	80	84	55
Ukraine	81	80	82
Vietnam	82	83	77
Bulgaria	83	81	95
Dominican Republic	84	86	79
Algeria	85	82	112
Serbia and Montenegro	86	85	110
Macedonia, FYR	87	87	90
Uganda*	88	80	87
Burkina Faso*	89	88	98
Moldova	90	91	91
Mali*	91	89	100
Gambia	92	92	85
Venezuela	93	94	81
Armenia	94	93	101
Benin	95	95	94
Bosnia and Herzegovina	96	96	107
Madagascar	97	99	99
Tajikistan*	98	97	103
Mongolia	99	98	104
Georgia	100	101	97
Mauritania*	101	102	88
Nicaragua	102	100	109
Zimbabwe	103	104	84
Malawi	104	103	93
Ecuador	105	105	89
Honduras	106	106	92
Cambodia	107	107	96
Bangladesh	108	110	105
Suriname	109	108	115
Mozambique	110	111	103
Nepal	111	113	106
Kyrgyz Republic	112	112	114
Cameroon	113	114	102
Guyana	114	115	111
Lesotho	115	116	116
Zambia	116	109	123
Bolivia	117	117	120
Ethiopia	118	118	121
Albania	119	120	113
Paraguay	120	119	118
Chad*	121	121	124

Note: * Survey data for these countries have high within-country variance, until the reliability of survey responses improves with future educational efforts and improved sampling in these countries, their rankings should be interpreted with caution

Figure 14.3a The business competitiveness index explores a country's prosperity measure by its level of GDP per capital adjusted for purchasing power. Among the component variables are production process sophistication, per capita internet and cell-phone use, intensity of local competition, financial market sophistication, and intellectual property protection. Source: Porter, M. and Sala-i-Martin, X. (2007).

Global Competitiveness Index rankings and 2005 comparisons

Country/Economy	GCI 2006 Rank	GCI 2006 Score	GCI 2005 Rank	Country/Economy	GCI 2006 Rank	GCI 2006 Score	GCI 2005 Rank
Switzerland	1	5.81	4	Azerbaijan	64	4.06	62
Finland	2	5.76	2	Colombia	65	4.04	58
Sweden	3	5.74	7	Brazil	66	4.03	57
Denmark	4	5.70	3	Trinidad and Tobago	67	4.03	66
Singapore	5	5.63	5	Romania	68	4.02	67
United States	6	5.61	1	Argentina	69	4.01	54
Japan	7	5.60	10	Morocco	70	4.01	76
Germany	8	5.58	6	Philippines	71	4.00	73
Netherlands	9	5.56	11	Bulgaria	72	3.96	61
United Kingdom	10	5.54	9	Uruguay	73	3.96	70
Hong Kong SAR	11	5.46	14	Peru	74	3.94	77
Norway	12	5.42	17	Guatemala	75	3.91	95
Taiwan, China	13	5.41	8	Algeria	76	3.90	82
Iceland	14	5.40	16	Vietnam	77	3.89	74
Israel	15	5.38	23	Ukraine	78	3.89	68
Canada	16	5.37	13	Sri Lanka	79	3.87	80
Austria	17	5.32	15	Macedonia, FYR	80	3.86	75
France	18	5.31	12	Botswana	81	3.79	72
Australia	19	5.29	18	Armenia	82	3.75	81
Belgium	20	5.27	20	Dominican Republic	83	3.75	91
Ireland	21	5.21	21	Namibia	84	3.74	79
Luxembourg	22	5.16	24	Georgia	85	3.73	86
New Zealand	23	5.15	22	Moldova	86	3.71	89
Korea, Rep.	24	5.13	19	Serbia and Montenegro	87	3.69	85
Estonia	25	5.12	26	Venezuela	88	3.69	84
Malaysia	26	5.11	25	Bosnia and Herzegovina	89	3.67	88
Chile	27	4.85	27	Ecuador	90	3.67	87
Spain	28	4.77	28	Pakistan	91	3.66	94
Czech Republic	29	4.74	29	Mongolia	92	3.60	90
Tunisia	30	4.71	37	Honduras	93	3.58	97
Barbados	31	4.70	—	Kenya	94	3.57	93
United Arab Emirates	32	4.66	32	Nicaragua	95	3.52	96
Slovenia	33	4.64	30	Tajikistan	96	3.50	92
Portugal	34	4.60	31	Bolivia	97	3.46	101
Thailand	35	4.58	33	Albania	98	3.46	100
Latvia	36	4.57	39	Bangladesh	99	3.46	98
Slovak Republic	37	4.55	36	Suriname	100	3.45	—
Qatar	38	4.55	46	Nigeria	101	3.45	83
Malta	39	4.54	44	Gambia	102	3.43	109
Lithuania	40	4.53	34	Cambodia	103	3.39	111
Hungary	41	4.52	35	Tanzania	104	3.39	105
Italy	42	4.46	38	Benin	105	3.37	106
India	43	4.44	45	Paraguay	106	3.33	102
Kuwait	44	4.41	49	Kyrgyz Republic	107	3.31	104
South Africa	45	4.36	40	Cameroon	108	3.30	99
Cyprus	46	4.36	41	Madagascar	109	3.27	107
Greece	47	4.33	47	Nepal	110	3.26	—
Poland	48	4.30	43	Guyana	111	3.24	108
Bahrain	49	4.28	50	Lesotho	112	3.22	—
Indonesia	50	4.26	69	Uganda	113	3.19	103
Croatia	51	4.26	64	Mauritania	114	3.17	—
Jordan	52	4.25	42	Zambia	115	3.16	—
Costa Rica	53	4.25	56	Burkina Faso	116	3.07	—
China	54	4.24	48	Malawi	117	3.07	114
Mauritius	55	4.20	55	Mali	118	3.02	115
Kazakhstan	56	4.19	51	Zimbabwe	119	3.01	110
Panama	57	4.18	55	Ethiopia	120	2.99	116
Mexico	58	4.18	59	Mozambique	121	2.94	112
Turkey	59	4.14	71	Timor-Leste	122	2.09	113
Jamaica	60	4.10	63	Chad	123	2.61	117
El Salvador	61	4.09	60	Burundi	124	2.59	—
Russian Federation	62	4.08	53	Angola	125	2.50	—
Egypt	63	4.07	52				

Figure 14.3b The global competitiveness index focuses on nine broad measures that score a country for the quality of its institutions, infrastructure, macro economy, health and primary education, higher education and training, market efficiency, technological business sophistication, and innovation.

Source: Porter and Sala-í-Martin (2007: xvii)

United Kingdom

Key Indicators

Total population (millions), 2005	59.7
GDP (US$ billions), 2005	2,201.5
GDP (PPP) as share of world total, 2005	3.00
GDP (PPP) per capita (US$), 2005	30,470

GDP (PPP) per capita (US$), 1980–2005

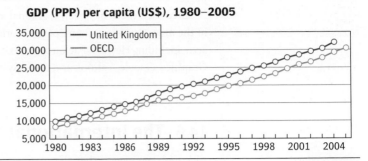

Global Competitiveness Index

	Rank (out of 125 countries/economies)	Score (out of 7)
2006–07	**10**	**5.5**
2005–06 (out of 117 countries)	9	5.5
Basic Requirements	**14**	**5.7**
1st pillar: Institutions	15	5.4
2nd pillar: Infrastructure	14	5.7
3rd pillar: Macroeconomy	48	4.7
4th pillar: Health and primary education	14	6.9
Efficiency Enhancers	**7**	**5.6**
5th pillar: Higher education and training	11	5.6
6th pillar: Market efficiency	3	5.6
7th pillar: Technological readiness	6	5.6
Innovation Factors	**10**	**5.4**
8th pillar: Business sophistication	6	5.8
9th pillar: Innovation	12	4.9

	Rank (out of 121 countries/economies)
Business Competitiveness Index	**8**
Sophistication of company operations and strategy	9
Quality of the national business environment	7

Stage of development

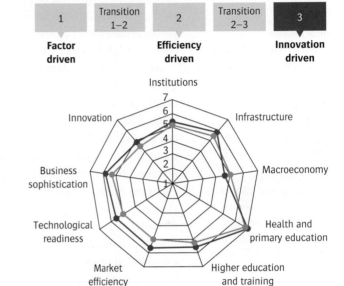

The most problematic factors for doing business

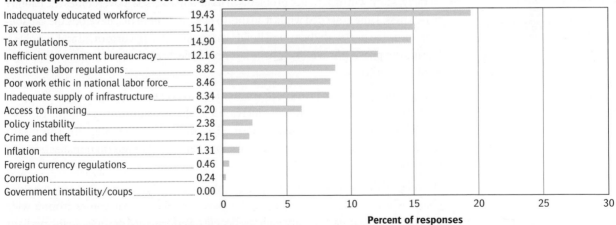

Inadequately educated workforce	19.43
Tax rates	15.14
Tax regulations	14.90
Inefficient government bureaucracy	12.16
Restrictive labor regulations	8.82
Poor work ethic in national labor force	8.46
Inadequate supply of infrastructure	8.34
Access to financing	6.20
Policy instability	2.38
Crime and theft	2.15
Inflation	1.31
Foreign currency regulations	0.46
Corruption	0.24
Government instability/coups	0.00

Note: From a list of 14 factors, respondents were asked to select the five most problematic for doing business in their country/economy and to rank them between 1 (most problematic) and 5. The bars in the figure show the responses weighted according to their rankings.

Figure 14.3c An example of a country competitiveness profile.

Source: Porter and Sala-í-Martin (2007: 378)

region, Terman persuaded Stanford to turn some of its land into a campus-like industrial park.[29]

Since then there has been a gradual agglomeration of innovation-supportive elements in the area. Nowadays many of the world's leading computing companies are based in the area, including Hewlett-Packard, Xerox's PARC research facility, Sun Microsystems, Silicon Graphics, Google, Yahoo!, and Cisco Systems.

14.6 **The international organization**

Although our view is that all organizations are affected by globalization, which is altering the rules of competition and industry structures across the world, that is not the same as saying that all organizations should themselves be global.[30] There are differences between a global product and a global firm or industry, although there are significant areas of overlap (we discuss global strategies in Section 14.6.2).

Some products, such as computer and aircraft components, are highly standardized and globalized. Some are purely local in terms of both customer focus and value chain—specific to the needs of a local population, and made locally. Perishable foods are an example, some utilities and some types of insurance are others. Others, such as automobiles, operate at a transnational, or regional, level. These products may be customized for regional customer preferences and different usage contexts, with one product range for North America, a second for western Europe, a third for Japan, and another for developing countries. However, many of their components may be standardized, and sourced or manufactured abroad. It is increasingly rare for products not to contain some internationally sourced elements.

Research suggests that internationalized firms on average perform better than those with a more local focus—as long as they are not *too* internationally diverse. In the same way as there are dangers in too much product diversification, too much international diversification appears to harm profitability.

There seems to be a typical pattern to this development.[31] (Figure 14.5)

- Initially, a firm will experience problems in its new markets as it overcomes the liability of newness. Time is needed while it adapts to new environments, develops the capabilities needed to deal with them, and builds its legitimacy with customers and suppliers. During this phase, a firm is likely to be less profitable than when it was just operating in its home market.

- In the second phase, the firm's performance improves as the investment in the markets it entered in phase 1 pays off. Sales increase and efficiency improves, and the capabilities it has built in the first phase can be used to penetrate further markets. This means that it is important for managers to take a long-term view of internationalization and not to be put off by initial setbacks.

- However, if the firm expands too quickly into too many countries, it enters the third phase, where the costs of managing the extra complexity that comes from a wide geographic spread start to outweigh the benefits. Performance declines again, perhaps to the levels of phase 1. Managers may be able to guard against this by making sure that their organization's architecture and capabilities keep pace with their expansion, so that complexity does not overwhelm them.[32]

Global product
A product that is uniform across the entire world.

Local product
A product that is different in each of the regions in which it is sold.

Global firm
A firm whose value chain activities are spread across the world.

Global industry
An industry in which there is a significant competitive advantage to integrating activities worldwide, and therefore whose constituent firms are global.

➜ We discussed diversification in Chapter 5, and the liability of newness in Section 3.4.

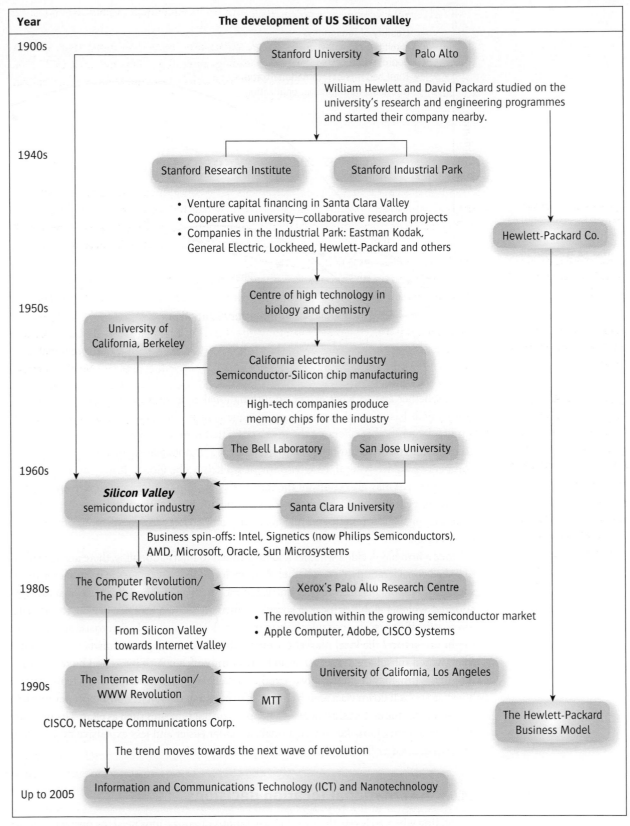

Figure 14.4 The development of Silicon Valley.
Source: Wonglimpiyarat (2006)

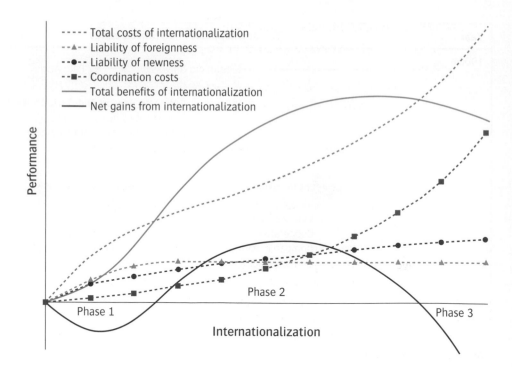

Figure 14.5
Multinationality
and performance:
a three-phase model.
Source: Lu and Beamish
(2004: 600)

So, whether and to what extent, to internationalize is an important decision for any company. It has to weigh up the likely management problems against the opportunities a much larger market offers, or the lower costs that it may achieve by locating in certain countries. It also needs to consider what happens if it does *not* expand abroad. Even if its competitive stance is local, its environment is likely to be global. It may be supplied by a global firm. It may also confront the threat of entry into its niche markets from international companies able to achieve low costs by operating on an international scale, and with sufficient financial strength and management competences to see off more purely local competitors.[33]

Once a firm has decided whether and how much to internationalize, there are a number of linked considerations. First, whether there are locational advantages in manufacturing or sourcing components in another country. Second, the type of generic international strategy adopted, whether global or local, or some intermediate form. A firm that decides to compete internationally must also consider how to market its offerings—whether to use agents, who might understand the local market conditions better, or to employ its own staff to set up fully owned subsidiary divisions, or find and communicate with interested buyers via the internet. A firm may decide simply to export a small part of its output, leaving it to interested buyers to track it down via a search engine, take payment only in its home currency and bill customers for the cost of shipment—as happens on auction sites such as eBay. The internet makes this form of low-key internationalization far easier and less expensive now than it used to be, since it offers any business a global shop window.

14.6.1 **International location decisions**

In deciding where to locate their various operations organizations need to consider:

- the characteristics of the product or service;
- the location and requirements of customers;

- whether the necessary resources are available in a particular region, such as:
  - sources of cost advantages like government incentives, low wages, or low property prices;
  - a suitable infrastructure, for example a supportive legal and regulatory environment, good transport, telephony, or IT facilities;
  - skilled workers;
  - suitable external links, for example suppliers, and sources of knowledge in the form of alliances;
- whether the necessary coordination of the value chain components can be achieved, for example if the firm has the requisite parenting competences or logistical infrastructure and capabilities.

Some organizations have turned the search for locational benefits into a source of competitive advantage in their own right. Organizational arbitrageurs[34] are firms that have the ability to exploit—rather than overcome or respond to—the differences between various countries by continually relocating their value chain elements to wherever is most beneficial. This requires them to have flexible architectures that can respond quickly to external changes in cost structures (see Real-life Application 14.6 later in this chapter). This is one of the reasons that H&M has so many suppliers; it has built in the option to move production to where capacity is highest or costs are lowest (because of exchange rate fluctuations perhaps) at little notice.

The characteristics of the product or service

The nature of the product/service is probably the most important determinant of location decisions:

- Products that have a short shelf-life, like some foodstuffs, or are difficult to transport because of their fragility, need to be manufactured close to their final market destinations.
- If a firm requires inputs that have a short shelf-life, it should put its production plant close to the source of the raw materials.
- Products that are expensive to transport, perhaps because of their bulk or special needs (live animals, for example) may also need to be manufactured close to their final destination. Packaging products, for example, are sold in similar form across a number of markets, but because the cost of shipping polystyrene foam or empty tin cans is high in comparison with the value of the goods, it is not economic to ship them more than 100 km or so.
- Other longer-lasting, robust products are suitable for mass production in a centralized location. For products that need to be produced in small batches, there are no aggregation benefits,[35] so manufacturing locations cannot usefully be centralized.
- Services need to be located where they are consumed.

The location and requirements of customers

A firm pursuing an international strategy will locate where it can reach customers who want—and are able—to buy its products. If consumers with similar needs are found in many different geographical areas, as for example are the customers for luxury goods, then it makes sense for a company to address all of them in the same way with an all-inclusive product that can be mass produced economically in a single location. But this then requires the firm to set in place a logistics system that gets these products to customers where and when they want them. In the luxury goods industry brands like Chanel and Louis Vuitton

Aggregation benefits
The advantages that come from gathering together value chain elements into the same location, thus making operations less complex, providing a single focus for customers, and achieving scale benefits.

have retail outlets or concessions in almost all of the major shopping centres and cities of the world. Their customers are international travellers, who are as likely to buy their Chanel bag in New York or Tokyo as in the company's home base of Paris.

Service organizations like hotels and fast-food restaurants, whose outputs are consumed as they are produced, obviously have to locate their outlets where the customers are. However, their supplies may come from other countries. Retailers, for example, may stock goods that are flown in from the other side of the globe, in which case how they communicate with key suppliers is an issue. Recently this has been made less of a problem by electronic communications.

Some firms, such as Levi Strauss and Hewlett-Packard, have been able to combine some of the aggregation benefits of centralized mass production with those of local customization by using regional centres to add local touches to global products.[36]

→ Virtual value chains and electronic commerce are discussed in Chapters 6 and 8.

Resource benefits

Cost advantage often comes from sourcing supplies and production in regions that have low costs, although this may be offset by disadvantages in other factors: a country may be located so far away from a firm's customers that the costs of transportation outweigh any savings on manufacturing or labour costs.

There are other trade-offs. Non-triad countries, whilst cheaper, often have fewer of the resources that companies need in order to develop innovation, or cannot staff units with competent managers (see Section 14.6.3 below). If the product needs high levels of expertise and requires partners with whom to exchange knowledge and ideas, then an expensive, but richly-resourced, triad location may be one that the company simply has to afford.

Low-cost countries often have a poor infrastructure, in the form of a strong legal framework or good transport links. Sometimes this gives local competitors an advantage, as they have had years to practice ways of getting round problems. In some cases they may use this as a springboard to become world-beating companies (see End-of-chapter Case Study 6.1). And countries like China or Bangladesh, which would otherwise be attractive on a cost basis, have to be judged against the possibility that the intellectual property rights of foreign companies will be weakly upheld (Real-life Application 14.3).

Real-life Application 14.3 Knowledge appropriation in China

When Gary Hamel[37] first introduced the notion of strategic alliances as a race to learn, the main threat (according to the Americans who felt they were the main 'victims') appeared to be from the less technologically sophisticated Japanese.[38] Now a similar threat is said to be under way from China, which has under-developed intellectual property laws, although its recent entry to the World Trade Organization is improving matters. But because of its enormous economic potential, many western firms feel that they cannot avoid doing business there.[39]

Eastman Kodak, one of the world's largest manufacturers of photography materials, encountered some difficulties with its Chinese partner, Lucky Film. Kodak owns a 20 per cent stake in its partner, although Lucky is still an independent company and also a direct competitor in the Asian markets. In 2006, Lucky hit the press because it was accused of infringing Kodak's brand and reputation.[40] Lucky was allegedly using a brand mark, printed on the back of photographic paper, which was very similar to the colour and font used on 'Kodak Royal Paper'. Kodak's studio proprietors were said to be using the cheaper Lucky paper but passing it off as Kodak's.

Although both companies say that the matter is resolved and that they have achieved much from their partnership, the incident was said to have caused 'some shock' in Kodak's US headquarters.[41]

14.6.2 Generic international strategies

Scholars have identified three basic ways in which companies deal with the various internationalization factors described in the previous section: global, locally responsive, and transnational strategies (Figure 14.6a and b).[42] These are ways of reconciling the pressures for cost minimization (e.g. through achieving global economies of scale) and for local responsiveness (because consumers in a particular area demand customized products).

Global products are standardized and usually sold under a single brand-name throughout the world, which is regarded as a single market and supplied worldwide from a small number of key locations.[43] There are a number of advantages to a firm adopting a global strategy:

- The firm can maximize any available economies of scale in, for example, advertising, product design, manufacturing, and purchasing.

- If up-front R&D costs are high and product life-cycles short, such as in microprocessors, then a global strategy allows the firm to recover these costs as quickly as possible.

- The organization can be exposed to developments in all key markets, so it is not taken by surprise by competitors who test a new product in one place before launching it globally.

- A company can fight competitive moves in one country with a counter-move in another. For example, if an American firm starts a price war in a firm's European home market, it can counter with a similar move in the USA.

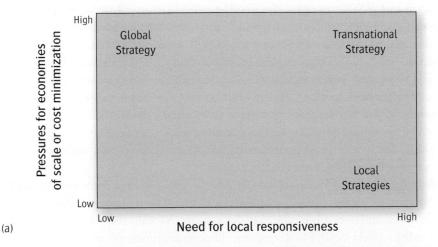

(a)

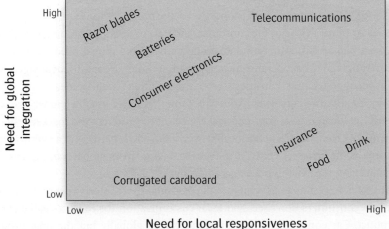

(b)

Figure 14.6 (a) International strategies. (b) Examples of international industries. Source: Bartlett and Ghoshal (1989)

- A firm can spread risk across a number of regions, reducing its vulnerability to an economic downturn in a single country

Of course it makes little sense to attempt to achieve economies of scale and standardize a product if people are unwilling to buy it. Products such as microprocessors, car components, or pharmaceutical ingredients can be identical anywhere in the world because, for the most part, their buyers are international businesses themselves. In the automobile industry, many companies even ask key suppliers to expand with them when they enter a new market. In industries like foodstuffs, on the other hand, consumers often have strong preferences for local products, although some global products like soft drinks have been made acceptable to a wide variety of tastes through subtle local adaptations and clever marketing.

Industries tend to globalize if consumers are aware of what is on offer in different countries. Some suggest that international travel appears to be making consumers more homogeneous in their tastes.[44] Travellers have been a major influence in helping brands like Canon (in cameras) and Gucci (in clothing) become global.

If one firm has been able to make a success of a global strategy, then it may change the industry recipe so that its competitors have to follow suit.[45] For example, in chocolate confectionery, Mars, the American industry leader, has followed a global strategy for a number of years. Nestlé–Rowntree, its main competitor, has gradually followed in making a more uniform selection of products available in different markets. This is despite the strong preferences that consumers in different countries have for chocolate with a particular cocoa, sugar, or milk content.[46]

In fact, a true global strategy is rare (see Theoretical Debate 14.1). Some of the most commonly cited global products (McDonald's and Coca-Cola, for example) change their packaging, advertising, or content, even if only slightly, to adjust to local taste. Coca-Cola is supposed to have a higher sugar content in some markets where consumers have a sweet tooth, and McDonald's offers Veggie and Chicken Maharajah burgers, rather than beef products, in its Indian branches. Even in electronic commerce, which some observers thought was likely to lead to further harmonization of tastes around the world, companies found they needed to respond to local differences. Internet retailer Amazon.com spends a great deal of time and money in adapting its website and inventory to take account of local customer preferences in each new country it enters.

At the other extreme, a locally responsive (sometimes known as a multi-local, or multi-domestic) strategy, allows a firm to serve each local market with products that are tailored specifically to it, and normally produced in that country. A locally responsive strategy may be adopted by a purely locally based company, although multinationals may also follow this strategy for some or all of their products.

Local strategies tend to need a high proportion of the product's value-chain activities to be located in each country close to the consumer, and because of duplication are likely therefore to have a higher cost structure than a company with a global product. Where cost drivers are strong, firms that operate on a purely national scale are at a disadvantage, so some theorists have suggested that industries are likely to be either global or local.[47]

However, an intermediate view, which became very fashionable under the slogan 'think global, act local', takes a transnational approach to products and markets[48] (Real-life Application 14.4). Here there is some localization of products, perhaps at a regional level, at the same time as the firm seeks cost advantages that come from global economies of scale. Some scholars have termed this objective 'ambitious'.[49]

The way that many companies achieve a transnational approach is to use global parts, the ones that end consumers don't see, and local customization for the noticeable elements of the product. Car components may be standardized globally but the final product is customized for local requirements, such as for left- or right-hand drive or automatic gearboxes.[50] Some scholars have suggested a model of a new global strategy,[51] which has some overlaps with a transnational one, which requires multinational enterprise (MNE) to integrate a worldwide network of differentiated affiliates, exploit the best location for each activity, manage financial activities globally, create political leverage in many countries and regions, and arbitrage cost differentials effectively. This means world-scale volume, world-class technology, world-class flexible processes *and* access to world-class production.

Under this model, the global MNE is a mechanism for transferring resources and capabilities, particularly tacit ones,[52] across borders when markets are 'insufficient to the purpose'.[53] The successful MNE is one that can develop capabilities in transferring such resources. This is almost certainly going to be a large firm, as only large organizations have the managerial and financial assets to build a network of wholly owned subsidiaries within which resources such as knowledge can be transferred relatively easily.

Real-life Application 14.4 Transnational strategies in GlaxoSmithKline

GlaxoSmithKline's primary global supply chain makes the active ingredients of drugs and ships them to the secondary supply chain facilities, which make the end product. *GlaxoSmithKline*

GlaxoSmithKline is a major international pharmaceuticals corporation. It is headquartered in the UK, with a very strong presence in the USA, where most of the world's drugs are sold. North America, Japan, and the EU are its primary markets.

The company was formed from the merger of Glaxo Wellcome, a UK pharmaceuticals company formed itself from the merger of Glaxo and Wellcome, and Smith-Kline-Beecham, a US firm, itself formed out of mergers between the companies that formed its name. Its shares are traded both in London and New York.

Its production is divided into a primary supply chain and a secondary supply chain.[54] The global primary supply chain manufactures the active ingredients of drugs, and ships them to the secondary supply chain facilities, which manufacture the end product. Its secondary supply chain is regional. There are facilities ➔

➜ in each of the triad regions as well as in Latin American and the Middle East, which make drugs for their regional markets. Whether a drug will be produced locally or imported is dependent on the regulations of the nation and regional trade treaties. Products are currently manufactured in some 37 countries.[55]

R&D is integrated globally. Drug research and development can take place in any of its network of R&D labs across the world, and best practice, wherever it is found, may be transferred and used anywhere else. R&D is spread around the world in order to take advantage of country-specific advantages, such as a university or research centre. It also locates its R&D in its major markets to learn about local requirements, and also where its major competitors are located. Its principal R&D facilities are in the UK, the USA, Japan, Italy, Spain, and Belgium.[56]

Theoretical Debate 14.1 Global products and international strategies

There are two main schools of thought regarding international strategy. One, which we call the global product school, believes that the tastes and needs of companies and consumers worldwide are converging, and that firms need to develop homogeneous products to serve them at low cost. The other holds that, although some tastes may converge, there will always be important differences between nations, which producers overlook at their peril.

One of the main proponents of the global product argument is a well-known American marketing expert, Theodore Levitt. In 'The globalization of markets' (Levitt, 1983), he suggested that the worldwide convergence was inevitable: 'the world's needs and desires have been irrevocably homogenized'. He said that this process was driven by technology, which facilitates communication, transport, and travel, and at the same time enables superior products to be produced at low prices. This leads to standardized products sold in standardized ways to customers the world over. Levitt cited, as examples of global products: McDonald's, which is found from the Champs Elysées to the Ginza; Coca-Cola and Pepsi-Cola which can be bought in Bahrain and in Moscow; and rock music, Greek salad, Hollywood movies, Revlon cosmetics, Sony televisions, and Levi jeans, which are found everywhere. More recently, middle-class consumers in countries such as India and China, increasingly affluent and numerous, appear to be attracted to the same brands and models of car, consumer electronics, and clothing as their peers in Europe or the USA.

George Yip, C. K. Prahalad, and Yves Doz are other prominent proponents of the idea of the global product. Johansson and Yip (1994) have found evidence that firms following a global product strategy perform better, on average, than those that do not.

Douglas and Wind (1987) are at the opposite end of the spectrum from these scholars—and advocate a countries or local approach to competition, which aims to customize products for local needs. They suggest that markets are not as homogeneous as Levitt claimed. They offer a range of examples of how customers in different parts of the world have differing needs that cannot be met by a standardized product. They also argue that the emphasis on economies of scale and production and marketing is not the irreversible driving force that Levitt emphasizes. Many new technologies actually lower the minimum efficient scale of production, and anyway, for many industries economies of scale are not a competitive success factor. In the local category are restaurants, local foodstuffs such as cheese, and many services or utilities, such as gas or water supply, car repair shops, and hairdressers.

Baden-Fuller and Stopford (1991) cite the European domestic appliances industry as an example where global strategies appear to be less effective than nationally based ones. Similarly Ford Motor pursued a global product strategy very single-mindedly in the late 1990s, developing a number of cars, such as the Mondeo, intended to sell in large quantities, with only minor modifications, throughout the world. In this, they were clearly influenced by the success in the 1980s of Japanese manufacturers such as Toyota, Honda, and Nissan, which had generated huge worldwide sales and profits from a limited product range. However, Ford has lost market share, most notably in Europe to Renault, which succeeded with models such as the Mégane, styled to appeal to European tastes.

There are writers who have taken a less polarized view of international competition. Ohmae (1989) suggested that customer needs around the world have become similar, whilst the fixed costs of meeting those needs have soared, making global products a necessity. But, in Ohmae's opinion, there are still sufficient differences in the needs of local markets to make totally universal products unrealistic. His may be classified as the transnational view, also favoured by Christopher Bartlett and Sumantra Ghoshal (Bartlett and Ghoshal, 1989).

Other researchers, led by Alan Rugman and his associates, believe they have demonstrated that global strategies are ➜

→ rather unusual, and that MNEs prefer regional strategies—focusing on Asia, the EU, or North America. They gathered data for 380 of the largest MNEs, and found that, for the vast majority (320) of them, an average of 80 per cent of sales came from the firm's home region (Rugman and Verbeke, 2004). Smaller studies of major retailers and automobile manufacturers showed similar patterns (Rugman and Girod, 2003; Rugman, 2004).

There are some indications, however, that the effectiveness of a regional or global strategy may to some extent be dictated by the stage of an industry's development. A 1998 study of the European domestic appliance industry (Segal-Horn et al., 1998) found a higher degree of globalization there than Baden-Fuller and Stopford observed in 1991. Schlie and Yip (2000) looked at car-makers' regional strategies, and concluded that automobile manufacturers did better if, like Toyota and Honda, they globalized first and then regionalized later. Globalization gained them bargaining power with their suppliers and allowed higher returns on expensive investments in R&D. They could then, from this profitable base, find ways to regionalize their strategies, whereas firms that competed purely at a regional level, such as Fiat, were at a disadvantage. Subsequent to this study, Renault, which had a successful regional strategy based on Europe, formed a close alliance with the Japanese firm, Nissan, in order to improve both firms' global competitiveness.

But there are those that suggest that trying to decide on either global or local products may be the wrong question. Ghemawat (2007) describes the assumption that firms face a trade-off between local responsiveness and global economies of scale as 'problematic'. He suggests, instead, that the major concern for firms pursuing any international strategy is to manage the 'large differences that arise at borders, whether those borders are defined geographically or otherwise'. Competitive advantage may come from exploiting these differences—arbitrage is the term he uses (see Section 14.6.3 below)—and moving value chain activities across the globe in order to benefit from any temporary local advantages.

These three generic strategies point out the ways in which firms may vary their offerings. But this does not necessarily tell us how the organization is configured: for example, where manufacturing takes place or the level of outsourcing that the firm chooses.

→ We introduced outsourcing, offshoring, and nearshoring in Chapter 6.

14.6.3 International organizational configurations

There are a number of factors that influence how an international firm is configured, size for example. A small firm has relatively few options, and is unlikely to be able to adopt a fully global strategy, although it still may contract out its manufacturing overseas and sell its products to international customers.

Managers must also decide how well they could handle a lot of diverse small operations spread across a number of time zones and national cultures, and whether they have parenting skills in managing such complexity.

→ We discussed diversification in Section 5.4 and parenting competences and the management of complexity in Chapter 9.

The international corporation's executives must use a parenting style in which they have competences, *and* which is suitable for international business units that may have very different cultures and business methods. The firm may be better suited to having fewer, larger operations in locations where its managers understand the people and their business practices. In a single operation in its home country, the organization might find it relatively easy to exert control and to ensure that information and learning are shared and acted upon. Coherence is an important consideration too—attempting to be simultaneously global for some products and locally responsive for others is likely to result in a complex organization that stretches managerial 'bandwidth' too far.

Firms may arrive at different location decisions for different elements of the value chain. A retail bank may centralize its cheque processing in Asia to take advantage of economies of scale and low labour costs. However, it may maintain an extensive network of small branches in Europe, so as to be close to its local customers, as well as serving its on-line customers through a telephone call centre, or via the internet.

International location decisions also depend on how possible it is for the different value chain elements to be linked with the others. For example, there is little point in locating in Silicon Valley or Paris in order to benefit from the knowledge that may be gained there, if this knowledge cannot be easily transferred to other parts of the organization. And, although costs may be saved by setting up manufacturing plants in China, as Sony has done, this may not mean that Sony in Japan will benefit from any new ideas that emerge there—unless the organization has a suitable architecture that allows this to happen.

International architectures

The problems of developing an architecture that we discussed in Chapters 8 and 9 are even more pronounced in international organizations. Although the internet has made it far easier to communicate between different countries and time zones, differences between national cultures and languages may still create problems of understanding. Tacit knowledge is best transferred from one part of an organization to another through frequent personal contact—and in international organizations this can be both expensive and time-consuming. One way of achieving knowledge transfer is through expatriate staff.[57] However, all will incur housing and relocation costs. Another is through requiring staff, especially managers, to travel abroad regularly—something that not everyone wants to do. And, again, this is costly.

Even when a firm makes global products, such as luxury clothes, which could easily be designed and produced at a single site, it may decide to keep departments in key additional locations. This helps the organization to stay in touch with the tastes and requirements of opinion formers, gives them credibility, and may help them gather information about what competitors are doing. This is why almost every information technology firm of any size has an office in Silicon Valley in California, and Kao, a Japanese cosmetics firm, has set up a centre of excellence for perfume development in Paris.

International organization structures

➔ We discussed organizational structures in Section 8.2 and Chapter 9.

International organizations, like nationally based firms, make use of a wide variety of hierarchical structures, including functional hierarchies, divisional hierarchies, global product units, and matrices. Companies may have portfolios of international business divisions that stand alone and make little or no attempt to relate to any other. Or there may be some attempt to develop synergies or share learning.

Partly, the choice of structure is dictated by the stage of internationalization of the firm. Initially, it is likely to use an exporting type of structure, in which overseas agents are used, to be followed in time by an overseas sales office. Or it may sub-contract manufacturing to a foreign firm without any thought of ownership of these assets. As international operations become more important to the organization, it may start to open overseas offices, acquire firms overseas, or enter into long-term alliances with international partners. In time, more complex forms emerge, such as product or area-based divisional structures, matrix, and network structures (see Chapter 10).

International companies have to decide whether they want to import their own home-based staff and impose their own employee management practices on their foreign unit, or use local labour and adopt local practices. Both have their advantages and disadvantages, and tend to be linked to the type of international strategy adopted (Real-life Application 14.5). Four basic approaches have been identified.[58]

A polycentric approach treats the multinational as a holding company; decision-making is decentralized to local managers in the foreign subsidiaries, who will almost always be from that country. Local structures and business conventions can be used, sometimes making it hard to tell that the company is owned by a foreign firm. This allows those people who are most informed about local conditions to make local decisions. This approach is particularly suitable for a locally responsive strategy, although the issue here then is what value the head office can offer. There is a danger that the local manager may feel too remote from the head office to keep them properly informed, especially if there are language barriers to overcome. In the same way as a diverse portfolio of businesses may find it hard to achieve synergies or knowledge-sharing between them, a polycentric approach can result in lack of coordination between the units, and a failure to achieve economies of scale.

An ethnocentric approach recreates local operations in the image of the home country; the top management in the local unit is dominated by home-nation personnel. The ethnocentric approach is used when local staff are not available or not sufficiently skilled, and is sometimes used as a temporary measure to train up and socialize local staff into the culture of the home organization. Companies that need to coordinate operations tightly, for example to adopt a global product strategy, as well as those that are worried about the loss of proprietary knowledge are likely to use an ethnocentric approach. However, this policy is expensive. There is also the danger of cultural imperialism: expatriate managers can be insensitive to local feelings, and can create a sense that the local operations are 'second-best' to the home country's units. There may be no sense of local 'belonging', loyalty, or commitment.

A geocentric approach is where the headquarters is the global centre of the organization's activity—financial planning and controlling decisions are centralized there. But in terms of staffing, the best person for the job, regardless of nationality, manages the foreign unit. The local manager may be from that country, from the parent company's country, or from a third country altogether. This is the approach often taken by the largest multinational companies, who spend a considerable amount of time and resources developing managers who can adjust to any business environment and to different cultures. It reduces the possibility for local personnel to feel put upon by the cultural imperialism of an ethnocentric HQ, whilst allowing managers that are loyal to the HQ's values to liaise with it.

A regiocentric approach blends the needs of headquarters with those of the local unit. It is similar to the geocentric approach, but utilizes the best people within a specific region.

In all cases, inter and intra-organizational transaction costs between international units are likely to be greater than between national units:

- Legal contracts taking account of the different national regulations and legislation will be complex and require greater legal expertise than in single-nation enterprises.

- The costs of policing and resolving any disputes are likely to be greater than for national firms.

- Cultural differences may make for misunderstandings and conflict, requiring considerable managerial oversight.

- Even though English has become the common business language in many parts of the world, this itself has costs:

  - International staff will need to be trained in English and any other language that the organization, and its suppliers and customers, use.

  - Documents, and even conversations between staff, may require translation.

  - There may be mistakes made as the result of poor translation, which will need to be rectified.

- Currency movements between the different national units make transfer prices hard to set.

Real-life Application 14.5 International structures in IBM and Procter & Gamble[59]

For most of its history, IBM served overseas markets by setting up a mini-IBM in each country, each of which pursued a nearly complete set of value chain activities. Since the 1980s IBM has aggregated its countries into regions and also created 'deal hubs' for its hardware, software, and services businesses. It has also relocated its procurement office from New York, to Shenzhen, in China.

More recently, however, IBM has taken to arbitrage. It has exploited wage differentials in some of its low-margin businesses by increasing the number of employees in India from 9,000 in 2004 to 43,000 by mid-2006. At the heart of IBM's arbitrage approach is a sophisticated algorithm that matches staff to assignments across all of IBM's locations according to the skills needed at any one time. This is said to represent a 'massive power shift'.

Procter & Gamble started out like IBM with locally responsive strategies and several 'mini-P&Gs' that adapted to local markets. It evolved differently, however. Early 'halting' attempts at European aggregation resulted in a matrix structure that proved unwieldy. In 1999, the new CEO brought in a structure in which global business units (GBUs) retained overall responsibility for profits, but sales were the responsibility of local market development organizations (MDOs).

However, it is said that problems arose in a number of areas, including the key GBU/MDO interfaces. Since then Procter & Gamble has adopted an approach that strikes more of a balance between local responsiveness and aggregation, allowing for differences between its business units and markets. Its pharmaceuticals division, which has its own distribution channels, has been left out of the MDO structure, and in emerging markets, profit responsibility continues to be held by country managers. It has also developed decision grids, which define how different decisions are to be made and by whom (GBU or MDO, for example). These are agreed after 'months of negotiation' and are reviewed regularly. Overall responsibility for profits (and the right to make decisions not covered by the grids) is still retained by the GBUs. This structure is helped by proximity: the GBUs' regional headquarters are often co-located with the regional MDO headquarters. Promotion to director level normally requires experience in both the GBU and the MDO, reinforcing the message that the two realms are equal, and safeguarding the MDOs' potential to feel marginalized by a lack of profit responsibility.

Arbitrage is also important to Procter & Gamble, and it achieves this mostly through outsourcing. However, in the faster-moving consumer goods industry, this is less important than aggregation.

Worked Example 14.1 Assessing H&M's international strategy and structure

Assessing H&M against the theory on international strategies and structures presented in this chapter requires us to make a judgement about its products, its market locations, and customer requirements, and to assess whether its value chain elements are located appropriately across the world. In this Worked Example we need to know how it is configured, and therefore will refer back to Worked Example 6.1 on H&M's value chain.

H&M is both a manufacturer and retailer. However, although it undertakes both types of operation, it has configured its value chain very differently in the two activities. The retailing arm is principally located within the European Union, with recent expansion into North America and tentative moves into other regions such as Dubai. It is untested whether H&M would be equally successful if it were to expand into fast-developing regions with very different cultures and economic profiles—China, India, Russia, or Brazil, for example. But it is currently dipping its toes into these new types of market. It is significant that for the first time it is using franchises, because of local trade restrictions, rather than wholly owned stores.

H&M's manufacturing, on the other hand, is carried out both in Europe and in developing countries, notably in east Asia—some

distance away from its core markets. To be successful, this requires its products to be easily and cheaply transportable, and for the company to have capabilities in logistics and supply chain management.

Its products are global, although there is some customization, in that stores are able to select clothes from the full range that they believe will sell best locally. In each of its markets it faces competition from local companies, as well as major international firms.

H&M acts as both an arbitrageur and an aggregator. It has a wide network of suppliers, which it switches between according to demand. It trades off its ability to be a fully-flexible arbitrageur with its desire to use suppliers that can adhere to the company's ethical code of practice—so there is some aggregation in a core group of suppliers, a trend that has accelerated in the last few years. There are signs in 2007 that the company is aggregating some of its logistics into a single transit centre in Hamburg, close to its major markets. This move in its own right appears to be the outcome of its ethical stance, in that it is attempting to transport more goods by rail or sea rather than air. It has reconfigured its product supply to allow non-fast fashion items to be →

→ manufactured in bulk and transported by 'greener' methods. Higher fashion items, which are made in smaller batches and in which speed to market is critical, are still transported by air and road. And aggregation is also taking place in the supply and buying function, as a small number of production offices are located close to suppliers.

Other aspects of its value chain are centralized and undertaken on a global basis—notably product design, which is carried out in its head office. And here we find an interesting choice of location. We suggested in Worked Example 6.1 that it was unusual in not locating the design function in Paris or Milan. Clothes design has not traditionally been one of Sweden's sources of national competitive advantage,[60] and in one study, none of Sweden's top 50 industries, with the very peripheral exception of textiles for machinery, had any obvious links to either apparel manufacturing or retailing, or indeed design. So, H&M appears to have developed in an environment with few factor advantages. But if we dig deeper, we find that Sweden has some benefits that may be relevant. It has had a strong logistics and transportation industry, and, recently, has shown that, along with Scandinavia as a whole, it actually does have a strong set of design industries and infrastructure.

Other research also shows that Sweden's national culture seems to be helpful in internationalizing. Hofstede's dimensions show Sweden to be high on individualism, low on masculinity, and low on uncertainty-avoidance.[61] This has been associated with organizational cultures and employment practices that favour relationship-building and cooperation, resulting in an ability to handle complex matrix organizational structures with dual bosses and numerous lateral relationships. Such lateral competences are associated with successful internationalization.[62]

One of H&M's defining characteristics is the attention it pays to ensuring that staff in new countries understand how it does business—it has a strong set of beliefs and values which may be at risk if it is now moving into countries with very different cultures and ways of doing business, and which are geographically distant from H&M's home base. H&M will probably have to use more resources, and reap lower rewards in the short term, than it is used to. These risks may of course be well worth taking in order to expand into large, new, and fast-growing, territories. But by moving into countries with different, and less stable currencies, H&M's treasury function has an increasingly important role.

Using Evidence 14.1 Assessing a company's international strategy

A good starting point when assessing a company's international strategy and structure is to draw a diagram of its locations and the connections between these. The value chain is a suitable model to use, which may then be extended to the wider value system to show linkages between the different locations, as well as suppliers' and other partners' value chains and locations. This should be as complete as possible, but realistically, for the largest and most complicated international organizations, this diagram needs to be selective—focusing on the largest locations and the most important relationships.

Using the theory in this chapter on, for example, economic stability, exchange rates, or country characteristics (using Porter's diamond as an organizing framework), an assessment can be made of the risks that an organization faces if it expands internationally. For example, H&M's move into the Middle East—a region that is predominantly shaped by theocratic, Islamic, laws, and which has not been the most stable of regions in recent years—provides some risks. We would want to know what those risks are, so evidence should be gathered on movements in the country's currency and exchange rates over, say, the last five years, the stability of the country or region's political systems (measured by how many changes of government there have been, and any press reports of trouble spots). We would also want to know about the national infrastructure—whether it has good road and rail links, and if it has an internationally recognized legal system able to deal with any copyright or IPR issues, for instance. We may also want to see how many foreign companies are already operating in the country, and if there have been any trade disputes in which the WTO or similar organizations have intervened.[62]

Practical dos and don'ts

Some large multinational organizations have operations in hundreds of locations worldwide and maybe a thousand different products. Some of these products may be global and some may be locally responsive. Given the time constraints that you are likely to be working under, it is important to prioritize—you will not be able to examine all aspects of the company or the countries in which it is to be found. Pick the largest and most strategically important.

You are looking especially for indicators of international value chain linkages which work well, or which work less well—perhaps because of geographic distance, perhaps because of cultural misunderstandings or language difficulties, or because senior managers do not have the necessary competences to manage a complex international firm. You are also looking for sources of value that are currently unexploited—such as the relocation of manufacturing to low-cost countries or to regions with a supportive infrastructure, or the aggregation of value chain elements into larger units where economies of scale may be achieved without loss of local responsiveness.

International alliances, mergers, and acquisitions

Alliances and mergers/acquisitions are common methods of internationalizing—edging into new geographic markets, or learning about a new environment with the help of a partner,[63] as in the Kodak/Lucky example above. Sometimes companies have no choice but to enter into strategic alliances with local partners if they want to enter a protected country. But often firms will choose international locations where they can be sure of finding suitable external partners. Increasingly, these are in developing countries.[64]

However, any of the cultural problems between alliance or merger partners that we discuss in Sections 9.3 and 17.5 are likely to be magnified by the sorts of national cultural differences that we introduced in Section 14.6.2.[65] In addition, international mergers/acquisitions and alliances have to cope with the very different laws that may operate in the companies' units. These may be solved in different ways, through an ethnocentric approach to the management of a joint venture perhaps, or through setting out a pre-nuptial agreement that spells out in as much detail as possible what will be the local unit's responsibility and what will be the parent's.

What Can Go Wrong 14.1 Outsourcing call centres to India

In the mid-1990s, when US and UK firms first started to outsource their call centres to India, the challenge was to convince sceptics that high-quality international outsourcing was feasible. However, what was at first a trickle of companies, soon became a flood aided by the USA and Britain's relatively liberal employment laws. Many of the companies who moved their call centres to India were financial services, such as the HSBC bank, Prudential, and Aviva (Norwich Union) insurance, or other service companies like airlines who located their booking offices there; others were computer hardware manufacturers, like Dell, Microsoft, and Hewlett-Packard, who set up telephone help centres there.

The reasons for outsourcing call centres were mainly to benefit from India's low wages: call centre staff in India earned approximately 10 per cent of equivalent salaries in the US or UK. The Prudential would have had to pay a one-off restructuring charge of £20m, but expected to achieve annual cost savings of £16 million.[66] However, the Prudential also cited other motives: it recognized that callers wanted 'to speak to real people' rather than an automated telephone, as well as flexibility in being able to talk to an operator outside working hours.[67] India's time is about five hours ahead of the UK, and about 12 hours ahead of the US.

Outsourcing to India was made possible because of significant improvements in the price and quality of international telecommunications. The cost of a telephone call from India to the US and UK fell by more than 80 per cent between 2001 and 2005.

India, on its side, appears to have been very happy to take on this work. Applications to work in call centres from graduates of India's universities (a typical call centre employee) ran into the thousands a month. Prudential received 25,000 applications when it first announced plans for the call centre, and then had to

conduct more than 8,000 interviews. There are plenty of reports telling of young women whose lives were revolutionized by call centre work and the new-found ability to earn good money: work represented 'modernity and freedom', in contrast to their normally conservative family life.[68] The regions where call centres have aggregated saw their economies and environment transformed. The outsourcing industry now contributes $17bn to India's economy: it employs 700,000 people.[69] US firms account for approximately 70 per cent of this business, followed by the UK.[70]

But there are now signs that optimism about outsourcing is beginning to sour—both in India as well as in the UK and USA. Some commentators put this down to distance—both physical and cultural—and suggest that although it is possible to manage a call centre badly anywhere, the effects of doing it badly in India are 'disproportionately great',[71] and companies do not fully understand what they are getting into. Because of this, the difficulty of maintaining the desired level of service may be much greater than anticipated.

Other complaints have included customer dissatisfaction with the service they receive from Indian units. These centre around problems of a lack of understanding of local culture and environment, as well as language problems. Although almost all Indian graduates speak English, only those from the best universities and some Indian regions speak it well enough to be able to cope with American and British callers. This has led to frustration and abuse of the call centre agent in some cases.[72]

Although some call centre operators have spent a lot of money training their staff on the American or British way of life, there is a limit to how much local knowledge can be imparted; staff can flounder when they have to deviate from the prepared script, →

→ and in any case, 'customers with complex queries requiring local understanding do not respond well to far-off operators repeating parrot-fashion a series of learned responses'[73] (not exclusively an Indian problem of course). Some companies' attempts to disguise the Indian location by giving call centre staff English-sounding names have misfired—accents give the game away, leading to accusations of deception and deliberate misrepresentation. There are also suggestions of racism—one survey found that 72 per cent of US consumers would rather use an automated system or the Web than talk to someone with a foreign accent.[74] Another, in the UK, found that only 5 per cent of respondents were happy to have their bank accounts serviced by an overseas call centre.[75]

There have been examples of data misuse. Although rare, fraudsters in overseas call centres have stolen details of customers, including their bank, passport, and mobile phone numbers,[76] with potentially devastating effects on the reputation of both Indian firms and their clients. And an organized ring of agents systematically deceived US customers of Capital One Financial Services at the Wipro Spectramind call centre in Mumbai, by making false claims about free gifts and membership fees.[77] Supervisors had apparently told the agents to spice up their sales pitch for the client—the result of 'pressure on the agents to make sales combined with insufficient training about acceptable ways of doing business'.[78] Capital One rescinded the contract with Wipro, and relocated in Virginia. As a result, there have been calls to extend data protection laws to cover overseas customer information.[79]

The loss of jobs to foreign workers has also caused concern. Perhaps 1 million US call centre jobs have been outsourced overseas. This has resulted in some considerable resentment from unions and some government agencies alike. Several American states have moved faster than the federal authorities in trying to halt this 'labour arbitrage'. The legislature in US states such as New Jersey, Connecticut, Missouri, Washington, and Maryland have already imposed bans on outsourcing or are in the process of doing so.[80]

India's telecommunications' infrastructure is still sometimes a problem—India jointly held last place among 16 countries that a McKinsey study assessed.[81] Floods in Mumbai recently caused internet services to go down for three days.

In India there are also increasing concerns. According to some reports, more than half of India's call centres are in financial difficulties and searching for buyers. Staff turnover is very high (up to 40 per cent a year), recruitment is becoming increasingly difficult because of the increasing competition from higher-paid jobs, and costs are escalating. These factors are linked. Call centre work is stressful at the best of times, made worse by hostility from dissatisfied customers.[82] In India this is made worse by the need to accommodate the time difference between the US/UK and India—staff often work long hours and at night.

Wages are lower than their young, well-educated, staff can increasingly get in other jobs—but cannot be improved because their international partners are squeezing margins as the rupee strengthens—increasing the pressure on service quality and staff stress yet more. Call centre operators are responding by recruiting older workers from the provinces, but one writer suggests that this translates as: 'Get ready for an even wider cultural and language gulf between workers and Western customers.'[83]

As a result many call centres are being repatriated to the UK or the USA, or relocated closer to home in Ireland, Jamaica, and Canada—a trend that is expected to continue.[84] Here, although they may be more expensive in terms of wages, head office executives do not have a ten-hour flight and jet lag to contend with, and can visit regularly—necessary to ensure standards in the foreign unit.

Other companies are experimenting with 'rightshoring'—placing simple queries offshore while retaining the more complex ones closer to the caller. Others are trying to manage their overseas operations better. In some cases, British or American top managers are being transferred into the foreign unit. And in what seems like a barely disguised dig at competitors, IBM says that it is not one of the companies that 'pride themselves on doing things cheaply'.[85] In fact, IBM is one company that has bought its Indian partner—Daksh, India's third-largest customer support services firm. And the Prudential also believes much of the success of its Indian operation is down to its 'captive'—wholly owned—subsidiary status: the call centre is an 'integral part of the UK operation and is treated as one of the company's five UK sites'.[86] It has, it says, few complaints about the unit.[87]

● CHAPTER SUMMARY

There are a number of important factors that are driving globalization, including an understanding of the economic benefits of trade, technological developments in communications and transportation, increasing international travel and inter-cultural awareness, a reduction in conflict, and the development of a legal and regulatory framework that governs international trade.

There are two major types of international trade—importing and exporting, and foreign direct investment—and a number of international arrangements that allow trade between nations. These include financial instruments such as interest and exchange rates. Differences between currencies provide a challenge for multinational firms, who have to translate profits accrued in one currency into consolidated accounts in the home currency. Without techniques such as hedging and currency options, international firms would face unacceptable fluctuations in their income.

Bodies such as the IMF, the World Bank, and the World Trade Organization set up rules and procedures governing international economic and political activities, with which member countries agree to comply. Other mechanisms that encourage international trade include economic unions, free trade areas, and common markets. Some of the best known are the European Union, ASEAN, and NAFTA. However, some countries still attempt to protect their own industries, through erecting barriers to trade including exchange and investment controls, embargoes, tariffs, quotas, and import licences. And there are some critics of globalization and the agencies that regulate it. They focus on global trade's negative effects on the world's poorest countries.

Most of world trade takes place within the countries in the 'triad'—Japan, the EU, and the USA—although a number of countries are catching up fast—China and India, for example. Different countries have different features that make them more or less attractive to firms, according to their specific requirements. There are legal and regulatory, socio-cultural, economic, and infrastructure issues that make some countries and regions more or less attractive to firms that wish to locate some of their activities abroad.

Which activities are located where depend on the organization's product and market strategies, based on the nature of the product, the location and requirements of customers, and the availability of inputs. There are three generic international strategies:

- global—in which a single, standardized, product, is sold worldwide. A global product is nearly always produced and administered in a small number of locations in which economies of scale can be achieved;

- locally responsive—in which products are developed for each market in order to take account of local tastes;

- transnational—products are manufactured at a regional level, although the product itself is customized for local markets.

Multinational firms can choose to configure their operations in a number of ways, depending on their size, parenting competences, and the type of product and market strategies adopted. There are four main approaches—polycentric, ethnocentric, geocentric, and regiocentric. International firms also engage in strategic alliances and mergers and acquisitions in order to enter new markets or learn about a new environment, although cultural differences between firms in different nations can make these hard to manage.

 Online Resource Centre
www.oxfordtextbooks.co.uk/orc/haberberg_rieple/

Visit the Online Resource Centre that accompanies this book to read more information relating to strategies in international contexts.

● KEY SKILLS

The key skills you should have developed after reading this chapter are:

- knowledge of the different bodies, instruments, and cross-national arrangements that encourage and regulate international trade;

- an understanding of the various advantages that different parts of the world have over others, and how these may change over time;

- expertise in appraising a firm's international product and market strategies, and whether these are appropriately matched with the organization's structure;

- the ability to evaluate a company's choice of international locations and show how they contribute to its success or failure.

REVIEW QUESTIONS

1. Hugo Chavez, Venezuela's president, has removed the country from the membership of the World Bank and the IMF. Do you think he is right to do so?

    What do you think will be the impact of his actions on:

    (a) A Venezuelan company that wishes to expand abroad?

    (b) A company that is hoping to trade with Venezuelan companies?

    (c) A company that is hoping to locate part of its operations in Venezuela?

2. Do you think that understanding national cultural characteristics will make you better at managing international acquisitions? If so, how? If not, why not?

3. Do you see any disadvantages to a firm moving to locate in a national or regional cluster?

4. You are the manager of a company that wishes to manufacture an innovative product in a low-cost country that does not yet have a fully-fledged IPR or regulatory infrastructure. What actions should you take to protect your product?

5. Do you think a major call centre industry in India will still exist in five years time? Explain your answer.

FURTHER READING

There are a number of excellent textbooks on international trade and management:

- Rugman, A. M., Collinson, S., and Hodgetts, R. M. (2006). *International Business*, 4th edn. Harlow: Pearson Education and Wild, J. J., Wild, K. L., and Han, J. C. Y. (2004). *International Business*. Harlow: Prentice Hall both cover the key issues to do with international trade bodies, the economics of international business, and the management of international companies.

- Hofstede, G. (1980). *Culture's Consequences: Comparing Values, Behaviors, Institutions, and Organizations across Nations*. Thousand Oaks, CA: Sage (and Hofstede 1991); Trompenaars, F. and Hampden-Turner, C. (1997). *Riding the Waves of Culture: Understanding Cultural Diversity in Business*. 2nd edn. London: Nicholas Brealey; and House, R. J., Hanges, P. J., Javidan, M., Dorfman, P. W., and Gupta, V. (eds) (2004). *Culture, Leadership and Organizations: The GLOBE Study of 62 Societies*. Thousand Oaks, CA: Sage are the leading authors on national dimensions of culture.

- Birkinshaw, J., Ghoshal, S., Markides, C., Stopford, J., and Yip, G. (eds). (2003). *The Future of the Multinational Company*. Chichester: Wiley is a book that brings together contributions from many of the pre-eminent authors on international management.

- Friedman, T. (2006). *The World Is Flat: A Brief History of the Twenty-first Century*. London: Penguin provides a readable and interesting account of the forces that are encouraging globalization.

Trade statistics and country information is available from any of the international trade organizations' excellent websites:

- IMF <http://www.imf.org>, international financial data—currencies, exchange rates, trade deficits/surpluses;

- International Labour Organization, *Yearbook of International Labour Statistics*—labour market data;

- OECD <http://stats.oecd.org>;

- UN COMTRADE database <http://unstats.un.org/unsd/comtrade/>;

- United Nations <http://www.un.org/Depts/unsd/>—national accounts data, Statistics Division;

- World Bank <http://worldbank.org>—country indicators and economic indicators;

- Porter, M. and Sala-í-Martin, X. (2007). *Global Competitiveness Report*. World Economic Forum—provides a comprehensive summary of countries' competitiveness factors. See World Economic Forum <http://www.weforum.org/en/initiatives/gcp/Global%20Competitiveness%20Report/index.htm> for research data on public institutions, laws, and corruption worldwide;

- World Trade Organization <http://www.wto.org>—international trade statistics and country data;

- Economist Intelligence Unit—produces a number of basic economic statistics on different economies of the world as well as a general risk rating.

Also see international organizations that develop standards including the UN and the International Institute for the Unification of Private Law.

UN:

- Food and Agriculture Organization, Statistical Yearbook—provides data on food production, soil quality, and other agro-economic indicators;

- Yearbook of National Account Statistics;

- Yearbook of International Trade Statistics.

US National Science Foundation <http://www.nber.org/papers/W5910>, Bowen-Feenstra-Lipsey Project.

● REFERENCES

Baden-Fuller, C. W. F. and Stopford, J. M. (1991). 'Globalization frustrated: the case of white goods'. *Strategic Management Journal*, 12/7: 493–507.

Bartlett, C. A. and Ghoshal, S. (1988). 'Organizing for worldwide effectiveness: the transnational solution'. *California Management Review*, 31/1: 54.

Bartlett, C. A. and Ghoshal, S. (1989). *Managing Across Borders: The Transnational Solution*. London: Century Business. 2nd edn (2001).

Benneworth, P. and Henry, N. (2004). 'Where is the value added in the cluster approach? Hermeneutic theorising, economic geography and clusters as a multiperspectival approach'. *Urban Studies*, 4/15–16: 1011–23.

Bernhofen, D. M. (2005). 'Gottfried Haberler's 1930 reformulation of comparative advantage in retrospect'. *Review of International Economics*, 13/5: 997–1000.

Boersma, A. (2006). 'Protecting intellectual assets in China: three stages to sustaining a strategic knowledge advantage'. *KM Review*, 9/3: 22–5.

Calori, R., Atamer, T., and Nunes, P. (2000a). *The Dynamics of International Competition*. London: Sage.

Calori, R., Melin, L., Atamer, T., and Gustavsson, P. (2000b). 'Innovative international strategies'. *Journal of World Business*, 35/4: 333.

Carr, C. (2005). 'Are German, Japanese and Anglo-Saxon strategic decision styles still divergent in the context of globalization?' *Journal of Management Studies*, 42/6: 1155–88.

Chng, P.-L. and Pangarkar, N. (2000). 'Research on global strategy'. *International Journal of Management Reviews*, 2/1: 91.

Collier, P. and Dollar, D. (2001a). *Globalization, Growth, and Poverty: Building an Inclusive World Economy*. New York: Oxford University Press for the World Bank (cited by Rodrik, 2001).

Collier, P. and Dollar, D. (2001b). 'Can the world cut poverty in half? How policy reform and effective aid can meet international development goals'. *World Development*, 29/11: 1787.

Conn, H. P. and Yip, G. S. (1997). 'Global transfer of critical capabilities'. *Business Horizons*, 40/1: 22.

Deardorff, A. V. (2005). 'How robust is comparative advantage?' *Review of International Economics*, 13/5: 1004–16.

Dieter, H. (2006). 'The decline of the IMF: is it reversible? Should it be reversed?' *Global Governance*, 12/4: 343–9.

Dolowitz, D. P. (2006). 'Bring back the states: correcting for the omissions of globalization'. *International Journal of Public Administration*, 29/4–6: 263–80.

Douglas, S. P. and Wind, Y. (1987). 'The myth of globalization'. *Columbia Journal of World Business*, 22/4: 19.

Earley, P. C. (2006). 'Leading cultural research in the future: a matter of paradigms and taste'. *Journal of International Business Studies*, 37/6: 922–31.

Ernst, D. (2002). 'Global production networks and the changing geography of innovation systems: implications for developing countries'. *Economics of Innovation and New Technology*, 11/6: 497.

Feitzinger, E. and Lee, H. L. (1997). 'Mass customization at Hewlett-Packard: the power of postponement'. *Harvard Business Review*, 75/1: 116–21.

Gerhart, B. and Fang M. (2005). 'National culture and human resource management: assumptions and evidence'. *International Journal of Human Resource Management*, 16/6: 971–86.

Ghemawat, P. (2003). 'Semiglobalization and international business strategy'. *Journal of International Business Studies*, 34: 138–52.

Ghemawat, P. (2007). 'Managing Differences'. *Harvard Business Review*, 85/3: 58–68.

Ghemawat, P. and Ghadar, F. (2000). 'The dubious logic of global megamergers'. *Harvard Business Review*, 78/4: 64–72.

Ghoshal, S. and Bartlett, C. A. (1987). 'Managing across borders: new organizational responses'. *Sloan Management Review*, 29/1: 43–53.

Gunter, B. G. and van der Hoeven, R. (2004). 'The social dimension of globalization: A review of the literature'. *International Labour Review*, 143/1–2: 7–43.

Gupta, A. K. and Govindarajan V. (1991). 'Knowledge flows and the structure of control within multinational corporations'. *Academy of Management Review*, 16/4: 768–92.

Hamel, G. (1991). 'Competition for competence and inter-partner learning within international strategic alliances'. *Strategic Management Journal*, 12/4: 83–103.

Helpman, E. (1999). 'The structure of foreign trade'. *Journal of Economic Perspectives*, 13/2: 121–44.

Hertel, T. W. and Reimer, J. J. (2005). 'Predicting the poverty impacts of trade reform'. *Journal of International Trade and Economic Development*, 14/4: 377–405.

Hitt, M. A., Hoskisson, R. E., and Kim, H. (1997). 'International diversification: effects on innovation and firm performance in product-diversified firms'. *Academy of Management Journal*, 40/4: 767–800.

van Hoek, R. I., Vos, B., and Commandeur, H. R. (1999). 'Restructuring European supply chains by implementing postponement strategies'. *Long Range Planning*, 32/5: 505–18.

Hofstede, G. (1980). *Culture's Consequences: Comparing Values, Behaviors, Institutions, and Organizations across Nations*. Thousand Oaks, CA: Sage. 2nd edn (2001).

Hofstede, G. (1991). *Cultures and Organizations: Software of the Mind*. London: McGraw-Hill. 2nd edn (2001); updated edition with G. J. Hofstede (2005).

Hofstede, G. (1993). 'Cultural constraints in management theories'. *Academy of Management Executive*, 7/1: 81–94.

Hofstede, G. (2002). 'Dimensions do not exist: A reply to Brendan McSweeney'. *Human Relations*, 55/11: 1355.

Hofstede, G. (2006). 'What did GLOBE really measure? Researchers' minds versus respondents' minds'. *Journal of International Business Studies*, 37/6: 882–96.

Hofstede, G, and Bond, M. H. (1988). 'Confucius and economic growth: new trends in culture's consequences'. *Organizational Dynamics*, 16/4: 4–21.

Hofstede, G., Neuijen, B., Ohayv, D. D., and Sanders, G. (1990). 'Measuring organizational cultures: a qualitative and quantitative study across twenty cases'. *Administrative Science Quarterly*, 35/2: 286–316.

Hoppe, M. H. (2004a). 'An interview with Geert Hofstede'. *Academy of Management Executive*, 18/1: 75–9.

Hoppe, M. H. (2004b). 'Introduction: Geert Hofstede's Culture's Consequences: International Differences In Work-Related Values'. *Academy of Management Executive*, 18/1: 73–4.

House, R. J., Hanges, P. J., Javidan, M., Dorfman, P. W., and Gupta, V. (eds) (2004). *Culture, Leadership and Organizations: The GLOBE Study of 62 Societies*. Thousand Oaks, CA: Sage.

Javidan, M., House, R. J., Dorfman, P. W., Hanges, P. J., and De Luquet, M. S. (2006). 'Conceptualizing and measuring cultures and their consequences: a comparative review of GLOBE's and Hofstede's approaches'. *Journal of International Business Studies*, 37/6: 897–914.

Johansson, J. K. and Yip, G. S. (1994). 'Exploiting globalization potential: US and Japanese strategies'. *Strategic Management Journal*, 15/8: 579–601.

Julian, S. D. and Keller, R. T. (1991). 'Multinational R&D siting'. *Columbia Journal of World Business*, 26/3: 46–57.

Kogut, B. (2002). 'International management and strategy'. In: Pettigrew, A., Thomas, H., and Whittington, R. (eds), *Handbook of Management and Strategy*. Sage, London.

Kogut, B. and Zander, U. (1993). 'Knowledge of the firm and the evolutionary theory of the multinational corporation'. *Journal of International Business Studies*, 24/4: 625–45.

Kwok, L. (2006). Editor's introduction to the exchange between Hofstede and GLOBE.

Journal of International Business Studies, 37/6: 881.

Larsson, R., Brousseau, K. R., Driver, M. J., Holmqvist, M., and Tarnovskaya, V. (2003). 'International growth through cooperation: brand-driven strategies, leadership, and career development in Sweden'. *Academy of Management Executive*, 17/1: 7–24.

Lee, E. and Vivarelli, M. (2006). 'The social impact of globalization in the developing countries'. *International Labour Review*, 145/3: 167–84.

Leknes, H. M. and Carr. C. (2004). 'Globalisation, international configurations, and strategic implications: the case of retailing'. *Long Range Planning*. 37: 29–49.

Levitt, T. (1983). 'The globalization of markets'. *Harvard Business Review*, 61: 92–102.

Lu, J. W. and Beamish, P. W. (2004). 'International diversification and firm performance: the s-curve hypothesis'. *Academy of Management Journal*, 47/4: 598–609.

McSweeney, B. (2002a). 'Hofstede's model of national cultural differences and their consequences: a triumph of faith—a failure of analysis'. *Human Relations*, 55/1: 89–118.

McSweeney, B. (2002b). 'The essentials of scholarship: a reply to Geert Hofstede'. *Human Relations*, 55/11: 1363.

Martin, R. and Sunley, P. (2003). 'Deconstructing clusters: chaotic concept or policy panacea'. *Journal of Economic Geography*, 3: 5–35.

Mowery, D. C. and Sampat, B. N. (2004). 'Universities in national innovation systems'. In Fagerberg, J., Mowery, D., and Nelson, R. (eds), *Oxford Handbook of Innovation*. Oxford: Oxford University Press, ch. 8.

Ohmae, K. (1989). 'Planting for a global harvest'. *McKinsey Quarterly*, 3: 46–59.

Porter, M. E. (1990). *The Competitive Advantage of Nations*. Basingstoke: Macmillan Business.

Prahalad, C. K. and Doz, Y. (1987). *The Multinational Mission: Balancing Local Demands and Global Vision*. New York: Free Press.

Reeve, T. A. (2006). 'Factor endowments and industrial structure'. *Review of International Economics*, 14/1: 30–53.

Rodrik, D. (1997). 'Has globalization gone too far?' *California Management Review*, 39/3: 3–53.

Rodrik, D. (1998). 'Globalisation, social conflict and economic growth'. *World Economy*, 21/2: 143–58.

Rodrik, D. (2001). 'Trading in illusions'. *Foreign Policy*, 123: 54–62.

Rugman, A. M. (2000). *The End of Globalization*. London: Random House.

Rugman, A. M. (2004). 'The regional nature of the world's automotive sector'. *European Management Journal*, 22/5: 471–82.

Rugman, A. and Girod, S. P. (2003). 'Retail multinationals and globalization: the evidence is regional'. *European Management Journal*, 21/1: 24.

Rugman, A. M. and Verbeke, A. (1992). 'A note on the transnational solution and the transaction cost theory of multinational strategic management'. *Journal of International Business Studies*, 23/4: 761–77.

Rugman, A. M. and Verbeke, A. (2003). 'Regional multinationals: the location-bound drivers of global strategy'. In Birkinshaw, J., Ghoshal, S., Markides, C., Stopford, J., and Yip, G. (eds), *The Future of the Multinational Company*. Chichester: Wiley.

Rugman, A. M. and Verbeke, A. (2004). 'A perspective on regional and global strategies of multinational enterprises'. *Journal of International Business Studies*, 35/1: 3–18.

Rugman, A. M., Collinson, S., and Hodgetts, R. M. (2006). *International Business*. 4th edn. Harlow: Pearson Education.

Schlie, E. and Yip, G. (2000). 'Regional follows global: strategy mixes in the world automotive industry'. *European Management Journal*, 18/4: 343.

Segal-Horn, S. (2002). 'Global firms—heroes or villains? How and why companies globalise'. *European Business Journal*, 14/1: 8.

Segal-Horn, S., Asch, D., and Suneja, V. (1998). 'The globalization of the European white goods industry'. *European Management Journal*, 16/1: 101–9.

Siebert, H. (1999). *The World Economy*. London: Routledge. 2nd edn (2002).

Sklair, L. (2006). 'Capitalist globalization: fatal flaws and necessity for alternatives'. *Brown Journal of World Affairs*, 13/1: 29–37.

Smith, P. B. (2006). 'When elephants fight, the grass gets trampled: the GLOBE and Hofstede projects'. *Journal of International Business Studies*, 37/6: 915–21.

Tallman, S. and Fladmoe-Lindquist, K. (2002). 'Internationalization, globalization, and capability-based strategy'. *California Management Review*, 45/1: 116–35.

Tarique, I., Schuler, R., and Gong, Y. (2006). 'A model of multinational enterprise subsidiary staffing composition'. *International Journal of Human Resource Management*, 17/2: 207–24.

Trompenaars, F. and Hampden-Turner, C. (1997). *Riding the Waves of Culture: Understanding Cultural Diversity in Business*. 2nd edn. London: Nicholas Brealey.

Vermeulen, F. and Barkema, H. (2002). 'Pace, rhythm, and scope: process dependence in building a profitable multinational corporation'. *Strategic Management Journal*, 23/7: 637.

Wielaard, R. (2007). 'EU offers to drop nearly all quotas, tariffs on imports from poor nations'. *Associated Press Newswire*, 4 April.

Wild, J. J., Wild, K. L., and Han, J. C. Y. (2006). *International Business*. Harlow: Prentice Hall.

Williamson, D. (2002). 'Forward from a critique of Hofstede's model of national culture'. *Human Relations*, 55/11: 1373.

Wonglimpiyarat, J. (2006). 'The dynamic economic engine at Silicon Valley and US Government programmes in financing innovations'. *Technovation*, 26: 1081–9.

Yip, G. S. (1989). 'Global strategy in a world of nations?' *Sloan Management Review*, 31/1: 29–41.

Yip, G. S. (1992). *Total Global Strategy*. Harlow: Prentice-Hall.

End-of-chapter Case Study 14.1 **Ranbaxy Laboratories Ltd**

Ranbaxy Laboratories is India's largest pharmaceuticals company and amongst the top ten drugs manufacturers in the world. *iStock*

Ranbaxy is India's largest pharmaceutical company and ranked among the top 10 generic drugs' manufacturers in the world. Generic drugs are identical but cheaper versions of branded, proprietary medicines. They are often produced under licence from the patent holder, although they are also manufactured when the patent on the original medicine has expired or is unenforceable, or are sold in countries where the patent is not enforceable.

Ranbaxy was founded in 1961 and was listed on the Indian Stock Exchange in 1973. Most of Ranbaxy's products are manufactured under licence from foreign pharmaceutical patent holders, although quite a high percentage of sales come from out-of-patent drugs. It exports its products to 125 countries and has an expanding international portfolio of affiliates, joint ventures, and alliances, ground operations in 50 or so countries, and manufacturing operations in 7 countries.[88] But at the same time as it has pursued its internationalization strategy it has also achieved the number one position in its home market, India (albeit with 5 per cent market share). The Indian pharmaceutical sector is forecast to grow in value by $10bn by the end of 2006 from $6bn in 2004. However, the Indian pharmaceuticals market, although the fourth-largest in the world by volume, by value is 13th, and so Ranbaxy is targeting the higher-spending consumers in the US and Europe. It is also aspiring to develop a significant business in proprietary prescription products and to be amongst the top five generic players with $5bn in sales by 2012.

In 1998, Ranbaxy entered the USA, now its biggest market. The USA and Canada, along with the so called BRICS countries (Brazil, Russia, India, China, and South Africa), accounted for two thirds of sales in the first half of 2007. Other key markets are Europe, especially the former Soviet Union countries.

Changing legal and social factors are driving growth in the generic markets in these international markets. Factors such as the Medicare Modernization Act and an ageing population are encouraging the move towards cheaper generics in the USA, and it is expected that by 2010, the share of generics could account for 70 per cent of all prescriptions dispensed, up from around 55 per cent at present (in value terms, the share is 15 per cent). American consumers are becoming increasingly unhappy about the price of the new generation drugs. For example one new drug, Lucentis (made by Novartis), which treats macular degeneration in the eye, costs $1,950 per injection. However finding blockbuster drugs has got a lot harder, as costs of R&D and compliance have increased. Some have estimated the costs of developing a drug in the US at between $800m and $1bn.[89] In most years in the 1990s, the industry spent $35–$40bn worldwide on R&D and introduced 35–40 new drugs. Now, annual spending has grown to $60bn, but the number of new drugs has not kept pace.[90]

Despite this, Ranbaxy's new CEO (appointed in 2005), Malvinder Mohan Singh, the former president of the Pharmaceuticals division, has set the company on a path of increased R&D with the intention of developing its own patented drugs. In fact Ranbaxy ➔

➔ was one of the first Indian pharmaceutical companies to recognize the importance of R&D and started investing in it in 1973. In 1994, it established its first R&D centre in Gurgaon on the outskirts of New Delhi.

The industry environment

There are perhaps 20,000 generic pharmaceuticals companies in India. Approximately 12 of these sell generic drugs in the major international markets. After Ranbaxy, the second largest Indian pharmaceuticals firm is Dr Reddy's, with sales of over $1bn. Like Ranbaxy, it is pursuing innovation and expansion through acquisitions.[91] Ranbaxy is competing fiercely with its rival to produce India's first new patentable drug molecule.[92] Ranbaxy's anti-malarial drug 'RBX11160' is facing Dr Reddy's 'DRF2593', an anti-diabetes drug, but this is not likely to be launched before 2011. Both companies have suffered setbacks in the past where new drugs have failed during clinical trials.[93]

Developing new drugs is now an expensive and risky business. For about ten years, the number of new patentable drugs has been steadily declining, despite the amount spent on research and development more than doubling from $17bn to $36bn.[94] There are fewer blockbuster drugs, regulations have become far more stringent, raising the amount of time and money drug-makers need to spend on development, and consumers have become much more litigious. As a result the drugs majors Pfizer and Merck alone have lost billions of dollars in market capitalization since 2000.[95]

Despite this, nine Indian firms have between them at least 35 new drugs in the pipeline, at different stages of development.[96] And the Indian pharmaceutical industry is forecast to grow in 2007 by 11 per cent to Rs600bn ($13.6bn). Half that figure is expected to come from exports—which are expected to increase by 18 per cent. By 2008, Indian companies are expected to have 30 per cent of the growing generics market globally (currently 22 per cent).[97]

R&D infrastructure

Historically, India has had the reputation of being rather inefficient, bureaucratic, chaotic, and somewhat cavalier with its enforcement of international patent laws. Its engineers had the reputation of being skilled at reverse engineering products made (and patented) elsewhere, and making copies. This is rapidly becoming less true, and India is now fast developing a reputation as an entrepreneurial place to do business, aided by government policies and investment programmes which are encouraging innovation and development.

India now has an extremely skilled educated middle class, almost all of whom speak fluent English. There are 16,000 hos-

pitals and 20,000 new doctors per year in India. It has six times the number of trained chemists as the US,[98] and produces 14 million undergraduates, 650,000 postgraduates, and up to 6,000 PhDs annually.[99] Many have spent some time living in the USA or Europe, but are now moving back to India, carrying with them 'western management methods, money, contacts and ambition . . . attracted by a potent cocktail—fast-growing markets, plentiful state funding for research and middle-class lifestyles in increasingly cosmopolitan cities'.[100]

Many of the major pharmaceutical innovators have not only started sourcing products from India, but are also setting up some of their custom manufacturing plants there. In 2005, the Indian contract research and manufacturing (CRAM) market was estimated at $532m, of which manufacturing accounted for 84 per cent and research the rest. The outsourced clinical trials market was estimated at $100m. Forecasts suggest that outsourced clinical trials sales are likely to reach $1bn by 2007, and that CRAM is to increase to $900m.[101] India now has the largest number of US Food and Drug Administration-certified plants outside the USA, which means that medicines manufactured in India can be sold in the US, as they meet the required quality standards.[102]

A critical factor in all of this is India's cost structure. The cost of manufacturing in India is probably up to 70 per cent lower than in western countries (depending on the nature of the product), and trained staff are available at one-tenth of what they would cost in the USA.[103] This is a critical matter for generic pharmaceuticals' manufacturers, as profit margins are much lower than proprietary medicines. Recent suggestions by the Indian government that it would impose price controls were met with a wave of protests from the country's drugs companies, who suggested that 'any move to bring intrusive price control measures will stymie the much-needed effort and capital required to augment crucial R&D efforts'.[104]

Ranbaxy's R&D

Some have suggested that the opportunities for Indian generics manufacturing are coming to an end, with margins becoming increasingly small, and with innovation the only way to achieve long-term success—a view that Ranbaxy appears to share. Over 7 per cent of its sales go towards new drug development.

Ranbaxy had the highest R&D expenditure of the Indian pharmaceutical firms in 2005.[105] This declined in 2006 by 21 per cent as part of a cost-cutting measure, but it increased again by over 20 per cent during 2007, from $85 million to $100 million, in line with the company's long-term plans to increase its investment in research.[106] It is Ranbaxy's stated goal to build a proprietary prescriptions business, based on its prowess in novel drug-delivery systems (NDDS) and new chemical entities (NCE) research.   ➔

→ The company opened a new R&D centre in August 2005, with 2,000 research scientists, and now has three 'state-of-the-art' multi-disciplinary research facilities on the same campus at Gurgaon, one of which is an exact copy of a Bristol-Myers Squibb facility in the US.[107] Two centres focus on the development of generics and NDDS research; the third is dedicated to new drug discovery research (NDDR).[108] NDDS research is focused mainly on developing enhanced performance of controlled-release oral medicines for European and US markets. The company's first significant international NDDS success came in 1999 when Ranbaxy licensed its once-daily ciprofloxacin formulation to Bayer AG.[109] Ranbaxy has developed four NDDS 'platform technologies' which have led to the development of several new drug applications (NDAs) based on these technologies. It also has ten NDDR programmes under development, including one in Phase-II clinical trials.

Ranbaxy received ten final abbreviated new drug application (ANDA) approvals in 2005, down from 14 in 2004, which was, however, more than any other company that year.[110] In 2005, Ranbaxy launched 49 products and filed 183 applications for generics with the US Food and Drug Administration, and filed 35 patents in India.[111]

In fact, the legal intellectual property rights (IPR) environment facing Indian pharmaceutical companies is currently going through considerable changes. There are three types of patent possible in pharmaceuticals: on the drug molecule (the product), on the process of manufacturing, and on the drug delivery system. In 1973, and under pressure from domestic companies, the government had decided against the type of product patent regime that operated in the developed world, and instead decided only to recognize process patents. This allowed Indian companies to reverse engineer drugs that had been patented abroad and develop copycat versions.

Eventually, in response to international pressure, product patent legislation was introduced in India in 2005 that was intended to comply with the World Trade Organization's Agreement on Trade-Related Intellectual Property Rights (WTO TRIPs), to which India is a signatory. But this legislation has caused more problems than it seems to have solved. Supporters argue that it will stimulate research investment in India. But others, including an expert committee set up by the Indian government itself to examine the law, have been extremely critical of it.[112]

Critics have suggested that under the new law, procedures are not only very complex, there are also no controls on the levels of royalties to be paid to patent holders, and some clauses are ambiguous and open to interpretation, which is forecast to lead to 'endless litigation and delays'.[113] It is now at the centre of a lawsuit by the Swiss drug major Novartis who is taking action against the Indian authorities for refusing to award a patent for its anti-cancer medicine Gleevec®/Glivec®. As Novartis says, 'the Indian patent law creates new hurdles for pharmaceutical innovation, unjustifiably and illegally narrowing what is patentable'.[114]

Ranbaxy is weighing into this debate, saying that patents should also be granted for incremental inventions—'molecules which have been slightly modified from their original form, or to which a new substance has been added':[115] the new legislation restricts patentability to entirely new chemical entities. Ranbaxy claims that the law prevents the 'necessary fillip to development of novel drug delivery systems' but is also worried that the new law would not allow it to patent its own low-cost version of Gleevec.[116] As companies like Ranbaxy are increasingly skilled and developing their own incremental innovations of new forms and derivatives of existing drugs and new delivery systems, they need patent protection from copycat manufacturers. In addition, as they increasingly enter into alliances with international firms, there is a need for Indian firms to repair their reputation as copycat manufacturers themselves.

Alliances and acquisitions

Ranbaxy is at the forefront of Indian pharmaceuticals in terms of the international alliances it has, and the acquisitions it has made. But it is not alone. India is now positioning itself as an 'inter-dependent innovator networked with the west'.[117] Indian companies made over 300 overseas acquisitions between 2000 and 2005, worth over $10bn.[118] Between 2000 and 2006, 62 companies in the healthcare and pharmaceutical sector abroad were acquired by Indian companies,[119] and five of these—Ranbaxy, Dr Reddy's Laboratories, Nicolas Piramal, Sun Pharmaceuticals, and Glenmark Pharmaceuticals—accounted for 30 of these acquisitions. Most were in Europe (36), followed by the US, where 17 companies were acquired.

Ranbaxy itself has made 15 acquisitions since 2004, including eight in 2006 (four in Europe, one in the US, two in India, and one in South Africa).[120] It is currently eyeing up 'its most ambitious acquisition bid yet'[121]—Merck's generic business, which, if successful, is likely to cost it $5bn (Rs22,500 crore)—more than three times its annual sales. But this would make it the number three global generics manufacturer, behind Israel's Teva and Novartis' German subsidiary Sandoz.

The major stimulus for Ranbaxy's acquisitions appears to be the search for scale. Ranbaxy is currently less than 20 per cent Teva's size. Generic prices have declined hugely as a result of commoditization, combined with increased competition from innovator firms who have started to make their own generic drugs, and the costs of fighting innovators' patents. This has meant increasing consolidation in the industry and a search for economies of scale and pricing power.[122] Acquisitions have formed a major part of Dr Reddy's Laboratories' strategy too. It recently acquired Germany's Betapharm Arzneimittel for →

→ $570m—the biggest pharmaceutical acquisition by an Indian company.[123]

In addition to acquisitions, Ranbaxy has many international strategic alliances. Many of these are co-development agreements, in which the Indian firm undertakes research or clinical data management on behalf of the major international pharmaceutical companies. An example is the relationship between Ranbaxy and the UK's GlaxoSmithKline. This alliance was originally signed in 2003, but was expanded In Feb 2007, giving Ranbaxy more drug development responsibilities beyond candidate selection to completion of clinical proof-of-concept.[124] At the same time, Ranbaxy is the subject of a patent infringement injunction taken out by GlaxoSmithKline against valacyclovir, Ranbaxy's generic version of GlaxoSmithKline's Valtrex antiviral drug.[125]

Case study questions

1. Ranbaxy has the choice of continuing as the manufacturer of imitative generic drugs or becoming the developer of proprietary medicines. Discuss the pros and cons of each strategy. Could it do both?

2. Should Ranbaxy focus its attention on developing markets, or the developed markets of the USA and Europe.

3. Does India have a suitable infrastructure for innovation?

● NOTES

1 Siebert (1999: 8).

2 Encarta Encyclopedia <http://encarta.msn.com/encyclopedia_1741588397/Globalization.html>, accessed 4 April 2007.

3 It is almost impossible to find articles that discuss these issues in a way that can be understood by non-econometricians. But a good review of the history of international trade theories is provided by Helpman (1999). See also Bernhofen (2005); Deardorff (2005).

4 Source: World Bank.

5 'Bank Boss Blues All Africa', 24 April 2007.

6 Economist (2006). 'Monetary misquotations'. 380/8492: 56–7.

7 Encarta Encyclopedia and Hitt, G. (2006). 'WTO at crossroads as failed talks cloud its future: risks fate of the League of Nations: a failed experiment in global governance'. *Wall Street Journal*, 31 July.

8 Rodrik, R. (2004). 'Rethinking Growth Strategies'. WIDER Annual Lecture 8. UNU World Institute for Development Economics Research. Available online at <http://www.wider.unu.edu/publications/annual-lectures/annual-lecture-2004.pdf>, accessed 10 April 2007.

9 Ravindran, P. (2005). 'India's water economy: World Bank prescription does not hold water'. *Business Line (The Hindu)*, 11 October.

10 Notably Rodrik, op. cit., and Collier and Dollar (2001a, 2001b).

11 Forero, J. and Goodman, P. S. (2007). 'Chavez builds his sphere of influence: Venezuelan spends to counter U.S.'. *Washington Post*, 23 February.

12 Mander, B. (2007). 'Chavez hails state control of Orinoco oilfields'. *Financial Times*, 2 May.

13 Forero and Goodman (2007) op. cit.

14 IMF data.

15 Economist Intelligence Unit (2007). 'Risk briefing, USA risk: legal and regulatory risk'. *Economist*, 8 March 2007.

16 See, for example, Porter (1990) and Wielaard (2007).

17 One of the most influential writers to question at least some of the premises of globalization is Dani Rodrik of Harvard University (see Rodrik 1997, 1998, and 2001). His criticisms focus around the unequal playing field, that globalization favours those countries that have the wherewithal to comply with dominant powers—those that cannot have probably been made worse by the WTO and other globalization-promoting bodies' policies. See also Dieter (2006); Dolowitz (2006); Gunter and van der Hoeven (2004); Hertel and Reimer (2005); Lee and Vivarelli (2006); Rugman (2000).

18 See, for example, Sklair (2006).

19 Tripathi, S. (2002). 'Adding to global penury'. *Wall Street Journal Europe*, 15 November. Also see the *Guardian* Saturday review of 4 August 2001 for a list of the 'Top 10 anti-capitalist books'.

20 Rugman et al. (2006), <http://www.wto.org/english/res_e/statis_e/its2006_e/section1_e/i07.xls>, and <http://www.wto.org/english/res_e/statis_e/its2006_e/section1_e/i05.xls> accessed 3 April 2007.

21 These examples come from Wild et al. (2006).

22 Ibid.

23 See, for example, PriceWaterhouseCoopers, who produce guides to the IAS <http://www.pwc.com/extweb/pwcpublications.nsf/docid/7289e4ba59312c28852570990060ccb8>, accessed 10 May 2007.

24 The ISO standards, which are regulated by a Swiss organization, may be found at <http://www.iso.ch/iso/en/ISOOnline.frontpage>, accessed 29 July 2007.

25 One consultancy, Transparency International (TI), based in Berlin, produces an annual Corruption Perceptions Index

26 The first and arguably most influential of these studies was undertaken by Hofstede (1980, 1991), who identified four dimensions. His work has since been extended and developed by Trompenaars and Hampden-Turner (1997), who distinguished seven dimensions of culture, and more recently the GLOBE project group (Javidan et al., 2006), who refined this further to nine dimensions. Hofstede's work has attracted an unusual amount of discussion, and also sometimes some extremely hostile criticism. An interesting excursion can be made to Geert Hofstede's 'official' website (there are imitators) to see the extent of the debate on these issues: <http://feweb.uvt.nl/center/hofstede/page3.htm>, accessed 16 April 2007. See also Earley (2006); Hofstede (1993, 2002, 2006); Hofstede and Bond (1988); Hofstede et al. (1990); Hoppe (2004a, 2004b); House et al. (2004); Kwok (2006); Smith (2006); Williamson (2002); McSweeney (2002a, 2002b).

27 It is beyond the scope of this book to discuss specific countries in any great detail. For that you should read any of the many good international management textbooks, some of which we suggest at the end of the chapter. The *Global Competitiveness Report* is an annual publication that summarizes many of the most important indicators and trends. See also Ernst (2002); Reeve (2006).

28 Porter identifies four stages that a country's national advantage goes through as it develops. These have, however, been strongly refuted by a number of critics, notably economic geographers such as Martin and Sunley (2003) and Benneworth and Henry (2004).

29 See also Mowery and Sampat (2004).

30 Bartlett and Ghoshal (1989). See also Chng and Pangarkar (2000).

31 See Hitt et al. (1997); Conn and Yip (1997); Schlie and Yip (2000).

32 Hitt et al. (1997); Vermeulen and Barkema (2002).

33 This important cautionary note comes from Prahalad and Doz (1987).

34 Ghemawat (2007).

35 This tem comes from Ghemawat (2007).

36 See, for example, van Hoek et al. (1999), and Feitzinger and Lee (1997). In the supply chain literatures this is termed a 'postponement' strategy.

37 Hamel (1991).

38 See also Julian and Keller (1991).

39 Boersma (2006). In a survey by the *Economist Intelligence Unit* in 2004, 39% of the western executives surveyed said that China was where they were going to spend most of their international R&D investments in the next three years. And in the same survey 38% cited intellectual property protection as their most critical challenge.

40 *SinoCast China Financial Watch* (2006). 'China Lucky Film delays stake delivery to Kodak'. 6 September; Jiang J. (2006). 'Lucky Film accused of infringing Kodak paper branding'. *China Daily*, 23 August.

41 Reuters News (2006). 'Kodak in brand dispute with China partner'. 24 August; and Jiang (2006) op. cit.

42 See for example Levitt (1983); Ghoshal and Bartlett (1987); Prahalad and Doz (1987); Tallman and Fladmoe-Lindquist (2002); Ghemawat (2003, 2007); Leknes and Carr (2004); Rugman and Verbeke (1992, 2003).

43 See Yip (1992).

44 Notably Levitt (1983) and Yip (1989).

45 Segal-Horn (2002); Calori et al. (2000b).

46 Calori et al. (2000a).

47 For example, Yip (1992).

48 The term was popularized by Bartlett and Ghoshal (1988).

49 Chng and Pangarkar (2000), for example.

50 See, for example, Carr (2005).

51 Tallman, S. (2005). 'Global strategic management'. In Hitt, M. A., Freeman, R. E., and Harrison, J. S. (eds), *The Blackwell Handbook of Strategic Management*. Oxford: Blackwell, 465ff.

52 Kogut and Zander (1993); Kogut (2002).

53 Tallman (2005) op. cit.: 487.

54 This section is adapted from Rugman et al. (2006).

55 <http://www.gsk.com/investors/reps06/annual-report-2006.pdf>, accessed 7 May 2007.

56 <http://www.gsk.com/investors/reps06/annual-report-2006.pdf>, accessed 7/57 May 2007.

57 Rugman et al. (2006); Gupta and Govinarajan (1991).

58 See for example Wild et al. (2006); Rugman et al. (2006); and Tarique al. (2006).

59 This example is adapted from Ghemawat (2007).

60 Porter (1990).

61 Hofstede (1980).

62 See Larsson et al. (2003).

63 Notably Ohmae (1989).

64 PricewaterhouseCoopers/World Economic Forum. See also Ghemawat and Ghadar (2000).

65 Although see Gerhart and Fang (2005) for a counter view.

66 *Economist* (2003). 'Relocating the back office'. 13 December, 369/8354: 67–9.

67 *Personnel Today* (2004). 'Prudential outlines good points of offshoring plan'. 18 May: 6.

68 Bidwai, P. (2003). 'The rise of the cyber-coolies'. *New Statesman*, 10 November: 32–3.

69 Kripalani, M., Lee, L., and Saminather, N. (2006). 'Call centre? That's so 2004: outsourcing shops are moving fast into higher-paying businesses'. *BusinessWeek*, 7 August.

70 *Economist* (2003) op. cit.

71 Heller, M. (2004). 'Outsourcing'. *Workforce Management*, 83/6: 95–7.

72 Tehrani, R. (2006). 'Keeping up with the call centre'. *Customer Interaction Solutions*, 24/11.

73 *Economist* (2003) op. cit.

74 Tehrani (2006) op. cit.

75 Bradley, A. (2005). 'It's good to outsource'. *Supply Management*, 10/16, 4 August: 28–9.

76 Hoffbrand, J. (2006). 'Is it safe to trust your data to an Indian call centre?' *Precision Marketing*, 18/43: 11.

77 *Financial Times* (2004). 'Capital One pulls out of Indian call centre deal'. 25 March; Krebsbach, K. (2004). 'Lessons from the dark side: avoiding mistakes in overseas outsourcing'. *Bank Technology News*, 17/5: 30–54.

78 Heller (2004) op. cit.

79 Thomas, D. (2004). 'MEPs warn of dangers of offshoring'. *Computer Weekly*, 13 April: 4.

80 Bidwai, P. (2003) op. cit.

81 *The Emerging Global Labor Market*—see <http://www.mckinsey.com/mgi>.

82 Marquez, J. (2006). 'Union cites high stress at call centres in India'. *Workforce Management*, 85/21: 14.

83 Fox, J. (2003). 'Hang-ups in India'. *Fortune*, 148/13: 16.

84 Bradley (2005) op. cit.

85 Brewin, B., Hamblen, M., Sliwa, C., and Songini, M. L. (2003). 'Offshore support questioned'. *Computerworld*, 37/49.

86 Bradley (2005) op. cit.

87 Ibid.

88 PR Newswire Europe (2007). 'PPD licenses Statin from Ranbaxy Laboratories'. 27 February.

89 Sharma, E. K., Mukherjee, A., Srivastava, P. (2007). 'Wanted: a booster shot'. *Business Today*, 11 February 2007.

90 Sinha, S. K. (2007). 'Indian pharmaceuticals majors take a dose of new molecule R&D'. *Business Standard*, 19 February 2007.

91 *Handelsblatt Wirtschafts- und Finanzzeitung* (2007). 'Chasing the blockbuster'. 21 February.

92 Sinha (2007) op. cit.

93 Ibid.

94 Sharma et al. (2007) op. cit.

95 Ibid.

96 Pharmaceuticals Marketletter, 1 March 2007.

97 Sharma et al. (2007) op. cit.

98 Ibid.

99 Leadbeater, C. and Wilsdon, J. (2007). 'South-East Asian economies herald a new dawn of technological innovation'. *The Times*, 17 January 2007.

100 Ibid.

101 Sharma, K., Mukherjee, A., and Srivastava, P. (2007). 'Wanted: a booster shot'. *Business Today*, 11 February: 146.

102 Pharmaceuticals Marketletter (2007) op. cit.

103 Chynoweth, E. (2007). 'An outbreak of opportunity'. *ICIS Chemical Business Americas*, 12 February; Sharma et al. (2007) op. cit.

104 Sharma et al. (2007) op. cit.

105 Source: Ranbaxy 2005 Annual Report.

106 Mathew, J. C. (2007). 'Ranbaxy to earmark 20% more for R&D'. *Business Standard*, 28 January.

107 Leadbeater and Wilsdon (2007) op. cit.

108 Source: Ranbaxy 2005 Annual Report.

109 Mathew (2007) op. cit.

110 MarketResearch.com (2007). 'Ranbaxy generics company intelligence report'. 16 January.

111 *Chronicle Pharmabiz* (2006). 'Indian business insight: the big time bet on research'. 3 December.

112 Chatterjee, P. (2005). 'India's new patent laws may still hurt generic drug supplies'. *The Lancet*, 365/9468: 1378.

113 According to a recent statement from India's Affordable Medicines and Treatment Campaign, MSF, Lawyers Collective /AIDS Unit, and Alternative Law Forum, cited in Chatterjee (2005).

114 See an 'open letter' written by Novartis to their Indian patients available at <http://www.maketradefair.com/assets/english/novartis-open-letter-organizations.pdf>, accessed 1 March 2007.

115 *Economic Times* (2007a). 'Copycat drug cos convert, back MNCs on patents'. 23 February 2007.

116 *Pharma Marketletter* (2007). 'Expert group warns India's govt on patents'. 9 February and *Economic Times* (2007a) op. cit.

117 Leadbeater and Wilsdon (2007) op. cit.

118 *Financial Express* (2006). 'The rise and rise of India's private sector'. 4 October.

119 *Financial Express* (2006). 'An insatiable appetite'. 10 November.

120 Sharma et al. (2007) op. cit.

121 Ibid.

122 *Economic Times* (2007b). 'The battle for generics: size matters'. 11 January.

123 Sharma et al. (2007) op. cit.

124 *Pharmaceuticals Marketletter* (2007). 'India's generic drug giants move into R&D'. 1 March.

125 <http://www.gsk.com/ControllerServlet?appId=4&pageId=402&newsid=964>, accessed 3 March 2007.

CHAPTER FIFTEEN

Strategies where Profit is not the Main Objective

LEARNING OUTCOMES

By the end of this chapter you should be able to:

➡ Explain the special characteristics of the environments confronting small firms, organizations in the public sector, and not-for-profit organizations, and how these differ from the environment in which most large firms operate

➡ Discuss the types of strategic options that are likely to be appropriate for small firms and for public and not-for-profit organizations

➡ Discuss the main issues confronting social enterprises

➡ Assess strategies currently being followed by organizations in these categories.

INTRODUCTION

Most of this book has been to do with large companies that are in the business of making money for their shareholders, and which compete with other firms in order to make profits. Not all organizations are like this, however. For some, financial considerations, although still important, may be subordinate to other objectives. Others do not have the size to implement the kinds of strategy we discuss elsewhere. So here we look at strategies for organizations other than large commercial firms.

We start this chapter by examining the strategic situations of smaller firms, a very important part of the organizational population. Two-thirds of the EU workforce is employed in small businesses, and nearly 30 per cent in organizations with fewer than ten employees. Of the 4.3 million businesses in the UK, over 99 per cent employed fewer than fifty people.[1]

We next look at the particular strategic choices that public sector organizations must make. In many state-owned concerns, competition and value for money have become increasingly important, and many of the principles outlined elsewhere in this book are equally appropriate there. But public sector organizations have constraints and opportunities all of their own and we shall consider some of these.

We move on to consider strategies for organizations, such as charities and foundations, in the not-for-profit sector. These also have to operate in an environment that is increasingly competitive, but all their income (after fund-raising and administrative costs) must go to their intended beneficiaries. In these circumstances there are particular issues relating to ethics, stakeholders, and reinvestment. Finally, we review issues in a relatively new but growing sector, social enterprise, where organizations are using business disciplines to achieve social ends, either by enhancing people's ability to fend for themselves or by generating profits that are used for social purposes.

All of these groupings—small firms, public sector organizations, the third sector, and social enterprises—embrace a wide variety of organizations of different sizes, objectives, and approaches. Some strive to be innovative and commercially minded, even entrepreneurial, looking to maximize the amount of income they can generate. Others make a virtue out of being conservative, perhaps bureaucratic, and see their assets as something to be conserved for future generations, rather than to generate financial returns.

15.1 **Strategic management for small firms**

Small firms are small for a number of reasons. Some are small only because they are new. They are owned and managed by entrepreneurs, whose objective is to grow them into large, profitable concerns—or perhaps to sell them to a larger enterprise.[2] The main challenges confronting these organizations, as participants in new or growing industries or as entrants into mature ones, have largely been dealt with in Chapter 13. Their capacity to overcome those challenges depends greatly on how effectively the owner can delegate responsibility and lead the organization, as it becomes larger and more complex.

Probably the majority of small firms, however, have no intention of becoming any larger. Many are what the Americans term 'mom and pop' concerns: organizations which provide employment for the owner and his or her family, together possibly with a few other employees. Most are to be found in the services or construction sectors, though about 10 per cent are manufacturers.

An important sub-category comprises firms which have no economic rationale for growing larger. These are found in professions such as design, architecture, consultancy, and accountancy, where only very small or very large firms are viable. This is because of the overheads costs associated with marketing, billing, quality assurance, and administration. In a small firm, these activities are carried out by the owner; in a large one their cost can be set against a revenue stream from a large number of employees, of whom a substantial proportion are likely to be earning fees at any given time. However, medium-sized professional firms have more difficulty in generating a consistent stream of fees to cover these potentially crippling overheads, so that their survival may be in doubt unless they can grow quickly.

15.1.1 The strategic characteristics of small firms

It will already be apparent that the term 'small firm' covers a wide variety of organizations operating in a large number of different contexts, so generalizations about them must be made with caution. A typical small firm, however, can be expected to have many of the following characteristics,[3] many of which derive from a lack of financial and human resources and of relational capital:

1. A sense of insecurity. Small enterprises have far less influence over their environments than large ones:[4] they have less lobbying power with politicians and regulators, and less capacity to ride out depressions or to respond to increases in demand. They are in industries which are either new and quite likely to be turbulent, or more mature and dominated by larger and more powerful firms. Environmental factors have been found to be the most important influence on their performance; however internal events, such as an illness to a key staff member, can also lead to severe disruptions.[5]

2. A focus on short-term survival rather than long-term strategy. This insecurity, and scarcity of resources, makes it difficult for small firms to see through a long-term strategy, or to find time to plan one. They are much more likely than larger firms to be opportunistic and short-term in their strategies and the way they seek to implement them, and less likely to look for innovation. Strategy may be driven by the owner's ideas or desires at the time.[6]

3. More weight given to short-term considerations of cash flow and liquidity than to the conventional definitions of business success that we have emphasized in this book, such as return on capital, growth in turnover, and profits.[7] The owners' main objectives might well be non-financial: to obtain an income free from the interference of colleagues or bosses, to provide an enjoyable way of spending the day, to perform a social service, or to maintain a business, such as a farm, that can one day be passed on to the next generation. In such cases, just the survival of the business may be an adequate gauge of success.

4. A tendency to grow sales in any manner possible rather than establish a clear market position. The temptation to take any work that comes along, in order to bolster cash flow, please a valued customer, and provide an alternative income stream in case of emergency, can be irresistible. In any case, small firms cannot afford the intensive advertising on TV and in the national press that large firms use to establish a clear positioning in the eyes of consumers. Since they are typically focused on local customers, other media such as local press and radio or the internet may be both more affordable and more appropriate.

5. A high degree of centralization, since most decisions are taken by the owner, together perhaps with family members or a few trusted associates. This also means that there are few principal/agent problems, since the principals are also the agents, or work closely alongside them.

6. An inability, on account of their size, to take advantage of economies of scale or scope in areas such as purchasing or manufacturing. This limitation may, of course, be self-imposed, and be offset by superior flexibility or customer responsiveness.[8]

➜ We examined the trade-offs inherent in organizations' choices of scale and scope in Chapter 5.

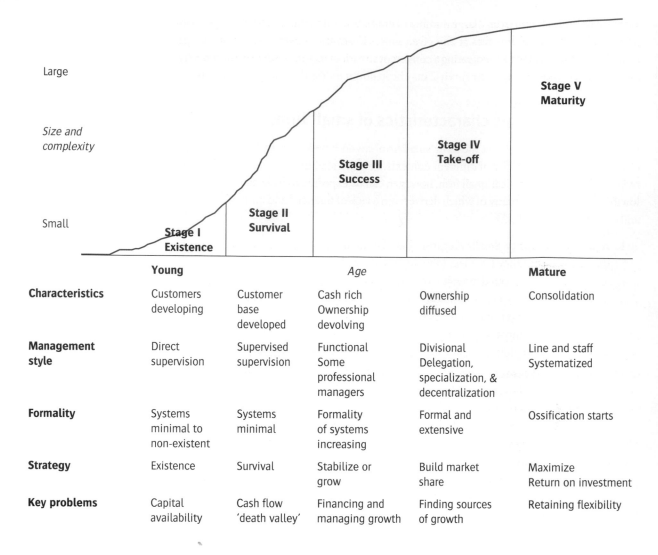

	Young		Age	Mature	
	Stage I Existence	**Stage II Survival**	**Stage III Success**	**Stage IV Take-off**	**Stage V Maturity**
Characteristics	Customers developing	Customer base developed	Cash rich Ownership devolving	Ownership diffused	Consolidation
Management style	Direct supervision	Supervised supervision	Functional Some professional managers	Divisional Delegation, specialization, & decentralization	Line and staff Systematized
Formality	Systems minimal to non-existent	Systems minimal	Formality of systems increasing	Formal and extensive	Ossification starts
Strategy	Existence	Survival	Stabilize or grow	Build market share	Maximize Return on investment
Key problems	Capital availability	Cash flow 'death valley'	Financing and managing growth	Finding sources of growth	Retaining flexibility

Figure 15.1 The five stages of company growth. Source: Churchill and Lewis (1983). *Reproduced with the kind permission of* Harvard Business Review

These characteristics will be most prominent in the smallest firms. As firms grow, they tend to acquire more of the architecture and strategic orientation associated with larger firms, as illustrated in Figure 15.1.

15.1.2 Factors influencing success and survival in small firms

Older firms, which have already demonstrated a successful capacity to adapt and develop, and have built competences and capabilities which allow this process to continue, are less likely to fail than new ones. Even amongst established firms, however, there are certain attributes that have an impact on survival and growth prospects.

a. Entrepreneurship[9]

Entrepreneurship
The process through which 'opportunities to create future goods and services are discovered, evaluated, and exploited'.[10]

Entrepreneurial firms are those that do at least one of the following: they strive for growth and/or profitability; they are strategic in their approach and they look for ways to innovate.[11] This makes their approach rather different from that of the 'typical' small firm discussed in Section 15.1.1. They are also managed in a somewhat different fashion. Entrepreneurs are typically risk-taking individuals, who are favourably disposed to change and innovation and are fiercely competitive with other firms. They derive a great deal of personal pleasure and satisfaction from performing their role well. They typically place great importance on managing the culture and vision in their organizations.[12]

Empirical studies indicate that, overall, an entrepreneurial orientation improves the performance of a small business.[13] This effect is especially strong when the environment is stable and capital is scarce—it seems that entrepreneurial ingenuity is particularly useful in these circumstances.

b. Management skills and practices

Although generic skills in managing finances and personnel are useful for organizations of all sizes, the management of a small business is very different from that of a large corporation. Flexibility and multi-tasking are important competences for small business owners/managers. For non-entrepreneurial businesses, strategy is typically a process of responding to changes in the environment, and using scarce financial and managerial resources so as to achieve the owner's objectives, whatever they might be, whereas an entrepreneur is likely to be more proactive.[14]

Having a strong and balanced management team is often a critical factor in the success of a small firm, especially if it is one whose owner wants it to grow. It is one of the reasons why venture capitalists (VCs) will often assess the strengths of the management team as a whole, rather than the owner alone. VCs will often appoint one of their own staff to work as part of the team and provide specialist expertise that may not be available elsewhere. However, obtaining suitable 'professional' and specialized managers, who have the skills that the original owner does not themselves possess, can be a real problem for small firms. They cannot provide the same level of salaries and benefits that managers could expect from larger organizations. The way that many small firms overcome this is by promising a share of the ownership of what is hoped will become a large and successful firm in the future.[15]

Research suggests that flourishing high-growth companies are more focused in their objectives, with a strong emphasis on forecasting and the management of financial data. On the other hand, inadequate accounting systems, lack of capital-budgeting abilities, poor stock control, poor record-keeping, and over-controlled and demotivated employees are known factors in small business failures. Under-capitalization—failing to obtain enough funding for start-up costs and working capital until the firm has an established customer base and a positive cash flow—is a particularly frequent cause of business failure. When large amounts of money are concerned, the founders are likely to make a more thorough assessment of the business' prospects.[16]

c. Environmental factors

Choices of sector appear to be important, with the manufacturing sector showing the highest annual bankruptcy rates (three times the average) compared with service and retail firms (approximately half the average rate for all businesses). Professional services firms have lower failure rates than other services, probably because they have to overcome hurdles before they are founded, such as industry accreditation.[17]

Small firms are, understandably, less able than large ones to penetrate industries where there are entry barriers, such as patents or large investment costs, that can only be overcome with the aid of substantial financial resources. However, they are better than large firms at establishing a presence in highly concentrated industries and in those where there is a high degree of vertical integration or product differentiation.[18]

15.1.3 Strategic options for small firms

Conceptions of what constitutes a 'strategic' option need to be scaled down in order to take account of the size, resources, and time frames of small businesses. Short-term practical issues that, for a large organization, would be minor, localized functional concerns become strategic when survival is a more important consideration than thinking five years ahead.

Similarly, the implementation of quite ordinary planning or administrative controls can become a strategic issue. This is because, even if they take up just a few hours per week of management time, they may have a substantial opportunity cost, since they eat into the time available for sales, production, R&D—or sleep. The implementation of *appropriate* planning and control systems appears, nonetheless, to yield performance benefits for small firms. Such systems can embrace strategic planning, competitor analysis, and performance measurement.[19]

There are a number of more general strategic prescriptions and options for small firms—see Real-life Application 15.1 for examples of a successful small business that uses some of them:

- They should aim to fill niches rather than actively confront larger firms in their smaller markets.[20]

- They should aim to be distinctive from larger firms *either* in terms of being more flexible *or* through being more efficient—for example, by using their limited capacity intensively, or by keeping overheads low. It is not yet clear whether flexibility is a better goal to pursue than efficiency, but firms that mix the two definitely perform worse than firms that are clearly oriented in one clear strategic direction.[21]

- They should actively consider internationalizing. As we have already mentioned in Section 13.2, technological and social changes have made internationalization a feasible strategy for smaller firms, and earlier in the industry life-cycle, than used to be the case—but some niches are inherently international in scope.

Small retailers may join buying consortia such as Spar. *Spar*

Table 15.1 Recommended strategic directions for small firms in the retailing, service and manufacturing sectors

Retailing	Services	Manufacturing
Negotiate good site close to attractor store	Involve staff in decision-making	Develop specialized understanding of products/customers
Price offerings below competitors'	Assess performance and reward accordingly	Acquire knowledge of competitors' activities
Emphasize efficiency	Invest in staff training	Establish market niche away from larger competitors
Emphasize high sales turnover	Emphasize high sales turnover	Make use of consultants and professional advisers
Find and use low-cost debt finance	Maintain large cash balances; avoid debt	Find cheap sources of finance
Manage cash flow and inventory effectively	Avoid high levels of inventory	
Check quality of offerings		

Source
Gadenne (1998)

- They should aim to build relational assets.[22] They can build networks with local organizations, through bodies like Chambers of Commerce or Rotary Clubs, or less formally as part of clusters of local firms such as those in the clothing and furniture industries in Italy. They may liaise with other small firms, in the same industry through industry associations or more generally through small business forums, in order to improve their lobbying or purchasing power. Small retailers may join buying consortiums, such as Nisa and Spar, which give their members access to a nationally recognized brand and negotiate on their behalf with suppliers of branded and own-label products and of services such as energy and vehicle leasing.

➜ We discussed relational assets in Section 7.3.6.

There are also certain strategic directions (summarized in Table 15.1) that appear to be associated with success in particular sectors. For example, the value-for-money factor in the retail industry suggests that small retail firms may only be able to compete successfully when both low price and good quality are achieved. Success in retailing is also strongly related to the ability to choose and negotiate a good site close to an attractor store. In other service industries, attention to employee welfare and motivation appears to be strongly related to success.[23]

Real-life Application 15.1 **A global niche in natural colorants**[24]

A picturesque village in southern France houses the world's leading supplier of natural red colorants, with annual sales of €5m euros. The product is derived, using a number of advanced technologies, from the pigment that gives red grapes their colour. The business is highly internationalized—around 70 per cent of inputs are imported and over 80 per cent of production exported. Customers, which include major multinationals in the soft drinks and pharmaceuticals industries, are located in over twenty countries. But the company serves them with just 40 employees—20 in France and 20 in Tunisia, where much of the production takes place.   ➜

→ The organization clearly exemplifies areas of good practice in small manufacturing businesses. It has a strong position in a product niche that is too small to be attractive to a larger competitor. It has a strong understanding of its customers and makes considerable use of consultants. It also has significant relational assets: alongside numerous alliances in Spain and Italy, it also enjoys an important relationship with France's Atomic Energy Committee, which collaborated in the development of much of the firm's technology.

Its international scope means, however, that the firm has to depart in important ways from the stereotype of the small business—most notably in its architecture. It is far more decentralized than one would expect from a firm with so few employees. Many employees enjoy a great deal of autonomy—not just the obvious key staff, such as the head of R&D and the managers of the Tunisian subsidiary, but also the employees who maintain the linkages with the far-flung networks of suppliers and customers. At the same time, it has invested in sophisticated reporting systems in order to keep track of events around the world, and in advanced quality systems to satisfy the expectations of its particular customers.

15.2 Strategic management in the public sector

The public sector is not a single, uniform entity. It includes, for example (Table 15.2):

- government departments of a number of different types, national, local, and international;
- agencies which are directly controlled by governments at either a national or local level;
- government agencies which are quasi independent in terms of their management and funding, and which are controlled principally by regulation.

There are also major differences—beyond the scope of this book—in the way that different nations set up, structure, and control these various bodies. One universal factor links them, however: they are all ultimately dependent on the state for their funds.

Table 15.2 Examples of public sector organizations

International bodies	The United Nations and its agencies (e.g. WHO, UNESCO) The World Bank NATO The European Parliament The European Commission ASEAN
National government bodies	Parliaments and Senates National civil services and ministries
Local government bodies	Borough, county and district councils (UK) Départements and Mairies (France); Länder (Germany)
Government agencies (directly controlled)	Armed forces Police forces Air traffic control Weather forecasters
Quasi-independent bodies	Universities Hospitals Utilities (in some countries)

15.2.1 The strategic characteristics of the public sector

Public sector organizations exist to provide a service, and their value chain will typically be of the 'professional services' type. Sometimes the client is the government that funds them, as in the case of the Civil Service in the UK or the federal agencies and bureaux in Australia and the USA. In many cases, however, the users of these services do not pay for them, except perhaps indirectly through various forms of taxation. Quite often, public sector organizations have two or more customers or user groups:

→ We examined the professional services value chain in Section 6.2.2.

- the actual consumers of their service—students at a university, patients at a hospital;

- other government or private agencies who refer individuals and may also contribute towards the cost of serving them—educational and health ministries and their local equivalents, health insurers;

- the broader set of stakeholders that benefit from the service being performed well and who may also contribute part of the cost, such as the families and the present and future employers of students and patients.

The main considerations affecting strategic management in the public sector are summarized in Figure 15.2. Not all of these are peculiar to the public sector. The challenges of what has been termed managing downward—managing human resources (quadrant A of the Figure) and day-to-day administration (quadrant B)—are equally applicable to private sector organizations. The public sector context does, nonetheless, give rise to some specific features —in most countries, for example, a high proportion of public sector employees belong to trades unions, and human resource management processes must take account of this.

The most singular challenges confronting public sector managers, however, relate to managing outward—working within the networks of which most public organizations are part—and managing upward—dealing with the elected politicians that set the policy frameworks.[25]

Managing outward is important because few public sector organizations exercise fully independent choice over what they do. Rather, they are participants in programmes—

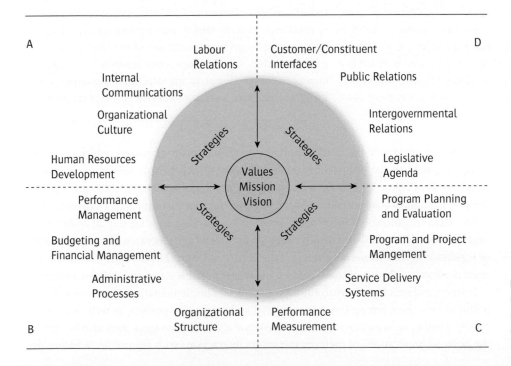

Figure 15.2 Strategic considerations in public sector organizations. Adapted from Poister and Streib (1999)

broad-based projects, designed to achieve policy goals such as reducing crime or poverty, or enhancing a region's attractiveness to inward investors. Some aspects of programme management appear in quadrant C of Figure 15.2. A typical programme is administered by multiple agencies, independently managed but interdependent in the services that they provide. It also involves networks: partnerships that cross traditional organizational and administrative boundaries.[26] This proliferation of customers and partnerships can make the architecture of public sector agencies very complex, both internally and externally (see Real-life Application 15.2).

Real-life Application 15.2   A complex architecture: the National Probation Service for England and Wales

The National Probation Service for England and Wales (NPS) is a UK government agency which supervises people who have been convicted of crimes. It has some 200,000 cases on its books at any given time. Its roles include:

- monitoring people who have been put 'on probation' after being convicted of a crime, sentenced to do unpaid community work as a punishment, ordered by a UK court to avoid certain types of behaviour, or released from prison on licence or parole;

- advising criminal courts on bail conditions and sentencing;

- giving welfare advice to offenders and their families;

- providing counselling to the victims of violent and sexual assaults;

- supervising the reintegration into society of prisoners after their release.

The National Probation Service (NPS) has to balance the protection of the public, and the proper punishment of crime, with the rehabilitation of criminals. It must please a number of different stakeholders at both national and local level. It has to satisfy the UK's central government that it is playing its part in a national strategy to reduce the incidence of re-offending by convicted criminals. The NPS must also show that it is giving value for the taxpayers' money that it is spending, for which the government is itself accountable to the public.

Its most direct customer is the National Offender Management Service (NOMS), an arm of the UK government's Home Office, which specifies the levels of service the NPS must deliver. The NOMS has the possibility of using private sector and not-for-profit organizations to deliver some of these services in the future. However, the head of the NPS sits on the NOMS Board and therefore has some influence over such decisions.

The NPS has other users that must be satisfied, although they do not pay directly for its services. It has to satisfy local communities, which have representatives on its local area management committees, that it is serving their interests effectively. On a day-to-day basis it has to provide the judges and magistrates in the courts with the information and service that they require. It must also ensure that offenders are receiving the high-quality services that *they* need.

The NPS is also required by statute to work within Multi-Agency Public Protection Arrangements (MAPPA) to manage the risk posed by sexual and violent offenders. Its main partners in these arrangements are the Prison Service (also part of the NOMS) and the police, but others include private sector providers of electronic monitoring ('tagging'), regional and local health authorities, and the housing, education, and social services arms of local authorities.

Managing upward is of crucial importance to public sector managers, which are more closely exposed to the political process than most of their private sector counterparts. Quadrant D of Figure 15.2 shows a few of the factors that they need to take into account. Periodic changes of government, and so of policy, mean that the immediate environment of public sector organizations alters more often, and more radically, than that of commercial organizations. It can also be affected by inter-governmental agreements, such as trade treaties or legislation agreed between members of the European Union. Effective public sector managers need to stay abreast of such changes, and where possible attempt to influence them.

Systems and structures have to allow for the efficient implementation of policies within a politically complex setting involving national and local party politics, as well as possible conflicts within an organization and between rival agencies. Managers must also be alert to the political implications of their organization's interactions with the public. Whether the public forms a good or a bad impression can affect the viability, not just of the organization, but also of a government or a local administration.

Because of the near-certainty of regular, radical environmental change, senior management decision-making in the public sector may be driven more by short-term expediency than a longer-term view of what will benefit the organization and its users.

Except in quasi-business units operating in competitive environments, for which the theory discussed throughout the rest of this book is largely applicable, concepts such as competitive advantage and competitive stance take on a different meaning in this sector. Many free-market thinkers in the UK and the USA believe that the public sector should only perform duties that the private sector is unable and unwilling to assume. From their point of view, a 'weakness' in a public sector organization is not necessarily a bad thing—it may represent a welcome opportunity to return that activity to the private sector.

a. The culture and architecture of public sector organizations

Cultures in the public sector vary widely, according to the type of department or agency and the country in which it operates. However, researchers have found a number of common traits.

Public sector managers must manage a wide variety of stakeholders and it may be difficult to find a common goal around which they can all unite, in the way that profitability can unite different factions in private firms. There may often be no direct personal or organizational benefit from collaborating with colleagues in other departments or agencies. This means that public sector organizations can be extremely political, and often feature small fiefdoms, which make it difficult to gain support and commitment to an overall goal. This is compounded by the fact that all public agencies or departments compete with one another for a share of a finite budget; there is no opportunity to increase income through increasing sales.[27] This tends to reduce risk-taking and creativity because of the potential for political conflict to develop when individuals step out of line.

Historically, public organizations have focused on cost management rather than profit generation, with little scope for creativity or entrepreneurship to be rewarded. Employees are promoted predictably within a fixed grading structure, with few bonus or performance-related rewards. This can make it hard for the public sector to attract entrepreneurial individuals or those who would introduce new and better working practices. Traditionally, public sector cultures have tended to notice poor rather than good performance. Few, however, have cultures whereby low standards are either measured or penalized. Sackings are rare and are usually only carried out for the most serious offences—such as criminal activities.

b. Trends in the public sector environment

Since the 1980s the most influential strands of economic and political theory have favoured 'small government'—reductions in government debt and spending—and the introduction of market mechanisms. These are held to lead to more efficient allocation and usage of resources, although the evidence that market structures improve public sector performance is not strong. This economic viewpoint is one underpinning of the new public management —a philosophy which sees the public sector mainly as a stimulator, through economic and social incentives, of action by the private and not-for-profit organizations, rather than an actor in its own right.[28]

This new orthodoxy has taken root most strongly in the USA and UK, but its influence has also been felt in many other countries.[29] It has shown itself in moves away from direct government control and funding of public sector service provision. These moves have included the introduction into public organizations of market mechanisms and partnerships with the private sector.[30]

The most radical means of introducing market mechanisms has been privatization—pushing organizations such as airlines and utilities out of the public sector altogether. Although there have been some cases where privatization has had to be reversed (see What Can Go Wrong 11.1 for an example in the UK rail network), there are other cases, such as BA, where it has led to improved service and lower prices. Privatization has met resistance in Latin America and certain parts of Asia, particularly in relation to energy and mineral assets. However, it has gradually gained ground in Europe. Even countries such as France and Italy that do not always favour Anglo-Saxon economic models have now privatized their national airlines, for example.

Where full privatization has been deemed inappropriate, departments have been turned into commercial quasi-businesses, or profit centres. They are given objectives by the government but are not subject to direct civil service control over their day-to-day operations. In some cases they have been encouraged to seek funding from lotteries and other non-government sources and to think of creative ways of generating revenues. For example, the UK Driving Licence Agency charges premium prices for car registrations that might be attractive as personalized number plates.

At the same time there have been moves towards the contracting out of an ever-increasing range of services, including waste disposal, prisons, and, in the UK, the management of schools.[31] Public sector departments are made to bid competitively against private sector rivals (or in some cases, public sector agencies from elsewhere in the country) if they want to keep on delivering such services. Extensive use has been made of the private finance initiative (PFI): agreements where the cost and the risk of large investments in public infrastructure are shared between the public sector body that will use the infrastructure and the private contractor that builds or refurbishes it. The private firm raises the finance for the project and bears the up-front costs, which it therefore has an incentive to find innovative ways of reducing. In return, it receives an agreed annual lease payment on the asset and, in some cases, an additional fee for maintaining or even operating parts of it.

The PFI is now the normal arrangement for building or rebuilding prisons, hospitals, and schools in the UK, and has also been used for programmes not directed around capital investment, such as training for the British armed forces. In other developed countries, including Finland, France, Italy, Ireland, Spain, Greece, Portugal, the Netherlands, Japan, and the USA, it has been used for the financing of transport, health, and water infrastructure. Critics of the initiative in the UK, however, contend that the savings from private sector efficiency do not cover the extra costs of PFI contracts (private sector firms must borrow at higher interest rates than governments pay, and must be compensated for the degree of risk they bear—for example, project overruns). Some also suggest, that by keeping the cost of the investment off the public accounts, the PFI is concealing the true extent of public sector debt.[32]

The privatization and commercialization of the public sector poses certain issues for governments. Privatized government departments can retain many of the advantages of a monopoly for some time following deregulation. This means they are very profitable, and their owners have no incentive to improve efficiency or service levels. Former state-owned airlines, in what is now a deregulated environment, still retain considerable control of key slots at major airports throughout the world, which predictably they are very reluctant to give up. For this reason, former government agencies in countries like the UK are heavily regulated in the period following privatization, being bound by rules as to prices, the functions and services they will provide, and how much they will invest. Only when they face meaningful competition in their core markets will the regulator back away from scrutinizing them.

With the introduction of economic and commercial disciplines from the private sector, public sector organizations have moved to adopt some of the strategies and management practices found there. Traditionally, they have focused on inputs and processes, ensuring that planning, budgeting, and evaluation and review processes were in place to implement government policy. Nowadays, there is a greater concentration on outcomes: efficient uses of resources and effective service delivery.[33]

They have also made increasing use of strategic planning procedures, suitably adapted to take account of the stakeholder management and political challenges in the public sector. Strategic planning encourages managers to consider longer-term objectives and any systematic change initiatives which might be necessary. This forces consideration of any long-term resource implications, such as the level of IT infrastructure that might help the coordination of effort across the organization and the multiple agencies involved in providing services. It also starts the process of moving the organization away from the ad hoc management that has tended to characterize public organizations in the past; and provides information that can be used to influence the political agenda for the future.[34]

15.2.2 Strategic challenges for public sector managers

The previous section highlighted the trend to involve private firms and, increasingly, the not-for-profit sector, in activities previously reserved for the public sector. This includes areas such as defence which were once thought to be too sensitive for such treatment. Managers everywhere in the public sector face the challenge of justifying their organization's continued existence.

This makes it vital that they have a clear understanding of who their stakeholders are, and of their attitudes, requirements, and power. It is these stakeholders who determine whether the organization grows or shrinks, and what resources are allocated to it. A stakeholder analysis thus plays much the same, fundamental role in strategy development in the public sector that environmental and competitor analysis do in the private sector.[35] Effective management, upwards and outwards, of these relationships with salient stakeholders is also a major challenge.

➡ We introduced the concept of stakeholders in Sections 1.1.4, 1.6.1, and 2.6, and examine detailed techniques of stakeholder analysis in Chapter 16.

Worked Example 15.1 **A stakeholder analysis for the Bank of Japan**

The Bank of Japan: Japan's central bank located in Tokyo   ➡

→ Here, we show how the Mitchell, Aigle, and Wood framework for stakeholder analysis, introduced in Chapter 2, can be used to appraise the situation of the Bank of Japan.

The Bank of Japan is Japan's central bank, located in Tokyo, near that city's main financial district, the Ginza. The bank is legally constituted as an autonomous 'legal person'—it is neither a government agency nor a private firm—whose main objectives are the issuance of currency, monetary control, the smooth running of a system for settling transactions between financial institutions, and the maintenance of an orderly financial system. In its monetary and exchange rate policies, the Bank is required to promote the sound development of Japan's economy by pursuing price stability.[36]

However, the bank over the past decade has had to cope with an unexpected phenomenon—falling prices, or deflation. This was the aftermath of a speculative bubble in shares and property in Japan that burst in 1990. It left consumers and companies holding assets that were worth a small fraction of what had been paid for them, often purchased with borrowed money. Meanwhile banks that had lent the money to buy the assets found themselves unable to make further loans until their reserves had risen to cover the bad debts. Spending and investment fell, and producers cut prices to try to persuade people to purchase their goods. However, consumers then held off purchasing in the expectation that prices would fall still further. The economy slowed and unemployment rose.[37]

Under its present governor, Toshihiko Fukui, the Bank of Japan has won considerable praise for the way it has handled the country's problems. Amongst its solutions have been the cutting of interest rates to zero and trying to stimulate borrowing through allowing the money supply to rise. There have been signs that the deflation has ended and mild price inflation and economic growth has returned. The Bank was emboldened to raise interest rates to 0.25 per cent in July 2006, and again, to 0.5 per cent in February 2007, in response to evidence that commercial property prices were rising again and that this was stimulating investment as firms used their property as security for loans. Its policy committee has indicated that it would like rates to rise further.[38]

Decisions like this are important, not just for Japan as a nation, but for the Bank of Japan as an organization. In January 2007, after having signalled to the markets that a rise in interest rates was in prospect, there was a change of mind at the last minute, and rates were left unchanged. Many observers saw in this the hand of the ruling politicians in Japan, and interpreted it as a blow to the Bank's credibility.[39]

For organizations such as the Bank of Japan, reputation is a crucial strategic resource. It needs to retain a reputation for professional competence (in the Bank's case, by making the right decisions on matters such as interest rates), and also an aura of authority and autonomy. If these reputational assets are eroded, then there are several potential dangers for a regulatory authority or government department. People and other organizations might begin to ignore its pronouncements, and to deal instead with other bodies, such as political parties or other ministries, that they perceive as the 'real' centre of power. The organization's ability to fight political pressures against the policies it believed were required to attain its objectives (such as economic stability in the case of the Bank), might also be compromised. This might lead to the erosion of other resources. People might be less eager to share up-to-date information, which might affect the organization's ability to take informed decisions, possibly degrading its reputation further. The best professionals might gravitate to organizations with greater perceived prestige or power. It might find its budgets being gradually eroded, and marginal powers allocated elsewhere.

The staff at the Bank of Japan are likely to believe (and there are commentators that agree with them) that their organization makes a worthwhile contribution, and that its continued authority and autonomy are worth sustaining. This makes it important that, in pondering monetary policy and some other key decisions, it takes account of the likely reaction of its stakeholders—its members' decision must be right for the economy, but the Bank must also be able to implement it. We list some of the main ones below, elaborate their requirements and assess the degree of power, urgency, and legitimacy that each commands.

- The Japanese government is anxious that nothing threatens the economy's recovery, since this would hurt its electoral prospects. The government has no formal power over the bank, whose independence is enshrined in law. However, the government clearly has urgency—it is partially dependent upon the bank for electoral success. It has pragmatic legitimacy, since the Cabinet, in conjunction with the two houses of Japan's parliament, appoints, and where relevant reappoints, the governor, deputy governor, and main members of the policy committee, and the minister of finance must approve the Bank's budget. It also has cognitive legitimacy, since the Bank is required to exchange views with the government and ensure that its monetary and exchange rate policies and the government's economic policies are in harmony.

- The Japanese people desire a flourishing economy in which there is full employment and stable prices. They cannot exercise direct power over the Bank, nor do they directly control its resources, except via the government. The peculiarities of Japan's electoral system, which almost always returns the Liberal Democratic Party to power, also diminishes their ability to exercise control over the Bank, since the electoral process rarely exerts real pressure on the government to change. However, they have urgency, since their →

→ well-being depends upon the Bank doing its job well. They have moral legitimacy, since they define the standards by which the Bank must work, and also cognitive legitimacy —their needs fit naturally with the bank's historic mission.

- The Japanese construction industry similarly has an interest in economic growth, which directly affects demand for its services. Arguably, it has the greatest urgency of all stakeholders reviewed so far, since in Japan's present economic situation, construction firms will feel the effect of any missteps by the Bank very strongly. It also has a degree of pragmatic legitimacy by virtue of the strong influence it has historically wielded within the Liberal Democratic Party.[40] It may well, however, have less moral or cognitive legitimacy than these other stakeholders, by virtue of what some people believe to be its role in promoting the asset bubble during the 1990s.

- Foreign speculators want low interest rates to continue and the yen to remain stable, since they have been able to make virtually risk-free profits by borrowing in Japan and investing the proceeds in countries where returns are higher. Their situation affords them only a limited amount of urgency, since if the Japanese situation changes they should be able to invest elsewhere. They have, moreover, no legitimacy in the eyes of the Bank's management—they have no influence over its resources, and their activities do not fit with its, or the country's, values or objectives.

To summarize, none of these stakeholders holds direct power over the Bank, although the Japanese government comes closest to doing so. Many observers felt that the Bank had bowed to government pressure in not raising interest rates in January 2007, though some also felt that this was the right decision.[41] Each of the stakeholders also manifests some degree of urgency, with the construction industry scoring highest on this factor, and the foreign speculators lowest.

The main factor that discriminates between the stakeholders, however, is legitimacy. The Japanese government, with its strong influence over resources allied to cognitive legitimacy, emerges as the most salient stakeholder, and the foreign speculators as the least salient. The extent to which the moral and cognitive legitimacy of the Japanese people scores more highly than the political influence of the construction industry will depend upon a number of factors. Amongst these might be the personalities of the decision-makers and whether or not a decision is close to or far away from an election.

Planning around the unpredictable political dimensions of the public sector environment represents a further challenge. Even though many public sector organizations are less dependent on government funding than they used to be, taking a long-term view is still more difficult than in commercial firms. Research in the mid-1990s found that 85 per cent of public sector agencies worked to time frames of less than five years, and many worked to one-year periods.[42] The relatively short-term appointments of governments and ministers, whose political priorities filter down eventually to most, if not all, public sector agencies, mean that environmental or regulatory change is regular and for the most part unpredictable.

For many public sector agencies, the move from government department to profit-generating entity has entailed a radical shift in culture and operating expectations. Even when not completely commercialized, most departments have had to become very much more business-like and accountable. The management of change has therefore been a continuing challenge for their managers.

→ We look at the challenges of executing change in Chapter 16.

15.2.3 Strategic directions for public sector organizations

'Strategic management in the public sector is concerned with strengthening the long-term health and effectiveness of governmental units and leading them through positive change to ensure a continuing productive "fit" with changing environments.'[43]

This implies:

- setting in place a value chain and architecture that will allow the agency's users to be served effectively and efficiently. This involves strengthening linkages between different parts of the agency, minimizing disruptive internal and inter-agency political activity, and minimizing the duplication and thus costs of particular elements. The way in which staff are managed and motivated appears to have a particularly significant impact on public organizations' performance, with good relational contracts and cultural controls being more effective than economic incentives;[44]

- developing relational assets in the form of cooperative relationships between agencies for implementing and evaluating policies. This implies that the organization needs to extend the internal architecture described in the previous paragraph to embrace external partners, with structures and a culture that facilitate inter-agency communication, as well as providing clear lines of responsibility and accountability;

- providing transparent accountability to both the public and politicians. This requires the development of clear financial systems, whose outputs may need to be made available for public scrutiny in a number of different formats. It also requires the creation of departments which have responsibility for monitoring public concern and reporting to the public on the work of the agency. Because public accountability has become so important, a core competence for many public sector departments is the management of relationships with various customer, client, and user groups. Public organizations have discovered benefit from incorporating these stakeholders' choices into their decision-making processes;[45]

- promoting the organization's values, mission, vision, and strategies. This is not only important in order to make the agency's services known to those that may benefit from them, but is also important in 'selling' the agency to those responsible for funding and controlling it. This counts as a 'problem acquisition' activity in the professional service value chain;

- seeking and obtaining sufficient resources to implement a politically set agenda. This is linked to the activities discussed in the previous paragraph, and is important because of the limited amount of funding available to agencies that may be in competition. The availability of resources is a major determinant of performance in public organizations.[46] The most successful in attracting funds may be those that are best able to 'sell' their work to those ultimately responsible for financing them, so that capabilities in communication and in managing customer expectations are important;

- developing knowledge assets and capabilities. The staff of the best-run public sector organizations invariably have a comprehensive understanding of the issues affecting the groups that use their services, and a knowledge of where to locate the resources to help them;

- developing innovative capabilities. There is some evidence that public sector organizations that develop innovative services or means of delivery out-perform those that do not.[47]

- influencing a future legislative agenda—another aspect of the problem acquisition activities in a public sector value chain. This is a tricky issue, because it can be argued that state agencies should be simply undertaking the work that the public requires them to do, without question. However, they are obviously in the best place to understand some of the key issues facing their particular clientele, and it is arguable that they would be failing in their duty if they were not to bring these issues to the notice of the wider public;

- putting in place an effective control and evaluation activity. This has two elements: performance measurement and feedback from external stakeholders. Performance measurement plays a crucial role, allowing the organization to adapt to changing circumstances, and allowing external stakeholders, from government ministers to the general public, to feel confident of its integrity and effectiveness.[48] Feedback—from

Environmental Types

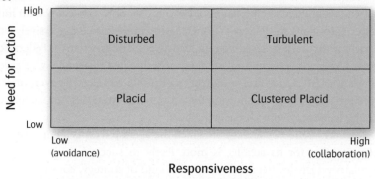

Strategy Types

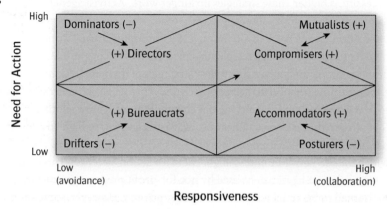

Figure 15.3 Matching strategy to public sector environments. Source: Nutt and Backoff (1995: 194). *Reproduced with the kind permission of Marcel Dekker Inc*

end-users, customers, and constituents, as well as the wider media and general public —has a similar function to that of market research data in commercial organizations, and similar systems are needed to obtain and evaluate it.

- Monitoring trends and changes in the agency's environment that might affect its policies or the ability to serve its mission. Given the radical and often unpredictable changes in the public sector environment, accurate predictions may be impossible to achieve, but managers in the public sector would be less than effective if they did not attempt to assess what might happen, and what they should do given different circumstances.

Public organizations confront a more general set of strategic choices regarding the degree to which they are proactive, rather than reactive, in driving change and influencing their stakeholders. Theorists have identified four different types of environment, in each of which (Figure 15.3) there are two different types of strategy, one (marked with a plus sign in the figure) being more suitable than the other (marked with a minus). These choices apply equally to not-for-profit organizations.

The four types of environment are determined, not just by the actual state of the environment but by perceptions of it within the organization. The organization may decide that the need for action is high or low, and that its responsiveness to stakeholders needs to be high or low. These decisions may be driven by events in the environment—melting icecaps and public concern about global warming—but also by preferences within the organization— whether to take a lead in becoming carbon neutral or to await a government policy directive, perhaps accompanied by some new funding for energy-efficiency.

In disturbed environments (high need for action, low responsiveness to shareholders) organizations may choose a dominator approach in which they drive through their desired polices with little regard for stakeholder views. Tax collection agencies may follow this strategy, changing their interpretation of tax rules at short notice and with little consultation. Under Elliot Spitzer, the New York Department of Justice aggressively pursued financial services firms that it believed were guilty of irregularities, when the Federal regulator for that sector favoured a less confrontational approach. The Department won several high-profile concessions from such firms—and Spitzer in 2006 was elected governor of New York State with a massive majority, showing that dominator strategies can sometimes succeed, and achieve legitimacy with a broader public.[49]

However, a director strategy, in which the agency accepts a minimal degree of external accountability for its actions, is more likely to succeed in this kind of environment. Regulatory agencies frequently adopt this kind of strategy, consulting with the people or firms they seek to regulate before promulgating rules and decisions.

In turbulent environments, where responsiveness to stakeholders, through preference or necessity, is higher, these strategies no longer work. Activist agencies must choose between a mutualist or a compromiser approach—otherwise, they will become vulnerable to political opposition (see What Can Go Wrong 15.1 for an example). Mutualists work with stakeholder groups to develop strategies that meet their evolving mutual needs—successful community schools and universities follow strategies of this nature. Compromisers, on the other hand, are more political in their approach: they try to meet a smaller set of requirements, and to deal with objections by playing one stakeholder off against another.

However, the need for action is not always perceived to be high. In a clustered placid environment (high responsiveness, low need for action) organizations may adopt a posture in which they do very little but highlight issues for action by others. This kind of strategy is most often, and most legitimately, used by not-for-profit pressure groups such as those pushing for human rights or increased action against poverty. However, some agencies may adopt it when formally charged with a task that their government does not really want to be completed. The implementation of EU regulations regarding opening markets to foreign competition has been through a posture strategy in certain countries. However, as the European Commission succeeds in using the courts to enforce market opening, the agencies in question must move towards an accommodator approach, in which there is some commitment to action.

In placid environments, the need for new actions is limited. Effective organizations in such circumstances use the strengths of bureaucracy—highly standardized and well-rehearsed routines—to execute their established tasks efficiently. Ineffective ones, by contrast, adopt a drifter approach in which they develop programmes that give an impression of action, but in fact achieve very little. The difference between a posture and a drifter approach is that a posture is an intentional approach, designed to postpone a specific action or persuade others to take it, while drifters may have little idea of what they are attempting to achieve, or avoid achieving. Organizations set up to implement vague and poorly drafted legislation may find themselves forced into a drifter approach, as may those that have achieved their primary mission and are regrouping before tackling another task.

15.3 Strategic management in the not-for-profit sector

This section deals with the not-for-profit (NFP), sometimes called the non-profit or 'third' sector. The not-for-profit sector is, if anything, even more varied than the public sector in the range of organizations that it embraces. NFP organizations are involved across the range of educational, research, welfare, economic, social, and spiritual activities and include:

- small organizations set up to provide services to a group of members, such as youth clubs, hostels for homeless people, parent–teacher associations, and residents' associations;

- larger organizations, such as hospices, schools, and universities, typically set up to provide social services in parallel with any state provision;

- organizations, such as religious bodies (e.g. churches or mosques), political parties, trades unions, employers' federations, set up to represent the interests of substantial numbers of individuals or organizations. These can be national or international in scope;

- charitable and quasi-political bodies that aim to raise money and marshal public opinion for a specific cause. In some cases, they actively intervene, through research or relief projects, to alleviate the issue that they are set up to address. Examples include educational and medical charities, hunger relief and aid organizations, and cause-related groups such as Greenpeace and Amnesty International. The largest of these are global in their fund-raising and operations. An unusual attribute of these NFPs is that their objective may, in theory, be to work themselves out of existence—by eliminating cancer, or poverty in Africa;

- foundations that exist to distribute money donated by philanthropists to worthy causes—often with clear guidelines as to which organizations or individuals are allowed to benefit. These can be very large: the Bill and Melinda Gates, Rockefeller, and Wellcome Foundations have assets of several billion dollars. Particularly in the USA, there is a strong tradition of philanthropy; rich business people there frequently give much of their fortunes away to fund worthy causes. There are also much smaller foundations set up to fund local projects.

Along with diversity, the sector shares other important features with the public sector. NFP organizations, like those in the public sector, generally provide a service to people who would otherwise not receive it.[50] They are sometimes used by governments instead of statutory agencies to provide a specialized service, such as training or housing advice, to particular constituents. This may be on a contractual basis, be funded through grants, or compensated through tax relief. In other cases it is the NFP's founders that create the organizations to provide something that they believe is lacking—whether this is financial aid, advice, or practical help to a particular group of people.

The NFP sector is large: in 2003/2004 there were 169,000 registered general charities in Britain, a country of about 57 million people. They had an income of £26.3bn, operating expenditure of £24.9bn, and a paid workforce of at least 608,000. If more specialized organizations such as housing associations and independent schools are included, these figures are considerably higher.[51]

Some NFPs are charities, and are regulated by governments in terms of what they can and cannot do. In many countries, charities are exempt from some sales, value-added or corporate taxes, and donors can reclaim income taxes on their contributions. Others, however, like Google's charitable foundation google.org, opt to forgo the tax concessions associated with registering as NFPs, in order to retain greater strategic freedom. In the case of google.org, this is to make seed-corn investment in social enterprises,[52] but others may want to do more political lobbying than local charity laws might permit.

15.3.1 The strategic characteristics of the NFP sector

The NFP sector shows an exceptional degree of polarization between very small and very large organizations. The smallest and most numerous have perhaps one or two workers and a limited income. In the UK, 56 per cent of general charities have incomes of less than £10,000, with an average of just over £3,000; 82 per cent have incomes under £100,000. At the other end of the scale, the largest 2 per cent of UK general charities have average incomes of £5.7m and account for around two-thirds of the sector's total income.[53] And the Bill and Melinda Gates Foundation, set up to distribute the fortune of Microsoft's co-founder, has assets of over $60 billion. Its size was doubled in 2006 when legendary investor Warren Buffet pledged his fortune to the foundation.[54]

The largest NFPs, international organizations such as Oxfam, or Médecins sans Frontières, employ many hundreds of paid and voluntary staff. Their management is, if anything, more challenging than managing corporations of similar size and scope, for reasons that we shall elaborate below. Nonetheless, the evidence from the UK is that a few (14 in the UK) of these very large (income over £100m) organizations are growing in public influence and becoming responsible for an increasing proportion of services delivered by the sector.

a. Volunteers and values

An important feature of NFP organizations is the primary role played by values. For NFPs that do not operate commercially, it is values that define the 'bottom line' against which internal and external stakeholders measure its performance.[55]

One reason for this can be found in the personal characteristics and motivation of the people that work in NFP organizations. The paid employees who undertake the management and administration of the organization often tolerate relatively low salary levels. And many of the people who work for and with them are volunteers. In the UK, for example, volunteers contribute around two-thirds of hours worked in general charities. All these people tend to be hugely committed to the cause which the NFP organization promotes, and are rewarded principally by the intrinsic nature of the work.

They may, however, display 'strategic delinquency': developing their own personalized version of the organization's goals and values, and being reluctant to acknowledge priorities that conflict with it. This sometimes leads to the internal management of the NFP being neglected—disadvantaging the client group it is supposed to help.

Volunteers are often even more difficult to control than 'normal' employees, since the sanctions which are used in commercial organizations, such as the threat of dismissal, have little force.[56] Volunteers will not work unless they want to, have little to lose if they leave, have a variety of alternative 'jobs' to go to, and so have to be interested and involved in the work. They tend therefore to either be highly active or become disenchanted, after which they either become inactive or leave.

These problems are further magnified in international NFPs. For tax and regulatory reasons, the individual national branches of these organizations are likely to be legally autonomous bodies. It is they that will raise most of the funds and recruit and manage the volunteers. There may be significant differences in outlook between these different national branches, over which the centre has no formal control—indeed, it is likely to depend upon them for funding and operational personnel. For example, the Anglican Church has had to reconcile differences between groups, most overtly in the USA, that favour the ordination of women and homosexuals as priests and the blessing of same-sex unions, and those, particularly in Africa, who vehemently oppose it. Some US parishes have sought to attach themselves to African dioceses because they share the views of the African bishops and cannot countenance the policies of their local ones.[57]

b. Corporate governance and stakeholder management

Like a public-sector organization, an NFP may have a large number of stakeholders that can in some way be considered customers. The most obvious are the users or purchasers of its services—government agencies that commission them, and the sponsors and donors that pay for them. But volunteers and staff also help to pay for the services through contributions of time and effort, either for free or at below market rates. And various partner organizations, together with people who benefit indirectly from the group's achievements (e.g. the families of its users), may also be in some way customers for information or other inputs.

Any of these stakeholders, together with others, such as regulators and the media, may have opinions as to the objectives and management of an NFP. A distinctive feature of the sector, however, is the degree to which these stakeholders are likely to have, not just legitimacy, but formal rights to be consulted, along with actual power. The ultimate governing body in an NFP is typically a management committee or board of trustees which has fiduciary responsibilities. It is quite likely to include:

- key donors who are powerful because of their control of funds, and very keen to see value for their money;
- representatives of the volunteers and/or staff;
- representatives from the client group which the NFP serves.

Board members have substantial power in setting policies and strategic direction. A management team may thus find itself overruled by well-meaning but unqualified trustees, following their own political or moral agenda, or by coalitions of customers and employees, in a way that would be unthinkable in most companies. Stakeholder analysis and management, and especially the management of relations with the board, are crucial skills for NFP managers. Board members may have valuable competences that complement those of the management team, but may also assume executive power unless the management is strong enough to prevent them.[58]

c. The changing nature of NFP funding

In general NFP managers spend considerable time in developing and maintaining sources of income. The NFP sector has seen something of a change in the way it is funded, mirroring the change in public sector management philosophy discussed in section 15.2.1. Historically, the prevailing model would be that an NFP, having identified an issue, would seek funding to address it. Some NFPs would solicit small donations in the street, through mailshots or through the media. However, even more important sources in many cases were governments, corporate sponsors, or charitable foundations. One of the skills of the successful NFP was to identify organizations or government programmes whose objectives fitted with those of the NFP, and to which it could then apply for a grant. These grants were given up front for a particular project or to set up a service, and were generally not dependent upon performance, although organizations would have to account for their use of the money and report back on the results. However, grants were often lower than requested, so that scarce resources had to be spent on reconfiguring plans to match available funding.

A number of funding programmes, such as those administered by the European Commission, still use this model. However, many governments and large private donors, such as the Bill and Melinda Gates Foundation and the Rockefeller Foundation (Real-life Application 15.3), now prefer to specify more precisely the objectives—such as the elimination of AIDS or malaria—which they hope to attain, and award contracts, rather than grants, to organizations that will undertake specific tasks—a testing or education programme or the development of a vaccine—to further those aims. These contracts contain performance milestones that must be met if funding is to continue, and may be awarded competitively.[59]

Real-life Application 15.3 The Rockefeller Foundation[60]

Heavily damaged New Orleans homes after Hurricane Katrina. The Rockefeller Foundation funded $3.5m towards planning the city's reconstruction. *iStock*

The Rockefeller Foundation was established in 1913 by John D. Rockefeller Sr, who made his fortune in the early days of the oil industry. Its founder directed it towards using science to address the root causes of the world's evils, and it helped fund major breakthroughs against yellow fever, a killer tropical disease, and in increasing agricultural productivity. More recently, it has directed its efforts to ensuring that the benefits of globalization are shared more equitably. It has assets of more than $3bn, making it one of the world's largest private foundations.

However, by the early years of the twenty-first century, the foundation had lost some of its early focus and energy. When a new president, Judith Rodin, arrived in 2004, she concluded that part of the reason for this lay in the way in which the foundation was structured as a number of programmes. The main ones were: Food Security (developing agricultural technology to improve the lives of the rural poor); Health Equity (reducing differences in death and disease rates across the world); Working Communities (reducing poverty in the USA); Creativity and Culture (support for individual artists and creative projects in the USA and elsewhere);

Global Inclusion (reducing the negative effects of globalization); and regional programmes in Africa, North America, and South-East Asia. It also ran a study and conference centre in Bellagio, Italy.

Each of these programmes was clearly worthwhile, and compatible with the Foundation's mission, to promote the well-being of humanity. However, some observers felt that the programmes had become individual fiefdoms and that this had stimulated unproductive political infighting.[61] Rodin also concluded that the fixed allocation of resources between programmes was inhibiting the foundation from taking the bold, transforming steps that it made in its early days, when it distributed more foreign aid than the US government. A typical grant under each of the programmes in 2005 was of the order of $200,000. The example of the Bill and Melinda Gates Foundation, which was underwriting massive, focused programmes to combat AIDS and malaria, was clearly a powerful one. Accordingly, Rodin took the decision to abolish the long-standing, broad-based programmes in favour of larger, more specific initiatives with a clearly defined time frame. In 2006, it announced it would fund:[62]   →

→
- $5m in low-interest loans for the purchase of affordable housing in New York;

- $3.5m of the nearly $8m required to plan the rebuilding of New Orleans after its devastation by Hurricane Katrina;

- access by selected NFPs to InnoCentive, a global online forum designed to bring the talent of scientists, technologists, and entrepreneurs worldwide. InnoCentive, which offers individuals rewards of up to $1m for a breakthrough idea, had up to then been open only to profit-making R&D-based concerns;

- a $150m initiative, in partnership with the Gates Foundation, to stimulate a green agricultural revolution in Africa through the adoption of higher-yielding seed varieties. This harks back to the Foundation's successes in transforming farming in Asia and Latin America, and builds upon work financed under the old programmes to develop seed varieties suitable for different parts of Africa.

Not everyone found it easy to adjust to this new way of working. According to the prestigious medical journal, the *Lancet*:

The pitch of anxiety has been so great that the Dean of an internationally famous northeastern US school of public health wrote to the chairman of Rockefeller Foundation's Board of Trustees, James Orr, on Oct 16, 2006, asking him 'to reconsider the decision to close the Foundation's health unit and activities'.[63]

Rodin responded with an interview to the Lancet, to rebut concerns that the abolition of its Health Equity programme meant that the Rockefeller Foundation was withdrawing from its commitment to health research. She reassured the medical profession that, in fact, the amount invested in their field was more likely to rise than fall. Internal stakeholders proved more difficult to manage.[64] Around one-third of the Foundation's staff left the organization in the first 21 months of Rodin's tenure.[65] However, a string of high-profile appointments in 2005 and 2006 testified to the persuasiveness of her vision: Sandra Day O'Connor, a recently retired US Supreme Court judge, joined the board; Peter Madonia, chief-of-staff to New York's Mayor Michael Bloomberg, became chief operating officer; and Derek Yach, a former executive director with the World Health Organization, joined as director of Global Health.

Traditional NFPs, particularly charities, may offer professional services that make them strong contenders for these contracts: Oxfam, a relief agency, provides services in hunger and famine relief, and manages projects for disaster relief. At their core, however, they have a network value chain—they exist to link donors and volunteers with the users who will ultimately benefit from their activities. Many charities have become extremely sophisticated in the marketing techniques they use to target potential donors, and database management and relationship marketing have become hugely important tools, although there are some indications that returns from them are diminishing as the general public is becoming tired of them. Trading activities—shops for second-hand books and clothing, or the sale of customized gifts and greeting cards—are a supplement to grant and donation income.

There are other organizations with charitable objectives, on the other hand, for which trading and competitive bidding are fundamental income generators. These organizations follow the social enterprise model (see Section 15.4 below).

It remains the case that many NFPs depend heavily on a single source of income, frequently government funding, which is the source of over 30 per cent of charitable revenues in the USA and 38 per cent in the UK. Governments often dictate the direction the NFP takes through the types of project that they will fund, and the performance criteria they set for renewing this funding. However, the proportion of that income that is earned, through sales or contracts, is now, at least in the UK, slightly higher than that obtained from donations and grants, at 48 per cent of the total.[66]

Trading NFP organizations may be more like commercial firms than traditional charities or public sector organizations. However, the reporting regime is generally less demanding than that of private firms, with no obligation to disclose directors' remuneration, and no powerful shareholders to mount a hostile takeover bid. This allows their managers considerable discretion as to how their organization's income is used. There is a case to be made for remunerating staff properly and investing in decent offices and other infrastructure.

There have, however, been controversial cases of charities whose entire income was swallowed up by administrative expenses, leaving almost nothing for the intended beneficiaries.

d. Judging effectiveness

Different NFP stakeholders vary in how they judge effectiveness. Donors are likely to judge success in terms of value for their money—but there are many ways of assessing this, and the most efficient charities are not necessarily those that win out in the competition for donations.[67] Governments, for example, will want to ensure that the money they put into a charity which is providing hostels and services for homeless people is actually and demonstrably taking people off the streets. The homeless people who use this charity will want the accommodation to be clean and safe. The employees and volunteers who staff the hostels will want to feel that they are doing a good job, and are appreciated by managers and users alike. Police and local hospitals and doctors may judge the charity by its effect on their workload; neighbours of the hostels will judge it effective if they are not hassled as they walk to their homes.

Some of these viewpoints are likely to be in conflict with others. For example, providing a large number of places for high-risk homeless people is almost inevitably going to lead to some degradation of neighbours' quality of life. Conflicting stakeholder objectives can make it difficult to define the level of service required or to be provided, and so to establish useable management targets.

It is often also difficult to assess whether an NFP's mission is being achieved. In the example above, it is a relatively easy task to assess whether the charity is providing accommodation; all it needs to do is count up bed occupancy. But if its mission is also to reduce long-term homelessness, how can it judge whether it has done this? Homelessness depends upon political and economic variables, and is affected by the actions of many different agencies, both statutory and voluntary. If the number of homeless falls or rises, it can be difficult to measure the impact of any one of them.

This is not to say that NFPs should not attempt such broad missions. Some of the biggest, best-known, and powerful NFP organizations have broad and ambitious political aims. Greenpeace and Friends of the Earth, both international organizations with a brief to crusade on ethical and 'green' issues, are campaigning bodies with large research and public relations arms. Both can legitimately claim to have been extremely effective in raising public awareness of their causes. Proving that they have been responsible for achieving any changes to corporate or government practice is, however, a much harder task.

 Using Evidence 15.1 Financial indicators of NFP effectiveness

Few NFPs seek to be judged by the same financial criteria as commercial firms. Profits or surpluses are not relevant except as a means to satisfying the NFP's mission. It is therefore quite difficult to judge these organizations' effectiveness using standard financial measures. An NFP with a growing balance sheet and money in the bank may, in fact, be failing in its mission to use those funds for the purposes for which they were donated. One recent study has found that large endowments tend to be a symptom of agency problems in NFPs.[68]

On the other hand, it is appropriate to look at some measures of fundraising efficiency (e.g. revenue/fundraising expenses), public support (e.g. public donations/total revenue) and overall financial performance (e.g. total costs/total revenue), if only to review how effectiveness is changing over time. Note, however, that an organization with a high ratio of fundraising expenses to income may be doing better by its stakeholders than one that spends less, but generates far fewer contributions.[69]

15.3.2 Strategic challenges for NFP organizations

As with public sector organizations, stakeholder management represents a key challenge for NFPs. The recognition and bridging of the competing demands of the different stakeholder groups, and the understanding of their individual objectives, cultures, and sources of power, is often vital to the organization's survival. A particular challenge at local level is ensuring that volunteers feel that they and their opinions and priorities are valued. For larger, in particular international, NFPs, the negotiation of a strategic consensus between different national and political factions is also a challenge, as is ensuring that the national organizations continue to subscribe enough money to allow the centre to function.

NFPs may also face change management challenges similar to those in the public sector. They may be required to move from the traditional model, in which grants are applied for and given, to a more commercial model, in which programmes are commissioned and contracted for, and to cope with the more commercialized environment that results. This can lead to dissent and departures among the staff (see Real-life Application 15.3).

The increased competition from other NFPs and an increasingly charity-sated public mean that traditional, donation-based NFPs need to pay considerable management attention to wooing, and keeping, donors, and to positioning the organization so that it can attract a sufficiently wealthy and committed group of supporters.

Creative Strategizing 15.1

You are the director of a modest charitable foundation with a remit to raise and distribute funds to support medical research. How would you position your organization to take advantage of the change in strategy by the Rockefeller Foundation (Real-life Application 15.3)?

15.3.3 Strategic directions for NFP organizations

Some choices to be made by NFPs mirror those in the public sector. They too select their strategic direction from the types of strategy shown in Figure 15.3. Large charitable foundations, like the Bill and Melinda Gates Foundation, which have both the cash and reputational assets to select their own agendas, may choose a director or even a dominator stance. Smaller pressure groups may opt for a posture stance, acting as advocates for action, until they acquire sufficient funds to move to a more activist stance.

Achieving legitimacy in the eyes of key stakeholders is a major concern. There is some evidence that adopting various professional management practices borrowed from commercial organizations, such as strategic planning, customer satisfaction surveys, cost-cutting and change management procedures are likely to enhance people's impressions of effectiveness. NFPs which are judged effective also tend to have management committees or boards of trustees with higher social standing. NFPs needing to raise their esteem in the eyes of the public, and key stakeholders might do well to upgrade the standard and status of their board's membership.[70]

Building relationships with local institutions and elites, and with other NFPs, has been shown to improve the survival and growth prospects of some traditional NFPs, which rely upon donations and volunteers.[71]

Bureaucratic controls may be needed to satisfy contributors that their money is being well used. If the organization cannot account for its money, there is a danger that donors, and even staff, will migrate to one that offers more transparency. A degree of bureaucracy may also reassure staff and volunteers that everyone is being treated fairly.

➜ Vision and values were discussed in Section 8.3.2.

Culture and architecture cannot be too formal, however, since they need to facilitate the particular style of motivation required for volunteers. The architecture must allow for two-way communication, and prominence be given to vision and values. This is a way of uniting disparate national groups in a large NFP and different stakeholder groups in a small one, bearing in mind that a lot of internal political bargaining goes on in many NFPs, with the management committee at its centre. It is also important that there is clear agreement among top managers regarding the organization's mission, since confusion on this point has been found to degrade the performance in NFPs.[72]

Many NFP organizations have started to separate into cost and profit centres. The cost centres deliver the services for which clients are not expected to pay. The profit centres are set up to raise funds through commercial activities, marketing, and managing investments —anything that will make money, which can then be used to fund the NFP's services.

A major strategic priority relates to the development of an infrastructure that allows income to be generated, in quantity, and in as regular, predictable, and reliable a form as possible. A traditional NFP, deriving income from donations rather than trading, may nonetheless require similar marketing and segmentation competences to those used in commercial firms. The broad thrust of marketing strategy will depend on whether the NFP is a 'has-been', 'celebrity', or 'star':[73]

- Has-beens, because they are perceived to be old-fashioned or out-dated, even though they may be well known, are at risk of losing both sponsors and clients. In order to achieve sufficient income, such organizations need to raise their public profile and be seen to be rejuvenating their operations and mission.

- A celebrity organization is usually well-known, but has not yet built up sufficient resources to meet demand. This type of organization should be able to attract new donors relatively easily, and this needs to be the area of most attention.

- A star organization already has a good public profile and high levels of financial support, and only needs to be worried about the threat of new competition for funds coming into its particular field.

The development of a strong brand orientation—an appreciation within the NFP that it is seen as a brand and that this is helpful to the organization—can also improve performance. An assessment needs to be made of the potential sources of funds. Charities with a diverse donor body, competing for a declining pool of available donations, are well advised to target specific stakeholders to build 'donor constituencies'—long-term relationships with key suppliers of funds.[74]

15.4 Social enterprises

➜ We examined the concept of corporate social responsibility in Section 2.7.

Social enterprises are firms that sell goods or services in the same way as profit-making companies, but which have an explicit social objective and which use any profits either to develop that social objective or to support one or more charities. Issues of corporate social responsibility play a significant role in deciding what they will do and how they will do it.

Many social enterprises are small firms with specific local aims, such as those that manage certain waste recycling and community transport schemes in the UK. Some of these may receive most of their money from public sector bodies or charitable foundations, although they may often need to tender competitively for them. However, some substantial and well-known firms also fall into this category. Examples include:

- the John Lewis Partnership, a prominent UK retail chain that is owned by its employees, who share in its profits;

- the Big Issue, an organization that works to give homeless people the ability to tackle their financial and social difficulties. Founded in London, it has spread throughout the UK and into Africa, Asia, and Australia. The homeless people become sellers of a professionally produced magazine, also called the *Big Issue*—but they must purchase the copies that they sell from the organization, and must therefore acquire the skills to organize their business;

- CaféDirect, a UK member of the Fairtrade movement, sells tea and coffee, bought direct from producers at a premium price designed to offer them a decent living and to make an investment in local training and infrastructure. Its products are sold in direct competition with those of corporations such as Nestlé;

- social cooperatives that perform a variety of functions in the Italian economy;[75]

- Easybeinggreen, an Australian company set up to tackle climate change and CO_2 pollution, offers advisory services on pollution reduction as well as energy-saving products and packages for offsetting the carbon used in everyday activities;[76]

- Grameen Bank, a Bangladeshi provider of finance to borrowers considered not to be credit-worthy by traditional lenders (Real-life Application 15.4);

- the Children's Investment Fund (TCI), a hedge fund whose founder is committed to giving a proportion of its profits to a charitable foundation for children in developing countries. The foundation had, by mid-2007, amassed assets of over \$1bn.[77]

Real-life Application 15.4 Grameen Bank: a social enterprise[78]

Bangladesh's Grameen Bank was born in 1976 as a University of Chittagong research project to investigate the feasibility of a financial institution offering credit to the very poor. Its founder, Professor Mohammed Yunus, was convinced that extending lending facilities to such people would unleash their entrepreneurial spirit and enable them to break out of poverty. At the time, the only sources of funding available to them were moneylenders, who charged exorbitant interest rates, and charity, which Yunus believed made people dependent.

Grameen (the name in Bangla means 'rural' or 'village') reinvented traditional models of bank lending to fit the specific circumstances of Bangladeshi rural society. Since few borrowers had assets to pledge as collateral, none was demanded. Loans were secured, in essence, on the good name of the borrower, who was required to join a group of four others. Group members were not liable for one another's loans, but exerted social pressure to ensure that the money for weekly or fortnightly repayments was not diverted to other purposes. It brought its services to the doors of its borrowers, rather than making them travel to its branches. It quoted its interest rates as simple, rather than compound, interest, which is easier for its clients to understand and monitor.

The experiment proved successful—the proportion of borrowers that default has turned out to be only 1 per cent. With the backing of Bangladesh's central and main commercial banks, and later with aid donor funding, Grameen Bank expanded rapidly. However, it encountered a setback when Bangladesh suffered from bad flooding in 1998 and borrowers were unable to meet their repayment schedules. It responded by moving to a model which encouraged people to save with the bank as well as borrow from it. Its outstanding loans are now comfortably exceeded by deposits.

In 2006, it had nearly 2,300 branches and operated in 76,000 villages. A typical loan is for around \$100, and might be put towards a solar panel to provide electric power and lighting, or to enable a 'telephone lady' to buy a mobile phone, which she can then lend out, for a fee, to other people in her village. The lady earns a healthy profit on her investment, and the village benefits from improved communications.

This is an example of Grameen Bank's prominent social agenda. As well as preaching the virtues of entrepreneurship and self-reliance, it also provides its 7 million members with experience of the democratic process—they elect local and national bank ➔

→ officers on a regular basis. Some have been encouraged to stand for local government office. It supports education through scholarships and student loans. It encourages members to abide by its Sixteen Rules, which include the use of latrines and of pure sources of drinking water, but also, more controversially, a refusal to accept or give dowries when their children marry. It challenges some tenets of male-dominated Bangladeshi society: 97 per cent of its borrowers are women.

Nonetheless, the Bank does not operate as a charity; it has always aimed to be a sustainable business. It charges market rates, which can typically be around 20 per cent, to its borrowers —even though it is 94 per cent owned by them. It has reported profits (which are put into a Rehabilitation Fund to cope with natural disasters) for all but three years of its existence, and for every year from 1993 onwards. Its 2005 return on assets was a creditable 22 per cent and it comfortably meets international banking standards for capital adequacy. And in 2006, the Bank and Mohammed Yunus were jointly awarded the Nobel Peace Prize.

Creative Strategizing 15.1

1. How might Grameen Bank diversify further? (Think of what strategic resources it has accumulated.) Should it limit its activities to Bangladesh? What risks and compromises are involved in further expansion?

2. You work for an orthodox bank in Bangladesh, offering a good service, but with no pretensions to being a social enterprise. How would you position your firm to compete with Grameen Bank?

It can be quite difficult to identify what is and what is not a social enterprise.[79] Some, such as the Big Issue or Grameen Bank, believe that acting as a profit-making business is actually the best way of achieving their social aims.[80] Involving people in a social business is argued to be more effective at making people self-reliant than charitable giving would be, and social enterprises have been found to be more effective than other types of organization in generating employment.[81] Others, such as John Lewis, act very much like 'normal' firms, except that social principles appear to be deeply embedded in their corporate values, in a way that clearly affects the manner in which they deal with staff, customers, and other stakeholders. Still others manifest their social principles mainly in the way that they distribute their profits; in generating those profits, they can be quite aggressive towards other stakeholders. TCI, for example, was instrumental in pressurizing the Deutsche Börse to abandon its 2005 bid for the London Stock Exchange, and in triggering the reorganization at ABN Amro, a Dutch bank that then, in 2007, became the subject of two competing takeover bids.[82]

These problems in defining social enterprises, together with the fact they have only recently become widespread, means that little theory has been developed for them. We are therefore not able to follow the pattern of the rest of this chapter, where we examine the strategic characteristics, the distinctive challenges that they face, and the directions that they should follow.

In particular, it is not yet clear whether they should be managed like profit-making firms or like NFPs.[83] One approach would be to treat them fundamentally as profit-making enterprises whose social values also allows them to benefit from increased legitimacy in the eyes of consumers, employees, and other stakeholders. This might improve employee motivation, or allow them to charge a price premium—which would increase the profits that could then be passed to the organization's social beneficiaries. Some early theories suggest that this is more likely to succeed than the alternative approach, which is to manage the organization as an NFP, and treat the commercial activities mainly as a way of raising funds.[84]

In either case, the challenge is to manage the trade-off between commercial and social issues. If the firm orients salary levels and service levels too far towards its social values, it may risk making itself commercially uncompetitive. If, on the other hand, the firm becomes too commercially cut-throat, it may undermine the values that give the organization its purpose and cohesion.

One source of seedcorn resources for the launch of a social enterprise might be a 'venture philanthropist'. These are individuals or foundations, such as google.org and the Skoll foundation (set up by an ex-president of eBay), that function as venture capital funds for the sector, and may contribute time and expertise as well as funds.[85] On the other hand, networks of local worthies, of the kind that promote the growth of traditional NFPs, have been found to slow the growth of social enterprises.[86]

Theoretical Debate 15.1 How different are these sectors—really?

One of the underlying assumptions in this chapter is that the three sectors considered here—small business, public sector, and not-for-profit—are sufficiently different, in strategic management terms, to warrant special treatment. In this theoretical debate, we examine how justified that assumption might be.

For small firms, the claims for underlying differences were made most stridently in a number of articles published from the late 1970s onwards (Dandridge, 1979; Welsh and White, 1981). Such articles, and those that followed them, pointed out the very real differences in management behaviour and perspectives between small and large businesses, which we have discussed in Section 15.1. In a more measured fashion, Gartner et al. (1992) pointed out that entrepreneurship could be considered as the process whereby organizations 'emerge'. It was not necessarily the case, therefore, that they would follow the same behaviour patterns as those that had already settled down. However, some researchers have found instances of small firms resembling large ones in terms of the sophistication of their architecture (Torrès and Julien, 2005).

It does not follow, however, that the different perspective found in small firms would mean the fundamental importance of issues like fit, distinctiveness, and sustainability no longer applied. Sandberg (1992) concluded that the basic tenets of strategic management were in fact as valid for small firms as large ones. And Torrès and Julien (2005) went further, suggesting that the claims that small businesses were a distinctive sector stemmed from a desire by researchers in that field to stake out their own territory.

The story for the public and not-for-profit sectors is a different one. Theory in these areas has grown up through a distinct body of research that places less emphasis on the behaviour of individual organizational units than strategic management theory does. Organizational effectiveness matters most, for scholars in these fields, as a factor that affects the extent to which public policy objectives can be attained. There have been very few studies of strategic management in the public sector, and most of those have focused on the adoption of strategic planning by public organizations and NFPs (e.g. Poister and Streib, 1999; Vinzant, 1996; Vinzant and Vinzant, 1996), rather than on their management.

The assumptions that firms and their managers are seeking profits is fundamental to the economic theories that are a major underpinning of strategic management theory. It is logical to expect public organizations and NFPs, which tend to have this motivation, if at all, only in a diluted form, to show differences in their strategic behaviour. There have, however, been very few studies of what these differences are, and researchers (e.g. Burns and Wholey, 1993; Oliver, 1988; Westphal et al., 1997) have been happy to use public sector organizations or NFPs to test some theories, such as those relating to the diffusion of practices across organizations, that have then been applied to a broader population.

Andrews et al. (2006) have demonstrated that in public sector organizations, prospector organizations that seek out expansion and innovation perform better than their peers, and organizations that just react to changes in their environment do worse. These findings match those for private sector firms (Miles and Snow, 1978), although in the private sector, defenders, which focus on improving the efficiency of existing operations, perform as well as prospectors; in the public sector, they are less successful. Andrews et al. (2006) also find a negative correlation between the degree of diversity of an organization's activities and performance, which mirrors the findings of early studies of diversification in private firms.

It is logical to expect some parts of strategic management theory to apply across all sectors. These include the importance of relatedness in diversification, the resource-based view, and theories about structure and organizational learning. These are theories that are derived from observations regarding managers' cognitive limitations, and do not assume that those managers are striving for profit, as against some other objective. But this remains to be tested.

What Can Go Wrong 15.1 The UK Home Office—unfit for purpose?

Rarely has an indictment been delivered so bluntly in the polite world of the British civil service. Appearing on 23 May 2006 before the select committee of the UK parliament that oversaw his department's activities, the UK Home Secretary, Dr John Reid, pulled no punches. 'Our system is not fit for purpose', he told the committee. 'It is inadequate in terms of its scope, it is inadequate in terms of its information technology, leadership, management systems and processes.' He was speaking about the directorate that dealt with immigration into the UK, but he was widely quoted as referring to the whole of his department, the Home Office.

The trigger for his admission was the revelation, a few days earlier, that over 1,000 prisoners from outside the country, who were due to be deported after serving their sentences, had absconded and were at large in the UK. Amongst them were 186 serious offenders, including 37 murderers and rapists. Two hundred of the absconders had committed further crimes in the UK.[87] Reid's predecessor, Charles Clarke, resigned shortly after this emerged.[88] The head of the same directorate had also admitted to having no idea how many illegal immigrants were in the country.[89]

Two months later, an external review of a number of government departments found that the Home Office, alone of the four departments reviewed, failed to achieve good assessments on any of ten measures of leadership, strategy, and delivery, and was given the lowest possible rating on two: 'nurturing and handling talent' and 'planning priorities for delivery'.[90]

That report appeared the day after Reid's plans for reforming the Home Office. In those, the Immigration and Nationality Directorate was earmarked for transformation into an executive agency with greater operational autonomy. Other large Home Office units were also offered more independence in return for a higher degree of accountability. Fifteen of the department's 60 directors were to be replaced, the remainder, along with 250 other top staff, would undergo capability assessments to confirm their suitability. Staff numbers would fall from 8,000 to under 6,000 by 2010, with 3,300 head office staff being returned to front-line duties.[91]

But worrying facts continued to emerge, with morale amongst staff reported to be plummeting with each new revelation. That same July day, the Home Office admitted that the number of failed asylum seekers still in the country was, at 450,000, double what had previously been admitted to. In November it was revealed that the number of people absconding from open prisons had doubled since Reid took over the department. In December, the department reported missed targets on cutting drugs use and reoffending by young people.[92]

In January 2007, the department's permanent secretary—its most senior civil servant—admitted that almost 20 per cent of its 160 sets of data were not of an appropriate standard. And the Association of Chief Police Officers reported that 27,000 paper files relating to convictions of UK citizens in other countries had, since 2001, been left unprocessed, with none of the details being passed to relevant agencies in the UK. This meant that there was nothing to prevent such people gaining employment in sensitive posts, such as those dealing with children. The head of a CV-checking firm told the press that one in ten checks run by his company found that the applicant had a criminal record—the fact that those applicants were prepared to give permission for the checks to take place showed their low opinion of the Home Office's record keeping.[93]

Opinions differed as to why the Home Office was in such apparent disarray. IT was felt to be part of the problem, with systems in different areas that did not communicate with each other, or use common reference numbers for the same individual. Some commentators suggested that the Home Office's problems were symptomatic of deeper cultural issues within the civil service, where both civil servants and ministers reported that there was little accountability for poor performance or scope to sack poorly performing individuals.[94]

Others placed blame at the door of the Cabinet—the UK Government's top decision-making body, comprising all senior ministers. They pointed to the sheer volume of criminal legislation—over fifty pieces between 1997 and 2004—and strategic plans—three since 2001—introduced by Reid's predecessors. Keeping up with this pace of legislative change had undoubtedly stretched the Home Office and its main services. Critics also felt that certain Cabinet initiatives had little substance, but were intended to reassure a public and press anxious about law and order and immigration. Reid himself, in an early meeting with his officials, was said to have asked for headline-catching 'quick win' initiatives.[95]

Still another diagnosis pointed to the Home Office's sprawling remit. Originally set up in 1782 to deal with all domestic affairs, it retains responsibility for a range of policy areas that have not been ceded to newer ministries such as Health or Education. Although law and order and national security are its main responsibilities, it also regulates charities, voluntary organizations, animal experiments, and British Summer Time. Mastering such a wide-ranging brief is acknowledged by past and present ministers to be extremely difficult.[96]

John Reid seemed to agree with this last diagnosis. On 21 January 2007, he announced a plan to split the department in two, with one part looking after criminal justice and the other responsible for national security—counter-terrorism and immigration. But critics queried whether this would address the communications problems, such as those between immigration and prison service officials, that were at the root of some past mistakes. And Reid himself admitted that he expected other problems to emerge before the Home Office was fully turned around.[97]

● CHAPTER SUMMARY

In this chapter, we have reviewed the strategic characteristics, the main challenges, and the choices of strategic direction available to four types of organization other than the large profit-making corporations for which mainstream strategic management theory was developed.

Small firms in general tend to be more short-term and opportunistic than larger firms in their strategic orientation, more focused upon survival and cash flow than on growth and profit, and more centralized. Small firms are more likely to be successful if:

● they and their founders have an entrepreneurial orientation, favouring growth, innovation, and change;

● their management team is strong and balanced;

● they have focused objectives;

● they are adequately capitalized.

In order to enhance their firm's performance, the managers of small companies might consider:

● implementing appropriate planning and control systems;

● focusing upon a small niche where they do not directly confront larger competitors;

● being distinctive from larger competitors in terms either of flexibility or efficiency—but not to attempt both;

● internationalizing.

Public sector organizations typically have a wide variety of stakeholders, several of which might legitimately be considered customers. They face the challenge of simultaneously:

● managing downward—dealing with internal issues, such as human resource management;

● managing outward—dealing with partner organizations. Most public sector agencies are involved in complex programmes which embrace a network of private, public, and not-for-profit organizations;

● managing upward—dealing with elected politicians. The electoral process means that the identity and objectives of this group of stakeholders is likely to change radically every few years.

Stakeholder management is a key challenge for public sector managers, along with the management of change, as many public organizations are called upon to adopt a more commercial orientation. The strategic directions that have been pursued to meet these challenges include:

● strengthening internal linkages, using good relational contracts and cultural controls, so as to minimize needless duplication of effort and disruptive political activity, and reduce the duplication and thus costs of particular elements;

● developing cooperative relationships between agencies for implementing and evaluating policies;

● improving the organization's image with the public and politicians by making it clearly accountable, building user choices into decision-making processes, and promoting the organization's values, mission, vision, and strategies. Good performance measurement and feedback systems may also help reinforce the organization's legitimacy;

● developing knowledge assets and innovation capabilities;

● monitoring trends and changes in the agency's environment and influencing the legislative agenda where appropriate.

The NFP sector is a highly diverse one that is often used by governments to supplement their own services. It has historically been funded by donations and staffed by volunteers. Increasingly there is a move towards a social enterprise model where organizations earn money through trading and contracting in competitive markets, and plough profits into their chosen cause.

NFPs face important challenges in sustaining their values, which are important in uniting their diverse stakeholders, including volunteers over whom it has few controls other than cultural controls. Stakeholder management is a key challenge, made more complicated by the fact that many stakeholder groups may have genuine power through representation on the NFP's board. Finding effective systems to measure performance and sustaining funding levels are other major challenges, particularly for traditional, donation-led NFPs. The NFP's value chain and architecture need to be shaped accordingly.

Social enterprises are a sector of emerging importance, comprising organizations that have strong social aims which they use business and the profit motive to fulfil. It is as yet unclear whether they are best managed as profit-making enterprises or as NFPs. A class of venture philanthropists has grown up to furnish start-up capital to them.

 Online Resource Centre
www.oxfordtextbooks.co.uk/orc/haberberg_rieple/

Visit the Online Resource Centre that accompanies this book to read more information relating to strategies where profit is not the main objective.

● KEY SKILLS

The key skills you should have developed after reading this chapter are:

● the ability to appraise the strategies followed by organizations in the small company, public, not-for-profit, and social enterprise sectors;

● the capacity to develop strategic options for organizations in those sectors.

● REVIEW QUESTIONS

1. What would the owner of a small but fast-growing manufacturing firm need to do to minimize the risk that the firm fails? How would your answer be different if this was a service firm? Or a retailer? Or a social enterprise?

2. What are the particular risks that small firms run when they internationalize?

3. To what extent do private sector firms and NFPs need to manage outwards and upwards, as public sector bodies must do?

4. Why might the chief executive of a public sector agency wish for their organization to be privatized?

5. Undertake a stakeholder analysis for the Probation Service of England and Wales (Real-life Application 15.2) and for Grameen Bank (Real-life Application 15.4).

6. Many NFPs are small organizations. In what ways does their small size affect their ability or need to act like a 'typical' NFP? In what ways does their NFP status affect their ability or need to act like a typical small firm?

7. You are the chief executive of a well-regarded charity that raises money for and undertakes research into a rare but deadly disease. Another charity in the same field, with which you have collaborated in the past, has just announced that it has found a vaccine that cures 98 per cent of all occurrences of the disease and, if administered to non-sufferers, will prevent them from catching it. What are your main strategic options, and which should you choose?

● FURTHER READING

- Chen, M. and Hambrick, D. (1995). 'Speed, stealth and selective attack: How small firms differ from large firms in competitive behavior'. *Academy of Management Journal*, 38/2: 453–82. A learned review of where small firms do, and do not, win out over large ones.

- Wiklund, J. and Shepherd, D. (2005). 'Entrepreneurial orientation and small business performance: a configurational approach'. *Journal of Business Venturing*, 20: 71–91. Examines the complex ways in which entrepreneurship affects performance in small businesses.

- Crosby, B. and Bryson, J. (2005). 'A leadership framework for cross-sector collaboration'. *Public Management Review*, 7/2: 177–201 looks, through an in-depth case study, at the complexity of social problems and at the types of leadership that public sector and NFP managers may need to display in order to make an impact upon them.

- Harding, R. (2004). 'Social enterprise: The new economic engine?' *Business Strategy Review*, 15/4: 39–43. A review of the issues regarding social enterprises.

- Huxham, C. (2003). 'Theorizing collaborative advantage'. *Public Management Review*, 5/3: 401–23 gives a penetrating account of the difficulties that can be experienced in managing partnerships in the private and NFP sectors, and some practical conclusions on how to overcome them.

- Kaplan, R. (2001). 'Strategic performance measurement and management in nonprofit organizations'. *Nonprofit Management & Leadership*, 11(3): 354–71 examines the problems of performance measurement in NFPs, with emphasis on the use of the balanced scorecard, a technique we examine in Chapter 17.

- Nutt, P. and Backoff, R. (1995). 'Strategy for public and third-sector organizations'. *Journal of Public Administration Research & Theory*, 5/2: 189–211. Gives a rounded framework for public and not-for-profit strategies.

- Torrès, O. and Julien, P.-A. (2005). 'Specificity and denaturing of small business'. *International Small Business Journal*, 23/4: 355–75. A review article that poses the question: how different are small businesses really?

● REFERENCES

Aberbach, J. and Christensen, T. (2005). 'Citizens and consumers'. *Public Management Review*, 7/2: 226–45.

Agranoff, R. and McGuire, M. (2003). *Collaborative Public Management: New Strategies for Local Governments*. Washington, DC: Georgetown University Press.

Aiken, M. (2004). 'What strategies do value-based organisations adopt in order to resist incursions on their organisational values from public or private sector markets?' In Chandler, J. and Barry, J. (eds), *Dilemmas Facing the Public Sector: Issues for Professionals, Managers and Users*. London: East London Business School, University of East London.

Aiken, M. (2006). 'Towards market or state? Tensions and opportunities in the evolutionary path of three types of UK Social Enterprise'. In Nyssens, M. (ed.), *Social Enterprises in Europe: Between Market, Public Policies and Communities*. London: Routledge.

Andersen, D., Belardo, S., and Dawes, S. (1994). 'Strategic information management: conceptual frameworks for the public sector'. *Public Productivity and Management Review*, 17/4: 335–53.

Andrews, R., Boyne, G., and Walker, R. (2006). 'Strategy content and organizational performance: an empirical analysis'. *Public Administration Review*, 66/1: 52–63.

Armstrong, M. (1992). 'A charitable approach to personnel'. *Personnel Management*, 24/12: 28ff.

Audretsch, D. and Lehmann, E. (2006). 'Entrepreneurial access and absorption of knowledge spillovers: strategic board and managerial composition for competitive advantage'. *Journal of Small Business Management*, 44/2: 155–66.

Baron, R. and Markman, G. (2000). 'Beyond social capital: how social skills can enhance entrepreneurs' success'. *Academy of Management Executive*, 14/1: 106–16.

Baum, J. and Oliver, C. (1992). 'Institutional embeddedness and the dynamics of organizational populations'. *American Sociological Review*, 57/4: 540–59.

Berry, F. (1994). 'Innovation in public management: the adoption of strategic planning'. *Public Administration Review*, 54/4: 322–30.

Berry, F. and Wechsler, B. (1995). 'State agencies' experience with strategic planning: findings from a national survey'. *Public Administration Review*, 55: 159–68.

Boyne, G. (1998). 'Bureaucratic theory meets reality: public choice and service contracting in US local government'. *Public Administration Review*, 58/6: 474–84.

Boyne, G. (2003). 'Sources of public service improvement: a critical review and research agenda'. *Journal of Public Administration Research and Theory*, 13/3: 367–94.

Boyne, G. and Gould-Williams, J. (2003). 'Planning and performance in public organizations'. *Public Management Review*, 5/1: 115–32.

Brouthers, K., Andriessen, F., and Nicolaes, I. (1998). 'Driving blind: strategic decision-making in small companies'. *Long Range Planning*, 31/1: 130–8.

Brown, T. and Potoski, M. (2003). 'Managing contract performance: a transaction costs approach'. *Journal of Policy Analysis & Management*, 22/2: 275–97.

Brown, T. and Potoski, M. (2006). 'Contracting for management: assessing management capacity under alternative service delivery arrangements'. *Journal of Policy Analysis & Management*, 25/2: 323–46

Brown, T., Potoski, M., and Van Slyke, D. (2006). 'Managing public service contracts: aligning values, institutions, and markets'. *Public Administration Review*, 66/3: 323–31.

Brudney, J., Fernandez, S., Ryu, J., and Wright, D. (2005). 'Exploring and explaining contracting out: patterns among the American states'. *Journal of Public Administration Research & Theory*, 15/3: 393–419.

Bryson, J. (2004a). *Strategic Planning for Public and Nonprofit Organizations*. 3rd edn. San Francisco: Jossey-Bass.

Bryson, J. (2004b). 'What to do when stakeholders matter'. *Public Management Review*, 6/1: 21–53.

Burns, L. and Wholey, D. (1993). 'Adoption and abandonment of matrix management programs: effects of organizational characteristics and interorganizational networks'. *Academy of Management Journal*, 36/1: 106–38.

Carland, J., Hoy, F., Boulton, W., and Carland, J. (1984). 'Differentiating entrepreneurs from small business owners: a conceptualization'. *Academy of Management Review*, 9: 354–9.

Chandler, G. and Hanks, S. (1994). 'Founder competence, the environment, and venture performance'. *Entrepreneurship Theory and Practice*, 18/3: 77–89.

Chapman, P. (1999). 'Managerial control strategies in small firms'. *International Small Business Journal*, 17/2: 75–82.

Chell, E. (2007). 'Social enterprise and entrepreneurship'. *International Small Business Journal*, 25/1: 5–26.

Chen, M. and Hambrick, D. (1995). 'Speed, stealth and selective attack: how small firms differ from large firms in competitive behavior'. *Academy of Management Journal*, 38/2: 453–82.

Churchill, N. and Lewis, V. (1983). 'The five stages of small business growth'. *Harvard Business Review*, May/June: 30–9.

Coble, R. (1999). 'The non-profit sector and state governments: public policy issues facing non-profits in North Carolina and other states'. *Non-profit Management and Leadership*, 9/3: 293–313.

Core, J., Guay, W., and Verdi, R. (2006). 'Agency problems of excess endowment holdings in not-for-profit firms'. *Journal of Accounting & Economics*, 41/3: 307–33.

Covin, J. and Slevin, D. (1988). 'The influence of organizational structure on the utility of an entrepreneurial management style'. *Journal of Management Studies*, 25/3: 217–34.

Crosby, B. and Bryson, J. (2005). 'A leadership framework for cross-sector collaboration'. *Public Management Review*, 7/2: 177–201.

Curran, J. (2006). ' "Specificity" and "Denaturing" the small business'. *International Small Business Journal*, 24/2: 205–10.

Curran, J., Blackburn, R., and Woods, A. (1991). *Profiles of the Small Enterprise in the Service Sector*. London: ESRC Centre for Research on Small Service Sector Enterprise.

Dandridge, T. C. (1979). 'Children are not "little grown-ups": small business needs its own organizational theory'. *Journal of Small Business Management*, 17/2: 53–7.

Dayton, K. (2001). *Governance is Governance*. Washington, DC: Independent Sector.

Dean, T., Brown, R., and Bamford, C. (1998). 'Differences in large and small firm responses to environmental context: Strategic implications'. *Strategic Management Journal*, 19/8: 709–28.

Denhardt, R. and Denhardt, J. (2001). 'The new public service: putting democracy first'. *National Civic Review*, 90/4: 391–400.

Department of Trade and Industry (2005). *Statistical Press Release*. London: Department of Trade and Industry/National Statistics, August.

Drucker, P. (1995). *Managing the Non-profit Organization*. Oxford: Butterworth-Heinemann.

Ebben, J. and Johnson, A. (2005). 'Efficiency, flexibility, or both? Evidence linking strategy to performance in small firms'. *Strategic Management Journal*, 26/13: 1249–59.

Eurostat (2006). *Key Figures on European Business*. Luxembourg: Office for Official Publications of the European Communities.

Farmer, S. and Fedor, D. (1999). 'Volunteer participation and withdrawal'. *Nonprofit Management & Leadership*, 9/4: 349–68.

Farmer, S. and Fedor, D. (2001). 'Changing the focus on volunteering: an investigation of volunteers' multiple contributions to a charitable organization'. *Journal of Management*, 27/2: 191–211.

Feldman, M. and Khademian, A. (2002). 'To manage is to govern'. *Public Administration Review*, 62/5: 541–54.

Fenwick, G. and Strombom, M. (1998). 'The determinants of franchisee performance: an empirical investigation'. *International Small Business Journal*, 16/4: 28–45.

Forbes, M. and Lynn, L. (2005). 'How does public management affect government performance? Findings from international research'. *Journal of Public Administration Research & Theory*, 15/4: 559–84.

Frumkin, P. and Kim, M. (2001). 'Strategic positioning and the financing of nonprofit organizations: is efficiency rewarded in the contributions marketplace?' *Public Administration Review*, 61/3: 266–75.

Gadenne, D. (1998). 'Critical success factors for small business: an inter-industry comparison'. *International Small Business Journal*, 17/1: 36–56.

Galaskiewicz, J., Bielefeld, W., and Dowell, M. (2006). 'Networks and organizational growth: a study of community based nonprofits'. *Administrative Science Quarterly*, 51/3: 337–80.

Garengo, P., Biazzo, S., and Bititci, U. (2005). 'Performance measurement systems in SMEs: a review for a research agenda'. *International Journal of Management Reviews*, 7/1: 25–47.

Gartner, W., Bird, B., and Starr, J. (1992). 'Acting as if: differentiating entrepreneurial from organizational behavior'. *Entrepreneurship: Theory & Practice*, 16/3: 13–31.

Geroski, P. (1999). 'The growth of firms in theory and in practice'. CEPR Discussion Paper no. 2092. London, Centre for Economic Policy Research <http://www.cepr.org/pubs/dps/DP2092.asp>, accessed 29 July 2007.

Gibb, A. (2000). 'SME policy, academic research and the growth of ignorance: mythical concepts, myths, assumptions, rituals and confusions'. *International Small Business Journal*, 18/3: 13–35.

Gumbus, A. and Lussier, R. (2006). 'Entrepreneurs use a balanced scorecard to translate strategy into performance measures'. *Journal of Small Business Management*, 44/3: 407–25.

Handy, C. (1988). *Understanding Voluntary Organisations*. Harmondsworth: Penguin.

Hankinson, P. (2002). 'The impact of brand orientation on managerial practice: a quantitative study of the UK's top 500 fundraising managers'. *International Journal of Nonprofit and Voluntary Sector Marketing*, 7/1: 30–44.

Harding, R. (2004). 'Social enterprise: the new economic engine?' *Business Strategy Review*, 15/4: 39–43.

Harding, R. (2006). 'Entrepreneurs: the world's lifeline?' *Business Strategy Review*, 17/4: 4–7.

Herman, R. and Renz, D. (1998). 'Non-profit organizational effectiveness: contrasts between especially effective and less effective organizations'. *Non-profit Management and Leadership*, 9/1: 23–38.

Hite, J. and Hesterly, W. (2001). 'The evolution of firm networks: from emergence to early growth of the firm'. *Strategic Management Journal*, 22/3: 275.

Horton Smith, D. (1999). 'The effective grassroots association, II: Organizational factors that produce external impact'. *Non-profit Management and Leadership*, 10/1: 103–16.

Hutchinson, K., Quinn, B., and Alexander, N. (2006). 'SME retailer internationalisation: case study evidence from British retailers'. *International Marketing Review*, 23/1: 25–53.

Huxham, C. (2000). 'The challenge of collaborative governance'. *Public Management*, 2/3: 337–57.

Huxham, C. (2003). 'Theorizing collaboration practice'. *Public Management Review*, 5/3: 401–23.

Jang, H. (2006). 'Contracting out parks and recreation services: correcting for selection bias using a Heckman Selection Model'. *International Journal of Public Administration*, 29/10–11: 799–818.

Jennings, P. and Beaver, G. (1997). 'The performance and competitive advantage of small firms: a management perspective'. *International Small Business Journal*, 15/2: 63–75.

Johnston, J. (1998). 'Strategy, planning, leadership, and the financial management improvement plan: the Australian Public Service 1983–1996'. *Public Productivity and Management Review*, 21/4: 352–68.

Kaplan, R. (2001). 'Strategic performance measurement and management in nonprofit organizations'. *Nonprofit Management & Leadership*, 11/3: 353–70.

Keeley, R. and Roure, J. (1990). 'Management, strategy, and industry structure: as influences on the success of new firms: a structural model'. *Management Science*, 36/10: 1256–67.

Kickert, W. J. M., Klijn, E.-H., and Koppenjan, J. F. M. (eds) (1997). *Managing Complex Networks: Strategies for the Public Sector*. London: Sage Publications.

de Lancer Julnes, P. and Holzer, M. (2001). 'Promoting the utilization of performance measures in public organizations: an empirical study of factors affecting adoption and implementation'. *Public Administration Review*, 61/6: 693–705.

Low, C. (2006). 'A framework for the governance of social enterprise'. *International Journal of Social Economics*, 33/5–6: 376–85.

Lozeau, D., Langley, A., and Denis, J. (2002). 'The corruption of managerial techniques by organizations'. *Human Relations*, 55/5: 537.

McNamee, P., Greenan, K., and McFerran, B. (2000). 'Shifting the predominant cultural paradigm in small businesses through active competitive benchmarking'. *Journal of Strategic Marketing*, 8: 241–59.

Mancino, A. and Thomas, A. (2005). 'An Italian pattern of social enterprise: the social cooperative'. *Nonprofit Management and Leadership*, 15/3: 357–69.

Maranville, S. (1999). 'Requisite variety of strategic management modes: A cultural study of strategic actions in a deterministic environment'. *Non-profit Management and Leadership*, 9/3: 277–91.

Meier, K. and O'Toole, L. (2001). 'Managerial strategies and behavior in networks: A model with evidence from US public education'. *Journal of Public Administration Research and Theory*, 11: 271–95.

Miles, R. and Snow, C. (1978). *Organisational Structure, Strategy, Process*. New York: McGraw-Hill.

Moore, M. (1995). *Creating Public Value: Strategic Management in Government*. Cambridge: Harvard University Press.

Napoli, J. (2006). 'The impact of nonprofit brand orientation on organisational performance'. *Journal of Marketing Management*, 22/7–8: 673–94.

Nicholson-Crotty, S. (2004). 'The politics and administration of privatization: contracting out for corrections management in the United States'. *Policy Studies Journal*, 32/1: 41–57.

Nicholson-Crotty, S., Theobald, N., and Nicholson-Crotty, J. (2006). 'Disparate measures: Public managers and performance-measurement strategies'. *Public Administration Review*, 66/1: 101–13.

Nutt, P. and Backoff, R. (1992). *Strategic Management of Public and Third Sector Organizations*. San Francisco: Jossey-Bass.

Nutt, P. and Backoff, R. (1995). 'Strategy for public and third-sector organizations'. *Journal of Public Administration Research and Theory*, 5/2: 189–211.

Oliver, C. (1988). 'The collective strategy framework: an application to competing predictions of isomorphism'. *Administrative Science Quarterly*, 33: 543–61.

Ospina, S., Grau, N., and Zaltsman, A. (2004). 'Performance evaluation, public management improvement and democratic accountability'. *Public Management Review*, 6/2: 229–51.

O'Toole, L., Meier, K., and Nicholson-Crotty, S. (2005). 'Managing upward, downward and outward'. *Public Administration Review*, 7/1: 45–68.

Parker, L. (1998). 'Non-profit prophets: strategy in non-commercial organisations'. *Australian CPA*, 68/6: 50–52.

Paton, R. and Cornforth, C. (1992). 'What's different about managing in voluntary and non-profit organizations?' In Batsleer, J., Cornforth, C., and Paton, R. (eds), *Issues in Voluntary and Non-profit Management*. Wokingham: Addison-Wesley.

Pepin, J. (2005). 'Venture capitalists and entrepreneurs become venture philanthropists'. *International Journal of Nonprofit & Voluntary Sector Marketing*, 10/3: 165–73.

Poister, T. and Streib, G. (1999). 'Strategic management in the public sector'. *Public Productivity and Management Review*, 22/3: 308–25.

Pollitt, C. (2001). 'Convergence: the useful myth?' *Public Administration*, 79/4: 933–47.

Power, B. and Reid, G. (2005). 'Flexibility, firm-specific turbulence and the performance of the long-lived small firm'. *Review of Industrial Organization*, 26/4: 415–43.

Provan, K. and Milward, H. (1995). 'A preliminary theory of interorganizational network effectiveness: a comparative study of four community mental health systems'. *Administrative Science Quarterly*, 40: 1–33.

Provan, K. and Milward, H. (2001). 'Do networks really work? A framework for evaluating public-sector organisational networks'. *Public Administration Review*, 61: 414–23.

Richbell, S., Watts, H., and Wardle, P. (2006). 'Owner-managers and business planning in the small firm'. *International Small Business Journal*, 24/5: 496–514.

Ritchie, W. and Kolodinsky, R. (2003). 'Nonprofit organization financial performance measurement: an evaluation of new and existing financial performance measures'. *Nonprofit Management & Leadership*, 13/4: 367–81.

Rivenbark, W. (2006). 'Evolutionary theory of routine: Its role in results-based management'. *Journal of Public Budgeting, Accounting & Financial Management*, 18/2: 224–40.

Sadler-Smith, E., Hampson, Y., Chaston, I., and Badger, B. (2003). 'Managerial behavior, entrepreneurial style, and small firm performance'. *Journal of Small Business Management*, 41/1: 47–67.

Sandberg, W. (1992). 'Strategic management's potential contributions to a theory of entrepreneurship'. *Entrepreneurship: Theory & Practice*, 16/3: 73–90.

Sandberg, W. and Hofer, C. (1987). 'Improving new venture performance, the role of strategy, industry structure and the entrepreneur'. *Journal of Business Venturing*, 2/1: 5–28.

Sargeant, A. and Kahler, J. (1999). 'Returns on fundraising expenditures in the voluntary sector'. *Non-profit Management and Leadership*, 10/1: 5–29.

Schindehutte, M., Morris, M., and Allen, J. (2006). 'Beyond achievement: Entrepreneurship as extreme experience'. *Small Business Economics*, 27/4–5: 349–68.

Shane, S. and Kolvereid, L. (1995). 'National environment, strategy, and new venture performance: a three country study'. *Journal of Small Business Management*, 33/2: 37–50.

Shane, S. and Venkataraman, S. (2000). 'The promise of entrepreneurship as a field of research'. *Academy of Management Review*, 25: 217–26.

Shelton, L. (2005). 'Scale barriers and growth opportunities: A resource-based model of new venture expansion'. *Journal of Enterprising Culture*, 13/4: 333–57.

Shoichet, R. (1998). 'An organization design model for nonprofits'. *Non-profit Management and Leadership*, 9/1: 71–88.

Spence, M. and Crick, D. (2006). 'A comparative investigation into the internationalisation of Canadian and UK high-tech SMEs'. *International Marketing Review*, 23/5: 524–48.

Tat-Kei Ho, A. and Ya Ni, A. (2005). 'Have cities shifted to outcome-oriented performance reporting?—A content analysis of city budgets'. *Public Budgeting & Finance*, 25/2: 61–83.

Thompson, J. and Doherty, B. (2006). 'The diverse world of social enterprise: A collection of social enterprise stories'. *International Journal of Social Economics*, 33/5–6: 361–75.

Tinkelman, D. (2006). 'The decision-usefulness of nonprofit fundraising ratios: Some contrary evidence'. *Journal of Accounting, Auditing & Finance*, Fall: 441–62.

Torrès, O. and Julien, P.-A. (2005). 'Specificity and denaturing of small business'. *International Small Business Journal*, 23/4: 355–75.

Vinzant, D. (1996). 'Strategic management and public organizations: lessons from the past and prescriptions for the future'. *International Journal of Public Administration*, 19/10: 1743–79.

Vinzant, J. and Vinzant, D. (1996). 'Strategic management and total quality management: challenges and choices'. *Public Administration Quarterly*, 20/2: 201–19.

Voss, Z., Cable, D., and Voss, G. (2006). 'Organizational identity and firm performance: What happens when leaders disagree about "who we are?"' *Organization Science*, 17/6: 741–55.

Walker, R. (2006). 'Innovation type and diffusion: an empirical analysis of local government'. *Public Administration*, 84/2: 311–35.

Walker, R. and Boyne. G. (2006). 'Public management reform and organizational performance: an empirical assessment of the U.K. Labour government's public service improvement strategy'. *Journal of Policy Analysis and Management*, 25/2: 371–93.

Walker, R., Jeanes, E., and Rowlands, R. (2002). 'Measuring innovation: applying the literature-based innovation output indicator to public services'. *Public Administration*, 80/1: 201–14.

Watson, J. and Everett, J. (1999). 'Choice of definition and industry effects'. *International Small Business Journal*, 17/2: 31–47.

Welsh, J. and White, J. (1981). 'A small business is not a little big business'. *Harvard Business Review*, 59/4: 18–32.

Westphal, J., Gulati, R., and Shortell, S. (1997). 'Customisation or conformity? An institutional and network perspective on the content and consequences of TQM adoption'. *Administrative Science Quarterly*, 42: 366–94.

Wiklund, J. and Shepherd, D. (2005). 'Entrepreneurial orientation and small business performance: a configurational approach'. *Journal of Business Venturing*, 20/1: 71–91.

Wisner, P., Stringfellow, A., Youngdahl, W., and Parker, L. (2005). 'The service volunteer-loyalty chain: an exploratory study of charitable not-for-profit service organizations'. *Journal of Operations Management*, 23/2: 143–61.

Zucchella, A. and Palamara, G. (2007). 'Niche strategy and export performance'. *Advances in International Marketing*, 17: 63–87.

End-of-chapter Case Study 15.1 Médecins sans Frontières in 2006

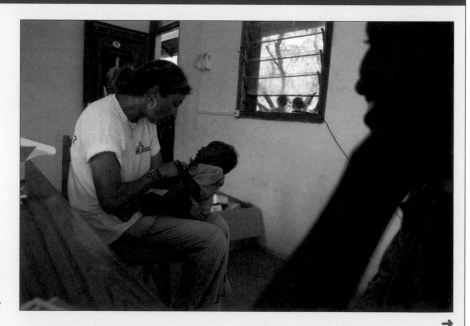

An MSF worker treats a child at the Dadaals refugee camp after the 2006 Somalian floods. *Brendan Bannon/MSF*

➜ Anyone reading or watching the news relating to the world's most troubled areas will have encountered the work of Médecins sans Frontières (MSF). The name translates as 'Doctors without Borders', the title under which it operates in the USA and some other countries. Whether a disaster is natural, such as the Asian tsunami of 2004, or man-made, like the wars in Afghanistan or Darfur, MSF's volunteers are to be found, braving physical hardship and often personal danger, ensuring that medical care is available to victims and survivors.

History

MSF was set up in 1971 by Bernard Kouchner (later to be a French government minister and UN high representative for Kosovo), Max Récamier, Jacques Bérès, and a group of other French doctors. They had volunteered for a mission of the International Red Cross in Biafra, a province of Nigeria where a bloody civil war was fought between 1967 and 1970. Part of the conditions of strict neutrality under which the Red Cross operated was that its staff were sworn to silence about the events they encountered while tending the sick and wounded. The 'French doctors' (another name by which the organization came to be known) could not accept this policy. They felt that seeing wartime atrocities, without speaking out against them, was equivalent to siding with the perpetrators.

On their return from Biafra, the doctors denounced what they termed the 'genocide' that they had seen in the conflict and formed an international committee to combat it.[98] They also formed a new organization whose aim would be to cut through political barriers to bring medical aid to the victims of conflict or disaster, regardless of their ethnicity or political or religious convictions. These two themes—ensuring that everyone had access to medical care, and publicly bearing witness ('témoignage') to the plight of the people they assist—have been the hallmarks of MSF since that time.

MSF's first international mission, ministering to victims of an earthquake in Nicaragua, came in 1972. It came to international prominence through its work from 1976 onwards in Lebanon, where it ministered without favour to both sides in the conflict. Since then, it has sent missions to practically every major conflict and disaster—sometimes, as in Afghanistan during the Russian invasion of 1980s, on donkey-back, and without the consent of all warring parties. In 1999, it was awarded the Nobel Peace Prize.

By the end of 2005, the organization had grown into a global movement with branches in 19 countries and operations in 70. It had 2,225 volunteers working with 25,850 locally hired staff. Key financial and other statistics are shown in Table 15.3 (please note that the 2005 income includes large sums raised shortly after the Asian tsunami at the end of 2004, and that funds raised in 2006 may be lower—these data were unavailable at the time of writing).

What MSF does

The classic MSF operation is a health centre serving a large population in a remote area affected by conflict and with no comparable medical facilities. While not a hospital, it has the capacity to treat the most common diseases affecting civilians in such circumstances, and to assist malnourished children and adults. It has perhaps ten qualified doctors and nurses from outside the affected country—all volunteers working for just a small monthly allowance, who serve for 6–12 months in any one place, though many sign up for other missions on their return home. They work together with up to 200 local staff, who along with their medical skills contribute an understanding of the region's culture and customs. They are able to explain treatments to the patients and follow up to ensure that medication is being properly administered and that there are no other people needing treatment.[99]

However, interventions are by no means confined to conflict zones. MSF takes pride in the logistical capability that enables it to be one of the first humanitarian organizations to organize relief in times of natural disasters, such as hurricanes and floods. The organization also works in refugee camps to provide health care and, no less importantly, facilities such as water and sanitation systems that can prevent disease taking hold. These projects are often collaborations with other non-governmental organizations (NGOs), with the United Nations High Commissioner for Refugees, or with local health services. Finally, MSF will work with local health ministries to build or revive health care systems that are inadequate. It will set up or rehabilitate hospitals and clinics, and put in place programmes for vaccinating the population and training local professionals.[100]

Logistics and preparation play a key complementary role to the courage and medical expertise of the volunteers. The organization has stocks of medical kits purpose-designed for various types of emergency in different parts of the world. These may include the supplies needed to treat a large cholera outbreak, or a prefabricated operating theatre, or even a prefabricated refugee camp. It also has the capability to project these kits and people into areas without transport links.[101]

MSF also has three research centres in areas such as epidemiology and health care programme management. One of these, Epicentre, undertakes disaster training for the World Health Organization.[102]

Témoignage

As well as assisting the victims, MSF continues to alert public opinion to their plight, with a particular emphasis on situations that it feels governments are trying to cover up or media are underplaying. Each year, it publishes a list of the ten most underreported humanitarian stories. It played a leading role in the ➜

→ **Table 15.3** Facts and figures, MSF International

Income	2005		2004	
	In M€	In %	In M€	In %
Private Income	543.0	83.7%	342.8	74.8%
Public Institutional ECHO*, EU & DFID**	44.8	6.9%	55.9	12.2%
Public Institutional Other	45.5	7.0%	47.0	10.3%
Other Income	15.7	2.4%	12.4	2.7%
Total Income	649.0	100.0%	458.1	100.0%

How was the money spent?				
Operations	*397.4*	*78.0%*	*321.5*	*76.3%*
Témoignage	*15.9*	*3.1%*	*14.5*	*3.4%*
Other humanitarian activities	*8.0*	*1.6%*	*7.9*	*1.9%*
Total Social Mission	421.3	82.7%	343.9	81.7%
Fundraising	59.8	11.8%	49.2	11.7%
Management, general & administration	28.2	5.5%	28.0	6.6%
Total Expenditure	509.3	100.0%	421.1	100.0%
Net exchange gains & losses (realized and unrealized)	4.1		−2.8	
Surplus/(deficit)	**143.7**		**34.2**	

* European Community Humanitarian Office
** UK Department for international Development

Balance sheet		In M€		In M€
(year-end financial position):				
Non-current assets		35.5		31.7
Current assets		66.6		91.2
Cash & equivalents		352.1		201.8
Total assets		454.2		324.7
Permanently restricted funds	*2.8*		*2.8*	
Unrestricted funds	*384.6*		*236.6*	
Other retained earnings	*1.5*		*−3.7*	
Total retained earnings and equities		388.9		235.8
Non-current liabilities		8.5		7.6
Current liabilities		49.9		43.3
Unspent temporarily restricted funds		6.8		38.0
Total liabilities and retained earnings		65.2		324.7

Where did the money go?

Programme expenses* by nature

- International staff 24.6%
- National staff 23.3%
- Medical & nutrition 19%
- Transport, freight, storage 17.3%
- Operational running expernses 8.4%
- Logistics & sanitation 5.6%
- Other expenses 1%
- Training & local support 0.9%

Programme expenses* by continent

- Africa 68%
- Asia 21.8%
- America 5.6%
- Europe 3.7%
- Non-allocated 0.9%

* project and coordination team expenses in country

→ **Table 15.3** (cont'd)

HR Statistics		In M€		In M€
International departures (full year):	**4,768**	100%	**3,803**	100%
Medical pool	1,276	27%	1,034	27%
Nurses % other paramedical pool	1,558	33%	1,257	33%
Non-medical pool	1,934	40%	1,512	40%
First time departures (full year):	**1,466**	(*) 31%	**1,340**	(*) 35%
(*) in % of the international departures				
Field positions:	**28,083**	100%	**24,666**	100%
International staff	2,227	8%	2,026	8%
National staff	25,855	92%	22,640	92%

campaign to make drugs for diseases such as HIV/AIDS available in the developing world at affordable prices. It was also voluble in alerting world opinion to the scale of the Sudanese crisis in Darfur.

Sometimes, its employees' outspokenness can get them into trouble. Two volunteers from the Dutch branch were briefly arrested by the Sudanese authorities after MSF had released a report alleging that rape was widespread in the Darfur region.[103] A French nurse was withdrawn from Niger after she shouted at a government minister who had arrived at short notice, with an entourage of journalists, at a feeding centre for children. She was concerned that the size of the group would be disturbing for the children and that the milk and dates the minister wanted to distribute would upset their nutritional regimes.[104]

Culture and structure

MSF has an unusual structure. Although it has an international headquarters in Brussels, five of its national 'sections' have the right, without reference to other parts of the organization, to initiate and terminate field projects and decide what measures are needed. These 'operational sections' are in Belgium, France, Holland, Spain, and Switzerland. The main activities of the remaining 14 MSF sections (Australia, Austria, Canada, Denmark, Germany, Greece, Hong Kong, Italy, Japan, Luxembourg, Norway, Sweden, UK, and USA) are fundraising, the recruitment of volunteers, and public relations and education.

Enforcing discipline in such a broad organization can be difficult. The Greek branch was expelled in 1999 (it rejoined in 2004) after it undertook a field operation in Serbia, without the consent of headquarters, under what appeared to be the Greek flag. The three largest and most influential sections of MSF (France, the Netherlands, and Belgium) won near unanimity for this move, which the Greek section maintained was unjustified. This reflected the deep significance the organization attached to maintaining its impartiality and probity.

This was not the first schism within the organization, which at the time admitted to 'constant bickering'. Kouchner, the best-known of the founders, split with MSF in 1979 to form Médecins du Monde after a disagreement over the chartering of a ship to rescue Vietnamese boat people. The French section took the Belgian section to court in the 1980s. Within the organization, this was seen as the inevitable consequence of recruiting people with the degree of uncompromising commitment and willpower needed to make its missions successful.[105]

This unwillingness to compromise sometimes led to conflicts from unexpected quarters. When MSF raised more money for Asian tsunami relief than it felt it could usefully spend in the region, it felt it had no choice but to offer donors the return of their contributions. Fewer than 1 per cent took them up on the offer—most elected to allow MSF to use the funds for its other projects. However, other charities undertaking longer-term work in the region were critical, saying that MSF's stance made them appear dishonest and undermined their appeals for further, much-needed donations.[106]

Challenges

In its 2006 Activity Report, Médecins sans Frontières was able to look back on a year when it continued to provide assistance to hundreds of thousands displaced in Sudan had treated 63,000 severely malnourished children in Niger, and had undertaken major relief operations in the aftermath of the tsunami in Indonesia and the earthquake in Pakistan. However, it faced a number of challenges.

One, common to all charities, was that the flood of donations that followed the tsunami and earthquake might dry up once these dramatic events had left the headlines. How were they to sustain public interest in places like Darfur, Congo, and Niger, where other catastrophes were unfolding?

Moreover, in some parts of the world, MSF was finding it increasingly difficult to guarantee the safety of its people. Although →

→ everyone who volunteered for an MSF mission recognized the dangers that might arise, MSF would never sustain a mission where its people, whether local or foreign, became objects of attack. Thus, in August 2004, the organization withdrew from Afghanistan, where it had operated for 24 years, after five of its staff were ambushed and murdered, the government appeared unwilling to tackle the gunmen responsible, and the Taliban claimed that MSF was a legitimate target. Relief operations in Iraq were suspended for similar reasons.

An MSF executive attributed this in part to the way in which US and other military forces in those countries had themselves started to distribute food and other aid in order to win the hearts and minds of the populace. Soldiers in civilian clothing were said to have presented themselves as 'humanitarian volunteers'. MSF prized its independence and refused to accept donations from governments with military involvement in Afghanistan. But it was becoming increasingly difficult to convince people in some parts of the world that they were not attached to what were perceived as occupying forces.[107]

Case study questions

1. Undertake a stakeholder analysis for Médecins sans Frontières.
2. Which of the Nutt and Backoff strategic types (Figure 15.3) is MSF using? Is this an appropriate choice?
3. How appropriate are MSF's culture and architecture for the achievement of its mission?
4. How well is MSF performing? What further performance measures other than those mentioned in the case do you feel might be appropriate?
5. What steps should the organization take to respond to the challenges confronting it in 2006?

● NOTES

1 The EU data are for 2003 and come from Eurostat (2006: 42). The definition of 'small business' is the standard one of having fewer than 250 employees. The UK data are from Department of Trade and Industry (2005).
2 Carland et al. (1984) give a helpful discussion of the differences between entrepreneurial and small business management.
3 For discussions of the singularities of small businesses, and of the extent to which it is legitimate to make generalizations between them, see Brouthers et al. (1998); Carland et al. (1984); Curran (2006); Gibb (2000); and Torrès and Julien (2005).
4 For discussions of this, see Curran et al. (1991).
5 In fact, all firms are subject to these shocks, and their revenue growth therefore tends to follow a random pattern (Geroski, 1999). Keeley and Roure (1990) show that external factors are a more significant influence on new venture performance than internal ones; see also Sandberg and Hofer (1987), Chandler and Hanks (1994), and Shane and Kolvereid (1995). However, there are some situations in which small firms are able to adapt more readily than large ones (Dean et al., 1998).
6 For examples of planning and strategy formation in small and medium-sized firms, see Richbell et al. (2006), and Spence and Crick (2006).
7 Small business owners' attitudes to profit were examined by Jennings and Beaver (1997).
8 See Shelton (2005) for a review of the impact of scale. The superior responsiveness of small businesses was noted by Chen and Hambrick (1995).
9 For excellent summaries of the literature on entrepreneurship and discussions of the concept, see Carland et al. (1984) and Shane and Venkataraman (2000).
10 Shane and Venkataraman (2000: 218).
11 This characterization is adapted from Carland et al. (1984: 358).
12 These characteristics of entrepreneurs are derived from Covin and Slevin (1988), Sadler-Smith et al. (2003), Harding (2006), and Schindehutte et al. (2006).
13 See Wiklund and Shepherd (2005) for a review. Entrepreneurship is not limited to small businesses; entrepreneurs can also be found in large firms, where they are sometimes termed 'intrapreneurs' or 'corporate venturers'.
14 See Sadler-Smith et al. (2003) for a review of the different management competences used in entrepreneurial and non-entrepreneurial firms.
15 See Sandberg and Hofer (1987).

16 See, for example, Gadenne (1998); Watson and Everett (1999); Chapman (1999); Jennings and Beaver (1997); Fenwick and Strombom (1998); Sandberg and Hofer (1987); Shane and Kolvereid (1995); Chandler and Hanks (1994).

17 These differences are discussed by Watson and Everett (1999).

18 See Dean et al. (1995).

19 See Garengo et al. (2005); Gumbus and Lussier (2006); McNamee et al. (2000); Richbell et al. (2006).

20 See Dean et al. (1998).

21 Ebben and Johnson (2005) pointed out the dangers of mixing the strategies, but found no significant differences in the performance of the two. However, Power and Reid (2005) found that small firms that pursued flexibility outperformed those that did not.

22 See Baron and Markman (2000), and Hite and Hesterley (2001).

23 These conclusions are derived from research in Australia by Gadenne (1998).

24 This example is derived from Torrès and Julien (2005). They do not name the company in question.

25 The distinction between managing downward, outward, and upward comes from Moore (1995). Empirical work by O'Toole et al. (2005) shows how each of these three management aspects is important for performance in the public sector.

26 For discussion of the importance and complexity of programmes and partnerships, see Agranoff and McGuire (2003); Andersen et al. (1994); Huxham (2000, 2003); Kickert et al. (1997); Meier and O'Toole (2001); and Provan and Milward (1995, 2001).

27 See Johnston (1998).

28 See Boyne (2003) for a discussion of the main factors affecting public sector performance and Walker and Boyne (2006) for an assessment of the impact of the introduction of contestable markets in the UK public sector. For a discussion of the 'new public management' and other current philosophies of public sector action, see Denhardt and Denhardt (2001).

29 For discussion of the evidence regarding international convergence in public sector management practices, see Pollitt (2001), and Forbes and Lynn (2005).

30 See Johnston (1998); Berry (1994); Poister and Streib (1999); Berry and Wechsler (1995); Nutt and Backoff (1992); Andersen et al. (1994).

31 Generally speaking, the empirical evidence supports the predictions of economic theory that these moves are effective, although the extent of the benefits depends on the way the contracts are managed. See Brown and Potoski (2003, 2006); Brown et al. (2006); Jang (2006); and Nicholson-Crotty (2004) for broadly positive assessments. Boyne (1998) and Brudney et al. (2005) take a rather more sceptical view.

32 See, for example, *Economist* (2006a). 'Rent-a-tanker'. 12 April and Kay, J. (1997). 'Private finance initiative'. *Financial Times*, 31 January.

33 For an American example of how far this trend has gone, see Tat-Kei Ho and Ya Ni (2005).

34 See Bryson (2004a) for a strategic planning process for public and not-for-profit organizations, and Boyne and Gould-Williams (2003), and Walker and Boyne (2006) for empirical evidence that planning helps improve performance.

35 See Feldman and Khademian (2002). John Bryson (2004a, 2004b), a leading theorist in this area, suggests that, even if managers do no other form of strategic planning, a stakeholder analysis is vital.

36 <http://www.boj.or.jp/en/type/exp/about/expboj.htm>, accessed 1 July 2007.

37 Garger, I. (2006). 'Japan's zero-rate policy helpful, but not decisive: economists'. *Dow Jones Business News I*, 13 July.

38 *Economist* (2007). 'A hiker's guide to Japan'. 21 February; *Nikkei Report* (2007). 'Interest hike moves rates closer to normal levels'. 21 February; *AFX Asia* (2007). 'Bank of Japan to hike rates gradually as economy improves—May meeting minutes'. 20 June.

39 *Economist* (2007) op. cit.; Rowley, A. (2007). 'Japan needs governance, not politicians'. *Business Times Singapore*. 8 February; *Nikkei Weekly* (2007). 'Political pressure only erodes trust in BOJ'. 22 January; Agence France Presse (2007). 'Dollar keeps rising after BoJ keeps rates on hold'. 22 January.

40 See, for example, Fackler, M. (2005). 'Koizumi spurs a samurai drama'. *International Herald Tribune*, 29 August; Watts, J. (2001). 'Rural Japan braced for new riches'. *Guardian*, 27 September: 19.

41 See, for example, Nakamoto, M. and Turner, D. (2007). 'BoJ decision casts doubt on its autonomy'. *Financial Times*, 19 January: 5; Evans-Pritchard, D. (2007). 'World economy—Japan's rate

rise delayed as bank bows to pressure'. *Daily Telegraph*, 19 January: 5; *Nikkei Weekly* (2007) op. cit.; Agence France-Presse (2007) op. cit.

42 Berry and Wechsler (1995).

43 The quotation is from Poister and Streib (1999).

44 Boyne (2003) and Walker and Boyne (2006) highlight the importance of HR and organizational factors.

45 See Aberbach and Christensen (2005), and Walker and Boyne (2006).

46 Boyne (2003).

47 The link between innovation and performance in the public sector was established by Andrews et al. (2006). For discussion of the nature of innovation in the public sector see Walker et al. (2002) and Walker (2006).

48 De Lancer Julnes and Holzer (2001) and Ospina et al. (2004) review the broader benefits of performance measurement in public sector organizations. For discussion of the difficulties in choosing and implementing appropriate measures, see Nicholson-Crotty et al. (2006) and Rivenbark (2006).

49 *Economist* (2007). 'You ain't seen nothing yet'. 22 March; *Economist* (2005). 'Curtain call'. 2 June; Elkind, P. (2005). 'Satan or Savior?' *Fortune*, 28 November: 86.

50 For more information on NFPs see Armstrong (1992); Coble (1999); Farmer and Fedor (1999); Handy (1988); Herman and Renz (1998); Horton Smith (1999); Maranville (1999); Parker (1998); Sargeant and Kahler (1999); and Shoichet (1998).

51 Wilding, K., Clark, J., Griffith, M., Jochum, V., and Wainwright, S. (2006). *The UK Voluntary Sector Almanac 2006: The State of the Sector*. London: National Council for Voluntary Organisations. Data for other countries are not readily available.

52 Jack, A. (2007). 'Beyond charity?' *Financial Times*, 5 April: 13.

53 Figures are for 2003/2004 and are taken from Wilding et al. (2006) op. cit.

54 Loomis, C. (2006). 'Warren Buffett gives it away'. *Fortune*, 10 July.

55 For discussion on this point, see Aiken (2004), and Paton and Cornforth (1992).

56 The term 'strategic delinquency' was coined by Charles Handy (1988). Farmer and Fedor (1999, 2001) and Wisner et al. (2005) discuss the challenges of managing volunteers.

57 LaFraniere, S. and Goodstein, L. (2007). 'Anglicans rebuke US branch on blessing same-sex unions'. *New York Times*, 20 February: 1; Grossman, C. (2007). 'Anglicans seek a middle way'. *USA Today*, 20 February: D5.

58 See Dayton (2001) for a discussion of this issue by an experienced NFP executive and board member.

59 *Economist* (2006b). 'The birth of philanthrocapitalism'. 25 February.

60 Source: Economist (2006c). 'Rockefeller revolutionary'. 16 December: 84; Jack, A. (2006). 'Manna from Omaha: a year of "giving while living" transforms philanthropy'. *Financial Times*, 27 December: 11.

61 *Economist* (2006c) op. cit.

62 Lee, J. (2005). 'Foundations join city's effort on affordable housing loans'. *New York Times*, 14 October: 2; Ascribe News (2006). 'The Rockefeller Foundation to provide $3.5 million to accelerate recovery planning for City of New Orleans'. 20 April; *Business Wire* (2006). 'The Rockefeller Foundation to extend InnoCentive's online, global scientific platform for technology solutions to global development problems'. 18 December; Jack (2006) op. cit.; <http://www.rockfound.org/about_us/press_releases/press_releases.shtml>, accessed 25 January 2007.

63 *Lancet* (2006a). 'Change at the Rockefeller Foundation'. 368/9548: 1623.

64 'Change at the Rockefeller Foundation' <http://www.lancet.com>, posted on 7 November.

65 *Economist* (2006c) op. cit.; Strom, S. (2007). 'Charities try to keep up with the Gateses'. *New York Times*, 14 January: 18; Beatty, S. (2006). 'Rockefeller adds three to board'. *Wall Street Journal*, 17 October: B11.

66 UK figures are for 2003/2004 and are taken from Wilding et al. (2006) op. cit. USA figures are for 1997 and are taken from Independent Sector (2001). *The New Non-profit Almanac in Brief*. For an Australian perspective see Parker (1998).

67 This finding comes from Frumkin and Kim (2001).

68 Core et al. (2006).

69 See Ritchie and Kolodinsky (2003) for a justification of this choice of measures, Tinkelman (2006) for a cautionary view, and Kaplan (2001) for a review of the issues.

70 See Herman and Renz (1998) and Horton Smith (1999).

71 Baum and Oliver (1992) and Galaskiewicz et al. (2006).

72 See Voss et al. (2006).

73 This categorization comes from Parker (1998).

74 See Hankinson (2002) and Napoli (2006) for evidence on the importance of brand orientation. The advice on building donor constituencies comes from Drucker (1995).

75 See Mancino and Thomas (2005).

76 See Thompson and Doherty (2006).

77 Mendick, R. (2007). 'City hedge fund boss gives record £230M to charity'. *The Evening Standard*, 2 July: 11.

78 Sources: <http://www.grameen-info.org/bank/GBGlance.htm>, <http://www.grameen-info.org/bank/the16.html>, and <http://www.grameen-info.org/bank/performaceindicators.html>, all accessed 22 January 2007; *Economist* (2006d). 'Macro Credit'. October 19.

79 See Harding (2004) and Chell (2007) for a review of the issues.

80 <http://www.bigissue.com/magazinesite/about.html>, accessed 2 July 2007.

81 Harding (2004).

82 *The Times* (2007). '£230m donation to charity'. 2 July: 27; Reguly, E. (2007). 'Europe's activist shareholders stir the pot'. *The Globe and Mail*, 16 June: B2; Quinn, J. and Griffiths, K. (2007). 'The equity rebels with a cause'. *The Daily Telegraph*, 12 June: 007.

83 See Aiken (2006) for a review and some examples.

84 See Low (2006).

85 For further details see Jack (2007) op. cit. and Pepin (2005).

86 Galaskiewicz et al. (2006).

87 Phillips, M. (2006). 'It's not only the foreign criminals who've vanished, but also any pretence that Britain controls its borders or, indeed, its very destiny'. *Daily Mail*, 26 April: 12; Morgan, V. and Moncrieff, C. (2006). 'Deportation blunder "deeply regrettable" says Clarke'. *Press Association National Newswire*, 26 April; Crichton, T. (2006). 'Lost: 1023 criminals . . . and one career'. *Sunday Herald*, 30 April: 1.

88 Eaglesham, J. (2007). 'Reid goes beyond cosmetic in radical Home Office makeover'. *Financial Times*, 22 January: 2; *Guardian* (2007). 'The Home Office: a year in crisis'. *Guardian Unlimited*, 10 January; Barnett, A. and Doward, J. (2006). 'Revealed: bonuses paid to Home Office bosses'. *Observer*, 3 September: 9.

89 *Guardian Unlimited* (2006). 'System "not fit for purpose", says Reid'. 23 May; Stringer, D. (2006). 'British home secretary says 85 serious foreign criminals still at large'. *Associated Press Newswires*, 23 May; Johnston, P. (2006). 'Confessions of the removal man'. *The Daily Telegraph*, 17 May: 1; Ford, R. (2006). 'Officials "haven't faintest idea" of immigrant count: Factbox'. *The Times*, 17 May: 11.

90 Riddell, P. (2006). 'Ministers are the elephant in the room'. *The Times*, 20 July: 8; Tapsfield, J. (2006). '"Red Mark" review blow for Home Office'. *Press Association National Newswire*, 19 July; Morris, N. (2006). 'Reid promises cull of senior Home Office staff'. *The Independent*, 20 July: 17; Ford, R. (2006). 'Reid ousts top staff as report shows failings'. *The Times*, 20 July: 29.

91 Green, M. (2006). 'Reid announces Home Office shake-up'. *FT.com*: 19 July; Ford (2006) op. cit.; Bentham, M. (2006). 'Heads roll in big shake-up at Home Office'. *The Evening Standard*, 19 July: 1; Morris (2006) op. cit.

92 Leppard, D. (2006). 'Escape from the ministry of madness'. *Sunday Times*, 23 July: News Review 8; Sowden, S. (2006). 'MP slams "terrible" figures'. *Newsquest Media Group Newspapers*, 23 November; Bentham, M. (2006). 'Home Office admits failure to meet targets'. *Evening Standard*, 8 December: 6.

93 MacNamara, W. (2007). 'Police chiefs say Home Office negligent over convicts' files'. *Financial Times*, 10 January: 2; Pitcher, G. (2007). 'Home Office record blunder leaves employers at risk of hiring criminals'. *Personnel Today*, 16 January.

94 Settle, M. (2006). 'Civil service "lacks leadership and plagued by amateurism"'. *The Herald*, 8 August: 6; *Guardian Unlimited* (2006). 'Top civil servants are "unaccountable"'. 7 August.

95 Cohen, N. (2006). 'John Reid's no-win quick-win situation'. *New Statesman*, 31 July: 22; Leppard, D. (2006) op. cit.

96 Leppard (2006) op. cit.

97 Eaglesham (2007) op. cit.; Reid, J. (2007). 'This won't be the last of it'. *Guardian*, 29 January: 29.

98 Aeberhard, P. and Deloche, A. (1999). 'Rebonds—Le nouvel horizon humanitaire'. *Libération*, 10 December. Langellier, J.-P. (2001). 'Humanitaire médecins sans frontières—Le savoir-faire des "French doctors", prix Nobel de la paix'. *Le Monde*, 21 June.

99 Steele, J. (2003). 'Oasis of medical care in desert of destruction'. *Guardian*, 10 December: 18 <http://www.doctorswithoutborders.org/aboutus/what.cfm>, accessed 24 January 2007.

100 <http://www.doctorswithoutborders.org/aboutus/where.cfm>, accessed 24 January 2007.

101 <http://www.doctorswithoutborders.org/aboutus/index.cfm>, accessed 24 January 2007; Suter, D. (2005). 'Ein leeres Flüchtlingslager mitten in der Stadt Zürich'. *Tages Anzeiger*, 5 November: 13.

102 <http://www.doctorswithoutborders.org/aboutus/org.cfm>, accessed 29 July 2007.

103 *Associated Press Newswires* (2005). 'Sudan prosecutor confirms dropping of charges against two Dutch aid workers over rape report'. 22 June.

104 *All Africa* (2005). 'Niger: MSF withdraws French nurse who shouted at minister'. 27 June.

105 Pilling, D. (1999). 'Doctors without fear or favour'. *Financial Times*, 16 October: 15; Zinoviev, S. (1999). 'Doctors operating in a divided house'. *Financial Times*, 4 December: 10.

106 Bennholt, K. (2005). 'Charity irks other groups by refusing tsunami aid'. *International Herald Tribune*, 7 January: 3; Agence France (2005). 'MSF a remboursé moins de 1 per cent des dons récoltés pour le tsunami'. 11 May.

107 Walker, W. (2001). 'Medecins sans donations'. *The Australian*, 10 October: 3; Dow Jones International (2004). 'Medécins sans Frontières quits Afghanistan'. 28 July; Parmar, T. (2004). 'Why we're leaving Afghanistan'. *National Post*, 4 August: A14.

Strategy Implementation

Once managers have determined which strategy they believe their organization should follow, they confront the challenge of steering the organization towards executing it. This is a considerable challenge, and many plausible strategies founder because they have proven impossible to implement effectively.

In Part Five, we examine the various aspects of this implementation challenge. We look at the challenges of executing substantial change in organizations, and at best practice in so doing. We examine the personal qualities that are required in effective change agents, and in the people who lead organizations both during and after change. We review the different ways in which organizations can finance their strategic proposals. Finally, we examine the specific challenges that managers confront when trying to turn around failing organizations, and in implementing mergers and acquisitions.

CHAPTER SIXTEEN

Effecting Organizational Change

LEARNING OUTCOMES

After reading this chapter you will be able to:

→ Explain the main stimuli for change and the different types of change to which they lead

→ Identify the main cultural and other obstacles to change in a particular organization

→ Identify the elements which will need to alter to support a future change in strategy

→ Identify actions that might be undertaken in order to bring about a desired change

→ Assess the acceptability of a proposed strategic option

→ Assess an organization's change programme in the light of what theory tells us about best practice in change management

→ Describe the attributes of effective change agents, and assess the suitability of a person for a change agent role.

> **INTRODUCTION**
>
> Previous chapters have shown you how to analyse an organization's strategic situation and identify appropriate strategic options. However, for managers in the real world, the most difficult part of the strategy process is often translating the selected options into practice. As we mentioned in Chapter 11, they frequently encounter issues of acceptability, which research has shown to be one of the two factors that significantly influences successful achievement of strategic proposals.[1] A proposal that seems good, even obvious, to the person who developed it may appear dangerous, or stupid, to a member of another stakeholder group with different objectives and preconceptions.
>
> In the following sections we look at some of the factors which might influence the success of an attempt to move an organization to a new strategic position. First, we review the concept of organizational change: the different internal and external stimuli that provoke it, and the different magnitudes and patterns of change that have been identified. Next, we identify the types of obstacle that change proposals typically encounter, and show how to anticipate them, and assess which are likely to be important. Finally, we look at best practice in implementing change so as to maximize the probability of success, and avoid the most common pitfalls. We do this first for change programmes in general, and then for two particularly important categories of change: when the organization needs to be turned around from being close to failure, and when two organizational cultures need to be brought together following a merger or acquisition.
>
> Effecting change in any organization is a tricky process, and obstacles may appear from any number of angles. Carefully thought-out actions designed to win over key stakeholders may end up being misinterpreted, and have the opposite effect to that intended. Brilliantly conceived strategies may be overtaken by unexpected economic or technological developments that render them irrelevant. This explains why, overall, the success rate for major change initiatives is low, at around 20–30 per cent.[2] Managers can, by being vigilant and flexible, reduce the likelihood of failure. However, theorists have come to recognize that there is no single series of logical steps that enables people to guarantee the successful 'management' of any organizational change.

16.1 **Stability and change in organizations**

Organizations are paradoxical entities. As we showed in Chapter 1, they become effective by developing routines. Without repetitiveness and stability they could not learn or become 'organized'. The key routines that define the value chain, architecture, and culture show inertia —they change slowly, if at all. On the other hand, every day, every organization is slightly different from the way it was the day before—it has found a new customer, an employee has left, a new product has been developed, or a process or ritual has been tweaked slightly.[3]

➜ We introduced the concept of inertia in Section 2.8.1.

The reason for this is that the process of organizing involves a constant interaction between the people in organizations—the 'actors'—and the routines in which they participate. Routines strongly influence the ways in which members of an organization think and act, but do not, except in extreme cases, constrain them completely. If new actors join the organization, at any level, they may subtly influence the routines, even as they are learning them. Even existing actors may change the way they behave at work, in response to influences from outside the organization—customers, suppliers, friends, or family—or just out of a desire to experiment.[4]

This means that, even in the absence of strategic change, most organizations do not stand still. Unless the culture and architecture are highly dysfunctional, individual actors are likely to make efforts to improve the way that they work, and share the results with their workmates. Sometimes there are suggestions schemes that encourage people to bring ideas forward, and sometimes they will just experiment with their own work routines until they think they have got them right. These efforts will mostly take place within the framework of the existing strategy, as those people interpret it, but may contribute to an alternative strategy emerging, although research indicates that this is quite rare.[5]

→ The concept of emergent strategy was introduced in Section 2.1.2.

In this chapter, however, we are concerned about what managers should do if they want to move the organization in a particular direction, so as to implement a specific strategic option. He or she will then need to persuade people to change their routines in a way that will make that option happen. If quality is to improve, people who are taking orders, producing goods and services, making deliveries, or even sending out invoices may need to change the way they work individually and collaboratively. If the organization wants to move its products up-market, then its designers will have to change what they design, and the salesforce will need to alter the things they say to customers when trying to close orders.

It will enhance the managers' chances of success if they have a clear idea of the obstacles they are likely to encounter. This means understanding:

- the magnitude and difficulty of the change that they are trying to achieve, and in particular the extent to which it will involve a change in the organization's culture;

- the strength, within the organization, of the main forces that might move it towards the desired strategic change;

- the extent to which different stakeholder groups are likely to favour or oppose the desired change, and the extent to which their support or opposition will matter. This in turn involves an understanding of the main reasons why people might end up opposing change that is intended to benefit their organization.

16.1.1 Magnitudes of strategic change

Table 16.1 shows the different magnitudes of change an organization might undergo, in order of the degree of disruption involved:[6]

- Fine tuning the workings of the existing strategy and business model. An example would be BA's system, introduced in 2007,[7] for charging for checked baggage, to discourage passengers from checking in more than one item, in order to reduce workload and security risks, and lessen the chances that suitcases will go astray.

- Incremental adjustment to reflect changes in the environment. This will involve noticeable adjustments to competitive stance, value chain, or architecture. An example would be H&M's extension of its product range to include childrenswear and perfume. Changes like this do not involve a fundamental reconsideration of the organization's strategy and values, though it may require some revision to the way the mission is articulated to employees.

- Modular transformation—radical change at the level of the business unit, rather than at corporate level. McDonald's moves to localize its menus fall into this category, since it requires each regional tier of management to assume new responsibilities and to develop the resources needed to generate its own menus. It also requires executives at the centre of the firm to change the way in which they exercise power; however, the corporate mission and values are largely unchanged.

- Corporate transformation—radical change to business and corporate strategies, and to values and belief systems, affecting the whole organization. This often comes about because of the need to turn around an under-performing organization. In 2006, BP (see What Can Go Wrong 8.1) and Sony (What Can Go Wrong 6.1) both announced changes to their structures and top management that indicated the desire to transform themselves in response to their recent problems.

Table 16.1 Magnitudes of organizational change

Type of change	Levels affected	Examples of changes involved
Fine tuning	Business unit, Department	Refining existing routines, control and reward systems; clarifying roles and responsibilities; training and development; fostering commitment to mission and values; minor reorganization (e.g. new specialist units, improved coordination between units)
Incremental adjustment	Business unit and functions	Improving production technology or product/service delivery; major product or market initiative; structural changes within and between business units to enhance synergies
Modular transformation	Business unit	Major restructuring of particular units or departments; major changes to management roles or personnel; significant downsizing; mission, goals, and strategy
Corporate transformation	Entire organization	Reformed mission, values and belief system; major changes to architecture, procedures, and work flows; outside appointments to key executive positions; new decision procedures and responsibilities resulting in changes to power structures

Source
Adapted from Dunphy and Stace (1993: 917–18)

Just as most people do not have major heart surgery every week, few organizations regularly undergo modular or corporate transformation. Most new products are incremental improvements on existing ones—breakthroughs tend to be developed by new, break-away firms, or in semi-independent new venture units. The types of change that organizations encounter regularly are typically small-scale localized fine-tuning or incremental adjustments, which are relatively cheap to implement.

Radical transformation (another term used is 'frame-bending change') is, on the other hand, difficult, costly, and demanding of staff time and energy and of organizational resources. Like major surgery, it can be dangerous. It risks sucking resources away from everyday operational activities, upsetting the routines that make organizations effective, destroying the sense of identity that holds it together, and so making it, at least temporarily, more vulnerable to competition.[8] Moreover, the greater the extent of disruption to people's daily working lives, the more likely they are to resist. So it is important, when gauging the acceptability of a strategic proposal, to recognize the extent to which these routines will need to change in order for it to succeed.

In doing so, it is important to bear in mind that apparently small changes in one area often involve change in another. A new product may end up being a runaway success that transforms the organization. The success of Apple's iPod has converted what, for twenty years, had been a niche firm in computing into a mainstream player in consumer electronics; the word 'computer' has been removed from the company name. An organization launching a new product may also need to invest in new skills (people), a new plant (technology), and a new structure (administrative changes). When Carphone Warehouse, a leading UK mobile phone retailer, began to bundle unlimited broadband internet at no extra cost with its 'TalkTalk' telephone service in April 2006, it needed people to take the orders, engineers to connect the new subscribers, and people to deal with customer enquiries. Taken by surprise by the extent of demand, it was overwhelmed by requests for new connections and then by enquiries and complaints from customers who had paid for the new service, but not received it. Three months after the launch, the firm's CEO admitted that, in particular, it lacked call-centre capacity, but critical press coverage of the firm persisted until the end of 2006.[9] Anticipating linkages like these can ease the path towards successful change.[10]

It is important, therefore to consider the whole picture, even when recommending change in only one part of the organization. However, there are also instances when organizations simply have to risk major change programmes, or even turnarounds.

16.1.2 Speed of change

Along with the magnitude of a proposed change, managers need to be alert to the speed at which the organization will be asked to change. Fine-tuning and incremental adjustment will normally be gradual, or evolutionary, although it will be faster in growing, turbulent, or hypercompetitive industries than in progressive, mature, or declining ones.

Modular and corporate transformations may also be evolutionary—periods of 3–7 years are not uncommon. But sometimes they are revolutionary, involving massive change in a short time. Revolutionary changes may be necessitated by the environment—for example, if an industry moves suddenly from a state of progressive or creative maturity into turbulence or decline. But they may also be triggered by internal factors, such as the arrival of a new leader with a fresh paradigm.

It used to be widely believed that evolutionary change was more desirable than revolutionary, but theorists now believe that both have their role to play. Many organizations intersperse long periods of evolutionary change with shorter phases of revolutionary change —the phenomenon of punctuated equilibrium we introduced in Section 2.8.3.[11] However, people who are used to relative stability may well have difficulties coming to terms with revolutionary change, and therefore resist it.

→ The different types of industry, and in particular of industry maturity were defined and discussed in Chapter 13.

16.1.3 The cultural adjustment required

Any change, whether revolutionary or evolutionary, is likely to be difficult to implement if it does not fit with the belief system of the parts of the organization that are affected. If the issue that is being addressed is not one that the organization has historically seen as important, then people may downplay it, and be reluctant to take action to deal with it. Similarly, if the solution being proposed challenges people's assumptions about what the organization stands for and what makes it successful, they may react against it.[12]

As we showed in Chapter 8, belief systems are built up gradually as a result of an organization's successes and failures, and are reified in its products and services, buildings and their contents, and structures and systems. These are not changed easily or quickly, so strategic options need to be reviewed in the light of the cultural shifts that they imply. This might entail:

- a review of how far the organization must move on the Goffee–Jones classification of cultures. A strategic option that requires a substantial increase or decrease in the degree of sociability or solidarity is likely to be more difficult to implement than one that does not require major change in either area. An option that requires change to both sociability and solidarity—a move from a fragmented to a communal culture, or from a networked to a mercenary one—is likely to require great care in its implementation, because of the degree of change needed in attitudes and behaviour patterns;

- a review of what the organization's belief system needs to be, in order for the new strategy to be effective, and how deeply it differs from the current one (Real-life Application 16.1). The greater the differences, the more radical the changes in culture and cultural artefacts that are implied, and the greater the implementation difficulties.

→ We introduced the Goffee–Jones and other models for analysing culture and belief systems, along with the notion of cultural artefacts, in Section 8.4.

Real-life Application 16.1 Strategic change at Hay Management Consultants in 1994[13]

Hay Management is a large and successful human resource consultancy. *iStock*

Hay Group is a large and successful specialist human resource (HR) consultancy, offering clients a wide range of HR advice. In the mid-1990s, its UK practice was facing a number of problems—most notably how to respond to strong market growth in areas, such as organizational change management, and HR planning and development, that were outside its traditional areas of expertise. Meanwhile its traditional core businesses, job evaluation and advice on pay structures, were forecast to grow more slowly.

The strategy that was decided upon involved doubling in size over a five-year period, and expanding strongly into the market growth areas. This posed a number of challenges to the belief system that the firm had built up over time, which would need to change in ways that are summarized in Table 16.2.

First, there remained a strong but outdated belief that job evaluation, the business in which Hay had made its name, was core; in fact it accounted for only 25 per cent of revenues. Second, some of the firm's best fee-earners in the past had been the so-called 'lone rangers'—consultants with strongly individualistic methods who had offered a broad range of advice to 'their' clients. While their broad awareness of HR issues was a strength, Hay, in order to compete in the developing industry, would need ➜

Table 16.2 Established and desired belief systems at Hay Management Consultants

The existing belief system in 1994	The desired new belief system
The core business is job evaluation	We have an integrated HR offering, enabling clients to realize their strategy through people
The client is all-important, and most behaviours can be excused if in the client's interest	The client is all-important (unchanged)
Our people are generalists who can consult in any HR field	Our people combine deep specialist expertise with a broad understanding of HR
We prize individualism and encourage people to think and act autonomously	Our experts work in teams that have a high degree of autonomy
Strategy should be adjusted regularly so that the need for radical change is avoided	Organizations are well served through periodic transformational change

Source
Heracleous and Langham (1996)

→ its people to be genuine experts in particular fields, who would then have to work as teams rather than individuals.

In order to avoid complacency and stagnation, Hay had got into the routine of announcing annual changes—nicknamed the 'autumn manoeuvres'—to its strategy. But if the firm was to grow at the pace required, its people would need to believe that this comfortable evolutionary change was no longer adequate.

Not every element of the belief system needed to be discarded, however. The firm's strong belief in putting the customer first was clearly consistent with the new strategy, and would form a link between the old and the new cultures. But to make the new culture a reality, cultural artefacts such as stories, symbols, and ways of working would need to be transformed, in ways we discuss in Real-life Application 16.4 below.

16.2 Change triggers and barriers

At the level of the organization, theorists have identified a number of factors that influence the likelihood of organizational change, which we examine in Section 16.2.1. In Section 16.2.2, we show how stakeholders act either to encourage or block change, and discuss how the most salient stakeholders—the ones who really must be persuaded to go along with the change—may be identified. In Section 16.2.3 we look at the reasons why particular stakeholders may decide to resist or promote change. This enables us to assess their likely attitude. Finally, we look at some tools that can be used to bring these different analyses together to assess the likelihood of a change initiative being resisted, and to identify the areas where a manager may need to take action in order to bring it about.

16.2.1 Organizational triggers and barriers

A good strategic proposal, particularly one that requires revolutionary or transformational change, is, as we point out in Chapter 11, a response to one or more strategic issues. These issues are the main triggers for change, and may also determine whether an organization is prepared to go along with it. Stakeholders will often differ, however, in the degree of priority they attach to an issue—or indeed, in the extent to which they notice it at all. At the same time, there are a number of factors, such as those that contribute to inertia, which must be taken into account. We have already looked at one of these, the belief system or paradigm, in Section 16.1.3.

a. Performance

Poor or disappointing financial or market performance will often lead to a consensus within an organization that change is necessary. Moreover, poor results are likely to lead to declining share prices and aggressive initiatives from competitors who perceive an opportunity. In extreme cases, lenders may refuse to extend existing credit or issue new debt. Top management may therefore detect pressure to change from colleagues, shareholders, and financial commentators. If they feel that there is a threat to their control of the organization, perhaps because of the possibility of a takeover which would threaten their personal status, then they are more likely to contemplate internal changes to the organization.[14]

Companies can therefore find that poor performance provides the spur to taking the necessary, but difficult, decisions to fix the underlying causes. A branch of behavioural economics known as 'prospect theory' has shown that when individuals believe that they have experienced a loss, they are more willing to take risks to redeem their situation. At the organizational level, when performance is poor, people show a greater willingness to consider risky, radical change.[15]

On the other hand, in circumstances where the organization is still profitable, it can be difficult to persuade people of the need to suffer the risk and personal discomfort of transformational change. Organizations that identify the need for radical change early, and embark upon it before they are in crisis, are rare. Xerox Corporation embarked upon a massive change in culture and manufacturing systems while its share of the world photocopier market was still 40 per cent, and Microsoft initiated major changes to its culture and architecture while highly profitable and dominant in computer operating systems and office software.[16] But, in both cases there was a clear threat emanating from the business environment.

b. The business environment

We showed in Chapter 3 the importance of an organization maintaining a fit with the developing business environment. Not everyone in every organization will spot such changes or be able to appreciate their importance. However, external stakeholders, such as customers, suppliers, and shareholders, may make new demands on the organization as their own requirements alter, and their concerns may be relayed upwards by the staff that they deal with, such as the salesforce or logistics teams. In such cases, these internal stakeholder groups can help persuade the rest of the organization to adapt.

In the case of Xerox, the market gains being made by Japanese competitors had become very plain, and its salesforce and business unit managers across the world were keen that something should be done. Microsoft had lost a high-profile court case regarding the way it had discouraged use of Netscape's competing internet browser.[17] In addition, a slump in the market for high-technology shares had made it more difficult for employees to become millionaires through owning share options. These events appeared to trigger a rethinking of the firm's hard-driving culture.[18]

The business environment can act as a brake on internally generated change, as well as a trigger for it. The same internal and external stakeholders can inhibit the organization from committing resources to disruptive technologies that do not serve their immediate needs, or to new customer groups.

c. The institutional environment

Other elements in the organization's environment can exert a strong influence upon it, and its ability to undertake certain types of change—particularly revolutionary and transformational change. These are known collectively as its institutional environment, and consist of:

- governments, regulators and other public institutions, which set the legal and regulatory framework within which firms operate. They also have large contracts which they can award to firms that meet their preferred ways of doing business and withhold from those that do not. They have been shown to be influential in firms' adoption of HR practices, for example;[19]

- the organizational field—the other organizations in the same locality and/or the same industry with which a firm and its managers have regular contact. These can influence the firm through peer-group pressure and other forms of legitimation. The speed with which many accountancy firms diversified into management consultancy and legal practice seems to have been strongly influenced by the attitude of the associations that set standards within the accountancy profession, as well as the actions of the largest and most prestigious firms. When those attitudes changed, in part as a result of what commentators outside the field felt were conflicts of interest, most such diversifications were reversed. Organizations which, like accountants and lawyers, have tight links to others in their field are likely to find it more difficult than others to break free of convention and undertake radical change.[20]

d. The organization's resources

Resources are both enablers of and constraints on change. On the one hand, without resources—management attention, human and financial resources—significant change is impossible. On the other hand, resources are a source of inertia in organizations. Significant time, effort, and money will have gone into developing routines and resources, and the people involved will think twice before allowing them to be disrupted. This may be why studies find that an abundance of resources in organizations does not have any measurable effect on the likelihood that they will act to take advantage of opportunities. However, it does appear to make them more ready to take strategic action in response to threats.[21]

e. Interest groups and power structures

Even if, overall, there is strong congruence between the goals of the organization and the people that work for it, different business units, departments, and functions often have different subcultures. Moreover, groups may compete to attract new investment to their unit, or to prevent staff being allocated elsewhere. This competition may be due to the self-interest of the individuals in the different groups, or to differing perceptions of the importance of a strategic issue and of how urgent it is to act to address it. We explore these possibilities further in Section 16.2.3.

Whatever the pressures from the business and institutional environments, major change—that is to say, anything beyond the level of fine-tuning—is unlikely to occur unless at least one powerful group in the organization feels such change is in its interest.[22] However, the most powerful individuals and groups will probably have had a significant say in the organization's present strategy. They are also likely to be tied particularly strongly into its belief system, and to play a major role in its development over time. This makes them likely sources of inertia.

An organization's dominant 'power echelons' develop over time, emerging around the founder as he or she recruits like-minded people. As a formal architecture is put in place, they will be put in positions where they can control resources and information, and take the kind of decisions that the founder, or a subsequent CEO, agrees with. Over time they are also likely to become increasingly numerous and gain influence through their connections to external stakeholders and to important individuals in other parts of the organization. While all employees hold power to some extent, these groups hold relatively more, and so have a disproportionate influence on organizational strategy.[23]

It is unlikely that all of the members of a dominant echelon will perceive the need for change at the same time, particularly if their power and control over events is threatened by it. One circumstance when they may do so, however, is when a newly arrived chief executive or management team has disrupted established power structures. Their appointment may be the result of poor organizational performance, but new managers also make considerable changes even when this is not the case. The greater the difference between their previous experience and the new situation, the greater the number of changes they typically make—not always successfully.[24]

➜ We introduced the concepts of power, legitimacy, and urgency in Chapter 2.

Considerations such as these make it important to identify key interest groups and assess their likely reactions to a proposed change. A careful analysis of stakeholders is needed to establish how salient they are to a particular strategic proposal. This topic is important enough to deserve a section to itself.

16.2.2 Stakeholder analysis

Change will affect interest groups both within the organization—groups of employees and managers—and outside it. In the public and not-for-profit sectors, or in industries like

→ For a longer set of examples of stakeholder groups see Section 1.6.1.

banking or defence, external stakeholders can be extremely powerful. Those that might influence change include:

- customers who might see changes to long-standing and critically important buyer–supplier relationships;
- suppliers whose income might be threatened, or who might find themselves needing to make large investments in order to cope with a firm's planned expansion;
- governments or government agencies whose concerns might include the effect of an organization's proposals upon tax income, consumer welfare, the environment, local communities, or a region's economy;
- competitors that may find themselves facing fiercer or laxer competition for customers, personnel, or key inputs such as energy;
- residents and neighbours whose concerns will include traffic, noise, pollution, and employment prospects.

The extent to which such stakeholders make their feelings known, and whether they are effective in modifying a strategic proposal, depends on several factors. The first is the saliency—power, legitimacy, and urgency—of each stakeholder with respect to the proposal in question. The second is the degree of interest in the proposal in question. The third is their ability to make common cause—form 'coalitions' with other interest groups.

a. Power

Most of the time, the chief executive and top managers are the most powerful people in an organization and in some cases are able to operate for long periods seemingly without reference to anyone. But in some western corporations, shareholders exert considerable power, and in many Chinese companies, ultimate power rests with external stakeholders in the government or Communist party. Apart from authority, power may be based on:

→ We defined power, and the associated concepts of influence and authority, in Section 2.2.6.

- Expertise that is valued by people in the organization: This may be the ability to make appropriate strategic decisions, or to perform technically difficult tasks. In a hospital, the top surgeons have power. The power that Bill Gates has been able to exert for decades in Microsoft[25] resides partly in his ability to envision the possibilities of new technologies, and partly in the fact that his computing skills remain second to none.
- Control over or access to valuable resources: In a commercial firm, these will include money; for this reason, finance departments are often powerful. Other valuable resources might be proprietary technology or knowledge that is critical to a particular aspect of the company's work.
- Control of or access to information: In a commercial company, important information may relate to customer requirements, future regulatory changes, or the profitability of certain divisions and activities.[26]
- Physical strength: It is a simple fact that physically stronger individuals are more likely to be able to achieve their objectives than weaker ones. In human society, physical strength is less important than in some areas of the animal world, but physical fitness and stamina remain a source of advantage in situations involving lengthy, complex, or hostile negotiations.
- Force of personality: Individuals can get power because no one wants to oppose them. One reason may be because they are prepared to initiate conflict and confrontation, which gives them power over the more numerous people who prefer to avoid such circumstances. They may also have charisma, a personal quality which inspires devotion. Charisma gives people 'referent power' over those who want to be associated with them as part of their 'gang'. Although it is easily recognized in many of the great warrior or religious leaders of the past and the political or business leaders of the present, it is

extraordinarily difficult to isolate or define. The extent to which it is necessary, or even desirable, in a leader has recently been questioned—we review this in Chapter 17.

- Relationships: Good relationships give people access to a wider base of resources, information, or expertise. It also typically allows them to call on others to return favours that they have performed in the past.

b. Legitimacy

As we mentioned when we introduced the concept of legitimacy in Chapter 2, it takes three forms, each of which may influence the saliency of a stakeholder regarding a particular strategic option.

A stakeholder group has pragmatic legitimacy when it has a clear influence upon an organization's access to important resources. The difference between this and power is that powerful stakeholders can have a direct impact upon decision-making in the firm, while the influence that comes from pragmatic legitimacy is less direct and vaguer. Individual consumers, for example, do not exercise a great deal of direct power over the decisions of a retailer, such as Tesco. However, as a stakeholder group, they have pragmatic legitimacy—if they are not satisfied, then they can turn to a competitor or a substitute, and the firm will lose resources. They have also been known to lobby government at national or local level, which may prevent Tesco from expanding as it would wish.[27]

Customers in most firms, and service users in many public and not-for-profit organizations, also have cognitive legitimacy. They figure strongly in the organization's belief system as the people that they were set up to serve. Depending on the organization, different staff groups may also have strong cognitive legitimacy because of their status in the belief system. McDonald's, as we showed in Worked Example 8.1, believes strongly in the education of the employees in its stores, and this group therefore has a degree of cognitive legit-imacy, although little power. The software engineers at Microsoft or Google enjoy a high status and great cognitive legitimacy.

Moral legitimacy attaches to two main classes of stakeholder. First, there are certain individuals in some organizations that function as a kind of conscience, reminding colleagues of their social and moral obligations and of the organization's mission and values. Their saliency, of course, depends upon the extent to which the organization takes those obligations and values seriously. The other class of morally legitimate stakeholder consists of outsiders that are held in high esteem by society at large. Pressure groups such as Médecins sans Frontières and Greenpeace are able, sometimes, to gain a strong influence over particular decisions as a result (Real-life Application 16.2).

Real-life Application 16.2 Shell's clash with Greenpeace

In 1995 Royal Dutch Shell announced a decision to dispose of a redundant oil storage facility in its Brent oilfield, by towing it from the North Sea to deep water in the Atlantic Ocean and there destroying and burying it.[28] Greenpeace, the environmental group, mounted a strong campaign to raise public concern about the effects of this decision on wildlife. Its moral legitimacy was such that people started to boycott Shell petrol stations in protest.[29] The company was eventually forced to reconsider its policy, and decided to bring the oil rigs ashore and dispose of them there.[30]

Greenpeace had no formal role in the decision process, but it did have a track record in issues of this kind. Royal Dutch Shell, however, failed to anticipate its interest in the situation, or the strength of the public feeling it could stir up. It also appeared to underestimate the degree of legitimacy that Greenpeace commanded, and accorded greater legitimacy to its own scientists, who had advised that the proposed solution was in fact not just the least expensive but also the least harmful to the environment. The fact that those scientists were probably correct[31] did not make the decision acceptable to the general public, whose pragmatic legitimacy was, in the end, the decisive factor.

c. Urgency

Urgency is, in some respects, the opposite of power. A stakeholder has urgency when it will suffer significantly from an organization's strategic change. This may be because it has made investments in the relationship, such as the purchase of specialized equipment, that have no alternative value. Car manufacturers increasingly demand that their component suppliers set up specialized factories inside or next to their production complexes, to ensure prompt deliveries of key components. Those investments make the component suppliers urgent stakeholders, exposed to risk if the car-maker withdraws from the markets the factory is intended to serve.

Other examples of urgent stakeholders include employees who have little chance of finding other jobs if the organization makes them redundant, beneficiaries in a company's pension scheme, their families, and perhaps the communities in which they live.

Using Evidence 16.1 Assessing saliency

There are a few quantitative indicators of power, such as the number of people and the size of budget that someone controls. These apply mainly to managers and operating units, but also to certain external stakeholders, such as unions. Easier to find are qualitative indicators of power and legitimacy, particularly if you are actually inside the company in question. Some of these, like large cars and offices, are ambiguous: often, they are evidence of power, but sometimes they are given to people with little power, except possibly the power to disrupt; these status symbols can soothe their egos and make conflict less likely. More conclusive evidence of power, or possibly of pragmatic legitimacy, comes from seeing who gets invited to important meetings and consulted over major decisions. Sometimes, these people rank quite low in the formal hierarchy, but their experience or expertise makes them indispensable—or they may have moral legitimacy, so that getting their agreement to a proposal will help persuade others.

When it comes to cognitive legitimacy, it is useful to start with any stakeholders—staff, customers, shareholders—mentioned explicitly in mission statements and similar policy documents. It is best, however, to check on the sincerity of these public statements, by looking for actual actions that the organization has taken to benefit those stakeholders.

Stakeholders with urgency may not manifest themselves until their interests are threatened. This means that there may not be direct evidence of their existence, and identifying them will require thorough analysis and a degree of intuition.

d. Linking saliency and interest

However salient a stakeholder may be, they are only likely to affect the success or failure of a strategic change if they are, or are persuaded to become, interested in it. Interest in this sense means something more than mere curiosity—it implies a willingness to take some form of action, such as:

- contributing or withdrawing resources;
- lobbying powerful outside stakeholders—governments, pressure groups, customers, suppliers—and power echelons within the company to take account of their objections;
- attempting to sabotage the change through strikes or overt refusal to do what they are told. Similar tactics can be used to push through a change to which management is resistant;

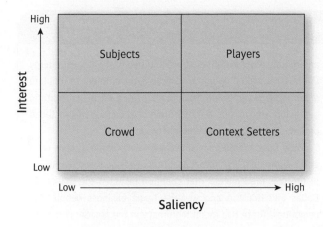

Figure 16.1 Saliency interest grid.
Source: Eden and Ackermann (1998: 122). *Reproduced with the kind permission of Sage*

- simply ignoring the proposals and quietly carrying on with their established routines. The people concerned may not see this as actual resistance—it may be a natural human reaction to prolonged or fast change, or to proposals that have not been effectively planned or communicated.

These actions are most likely where a stakeholder believes that they are affected, positively or negatively, by the change in question. The combination of saliency and interest (Figure 16.1) determines the degree of effort that must be made in respect of a particular stakeholder when trying to effect a change:

- Players are the people or groups that cannot be ignored. If the change is to take effect, they must be either kept happy or confronted.

- Context setters have the potential to influence the outcome but will not become involved spontaneously. A proponent or opponent of a particular course of action may therefore try to lobby them to persuade them that it is in their interest to intervene—or to take steps to avoid provoking them into an intervention.

- Subjects may have a degree of urgency but are unlikely to be salient in any other way. They are strongly affected by the change, and may attempt to persuade players or context setters to intervene on their behalf.

- There will be a crowd of stakeholders that are unaffected by the change and, in any case, unable to influence the outcome. They can largely be ignored when evaluating the acceptability of a proposal.

e. Mapping coalitions

Once the main stakeholders have been mapped, it becomes easier to envisage ways in which they might combine into coalitions that have a common point of view on an issue. By becoming part of a coalition, one stakeholder group may be able to tap into the power or legitimacy of another. Coalitions can be formed formally, through negotiations between representatives of different interest groups, or informally.[32] In Real-life Application 16.2, for example, Greenpeace and consumers became part of a coalition that combined pragmatic and moral legitimacy in combating Shell's plans for its Brent Spar platform.

Awareness of potential coalitions is important for someone trying to effect change:

- By bringing together stakeholders that favour a particular change at an early stage in the change process, it may be possible to build momentum for successful implementation.

- By being alert to possible coalitions against change, it may be possible to forestall their creation. We discuss ways in which this might be done in Section 16.3.

Real-life Application 16.3 Stakeholders and coalitions in the US electricity industry[33]

In spring 2006, TXU, an electricity utility based in Dallas, Texas, announced plans to invest over $10bn in 11 new power generating plants. The plants were needed to meet burgeoning demand for electricity in the state, and to replace some older ones. However the new plants, like those they were to replace, were coal-fired.

Coal as a fuel had a number of advantages over other potential fuels: it was plentiful, could be sourced cheaply and reliably from the USA—important, given that country's reluctance to become any more reliant on foreign energy producers—and it was cheaper than most alternatives.

However, coal-burning produced a number of pollutants. The new plants would employ the latest technology to ensure that they met all emissions standards relating to mercury, and to oxides of sulphur and nitrogen. However, people who lived and farmed in the area around Waco, where many of the plants would be sited, were not convinced that these standards were tight enough. And there remained the issue of carbon dioxide (CO_2), the main greenhouse gas and contributor to global warming. Burning coal produced more of this gas per unit of energy output than any competing mode of power generation. Moreover, the CO_2 could not be captured and stored, as was possible in, for example, gas-fired plants, though TXU's chosen designs allowed for this technology to be retrofitted once available.

Since TXU's proposals had been announced, public opinion in the USA was becoming increasingly sensitized to issues of global warming. A number of large firms, including Dell and Wal-Mart, had announced plans to reduce their carbon footprint, while the CEOs of others, including major users of energy in the chemicals and metals-processing industries, and two of the largest energy utilities, had called upon the US federal government to regulate greenhouse gas emissions from fossil fuels—coal, oil, and natural gas. In lobbying for this, they were part of a coalition that included prominent environmental pressure groups.

These same, normally business-friendly, pressure groups were at the centre of a less formal coalition opposing the construction of the coal-fired plants. That coalition included the mayors of Dallas and Houston and wealthy Texan business people and celebrities. These had moral legitimacy in the broader community, and the resources to acquire pragmatic legitimacy as well. They were applying pressure, through lobbying and lawsuits, to context setters in the Texan and federal legislatures, and to players in the Wall Street banks that were underwriting TXU's investment. The aim was to get them to withdraw resources, or to persuade the local government to do so. TXU had, however, the support of the governor of Texas, Rick Perry, who had given fast-track approval to four of the plants, and the state's energy regulators.

Events took an unexpected twist in February 2007, when two private equity (PE) funds, Kohlberg Kravis Roberts and Texas Pacific, announced a plan to acquire TXU for $44bn—the largest such takeover to date. These highly acquisitive funds had themselves become controversial as the proportion of the US and UK economies that they controlled had grown. In the UK, two major trades' unions had been lobbying to constrain their activities, which they felt were disadvantageous to the employees of the acquired companies. But the environmental coalition in Texas was in favour of the proposed acquisition; the two PE firms, in ➔

Trades unionists lobbied on behalf of existing staff when the planned acquisition of TXU was announced. *iStock*

→ preliminary talks with them, had offered to scrap seven of the proposed eleven new stations and to implement clean air policies. As well as benefiting from TXU's cash flow, the two firms stood to bolster their moral legitimacy within US society.

This did not mean, however, that they would have an easy time changing the mindset inside TXU. For example, the CEO of its wholesale electricity division had gained a degree from a mining college, financed by one of America's premier coal mining firms, and had spent much of his career prior to joining TXU in coal-related businesses. Moreover, the financial case for using coal rather than alternative energy sources was very robust, and PE firms have historically encouraged the businesses that they own to maximize cost-saving and profit-making opportunities of this kind. It is therefore quite possible that people in TXU, if they wanted to press for a reversion to coal-fired expansion, might find stakeholders in their new owners who agreed. The coalition-building opportunities would be greater because TXU was being bought by two firms, and not just one.

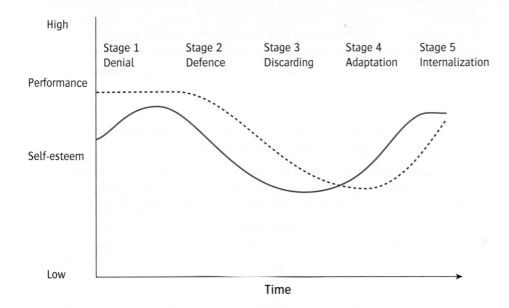

Figure 16.2 The coping cycle. Source: Carnall (2007). *Reproduced with the kind permission of FT Prentice Hall*

16.2.3 **Individual reactions to change**

Having established who the key stakeholders are, the next step is to try to anticipate their reaction to any proposed change. This requires an understanding of how individuals react to change and the reasons why they may favour or resist a particular proposal.

a. The coping cycle

Even where people initially resist organizational change, they typically adapt to it in time. This is a process known as the coping cycle (Figure 16.2) which has five stages:[34]

- Denial: Individuals pretend to themselves that externally imposed change is not happening, and remain attached to traditional approaches even if they are clearly problematic. Behaviour remains unaltered, even though it may be becoming increasingly inappropriate. There is a refusal to recognize either that change may be occurring at all, or that it could be beneficial.

- Defence: Externally imposed change has been recognized, but not accepted. People cling to and defend old ways, refusing to consider that new approaches might be beneficial. Paradoxically, self-esteem may actually rise at this stage. There can be a sense of bonding with colleagues as they fight a 'common enemy'—the managers who have introduced change. However, depression can also start to bite and behaviours sometimes become defensive and negative, as is common during periods of uncertainty. During a period of, essentially, grieving for the old ways, and a gradual acceptance of

Table 16.3 'Negative power': defensive behaviour in organizations

Over-conforming	Never bending rules or challenging senior managers
Buffing	Rigorously documenting or fabricating documents
Passing the buck	Attempting to reduce the chance of being blamed for a mistake
Playing dumb	Pretending not to know something
Stalling	Pretending to do something when not doing so
Playing safe	Not taking risks
Justifying	Providing excuses for behaviours
Scapegoating	Blaming others
Misrepresenting	Failing to tell the whole truth
Protecting 'turf'	Defending one's position or staff, even when unjustified
Escalating commitment	Continuing to defend a mistake after it has become clear it is a mistake

Source
Ashforth and Lee (1990)

the new, there may be resistance to, or even sabotage of, the efforts of those imposing the change, using some of the behaviours in Table 16.3.

- Discarding: People start to accept that change is going to happen and may even have some benefits, and begin to 'disengage' from the old ways. They acknowledge that perhaps earlier approaches had flaws, and the new ones are not as bad as was first thought.

- Adaptation: Behaviour changes and people accept change as a reality that has to be made to work. They disengage further with the old approaches, and may even start to 'sell' some of the benefits of the new approaches to others who are further behind in the adaptation process.

- Internalization: Individuals have adapted totally to their new environment. It has become increasingly difficult to imagine any other approaches. Old ways are but a distant memory—and it may seem incredible that they were clung to for so long.

By understanding the stage that important individuals and stakeholder groups have reached in the coping cycle, you can get clues about how likely they are to resist further change, and what form that resistance might take.

b. Factors influencing adaptation and resistance

It is impossible to say how long the coping cycle takes, or indeed if everyone will go through it completely. Some people never get beyond the denial stage—one reason why change programmes are characterized by high levels of staff turnover. Many different factors will influence the process of adaptation. Some of these are based on rational calculation of costs and benefits. People who stand to gain power, status, or money from a change are likely to favour it, while those who are likely to lose in these areas will oppose it.

But there are other, more emotional influences on people's attitudes to change. Some of these will relate to the individual's personality and circumstances—whether they are adventurous or conservative, and whether their family, social circle, and financial circumstances will allow them to leave the firm if something happens that they do not like. Others will relate to people's natural reaction to the change process itself.

Many individuals find substantial change stressful, since most of us have only a limited ability to take on and cope with new things. We all differ, according to our individual constitutions and experiences, in the levels of stress or strain we experience and in our ability to deal with it. Nevertheless, at some point most people begin to feel uncomfortable, even to the point of ill health, if change is excessive.[35] In these circumstances resistance and conflict can result, manifested in high levels of hostility, increased politicking, increased absenteeism, and high staff turnover rates. Negative or dysfunctional activities such as 'stalling', pretending to work but not doing so, or stretching tasks much longer than necessary become more prevalent.[36]

Moreover, individuals seem only to be able to cope with a limited amount of stimulation before they become disoriented or dysfunctional. A psychological mechanism kicks in which acts to block off new stimuli and prevents the individual from taking on board further novelty. In demanding situations people retreat into familiar, and thus psychologically comfortable, territory, and take conservative decisions.[37]

For these reasons, substantial change may give rise to anxiety and personal resistance. Potential triggers for this include:

- Fear of the new: Many people prefer certainty in order to plan for the future of children, or to take on an expensive commitment, such as a mortgage. Change erodes that certainty, while bringing the promise of a period of considerable disruption and hard work, as 'bugs' are ironed out, and employees and others around them learn to cope with new routines.

- Loss of autonomy: Change that is imposed by others also reduces our sense of autonomy or control of our own destinies—and the sense of not being in control is a well-known factor in stress-related illnesses. This is particularly so for people who do not agree with the proposed change—bearing in mind that some people invariably lose out from radical change, even if the organization as a whole benefits.

- Fear of incompetence: If what the future holds is different from the way we work now, we may become anxious about whether we have the skills to cope with it. This is why experienced and capable staff have in the past resisted the introduction of IT into their work, particularly when more junior people around them seemed to find it easier to cope.

- Change fatigue: Where an organization has changed repeatedly, or where a single change programme has lasted a long time, people may simply become overwhelmed and unable to cope with further change. Sometimes, these changes will appear to be the result of managers responding to successive 'fads'—new techniques that appear to offer a quick fix for common organizational problems, and which gain widespread acceptance only to be discarded quickly by the majority of adopters, once the implementation difficulties become clear. In such cases, employees may become cynical, and react by doing the minimum needed to placate their managers, while waiting for this round of change to blow over.[38]

People can also resist change on other grounds. They may feel aggrieved that they were not consulted about the proposals, or asked to be involved in the implementation. They may genuinely believe that the proposals are mistaken, and would make the organization's position worse. Or they may simply not care enough about the organization to make the effort needed to change their existing routines. This may be because they are not committed to its values or, in a fragmented culture, they may feel more committed to their personal or professional goals than to the organization's. Software engineers or researchers, for example, may feel more deeply about developing 'cool' technology and about their status in their peer groups of hackers or scientists than about making money for their firm—particularly if their company is not itself highly regarded by that peer group.[39]

As a counterbalance, there will in most organizations be some people who are enthusiasts for novelty, and are happy to try out new ways of working. Depending upon the size and influence of this 'early adopter' group, it can be a powerful force in favour of change. Others will fall in behind a change proposal because their commitment to the firm outweighs considerations of personal gain or loss.

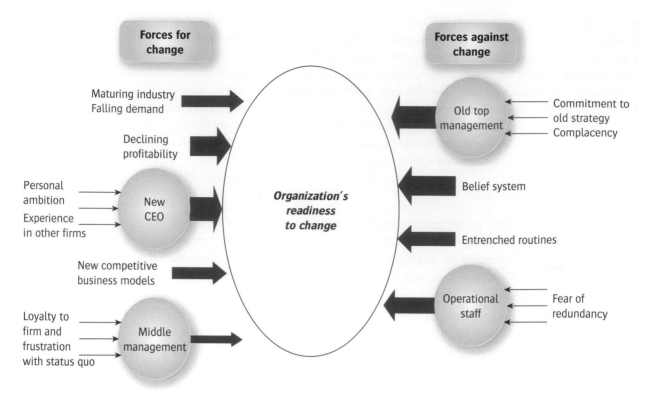

Figure 16.3 Example of a force field (thickness of arrow indicates strength of force)

16.2.4 **Force fields**

A useful way of picturing and summarizing the influences operating for and against change is as the force field shown in Figure 16.3.[40] On the right-hand side you will see examples of factors that might act to block change, countered, on the left-hand side by elements that might promote change. The relative strength of the two sets of factors dictates whether change from the current situation (shown in the middle of the diagram) will be more or less likely.

A force field might feature any of the organizational or stakeholder triggers or barriers featured in Section 16.2, plus others that are specific, and have a genuine influence upon the organization, issue, and option being examined. It can serve to highlight the most important factors that could tip the change process one way or the other, and so need particular attention. Where the reaction of a particular stakeholder group is unclear, a separate force field, looking at the individual reactions within that group, can be drawn up and will become an input into the main force field.

Using Evidence 16.1 **Force fields**

Where possible, it is good practice to cite precise evidence for the force field factors you identify. This might include financial performance figures over time—to identify trends, or allow comparisons with other similar firms—or evidence that particular stakeholders have power, and might gain or lose from the proposal.

Some people like to weight the various factors, which can help give a crude assessment of the relative strength of the forces for and against the change. This can be helpful, as long as you bear it in mind that such weightings can only be subjective guesses.

Worked Example 16.1 Assessing the acceptability of introducing greater autonomy for staff in McDonald's restaurants

Table 16.4 Profit margins in McDonald's company-owned restaurants

Percent of sales	2003	2004	2005
USA	17.7%	19.1%	18.8%
Europe	15.7%	15.6%	14.9%
APMEA*	9.9%	11.0%	10.9%
Latin America	6.1%	9.5%	11.4%
Canada	14.6%	15.3%	13.9%
Global total	**14.5%**	**15.3%**	**15.0%**

Note

* APMEA = Asia-Pacific, Middle East and Africa

Source

McDonald's Corporation Financial Report (2005: 9)

In this Worked Example, we examine the acceptability of introducing greater autonomy for staff in McDonald's restaurants, so that they would work to routines that are less tightly defined and have greater flexibility to vary products and behaviour to meet customer demands. We have no evidence that, at the time of writing, this strategic option is under consideration by McDonald's management—and we are not necessarily advocating that it should be. However, it is, for reasons that will become plain below, quite a plausible option for them to look at, and makes a good platform for us to review how the mass of theory in this chapter can be deployed in practice. You will also see how this part of a strategic analysis links back to earlier analyses of the competitive environment, culture, and architecture.

We first note that this is quite a substantial transformation of McDonald's working practices. It also represents a challenge to the paradigm which, as we saw in Worked Example 8.1, includes beliefs regarding the importance of controlling the environment, and also that most people are interested only in short-term relationships. Changing the routines so as to encourage greater personal autonomy may succeed in fostering greater commitment to the firm among a broader group of staff. However, not all stakeholders will agree that the rewards will justify the risks.

Triggers for change

As we mentioned in Worked Example 3.1, McDonald's performance in competitive terms has been quite strong. Its profit margins in 2005, the most recent year for which we have figures, were higher than those of its major competitors. However, as Table 16.4 shows, the profit margins in its company-owned restaurants slipped somewhat between 2004 and 2005, indicating that improvement might be possible and desirable, and the increasing intensity of competition in the industry will also inject some pressures for change. Worked Example 3.1, where we noted this trend in the environment, of course refers to the USA—this is not only McDonald's largest market, but also the one to which key top management stakeholders are most strongly exposed.

Stakeholders may also have noted Yum! Brands apparently successful experiment with cultural change (see Section 8.4.2). Although our proposal is different from Yum! Brands', which emphasized recognition rather than autonomy, the institutional environment might be favourable to experimentation with novel practices. The organization's breadth of resources is favourable to the testing of new practices in a few restaurants or regions. However, because there has been so much investment in honing the existing, tightly managed, restaurant routines, the sunk cost of the resource base is a likely source of inertia.

Interest groups and stakeholder reactions

Table 16.5 summarizes the saliency of the most important stakeholders. Some have been omitted for the sake of brevity, such as various layers of middle management, debt-holders, local communities, health and anti-globalization pressure groups, and the families of staff members. They would be included in a thorough analysis, which might also break down customers into the main segments discussed in relation to McDonald's in Chapter 5. Since, however, there are few likely differences in the different customers' reaction to the proposal we are considering in this example, they can be treated here as a single, homogeneous, stakeholder. ➔

→ **Table 16.5** Saliency of main McDonald's stakeholders

	Power	Legitimacy	Urgency
Shareholders	Theoretically extremely high, but few signs of influence on decision-making. Can be enlisted on major issues of public interest	Very high cognitive and moral legitimacy—in American firms of this kind, everything is done in their name	Low. For most, McDonald's will be a small part of a diversified portfolio of investments
Central Management	Very high: authority and control of resources. Have been able in the past to force through policies as required	High cognitive legitimacy by virtue of operational experience. Central control important in McDonald's belief system	High. Reputation and self-esteem vested in success of firm
Regional Management	High. Delegated authority in their own region; can probably delay implementation of measures not seen as compatible with regional policy	High. As per central management	High. As per central management
Restaurant Managers	Moderate. Have control of own restaurant but constrained to obey directives. Can threaten to quit firm but there are many people at lower levels who will be willing replacements	High cognitive legitimacy since they are important in motivating, controlling, and educating employees. Also have pragmatic legitimacy through interface with customers	Moderate. May have invested a lot of energy and emotion in the firm. But skills make them employable elsewhere if necessary
Franchisees	Medium. Can delay initiatives that require their investment unless they agree to them, but in the past not able to block central decisions	As per restaurant managers	High. Stand to lose income plus capital they have invested in franchise if firm founders
Restaurant Staff	Low. Have negligible input into decisions. Some blocking power in times of labour shortage	High cognitive legitimacy by virtue of central status in paradigm. Also have moral legitimacy—society sees their interests as important	Moderate in times of high unemployment. Low when unemployment low
Customers	Low. No one customer or group of customers has enough clout to influence firm	High. They are the ultimate source of the firm's resources. Also have moral legitimacy	None. Ample alternatives available if McDonald's fails them
Suppliers	Low. Firm holds balance of power (see Worked Example 3.1 for reasoning). Some short-term blocking power	Medium. Control access to and quality of key inputs—pragmatic and cognitive legitimacy	High. Many depend on McDonald's for much of their livelihood

The most salient stakeholders emerge as McDonald's central and regional management, and its franchisees. Restaurant managers and suppliers have a lower degree of saliency, while restaurant staff, shareholders, and customers emerge with the lowest saliency by this measure. Note that we are not saying here that McDonald's does not, or should not, care about its staff, shareholders, or customers—it clearly does, and should. Our analysis shows, however, that when it comes to a *realistic* assessment of the impact of *particular* decisions, there are other stakeholders who (in our judgement) will figure more prominently, by virtue mainly of their power to promote or block specific actions.

We next move on to assessing stakeholder reactions to this proposal (Table 16.6). These appear broadly negative—there are reasons why just about all of the salient stakeholders, particularly at franchisee and restaurant manager level, might resist the proposed change. This implies that it will be difficult to build a coalition for change, though within every interest group there might be a set of enthusiasts, as we have noted specifically for the restaurant staff. The positions of the different stakeholders can be summarized on the saliency-interest grid (Figure 16.4).

Assessment of acceptability and possible ways forward

The overall situation regarding the change is summarized in the force field in Figure 16.5. A striking feature is the absence of a salient stakeholder likely to favour change—the only stakeholder likely to do so is a sub-group of restaurant staff, and they lack →

→ **Table 16.6** Reactions of main McDonald's stakeholders to proposal to give more autonomy to restaurant staff

	Saliency	Degree of interest	*Likely Attitude*
Shareholders	Moderate, due to high legitimacy. Potentially powerful. Can be enlisted on major issues	Low, unless there is evidence that proposal will affect profits. In this case, evidence ambiguous	Neutral
Central Management	Very high. Power, legitimacy, and urgency	Very high. Significant change implied	Those who have risen through restaurants likely to be sceptical—runs counter to belief system. Others may be enthusiasts
Regional Management	High. Power, legitimacy, and urgency. Substantial power to promote or delay implementation in own region	Very high. As per central management	As for central management, but greater likelihood of finding director prepared to champion change in own region
Restaurant Managers	Moderate. High legitimacy but limited power or urgency	Very high. They will be intimately involved in developing and implementing new routines	Opposed. Proposal challenges beliefs and will require them to learn new ways of managing. May be seen as loss of power. Fear of new and of incompetence
Franchisees	High. Have blocking power alongside legitimacy and urgency	Very high. As per restaurant managers, plus may require financial investment as well	Opposed. For same reasons as restaurant managers, plus fear of loss of livelihood if initiative a failure
Restaurant Staff	Moderate. High legitimacy. May have some power or some urgency—but never both together	Very high. Substantial change in way in which they work	Two likely groups. Better educated and more ambitious staff will welcome greater opportunity to display initiative. Others may not care enough about firm to make efforts required. Fear of new, fear of incompetence may also be factors
Customers	Moderate. High legitimacy	Low unless quality of food or service threatened. May react if they feel staff being unfairly treated	Indifferent to McDonald's internal organization
Suppliers	Medium. Some short-term blocking power. Medium legitimacy, high urgency	Low. This is unlikely to affect them unless sales drop	Indifferent

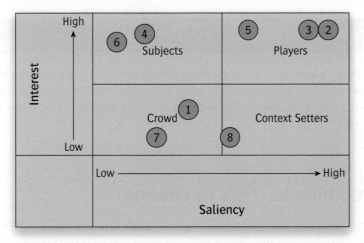

1) Shareholders
2) Central management
3) Regional management
4) Restaurant managers
5) Franchisees
6) Restaurant staff
7) Customers
8) Suppliers

Figure 16.4 Saliency–interest matrix for McDonald's 'increased autonomy' option →

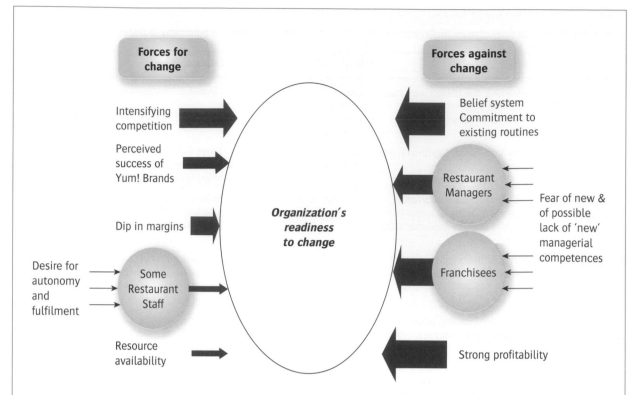

Figure 16.5 Possible force field for proposed change at McDonald's (thickness of arrow indicates strength of force)

➡ power. This, combined with the fact that the firm is performing quite strongly, means that it would be difficult to build a consensus for change, or a strong coalition in its favour. This would probably lead us to reject the option.

Another factor that would act against this option is the possibility of a strong coalition emerging against it. The franchisees, restaurant managers and many of the restaurant staff all have a vested interest in the status quo. If they were able to portray the proposed changes as being against the interests of the staff

in some way—for example, if they were to make it appear that the firm was trying to get people to do more demanding work for the same pay—then they might be able to raise interest levels amongst customers to the point where it affected their attitudes towards McDonald's, and their purchasing behaviour. This in turn might raise shareholder interest to the point where they decide to use their latent power—moving from the 'crowd' quadrant of Figure 16.4 to the 'players' quadrant—to quash the idea.

Creative Strategizing 16.1

If you were a McDonald's executive who strongly believed that greater autonomy was the way to go, what would you do? Which stakeholders might you try to mobilize to help you, and how? How would you try to address the concerns of likely opponents, or make it less likely that they form a coalition against you?

16.3 Overcoming barriers to change

Once the analyses in the previous two sections have been completed, it should be clear how great the obstacles are to the proposed change and from where in the organization they will come. What remains is to develop a programme for moving the organization in the desired direction.

Table 16.7 The TROPICS test for hard versus soft change

'Hard', planned change possible		'Soft', developmental change probably required
Clear, constrained; Short-/medium-term	**TIMESCALES**	Unclear, medium- to long-term
Clearly delineated and unlikely to change greatly	**RESOURCES required**	Uncertain; may alter substantially as programme unfolds
Clear and quantifiable	**OBJECTIVES**	Subjective, qualitative, couched in terms of overall vision
Shared by all salient stakeholders	**PERCEPTIONS of issue/solution**	No consensus; potential conflicts of interest
Limited group, clearly defined membership	**INTERESTED stakeholders**	Broad-based group, membership difficult to determine
Exercised by managing group	**CONTROL**	Shared outside managing group—perhaps outside organization
Internal to organization	**SOURCE of issue**	External

Source
Adapted from Paton and McCalman (2000: 24)

16.3.1 **Hard and soft change: the TROPICS test**

Change programmes can be divided into two categories: hard and soft. Hard change programmes are simpler, and can be planned within precise time horizons. Soft change, by contrast, is slower, more difficult, and typically requires changes to be developed to the organization's belief system. The TROPICS framework (Table 16.7) can be used to determine into which category the proposed change is likely to fall.[41]

Changes that are clearly bounded in respect of time-frames, resources, and stakeholders are best addressed through hard, planned change. Much fine-tuning and incremental change will fall into this category, although, as we mentioned in Section 16.1.3, some apparently small changes have broader ramifications which mean that a soft approach is needed. Some modular transformations, such as major product introductions, can also be handled through the hard approach, as long as there is sufficient consensus in their favour among interested stakeholders. We discuss the project management techniques needed to monitor the progress of hard change in Chapter 17; the rest of this chapter is concerned mainly with the trickier, soft change.

16.3.2 **Holistic change and the three types of power**

An important principle of soft change is that it must be holistic—that is, it must deal with all aspects of the organization, or as many as is humanly possible. This is because, as we showed in Chapter 8, the belief system and the cultural artefacts that underpin it are all mutually interdependent. In order to achieve genuine, lasting change in people's ways of working, the values and belief system must change. Quality initiatives aim to achieve, not just improvements in the quality of products or services, but also changes in people's beliefs and attitudes towards quality. This in turn implies changes in the architecture, power structures, and stories and symbols.

Think back to any organizations where you have worked, however briefly. It is the stories, symbols, and ways of working that you will remember most vividly, because they shape the reality of most people's working lives. Thus, these need to be worked on, if a change programme is to succeed. Unfortunately, these elements of the belief system, commonly referred to as 'soft factors', are the trickiest to influence in a way that leads to predictable results. Partly because of this, they are also the ones on which many traditional, 'rational', 'hard-headed' managers find it most difficult to justify spending time and money. They prefer to confine their efforts to elements such as the structure and control systems, where it is possible to produce concrete evidence of how they have been spending their time.

However, a change programme that is limited to these elements alone is likely to fail to overcome inertia within the organization. Success is far likelier if use is made of all of the following three types of power:[42]

- Power of meaning comes from the ability to shape the language and jargon that people use in referring to their work, colleagues, and other stakeholders, the stories that they tell, the symbols that are on display, and the rituals that they indulge in at work. Changes to these can subtly alter people's ideas of what constitutes acceptable behaviour in the organization and lay the foundation for a change in values and routines. Named change programmes, such as 'Putting People First' at British Airways in the 1980s or TOP ('time-optimized processes') at Siemens in the 1990s are examples of how language can be used in an attempt to influence attitudes and behaviour.

- Power of processes gives control over the routines, control systems and structures that determine how decisions are made. Changes to these enhance people's awareness that there has been a genuine shift in strategy. However, some experts caution that changes to the hierarchical structure are not always necessary, and should be avoided unless vital.[43]

- Power of resources enables managers to give money, information, and other scarce resources to some people and withhold them from others. It includes the power to decide which stakeholders are rewarded with money, authority, and prestige—or punished by their withdrawal. This type of power can thus be used to encourage or discourage specific behaviours. It also allows routines to be altered by bringing in new actors and, if need be, expelling existing ones.

→ We examine the use of power, in particular the power of resources, by organizational leaders in more detail in Chapter 17.

Together, these three types of power influence all aspects of the belief system (Figure 16.6). They are not independent of one another—for example, using the power of resources to dismiss or promote selected people will have a strong symbolic impact on the organization. If certain directors are fired while others who are widely trusted are retained, this may give people confidence in the change process. If all top managers retain their posts while there are significant redundancies at lower levels, then this also sends messages regarding the willingness of the top team to bear responsibility for organizational problems.

The different aspects of power are often deployed as part of the change process—managers can be nominated to a change task force (power of resources), which runs a number of strategy workshops (processes), during which participants start to develop a specific jargon for the change process and its desired outcomes (meaning).

16.3.3 Establishing the desired outcome

A more important use for the three types of power is to change the way the organization works—a new vision is formulated (meaning), control systems are altered to monitor its achievement (processes), and new units, headed by managers friendly to the change, with impressive job titles (meaning) are carved out of divisions headed by people that resist it (power of resources).

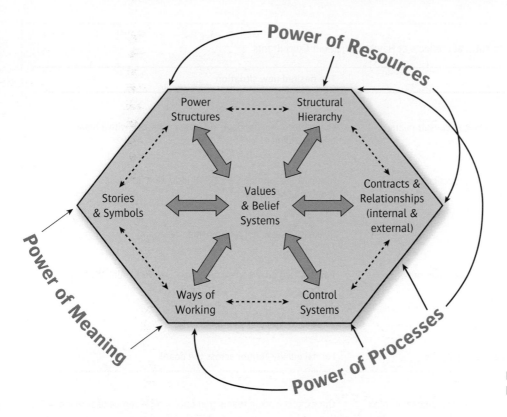

Figure 16.6 Power and belief systems

For this to be effective, it will be necessary to envisage the belief system the organization will require after the change. This can then be used to target specific changes to the various cultural artefacts (Real-life Application 16.4).

Real-life Application 16.4 Changes to the cultural artefacts at Hay Management Consultants[44]

In Real-life Application 16.2 we showed how Hay Management Consultants embarked upon a transformational change in response to issues in its competitive environment. With the aid of external consultants, its managers drew up a picture of the significant changes needed to the firm's belief system (some of which are summarized in Table 16.2). They also determined how the cultural artefacts needed to change to reflect the new belief system. Table 16.8 gives examples supporting a change in the old belief in the superiority of individualistic, generalist consultants to a belief that the firm needs specialists who can collaborate in teams.

The changes required touched many aspects of the firm and different aspects of power. The power of resources and processes were brought to bear on recruitment and induction practices, in order both to pick the people with the right attitudes and skill, and also to imbue them, from the word go, with the importance of expertise and professionalism. Power structures needed to alter—people without expertise should not be able to command power.

The power of meaning was also to be harnessed. Apparently trivial rituals, such as the speeches at the firm's annual Christmas gathering, were to be thought about, to make sure that they did not send the wrong message by praising behaviours that belonged to the old paradigm. And in the longer term, the stories that circulated within the firm would change, so that their heroes were no longer the individualists of old.

New stories, beliefs, and cultures, of course, do not spring up overnight. But the change process itself could be designed in a way that, hopefully, would push them in the desired direction. The firm's leaders took care to act in ways that demonstrated commitment to the change process and reflected the new paradigm. Senior consultants were sought out who could act as role models for the new routines. A working group was set up to address how the individual expertise required could be developed. This was not just a model for new collaborative ways of working; it could also demonstrate, through the meticulous analytical methods that it deployed, the power of 'new-style' professional expertise. →

→ **Table 16.8** Changes to cultural artefacts at Hay Management Consultants

The situation in 1994	The desired new situation
Belief 1	
Our people are generalists who can consult in any HR field	Our people combine deep specialist expertise with a broad understanding of HR
Ways of working	
Extensive recruitment, minimal induction processes Rushing around looking busy	Intensive recruitment, excellent induction processes Purposeful behaviour
Stories	
'Lone ranger' consultants	Successful customer relationship managers
Power structure	
Power based on position, expertise, client network	Power based on expertise and client network (but not position)
Contracts and relationships	
Unfocused, 'chaotic' accountabilities	Focused, clear accountabilities
Control systems	
Quality control for job evaluation projects	Formal quality control across the board
Belief 2	
We prize individualism and encourage people to think and act autonomously.	Our experts work in teams that have a high degree of autonomy
Ways of working	
Minimal induction processes Poor information flows across departments Praising high-billing individuals at Christmas party	Excellent induction processes Excellent internal information flows Praising teams involved in successful projects at Christmas party
Stories	
'Lone ranger' consultants competing with one another	Successful Hay teams

Source
Heracleous and Langham (1996)

16.3.4 The practicalities of effecting change

As we mentioned in our introduction to this chapter, there is no 'magic formula' that can guarantee successful change. However, academics and consultants that work with companies to help them change have found that successful change programmes have a number of factors in common.[45] The lessons from these studies are summarized in Table 16.9 as sets of measures that managers can take to improve the probability of successful change and avoid the most common known causes of failure.

The list in Table 16.9 can be thought of as a kind of checklist against which to assess whether a change programme or programme proposal contains the relevant elements. These elements should not, however, be thought of as distinct 'phases' in a change process, since they overlap and should not be expected always to occur in the same sequence. For example, while 'Building a sense of need, urgency, and commitment' and 'Developing and communicating a shared change vision' are both likely to be initiated at the very beginning of a change programme, there is no fixed rule about which should start first, and both activities are likely to continue until the new routines have been institutionalized.

Table 16.9 Best practice in organizational change

Change measures	Power of meanings	Power of processes	Power of resources
Building sense of need, urgency, and commitment	Diffuse dissatisfaction Uncompromising straight talk Stories illustrating top management commitment to new ways	Joint diagnosis of problems Information sharing Benchmarking Target-setting	Commit top management time Divulge information Withdraw resources from dissenters and poor performers Introduce consultants and/or new managers
Developing and communicating shared change vision	Mission and vision statements	Fostering consensus Building coalition for change	Invest in communications media
Empowering and building competence and confidence	Language of optimism Stories of early successes Stories of top managers learning new behaviours	Planning for quick wins Counselling Training in new behaviours Monitoring extra commitments Relaxing controls to encourage new 'bottom-up' initiatives Progress reviews	Invest in 'quick win' projects Invest in facilities such as help-lines to combat fear Commit top management time to training and counselling Rewards for successful adopters Recruitment to fill skills gaps
Spreading and consolidating change	Success stories Successful adopters as role models Tales of setbacks overcome	Sharing of best practice Refining systems and structures Checking for problems and reversion to old behaviours Progress reviews	Promotion and financial rewards for successes 'Blockers' disciplined or fired Consultants' presence reduced
Institutionalizing new routines and preparing for next round of change	New unit names and job titles New formal policies Warnings against complacency Lessons learned	New control systems to monitor new behaviours Environmental scanning Reflections on change process	New structure with pro-change managers at the top

a. Building a sense of need, urgency, and commitment

We remarked earlier that change will not occur unless an influential group believes that it is in their interests. When influential stakeholders are comfortable with the status quo, or cannot readily see a way to improve it, then organizational inertia can be difficult to overcome. Even if there are genuine threats emerging from the environment, they may fail to spot them or underestimate their importance.

It is therefore important to use the power of meaning to 'diffuse dissatisfaction' with the status quo and instil a sense that change is necessary and urgent. A number of processes and resources can be harnessed to do so. Information on performance and competition can be shared with stakeholders, such as unions, who would not normally have access to it, to convince them that drastic responses are needed. High-performing organizations in other industries or sectors can be invoked as benchmarks to convince people that improvement is possible. Stretch targets for cost or revenue improvement can be used to force people to think of new methods of working, with budget cuts or other sanctions for managers that fail to meet the targets.[46]

Complete honesty about the organization's situation can also be important in building the need for change. The power of processes can be important in persuading people to this position of 'uncompromising straight talk'. Views from customers and from all levels of the organization may need to be fed back to top management and other stakeholders in a form that they cannot ignore. Strategy workshops may be helpful in getting people to confront the reality of environmental change. However, the processes need to be structured to encourage free flow of information and to avoid participants, whether top managers or from further down the organization, being placed in a position where they feel threatened.[47]

Consultants can be introduced into the organization to help diagnose issues, gather objective data, and introduce an alternative point of view. However, many organizations that are seen as 'able' at change are sparing in their use of consultants, and using a task force of respected managers to gather data within the firm will send a stronger signal about management commitment to the change process.[48]

Top management commitment is almost universally regarded as critical—without it, any change programme is very likely to founder. It must therefore be signalled clearly right from the start and restated periodically until the change is fully institutionalized. It is also important that top management 'walk the talk'—i.e. they make sure that their everyday behaviour and conversations are compatible with the envisaged change. In one firm, shortly after a customer service initiative was launched, a senior director was reported to have lost his temper with a customer and literally thrown him out of the door. For some time afterwards, managers visiting stores to emphasize the importance of customer service were (jokingly) threatened with the same fate![49]

b. Developing and communicating a shared vision of change[50]

Along with top management commitment, the existence of a compelling and easily articulated vision is probably the most widely cited prerequisite for successful change. Without it, there is a danger that change initiatives at lower levels will fail to add up to a consistent strategy—indeed, there have been cases where different departments have developed policies that actually contradict each other—or that behaviours will not change at all. The vision should be easy for people to communicate and understand in a short time.

The vision should not, however, be the work of one person. An important pre-requisite is building a coalition to guide change. The coalition may consist of a group of senior managers, along with people who may have been held back in the previous regime. It may start small, but in a large organization may grow to 20–50 people as the change programme gathers momentum. It can provide a particularly important symbol of the future, undertaking the change management tasks, and acting as a bridge between the old and the new, and between staff and senior management.

A number of meetings, workshops, and off-site retreats may be needed to arrive at a consensus within the guiding coalition regarding the vision. Once the vision has been developed, it then needs to be extensively communicated to people outside the coalition, in order to obtain their commitment to the sacrifices needed in achieving major change. In one retailer, the various dimensions of the vision and strategy that emerged from a series of workshops and discussions were summarized on a 'seven-sided cube'—a normal cube with a slice cut into the top. Ten thousand of these striking-looking objects were distributed around the firm's head office, retail outlets, and suppliers, and an electronic version distributed as a PC screensaver. This successfully brought the vision and strategy into people's discussions.[51] Although there is a risk that undue repetition of the change message may provoke jokes and cynicism, the risks involved in under-communicating appear to be greater.

c. Empowering and building competence and confidence

Successful major change is rarely a purely top-down exercise in which a deliberate strategy set out by the CEO and top management team is implemented according to their specifications. The change coalition must, to some degree, specify the types of practice that the organization will end up adopting. However, it is often important to involve employees in developing the precise routines needed to meet the challenges set out in the change vision—one reason why effective communication of that vision is important. As with other aspects of the management of complex organizations, therefore, there is a balance to be struck between local delegation and central control.[52]

If there is insufficient local input in developing the programme, then the result may be an 'ivory tower' change, which appears unrealistic or irrelevant to some parts of the organization, or which misjudges people's attitudes and morale. One clothing retailer, involved in rationalizing its outlets into fewer, larger stores, offered many of its existing store managers the opportunity to become voluntarily redundant. It was aiming to reduce store manager numbers by 50 per cent—but managers were so disgruntled with the firm that they all took up the offer. The resulting exodus of expertise led to profits halving over 12 months. On the other hand, if the change is not tightly enough specified from the centre, then local managers may mistake the aim of the programme—for example, making a broad-based transformation towards team-working and higher quality into a narrower initiative to improve efficiency.[53]

In order for the bottom-up element of change to be possible, however, employees must be given the autonomy to develop and test their own ideas for improvement. They must also be given the skills needed to develop these ideas, and to operate once they have been implemented. Finally, they must be given the confidence to take on new challenges, since, as we mentioned in Section 16.2.3, fear of the unknown and of incompetence are common in times of change.

One way of building confidence in the proposed change is to seek out, and publicize, 'quick wins'—new products or cost-saving initiatives that will produce concrete evidence, within 12–14 months, of the effectiveness of the change programme. These provide the evidence that will help recruit new people to the change coalition and hurry others through the defence stage of their coping cycle.[54]

Meanwhile, resources need to be committed to ensuring that people understand precisely the behaviours that are expected of them, and how to execute them. People who are not used to working in teams or technical staff who are to be called upon to be customer-sensitive may need training in relevant interpersonal skills (See Real-life Application 16.5). Resources also need to be allocated to dealing with people's anxieties, for example by providing access to counselling services or ensuring that supervisors are available to offer support to their subordinates—and have the necessary skills.

It is important to manage the extra efforts that employees are called upon to make during a period of organizational change. If the extra commitments amount to more than about 10 per cent of normal workload, then people may become overwhelmed, morale may fall, and either the change programme or normal work routines may suffer. It will help if they feel that they achieve appropriate rewards for their inputs. These may take the form of salary and bonuses, improved employability and career prospects, or greater job satisfaction. However, it may also be necessary to postpone non-urgent projects or bring in extra employees or recently retired staff on a temporary basis to alleviate the load and stress on key staff.[55]

New permanent staff may be needed if specific skills—technical competences or languages—are required and there are not enough internal staff who can provide them, or be trained to do so. New staff also bring in different attitudes and mindsets; research suggests that such benefits remain potent for a period of about two years.[56]

Although, as we showed in Section 16.1, change does bring risks, it also gives organizations an opportunity to explore a greater range of practices and determine which are the most effective. To make best use of that opportunity, the control systems that were part of the old architecture may need to be relaxed, so that people have a degree of liberty to explore new, even innovative, ways of working. Although it may be possible, quite early on, to envisage the basic control systems that will eventually be needed to support the new belief system, it may be best to delay their full implementation. There is evidence that, in organizations with several, interdependent departments or businesses, relaxing and then tightening central controls leads to better performance than either keeping them constantly in place or removing them permanently.[57]

Control systems are needed, however, to monitor the progress of the change itself. The frequency of formal project reviews has been shown to have a significant effect on the success of the project—far more so than the total duration of the change programme. Long programmes with frequent reviews are less likely to fail than shorter projects that are assessed at longer intervals. Ideally, reviews should be no more than two months apart, while intervals greater than eight months are a strong danger signal.[58]

One factor to monitor during such reviews is the capacity of the team heading the change programme, another major determinant of success. Ideally, the project team should be led by a capable and respected individual, contain all the skills needed, and be able to call on at least 50 per cent of its members' working time.[59] The skills needed by change agents are discussed in Section 16.4.

d. Spreading and consolidating change[60]

Once the change programme has developed to the stage where some genuine successes are in place, two further challenges appear. The first is to spread the change into other parts of the organization. The early successes can be used as models of good practice and as evidence to win over doubters, but their methods may not be entirely applicable to units with different national or professional subcultures. Theorists recommend that each unit should be allowed to invent its own way of adopting new practices.

The second challenge is to avoid mistaking early successes for complete triumph and disbanding the programme management structure. Although there is a good case for the firm gradually reducing the input of any consultants and for the managers to take ownership of the change, there may still be setbacks and opponents of the change who are looking for ways to fight back. If these emerge after the change management team has been dissolved and its members are allowed to resume their normal duties, then it may be difficult to reassemble it, remotivate its members, and recover lost momentum. There are several types of setback for which people need to be alert:[61]

- Change that extends over a protracted period may come to be seen as little more than a ritual; as the novelty fades, change fatigue sets in. This had occurred in Hay Management Consultants in Real-life Application 16.1.

- Managers get sucked back into their daily operational routines, and lose sight of the need to behave differently and to reinforce new behaviours in others. This presents change programme leaders with a dilemma: if they reinforce the change message regularly, then they risk it becoming a ritual and losing impact, but if they do not, then people may lose focus. This can be a particular problem in industries like hotels, where there is high staff turnover, so that if the message is not reinforced regularly, a large proportion of employees will never have been exposed to it at all.

- One interest group is able to hijack the change process for its own ends, diverting the resources dedicated to the process to obtain different goals, or reinterpreting the new vision to be just an alternative perspective on existing ways of working. For example, a clothing retailer launched a change programme designed to move its emphasis from product quality to the quality of customer service—putting the customer first. However, influential stakeholders were able to argue that what the customer really wanted was excellent products, so that no real change was apparent.

One possibility is to sustain momentum by seeking new areas to which to broaden the change programme. Ideas for new areas may appear if the change team and coalition are alert to unexpected outcomes from the change process—for example, people finding new and unplanned uses for newly installed information systems, or collaborative networks

It is difficult to effect change in industries with a high staff turnover, like hotels. *iStock*

growing up between business units that have hitherto not been in contact. Team and coalition members will need to use their personal networks to check for signs of these—and also of potential setbacks, which may need to be met by further training, or fine-tuning of new procedures.[62]

Top management, meanwhile, will need to be prepared to take action against stakeholders who appear to be deliberately blocking the change or who are simply unable to adjust. Moving, disciplining, or dismissing such people early in the change process, before they have had a chance to be trained in new skills and move through the coping cycle, would suggest to other employees that any previous relational contracts had been broken, and cause them to reconsider their own commitment to the firm. However, tolerating inappropriate behaviours beyond a certain point would symbolize a lack of commitment to the change process and risk killing it.[63]

Nonetheless, such actions need to be thought through carefully. The removal of chosen opponents is one effective way to break up groups that are hostile to change. However, it also risks disrupting relationships and communication channels that are necessary for organizations to be effective—and for change to be seen as successful. Moreover, it often adds considerably to the anxiety and stress that accompany change when employees see colleagues and friends forced to leave, perhaps to an uncertain future. Morale might suffer even among people who understand and even sympathize with managers' reasons for taking such action. This may result in many of the best employees—those who are most marketable—departing, leaving the organization with a skills shortage that may undermine the effectiveness of the change.[64]

One possible tactic, however, is to keep people within the organization but remove them from decision-making committees. Sidelining people—or giving them a 'sideways push'—is one well-established way of moving people away from key roles while at the same time allowing them to retain their job and dignity.

e. Institutionalizing the new routines

The climax to a change programme comes when almost all operating units have modified their behaviour and routines in the desired fashion, and most people have moved through the coping cycle to the internalization stage. The change can now be institutionalized—the new behaviours become the norm and the architecture is formally changed in a way that will cement them and the new belief system in place.

Major changes to the structure, as mentioned earlier in this section, may be best avoided unless they are vital, but symbolic changes to the titles of jobs and departments may be in order. The most substantial changes are likely to come to control systems, as managers begin to develop expectations as to how units should be performing, and work out how to measure their performance. Information systems can also be put in place to link newly formed work groups and support new ways of working.

→ The design of control systems is discussed in Section 17.2.

While institutionalizing the results of one round of change, it is advisable to give some thought to readying the organization for subsequent change. This may imply putting in place improved procedures for scanning the environment, and circulating stories about the dangers of being complacent about future threats. Some researchers advocate the development of new routines to enhance employees' 'strategic intuition'—their ability to recognize new patterns in the environment and help the organization adjust. The change team and top management may also wish to reflect on lessons learned from successes and setbacks. Companies that learn from change in this way are more capable of handling change in the future.[65]

f. Behavioural compliance: a sub-optimal outcome

Even if all change activities have been carried through with attention and energy, the programme may not be counted a complete success. It is possible that the organization may achieve nothing better than 'behavioural compliance' from employees—that is, they will do and say the right things in order to please their managers, but their underlying beliefs may not have changed in the way that the change coalition might have envisaged. Even apparently highly successful change projects, like that at British Airways, can suffer from this to a degree (Real-life Application 16.5).[66]

Real-life Application 16.5 Cultural change in British Airways[67]

In 1981, British Airways lost almost £140m. In the words of Colin Marshall (later Sir Colin), who joined the company from Avis as chief executive: 'Horror stories abounded. Passengers complained of grubby, uncared-for aircraft, while cabin crews in turn told tales of woe about broken trolleys and ovens that would not heat the meals. The complaints about our staff were, if anything, even worse.'[68]

Five years later, however, BA's profits were the highest in the industry, and 94 per cent of its employees bought stock in 1987 when the firm went public. With essentially the same workforce, flying largely the same routes, British Airways became one of the world's leading airlines. A major element of this transformation was what has been described as a 'cultural revolution', engineered by the airline's chairman and chief executive, Lord King and Sir Colin Marshall. The company is often held up as an example of one of the few companies to have successfully achieved a major cultural change, but it took a very long time, and considerable expense and top management support and encouragement.

Between 1983 and 1986, virtually the entire 37,000-person workforce was put through a two-day culture change training programme entitled 'Putting People First' (PPF). Almost all of the →

→ 1,400 managers went through a five-day version entitled 'Managing People First'. What separated these from most normal management training sessions were their magnitude, the consistency with which they were applied throughout the organization, and the commitment of money and top management time.

Although sometimes mocked as the 'learn to smile' sessions, PPF contained advice, not just on customer care, but on managing stress and achieving confidence and personal growth. It also made strong use of the power of meanings to attack BA's traditional culture which resembled that of the armed forces, where many of the pilots had received their initial training. People wore military-style uniforms, worked according to strict rules, and deferred to those of higher rank. However, at PPF sessions, they were told that they were in a highly competitive situation, and needed to use personal initiative to ensure the quality of service they offered customers. Uniforms were not worn and employees worked in groups that crossed traditional boundaries of rank and department.

Colin Marshall is said to have personally attended 95 per cent of the PPF sessions to explain his vision for the airline and answer questions, and to have worn his 'We're putting people first' lapel badge for two years. Furthermore, he conspicuously and assiduously 'walked the talk', going out of his way to get feedback from customers and crew whenever he flew BA, and on one occasion serving breakfast to customers queuing for a new service.

The programme was followed by a variety of follow-on courses and supported by other changes. An appraisal scheme was instigated that measured not only what managers did but how they did it, and a new compensation programme was brought in which paid bonuses of up to 20 per cent of salary based on how managers behaved. Crew schedules were changed so that people would work regularly with the same 'family' of colleagues. An extensive system for briefing employees on developments at BA was put in place, with special arrangements, eventually including daily TV broadcasts, for staff who were travelling or alone.

The cultural change at BA was clearly enduring. Some 75 of the 100 teams formed to spread the message of PPF were still active in the 1990s. But it was not the only reason for BA's revival. Between 1981 and 1983 the airline had slashed its cost base, making some 40 per cent of staff redundant—on generous terms—and had embarked on investment in new aircraft, facilities, and systems, although those could also be seen as symbolizing management commitment to the change programme. Engine maintenance and IT were outsourced.

And when Marshall's successor attempted a 'second revolution' to shrink the cost base further, in response to new competition from low-cost airlines, cracks appeared in BA staff's unity. Negotiations on new contracts stalled, and the airline's heavy-handed attempt to dissuade crew from striking led to a period when some 2,000 employees called in sick, leading to extensive flight cancellations.[69] The Transport and General Workers Union recruited several thousand new members at BA at a time when union membership was falling elsewhere in the UK private sector.[70] Although BA's reputation for customer service has stayed strong, industrial relations have remained fragile, with a threatened strike in February 2007 being only narrowly averted.[71]

Theoretical Debate 16.1 Can change be 'managed'?

In this chapter, we have carefully avoided using the term 'managing change', although it is in common use in textbooks and journals. This is because there is genuine debate as to the extent to which change is susceptible to being managed—in the sense that a set of managerial inputs can be conceived that will lead to a specified outcome.

The concept of managing change arose out of the organization development (OD) movement. This was founded, starting in the 1940s, by a group of theorists including Kurt Lewin and Warren Bennis who sought to apply psychological insights in an organizational context. They believed that, by using team-building and other interventions to enhance interactions between people, an organization could be readied for change. By tailoring those interventions to encourage or discourage particular behaviours, change could be steered in a particular direction. Gradually OD theorists started to produce 'rule books' and templates for successful change. The writings of Michael Beer and his associates (Beer and Eisenstat, 2000, 2004; Beer et al., 1990; Beer et al., 2005) and of John Kotter (1995) can be seen as arising from this tradition.

Interventions in this planned vein scored some spectacular successes, such as the one at British Airways (Real-life Application 16.5). Not all of them worked so well, however: Customer First, an initiative introduced at British Rail after BA's successful change programme, had a much smaller impact on that organization's problems.[72]

Other obstacles to planned change come from the way that power is used in organizations. Theorists in the field of power and resource dependency (Pfeffer, 1992; Pfeffer and Salancik, 1978; Kanter, 1983; Pettigrew, 1973, 1977, 1985) point out that powerful stakeholders have the capacity to block change or divert it →

→ to their own ends. Hodgkinson and Wright (2002) give an example of a CEO undermining, apparently as a demonstration of her own power, an intervention she had herself commissioned from outside change agents.

Some postmodernist organization theorists go further, drawing upon the writings of philosophers such as Foucault and Habermas (see Manki, 2003 and Tsoukas, 2005 for explanations). They suggest that organizations are just part of a web of power and discourse that is shaped by the society in which they are embedded. These societal influences will shape the thought processes of people in the organization, sometimes in conflicting ways, and so will mould, and may prevent, attempts at change on the organizational level. Institutional theorists also point to the power of the institutional environment to constrain thinking in a way that may limit change outside parameters that are regarded as legitimate within an organization's field (DiMaggio and Powell, 1983; Greenwood and Hinings, 1996).

However, there are researchers who suggest that these influences, while real, do not totally constrain managerial action or the ability to induce a desired change. Hardy (1996) and Balogun et al. (2005), while clearly having absorbed postmodernist ideas on the pervasive nature of power, nonetheless suggest ways in which it can be used to bring about change as well as prevent it. Once the importance of power has been recognized and the power-holders identified, then it can perhaps be treated as one more item to factor into plans for change. Practices that have become institutionalized can become deinstitutionalized (Oliver, 1992) and new practices and organizational forms do spring up alongside established ones (Lee and Pennings, 2002; Kraatz and Zajac, 1996).

Thus, a determining factor in managers' ability to influence change may be the extent to which their organization is an independent culture, decoupled from its organizational field and from pervasive societal influences. However, once change is under way, current theory points to the likelihood of its having unintended consequences, as managers' cognitive processes and beliefs are reshaped in unpredictable ways by the change process. This in turn implies that managers need to be prepared to cope with these consequences as they arise (Harris and Ogbonna, 2002; Balogun, 2006; Balogun and Johnson, 2004, 2005).

Even this lesser degree of predictability is too much for some scholars to swallow. Complexity theorists—see Burnes (2005) for a review—take the view that organizations are too unpredictable as entities for such logical steps to be feasible. Organization ecologists, such as Hannan and Freeman (1977), as we have noted in earlier Theoretical Debates, emphasize the extent to which inertia limits organizations' capacity to change. They suggest that only a minority of firms will acquire the resources needed to adapt to a given competitive environment. Both schools hold that the impact of managerial action upon firm survival is at best unclear and at worst an illusion. Some researchers (e.g. Rosenzweig, 2007) believe that many acclaimed managerial triumphs can in fact be traced back to fortuitous environmental factors, but that they have become, erroneously, attributed to the change management practices current in the organization at the time, through what is termed a 'halo effect'.

16.4 **Change agents**

Change agent

A person (more rarely, a group of people) who takes on the role of promoting change within an organization and of enlisting other people to support that change.

→ Different styles of organizational leadership are reviewed in Section 17.1.

Many writers on change have suggested the activities of the person acting as the change agent are critical to the success or failure of change programmes. In this section, we explore the characteristics of such 'champions' of change, the different approaches that they may adopt, and the attributes and competences that they typically possess. Four different classes of change agent have been identified:[73]

- Leaders or senior managers. A significant proportion of CEOs see change agency as their primary task, and the instigator of transformational change is often the chief executive or managing director, since few other actors have the power of resources and processes to carry it through against significant opposition. Colin Marshall at BA (Real-life Application 16.5) was a good example of a change agent CEO, and Howard Stringer is also attempting to achieve a change in attitudes and behaviours at Sony.

- Middle managers and functional specialists who typically are nominated by their superiors to lead change in their own business units, or across several. Sometimes managers may nominate themselves as change agents: in Lufthansa in the 1990s, change was initiated by a group of managers who met at a corporate workshop, discovered that they shared a desire for urgent action, and nominated themselves the 'Samurai of Change'.[74] The credibility of such change agents is greater if they have considerable experience across many units and locations, and in-depth industry experience.[75]

- Consultants who provide specialist advice or skills to facilitate the change process. They may be professionals hired specifically for the purpose, academics, or internal staff with the requisite know-how. The expertise required is typically in areas like project management, change management, and process consulting—observing and enhancing the group processes within the top management or change programme teams.

- Teams operating across a number of levels in the organization and embracing people with a range of skills and backgrounds, including those in the other three categories.

Change agents need to be able to assume a variety of roles during the course of a change programme.[76]

- They will need to 'sell' the change of vision to key stakeholders, a process that requires sensitivity to those people's needs and fears. Introducing the wrong topic at too early a stage may provoke a wave of protest that will stop the change in its tracks. Skilled change agents understand how to use the power of meanings, what language to use for controversial proposals, and which topics to leave until people have started to buy into the need for change. This role is important if change is to be implanted in the culture, but requires the change agent to be patient, empathetic, and take a long-term perspective.

- They will sometimes need to dictate the overall direction that the change programme will take and to sideline or eliminate objectors. This is particularly the case where the organization is under pressure to produce quick financial wins, and calls upon the change agent to be autocratic and ruthless.

- They may need to undertake detailed engineering of new routines, or to oversee the people who are doing so. This may require competences, or at least credibility, in areas such as production engineering or IT. This type of intervention is important if visible results are required reasonably quickly.

- They may need to educate the people around them so that attitudes and beliefs are changed as a way to developing new capabilities over the medium to long term.

Change agents need not only to be able to function in all these roles, but also to judge when the time is right to move from one to the other. This involves a sophisticated appreciation of the context in which they are operating. In firms where people are used to a great deal of autonomy, autocratic styles are likely to encounter considerable resistance. The change agent perhaps needs to start with a more laid-back style, paying attention to altering important symbols such as reward systems, or persuading his or her colleagues about the benefits of change and the need for urgency. In contrast, in an organization with strong bureaucratic controls and centralized decision-making, a more dictatorial style might be effective—and even expected.

Change agents therefore need to be special people: both practical and visionary; detailed and broad; considerate and ruthless; team players and individualistic; empathetic and detached; and resistant to stress. They need to have the necessary expertise to make correct decisions, to know when people are trying to pull the wool over their eyes, and to understand the art of what is possible. Political astuteness and the ability to build and make use of different dimensions of power and internal networks of contacts appear to be particularly important attributes. Table 16.10 lists 15 competences that characterize effective change agents at all levels in an organization.[77]

Table 16.10 The fifteen competences of change agents

Goals cluster

Sensitivity to changes in personnel, top management perceptions, and market conditions, and how these impact the goals of the project in hand

Clarity in specifying goals and defining the achievable

Flexibility in responding to changes outside the control of the project manager

Roles cluster

Team-building abilities to bring together stakeholders and develop effective groups and allocate responsibilities

Networking skills in establishing and maintaining contacts within and outside the organization

Tolerance of ambiguity to be able to function comfortably and effectively in an uncertain environment

Communication cluster

Communication skills to be able to transmit effectively to colleagues and subordinates the need for change and challenges to individual tasks and responsibilities

Interpersonal skills, including selection, listening, collecting appropriate information, identifying the concerns of others, and managing meetings

Personal enthusiasm in expressing plans and ideas

Stimulating motivation and commitment in others

Negotiation cluster

Selling plans and ideas to others; creating a desirable vision of the future

Negotiating with key players for resources or changes in procedures, or to resolve conflict

Managing up cluster

Political awareness in identifying coalitions, and in balancing goals and perceptions

Influencing skills to gain commitment to projects from potential sceptics or resisters

Helicopter view, to take broader view of priorities

Adapted from Buchanan and Boddy (1992)

What Can Go Wrong 16.1 Planned change backfires at Morgan Williams[78]

Few firms are eager to publicize their failures and it is therefore difficult to find current examples of well-known firms whose change programmes have gone awry. Some anonymous examples can be found in Harris and Ogbonna (2002) and in Abrahamson (2004). But the following is instructive for a number of reasons.

A new chief executive, Paul Wilson, arrived in 1990 at Morgan Williams, a British equipment-hire firm, with a brief to arrest a decline in performance and to integrate the company into a coherent whole. Morgan Williams was the product of a merger between two established firms, Morgan and Williams, with radically different cultures. The strategy he formulated drew upon his past experience in another hire operation that he had success-

fully managed. It revolved around allowing latent talent in the organization to flourish, rationalizing the IT and control systems, and putting all the firm's diverse hire operations under a single corporate brand.

He communicated this strategy through a formal, regularly updated strategy document, the first in the firm's history. He backed this up with a series of training courses for managers at all levels and for sales representatives, which he personally led. He also made a point of visiting the company's many sites, and holding meetings with a broad team of 30 managers, to explain the strategy. He also removed a layer of regional management and made changes to the firm's planning, purchasing, and ➜

→ management information systems. He brought in a common scale of salaries and benefits across the entire firm, and introduced performance related pay and a share options scheme.

Wilson selected a management team with two operations directors, one ex-Morgan, the other ex-Williams, a finance director who was also a major shareholder in the firm, and a marketing director who was a colleague from Wilson's previous employer. Other appointees from the chief executive's previous company replaced managers who were unwilling or unable to accept the new terms, or who appeared unlikely to help the company to move forward.

The removal of the regional management and the new management information systems were intended to empower lower-level managers, encourage innovation, and promote healthy competition between business units. Some lower-level managers embraced this change wholeheartedly, and began to generate ideas for new products that they transmitted upwards, just as the chief executive had hoped they would. However many were less enthusiastic; they saw the changes in terms of the centre asserting greater operational control, not less. The majority played along, acting as the strategy demanded, while communicating their reservations to those who would listen. A few individuals, such as those who ran the most profitable business units, were able to reject elements of the strategy. In particular, they resisted the application of the corporate brand to their business units, and lobbied senior managers for change in the strategy.

Wilson took encouragement from the signs of creativity from the most enthusiastic adopters and was also enthused by a number of new market and product opportunities, notably in eastern Europe. In 1993, he announced ambitious new growth targets. But he also undertook some changes that gave mixed messages. He fired two of the top management team, including one person he had hired the previous year. He promoted a number of junior managers into positions that looked very similar to those in the management layer he had recently abolished.

To the CEO and his allies at top level, these changes were simply fine-tuning to the new strategy. Further down the organization, however, they were perceived as a reversal of direction and a sign of top management uncertainty, which added to some people's dissatisfaction with some of the systems that had been imposed in the first round of change. As a result, middle and lower-level managers started to lobby determinedly against the CEO's expansion targets, suggesting that a period of consolidation was needed first.

There were also signs of disquiet at the performance of some of the newly external appointments, including the marketing director, who were seen in the organization as inferior to the insiders that they had replaced. Wilson's loyalty to those people was contrasted with the tougher treatment that had been accorded to established Morgan Williams employees.

After heated debate with his fellow directors, Wilson agreed to dismiss the marketing director, at about the same time as some of the other most problematic of his former colleagues were also dismissed. The removal of these managers appeared to symbolize a significant decline in the chief executive's power within the organization. In May 1995, following publication of the first major loss for the company, an emergency board meeting was convened, at which Paul Wilson resigned.

This example illustrates how difficult it is to get change right. Many of the actions that Paul Wilson took were well in line with best practice in strategy and change management. But empowerment and flexibility only work if people want to be empowered, and do not see delegation as a sign of weak leadership. It may be that he was too ready to apply the solutions that had worked for him elsewhere to the unusual context of Morgan Williams—a criticism that some employees levelled at his marketing strategy.

It may also be that he underestimated some of the people he dismissed and did the opposite with some of their replacements, and thus sent the unintended message that loyalty was more important than competence. Moreover, few of the trusted people with whom he surrounded himself were able to build good networks inside the firm, and that made it difficult to monitor how the changes were being received further down the hierarchy. This led him to give too much weight to the responses of people who favoured his new strategy, and overlook the disquiet and behavioural compliance that was the majority view. And it also meant that his change coalition lacked depth in comparison with the coalition that emerged to combat him.

● CHAPTER SUMMARY

In this chapter we have surveyed the organizational and individual factors which might influence the success or failure of a strategic proposal. Organizations combine a tendency to change gradually over time with a basic inertia, which means that major change tends to happen infrequently and with difficulty. The four broad types of change, listed in order of potential disruptiveness to established ways of working, are:

- fine-tuning the workings of the existing strategy and business model;
- incremental adjustment to reflect changes in the environment;
- modular transformation at the level of the business unit;
- corporate transformation of business and corporate strategies.

Any of these may be either evolutionary or revolutionary in nature. Many organizations exist in a state of punctuated equilibrium, with long periods of evolutionary change alternating with shorter phases of revolutionary change. Revolutionary change is the more difficult to implement, particularly if it involves a major shift in an organization's culture and belief system.

Change will not occur in an organization unless it is in the interests of one or more salient stakeholders. They may be induced to favour change by poor organizational performance, or changes in the competitive or institutional environment. However, the organization's existing routines and power structures will often act to reinforce its inertia.

People who are seeking to implement a particular strategic proposal therefore need to be aware of who the salient stakeholders are, the degree of interest they are likely to show vis-à-vis the proposal, and the likelihood of their forming coalitions to promote or oppose the strategy. This in turn will be influenced by the way in which individuals within a stakeholder group will view any proposed change.

Although most people find major change stressful and threatening, their reactions will vary according to their individual attributes and situations—for example, whether they stand to gain or lose power, status, or money from a change. Individuals internalize and accept change gradually, going through a coping cycle. Many of the individual factors that act to block the acceptance of change at the early stage of that cycle are emotional. They may derive from uncertainty regarding the future, from fear of not being able to cope or of losing autonomy, from change fatigue, from a belief that the proposals are wrong, or from annoyance at not having been sufficiently involved.

The balance between forces which encourage change and those that act to block it can usefully be summarized in the form of a force field.

Programmes to effect strategic change and overcome barriers to it can take two forms. Less complex changes in which outcomes, time-scales, resources, and stakeholder interest are clearly defined can be handled as 'hard' change, using classic disciplines of project management. More complex changes, where the precise outcomes are not immediately clear and where both outcomes and processes may need to be negotiated with internal or external stakeholders, require a different range of techniques.

Such changes must be holistic, working at the level of the organization's belief system and the associated cultural artefacts. In order to do so, they must make use of all three potential types of power:

- the power to give or withhold resources within the organization or the change process;
- the power to alter processes followed by the organization, both within the change process and in its everyday operations and decision-making;
- the power to influence meanings—the language and symbols used by people in the organization.

Successful change cannot be guaranteed, but the chances of its occurring can be enhanced by including the following activities within the change programme:

- building a sense of need, urgency and commitment;
- developing and communicating a change vision;
- empowering and building competence and confidence;
- spreading and consolidating change;
- institutionalizing the new routines;

Within this framework, a number of tricky decisions need to be made. The right balance must be struck between mandating specific changes from the centre and empowering people to develop the routines they need to achieve the change vision. The use of the power of resources to deal with people who are blocking the change must be carefully timed, and the way in which they are treated carefully thought through in order not to discourage their colleagues and undermine the change process. There remains a danger that at the end, the outcome may be no better than behavioural compliance, rather than full cultural change.

The change agents that make these and other decisions require a range of skills, and the ability to know which skills to employ at a given point in the process. They must be politically astute, and able to move between selling the idea of change to doubters, being dictatorial about which practices to adopt, designing or supervising the design of new routines, and educating people about the kinds of behaviour and attitudes that are needed.

 Online Resource Centre
www.oxfordtextbooks.co.uk/orc/haberberg_rieple/

Visit the Online Resource Centre that accompanies this book to read more information relating to effecting organizational change.

● KEY SKILLS

The key skills you should have developed after reading this chapter are:

- the ablity to identify forces that militate for and against change in an organization;
- the ability to anticipate likely obstacles to a change proposal—their nature, and the stakeholders from which they will emanate;
- the ability to assess a change programme—proposed or already undertaken—and critique its appropriateness for the organization and change in question;
- the ability to specify the measures needed to effect a specific, desired change in a given organization;
- the ability to assess whether a change agent has the skills needed and is applying them well.

● REVIEW QUESTIONS

1. Some firms embrace change as a continuous and ongoing part of their culture. To what extent do the issues and problems described in this chapter apply to these types of organization?

2. Are there any stakeholders who should always have a veto over the strategy an organization follows?

3. Section 16.3.4 sets out a number of steps in the change management process, in a plausible order. However, sometimes that order may need to be altered. Under what circumstances might it be appropriate to:
   - dictate the details of a change before developing and communicating the change mission?
   - spread the change through the organization before it is fully entrenched in the initial implementation sites?
   - begin putting in new control systems before the change is fully developed?

4. 'Change which is imposed on an individual by his or her manager is always going to be resisted.' Discuss.

5. How can you judge whether someone has the right skills and personality to be a change agent?

● FURTHER READING

- Beer, M., Eisenstat, R., and Spector, B. (1990). 'Why change programs don't produce change'. *Harvard Business Review*, 68/6: 158–66. Kotter, J. (1995). 'Leading change: why transformation efforts fail'. *Harvard Business Review*, 73/2: 59–67. Two classic, much cited, and highly practical articles on the pitfalls that can befall major change programmes, both based on substantial empirical research in organizations that had attempted transformational change. Michael Beer and John Kotter are both accepted gurus of change management.

- Sirkin, H., Keenan, P., and Jackson, A. (2005). 'The hard side of change management'. *Harvard Business Review*, 83/10: 108–18. Written by a group of senior vice-presidents from the Boston Consulting Group, a leading strategy consultancy, this article describes a set of four measurable factors, derived from studies of over 200 projects, which the authors claim can predict with considerable accuracy whether a change programme is likely to succeed or fail.

- Lawrence, T., Dyck, B., Maitlis, S., and Mauws, M. (2006). 'The underlying structure of continuous change'. *MIT Sloan Management Review*, 47/4: 59–66. An interesting attempt to define a cycle in organizational change and the change agent roles that are appropriate to each stage in it. Although based upon the authors' own empirical research, it echoes earlier work by Dunphy and Stace (1993) and Huy (2001).

- Balogun, J. and Johnson, G. (2005). 'From intended strategies to unintended outcomes: the impact of change recipient sensemaking'. *Organization Studies*, 26/11: 1573–601. A more learned article which gives a deep and rounded picture of how even a well-planned change can encounter setbacks, as staff misinterpret the signals that their managers are sending out.

- Harris, L. and Ogbonna, E. (2002). 'The unintended consequences of culture interventions: A study of unexpected outcomes'. *British Journal of Management*, 13/1: 31–49. Contains some classic examples of how change interventions can backfire.

- Buchanan, D. and Boddy, D. (1992). *The Expertise of the Change Agent: Public Performance and Backstage Activity*. Hemel Hempstead: Prentice Hall. Definitive work on what change agents do.

- Balogun, J., Gleadle, P., Hope Hailey, V., and Willmott, H. (2005). 'Managing change across boundaries: boundary-shaking practices'. *British Journal of Management*, 16: 261–78. A more up-to-date scrutiny of how change agents operate, in particular those operating across several business units. Some interesting examples of how people below senior management level build or plug into power networks.

● REFERENCES

Abrahamson, E. (2000). 'Change without pain'. *Harvard Business Review*, 78/4: 75–9.

Abrahamson, E. (2004). 'Avoiding repetitive change syndrome'. *MIT Sloan Management Review*, 45/2: 93–5.

Amburgey, T., Kelly, D., and Barnett, W. (1993). 'Resetting the clock: the dynamics of organizational change and failure'. *Administrative Science Quarterly*, 38: 58–73.

Armenakis, A. and Fredenberger, W. (1995). 'Process strategies for turnaround change agents: crisis and non-crisis situations'. *Journal of Strategic Change*, 4/1: 19–31.

Armenakis, A., Fredenberger, W., Cherones, L., and Feild, H. (1995). 'Symbolic actions used by business turnaround change agents'. *Academy of Management Journal*, Special Edition (Best Papers Proceedings, p. 229).

Armenakis, A., Fredenberger, W., Giles, W., and Cherones, L. (1996). 'Symbolism use by business turnaround change agents'. *International Journal of Organizational Analysis*, 4/2: 123–34.

Ashforth, B. and Lee, R. (1990). 'Defensive behaviour in organisations: A preliminary model'. *Human Relations*, 43/7: 621–48.

Ashforth, B. and Mael, F. (1996). 'Organizational identity and strategy as a context for the individual'. In Baum, J. and Dutton, J. (eds), *Advances in Strategic Management*, vol. 13. Greenwich, CT: JAI Press, 17–72.

Bacharach, S., Bamberger, P., and Sonnenstuhl, W. (1996). 'The organizational transformation process: the micropolitics of dissonance reduction and the alignment of logics of action'. *Administrative Science Quarterly*, 41/3: 477–506.

Balogun, J. (2006). 'Managing change: steering a course between intended strategies and unanticipated outcomes'. *Long Range Planning*, 39/1: 29–49.

Balogun, J. and Johnson, G. (2004). 'Organizational restructuring and middle manager sensemaking'. *Academy of Management Journal*, 47/4: 523–49.

Balogun, J. and Johnson, G. (2005). 'From intended strategies to unintended outcomes: the impact of change recipient sensemaking'. *Organization Studies*, 26/11: 1573–601.

Balogun, J., Gleadle, P., Hope Hailey, V., and Willmott, H. (2005). 'Managing change across boundaries: boundary-shaking practices'. *British Journal of Management*, 16: 261–78.

Baron, J., Dobbin, F., and Jennings, P. (1986). 'War and peace: the evolution of modern personnel administration in U.S. industry'. *American Journal of Sociology*, 92/2: 350–83.

Beech, N. and Johnson, P. (2005). 'Discourses of disrupted identities in the practice of strategic change: the mayor, the street-fighter and the insider-out'. *Journal of Organizational Change Management*, 18/1: 31–47.

Beer, M. and Eisenstat, R. (2000). 'The silent killers of strategy implementation and learning'. *MIT Sloan Management Review*, 41/4: 29–40.

Beer, M. and Eisenstat, R. (2004). 'How to have an honest conversation about your business strategy'. *Harvard Business Review*, 82/2: 82–9.

Beer, M. and Nohria, N. (2000). 'Cracking the code of change'. *Harvard Business Review*, 78/3: 133–41.

Beer, M., Eisenstat, R., and Spector, B. (1990). 'Why change programs don't produce change'. *Harvard Business Review*, 68/6: 158–66.

Beer, M., Voelpel, S., Leibold, M., and Tekie, E. (2005). 'Strategic management as organizational learning: developing fit and alignment through a disciplined process'. *Long Range Planning*, 38/5: 445–65.

Bhaskar, R. (1978). *A Realist Theory Of Science*. Sussex: Harvester Press.

Birnbaum, R. (2000). 'The life cycle of academic management fads'. *The Journal of Higher Education*, 71/1: 1–16.

Brock, D. and Powell, M. (2005). 'Radical strategic change in the global professional network: the Big Five 1999–2001'. *Journal of Organizational Change Management*, 18/5: 451–68.

Bruch, H. and Sattelberger, T. (2001). 'Lufthansa's transformation marathon: process of liberating and focusing change energy'. *Human Resource Management*, 40/3: 249–59

Buchanan, D. and Boddy, D. (1992). *The Expertise of the Change Agent: Public Performance and Backstage Activity*. Hemel Hempstead: Prentice Hall.

Burnes, B. (2005). 'Complexity theories and organizational change'. *International Journal of Management Reviews*, 7/2: 73–90.

Caldwell, R. (2003). 'Models of change agency: a fourfold classification'. *British Journal of Management*, 14/2: 131–42.

Carnall, C. (2007). *Managing Change in Organizations*. 5th edn. Harlow: FT Prentice Hall.

Chatterjee, S., Lubatkin, M., Schweiger, D., and Weber, Y. (1992). 'Cultural differences and shareholder value in related mergers: linking equity and human capital'. *Strategic Management Journal*, 13/5: 319–34.

Chattopadhyay, P., Glick, W., and Huber, G. (2001). 'Organizational actions in response to threats and opportunities'. *Academy of Management Journal*, 44/5: 937–55.

Chattopadhyay, P., Hodgkinson, G., and Healey, M. (2006). 'Of maps and managers: toward a cognitive theory of strategic intervention'. *Academy of Management Proceedings*, B1–B6.

Chia, R. (1999). 'A "rhizomic" model of organizational change and transformation: perspective from a metaphysics of change'. *British Journal of Management*, 10: 209–27.

Chreim, S. (2006). 'Postscript to change: survivors' retrospective views of organizational changes'. *Personnel Review*, 35/3: 315–35.

Courpasson, D. (1990) 'Les nouvelles pratiques d'acces à l'emploi bancaire'. *Annales des Mines*, June: 42–8.

Dahl, R. (1957). 'The concept of power'. *Behavioral Science*, 2: 202–10.

David, K. and Singh, H. (1993). 'Acquisition regimes: Managing cultural risk and relative deprivation'. *Corporate Acquisitions: International Review of Strategic Management*, 4: 227–76.

Day, G. (1999). 'Creating a market-driven organization'. *Sloan Management Review*, 41/1: 11–22.

DiMaggio, P. and Powell, W. (1983). 'The iron cage revisited: institutional isomorphism and collective rationality in organizational fields'. *American Sociological Review*, 48: 147–60.

Dobbin, F., Sutton, J., Meyer, J., and Scott, R. (1993). 'Equal opportunity law and the construction of internal labor markets'. *American Journal of Sociology*, 99/2: 396–427.

Dunphy, D. and Stace, D. (1993). 'The strategic management of corporate change'. *Human Relations*, 46/8: 905–20.

Durand, R. and Calori, R. (2006). 'Sameness, otherness? Enriching organizational change theories with philosophical considerations on the same and the other'. *Academy of Management Review*, 31/1: 93–114.

Eden, C. and Ackermann, F. (1998). *Making Strategy: The Journey of Strategic Management*. London: Sage.

Espedal, B. (2006). 'Do organizational routines change as experience changes?' *Journal of Applied Behavioral Science*, 42/4: 468–90.

Fineman, S. (ed.) (1993). *Emotions in Organizations*. London: Sage.

Gabarro, J. (1987). *The Dynamics of Taking Charge*. Boston, MA: Harvard Business School Press.

Gabarro, J. (2007). 'When a new manager takes charge'. *Harvard Business Review*, 85/1: 104–17.

Ghoshal, S. and Bartlett, C. (1996). 'Rebuilding behavioral context: a blueprint for corporate renewal'. *Sloan Management Review*, 37/2: 23–36.

Giddens, A. (1984). *The Constitution of Society: Outline of the Theory of Structuration*. Cambridge: Polity Press.

Goodman, P. and Rousseau, D. (2004). 'Organizational change that produces results: The linkage approach'. *Academy of Management Executive*, 18/3: 7–19.

Gray, C. and Larson, E. (2006). *Project Management: The Managerial Process*. London: McGraw-Hill/Irwin.

Greenwood, R. and Hinings, C. (1996). 'Understanding radical organizational change: bringing together the old and the new institutionalism'. *Academy of Management Review*, 21/4: 1022–54.

Greenwood, R., Suddaby, R., and Hinings, C. (2002). 'Theorizing change: the role of professional associations in the transformation of institutionalised fields'. *Academy of Management Journal*, 45/1: 58–80.

Greve, H. (1998). 'Performance, aspirations and risky organisational change'. *Administrative Science Quarterly*, 43: 58–86.

Grugulis, I. and Wilkinson A. (2002). 'Managing culture at British Airways: hype, hope and reality'. *Long Range Planning*, 35/2: 179–94.

Hambrick, D. and D'Aveni, R. (1988). 'Large corporate failures as downward spirals'. *Administrative Science Quarterly*, 33/1: 1–23.

Hambrick, D. and D'Aveni, R. (1992). 'Top team deterioration as part of the downward spiral of large corporate bankruptcies'. *Management Science*, 38/10: 1445–66.

Hambrick, D. and Mason, P. (1984). 'Upper echelons: the organization as a reflection of its top managers'. *Academy of Management Review*, 9: 193–206.

Hannan, M. and Freeman, J. (1977). 'The population ecology of organizations'. *American Journal of Sociology*, 82/5: 929–64.

Hannan, M., Baron, J., Hsu, G., and Koçak, O. (2006). 'Organizational identities and the hazard of change'. *Industrial & Corporate Change*, 15/5: 755–84.

Hardy, C. (1996). 'Understanding power: bringing about strategic change'. *British Journal of Management*, Special Issue (March): S3–S16.

Harpaz, I. and Fu, X. (2002). 'The structure of the meaning of work: a relative stability amidst change'. *Human Relations*, 55/6: 639–67.

Harris, L. and Ogbonna, E. (2002). 'The unintended consequences of culture interventions: a study of unexpected outcomes'. *British Journal of Management*, 13/1: 31–49.

Heracleous, L. and Langham, B. (1996). 'Strategic change and organizational culture at Hay Management Consultants'. *Long Range Planning*, 29/4: 485–94.

Hodgkinson, G. and Wright, G. (2002). 'Confronting strategic inertia in a top management team: learning from failure'. *Organization Studies*, 23/6: 949–77.

Howell, J. and Higgins, C. (1990). 'Champions of change: identifying, understanding and supporting champions of technological innovations'. *Organizational Dynamics*, 19/1: 40–55.

Huy, Q. (2001). 'Time, temporal capability, and planned change'. *Academy of Management Review*, 26/4: 601–23.

Kahneman, D. and Lovallo, D. (1993). 'Timid choices and bold forecasts: a cognitive perspective on risk taking'. *Management Science*, 39/1: 17–31.

Kahneman, D. and Tversky, A. (1979). 'Prospect theory: an analysis of decision under risk'. *Econometrica*, 47: 263–91.

Kanter, R. (1983). *The Change Masters: Innovations for Productivity in the American Corporation*. New York, NY: Simon and Schuster.

Kraatz, M. and Zajac, E. (1996). 'Exploring the limits of the new institutionalism: the causes and consequences of illegitimate organizational change'. *American Sociological Review*, 61/5: 812–36.

Kotter, J. (1995). 'Leading change: why transformation efforts fail'. *Harvard Business Review*, 73/2: 59–67.

Lamarsh, J. and Potts, R. (2004). 'Sustain the change'. *Industrial Management*, 46/3: 14–19.

Lawrence, T., Dyck, B., Maitlis, S., and Mauws, M. (2006). 'The underlying structure of continuous change'. *MIT Sloan Management Review*, 47/4: 59–66.

Leana, C. and Barry, B. (2000). 'Stability and change as simultaneous experiences in organizational life'. *Academy of Management Review*, 25/4: 753–9.

Lee, K. and Pennings, J. (2002). 'Mimicry and the market: Adoption of a new organizational form'. *Academy of Management Journal*, 45/1: 144–62.

Leppitt, N. (2006). 'Challenging the code of change: Part 1. Praxis does not make perfect'. *Journal of Change Management*, 6/2: 121–42.

Lewin, K. (1952). *Field Theory in Social Science*. London: Tavistock/Routledge & Paul.

Liu, Y. and Perrewé, P. (2005). 'Another look at the role of emotion in the organizational change: A process model'. *Human Resource Management Review*, 15/4: 263–80.

McKinley, W. and Scherer, A. (2000). 'Some unanticipated consequences of organizational restructuring'. *Academy of Management Review*, 25/4: 735–52.

Maitlis, S. and Lawrence, T. (2003). 'Orchestral manoeuvres in the dark: Understanding failure in organizational strategizing'. *Journal of Management Studies*, 40/1: 109–39.

Manki, M. (2003). 'Power, subjectivity and strategies of resistance: The case of the Acme School'. *TAMARA: Journal of Critical Postmodern Organization Science*, 2/4: 52–75.

Meyer, C. and Stensaker, I. (2006). 'Developing capacity for change'. *Journal of Change Management*, 6/2: 217–31.

Mike, B. and Slocum, J. (2003). 'Slice of reality: changing culture at Pizza Hut and Yum! Brands, Inc.'. *Organizational Dynamics*, 32/4: 319–30.

Miles, R. and Snow, C. (1978). *Organisational Structure, Strategy, Process*. New York: McGraw-Hill.

Miller, D., Hartwick, J., and Le Breton-Miller, I. (2004). 'How to detect a management fad—and distinguish it from a classic'. *Business Horizons*, 47/4: 7–16.

Miller, S., Wilson, D., and Hickson, D. (2004). 'Beyond planning: strategies for successfully implementing strategic decisions'. *Long Range Planning*, 37/3: 201–18.

Nahavandi, A. and Malekzadeh, A. (1988). 'Acculturation in mergers and acquisitions'. *Academy of Management Review*, 13/1: 79–90.

Ogbonna, E. and Harris, L. (2002). 'Organizational culture: a ten year, two-phase study of change in the UK food retailing sector'. *Journal of Management Studies*, 39/5: 673–706.

Ogbonna, E. and Harris, L. (2003). 'Innovative organizational structures and performance: a case study of structural transformation to "groovy community centers"'. *Journal of Organizational Change Management*, 16/5: 512–33.

Oliver, C. (1992). 'The antecedents of deinstitutionalization'. *Organization Studies*, 13/4: 563–88.

Orlikowski, W. and Hofman, J. (1997). 'An improvisational model for change management: The case of groupware technologies'. *Sloan Management Review*, 38/2: 11–21.

Pascale, R., Millemann, M., and Gioja, L. (1997). 'Changing the way we change'. *Harvard Business Review*, 75/6: 126–39.

Paton, R. and McCalman, J. (2000). *Change Management: Guide to Effective Implementation*. 2nd edn. London: Sage Publishing.

Pettigrew, A. (1973). *The Politics of Organizational Decision-making*. London: Tavistock.

Pettigrew, A. (1977). 'Strategy formulation as a political process'. *International Studies of Management and Organisation*, Summer: 78–87.

Pettigrew, A. (1985). *The Awakening Giant*. Oxford: Blackwell.

Pettigrew, A. and Whipp, R. (1991). *Managing Change for Competitive Success*. Oxford: Blackwell.

Pfeffer, J. (1992). *Managing with Power: Politics and Influence in Organizations*. Boston, MA: Harvard Business School Press.

Pfeffer, J. and Salancik, G. (1978). *The External Control of Organisations: A Resource Dependency Perspective*. New York: Harper & Row.

Reay, T., Golden-Biddle, K., and Germann, K. (2006). 'Legitimizing a new role: Small wins and microprocesses of change'. *Academy of Management Journal*, 49/5: 977–98.

Reichers, A., Wanous, J., and Austin, J. (1997). 'Understanding and managing cynicism about organizational change'. *Academy of Management Executive*, 11/1: 48–59.

Rieple, A. (1998). 'An analysis of the structural factors which led to the enforced departure of a chief executive'. Unpublished doctoral thesis, Cranfield University, England.

Rivkin, J. and Siggelkow, N. (2006). 'Organizing to strategize in the face of interactions: Preventing premature lock-in'. *Long Range Planning*, 39/6: 591–614.

Rodrigues, S. (2006). 'The political dynamics of organizational culture in an institutionalized environment'. *Organization Studies*, 27/4: 537–57.

Romanelli, E. and Tushman, M. (1994) 'Organizational transformation as punctuated equilibrium: An empirical test'. *Academy of Management Journal*, 37/5: 1141–66.

Rouleau, L. (2005). 'Micro-practices of strategic sensemaking and sensegiving: How middle managers interpret and sell change every day'. *Journal of Management Studies*, 42/7: 1413–41.

Rosenzweig, P. (2007). 'The halo effect, and other managerial delusions'. *McKinsey Quarterly*, 1: 76–85.

Rumelt, R. (1995). 'Inertia and transformation'. In Montgomery, C. (ed.), *Resource-based and Evolutionary Theories of the Firm*. Cambridge, MA: Kluwer Academic Publishers, 101–32.

Schatzki, T. (2006). 'On organizations as they happen'. *Organization Studies*, 27/12: 1863–73.

Sirkin, H., Keenan, P., and Jackson, A. (2005). 'The hard side of change management'. *Harvard Business Review*, 83/10: 108–18.

Spector, B. (1989). 'From bogged down to fired up: inspiring organizational change'. *Sloan Management Review*, 30/4: 29–34.

Taplin, I. (2006). 'Strategic change and organizational restructuring: how managers negotiate change initiatives'. *Journal of International Management*, 12/3: 284–301.

Tsoukas, H. (2005). 'Afterword: why language matters in the analysis of organizational change'. *Journal of Organizational Change Management*, 18/1: 96–104.

Tushman, M. and O'Reilly, C. (1996). 'Ambidextrous organizations: managing evolutionary and revolutionary change'. *California Management Review*, 38/4: 8–30.

Tushman, M. and Romanelli, E. (1985). 'Organizational evolution: a metamorphosis model of convergence and reorientation'. In Cummings, L. and Staw, B. (eds), *Research in Organizational Behavior*. Greenwich, CT: JAI Press, 171–222.

Tushman, M., Newman, W., and Romanelli, E. (1986). 'Convergence and upheaval: Managing the unsteady pace of organizational evolution'. *California Management Review*, 29/1: 1–16.

del Val, M. and Fuentes, C. (2003). 'Resistance to change: a literature review and empirical study'. *Management Decision*, 41/2: 148–55.

Vince, R. and Broussine, M. (1996). 'Paradox, defense, and attachment: accessing and working with emotions and relations underlying organizational change'. *Organization Studies*, 17/1: 1–21.

Weick, K. (1995). *Sensemaking in Organizations*. Thousand Oaks, CA: Sage.

Whittington, R., McNulty, T., and Whipp, R. (1994). 'Market-driven change in professional services: problems and processes'. *Journal of Management Studies*, 31/6: 829–35.

Whittington, R., Molloy, E., Mayer, M., and Smith, A. (2006). 'Practices of strategising/organising: broadening strategy work and skills'. *Long Range Planning*, 39/6: 615–29.

End-of-chapter Case Study 16.1 Reinvigorating Renault

The trend in 2005 for Renault SA, the French car manufacturer, was certainly disturbing. Granted, it was still Europe's most popular car brand, and the flagship Mégane range, which accounted for 60 per cent of its operating profit, remained popular. The low-cost Logan saloon, manufactured in Romania by its Dacia subsidiary, had exceeded expectations in generating demand, not only in developing countries but also in some developed ones. However, by late 2005, it had become clear that the company was gradually losing share in the western European markets that accounted for nearly three-quarters of its sales. Gross margins, a key indicator of profitability in automobile manufacturing, were also slipping (see Table 16.11 for a summary of Renault's financial position in 2005).

Carlos Ghosn

There was little dispute that in Carlos Ghosn, the newly appointed president/CEO, Renault had the man to tackle such issues. Born in Brazil to Lebanese parents, educated in Beirut and later, as an engineer, at two of France's Grandes Ecoles, Ghosn had built a formidable track record in addressing tough situations. As chairman and CEO of Michelin North America, he had presided over the integration of newly acquired rival Uniroyal Goodrich. He joined Renault in October 1996 as executive vice-president in charge of purchasing, manufacturing, and R&D. The tough measures he took then, involving a number of plant closures, laid the foundations for Renault's prosperity in the 1990s, giving the firm a competitive cost base and earning him the nickname 'le cost killer'.[79]

The achievements that raised him to near-mythical status in the automobile industry came after he was dispatched in 1999 to run Nissan, in which Renault had taken a 36.8 per cent stake. In order to save that company from bankruptcy, Ghosn put in place a change programme that broke with several traditions cherished both by Nissan and Japanese industry in general. He dissolved linkages with long-standing suppliers, and cross-shareholdings with other firms. He closed down plants, made several thousand workers redundant, and changed the basis of promotion from seniority to performance. He announced a set of demanding

financial targets and declared he would resign if they were not met.[80]

He took some bold gambles in pursuit of these targets, building a brand new plant in a part of the US with no established supplier network or automaking tradition. Nearly 6,000 people with no car manufacturing experience were recruited to make four completely new models of pickup, minivans, and SUV—vehicles that commanded high margins in north America. When quality problems materialized with vehicles from the plant, Ghosn diverted over 200 American and Japanese engineers from their normal jobs to troubleshoot the source of the problems.[81]

Nissan's workers, dispirited after many years of poor profitability, responded strongly to these new challenges. They surpassed not only Ghosn's original targets but the successively more demanding ones that he announced as each previous set of goals was exceeded. Nissan's return to profitability was so pronounced that by 2005 some two-thirds of Renault's net income came from its share of the Japanese auto-maker's profits. His status was such that in Japan a comic book character was modelled on him, while in the UK he received an honorary knighthood. And in May 2005, he was promoted to the post of Président Directeur Général (PDG) at Renault, while retaining his CEO role at Nissan. (A French PDG is broadly the equivalent of a CEO, but has greater power to act autonomously.)

Taking over at Renault

While Renault and Nissan were strongly linked through cross-shareholdings, an alliance management structure and a number of collaborative initiatives in areas such as purchasing, they remained legally and culturally separate. Ghosn was to divide his time more or less equally between France and Japan, while setting aside one-fifth of it for the US and other markets. That time needed to include personal visits to dealers, suppliers and manufacturing facilities, to which Ghosn attached great importance; he also served on the boards of Sony, IBM, and Alcoa.

Ghosn was the first PDG not to have been nominated by the French government, which had held a controlling shareholding ➔

→ **Table 16.11** Renault SA financial performance 2002–2005

	Units	2002	2003	2004	2005
Vehicle sales					
Worldwide volume sales (Group)	M units	2.40	2.39	2.49	2.53
% growth year-on-year		(0.3)%	(0.7)%	4.3%	1.8%
of which passenger cars	M units	2.06	2.06	2.11	2.14
Western Europe	M units	1.87	1.81	1.81	1.74
Market Share in Western Europe		11.3%	11.1%	10.8%	10.4%
Passenger cars		10.7%	10.6%	10.3%	9.8%
Selected P&L items					
Group revenues	€ billion	36.3	37.5	40.3	41.3
% growth year-on-year		0.0%	3.3%	7.4%	2.6%
Automobile division	€ billion	34.5	35.5	38.4	39.5
Cost of sales	€ billion	30.9	33.3	31.3	30.5
Selling, General & Admin costs	€ billion	4.5	4.8	4.5	4.4
Group operating margin	€ billion	1.5	1.4	2.1	1.3
% of revenues		4.1%	3.7%	5.2%	3.2%
Automobile division	€ billion	1.2	1.0	1.6	0.9
% of revenues		3.5%	2.9%	4.3%	2.2%
EBITDA	€ billion	3.2	3.4	4.6	4.2
% of revenues		8.7%	8.9%	11.5%	10.2%
Operating income (EBIT)	€ billion	1.2	1.2	1.9	1.5
% of revenues		3.3%	3.3%	4.6%	3.7%
Automobile EBIT	€ billion	0.9	0.9	1.4	1.1
% of revenues		2.7%	2.4%	3.7%	2.7%
Group share of Nissan/Volvo net income	€ billion	1.3	1.9	1.9	2.6
Group net income	€ billion	2.0	2.5	2.8	3.4
Selected balance sheet items					
Inventories	€ billion	4.8	4.9	5.1	5.9
Total Assets (= total liabilities)	€ billion	53.2	58.3	61.8	68.4
Shareholder's equity	€ billion	11.8	13.6	15.9	19.7
Net automobile financial indebtedness	€ billion	2.5	1.7	1.6	2.3
Cash Flow (automobile)	€ billion	3.2	3.2	4.6	4.1
Capital expenditure and R&D (Auto)					
R&D cash spent	€ billion	1.8	1.7	2.0	2.3
% of auto revenues		5.1%	4.9%	5.1%	5.7%
Capital expenditure net of disposals	€ billion	3.0	2.5	3.2	2.9
% of auto revenues (1)		8.6%	7.1%	7.9%	7.0%
Return on Equity		19.8%	22.3%	20.7%	21.8%
Financial leverage (Net auto debt/Equity)		21.1%	12.9%	9.9%	11.5%
Workforce at year-end	thousand	132.4	125.1	124.3	126.6
Market capitalization at year-end	€ billion	13.3	15.7	18.0	19.6

Source
<http://financial-analyst.renault.com>, accessed 14 March 2007

in Renault until 2002. Although it was normal for the government to take an active interest in industrial policy, and although it still held 15 per cent of the company's shares, Ghosn made it clear in interviews that he would not suffer interference from that, or any other quarter.[82]

He took other steps that some observers interpreted as distancing himself from his predecessor, Louis Schweitzer. The Director of Information Services, Jean-Pierre Corniou, left his post in June 2006. The Executive Committee member who replaced him, Christian Mardrus, would report to Jean-Louis Ricaud, Director of Quality and Engineering, rather than Thierry Moulonguet, Director of Finance. Both Moulonguet and Corniou were, like Schweitzer, graduates of France's elite Ecole Nationale d'Administration, whose graduates fill most of the top slots in politics and government, and many in French business. Mardrus and Ricaud, by contrast, came, like Ghosn, from an engineering background. →

→ By February 2006, one observer was remarking that Schweitzer was no longer mentioned by name in Ghosn's public utterances.[83]

One of Ghosn's first acts in July 2005 was to set up seven cross-functional task forces with titles such as 'Business Development', 'Mastering Product Complexity', and 'Service Effectiveness'. Four further task forces followed early in 2006. Each comprised around ten staff members, a leader drawn from the six-member Executive Committee that was Renault's highest decision-making body, and a facilitator nominated by Ghosn in person. Each had a brief to identify risks, opportunities, and untapped areas of potential. Similar teams had successfully identified €3bn of efficiency gains for Renault in the late 1990s.[84]

Commitment 2009

When Ghosn took the stage on 9 February 2006 for a major presentation of his plans for the future, there were fears in France that, given his track record as a cost-trimmer, he might be about to announce a further round of cuts and closures. With typical frankness, Ghosn did not rule restructuring out entirely, but said that, given the firm's genuine strengths, it would only be needed if his planned growth offensive failed.

He started with his diagnosis of the firm's situation, which he described as 'precise, methodical, and the outcome of a collective process'. Renault was not in crisis, but remained fragile, he said. The problem was not one of costs: the product range was too narrow and the brand image had weakened in the last few years. He then unveiled his programme to address these issues; entitled 'Renault Commitment 2009', it focused on three areas:[85]

- Quality: The company saw this as a key customer requirement. The most specific target was that Renault's top-of-the range Laguna would figure in the top three in its segment for product and service quality. The new version of the Laguna, due to be launched in 2007, was positioned against redoubtable competitors: the BMW 3 Series, Mercedes C Class, Audi A4, and Toyota Avensis. In meeting this objective, Renault aimed to symbolize a broader commitment to quality that would be reproduced across the range.

- Profitability: Ghosn set Renault an objective for 2009 of nearly doubling its operating profit margin from its 2005 figure of 3.2 per cent of sales to 6 per cent, a level it had not attained since 1999. It would thereby become the most profitable volume producer of cars in Europe. It recognized that margins would drop in the short term as the change programme took effect, but set intermediate milestones for them to be no lower than 2.5 per cent in 2006 and 3 per cent in 2007.

- Growth: The firm was to grow sales at an unprecedentedly high rate, with 2009 sales being 0.8 million units above the 2005 level of 2.54 million. Two subsidiary targets underpinned that growth figure. No fewer than 26 models were to be launched by 2009, a 50 per cent increase on the firm's previous rate of new product introduction. Half of these would be upgrades of existing offerings, while others would be entirely new, expanding the range into areas such as sports cars, pickups, and 4x4 vehicles. And sales in markets outside Europe were to grow by 80 per cent and to constitute 37 per cent of total sales, as against 27 per cent in 2005.

It was typical of Ghosn to express the strategy in this precise fashion, with quantified objectives and milestones. But buried within these targets were a number of hidden challenges. It had proved extremely difficult for any car producer to raise sales volumes without cutting prices, and hence margins. Achieving the growth and profitability targets together would therefore be doubly difficult, particularly as so much of the sales growth was likely to come from low-cost vehicles, such as the Logan, sold in developing markets. Unlike Nissan, Renault had no presence in the USA, the world's most profitable car market, though it had operations in Brazil and South Korea.

This reinforced the importance of the quality and product development targets. Renault's strengths were in producing stylish vehicles at low and medium prices. In order for the strategy to be achieved, it would need to produce distinctive vehicles that commanded a price premium, and to improve its position at the top end of the market, with products such as the Laguna. Commitment 2009 called for sales of high-end cars to double from the 2005 level.

'Le cost killer' had not, however, completely disappeared from view. The plan contained further targets for a 9 per cent cut in logistics costs—notwithstanding increases in energy prices—a fall in overheads from 5.1 per cent to 4 per cent of sales, an 8 per cent reduction in distribution costs and a 14 per cent reduction in purchasing costs. The company was to change its approach to fixed investment in ways that would allow it to do twice as much with the same money. This would involve focusing expenditure upon its core skills, and opening up other areas to potential partners. Intriguingly, these targets incorporated less than a third of the €1bn of gains identified by the cross-functional teams.

Stakeholder reactions

Reactions to the proposals were broadly supportive. The unions, powerful in Renault, were reportedly relieved. The PDG of Valéo, France's largest manufacturer of auto components, expressed his firm's readiness to help Renault fulfil its plans to cut purchasing costs; Renault accounted for 15–20 per cent of Valéo's €10bn turnover. →

→ In December 2006, Renault published the results of an employee survey, administered by an independent American research institute, on the quality and commitment of the firm's management. Over 100,000 employees, 87 per cent of the total, completed the survey. Renault was rated highly by its staff for employee commitment, clarity of objectives and the way it adhered to its overall strategy. Staff, on the other hand, were less satisfied than in the previous year's survey with the extent of inter-departmental collaboration, with the way their personal performance was evaluated, and with the firm's image in relation to its competitors.[86]

Setbacks

In a change programme of this magnitude, setbacks were to be expected. One arose in Renault's IT function, which was implementing a plan to save €100m annually by outsourcing much IT provision and support and by rationalizing numbers of IT subcontractors from over 300 to just three. By mid-2006 one specialist IT publication was reporting that the plan, which had been set up under Schweitzer but initiated under Ghosn's leadership, was not getting the desired results in the planned time frames. Service levels in areas such as user support helplines—which had been offshored to Tunisia by the new contractor—were alleged to have fallen, while IT costs had actually risen to 1.9 per cent of turnover, against a target of 1.5 per cent. It was proving difficult to trim the subcontractor base as quickly as planned, and those that had left had taken with them tacit knowledge, accumulated in some cases over 10–15 years with Renault, that was proving difficult to replace.[87]

A phenomenon that attracted greater public attention, however, was an unprecedented number of suicides amongst the 12,000 staff at its Technocentre product design complex. The centre, located on a carefully landscaped site in pleasant countryside near Versailles, to the west of Paris, boasts state-of-the-art facilities alongside on-site restaurants and a bank. The engineers and technicians employed there were highly qualified and motivated. However, between October 2006 and February 2007, three had committed suicide, the first in a highly visible fashion that traumatized those unfortunate enough to witness it. After the second body was discovered—ironically, the day after a seminar on managing stress at work—a cortege of several hundred employees observed a minute's silence beside the lake where it had been found.[88]

The suicide rate at the Technocentre was not, statistically, abnormal for a population of 12,000 people. However, questions were naturally asked as to whether working conditions at the centre were becoming intolerable; indeed, a local prosecutor had opened a criminal investigation to ascertain whether the company was culpable in any of the deaths. Representatives of the CGT and the SUD, two of Renault's four unions, were forthright in their insistence that working conditions had deteriorated since Ghosn's arrival. The company's use of targets was said to have fractured working relationships and increased stress. Cases were cited of people coming out of individual meetings in tears, having problems sleeping, and taking tranquillizers. Other unions, however, were less ready to blame the firm, and responses to the feedback questionnaire indicated that most staff backed the strategy.[89]

A number of factors might plausibly have contributed to raised stress levels at the Technocentre. An expansion of engineer numbers, predating Ghosn's arrival, was said to have led to increased competition for a limited number of promotion opportunities, which had weighed heavily on the most experienced engineers. The ambitious product development targets within Renault Commitment 2009 might also have been a factor, with some people suggesting it had led to a blurring of lines of responsibility and to people being bounced from department to department.[90] An announcement that Renault would open a new product development centre in Romania, its first outside France, might have led to fears regarding job security, though the company had indicated that the work to be done there, specifically on the Logan, was additional to that undertaken elsewhere, and not a replacement for it. The CGT had nonetheless denounced the move.[91]

On 1 March 2007, Carlos Ghosn, at an internal seminar for 2,500 engineers, paid tribute to the colleagues who had died. He said that the situation needed to be grasped with both humility and firmness, and that a period of serious and deep reflection was needed—but that it should not go on forever. He announced that he had asked Jean-Louis Ricaud and the director of the Technocentre to report back to him by 15 March on the concrete measures to be taken to improve the situation. The nomination of an Executive Committee member to review the Technocentre was seen by observers as significant; interestingly, Ricaud was preferred to Michel de Virville, the HR director who was also in charge of the cost reduction aspects of Commitment 2009.[92]

At an executive meeting the previous day, Ghosn had given another indication of his feelings on the matter. 'Renault has no right to fail—but an individual employee has', he said, going on to emphasize the crucial role that individual men and women played in the success of the enterprise.

The 2006 results[93]

In February 2007 the results for the first year of Renault Commitment 2009 were unveiled. As predicted, 2006 had turned out to be a difficult year for the company. Worldwide sales volumes had fallen 4 per cent, and revenues by 0.8 per cent, though these statistics concealed considerable regional variations. Sales in Latin America, eastern Europe, and North Africa had risen by nearly 13 per cent, with demand for the Logan model in particular →

→ increasing by 70 per cent during the year. However, sales in the French home market declined by 5 per cent and in the rest of western Europe by 11 per cent. In Asia and Africa (excluding North Africa), there was a 3 per cent fall in sales volume.

The decline in volumes was one reason why operating profit margins had also fallen to 2.6 per cent, below the 3 per cent recorded in 2005 but slightly ahead of the 2006 target set a year previously. Here again there were bright spots, with progress being made on containing logistics, purchasing, overheads, and investment costs. However, manufacturing costs had risen, in part because of increased raw material costs, as had distribution costs. Savings of €200m were attributed to the work of the cross-functional teams.

The company was pleased with a 30 per cent improvement in the costs of fulfilling customer warranties which, it believed, showed that Renault was making advances in the key area of product and service quality. And it showed figures that indicated that development of the Laguna and other new products was firmly on track.

Case study questions

1. Analyse the main stakeholders in relation to the change programme at Renault. Which are the salient stakeholders, what level of interest are they likely to have and to what extent are they likely to oppose or support the proposed changes. What are the likely coalitions for and against the change?

2. Appraise Ghosn's handling of the change programme at Renault. Were the setbacks predictable? What do you suggest he should have done differently, and why?

3. To what extent is Ghosn the ideal change agent for Renault in 2005?

● NOTES

1 The other factor is the degree of priority the proposal is given by management (Miller, Wilson, and Hickson, 2004).

2 *Economist* (2000). 'An inside job'. 15 July: 87. See also Pascale et al. (1997).

3 This interplay between stability and change is explored in greater depth by Chia (1999); Leana and Barry (2000); Harpaz and Fu (2002); and Durand and Calori (2006).

4 The sociological theory on which this paragraph is based was set out by Roy Bhaskar (1978) and Anthony Giddens (1984). We have used the term 'routine' to be consistent with other chapters and to avoid confusion—sociologists prefer to call them 'structures'. For a further discussion of the relationship between the organization's unfolding present and its past, see Schatzki (2006). Espedal (2006) and Reay et al. (2006) show how actors bring about changes in routines.

5 Romanelli and Tushman (1994).

6 This classification was developed and empirically tested by Dunphy and Stace (1993). It builds on earlier work by Tushman et al. (1986).

7 <http://www.britishairways.com/travel/bagunacc/public/en_gb>, accessed 4 July 2007; Butler, S. (2007). 'Travel advice from the expert: airlines are increasing their charges for checked baggage—and damaging or losing more of it'. *Sunday Telegraph*, 25 March: 15.

8 See Amburgey et al. (1993) for a famous study of this effect in the Finnish newspaper industry, and Hannan et al. (2006) for a review of the literature and further empirical evidence.

9 Attwood, K. (2006). 'Talk Talk overwhelmed with broadband orders'. *Press Association National Newswire*, 6 June; Bachelor, L. (2006a). 'Cash: In brief: Talk Talk struggles to fulfil "free" broadband promise'. *The Observer*, 11 June: 16; Durman, P. (2006). 'Broadband "nightmare" for Talk Talk'. *Sunday Times*, Business, 23 July: 3; Bain, S. (2006). 'Navigate your way through the broad web of confusion'. *The Herald*, 15 August: 6; Francis, C. (2006). 'Fury over Talk Talk's broken promises'. *The Sunday Times*, Money, 10 September: 6; Coney, J. (2006a). 'Frustration as TalkTalk fails the customer service test'. *Daily Mail*, 13 September: 49; Greek, D. (2006). 'TalkTalk admits service strife'. *Computeractive*, 12 October: 226; Bachelor, L. (2006b). 'Cash: calling time on the Talk Talk fiasco: why are we waiting?' *The Observer*, 17 December: 13; Francis, C. (2006b). 'TalkTalk is top villain'. *The Sunday Times*, Business & Money, 24 December: 13.

10 Whittington et al. (1994) give examples of these linkages for professional services. Goodman and Rousseau (2004) describe a method for analysing them.

11 Dunphy and Stace (1993) summarize the debate regarding the relative merits of revolutionary and evolutionary change.

12 See Chreim (2006) for some empirical evidence on this.

13 Source: Heracleous and Langham (1996).

14 Chattopadhyay et al. (2001); Chattopadhyay et al. (2006).

15 The underlying economics and psychology of prospect theory are well summarized in Kahneman and Tversky (1979) and Kahneman and Lovallo (1993). Greve (1998) has provided empirical evidence that this effect translates from the individual to the organizational level.

16 Rushe, D. (2002). 'They're smart, they're rich, they're . . . geeks—New Microsoft'. *Sunday Times*, Business focus, 23 June; Guth, R. (2003). 'Cultural evolution'. *Wall Street Journal*, 10 July: B1.

17 Wigfield, M. (2001). 'A primer on the Microsoft antitrust case settlement'. *Dow Jones Newswires*, 15 November; Warsh, D. (2001). 'Fighting back'. *Boston Globe*, 6 November: D1; Krim, J. (2004). 'Microsoft settlement upheld: appeal for tougher sanctions rejected'. *Washington Post*, 1 July: E01; Clark, D. and Greenberger, R. (2004). 'Microsoft wins approval of pact in antitrust case'. *Wall Street Journal*, 1 July: A3.

18 Rushe (2002) op. cit.; Guth (2003) op. cit.; Schendler, B. (2004). 'Ballmer unbound'. *Fortune*, 26 January: 116.

19 See Baron et al. (1986) and Dobbin et al. (1993). For a more recent example of the effect of institutions on strategic change, see Rodrigues (2006).

20 This effect is discussed by Greenwood and Hinings (1996). Greenwood et al. (2002) provide a specific example of the power of industry associations in the accountancy field. See also Brock and Powell (2005).

21 This strange-looking result, noted by Chattopadhyay et al. (2001), is in fact consistent with the predictions of prospect theory (see n. 15).

22 See Greenwood and Hinings (1996) and Maitlis and Lawrence (2003).

23 A number of writers, for example Miles and Snow (1978), have found contingent links between organizations' strategies and the characteristics of their dominant managerial echelons. Hambrick and Mason (1984) go further, suggesting that organizations are largely a reflection of their top managers.

24 Gabarro (1987, 2007) provides an interesting summary of some of these issues.

25 See Schendler (2004) op. cit.

26 For a famous example of exercise of power through the manipulation of information, see Pettigrew (1973).

27 See, for example, Bar-Hillel, M. (2007). 'People power defeats Tesco'. *Evening Standard*, 21 February: 1; Hall, J. (2006). '"Turkey" Tesco told to get stuffed by Torrington'. *The Sunday Telegraph*, 17 December: 3; Lundy, I. (2007). '"Tesco town" opponents to petition Tony Blair'. *Evening Times*, 14 March: 21.

28 Urquhart, F. (1995). 'Shell wins go-ahead to dump platform'. *The Scotsman*, 17 February: 3.

29 Kearney, J. and McKie, R. (1995). 'Motorists shun Shell over sinking of rig'. *Observer*, 18 June: 1; *Independent on Sunday* (1995). 'They lose even when they win'. 18 June: 26; Nacheman, A. (1995). 'Greenpeace savours environmental victory against multinational giant Shell'. Agence France-Presse, 21 June.

30 Nacheman (1995) op. cit.; Boulton, L. and Lascelles, D. (1995). 'Shell confronts disaster at sea'. *Financial Times*, 21 June: 10; *Economist* (1995). 'Oil platforms: Greenpeace's irrational victory'. 24 June.

31 *Independent on Sunday* (1995) op. cit.; *Economist* (1995) op. cit.; Schoon, N. (1995). 'Scientist backs sea dumping'. *The Independent*, 19 July: 3.

32 Bacarach et al. (1996) is an interesting study of how coalitions can form and dissolve during a long process of organizational change.

33 Sources: Clark, A. and Inman, P. (2007). 'Private equity plays the green card in US'. *Guardian*, 26 February: 25; Gunther, M. (2007). 'A Texas coal rush'. *Fortune*, 19 February: 47–50; *Project Finance* (2007). 'New TXU, new coal plans'. 1 March; *Energy Trader* (2007). 'Canceling plans for new TXU coal-fired plants will add to Texas' demand for gas: consultant'. 6 March: 1; Smith, R. (2007). 'TXU sheds coal plan, charts nuclear path'. *Wall Street Journal*, 10 April: A2. Steffy, L. (2007). 'System encourages coal-fired power plants'. *Houston Chronicle*, 4 March. *Dow Jones International News* (2007). 'TXU bidders offer $30m to end opposition to coal-fired plants'. 8 June.

34 This model comes from Carnall (2007: 241).

35 Writers who have examined emotions and change include Weick (1995); Armenakis et al. (1995, 1996); Armenakis and Fredenberger (1995); Vince and Broussine (1996); Fineman (1993); and Liu and Perrewé (2005). A lot of the writing on the after-effects of mergers is also interesting in terms of looking at the emotions of uncertainty; see, for example, Chatterjee et al. (1992), Nahavandi and Malekzadeh (1988), and David and Singh (1993).

36 See, for example, Gabarro (1987, 2007), Pfeffer (1992), and Rieple (1998). For more detail on the underlying theory see Ashforth and Lee (1990), and Ashforth and Mael (1996).

37 See Weick (1995).

38 Management fads are not necessarily worthless, but are often adopted by organizations that lack the capacity or the commitment to stick with them once the initial difficulties become clear. Recent examples include benchmarking, total quality management, business process reengineering, the balanced scorecard, and customer relations management. For reviews, see Birnbaum (2000) and Miller, Hartwick, and le Breton-Miller (2004). Change fatigue is discussed by Abrahamson (2000, 2004), and cynicism by Reichers et al. (1997).

39 For a more detailed review of the different reasons for resistance to change, see del Val and Fuentes (2003).

40 This very famous technique was pioneered by Kurt Lewin (1952).

41 This framework comes from Paton and McCalman (2000).

42 This three-fold classification of power was set out by Cynthia Hardy (1996). See also Balogun et al. (2005).

43 Beer et al. (1990) and, in particular, Miller, Wilson, and Hickson (2004).

44 Source: Heracleous and Langham (1996).

45 Papers based upon observations of change in practice include: Beer and Eisenstat (2000, 2004); Beer et al. (1990); Beer and Nohria (2000); Beer et al. (2005); Day (1999); Ghoshal and Bartlett (1996); Kotter (1995); Lawrence et al. (2006), Miller, Wilson, and Hickson (2004); Orlikowski and Hofman (1997); Pascale et al. (1997); Sirkin et al. (2005); and Spector (1989). See also Leppitt (2006), and Meyer and Stensaker (2006) for useful syntheses.

46 See Spector (1989); Hardy (1996); Lawrence et al. (2006); and Pascale et al. (1997).

47 Day (1999), Beer and Eisenstat (2004), and Beer at al. (2005) give examples of how these processes can succeed, and Hodgkinson and Wright (2002) an example of how things can go wrong.

48 *Economist* (2000) op. cit; Beer and Eisenstat (2004). The appropriate use of consultants is discussed by Beer and Nohria (2000).

49 See, for example, Beer and Eisenstat (2000), Day (1999), and Sirkin et al. (2005), who also place great importance on the commitment of other affected stakeholders. Kotter (1995) points out the importance of 'walking the talk'. The example is from Harris and Ogbonna (2002).

50 The empirical basis for this section comes from Beer et al. (1990), Beer and Eisenstat (2000), Day (1999), and in particular Kotter (1995). Sirkin et al. (2005) also emphasize the importance of consistent top management communication of the purpose of the change, while Harris and Ogbonna (2002) have some examples of what happens if different departments are able to interpret the vision in different ways.

51 This example comes from Whittington et al. (2006).

52 The research of Lawrence et al. (2006) points to two distinct phases. First, practices are imposed from above, then routines are developed to make them work.

53 The first example comes from Harris and Ogbonna (2002), while the counter-example is from Taplin (2006).

54 Kotter (1995).

55 Sirkin et al. (2005) emphasize the importance of containing the extra effort, and Pascale et al. (1997) of giving an appropriate 'quid pro quo'.

56 See Courpasson (1990).

57 This sequence of change was suggested by Ghoshal and Bartlett (1996) on the basis of their research in companies. The results of simulations undertaken by Rivkin and Siggelkow (2006) support their observations.

58 Sirkin et al. (2005).

59 Sirkin et al. (2005). Whittington et al. (2006) give an interesting example (in Exhibit 2) of an able and successful change project manager.

60 Beer et al. (1990), Kotter (1995).

61 These were identified by Harris and Ogbonna (2002); Lamarsh and Potts (2004) have some interesting examples.

62 Balogun (2006), Balogun and Johnson (2005), Harris and Ogbonna (2002), and Orlikowski and Hoffman (1997) all describe how unintended practices and outcomes, both beneficial and catastrophic, can arise from planned change efforts.

63 Beer and Eisenstat (2000).

64 If you are interested in learning more about this, then articles by Hambrick and D'Aveni (1988, 1992) make interesting reading.

65 Lawrence et al. (2006) emphasize the importance of strategic intuition. For evidence of the importance of learning how to change, see *Economist* (2000) op. cit. and Pascale et al. (1997).

66 See Harris and Ogbonna (2002), who coined the term 'behavioural compliance', and Ogbonna and Harris (2002) for some examples.

67 Based on Tushman and O'Reilly (1996); Grugulis and Wilkinson (2002); Pike, A. (1984). 'Putting on a human face'. *Financial Times*, 25 May: 12; Parkes, C. (1985). 'How BA is creating its "lasting asset"'. *Financial Times*, 10 May: 16; Marshall, C. (1988). 'Two wings and a prayer: British Airways: inside story'. *The Times*, 17 September; Moseley, R. (1986). 'British Airways scores big profit turnaround'. *Toronto Star*, 12 January: A2.

68 Marshall, C. (1988). op. cit.

69 Bolger, A. (1997). 'BA staff sickness delays return to normal service'. *Financial Times*, 7 August: 8.

70 Grugulis and Wilkinson (2002).

71 Warner, J. (2007). 'British Airways averts strike threat'. *The Independent*, 30 January: 37; Evans, G. (2007). 'Strike threat likely to cost BA £80 million'. *Press Association National Newswire*, 2 February; Ashworth, J. (2007). 'BA faces new strike threat over £2bn pension hole'. *The Business*, 3 February.

72 Lorenz, C. (1987). 'The design connection in corporate renewal'. *Financial Times*, 26 March; *Financial Times* (1988). 'The struggle for quality'. 8 August: 10; *Marketing Week* (1985). 'Cover story on customer service in the UK'. 10 May: 32.

73 These categories come from Caldwell (2003) whose paper also contains an excellent review of the literature on change agents.

74 Bruch and Sattelberger (2001).

75 Howell and Higgins (1990).

76 Pettigrew and Whipp (1991) and Dunphy and Stace (1993) found that effective change leadership required leadership approaches that varied over time and according to the organizational context. The approach in this section follows Huy (2001). Lawrence et al. (2006) come to similar conclusions from their empirical research, but suggest that change invariably follows the sequence set out in the following bullet points.

77 This list comes from Buchanan and Boddy (1992). Balogun et al. (2005) also emphasize the importance of political awareness in a change agent. See Howell and Higgins (1990) for a more general set of characteristics.

78 This company name is a pseudonym. The data come from Rieple (1998).

79 Faiola, A. (2006). '"Cost killer" whose methods may not translate'. *Washington Post*, 3 August: D01.

80 Taylor III, A. (2005). 'Double duty'. *Fortune*, 7 March; Taylor III, A. (2006). 'The world according to Ghosn'. *Fortune*, 30 November.

81 Taylor III, A. (2005) op. cit.

82 Débouté, A. (2006). 'Le grand oral maîtrisé du président de Renault'. *Stratégies*, 16 February.

83 Débouté, A. (2006) op. cit. Biseul, X. and Discazeaux, O. (2006). 'Externalisation: des ratés chez Renault'. *01 Informatique*, 5 May; <http://www.lemondeinformatique.fr/actualites/lire-christian-mardrus-remplace-jean-pierre-corniou-a-la-dsi-de-renault-19956.html>, accessed 15 March 2007.

84 *Les Echos* (2006). 'Renault met le cap sur la transversalité'. 5 May: 11.

85 <http://www.renault.com/renault_com/en/main/10_GROUPE_RENAULT/30_Strategie/05_Renault_contrat_2009/Engagements/index.aspx>, accessed 15 March 2007. Newspaper articles often refer to this as Contract 2009, which is the literal translation of its French title. 'Renault

Commitment 2009' is the company's own preferred English nomenclature. Supplementary detail from Bembaron, E. (2006). 'Carlos Ghosn redessine Renault pour en faire le constructeur européen le plus rentable'. *Le Figaro*, 10 February; Fainsilber, D. (2006). 'Carlos Ghosn impose des objectifs réalistes à Renault pour 2009'. *Les Echos*, 10 February: 17; *Automobile & Composants* (2006). 'Renault contrat 2009: Un plan tout en nuances'. 23 February: 2.

86 Fainsilber, D. (2006). 'Renault: les salariés jugent le management'. *Les Echos*, 19 December: 25.

87 Biseul and Discazeaux (2006) op. cit.

88 Lauer, S. (2007a). 'Le deuil au coeur de Renault'. *Le Monde*, 2 February: 3; Willsher, K. (2007). 'Heading for a breakdown: French workers used to be envied, but after suicides at car-maker Renault, unions are blaming US-style methods for shattering the harmony'. *Guardian*, Work, 10 March: 1.

89 Lauer (2007a) op. cit. Terrier, N. (2007). 'Colère après les suicides au Technocentre Renault'. *Le Parisen*. 30 January: 1.

90 Lauer (2007a) op. cit. Terrier (2007) op. cit.

91 Agence France-Presse (2006). 'Renault crée une filiale en Roumanie, la CGT dénonce une "délocalisation"'. 5 April.

92 Lauer, S. (2007b). 'M. Ghosn monte en première ligne après la série de suicides chez Renault'. *Le Monde*, 3 March: 14.

93 Renault press release <http://13322%2013322_Resfi_final_presse_statique_web_0702_GB_tcm1120-561658>, downloaded 14 March 2007.

CHAPTER SEVENTEEN

Making Strategy Happen

LEARNING OUTCOMES

After reading this chapter you will be able to:

→ Explain the importance of leadership to an organization, describe the different styles of leadership that exist, and discuss their appropriateness to different types of situation

→ Describe the attributes of successful leaders and assess the skills of a particular leader

→ Discuss the manner in which different forms of control mechanism interact to influence strategic performance

→ Describe the key elements of value-based management and the balanced scorecard

→ Describe the main components of a project control system and explain when and why it is appropriate to use such a system

→ Discuss the advantages and disadvantages of the main means of raising finance

→ Explain the main steps that managers should take to turn around an underperforming organization

→ Describe the main pitfalls that can arise during mergers and acquisitions, and explain best practice in managing such transactions.

In the previous chapter, we looked at the issues related to changing an organization's strategy, with particular reference to the issues involved in major, transformational change. This chapter follows on from that in several ways.

First, the style and quality of the organization's leadership will influence its ability to change —and also its effectiveness as a social system and economic actor, whether it is changing its direction or proceeding with an established strategy. Second, an organization requires systems for monitoring performance and progress. If it is going through a change programme, monitoring will be against objectives specific to that programme. Once any change has been institutionalized, performance is then monitored against the organization's broader strategic objectives. Control systems of this kind are, as we mentioned in Chapters 8 and 9, key elements of the architecture that also have broader implications for the motivation of employees and the organization's capacity to learn. In this chapter, we look in detail at the specification of appropriate measurement and control systems. Third, the implementation of strategy requires access to financial resources, so in this chapter we review the different options for raising finance.

Finally, we look at two strategic situations that call upon specific planning, financial implementation and, in particular, leadership skills: the management of turnarounds and of mergers and acquisitions.

17.1 Leadership

Leadership plays a key role in the way in which strategy unfolds in an organization— indeed, the whole discipline of strategic management grew out of the study of what distinguished effective leaders from the rest. As we noted in Section 1.6.4, an organization's culture, vision, and values are frequently the legacy of a strong leader, past or present. Akio Morita at Sony, Ray Kroc at McDonald's, Lord King and Colin Marshall at British Airways, and Erling Persson at H&M have all left a lasting imprint on the companies that they helped found or led at key moments in their development. The personal qualities and ambition of the leader are important in gaining, and keeping, organizational commitment to a particular strategic direction, and also in changing that direction when necessary.

Leadership
The capacity to develop and shape organizational routines, or to maintain commitment to existing routines.

17.1.1 Who are the leaders?

However, it is a mistake to think of leadership as occurring only at top management level. In fact, a number of leadership levels has been identified (see Table 17.1). At top management level, level 5 leadership has been identified by some researchers[1] as a necessary factor if an organization is to deliver sustained, exceptional performance; we discuss the attributes of level 5 leaders in Section 17.1.3. However, the other levels of leadership, exercised right through the hierarchy, also contribute to an organization's success.

Middle managers, in particular, have been recognized as playing specific leadership roles that contribute significantly to successful strategy implementation:[2]

- the obvious role of implementing the deliberate strategies set out by top management. This involves significant challenges in interpreting what these strategies mean in their local context, juggling resources, and motivating people to carry out the strategy. On occasion, this may mean reinterpreting the strategy significantly, or setting up local programmes to make it easier for people to adapt to the strategy;[3]

Table 17.1 Levels of leadership

Level	Description	Contribution to organization
Level 1	Highly capable individual	Talent, knowledge, skills, good work habits
Level 2	Contributing team member	Works effectively with others; helps achieve group objectives
Level 3	Competent manager	Organizes people and resources to meet objectives in efficient and effective manner
Level 4	Effective leader	Builds compelling vision, evokes commitment to it, stimulates high performance
Level 5	Executive	Builds enduring greatness

Source
Collins (2001)

- gathering and pulling together information for senior managers. The 'spin' that they decide to give to this information—whether to present something as a threat or an opportunity, for example—can be important in shaping strategic responses, and in pushing top management into overcoming caution and inertia;[4]

- championing innovative ideas and business opportunities. Middle managers can use their experience to decide which ideas are worth testing, provide them with seedcorn resources to help get them off the ground, and use their relationships with senior managers to gain formal support for them.[5]

17.1.2 **Leadership approaches**

Theorists have identified two main styles of leadership. Transformational leaders use charisma and enthusiasm to inspire people to exert themselves for the good of the organization. They offer excitement, vision, intellectual stimulation, and personal satisfaction. Some researchers believe, however, that leaders who rely too heavily upon charisma are not always effective in the long term.[6] This is because few individuals, however talented and energetic, are able to handle all types of business problems alone. They require people around them who are able to support them, and who are prepared to tell them when things are going wrong. Charismatic leaders are not always willing to listen to bad news, or to let talented people flourish if they may one day turn into rivals.

Transformational leaders will challenge established paradigms and ways of working, whereas transactional leaders, on the other hand, look to build on the existing culture and improve current practices. They prefer a more formalized approach to motivation, setting clear goals with explicit rewards or penalties for achievement or non-achievement.

Neither style of leadership is suitable for all circumstances. Transformational leadership may be appropriate in turbulent environments, in industries at the very start or end of their life-cycles, in poorly performing organizations, or generally when there is a need to inspire a company to embrace major change. The use of charismatic behaviours to make people feel important and cherished is arguably important during periods of uncertainty when people are generally feeling quite distressed. In a settled environment, in growing or mature industries, and in organizations that are performing well, a transactional leadership style may be better suited to persuading people to work efficiently and run operations smoothly.[7]

As well as different styles of leadership, there are also different approaches, each implying a different notion of what the leader's job entails. Effective executives use a leadership approach that is appropriate to the needs of the organization and its business situation. Research has identified five such approaches:[8]

- The **strategy approach** is used in firms like Dell Computer. Leaders with this style believe that their position at the top of the organization makes them uniquely qualified to take strategic decisions. They spend their time gathering competitive, market, and technological data to inform those decisions.

- The **human-assets approach** starts from the notion that if the organization has the right people, then it will develop an appropriate strategy. The leader spends a lot of time travelling around the organization, becoming involved in recruitment and career planning for even quite junior staff. Jack Welch, legendary CEO of General Electric in the 1990s, was renowned for his use of this approach, though he used others as well.

- The **expertise approach** was the least common in the research sample. It involved leaders devoting their time to championing the adoption of certain vital skills and knowledge within the organization. Jamie Dimon, the President of US bank JP Morgan Chase, is an example of this approach (Real-life Application 17.1).

- The **box approach** was the most common among the firms researched. It was employed by British Airways, and by France's AXA, the world's largest insurer. Leaders using this approach see their main task as building a 'box' of control systems that defines the norms that people in the organization must conform to. These might be financial systems, corporate values, expected behaviours, or even a common language to link different units across the world.

- The **change agent approach** was used by leaders who see it as their role to reshape their organization from top to bottom, and to create a climate of continual reinvention, even at the cost of a degree of change fatigue, which may lead to some strategic misjudgements and short-term falls in financial performance. Such leaders travel widely through the organization, holding meetings and giving motivational speeches.

→ Change fatigue, and the qualities of an effective change agent were reviewed in Chapter 16.

17.1.3 Attributes of effective leaders

Almost by definition, effective leaders display vision, energy, and authority. A number of other attributes have been cited for them, including:[9]

- a deep understanding of the business. Sir Colin Marshall, who along with Lord King built British Airways into a major force, and Sam Walton, founder of Wal-Mart, the world's largest retailer, were both renowned for their attention to the detail of everyday operations;

- the ability to empathize with fellow members of the organization, to speak their language and genuinely care about the problems that confront them. This was one reason why Rod Eddington, whose character enabled him to mingle and chat easily with British Airways' flight and cabin crew, was better accepted than Bob Ayling, the more reserved person that he succeeded as BA's CEO. Deep business understanding helps in this regard, but also important is the ability to convey authenticity—false bonhomie will be noticed. Empathy of this kind should not be taken too far, however. Strong leaders also show a measure of ruthlessness when necessary, including a preparedness to get rid of people when it is clear that they cannot perform;

- the ability to choose and motivate people. This may include coaching people so that they grow into their jobs—though not all authorities agree that great leaders must be good coaches;

- the ability to listen, and to understand what is going on in the organization and its environment. Good leaders appear to be particularly strong at gathering 'soft' data —they have networks and pick up gossip and rumours, but they are also skilled at interpreting non-verbal messages, such as when people stop communicating for no apparent reason. Their intuition is strong;

- a willingness to show their human side, revealing differences, eccentricities, and, paradoxically, weaknesses. This must not be taken too far—differences that make people appear intolerably arrogant, or unable to listen, or incompetent in their specialist role will weigh against them. But an obsession with sport, an unusual accent or dress sense, even a refusal to use email, can help a leader to appear genuine and human. Virgin's Richard Branson, for example, was said to be ill-at-ease when interviewed, and to fumble constantly.[10]

The exceptionally effective 'level 5 leaders' have two further characteristics.[11] The first is personal humility. They do not conform to the stereotype of the charismatic leader, although they can inspire great loyalty, partly because they are content to credit their organization's success to those around them, while taking personal responsibility for any setbacks. They avoid adulation and media attention, and while they are clearly ambitious, that ambition is channelled towards their organization's success, rather than their own.

In pursuit of that ambition, they are however implacable. They set the highest standards, for themselves and those around them, and are willing to take whatever action is needed for long-term success, even when it involves breaking with cherished traditions or withdrawing from long-established businesses.

17.1.4 Power, politics, and effective leadership

→ We introduced the concept of power and politics in Section 1.6.2, and looked at the nature and sources of power in Section 16.2.1.

Regardless of the style they adopt, leaders will achieve little unless they are able to use power effectively. Power and politics are crucial, both when leading change, as we noted in Chapter 16, and when trying to keep an organization on course with an established strategy. A leader who fails to master the exercise of power risks losing the 'consent of the governed'—the acceptance by people lower down the hierarchy of the authority of a manager at higher level.[12] Those people may resist the exercise of authority by industrial action, sabotage, working to rule, or political lobbying for the leader's removal.

Developing a power base and nourishing through political activity are therefore increasingly important the higher one rises in an organization. There are very few chief executives who are not skilled in the politics of management—the deliberate manipulation of factors in order to improve their own position, or that of their allies.[13] Often, in so doing, they also weaken the position of others who oppose them. As we noted in Section 16.3.2, there are three forms of power: power of resources, power of processes, and power of meaning.

One key area where the power of resources is exercised is in the selection of people for key roles. Potential troublemakers can be marginalized from decision-making and removed from the control of resources. They can be replaced with people who are likely to be supporters of the chief executive, acting as their agents and as their eyes and ears. A common practice among new chief executives, for example, is to replace existing management with their own chosen employees.[14]

Power of processes can be harnessed through the deliberate alteration of channels of communication, so that only chosen individuals get to hear about important pieces of information, or at least hear of them in time to do anything about them.[15] Employees can also be deliberately moved from one function, location, or role to another. This breaks up subcultures and brings people in contact with entirely different ways of seeing things. This can promote organizational change if required, but can also serve simply to transfer learning, and promote innovation.

The astute use of the power of meanings is another important capability for a leader, including:

- The presentation of facts and figures in such a way as to give the correct impression of the organization's situation. Normally, this will be positive, although, as we noted in Chapter 16, there will be occasions when negative features will be emphasized as a prelude to change;
- the manipulation of organizational and personal images. The organization's performance and policies can be presented to best effect with chosen stakeholders. Leaders, too, should take care in respect of their appearance, in what they say, and in how they say it.

Leaders cannot operate alone except in small organizations or for short periods of time. Allies can be an important source of personal support, as well as acting, where appropriate, as agents of change in their own right. Alliances need most urgently to be forged with important power holders within the organization. People or groups that command a high degree of cognitive legitimacy—outstanding salespeople or researchers, for example, who epitomize the organization's values—can also help legitimize leaders and their policies in the eyes of the organization as a whole. Allies in the outside world can also be very helpful if they can bring in resources or useful information.

One problem encountered by newcomer chief executives is that they cannot know all the hidden aspects of the organization they have inherited—the relationships, the favours owed, the jealousies and dislikes. Most importantly of all, they do not know the hidden holders of power, who perhaps lack formal authority, but who have particular knowledge or understanding of how the informal organization operates. These types of hidden structure can mean the difference between success and failure—see What Can Go Wrong 16.1 for an example.

Finding good people to be on your side is therefore critical, and new executives need quickly to build a network of supporters around them. This can be done by picking out key people and cherishing them—through the use of charismatic behaviours, but also by rewarding them tangibly with, for example, enhanced salaries, and by promoting them to key posts, where they can control resources or important information. Rewarding key allies at the same time removes unwanted individuals from key decision-making roles, and removes resources from their control. Both are important factors in achieving change, both symbolically and practically.

Real-life Application 17.1 Jamie Dimon in 2006: transformational leadership in a fragmented bank[16]

Jamie Dimon's leadership skills are highly prized—to the extent that they were a major factor in the 2004 purchase, by JP Morgan Chase, of Bank One, whose market capitalization Dimon had doubled in four years as CEO. Dimon was nominated president and chief operating officer, and was promoted to CEO at the end of 2005 and then chairman as from 31 December 2006. Analysts described his 2006 remuneration—$1m salary, $26m bonus, and $36m from exercising stock options—as fair, given the shareholder value he had created.[17]

Dimon has made considerable progress in improving the bank's revenues, in particular by enhancing opportunities for cross-selling between divisions. But the most prominent feature of his leadership approach is his expertise in two areas: IT and cost control. First in Bank One, and then in JP Morgan Chase, he oversaw the integration of IT systems. Both companies had grown through mergers, and were burdened by the legacy of a variety of incompatible systems from the banks from which they had been formed. At JP Morgan Chase, this incompatibility had led to →

→ high costs while preventing branch staff from accessing more than basic details about a customer. In 2004, Dimon called together the bank's main IT personnel for a Saturday meeting and, having demonstrated an expert grasp of IT, told them that they had six weeks in which to choose a standard system for the whole bank to use in each of its main areas. If they could not reach agreement, he would make the choice himself. Faced with this highly credible threat, the IT managers met the deadline.

Dimon also takes a notably hands-on approach to controlling costs. Early on in his tenure, he determined that many JP Morgan Chase managers were being paid far more than their Bank One counterparts, and implemented salary reductions of 20–50%. Most of the hundreds of managers affected remained with the firm—according to Dimon, they knew they were overpaid.[18] He also eliminated 2,000 central support jobs on the way to bringing the number of back office staff per branch closer to levels achieved at Bank One. Divisional managers submit 50-page monthly reports embracing not just top-level operating ratios, but details such as the bills for hand-held computer usage. Their meetings with Dimon to discuss these reports can last several hours.

This illustrates the way in which Dimon has deployed both the power of processes and the power of resources at JP Morgan Chase. He has used the latter to replace several top JP Morgan Chase directors with trusted lieutenants from his Bank One days.

But he is also adept at using the power of meaning. He symbolized the importance of cost-cutting through closing down JP Morgan's gyms and ending the use of fresh flowers in its offices. There are rumours that he asks the drivers of limousines parked outside the corporation's HQ whom they are waiting for—and then summons the executives concerned for a lecture on cost control. The stories are untrue—but Dimon says he is happy for them to remain in circulation.[19]

Dimon is by no means the bookish accountant or computer expert that his expertise might lead one to expect. His personality is abrasive, even with long-standing colleagues, something that contributed to a well-publicized break-up with Sandy Weill, a friend and mentor with whom he was co-CEO at Citigroup in the 1990s.[20] However, he also inspires great trust and admiration and insists that subordinates make time for their personal life.

He leads by example, flying back from JP Morgan Chase's New York headquarters to Chicago each weekend to be with his wife and youngest daughter—they will not move to New York until the daughter finishes high school. He eschews executive perks like golf (he cancelled the bank's sponsorship of golf's Masters' tournament) and expensive clothes and restaurants. His tastes are simple, and rather than waste his Citigroup T-shirts, he continued to wear them long after that company had sacked him.[21]

Theoretical Debate 17.1 Organizational conflict and politics: problems or necessary evils?

We have said in this section that leaders, in order to be effective, need to be astute political animals. This implicitly assumes that micro-politics are an unavoidable feature of organizations—that there are no 'ideal' organizations that proceed without political bargaining and wrangling. In this theoretical debate, we examine that assumption.

Organizations, as we noted in Section 1.2, are collections—coalitions—of individuals and stakeholder groups. It is almost inevitable that, in an organization of any size, the outlooks and goals of the different stakeholders will conflict.

Conflict is not, of itself, necessarily a bad thing; it can be a useful antidote to 'groupthink' (Janis, 1982), where no one in a group of decision-makers challenges the logic of a flawed decision because everyone shares the same background and belief system. Conflict can improve the quality of decisions, even when it is built artificially into the decision-making process, for example by nominating somebody to act as 'devil's advocate' and challenge the consensus view. However, it can be unpleasant: managers tend to dislike it, and to be more satisfied and committed to

decisions reached through consensus (Schweiger et al., 1986; Schwenk, 1989). This is because 'cognitive conflict'—clashes between different points of view—can spill over into 'affective conflict'—conflict which disrupts the social ties between people, and which undermines both the quality and the acceptability of strategic decisions (Amason, 1996).

Political manoeuvring and bargaining between stakeholders constitutes one way of managing conflict in organizations. There are, however, two conflicting views of how politics figure in decision-making (Eisenhardt and Zbaracki, 1992).

On the one hand, some theorists hold that politics are a dysfunctional and time-wasting activity that people adopt only as a last resort (Eisenhardt and Bourgeois, 1988; Pettigrew, 1973). There is some empirical evidence (Dean and Sharfman, 1996) that self-serving political behaviour leads to less effective strategic decisions.

The opposing view (Quinn, 1980; Pfeffer, 1981, 1992) is that politics are an indispensable, useful, part of the way that organizations change and adapt. There are certainly organizations, →

→ notably in the public sector, where political behaviour is very prominent in the strategy process (Bailey and Johnson, 1995), and few, if any, organizations of any size have been found where it is absent. Paul Nutt (2002) argues that, for certain types of strategic decision, where it is clear *how* the organization might move forward, but stakeholders have yet to agree what the objectives should be, political bargaining is the most natural form of decision process.

Postmodernists such as Foucault (1980) would argue, however, that the debate as to whether political behaviour is good or bad is an irrelevant one. Politics, in their view, are simply the exercise of power, and power is a pervasive feature of society. Under this view, therefore, politics are a fact of life, with which managers, like everyone else, must deal.

17.2 Strategic control and performance measurement

Once a strategy, or a change programme, is in place, it is crucial that the architecture is developed to monitor progress against the relevant objectives. Historically, the emphasis on designing this part of the architecture has been on controlling people's behaviour, giving them incentives for activities that further the strategy and penalties for those that do not.

Equally important, however, is the extent to which managers at all levels are able to monitor whether an action is having the desired effect, and to take swift corrective action if it is not. The timeliness of information is an issue here. The longer the delay between an action being taken and management learning of its effects, the greater the danger that they will persist with an initiative that is not working, or fail to implement change because they are not aware that it is needed.

A final benefit from these systems is the way in which they help organizations to learn. By analysing data performance, it is possible to show how different elements of strategy have interacted. For example, a study of Sears, a major American retail chain, showed that a '5 point improvement in employee attitudes will drive a 1.3 point improvement in customer satisfaction, which in turn will drive a 0.5% increase in revenue growth'.[22] This enables managers to test their assumptions about the way their business works and make educated forecasts about the impact of proposed strategic actions.

Control is exerted on the actions of organizations, and of the people within them, through a variety of influences (Table 17.2), some from outside stakeholders, others imposed by managers.

Table 17.2 Ways in which organizations are controlled

External controls		Internal controls				
Societal control	Market control	The system of authority	Bureaucratic control	Cultural control	Reward systems	Output controls
Institutional environment	Competitor actions	Rewards and punishments	Rules and procedures	Recruitment	Salary	Goal setting
Legislation and regulation	Investor expectations	Hierarchy	Standardization	Socialization	Bonuses and share options	Measuring and evaluating
Customer demands	Market for corporate control	Appraisals	Management information systems	Norms Shared values	Fringe benefits Performance-related pay	

17.2.1 **External controls**

a. Societal controls

→ We defined the institutional environment in Section 16.2.1.

Controls are placed upon an organization by the society in which it is rooted, and in particular its institutional environment. It must take account of the expectations of society at large, and of the elements in society—other organizations in the same industry, local people —with which it is most in contact. Society may impose norms regarding ethics, social responsibility, economic performance, or anything else an organization does, or might wish to do. It may also determine the systems of corporate governance that are used.

→ We examined the influence of governments and regulatory bodies in Sections 2.7 and 3.2.1.

Governments, which are an important part of the institutional environment, may formalize some of those norms as laws and regulations. Customers are also frequently in a position to impose their own requirements regarding what the organization produces and how it acts in producing it.

→ We looked at the reasons why customers may be powerful in Section 3.5.2.

b. Market controls

Two types of market exert controls upon organizations—the markets where it competes with its offerings and the market for corporate control, of which stock markets are the most prominent part.

Competitors control a firm's strategy by limiting its options and activities. They may take potential customers, charge lower prices, or seize control of key locations or scarce resources. This in turn affects the firm's ability to meet the expectations of its investors.

The most important of these expectations relates to its profitability, though increasingly managers are targeting a triple bottom line in which targets for return on investment or shareholder returns stand alongside those measuring its impact upon the natural environment and upon society. The extent to which those expectations are being met is reflected in the firm's share price. If the share price falls to unacceptable levels, then the market for corporate control means that the firm is likely to find itself with new owners—and new managers.

Market expectations can influence not just the type of performance that is expected, but also the systems that are used to measure it. The film industry, for example, has had to reform the unusual and opaque way in which it had traditionally reported the profits made by a film. Otherwise, it would be unable to attract the new investors, such as hedge funds, who are becoming increasingly important as sources of motion picture finance, and who expect to share in those profits.[23]

Economic theory assigns a lot of importance to market controls, and this has led some organizations to apply them internally. Internal units can be forced to compete with external suppliers for custom, or encouraged to sell some of their output on the open market. Bertelsmann, the German media conglomerate, makes its CD-pressing subsidiary do both, while British Airways offers pilot training to other airlines. But market controls can be applied to purely internal transactions, since they are believed to give the best signals about how to make the most effective use of resources.

There are risks when one internal unit (unit A) sells outputs to another in the same firm (unit B) at prices that do not reflect external market conditions. Unit A may produce too much if the price is artificially high, especially if unit B is forced to buy its entire output; B may also get poor levels of service. Alternatively if unit B gets the inputs at lower than the market price, it may be tempted to buy more of them than it really needs, diverting resources in unit A that might be more profitably employed for internal or external customers. And, depending on whether the price is too high or too low, either A or B will appear more profitable than it really is, and may attract investment that would be better diverted elsewhere.

These risks can be reduced if units A and B trade with one another at 'arm's length'—at market prices, with a 'service level agreement' to specify what B can expect in terms of lead times and service quality. Relationships like this are quite normal for commonplace services like photocopying and computer maintenance. If A fails to deliver on that agreement, it may face financial penalties, or B may gain the right to buy from an outside supplier. And if A or B consistently operates at a loss, then the firm's managers have a signal that they might be better off outsourcing the service in question. Very large organizations may set up internal markets, where different supplier units bid against one another. In the UK health service, different hospitals may compete with one another, or with private suppliers, for contracts to provide hip replacement operations or orthopaedic services in their locality.

These pseudo-market arrangements are not always feasible or desirable. Sometimes there is no real market for the kind of resource that is being supplied, because it is so rare. Sometimes a firm sets up an internal supplier precisely because its managers believe that the market price is unrealistically high or that outside suppliers have too much power. And sometimes putting internal relationships on an arm's length basis may destroy cooperation between different units, or even lead them to try to cheat one another. Internal control systems are needed to mitigate such risks.

17.2.2 **Internal controls**

Broadly speaking, external controls define expectations regarding the way the organization is expected to perform. Not all managers or employees are directly exposed to these external factors, however; internal rules, norms and performance measures typically have a greater influence on the way they approach their everyday tasks. Internal systems, therefore, need to convey the organization's priorities and reflect external expectations, so that these inform employee behaviour and actions.

Internal control systems are rooted in the system of authority—the formal right of some individuals—managers—to take decisions which affect others. Most human beings appear instinctively to accept these, perhaps recognizing the advantages of working as a group. Employees accept the duty to comply with the rules of the organization—unless they are overruled by the law of the land—and the organization's right to reward them if they do and punish them if they do not.

In most organizations there is a formalized chain of command—the hierarchy—with managers at senior levels normally having broader powers than those lower down. A chief executive, for example, will have the right to close down a whole factory, or relocate an office from one country to another. A design manager might only have the right to spend a certain budget and take decisions that relate to a specific product development project.

People higher up the organization administer rewards and punishments to their subordinates, and also typically formally appraise the performance of those who report to them on a regular basis—normally annually. These appraisals should help employees to understand how to improve their performance, and the company to programme training and other measures to help them. A newer development is 360-degree appraisal, where managers are appraised by both superiors and subordinates.

The system of authority may fail if managers are unable to recognize that performance is poor, or to admit their responsibility for it. Authority can sometimes breed complacency and arrogance, so its effectiveness ultimately depends on external controls wielded by stock markets or boards of directors to force out underperforming managers.

Authority is often expressed in the form of bureaucratic controls that specify what an individual employee should do if and when a particular type of situation is encountered. Examples of bureaucratic procedures include formal job descriptions, standardized

→ We examined the
nature, advantages
and disadvantages of
bureaucratic and cultural
controls in Section 8.2.1.

specifications of the materials required and the activities to be carried out to produce a particular product or service, and procedures for collecting and distributing information.

Bureaucratic controls are often formally specified in writing. However, dress codes, time-keeping practices, and the use of company computers for private activities are examples of routines that may be established, or varied, by local custom and practice. This illustrates how bureaucratic and other formal control procedures are to some extent subordinate to cultural controls—the shared norms and values of the organization, business unit, or department.

As we noted in Chapter 8, there is an interdependence between bureaucratic controls, cultural controls, and economic incentives in influencing behaviour in organizations. Reward systems and sanctions—the way people are paid, given incentives to perform well, and disciplined if they do not—are strong shapers of behaviour. The threat of dismissal is the ultimate deterrent, while reward systems can be tailored to encourage particular behaviours that further the chosen strategy. A firm pursuing an entrepreneurial strategy and dependent on a stream of innovative products would reward people for the number and quality of new ideas they produce, as 3M does. A firm pursuing a low price strategy will want to reward people for behaving in ways which reduce costs.

People's rewards can simply be related to the time they spend in the workplace—working hours or overtime, with the organization relying upon authority, bureaucratic controls, or cultural controls to ensure that time is productively spent. Fringe benefits, such as company cars, loans at preferential rates, and discounts on the firm's own offerings, may foster commitment to the organization. There may also be an element related to individual performance—how much a person produces or sells—or to the performance of the work group, business unit, or organization as a whole. Managers' pay is often linked to the performance of the department they supervise.[24]

These incentives may take the form of bonuses—giving management discretion as to how generous they should be to a given individual or group—or performance-related pay, which links rewards to outcomes in a more formal and predictable way. Sometimes, firms will use non-monetary incentives—exotic holidays or the use of flashy cars—designed to strike a chord with a specific group of people. The head of one UK retailing concern offers high performers a holiday on his private island. Shares or share options are a common form of incentive, particularly for high-level executives, with a view to giving agents (managers) a financial interest in behaving in ways that benefit their shareholder principals.

In order for performance to be rewarded, however, it must first be measured. The output controls or performance measures that enable managers to do this are also crucial to the strategic management of the firm, since they determine the information that managers have at their disposal when monitoring the organization's progress.

17.2.3 Strategic performance measurement and output controls

Organizations gather and process data for two reasons:[25]

- to reduce the degree of uncertainty regarding their circumstances. For example, if they are uncertain as to the level of their sales, client attitudes, or employee productivity, they can gather quantitative data on revenues, satisfaction, or output levels. Formal information systems are needed to do this on a regular, timely basis;

- To resolve ambiguities as to what the data mean: why sales might be falling, what precisely the organization might be doing that particularly appeals to some clients, but not others. 'Soft' qualitative data—opinions and interpretations of what particular

Organization's goals—most accessible and
comprehensive online video provider

Infrastructure division targets—**e.g.** *no user to wait more than 5
seconds for a response; zero down time overall*

Procurement department target for number of servers
to install to meet expected demand growth
Maintenance department targets for average down time per server

Individual maintenance engineer targets: response time for
maintenance call-out; number of jobs completed per day

Figure 17.1 Hierarchy of targets.

events signify—can help managers reach consensus on these tricky factors. Good leaders and managers spend a lot of time personally gathering and processing soft data.[26]

Making sense of quantitative data requires some idea of what the level ought to be. Hence, organizations develop plans and budgets containing targets against which actual performance is monitored. Rewards, such as bonuses, are given accordingly, and corrective action can be taken if performance does not appear to be matching expectations. Top managers will typically set a number of overall goals for the organization, embracing factors like return on assets or shareholder returns, and then translate them into a set of more detailed key performance indicators (KPIs) for divisions, functions, and individual employees (see Figure 17.1 and Real-life Application 17.2 for examples).

➜ We looked at measures of strategic performance in Chapter 11.

Real-life Application 17.2 Linking mission, vision, corporate goals, and operational KPIs and procedures at c2c[27]

c2c is a subsidiary of the National Express group, a quoted UK bus and rail company with interests in the UK, Spain, and the USA. It runs services, mostly for commuters, between Shoeburyness and Southend on the east coast of England and Fenchurch Street in the City of London.

In conjunction with its headquarters, c2c issues a booklet to every employee that sets out its vision, its values, its business objectives, and targets for the year ahead. The company's mission is 'to be the 1st choice of travel in the areas we serve'. The vision is 'joining up people and places—by creating the best possible connections and thinking of the whole journey from the moment our customers decide to travel and book their ticket to when they arrive at their ultimate destination'.

The company has developed six objectives that cover the most important elements of its business: people, customers, operational excellence, safety, partnership with stakeholders, and profitability to enable future investment. The full objectives

are set out in Table 17.3. For each objective, the company has put in place a range of more specific objectives, some expressed qualitatively and some as quantitative performance indicators. Examples are given in Table 17.3.

c2c has targets based around these Key Performance indicators. For operational excellence, for example, the key measure is the Public Performance Measure (PPM), so called because it is used to compare the performance of rail operators across the country. It is the proportion of trains that arrive within 4 minutes, 59 seconds of the timetabled arrival time—since cancelled trains are counted as missed arrivals, this metric measures both reliability—what proportion of trains run—and the punctuality of those that do run. For the 12 months finishing 3 March 2007, c2c led the UK industry on this measure, with a score of 94.1%, compared with an average for all rail franchise operators of 88.0%.

In order to achieve this result, c2c monitors a number of subsidiary performance indicators. One crucial indicator is the total ➜

➜ number of minutes of delay on the line during a given period. Systems are in place to measure these, and also to allocate responsibility for the delay to c2c, to other operators using the same railway tracks, and to Network Rail, the body that owns the rail infrastructure along which c2c runs its services. For delays attributable to c2c, the company can track the fleet depot and stations involved.

Specific managers have primary responsibility for managing the consequences of a delay. c2c measures the ratio of the initial delay to the total of all the delays that come about as a result— for example, by having to wait behind the delayed train, or at signals for it to pass. This helps the company assess, and improve, the quality of its contingency planning.

Alongside this set of targets, the company has a framework of systems and procedures that reflects the complexity of the system it manages. This specifies, for instance, what data should be collected by what method, and how it should be coded (e.g. so it can be seen where responsibility for a delay lies) and analysed. Procedures are laid down for regular meetings related to performance, where other parties are involved, such as Network Rail and the company from which c2c leases its rail carriages. There are clear procedures as to how often these parties should meet, who should attend, and what matters may be discussed at the meeting. These contribute to c2c's success in managing its stakeholder relationships.

Table 17.3 Objectives and examples of performance indicators at c2c

Main objective	Example of quantitative performance indicator	Example of qualitative aim
Be a great place to work that develops and recognizes people	Attendance and sickness levels Employee satisfaction with management style	Reward, recognize, and celebrate success
Understand and exceed our customer expectations	Customer satisfaction scores on National Passenger Survey	Provide clear and informative communications
Deliver operational excellence and be best in class	Proportion of trains arriving punctually Minutes of delay Be first or second in industry performance league table	Robustly manage all aspects of train planning systems
Create a culture of safety in a healthy environment	Numbers of trips, falls, staff assaults	Ensure every staff member has Safety Responsibility Statement
Work in partnership with our stakeholders	(Depends on partner objectives)	Earn support and trust of stakeholders
Deliver profitability to invest in the future	Market share Profit and cash flow targets set by National Express	Ensure value for money in everything we do

Systems must then be put in place for collecting the data. A fast-food restaurant may set the target of serving every customer within a given period. The procedure for measuring this might be through observation from time to time, or by checking time stamps on till receipts. IT systems, such as barcode readers, can help to measure output in a factory or a supermarket. Well-designed management information systems will then help managers spot if anything is amiss. Good managers will often supplement the formal systems with informal conversations and regular walks around their office or factory, to see how things are going.

Difficulties arise, however, in measuring more intangible activities, such as research or design, where satisfactory payback or measurable success may be years away. Even for more common targets, such as customer satisfaction or market share, the collection of the necessary data can be laborious and expensive.

Table 17.4 Factors affecting successful implementation of performance management systems

Areas of attention	Behavioural factors
Managers' understanding—a good understanding by managers of the nature of performance management	Managers understand the meaning of KPIs Managers have insight into the relationship between business processes and CSFs/KPIs Managers' frames of reference contain similar KPIs Managers agree on changes in the CSF/KPI set
Managers' attitude—a positive attitude of managers toward performance management, toward a performance management system and toward the project	Managers agree on the starting time Managers have earlier (positive) experiences with performance management Managers realize the importance of CSFs/KPIs/BSC to their performance Managers do not experience CSFs/KPIs/BSC as threatening
Performance management system alignment—a good match between managers' responsibilities and the performance management system	Managers' KPI sets are aligned with their responsibility areas Managers can influence the KPIs assigned to them Managers are involved in making analyses Managers can use their CSFs/KPIs/BSC for managing their employees
Organizational culture—an organizational culture focused on using the performance management system to improve	Managers' results on CSFs/KPIs/BSC are openly communicated Managers are stimulated to improve their performance Managers trust the performance information Managers clearly see the promoter using the performance management system
Performance management system focus—a clear focus of the performance management system on internal management and control	Managers find the performance management system relevant because it has a clear internal control purpose Managers find the performance management system relevant because only those stakeholders' interests that are important to the organization's success are incorporated

CSF = Critical success factor
KPI = Key performance indicator
BSC = Balanced scorecard

Source
De Waal (2003: 694)

Implementing a new performance management system typically takes 18 to 24 months. The organization has therefore to decide whether the gains from reducing uncertainty and ambiguity outweigh the cost of acquiring the information. These are not just the cash costs of consultants, hardware, and software, but the opportunity cost of the employee time spent in compiling the data, and management time spent making sense of it, and discussing it. There is also, as with every major change programme, a significant risk of failure.

Research has shown that a number of factors are of great importance to the effectiveness of a performance measurement system (Table 17.4).

a. Value-based management

Early systems of 'management by objectives' tended to focus upon one or two key performance measures, such as return on investment, in order to give managers a clear, unambiguous goal to aim for. However, agency problems then started to appear, as cunning

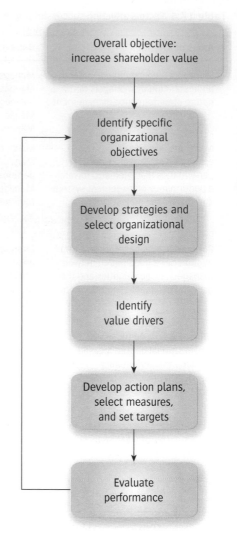

Figure 17.2 Value-based management.
Source: Ittner and Larcker (2001: 353)

managers found ways of achieving their targets without working too hard in pursuit of the organization's strategic aims. For example, they might reduce spend on important items like research, training, marketing, or maintenance, apparently improving profits in the short term but building up problems for the future.

There has therefore been a move towards systems of targets intended to motivate people to enhance their organization's value, investing for the long term while sustaining profits in the short term. Organizations adopting this philosophy of value-based management (VBM) typically go through six steps (Figure 17.2). It is not yet clear whether adopting VBM improves organizational performance; the most recent studies suggest that it does, although more for small than for large firms. As with many, relatively new, management methods, there are some case studies of successful adoption, but also a large number of instances where firms have been unable to implement it correctly.[28]

Many supporters of VBM advocate that the organization's primary objectives should be expressed in terms of economic value added (EVA) or shareholder value added (SVA). However, the VBM philosophy can be applied to any concept of value, so that it can be used in public sector and not-for-profits (NFP) organizations, and can embrace many stakeholders other than just shareholders. Moreover, while EVA and SVA may be the most precise theoretical measures of firm performance, this does not make them the best metrics for everyday

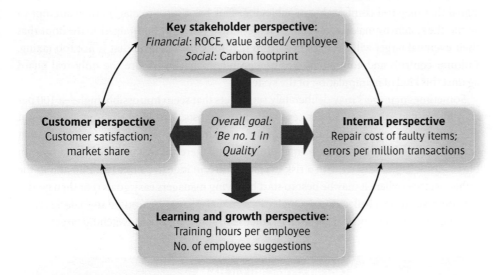

Figure 17.3 Examples of measures in a balanced scorecard

use. In practice, many high-performing users of VBM set business unit objectives in terms of return on capital employed or similar, well-understood, accounting ratios.[29]

b. The balanced scorecard

Once the overarching goal has been established, it is necessary to develop sets of KPIs that enable managers to monitor how well the organization is performing at present and how well placed it is to cope with the future. Many frameworks for performance measurement have been developed, but by far the best known is the balanced scorecard (Figure 17.3), which incorporates four sets of factors that assess:[30]

- learning and growth—the extent to which the organization is developing the intellectual and other resources needed for future innovation and expansion;
- the customer perspective—how well the organization is serving its customers and users, how satisfied they are at present, and how likely they are to use its products and services in future;
- the internal perspective—the efficiency and effectiveness of key processes in the value chain, and how quickly these are improving;
- the key stakeholder perspective—in most commercial balanced scorecard models, this perspective will relate to shareholders, and will be monitored using financial measures. However, the requirements of other key stakeholders—for example, for good corporate governance or environmental responsibility—can be incorporated in this perspective where appropriate.

Whatever the chosen framework, the individual measures need to be carefully chosen. They are typically based upon a strategy map, in which the value drivers (sometimes called 'critical success factors', CSFs) for the organization are identified, and relevant KPIs are developed. They should be meaningful and useful to managers whose performance is being controlled, and be clearly related to factors that they, and they alone, can influence.[31] Worked Example 17.1 shows how this might be done.

c. Setting targets

The levels at which targets are set may also be important for motivating employees. A typical practice is to set targets that are 'stretching'—in other words, just beyond what managers signal that they feel comfortable in achieving. This has risks—managers may attempt to 'game' the system by making forecasts that they know can easily be attained, in the hope that their eventual target will be 'stretched' from that forecast to a level that is not too taxing. Cultural controls and competent, knowledgeable, management are the only real guard against this kind of manipulation of the system.

Sometimes managers may deliberately set targets that seem impossibly high—a 100 per cent increase in sales, or a 50 per cent reduction in costs. This kind of target, even if not met in full, can push the organization towards the kind of radical process innovation that can give competitive advantage. On the other hand, there are instances—for example, in bureaucratic organizations with a risk-averse culture, in industries like banking and in the public sector—where it may be best to start by giving managers easy goals that then gradually are made more challenging. In such cases, managers may be unused to making entrepreneurial decisions, and feel paralysed, rather than stimulated, by a stretching target.

Worked Example 17.1 A possible balanced scorecard for H&M

We have no evidence as to whether H&M is using, or contemplating, a balanced scorecard. Nonetheless, in this worked example, we give our ideas on what its scorecard might look like if its managers did opt to employ one.

The first stage is to draw up a map of how the strategy works (Figure 17.4). The best place to start in H&M's case is with the customer perspective—essentially, its competitive stance—since this defines the crucial aspects of the company's strategy. People go to H&M for affordable and fashionable clothes in an attractive, funky retail setting. The key elements that need to be measured will therefore relate to price, to the extent to which the offer is fresh and up-to-date, and to the quality of the store environment.

We can now turn our attention to the internal perspective—the value chain that delivers these benefits to the customers. As we saw in Chapter 8, H&M's supply chain management has a huge impact on affordability of the products and the timeliness of their appearance in the stores. Two aspects of the firm's architecture are of particular importance to the functioning of that supply chain: the IT architecture and the management of the many partnerships and linkages within it, notably with key suppliers. The design activity is clearly crucial in getting clothes to market in time to catch the mood of the customer, and in making the garments affordable. It will also have a critical role in making the stores attractive. Last but not least, there is the need to nurture the property portfolio, ensuring that shops are in optimum locations—partnerships with property developers and professionals are likely to be important here—and kept in a good state of repair.

We can now look at where H&M needs to direct its attention in order to sustain these sources of competitive advantage. This tends to be the trickiest part of the strategy map (see Practical dos and don'ts below). In H&M's case, we can pick out three elements as important. Without comprehensive and up-to-date information on factors such as available suppliers and potential store sites, it

will not be possible to continue the firm's expansion. Unless the staff are strongly motivated, no improvements can be expected in the effectiveness of the supply chain, the degree of creativity, or the quality of the shopping experience, or in the quality of the specific skills that underpin each of the internal factors.

Finally, we can consider what the desired financial outcomes from a successful strategy are likely to be. According to our analysis, H&M's strategy is designed to give a high utilization of, in particular, fixed assets such as its stores—this is common in retailing. It does not appear to be aimed at generating high profit margins, but each tenth of a percentage point that can be added to margins is likely to have a large impact on overall profits, given the high sales volumes. And volumes themselves seem to be important to the success of the strategy; growth in volumes will be the primary driver of profit growth.

Figure 17.4 shows the key strategic elements for which, on the basis of the strategic analysis in the preceding paragraph, performance metrics would be needed. Now we need to think about what those performance measures should be—bearing in mind that they have to be easy for managers to understand, that there should not be too many of them, and that it should be possible to foresee a realistic way for the data to be collected.

For the key stakeholder perspective, we can use conventional metrics:

- Return on capital employed is useful to compare H&M's performance with competitors that use different business models: for example, those that are vertically integrated into manufacturing or that do not run their own retail outlets.

- Revenue per square metre is a normal industry-specific measure of asset utilization.

- Sales/employee is a useful measure of the productivity of H&M's staff.   ➔

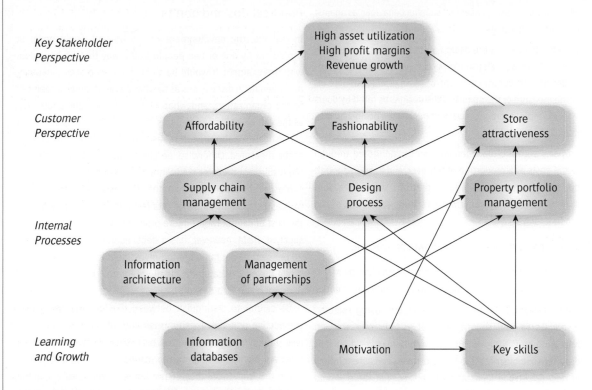

Figure 17.4 A possible strategy map for H&M

→

- Gross profit margin is a good, simple indicator of how revenue and costs compare for individual garments.

- Sales, general, and administrative costs as a percentage of sales allow us to track overheads.

For the customer perspective:

- The price of a bundle of commonly bought items could be tracked over time, and benchmarked against selected competitors, with a warning if H&M ranked below, say, second place for more than two weeks in a row.

- Fashionability can be measured quantitatively using the average time that items remain in store between delivery and sale. This measures both the allure of the garment and the effectiveness of the selling process. It can also be measured using customer surveys—average customer approval scores of a selection of items—perhaps the same as the bundle whose price is measured. And H&M can track the number of mentions of H&M garments in the fashion pages of selected publications known to be read by target customers.

- Store attractiveness can, like fashionability, be measured through customer surveys, but the time since a store's last refurbishment will give an indicator of how effective and

up-to-date its design is, especially if benchmarked against key competitors in the locale.

From the internal perspective:

- The effectiveness of the supply chain management could be measured in terms of inventory turnover—the faster, the better—and average time between order and delivery. This second metric would also be a measure of supplier commitment to H&M.

- The quality of the information architecture is trickier to measure. The percentage of down time is important, but once the system has achieved a certain threshold of reliability, it ceases to be a KPI—it should only be flagged if it reaches a level that is a trigger for emergency action. It may be more important to look at measures like average response time to user queries and to proportion of queries that are unanswered after, say, 1 minute.

- The quality of H&M's management of partnerships could be monitored using surveys of partners, and the proportions of highly satisfied and highly dissatisfied partners used as metrics. The average order delay time, or the proportion of orders delayed more than, say, three working days, could →

➔ be useful measures of actual supplier behaviour, as against proclaimed attitudes.

- The effectiveness of the design process can be measured in terms of average elapsed time between commencement of design and commencement of mass product deliveries. Some measure of the quality of the designs as rated by peers —for example, average placement in selected design awards, may also be helpful.

- Property portfolio management can be monitored through rental costs as a proportion of turnover, and average footfall per store, while acknowledging that this second measure may be distorted by variations in the attractiveness of the product range.

Finally we come to the learning and growth perspective:

- The quality and currency of H&M's databases can be measured in terms of average times between significant updates.

- Staff motivation can be measured directly, using selected responses to staff surveys, as well as indirectly, through reviewing staff turnover. Bear in mind, however, that it is desirable in a business like H&M to have a consistent inflow of new talent and ideas at all levels, so that there should probably be both a maximum and a minimum acceptable level set for staff turnover.

- Inputs into maintaining and upgrading key skills can be monitored, quite simply, as the number of days of training per employee.

Practical dos and don'ts

In real life, the development of a scorecard would never be carried out by one or two people in the way that we have done with this example. It would be a collaborative process, involving many people in discussions as to what drives strategy in their part of the organization, and what KPIs might be appropriate. Just as the exercise of power requires the consent of the governed, so sophisticated performance measurement requires the consent of the measured. Otherwise, people simply find ways of fiddling the results or otherwise subverting the system.

Metrics should be tailored to the circumstances of the firm and to its stakeholders. In other retailers, which are highly geared, the cost of capital might figure prominently in the financial perspective. H&M, however, has a debt/equity ratio of only about 20 per cent, and a fairly limited investment in fixed store assets. While the cost of capital is clearly of interest to the company, it does not count as a KPI.

Be careful to distinguish between the learning and growth perspective and the dynamic elements of the other perspectives. Improvements in internal processes or customer perceptions are highly likely to be the *results* of learning and growth, but in this framework they do not figure as *measures* of learning and growth. For the balanced scorecard, we emphasize the inputs that enable learning and growth to take place; typically, these relate to human resources, intellectual resources, and relational assets.

d. The performance measurement culture

Target setting is pointless unless the culture fosters the right responses. The managers who are being monitored must appreciate the importance of performance measurement, and see it as something that can help them improve, rather than as a threat. They must trust the data, and also believe that the organization is serious about using it. It helps if results are openly communicated so they can benchmark themselves against their peers, and see that good or disappointing performance is being treated in the same way for everyone.[32]

Managers need to be prepared to take action if a target is not being met. Depending upon the cultural norms in an organization, this may take the form of a quiet word of encouragement, an offer of help, a formal memo expressing concern, or a threat of dismissal. If a target is being surpassed, the appropriate action may be a front-page article in the company newsletter. On the other hand, people will soon realize if no one is really taking any notice of whether they achieve their targets or not, and may stop trying.

Putting such a culture in place may require extensive training—the most successful VBM implementers train 75 per cent of their managers in the meaning and use of relevant performance measures, and some even train 75 per cent of the entire workforce. More thoroughgoing change management measures, including changes to the management team, may also be needed.[33]

e. The drawbacks of output controls

Output controls suffer a number of potential problems. They will always encounter sharp-witted managers who may feel, almost as a matter of honour, that they have to find a way around them. Making the controls more sophisticated may simply increase the time that is spent in trying to outwit them. Furthermore, there is always the temptation to base targets on incremental improvements to past performance rather than on what should happen in the future.

The balanced scorecard was developed partly in response to such concerns, but it has potential drawbacks of its own. The strategy maps on which balanced scorecards are based take a long time to develop, and may not be updated frequently: if the environment changes rapidly, the organization risks basing its scorecard analysis on CSFs that no longer fit either the environment or the strategy. Another risk is that the scorecard may focus attention on the measurement process, and divert time and energy away from the actual management of performance.[34]

There are also doubts as to whether it is possible for organizations to set up a workable set of truly strategic output controls.[35] Most managers like to focus on short-term measures of performance, which are easier to achieve and lead to bonuses for the managers concerned. In contrast, strategic performance measures need to be 'softer' and more subjective. They must assess competitive strength and market positioning and look at unit performance over the long term in the light of changing circumstances. Uncertainty in the business environment demands flexibility and creativity when developing strategy—two factors that are difficult to measure.

17.2.4 **Controlling projects**

Projects are an important element of strategy in many organizations. In some industries, like construction and consultancy, every significant customer assignment is a separate project. Even outside these industries, most organizations encounter major, one-off projects on a regular basis. For example:

➜ We gave a definition of a project, and examined project-based structures, in Section 9.1.

- the construction by BAA of a fifth terminal at Heathrow Airport, and British Airways' moving of its Heathrow facilities into that new Terminal 5;
- H&M's launches of its Karl Lagerfeld, Madonna, and Stella McCartney clothing ranges;
- Sony's development and launch of its Blu-ray video technology and of its PlayStation 3 games console;
- the computerization of a hospital's medical records and the integration of its systems with those of its country or region's health services.

These examples include business development exercises and bounded, 'hard' change projects of the kind discussed in Section 16.3.1. Some writers believe that strategy implementation in many contexts can be improved by applying the disciplines of project management more widely in organizations.[36]

A successful major project can boost morale among staff and the organization's legitimacy with other stakeholders. One that exceeds its budgets, runs late, or fails to deliver at all can seriously hurt an organization's reputation and its competitiveness. There is a risk that delays in the launch of Sony's PlayStation 3 (PS3)[37] have damaged its position in a highly competitive market-place by making it more likely that prospective customers will defect to other suppliers.[38] Putting such problems right can consume a great deal of management attention and divert resources from other important activities, and it takes a very strong-willed manager to convince stakeholders to 'pull the plug' on a project that may have consumed hundreds of millions of pounds.[39]

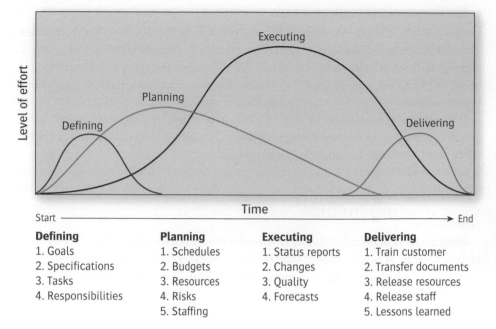

Figure 17.5 Phases in a project's life-cycle. Source: Gray and Larson (2006)

Defining
1. Goals
2. Specifications
3. Tasks
4. Responsibilities

Planning
1. Schedules
2. Budgets
3. Resources
4. Risks
5. Staffing

Executing
1. Status reports
2. Changes
3. Quality
4. Forecasts

Delivering
1. Train customer
2. Transfer documents
3. Release resources
4. Release staff
5. Lessons learned

Although projects differ according to their size and objective, almost all pass through the life-cycle shown in Figure 17.5. At the defining stage, the goals and specification of the project are established and the project manager appointed, who will lead the project through to completion. A key factor to be controlled at this stage is the degree of coherence between project objectives and the organization's business and corporate strategy, since it would be unwise to expend the resources, and take on the risks, inherent in a major project that did not further the organization's strategic aims.[40] Strategic considerations may affect the project specifications—the decision to incorporate Blu-ray into PlayStation 3 was taken to promote the adoption of Blu-ray as a global standard, as well as to enhance the attractiveness of the PS3.[41]

The success of a project is measured against three main criteria—timeliness, cost, and the extent to which outcomes meet the intended specifications. At the planning stage, detailed schedules and budgets are produced, which form the benchmarks against which subsequent progress is controlled. The project is broken down into discrete steps, and the outputs from each task are specified, along with the resources required. This enables projections to be made as to the time-scale and cost of each step, and interdependencies between tasks, and between projects, to be identified. The PlayStation 3 could not be brought to market in Europe until problems with some essential components had been fully resolved.[42]

The project plan will contain deadlines for the completion of each task, and milestones —dates at which progress will be assessed and where formal approval may be sought to commit the next tranche of resources to the project. Contributing departments will then be in a position to schedule their staff and other resource inputs; they may be involved in many projects, and have other ongoing work as well.

It is important at the planning stage to identify the key risks associated with each step in the project, and to make contingency plans for when things go wrong. Few, if any, projects run precisely according to plan—power cuts, price rises, or shortages for key inputs, or unexpected difficulties with particular tasks may trigger delays or cost overruns. Risk management is one of the most important project management skills. Particular attention is likely to be given to tasks that are on the 'critical path'—the sequence of tasks that together define how long the project is likely to take. Any delays to such tasks delay the entire project.

During the execution stage, each project task will need to be monitored regularly against the schedule and budget. Systems need to be in place to collect the necessary data, and to record any changes to the project specification that may be agreed by the client, and any agreed remedial work needed if a task does not meet its specification. Updated forecasts may need to be issued and recorded. There will also be handover points at which a task is formally completed, and accepted by the project manager, and eventually by the client or end-user.

Project management is a specialized discipline with a considerable literature of its own. Methodologies such as PRINCE2™ have been developed to give project managers access to a standardized body of procedures.[43]

17.3 Raising finance

Strategy implementation may require considerable financial resources. Some may be available from retained profits, but even big conglomerates sometimes need to obtain money from elsewhere. The potential sources of these funds include banks, equity markets, and venture capital.

17.3.1 Banks

The types of funds available from banks are usually loans of one sort or another. These often have a specified date by which time the loan has to be repaid and require regular payments of interest—an amount of money (typically between 5 and 30 per cent per year) which is roughly equivalent to the opportunity cost of the funds—in other words, its unavailability to the bank to be invested elsewhere. In some countries at different times (according to government tax policies), loans are a cheaper way of obtaining funds than the issuing of shares, although firms rarely want to over-extend their borrowings because of the risk that they could default on interest payments.

Loans can be long-term (usually more than ten years) or short-term, and may be secured or unsecured:

- A secured loan is given on condition that if the loan is not repaid the bank gains an asset such as a building or plant, which would probably be sold in order to recover the costs of the loan. This is like a private individual taking out a mortgage on a house purchase.

- An unsecured loan is given without any hold over tangible assets. Unsecured loans are quite rare, and would normally only be issued if the bank had considerable faith in the company's long-term viability. Interest rates on this type of loan would almost certainly be higher than for a secured one. There are a number of companies which carry out assessments of other firms' risk profiles, giving information about numbers and types of creditors, previous debts unpaid, and trading record as an aid to financiers making appropriate loans.

17.3.2 Equity markets

Equity markets are organizations set up to trade in publicly owned stocks and shares. They are almost always heavily regulated by the governments of the countries in which they exist, which delimit their activities and the types of financial instruments that they can administer.

The types of funding available from stock markets include shares, preference shares, and debentures. Most companies will use a range of these types of finance in order to spread risk and also vary the types of repayments that they have to make.

a. Shares

Shares, sometimes known as ordinary shares, are legal documents allocated by firms to individuals or other firms who become shareholders. They are the partial owners of the firm and can influence decisions about the firm's operations and personnel. Shares usually, although not always, attract annual payments known as dividends, and if the company is publicly owned, these shares can be traded on the open market. Shares form part of a firm's equity capital. Issuing new shares is subject to a number of rules about size and financial performance, and dilutes the company's balance sheet equity. Firms issue shares when their balance sheet is very strong, and when they have special projects that require large injections of capital. However, increasing the number of shares issued dilutes the percentage of the firm that other shareholders own, which they may not wish to allow, and has risks in the need for dividends to be paid in the future.

b. Preference shares

Preference shares are a variety of share in which dividend payments are usually of a fixed amount. This can be quite risky if a company's performance is unstable. Preference share-holders have to be paid first, before ordinary shareholders. A company chooses preference shares if the costs are less than those of raising other types of finance such as debentures.

c. Debentures, gilt-edged stocks or bonds

These are financial instruments which confer no ownership benefits on the holder, who cannot vote on company issues. Debenture holders obtain defined amounts of interest each year, which has to be paid even if the firm makes no profits. These types of instrument have a defined period of existence, at the end of which they must be redeemed (paid back).

17.3.3 Venture capitalists

Venture capitalists are individuals or organizations who specialize in providing finance to high-risk businesses that are relatively young and for which more traditional forms of finance are not available or are too expensive. They also invest in management buy-outs and buy-ins, and other types of company flotation. Venture capitalists usually fund their investments through a mixture of loans and the issuing of equity capital, some of which is normally bought by the managers of the new venture. Venture capitalists usually vet the management teams of the ventures very carefully, and often place one or more of their own staff on the management team until it has shown that it can manage the business properly.

An alternative to venture capital for small firms may be business angels—rich individuals that will take a stake in a promising business and lend it some of their own experience.

17.3.4 Issues in raising finance

Whenever finance has to be obtained, a number of critical issues will need to be considered:

- What amount of money can be obtained? Financiers will consider the availability of assets against which a loan may be secured and assess the viability of the project under consideration. This may involve a judgement as to the calibre of the management team concerned, including the team's historical performance, relative to competitors'. This will also be used to assess whether interest payments on the funds would be covered. The price/earnings ratios of other firms in similar industries may be used to estimate the amount of equity that can be raised, if this is the preferred source of funding.

- Can the firm repay a loan or debenture when it becomes due? For most companies in a healthy financial state this is not a problem—they can take out a new loan or issue new debentures—but circumstances can change and high levels of borrowing can push a company into not being able to afford to service the debt.

- Can interest payments or dividends be met? (The amounts called for will vary from country to country, and will also depend on the current cost of capital, which is partly dependent on inflation rates.) This will relate not only to the date that the finance is obtained, but to all times in the future until the debt is repaid, or shares withdrawn.

- The timing of payments, and when financing will be required. Venture capitalists talk of the 'death-valley curve', when income goes way below the break-even line. This happens when a firm is expanding so much that its costs are astronomical, and because of the, often large, lag in income, it may not be able to pay creditors or interest payments.

Real-life Application 17.3 Raising start-up finance: YouTube

YouTube was founded in February 2005 by two friends, Chad Hurley and Steve Chen. The idea was to create a simple website where people could share video clips in the easiest way possible, without having to pay a subscription fee or download any software.[44] It began, like many other internet companies, in a garage, with funding only from the founders' own credit cards.[45] This worked well for a while, as their capital requirements were low—all they needed was a website, which they designed themselves, and enough bandwidth and storage to allow users to upload and download video clips as quickly and efficiently as possible.

YouTube caught the enthusiasm of the time for internet services that used the latest interactive software, where much of the content was generated by its users, and an on-line social network was created.[46] After just a few months, it had signed up hundreds of thousands of users. With this massive growth came costs of more staff, administration, monitoring, and storage of millions of video clips.

Many internet companies generate revenues through advertising, with companies eager to pay for the potential of millions of users seeing their marketing material. However, this was not an option for YouTube, whose lack of advertisements and commercialism was key to its attracting so many users, and gaining its on-line community status.[47]

With the growing need for funds, Chad and Steve began looking for different ways to gain finance. Chad and Steve met whilst working for PayPal (the on-line payments system, now owned by eBay) during its start-up years. Many of that firm's former employees had gone on to create their own on-line businesses, and many had found advice and investment through former acquaintances at PayPal—it has been said that the bonds formed between employees during the early years at PayPal created a level of trust, and willingness to invest in each other's ideas.[48] In November 2005, Chad and Steve called upon their own social network, in particular Roelef Botha, who was the former chief financial officer at PayPal and now a partner at the venture capitalist company, Sequoia Capital. YouTube secured an investment of $3m, and a further $8m in April 2006.[49]

In October 2006, YouTube was bought by Google for $1.65bn. At this time it was estimated that YouTube had 72 million individual visitors each month, and 100 million videos viewed each day.[50]

17.4 Effecting turnarounds

In this section, we examine a particular type of strategy implementation, recovery strategies, or 'turnarounds', where an organization is taken from the brink of failure to a viable situation. Turnarounds pose particular problems, which have spawned a specialist literature and a dedicated consultancy association.[51]

17.4.1 Why turnarounds are necessary: causes of decline

One of the primary causes of organizational decline is poor management. Some writers on declining firms think that they begin their slide into problems up to ten years before they

Table 17.5 Managerial causes of organizational crises

Causes	Effects
Management blinded by previous success	Entrapment and self-deception
Loss of vision	Lack of clear goals
Small teams; stress	Impoverished decision-making
Autocratic management 'Tucked-away' manager	Lack of consultation of sources of expertise within the organization, lack of empowerment and commitment
'Cronyism'	Decisions based on politics rather than 'rational' competitive factors
Departure of most able staff	Loss of key skills
Hierarchy orientation	Outdated structures and poor communication Excess bureaucracy and administrative procedures
Concern for consensus and fear of conflict	Desire for acceptance leads to group think and impoverished decision-making Lack of creativity
Tolerance of incompetence	Excess personnel

finally fail—through bankruptcy, or takeover. Causes include small management teams, which reduce the quality of decision-making, autocratic management, and lack of consultation, all of which are often compounded by stress and the departure of the most competent managers (Table 17.5).[52]

Apart from these poor management practices, poor financial controls are the most common causes of corporate crisis. Falls in demand, increased competition, and other environmental problems, such as increases in input prices or interest rates, were a factor in 30–40 per cent of corporate crises. One-off errors, such as a failed large project or acquisition, can also reduce a firm to a critical state.[53]

17.4.2 Stages in a turnaround

Scholars have identified several phases in an organizational turnaround. During these the practitioner leading the turnaround—a new chief executive, or perhaps a specialist 'company doctor' or turnaround consultant—will go through a number of activities. The US Association of Certified Turnaround Professionals lists five such steps, summarized in Table 17.6.[54]

In the first phase, the turnaround practitioner (TP) assesses the situation of the organization, to determine if it possesses the strategic resources needed to bridge the gap between its current performance and that required for viability. If it does, then he or she will start to negotiate with key stakeholders—essentially, the holders of the company's debt—with a view to refinancing the company. At the same time, the TP will move to replace, or at least inject new skills and ideas into, the management team. Some 40 per cent of turnarounds involve the replacement of the CEO. The aim is to realign the expectations of management and creditors as to what they can expect from the company. If the debt-holders cannot be convinced that, under the new management, they can get an adequate return on their

Table 17.6 Stages in the turnaround process

Organization Phase	Turnaround practitioner actions
Realignment of managerial and stakeholder expectations	Situation analysis Management change/augmentation
Retrenchment	Emergency action
Recovery	Business restructuring Return to normal

investment, or that value can be realized from asset sales, then the turnaround will not proceed.

In the next phase, retrenchment, the business is cut back to its viable core. The crisis calls for fast and radical changes without the resources available in times of growth. This often requires the TP to take tough emergency action, including shutting down parts of the organization, selling assets to raise cash, and redundancies. Some form of legal shelter from the demands of creditors ('Administration' in the UK, 'Chapter 11' in the USA) may be sought. The TP may also need to negotiate some form of refinancing package, which requires considerable selling skills, and credibility with bankers and investors. If they cannot be convinced that the restructured firm can generate adequate returns on their new and existing investment, then the turnaround attempt will falter at this point—sometimes ignominiously. In the 1980s, following an unsuccessful acquisition, the UK defence electronics firm Ferranti ended up selling prized businesses to a long-time rival, GEC.[55]

In the third phase, the organization is set on the road to recovery. Table 17.7 lists the most common strategic elements used in this phase. A change of competitive arena is often required. This may imply moving products and brands up- or down-market, the identification of new customer groups, or the development of new brands to replace those with a

Table 17.7 Most common changes in strategy for firms attempting turnarounds

Change in strategy pursued	% of cases where used
Modernizing manufacturing capacity with equipment utilizing new technologies	(89%)
Increasing or decreasing the capital available for the commercial development of new products	(84%)
Changing priorities among the corporation's traditional set of businesses	(79%)
Introducing new products or services (other than by acquisition or joint ventures)	(68%)
Targeting new customer segments and/or eliminating existing segments	(68%)
Selling or closing inefficient or underutilized plants	(68%)
Increasing or decreasing the capital available for research on new products or processes	(68%)
Eliminating individual offerings from remaining product lines	(63%)
Eliminating entire product or service lines	(61%)
Selling off organizational units as going concerns	(61%)
Liquidating the assets of, or harvesting, units not divested	(55%)

Source
Barker and Duhaime (1997)

tarnished image. The TP must manage the balance between the old business, which needs to be maintained and milked as far as possible, and the move into new business areas.

A transformation of the culture and architecture—possibly the most demanding of all management tasks, as we described in Chapter 16—is also likely to occur, with a view to restoring pride to the organization under its new leadership. Sometimes, where funds have been made available, a judicious acquisition may also be a vital stage in an organization's recovery, since combining the firm's resources with those of another may be crucial to giving it a sustainable advantage.[56]

The TP, at this stage, may well withdraw discreetly, leaving the running of the business in the hands of its new management team.

However, none of the strategies listed above is guaranteed to succeed—unsuccessful turnarounds have been found to use the same strategic elements as successful ones. The difference in outcome arises from the quality of implementation and change management. Successful corporate recoveries are rare: during the 1980s and 1990s, it was over three times more likely for a very low performing firm to stay that way over five years than for it to be turned around into a very high performer. Only 3 per cent of the best performing businesses at the end of a given five-year period had been very low performers when the period started.[57]

Real-life Application 17.4 Allen Loren's 'turnaround' of D&B Corp.[58]

When Allen Loren arrived as CEO of D&B Corporation in May 2000, the company was in the process of unwinding the last of its diversifications of the 1980s and 1990s, by separating itself from Moody's, a provider of research and credit ratings. As Dun and Bradstreet, D&B was long-established as a leading provider of business information, such as mailing lists and detailed reports on companies for purposes such as credit control and supplier management. It had missed its earnings targets for 1999, a year in which its revenues and profits were lower than in 1998. While this was not a classic turnaround situation—the company was not in immediate danger of folding—it was clearly underperforming,[59] and a potential takeover target if performance did not improve.

In his analysis of the company's situation, Allen Loren concluded that several years of buying and selling businesses within the corporate portfolio had left D&B's core business with little direction or focus. Subcultures had proliferated across countries (D&B did business in over thirty) and business units. As a result, even though units might be serving common customers, pricing and competitive stance would often differ between them. This meant that, although the firm's brand was extremely well known, its brand values were not well understood, inside or outside the company. Frustration with the situation had led many talented people to leave the firm.

At the same time, although the company was not bankrupt, funds for investment were in short supply. As with any turnaround, tough measures would be needed to free up capital to take advantage of new business opportunities in areas such as e-business, which in 2000 was a new and fast-growing area. D&B, with its brand and information resources, was exceptionally well-placed to assist companies that wanted to find trustworthy suppliers and customers with whom to do business over the internet.

Having convinced themselves of D&B's long-term potential, Loren and his team needed to ensure that they did not lose control of the company before realizing it. The key stakeholders with whom they needed to negotiate were the shareholders who, if dissatisfied, might either press for a change of management or allow D&B to be taken over. They therefore approached the shareholders to explain that they would receive, as retained earnings, approximately 20 cents of each dollar of cost saved by restructuring the business. Of the remaining 80 cents, 20 would be needed to pay for the restructuring process and 60 would be reinvested. They were able to convince investors to support them during the turnaround.

There were also internal stakeholders to be won over. Loren found that while D&B's managers had plenty of ideas for growing the business, they also shared a conviction that those ideas were unaffordable, since there was no room to cut costs.[60] He therefore needed to effect an organizational change, as part of the turnaround. He started by building a sense of need and urgency, pointing out that if costs could not be cut, then the business should only be sold, since without growth it had no long-term independent future. This concentrated people's minds, and ideas for retrenchment began to surface.

The retrenchment, when it came, was substantial. By the end of December 2002, the company's numbers of employees had fallen to 6,600. The company's 'financial flexibility' programme, →

→ as it was called, had seen 2,400 people made redundant and a further 300 posts earmarked for elimination.[61] This was made possible by centralizing many administrative activities at global level, automating data collection, utilizing the web for data delivery, and eliminating duplications in sales and marketing networks. In Europe, 19 separate country operations were combined into one. Some non-core businesses were also sold off, liberating further funds for investment.

This allowed investments of several hundreds of millions of dollars in restructuring the business. Databases that had not been fully updated during the 1990s were brought fully up to date with details of new companies. The company's proprietary software was also updated. The database and software together formed the 'DUNSright' quality process, designed to allow customers to make decisions with confidence regarding prospective customers, suppliers, and marketing activities. All marketing literature worldwide was rewritten to emphasize DUNSright's unique advantages, and the brand became 'D&B: Decide with confidence'.

Meanwhile, the cultural change process continued. Loren had concluded that leadership skills in the organization needed to be enhanced, and D&B invested in coaching and development to help managers to improve them.[62] The firm's leaders drafted statements of values. Building on his own leadership experience as a senior executive at Apple Computer, Galileo International, and American Express, Loren himself drafted a set of 'guiding principles' about how leaders should behave: including open and honest communication, accepting when one has made mistakes, and seeking help to rectify them. These were intensively communicated, and read out at the start of every meeting, after which people discussed what they had learnt by applying them.[63]

Together, the rebranding, financial flexibility, and cultural change led to a substantial improvement at D&B. Earnings per share growth averaged 15–18 per cent per year between 2000 and 2005 (the original promise to investors was for just 10 per cent annual growth) and the firm's market capitalization increased from $1bn to $4bn. The strategy put in place under Loren's leadership remains largely unchanged following his retirement in May 2005.

Creative Strategizing 17.1

Now that D&B has stabilized its situation, how might it expand its geographic or product range in a way that makes good use of its strategic resources? What would be the risks of such an expansion?

17.5 Effecting mergers and acquisitions

One strategic method that poses particular leadership and implementation issues is mergers and acquisitions (M&A). The term 'merger' tends to be used where both firms' managements agree to combine (a 'friendly' merger) and often, although not always, implies a relative equality in the size and strength of the combining firms. The term acquisition or takeover usually refers to the purchase by a larger firm of a smaller one. Sometimes, however, a smaller firm will acquire management control of a larger or longer established company and keep its name (and often its stock market quotation) for the combined entity. This is known as a reverse takeover. If the managers of the target firm do not agree to recommend the acquisition to their shareholders, then the deal is termed a 'hostile' takeover, and the acquirer must approach the shareholders directly.

→ We examined the reasons why firms might undertake mergers and acquisitions in Section 12.2.2.

Both acquisitions and mergers can be financed by capital from the purchasing company (a 'cash bid'), by offering shareholders in the target shares ('paper') in the acquiring firm or in the merged entity, or by a combination of the two. Paper bids are more common in firms which are in public ownership and in mergers. Acquisitions are often purchases of small, privately owned firms, whose price can be met from existing financial resources.

Accountants and lawyers place great store on the formal difference between an acquisition and a merger. For strategists, the distinction is less clear-cut and not really important, so that the two words are often used interchangeably. Both pose similar management challenges, and it is sometimes impossible to tell whether a deal is really a merger or an acquisition. When in 1998, German engineering conglomerate Daimler-Benz merged with Chrysler, the American auto manufacturer, the deal was billed as a 'merger of equals', and the legal form of the combined entity reflected this, as did its name, DaimlerChrysler. However, it soon became clear that the German management was firmly in charge, and had always viewed the deal as an acquisition. (See What Can Go Wrong 17.1.)

17.5.1 The performance of mergers and acquisitions

Most of the many studies that have been conducted of M&As have found that over 50 per cent are unsuccessful, whether their impact is measured in terms of profitability or share price.[64] Typically, they fail to generate returns in excess of the cost of the capital required for the deal. The main beneficiaries, apart from the professionals who earn juicy fees for advising the participants, are the shareholders in the target firm, who normally will receive more for their shares—a 'bid premium'—than the quoted price before the offer is made. A 2006 study by Cass Business School and consultancy Towers Perrin, however, indicated that mergers since 2002 have on average shown positive returns. The researchers attribute this to participants having learnt from the pitfalls (see Section 17.5.2) experienced in implementing past mergers.[65]

In any case, the potential benefits that mergers offer mean that managers are prepared to take the risks. Acquisitions remain a constant feature of the business landscape, although M&A activity is cyclical, with recent peaks in 1989 and 1999—at the time of writing, a merger wave that began in 2002 has yet to abate. The most successful firms measured in terms of stock market performance tend, on average, to make fewer, but larger acquisitions than their peers. In high-technology industries, however, the most successful firms undertake twice as many acquisitions (and ten times as many alliances) as the less successful.[66]

Research has shown that certain types of takeover deal appear to have a higher probability of success than others. Friendly bids are more likely to generate positive financial returns (measured by cash flow) than hostile ones, partly because the bid premium is lower. These benefits are enhanced when the deal is financed through equity rather than debt. When there is a high degree of overlap between the businesses of the bidder and the target, there are higher average financial returns and a lower probability that the deal will be unprofitable.[67]

Stock markets also value different types of deal differently. Positive evaluations are accorded to acquisitions aimed at geographic roll-up, or expansions into products or markets that are close to existing areas of activity. The announcement of industry convergence mergers or deals involving similarly radical product moves, however, leads to falls in share prices. Firms that justify M&A activity as a means of growing sales volume and market share tend to have poorer stock market performance than those that focus more on a deal's profitability and economic value added.[68]

17.5.2 Pitfalls in mergers and acquisitions

Mergers and acquisitions have three phases, and pitfalls can emerge at any one of them. In the first phase, the acquisition target is identified. Sometimes the acquirer will initiate this in response to a business need, and sometimes an investment bank or other adviser will suggest a target to a client.

This is followed by establishing a price for the deal. The instigators of an acquisition, and their professional advisers, will calculate an offer price that they think appropriate, taking into account the target's current market capitalization, levels of debts and liabilities (e.g. to its pension funds), and the value of any synergies that might result. The two parties may then negotiate regarding price, and also who will hold key board and executive posts if the deal goes ahead. If the target's management is satisfied, they will recommend the bid to their shareholders—if the target is a small firm, then managers and shareholders may well be the same people. If they are not satisfied, the bidder may make a hostile offer directly to the target's shareholders, which may be raised several times as it becomes clear whether the proposed price is acceptable. If another bidder enters the fray, then there may be a competitive auction with several rounds.

This second phase culminates in the due diligence process, when the target allows bidders, or their representatives, limited access to its premises and to confidential information as to its business situation. This is the stage at which the bidder can finalize its estimates on how much the target is worth—or whether it should withdraw from the deal. In a genuine merger, due diligence needs to be carried out by both sides.

If the target's shareholders accept the offer (in some cases, the bidder's shareholders and relevant regulatory bodies must also give their approval) then the final phase involves the post-merger integration of the two organizations.

Where an acquisition involves diversification, then it may suffer from any of the problems that diversification entails, such as management attention being dissipated over too many businesses. These will be compounded if the acquisition process itself takes time, attention, and energy away from running the businesses. In the following sections, we examine other pitfalls that can arise.

➡ The benefits and risks of diversification were examined in Chapter 5.

a. The acquired firm's resources are less valuable than expected

There have been cases where firms have been acquired on the basis of a substantial overestimate of their operating capabilities, or in ignorance of severe weaknesses. When Ford Motor Company bought Jaguar plc for £1.6bn in 1989, it thought it was obtaining an up-market car manufacturer with good facilities. However, although Jaguar had been the subject of a much-praised turnaround in the 1980s, its factories turned out to be in a poor condition. Moreover, the classic designs on which its range was based were starting to lose their appeal. Ford was able to address the manufacturing issues with the help of a new purpose-built facility, but was estimated to have put in over £2bn of extra capital to sustain Jaguar between 1989 and 2006.[69]

There have even been cases where the target's resources turn out to be an illusion. When Ferranti, a UK engineering and defence firm, bought the US contractor International Signal and Control (ISC) for £420m in 1987, it did not find out until too late that much of ISC's declared profit came from 'confidential' defence contracts that in fact did not exist. ISC's chairman, James Guerin, was jailed for fraud in 1991, but Ferranti was driven into bankruptcy in 1993.[70]

b. The bidder overpays for the target

The Ferranti example illustrates the level of risk that attaches to a major acquisition. If, as frequently happens, debt is taken on to finance the deal, it becomes even more important not to overpay. Nonetheless, it can be difficult to estimate precisely what the correct price should be, particularly in cross-border deals, where different accounting standards and business practices may muddy the waters.

If a takeover bid is contested, managers may need to raise the price they offer several times—when Tata Steel acquired Corus Group, the price it offered rose from an initial 455p in October 2006 to 608p per share after a nine-round auction in March 2007, competing with Brazil's CSN. The difference amounts to some £1.6bn.[71] Time will tell whether the final price was a fair one—there have been other transactions where managers seem to have been carried away by the excitement of the deal and become determined to 'win' at all costs.

c. Difficulties in achieving operational or cultural fit

Strategic and cultural fit—the degree to which a target firm augments or complements its partner's market position, structure, technological competences, administrative practices, behavioural norms, and reward systems—appears to be an important determinant of acquisition success. However, in many cases, acquirers find that there are substantially more differences between the firms than expected and even in friendly mergers between two ostensibly compatible firms, cultural differences can be profound.

→ We discussed the concepts of belief system, paradigm, and cultural artefacts in Section 8.4.

What a suitor can get to know about a prospective partner is limited to what is known as its 'front-stage' or 'front-room' culture—things that can be made explicit and communicated. The 'back-stage' culture—less tangible things like belief systems, which may be hidden even to the firm's employees themselves, let alone an outsider—is much harder, if not impossible, to ascertain before the companies are brought together. An organization's cultural artefacts may give some clues as to its historical priorities and values, but not a full picture of its paradigm. This means that companies may perceive more similarities, and anticipate fewer problems, than in fact they encounter.

As we noted in Chapter 1, organizations in similar business areas often have idiosyncratic cultures, so will lack a common language or a proper understanding of each other. After the merger that created Japan's Kangyo Bank, the managers had to publish a dictionary of more than 200 words to ensure the correct interpretations of key terms. Even apparently straightforward words had had completely different interpretations in the two constituent banks. The risk of such misunderstandings is higher in international acquisitions because of national cultural differences.[72] Airbus (see What Can Go Wrong 6.1) shows how firms can experience problems because of differences of opinion between national factions.

→ Resistance to change was reviewed in detail in Section 16.2.

Merging two organizations can threaten established roles and economic security, and generate great uncertainty about the future, so that a degree of resistance would be expected, as in any change situation. These may make it difficult to get people to adopt common systems and standards, as staff from one or other of the companies lose out, and are forced to abandon their preferred way of doing things. Mergers provide plenty of opportunities for these feelings of relative deprivation to occur—when one group believes that its situation has worsened, or that others have had a better deal. Conflict is often the result, as people in one firm band together against the 'enemy' in the other. The stress that results can make people cling more strongly to their established habits. And even if senior managers get on well (the ones that brokered the deal), there may be multiple mini culture clashes throughout the combined firm, so that a 'merger of equals' may actually be seen as a takeover at local levels.

d. Demotivation, distraction, and customer neglect

These high stress levels can mean that employees leave for other jobs, or simply do not come to work with the same degree of commitment as previously. Absenteeism levels and staff turnover rise, and productivity can decline. This is a particular problem in companies where critical resources are lodged in the knowledge and skills of key members of staff. In industries with a high knowledge content, such as advertising and financial services, personnel are the firm's assets and, if they leave, the price which the acquirer has paid for the company can appear very poor value.

This can be made worse by employees' anxiety regarding future working arrangements for themselves and their colleagues. Mergers are typically negotiated by senior managers, whose concern is for the overall structure of the combined firm and their role within it. Considerations such as who, at lower levels, will be located where, whom they will report to, and who will be made redundant, are left until later—but are of primary importance to the people affected. These anxieties are likely to affect people's ability to concentrate on their everyday jobs, so that quality and customer service levels may decline. A typical merger results in the loss of 2–5 per cent of the combined firm's customers.[73]

The middle managers who would normally monitor such things may themselves be similarly distracted, or unsure of their remit. Slow decision-making is a common problem in the aftermath of mergers. There is also the danger that, without a sufficient appreciation of the skills of managers from the other side of the merger, top executives will appoint the wrong people to key jobs.[74]

e. Hoped-for benefits do not materialize

The change management, culture, and resource issues highlighted in the earlier points may mean that synergies, or other benefits that were factored in when the offer price was calculated may fail to materialize in practice. There may also be subtle, unanticipated differences in product or customer characteristics, which may make it impossible for two businesses to share logistics or marketing resources. Incompatibilities in IT systems are a frequent source of problems in realizing benefits from mergers in financial services.

f. Outside stakeholder intervention

Even if there are no internal problems in realizing the benefits from a merger, outside stakeholders may intervene. Some regulatory bodies, in particular the European Commission and the US anti-trust authorities, have the power to intervene to prevent a merger that they determine will threaten customer interests in their own jurisdictions. They even have the power to force companies to unwind mergers that have already been effected. In 2001, the European Commission refused, in the face of strong lobbying from the US government, to allow GE and Honeywell to merge.[75] Although both firms are American, and the US authorities had allowed the merger, the Commission determined that in one area of joint operations, aero-engines, the combined firms would have too much market power. The previous year, the UK monopolies and mergers commission compelled Interbrew, the Belgian brewer, to divest certain brands that it had acquired through its purchase of Bass, a UK brewer.[76]

Other stakeholders, such as consumer groups and competitors, may lobby regulators and attempt to stir up public opinion to prevent mergers or acquisitions. When British Airways was contemplating a merger with American Airlines in 1998, Virgin Airlines led protests against the deal.[77]

17.5.3 Best practice in mergers and acquisitions

Experienced M&A practitioners, like General Electric, Cisco, Intel, and Electrolux, develop capabilities in planning and implementing acquisitions that are important elements of their corporate parenting propositions. Often, they will have specialist units dedicated to seeking out, valuing, and then integrating acquired firms.

a. Identifying the target[78]

If an acquirer exercises due care in researching and selecting its targets, it can reduce the risk that resources will be misjudged or cultural differences underestimated. There are two main alternative approaches. In mergers between large firms, where the aim is typically to consolidate activities in mature industries, turn around an underperforming target, or, more rarely, industry convergence, the number of possible target firms is likely to be quite small. In such cases, practised acquirers may 'stalk' their acquisition candidates over several years, building up a picture of their strong and weak points and their culture from published sources and industry rumours. These insights can be brought to bear during the valuation and post-merger phases.

Smaller deals, for resource acquisition or expansion into related products or markets, are normally intended to further strategic objectives at business unit level that cannot be met through organic growth. Managers at the centre of a large acquirer will want to retain overall control of what is being acquired, to ensure that it is coherent with the corporate strategy. Nonetheless, it is sensible practice to involve strategic business unit managers in the choice of target, to ensure that they are genuinely committed to making the acquisition work and that it meets their precise strategic needs. Business-level expertise can contribute to the success of the deal; strong marketing capabilities, for example, have been found to help firms make better acquisition selections.

It is also good practice to consider a broad range of potential targets before homing in on the one that best suits business needs. This reduces the risk that people's business judgement will be clouded by enthusiasm for firms with whom they have good personal relationships, or that have exciting technologies. However, this needs to be balanced against the need sometimes to move quickly. Organizations that can close deals quickly can do more of them, be offered good quality companies by the target's managers or venture capital owners, and get sizeable discounts on the price. In high-technology industries, where the need for speed is most pressing, leading firms have streamlined their processes so that a group consisting of the CEO, chief financial officer, and just two to three other executives can approve transactions.

b. Valuation, negotiation, and bidding[79]

Firms use the data gathered during the target identification phase to assess precisely how much the company is worth to them. This means that they are able to strike quickly if, because of a temporary operational problem or a fall in the stock market, the target's share price dips. The acquirer can then move quickly to pick up the target firm cheaply. They are also in a position to judge whether to walk away from the deal if a bidding war starts to push up the price of the acquisition. It is important to have the strength of mind to set a maximum price, and not to get lured into exceeding it.

In setting this price, it is important to get realistic estimates of the likely cost savings and revenue increases that can be extracted through the merger, and of the costs of any necessary restructuring. Acquirers have been found to be particularly prone to optimism when forecasting likely revenue gains—for example, they underestimate the probability that customers may be lost as the merger unfolds. It is important to check their estimates of merger synergies against outside benchmarks to ensure that they are realistic. If the projected revenue growth is substantially greater than what outsiders forecast for the industry, or if projected cost savings greatly exceed those achieved through past mergers in the sector, then they should be revised downwards. The involvement of operational managers, with detailed knowledge of the areas where synergies are being sought, is also likely to improve the quality of the projections.

The involvement of such managers at the due diligence stage is also important, since it reduces the risk of overlooking important deficiencies in the target's resources or key facets of its business model. The legal and accounting professionals who have traditionally driven the due diligence process are rarely qualified to do this. In one banking merger, the due diligence process did not extend to customer habits, and did not spot that many of the target's customers were heavy users of its branch network. When the acquirer extracted its planned cost savings by closing 75 per cent of those branches, it was taken by surprise by the number of customer defections.

Given the dangers that arise from insufficient cultural fit (Section 17.5.2), it is now widely accepted that 'cultural due diligence'—an assessment of the degree of compatibility between the two organizations' cultures—is as important as the traditional legal and accounting audits. Acquirers can look at whether the target's management have in their past decisions shown judgement similar to their own, and whether they take too many—or too few— risks. The degree of compatibility that the acquirer will look for will depend, however, on what is likely to happen after the merger has taken place. GE Capital, a financial services organization, has tended to transform ways of working in the firms it acquires to fit its own mould. When selecting acquisition targets, it therefore places far less emphasis on cultural fit than other acquirers, who will allow the target's managers more autonomy, and so need them to be on the same wavelength as their new parent. This does not mean, however, that acquirers should look for clones of themselves. A degree of cultural incompatibility can be useful, since it can trigger discussions that help the two firms learn from one another.[80]

Once the bidder has firmed up its estimates for what it is prepared to pay, it will normally attempt to negotiate an acceptable price and other conditions with the target's management. If successful, it may be able to avoid the time and expense of a hostile bid, which might also harm personal relationships between the two sets of managers. To preserve these relationships, the acquirer's negotiators should avoid behaviours that might be seen as condescending or culturally insensitive. The negotiation process can also reveal important things about a target organization, such as the existence of conflicts between its managers, which may need to be taken into account when valuing the firm, and when planning post-merger integration.

Other stakeholders, such as customers and regulatory bodies, need to be taken into account at this stage. Regulatory approval should never be treated as if it is a foregone conclusion, so it is advisable in a major merger to sound out regulators beforehand on their likely attitude to a proposed deal, and the conditions they might impose for it to be allowed to go ahead. Two-way communication with key customers, so that they can voice concerns and requirements, is also good practice at this stage and through the post-merger integration.

c. Post-merger integration[81]

The post-merger integration process is fundamental to the success of any merger or acquisition. Excellent work in finding and valuing the target, and negotiating the deal, will be of no use if cultural conflicts and operational problems render the merger unworkable. Some authorities suggest that planning for this phase should start as soon as the merger is proposed, since integrating two firms poses substantial leadership and change management challenges. In order to capture synergies and other benefits, one or both parties must change their distinctive political, cultural, and technological structures—but such changes should not disrupt the idiosyncratic routines that are the basis of valuable competences and capabilities. Moreover, the time available to get it right is short and the top managers involved may be tired after negotiating the deal.

One early decision required is whether the two firms need to be fully integrated. Most horizontal mergers—for example, between banks—will require full integration if synergies and cost savings are to be extracted. In some cases, as with GE Capital, the acquirer will impose its culture on the newly merged entities, whilst in others, such as IBM's acquisition of Lotus, the parent may be seeking a cultural infusion from the new arrivals.

Other acquisition types may involve a lower degree of integration, depending upon the acquirer's parenting style, the degree of relatedness between the businesses, and the extent

➔ We examined relatedness in Chapter 5, parenting style in Chapter 9, and organizational learning in Chapter 10.

to which there is potential for inter-unit learning and other synergies. There may be variations in the degree of integration across different elements of the value chain—for example, purchasing activities may be integrated across the new firm, but R&D activities may be left separate. Marketing is a particularly sensitive area, since if left entirely separate, opportunities to cross-sell, leverage corporate brands, and use marketing assets more productively may be lost, but if it is integrated too quickly, then brand loyalty and other relationships with the target's customers may be damaged.

The consensus among modern writers on M&A is that any necessary changes, in particular redundancies and restructuring, should occur within the first hundred days of the merger. This minimizes the uncertainty and stress for employees and shows that the new management has a clear direction for the merged organization. It is also important to develop a vision for the newly combined business and communicate it effectively, along with the rationale for any changes that it entails.

There are two common approaches to managing the change process. One, in which a larger company is integrating a smaller acquisition, involves nominating an integration leader, normally from the acquiring firm. Such a person needs to have the capacity to inspire people from both sides of the merger to renewed efforts, and gain acceptance and trust from their new colleagues. They will also need strong change agent skills to bring about any structural or strategic changes. Particularly important will be the capacity to negotiate their way within the political structures of both the acquirer and the target, and to work around any power struggles that may result from the merger.

→ The skills of change agents were examined in Section 16.4. Leadership attributes were reviewed in Section 17.1.

The second approach, most common when two larger organizations are merging in a way that envisages substantial transformation of working practices, entails the use of a transition structure involving employees from both sides. Typically, this involves setting up cross-organizational teams, each with a specific remit such as IT or customer service—one pharmaceuticals merger in 1989 gave rise to over three hundred of them. As well as specifying in detail how the new organization will function, these teams can help to reduce conflict and create a new, common culture. They should ideally start functioning as soon as possible, without waiting for the merger deal to be finalized, and should be led by the person who will be in charge of the relevant unit or function in the merged firm.

Business units and major departments will need to develop or revise their own strategies in response to the changes in corporate strategy that the merger will almost certainly entail. This may entail off-site meetings where large numbers of people thrash out joint approaches, business plans, performance measurement and control systems, and action plans for the first hundred days.

While these lower-level activities are crucial to post-merger integration, it is also very important that top management gives a strong lead to the merger process. First of all, however, top management roles need to be clearly determined, which can be a challenge, given that there are likely to be several candidates for each post. Politically expedient compromises, like having joint heads of every major division or function, tend to perpetuate conflicts and rivalries, rather than resolving them, and also give people at lower levels the message that post-merger issues can be fudged.

Top management should also take the lead in communicating the overall strategy of the merged organization, to give people who will be absorbed in their own post-merger activities an understanding of the broader context. They should give a lead on values for the new organization, and ensure that everyone understands what kind of performance is expected of them and their colleagues. They should remind employees, who naturally may be tempted to turn their attention inwards, of the importance of attending to other stakeholders—customers, business partners, and local communities.

Real-life Application 17.5 Procter & Gamble's merger with Gillette

In July 2005, two global consumer goods giants agreed to merge. Procter & Gamble (P&G), based in Cincinatti, Ohio, agreed to pay $57bn, the largest deal in its history, for Gillette, headquartered in Boston, Massachusetts. The combined group had annual sales of $62bn and a market capitalization of $200bn.[82] It had 22 brands with sales of over $1bn: P&G's stable included Crest toothpaste, Ariel soap powder, Pampers nappies, Head and Shoulders shampoo, and the Clairol and Wella beauty ranges, while Gillette contributed its shaver brand, along with Oral B dental care, and Duracell batteries.[83]

Although most deals of this size attracted a degree of scepticism, based upon the poor track record of large mergers, the P&G/Gillette fusion was broadly welcomed. Famed investor Warren Buffett, a shareholder in both firms, was quoted as saying it was a dream deal.[84] Of the votes cast by P&G shareholders, 97 per cent favoured the deal, as did 96 per cent of those cast by Gillette's.[85] A year after the merger, the combined firm's shares had risen slightly faster than the stock market average, when most other major deals had resulted in substantial stock price falls.[86]

Even the regulators looked kindly on the deal. The US Federal Trade Commission insisted that Gillette's Right Guard toiletries and Rembrandt tooth-whitening businesses be sold, to which the European Commission added Crest's electric toothbrush business (which, if added to Oral B's, would have commanded 50 per cent of the market). However, the Commission brushed aside competitors' concerns that the merged firm would be in a position to force them out of prime retail space.[87]

In fact, there was very little overlap between the two firms' product lines. One of the great attractions of the combination to many observers was complementarity: Gillette sold overwhelmingly to men, while 80–90 per cent of sales of P&G products were to women.[88] There were other attractions to the deal as well: the combined buying power and other synergies were expected to generate annual cost savings of over $1bn.[89] And P&G's track record of managing recent acquisitions of Wella, Clairol, and Tampax

were cited as a reason to be optimistic about the integration of Gillette, although this was a rather larger company than the other three.[90]

Gillette and P&G were both highly regarded for their prowess in marketing and supply chain management.[91] This expertise, of course, would count for nothing unless the two sets of experts could be persuaded to work together. It quickly became clear that P&G understood that it could learn from Gillette, as well as vice versa. Rather than following the path taken with its earlier acquisitions, which were integrated into P&G's systems, the company looked to harness the best of both firms' practices, and appointed several Gillette executives to head divisions, such as dental care, where there were also strong P&G candidates.[92] Two years later, the benefits of that mutual learning were clearly apparent. P&G had learnt from Gillette about sports marketing, in-store advertising, and, perhaps most importantly, about how to sell global products with a single global message. Gillette, for its part, had learnt when there might be benefits in tailoring a global message or product to appeal to local consumers, something at which P&G excelled.[93]

This did not mean that the merger had been plain sailing. Although AG Lafley, the CEO of P&G, was able to boast in December 2005 that not a single one of Gillette's business category or brand managers had left in the wake of the merger,[94] a report from Boston suggested earlier that month that around 40 per cent of Gillette's top 135 managers had either turned down jobs in the merged firm, not been offered one, or retired.[95] Two years later, it was reported that three key ex-Gillette executives who had been appointed to head P&G businesses had left the firm. The report suggested that Gillette managers found it difficult to adapt to differences in the two firms' marketing and management cultures.[96] However, a company spokesman denied that there were cultural problems, pointing out that three further ex-Gillette executives remained at the head of significant businesses, and that 95 per cent of Gillette managers offered jobs by P&G had accepted them.

What Can Go Wrong 17.1 DaimlerChrysler—problems in pursuit of an ambitious vision

When Daimler-Benz merged with the American car firm Chrysler, it was hailed as a 'marriage made in heaven'. *DaimlerChrysler*

When Daimler-Benz, the parent company of Mercedes-Benz cars, merged in May 1998 with the American car firm Chrysler it was hailed as a 'marriage made in heaven'. Chrysler was the smallest of the American 'Big 3' car-makers, but its adventurous designs had given it first-mover advantage in niches such as people-movers and sports-utility vehicles, where its Jeep brand was highly prized. The potential benefits from melding this creativity with Mercedes-Benz's famed discipline and quality were seen as enormous. Moreover, there were economies of scale and scope to be had from jointly sourcing and sharing components, even engines, between the two model ranges. Other synergies could be had from sharing best practice, such as Chrysler's paperless design and supplier management capabilities.

This was, however, just the first step in realizing the ambitious vision of CEO Jürgen Schrempp to build a 'Welt AG'—a global automobile powerhouse. DaimlerChrysler forged links with Japan's Mitsubishi in March 2000, and with South Korea's Hyundai in June the same year. These partners, in which DaimlerChrysler purchased substantial minority stakes, were intended to give it an entrée into not just their large home markets but also emerging markets in China and elsewhere in Asia.[97]

Problems, however, soon emerged between Daimler and Chrysler, in part because of differences in national cultures and practices that had not been taken into account during pre-merger planning. American executives, flush with share options that the merger allowed them to exercise, found themselves working with counterparts or bosses who might earn one-quarter to one-half of their own salary, but spend more lavishly when travelling on company business. German executives came to meetings armed with 50-page reports that they expected to spend hours discussing; the Americans, by contrast, summarized the key issues on one side of A4 and agreed the outcomes in informal discussions prior to the meeting.

This was one area where mutual learning was quickly visible—Schrempp limited papers to two pages, but with the expectation that meaningful discussions would take place at the meeting itself.[98]

The deal was heavily advertised as a 'merger of equals', and the company initially strove, not always productively, for equality in its treatment of the two sets of managers. Quickly, however, this began to change. By 2000, it was clear that the Germans were firmly in charge, and in October of that year Schrempp, in an interview with the *Financial Times*, was able to talk of Chrysler as 'a division, like Mercedes cars or like Mercedes trucks'. By January 2004 ten board members were from Daimler and only one from Chrysler; originally, posts were split 50/50.[99]

By mid-1999, highly regarded Chrysler designers and managers were defecting in large numbers. By the end of 2000, the top 15 Chrysler executives at the time of the merger had all left, been fired, or retired, like the head of design, Tom Gale, whose work had been key to Chrysler's revival prior to the merger.[100]

Meanwhile, it was proving difficult to extract the promised synergies from the merger. It was decided early on to keep the two brands and dealer networks separate and not to share platforms between them. However joint manufacture was to take place where financial considerations favoured it, and joint committees were set up to coordinate plans for developing and producing cars. Surplus capacity in a Jeep plant in Austria was diverted to Mercedes production; Chrysler's Crossfire sports car, launched in 2002, was built in a Mercedes plant and incorporated a Mercedes engine and components. However, most proposals for sharing components foundered on Mercedes engineers' jealous protection of their marque's reputation for quality, and their poor opinion of Chrysler's. There was more concrete collaboration between Chrysler and Mitsubishi, who already had a relationship before the merger.[101]

→

→ In his 2000 *Financial Times* interview, Schrempp had said that he had been working from the outset towards a structure in which Chrysler was just one division among many. This exposed him to another unfamiliar facet of US corporate life—litigious shareholders. Several sued Daimler in the US courts, alleging that had they been made aware of Schrempp's true intentions, they would have demanded a premium for their shares as compensation for ceding control. While their claim was debatable for several reasons, they were able to force a number of DaimlerChrysler's top managers to defend their actions in court in 2003.[102]

This must have been an unwelcome distraction from the pressing problems that had emerged in the company since 2000. By the third quarter of 2000, the Chrysler division was making losses, and Schrempp despatched Dieter Zetsche to be its third president in little more than a year. Japanese firms had launched models that competed directly with Chrysler's once-innovative niche products, which were now showing their age. DaimlerChrysler were forced to offer discounts of $2,000 per vehicle to maintain sales.[103] The approachable Zetsche, equally at home mingling with workers in the staff canteen and with Detroit's wealthy set at charitable functions, proved a popular leader. His charm and humour helped him push through the closure of six plants, with the loss of 26,000 jobs. DaimlerChrysler also invested in a revitalized product range, and by 2004, the division was profitable again.[104]

By then, however, the unthinkable had happened—Mercedes cars were experiencing quality problems. Mostly, these related to malfunctions in the advanced electronics that the firm used to differentiate its vehicles, but some German taxi drivers, important customers, complained of faulty paintwork. These issues depressed profits at Mercedes, while the Smart small-car operation was losing money and the Maybach limousine, a prestige product, had achieved barely half its target sales.[105]

Meanwhile, the Asian part of the strategy had also experienced setbacks. Mitsubishi, despite the efforts of the German executive sent to run it, remained a persistent loss-maker. Schrempp's leadership style was always to listen to arguments, then take the final decision himself, forcing opposition aside if necessary.[106] But in April 2004, his board refused his proposal to inject more capital into Mitsubishi; the funds were provided by other Mitsubishi partners and DaimlerChrysler's stake heavily diluted. And in August 2004, after a disagreement regarding strategy in China, the Hyundai stake was sold.[107]

In July 2005, Jürgen Schrempp unexpectedly resigned as DaimlerChrysler's CEO. The company's share price rose 10 per cent on the news, though its market capitalization remained at little more than half of the value of DaimlerChrysler at the time of the takeover. Dieter Zetsche was nominated as his replacement. Amongst his first acts on taking office in January 2006 was to cut 8,500 manufacturing jobs at Mercedes and 6,000 posts at the Stuttgart headquarters—and to announce further plans to push Mercedes and Chrysler towards using more common components.[108]

In September 2006, however, he was forced to issue a profit warning as Chrysler went $1.3bn into the red. With costs already pared back by Zetsche when he was in charge there, it was unclear how the American operations could be returned to profitability. In February 2007, it announced the closure of two factories and the loss of 13,000 jobs. When asked, at the press conference announcing DaimlerChrysler's 2006 results, whether he would consider selling Chrysler, he replied 'All options are on the table.'[109]

Creative strategizing 17.2

Other than spinning off Chrysler, what measures might Zetsche consider to rescue the situation?

● CHAPTER SUMMARY

In this chapter, we have examined a number of facets of the implementation of strategy.

The quality of leadership in an organization has a major role to play in the way in which strategy unfolds there. Leadership can be found at all levels in an organization. As well as top management, middle managers have important roles to play in making strategy happen. They reinterpret strategies so that they can be effectively implemented in their units, pull together information to transmit to senior managers, and champion new ideas, providing them with the resources needed for initial testing.

Leaders can be transformational—inspiring people through their charisma and enthusiasm, and challenging established practices—or transactional, aiming to build on existing ways of working, and motivating through formal targets and rewards. It is important to match the style of leader to the demands of the organization's situation. Both transactional or transformational leaders can use one of several leadership approaches:

- the strategy approach—leaders take key strategic decisions themselves and spend time gathering data to inform them;
- the human-assets approach—making sure that the organization has the right people, and becoming involved in recruitment and career planning;
- the expertise approach—leaders championing the adoption of certain vital skills;
- the box approach—building a 'box' of control systems that define norms and corporate values;
- the change agent approach—creating a climate of continual reinvention.

Effective leaders display vision, energy, and authority, a deep understanding of their business, and the capacity to empathize with their colleagues but also the ability to be ruthless where necessary. They are able to choose and motivate people, to listen and gather soft data, and to show their human side by displaying selected weaknesses. 'Level 5' leaders, in addition, combine personal humility with an implacable will to achieve what is needed for their organization. They are able to transform good firms into exceptional performers.

Effective leaders must also be able to use power effectively. They use the power of resources to place allies in key roles, the power of processes to determine who gets what information and when, and the power of meanings to present organizational and personal performance in its best light. They are astute in choosing, motivating, and rewarding allies—particularly important where the leader is new to the organization.

Effective strategic control and performance measurement systems allow behaviour to be controlled, performance monitored, and effective corrective actions to be taken where necessary. Controls can be internal or external to the organization. Some external controls are imposed by society, in particular societal and institutional norms, which may be expressed as laws and regulations. Customer requirements also impose controls upon organizations, as do the markets in which they compete, and the financial markets from which they may draw their funds. Managers must meet the requirements of their company's investors, otherwise the market for corporate control will pass the firm into the hands of different managers.

Internal control systems need to translate these external controls into a form that influences the everyday behaviour of managers and employees. All internal controls derive ultimately from the system of authority to which people submit when they join an organization. The organization's hierarchy may set up bureaucratic control systems—rules and procedures, standards, and information systems —but cultural norms and values will have at least as strong an influence on behaviour. Behaviour will also be shaped strongly by the rewards and sanctions, both financial and non-financial, given for particular types of conduct. The effectiveness of reward systems will depend on the way in which performance is measured, and the way that managers use that performance information.

Managers need, and collect, both 'hard' quantitative data and 'soft' qualitative information for use in assessing performance. Overall goals for the organization are translated into detailed key performance indicators (KPIs) for divisions, functions, and individuals. However, cunning managers, given a single target, often devise ways of hitting it without necessarily achieving the organization's strategic aims. Cultural controls are the only real guard against this, but performance measurement systems have been developed to help balance short-term and long-term considerations. The most popular is the balanced scorecard, which contains measures of efficiency, quality, innovation, and customer responsiveness.

Targets are typically set at levels that stretch managers to achieve slightly more than they feel is comfortably attainable, but there can be cases when targets can be set either 'impossibly' high or at comfortably attainable levels. It is important to have a performance measurement culture in which the measures are accepted and trusted, action is taken if targets are not met, and positive feedback given where they are exceeded.

Projects require particular, specialized, systems of controls that focus on their timeliness, cost, and the extent to which outcomes meet the intended specifications. Projects are broken down into tasks, each with its own specifications, schedules, and budgets, against which performance is measured. Particular attention should be given to the management of the risks associated with each task.

Strategy implementation requires financial resources, of which the main sources are banks, equity markets, and venture capital. The amount of finance that can be raised depends on the firm's asset base, the quality of the management team and its past performance.

Firms typically descend into crisis because of poor management practices, poor financial controls, or environmental change. Turnarounds from such situations are difficult to achieve. The steps in a turnaround process are:

- an analysis of the firm's situation, to see what has led to the crisis and whether anything can be saved from it;
- changes to or augmentation of the management team, often including a new CEO;
- emergency action—retrenchment—to stabilize the situation, raise cash from asset sales, and cut costs, often through redundancies and closures;
- restructuring of the remaining parts of the business to perform profitably, often including a change in competitive stance,
- a return to stable profitability.

Mergers and acquisitions (M&A) generate particular implementation problems. They typically fail to generate adequate returns on investment, though there is limited evidence that more recent M&A activity has been more successful. Mergers have three main phases: target identification, price negotiation (including the due diligence process which helps the bidder establish the target's true worth), and post-merger integration. Problems may arise at any of those phases:

- the acquired firm's resources may be less valuable than expected;
- the bidder pays more than those resources are actually worth;
- there are difficulties in establishing cultural and operational fit between the merger partners;
- the stress and distraction associated with the merger may lead employees to become demotivated and customer service and operational duties to be neglected. This may be exacerbated if the wrong managers are appointed to key posts;
- the above factors or other unforeseen differences between the firms leads to difficulties in extracting the expected synergies;
- regulators may intervene, perhaps egged on by competitors and customers.

Experienced M&A practitioners have processes designed to minimize these risks. At the candidate identification stage, they may gather intelligence regarding large merger targets over many years. For smaller acquisitions, they ensure that there is a business unit ready to take responsibility for the acquisition, and involve its managers in the selection process. Where time permits, they will scan a number of targets rather than opt for the first one that appears attractive.

Any data gathered on the target will help with the valuation, negotiation, and bidding phase, and help ensure that negotiators are not carried away with the momentum of the deal. It is important also to ensure that estimates of merger synergies, and of the costs of achieving them, are realistic. Business unit managers should be involved in the due diligence process, to ensure important operational details are not overlooked, and due diligence should cover cultural fit as well as the legal and financial aspects of the business. Negotiations on price should be undertaken diplomatically, with post-merger integration in mind, and customers and regulatory bodies should be consulted.

The first hundred days after the deal are crucial for post-merger integration, although not all deals will require the participants to be fully integrated. All major changes, in particular redundancies and restructuring, should take place within this period if possible. When a large firm is acquiring a smaller one, a change agent may be appointed as integration leader. When two large organizations are merging, it is more common to set up transitional structures, such as joint task forces, to finalize new working arrangements—these should start working before the deal is finalized. Top management needs to take a strong lead to ensure that the new organization's objectives and values are clearly understood, and that customers are not neglected as people focus on restructuring.

 Online Resource Centre
www.oxfordtextbooks.co.uk/orc/haberberg_rieple/

Visit the Online Resource Centre that accompanies this book to read more information relating to making strategy happen.

● KEY SKILLS

The key skills you should have developed after reading this chapter are:

- the ability to identify the style and approach adopted by a leader and to assess its appropriateness;
- the ability to analyse the control systems in an organization and appraise their appropriateness for that organization's chosen strategy;
- the ability to propose key performance indicators relevant to an organization's strategy, within the framework of a balanced scorecard;
- the ability to identify appropriate ways for an organization to raise finance;
- the ability to appraise the turnaround strategy adopted by an organization and to propose relevant enhancements to it;
- the ability to appraise a firm's track record on mergers and acquisitions and critique the methods it has used in planning and executing them.

● REVIEW QUESTIONS

1. Which leadership approaches might be particularly suited to:
   (a) a small design consultancy or architectural practice?
   (b) a high-technology firm in an emerging industry?
   (c) a firm that is the product of a recent merger between two large players in a highly competitive, mature industry?
   (d) a medium-sized manufacturing company, in a growing industry, which has run out of cash because of ambitious expansion and poor financial controls?

2. What performance measures would you suggest for the firms listed in Question 1, and how might they gather the relevant data? For firms (c) and (d), look at both the control systems used during the merger/turnaround process and those to be implemented afterwards.

3. Which sources of finance would be best suited to firms a–d above?

4. You are considering the acquisition of a company that is in a turnaround situation. Which are the factors to which you would give particular attention at each of the three phases of the merger process?

5. Why do people try and rescue failing companies, rather than simply buying up the assets cheaply after they have gone bankrupt? What does your answer imply for the people leading an attempted turnaround?

● FURTHER READING

- Collins, J. (2001). 'Level 5 leadership'. *Harvard Business Review*, 79/1: 66–76 is a report of a wide-ranging study on what makes the difference between organizations that perform well and those that perform exceptionally, with leadership being identified as a key component.

- Vera, D. and Crossan, M. (2004). 'Strategic leadership and organizational learning'. *Academy of Management Review*, 29/2: 222–40 is a more scholarly, but still quite approachable, paper that summarizes current leadership research.

- Neely, A. and Al Najjar, M. (2006). 'Management learning not management control: the true role of performance measurement'. *California Management Review*, 48/3: 99–114. Summarizes the current understanding of the role of performance measurement in an organization's architecture.

- Kaplan, R. and Norton, D. (2006). 'How to implement a new strategy without disrupting your organization'. *Harvard Business Review*, 84/3: 100–9. Summarizes these two influential authors' recent thinking on balanced scorecards, strategy maps, and their implementation.

- Gray, C. and Larson, E. (2006). *Project Management: The Managerial Process*. London: McGraw-Hill/Irwin is a well-written guide to the topic.

- Burbank, R. (2005). 'The classic five-step turnaround process: case study of ProdiGene, Inc'. *Journal of Private Equity*, 8/2: 53–8 is a very useful practitioner's guide to turnarounds.

- Boyne, G. (2006). 'Strategies for public service turnaround: lessons from the private sector?' *Administration and Society*, 38/3: 365–88. A thorough review of the academic literature on turnarounds, aimed at people who might want to use it in the study of public sector organizations, but of interest to all.

- DiGeorgio, R. (2002). 'Making mergers and acquisitions work: what we know and don't know', pt 1. *Journal of Change Management*, 3/2: 134–48; (2003). pt 2. *Journal of Change Management*, 3/3: 259–74. Together these two papers form a comprehensive and readable survey of what is known about M&A, combining academic research with the practical insights of the author, who is a consultant in this area.

● REFERENCES

Adams, C. and Neely, A. (2002). 'Prism reform'. *Financial Management*, May: 28–31.

Amason, A. (1996). 'Distinguishing the effects of functional and dysfunctional conflict on strategic decision making'. *Academy of Management Journal*, 39/1: 123–48.

Ambos, B. and Schlegelmilch, B. (2007). 'Innovation and control in the multinational firm: a comparison of political and contingency approaches'. *Strategic Management Journal*, 28/5: 473–86.

Armenakis, A., Fredenberger, W., Cherones, L., and Feild, H. (1995). 'Symbolic actions used by business turnaround change agents'. *Academy of Management Journal*, Special Edition (Best Papers Proceedings, p. 229).

Armenakis, A., Fredenberger, W., Giles, W., and Cherones, L. (1996). 'Symbolism use by business turnaround change agents'. *International Journal of Organizational Analysis*, 4/2: 123–34.

Ashton, R. (2007). 'Value-creation models for value-based management: review, analysis, and research directions'. *Advances in Management Accounting*, 16: 1–62.

Bailey, A. and Johnson, G. (1995). 'Strategy development processes: a configurational approach'. *Academy of Management Journal*, Best Paper Proceedings: 2–6.

Balgobin, R. and Pandit, N. (2001). 'Stages in the turnaround process: the case of IBM UK'. *European Management Journal*, 19/3: 301–16.

Balogun, J. (2003). 'From blaming the middle to harnessing its potential: creating change intermediaries'. *British Journal of Management*, 14/1: 69–83.

Barker, V. and Duhaime, I. (1997). 'Strategic change in the turnaround process: theory and empirical evidence'. *Strategic Management Journal*, 18: 13–38.

Barker, V. L. and Mone, M. A. (1994). 'Retrenchment: Cause of turnaround or consequence of decline?' *Strategic Management Journal*, 15/5: 395–406.

Bass, B. and Avolio, B. (1990). 'The implications of transactional and transformational leadership for individual, team, and organizational development'. In Staw, B. and L. Cummings (eds), *Research in Organizational Change and Development*. Greenwich, CT: JAI Press, 231–272.

Bibeault, D. (1982). *Corporate Turnaround: How Managers Turn Losers into Winners*. New York: McGraw-Hill.

Bieshaar, H., Knight, J., and Van Wassenaer, A. (2001). 'Deals that create value'. *McKinsey Quarterly*, 1: 64–73.

Bourne, M., Neely, A., Platts, K., and Mills, J. (2002). 'The success and failure of performance measurement initiatives: perceptions of participating managers'. *International Journal of Operations and Production Management*, 22/11: 1288–310.

Boyett, I. and Currie, G. (2004). 'Middle managers moulding international strategy: an Irish start-up in Jamaican telecoms'. *Long Range Planning*, 37/1: 51–66.

Brass, D. and Burkhardt, M. (1993). 'Potential power and power use: An investigation of structure and behavior'. *Academy of Management Journal*, 36/3: 441–70.

Buono, A. and Bowditch, J. (1989). *The Human Side of Mergers and Acquisitions: Managing Collisions between People, Cultures, and Organizations*. San Francisco: Jossey-Bass.

Buono, A., Bowditch, J., and Lewis III, J. W. (1985). 'When cultures collide: the anatomy of a merger'. *Human Relations*, 38/5: 477–500.

Burbank, R. (2005). 'The classic five-step turnaround process: case study of ProdiGene, Inc'. *Journal of Private Equity*, 8/2: 53–8.

Burgelman, R. (1983). 'A process model of internal corporate venturing in the diversified major firm'. *Administrative Science Quarterly*, 28/2: 223–44.

Burns, J. (1978). *Leadership*. New York: Harper & Row.

Carey, D. (2000). 'Making mergers succeed'. *Harvard Business Review*, 78/3: 145–54.

Cartwright, S. and Cooper, C. (1993). 'The role of culture compatibility in successful organizational marriage'. *Academy of Management Executive*, 7/2: 57–70.

Cartwright, S. and Cooper, C. (1996). *Managing Mergers, Acquisitions and Strategic Alliances*. 2nd edn. Oxford: Butterworth Heinemann.

Charan, R. and Colvin, G. (1999). 'Why CEOs fail'. *Fortune*, 21 June: 31–7.

Chatterjee, S., Lubatkin, M., Schweiger, D., and Weber, Y. (1992). 'Cultural differences and shareholder value in related mergers: linking equity and human capital'. *Strategic Management Journal*, 13/5: 319–34.

Christofferson, S., McNish, R., and Sias, D. (2004). 'Where mergers go wrong'. *McKinsey Quarterly*, 2: 92–9.

Collier, N., Fishwick, F., and Floyd, S. (2004). 'Managerial involvement and perceptions of strategy process'. *Long Range Planning*, 37/1: 67–83.

Collins, J. (2001). 'Level 5 leadership'. *Harvard Business Review*, 79/1: 66–76.

Daft, R. and Lengel, R. (1986). 'Organizational information requirements, media richness and structural design'. *Management Science*, 32/5: 554–71.

Daft, R. and Macintosh, N. (1984). 'The nature and use of formal control systems for management control and strategy implementation'. *Journal of Management*, 10/1: 43–66.

David, K. and Singh, H. (1993). 'Acquisition regimes: managing cultural risk and relative deprivation'. *Corporate Acquisitions: International Review of Strategic Management*, 4: 227–76.

Dean Jr, J. and Sharfman, M. (1996). 'Does decision process matter? A study of strategic decision-making effectiveness'. *Academy of Management Journal*, 39/2: 368–96.

De Waal, A. (2003). 'Behavioral factors important for the successful implementation and use of performance management systems'. *Management Decision*, 41/8: 688–97.

DiGeorgio, R. (2002). 'Making mergers and acquisitions work: what we know and don't know—Part I'. *Journal of Change Management*, 3/2: 134–48.

DiGeorgio, R. (2003). 'Making mergers and acquisitions work: what we know and don't know—Part II'. *Journal of Change Management*, 3/3: 259–74.

Eisenhardt, K. and Bourgeois, L. (1988). 'Politics of strategic decision making in high-velocity environments: towards a mid-range theory'. *Academy of Management Journal*, 31: 737–70.

Eisenhardt, K. and Zbaracki, M. (1992). 'Strategic decision making'. *Strategic Management Journal*, 13: 17–37.

Ernst, D. and Halevy, T. (2004). 'Not by M&A alone'. *McKinsey Quarterly*, 1: 68–9.

Farkas, C. and Wetlaufer, S. (1996). 'The ways chief executive officers lead'. *Harvard Business Review*, May–June: 110–22.

Filatotchev, I. and Toms, S. (2006). 'Corporate governance and financial constraints on strategic turnarounds'. *Journal of Management Studies*, 43/3: 407–33.

Fletcher, H. and Smith, D. (2004). 'Managing for value: developing a performance measurement system integrating economic value added and the balanced scorecard in strategic planning'. *Journal of Business Strategies*, 21/1: 1–17.

Floyd, S. and Wooldridge, B. (1994). 'Dinosaurs or dynamos? Recognizing middle management's strategic role'. *Academy of Management Executive*, 8/4: 47–57.

Floyd, S. and Wooldridge, B. (1997). 'Middle management's strategic influence and organizational performance'. *Journal of Management Studies*, 34/3: 465–85.

Foucault, M. (1980). *Power/Knowledge: Selected Interviews and Other Writings 1972–1977*. Brighton: Harvester Press.

Franco, M. and Bourne, M. (2003). 'Factors that play a role in "managing through measures"'. *Management Decision*, 41/8: 698–710.

Frick, K. and Torres, A. (2002). 'Learning from high-tech deals'. *McKinsey Quarterly*, 1: 113–23.

Fubini, D., Price, C., and Zollo, M. (2006). 'The elusive art of postmerger leadership'. *McKinsey Quarterly*, 4: 28–37.

Furman, J. and McGahan, A. (2002). 'Turnarounds'. *Managerial and Decision Economics*, 23: 283–300.

Gabarro, J. (1987). *The Dynamics of Taking Charge*. Boston, MA: Harvard Business School Press.

Gabarro, J. (2007). 'When a new manager takes charge'. *Harvard Business Review*, 85/1: 104–17.

Gadiesh, O., Pace, S., and Rogers, P. (2003). 'Successful turnarounds: three key dimensions'. *Strategy & Leadership*, 31/6: 41–3.

Garvin, D. (1993). 'Building a learning organization'. *Harvard Business Review*, July–August: 78–91.

Goffee, R. and Jones, G. (2000). 'Why should anyone be led by you?' *Harvard Business Review*, 78/5: 62–70.

Goffee, R. and Jones, G. (2005). 'Managing authenticity'. *Harvard Business Review*, 83/12: 86–94.

Goold, M. and Quinn, J. (1990). 'The paradox of strategic controls'. *Strategic Management Journal*, 11: 43–57.

Gopal, R. (1991). 'Turning around sick companies—the Indian experience'. *Long Range Planning*, 24: 79–83.

Gouldner, A. W. (1954). *Patterns of Industrial Bureaucracy*. New York: Free Press.

Gray, C. and Larson, E. (2006). *Project Management: The Managerial Process*. London: McGraw-Hill/Irwin.

Grinyer, P, Mayes, D., and McKiernan, P. (1990). 'The sharpbenders: achieving a sustained improvement in performance'. *Long Range Planning*, 23: 116–25.

Grundy, T. (1998). 'Strategy implementation and project management'. *International Journal of Project Management*, 16/1: 43–50.

Hambrick, D. and D'Aveni, R. (1992). 'Top team deterioration as part of the downward spiral of large corporate bankruptcies'. *Management Science*, 38/10: 1445–66.

Hanessian, B. (2005). 'Leading a turnaround: an interview with the chairman of D&B'. *McKinsey Quarterly*, 2: 83–93.

Haspeslagh, P. (1989). 'Emphasizing value creation in strategic acquisitions'. *Mergers and Acquisitions*, 24/2: 68–71.

Haspeslagh, P. and Jemison, D. (1986). *Managing Acquisitions: Creating Value Through Corporate Renewal*. New York: Free Press.

Haspeslagh, P., Noda, T., and Boulos, F. (2001). 'It's not just about the numbers'. *Harvard Business Review*, 79/7: 64–73.

Healy, P., Palepu, K., and Ruback, R. (1997). 'Which takeovers are profitable? Strategic or financial'. *Sloan Management Review*, 38/4: 45–57.

Hickson, D., Hinings, C., Lee, C., Schenk, R., and Pennings, J. (1971). 'A strategic contingencies theory of intraorganizational power'. *Administrative Science Quarterly*, 16/2: 216–29.

Hubbard, N. (1999). *Acquisition: Strategy and Implementation*. London: Macmillan.

Ingham, H., Kran, I., and Lovestam, A. (1992). 'Mergers and profitability: a managerial success story?' *Journal of Management Studies*, 29/2: 195–208.

Isaksen, S., Babij, B., and Lauer, K. (2003). 'Cognitive syles in creative leadership practices: exploring the relationship between level and style'. *Psychological Reports*, 93/3: 983–94.

Ittner, C. and Larcker, D. (2001). 'Assessing empirical research in managerial accounting: a value-based management perspective'. *Journal of Accounting and Economics*, 32: 349–410.

Janis, B. (1982). *Groupthink: Psychological Studies of Policy Decisions and Fiascos*. Boston: Houghton-Mifflin.

Kanter, R. (1983). *The Change Masters: Innovations for Productivity in the American Corporation*. New York: Simon and Schuster.

Kaplan, R. and Norton, D. (1992). 'The balanced scorecard—measures that drive performance'. *Harvard Business Review*, 70/1: 71–9.

Kaplan, R. and Norton, D. (1996). 'Using the balanced scorecard as a strategic management system'. *Harvard Business Review*, January–February: 75–85.

Kaplan, R. and Norton, D. (2000). 'Having trouble with your strategy? Then map it'. *Harvard Business Review*, 78/5: 167–76.

Keegan, A. and Turner, J. (2002). 'The management of innovation in project-based firms'. *Long Range Planning*, 35/4: 367–88.

Keil, M. and Montealegre, R. (2000). 'Cutting your losses: extricating your organization when a big project goes awry'. *MIT Sloan Management Review*, 41/3: 55–68.

Kenny, J. (2003). 'Effective project management for strategic innovation and change in an organizational context'. *Project Management Journal*, 34/1: 43–53.

Lawler III, E. (1998). 'Strategic pay systems'. In Mohrman, S., Galbraith, J., Lawler III, E., and associates (eds), *Tomorrow's Organization*. New York: Jossey-Bass.

Lohrke, F., Bedeian, A., and Palmer, T. (2004). 'The role of top management teams in formulating and implementing turnaround strategies: a review and research agenda'. *International Journal of Management Reviews*, 5–6/2: 63–90.

Lorange, P. and Nelson, R. (1987). 'How to recognize—and avoid—organizational decline'. *Sloan Management Review*, 28/3: 41–8.

Lynch, R. and Cross, K. (1991). *Measure Up!* Cambridge, MA: Blackwell Publishers.

Maitlis, S. (2004). 'Taking it from the top: how CEOs influence (and fail to influence) their boards'. *Organization Studies*, 25/8: 1275–311.

Mair, J. (2005). 'Exploring the determinants of unit performance: The role of middle managers in stimulating profit growth'. *Group and Organization Management*, 30/3: 263–88.

Malmi, T. and Ikäheimo, S. (2003). 'Value based management practices—some evidence from the field'. *Management Accounting Research*, 14/3: 235–54.

Marks, M. and Mirvis, P. (1998). *Joining Forces*. San Francisco: Jossey-Bass.

Marr, B. and Schiuma, G. (2003). 'Business performance measurement—past, present and future'. *Management Decision*, 41/8: 680–7.

Martin, A. (2007). 'The future of leadership: where do we go from here?' *Industrial & Commercial Training*, 39/1: 3–8.

Milosevic, D. and Srivannaboon, S. (2006). 'A theoretical framework for aligning project management with business strategy'. *Project Management Journal*, 37/3: 98–110.

Mintzberg, H. (1975). 'The manager's job: folklore and fact'. *Harvard Business Review*, July–August: 49–61.

MIT Sloan Management Review (2004). 'The benefits of managing for value'. 45/2: 8.

Morris, P. and Jamieson, A. (2005). 'Moving from corporate strategy to project strategy'. *Project Management Journal*, 36/4: 5–18.

Morrow Jr, J., Sirmon, D., Hitt, M., and Holcomb, T. (2007). 'Creating value in the face of declining performance: firm strategies and organizational recovery'. *Strategic Management Journal*, 28: 271–83.

Nadler, D. and Tushman, M. (1988). 'What makes for magic leadership?' *Fortune*, 6 June: 115–16.

Nahavandi, A. and Malekzadeh, A. (1988). 'Acculturation in mergers and acquisitions'. *Academy of Management Review*, 13/1: 79–90.

Neely, A. (2005). 'The evolution of performance measurement research: developments in the last decade and a research agenda for the next'. *International Journal of Operations and Production Management*, 25/12: 1264–77.

Neely, A. and Al Najjar, M. (2006). 'Management learning not management control: The true role of performance measurement'. *California Management Review*, 48/3: 101–14.

Neely, A., Gregory, M., and Platts, K. (2005). 'Performance measurement system design: A literature review and research agenda'. *International Journal of Operations and Production Management*, 25/12: 1128–63.

Nutt, P. C. (2002). 'Making strategic choices'. *Journal of Management Studies*, 39/1: 67–96.

O'Reilly, B. (1999). 'The mechanic who fixed Continental'. *Fortune*, 140/12: 176–86.

Palter, R. and Srinivasan, D. (2006). 'Habits of the busiest acquirers'. *McKinsey Quarterly*, 4: 18–27.

Pant, L. (1991). 'An investigation of industry and firm structural characteristics in corporate turnarounds'. *Journal of Management Studies*, 28/6: 623–41.

Pearce II, J. and Robbins, D. (1994). 'Retrenchment remains the foundation of business turnaround'. *Strategic Management Journal*, 15/5: 407–17.

Pellegrinelli, S. and Bowman, C. (1994). 'Implementing strategy through projects'. *Long Range Planning*, 27/4: 125–32.

Pettigrew, A. (1973). *The Politics of Organizational Decision-making*. London: Tavistock.

Pettigrew, A. and Whipp, R. (1991). *Managing Change for Competitive Success*. Oxford: Blackwell.

Pfeffer, J. (1981). *Power in Organizations*. Marshfield, MA: Pitman.

Pfeffer, J. (1992). *Managing with Power: Politics and Influence in Organizations*. Boston, MA: Harvard Business School Press.

Pfeffer, J. and Salancik, G. (1978). *The External Control of Organisations: A Resource Dependency Perspective*. New York: Harper & Row.

Pun, K. and White, A. (2005). 'A performance measurement paradigm for integrating strategy formulation: a review of systems and frameworks'. *International Journal of Management Reviews*, 7/1: 49–71.

Quinn, J. B. (1980). *Strategies for Change: Logical Incrementalism*. Irwin, IL: R. D. Irwin.

Ranson, S., Hinings, B., and Greenwood, R. (1980). 'The structuring of organizational structures'. *Administrative Science Quarterly*, 25/1: 470–4.

Rieple, A. (1997). 'The paradoxes of new managers as levers of organizational change'. *Strategic Change*, 6/4.

Rieple, A. (1998). 'An analysis of the structural factors which led to the enforced departure of a chief executive'. Unpublished doctoral thesis, Cranfield University, England.

Rieple, A. and Vyakarnam, S. (1996). 'The case for managerial ruthlessness'. *British Journal of Management*, 7/1: 17–33.

Roach, C. (2007). 'Taking the lead during a merger'. *Strategic Communication Management*, 11/1: 8.

Robbins, D. and Pearce, J. (1992) 'Turnaround: retrenchment and recovery'. *Strategic Management Journal*, 13/4: 287–309.

Rouleau, L. (2005). 'Micro-practices of strategic sensemaking and sensegiving: How middle managers interpret and sell change every day'. *Journal of Management Studies*, 42/7: 1413–41.

Rucci, A., Kirn, S., and Quinn, R. (1998). 'The employee-customer-profit chain at Sears'. *Harvard Business Review*, 76/1: 83–97.

Ryan Jr, H. and Trahan, E. (2007). 'Corporate financial control mechanisms and firm performance: the case of value-based management systems'. *Journal of Business Finance & Accounting*, 34/1–2: 111–38.

Salancik, G. and Pfeffer, J. (1977). 'Who gets power—and how they hold on to it'. *Organizational Dynamics*, 5/3: 3–21.

Schweiger, D., Sandberg, W., and Ragan, J. (1986). 'Group approaches for improving strategic decision making: a comparative analysis of dialectical inquiry, devil's advocacy, and consensus'. *Academy of Management Journal*, 29: 51–71.

Schwenk, C. R. (1989). 'Linking cognitive, organizational and political factors in explaining strategic change'. *Journal of Management Studies*, 26/2: 177–87.

Shenhar, A., Dvir, D., Levy, O., and Maltz, A. (2001). 'Project success: A multidimensional strategic concept'. *Long Range Planning*, 34/6: 699–725.

Slatter, S. (1984). *Corporate Recovery*. London: Penguin.

Slatter, S. and Lovett, D. (1999). *Corporate Turnaround*. London: Penguin Business.

Sorescu, A., Chandy, R., and Prabhu, J. (2007). 'Why some acquisitions do better than others: product capital as a driver of long-term stock returns'. *Journal of Marketing Research*, 44/1: 57–72.

Srivannaboon, S. (2006). 'Linking project management with business strategy'. *Project Management Journal*, 37/5: 88–96.

Srivannaboon, S. and Milosevic, D. (2006). 'A two-way influence between business strategy and project management'. *International Journal of Project Management*, 24/6: 493–505.

Sudarsanam, S. and Lai, J. (2001). 'Corporate financial distress and turnaround strategies: An empirical analysis'. *British Journal of Management*, 12/3: 183–99.

Vera, D. and Crossan, M. (2004). 'Strategic leadership and organizational learning'. *Academy of Management Review*, 29/2: 222–40.

Von Krogh, G., Sinatra, A., and Singh, H. (eds) (1994). *The Management of Corporate Acquisitions. International Perspectives*. New York: Macmillan.

Vroom, V. and Jago, A. (2007). 'The role of the situation in leadership'. *American Psychologist*, 62/1: 17–24.

Waggoner, D., Neely, A., and Kennerley, M. (1999). 'The forces that shape organizational performance measurement systems: an interdisciplinary review'. *International Journal of Production Economics*, 60–1/3: 53–60.

Watson, A. and Wooldridge, B. (2005). 'Business unit manager influence on corporate-level strategy formulation'. *Journal of Managerial Issues*, 17/2: 147–61.

Wooldridge, B. and Floyd, S. (1990). 'The strategy process, middle management involvement, and organizational performance'. *Strategic Management Journal*, 11/3: 231–41.

Zweig, P. and Perlman, J. (1995). 'The case against mergers'. *Business Week*, 30 October: 122–30.

End-of-chapter Case Study 17.1 The turnaround at Philips 2001–2007

Dutch conglomerate Royal Philips Electronics has a proud history of innovation in electrical goods and electronics. From its foundation by Anton and Gerard Philips in 1891, as a manufacturer of light bulbs, it had pioneered such products as X-rays, rotary electric shavers, compact cassette tapes, CDs, and DVDs, accumulating some 126,000 patents.[110] Its innovativeness made Philips the largest consumer-electronics group in Europe, and a mainstay of the Dutch economy. The philosophy of Frits Philips, the much-respected son of Anton, who ran the company from 1940 until 1971, was to encourage inventiveness on the part of Philips' engineers; the company would then manufacture and attempt to sell the resulting products.

The firm's unbridled passion for technology led it to become a highly diversified conglomerate that produced lighting, medical systems, computers, semiconductors, TVs and their components, and a variety of other electronics items for consumer and business use. However, it also ventured into other areas not strongly connected to electronics, such as fertilizers, vitamin pills, furniture, and trumpets. Eventually, this diversity became difficult to manage, and in 1990 the company was close to bankruptcy.[111]

The 1990s were marked by attempts by first Jan Timmer and then Cor Boonstra to rationalize Philips' portfolio, trim bureaucracy, and enhance profitability. These culminated in record profits in 2000, when its semiconductor and consumer businesses in particular →

In June 2007, it was announced that Philips would acquire Color Kinetics to strengthen its leading position in LED lighting systems, components, and technologies. *Royal Philips Electronics*

➜ performed strongly in buoyant economic conditions. However, the following year, the Al-Qaeda attacks on New York in September, and the unwinding of the internet boom, led to a much tougher environment, and the firm recorded its worst ever loss (see Table 17.8 for a summary of financial results). On 30 April 2001, Gerard Kleisterlee was announced as Philips' new President and CEO.[112]

Gerard Kleisterlee

An engineer by training, Kleisterlee, like his father before him, had spent his entire career at Philips, whose medical systems division he had joined in 1974. His experience at the company had included senior positions in divisions marketing consumer products and components. He had also had considerable experience in Asia, culminating in his taking charge of Philips' operations in China.[113]

He lives the Philips brand and its products. As he explained to a German interviewer:

> I am woken in the morning by a Philips radio-alarm, clean my teeth with a Philips toothbrush, shave with a Philips razor, and am made a cup of coffee by my wife in a Senseo machine. After that, I watch the morning news on a Philips flat-screen TV and go to the office, which—depending on the time of year—may be lit all day by Philips lighting systems.[114]

Kleisterlee is an imposingly tall man, impeccably dressed, with piercing blue eyes. A Catholic by upbringing, he acquired, during his time in Asia, an affinity with the teachings of the Chinese philosopher Confucius, with whom he shares a birthday. He also draws inspiration from Mahatma Ghandi and the Dalai Lama, in particular the way in which they combine leadership and humility. A French journalist described him thus: '... reserved but accessible. As rigorous as he is meticulous, he can become blunt when confronted with imprecision.' However, he claims to have mellowed over time.[115]

In his first Annual Report, he gave a clear message to people who might be tempted to explain away the 2001 performance. In a section headed 'Facing the Facts', he wrote:

> It would be too easy to attribute all our problems to the general economic situation. Despite the excellent year we had in 2000, several problems were already beginning to surface. Some of our processes are not up to benchmark standard, our fragmented organization makes us carry too high costs for infrastructure and overhead, and we've allowed too many low growth, low-margin businesses to develop. They account for an unacceptably high percentage of our total portfolio. Consumer Electronics, for instance, which accounts for around a third of Group sales, hasn't been performing well enough for several years.[116]

➜

Table 17.8 Royal Philips Electronics: selected financial results 1998–2001

	1998[a]	1999	2000	2001[c]
Sales	30,459	31,459	37,862	31,725
Percentage increase over previous year	3	3	20	(16)
Income (loss) from continuing operations	1,025	1,595	9,577	(2,331)
As a % of stockholders' equity (ROE)	9.7	10.9	48.5	(11.2)
Discontinued operations[bc]	4,891	–	–	(144)
Cumulative effect of a change in accounting principle	–	–	85	–
Net income (loss)	5,900	1,590	9,662	(2,475)
Earnings before interest and tax	1,289	1,553	4,258	(1,251)
As a % of sales	4.2	4.9	11.2	(3.9)
Total employees at year-end (in thousands)	234	227	219	189
Inventories as a % of sales	13.2	13.6	13.9	13.4
Outstanding trade receivables, in months' sales	1.3	1.4	1.5	1.5
Total equity and liabilities = Total assets	**28,009**	**31,673**	**39,524**	**39,202**
Net debt : group equity ratio	(25):125	5:95	11:89	26:74
Market capitalization at year-end	20,631	44,942	50,098	42,532

Notes

a The Company has applied US GAAP since January 1, 2002. The years from 1998 onwards have been restated accordingly

b Discontinued operations until 1998 reflect the effect of the sale of PolyGram N. V. in 1998 in order to present the Philips Group accounts on a continuing basis

c Discontinued operations from 2001 onwards reflect the effect of the sale of MDS in 2006, for which previous years have been restated

Source

<http://www.annualreport2006.philips.com/>, accessed 17 April 2007

→ The consumer electronics (CE) business, indeed, was barely profitable, and its chronic weakness in the US, where its brands— Marantz in audio, Magnavox in video, Norelco in shavers—were not readily associated with Philips, was particularly bothersome. It was made known in 2001 that if the American CE business was not profitable within two years—it had not made a profit since 1991—it would be closed down. Without the world's largest consumer market, it was unlikely that the CE business would have a future. Although this ultimatum was later relaxed when it became plain that the deadline was unrealistic—in fact, the US operation was reinforced through an acquisition—it served to focus minds. Losses in the US were cut through a disciplined weeding out of unprofitable small customers and orders, and improved logistics. However, in 2004, Kleisterlee could still tell a German newspaper that he 'could not rule out' the sale of low margin parts of the CE division.[117]

Rebalancing the cost base

One issue to which Kleisterlee gave immediate priority was to bring Philips' cost base more in line with industry norms. He started by asking the staff for suggestions, which generated an immediate €150m of savings on services such as consultancy and telecoms. He also closed Philips mobile phone manufacturing facilities and outsourced production to a collaborator in China. Outsourcing deals for other production units, and for selected administrative functions, followed: the last two years of Boonstra's term and the first two of Kleisterlee's together saw the number of Philips factories reduced by one-third, to 160, with the loss of over 19,000 jobs, and by 2007 almost all of the CE business' production had been outsourced.[118]

Outsourcing was not the only way in which costs were reduced, however. By reorganizing the way in which the group bought in goods and services, whose total cost amounted to 66 per cent of revenues, Philips was able to trim this expenditure by over 12 per cent. This was done through a mixture of centralization—business units were no longer allowed to buy their own supplies—and decentralization. Each business division was given responsibility for purchasing particular inputs on behalf of the whole group—the CE business bought all the plastics, for example—while members of its purchasing department were spread around the other businesses to liaise with product developers there. This gave the group the benefits of scale in negotiation while ensuring the users got precisely the materials they needed.[119] →

→ Towards one Philips

This was an example of Kleisterlee and his team tackling what he had long regarded as one of Philip's most pressing problems. The six business divisions—lighting, consumer electronics, domestic appliances and personal care, components, medical systems, and semiconductors—were 'silos' that communicated little amongst themselves. This severely limited the benefits that the company could draw from its diversity.

One of Kleisterlee's first initiatives, therefore, was an initiative entitled 'Towards One Philips' in which people were encouraged to participate in 'strategic conversations'. The themes he defined for these conversations were uncontroversial technologies where Philips could hope for competitive advantage. People at all levels and from all divisions were invited to participate, and realized that to win with these technologies, they would need to collaborate. For example, to stand a chance of winning the competitive race in optical storage, the firm would need to be first to market with a DVD recorder. Collaboration between the semiconductors, CE and components divisions trimmed nine months from the normal product development cycle and enabled the firm to grab 60 per cent of the US market.[120]

These changes had an uplifting effect at a time when financial results were disappointing. One senior manager spoke warmly of how Kleisterlee was holding together a company that had become bitterly divided, saying that he knew of many people whose faith in the chief executive was the main reason why they were sticking with the firm.[121]

Kleisterlee also fostered outside collaboration, creating, for example, a joint-venture with Korean conglomerate LG to make first cathode ray tubes and later flat-screen panels for TVs. It cooperated with Sara Lee, owner of the Douwe Egberts coffee brand, to design and market the Senseo, an easy-to-use espresso machine, and with consumer electronics rival Sony on wireless technology for consumer devices.[122]

This new openness found expression in a new corporate R&D campus where 1,500 Philips technologists were to interact with some 3,500 employees of the dozens of other firms that had taken space there. Not all the research conducted there would lead to products marketed under the Philips brand—some, in 2007, was being conducted on disc players, a product from which the firm had exited. However, it aimed to incubate such products to a stage where another firm would take them on and Philips would get a return on its share of the investment.[123]

At the same time, the CEO moved to coordinate certain vital functions from the centre. As well as procurement, human resources, payroll, and finance were centralized, and Andrea Ragnetti was appointed as the firm's first chief marketing officer. It was Ragnetti, an Italian with no prior experience in Philips, who was to help Kleisterlee, the insider, to achieve perhaps the most important coup in Philips' recent history.

Sense and simplicity

Like many important strategic moves, this was born from apparent adversity. In December 2003, Philips executives got a call from an American news programme, which was running an item about the experiences of a man that they had left in a room full of consumer electronics devices. The poor victim had been unable to persuade any of the gadgetry to function using the Philips universal remote control with which he had been provided. Later that year, 100 top Philips managers were given various products to take home and tasked with getting them to work. A number returned frustrated at their inability to do so.[124]

Philips had already conducted focus groups with 2,000 people in eight countries and had discovered that fascination with the potential of new technology was tainted by frustration at over-specified products that failed to work as promised.[125] In January 2004, Kleisterlee, in a speech at the Consumer Electronics Association, rebuked the assembled industry executives for failing to deliver the benefits of new technology in usable form. And in September that year, Philips unveiled its new marketing slogan, 'Sense and Simplicity', promising advanced technology that was easy to experience and designed around the user.

Backed with a suitably minimalist $100m advertising campaign, the rebranding was a stunning success, raising the value of the Philips brand from $4.5bn to $6.7bn within three years. Marketing had been an area where Philips had admitted it needed to improve, but this time the execution of the campaign seemed impeccable, with innovative touches, such as purchasing blocks of prime advertising near the contents page of prestigious magazines or during live TV sporting events—and then not using them, but 'donating' them to the reader or viewer, to make their life simpler.[126]

The products, of course, had to deliver on the brand promise, so were exhaustively tested to ensure that the manuals and software made for easy setting up and usage. The Senseo was an early example: ten million were sold in just four years. Other easy-to-use products that crossed divisional boundaries appeared, such as a heart defibrillator that anyone, guided by audio instructions, could use to treat a heart attack in the home.[127]

No less importantly, 'Sense and Simplicity' seemed to become a rallying cry within the organization itself, shaping not just the way that the products were designed but the way Philips did business. Presentations to top management, for example, which had been known to last hours, were capped at ten PowerPoint slides.[128]   →

→ A simpler portfolio

This new attitude paved the way for a simplification of the portfolio, something that outside observers and analysts had been advocating for many years. In December 2005, the global semiconductor activities were transferred to a new legal entity, NXP Electronics, 80.1 per cent of which was sold to a private equity consortium in September 2006. The firm also committed to selling off its stake in TSMC, a Taiwanese chip-maker by 2010.[129]

After its exit from semiconductors, combined with earlier factory closures and transfers of mature product lines, such as VCRs, to outside partners, Philips could term itself 'asset-light'. It retained manufacturing capability only in businesses where it had distinctive production capabilities, such as domestic appliances, lighting, and medical systems.

Lighting and medical systems, two of the oldest businesses in the portfolio, were also the ones where the capital freed up by these disposals was being reinvested. Modern lighting technologies, such as light-emitting diodes (LEDs), which consumed far less energy than classic tungsten filament lights (Philips was able to cut the energy consumed in illuminating the Eiffel Tower by 38 per cent), were seen as having great promise as awareness of the threat of global warming became more widespread. An ageing population in the developed world and greater economic prosperity in large developing countries were already leading to an increase in demand for medical systems, where Philips was the number three player behind GE and Siemens. Products to address these sectors included Motiva, a product that could take key medical readings and send them to a doctor via a TV set-top box, and a mobile clinic, designed to serve rural areas in India, with basic diagnostic equipment and a satellite link to a top urban hospital. Kleisterlee seemed to take special pride in the latter, mentioning it frequently in interviews.[130]

Control systems

Along with the new marketing vision, Philips' management made comprehensive changes to the control systems in an organization where financial discipline had not always been strong. One senior manager recalled how '... in the 1980s... I wasn't making my numbers. But nobody asked. Philips money wasn't real money.'[131]

The changes were driven, in part by the desire to simplify and harmonize systems in line with the 'Towards One Philips' initiative, and partly by regulatory changes, such as the Sarbanes-Oxley Act in the USA. The new Internal Control Standard (ICS) was put in place in 2004, and the company claimed that it gave 'full transparency of our control environment. The Internal Control Standard has been deployed in 900 reporting units, where business process owners perform approximately 90,000 controls each quarter.'[132]

The company's top managers themselves led the training of Philips' top 200 divisional and functional managers in the concepts underlying the new system, with comprehensive training being given to regional financial controllers and managers. The new system meant that Kleisterlee and his team were able to display an impressive grasp of the business when discussing it with journalists and financial analysts.

The key indicators of performance used varied from unit to unit. The design unit, for example, although it charged its service out at market rates to both internal and external customers, was not expected to make a profit. On the other hand, when discussing the CE business with visiting financial analysts at the end of 2006, Rudy Provoost, CEO of that business, discussed two measures of profit, EBIT and EBITDA, along with sales and the net working capital for the business—negative, as a result of the asset-light strategy. He also homed in on employee productivity, measured using sales/employee and added value/employee.

Other elements of the division's balanced scorecard were less predictable. Provoost took pride in its staff showing the highest average score in Philips' annual people engagement survey. The firm had also begun to use 'net promoter scores'—it measured the proportion of people who were strongly convinced that they would recommend the Philips brand, and subtracted from that the proportion who responded in a way that was apathetic or unfavourable. A number of top-selling CE products had scores above 60, putting them in the top tier of all brands. It was intended to extend this metric to gauge, not just products, but also a variety of internal processes.[133]

Mergers and acquisitions

By 2005, Philips was solidly profitable (Table 17.9) and had the funds available to develop promising businesses. Its Indian and Chinese operations were developing and testing low-cost versions of its successful consumer items from Western markets. It also let it be known that it was constantly looking to make selected acquisitions for its key businesses both in its established markets and in Asia. In 2005, Philips made the first of a series of acquisitions (Table 17.10), all of market-leading firms in specialized fields; Lumileds, for example, held over 200 patents related to LED technology.[134]

Philips had made acquisitions before, notably when putting together its semiconductors business, and its management team prided itself on its disciplined approach to them. They established lists of potential targets, and were prepared to take their time in order to get the target and the process right. In screening a potential acquisition, they assessed many factors, including its market position relative to Philips', the competitiveness and location of any manufacturing operations, the strength of management, and not least the culture.

→

Table 17.9 Royal Philips Electronics: selected financial results 2002–2006

	2002[a]	2002[ab]	2003[ab]	2004[ab]	2005[ab]	2006[ab]
Sales	30,983	26,788	24,049	24,855	25,775	26,976
Percentage increase over previous year	(2)	(2)	(10)	3	4	5
Income (loss) from continuing operations	(3,184)	(2,863)	100	2,584	2,831	919
As a % of stockholders' equity (ROE)	(19.1)	(15.3)	1.0	18.5	18.1	4.4
Discontinued operations[bc]	(22)	(343)	609	252	37	4,464
Cumulative effect of a change in accounting principle	–	–	(14)	–	–	–
Net income (loss)	(3,206)	(3,206)	695	2,836	2,868	5,383
Earnings before interest and tax	442	943	830	1,156	1,472	1,183
As a % of sales	1.4	3.5	3.5	4.7	5.7	4.4
Total employees at year-end (in thousands)	170[c]	170[c]	164[c]	162[c]	159[c]	122
Inventories as a % of sales	11.1	10.7	10.3	10.1	10.9	10.7
Outstanding trade receivables, in months' sales	1.3	1.3	1.3	1.3	1.4	1.5
Total equity and liabilities = Total assets	32,289	32,205	28,989	30,739	33,905	38,497
Net debt : group equity ratio	27:73	27:73	18:82	1:99	(5):105	(10):110
Market capitalization at year-end	21,309	21,309	29,648	25,003	31,536	31,624

Notes

a Discontinued operations from 2001 onwards reflect the effect of the sale of MDS in 2006, for which previous years have been restated

b Discontinued operations from 2002 onwards reflect the effect of the sale of Semiconductors in 2006, for which previous years have been restated

c Including discontinued operations

Source

<http://www.annualreport2006.philips.com/>, accessed 17 April 2007

Table 17.10 Acquisitions by Philips since January 2005

Date	Target	Price	Activity
2005			
July	Stentor Inc.	$280m	Technology for digital medical images
August	Lumileds Lighting BV*	$950m	LED lighting technology
2006			
January	Lifeline Systems Inc	$750m	Personalized emergency call systems for people with health problems
March	Witt Biomedical Corp	$165m	Equipment for cardiology catheterization laboratories
May	Advent Holdings Ltd	€675m	Baby feeding systems and breast pumps
June	Intermagnetics	€1bn	Superconducting magnets for MRI medical scanning systems

* This deal was for the partner's 47% stake in an existing joint venture

→ Every acquisition, no matter how large or small, had to be able to demonstrate a payback period no longer than two to three years. If the price was not right, then Philips were 'absolutely capable of staying away' from a potential deal. They believed that they could also demonstrate a good track record in integrating Philips' larger acquisitions, though their experiences with smaller deals, undertaken to fill temporary gaps in the portfolio, had been less positive—it had proved difficult to hold on to key people. They were nonetheless proposing to continue with such small, bolt-on acquisitions to bolster the consumer electronics business.[135]

Observers by and large agreed with the company's strategic direction, noting its 'formidable' track record in M&A. Some suggested, however, that Philips paid a full price for certain of its acquisitions, such as that of Avent and, in particular Intermagnetics. Philips, having been Intermagnetics' largest customer, would have good knowledge of the firm, and one analyst suggested that the logic for the deal would have been as strong, and the price →

→ much lower, two or three years beforehand. Another suggested that Philips might have been able to replicate Lifeline's personal emergency technology, which complemented its existing Motiva product, in-house.[136]

The situation in 2007

By April 2007, Philips had clearly come a long way since the torrid times of 2002. The portfolio had been simplified; intriguingly, as one journalist pointed out, this left the firm with a structure that the founding Philips brothers would have found familiar. The people that had criticized Philips for sticking to its low-margin CE business 'despite having had their ass kicked so many times' had fallen silent. Philips' management, for its part, was convinced that consumer electronics gave it vital leverage in negotiations with powerful retailers, such as Wal-Mart, that were crucial to the distribution of its other products.[137]

No longer exposed to the highly cyclical semiconductor industry, Philips could look forward to stable profitability. In fact, one key issue preoccupying its management was how to use the funds at its disposal; the company was debt-free, with further cash injections to be expected as it sold off its remaining stakes in some of the businesses from which it had withdrawn. It was committed to either returning the cash to shareholders or spend-

ing it on M&As, but pressure was mounting for it to pull off a really large deal—€3bn or more—of the kind already achieved by its main competitors in medical systems.[138]

Fortune, the top American business publication, had named Gerard Kleisterlee as its Europe Businessman of the Year for 2006. He had welcomed the honour of having his photograph on the magazine's front page, suggesting that it would help the company's sales in the USA, and that it demonstrated to Americans that Europe was truly capable of change—but that 'his' achievement was really that of the entire group. In March 2007, his tenure as CEO was extended from October 2008 until April 2011.[139]

Case study questions

1. What attributes made Gerard Kleisterlee an effective leader for Philips? Was the company right to renew his contract in March 2007 when it still had over a year to run?

2. Critically appraise Philips' approach to mergers and acquisitions. Are people right to expect them to do a larger deal?

3. Critically appraise Philips' control and performance measurement systems. What other performance measures might you propose for the CE business?

● NOTES

1 Level 5 leadership and its importance was identified by Jim Collins (2001), who looked at matched pairs of companies in the same industry, one moderately successful, the other a firm that had moved from moderate success to industry leadership.

2 The definitive studies on the strategic role of middle managers are those of Steven Floyd and Bill Wooldridge (1994, 1997; Wooldridge and Floyd, 1990). Mair (2005) demonstrated that the behaviours of middle managers significantly affected strategic performance.

3 Balogun (2003) and Rouleau (2005) both give detailed accounts of the reality of middle management life. Kanter (1983) and Boyett and Currie (2004) contain case studies of middle managers taking the initiative.

4 Watson and Wooldridge (2005) show how middle managers exert upward influences on corporate strategy, while Collier et al. (2004) found that their participation significantly improved the strategy development process.

5 Burgelman (1983) remarked on middle managers' role in new venture development.

6 For example, Pettigrew and Whipp (1991) and Nadler and Tushman (1988).

7 The distinction between transactional and transformational leadership comes from Burns (1978); see also Bass and Avolio (1990). The propositions in this paragraph as to which styles of leadership suit which circumstances were derived by Vera and Crossan (2004).

8 Farkas and Wetlaufer (1996) derived this from a sample of 160 CEOs of various nationalities. For alternative views, see Ambos and Schlegelmilch (2007); Isaksen et al. (2003); Martin (2007); and Vroom and Jago (2007).

9   Charan and Colvin (1999); Goffee and Jones (2000, 2005); Pettigrew and Whipp (1991); and Rieple and Vyakarnam (1996).

10 This comment about Branson comes from Goffee and Jones (2000). His recent TV appearances have become more assured.

11 Collins (2001).

12 The notion of the consent of the governed dates back to eighteenth-century philosophers Jean-Jacques Rousseau and David Ricardo. The issues surrounding the exercise of power have been discussed more recently by the French philosopher Michel Foucault (1980) and, specifically in an organizational context, by American academic Jeffrey Pfeffer (1992).

13 The classic work on the exercise of power remains the sixteenth-century treatise *The Prince*, by Niccolo Machiavelli <http://www.gutenberg.org/etext/1232>, accessed 20 July 2007. Some interesting modern studies of the exercise of power can be found in Brass and Burkhardt (1993), Maitlis (2004), and Salancik and Pfeffer (1977).

14 See Gabarro (1987); Gouldner (1954); Rieple (1997, 1998); Pfeffer and Salancik (1978).

15 The importance of the control of resources and information are explored further in, for example, Pettigrew's (1973) writing on information centrality; Pfeffer and Salancik's (1978) work on resource dependency; Hickson et al. (1971); and Ranson et al. (1980).

16 Most of the facts cited in this example are drawn from Tully, S. (2006). 'In this corner! The contender'. *Fortune*, 3 April and *Economist* (2007). 'The careful climber'. 27 January. Some biographical details are from <http://www.jpmorgan.com/cm/cs?pagename=Chase/Href&urlname=jpmc/about/governance/members/dimon> accessed 5 April 2007.

17 Bloomberg News (2007). 'JPMorgan boss collects $63M'. 31 March. The stock options were related to Dimon's tenure as CEO of Bank One.

18 Tully (2006) op. cit.

19 Ibid.

20 Rose, C. (2006). 'A series of conversations about finance, philanthropy and innovation'. *PBS: The Charlie Rose Show*, 28 December. Weidner, D. (2006). 'Before Brad and Jen, there was Sandy and Jamie'. *Dow Jones Business News*. 2 November.

21 Tully (2006) op. cit.

22 For an examination of how performance measurement can help organizational learning, see Garvin (1993) and Neeley and Najjar (2006). The quoted example is from Rucci et al. (1998: 91).

23 *Economist* (2007). 'Hollywood's new model'. 17 March: 81.

24 For an overview of issues relating to rewards, see Lawler (1998).

25 This important insight comes from Daft and Lengel (1986). For reviews of performance measurement in organizations, see Daft and Macintosh (1984), Marr and Schiuma (2003), and Waggoner et al. (2002).

26 See Mintzberg (1975).

27 Data for this Real-life Application were kindly provided by Roger Lewis of c2c.

28 See Ryan and Trahan (2007) and Haspeslagh et al. (2001).

29 For a reviews of the theory of VBM see Ashton (2007) and Ittner and Larcker (2001). For insights into how VBM is used in practice, and the differences between successful and unsuccessful adopters, see Haspeslagh et al. (2001), Malmi and Ikäheimo (2003), and MIT Sloan Management Review (2004).

30 The balanced scorecard (Kaplan and Norton, 1992, 1996) accounts for over one-half of all article citations in this field. For alternative frameworks, see Adams and Neely (2002) and Lynch and Cross (1991). For comprehensive reviews of the performance measurement literature see Neeley et al. (2005), Neely (2005), and Pun and White (2005).

31 The idea of the strategy map was introduced by Kaplan and Norton (2000). For a discussion of the properties of KPIs see De Waal (2003) and Franco and Bourne (2003). Fletcher and Smith (2004) give an interesting case study of a strategy map and a balanced scorecard.

32 Bourne et al. (2002) de Waal (2003) and Franco and Bourne (2003).

33 See Haspeslagh et al. (2001).

34 See Neely (2005).

35 See Goold and Quinn (1990).

36 See, for example, Shenhar et al. (2001), Grundy (1998), and Pellegrinelli and Bowman (1994), although Keegan and Turner (2002) caution that the project management mindset does not always promote innovation. Kenny (2003) gives an example of project management disciplines applied to change in the public sector.

37 Agence France-Presse (2007). 'Recovering Sony won't make same mistakes again: Stringer'. 21 June.

38 See, for example, Moulds, J. (2007). 'Sony dented by PlayStation costs'. *Daily Telegraph*, 17 May; Wray, R. (2007). 'Game over for creator of Sony's Playstation'. *The Guardian*, 27 April: 27; Kageyama, Y. (2007). 'Sony European video game unit cutting jobs'. *Associated Press Newswires*, 19 April.

39 For some examples, see Keil and Montealegre (2000).

40 More detailed arguments and frameworks in this connection are put forward by Milosevic and Srivannaboon (2006); Morris and Jamieson (2005); Srivannaboon (2006); and Srivannaboon and Milosevic (2006).

41 Schendler, B. (2007). 'The trouble with Sony'. *Fortune*, 5 March: 46; *Economist* (2006). 'Playing a long game'. 18 November.

42 Kageyama (2007) op. cit.; Wray (2007) op. cit.; *Economist* (2006). 'Business this week'. 9 September.

43 PRINCE2 was developed by a group of experienced project managers under the auspices of the UK Government and is a trademark of the Office of Government Commerce. See <http://www.ogc.gov.uk/methods_prince_2.asp>, accessed 20 July 2007.

44 Gardner, D. (2006). 'All these two geeks wanted to do was share a funny video with friends, instead they made a $2.2b internet giant'. *Sunday Times (Perth)*, 15 October.

45 Delaney, K. (2006). 'Garage brand'. *Wall Street Journal*, 27 June A1.

46 Auchard, E. (2007). 'Web 2.0 funding doubled in 2006, but few rich yet'. *Reuters News*, 21 March.

47 Cloud, J. (2006). 'The YouTube gurus'. *Time*, 25 December.

48 Helft, M. (2006). 'It pays to have pals in Silicon Valley'. *The New York Times*, 17 October.

49 Bloch, M. 'YouTube—an on-line success story'. <http://www.tamingthebeast.net/articles6/youtube-success.htm>, accessed 22 March 2007.

50 BBC News (2006). 'Google buys YouTube for $1.65bn", 10 October <http://news.bbc.co.uk/1/hi/business/6034577.stm>, accessed 22 March 2007.

51 For further reading on the subject of turnarounds, see Barker and Duhaime (1997), and *Economist* (1999). 'Ma Bell restored', 11 December 1999: 53–4; Barker and Mone (1994); Pearce and Robbins (1994); Armenakis et al. (1995, 1996); Pant (1991); Robbins and Pearce (1992); O'Reilly (1999).

52 See, for example, Hambrick and D'Aveni (1992). Lorange and Nelson (1987) in their work on corporate crises, John Gabarro (1987, 2007), in his work on new managers who fail to take charge, and Alison Rieple, in her research on managerial ruthlessness (Rieple and Vyakarnam, 1996), also make some pertinent points on factors that lead to organizational failure. See also Lohrke et al. (2004).

53 This list comes from Slatter (1984), but other sources, including Grinyer et al. (1990) and Gopal (1991) agree—see Balgobin and Pandit (2001) for a review. Slatter has updated his work in Slatter and Lovett (1999).

54 The three-phase model is from Filatotchev and Toms (2006). The five-step programme derives from Bibeault (1982) and is cited by Burbank (2005). The list of successful recovery strategies comes from Slatter (1984), Burbank (2005), and a study by Bain, a prominent management consultancy (Gadiesh et al., 2003).

55 *Financial Times* (1993). 'Declining fortunes of Ferranti'. 27 October: 20.

56 The use of acquisitions in turnarounds was noted by Slatter (1984), and a more recent study by Morrow et al. (2007) has verified its impact.

57 Furman and McGahan (2002); Sudarsanam and Lai (2001).

58 The facts in this example are from Hanessian (2005).

59 The company openly admitted its shortcomings in Loren's letter to shareholders on page 2 of its 2000 Annual Report.

60 Hanessian (2005).

61 D&B Annual Report 2002: 31.

62 Hanessian (2005).

63 Ibid.

64 See, for example, Bieshaar et al. (2001); Buono and Bowditch (1989); Buono et al. (1985); Cartwright and Cooper (1993, 1996); Chatterjee et al. (1992); Christofferson et al. (2004); David and Singh (1993); Haspeslagh (1989); Nahavandi and Malekzadeh (1988); Ingham et al. (1992); and Zweig and Perlman (1995). DiGeorgio (2002) has a useful summary.

65 Cass Business School press release, 3 April 2006. We have been unable to locate a refereed journal article incorporating these findings, which exclude small deals, below $0.4 billion in value, and very large ones with a value in excess of $1.5 billion.

66 The use of M&A by stock market 'outperformers' is reviewed in *MIT Sloan Management Review* (2004). Frick and Torres (2002) surveys the practices of leaders in high-technology industries.

67 Healy et al. (1997).

68 Bieshaar et al. (2001); *MIT Sloan Management Review* (2004).

69 Hutton, R, (2006b). 'Jaguar needs to show its teeth'. *The Sunday Times*, Business, 29 October: 7; Hutton, R. and O'Connell, D. (2006). 'Land Rover may go in Jaguar sell-off'. *The Sunday Times*, Business, 6 August: 7; Hutton, R. (2006a). 'The engineering may be innovative but the styling is stuck in the 1980s'. *The Sunday Times*, Business, 6 August: 5; O'Connell, D. (2006). 'Wanted: buyer for Jaguar'. *The Sunday Times*, Business, 6 August: 5; Taylor, A., III (1993). 'Shaking up Jaguar'. *Fortune*, 6 September: 65.

70 Friedman, A. and Donkin, R. (1992). 'The Ferranti saga: the man who used CIA tools to commit a $1.1 bn fraud'. *Financial Times*, 12 June: 7; Mackay, A. (1992). 'Ferranti slims down under doctor's orders'. *The Times*, 31 October; Meekel, A. (2005). 'Guerin "home" to complete sentence'. *Lancaster New Era/Intelligencer Journal/Sunday News*, 13 January.

71 Leahy, J. (2007). 'National pride had Tata near tipping point: steel group paid close to its "top price" for Corus'. *Financial Times*, 3 February: 1; *Financial Times* (2007). 'Tata takes Corus: Lex Column'. 1 February: 16; Organization of Asia-Pacific News Agencies (2007). 'Corus shareholders approve Tata Steel offer'. 8 March.

72 The Kangyo Bank example comes from Haspeslagh and Jemison (1986). Von Krogh et al. (1994) have some interesting examples of the effect of national cultural differences.

73 These issues are well handled by Hubbard (1999). The figures on customer retention are from Christofferson et al. (2004).

74 These issues were highlighted in a survey by consultancies Towers Perrin and SHRM, cited by DiGeorgio (2002).

75 *Economist* (2001). 'A $40 billion merger is in trouble with Europe's antitrust authorities'. 12 May; Novak, M. and Lawsky, D. (2001). 'EU slams pressure over GE: White House denies interfering in review'. *Reuter News Agency*, 19 June; Shishkin, P. (2001). 'EU makes it official: no Honeywell for GE'. *Wall Street Journal Europe*, 4 July: 1.

76 Osborne, A. (2001). 'Interbrew must dispose of Carling lager offshoot'. *The Daily Telegraph*, 19 September: 31.

77 Agence France-Presse (1996). 'Branson to fly to Washington to protest against BA–American alliance'. 24 June.

78 See Frick and Torres (2002), Palter and Srinivasan (2006). The research on the relationship between marketing capabilities and acquisition performance comes from Sorescu et al. (2007).

79 See Christofferson et al. (2004)—the source of the example relating to banking branch closures—and DiGeorgio (2003).

80 This insight comes from Marks and Mirvis (1998). See also Cartwright and Cooper (1996) and von Krogh et al. (1994).

81 For further details on this topic, see DiGeorgio (2003); Fubini et al. (2006); Haspeslagh and Jemison (1986): Marks and Mirvis (1998): Roach (2007): and von Krogh et al. (1994).

82 Teather, D. (2005). 'Profile of a giant'. *The Guardian*, 27 October: 28.

83 Ibid.; Grant, J. (2005). 'P&G learns lessons as it integrates $57bn Gillette'. FT.com, 21 December.

84 Teather (2005) op. cit.

85 *AFX International Focus* (2005). 'European regulators clear P&G's acquisition of Gillette'. 15 July.

86 Carrick, R. (2006). 'Big merger wins point to investor losses'. *The Globe and Mail*, 1 July: B8.

87 Abelson, J. (2005). 'Gillette losing 40% of its top managers'. *Boston Globe*, 7 December; Dow Jones International (2005). 'EU clears P&G to buy Gillette with dental concession'. 15 July.

88 Teather (2005) op. cit.; *AFX International Focus* (2005) op. cit.; *Marketing* (2006). 'Last to the table'. 19 April: 24; Story, L. (2007). 'Procter and Gillette learn from each other's marketing ways'. *New York Times*. 12 April: 3.

89 Teather (2005) op. cit.

90 Ibid.; *Marketing* (2006) op. cit.

91 *Logisticstoday* (2005). 'Top ten supply chains of 2005'. 1 December: 18; *Marketing* (2006) op. cit.

92 *Marketing* (2006) op. cit.; Grant (2005) op. cit.

93 Story (2007) op. cit.

94 Grant (2005) op. cit

95 Abelson (2005) op. cit.

96 Neff, J. (2007). 'P&G struggles to hold on to top Gillette talent'. *Advertising Age*, 28 May: 4.

97 *Economist* (2000a). 'The DaimlerChrysler emulsion'. 29 July.

98 Tait, N. (1999). 'Beware, steep learning curve ahead'. *Financial Times*, 4 May: 26; *Economist* (1999). 'DaimlerChrysler: crunch time'. 25 September; *Economist* (2000a) op. cit.

99 Tait (1999) op. cit.; *Financial Times* (2001). 'Interview: DaimlerChrysler's Jürgen Schrempp'. FT.com, 14 February; Politi, J. (2004). 'The battle of DaimlerChrysler'. FT.com, 1 January.

100 *Financial Times* (1999). 'DaimlerChrysler pushes radical overhaul of senior management'. 28 September; Harnischfeger, U. and Tait, N. (1999). 'Real tests still way down the road for DaimlerChrysler'. *Financial Times*, 19 March: 30; Tait, N. (1999). 'Beware, steep learning curve ahead'. *Financial Times*, 4 May: 26; *Economist* (1999) op. cit.; Economist (2000a) op. cit.; Burt, T. (2000). 'Colliding with Chrysler'. *Financial Times*, 10 October; Burt, T. and Tait, N. (1999). 'In search of more equal partnership'. *Financial Times*, 6 October: 23.

101 Büschemann, K.-H. (2007). 'Notbremse am Valentinstag; Von Anfang an hat die Fusion von Daimler und Chrysler nicht funktioniert—jetzt weiß jeder, warum'. *Süddeutsche Zeitung*, 15 February: 2; Burt, T. (2000) op. cit.; *Economist* (2000a) op. cit; *Economist* (2000b). 'DaimlerChrysler marital problems Auburn Hills, Michigan'. 14 October; *Financial Times* (2001) op. cit.; Harnishfeger (1999). 'Push for synergies is taking its toll'. *Financial Times*, 27 May: 2.

102 Burt, T. and Harnishfeger, U. (2001). 'Schrempp starts his repair job on DaimlerChrysler'. *Financial Times*, 21 February; Burt, T. (2001). 'DaimlerChrysler agrees radical restructuring'. *Financial Times*, 24 February; Politi, J. (2003a). 'Schrempp admits Chrysler was a "division"'. *Financial Times*, 11 December; Politi, J. (2003b). 'With equals, someone is always first'. *Financial Times USA Ed2*, 20 December: 12.

103 Burt (2000) op. cit.

104 Simon, B. (2005). 'Detroit's local hero who "walks the talk"'. *Financial Times USA Ed2*, 30 July: 8; Wihofszki, O. and Clark, T. (2006). 'Der Sterndeuter'. *Financial Times Deutschland*, 2 January: 25.

105 Deckstein, D. (2005). 'Zetsches einfache Formel'. *Süddeutsche Zeitung*, 29 December: 21; Jenkins, P. (2005). 'Smart solution to cost Euros 1bn'. *Financial Times*, 27 March: 25; Mackintosh, J. and Simon, B. (2005). 'Survey a blow to Mercedes-Benz image'. *Financial Times Ed3*, 7 March: 28; Milne, R. (2005). 'Even German taxi drivers no longer hail a Mercedes—The reputation of the icon carmaker lies in tatters as it is forced to admit its vehicles are prone to breakdown'. *Financial Times Ed1*, 17 February: 18; Taylor, A. (2005). 'The nine lives of Jurgen Schrempp'. *Fortune*, 10 January: 86.

106 *Economist* (2000a) op. cit.

107 Betts, P. (2004). 'DaimlerChrysler and the sum of its parts'. *Financial Times Europe Ed1*, 18 August: 15; *Financial Times* (2004). 'Daimler debacle: A failed investment points to problems of corporate culture'. 26 April: 18; *Economist* (2004). 'The wheels come off: DaimlerChrysler'. 1 May; Taylor, A. (2004). 'For Schrempp, it was a cruel April'. *Fortune*, 17 May: 36; Taylor (2005) op. cit.

108 Büschemann (2007) op. cit.; Hawranek, D. (2006a). 'Der große Kommunikator'. *Der Spiegel*, 14 August: 72; Jenkins, P. (2005). 'Board oustings start to bear fruit'. FT.com, 29 July; Mackintosh, J. (2006). 'Zetsche delivers a slick new model'. *Financial Times*,

109 Büschemann (2007) op. cit.; *Financial Times* (2007). 'Daimler open to partial sale of Chrysler'. FT.com, 14 February; Hawranek, D. (2006b). 'Amerikanisches Trauerspiel'. *Der Spiegel*, 30 October: 116; Milne, R. (2006). 'Reputation of man at the wheel badly dented: analysts are disappointed because Dieter Zetsche of DaimlerChrysler promised a fresh start'. *Financial Times London Ed2*,

19 September: 25; Wihofszki, O., Spiller, K., and Milne, R. (2007). 'Börse feiert Zetsches Trennungsplan'. *Financial Times Deutschland*, 15 February: 33.

110 Canonici, A. (2006). 'Un campus fertile per nuove sfide'. *Il Sole 24 Ore*, 22 November.

111 Palmer, J. (2006). 'Philips' higher definition'. *Barrons*, 29 May: 14; *Economist* (1994). 'A brighter future?' 13 August: 60–3.

112 TWICE (2000). 'Boonstra To Leave Philips In '01, Kleisterlee Elevated To Top Spot'. *This Week in Consumer Electronics*, 15/20: 8; Philips (2001). Annual Report—Management Report: 5–6; *Economist* (1993). 'A brighter spark'. 21 August: 51–2; *Economist* (1997). 'The dimmest bulb of all'. 6 July: 69–70; *Economist* (2002). 'Struggling with a supertanker'. 9 February: 52–3; Holstein, W. (2005). 'Philips' big idea'. *Chief Executive*, 1 November: 38.

113 <http://www.philips.com/about/company/management/boardofmanagement/article-14667.html>, accessed 20 April 2007.

114 Dohmen, F. and Kerbusk, K.-P. (2006). 'Spiegel-Gespräch—"Der Verbraucher will Emotionen"'. *Der Spiegel*, 21 August: 90.

115 The quote is from Fontaine, G. (2007). 'Ce rénovateur d'exception la joue collectif'. *Challenges*, 15 February: 67. Other material from Ahmad, T. (2003). 'Fillip or folly?' *Strategic Direct Investor*, June: 11–15; Chellam, R. (2005). 'A giant in Asia'. *Business Times Singapore*, 8 October; *La Tribune* (2005a). 'Le nouveau gourou du bien-être'. 23 May.

116 Philips (2001). Annual Report—Management Report: 6.

117 Armstrong, D. (2006). 'Move into the light'. *Forbes*, 178/3: 106; Agence France-Presse (2004). 'Philips mulls selling consumer electronics business'. 20 October; AFX News (2004). 'Philips has no plans to sell parts of its consumer electronics division'. *AFX International Focus*, 20 October.

118 Philips (2001) op. cit.; *Economist* (2002) op. cit.; Ahmad (2003) op. cit.; Heuzeroth, T. (2007). 'Philips—Nür ein Atempause'. *Berliner Morgenpost*, 23 January: 5; Dohmen and Kerbusk (2006) op. cit.; Meredith, R. (2005). 'A tale of two strategies'. *Forbes Asia*, 1/3 (3 October): 30A.

119 Marsh, P. and Bickerton, I. (2005). 'The art of knitting together a loosely woven web'. *FT.com*, 17 November.

120 Wylie, I. (2003). 'Can Philips learn to walk the talk?' *Fast Company* 66 (January): 44–5; *Economist* (2001). 'Philips' new frontiersman'. 5 May: 58.

121 Wylie (2003) op. cit.

122 Jones, D. (2002). 'Philips CEO expects spirit of cooperation to pay off'. *USA Today*, 19 November: B04; *La Tribune* (2005b). '"Le modèle de l'entreprise qui réalise tout elle-même est mort"'. 23 May; Ahmad (2003) op. cit.

123 Fontaine (2007) op. cit.; Truttmann, M. (2007). 'Zweite Geburt der Philips-Stadt'. *Der Bund*, 13 February: 15; Voxant FD (Fair Disclosure) Wire (2006). 'Royal Philips Electronics analyst day: DAP, CE, marketing and adding value through the corporate center & corporate technologies'. 5 December.

124 Endt, F. (2004). 'It is rocket science'. *Newsweek*, 18 October, 144/16: E8.

125 Voight, J. (2007). 'Why "Less is More" is fit for the Zeitgeist'. *Adweek*, 26 February.

126 Ibid.; Reingold, J. (2006). 'Design intervention: At Philips, a place long known for big ideas and small numbers, can there be too much of a good thing?' *Fast Company*, 1 October: 88; Capell, K. (2006). 'How Philips got brand buzz'. *BusinessWeek On-line*, 1 August.

127 *Dutch News Digest* (2005). 'Dutch Philips sells 10 mln Senseo'. 25 September; Capell (2006) op. cit.

128 *Institutional Investor—Americas* (2006). 'Gerard Kleisterlee of Royal Philips Electronics'. 15 June.

129 Voxant FD (Fair Disclosure) Wire (2005). 'Royal Philips Electronics "To create a separate legal structure for its Semiconductors business" Conference Call—Final'. 15 December; Reuters News (2007). 'Philips board gets bonus for sale of chip unit'. 19 February. *La Tribune* (2007). 'Philips tourne définitivement la page des puces'. 12 March.

130 Palmer, J. (2006). 'Philips' higher definition'. *Barron's*, 29 May: 14; Arndt, M. (2005). 'The new face of Philips'. *BusinessWeek On-line*, 1 December; Meredith (2005) op. cit.; Business Line (The Hindu) (2005). 'Philips CEO sees India as engine of growth'. 15 November: 02.

131 Schwartz, N. (2007). 'Lighting Up Philips'. *Fortune*, 155/1: 30–35.

132 Philips (2004) Annual Review: 15.

133 Voxant FD (Fair Disclosure) Wire (2007a). 'Q4 2006 Royal Philips Electronics Earnings Conference Call—Final'. 22 January.

134 Business Line (2005) op. cit.; Meredith (2005) op. cit.; Singer, J. and Karnitschnig, M. (2005). 'Europe gets merger mania'. *Wall Street Journal Europe*, 9 September: M1. Fortson, D. (2005). 'Royal Philips bets on LEDs'. TheDeal.com, 16 August; *Dow Jones Business News* (2007). 'Philips Electronics reviewing a "number" of possible deals'. 29 March; Schiffers, M. (2006). 'Philips exec considers buys to bolster consumer elec ops'. *Dow Jones Capital Markets Report*, 31 August; Simons, S. (2006). 'Philips buys Intermagnetics for Eur1b in cash'. *Dow Jones International News*, 15 June; Cordes, R. (2006a). 'Philips reaches for lifeline'. TheDeal.com, 20 January; Pantulu, C. (2006). 'Philips prowls for M & As'. *DNA—Daily News & Analysis*, 5 December.

135 Voxant FD (Fair Disclosure) Wire (2005, 2006) op. cit.; *La Tribune* (2005b) op. cit.; Voxant FD (Fair Disclosure) Wire (2007a) op. cit.

136 Cordes (2006a) op. cit.; Cordes, R. (2006b). 'Philips pays high for Intermagnetics'. TheDeal.com, 16 June; Pisa, K. (2006). 'Charterhouse sells baby-goods company'. TheDeal.com, 24 May; Simons (2006) op. cit.

137 The quotation is from Marsh and Bickerton (2005) op. cit. Other information from *Les Echos* (2007). 'Retour aux origines'. 17 April and *Institutional Investor—Americas* (2006) op. cit.

138 Schiffers, M. (2007). 'Philips needs route to drive growth, boost stock'. *Dow Jones International News*, 28 March; Bickerton, I. (2007). 'Philips looks to step up pace of takeovers'. *Financial Times*, 30 March; 22.

139 Schwartz (2007) op. cit.; Fontaine, G. (2007) op. cit.

Glossary

absorptive capacity An organization's capacity to absorb new knowledge, disseminate it, and implement it in new products or practices.

acquisition or takeover The buying of one company (the 'target') by another.

agency costs The cost to an organization of making sure that its employees are acting in its interests and those of its owners, together with any profits lost because of ineffective control.

aggregation benefits The advantages that come from gathering together value chain elements into the same location, thus making operations less complex, providing a single focus for customers, and achieving scale benefits.

architecture The structures, systems, and practices that shape information flow into and out of the organization, and the way that decisions are taken (or avoided) on the basis of that information.

authority The formal hierarchical position to which society (the organization itself or the wider social environment) has allocated certain power elements.

barrier to entry Any advantage that firms already operating in an industry hold over other firms that might potentially decide to enter it.

benchmarking Measuring products or practices against those of top-ranking competitors or of organizations seen as industry leaders. Sometimes undertaken on best practices in unrelated sectors to make comparisons with world-best performers.

bounded rationality A reasoning process determined—or *bounded*—by factors such as preconceptions, or lack of time or information, which make particular ways of problem-solving much more likely than others.

business model The combination of competitive stance, value chain, and administrative structure (architecture) of an organization.

change agent A person (more rarely, a group of people) who takes on the role of promoting change within an organization and of enlisting other people to support that change.

common market A form of free-trade area.

competitive stance The visible aspects of a strategy that customers and users see when dealing with an organization.

It comprises the organization's chosen markets, products, and services, and their positioning.

contingency A feature of an organization or its environment that influences something else. E.g. an organization's size and environment appear to influence the structure that its managers are likely to choose.

corporate social responsibility (CSR) An umbrella term for corporate policies to ensure ethical behaviour and address social problems inside and outside the organization.

creativity The production of novel or original ideas in a domain. Some authorities regard creativity as a necessary precursor to innovation.

customers The people or other organizations that pay for an organization's services or products.

deliberate strategy A strategy conceived by senior managers as a planned response to the challenges confronting an organization. Often the result of a systematic analysis of the organization's environment and resources.

differentiation Distinguishing a product, service, or brand from its competitors in ways that customers find valuable, so that they will pay a price premium or show greater loyalty.

diversification A substantial extension of an organization's activities through the introduction of new varieties of product or service and/or moves into markets which the organization has not penetrated to any great extent.

divestment The selling off or closing of parts of a business in order to concentrate on core business areas, or to raise the funds to invest in expansion.

dominant design A configuration for a product or service that becomes accepted and expected by producers and customers. It may embrace the appearance, functionality, basic features, and sometimes also the production technology.

economic rents The returns from a given investment that an organization is able to achieve, over and above those expected by stockholders for a given level of risk.

economic union Characterized by the free movement of goods between member countries and the integration of economic policies; it implies a common fiscal regime and currency, or at least a fixed exchange rate.

economies of scale When for each 1% increase in production volume, the total cost of production increases by less than 1%, and the organization's average cost per unit of output falls.

effectiveness An output or activity is effective if it does what the intended user or beneficiary, inside or outside the organization, requires it to do.

efficiency Getting or keeping the cost of an output or process as low as possible, minimizing wastage and unnecessary activities.

emergent strategy A strategy that 'emerges' from lower down the organization without direct senior management intervention.

entrepreneurship The process through which 'opportunities to create future goods and services are discovered, evaluated, and exploited' (Shane and Venkataraman, 2000).

exploitation Utilizing and refining existing knowledge and capabilities, in order, for example, to increase the efficiency or effectiveness of existing activities.

exploration The search for new possibilities through activities such as experimentation, risk-taking, and innovation.

first-mover advantage The advantages the first major entrant to a new industry/market can obtain, e.g. by appropriating locations, obtaining patents and reputational resources, and moulding customers' processes to suit its value chain.

free-trade area Not as extreme in terms of integration as an economic union, but involves the agreement of member countries to reduce or eliminate barriers to trade, such as tariffs or quotas. A common market is a form of free trade area.

global firm A firm whose value chain activities are spread across the world.

global industry An industry in which there is a significant competitive advantage to integrating activities worldwide, and therefore whose constituent firms are global.

global product A product that is uniform across the entire world.

global strategy Where a firm uses a single set of brands worldwide, sources key inputs internationally, and exerts strong central control over many aspects of the business.

globalization A reduction in market segments, and increasing inter-dependence of national markets worldwide (Siebert 1999: 8).

goal congruence Compatibility ('congruence') between the goals of the organization and the personal goals of the individuals that work for it or with it.

hierarchy The shape or format of reporting and decision-making relationships in an organization. Hierarchies may be *tall* with many layers of management, or *flat*, with few.

hold-up One partner's potential to blackmail the other, e.g. by raising prices or demanding other concessions. This is more likely to happen when the victim is irrevocably committed to the project.

imposed strategy A strategy that an organization's managers would not otherwise have chosen, but is forced on them.

industry A group of firms (competitors) that produce a set of similar outputs—products and services that fulfil the same broad function.

industry life-cycle A model of how a typical industry progresses from its birth, with the creation of a new product type, to its demise, with the sale of its very last product.

influence The ability to *persuade* someone to do something that they would not otherwise have done.

innovation The implementation of a significantly new idea in a specific context. This may apply to products, technologies, or processes. Some further subdivide it into radical (or transformational) and incremental innovation.

insourcing When a separate firm carries out part of the organization's operations, but undertakes them in the organization itself, rather than on its own premises.

intellectual property The product of intellectual endeavour. It includes written material (words or music), designs, works of art, trade marks and logos, and databases.

invention The first occurrence of an idea for a new product or process (Fagerberg et al., 2005: 4).

knowledge management The process of turning unrecognized or inaccessible knowledge into recognized and accessible knowledge through mechanisms that facilitate the emergence, storage, and transfer of knowledge within an organization.

leadership The capacity to develop and shape organizational routines, or to maintain commitment to existing routines.

legitimacy '[A] generalized perception or assumption that the actions of an entity are desirable, proper or appropriate within some socially constructed system of norms, values, beliefs and definitions' (Suchman, 1995: 574).

local product A product which is different in each of the regions in which it is sold.

macro-environment The set of factors and influences that are not specific to an organization or the industry in which it operates, but that nonetheless affect them.

market A group of customers.

merger The creation of a new legal entity by the bringing together of two or more previously independent companies.

mission The set of goals and purposes that an organization's members and other major stakeholders agree that it exists to achieve. It is often expressed in a formal, public mission statement.

nearshoring The outsourcing of value chain activities to companies located in a foreign country, but one that is closer geographically to the home organization.

offshoring The outsourcing of value chain activities to companies in another country, distant from the home organization, and usually one that offers lower costs or other benefits.

organizational culture Culture is 'how things are done around here'. It is what is typical of the organization, the habits, the prevailing attitudes, the grown-up pattern of accepted and expected behaviour.

outsourcing The contracting out of part of an organization's operations to a separate company.

parenting skills Corporate-level competences that add value to individual businesses, and/or to the company overall.

portfolio The range of products, services, or brands offered by a business. Also, the range of strategic business units (SBUs) controlled by a diversified corporation.

position The choices that an organization makes about the price and quality levels of its products and services, as well as the ways and places in which they are sold.

positioning The building of an image of a product, service, or brand in the mind of the customer as to what it promises and what values are associated with it.

power The ability of one person to *induce* another to do something they would not otherwise do.

project The commitment of resources over a defined time-scale to produce a one-off output: a product such as a new airliner, or a service such as a major consultancy investigation and report.

realized strategy The strategy the organization actually ends up implementing. It may be deliberate, emergent or imposed.

resource Something that an organization owns, controls, or has access to on a semi-permanent basis. It may be a physical object, a person, money, or something intangible, such as a capability or reputation.

share buy-back When a company buys back its own shares from shareholders.

share split Issuing new shares to each shareholder, and reducing each share's nominal value. For example, a company may issue 10 shares of nominal 10p value to replace each £1 share.

shareholder value Shareholder value theory states that organizations belong to their shareholders, whose interests supersede those of any other stakeholders, and that it is the managers' duty to maximize the firm's economic value.

stakeholders People with an interest in an organization's success, failure, or activities, and therefore a desire to influence its behaviour.

strategic business unit (SBU) A part of a firm that operates in a distinct industry, or sometimes a substantial sub-sector within an industry: an independent subsidiary company, an operating division, or part of a division.

strategizing The processes of strategy development, and in particular the way in which the practices that make up organizational life contribute to them and their outcomes.

switching costs Costs that a firm incurs when it changes from one supplier or type of product to another.

synergy '[T]he ability of two or more units or companies to generate greater value working together than they could working apart' (Goold and Campbell, 1998).

tacit knowledge Tacit (literally, 'silent') knowledge is knowledge that exists within an organization, but about which its members are unconscious or unaware.

transaction costs The costs (many of which may be hidden) of doing business with other organizations.

transnational strategy When a firm uses regional brands for its otherwise global products, and allows its businesses considerable local autonomy—but exerts central control over key aspects of the business.

users The people or other organizations who actually use an organization's products or services.

values The philosophical principles that the great majority of an organization's members hold in common.

value chain The way an organization decides to undertake the important activities at each stage in the development, production, and delivery of its products and services.

vertical integration The extent to which an organization extends control over its activities 'forwards' towards the customer or end user, and 'backwards' or 'upstream' towards the production of its raw materials.

vision A description of what an organization's leaders aspire to achieve over the medium/long term, and of how it will feel to work in or with the organization once this has taken effect.

Index